# COMBINED
# FLEET
# DECODED

# COMBINED
# FLEET
# DECODED

## THE SECRET HISTORY OF

## AMERICAN INTELLIGENCE

## AND THE JAPANESE NAVY

## IN WORLD WAR II

# JOHN PRADOS

RANDOM HOUSE / NEW YORK

All rights reserved under International and Pan-American
Copyright Conventions. Published in the United States by
Random House, Inc., New York, and simultaneously in Canada by
Random House of Canada Limited, Toronto.

Library of Congress Cataloging-in-Publication Data
Prados, John.
Combined fleet decoded : The secret history of American intelligence
and the Japanese Navy in World War II / by John Prados.
p. cm.
Includes bibliographical references and index.
ISBN 0-679-43701-0
1. World War, 1939–1945—Naval operations, Japanese. 2. World
War, 1939–1945—Military intelligence—United States. 3. World War,
1939–1945—Cryptography. 4. Japan. Kaigun—History—World War,
1939–1945. I. Title.
D810.C88P73 1995
940.54′8673—dc20      94-20784

Manufactured in the United States of America on acid-free paper
24689753
First Edition
Book design by Jo Anne Metsch

To Bill Fox,
W.T.R.
Professor and Friend

For knowledge, too, is itself power.

—FRANCIS BACON

# N O T E   T O   T H E   R E A D E R

A N EXTRAORDINARY RANGE OF INCONSISTENCIES EXISTS WITH RESPECT TO MANY ITEMS one might consider conventional in this account that spans the Pacific Ocean. These variants range from standards for translation to conventions pertinent to usage to simple listings of time and date. In wading through the mass of sources and assembling a narrative I have attempted to create a degree of uniformity. In translations from the Japanese some sources use diacritical marks, some do not; some use Western name order, some do not. There are numerous variations of spelling. I have written names in the Japanese fashion—family name first, given name following—but have used spellings familiar to the Western reader and have omitted diacritical marks. Where names appear in a quotation these standards have been imposed. I have not otherwise altered quotations. I have not invented quotations. Some usages have changed since World War II; for instance, "Formosa" was the most common name given to the island also called Taiwan, but the latter name is more familiar today and I have used that instead. Conversely, Chinese transliteration systems have entirely changed since the 1970s, but I consider place names in use during World War II more familiar, and have retained them. All distances are given in nautical miles and yards. All times are local unless otherwise stated. I have attempted to reconcile differences among sources as to time and measures, and figures I use represent my best assessments.

# A C R O N Y M S
# A N D
# A B B R E V I A T I O N S

| | |
|---|---|
| ABDACOM | American-British-Dutch-Australian Command |
| AIB | Allied Intelligence Bureau |
| A.I.F. | Australian Infantry Force |
| ASW | antisubmarine warfare |
| ATIS | Allied Translator and Interpreter Section |
| | |
| BAMS | Broadcasting Allied Movement Ships |
| BB | battleship |
| BD | battleship division |
| | |
| CA | heavy cruiser |
| CAP | Combat Air Patrol |
| CBI | combat intelligence |
| CD | cruiser division |
| CIA | Central Intelligence Agency |
| CIC | Combat Intelligence Center |
| CIC | Counterintelligence Corps |
| CINCPAC | Commander in Chief, Pacific |
| CINCPOA | Commander in Chief, Pacific Ocean Area |
| CIU | combat intelligence unit |
| CL | light cruiser |
| CO | commanding officer |
| COMAIRSOLs | Commander Air Solomons |
| COMINCH | Commander in Chief, U.S. Navy |

| | |
|---|---|
| COIS | chief of intelligence staff (British usage) |
| CV | aircraft carrier |
| CVL | light aircraft carrier |
| CVE | escort aircraft carrier |
| CNO | chief of naval operations |
| | |
| DD | destroyer |
| DE | destroyer escort |
| DF | destroyer flotilla |
| DF | direction finder/finding |
| | |
| FECB | Far East Combined Bureau (British usage) |
| FRUMEL | Fleet Radio Unit Melbourne |
| FRUPAC | Fleet Radio Unit Pacific |
| | |
| G-2 | U.S. Army Intelligence |
| | |
| HF/DF | high-frequency direction finder |
| | |
| ICPOA | Intelligence Center Pacific Ocean Area |
| IGHQ | Imperial General Headquarters (Japanese usage) |
| IJN | Imperial Japanese Navy (Japanese usage) |
| | |
| JAAF | Japanese Army Air Force (U.S. intelligence term for Japanese armed force) |
| JANAC | Joint Army-Navy Committee on Assessment of Loss or Damage on Enemy Naval or Merchant Vessels (later simply Joint Army-Navy Assessment Committee) |
| (j.g.) | junior grade (U.S. Navy rank of sublieutenant) |
| J.I.C. | Joint Intelligence Committee |
| JICPOA | Joint Intelligence Center Pacific Ocean Area |
| JNAF | Japanese Naval Air Force (U.S. intelligence term for Japanese armed force) |
| | |
| LST | landing ship tank |
| | |
| NBK | Nanyo Boeki Kaisha (South Seas Trading Company; Japanese usage) |
| NCO | noncommissioned officer (often a "petty officer" in naval terminology) |
| NEFIS | Netherlands Foreign Intelligence Staff |
| NGS | Naval General Staff (Japanese usage) |
| NKK | Nanyo Kohatsu Kaisha (South Seas Development Company; Japanese usage) |

| | |
|---|---|
| NYK | Nippon Yusen Kaisha (Japan Mail Lines; Japanese usage) |
| OKW | Oberkommando der Wehrmacht (Armed Forces High Command, German usage) |
| ONI | Office of Naval Intelligence, U.S. Navy |
| OpNav | Office of the Chief of Naval Operations |
| OP-20-G | Communications Security Section, U.S. Navy |
| OSS | Office of Strategic Services |
| PRISIC | Photographic Reconnaissance and Interpretation Section Intelligence Center |
| PT | patrol torpedo boat |
| RAN | Royal Australian Navy |
| RDF | radio direction finder |
| RI | radio intelligence |
| RIP | registered intelligence publication |
| RN | Royal Navy |
| RNR | Royal Naval Reserve |
| RNZN | Royal New Zealand Navy |
| SIGINT | signals intelligence |
| SIS | Special Intelligence Section, U.S. Army Signal Corps |
| SNLF | Special Naval Landing Force (Japanese usage) |
| SOPAC | South Pacific Command |
| SOWESPAC | Southwest Pacific Command |
| SS | submarine |
| TBS | talk-between-ships |
| USMC | United States Marine Corps |
| USN | United States Navy |
| VMF | Marine Fighter Squadron |
| ¥ | yen (Japanese currency) |

## MAP SYMBOL KEY

### BASES

U.S.    U.K.    Neth.    Japan

### NAVAL FORCES

Allied    IJN

○    ◉    Surface Action Group
             Combined force-all types

▭    ▮    Carrier Group

### Individual Ships

BB    CA    CL    DD    CV

### ACTIONS

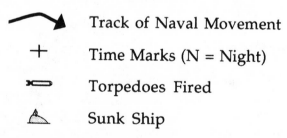

Track of Naval Movement

Time Marks (N = Night)

Torpedoes Fired

Sunk Ship

### AREA OF AIR SEARCHES

Day     Night

Note: Map scales are given in Nautical Miles.
Unless otherwise noted, positions are for 12 Noon.

# CONTENTS

# LIST OF MAPS

"COMBINED FLEET" (RENGO KANTAI) WAS THE NAME JAPAN GAVE TO THE UNITED OPER-
ating forces of its navy during the era of imperial government that ended
with World War II. That cataclysmic conflict brought about the end of the
Japanese Empire, the destruction of much of historical Japan, and untold
suffering and grief in every corner of the Pacific. The war was so hard
fought, and seemed so fierce, that with few exceptions no one was willing to
see the adversary as a people, as a nation, with interests and ideals,
strengths as well as weaknesses. Instead the stereotypes prevailed: The
enemy was ten feet tall or, once bested, ten inches small. The Combined
Fleet was invincible or enfeebled; the U.S. Pacific Fleet was puny until it
became omnipotent.

Stereotypes can be useful in propaganda, and as intellectual devices can
perhaps simplify complex issues, but they can be dangerous in warfare, an
ultimate reality test. Powers wisely employ intelligence organizations to
appreciate the opponent, to reach beyond the stereotypes. It is no accident
that intelligence officers on both sides of the Pacific war are prominent
among those who refused to accept the wartime stereotypes. Nor is it coincidental that former intelligence people produced some of the most perceptive analyses of what transpired. While these analyses have helped us
understand what happened, however, strictures of secrecy have prevented
many of these people from telling us about themselves.

Today we have a history of the Great Pacific War but also a hidden
dimension to the story. We know what the Combined Fleet did and when;
we know how many ships were involved. We know much less of the hidden

story, the underlying framework of victory or defeat. After half a century it is time that story be told, in relation not just to single episodes like Pearl Harbor but to the entire Pacific war. It is time to reassess the outcomes of battles and campaigns in terms not just of troops or ships but of how the secret war played out. The story is intrinsically important because it lends unparalleled depth and scope to our understanding of how World War II turned out the way it did. An account of intelligence in the Pacific war will help identify strengths and weaknesses of the adversaries and will record important facets of history before they are completely lost to the mists of time.

A history of intelligence in World War II also helps us understand modern practices in this subtle and very secret field of endeavor. World War II proved the formative era for virtually every element in the panoply of modern intelligence practice, from analytical estimating to covert action. A certain way of framing questions for analysis, and certain standards for adequacy of information collection, for documentation of conclusions, were established during this war. Even procedures for conducting paramilitary operations emerged from World War II. The war provided a powerful stimulus for the growth of communications intelligence entities and their sophisticated techniques. In recent years considerable attention has been given these subjects in the European context, witness all the work on the Germans and their Enigma coding machine, yet the Pacific conflict (as always, excepting Pearl Harbor) remains almost untouched. Nevertheless it is precisely in the Pacific that the synergism of evolving intelligence techniques shows to best effect. The story of Pacific intelligence operations is also one of unparalleled personal achievements, of brilliant responses to true crises, and of misfortune and miscalculation on both sides. Techniques that in the short run brought the demise of the Combined Fleet predominate in the intelligence world of today. It behooves us to understand them better. As for the men and women who brought us those techniques, it rewards us to know them better.

Much of the recent interest in intelligence has revolved around one single aspect of the work: codes and codebreaking. While this is important— and especially so in the Pacific war, as I hope to show in great detail— communications intelligence is by no means the whole of the subject. Reports from attachés in foreign lands, translation of documents, interrogation of prisoners, technical intelligence, and aerial photography were all vital aspects of an overarching effort to understand the adversary. What has been missing, even in intelligence histories, is an approach that brings together the mundane as well as the exalted, the low and the high, and shows how all together influenced the course of the war. I hope to do this, insofar as possible for *both* sides, for the naval war in the Pacific.

Obviously this is a large subject, involving a huge range of material. But restricting the narrative to just one aspect does not seem a satisfactory alternative—it prevents us seeing the war and the intelligence effort as an organic whole of interrelated parts. I prefer to choose different boundaries, for the most part excluding land warfare and armies except where ground combat requirements directly affected the naval campaign. Within the naval focus I have tried to emphasize matters unreported or underreported in the past without bogging down in those that have been the subject of serious research. Pearl Harbor, Midway, and the submarine war are cases in point, being almost the only episodes of the Pacific war with respect to which even knowledgeable readers have any idea of the impact intelligence had on the conflict. This narrative brings out interesting facets of those events, but goes far beyond them to provide a coherent account of the influence of intelligence on aeronaval warfare in the Pacific and the destruction of the Combined Fleet.

One more benefit of the focus here on naval war in the Pacific is that it permits us to use the eyes of Allied intelligence, those least affected by the dangerous stereotypes of wartime, to view the Imperial Japanese Navy. Western readers in particular have long lacked a history that goes beyond enumerations of numbers of ships and planes to view the Japanese Navy as an entity made up of people with their own hopes and dreams, internal cleavages and struggles, technical achievements and doctrinal dogmas. This book hopes to help remedy that lack, and to do so using the contemporary appreciations of Japanese participants and of foreign intelligence observers. I believe the result lends new depth to our previous understanding of the Japanese side of the war.

This book is based on the best available material and makes an effort to go beyond the wooden stereotypes of the past. At one point I had hoped to rely entirely upon Japanese-language sources for the Imperial Navy portions of the narrative, but sadly I was to be disappointed. It turns out that media outlets and corporations have put such a premium on Japanese-language translation as to bid me right out of the market. I posted requests for translation help at three major Eastern universities in the United States; for what I could afford to pay there was not a single expression of interest, not even an inquiry, not even from a beginning student of the language.

The language problem turned out to be a blessing in disguise. For example, I knew there was a collection of captured Japanese materials in the hands of the U.S. Navy. I had always intended sampling this material, but when beginning this book I supposed I would rely more upon the recently declassified records of the codebreakers, released by the National Security Agency. Of course the latter proved highly useful, as the reader will see, but the captured records included exactly the kind of materials I had hoped to get from Japanese-language sources. There were seamen's diaries, ship logs, after-action reports, debriefings of prisoners, official Imperial Navy manuals, and the like. There were other documents the United States held as well, including translations of official Japanese records held by the Washington Document Center established toward the end of the war, and a series of operational monographs commissioned by Allied authorities, written by Japanese officers after the war. Then there were the extensive interrogations conducted by the U.S. Strategic Bombing Survey with surviving Imperial Navy officers. In the end I encountered too much rather than too little material. This has enabled me to present wholly new accounts of certain episodes, such as the Japanese side of the surface action at the battle of Samar, part of the big Leyte Gulf engagement.

Use of translations of captured records presents a problem in that the narrative may fall victim to translation errors made by wartime linguists. That is unavoidable. However, the narrative would have been equally vulnerable to translation errors made today by a linguist hired for this project, and unfamiliar with the terminology of the Imperial Navy, which used British-derived terms rather than the American ones standard in the Maritime Self-Defense Forces today. The wartime translators at least were making a conscious effort to understand Japanese naval usage. Moreover, readers today, with access to Japanese archives, may be able to show the kinds of error to which Allied intelligence was prone as a result of its translation problems. Postwar translations of official Japanese records no doubt contain similar errors. Both sources, however, make official data available for analysis. Coping with errors in the sources is not different in principle from coping with self-serving recollections or justifications contained in memoirs from participants.

In addition, the more wide-ranging canvass for captured documents and translations that was forced on me by the language problem brought me into contact with a wider range of this material. It made me realize that standard, old-fashioned combat intelligence—such as interrogation of prisoners and capture of documents—was far more valuable to the intelligence effort in the Pacific than has ever been recorded. That was a thread worth following in the research, and I have made it a theme in this narrative, which I believe to be richer as a result.

One special resource that deserves mention is the set of interviews conducted in Japan in the mid-1960s by historian John Toland for his fine book *The Rising Sun*. Done while many of the key participants were still alive, the interview tapes and notes, which Toland has deposited at the Franklin Delano Roosevelt Presidential Library, constitute an invaluable collection of oral history. I stand indebted to Toland for yet another contribution to the field, as will any other historian who uses the collection.

Other sources consulted include records of the U.S. Navy, of intelligence organizations, of the Naval Technical Mission to Japan after the war, of the

Pearl Harbor investigation, and of the International Military Tribunal for the Far East. I have made use of memoir and periodical literature and of secondary sources as appropriate. The interested reader can find these listed in the bibliography. I made an effort also to use official Dutch historical sources for this work, but the Dutch armed forces historical office proved unhelpful, while two Dutch researchers whom I encountered at different times proved initially enthusiastic but ultimately unresponsive.

I repeat what I have said on other occasions, that this work would have been impossible but for help, friendship, and cooperation offered by many persons. Among them I wish to thank first those who agreed to interviews on one aspect or another of the subject. For helpful discussion or clarification of certain matters I am indebted to Asada Sadao, Michael A. Barnhart, Roger V. Dingman, James W. Morley, and Grace Murakami. Assistance with certain sources was graciously provided by Edward C. Drea, David C. Isby, Mark Jacobsen, David Kahn, and Paul Stares. Thanks are due also to the helpful librarians and other staff of the Library of Congress, Columbia University libraries, New York Public Library, Martin Luther King Library, and Wheaton Regional Library of Montgomery County.

Special thanks are due John E. Taylor, Judy Thorne, and Richard von Doenhoff at the National Archives. Elizabeth Mays of the Navy Department Library, Linda O'Doughda of the U.S. Naval Institute, and Edward Finney, Jr., of the Naval Historical Center all provided key assistance. At the Naval Operational Archives I am indebted to Michael Walker in particular, as well as to John Hodges, Kathleen Lloyd, and Gina Akers. At the Franklin D. Roosevelt Library, National Archives and Records Administration (NARA), I wish to thank Susan Y. Elter, John C. Ferris, and Robert Parks. The Center for Cryptologic History of the National Security Agency also deserves thanks. Other persons who gave generous help and assistance include Larry Bowers, Lenny Glynn, Abbot and William Kominers, and Scott Wallace.

For his fine map work I am again indebted to Kevin Zucker, who makes it look so easy.

I also want to take this opportunity to say a special word about a fine man, W.T.R. Fox, who passed away as I was setting out on this project. At the beginning of the war that is the subject of this book, Bill Fox was a member of a special seminar at Princeton held by Edward Mead Earle that produced a study on makers of modern strategy which was famous in its time. While the book's contribution on the Japanese Navy proved rather badly dated, overall it was a landmark advancing the notion that strategy could be studied, put under a microscope, made a subject of analysis. At the end of World War II Fox penned an essay for Bernard Brodie's pathbreaking atomic-bomb study, *The Absolute Weapon*. It was Fox who coined the term "superpower." In Australia and at Yale, Columbia, and elsewhere, for four decades after World War II Fox taught generations of neophyte strategic thinkers that contributing to understanding requires more than just research. I owe him a special debt. We are all of us worse off for having lost Bill Fox.

These people, individually and together, are responsible for much of what is good about this book. I alone contributed its errors and omissions.

—John Prados
Washington, D.C.
December 29, 1992

# PART I

## SAILORS,

## SPIES,

## AND

## STRATEGIES

**M**OST CLOCKS STOPPED AT PRECISELY 11:59 A.M. A FEW, BETTER ABLE TO WITHSTAND shock, carried on for minutes or hours or until they wound down. People around Tokyo had not much time for their clocks that day, that disastrous Saturday, September 1, 1923. The nightmare began with barely noticeable tremors, which built to such a degree that survivors swore the land had swayed like the sea. Seismic instruments at the Imperial University recorded shocks so powerful they went right off the top end of the scale. The earthquake's epicenter was found to lie in the extinct volcano Mount Fuji, west of Tokyo.

Although the earthquake ended within minutes, its impact was devastating and its effects endured much longer. Streets, roads, and railroad lines were severed; indeed, hundreds of people had been injured or killed in the collapse of two railroad stations. Water mains broke. Hardest hit were Tokyo and Yokohama, but towns throughout the surrounding Kanto Plain shared in disaster. Because of the time of day at which the earthquake struck, many families had been cooking their midday meals. Conflagration spread quickly through both Tokyo and Yokohama as highly flammable houses, built of wood and paper, collapsed onto overturned stoves and open cooking fires. With water and electricity disrupted, firefighters were helpless even to communicate the extent of the danger. Before the fires burned out there were 140,000 dead, a half-million homes destroyed, countless Japanese left destitute. At ¥3 billion, the estimated value of damage exceeded the combined total of Japan's specie reserves, its foreign investments, and the money the nation had spent in all World War I. Two thirds of Tokyo and over three quarters of Yokohama were destroyed.

One of the more ghastly scenes occurred at Yokosuka Naval Base, a major Imperial Navy facility near Yokohama. There tanks ruptured, sending stockpiled oil into Tokyo Bay where it caught fire, burning Japanese who thought they had escaped by taking to the sea. Some 100,000 tons of oil were lost in the earthquake. The quake also smashed the 40,000-ton Imperial Navy ship *Amagi*, which had been under construction for almost three years. *Amagi* began as a battleship but was being converted to an aircraft carrier. Her hull was thrown into the air, then slammed into the ground like a baseball bat after a missed third pitch. (Her keel and plates strained, the *Amagi* would be scrapped.) In Yokohama and Tokyo several merchant vessels were actually washed up onto dry land.

Not far away from the big Japanese naval base stood Yokohama's commercial piers. A young American naval officer named Ellis M. Zacharias, in Japan to learn the language, had come that morning to see off friends leaving for home aboard the liner *Empress of Australia*. Zacharias appreciated the feverish activity as the ship prepared for departure and, having already made a quick trip to Tokyo that morning to pick up his paycheck, was ready to join the festive revelers on the dock. Streamers waved in the breeze on the liner's shrouds; there were smiles and much shouting and waving. Suddenly all frivolity disappeared. The pier, a huge thing—a thousand feet long and quite wide—made of reinforced concrete, shook uncontrollably. No one could stand. Before Zacharias could escape from the dock came a second shock. By then his view of the city beyond had already become obscured by a wall of gray dust in the sky; Zacharias realized the loud roar he heard was the city of Yokohama collapsing. Billowing smoke revealed ruins already afire.

The American officer used his head, then did what many thoughtful people did that day. First Zacharias leaped from the pier into Yokohama harbor; then he scrambled aboard a sampan, using which he and others began rescuing frightened survivors. Heat and gale-force winds whipped up by the firestorm hindered rescue work, forcing a halt for a time, but soon the desperate deliverers again bent to their task. Zacharias noticed that the foreigners among the crowd seemed to regain their senses first, spearheading emergency crews, while many Japanese appeared incapable of grasping their situation and responding appropriately. That Japanese did not respond was a wild exaggeration, of course—there were only about 5,000 foreign residents among the 350,000 who lived in Yokohama and just 3,000 among the much larger population of Tokyo. Foreigners might have reacted more quickly, but there was no way they could have outworked Japanese in relief efforts. Nevertheless the perception that foreigners formed the backbone of response to the earthquake would be widespread among Ellis Zacharias's colleagues.

One colleague, one of Zacharias's first friends in Japan, was American army officer Sidney F. Mashbir. That morning Mashbir happened to be at the seaside resort of Oiso, where it was his custom to go each weekend for the fine swimming with which he complemented the judo he did for exercise. Mashbir's experience proved very similar to Zacharias's: He effectively took charge of rescue activities in Oiso. More than 60 percent of the town's inhabitants died in the tragedy. Not until the fifth day, Mashbir recalled, did he even discover, from survivors, that the disaster reached farther than the town in which he then found himself.

All over Japan, American officers sprang to do what they could for others around them. One naval officer, a former captain of the Annapolis water polo team, was sitting in the barber's chair at Yokohama's Grand Hotel when the fateful moment came. The earthquake shook him out of his chair. At some point during the disaster he was told of a woman upstairs trapped under a bathtub; people wanted her put out of her misery before the fires got to her. The American raced to the woman, pulled her naked from the bathtub (unfortunately her leg broke as she came free), and got out of the hotel. The officer raced across the bund, or waterfront, where the hotel stood, and jumped into the harbor with the woman rescued from her bath. He won a medal for swimming her out to the French liner *André le Bon*. There were many like stories that day.

From Washington came expressions of sympathy on the part of President Calvin Coolidge, who simultaneously ordered the U.S. Asiatic Squadron, then near Port Arthur on the Chinese coast, to render assistance. Within a couple of days the armored cruiser *Huron* with a few destroyers was on the scene. Arthur H. McCollum, a young officer in Japan for language training, recalled that when Japanese saw the American warships their first reaction had been to open fire. An Imperial Navy rear admiral who had just steamed into Yokohama aboard the light cruiser *Tama* understood the delicate situation and convinced his countrymen to permit the Americans to help.

Days stretched into weeks as the rescue work went on. McCollum became a liaison between the fleet at Yokohama and the ambassador, who moved a rump diplomatic team into a small suite at the Tokyo Imperial Hotel, a Frank Lloyd Wright creation that had been one of the few buildings to withstand the earthquake perfectly. With roads and railroads completely destroyed, the short round-trip that had taken Ellis Zacharias half a morning on September 1 became an ordeal of several days for McCollum each time he made the journey. Japanese suspicions remained a major stumbling block. Each of the seventeen American military or naval officers in Japan at the instant of the tragedy encountered such suspicions. At Yokohama, where the American Navy set up a field hospital and then, realizing that all the water mains had been destroyed, had to ask leave to drive new pipes into the city reservoir, the mask of courtesy almost fell off. Dark ruminations were heard about foreigners poisoning the water, but permission would finally be given. The American humanitarian assistance proved entirely inoffensive.

Though one may doubt the objectivity of American reminiscences of the Tokyo earthquake, there are plentiful data to suggest, first, that the relationship of the sides was truly as delicate as it seemed; and second, that despite the racial stereotypes, Americans and Japanese were capable of close cooperation and effective action. It is an irony of the earthquake experience, however, that many of the same Americans so intimately laboring alongside the Japanese in 1923 would, two decades later, be at the center of American efforts to frustrate them. Many of these men were Japanese-language officers, men quite consciously groomed by the U.S. military to be experts on Japan.

# "Your Message, Affirmative"

FRED ROGERS SAT, ANNOYED, AT THE FOOT OF THE TABLE. LUNCH HAD NOT BEEN SERVED and, as mess treasurer for officers of the U.S. battleship *Virginia*, Rogers was responsible. Rogers called the steward and addressed him in a foreign tongue, demanding that the meal be produced. The steward happened to be a Japanese national, the language of their conversation Japanese. Their exchange was possible only because Lieutenant Fred F. Rogers was a Japanese-language officer, the only one in the whole U.S. Navy that fall of 1913. At one time there had been another officer fluent in Japanese but that man had resigned, and the Navy had not seen fit to replace him.

Witness to the exchange in the *Virginia* wardroom was Ellis Zacharias, then a twenty-three-year-old ensign on his first extended-duty assignment. Fascinated with the idea of learning Japanese, and with the whole concept of a language officer, Zacharias became close to Rogers, thriving on his tales of life in Japan and of the difficulty of mastering the language.

In 1917 Zacharias moved on to the engineering department of a survey ship, and in World War I he served as engineering officer of a light cruiser, then as gunnery officer of a bigger cruiser in the Atlantic. After the war Zacharias taught engineering at Annapolis; he accompanied the midshipmen on their summer cruise, which had reached Honolulu when Zach, as he was called, received a cable that changed his life.

Long before, Zach had asked Fred Rogers how to go about becoming a Japanese-language officer. The word had been that there was no chance; the Navy had no intention of expanding its cadre of Japanese linguists. Now, in 1920, the Navy planned to send two new men to Japan for language training—and Rogers was in Washington, on the Japan desk of the Office of Naval Intelligence, which made the personnel selections. Commander Rogers's cable to Zacharias asked if he was still interested in going to Japan as a language officer.

"Your message, affirmative," Ellis Zacharias replied.

So began an oriental adventure for the thirty-year-old Floridian Zacharias, an experience repeated by sixty-five other young Americans over the next two decades. Officially the language officers were assigned to the naval attaché's office at the U.S. embassy, but except in special instances like that of the Tokyo earthquake, their duty focused simply upon learning Japanese. Zacharias himself rose to become deputy director of naval intelligence and it was he, under the press of war requirements, who established a regular routine for the language officers. During those earlier years things were very much more catch-as-catch-can.

The informality of the programs did not prevent learning, however. The accounts of Zacharias himself and other early language officers such as Arthur McCollum, Henri Smith-Hutton, and William J. Sebald describe a remarkably similar experience. Many roomed in the same houses, used the same teachers, followed the same program. Periodically they submitted to language examinations given by State Department officials. Through much of the interwar period the diplomat administering the tests was Eugene H. Dooman, who by 1941 had risen to embassy counselor, a rank that made him one of the most senior American officials dealing with Far Eastern affairs.

In the beginning there were very few students. Zacharias and Hartwell C. Davis became the first of the new breed. Until 1927 the Navy sent over one more man each year; then it assigned three language officers annually. Gradually the program evolved into a three-year course with examinations every six months. The slow pace of assignments was partly accounted for by the lack of need for numbers of Japanese linguists during the early years, but also by the Navy's limited budgets and difficulty finding good candidates. By 1927 policy was to have some officers in training at all times. The pace increased with the perception of a Far Eastern crisis after the Manchurian Incident of 1931, and 1932–1935 became the peak for language-officer assignments, although as many as eight men in various stages of learning would be sent home when hostilities clearly impended.

"Quaint" might be the best adjective for the life of officers in the early language program. Bill Sebald, for example, got interested in becoming a Japanese linguist while serving aboard the battleship *Texas* at Guantánamo Bay, where he met Ellis Zacharias and felt the pull of foreign places. A friend at ONI put in a good word, and Sebald got orders to Japan in the summer of 1925. He roomed with three other linguists in a house in Karuizawa. David Wells Roberts, whose mother had gone to Japan with him and kept up the house at Karuizawa, helped show Sebald around. The house was rented from Dr. Benninghoff, a missionary teacher at Waseda University. Arthur McCollum ended up marrying Benninghoff's daughter; both had been born in Japan. Sebald met his future wife in Japan too. Officers would arrive in the country, be presented to Japanese officials in dress uniform with cocked hats—the naval equivalent of tie and tails—then venture all over the country, surfacing occasionally for a diplomatic function or a work assignment. One student who arrived in 1926 was Henri ("Hank") Smith-Hutton, whose rapid progress astounded Dooman and others. Sebald, Smith-Hutton, and McCollum, who roomed for a time with Eugene Dooman, have all left oral histories describing their training.

Each officer had a fund from which he employed tutors, usually two, and bought texts. The most useful Japanese grammars were one in English by a German named Lange, and another by the Englishman Basil Hall Chamberlain, professor of philosophy at Imperial University. Most popular tutor was a Professor Naganuma who, Sebald tells us, preferred the "direct" method, in which students memorized so-called "type" sentences. Naganuma illustrated his points by repeating the sentences and he and the students, working two hours a day at their homes, would sometimes go over the same ones for days on end. Naganuma would begin with conversation, gradually ease the language students into grammar, and start them reading the katakana and hiragana written characters.* Written Japanese using the *romaji* system with Western-style roman letters would be introduced only after the students were familiar with the native Japanese styles. Professor Naganuma's methods proved so successful that they were copied by Berlitz, and he was in such demand that he was obliged to hire several assistants. Naganuma ended up teaching Army language officers and diplomats too, and worked for the Americans right through 1941. After the war he opened

---

*Katakana and hiragana are both syllabic forms of writing developed in the ninth century to simplify written Japanese, which in its classical form used ideographs called kanji that were borrowed from the Chinese system of writing. In 1946 the Japanese government issued an official list that accepted for standard use some 1,850 kanji (the number is even greater today). Katakana and hiragana each reduce these kanji to more acceptable numbers of characters (currently both use forty-eight), with the former, the most abbreviated and simplified form, typically used to write foreign words. Hiragana, more cursive, is more directly related to the Chinese, and would be used for native Japanese words and concepts. This distinction would be academic except for naval radio communications, which require standardized language to simplify transmission, and for intelligence, which obviously requires translation in order to draw the meaning from intercepted or captured materials. The terms are explained here since points pertinent to translation may arise at several places in this narrative. The Imperial Navy prior to and during World War II developed a form of Morse code which used a syllabary of seventy-three kana, each with one of two suffixes that might alter its meaning.

a language school for Americans from the occupation forces. Naganuma died in 1973, still revered by many former students.

There were several teachers in addition to Naganuma. William Sebald recalls as many as six Japanese who made their living by teaching for the United States Navy. At times Sebald worked with three tutors at once, though he felt that two was an ideal number and one instructor, if good, could be ample. Sebald worked on his Japanese six days a week and thought he was doing well learning as many as ten written characters in a day. He and the other students had allowances of $50 a month to pay their tutors.

In addition to learning the language, indeed precisely because they were learning it, the students received occasional assignments from the American naval attaché at the embassy. One early job was to translate navigational instructions in the *Japan Pilot*, a project undertaken by Bill Sebald and Hank Smith-Hutton. Another typical work assignment, handed out in March 1927, called for papers reviewing evidence on various subjects. That time Sebald was to study the Japanese shipbuilding industry, and Smith-Hutton the chemical industry; Franz B. Melandy was to compare the gun power of the U.S. and Japanese battle fleets, and David Roberts to review the Japanese steel industry. The officers worked from naval attaché files, military attaché reports, trade journals, Japanese government releases, consulate-general files, and conversations with knowledgeable individuals. These sources, in fact, were the basic stock-in-trade for the naval attachés on all subjects all the time.

The essential value of the language-officer program was to provide both naval attachés and the Office of Naval Intelligence with a pool of trained linguists who could use original source materials in a difficult language. As naval officers these men knew the technical meanings and importance of things; as linguists they learned of corresponding things Japanese. Washington never imagined how important its language-officer program would turn out to be.

It should not be surprising that in the early 1920s the United States saw only limited need for Japanese-language officers. In the late twentieth century it is difficult to recollect the mood of that era; almost no one is now left who was a direct observer; the events of subsequent years have crowded in to such an extent that those days seem shrouded in the mists of time. To the degree that we recall anything, it is the social history of the 1920s that commands attention—the "Roaring Twenties," a brassy, beaming era when anything seemed possible and everything appeared to be in place. In fact, international relations followed broader trends, and the world, which had just put the global 1914–1918 war behind it, dared to dream of universal peace. In international relations the 1920s became the decade of accommodation, of the League of Nations, of the Kellogg-Briand Pact outlawing war; the newsreel films with their jerky footage captured the images of diplomats shaking hands over the latest diplomatic agreement. Above all the 1920s were the age of naval arms control, and that fact was of specific importance to both the United States and Japan.

In the period prior to World War I there had been competition in naval armaments as Great Powers each strove to acquire the strongest, most technologically advanced battle fleet. So fierce became competition for navies that people spoke of a "race." The experience brought to language the terms "naval race" and "arms race." The Anglo-German race to build dreadnought battleships is the best-remembered aspect of this competition, but France, Italy, the United States, and Japan were also participants. After the war, when Germany no longer figured as a significant naval power, the stage seemed set for a race between the United States and Great Britain, while Japan also engaged in a naval building program that put it in a strong third-place position. Not only was this competition for armaments costly, but analysts increasingly agreed that the Anglo-German naval race had figured as one of the direct causes of World War I. It seemed worthwhile to head off similar postwar competition.

Complex political factors also helped create conditions for accommodation. Most important was the revulsion everywhere after the incredible carnage of World War I. Many felt it necessary to avoid future war at all costs, and if naval racing was leading to war, then such competition had to be stopped. In the United States the administration of Warren G. Harding found it politically expedient to host a grand negotiation, capitalizing on the rise of isolationist sentiment in this country. There were also outstanding differences with Japan over, for example, Japanese encroachments in China during the war years, which had created a perceived threat to the American policy of an "Open Door" in China. Political leaders in Japan saw a grand accommodation in the Pacific, which included naval arms limits, as a way to restrain the political power and continental ambitions of the Japanese Army. Japanese Navy commanders felt naval limits might be acceptable to prevent the Army from increasing its influence. In Britain political factors also applied. In all three countries many considered the cost of a naval arms race prohibitive; this created powerful inducements to accommodation.

As a result of these varied pressures, in the summer of 1921 the United States proposed an international conference in Washington to consider arms limitations plus Far Eastern issues. Following some delay the grand negotiation opened in November. On the second day of the conference American secretary of state Charles Evans Hughes made public a plan that became the basis for agreement. The plan acquired immense popularity because it provided for wholesale scrapping of major warships: battleships, considered the most important combatant vessels, or "capital ships," of that day. As finally agreed upon, the "battleship burning" encompassed some sixty-eight warships aggregating 1,861,643 tons.

The American proposal also introduced the concept of naval "ratios," by which the tonnage of each naval power's capital ships would be set at a fixed proportion of the tonnage of the strongest ones'. There would be specific rules governing when ships could be replaced and what characteristics new battleships could have.

The powers clearly anticipated a proposal embodying some of these elements. In Tokyo, for example, authorities delayed accepting their invitation to the Washington conference while an Imperial Navy expert group compiled technical studies comparing aggregate tonnage of Japanese warships in service and building with those other navies had or planned. In 1907 the Japanese Navy designated the United States its hypothetical enemy for budget purposes. From that time Japanese naval thinking considered that the fleet needed to equal 70 percent of the U.S. Navy to be adequate for national security. But the expert group formed to consider arms limits in advance of the Washington Arms Limitation Conference discovered that the Imperial Navy had never attained that strength. The figures showed that at the end of 1921 Japanese tonnage would be just 52 percent of American. By 1925, when the Americans completed a massive building program, Japan would have increased its naval tonnage only slightly. In 1927, when the Imperial Navy finished building its own program of eight battleships and eight battle cruisers, the fleet would still aggregate 200,000 tons less than the American.

Thus technical studies in Tokyo suggested that Japan could not meet its minimum standard for national security against the United States, much less build a fleet equal to the American. That realization implied a need to prevent the United States from completing its own program. Far from a luxury, naval arms limitation suddenly seemed imperative. Similar calculations were made in Washington and in London.

In his speech to assembled delegates at the Washington Arms Limitation Conference, Secretary of State Hughes set down quotas the powers might be allowed: For every five British battleships there could be five American and three Japanese—or, stated as a ratio, 5:5:3. The Japanese held out for their 70 percent formula, which meant a ratio of 5:5:3.5, usually rendered as 10:10:7. Western powers resisted this concession.

About two weeks into the conference the Americans enjoyed a demonstration of good intelligence work. It happened that the War Department had a small codebreaking unit under Herbert O. Yardley, which had labored on the Japanese codes for a long time. By the summer of 1921 Yardley's so-called Black Chamber had mastered the Japanese diplomatic code and was reading Tokyo's communications with its Washington embassy. During the conference the Black Chamber read the Japanese cables instructing its delegation. On November 28 Tokyo informed delegates that the Foreign Ministry agreed with their advice to avoid any open break with the British and Americans on naval limits even if this meant making concessions on strength. Yardley's Black Chamber decoded this cable, which revealed for the first time that Tokyo might abandon its insistence on a 10:7 ratio. The message mentioned ratios of 10:6.5 and 10:6 as possible fallback positions, the latter in conjunction with agreement not to fortify islands in the Pacific Ocean and to maintain the status quo in other respects.

There would be long negotiations before details were arranged, but the basic compromise that created the Washington treaty system was prefigured in that cable. The Japanese insisted on some changes, such as substituting the battleship *Mutsu,* completed and commissioned during the conference and partly paid for by fund-raising among Japanese schoolchildren, for another vessel Japan was supposed to retain under the agreement. Japan opposed the British desire to outlaw submarines in the agreement, while several powers got the British to give up their effort to restrict battleships to no more than 30,000 tons. The final naval treaty, signed in Washington on February 6, 1922, permitted battleships to be replaced after twenty years, replacement vessels to be not over 35,000 tons' displacement and to carry no guns of larger than 16-inch caliber. There was also a Four Power Treaty, signed December 13, 1921, intended to preserve peace in the Pacific, and a Nine Power Treaty, also signed in February 1922, concerning extraterritorial rights and duties in China.

By February, in support of the U.S. negotiators at the conference, Herbert Yardley's Black Chamber deciphered more than 5,000 foreign communications. Yardley and most of his people were wrecks from nervous exhaustion. The boss took to bed and was then ordered to Arizona by anxious doctors. In June, when Yardley returned to Washington, it seemed a new world, one in which naval arms competition had been banished and the Pacific subjected to a security regime. Small wonder the Navy did not see great need for Japanese-language officers.

Unfortunately, the seeds that led to a far different situation were already in the wind. One Japanese concern not dealt with at the conference had been desire to redress discrimination in America against Japanese citizens and persons of Japanese descent. Not only were no measures taken to address these concerns, but court cases in the mid-1920s and an immigration law Congress passed in 1924 greatly inflamed the situation. California discrimination laws were held constitutional, Japanese nationals were denied American citizenship. These developments confirmed Japanese fears that their country was not going to be accepted into the club of developed nations.

Narrow military considerations added to prospects for rising tension.

Regardless of Japan's lack of resources, money, and shipbuilding capacity to compete in a naval race, many Imperial Navy officers considered agreement on a 5:5:3 ratio an excessive, even unpatriotic act. Nor was this feeling confined to the officer corps; a hint of the state of opinion among Japanese seamen lies in the sudden popularity of a brand of cigarettes called "5:5:5," the name of which was held to signify the yearning not just for a higher relative ratio but for full equality. More seriously, Admiral Kato Kanji, chief of the naval expert group at the Washington Conference, a man who had argued *against* defining Japanese security in terms of any particular ratio, returned from Washington to voice strong complaints. Around Kato coalesced a cohort of like-minded officers eventually called the fleet faction. Those advocating arms limitation became known as the treaty faction. This cleavage within the officer corps became a central feature of Japanese naval politics for the next two decades.

Naval difficulties became apparent as a result of new construction of warships not limited, or only minimally limited, by the Washington treaty. Aircraft carriers fell in this category, as did a whole new class of ship, the "treaty cruiser," later called a heavy cruiser because it was bigger than conventional (soon called light) cruisers and mounted heavier guns (typically 8-inch guns instead of the 6-inchers common to light cruisers). Treaty cruisers were only restricted as to size. Aircraft carriers had size restrictions and tonnage limits, but few had previously been built and more could be. Probably as a sop to the fleet faction, in mid-1922 Japan announced a new building effort in the heavy-cruiser class. Britain and the U.S. initiated heavy-cruiser programs by the end of 1924. A brand-new naval race suddenly loomed.

Desultory negotiations on the cruiser question took place at Geneva under League of Nations auspices in 1925 and 1927. These brought no agreement, though they did reveal the basic positions of the powers. Japan seemed most flexible, having no objection to extending the ratio system to cruisers so long as the specific ratio would be 10:10:7. The British opposed ratios this time, insisting that they needed a very large number of cruisers for trade protection. The Americans insisted upon both the ratio—the same ratio as in the Washington treaty—and a much smaller total tonnage in cruisers than the British desired. The impasse endured into 1930, when another naval conference occurred in London.

At the London Conference, agreement proved surprisingly easy, even though in the interim the Japanese position had solidified behind a 10:10:7 ratio. The chief Japanese technical expert, Rear Admiral Yamamoto Isoroku, made it quite clear that his government would be unable to ratify any agreement providing less than the stipulated ratio. British and American desire for an agreement made the decisive difference. The British accepted a smaller number of ships than they claimed were necessary. The

Americans agreed to delay building new heavy cruisers, so the Japanese would secure an *effective* 10:7 ratio if they agreed to the official 5:5:3 ratio written into the treaty. With a term of five years, the London Naval Treaty also extended until 1935 the freeze on battleship construction begun by the Washington agreement.

Where the 1920s had been a decade of accommodation, however, the thirties would be one of confrontation. Early hints of this trend appeared as soon as the Japanese government attempted to ratify the London Treaty. The fleet faction and its parliamentary allies argued vociferously against this extension of treaty ratios to the cruiser classes. In the midst of the political debate, the Japanese Army embarked on an adventure of its own in China, beginning with the 1931 takeover of Manchuria. Extremists inspired by the Army's actions assassinated the Japanese prime minister when Tokyo opposed what had been done in Manchuria.

Japan did ratify the London Treaty, but at exorbitant political cost. Early in the decade it thus became apparent that Japanese adherence to further arms agreements could not be taken for granted, while the Japanese military began demonstrating ambitions in Asia that could threaten peace. At the same time the peculiarities of the Japanese constitution, under which only a military officer on active duty was permitted to be war or navy minister, conferred additional power on the armed services, enabling them to bring down any cabinet with which they disagreed. This put the armed services in a unique position to drive government policy. With the Army and Navy co-equal but not cooperative partners, each would typically permit the other a free hand in matters of particular interest.

Any remaining goodwill the West might have toward their nation, the Japanese squandered through alliance with fascism in Europe. In November 1936 Japan joined Germany in the Anti-Comintern Pact, a treaty of cooperation ostensibly aimed at communism but with overtones of a fascist alliance. The five-year treaty was extended a further five years in November 1941, by then overshadowed by the Tripartite Pact, an extension of the Italo-German "Pact of Steel," or Axis. The Japanese entered into the Tripartite Pact in November 1940; the move seemed a clear stepping-stone to war. The Imperial Navy was uncertain about the pact, and Navy opposition prevented Japan's joining for some time, but when anti-Pact navy minister Admiral Yoshida Zengo suffered a heart attack and stepped aside in September 1940, the Navy's internal divisions were papered over. Although on paper the Tripartite Pact remained a defensive alliance, not requiring Japan to attack the West, it formally aligned the Japanese with the Axis powers, which were already at war in Europe.

The Japanese Army proved most enthusiastic regarding the Tripartite Pact. Army strategists saw it as a free hand to pursue the China Incident. This followed agitation to occupy northern French Indochina, in September

1940, and led to Japanese pressure on Great Britain to halt the flow of military supplies to China through Burma. Both moves became further stepping-stones toward war. The final break, in July 1941, came when the Japanese went ahead to occupy the southern portion of Indochina. The United States and the Netherlands East Indies (today Indonesia) retaliated by cutting off oil sales to Japan. Without oil the Japanese economy was condemned to ruin, so Japanese leaders faced a choice for war as the ultimate way to seize the oil they needed.

These moves played out against a backdrop of interservice rivalries between the Japanese armed forces. The Army's traditional enemy had been Russia, so the Army favored a "Strike North" policy of continental expansion. The Imperial Navy sought to avoid war by advocating a "Strike South" policy but had only vague notions about how this might be accomplished without resort to hostilities. Both services rationalized events without thought to longer-term implications. Japan slid down the slope toward war. Intrigues by middle-level staffs, who frequently confronted their superiors with a choice between supporting an outrageous gambit or losing face, further impelled the leaders. There were also extremists, especially on the political right; these had already launched one abortive military coup, in February 1936, and over the decade had murdered so many politicians and senior officers that one Western observer described the Japanese political system as "government by assassination." Behind all the surface maneuvers now lurked real fear that making concessions could also mean losing one's life. Under the circumstances, changing Japan's political course would have amounted practically to a superhuman deed.

As the resentments of the 1920s and antagonisms of the 1930s propelled the powers toward war in the Pacific it was the task of intelligence organizations on both sides of that great ocean to interpret events and keep track of the military and naval developments of the potential adversaries. The language officers were necessary adjuncts to the eyes and ears of this prewar intelligence system, who were the naval attachés. With language officers to interpret the other culture and society, the naval attachés (and military attachés for land forces) represented the front line in information-gathering efforts.

SINCE REGULAR EXCHANGE OF AMBASSADORS BEGAN, IN RENAISSANCE ITALY, ONE OF THE main fears of host countries has always been that envoys would be spies in their midst. To a degree that fear is well-founded. An important aspect of an ambassador's job is to observe and report all kinds of conditions in the host country. Diplomatic spying is tolerated because other advantages accruing from the presence of envoys are considered more important. Nations deem it so advantageous, in fact, that international custom grew to include specialized representatives called attachés, who ranked below the ambassador. Armed services acquired direct representation through military and naval attachés abroad. These diplomats in uniform were active officers but carried diplomatic passports, attended diplomatic receptions and functions, and handled occasional diplomatic communications or other business. Attachés made official contacts between their armies or navies and those of the host countries. Even more so than diplomats, however, military and naval attachés are sanctioned spies.

The naval attachés in Tokyo before World War II were no exception. The American ones, from Captain Edward H. Watson just after World War I, to Commander Henri Smith-Hutton just before Pearl Harbor, worked hard to observe the Imperial Japanese Navy. Japan had actually been the leading collection target for the Office of Naval Intelligence (ONI) since after the Russo-Japanese War of 1904–1905. It was ONI that made attaché assignments and supplied attachés with letters of introduction.

Key intelligence questions introduced in the 1920s which endured through the coming of war included the search for evidence that the Japanese might be violating the naval treaties, and the question of Japanese activities in the Mandated Islands, former German possessions in the Pacific, in the Marianas, custody of which had passed to Japan under a League of Nations mandate. The need for such special assignments as finding intelligence on these matters often had to be intuited by the naval attaché from the tone of communications received from ONI; specific requests came rarely, while the attaché's formal task would simply be to assemble materials for the ONI monograph on his country. These ONI monographs were massive compendiums of data, including everything from the most basic information, such as population, names of ports, and the state of land communications, to material on political systems and trends and on military forces. Before assuming his post as attaché an officer would spend weeks with ONI becoming familiar with the files on his host country, the relevant ONI monograph in its current edition, and the equally massive—almost telephone-book size—ONI guide to information collection. The guide assigned special numbers to every category of intelligence so that ONI analysts could easily integrate reports into the monographs.

Much as an ambassador upon arrival presents credentials to the host government's head of state, the naval attaché has an audience with a senior officer. In Tokyo the custom was to meet the navy minister. Those so introduced included not just attachés themselves, who mainly held captain's rank during the interwar period, but also assistant attachés, who were more junior—lieutenant commanders, or even lieutenants. Thus senior Japanese admirals were meeting subordinate officers of far lesser rank, as happened when Yonai Mitsumasa, Japanese navy minister from 1937 to 1939, was introduced to newly arrived assistant attaché for air Stephen Jurika. The American later recalled, "He was not only gracious—remember, I was a lieutenant, junior grade, and he was an admiral—but he considered every American naval officer he came in contact with . . . as a representative of a great country." Admiral Yonai asked indirect but very perceptive questions, and went beyond a simple exchange of pleasantries. Jurika found Yonai an interested interlocutor each of the dozen or so times they came into contact.

The reality that gives meaning to the notion of sanctioned spying lies in the fact that most of the intelligence American attachés got about the Imperial Navy came from the Japanese themselves. A meeting with Admiral Yonai, for example, would become the subject for a report to ONI on the views of the Japanese navy minister. The Americans would ask for and receive tours of Japanese warships, naval bases, naval air stations, and so forth. In a spirit of reciprocity, Japanese attachés in the United States would be accorded the same visiting privileges.

During the heyday of the Washington Treaty system, when Captain Lyman A. Cotten was U.S. naval attaché in Tokyo, the sides also exchanged tours of each other's shipyards. An ideal way to verify that treaty limits were being observed, this was the kind of measure that, had it been taken in the 1908–1911 period, might have helped slow the Anglo-German naval race. Of course, shipyard visits became occasions for all manner of chicanery; on one occasion in the late 1920s, for instance, then–assistant attaché Commander George Courts toured the Kure Naval Shipyard in company with one of the language officers. Courts was received by the dockyard commander, a full admiral, given a long introductory talk in the august presence, and then left with little time to complete his itinerary.

As a general practice the Japanese also did not volunteer information unless Americans asked the right questions. Still, American personnel got to visit all the major Japanese shipyards, including the naval dockyards at Yokosuka and Maizuru, and supplemented their observation by comparing notes with other observers, such as British attachés. Much Japanese dockyard equipment, including locks and heavy-lift cranes, had been imported from British manufacturers. British authorities could therefore supply knowledge of specifications that led directly to an understanding of Japanese shipyard capabilities. Moreover, individuals might have especially useful knowledge. For example in the late 1930s the British attaché's office had an engineering specialist, Commander A. C. Ross, who could reliably estimate the horsepower of a vessel's engines and the volume of space devoted to machinery simply from looking at the ship's propellers.

The real drawback in the treaty system lay not so much in the powers' temptation to cheat but in the treaty's failure to regulate all classes of ships. Thus the 1922 agreement limited battleships but created an incentive for an arms race in "treaty cruisers," vessels displacing up to 10,000 tons with guns of 8-inch caliber. When the 1930 agreement extended treaty ratios to these heavy cruisers, the incentive switched to light-cruiser classes. Both the United States and Japan then designed and built light cruisers with armaments of twelve or fifteen 6-inch guns and displacements up to 10,000 tons. These warships were heavy cruisers in all but name, even throwing broadsides with the weight of a treaty cruiser, simply using smaller guns. Once the treaty had been abrogated, the Japanese abandoned pretense and, when ships of this class were in the yard for other work to improve their stability at sea, replaced the 6-inch guns with weapons of the larger caliber.

Attaché visits to the dockyards grew less frequent as hostility grew and the powers began to press at the constraints in the naval treaties. In the mid-1930s the Americans might have been embarrassed by the disclosure that their *Baltimore*-class "light" cruisers were really heavy ones in disguise, or that the *North Carolina*–class battleships begun about this time might also have questionable aspects from the standpoint of treaty compliance. Naval attaché Captain Harold M. Bemis is said to have been told quietly in about 1938 that the United States would prefer not to give Japanese officers permission to visit American shipyards. Bemis told his successor in Tokyo that the U.S. attaché should *avoid* insisting on yard visits to prevent giving the Japanese any pretext to insist upon reciprocal rights. For its part, the Imperial Navy had designed and begun the huge *Yamato*-class battleships, which far exceeded treaty specifications for size and armament, and were perfectly happy to deny the United States visitation rights.

Although Japan remained a very private and ingrown society, it was not a closed society, a "denied area" in the jargon of intelligence work. The Japanese parliament, or Diet, received budget proposals each year from the Imperial Navy and debated them extensively, including the shipbuilding program. There were official declarations from the Navy, speeches by officers, statements to the press, and an extensive array of special-interest media such as the publications of the Navy League, with such semi-official material as articles and speeches by retired senior officers—for example, Admiral Suetsugu Nobumasa. American attachés could, and did, exploit these sources for intelligence purposes.

Diet debates were reprinted in the official *Tokyo Gazette*, which the U.S. embassy procured routinely. Portions of interest to the naval attaché were translated by one of his employees, a Japanese man named Iwamoto who had graduated from Harvard and married an American woman. Budget data from the *Gazette* became the province of Leonard Wagner, who had gone to Tokyo in 1920 as a career Navy yeoman and was still there two decades later as a Navy civilian employee. These two (with help during the busiest months from language officers) provided the nucleus of a body of data that enabled the U.S. attaché to send Washington a stream of reports with considerable value.

In January 1937, when the Imperial Navy presented the Diet its proposal for a Third Replenishment Program, which authorized the *Yamato*-class battleships, the aircraft carriers *Shokaku* and *Zuikaku*, and sixty-three other ships, the attaché was able to report to Washington within days, outlining the costs of the five-year program (¥86.3 million for dockyard expansion and another ¥837 million for the ships) and analyzing the apparent cost per ton for warships of various classes. Washington also received a summary of all Imperial Navy vessels built, building, or authorized. In mid-February, Admiral Yonai responded to questions in the Diet; within two weeks a translation of the navy minister's remarks was on its way to U.S. Navy headquarters. The dispatch included coverage of Yonai's secret remarks at a February 19 Diet session which leaked to the Japanese newspaper *Miyako Shimbun*. In the latter, Yonai claimed that Japan had had an effective naval ratio against the United States of 10:9 at the time of the Shanghai Incident (1932); this ratio had declined to 10:8 by 1937 and, he estimated, would be less than 10:6 by the end of 1941. The minister saw no reason any longer for Japanese adherence to limits on battleship armaments or size, and declared that progress in the technological development of the airplane had made obsolete the Pacific nonfortification agreement. Yonai's declaration in secret session that "it is the policy of the Navy to maintain an adequate fighting strength in the Western Pacific" seemed quite similar to his public assertion that "Japan's fundamental naval policy . . . [is] the maintenance of the minimum independent naval strength necessary to preserve peace in the Far East."

Just a few days later Captain Bemis informed Washington of a radio speech by Imperial Navy vice minister Admiral Yamamoto Isoroku in which the admiral emphasized that Japan had entered a "treaty-less period" now that "repeated efforts to correct the defects of the treaties [lay] shattered." Yamamoto noted that both the United States and England had added battleships to their building programs, and he implied that Japan could do no less. There were also British and American activities "strengthening advance bases" and creating air bases and air routes "on and around the Pacific."

Yamamoto declared that the expiration of the treaties enabled Japan to "have a navy best suited to her needs and national characteristics." This formulation was remarkably like Yonai's comment in the Diet that "we are free to choose what types of ships we wish to construct," which was followed by his assertion that "it is the policy of the Navy to select those types best suited to Japan's needs." Both officers made veiled references to the inclusion of new battleships in the building program, and possibly to the greatly increased tonnage and armament of the *Yamato*-class vessels.

Naval attaché reporting from Tokyo reflected Japan's effort to minimize the importance of its building program, recording Yamamoto's statement that "Japan has no intention of constructing a navy which will be a menace to other nations." Two months later, in May 1937, the attaché dutifully reported Navy Minister Yonai's written replies to questions posed by *New York Times* correspondent Hugh Byas; these replies included the affirmation that "the Japanese Navy declares without reserve that it contemplates no armament programs whatever that might menace other countries."

The Diet approved the building program. Workers laid the keel for battleship *Yamato* at Kure that November, and for aircraft carrier *Shokaku* at Yokosuka a month later. A second huge battleship, *Musashi*, was begun at the Mitsubishi shipyard in Nagasaki in March 1938, while a keel for carrier *Zuikaku* followed in May at the Kawasaki yard in Kobe. In the interval, worried Japan was about to exceed Washington treaty limits on battleship size, the Western powers delivered a joint démarche demanding data on characteristics of the new ships. The Japanese refused. Naval attaché Bemis reported to ONI the tenor of Japanese press reporting on the joint note.

One means for counteracting the restricted information the Japanese circulated was the so-called Attachés' Club. This was simply the circle of various nations' naval attachés, who would lunch together periodically to trade notes, ask about suspicions, or discuss news and technological developments. French attaché De le Noye, by virtue of having been longest in Tokyo, was doyen of this group in the mid-1930s. It also included British attaché Captain Guy Vivian (who maintained a parallel independent relationship with the Americans) and officers of the Soviet, German, Italian, and Chinese navies. This informal group discussed the new Japanese battleships and reached conclusions Captain Bemis reported in January 1938: "Japan now has under construction two 16-inch battleships of considerably greater tonnage than 35,000 tons and is planning to lay down a third and possibly a fourth." The *Yamato* class eventually comprised four ships, the last two included in the 1939 program.

The range of opinion among the naval attachés regarding the Imperial Navy battleships is worth examining in a little more detail. Bemis's predecessor, Captain Fred F. Rogers, the original Japanese-language officer, had already predicted in 1936 that Japan had designs for warships of 45,000 to 55,000 tons, then that the Imperial Navy would not hesitate to build ships of at least 35,000 tons, finally that Japan would not revert to the Washington restriction on tonnage or its limit for guns. Captain Rogers had also reported secret Diet testimony, from then–Navy Minister Admiral Nagano Osami, that

> as a result of the coming no-treaty period we shall enjoy freedom of action in construction of warships in respect to category, quality and characteristics. With this freedom we may construct those ships particularly adapted for our national requirements, thereby gaining an advantage which obviates the necessity for numerical equality.

In fact the Imperial Navy had put out a request for design of the new battle-ships in 1934 with specifications for a ship mounting 18-inch guns that could steam at about 30 knots. The first plan, in March 1935, proved unacceptable, and twenty-one more followed before Admiral Yonai accepted a final design in March 1937, at roughly the time of his Diet statements already quoted. The actual Japanese design provided for ships of 62,000 tons with nine 18-inch guns and a speed of 27 knots. These were to be the biggest battleships in the world.

Members of the Attachés' Club were largely agreed that the new Japanese ships would exceed treaty limits. The British, Germans, and French all believed the warships would displace 45,000 tons. An article in the Italian newspaper *Giornale d'Italia* (November 7, 1937) had held out for 46,000 tons with twelve 16-inch guns. The Italian attaché, who claimed he had had nothing to do with this article, also felt that the tonnage would be 46,000 and might later increase to 50,000. The Soviet attaché thought the ships would be only 35,000 tons "or slightly larger."

As for armament, the attachés were in entire agreement on 16-inch guns, and almost all said the Japanese ships would have a dozen of them. However, they were aware of Japanese interest in 18-inch guns. An Imperial Navy junior officer unwittingly disclosed the development of such a weapon in early 1937, and it was also generally known that the ships Japan had planned for its 8:8 Program before the naval treaties were to mount this armament. The Soviet attaché placed development of the 18-inch gun at a Japanese research facility in Muroran in February 1937. A year later the Soviets held the opinion that Japan could not produce guns of 18-inch caliber because they lacked lathes large enough to handle them and would have to import such equipment. The Italian attaché reported that the 18-inch gun had failed its tests, blowing out its powder chamber when discharged. In fact, the Japanese were far advanced in their work on the weapons, which, to mislead Western intelligence officers, they referred to as "special-type 16-inch guns." A single one of *Yamato*'s gun turrets would weigh as much as a destroyer.

Aside from the club's exchanges on the new Japanese battleships there were other services members performed for one another. When Commander Henri Smith-Hutton, who had been assistant attaché in the early 1930s, returned in the top position from 1939 to 1941, the Russians asked him to provide them a copy of his weekly translations of navigational data the Japanese regularly published. One of Smith-Hutton's subordinates also gave the Soviets general material on Japanese warships, largely culled from the press, in exchange for intelligence on industrial facilities and military production centers. In addition, the Americans and British had a wide-ranging exchange of intelligence in progress on all subjects.

Such intelligence exchanges were always useful, but in Tokyo they were especially necessary because working conditions were so poor. To start with, the U.S. attaché's office was a small one to cope with the ground it had to cover. In addition to the attaché, there was an assistant, plus the yeoman, Wagner, and the Japanese translator, Iwamoto. There was also a messenger. At first on temporary duty for a special report, but then (from about the mid-1930s) on a regular basis, the office added an assistant attaché for air. Upon his arrival Smith-Hutton found the best reporting in the files of this officer. It happened that the air attaché outranked Smith-Hutton, however, and had to be sent home to prevent seniority problems. Fortunately Lieutenant Stephen Jurika, the replacement, proved a very capable aviation officer and did excellent work in Japan. In the last year or so before the war, the attaché's office received the help of a part-time employee, a woman who divided her time with another embassy office, to complete its complement.

The assistant attachés through the 1930s were consistently among the top Japanese-language officers ONI could find. They included Smith-Hutton, Ethelbert Watts, Franz Melandy, and Daniel McCallum, all of whom would have prominent careers as intelligence officers. With such skilled language officers for assistants, the attachés had the best possible window on Japanese society. Still, the Japanese did not make anything easy. The Americans' last official visit aboard an Imperial Navy warship occurred as far back as April 1934, celebrating the eightieth anniversary of the treaty signed between Japan and the United States as a result of the visit of Commodore Matthew C. Perry. On that occasion Ambassador Joseph C. Grew and his party rode the destroyer *Shimakaze* to the town of Shimoda, where the treaty had been negotiated. Grew witnessed a lantern parade by 20,000 Japanese, but his naval attaché saw nothing very impressive, for the *Shimakaze* was an obsolescent vessel nearing the end of her service life and would later be rerated a mere patrol boat.

An evident token of the Japanese attitude was a vehicle parked outside the American embassy that Western reporters took to calling the "spy wagon." Supposedly broken down, this huge limousine sat across the street so long its tires all went flat. When someone investigated, he found that no engine was under the hood, that the curtains were pulled down in the windows, and that there were several Japanese policemen inside, who jumped out when a reporter one day tried to take pictures of the 1920-vintage automobile. The Japanese had been so hot inside they had stripped to their underwear, but their role was clear from the notebooks they bore. The car sat outside the embassy for almost two years.

Japanese authorities were ultra-sensitive regarding cameras and photography. Reporter James Young was constantly harassed and ultimately arrested, a hostility that escalated, he was convinced, after he printed pictures of Japanese bombers flying over Taiwan that had been given out by official spokesmen.

A case that may be the perfect illustration of Japanese touchiness occurred in Osaka in 1934. There the local branch of the First National City Bank received instructions from its New York head office to obtain photographs of various Osaka companies the bank served, with the intent of illustrating advertisements. The Osaka bank branch forged ahead and began the photo program, which included some buildings so beautiful the staff posed in front of them for formal portraits. Japanese military police became infuriated, confiscated the photographs, and began a campaign to portray First National City Bank as an agent of the U.S. government.

Such were the vagaries of attaché work in Tokyo. Under the circumstances it became quite difficult to judge the veracity of claims, whatever they might be. Who could know, even if given the most accurate information? One officer told Captain Bemis he had "reliable information" the Japanese had begun construction of 50,000-ton capital ships mounting 18-inch guns that had been *successfully* tested at Muroran. Bemis reported to ONI his source had been "a foreign Naval Officer, whose opinions are not valued any too highly." Then there was the very suggestive article published by naval writer Ito Masanori in the January 1936 issue of the magazine *Kaizo*. Ito hypothesized that Japan's new battleships would displace 50,000 tons and have 18-inch guns, and that Japan would build to a strength of twelve battleships, or even sixteen if the British and Americans initiated large programs. When the substance of Ito's article appeared abroad he was summoned to the Navy Ministry and threatened with prosecution for disclosing national secrets. The writer protested, demonstrating that he had given authorities his manuscript and they had approved it. A junior officer in the Navy Ministry press section was dismissed in disgrace.

The details of this incident became known to the American naval attaché. It was the leak of a lifetime, one that said a very great deal about Japanese weapons development. A professional intelligence officer running good agent networks could have had a field day working from an indication like this. Captain Bemis merely reported what he had heard. At the end of his tour Bemis told his successor he had been poorly served in Tokyo and had had no good sources. It might be more accurate to say that the attaché was a poor judge of the sources he did have. Henri Smith-Hutton *was* a professional intelligence officer; it remained to be seen what he could learn in Japan.

# Watching the Japanese

WHERE THE JAPANESE ARMY TENDED TO BE CONSERVATIVE, INGROWN, AND TECHNOLOG-ically hidebound, the Imperial Navy had always been relatively modernist and comparatively internationalist. Though the Navy, crippled by factional struggle, regressed politically between the wars, technologically speaking the Japanese remained attentive to the possibilities and in fact created a supple, sophisticated instrument of war. In many ways the Imperial Navy would be the most advanced fighting force in the Pacific when hostilities began. Actual Japanese achievements stood in marked contrast to the Western image of a poorly trained and ill-equipped adversary. This much is fairly familiar ground. What is startling, even disconcerting, is that American intelligence *knew* of Japanese technological developments, but the image persisted despite that knowledge. This becomes apparent in examining evaluations of the Japanese surface fleet, naval aviation, and certain technical matters such as torpedo design. In each case American intelligence was better than is usually assumed in our histories of the Pacific war.

There is no doubt that tracking the evolution of Japanese naval ship-building was an onerous task. The Japanese were well aware of ways to gain information about naval construction and tried to cover all of them. The most concentrated and detailed source was obviously the presentations the Navy made to the Diet when asking for money to build warships. In 1935 and 1936, before even presenting their construction program, Japanese officers were asking Diet members to help prevent information from becoming public. The data the Imperial Navy presented were deliberately askew—ships were slightly faster, displaced more, and were armed somewhat differently than the Diet was told.

At the shipyards came the true struggle to preserve secrecy. Halting visits by American naval attachés figured only as an initial measure. The Japanese built tall brick walls around the construction ways to block the view at key locations such as Kure, where the *Yamato*'s keel had been laid. At Yokosuka a similar wall completely enclosed the base. To impair visibility from any direction, inside the walls wire and bamboo mesh would be hung from scaffolding used by dockyard workers. Foreigners who took trains on the Tokkaido line, which passed through both Yokohama and Kobe, would be instructed by railroad personnel to pull down their window shades while passing those places, and to keep them down until told otherwise. On one occasion at least, this care extended down to the selection of hotel rooms. When Henri Smith-Hutton and his wife took a vacation on Miyajima, an island near Kure, they were given a room that faced away from the naval base, and an escort of two policemen to boot. There were plenty of obstacles to gathering intelligence on Japanese naval construction.

Nevertheless, with imagination, persistence, and effort, the attachés gained surprising knowledge of Japanese activities. At their embassy office the Americans clipped every article about or photograph of a ship launching, and attended as many of these as they could, taking pictures to supplement those in the media. Whenever naval air attaché Stephen Jurika was assigned to attend one of these events in Kobe he registered at one of two hotels, the German Tor, on a hill overlooking the harbor, or the Oriental, right downtown, where he could get rooms overlooking the Mitsubishi shipyard. Even from inside and far away, a camera with a telephoto lens could get quite reasonable pictures.

The waterside was one of the best angles from which to view the building yards. One time before 1938 a U.S. naval courier on his way home simply hired a boat at Kobe and sailed out into the harbor to have a look at the Kawasaki yard, where the carrier *Zuikaku* was building. Warned by lawyer and former naval officer William J. Sebald that he was taking a big chance, the man went anyway. Similarly, in January 1939 a British assistant attaché returned from a visit to Nagasaki to assure the Americans that Japan had a battleship building on the number two way of the Mitsubishi yard there (he was correct; the ship was *Musashi*). From a boat at dusk the Englishman could see welding lights through the screens; he calculated that the vessel inside had to be more than 720 feet long. He also noted enlargement of the construction building—which, presumably, could have been done only for the purpose of constructing an especially large warship—and saw screening at one end of the number one way, probably for assembly of plates, armor, and armament. The British learned that workmen on the project had been sworn to secrecy and were not being replaced when ill; rather, their jobs were held open while they recovered.

Assistant attaché Stephen Jurika innovated a technique for getting actual photographs of warships under construction at the Mitsubishi yard at Kobe. As a pilot Jurika had to log a certain number of hours in the air every year to maintain his proficiency rating, so the embassy had an arrangement with the Asiatic Fleet whereby air attachés would go to the Philippines several times a year to fly. On these trips Jurika made a point of taking U.S.-flag ships from Kobe—the American President Lines served Japan—both because the captains were reserve officers and because the vessels were U.S. territory and immune to Japan's spy fever. Jurika would identify himself to the captains and ask that as they exited harbor into the Bungo Strait they sail as close to shore as possible. The Mitsubishi yard happened to be located right near the Bungo entrance. Jurika would get a cabin on the port side of the liner; on a tripod a few feet back from the porthole stood his Leica camera with its telephoto lens. For the few moments during which the camera was aligned as the ship steamed past the yard, Jurika would snap as fast as he could wind film. His pictures showed vessels behind netting or fitting out, but were good enough over time to show the progress of construction. Later ONI could go back and calculate just how long it had taken to construct a given warship and could then apply this information to other vessels of the same type or class.

At Sasebo, attaché observers could stay at an inn, perched above the harbor, that would later become famous among American airmen during the Korean War. At Yokohama, Americans who worked for the Standard Oil Company owned houses high on a bluff and let officers come up to watch the harbor. Until forced to leave Japan in 1938, William J. Sebald lived in a house similarly situated above Kobe. He would pass tidbits along to the naval attaché. Mostly Sebald saw freighters and troopships on the China run, but once there was a naval review during which a good portion of the Imperial Navy sailed beneath his window. Not until 1941, when one of Smith-Hutton's officers was detained at Yokosuka, did Japanese authorities act directly against a naval attaché.

Beyond the Japanese media, the Attachés' Club, and direct observation, a further intelligence resource was the most traditional one: espionage. The attaché office had a small fund of perhaps $300 a year for the purchase of information, beyond which special requests had to be made to ONI. Such money sufficed for not much more than covering expenses entailed in operations. Where money was an object, usually the point was entrapment and the scheme had been thought up by the *kempeitai*, the Japanese military police. Ellis Zacharias, George Courts, and Henri Smith-Hutton were all tested this way, and each refused the proferred bargain. Through the club Smith-Hutton, at least, also knew that other nations' attachés had been targets of such intelligence-for-money offers. The only person known to have succumbed had been an Italian air attaché, whom the Japanese exposed in 1938 and expelled from the country.

There was one offer that could have been genuine, whose reality could never be established. A German engineer employed at the Mitsubishi shipyard in Kobe approached Bill Sebald, who contacted the naval attaché, at that time either Fred Rogers or Harold Bemis. The engineer wanted to sell plans for a submarine he said was going to be the biggest in the world. The German wanted big money, too—perhaps $25,000, a huge amount in those days and much more than the attaché had at his disposal. Queries to ONI brought only rejection. Mitsubishi-Kobe in fact built units of two Japanese submarine designs, the *I-16* and *I-9* classes, which with tonnages of 2,200 to 2,400 were far larger than German U-boats and about a third bigger than later U.S. fleet submarines.

Most information the attaché received came gratuitously. Whether it was a revelation dropped during a dinner or casual conversation with Imperial Navy officers, or a fanciful report from some person who claimed to know, a source usually had reasons for the contacts made. Reasons could be as simple as the desire of a Japanese naval officer to brag, or as convoluted as those of a White Russian in Shanghai hoping to encourage war between Japan and the Soviet Union to overthrow Stalin.

One typical case occurred through 1938–1939, during which the U.S. naval attaché had a series of contacts with one or more diplomats representing the puppet government the Japanese had formed in Manchuria and called Manchukuo. Now, these Chinese were ostensibly allied to Japan, but the relationship remained uncomfortable since Japanese ambitions unmistakably clashed with Chinese nationalism. In July 1938 the Chinese diplomat warned of an intentional attack against some ship of the U.S. Asiatic Fleet and of Japanese fishing boats undertaking "naval infiltration" of the Aleutian Islands and the coast of El Salvador. A few months later he volunteered a copy of the closely held trade agreement between Germany and Manchukuo. In February 1939 a Chinese secretary at the Manchukuo embassy supplied an American details of his visit to the naval yard at Yokosuka (where the aircraft carrier *Shokaku* was then under construction) and the naval air station at Tachikawa, plus information on raw materials and on German-Japanese exchanges regarding relations with the Soviet Union. At one point the naval attaché reported to ONI that the source "has prejudiced his value somewhat in the eyes of this office" by discussing the information given with many other people, fortunately all of them American.

While most intelligence gained in this fashion seemed of dubious authenticity, it was the job of the attaché to be open to possibilities. Fred Rogers added a dining room to the Tokyo house used by the naval attaché, precisely to be able to entertain more. Henri Smith-Hutton used to tell subordinates that it was time for them to bring around some Japanese friends. Smith-Hutton did substantial entertaining on his own, including of Imperial Navy officers, and was considered a friend of Admiral Nomura Kichisaburo. Some years before, when Captain Joseph V. Ogan had been attaché, the Americans got the only visit recorded to the Japanese naval academy at Etajima as a result of his entertainment of Admiral Nagano Osami, who was then superintendent there.

Probably the most valuable espionage contact the Americans made in prewar Japan came in 1940, coincidentally as a result of tennis. Henri Smith-Hutton used to play almost daily at the Tokyo Tennis Club, just three blocks from the U.S. embassy. The club brought together Japanese and Westerners, with half its memberships reserved for each group, and stiff competition among Japanese to fill their membership list. The competitive spirit extended to matches with other clubs; one day early in 1940 came a tournament with a team from Yokohama, followed by a dinner at which Smith-Hutton sat next to a young Japanese who impressed him as personable and intelligent. Occasionally after that the youth appeared at the Tokyo club by invitation of one member or another, until one summer day Smith-Hutton found him at the club without a partner and played with him.

That evening they had dinner and then strolled home together, as both were going to nearby places. Suddenly the youth asked the American attaché if he would be interested in learning more about the Japanese Navy. Smith-Hutton expressed interest, but also doubt, and questioned the youth's motive. The man explained that he was not Japanese at all, but Chinese, raised by an uncle after his parents died in the great earthquake. He had taken a Japanese name, like his uncle, and no one knew him as anything but Japanese. Now he was a medical student and member of a club that arranged visits to Imperial Navy bases and ships. With Japan at war in China the youth wanted to do everything he could.

As a result of this contact the U.S. naval attaché received information regarding Imperial Navy aircraft carriers, although nothing very startling, and heavy cruisers. In the latter case the spy reported after a visit aboard a *Mogami*-class cruiser that the ship's armament consisted of 8-inch guns, two per turret, in five turrets. That year's edition of *Jane's Fighting Ships* showed the *Mogami* armed with 6-inch weapons only, in five triple turrets. Similarly, professional journals such as the *U.S. Naval Institute Proceedings* agreed in commentaries on the Japanese fleet that *Mogami*-class ships carried 6-inch armament and even debated whether three of these weapons had been removed to improve the vessels' seaworthiness. In fact the 6-inch gun turrets had been removed in 1939 and replaced by 8-inch weapons. Admiral Hiraga Yuzuru, who had designed the *Yamato*-class battleships, affirmed publicly (in an interview with the *Asahi Shimbun* newspaper chain) that *Mogami* had the bigger guns. Smith-Hutton reported both items from Tokyo. In Washington the reaction at the Navy's Bureau of Ordnance was that it did not seem possible for the Japanese to put 8-inch guns on a ship designed for smaller weapons.

Intelligence reported by the U.S. attaché in Tokyo during 1940 and 1941 featured a considerable body of material on the Japanese merchant marine, shipping conditions, naval personnel strength, biographies of senior officers, and Japanese reactions to American military measures. In January 1940 the attaché sent an analysis that showed Japanese warships to be two or three knots faster than indicated by published data. There were several reports through the spring of 1941 on German merchant raiders and other vessels using Japanese ports or facilities. There was also a specific report in April, within eight months of the beginning of this work, that the Japanese were converting liner *Kasuga Maru* into an aircraft carrier (it became the *Taiyo*). This was all valuable intelligence, a far cry from the episode, early in Smith-Hutton's tour, when an October 1939 memo went all the way to President Franklin D. Roosevelt denying reports that a battleship was under construction at Mitsubishi-Nagasaki, where in fact the *Musashi* was being built. As for the armament of *Mogami*-class cruisers, not until the battle of Midway, when U.S. aircraft got aerial photographs of two of these ships, did the truth become known: The Tokyo attaché had been right all along.

It is interesting to contrast the American naval attaché's reporting with that of the Germans, who were moving toward actual military alliance with Japan during this period and therefore had much better access to official Japanese circles. The Germans also had, in Henri Smith-Hutton's judgment, a better espionage network, based upon German proprietors of hotels and other businesses. Official diaries of the German attachés show little reporting on Japanese military technology, fleet organization, naval construction, or leadership. There is a certain detail in the German reports on Japanese strategic policy, but entirely based on assertions by official Japanese sources, who were not entirely candid with their soon-to-be allies. Finally, as might be expected for a power already at war, the German attaché remained clearly preoccupied with organizing a campaign by merchant raiders and with securing Japanese cooperation on that and on raw materials that could be sent home in the face of British blockade.

One American attaché's opinion in retrospect is that all along it was the British who had the second-best spy networks in Japan, networks based upon the many offices of their shipping and maritime-insurance agents throughout the country. The British naval attaché, Captain David Tuffnell, also had a bigger staff and many more language officers than available to Smith-Hutton. The British and Americans did not exchange intelligence so much as compare information to see if each attaché had heard a given report and how he evaluated its credibility. According to Stephen Jurika, the Soviets had by far the best networks in Japan, using Japanese Communist party members; but judging from Jurika's own intelligence exchange with the Russians, Soviet information collection was haphazard at best.

With their sensitivity to espionage and virtual national hysteria over spying, the Japanese still proved unable to prevent foreign governments from gaining real knowledge of important aspects of their capabilities, if not their intentions. In early 1939 a law for the protection of military secrets classified a broad range of information as secret and provided penalties for disclosure, stiffening already draconian provisions existing under the national general mobilization law. Legal statutes reinforced xenophobic tendencies among the Japanese people, encouraged by periodic government pronouncements and a cooperative press. In the summer of 1940 an Englishman, Mr. V.O.W. Peters, was arrested and charged with espionage by the *kempeitai*, a strong organization that grew constantly and would reach a strength of 75,000 before the war played itself out. The Peters affair stoked spy fever. For three days in January 1941 the Osaka-Kobe region became the locale for actual anti-espionage "drills" in which the authorities practiced catching spies. From May 12 to May 17 came National Anti-Espionage Week. Typical of the fever was a July article in the magazine *Nippon Kaiun* advocating that foreigners be prohibited from raising or keeping carrier pigeons. In the midst of all this real spies, like Soviet master spy Richard Sorge, worked undetected.

Commander Smith-Hutton's Chinese-Japanese agent was no Sorge, but it appears he was capable of major accomplishments. Perhaps his most significant discovery concerned the Japanese Type 93 torpedo, the "Long Lance," a 24-inch-diameter, oxygen-driven torpedo with unprecedented speed, range, and destructive power. This was a super-secret weapon, originally developed at Kure between 1930 and 1933 by a team under Admiral Oyagi Sadamu, who had gotten the idea working at the Whitehead Torpedo Works in Weymouth, England. Later the design was perfected by Captain Kishimoto Kaneji and Admiral Asaguma Toshihide at the Kure Naval Arsenal. Then–Rear Admiral Ozawa Jisaburo, author of a key Japanese text on torpedoes and long a proponent of the oxygen torpedo, was instrumental, along with Admiral Sawamoto Ikuta, in the adoption during 1939–1940 of a tactical doctrine for use of the Type 93, a weapon that possessed key advantages.

One day Smith-Hutton's Chinese-Japanese agent came to him to explain that his school club had scheduled a visit to an Imperial Navy destroyer. The attaché had a keen interest in discovering whether the Japanese had torpedoes larger than 21 inches in diameter—that is, new-type torpedoes. Smith-Hutton figured out a way his spy could estimate diameter quickly and unobtrusively. The agent reported not only that the torpedoes *were* bigger than 21 inches, perhaps as big as 25 inches, but that Japanese torpedomen had proudly explained that the Imperial Navy no longer used air in its torpedoes, only oxygen. Smith-Hutton reported the details to ONI on April 22, 1940. There was no reply. Three years later, after many U.S. and Allied ships had succumbed to the infamous Long Lance, ONI report 44-43 of April

20, 1943, concluded on the basis of prisoner interrogations that Japanese cruisers and destroyers were armed with 24-inch torpedoes.

Despite Japanese sensitivities and regardless of the limitations on information available to the public, U.S. naval attachés were surprisingly well informed on the Imperial Navy, its ships, men, and weapons. Given the inherent difficulties of intelligence gathering in that age, and the less sophisticated technical collection systems then available, perhaps one should conclude that the Tokyo attaché provided *remarkable* intelligence. But the quality of intelligence did not matter much if it was not believed by consumers—in 1940–41, by the White House and the U.S. Navy. Nowhere did this problem become more apparent than with respect to intelligence on Japanese naval aviation.

IN PARALLEL TO THE VERY RECENT ADVENT OF AIRPOWER AS A MILITARY FACTOR, SO IT WAS that only in the last few years before war came did the naval attaché in Tokyo benefit from an assistant specializing in air matters. It was not that the Office of Naval Intelligence completely ignored the subject; rather ONI wished to husband its manpower. Instead the arrangement was that the Asiatic Fleet would send an aviation officer to Japan for about two months a year, to give expert opinions to the attaché during the annual round of visits to Japanese naval air stations. The first officer so assigned, Lieutenant John J. Ballentine, was a skilled aviator who would go on to command a carrier and a carrier division in the Pacific and would be chief of staff to the U.S. Navy's Pacific air command. Ballentine spoke no Japanese, however, so here again the contributions of language officers proved crucial.

When the Tokyo embassy got a full-time aviation expert in 1935, this officer would be called the assistant naval attaché for air. The first air attaché, as we shall call him here, in Tokyo for a two-year tour of duty, was Lieutenant Commander Ralph A. Ofstie, fresh from command of an aircraft squadron aboard the carrier *Saratoga*. Lieutenant Commander Francis J. Bridget succeeded him, but in 1939, shortly before Smith-Hutton returned to Tokyo as top attaché, Bridget was sent to the Philippines. Lieutenant Stephen Jurika then got the assignment. Jurika had been born in the Philippines, had plenty of Far East background, and was an experienced pilot, but happened to be a junior officer, clearly subordinate to the new naval attaché. (In a sense, Bridget and Jurika later traded places, for the former air attaché would end up in charge of the Asiatic Fleet's air arm, trying to cobble together some kind of air effort during the dark early days of the war.)

Individually and collectively the few officers who held the post of naval air attaché would be responsible for much of what the U.S. Navy knew about the Japanese naval air force (JNAF) in 1941. Several aspects figured in the overall state of American knowledge, including estimates of the size of the JNAF, of the productive capacity of Japanese aviation industry, and of the degree of technological sophistication the JNAF had attained. Popular writers such as Fletcher Pratt and William D. Puleston, himself a former director of naval intelligence, were filling the public mind with images of Japanese who couldn't fly straight, so to speak—pilots handicapped by poor eyesight and fluid imbalances in the inner ear (which precluded their making acute turns). Claims of physical handicaps were often matched by allegations the Japanese were incapable of producing advanced aircraft on their own, instead copying foreign designs. It is important to discover how such views were reflected in the secret intelligence reporting.

As far as attributes of pilots are concerned, search thus far has disclosed a couple of passing notes regarding the typical educational attainments of JNAF flight crewmen, but no detailed treatment of this entire subject. *British* attaché reporting on the other hand, cited by the late Arthur Marder, includes several instances of seemingly racially biased reports regarding Japanese airmen. However, the size of JNAF pilot classes remained so small in the prewar years that the Japanese could hardly help but be highly selective, and indeed the accounts we have of training demonstrate the Japanese as very concerned to produce quality aircrews. A copy of the actual physical standards the Japanese used in selecting prospective trainees, together with subsequent alterations the JNAF issued, became available to U.S. intelligence during the war. These documents demonstrate not only that the Japanese had had quite stringent standards, but that even under wartime pressures they lowered their physical standards only slightly.

Nevertheless, American attachés were capable of entertaining prejudices akin to those of their Western colleagues. One 1939 report talked of seeing seventeen wrecked aircraft fuselages sitting at a railway siding, then about the same number of planes being decrated at the base; the writer concluded from these observations that "accidents at training stations are apparently quite high." On the technical side, Americans seemed quite willing to believe Japanese advances were few and their propensity to copy great. Year after year the air attaché reports note deficiencies, starting with one in late 1937 which asserts that the Japanese had trouble establishing facts in their wind tunnels and labs, and difficulty applying data to the engineering of actual airplanes. This report, noting the success of the Nell* bomber design, which entered production in 1936, attributed it to the plane's "seem[ing] originally to be a commercial product of Junkers." In fact the requirements for the Nell

---

*The Japanese Navy used at least three different systems for designating aircraft. The alphanumeric arrangement (for example, "A6M2") used the initial letter to show type ("A" for fighter, "G" for land-based bomber, "B" for carrier attack plane, "D" for dive-

had been issued by JNAF headquarters when Admiral Yamamoto Isoroku headed research and development there, and the design had been the product of a team consisting of Honjo Sueo assisted by Kubo Tomio and Kusabake Yoshitaka, who owed no special debt to the Germans.

Meanwhile, as a consequence of the Anti-Comintern Pact, the air attaché warned in 1937 that Germany, Italy, and Japan had reached a private understanding whereby complete aircraft, together with sets of blueprints and design data, were to be made available to Japan. The 1939 annual naval aviation digest claimed that the Japanese "have not designed, by themselves, any [aircraft] types now in production for the armed services." In reality, aside from versions of a trainer aircraft and several transports (the Lockheed Electra and Douglas DC-2 and DC-3), *all* aircraft manufactured in Japan were of indigenous design.

The British liked to claim that the Japanese Emily (H8K) flying boat had been copied from their own Sunderland, built by the Short aircraft company. True, the JNAF aircraft requirement specified a plane that would outperform the Sunderland, but that must have been based upon news of the Short flying boat rather than experience with aircraft, for the first Sunderland came off the production line only a few months before the Japanese began to design their aircraft. Moreover, the Emily would eventually be longer and lower than the Short plane, with a longer wingspan and considerably greater airspeed. The Emily was not a copy.

The Japanese Navy did import a variety of foreign aircraft, primarily for test purposes; most of the aeronautical research flying was performed at the Yokosuka Naval Air Station. The imports included six types of German aircraft, but eleven American ones. There were also a few British types. During the China Incident the JNAF briefly fielded a unit of American two-seat fighters and one of German Heinkel He-112s. The latter, failed competitor for Luftwaffe procurement against the Messerschmidt Bf-109, proved unlucky in Japanese service as well. The JNAF reduced its order for thirty fighters to just a dozen, enough to equip a single squadron. The He-112

---

bomber, and so on) and a second to specify manufacturer (here "M" for Mitsubishi). The first number stood for the order in which planes of that type were adopted for fleet service, the last number for the model or modification of the aircraft.

Another method of nomenclature was based upon the year since the Emperor Meiji's reign began; thus the A6M2 was the Type 0 (for 100 years) fighter. Since the same type number could be used for different aircraft, this narrative does not rely upon that system, nor does it use the third sort of nomenclature, which the JNAF used for experimental designs. Yet a fourth style of nomenclature was introduced by Allied intelligence authorities, who referred to Japanese aircraft by male and female names; most Western accounts utilize the Allied style. To prevent confusion, for the most part I do too, except for occasional use of the JNAF alphanumeric system, and for consistent use of "Zero" to designate the A6M series fighters, a name that should be familiar to readers.

quickly went out of service in favor of the Claude, a fixed-landing-gear, home-grown design that became the Imperial Navy's standard fighter until the advent of the renowned Zero. American air attachés reported the A5M Claude as heavy in the nose, but the JNAF considered it a complete success.

Western lack of appreciation for Japanese aviation developments was by no means wholly due to cultural bias, however. Imperial Navy officers played the same games of deception with the attachés on air matters that they did during visits to shipyards or naval bases. A typical instance occurred in March 1937, when naval attaché Bemis plus air attaché Ofstie visited Yokosuka Naval Air Station along with language officer Joe Finnegan. Captain Mitsunami Teizo, the base commander, delivered himself of the usual preliminary remarks, resulting in "some haste in getting over the station, and numerous hangars not visited." Among the bypassed hangars were all those containing experimental aircraft or foreign ones. Asked about tests, the Japanese responded that any dangerous ones, such as spins or dives, were conducted at an Army airfield. When the Americans saw an instrument flight trainer they were told it was hardly ever used because advanced flight training had been moved elsewhere. Then the Americans saw a cruiser- or battleship-type catapult mounted on a seawall, but an escort officer promptly volunteered "the positive statement" that "no training whatsoever was given future catapult [control] officers." The Americans saw only old planes "of little interest" with no evident additions in the fifteen months since U.S. officers had last visited Yokosuka.

If this was what Americans could learn visiting Japan's premier aeronautical research center, then perhaps it is not so surprising that Western impressions of Japan's aviation prowess were wide of the mark. In fact, what *is* surprising given this context is that the Americans were pretty close to the truth in estimating the overall strength of the JNAF, and that before the war our air attaché and others developed good data on the Zero fighter, often held to be a surprise sprung on the Allies with the onset of hostilities.

As we turn to the growth of the JNAF it is useful to sketch the history of aviation in the Imperial Navy, with antecedents to the 1870s, during the reign of the Emperor Meiji, when the Japanese experimented with hot-air balloons. With the invention of airplanes Japanese interest again flared, and in 1911 six officers went abroad for training as pilots while the Imperial Navy established its first air station, Oppama, subsequently renamed Yokosuka. In 1912 the Navy formed an Aeronautical Research Committee, and the next year put in service a seaplane tender. Aircraft flew missions from this ship against the German defenders of Tsingtao on the China coast in World War I, possibly history's first combat sorties flown by aircraft based at sea.

The Imperial Navy activated its first land-based air group in 1916 at Yokosuka, with a second at Sasebo in March 1918. The first Japanese-designed aircraft for the Imperial Navy was a 1917 product of the Yokosuka

Naval Air Arsenal. The Japanese achieved their first takeoff from the deck of a warship when a pilot flew a British plane off a platform constructed on the seaplane tender in June 1920. In 1918 the Imperial Navy adopted a long-range expansion plan for new air bases and additional air groups plus construction of the light aircraft carrier *Hosho*, the world's first warship built from the keel up to handle aircraft at sea. *Hosho* joined the fleet in 1922. Lieutenant Kira Shunichi made the first carrier landing aboard her on March 16, 1923. By then the JNAF had ten aircraft squadrons, and further expansion programs were adopted in 1926 and 1931.

As in the United States, in Japan air enthusiasts conducted experiments attacking warships. The American general Billy Mitchell used aircraft to sink the former German battleship *Ostfriesland*. The Japanese began their experiments with a vessel originally sunk at Port Arthur during the Russo-Japanese War, the battleship *Retvizan*, salvaged and refloated by a team under young Nagano Osami, then refurbished in a Japanese shipyard. The Washington Treaty made *Retvizan* just more scrap, so the Imperial Navy decided to use her as a target instead. She sank under combined attack by Navy and Army aircraft in Sagami Bay in July 1924. Several months later, the Navy chose another surplus battleship, the 1909-vintage *Satsuma*, expending her as a target for bombing and surface-torpedo attack. In addition the Navy took the battleship *Settsu*, originally to be preserved under the Washington Treaty, but traded in to keep the *Mutsu*, and converted this vessel also into a target, albeit one not permitted to sink. In 1927 the Imperial Navy created a Bureau of Aeronautics under Rear Admiral Yamamoto Eisuke, a prime exponent of aerial bombardment. This made the JNAF an independent service branch directly responsible to the navy minister. Yamamoto Eisuke planned further aerial bombing experiments in Tokyo Bay in August 1930, when the old protected cruiser *Akashi* was the target. This Russo-Japanese War veteran, however, survived both aerial-torpedo attacks (which missed) and numerous bomb hits. *Akashi* would finally be dispatched by destroyer torpedoes.

Much as happened in other lands, not least the United States, the Japanese faced the necessity of popularizing aviation. Even civil aviation then seemed primitive and dangerous. Taxpayers had to be convinced not so much of the need, for the Japanese were intensely patriotic and willing to pay for a strong navy, but the practicality of naval aviation. Part of the task fell to the Navy League, a public support group formed in 1917. Japanese naval aviators did the rest, a great deal, encouraging interest in flying. Very prominent throughout this period were the stunt fliers of "Genda's Flying Circus," JNAF pilots Genda Minoru, Okamura Motoharu, and Aoki Atae, who barnstormed the length and breadth of Japan performing acrobatics at air shows.

Yamamoto Eisuke's contribution was the energy he brought to JNAF development. Under his leadership the naval air arm in 1930 reached expansion goals set a decade earlier. By then JNAF had thirteen air groups, with 112 first-line aircraft and sixty-two in reserve. A decision to add fourteen more groups followed in 1931, and a year later the plan expanded by eight units. By then Vice Admiral Matsuyama Shigeru had become chief of the bureau, with Rear Admiral Yamamoto Isoroku (no relation to Eisuke) as technical section chief. This Yamamoto shared deep enthusiasm for airpower. He had been captain of the carrier *Akagi* and had been quoted as far back as 1915 declaring that the most important ship of the future would carry planes. Throughout the 1930s, as section chief, as vice minister of the Navy, and as director of the Bureau of Aeronautics, Yamamoto played a key role in the evolution of naval aviation. He pushed successfully for development of a full generation of new carrier aircraft, including a fighter type, a dive-bomber, and a torpedo bomber, as well as a land-based medium bomber design. Public attitudes changed to such a degree that in both 1938 and 1939 American air attachés calculated that private donations to the JNAF were sufficient to purchase about a hundred new aircraft.

For present purposes the point of all this is that America began sending naval air attachés to Tokyo at precisely the moment when the Japanese Naval Air Force had passed its infancy and begun a stage of rapid growth. Thus, given Japanese reticence regarding information plus sustained increases in JNAF strength, there is little reason to suppose that U.S. attaché estimates had any accuracy. Yet Ralph Ofstie, Francis Bridget, and Stephen Jurika rendered reports that came close to overall JNAF numbers.

This conclusion is based on comparisons between postwar data assembled for the Supreme Commander Allied Powers, and annual digests on Japanese naval aviation for 1937, 1938, and 1939. For 1938, when the postwar data set shows 961 first-line aircraft, the U.S. naval air attaché reported 958 to ONI. The following year, when postwar data tabulate JNAF strength at 1,005 aircraft, the air attaché estimate is 1,002 or, counting fleet-based aircraft not on carriers, 1,237. Other features of the air attaché data include an estimate that the average JNAF pilot was receiving about 200 hours of flight time per year, and the assertion that the Japanese had two patrol planes stationed at Jaluit in the Mandates. In any case, numerically at least, American assessments of JNAF strength were close to reality or even overestimates.

Effectively the pattern was one of *qualitative* underestimate but *quantitative* near accuracy. Interestingly enough, this pattern was replicated in the professional press as exemplified by the *U.S. Naval Institute Proceedings.* In its May 1941 issue the "Professional Notes" section of this journal carried a report that Japan was reorganizing its air force along German lines. The same section a month later noted Japanese "claims" that recent aircraft types were superior to those of potential adversaries, but then went on to say that "other [Japanese] types follow the Western fashions, though somewhat tardily, and have the performance of European designs of 1932 and thereabouts. . . . The newest types compare favorably with European practice in 1934–35." While the report noted that the Japanese rate of commissioning new pilots was slow, it mistakenly added that "the standard of efficiency is not high, and is certainly below that of all the bigger nations." Finally the report contained a figure for Japanese carrier-based aircraft strength (330) virtually identical to what the Tokyo air attaché had reported in 1939 (333). In November 1941, during the final slide into war, *Proceedings* gave the figure 1,000 for JNAF first-line aircraft strength. This number, though an underestimate (actual JNAF strength was 1,381), included a figure for carrier air strength (400) almost precisely matching the actual number (418).

In any case the view in Washington of Japanese aviation prowess was complacent. Efforts to break the stereotype met frustration, and two notable such efforts ought to be mentioned. In 1937 Frank Bridget, who had a home from which he could watch JNAF planes using Yokosuka, wrote an extensive report on the quality of the Japanese aircraft—in particular, their medium bomber force, which was actually flying bombing missions in support of the fighting in China from faraway bases on Taiwan. Bridget discussed the quality of pilots and planes, assessing both as very good. After presenting his report to Captain Bemis, Bridget celebrated with a night on the town, drinking too much, so much that Bemis put him under arrest, wrote a bad efficiency report on him, and refused to forward his study. Thus ONI remained in ignorance of a crucial bit of intelligence.

Another inveterate watcher of air activity was Bridget's successor, Stephen Jurika. This air attaché played a great deal of golf in Japan, particularly in groups with members of the British embassy, including Ambassador Sir Robert Craigie. His British friends, with their own intelligence interests, readily agreed to play at courses near Japanese military and naval airfields, but kept wondering why Jurika didn't concentrate on his game. One day it became obvious the American was really observing Japanese aircraft operating around their bases.

Jurika believed that if you wanted to understand the Japanese you had to get out of the embassy, so he took every opportunity to attend a Japanese function, whether ship launching, garden party, or base visit. Once this even led to Jurika lecturing to a Japanese audience at Imperial University about American naval strategy in the Pacific.

Jurika's break of a lifetime came when he heard that the Japanese Army was sponsoring a show at Haneda field outside Tokyo.* He went, of course.

---

*In his recollections, Jurika does not give a date for this air show, but the Japanese customarily held an annual contest between Army and Navy aircraft, contests begun in 1934, and such an event occurred in January 1941. An airplane display open to the public in conjunction with the contests is likely the event Jurika remembers. Incidentally, in the January 1941 contests the Zero outperformed three different Japanese Army aircraft in all but one event.

There in front of him stood a static display—a parked aircraft of novel configuration. It was the Zero fighter, developed in the usual Japanese secrecy by the veteran Mitsubishi design team under Horikoshi Jiro, who had also designed the A5M Claude, Japan's first low-wing monoplane aircraft. Jurika walked right up to the plane and climbed into the cockpit. He found a plaque in English bearing such essential specifications as the plane's weight and engine horsepower. Jurika also looked at the metal used, the type of landing gear, the construction of wing covers, and other features. Henri Smith-Hutton naturally seemed startled by the detail in Jurika's subsequent report, but the air attaché explained that he had taken the information right out of the plane. The report went off to ONI. Several months later a note came back saying that the attaché ought to be more careful in reporting characteristics of aircraft—this one weighed so much less than others and had such high performance that the United States had nothing with which to compare it. Washington assumed the report had to be wrong. Jurika remembers this as about the only time ONI responded to any report sent from Tokyo.

In the summer of 1941, seeing the rush toward war, Smith-Hutton got all his language officers out of Japan and recommended that no one be sent to replace attaché staff as they finished their tours. Among the evacuees were Navy and Marine officers who would play key roles in wartime intelligence work, including attaché Daniel J. McCallum, who would serve on Guadalcanal; Stephen Jurika himself, later to have a variety of assignments; plus Gilven M. Slonim and Bankston T. Holcomb, leaders of intelligence units sailing with the fleet. Lieutenant Jurika received orders to join the new aircraft carrier *Hornet*. On his way, Jurika spent several weeks at the ONI head office, examining the current Japan monograph and writing several updates to supplement it. Jurika found that ONI had done a fair job of incorporating intelligence its staff believed from the Tokyo reports, but he kept waiting for someone to debrief him on his tour in Japan. No one did. "It is most unfortunate that the reports sent back to our Navy Department by experienced observers . . . didn't receive wider circulation," Henri Smith-Hutton commented later. The Navy's officers thus did not know the opinions of its experts. Stephen Jurika himself, for example, would have been surprised to hear that his intelligence on the A6M Zero fighter had even been matched—by information the ONI received from China.

# "Four Years on a War Footing
# and Unlimited Budgets"

A LTHOUGH JAPANESE ARMY PROVOCATIONS AND INTRIGUES BROUGHT ON THE CHINA
Incident, the Imperial Navy remained more than an interested observer; it
had ready suggestions and burning ambitions. Some naval officers, fearing
that the Army's continental aspirations would lead to conflict with Russia,
felt war in China might be the lesser evil. Others did not mind letting the
Army have its way, or simply wanted to ignore the whole problem, or
envied the Army getting all the glory and wished to line up for a share of the
spoils. Then too there were officers who opposed the Japanese adventure in
China.

An event revealing something of which way the wind blew was the purge
of several admirals; those sacked were primarily officers who favored the
arms treaties, but the action had a China connection. Among the victims
stood Admiral Horie Teikichi, a member of the Japanese delegation at the
Washington Conference. A classmate and good friend of Yamamoto
Isoroku, Horie was chief of the Naval Affairs Bureau when Yamamoto
helped negotiate the London Treaty in 1930. Reputedly the most brilliant
brain ever produced by the Imperial Navy, Horie made vice admiral a year
ahead of Yamamoto. In 1932 Horie had commanded warships off Shanghai
during brief hostilities there, and held his fire against some Chinese batteries
because he could see civilians near them. Things turned out all right for
Japan, but not for Horie, who later found himself accused of cowardice. The
Navy personnel office, headed at the time by Rear Admiral Nagumo
Chuichi, a colleague on the Washington Conference delegation, forced
Horie into retirement even though the mandatory retirement age for a vice

admiral in the Imperial Navy happened to be sixty-two and Horie was just fifty-one years old.

The watershed probably came in 1936. By then senior Navy officers were quite willing to join the intrigues in progress, as became evident that spring when the commander of the Third Fleet, the Imperial Navy's force along the China coast, exchanged messages with Tokyo regarding the desirability of allowing free rein to the already expanding activities of smugglers in Taiwan, Hong Kong, and eastern Hopei province. The Japanese entertained hopes that smuggling might undermine Chinese government customs collections, until then rather efficient, and bring reduction in high import tariffs.

That summer came an incident at Pakhoi on the south-central Chinese coast, which fell under control of a Chinese nationalist faction that opposed accommodation with Japan. A Japanese pharmacist was murdered in his store; there followed a storm of protests, including a strong note from Third Fleet commander Admiral Oikawa Koshiro. The reaction of the Naval General Staff and Navy Ministry was to dispatch reinforcements and demand investigation. These measures ultimately provided for movement of Nell bombers to Taiwan; of aircraft carriers, cruisers, and other ships to the China coast; and of Japanese marines, whom the Imperial Navy called Special Naval Landing Forces (SNLFs), for prospective ground operations. By then further incidents had occurred at Hankow and Shanghai, the latter involving the murder of a crewman of the Third Fleet flagship, armored cruiser *Idzumo*. The SNLF reinforcements ended up at Shanghai, where 2,200 SNLF troops were garrisoned, and a detachment of 300 more landed at Hankow. The Third Fleet was increased in strength to six cruisers, twenty-four destroyers, and ten gunboats plus auxiliaries.

Spurred by the Pakhoi crisis, Navy leadership came to the realization that Japan, or at least the Imperial Navy, needed a whole new policy for China. The Naval Affairs Bureau, under a fifty-one-year-old vice admiral named Toyoda Soemu, who rose to command the Combined Fleet, produced a basic policy paper after consultations with the Naval General Staff and the Foreign Ministry. Completed in late September 1936, the paper presumed that diplomatic negotiations could be "expedited" by military preparations, and spoke of an "ultimatum" to the Chinese for some Japanese demands. Most tellingly, the Navy Ministry began talking about "a national consensus in support of the chastisement of China." As part of this, the Imperial Navy and Japanese Army agreed that the latter would provide troops to reinforce SNLF garrisons at Shanghai and Tsingtao in the event of further trouble.

Thus matters stood in July 1937 when shots were fired at Japanese troops near the Marco Polo Bridge outside Peking. This affair, often said to have been engineered, or at least manipulated, by the Japanese Army, is usually taken as the beginning of the China Incident. Mediation might have cooled tempers, argue modern Japanese scholars, but this time the Imperial Navy stoked up the tension, its previous agreement with the Army about troops for Shanghai suddenly a trigger for escalation. Japanese scholars have uncovered documents showing that in mid-July Third Fleet commander Admiral Hasegawa Kiyoshi opined that the Navy was "fully prepared to engage in an all-out war against China" and told representatives of the Naval General Staff that the Army should mobilize five infantry divisions to prepare a campaign to occupy the Chinese capital, Nanking. Within the month the NGS had begun taking more forceful action in China.

As often happened in prewar Japan, views from the field differed markedly from those at the highest levels of government, where efforts were made to avoid conflict. At a cabinet meeting after the initial fighting at the Marco Polo Bridge, Navy Minister Admiral Yonai Mitsumasa opposed dispatch of troops to China, and continued to do so at sessions among ministers most directly involved with China matters. Yonai's opposition was undermined partly by more aggressive subordinates, and partly by events in China, this time at Shanghai.

In the summer of 1937 the Chinese strengthened their forces outside Shanghai and moved two divisions to positions the Japanese claimed were within the demilitarized zone. On August 6 the Japanese consul ordered all nationals of his country into the International Settlement; there were rumors the Chiang Kai-shek government had decided for war with Japan. On August 9 Imperial Navy lieutenant Oyama Isao and seaman Okamoto Suemasa, on an assignment to survey potential airfield sites, were shot and killed by Chinese troops. The next day Tokyo accorded full freedom of action to its Third Fleet commander.

Admiral Hasegawa reported on August 12 that "the situation in Shanghai could explode at any moment." By then the Naval General Staff had adopted the assumption that force would be required. Pressed to activate contingency plans to send Army troops to supplement the SNLF at Shanghai, on August 10 Minister Yonai asked the cabinet to authorize mobilization. Hasegawa's fleet grew by fifteen warships including an aircraft carrier. On the ground were 2,000 SNLF troops, quickly strengthened to 3,500, and many civilian militia; journalists recorded overall Japanese strength at 7,000 to 9,000. In Tokyo the cabinet met on August 13 to approve sending two Army divisions; soldiers began to embark at Sasebo and Nagoya the same day.

That day in Shanghai the pot boiled over, with Chinese troops openly attacking the Japanese. For more than a week, until the Army began arriving, SNLF troops were in great danger. The Chinese came close to a position from which they could have captured SNLF headquarters during the period from August 16 to 19.

Air operations were especially critical during these days, for the Imperial

Navy had no airfields at Shanghai. On the night of the thirteenth, Third Fleet intelligence intercepted and decoded a Chinese message that ordered large-scale bombing against the Japanese fleet for the next day. The Imperial Navy immediately decreed a preemptive strike by medium bombers based on Taiwan and Kyushu, but bad weather prevented any missions from being carried out until August 15. The Chinese went ahead with their bombing but completely missed the fleet, hitting the International Settlement instead. More than a thousand civilians died under the hail of bombs. Japanese bombers retaliated; in addition there came a carrier air strike from the *Kaga* as early as August 17, though after that the aircraft carrier returned to Sasebo to receive some of the then-new A5M Claude fighters.

The tide turned during the night of August 22–23 when the Imperial Navy landed elements of two Army divisions at Woosung. More than twenty warships and five transports participated. Initial Chinese resistance would be quelled. Lieutenant Commander Hara Tameichi commanded one of the destroyers in the operation, Lieutenant Commander Ohmae Toshikazu another. Both will be met again later in this narrative. There were Chinese counterattacks and fierce fighting for two weeks afterward, but the Japanese gradually gained the upper hand, bringing in three more Army divisions plus an independent brigade, troops who would set out on a march to Nanking, which they would capture and gut in an orgy of atrocities.

For the first six months of the war the Imperial Navy furnished all air support to Japanese forces in China, whether medium bomber strikes flying from Taiwan (a significant technical feat at that stage in aviation history) or shorter-range tactical operations from airfields behind the front. Genda Minoru, of Flying Circus fame, went to Shanghai with the 2nd Combined Air Flotilla and became instrumental in innovating a system whereby air units could leapfrog to new forward bases to keep up with Army and SNLF troops. Genda also served as air officer aboard the carrier *Kaga* during the period of task force operations off Shanghai. Also on the scene were Captain Kusaka Ryunosuke, commanding light carrier *Hosho*, and Rear Admiral Takasu Shiro, in charge of Carrier Division 1.

After Shanghai there would be no turning back. Chinese forces suffered as many as 200,000 casualties in the campaign, the Japanese perhaps 20,000. There were losses of territory, atrocities, the very stuff from which unalterable enmities are made. A mediation effort by the German ambassador, which in December 1937 finally received Navy approval—both from Minister Yonai and NGS vice chief Admiral Koga Mineichi—was judged insufficient by other Japanese. As for the Chinese, it was about that time that Nanking fell and was pillaged.

·　　·　　·

For JAPAN, CHINA BECAME MORE THAN SOME PERIPHERAL AFFAIR. AS LATER PRACTITIONERS of coercive diplomacy have also discovered, mere strategic interests have a way of turning into obsessive involvements. China also represented a far different stage upon which to act. Though Chinese society seemed as closed as Japanese, in China the extraterritorial powers—Great Britain, the United States, France, Germany, and Italy—were already in place. Even Portugal had its little enclaves, such as Macao on the China coast. Japan could not act secretly. Only diplomatic solutions could be pursued confidentially, and in those Japan evinced little interest. The other treaty powers could all observe Japanese acts of force, not to mention record their analyses of Japanese strategies, tactics, and technologies. The China Incident was not going to be a secret war.

American presence in China had long been established by 1937. The "Open Door" policy had by then become a tradition, with the door opened not only to U.S. investment but to missionary work and to all sorts of odd characters attracted by the exotic East. American portfolio holdings in China totaled something over $432 million in 1933, with direct investment in all of East Asia (including Japan but excluding the Philippines) of $310 million. In 1931 U.S. interests controlled about 6 percent of foreign investment in China, and held 7 percent of Chinese foreign debt. This hardly compared to the British, who had 39 percent of investments in China and held 36 percent of China's debt, or the Japanese, whose share of investment amounted to 37 percent as they held 38 percent of Chinese debt. Still, excepting the Japanese, through the 1930s the values of all other nations' investments in China fell while those of the United States increased by a factor of six. America seemed Japan's most dynamic competitor, though Great Britain remained strongest at that point in time.

With Shanghai at the mouth of the Yangtze River, and Hankow 585 miles upstream of it, geographical factors naturally increased the difficulties of American military authorities working to protect the extraterritorial rights of Americans in China. The two major features of the U.S. presence in China were the garrisons located in certain places and the ships of our Asiatic Fleet, which peripatetically steamed among the Philippines, Shanghai, points upstream, and other Chinese ports. The Asiatic Fleet usually consisted of one big treaty cruiser, one or two smaller cruisers, a number of destroyers, submarines, and a couple of dozen gunboats known as the Yangtze Patrol. On land the major U.S. garrison stood at Shanghai, built around the 4th Marine Regiment, and numbered 2,701 marines once reinforcements arrived after the Japanese and Chinese began fighting. Also, since the Boxer Rebellion (1900), the United States had maintained a Marine legation guard at Peking and an Army contingent at Tientsin, the main port for the former Chinese capital. In 1937 these garrisons numbered

527 and 784 respectively. The American military presence in China, while not huge, was significant.

In addition to actual military forces, in China the United States maintained the same sort of naval attaché setup that existed in Japan. The official attachés were attached to the Chinese nationalist government at Nanking, but there were assistants at both Peking and Shanghai. American combat units in China also had standard staff sections for intelligence work. Thus when the China Incident began U.S. forces in the theater had not only opportunity but capability to score an intelligence windfall by observing the Japanese in action.

This was even more true since in China the Americans had radio intelligence—watching Japanese moves by intercepting Japanese communications. This technique, whose inception we shall examine presently, had been available in China since the mid-1920s, when self-trained radiomen at Shanghai began to use their receivers to intercept Japanese naval communications traffic. Radio intelligence had the important advantage that it consisted of collecting the target nation's *own* secret messages, and thus represented information straight from the horse's mouth, as it were. It was a technical collection method that did not depend on success at infiltrating the adversary with spies or on the broadness of one's canvass of the open literature. In any case, even with this technique in its infancy in the U.S. Navy, someone thought to utilize it at Shanghai.

Not for long, however. The intercept station established in about 1924 relocated three years later aboard an Asiatic Fleet accommodation ship, and then phased out completely in March 1929. What remained at that point was the presence on Asiatic Fleet staff of one officer attached from the Navy's central radio intelligence organization in Washington, a unit known as OP-20-G. In 1931 this officer, Lieutenant Joseph Wenger, a very enthusiastic advocate of radio intelligence techniques, prepared plans for an expanded intercept network in conjunction with then-Lieutenant Henri Smith-Hutton, who at that time was fleet intelligence officer on the same staff. Both were with the Asiatic Fleet in 1932, when an early crisis brewed up at Shanghai. The fleet hurriedly left Manila for the China coast, anchoring at Shanghai to safeguard Americans there.

Four years later, after his tour as assistant attaché in Tokyo, Smith-Hutton returned to the China station as chief communications officer aboard heavy cruiser *Augusta,* flagship of the Asiatic Fleet. Once again he worked with Joe Wenger, now assistant communications officer on the fleet staff. Wenger supervised half a dozen radiomen specifically to intercept not only Japanese communications but also those of Britain, France, the U.S.S.R., and other nations with regular radio stations.

In the meantime another radio intercept section had been located in Peking with the Marine detachment guarding the legation there, and in late

1934 authorities recommended the transfer of the unit to Shanghai. An intercept unit at Shanghai actually came into being in the summer of 1935 under Marine captain S. C. Zern, with one Navy chief petty officer and nine Marine enlisted men. The station was located in a small wooden shack atop a two-story building on Haiphong Road. Later it moved to a new location in the Marine compound at the corner of Hart and Sinza roads, in the International Settlement at Shanghai away from the bustle of the Bund.

In the summer of 1937 the main action at the Shanghai station, formally known as the Fleet Intelligence Unit attached to the 4th Marines, was preparation to cover Japanese fleet maneuvers. It was not long before the advent of the China Incident brought work of even more critical importance. The United States set up its Shanghai station just in time.

Several Japanese measures were of direct importance to the United States. One was Japan's dispatch of its 5th Infantry Division to reinforce Imperial Army units at Tientsin, where 5,500 Japanese troops, 1,500 technicians, and 10,000 residents plus a further 10,000 indigenous workers, though a powerful garrison, felt threatened. This Boxer treaty port also had U.S. and British contingents, for whom Japanese activities had dire implications. Tensions at Tientsin rose until eventually the Americans, then the British, withdrew their own forces and nationals. Meanwhile, Americans learned much about Japanese military doctrine and tactics by watching the Imperial Army and Navy and intercepting their communications.

The Imperial Navy and Army coordinated operations by means of so-called central agreements which laid out the responsibilities of each service in a common situation. The central agreement of July 11, 1937, governed activities in China and provided the Navy the main responsibility for "security measures in Central and South China." Initially the Naval General Staff foresaw a campaign restricted to Shanghai and Tientsin, but its July 12 plan envisioned actions should the war spread, as it did. One provision directed that "Navy air strength will be employed for the neutralization of the enemy air strength." Another paragraph of the directive mandated that

> a blockade will be enforced along the lower reaches of the Yangtze and the coastal area of Chekiang Province as well as in other areas where our troops are stationed. The blockade will be enforced only on Chinese ships in order to avoid any conflict with third powers. However, should the progress of the war so require, it will be enforced more intensively and extensively.

In keeping with directives from the high command, Admiral Hasegawa Kiyoshi duly began to blockade an 800-mile stretch of the China coast. The blockade, declared on Wednesday, August 25, would be effective that same day. Hasegawa stated his purpose as preventing the Chinese from moving supplies by sea into the Shanghai area where, just three days before, his fleet had fought a pitched battle covering the amphibious landing at Woosung. From that day on Japanese warships were constantly on blockade duty, as the Imperial Navy repeatedly lengthened its blockade zone until eventually covering the full China coast.

The United States remained neutral in the China Incident but sympathetic to the Chinese. Two days after the Japanese declaration of a blockade, the U.S. government–owned motorship *Wichita* left Baltimore with a cargo of aircraft destined for the Chinese air force. On September 10 the United States gave official warning of the blockade to American shipping in the Far East. Following Japanese protests, President Franklin D. Roosevelt ruled that government-owned vessels would no longer be allowed to carry arms to China. Privately owned ships could still sail at their own risk. In October FDR gave a speech in Chicago in which he declared a "quarantine" of China restricting sales of weapons to both sides.

Japanese warships plied the East China Sea, stopping ships at their pleasure. They did make efforts to avoid problems with the other Powers. When the American liner *President Hoover* staved in her bottom on rocks off the coast of Taiwan, the Imperial Navy sent a cruiser and a destroyer to assist while a Japanese merchantman aided in the rescue. In September the Imperial Navy accepted a British proposal that required searches be carried out by *British* officers when Royal Navy vessels sailed in company with merchant ships bound for Chinese ports. The United States adopted similar procedures. Western navies suddenly found themselves escorting ships to China.

Difficulties were inevitable. Learning that Chinese shipping had been disguised under neutral flags of convenience, Admiral Hasegawa ordered searches regardless of nationality. In mid-September Hasegawa declared that the Japanese would not recognize any transfer of a Chinese ship to foreign registry made after inception of the blockade. The Imperial Navy extended its blockade to all ports except Tsingtao, Macao, Hong Kong, and the French concession at Kwangchowan. Hong Kong fishermen protested the blockade impeded their work, keeping 200 boats and 100,000 fishermen in port. In November a Japanese warship opened fire on aircraft from the British carrier *Eagle*. On November 30 an Imperial Navy boarding party seized steamship *Feitung*, an American flag vessel. Asiatic Fleet commander Admiral Harry E. Yarnell protested vigorously. Hasegawa's chief of staff, Admiral Sugiyama Rokuzo, apologized and the *Feitung* was released. The situation remained quite tense.

This activity provided grist for the mill of the Asiatic Fleet radio intercept units. They monitored Hasegawa's Third Fleet circuits during all Japanese operations, particularly those up the Yangtze. It was there that occurred an incident, resulting from the offensive by combined Japanese Army-Navy forces, an ancillary operation to the march on Nanking.

The river campaign became a major feature of Imperial Navy activity in this first year of the China war. At first Japanese maneuvers were defensive: evacuations of nationals from such exposed cities as Hankow. These evacuations began about a week after the fighting broke out. As Japanese gunboats moved downriver the Chinese followed, establishing a defense above Nanking. The Chinese had no plans initially and had not prepared any special weapons, but finally built a river barrier backed by a small flotilla of gunboats.

For a few brief months, Nanking became the prize, with the Japanese hoping China would sue for peace if her capital were captured. On September 19, 1937, the British cruiser *Capetown*, anchored at Nanking, was warned by a Japanese officer that the JNAF would begin bombing two days later, and that all foreign warships on the Yangtze should move upriver to avoid becoming targets. The bombing of Nanking duly began, while the Treaty Powers' ships tried to stay out of the way. Maintaining their correct attitude, the Americans, at least, kept their diplomats at Nanking until Chiang Kaishek's government left for Hankow, 350 miles upriver, on December 7. The Americans and British began to evacuate their nationals and any Europeans who wished to escape the conflict.

With the Japanese Army approaching, the situation became extraordinarily tense. On December 5 someone fired machine guns at the British gunboat *Ladybird*, while Japanese artillery sank two cargo ships. *Ladybird* herself became a target for artillery fire a week later. The American gunboat *Panay*, under Lieutenant Commander James J. Hughes, was also in the area, with evacuees aboard and escorting three Standard Oil tankers. Meanwhile, in the belief Chinese ships were evacuating Chinese nationalist troops upriver, Japanese Army officers asked for air strikes on river shipping. Colonel Hashimoto Kingoro, local Japanese commander and a reserve artillery officer, who had been founder of the ultra-right-wing Cherry Blossom Society, had his artillery fire on ships in the Yangtze. At Shanghai the men of the Fleet Intelligence Unit were listening to the whole thing.

The JNAF took center stage in ensuing events. The 2nd Combined Air Group was conducting the Yangtze campaign, its headquarters in Shanghai under Rear Admiral Mitsunami Teizo, the same man who had misled American naval attachés in Japan about the Yokosuka Naval Air Station. Mitsunami's units were establishing a whole new doctrine of theater operations for the JNAF. Air officer Genda Minoru innovated a technique for rapid advance of planes that was being implemented at that moment as fighter and dive-bomber units flew into the newly captured base at Changchow. In a bit of surreptitious spying, Henri Smith-Hutton induced Admiral Yarnell to assign an aviation officer to command security at the Shanghai Electric Company, an American-owned facility located right next to JNAF's Shanghai base. That officer, having observed Japanese flight activity for three weeks, reported that "if we had sent an air group ashore to establish a field as the Japanese did and operated it in the fac[e] of enemy attacks as well as they did, our officers would have considered that they had done a fine job." An object demonstration would now be rendered.

Lieutenant Okumiya Masatake arrived from Japan with his dive-bomber unit on December 4, 1937. One of the JNAF's sharpest young pilots, seven years out of Etajima, four out of flight school, Okumiya intended to prove himself in combat. On December 12 Okumiya led his formation from Shanghai to attack Chinese army positions. Landing at Changchow to rearm, Okumiya was summoned to headquarters where base commander Captain Miki Morihiko told him the Army wished JNAF to attack Chinese ships fleeing Nanking. The latest word from the Navy liaison officer at Army headquarters, Aoki Takeshi, had been that seven large and three smaller ships were involved. Captain Miki ordered an immediate attack. By 1:00 P.M. Okumiya with his formation and three other JNAF units was flying west along the Yangtze about twenty miles south of Nanking. The pilots were very excited: This was going to be the first time Japanese aircraft had ever attacked, in combat, for real, ships under way. "Peaceful beneath us lay the rich river valley," Okumiya recalled later, "the serenity of the vista broken only by bomb-born columns of smoke rising from the city of Nanking on our right and from the Kuchow–Wuhu highway on our left."

Ahead of Okumiya, Lieutenant Murata Shigeharu's unit sighted ships and began to attack. Okumiya instructed his own pilots to hit the biggest ship, and followed. Murata's planes bombed a smaller vessel at the south end of the group—the gunboat *Panay*. Apparently no one noticed the large American flags painted atop her canvas awnings. Okumiya saw at least two hits by Murata's group, but then became absorbed in his own attack, in the midst of which he found to his horror that the ship sported a British flag. "I was struck with terror at the thought of the blunder I had committed," says Okumiya.

Though Okumiya himself saw no bombs strike the tankers, two of those ships were hit, and fighters strafed the targets for good measure. Then, from the Yangtze banks, Colonel Hashimoto's artillery opened fire as well. The *Panay* sank; its captain and one seaman from the tankers were killed; seventy-four more persons were wounded. With *Panay* abandoned and set-tling in the Yangtze, two motor launches of Japanese Army soldiers machine-gunned the gunboat, then boarded her for about five minutes before leaving. This added insult to injury.

*Panay* had been transmitting on the Yangtze Patrol's main radio circuit at the instant of the raid. Rear Admiral William A. Glassford lost contact in mid-message at exactly 1:35 P.M. Glassford informed Yarnell, who conferred with the consulate in Shanghai. Within hours inquiries were made of the Japanese Third Fleet command. The Americans actually had quite good information on what had happened. The Shanghai station had intercepted the radio messages sent by the JNAF squadron leaders and their ground controllers. Aboard the *Panay* newsreel cameraman Norman Alley filmed parts of the JNAF attack while Italian war correspondent Luigi Barzini watched it. Barzini, a journalist trained at Columbia University who had covered the Italian invasion of Ethiopia in 1935–1936, knew something of the power of the airplane and got under cover. He ended up with bullet holes in his jacket but miraculously emerged unharmed. (Barzini would go on to an illustrious political career in Italy after World War II.)

American authorities introduced portions of Admiral Mitsunami's radio dispatches as evidence in their court of inquiry on the *Panay* affair. Admiral Hasegawa held inquiries too, beginning the day after the sinking, when Okumiya and other JNAF commanders reported aboard Third Fleet flagship *Idzumo*. In fact Hasegawa had been told the *Panay*'s location by Yarnell on December 11, while on the twelfth the U.S. consulate at Shanghai warned the ship was going to move. Commander Takata Toshitane, Hasegawa's senior staff officer, had wanted his air staff to inform Mitsunami's command, but Lieutenant Commander Toibana Kurio, who had long experience in China, convinced him to wait to see what the *Panay* actually did. The delay proved fatal, especially since the 2nd Combined Air Group's planes had advanced to a forward base: As a result, any notice had to pass through two layers of command at two remote locations. Air officer Toibana only learned *Panay*'s new location an hour and a half after the gunboat sank. There could be no doubt the Japanese stood in the wrong. Hasegawa sent chief of staff Sugiyama Rokuzo to the Americans to make apologies. It was the second time in two weeks. Sugiyama's deputy, Captain Kusaka Ryunosuke, must have hung his head in shame.

Infuriated by the *Panay* affair, Franklin Roosevelt could do more than demand apologies. In October he had been given a suggestion, originated by Admiral Yarnell, for the economic strangulation of Japan. Now, the day of the attack, chief of naval operations Admiral William D. Leahy recorded his opinion that the time had come to get the U.S. fleet ready and talk to Britain about a demonstration of power in the Far East. The British were not prepared to go that far, however, and shortly after the U.S. Navy rendered its detailed report on the *Panay* sinking, FDR learned that the Japanese government was making a formal apology. Ambassador Grew told reporters, "I had been working for five years to build up Japanese-American friendship and . . . this incident seemed to risk shattering the whole structure."

In Tokyo the Imperial Navy high command felt equally threatened by the affair. Rear Admiral Inoue Shigeyoshi, director of the Navy Ministry's Military Affairs Bureau, visited the vice foreign minister to ask that personal condolences be sent to President Roosevelt and the King of England. Foreign Minister Hirota Koki went to the U.S. embassy to commiserate with Joseph Grew, had his ambassador in Washington call on U.S. officials, and prodded

Imperial Navy commanders to express regrets. Minister Yonai and Vice Minister Yamamoto were both mortified. Yamamoto, realizing that further incidents could occur so long as the British and Americans used the Yangtze, sent a skilled translator to Shanghai as intermediary between Hasegawa's fleet and the Westerners. Yamamoto also called at the U.S. embassy, some say in tears, and not only expressed regrets but, on December 22, presented an unprecedented detailed reconstruction of the Japanese moves that led to the attack. Ambassador Grew held this conference in his study; it was attended by naval attaché Captain Bemis, military attaché Major Harry I. Creswell, and other officials. The floor was strewn with maps as Yamamoto's briefers, principally Commander Takata, described events on the Yangtze.

"We were all impressed," noted Grew in his diary, "with the apparent genuine desire and efforts of both Army and Navy to get at the undistorted facts, but for a good many reasons this has not been easy."

Even before this meeting the Japanese recalled Admiral Mitsunami of the 2nd Combined Air Group. Minister Yonai issued reprimands to Okumiya, Murata, and the other squadron commanders. Japan paid reparations of $2,214,007 for the sunk and damaged ships. The Imperial Navy assumed the Japanese Army would similarly discipline its Colonel Hashimoto, but that never happened. As Admiral Nomura Kichisaburo later wrote, the *Panay* affair became a major "stepping stone to war."

In the field in China, fighting continued, including the campaign up the Yangtze. Hankow fell in the fall of 1938, after a major JNAF long-range bombing campaign. During the first year of the China Incident the Imperial Navy suffered almost a thousand dead, though Army dead numbered fifty times that and Chinese war dead two and a half times the Japanese total. Thereafter the Japanese Navy averaged about 1,500 deaths a year in China, for a total of 6,914 dead before December 1941. In the same period there were 320,000 dead for the Japanese Army, and the official Chinese figure amounts to 1,028,440. However, by the end of 1941 China seemed as strong as it had been in 1937. Chiang Kai-shek moved his capital to Chungking, made a common front with the Chinese Communists to prosecute the war, and solicited aid from the West. American arms to China, measured by the value of export licenses, amounted to $35.6 million by June 1941. Equally—if not more—important, American pilots constituted themselves as an air unit that became the backbone of the Chinese air force—the American Volunteer Group, popularly known as the Flying Tigers.

The American pilots, along with intelligence sources already noted, continued to collect data on the Japanese military machine. The *Panay* affair actually helped the intelligence effort, not only providing an occasion on which Japanese communications surged, meaning there were more messages to intercept, but also indirectly. Kenneth E. Carmichael, then with the radio intercept station at Shanghai, remembers that a couple of former *Panay* radiomen came to augment the fleet intelligence unit. One, Radioman First Class "Speed" Adams, had passed ammunition during the air attack; the other, a man named Peterson, had barely had time to escape the sinking ship. Carmichael notes that they did not know anything about Japanese code practices, but the former *Panay* crewmen could stand watch, and they did good work on Japanese diplomatic traffic.

Shanghai, called Station E in the Navy's secret network of radio intercept facilities, remained a key link in the U.S. intelligence effort. There were other intercept stations, at Guam and in the Philippines—first at Cavite, then at Corregidor—and when the Navy eventually closed Station E they expected to do the same work from Corregidor. Shanghai veterans disagreed; coverage would never be as good from the Philippines; the Shanghai men had transferred from there and felt they knew better. For one thing, the Imperial Navy tightened up communications security a great deal—before the *Panay* sinking, a lot of Japanese communications, right down to fleet and ship movement reports, had been sent in plaintext. Afterward, not only were the messages in code but also there were extra security measures such as regular changes of the call signs utilized by each specific radio set on a network. Fancy security made it especially important to intercept every Japanese message, and there Shanghai excelled.

After reviewing Naval Security Group histories of both these intercept stations, Radioman Clarence P. Taylor observed:

We could not do the job at Corregidor that we did at Shanghai. . . . Maybe they should have let [Shanghai station] go on and get captured with the Fourth Marines [in 1941]. They would have had the benefit of almost another year of traffic which would have been very worthwhile and which they definitely could not get at Corregidor. They were limited at Corregidor. You could get some of the traffic out of Tokyo to the net, but they would be limited to some of the southern stations like Amoy picking up the net. In Shanghai, most of the time, we could copy every station on the net and, if we missed a message, somebody else had missed it [too] and it would have to be relayed to them . . . and then we would get it. As I say, we had them cold, 100%. We got every dot and dash, almost, that was sent on that net.

Roy Sholes, who served with Taylor at Shanghai in 1940, recalls that one of Station E's big assignments had been monitoring Tokyo–Moscow diplomatic communications, and when those stopped the U.S. interceptors typically switched to Imperial Navy messages on the Yangtze River network.

Shanghai would be sought-after duty until the place closed down in

December 1940. The small band of Station E men were very close. "It was a great bunch of people," Clarence Taylor remembers. The whole station never had a single security lapse. "It was a tight-knit organization and, as I say, we were very dedicated, proud of what we were doing . . . and we just worked together, doing what had to be done."

It helped, of course, that life was easy in prewar China, at least for someone paid in American dollars. Taylor and Sholes, who were married, had apartments about eight long blocks from Marine headquarters, where Station E was located. For less than $25 a month they had housing on Seymour Road with food, electricity, heat, other household expenses, a Chinese "boy," and a coolie all included. Tickets to the movies cost less than 4¢, which was also the price of good Chinese lime beer. A rickshaw went for 17¢ a night. Sholes found himself walking to work sometimes just for the exercise. Occasionally, until families were evacuated early in 1940, the two couples from Seymour Road would bicycle around Shanghai. At the gates of the International Settlement, Japanese guards moved aside the barbed-wire barriers and waved them through.

Single sailors (for the Navy had taken over from the Marines) lived in a barracks closer to the station and life was a little different, but still Shanghai beckoned. At Cavite in 1939, when authorities asked for volunteers to go to Shanghai, despite the China Incident every man but one raised his hand!

It was different for Chinese. "In the winter," recounts Roy Sholes, "it was not unusual to pass, oh, within that eight blocks, five to eight corpses in the street. Frozen, and they had just been put out to be picked up by the truck that the city sent around." From what he saw the Navy radioman concluded that "they were really ripe for communism." Others saw the same squalor and frustration as tools to turn against Japan, as did Marine major Gregon Williams, whose cover was as assistant naval attaché in Shanghai but whose real job happened to be running agents against Japan. Williams worked in parallel to the intelligence section (S-2) of the 4th Marines, with wider interests than simple combat intelligence, which trade he had learned previously with Marines in the Dominican Republic. Williams used to regale visiting attaché Stephen Jurika with stories of his preparations to escape once the Japanese took over, and to leave behind agents who would continue reporting to the Americans. (Despite his advance preparations, when war came Williams did not make it. Captured by the Japanese, he would be held separately from other Americans. The Office of Naval Intelligence spent months trying to find out what had happened to him. He eventually was repatriated in a diplomatic exchange.)

Tokyo attaché Stephen Jurika liked his Shanghai visits, not only because he compared notes with Major Williams. In Shanghai, Jurika garnered Asiatic Fleet scuttlebutt, observed the Japanese in a setting where they, too, were away from home, and got news, magazines, books, and all manner of information in a place free of Japanese press controls. In fact, what Stephen Jurika did on a small scale became an official activity for the U.S. naval attaché in Japan. That is, wholly apart from the American attachés assigned to China, the Tokyo attachés began to make Shanghai visits specifically to watch the Japanese. Unlike Jurika's informal sojourns, these visits were made with the cognizance and specific approval of the Japanese Navy Ministry.

One typical instance came in June 1938, when Captain Bemis made his second Shanghai visit. He stayed two weeks, met with top Asiatic Fleet officers and American diplomats, the naval attaché from Peking, businessmen, local Chinese, and foreign naval officers. There was a trip up the Yangtze aboard the gunboat *Isabel* with the Asiatic Fleet commander and his staff. In the nine months since Bemis's previous visit much had changed as the pace of the Sino-Japanese war accelerated. "Almost instantly," Captain Bemis noticed "the magnitude of the preparations that Japan had made to prosecute the war." Bemis reported on Shanghai, on the Japanese campaign along the Yangtze, on Japanese cabinet changes, and on potential Chinese strategies.

These visits were snapshots of the Imperial Navy at moments in the China Incident. Following a similar visit in November 1938 Captain Bemis reported:

> The Japanese Navy has been engaged in a quasi-naval war for the past sixteen months. . . . Its training has probably been that of a fleet which must be ready at any moment to meet an enemy. It is known that it cruises at high speed during daylight and darkened at night. Parts of it have been on blockade duty winter and summer. The smaller units have been in actual combat with an enemy. Certain parts of the fleet have carried out joint operations with the Army. A very high technique in convoy work, in supporting a landing and in actual landing operations has undoubtedly been developed.

The attaché reminded ONI readers that Imperial Navy activities encompassed all types of action, from minesweeping, to defense against torpedo boat and air attacks, to amphibious operations. Combat gave the Japanese Navy an opportunity to demand larger budgets and increase its strength. Most important, the Japanese had had occasion for combat employment of their naval air arm, the JNAF. As Bemis noted, "No other Naval Power has had similar war experience or anything even approaching what Japan has enjoyed."

This seemed a most ominous aspect of the Tokyo attaché's report. In fact, Captain Bemis wrote: "Where, before the war, it could truthfully be stated that Japanese naval aircraft were several years behind our own, it would be most unwise to hold such an opinion today." This became one more attaché report that went unheeded.

It should be noted that Army attachés in China were also filing reports on Japanese airpower, and these seem to have received rather more attention from the home office. As early as October 1937 General Henry H. (Hap) Arnold, future head of the U.S. Army Air Forces, called Japan a "first rate air power which knows how to use its air strength." Technical experts opined that JNAF Claude fighters completely outclassed the U.S. aircraft they faced at that time. Claire Chennault, head of the Flying Tigers, sent commentaries on the Japanese aircraft they encountered. Even the Zero fighter, which the JNAF introduced to combat in China in September 1940, was pictured in reports by the Chinese, based on commentary by captured Japanese pilots. Army chief of staff George C. Marshall referred to this aircraft, and gave accurate technical characteristics, in February 1941 letters to air commanders in the Philippines and Hawaii. The last prewar edition of the Army's standard reference on Japanese planes, which appeared in March 1941, contained an entry on the A6M with accurate details and even the notation that it was being called the "Zero type." In May the Chinese actually recovered relatively intact Zero fighter wreckage near Chengtu and prepared a foreign-technology report on the plane.

Once again the Navy had some of the same information. The assistant naval attaché at Peking, Captain James H. McHugh of the Marines, received a copy of the Chinese technical report and sent it to ONI. In late July 1941 Major Ronald A. Boone of the Marines released an ONI study of Japanese air combat tactics noting the Zero fighter's speed, range, and weapons, but discounting it as not very maneuverable. The intelligence circulated more widely within the Navy pilot community, however. Lieutenant Commander John S. Thach, who conceived the most effective tactic for countering the Zero's advantages, later recalled that the information on which he based his "Thach weave" maneuver came to him in the spring of 1941. Things known at working levels are sometimes missed or not believed higher up the intelligence chain, and the Zero became a technical surprise due to this phenomenon.

China was the mixing pot for a whole stew of Japanese tactics and techniques. Air warfare became a most vital function for the Imperial Navy, whose units in China grew to as many as 400 to 500 aircraft after 1938. Admiral Oikawa Koshiro, Third Fleet commander during 1938–1939, later said of the JNAF effort, "I believe that it made a very important contribution to our operation." Other activities in China also increased Japan's war preparedness. Imperial Navy task forces convoyed and furnished fire support for at least sixteen major amphibious assaults between 1937 and 1941. Some were quite large affairs involving three or more divisions of Japanese Army troops. Some Army troops, especially those of the 5th Division, which participated in eight invasions during this period, and the 18th, which had been in three, acquired considerable amphibious experience, put to use later invading Malaya. The Imperial Navy improved fleet readiness, gained sea time and combat exposure, and learned the proclivities of its sister service. The Sino-Japanese War provided Japan with background for its Great Pacific War.

Thus matters stood when, far across the Pacific, the American war began. Later the importance of China would be diminished by historians who largely ignored it in their work on the Pacific war. At the time, however, the China factor was well recognized. "The Army may be bogged down," wrote Hugh Byas, a former *New York Times* correspondent in Tokyo, "but the Navy has had four years on a war footing and unlimited budgets, all spent in preparation for the struggle now on." Perhaps Japan's Chinese adventure was neglected because it seemed somehow a sideshow; Imperial Navy sailors, like sailors in all large fleets, dream of blue water. The true metier of these navies was to be sought in an ultimate confrontation across the broad expanse of the Pacific.

# Like an Athletic Competition

O NE INDICATOR OF THE RISE OF HOSTILITY ACROSS THE PACIFIC CAN BE FOUND IN COMparing the Japanese League of Nations Association and its Navy League. Both entities were voluntary organizations of private citizens, formed at nearly the same time. Their histories, however, are like a photograph and its negative, reversed images. These organizations' evolution presents a microcosm of political trends in Japan from the 1920s into the decade before the war.

Japan had been perfectly content to join the League of Nations in the heyday of internationalism following World War I. The Japanese government even helped fund that country's League of Nations Association, created in 1920 under the auspices of a prominent industrialist, followed by Ishii Kikujiro, a former foreign minister. Membership grew from 683 in 1920 to almost 12,000 by 1932. The high point for the association probably came in 1929, when the Institute for Pacific Relations (IPR) held its third annual conference at Kyoto with substantial assistance from the Japanese League association. Japan's delegation was headed by Itobe Inazo, a prominent association member and former undersecretary of the League of Nations itself. Despite its membership growth and the presence of opinion-makers such as Diet members, businessmen, and diplomats, not to mention early support the group had had from members of the imperial family, the organization shattered under the strain of Japan's growing intervention in China.

In 1931, when Itobe led another Japanese delegation to the Institute for Pacific Relations conference at Shanghai, he found himself under pressure to explain Japanese policy in Manchuria, where the Imperial Army had inaugurated a decade of force by seizing control on a pretext, the first of many such coups. Itobe did the best he could to put a rational face on the Army's actions, then, after the IPR conference, embarked on a tour of the United States to bring his arguments to a wider American audience. He gave a national radio address on Japan and the League of Nations. While Itobe continued his U.S. tour, fighting broke out in Shanghai, with Japan implicated as aggressor in events that cut the ground from under Japanese internationalists.

After the 1932 Shanghai affair, the League of Nations formed an investigating commission chaired by British Lord Lytton, a former viceroy in India and son of another, grandson of the author of *The Last Days of Pompeii*. Lytton's commission, including members from four other nations, concluded that Japan had been responsible for the troubles in China. A debate at the League was scheduled. The Japanese League of Nations Association obtained a delay for the purpose of making an independent translation of the Lytton Report, but when the League debate actually came, Japan found herself condemned by unanimous vote, 42–0. Ambassador Matsuoka Yosuke stalked out of the meeting chamber; Japan withdrew from the League. The date was February 24, 1933. Japan's League of Nations Association never recovered. It subsequently reorganized as the International Association of Japan, but before the China Incident reached full intensity the group had effectively lost its influence.

Japan's Navy League presents a study in contrasts. Like the League of Nations Association, the Navy League had been formed by businessmen. The Navy League founders were a group from the Chamber of Commerce and Industry, meeting in Tokyo on October 3, 1917. That year the League had 444 members. In 1918 it began to publish its own magazine and held public activities on Japan's Navy Day, May 27, the anniversary of Japan's victory over Russia at the 1905 battle of Tsushima. In 1921, during the fund-raising drive that paid for battleship *Mutsu*, the Navy League published a children's book of tales of the sea and warships. Of course, that happened to be the year of the Washington Conference and the naval treaty. Membership in the League, which had risen to over 4,500, remained stagnant. In fact the membership figure for 1922 is not available in the source document, which was prepared for U.S. occupation authorities by Navy League officials in 1945. That this is the only year for which data are missing suggests the Navy League either became too demoralized to keep its figures for 1922, or suppressed the data, or perhaps lost them in the 1923 earthquake. In any case, 1923 membership was below that for 1921, the last pre-treaty year, and recovered to pre-treaty levels only in 1926, the year the League held an exhibition on Tokyo's Ginza that attracted over a million visitors.

After the initial session of the London Naval Conference, the Navy League formed a committee to write a report on the negotiations, the first of a series of more overtly political actions. In 1932, when the League of Nations Association was being eclipsed by the Shanghai Incident, the Navy League collected donations for relief of disabled Imperial Navy veterans and surviving kin. It became the first of the regular donation drives mentioned in a previous chapter. Navy League membership mushroomed at this time, increasing from 10,000 to 25,000 in 1933, to 64,000 in 1934, and to 154,000 in 1935. In the first year of the China Incident, membership stood at almost 183,000, and in the year of Pearl Harbor the Navy League members numbered 422,000. In October 1945 there were 1,700,000 members. By then the director of the League's activities (since December 1939) was Admiral Prince Fushimi Hiroyasu, retired chief of the Naval General Staff. The League thus evolved into an effective Imperial Navy support group, a manifestation of the political power of Japanese navalism, sharing the dreams and aspirations of the Navy itself.

IF THERE WAS A DREAM AMONG OFFICERS OF THE IMPERIAL NAVY, ONE DREAM, WIDELY HELD, a fundamental basis for the tactics and doctrine the Japanese developed, that has to be the vision of a "decisive" naval battle. Not just any decisive naval battle, mind you, for battles can be decisive or not depending upon outcomes, but a particularly shaped and designed battle. The Japanese fleet was built to engage in this Decisive Battle, trained to conduct it, and officers and men were imbued with the idea of the Decisive Battle almost as a tradition, an ideology, a cult. Tear away a few layers of the education and modernist orientation that characterized the naval officer corps and not too much separated the Imperial Navy's cult of the Decisive Battle and the cargo cults of some primitive societies on the South Sea islands Japan sought to dominate.

In small societies, legend serves to explain and justify current hardship and to give hope of future fulfillment. In exactly this way the doctrine of Decisive Battle explained how the inferior fleet permitted under the naval treaty system could emerge victorious from the future war. In both cases cultism started from, and made use of, hard realities of current conditions. For the Imperial Navy these conditions were its restriction to a fraction of U.S. fleet strength and its desire to attain absolute superiority in Far Eastern waters, a desire that stood to be vitiated by intervention of a U.S. fleet which by definition had superior strength.

For Japanese doctrine the question was and remained how to square this circle. The answer owed something to the experience of the Russo-Japanese War, when czarist Russia assembled in Europe a force to break the Japanese stranglehold in the Far East and then sent it around the world to eventual defeat at Tsushima. There was some question in the case of Tsushima as to which fleet should be judged materially superior, but that was not the point. The Russians had arrived in the Far East in an exhausted condition after tribulations all over the world. They had even frightened themselves with rumors of Japanese ambushes in the North Sea, the Indian Ocean, and the South China Sea.

What if the fancied attacks that had frightened the Russians had been real? Japan's preeminent naval strategists after 1905 were discriminating observers of the Russo-Japanese War. Sato Tetsutaro originated a concept of offensive-defense operations, like the Port Arthur torpedo-boat raid at the outset of the 1904–1905 war, attacks to which Japan might commit limited forces for large payoffs. Akiyama Saneyuki, who incidentally had been the Imperial Navy's observer with the U.S. fleet off Cuba in the Spanish-American War, emphasized the advantages of night attacks, proper use of light forces, fleet formations, and principles of engagement. Both Sato and Akiyama taught at the Naval Staff College in the period just before World War I when many of the Imperial Navy's key commanders did the course there.

The strategic problem of a naval war with the United States appeared very similar to that of 1904–1905 and amenable to the kinds of tactics taught by theorists like Akiyama and Sato. The United States possessed a Far East bastion in the form of the Philippines, but its main battle fleet had never been based there. In all probability the American fleet would have to advance across the Pacific before it could even engage. Such a lengthy preliminary provided the Imperial Navy numerous opportunities to whittle down America's fleet with torpedo attacks by submarines and destroyer flotillas. As the airplane gained stature it, too, fit perfectly into place as a component of what came to be called *yogeki zengen sakusen,* or the strategy of interceptive operations.

As the concept was written into war plans in the treaty era it acquired a concrete operational character. At the outset of a war, Imperial Navy and Army forces would cooperate to overwelm the Philippines, robbing the United States of its potential Far East base. Guam, an American possession in the Marianas, and an intermediate point with base potential, would also be captured. The other Mariana Islands, together with many of the Marshalls and Carolines, by then embodied in a League of Nations mandate administered by Japan, offered a countervailing advantage to the Imperial Navy as bases for the attrition forces to reduce the Americans. In particular, submarines and aircraft could be used in this endeavor; in a late prewar development, midget submarines became available as well.

When the U.S. fleet came within striking range of Japan, the Imperial Navy could prepare the ground, so to speak, for the final encounter, by a night attack with cruisers and destroyers supported by fast battleships. In particular, torpedo runs with fast, lethal Type 93 oxygen torpedoes would create havoc among hapless Americans. Some Japanese authorities went so far as to estimate that 25 percent of the torpedoes (an uncommonly large fraction) could be expected to strike home.

At dawn the Imperial Navy's battle line would draw over the horizon to begin the Decisive Battle per se. By that time an adversary would presumably be exhausted, weakened by substantial losses, far from repairs or support, and probably confused as well. In short, an American fleet ripe for annihilation at the hands of the Imperial Navy. At that point the Japanese battle line—fresh battleships supported by great numbers of fully armed destroyers and, shortly before the war, even some innovative torpedo cruisers—would be well prepared to deal the final, fatal blows.

That was the Imperial Navy's vision. It was not some top-secret contingency plan gathering dust in a safe. Not only were the Japanese constantly exercising aspects of the plan and designing their warships accordingly, but in its broad outlines the plan was known to the public. Naval commentators discussed principles of interceptive operations; former officers wrote about them; articles in Navy League publications extolled the perfection of the concept. In fact, so widely known did the strategy become that mention of it, as already quoted, could be found in the reports of the U.S. naval attaché in Tokyo.

Always prepared to seize upon any element it might use to advantage, the Imperial Navy, which intended to conduct its Decisive Battle in the region of the Bonin Islands, performed weather studies and estimated that foul weather was roughly eight times more common in that region than in the typical U.S. fleet training areas off Hawaii, the American West Coast, and the Caribbean. As a result, the Japanese adopted a program emphasizing training exercises precisely during rough-weather periods. In 1935, when Admiral Prince Fushimi headed the Naval General Staff and Captain Fukudome Shigeru was his chief of operations, the NGS deliberately planned that year's major fleet maneuver for when the weather would be worst. When the maneuver duly took place it coincided with a typhoon; seas became so rough that the torpedo boat *Tomodzuru* capsized and sank. Western observers focused on the supposedly inferior sea-keeping quality of Japanese ships that could be sunk so. Though better aware of the rationale for these maneuvers, Japanese were scandalized at the heavy loss of life that occurred.

Another feature of Japanese practice was the constant driving of seamen to get the most from them. Americans are most familiar with accounts of the use of corporal punishment by Imperial Navy officers and petty officers that appear in the narratives of JNAF aviator Sakai Saburo and destroyerman Hara Tameichi. But Imperial Navy practice happened to be to work as hard as possible as long as possible. It was a saying in the Japanese fleet that the week consisted of "Monday, Monday, Tuesday, Wednesday, Thursday, Friday, Friday." Admiral Suetsugu Nobumasa, who commanded the Combined Fleet from 1933 to 1935 (and found himself forced to resign in the *Tomodzuru* affair) was known as "Seven Days" for the way he worked the fleet. The feeling was that crews inured to the pace would be the most capable on the day of the Decisive Battle.

Much activity by Japanese warships revolved around naval maneuvers in which vessels were played off against each other in mock combat. There were several classes of these maneuvers, including "special grand" exercises; "grand" exercises, usually timed at three-year intervals; and minor maneuvers, involving just a few ships or flotillas. Thus in 1930 there was a "special grand" maneuver that included a complete mobilization of the Imperial Navy *and* reserve personnel plus the recommissioning of every ship on the Navy list, all with such secrecy that the U.S. naval attaché remained unaware anything unusual was up.

In 1929 the Imperial Navy had designated its cruiser commander, the chief of the Second Fleet, as night attack commander, with the tactical title of commander, Advance Force. Very likely the 1930 maneuvers constituted the first major rehearsal of his role, for the exercise involved the assembly of a hypothetical Philippine invasion fleet in Taiwan, which was subsequently covered en route by the Advance Force. As the ships playing the U.S. fleet steamed forward to respond to the supposed invasion, the Advance Force retired while making nightly torpedo attacks. The First Fleet, Japan's battleship force, remained in Empire waters until the hypothetical U.S. units were judged worn out by Advance Force attacks. This sequence bears a clear relationship to the *yogeki zengen sakusen* concept already detailed.

So-called minor maneuvers were actually of relatively large size and were conducted on the average twice a year. One of those would be of a magnitude equivalent to the "fleet problems" conducted by the U.S. Navy. Typically vessels of the Third Fleet in China, ships on detached duty, and ships in the yards for routine servicing did not participate. In each of the years 1931, 1932, 1934, and 1935, the Imperial Navy's First Fleet opposed its Second Fleet. Put another way: Each time, the battle line fought the Advance Force in a simulation of the attrition of the U.S. enemy to be exacted prior to the great Decisive Battle. As early as 1927 maneuvers, aircraft carriers were introduced in a scouting role; in 1930 carriers were judged to have sunk some battleships of the opposing fleet. The carriers were initially considered an adjunct to attrition operations against the adversary.

During 1933 the Imperial Navy again held grand maneuvers like those in 1930. Again there was a mobilization, a period of strategic operations, one of tactical exercises, and a critique and fleet review. During the tactical maneuvers held between August 15 and 19, Emperor Hirohito embarked on the battleship *Nagato* to observe personally. For these maneuvers the Imperial Navy created a Fourth Fleet, an entity that here acted as a defending force but that would soon acquire rather different responsibilities, as we shall see. The Third Fleet simulated a blockade of the China coast. The First and Second fleets escorted troop convoys to Palau from Taiwan. The Fourth Fleet defended against the U.S. riposte from the Bonin Islands. Admiral Suetsugu commanded the simulated U.S. force from the flag bridge of battleship *Mutsu.*

Japan's 1934 minor maneuver had similar premises, but for the 1935 exercise the Imperial Navy assumed the approach of a U.S. fleet from the Aleutian Islands–Kurile Islands sector, a factor that made it easier for the Japanese fleet to encounter rough weather in the course of its operations. Starting late in July the maneuver extended into October. The final stage of this "minor" exercise involved 180 vessels! Maneuvers the following year were interrupted by the so-called February 26 Incident and by upheavals in Japanese internal politics that required attention from Navy leaders, but there were still reasonably extensive practices. Another grand maneuver was intended for 1937 but was preempted by the outbreak of the China Incident. That year, for the first time, a question arose as to whether Combined Fleet headquarters might not be better located ashore.

It seems clear from what is known of the Imperial Navy maneuvers that these were intended precisely to practice and refine aspects of the basic war doctrine, the concept of the Decisive Battle. With great purpose and single-mindedness the Japanese conceived their strategy, refined it, built forces optimized to execute it, and practiced, repeatedly and in detail, how they were going to implement it. American intelligence through its radio interception observed all the big Japanese maneuvers.

Japan's plan had one great weakness, perhaps not apparent at the time, but in fact so obvious that it formed the theme of a manuscript written by Imperial Navy officer Chihaya Masataka within months of the final defeat. The weakness was the assumption that the action to be prepared for would take place within the space of a day, or a few days, or a few months at most. This was going to be a battle, hardly a *campaign,* certainly not a *war.* Long-term factors such as America's production base were barely expected to come into play. Japanese planners resisted thinking through that portion of their strategic problem, apparently assuming that America would choose a compromise peace instead of a fight to the finish. In a typical formulation, naval officer Matsuo Kinoaki wrote: "If the United States–Japan war develops into an endurance war, the United States strategical position will become more and more difficult. . . . There is no prospect of a United States victory in such a case." This was wishful thinking. How could the Japanese have held such a view, especially in view of their intelligence sources? The answer has to do with Imperial Navy intelligence, and with the use of that function in the Japanese command system.


IN MANY WAYS CAPTAIN YOKOYAMA ICHIRO, JAPAN'S LAST PREWAR NAVAL ATTACHÉ IN the United States, seems to have been atypical. Where Japanese attachés, selected by the Navy personnel bureau after consultation with the Third Bureau of the Naval General Staff, usually regarded their posts simply as way stations on the road to higher command, Yokoyama took his work seriously. A 1919 graduate of the naval academy at Etajima, Yokoyama went to America as an English-language student in May 1931. A year later he became assistant naval attaché at the embassy, standard practice for a Japanese officer and one of the ways their language program differed from the American. For several years after his 1933 return to Japan, Yokoyama worked in the Navy Ministry; he then held staff billets with the 5th Destroyer Flotilla and the 2nd China Fleet, and after those postings headed the Third Bureau's 5th Section, which had primary responsibility in the Imperial Navy for collecting intelligence on the United States. In late 1940 Yokoyama was appointed naval attaché in Washington, his second tour, and he was there at the moment of Pearl Harbor.

Where some Japanese naval attachés leaped into the role of spy with alacrity, Yokoyama appreciated the subtle connections between intelligence officer and diplomat. He cultivated contacts among American officers in the belief that the best information came from casual repartee with acquaintances. Thus Captain Yokoyama numbered among his American contacts intelligence officers such as Ellis Zacharias and Henri Smith-Hutton, aviation specialists like Stephen Jurika, and even naval planners like Richmond Kelly Turner. When the latter, as captain of the cruiser *Astoria* in 1939, sailed to Japan carrying the ashes of deceased Japanese ambassador Saito Hiroshi (plus a secret contingent of radio intelligence monitors), Yokoyama was on hand to entertain his American friend. Similarly, it was Yokoyama who invited attaché Stephen Jurika to lecture at Imperial University on American strategy in the Pacific. One never knew what gems might flow from informal contacts. Even if none did, the range of acquaintances and friendships thus developed might prove useful in other ways.

Japanese attachés received no special training for their assignments, but they could be given instructions by the Navy Ministry or the Third Bureau of NGS, which was the Imperial Navy's formal intelligence organization. Captain Yokoyama thus found himself received by Admiral Oikawa Koshiro, Navy minister at the time of Yokoyama's late 1940 appointment to Washington. "You are not the usual sort of naval attaché," Yokoyama recalls Oikawa telling him, "so please don't work hard to collect military information. You should help Ambassador Nomura to prevent war with the United States."

Though Yokoyama's main task may have been striving to prevent war, he supervised a staff of assistant attachés who *were* supposed to gather information, and he had general cognizance of the activities of the Naval Inspector's Office, which had a similar function in addition to its duty of contracting for and supervising Imperial Navy purchases in the United States. Captain Yokoyama's own staff was made up of three lieutenant commanders and several specialist officers. It included Sanematsu Yuzuru, Tachibana Itaru, Okada Shiro, and specialists Imai, Takita, and Shijo. Though Yokoyama was himself a gunnery officer, in fact an expert on large-caliber naval guns, one of his subordinates in Washington happened to be an ordnance specialist.

The last fact indicates the importance the Japanese really attached to collecting technical information of all kinds regarding their probable adversary. The mission of the Naval Inspector's Office underlines this concern. The flavor is conveyed by a document the U.S. captured in Europe (there were also Naval Inspector's Offices in Great Britain, France, Germany, and Italy) toward the end of the war, which listed the specific information the Navy Ministry wanted obtained during the 1940–1941 fiscal year. Given the very top priority was intelligence on the armament of newly designed capital ships and cruisers, followed by details of that armament and details of anti-aircraft armament. The top fifteen priorities included information on extent and use of shipboard equipment to counter poison gas, trends in research on chemical warfare compounds, uses of powder-type timed fuses, special shells for anti-aircraft guns, and details of steel production capacity.

These were universal targets, information the Imperial Navy wanted from every country in which it was represented, but there were also other, even more specific collection objectives. For the United States, for example, three of the top priorities concerned torpedoes and three others mines. The Japanese wish list included blueprints for American turbine-driven torpedoes, information on U.S. torpedo detonators, and material on magnetic mines. Priority number seven (remember, this was 1940) was for intelligence on "the condition and capabilities of underwater sound locators and radar equipment." Another priority was information on research into "oxy-hydrogen torpedoes." In other areas the Navy Ministry's bureau of construction wanted details on electric welding for the hulls of ships, on the seaworthiness of destroyers, and on methods of aircraft stowage on ships at sea. The top priority in the field of radio equipment was for intelligence on U.S. advances in underwater sound detectors and sound communication systems, and a further priority was results of U.S. use of such equipment by surface craft.

Located in a Manhattan office building near the Forty-second Street

Library, the naval inspector drew his information from contacts with American manufacturers, liaison with U.S. naval shipyards, and old-fashioned open-source research at a good library. Engineer Captain Ishikawa Yasutaro was naval inspector in the United States at the beginning of 1941. In Britain the senior naval attaché doubled as inspector.

The kind of thing the naval inspectors did typified the genteel espionage Captain Yokoyama believed in. Predecessors and subordinates, not to mention colleagues elsewhere, were not necessarily of the same view. There was also a certain brash, ebullient, sometimes even swashbuckling variety of Imperial Navy attaché who went about intelligence-gathering as if engaged in athletic competition. Yamaguchi Tamon, attaché from 1934 to 1936, had a finger in some West Coast spy cases about which more shortly. *His* predecessor, Kobayashi Masahi, had raised a stink in 1934 when FDR held a presidential review of the U.S. fleet: Kobayashi openly went aboard carrying a heavy load of film, cameras, and telephoto lenses.

In a class by himself was Ogawa Kanji, who had been naval attaché in Washington between 1938 and 1940. Ogawa rose to admiral and later headed Japan's Total War Research Institute; he was one of the small band of real intelligence experts in the Imperial Navy. He graduated first in his class from Etajima, became a gunnery expert, and gravitated to delicate staff jobs, moving back and forth from the Military Affairs Bureau of the Navy Ministry to the Third Bureau of NGS. In 1935 Ogawa visited North America and that October accompanied several other Imperial Navy officers then serving in the United States to Cuernavaca, Mexico, where they met with German intelligence officials, according to one account, to cook up a spy alliance against the United States. In any case Ogawa moved smoothly from deputy chief of the Third Bureau's American section, to chief of the section, to attaché, and back. He would head the American section again for six months in 1942, when Japanese espionage in North America had ground to a complete halt.

Such as they were, Japanese networks in the United States seem to have been based on the extracurricular activities of language officers. This is logical in a way, since the lowly students presumably attracted less attention, but it was also detrimental since the Imperial Navy usually assigned students for only a single year of language study, often at a college (Princeton, Harvard, and the University of California seem to have been popular), and combined their language training with study of formal academic subjects, such as American history or political science. Moreover, the Navy Ministry assigned students for their general promise as naval officers, not any particular potential as intelligence specialists. The Americans soon organized themselves to follow the activities of all official Japanese closely, and under ONI's general direction district intelligence officers assigned to each U.S. naval district monitored local foreign nationals.

In Los Angeles in the early 1930s there had been an Imperial Navy language student named Torii who was hit by a car and killed. The officer's briefcase contained documents suggesting that he had done more than learn English. Although the connection cannot be positively established, Lieutenant Commander Miyazaki Toshio entered the U.S. in August 1933, registered as a student at Stanford, then moved to Los Angeles, where he began to run an American agent, one Harry T. Thompson, a former U.S. Navy enlisted man, who impersonated a petty officer and cadged information from sailors to sell to the Japanese. Thompson's act became known when his roommate went to Pacific Fleet commander Admiral Joseph Reeves with information that the man had been handing papers over to a Japanese after impersonating sailors.

Admiral Reeves had as fleet intelligence officer a young lieutenant named Joseph J. Rochefort, a Japanese-language officer and radio intelligence expert whom Reeves took from official (cover) duty as assistant district intelligence officer. As an admiral's aide, Rochefort had been spending much time arranging social engagements and finding out about people who wanted to see Reeves; the Thompson case seemed an opportunity to get back toward his main interest. Admiral Reeves brought in an amateur sleuth, Cecil H. Coggins, an obstetrics specialist at Long Beach Naval Dispensary who had been delivering sixty to eighty babies a month. Rochefort brought in Arthur H. McCollum from ONI, and contrived some doctored information that could be fed to Thompson to see where it went. Then McCollum took over the investigative phase, getting a lucky break when watchers saw Commander Miyazaki's car at the site of a failed rendezvous. Incredibly, the vehicle had been registered in Miyazaki's own name and led immediately to the Imperial Navy officer. As investigators worked to develop the case, Harry Thompson got scared and tried to resign as a spy. With his agent shying away, Commander Miyazaki felt there was little point continuing his ostensible language study and left for Japan. Thompson would be sentenced to fifteen years in prison.

Published accounts indicate that the intelligence the Japanese got from Thompson was routine stuff. Navy documents confirm this: ONI established that Miyazaki had *asked* for data on floating mines, smoke screens, and the power of U.S. torpedoes. Thompson admitted *providing* information on anti-aircraft guns aboard the light cruiser *Milwaukee*, specimen .50-caliber bullets, and Pacific Fleet target-practice results. Ironically, the Japanese succeeded in penetrating the *Milwaukee* again, for Oliver A. Kirkeby, a gunner's mate aboard the cruiser, was later found to have passed certain information to a Japanese resident of San Francisco. Letters signed by "Oliver" turned up in the briefcase of Lieutenant Commander Ohmae Toshikazu, as did a Naval General Staff document containing instructions along with requests for data on naval tactics, identification of units, communications, and U.S. Navy training and education. (Ohmae's briefcase reportedly had been surreptitiously opened one night in Davenport, Iowa, while the officer tarried with an inviting young woman.) After delivering fresh code material to the Japanese embassy in Washington, Ohmae spent a year at the University of Pennsylvania as language officer, then a second year in San Francisco, leaving the United States on April 29, 1937.

It may have been that Commander Ohmae was intended as the replacement for Miyazaki on the American West Coast, since he is known to have visited Seattle and Portland and to have given a Japanese bank in Los Angeles as his home address. It may also be that the West Coast spy network functioned under direct control of the Third Bureau and NGS, since Ellis Zacharias reports that Washington initially proved loath to prosecute Thompson because the Miyazaki evidence led straight to senior Imperial Navy officers.

The Third Bureau did run espionage operations unilaterally, outside the purview of the attaché system, and other examples of this have come to light. One was an affair in Singapore in 1934, when British authorities arrested Lieutenant Commander Kaseda Tetsuhiko, who sought intelligence on the British naval base, posing as a construction expert under the alias Kashima Teizo. Another apparent NGS unilateral operation was the 1937 U.S. sojourn of Commander Togami Ichiro, who landed at Seattle together with a radio specialist, spent six months at the Japanese embassy familiarizing himself with American communications procedures, and then began an eighteen-month road trip with sophisticated (for those days) radio equipment in the trunk of his car. Togami became, in effect, a mobile radio interception unit, following the U.S. fleet to its exercise areas and observing their radio messages. The details of this operation could never be fully established since Togami went on to command a submarine in the war and perished at sea.

It is likely that Togami's radio espionage had its origin not in the Third Bureau of the Naval General Staff but in the Fourth. In the Japanese system the Fourth Bureau controlled naval communications, including radio intelligence. First created in the heat of the Russo-Japanese War, moribund afterward, then temporarily abolished in 1916, the Naval General Staff communications unit had had poor prospects until the mid-1920s, when the use of radio burgeoned in Japan. Formal communications intelligence began with the creation of a "special section" (*tokumu han*) in either 1925 or 1929, depending upon the authority cited. The earlier date seems more likely in view of reports that Imperial Navy ships bearing special equipment were dispatched to observe U.S. maneuvers during 1924. Initially the *tokumu han*, located in the Navy Ministry building, had a total of six personnel, including administrative staff.

Imperial Navy codebreakers cooperated with Japanese Foreign Ministry and Army counterparts on U.S. State Department codes, and they gained entry into some of them. Success followed against certain temporary codes the U.S. Navy used only during fleet maneuvers, and against Chinese code systems. In fact, American codebreaker Herbert Yardley, of Washington Conference fame, ended up in China trying to perfect the Nationalists' communication security but this time had little success against *tokumu han.* Rundown, passed by, distracted by a passion for gambling, Yardley ended his career in China.

Meanwhile the Imperial Navy forged ahead, in a technical sense, though its measure of success did not increase much. In 1932 the Japanese converted their oiler *Erimo* into a specialized intelligence-collection vessel; American naval officers repeatedly worried later that Japanese fishing boats were moonlighting as radio intercept stations. Such fishing boats were said to have the latest radio gear where similar American ships usually carried just a primitive receiver.* Imperial Navy officers were also said to be on detached duty with the fishing fleet. In at least one instance an agent reporting to the U.S. naval attaché in Tokyo warned that El Salvador had become a covert base for fishing-fleet spy activity. Other reports warned of Japanese interest in such facilities in Mexico, especially at Guaymas on the Gulf of California, or at Mazatlán.

At this late date it is difficult to separate anxiety from realism in these prewar apprehensions. American views have been inescapably colored by the real intelligence competition of the Cold War, in which Soviet fishing boats definitely served as intelligence collectors and both sides used supposedly innocent tourists to obtain information of intelligence value. Some Americans profess to remember, and even still insist, that every Japanese boat was a communications monitor and every tourist with a camera a budding spy. Knowing the Japanese passion for gadgets, however, including precisely such items as electronics and cameras, it is difficult today to picture mere possession of these things as criteria exposing someone as an agent. More likely, a certain hysteria prevailed that went far beyond the actual depredations of Japanese agents.

This is not to say that Japanese did not carry out real espionage. In the communications intelligence field, for example, during the early 1930s there were a series of clandestine break-ins at British and American consulates in Kobe to obtain code material. The technical collection effort, however, outweighed espionage endeavors, exactly as became the standard in the Cold War era. It was in 1936 that *tokumu han* opened its big radio inter-

---

*It is not generally known that at one point during this period the Pacific Fleet staff permitted a cryptanalyst who wished to look at the fishing-boat question to work on the Japanese codes involved. The expert, who was the talented Ham Wright, solved the code and recovered a set of messages. Once translated, the Japanese fishing-boat traffic turned out to concern the locations and behavior of schools of fish. See Admiral Edwin T. Layton et al., *And I Was There: Pearl Harbor and Midway—Breaking the Secrets* (New York: William Morrow & Company, 1985).

ception center at Owada, about twenty miles northeast of Tokyo. In 1938 the Navy established a special section (*L kikan*) of its attaché staff in Mexico as a forward intercept post watching the U.S. fleet, including the U.S. Navy's main radio transmitters in Washington and the Atlantic Fleet as well as RCA commercial radio transmissions from New York City. The Owada facility by that time had as many as 181 receivers and 20 radio direction-finding units. The Imperial Navy network was also increased with the addition of stations on Marcus Island in the Pacific; at Wakkanai, Ominato, and Maizuru in the Home Islands; Chinkai in Korea; and Takao in Taiwan. The 11th Section of the Naval General Staff processed and analyzed the intercepts, converting them into intelligence useful to the Japanese fleet.

Such raw intelligence as resulted from intercept reports, radio direction finding, and the analysis of foreign communication networks, so-called traffic analysis, went to the Naval General Staff and the Combined Fleet. The Third Bureau of NGS became the most prominent consumer of communications reporting, contributing to its all-source intelligence. The Third Bureau held pride of place as top Japanese naval intelligence outfit, having been created as early as 1896. The intelligence bureau, or *joho kyoku*, comprised several subordinate units with geographic responsibilities: The 5th Section handled both North and South America; the 8th produced intelligence on British and Indian subjects; and the 6th Section became chief *joho kyoku* player in the China Incident. These are the key naval intelligence components for our purposes, though it should also be noted that the 7th Section maintained files on the Soviet Union plus European powers other than Great Britain. The *joho kyoku* supervised the naval attachés, interacted with naval planners, and controlled a group of resident naval officers who looked out for Imperial Navy interests in Shanghai, Hankow, Manchukuo, and so forth.

Though the Japanese clearly recognized the role of intelligence, their view of its proper scope and importance differed from the Americans'. One crude measure of the relative value attributed to intelligence by the several naval powers lies in comparison of the number of officers assigned to central intelligence units as of 1941. The U.S. Office of Naval Intelligence had 230 officers in 1941; the British Royal Navy's Naval Intelligence Division had 161; in the Third Bureau in Tokyo there were just 29 officers.*

---

*The comparison is even more stark if one takes the full complement of the Office of Naval Intelligence instead of just counting its Washington headquarters. In all, in Washington there were 230 officers, 175 enlisted men, and 300 civilians. Posted abroad were another 133 officers and 200 enlisted men. Naval district offices had another 100 officers, but employed an additional 900 enlisted men, 100 civilians, and 135 civilian agents. Thus total ONI manpower was about 2,200, with the proportion devoted to foreign intelligence or administration—a range of functions comparable to those of *joho kyoku*—roughly half.

This comparison is misleading in part because the Imperial Navy believed itself a lean, mean, seagoing fighting machine, with a minimum of shore-based tail that provided maximum support functions. This amounted to parsimony. About half the Japanese Navy's total personnel served aboard ship or in operating air units. Competition for duty in these desirable assignments remained so great that annual rotations transferred almost everyone *except* those officers in intelligence or staff posts. These officers, sometimes relegated to limited duty due to handicaps, more often considered specialists, tended to have much longer tours of duty than the average elsewhere in the Navy.

Another factor that helps account for the small size of Japanese intelligence organizations is simply the number of officers in the Imperial Navy. For 1936, the last year the Japanese and United States exchanged official data, there were just over 5,300 officers in the Imperial Navy. This cadre had to man not only a fleet and an air force, but a marine corps (the Special Naval Landing Force) estimated to number almost 30,000 (the size of a small army corps), a network of bases and support units in China, and a shore establishment including shipyards, technical research centers, naval bases, air stations, and training and logistics facilities. In short, the Japanese naval officer corps had to stretch to its fullest to cover the range of its duties. It is worth noting that the size of *joho kyoku* compares favorably, for example, with that of the naval operations staff, which in fact had even fewer officers assigned.

The small size of the Japanese naval intelligence organization is also partly accounted for by functional differences between it and Western counterparts. In Washington much of ONI's activity aimed at creating and maintaining massive compendiums of basic information. This included, most noticeably, the ONI monographs, but also aircraft and ship recognition manuals and encyclopedic materials on adversaries. The Third Bureau did not produce such publications. Rather, *joho kyoku* issued occasional reports based upon whatever information it had in hand. This difference helped limit personnel requirements and also reduced the need for comprehensive intelligence collection by attachés abroad.

American interrogators would be surprised *after* the war to learn that Japanese attachés were not required to submit *any* regular reports, and they also could not quite believe that Imperial Navy officers selected to become attachés did not receive special training or indoctrination by *joho kyoku*. As with the Americans, language officers formed the basis of the attaché system. Unlike the Americans, Japan's language officers also conducted espionage, although assistant attachés and even attachés could also be involved. In the most important interwar espionage case, that of John S. Farnsworth, the agent had been handled successively by assistant attachés Ichimiya Yoshiyuki and Yamaki Akira under supervision of Captain

Yamaguchi Tamon, senior naval attaché.* In the case of the West Coast espionage effort, assistant attachés Otani Inao and Tachibana Itaru were involved. Tachibana was actually deported in June 1941.

Conversely, there are many distinguished officers who served as attachés in the United States and went on to high command without having been linked to espionage efforts. This list includes such officers as Yamamoto Isoroku (attaché between 1925 and 1927 and assistant attaché earlier than that), Nagano Osami, Hoshina Zenshiro, Hasegawa Kiyoshi, Ito Seiichi, Fukudome Shigeru, Sakano Yasaburo, and so on. Admiral Nomura Kichisaburo, a Russian-language officer who probably achieved some kind of record by serving as senior attaché in four important nations, including the United States, stood at the center of one of Japan's final attempts to avoid war with America, a set of negotiations held in 1941.

By that time Captain Yokoyama had become attaché, with Commander Sanematsu Yuzuru as his top assistant. Sanematsu graduated from Etajima with the class of 1923, one that seems to have been especially important to the annals of Imperial Navy intelligence. Classmates included attachés Otani Inao and Usui Yoshiro (assigned to the U.S.S.R.), language officer Kisaka Yoshitane (in America during 1939–1940), and communications intelligence experts Wada Yushiro and the unfortunate Togami Ichiro; not to mention several officers who held important posts on the staffs of the Combined Fleet or NGS. Born in Saga prefecture in November 1902, Sanematsu, like his boss Yokoyama, represented the Imperial Navy putting its best foot forward. He had been at the Naval War College with Genda Minoru and Fuchida Mitsuo, had been aide to navy ministers Nagano Osami and Yonai Mitsumasa, and had studied politics and history at Princeton. In the Imperial Navy Sanematsu rose to captain and wartime chief of the *joho kyoku* section responsible for intelligence on the United States, so his impressions are important. Most memorable is Sanematsu's recollection of an auto tour through the U.S. in 1940. As he drove up into the Rocky Mountains, at 12,000 feet Sanematsu encountered a work crew using a power shovel and a dump car. There were only three men using the machines, and Sanematsu knew that in Japan a similar job would have been given to thirty or forty. "I felt in my guts that it would be a real trouble if Japan had to fight with such a country," Sanematsu later recalled.

On the day war began, Sunday, December 7, 1941, Sanematsu happened

---

*According to Edwin T. Layton, the first inkling that the Japanese were getting intelligence on the Pacific Fleet actually came from a message decoded and translated in Washington. In his own oral history, Arthur McCollum alludes to this episode by saying that Joe Rochefort's assignment to the district intelligence office was conceived by ONI strictly for purposes of cover. In his own interviews, however, Rochefort is silent regarding the provenance of his assignment.

to arrive early at the Japanese embassy in Washington. In front of the door were several piles of newspapers, a collection of milk bottles, and such a number of letters and telegrams that they overflowed the mailbox. One of those telegrams happened to be an instruction for the ambassador to deliver Japan's final ultimatum at a precise hour to coincide with the attack on Pearl Harbor. Sanematsu could find no one to decode the crucial instruction. The delay helped retard Japanese diplomacy that day. In the long run the Imperial Navy would suffer the consequences, and Japanese intelligence bore a share of the blame. Years afterward Sanematsu would still be writing in an attempt to understand what had happened.

BEHIND THE OPEN, DISCREET, QUASI-DIPLOMATIC SPIES AMONG THE NAVAL ATTACHÉ CORPS stood others, the technical intelligence collectors, men and women who labored to divine the adversary's innermost secrets. Where the attachés more or less openly sought information host countries considered secret, the people in communications intelligence, the main technical program in this dawn of the machine intelligence age, very secretly sought information that could be openly plucked from the airwaves. This quest for vision into the adversary's heart caught on among Americans just as among Japanese— perhaps more so, for Americans tended toward a different view of the role of intelligence. The Japanese seemed to take the intelligence as informing them of obstacles to be overcome in pursuing a goal, Americans utilized intelligence as an actual planning factor more than an ethereal quantity. This practical approach dictated a more systematic effort to exploit the techniques available. Where intelligence had begun in almost the same place in both navies, in time differences in attitude led to an American effort that burgeoned as the Japanese languished.

Communications intelligence illustrates the difference in national efforts. If anything, the Imperial Navy initially had the lead in this field. Of course the U.S. Navy had for a long time compiled special signal books, and it began inventing codes when telegraphic communications came into widespread use in the mid-nineteenth century. The Navy's first signal code dates from 1863. Between then and 1913 there would be at least eleven code or signal books adopted by the United States. Though creating all these codes, during this period the Navy exhibited little interest in delving into others' codes. Thus the Japanese had a codebreaking unit within their Naval General Staff before the United States possessed any equivalent entity.

This is not a technical history of codebreaking and will not burden the reader with detailed examinations of the features of various codes and ciphers, but it *is* important to introduce a few concepts and terms. Interest in secret writing and communications goes back many centuries, but for the

U.S. Navy the advent of telegraphic communication marked an important watershed, in that using this method required reducing the alphabet to a series of signals. The short and long dots of Morse code used for telegraph messages are themselves a simple cipher. Morse code found wide, indeed universal, acceptance in telegraphy, was carried over into radio, and is still with us today.

Having once reduced the alphabet to a code, the Navy found it easier to develop additional codes to protect the true meaning of its messages, the "plaintext" in the term of art. Plaintext could be protected not only by letter or digital transposition code, but by substitutions for whole words and even phrases. These were usually collected in books and hence the term "book code." If one was interested—and most users were—in additional protection for plaintext, the simple code characters could be recorded or, if the code being used was numeric, could be given an "additive," an additional random number added to the base value to disguise it. Thus there could be two-stage (or multiple-stage) codes. Messages with additives were considered "enciphered" or "encrypted."

Reconstruction—"recovery"—of the plaintext of a message necessitated getting rid of the additives, stripping them off in the process called deciphering. Mathematical techniques could be applied to decode the message. The frequency in the use of letters or characters in a given language could be calculated and the result applied to decoding. Making one break (often called an entry) in a code facilitated more. Comparing many messages and observing their commonalities also enabled the codebreaker to make informed judgments as to the identity of some code groups, or units of numbers or characters in a message. Conversely, mathematical or other techniques for generating random numbers were important to the process of compiling codes and additive lists. In principle, both the sender and receiver of a plaintext message would be working from identical lists of additives and codebooks. A receiver would recover the message by subtracting the listed additives and then using the codebook to derive the actual text. Unauthorized persons would be unable to interpret a message except by breaking the code (or otherwise gaining access to it).

As long as coded messages were transmitted only by telegraph the U.S. Navy felt little incentive to create an organization specifically to break enemy codes. This evidently stemmed from the problem of gaining access to the coded messages themselves, for telegraphy made use of landlines that had to be physically tapped for interception to occur. In addition, the Navy, yet to be engaged in global operations, felt only modest anxiety over the activities of other countries. This all changed with radio communication, at first called wireless telegraphy, in the early twentieth century. Radio made it possible to communicate between shore stations, including command posts, and ships at sea, and made remote direction of fleets practical. By the same token, however, radio made those commands accessible to anyone who could pick them up, putting a new premium on codes and ciphers.

In addition to its actual content a message also has certain "external" features. These include its point of origin, its address (or addressees, who may be either "for action" or "for information"), its format, and (for a military service) its degree of classification or secrecy. The earliest American efforts in the radio intelligence field actually began as attempts to exploit the external features of communications traffic. For instance, by detecting the direction from which radio waves came one could get a bearing on the source. This, if combined with a second bearing from another (remote) receiver, could generate an actual position for the transmitter. If the transmitter's position could be repeatedly identified, one established if an emitter was fixed or mobile, whether it was a ship (or later, an aircraft), and even its general course and speed. Radio direction finders, essentially radio receivers linked to special directional antennae, were first invented in Europe in 1907; the U.S. Navy began experimenting with them by 1912. A naval communications station at Bar Harbor, Maine, became the location for the first American radio direction finder. By 1924 there were twenty-four U.S. Navy direction-finder stations operating or under construction.

Meanwhile radio technology progressed rapidly, moving into high-frequency bands that offered both longer range and a higher rate of transmission. Coping with the technology required a whole new generation of direction-finding equipment, innovated at Washington's Naval Research Laboratory, where a first experimental antenna would be installed in January 1931. The equipment reached units after perfecting directional loop antennae on which patents were actually issued. An initial high-frequency direction-finding (HF/DF, or "huff-duff") station was installed at Cavite Navy Yard in the Philippines in May 1937, with another station established at Guam that summer. By 1940 the Navy had a HF/DF net of sixteen stations with sixty-five operators, all under OP-20-G, supplemented by an even more extensive network in the United States operated by the Federal Communications Commission.

One of the earliest reporting responsibilities of American naval attachés in Japan became tracking Japanese development of radio. Each time news reached attaché ears of construction or opening of a new radio station it would be reported to Washington together with particulars of the station's antenna array, power capacity, and frequency spectrum. Occasionally American warships cruised offshore to verify reported details of radio installations, in particular one on the Taiwan coast in early 1923.

That American officers watched Japanese fleet communications even at this early date, when radio was in its infancy, is apparent from a report filed in May 1916 by Ensign Thomas A. M. Craven, then Asiatic Fleet communications and intelligence officer. With sources including a Japanese communications officer, with whom he had gone out drinking, Craven acquired surprising detail on Imperial Navy communications. His report included such items as the general method of sending and acknowledging tactical signals from the Japanese fleet flagship *Settsu;* details on radio equipment aboard the *Fuso-, Kongo-,* and *Settsu-*class battleships and battle cruisers; Imperial Navy battleship radio call signs, verified by his drunken Japanese friend; biographical information regarding the Japanese fleet communications officer, a graduate of Harvard and M.I.T. with a thorough knowledge of the physics and theory of radio; data on communications training in the Imperial Navy; and information on radio facilities available to the Japanese Navy Ministry. At that time the ministry had no radio equipment on premises, but there was a powerful station on the outskirts of Tokyo, and the main Navy transmission facility was at Yokosuka base. Data like these furnished ONI, and later OP-20-G, a solid understanding of the Imperial Navy's communications establishment, helping them interpret the external elements of messages.

Work on the Japanese naval codes, which became perhaps the best-known feature of American naval intelligence in World War II, began rather later than the effort to make use of the external features of communications. Part of the impetus was simply having access to the code. In an incident whose details remain obscure, ONI specialists photographed the Imperial Navy's 1918 code in about 1921. According to Ladislas Farago, who collaborated with Ellis Zacharias on the latter's memoir of ONI service, Zacharias discovered that the Japanese naval attaché, then Commander Uyeda Yoshitake, who had the apartment immediately below him in a Washington building, was dating Navy secretaries to gain secret information. Then ONI baited a trap for the Japanese only to discover from Uyeda's subordinate that the attaché worked out of his apartment and actually kept a copy of the naval code there, and that another copy existed at one of the Japanese consulates in the United States. (Though Farago does not say so, the likelihood is that a codebook would have been kept in New York, where the Japanese naval inspector had his offices.) A break-in at the relevant consulate then provided access to the code.

The Americans made only a few copies of the Japanese fleet code, which they encased in red binders and thereafter called the Red Code. The Imperial Navy continued to use its Red Code until 1930; this longevity provided the U.S. Navy an incentive to take advantage of its knowledge. In December 1923 the Navy established a research desk within the Code and Signal Section of the Office of Naval Communications. Officially charged merely with safeguarding the security of *American* fleet codes, the unit was quietly given the task of penetrating the Japanese ones. Naval Communications was called OP-20 in the abbreviation system begun when Congress in 1915 approved creation of the Office of the Chief of Naval Operations (OpNav); its communications security section carried the designation OP-20-G from the time the very first organization chart for naval communications was drawn up in 1926.

The first director of the Research Desk, which indeed started as a single desk in the old Navy Building on Constitution Avenue in Washington, was Lieutenant Laurence Frye Safford. Beginning a two-year tour of duty with OP-20-G (which, for brevity, we shall hereafter use as the sole title for the Navy's radio intelligence unit), Safford was a thirty-one-year-old Yankee, a native of Massachusetts, with a Yankee's ingenuity, a way with machines, and an above-average aptitude for mathematics. Graduating from Annapolis with the U.S. Naval Academy's class of 1916, Safford was an avid chess and soccer player and an expert marksman. He had served aboard battleships and troop transports in World War I, with destroyers and submarines afterward. Having navigated a submarine out to the Philippines to join the Asiatic Fleet, Safford received command of a minesweeper from which he would be called to code work.

So began Laurence Safford's romance with cryptology, which endured throughout his active career (until 1953) and indeed to his death. Along the way Safford became instrumental in a number of key developments in codebreaking, including the introduction of machines to help solve codes, and the invention of a specialized typewriter able to tap out Japanese kana characters. Safford also innovated a machine the Navy used to encrypt its own messages, contributing importantly to American communications security throughout the war.

Seconding Safford, preceding him and remaining with OP-20-G past his first tour, were the earliest of what became a dedicated band of brothers and sisters, in this case Dr. Emerson J. and Mrs. Haworth. Between 1922 and 1927 the Haworths completed an English translation of the Red Code, while over the next three years they continued translating messages in that code. The cryptanalysts completed the early American cadre. Between 1924 and 1931 twenty naval officers received some training in cryptanalysis. Some went on to become Japanese-language officers; others left the service or were assigned to sea duty. Safford was himself assigned to the battleship *California* in February 1926, to be replaced by Joseph J. Rochefort. So uncertain was the situation during this early period that Dr. Haworth and his wife were paid in part from an unvouchered slush fund established for ONI during World War I.

In 1931 only Safford and Rochefort were considered capable of instructing new cryptanalysts, though the latter had branched out to train himself to be a Japanese-language officer. Only one of the other five officers considered the Navy's most competent cryptanalysts by OP-20-G had had more than six months' training, and that was Lieutenant Joseph N. Wenger, then completing a year-long program. The other four naval men, all of them lieutenants or lieutenants junior grade except for an ensign named Leahy, were Eugene Anderson, Thomas H. Dyer, and Thomas A. Huckins. Anderson, who briefly headed the Research Desk, by then had gone to sea as communications intelligence chief on the staff of the Asiatic Fleet. The others served in Washington under the wing of the formidable "Miss Aggie," Agnes Meyer Driscoll, a thirtysomething wonder who believed that any code devised by man could be broken by a woman. Miss Aggie sported tailored clothes and was married to a lawyer but could use language as salty as any sailor's. She had taught mathematics and music, had been brought to OP-20-G by Safford during his first tour there, and became the instructor who initiated many of the Navy's best cryptanalysts.

Tom Dyer, an informal, jovial sort of fellow who hardly seemed a naval officer, joined OP-20-G in the spring of 1931. At Annapolis with other kindred souls who called themselves the Radiator Club, Dyer had whiled away wintry days sitting on a heater and telling off-color stories. At OP-20-G Dyer got three months' training and became a neophyte codebreaker under Joe Wenger, frustrated that Japanese messages seemed to resist his efforts at cryptanalysis. Agnes Driscoll looked over his shoulder one day that fall and made the sudden observation that the Japanese were using a new code. This marked the end of success with the Red Code, the beginning of a struggle to break the Blue Code, as OP-20-G termed the new Japanese system.

For several months the Japanese code resisted efforts to break it. The Americans had certain advantages accrued from their knowledge of Red, however, including an idea of the structure the Japanese typically used for their codes, a list of the terms given code phrases, a list of characters and kana the Japanese used for English-equivalent place-names, and the pattern in which Japanese codemakers arranged all this material. Still, Blue was a four-kana code in place of the three-kana Red and thus considerably more complex. The Research Desk worked away at the new Imperial Navy code by simultaneously solving the transposition table the Japanese had added and recovering code groups one by one. The Japanese attempted to further complicate their code by inserting material from other sections on each page, thus breaking up the progression of vocabulary in the old code, but the Americans eventually discovered that the inserts themselves were in identical order to their listings in the old code, which facilitated OP-20-G's work. A few mistakes in transmission, inevitable in the introduction of any new code, permitted crucial early entries into the new system. OP-20-G entered recovered code groups on pages placed into a blue looseleaf binder (hence the name the Research Desk gave the Japanese code).

Americans further matched the increased complexity of the Japanese code with a technological advance. This was application of business machines to the codebreaking task. Though computers were then still in gestation, not yet even in infancy, frequency counters, card sorters, keypunch machines, and the like had already been invented to simplify routine business tasks. Such machines had potential for codebreaking in two ways: by helping identify the frequencies with which letters, words, or expressions appeared in radio traffic or ordinary language; and by helping match given code groups to corresponding letters, words, and so on. Most important, the machines increased the speed with which this could be accomplished. Joseph Wenger early on appreciated the potential of the machines and pressed OP-20-G to adopt them. Laurence Safford, back on the Research Desk for another tour, and Agnes Driscoll at first resisted them. Wenger and other advocates convinced their superiors of the advantages; then the Research Desk sold the idea to the Navy Department. The initial set of machinery would be rented for $400 a month. Lieutenant Dyer developed detailed procedures for using it.

The actual attack on the Blue Code only began in about September 1931, for OP-20-G previously occupied itself with recovery of stacks of radio messages in Red Code collected during the Japanese Navy's 1930 grand maneuvers. Work on the Blue Code coincided almost perfectly with introduction of the machine tabulators. It was a huge job, since the new system contained some 85,184 code groups (actually fewer than the Red Code, which had had 97,330). Miss Aggie made the first entry into Blue, and continued to focus on this project until the solution was well along; Thomas Dyer labored full-time on it for five months, and Safford put as much time as he could spare into the project for eight months until, in May 1932, he was reassigned to help commission the heavy cruiser *Portland,* then building in Quincy, Massachusetts. Solution of the Blue Code would be completed under the tenure of Commander Howard F. Kingman, who led OP-20-G from mid-1933 through mid-1935. The solution provided the U.S. Navy with important information on the Japanese including, according to Safford, data on the postmodernization characteristics of the Imperial Navy's *Mutsu*-class battleships. The Japanese continued to employ this code system until November 1938.

At that point the Japanese introduced a new set of codes, for the first time distinguishing between general operational signals and very sensitive communications among senior officers. These codes became known respectively as the Fleet and Admirals' systems. Demonstrating greatly increased concern regarding their message traffic, the Japanese went on to change their Fleet Code to a novel five-kana system in June 1939. Before introducing a major revision of the Fleet Code the Japanese successively used five books of additives to encipher coded messages. The Japanese actions posed a new challenge to OP-20-G, which confronted potential disaster. Still, the Americans had solved the major Japanese Red and Blue codes and their variants, as well as several lesser systems like shipping, weather, and harbormaster codes, so a certain optimism remained. Agnes Driscoll led the attack from November 1939. In eleven months she made so much progress that OP-20-G felt able to allow Miss Aggie to continue on to German Navy systems, leaving two full-time officers, two student officers, two yeomen or radiomen, and two cryptologic clerks to labor on the Japanese system. About the end of 1940 the Imperial Navy switched to a new variant of the Fleet Code, a setback for OP-20-G. This happened to be the twenty-fifth Japanese Navy code the Americans had tackled, so OP-20-G called it JN-25. When the Japanese moved to a fresh variant, OP-20-G distinguished that by terming it JN-25(b). The attack on JN-25 and its variants would become a major feature of American codebreaking activity throughout the war.

As work continued on solving Japanese codes the entire fabric of American communications intelligence was woven into a bigger, stronger unit. It grew from literally one desk to a covey of rooms plus radio stations scattered around the world. Shedding the name Research Desk, OP-20-G became the Communications Security Group until early 1939, then the Radio Intelligence Section, then, from October 1939, the Communications Security Section. It grew to have separate subsections on cryptography (providing new codes and security techniques for the U.S. fleet), research and training (the actual codebreaking unit), radio intelligence (managing direction finding and traffic analysis), cryptologic intelligence (translating and analyzing intercepted messages), and enemy information. The cryptologic intelligence unit, known as OP-20-GY, was operated jointly by the directors of naval communications and naval intelligence and constituted the largest single component of OP-20-G. Its chief served simultaneously as an ONI staffer. In September 1939, OP-20-GY worked out of Room 1643 in the Navy Department and had twenty-three of the total of forty-nine staffers serving in the Washington headquarters of communications intelligence.

From this time, with war having broken out in Europe, plus Japan as embroiled as ever in China, OP-20-G began expanding rapidly to meet growing demand for intelligence material. Authorized personnel increased 50 percent during the first year of the European war; the growth trend continued. Actual personnel stood at about 90 at the start of 1941, 105 by the end of March, 135 by the end of June, 181 at the end of September, and about 231 by the beginning of 1942.* By late 1941 the Navy's plans for the following year provided for 447 enlisted personnel in the United States alone, with another 318 enlisted men planned for Asia and the Pacific. That did not count officers or civilian employees, of whom there were a significant number.

---

*These figures are from an official account, SRH-355, *Naval Security Group History to World War II* (NARA: RG-457). Unaccountably, however, my numbers differ from those given by Layton et al. (p. 527), who list 543 personnel at the beginning of 1941, rising to 740 that December. Those figures are supposed to have been drawn from SRH-355 also.

Only a minority of enlisted personnel were destined for communications intelligence headquarters. In Washington OP-20-G employed in 1939 almost as many officers as enlisted men. Cryptologic clerks assisted supervisors or encoded American messages. Yeomen provided a variety of services. Men from both groups worked in the machine room, where the card sorters held sway; in January 1941 there were sixteen machines at OP-20-G operated by nine men for eight hours a day. Most enlisted personnel in fact were connected with the radio nets, even in Washington, where radiomen were trained in classes that met in an addition built on the roof of the Navy Department building, and were therefore called the On-the-Roof Gang.

Training was and remained careful, because the Navy realized that communications intelligence required specialized radio facilities and personnel. In dealing with the Japanese, for instance, the Navy used men who were not only experienced radio operators but knew *Japanese* communications procedures, Japanese kana and Morse, and Japanese fleet organization. Successive classes of On-the-Roof Gang specialists learned these arcane subjects in Washington. The initial class of seven men graduated in 1929 and found themselves sent as a group to Guam where they augmented Station B, previously a one-man listening post. By September 1930 four classes had been trained. Though men left the service from time to time or moved away from intelligence work, the number of radio operators gradually increased. There were 55 in 1935, 70 in 1937, and 78 at the beginning of 1939. In early 1941 there were a total of 103 intercept operators, including 40 on the Asiatic station and 29 in Hawaii. Twelve more were in training, and there also existed the network of direction-finding stations mentioned previously, which comprised eight stations with 85 operators and 116 radio receivers. The contributions of this early band were subsequently considered so vital that in 1983 the Naval Security Group erected and dedicated a plaque honoring the On-the-Roof Gang.

The Washington classroom where operators trained contained blackboards and all sorts of practice equipment, including eight stations at which students could receive Morse code. It was housed in a concrete-block structure on the roof, which, Elliot Okins remembers, could only be reached by going up to the third floor, or "deck," of the Navy Department building, crossing a crosswalk between two buildings, then climbing a vertical ladder. Secrecy could be preserved relatively easily, important because a few operators actively worked in the twenty-foot-by-twenty-foot room intercepting diplomatic traffic. The Japanese course began with an overview, then familiarization with Imperial Navy organization and procedures, followed by learning Japanese Morse and writing, both the katakana and Westernized *romaji* forms. Intercept operators had to be able to copy twenty-three to twenty-five words a minute in Japanese.

Once the students attained proficiency by hand they were introduced to the RIP-5. Famous among communications intelligence veterans, the RIP-5 was a machine that greatly simplified interception of Japanese transmissions. Though its acronym stood for "Registered Intelligence Publication," the RIP-5 consisted of a typewriter modified to reproduce the kana for which Japanese Morse code letters stood. It had been developed at the initiative of Laurence Safford in 1924, paid for from the ONI slush fund, and made by the Underwood Typewriter Company, whose officials worked out the mechanism in cooperation with Safford. The first ones cost $160 each. Intercept veterans recall using RIP-5s in Shanghai as early as 1929. Operators could record Japanese radio transmissions more easily, often faster than Imperial Navy radiomen could draw the kana themselves. Of course there were not enough RIP-5s for all posts at every intercept radio station, and plenty of pencil-and-paper work remained for the intercept operators. Still, both the kana typewriter and the machine card-sorter and keypunch equipment illustrate key features of the U.S. communications intelligence effort even during the relatively somnolent years before World War II: Americans were alert for novel ways to surmount obstacles before them, and did not hesitate to apply in new ways methods or machinery invented for other purposes.

On-the-Roof Gang intercept operators could well testify to the ingenuity of the OP-20-G effort. Elliot Okins, for example, would be commandeered every afternoon during training to help the codebreakers. Stewart T. Faulkner, who took the intercept course in 1939, remembers that every other day he and classmates spent the afternoon either keypunching newly received messages or using the card sorters to identify items requested by the officer cryptanalysts. The "cryppies," as they were known familiarly, did not explain why they wanted certain things a certain way, but good radiomen understood the principle and could figure out much themselves.

Naturally good cryptanalytical work depended in great part on the radio traffic and its interception. Without sufficient messages in a given code to compare and pick up repetitions, chances were minimal of making an entry into the system. If the messages did not exist or were not intercepted, the problem began right there. Thus the Imperial Navy's Admirals' Code, rarely used, would never be broken. But Fleet Code (JN-25) traffic remained considerable, and there the more important factor would be the effectiveness of the U.S. radio intercept network.

The intercept network comprised a number of stations each of which might or might not have some cryptanalytical capability as well. The station at Shanghai has been discussed already. Station Baker ("B") at Guam has been mentioned only in passing. It had been established at Agana in March 1929 but moved four miles away to the Navy transmitter site at Libugon in 1934. Baker was manned entirely by eight enlisted men with no cryptanalysts and mostly outmoded equipment, though it did have three of the RIP-5 typewriters. It achieved notable successes during the Imperial Navy fleet maneuvers of 1929 and 1930. The Philippines were the location of Station C—or Cast, as it would be known in the phonetic alphabet current in 1941–42. Cast provided major intelligence support for the Asiatic Fleet, with interception and cryptanalytic capacity, a direction-finding capability installed at Sangley Point in the spring of 1937 by Jack Holtwick and radioman Meddie J. Royer, plus extensive liaison with fleet headquarters. Safford informed Cast after Sangley Point began its work that it had made history, becoming the first U.S. unit to track a foreign (Japanese) warship entirely by means of monitoring communications. Most Cast facilities were at Cavite Naval Base, but beginning in 1939 the Navy spent $45,000 to construct a bombproof tunnel on Corregidor, and the station moved there in 1941. In the fall of 1941 Cast had forty-one radiomen, nine yeomen, and ten cryptanalytical personnel. By that time Hawaii, or Station H (Hypo) had sixty-nine radiomen. There was also a significant cryptanalytical facility, begun as a one-man show by Thomas Dyer in 1936, about which more will be heard presently.

These mid-Pacific stations were complemented by others in the continental United States, including Alaska, and by the direction-finding network. The Alaskan contingent, for example, included five-man detachments established at Dutch Harbor and at Sitka in 1940. These were primarily direction-finding stations at that time. Robert L. (Buck) Dormer worked as a direction-finding operator at Dutch Harbor and remembers tracking Japanese vessels from Empire waters right into the Mandated Islands, to places like Truk, Saipan, Tinian, and Kwajalein. Buck and his comrades even identified types of ships and specific islands that responded to given radio call signs. "We had them pretty well covered," Dormer says. He suspected the Japanese had to be getting ready for something because many merchant ships in the area sent or received messages for armed guard commanders. "For goodness' sakes," Buck Dormer said to a friend, "Look at this. The people in Honolulu really must know that something is coming on . . . they must realize that [the Japanese] must be building something up on the so-called Mandated Islands." Here was a piece in the puzzle of the Mandates, a puzzle that preoccupied the U.S. Navy throughout the prewar period and that connected directly to Imperial Navy doctrine and war plans, a puzzle at the heart of the spiral of rising hostility between the Pacific powers.

# "The First Time It Flies I Want to Be on Board"

ONE IRRITANT IN THE HOSTILITY IMPELLING THE POWERS TOWARD WAR WAS THE QUEStion of Japanese activities in Micronesia. Though it may have started as a minor irritant, the controversy over Micronesia became a real problem, compounded about equally of Japanese secretiveness and notions of exploration and colonization, American ignorance of Tokyo's actions, and American fears that the Pacific islands would be used against the United States in war. A geographic region of thousands of square miles, not a national state or other entity, Micronesia was a collective term for the various island groups in the mid-Pacific, places with exotic names like the Ellice and Marshall islands, the Carolines, the Marianas. Most had been "discovered" centuries earlier by Spanish explorers, some by the British during the nineteenth century. For the most part indigenous peoples inhabited the islands until Europe's push for colonies before World War I.

As much as anything else it was technology that made Micronesia interesting to the world outside. The islands were ideal way stations for the transoceanic cables laid during this period to permit rapid transmission of messages (in Morse code) between continents. Cable stations on the islands simplified maintenance and generated the power to make the cables work. When radio was invented it at first just supplemented cables—early transmitters lacked transoceanic range. Radio repeater stations on the islands became as necessary as cable stations. Adding a few Micronesian islands with natural resources, such as the phosphate of Nauru and Ocean Island, and the need for coaling facilities in the age of coal-fired steamships, there seemed at least some reason in strategy for attempts to control the islands. The drive to empire characteristic of the age found sustenance in such presumably practical reasons for the desire to dominate Micronesia.

The British and Germans came first, with the latter establishing themselves in the Marshalls and buying the Marianas and Carolines from Spain in 1898. This was by no means a militarily organized colony; the few Germans in the area were mostly colonial administrators or cable-company employees with a sprinkling of missionaries and traders. Meanwhile Japan had been coming of age as a European-style nation-state with a blue-water navy, and in 1875 the screw sloop *Tsukuba* explored Micronesia for the first time. Nine years later the corvette *Ryujo* dropped anchor at Kusaie in the Carolines, becoming the first Japanese vessel to visit any of the islands. By that time Imperial Navy ships on training cruises regularly plied the South Seas, or *nanyo*, as they termed this region. In 1914, with the Japanese allied with the British in World War I and a German cruiser squadron on the loose in the Pacific, the Imperial Navy found itself encouraged to search for the common enemy. Strategic thinkers at the Naval General Staff, plus Japanese business interests, urged occupation of German Micronesia. In the fall of 1914 naval forces captured Palau, Angaur, Saipan, Truk, Ponape, Kusaie, and Jaluit in just about a month. Yap and Pagan followed. By December 1914 there was a South Sea Islands Defense Force (Nanyo Gunto Bobitai) under the Yokosuka Naval District. Japan retained control through the war, and after it received a League of Nations mandate to govern occupied Micronesia, henceforth known as the Mandated Islands or simply the Mandates.

Beginning in 1918 the Navy Ministry progressively gave up its occupation role in the Mandates. Administration became the province of a Nanyo Cho (South Seas Bureau) with headquarters on Palau. Already in the area was the Nanyo Boeki Kaisha (South Seas Trading Company), active since 1908, supplemented in 1921 by the Nanyo Kohatsu Kaisha (South Seas Development Company), a private nongovernmental corporation whose stock was traded on the Tokyo exchange. Cultivation of sugar, tapioca, and coconuts emerged as major agricultural activities, with mining phosphates a key industrial activity of the development company; the trading company held a monopoly on shipping. Japanese citizens settled in the islands, while limited education and opportunities were provided to the natives. By 1939 population figures showed 73,028 Japanese residents in the Mandates compared with 40,406 indigenous ones. There were Japanese boomtowns on Palau, Saipan, Tinian, Truk, Ponape, and Jaluit. According to a French observer assembling a 1933 report for the League of Nations, over half the Japanese moving to the islands came from the Ryukyu Islands, primarily Okinawa.

American fears regarding the Mandates arose from their location squarely upon the shortest routes among Hawaii, Guam, and the Philippines.

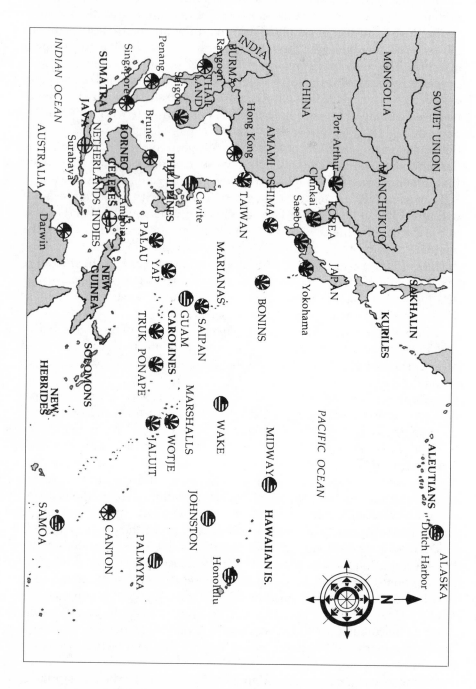

I. Pacific, 1941 (Showing Mandated Islands)

Japanese naval and air forces in the Mandates would be well positioned to interdict American attempts to reinforce U.S. possessions in the Western Pacific. Such fears did not simply appear in a vacuum. Japanese commentators spoke of the islands as "unsinkable aircraft carriers." More than once, authorities described the principles of conducting attrition operations against a U.S. fleet advancing across the Pacific. In the doctrine of the Decisive Battle these attrition efforts were to lead to a final fight in which an exhausted, reduced American force would be annihilated. General statements of this strategy appeared in articles and speeches, in the press, and in attaché reports to the Office of Naval Intelligence.

One typical formulation would be published in 1940 by Commander Matsuo Kinoaki, who postulated an Imperial Navy "surprise attack fleet" that would strike the Americans once they reached a point 2,500 miles from Hawaii, roughly equal to the distance between there and the Marshalls, the outermost of the Mandates.

At the top-secret level of war planning it appears that early American plans dovetailed rather dangerously with Japanese intentions but that the whole U.S. approach changed well before the outbreak of hostilities. In the U.S. Navy's procedure for contingency planning the United States was always termed Blue, and other nations received color designations too. Japan would be called Orange, and the hypothetical war plan against the Japanese was War Plan Orange. From its inception in 1906, War Plan Orange assumed an initial phase of Japanese offensive and American mobilization; a second phase of American offensive into the Western Pacific, including both attrition warfare and a decisive battle; and a final phase in which Japan would be strangled by blockade and economic warfare.

The plan supposed that during the early period these actions would occur at a fast pace, so quickly that some planners thought of the effort as encompassing a "Through Ticket to Manila." Such an operation corresponded to the Japanese Navy's notion of a short campaign leading to Decisive Battle. But in 1930 the Americans achieved substantial radio intelligence coverage of the Imperial Navy's grand maneuvers, and in 1933 the United States completed the process of decoding, translating, and analyzing this material. All of a sudden, in 1934, War Plan Orange was revised to provide for a number of intermediate stages in which the U.S. fleet seized islands and set up advance bases on its way across the Pacific. It was about this time as well that the role intended for the Asiatic Fleet changed from attempted defense of the Philippines to flight from that theater on the first day of mobilization.

If the intelligence did not scotch the rapid-advance version of War Plan Orange, the logistical difficulties were enough to sink it. Coal-burning ships predominated in the fleet in the early days of Orange planning, with oil-fired vessels taking over in the period after World War I. For either coal or oil the quantities necessary to concentrate an American fleet in the Western Pacific and push it to the Philippines were enormous. In the days of coal, U.S. planners estimated a requirement of 197,000 to 480,000 tons of fuel for the movement, with the entire endeavor useless unless the fleet still had fuel for a month or so of operations once it arrived in the Philippines. (This amounted to another 125,000 tons, or 225,000 if two months' operations proved necessary.) No coaling stations were available in Micronesia, either in the Mandates or in the American and British possessions (Guam and the Gilberts respectively). The 1917 edition of the Orange plan postulated the necessity for 494 colliers or tankers. Rapid advance would have been a nightmare.

These factors were apparent to planners on both sides of the Pacific, and even to the informed public. In 1921 journalist Hector Bywater published calculations estimating that 242,000 tons of coal and 41,600 of oil would be necessary to move a U.S. fleet from Panama to Manila. Subtracting fuel consumption for a ten-day stay in port at the destination, Japanese Commander Matsuo in 1940 used the figures 232,000 tons of coal and 39,200 of oil. Both sets of consumption data lie within the range secretly postulated by U.S. war planners.

Faced with undeniable supply difficulties, American planners confronted intelligence knowledge of a Japanese intention to respond to the fleet's advance in a fashion keyed to the "Through Ticket" scenario. To some degree the effectiveness of Japanese attrition operations would hinge upon the extent and capacity of naval and air bases the Imperial Navy might have in the Mandates, and about those factors Washington was wholly ignorant. True, it was the Japanese themselves who had insisted upon nonfortification in the Washington Naval Treaty; nevertheless, many thought it expedient to assume the worst. Discovering the truth about the Mandates—"Japan's Islands of Mystery," as one writer called them—became major business for the Office of Naval Intelligence. In the meantime, the U.S. Navy began rethinking War Plan Orange, providing for a war of years' duration and the seizure of intermediate bases during the advance. The Americans readjusted their planning; the Imperial Navy never did.

As HAPPENS MORE FREQUENTLY THAN IT SHOULD, HOSTILITY IN THE PACIFIC WOULD BE increased by plain misunderstanding. The Mandates became a prime locus for this. Japanese authorities proved loath to permit visits there, and over time it became almost an article of faith, especially among American naval officers, that the reason was because the Imperial Navy was fortifying the Mandates. Americans were ignorant of an important difference between U.S. law and Japanese: In the U.S., shipping and people enjoyed free access to ports unless these were expressly prohibited. Only a few ports, such as

Pearl Harbor, fell in that category. In Japan, as in China too, access to ports was prohibited unless specifically approved. This was exactly the reason why the "opening" of Japan by Commodore Matthew Perry had been important: The Japanese were induced to approve a permanent opening to Western commerce. League of Nations mandates required that the territories subject to them be governed under the domestic law of the mandatory country. Thus the Mandated Islands were governed under Japanese law, which closed ports except by permission.

From the Japanese standpoint there was much to recommend this stance, especially in the age of coal. During the 1914–1918 war, port visits were discouraged for reasons of military security, making it possible to identify non-Japanese vessels in the area as enemy. Identification was otherwise difficult and communications facilities meager. The Navy erected radio stations on Palau, Saipan, Truk, and Jaluit in 1916, on Ponape the following year, and on Wotje in 1923, but there were many islands with no communications to summon help. Fresh water could be a problem. There were also no coal stocks to refuel ships that might visit, a condition persisting into the mandate period. In conferring its mandate the League of Nations essentially agreed with the Japanese argument that they lacked adequate facilities to host visiting ships. Nevertheless the Japanese designated Saipan, Truk, Ponape, and Jaluit as ports open if given advance application for visits.

From the beginning of the League mandate the U.S. Office of Naval Intelligence received reports of fortification work in the islands. One typical report in 1920 came from two marines beached in the Carolines who, before they were repatriated by the Japanese, heard from local inhabitants that huge gun emplacements were being built. In Tokyo the Japanese actually contacted the U.S. embassy and offered permission for a visit to the open-port islands by young language officer Ellis Zacharias. The Navy ordered Zacharias to decline the invitation, however, and the opportunity passed. By far the most successful expedition during this period was the voyage of light cruiser *Milwaukee* in 1922–1923. She was supposed to conduct shakedown training while en route to the Asiatic Fleet; ONI wanted her to observe the Mandates along the way. Ship's skipper Captain Luke McNamee requested and received ONI specialists and photographic equipment, and *Milwaukee*'s navigator was briefed on exactly what ONI wanted to learn. The voyage yielded excellent pictures and other data. Its low point occurred when the cruiser made an unannounced visit to Truk, where the Japanese were polite but unhappy. Intelligence from the trip indicated extensive dredging of harbors but no evidence of fortifications.

An espionage disaster of this period followed in the mission of Marine lieutenant colonel Earl Hancock (Pete) Ellis, who ostensibly worked without the knowledge or approval of ONI. Ellis had done a seminal bit of war planning himself—a paper on creating advanced bases in support of transpacific operations—and naturally had an interest in visiting the islands that had been the subject of his inquiry. Colonel Ellis has been shown to have had a direct relationship (by back channels) to the director of naval intelligence. In any case, in August 1921 Ellis left on a mission to Australia, then the Philippines, Japan, and the Mandates. He never returned.

It is pertinent to what happened to note that Pete Ellis had serious difficulty with alcoholism, including both depression and kidney problems. In fact, he ended up hospitalized in almost every port he touched on the way to Japan. There too he had to be hospitalized, but while outside cut a wide swath through the sake parlors and geisha houses. Ellis Zacharias, who was in Japan at the time and probably smarting because his own request to visit the Mandates had been refused, notes that he and the naval attaché heard that in his cups Pete Ellis was openly bragging about an espionage mission to the Mandates. When Colonel Ellis learned that the attaché had plans to send him home on the next liner, he booked passage on a Nanyo Boeki Kaisha vessel instead, leaving Tokyo in October 1922. Residents of the islands have been found who recall Ellis on Saipan, Yap, Kusaie, and Jaluit. From the latter Pete Ellis apparently took a smaller inter-island sloop to circumnavigate the Marshalls, claiming to be a copra buyer for a New York firm, the John A. Hughes Trading Company. Angering Japanese officials on Jaluit, who reportedly discovered that he had extensive notes on places he had visited, and became convinced he was a spy, the marine left for Ponape and Palau, on the latter taking up with an indigenous woman.

On several islands, once again, Pete Ellis had to have treatment for conditions arising from inability to stay away from alcohol. On Palau, in May 1923, Ellis died. According to his Palauan wife, Metauie, who was with him during his last hours, Ellis had been violently sick for days from alcohol-induced blood poisoning, but refused to take medication or stop drinking. Others believe that Ellis was poisoned or killed by Japanese who had learned of his spy mission. When the U.S. attaché in Tokyo learned, approximately a week later, of the officer's death, he determined to do some snooping in the guise of recovering the remains. Chief pharmacist Lawrence Zembsch, who had attended Ellis at Yokohama Naval Hospital, was sent in July to bring back the remains.

The fate of Lawrence Zembsch became the second part of the Ellis mystery. Zembsch returned after about five weeks in a completely distracted state bordering on psychosis. He had the remains of Colonel Ellis, exhumed and cremated, but Zembsch himself proved completely incoherent, unable to say what had happened. Commander Ulys R. Webb, the naval doctor at Yokohama who treated both men and for whom Zembsch had worked, became convinced his subordinate had been drugged. Zembsch gradually improved with the watchful care of Dr. Webb and loving ministrations of his wife. Then came the great earthquake of September 1923. The Yokohama hospital collapsed, killing both Zembsch and his wife, who had been visiting that morning. Dr. Webb had had another session with Zembsch scheduled for that afternoon. The Ellis-Zembsch mystery has never been solved, though recent historians seem to agree that Colonel Ellis, at least, died of natural causes.

None of the notes Colonel Ellis allegedly compiled, or the navigation and codebooks he carried, survived to be examined by ONI. The primary evidence on Ellis came from American missionaries and other Western residents of the Mandates who met him during his sojourn. It was those individuals, with their knowledge of Japanese, who did much translation for U.S. intelligence in those early days. "Any time you worked at [the] hush-hush section," recalled William A. Worton, a Marine intelligence officer, "the name Ellis always came up."

Still, Pete Ellis was not the only American who tried to penetrate the Mandates. Another marine, a friend whom Ellis made plans to meet but never did, was active in the northern Marianas. This was Hans Hornbostel, who sailed from Guam and made several visits to Japanese islands in this group between 1922 and 1925. In 1927 Marine colonel Richard M. Cutts investigated the Tawitawi group, which lay outside the Mandates proper but was equally inaccessible.

Another abortive scheme for gathering data involved a scientific ruse. In 1921 ONI recommended formation of a bogus zoological survey, a variant on an effort the previous year to explore the suspected Ryukyu Islands base Amami O Shima by sending an expedition that was supposed to mark the graves of members of Matthew Perry's crew who had perished during the momentous events of 1857. The Japanese approved the expedition but permitted it to land only at small ports on Okinawa. The scheme collapsed when ONI proved unable to create a suitable relationship with a credible academic who would deal directly with them.

In the mid-1930s this approach was resurrected in the context of an anticipated total eclipse of the sun, expected to be best visible from the region of the Mandates. An international team of forty scientists, including Russians, Germans, Canadians, and Americans, was to observe the event from an atoll about midway between Truk and Ponape. Opportunities for intelligence gathering were minimized, however, when the Imperial Navy volunteered to carry the scientific mission itself and provided the old cruiser *Kasuga* to do it.

Serendipity played some role in knowledge regarding the Mandates. A Major Bodley from the British embassy happened to be aboard a vessel wrecked on reefs at Yap. Survivors spent days ashore before a Nanyo Boeki Kaisha (NBK) steamship arrived to take them away. In transpacific crossings liners sometimes transited the Mandates, as was the case when Alexander H. Ford, director of the Pan Pacific Union, a friendship association, visited Japan in the mid-1930s. Ford's ship stopped at some of the islands, but he made no effort to go ashore.

Willard Price proved more enterprising. Price, an American freelance journalist, had gone everywhere in the Far East *except* the Mandates. Now he wished to see them too. At the Nanyo Boeki Kaisha offices, he was repeatedly told the steamships were full and no tickets were available. One day Price persisted, demanding to see the passenger list, which showed the latest steamer not full at all, but NBK officials then warned him that the trip was too dangerous, what with storms, treacherous reefs, tropical diseases; besides, "the natives were savage head-hunters." Added to that was the fact that NBK ships served only simple Japanese food. And the islands lacked hotels. When Price insisted, he received a visit from *kempeitai* agents who wanted full details on his reasons for wishing to visit the *nanyo*.

Suddenly, when awkward questions were asked at the League of Nations about why the Japanese, in the context of the impending solar eclipse, did not wish foreign scientists to sail in their own ship, Price got called to the Nanyo Cho, the South Seas Bureau. There smiling officials presented him steamship tickets for both himself and his wife.

For the most part Willard Price's visit to the South Seas proved anticlimactic, save for his energetic efforts to escape the steamer upon which the Japanese attempted to confine him. This byplay proved the main substance of the trip; there was little to report in terms of Japanese military activity. For example, Price's description of military development on Saipan was simply that the Japanese were dredging the harbor. On Yap Price found a dozen kings but no Japanese bases. On Palau, headquarters of the Nanyo Cho, where an Imperial Navy officer was actually assigned as adviser to the administrator, Price found an airfield, but an anchorage at Koror that "no money could convert . . . into a really formidable fleet base." On Angaur Price could not even find a bay, much less a fleet base, as claimed in one 1925 book. At Truk, fabled Combined Fleet stronghold of the coming war, of whose fine harbor Price remarked that "Truk was born to be a fleet base," the only defenses he found were those of nature: the rugged terrain. Price writes that while there, however, he witnessed "the reduction by noisy bulldozers of an island three hundred feet high into a level field for landplanes." On Ponape, where Price found "a fortified island," the defenses turned out to consist of the 900-foot height of the islet. The real fortress, on the islet of Nanmatol, with walls up to forty feet high, had been constructed in ages past as a tomb for kings. On Kusaie Price met several Americans, including missionary Jesse Hoppin, who had befriended Pete Ellis, but again there were no fortifications.

Another seaborne adventurer would be Vincent Astor, an intimate of Franklin D. Roosevelt, whom FDR occasionally used for confidential business he deemed necessary. Although it is unknown whether FDR authorized, or even knew of, the mission, Astor sailed into the Central Pacific in late 1937. Aboard his yacht, *Nourmahal,* Astor retraced some of Pete Ellis's steps, circulating among the Marshall Islands. Astor became convinced that Japan intended to build bases there; he collected information regarding fuel stores, docks, and airfields, particularly on Wotje and Eniwetok. In January 1938 Astor cabled the President: "The information gathering side of our cruise has proved interesting, instructive and, I hope, will be helpful." (Kermit Roosevelt, grandson of Teddy Roosevelt and a second cousin of FDR, accompanied Astor on this cruise and developed such a taste for cloak-and-dagger escapades that he went on to work for the Office of Strategic Services and then the Central Intelligence Agency.)

Probably the most notable adventure connected with the Mandates, at least in the public mind, would be the 1937 attempt at a round-the-world flight by aviator Amelia Earhart. Likely as not, Vincent Astor's cruise began with the notion that he could find Earhart, who disappeared together with her navigator, Fred Noonan, after taking off on a leg of their flight from Lae, New Guinea, on July 2. The two vanished in the area of the Mandates en route to Howland Island; their last communication, with a U.S. Coast Guard cutter, came some twenty-one hours into the flight.

Former Air Force pilot Vincent V. Loomis and aviation writer Jeffrey Ethell, who have made a detailed examination of the Earhart mystery, have reconstructed a flight path that led Earhart to ditch the plane, practically out of gas, on a reef off Mille Atoll in the Mandates. According to this scenario the Japanese survey ship *Koshu,* under Captain Takagi Hachiro, recovered the Electra aircraft the aviator had flown and carried Earhart and Noonan to Jaluit for medical treatment. Loomis found a Japanese medical corpsman who claimed he had treated Noonan at Jaluit, and posits that the *Koshu* then took the Americans to Truk, whence they were flown to Saipan by seaplane and incarcerated, given Japanese fears of what they might have found out. Having found a number of indigenous people who saw an American man and woman on Saipan, and having discovered that two U.S. marines later dug up a grave they believed to contain the remains of Earhart and Noonan, the authors conclude that this resolves the mystery.

Interestingly, this investigation disclosed additional evidence that can be read to indicate Japanese sensitivity to penetration of the Mandates. On the one hand the authors document that the Imperial Navy unit supposedly sent to search for the flier, according to logbooks and interviews with a former crewman of the seaplane tender *Kamoi,* actually *left* the Mandates at this time and returned to Ise in Japan.* Claims that a search was conducted

---

*According to Admiral Suzuki Suguru, then a young Naval General Staff officer, who later gave evidence at the Tokyo war-crimes trials on this point, when news of the Earhart disappearance reached Tokyo, Prince Takamatsu, then also at NGS, argued

therefore may have dissuaded other searchers, while failure actually to conduct a search suggests that the Japanese knew Earhart's whereabouts already. A second interesting find by Loomis and Ethell was press reports in Australia and Britain, and Japanese diplomatic cable traffic pertaining to them, indicating that the U.S. aircraft carrier *Lexington,* in its own search for the missing Earhart plane, sent aircraft to take aerial photographs of some of the Mandates. These reports also claimed that the United States shared this intelligence with Australia.

As in so much else, the Tokyo naval attachés' club proved useful to ONI in the search for knowledge about the Mandates. In 1938 the French attaché lent the Americans a report of a visit to the Mandates five years before by a French naval officer preparing a study for the League of Nations. The Tokyo naval attaché's dispatch to ONI, based on a translation of this report, is much the most detailed intelligence on the Mandates so far found in official records.

Unlike casual observers such as Willard Price, the French officer, Commander Robbe, not only was a discerning witness but also had the authority of the League to go anywhere, specifically to look for evidence of military preparations. Like Price, however, Robbe found very little to report. There were few stocks of fuel, and liners were making the thirty-eight-day round trip from Yokohama to Jaluit and back without taking on fuel (or water) at any local port. Even provisions seemed in short supply. In some respects the islands seemed quite comfortable: For example, while as late as 1930 the French possession Nouméa in New Caledonia had light only from an inefficient gas system, the *nanyo* islands got electricity from diesel power plants. In some cases power came from the machinery used to run Imperial Navy radio stations. Commander Robbe described large "playing fields" on Ponape that could easily be converted to airfields, and he did not visit Palau,

---

strongly that a search effort should be made. Admiral Prince Fushimi, the chief of staff, issued requisite orders to seaplane tender *Kamoi,* then closest to Howland Island, but the effort had to be given up because of lack of clues and distance from the presumed crash site. Admiral Kozaka Kanae, who as a captain commanded the *Kamoi* in 1937, affirms that he learned of the crash from a newscast: "A few hours later, I received orders for a search for the missing American fliers. No grid positions and no clues were given in the orders. I was still trying to dispatch seaplanes for the search when I received another message saying Earhart's plane [had] headed for Howland. That was several hundred miles away from my position. Tokyo rescinded the orders when it found out my situation. So I turned for Japan." The *Kamoi* arrived at Ise on July 10, 1937. (Okumiya Masatake, "For Sugar Boats or Submarines?" *U.S. Naval Institute Proceedings,* August 1968, quoted on p. 70.)

but his general conclusion was that "no evidence is found anywhere, from a military point of view, of the Japanese acting in public contravention of the terms of the Mandate."

By and large this describes the status of the Mandates through most of the interwar period. In 1937, that is, after expiration of the Washington Treaty and its nonfortification clause, the Imperial Navy stopped contracting private builders and began to rely on its own construction corps for work in the *nanyo*. That year the *Kamoi* carried a naval engineer, one Itsumi Naoyoshi, to survey the islands for potential military sites. A postwar study by Thomas Wilds, investigator for the American occupation authorities on the Japanese in the Central Pacific, could identify only a handful of installations begun before 1939: an airfield (1934) and a seaplane ramp (1935) on Saipan; an airfield (1938) and a seaplane ramp (1934) at Palau; and an airfield (1935) at Truk. Admiral Kozaka Kanae recalled the surveys *Kamoi* made between 1935 and 1937; there were drying yards Saipan made on in 1933 and at Truk in 1935 (by Nanyo Kohatsu Kaisha, the South Seas Development Company), as well as two or three suitable sites on Palau and elsewhere. Imperial Navy units were never stationed in the *nanyo* until December 1939, when the Fourth Fleet was organized at Truk. The initial units based there were seaplane tenders *Chitose* and *Kinugasa Maru*, twenty-four flying boats of the Yokohama Air Group, and, later, the 6th Destroyer Flotilla and 7th Submarine Flotilla. No land-based medium attack planes were stationed in the Mandates until the spring of 1941.

After the war the U.S. Strategic Bombing Survey conducted extensive studies of a number of the Mandated Islands, including Truk, Jaluit, Wotje, Mille, and Maloelap. At none of these did the survey uncover fortifications or naval or air facilities built prior to 1940–1941. One of the survey reports asserted that Kwajalein had been developed in the 1930s, but intelligence analyst Thomas Wilds lists facilities there as having been begun in 1940 as well. Takeuchi Kaoru, a staff officer in the Marshalls who inspected the islands in the summer of 1941, returned to Kwajalein furious. "There are no defense systems or defense equipment at all in the whole area of the Marshalls," he thundered. "I doubt the mentality of the High Command."

In August 1941 the Fourth Fleet received a new commander with a modern outlook. Vice Admiral Inoue Shigeyoshi was being shunted out of his Navy Ministry post as chief of the Bureau of Aeronautics; earlier in the year he had argued against a naval construction plan that (once more) overemphasized battleships and tried to attain a certain ratio (5:4) against the anticipated size of the U.S. fleet. Inoue instead thought the real threat would be blockade of Japan; the key weapons for procurement, he believed, were submarines and aircraft, to attempt three-dimensional control of the sea. At Truk Admiral Inoue soon energized efforts to erect base facilities. The number of construction workers in the Mandates increased from 4,000 to

10,000 and a good dozen airfields or seaplane ramps were completed on various islands. One of the last dispatches to reach ONI from the U.S. attaché in Tokyo, a report of November 27, 1941, noted that three ships had been used since September exclusively to move oil, building supplies, personnel, and materials to the Mandates, including two trips to the Carolines and one to the Marshalls. The report estimated that there were now 3,000 workers in the Marshalls, mostly at Jaluit, and that in Japan 8,000 tons of oil in barrels on piers awaited shipment to the Mandates. Imperial Navy war plans in fact called for monthly allocations of 17,000 tons of oil (7,000 of them to Truk) and 12,500 kiloliters of aviation gas to the Mandates.

Meanwhile, inspired by Willard Price's story, in an early edition he had gotten in Shanghai, American air attaché Stephen Jurika determined to visit the Mandates himself. Jurika seized on the fact that Japan had stopped filing reports with the League of Nations in 1938 and insisted that a visit was necessary. Attaché Smith-Hutton had some thoughts on how to get intelligence from the Mandates in 1938 and 1939 and figured "the only way to get the information . . . was to take aggressive, positive steps." Smith-Hutton's notion of such a step was for an aircraft carrier to appear off Truk, have its planes take pictures, and be off. But Jurika's idea looked aggressive and positive too, so the attaché told him, "I don't think you'll make it, but fine."

Lieutenant Jurika tried to get a seat on the weekly flight, a four-engine Kawanishi flying boat, sending his Japanese clerk over to the South Seas Development Company offices to buy a ticket. Next day the clerk told Jurika he could not obtain the ticket because the company said its scheduled plane had engine trouble. After several weeks of interesting excuses, Jurika tried himself. The Japanese asked for his passport and diplomatic card, then told him why the Kawanishi was not going to fly.

"Fine," Jurika shot back. "The first time it flies I want to be on board."

Again that did not happen, and Jurika went back with newspaper clippings reporting the visit of a touring or fishing commission or such to Truk or Ponape, obviously having gone by plane. The Japanese had no real answer to this. They finally put it in writing that the American naval officer was not eligible to visit the Mandates, which was a violation of the League of Nations guidelines except that the question became moot as war loomed over them all. Jurika never got his trip to the islands. Instead, he and the language officers were all sent home or to the Philippines, out of harm's way.

ALL THESE EFFORTS TO COLLECT INTELLIGENCE ON THE MANDATES WERE INTENDED TO INFORM the Office of Naval Intelligence in Washington. It was there, in the Navy Department on Nineteenth Street and Constitution Avenue, that it all came together. Attaché reports were good, ship visits better; all volunteered reports from private individuals had to be used with great caution. During the crucial latter half of the 1930s the Far East Division of ONI would be successively headed by Ellis Zacharias, Jack M. Creighton, and Arthur H. McCollum. It was McCollum's second tour in the division, the first having been in charge of the Japan desk. Zacharias and McCollum, of course, were both Japanese-language officers. If anyone had a basis for judgment, they did.

Arthur McCollum tried to keep things in perspective. "If you pick up every rumor and start believing it," he said, "you can go into a complete tailspin." The Mandates fortification issue furnished a good example. It happened, for example, that in 1933 the naval attaché in Rome had forwarded reports containing very precise drawings of heavy gun emplacements alleged to be in the Mandates. The drawings were on a transparent type of paper. McCollum got to looking at the drawings one day; and he knew something about guns, having once been in charge of a 16-inch gun turret on the battleship *West Virginia.* Now, ONI lacked much, but it did have elevation drawings and topographic maps for the islands, and McCollum could not see how big coastal guns (a 16-inch gun weighed about a hundred tons all stripped down and had about eighty feet of barrel length) could be moved up jungle-covered hills without railroads, cables, or some other heavy haul mechanism. How such guns could even be landed without wharves and cranes constituted another mystery. In 1935 and 1936, while Zacharias headed the Far East Division, he made an effort to get the State Department to propose naval visits to the Japanese, but without success.* Nevertheless, ships were going out to the Asiatic Fleet or coming back all the time, and it was a simple matter to have them take photographs along the way. Photographs of the particular island at issue showed that no gun emplacements existed.

McCollum found out later that the British were also getting this intelligence and that both countries were buying it. The progenitor was thought to be a Hungarian living in Latin America, described as a "deranged mercenary . . . informer." Toward the end of 1937 the director of naval intelligence wrote his Rome attaché regarding the original claims:

---

*In his memoir Ellis Zacharias makes a great deal (*Secret Missions,* p. 49) of his proposals for naval visits, alleging that they were scuttled by Eugene Dooman, then chief of the State Department's Japanese section, who believed no useful purpose would be served by pressing the issue at that particular time. State Department records show the Japanese were in fact approached, however. Zacharias gives the State Department no credit for its effort to propose an exchange of visits in the summer of 1936, or for State's reciprocal denial of visiting privileges to a Japanese training ship that wished to visit an off-limits Hawaiian port. Zacharias also does not note that State permitted the U.S. naval attaché in Tokyo to make a further proposal for visits directly to the Imperial Navy.

I must tell you that the reports referred to are the only ones in our office stating that guns are actually installed in the Mandated Islands and that we have other reports of approximately the same date from persons who have visited or who were actually living in the islands at that time stating that no fortifications of any sort existed there.

The gun claims had been concocted from whole cloth.

That did not still the fears, however. Arthur McCollum again: "A lot of people in the Navy Department didn't like to believe the Japanese weren't arming those islands, and I will say here and now, I never believed they were myself. I didn't think it was possible or practical." In the Mandated Islands during the war that followed, the United States encountered no coastal gun larger than 6-inch and no fortification of prewar vintage.

Meanwhile, separating wheat from chaff among intelligence reports remained as difficult as ever. Several 1941 reports from the attaché in Tokyo are worth mentioning. One in January informed ONI that the Japanese fleet in the Mandates had an unusually large number of patrol planes, light cruisers, and torpedo-carrying ships (in fact, the Fourth Fleet remained a minor force). In early March the attaché passed along British data that Jaluit had become headquarters for Japanese naval and air operations (in fact, headquarters was at Truk). Several weeks later the attaché reported the statement of a Navy Ministry official who told a Diet committee that the Imperial Navy had taken measures adequate to cope with "any" situation that might arise in the South Seas. Just what was that supposed to mean?

In December 1941 ONI rated as "unconfirmed" its information regarding Wotje, Jaluit, Kwajalein, Eniwetok, Rongelap, Kusaie, Ponape, Truk, Yap, Palau, Saipan, and Rota. Needless to say, the preponderance of real Japanese strength was located in these very places, about which the Americans had the least information. When Pearl Harbor found itself devastated by surprise attack from Imperial Navy aircraft carriers, many Americans found it easy to believe the Japanese fleet must have come from the Mandates.

# PART II

## YAMAMOTO'S

## WAR

T HE PALPABLE INCREASE IN HOSTILITY ACROSS THE PACIFIC FORCED THE UNITED STATES TO grapple with the dilemma of what to do in case of a war with Japan. Following 1940 naval maneuvers President Roosevelt ordered the fleet to remain at Pearl Harbor, halfway over the ocean from its harbors in California. Pearl Harbor had been a useful forward facility since a dry dock was completed there before World War I, but it had never served as a primary fleet base. Roosevelt clearly intended the move as a deterrent to Japan, a warning of possible measures beyond even the more and more stringent economic sanctions he had been imposing.

Some American naval officers did not at all appreciate FDR's coercive gesture. Admiral James O. Richardson stood among them, a fleet commander who felt that Pearl Harbor lacked both the capacity to handle his ships and the defensive capability to protect them. Admiral Richardson took his dissent up the chain of command, right to the President, returning to Washington to meet with Roosevelt. Afterward Richardson found himself without any command at all, relieved on FDR's orders for his pains. His successor was Admiral Husband E. Kimmel, formerly a flag officer with cruisers. In time Kimmel would probably come to wonder whether, in fact, it had not been Richardson who was the lucky one, his relief saving him from the fate of the commander defeated in wartime.

For 1941, however, there were problems of the present to face, not least among them the Mandates. Commander Edwin T. Layton, briefly fleet intelligence officer for Richardson and then serving Kimmel in the same post upon the latter's January 1941 appointment, was one who felt keenly the mystery of the islands. Layton had volunteered to help the hard-pressed codebreakers of Station Hypo in his spare time, and was assisting in work on a Japanese address code. Messages using the code Layton helped solve contained many references to islands and units in the Mandates, leading the fleet intelligence officer to conclude that the islands were a major center of Japanese strength. Commander Layton began to pay the Mandates special attention, and over some months of 1941 he assembled a special briefing on the Mandates that not only worried Admiral Kimmel but also brought expressions of interest from Washington.

In fact, the Mandates figured so much in Japanese communications in 1941 precisely because the Imperial Navy had begun its buildup in the *nanyo*. It is significant that when the buildup got under way suspicions were triggered almost immediately at Pearl Harbor, and indications were also reported by both the U.S. attaché in Tokyo and American radio direction finders in Alaska. Suspicions aroused, the Americans made arrangements to get aerial photographs of the Mandates, using specially equipped B-24 bombers flying from Wake and Midway islands. Both Ponape and Truk were slated for photographic coverage as part of a transpacific movement of heavy bombers to reinforce the Philippines in December 1941. As it turned out the project would be preempted by the onset of the war, but in the meantime intelligence officers at Pearl Harbor remained fascinated by the mystery of the Mandates. Communications intelligence in November 1941 reported indications that the Imperial Navy had some of its aircraft carriers in the Mandates. As a result, when Pearl Harbor was attacked from aircraft carriers, many were mesmerized by the notion that the attackers must have come from there. How Japan decided for war, the origins of the plans to attack Pearl Harbor, and the execution of those designs have everything to do with the Imperial Navy, its fears and doctrines, and the power of its senior officers. Ensuing events provided great impetus for Allied naval intelligence. Those events initiated a dark period of Allied defeat that can be called Yamamoto's war.

# "We Have a Chance to Win
# a War Right Now"

ONE IMPERIAL NAVY OFFICER WHO HAD A MAJOR, PERHAPS PREDOMINANT VOICE IN Japan's decision for war, Admiral Nagano Osami, figured among the treaty faction favoring good relations with the United States. During critical months of 1941 Nagano sat in the highest councils of government as chief of the Naval General Staff; he was a full admiral, indeed the oldest officer then on the Navy's active list. Nagano's April 1941 appointment to head the NGS represented a comeback for a man who had already experienced the full perquisites of command in the Japanese Navy. He had led the Combined Fleet from 1937 to 1939 and preceeded Yonai as Navy minister. In 1941 Admiral Nagano held powers of decision greater than ever due to the China Incident, which had led Emperor Hirohito to activate Imperial General Headquarters (IGHQ), a high command unit linking the Navy and Army general staffs. Nagano served as the voice of the Navy on operational matters, and a decision for war would be an operational matter par excellence.

It was ironic that Nagano should be cast in the role of war advocate, as much so as in the case of Yamamoto Isoroku, who also opposed war with America. While Yamamoto once joked that such a war would have to be ended by dictating peace terms in the White House, Nagano had actually dined there, having been to lunch along with the Japanese midshipmen during the 1927 training cruise he commanded. Nagano had been a language officer in the United States in 1913; he had studied international law at Harvard for seven months and had been attaché in Washington from 1920 to 1923, rendering important service during the Naval Conference, subsequently heading the intelligence component of the Naval General Staff. In 1931 he had been chief of the Japanese technical delegation to disarmament talks at Geneva under League of Nations auspices, and in 1935 he headed the Japanese delegation to the last, abortive London Naval Conference. His eldest son went to the American Methodist school in Tokyo.

Though he hailed from Kochi prefecture, born in 1880, the fourth son of Nagano Harukichi, a samurai, the family had ties to Satsuma province in southern Kyushu. Men from Satsuma had been dominant among officer ranks of the Imperial Navy. Kagoshima anchorage, one of the Navy's most frequently used mooring places, was in Satsuma, as were some of the ports and landing places where Portuguese and other Western traders and missionaries had made the earliest contacts with Japan. Nagano reflected the Western influences that had seeped into Japan through Satsuma. He had many friends among Americans and other pro-Western Japanese officers such as Nomura Kichisaburo. All told Nagano had spent five years in the United States and considered New York City a second home. Some regarded Nagano Osami as the Japanese Navy's foremost expert on the United States.

Americans perceived Nagano's qualities and responded to them. Office of Naval Intelligence biographies called the admiral an excellent administrator and strategist; a strong, virile, and forceful officer. Arthur H. McCollum got to know Nagano when at the Naval War College. When Nagano led his student cruise to the United States, McCollum was assigned as the admiral's American aide. In Japan a couple of years later McCollum accompanied attaché Joseph Ogan on a reciprocal visit to the Etajima naval academy, of which Nagano had become president. The Japanese admiral entertained them nicely and personally prepared a sukiyaki dinner. The next morning Nagano showed them the Etajima cadets at rifle practice.

"You know, we make them yell to increase their warlike spirit," Nagano said with a laugh. "They don't have enough of it!"

Toward the end of the Americans' inspection trip, Admiral Nagano said, "You people have got to make out a big report on this. If there's anything I can give you to fatten it up, it's fine by me."

During those years Admiral Nagano gave Etajima cadets the impression that he was a superman, everywhere, monitoring every facet of education and training. In 1933 his handling of the simulated "American" fleet during grand maneuvers earned high praise, and Nagano's career seemed on a meteoric trajectory, culminating in promotion to full admiral in March 1934 and in the Navy Ministry and Combined Fleet posts already noted. But seniority injected Nagano Osami into the Imperial Navy's high command system with all its drawbacks. Young Fuchida Mitsuo, then observing from the perspective of the War College, felt the admiral was not the man to actively direct subordinates' planning activity. That left the field to the ambitions and energy of middle-level staff officers. Nagano's own energy seemed to flag as well. Perhaps it was the drinking parties he enjoyed, which lasted late into the night; perhaps it was the attention claimed by three successive wives, all much younger than he; perhaps it was the toll of siring three sons and two daughters; for whatever reason, Nagano visibly slowed down in the 1930s. Soon he became known for falling asleep in meetings and for a perpetually tired appearance. In 1939 Admiral Nagano stepped down from the Combined Fleet to less demanding duty as special naval inspector.

In Nagano's opinion, expressed to American interrogators after the war, the main reason for his appointment to the Naval General Staff was the recommendation of the incumbent, Admiral Prince Fushimi Hiroyasu. Chief of the Naval General Staff for nine years, Prince Fushimi presided over the Navy's agreement to go along with the Tripartite Pact. Although considered pro-German and associated with the fleet faction, Fushimi could not help but be aware of the substantial opposition to a German alliance within the Imperial Navy. Accordingly, at the point when the Navy stopped rejecting the pact, Prince Fushimi stated a number of conditions for his service's agreement that were designed to lessen the adverse effect upon Japanese-American relations. Fushimi's recommendation of Admiral Nagano for a successor appears to have been part of that design. Cosmetic measures could no longer halt the slide toward war, however, and the net effect of Nagano's appointment was to put peace advocates in the responsible positions at the onset of war.

THE MOST STRIKING ASPECT OF ADMIRAL NAGANO'S COMEBACK AS CHIEF OF THE NAVAL General Staff is the role reversal that occurred. As will become clear shortly, the NGS viewpoint expressed by the chief of staff would be far from the opinions one might expect from Nagano Osami. A man who, it has been recorded, turned up on the doorstep of the U.S. embassy in Tokyo in tears on the occasion of the *Panay* sinking, as chief of staff was telling top officials the time had come for war with America. As with Prince Fushimi before him, Nagano had to represent the broad outlook of the Imperial Navy, and a sea change of naval opinion had begun, imperiling the moderate views of Nagano and Yamamoto, or for that matter Admiral Nomura Kichisaburo, by this time appointed ambassador to the United States with the specific intention of negotiating a solution to the growing Far Eastern crisis.

Nomura's example is a poignant one. He had been brought out of retirement in the fall of 1940, a professional naval officer selected for what amounted to a diplomatic special mission. Rather than proceeding immediately to Washington, Admiral Nomura had spent weeks in Japan, Manchuria, and China touching base with key figures of the Imperial Navy, the Kwangtung and China Area armies, the Army General Staff, and Tokyo political figures. The intent clearly seems to make certain that the political factions would permit a negotiated settlement to emerge. Only then did Nomura travel to Washington; by the time he initiated conversations with Secretary of State Cordell Hull it was the spring of 1941.

Unfortunately, the critical miscalculations had already been made. Japanese foreign minister Matsuoka Yosuke underestimated the antagonism with which Americans would view Japan's entering into an alliance soon called the Rome-Berlin-Tokyo Axis. Japanese Army leaders overestimated their chances for defeating China, and erred especially in repeatedly anticipating the imminent end (a frequently used term was "liquidation") of that conflict. Japanese political leaders underestimated the degree to which their short-term maneuvers among factions would foreclose long-term prospects for a policy to lead the way out of the morass. Imperial Navy officers overestimated their ability to keep the nation out of a war that seemed to beckon with opportunity both to the north, where the Soviet Union was preoccupied by her fight against Germany, and to the south, where colonies cut off from conquered mother countries looked like fruit ripe for the plucking. The United States overestimated its ability to restrain Japan through economic measures or deter Tokyo by means of military deployments.

On both sides there was misperception of the terrain for negotiation. The rock-bottom American aim was really to reverse the China Incident, and that could not be done without a policy anathema to the Japanese generals, which in actuality meant overturning the entire political system. Japan's aim in the 1941 negotiations was to reach a settlement that left its gains intact, an objective with which no American government would have agreed. Thus in reality there remained very little to negotiate.

Admiral Nomura himself overestimated the impact of those cosmetic concessions he could offer, and underestimated the aversion military and even Foreign Ministry officials would eventually show to real bargaining.

Perhaps more realistic were the middle-level staff officers of the Navy Ministry. Many of these officers discounted the efforts to ameliorate the impact of the Tripartite Pact, and concluded as soon as it was signed that war was coming. Before the end of 1940, mobilization officials prompted the Imperial Navy to request permission to move to full war footing. Their request would be approved. Target date for completion of war preparations would be November 15, 1941. Admiral Nagano later likened the rush of events to the force of water pushing into Niagara Falls. This may indeed have been Nagano's rationalization for abandoning the moderate views he had previously held—abandoning them so completely that recent Japanese historians describe the admiral as the leader "closest to the war faction in the navy."

Next to Nagano the key Imperial Navy leader at this time, Admiral

Oikawa Koshiro, also numbered among the moderates. The fifty-eight-year-old Oikawa had been a staff officer with the NGS in 1930 who helped push through ratification of the London Naval Treaty. As naval commander in China in 1935 he had advocated a "strike north" against Russia in preference to hostilities in China, but as Navy minister in 1940–1941 advised Nagano against that same option. A study in contrasts to Nagano, Oikawa was handsome where Nagano reputedly numbered among the three ugliest admirals in the Navy, and erudite where Nagano seemed workmanlike. Oikawa had attended the Naval War College during its golden period, was a classical Chinese scholar, peppered his speeches with historical and philosophical allusions, and had been aide-de-camp to Emperor Hirohito when the latter was still crown prince. Japanese officers agree that Oikawa was gracious and gentlemanly, while American intelligence recorded an impression of him as a "Prussian son of a bitch." Oikawa made full admiral in 1939, a year ahead of Nagano. The only officer to have held command of the China Area Fleet twice, Oikawa was well versed in the aggressive tactics favored by the Japanese Army. Had he been a bit more of a Prussian, the Navy might have had a better chance of heading off war. Instead, according to his flag secretary, Oikawa seemed greatly influenced by the pro-German sentiment abroad in Japan and muted his opposition to the march toward war. At the liaison conferences, which brought together service ministers, chiefs of staff, the prime and foreign ministers, and other cabinet officials, Oikawa mouthed only ambiguities.

The liaison conferences, the more important of which sat in the presence of the Emperor, were the forum in which the Navy exhibited its attitude. Though the Imperial Navy's own records of these meetings, as well as those compiled by the cabinet, were destroyed during the war, Army records, including both transcripts of meetings and copies of policy documents discussed, survived. At the start of 1941 French Indochina became a featured subject as hostilities broke out between the French and Thais. At Imperial General Headquarters, according to Army operations staffer Colonel Hattori Takushiro, authorities had come to view as necessary bases in both Thailand and southern Indochina. Even if force in the south proved unnecessary, the Japanese wanted the raw materials available in Thailand and Indochina. Liaison conferences therefore decided to intervene in the French-Thai border war. The idea of acquiring bases was in mind even at this early date. Actual Japanese intervention included Imperial Navy demonstrations off the Indochinese coast, among them the dispatch of a carrier division plus its escort vessels.

By spring, just when Nomura reached Washington and began conversations there, the liaison conferences in Tokyo were actively considering more extensive penetration of French Indochina, demanding bases there. By June, about the time the Navy stepped up its air campaign in China, beginning night bombardments of Chungking, the liaison conferences were deciding on measures to be taken toward the "Southern Area," which included Indochina and Thailand, and maneuvers to expedite matters.

"We must build bases in French Indochina and Thailand in order to launch military operations," Admiral Nagano declared at a June 11 liaison conference. "We must resolutely attack anyone who tries to stop us."

Nagano spoke so forcefully on that occasion that General Sugiyama Gen, the Army chief of staff, said nothing, except to contradict Foreign Minister Matsuoka, who warned that moving into southern Indochina would provoke Britain and the United States. Sugiyama told Army staffers later that Nagano's words had made him uneasy.

Perhaps the Army leader had been thinking of the warnings from the Naval General Staff that March, shortly before Nagano took over, when Commander Onoda Sutejiro explained to Army opposite numbers at IGHQ that the Navy was not yet prepared to use force in the south because it feared this course would bring conflict with America.

Admiral Nagano pressed ahead regardless of the Navy's earlier reservations. At a session the day after his forceful declaration to the liaison conference, Nagano presented a plan to accelerate a "union" with French Indochina, in pursuit of which Japan would "not refuse to risk a war with Britain and the United States." At a meeting on June 16, when the Army objected that preparations it could initiate in terms of unit movement, mobilization, and organization were restricted by need for the Emperor's approval, Nagano posed an alternative: "How about making all preparations and then obtaining His Majesty's approval?"

Toward the end of June, Japan considered turning north against Russia, in support of the German blitzkrieg just unleashed, and despite the nonaggression pact Japan had signed with the Soviet Union in April 1941. Nagano opposed this, as did Navy Minister Oikawa. The chief of staff warned that the Imperial Navy would need fifty days to redirect war preparations against Russia. Nagano's vice chief, Admiral Kondo Nobutake, also warned that a campaign against the Russians could cost a hundred submarines. Not only was there no apparent rationale for predicting such high losses, but the figure given exceeded the Imperial Navy submarine force at that time.

At a July 2 liaison conference, where Sugiyama focused on the Russian question, Nagano mentioned only the south. "I believe that . . . our Empire, in order to secure our defenses in the South and attain a position of self-sufficiency . . . must take immediate steps to push steadily southward by coordinating political and military action," Nagano told his colleagues.

The Navy chief of staff anticipated trouble with Britain, the Netherlands, and the United States. "If they obstinately continue to obstruct us," Nagano rasped, "we may . . . have to go to war against Great Britain and the United

States." The Navy insisted that Japan should not be deterred by that possibility: "I believe it will be necessary for us to decide independently when and in what manner we should use armed force."

Around this time, lower levels of the Army General Staff were told by Rear Admiral Oka Takasumi, a Navy Ministry politico-military specialist, that if there were a strike north, operations would have to be carried out in the south also—in fact, especially in the south. The message was clear: The Navy not only preferred a war in the Pacific to one with the Soviet Union, but war in the Pacific *was the Navy's price* for agreement to fight Russia. The decision that emerged in early July, approved by the Emperor, involved war preparations both to the north and to the south, but the postponement of any immediate decision for either option.

In Washington, in the meantime, Admiral Nomura continued desultory talks with the United States. The naval ambassador adopted the practice of playing his cards for effect, softening harsh rhetoric where he could, delaying or suppressing some of the more inflammatory cables, casting American proposals in the most favorable light. It did not help that Ambassador Nomura seemed to have a very poor relationship with Foreign Minister Matsuoka, who frequently upbraided Nomura in their exchanges. On July 10 the frustrated admiral resorted to a back-channel message, sent through his naval attaché to Oikawa and Nagano, complaining that he had been getting little support for his peace efforts even though he had spoken with "everyone" at the time of his appointment. America had seemed to soften its criticisms, Nomura reported, but since the outbreak of the Russo-German war Nomura had heard talk that Tokyo and Berlin were inseparable.

The reaction in Tokyo was immediate. "According to Navy reports," Admiral Oikawa told a liaison conference on July 12, "it appears that Secretary of State Hull and others are not prepared to provoke a Pacific war. Since Japan does not wish to engage in a Pacific war, isn't there room for negotiation?"

"Is there room?" Minister Matsuoka shot back. "What will they accept?"

"Well, something minor," responded the Navy minister.

In fact Washington had no intention of accepting any minor concession; the American proposal seemed so outrageous to Matsuoka that the foreign minister wished to reject it out of hand. Suddenly Navy chief of staff Nagano came to Matsuoka's aid.

Said Admiral Nagano, "If it is true that the United States will not change its attitude no matter what Japan says, then won't it be all right to do as you [Matsuoka] propose?"

Thus Nagano undercut his own service minister, who had just spoken for accommodation, and indeed against the agreed Army-Navy policy, which called for continued negotiations. Navy specialist Oka immediately intervened.

"If we are going to break off negotiations, as His Excellency the Navy Chief of Staff proposes, won't those in the lower echelons lose all enthusiasm for their work?"

Nagano backed down.

Hopes for negotiations were set far back, however, when Japan made its move into southern French Indochina on July 25. The very next day, President Roosevelt froze all Japanese assets in the United States, halting further imports. With Japan dependent on imports for critical raw materials, Washington's action had disastrous implications. The situation appeared especially critical to Tokyo: Although the Imperial Navy had had a stockpiling program in place for some time, the Army had not. The Navy initially estimated it had a two-year stock of fuel, but found itself expending oil at a rate of 400 tons an hour and realized that its stockpile would run out in eighteen months. The Army had only recent imports in hand, sufficient for about four months' operations. This was stretched somewhat by conservation and diversion of civilian stocks, but the truth remained that the hourglass had begun to run out on Japan. One way or another, the crisis had to be resolved.

CLEARLY THE ROLE NAGANO OSAMI PLAYED IN TOKYO'S HIGH POLICY DISCUSSIONS WAS FAR from that of a moderate, anti-war officer. Nagano's need to reflect service opinion accounts for part of this change. An Imperial Navy perception that it stood on the brink of great achievement probably also had some influence, tempting Nagano to go along with proponents of action in the south. Most likely, however, cold calculation lay behind the positions the Navy espoused. Made by the Navy General Staff, aware of Japanese building programs as well as *joho kyoku* intelligence on American naval construction, the calculations showed that long-term trends did not favor Japan. It was no secret that in 1940 the United States had passed a massive building program to lead to a "Two Ocean Navy," and the Japanese also knew that Roosevelt had ordered a significant proportion of U.S. naval forces to the Atlantic. Officers at NGS could see that the balance of forces temporarily favored Japan, and also that any advantage would eventually be wiped out as new vessels joined the American fleet. The oil crisis merely sharpened the dilemma and gave it an urgent character. Admiral Nagano's new bellicosity likely owed much to this realization. Nagano's statements during the final months of negotiations contain echoes of his former moderate views but focus on this question of the adverse trends.

The basic analysis of the Naval General Staff Admiral Nagano presented to the liaison conference on July 21, four days *before* the fateful move into Indochina:

As for war with the United States, although there is now a chance of achieving victory, the chances will diminish as time goes on. By the latter half of next year it will already be difficult for us to cope with the United States; after that the situation will become increasingly worse. The United States will probably prolong the matter until her defenses have been built up, and then try to settle it. Accordingly, as time goes by, the Empire will be put at a disadvantage. If we could settle things without war, there would be nothing better. But if we conclude that conflict cannot ultimately be avoided, then I would like you to understand that as time goes by we will be in a disadvantageous position. Moreover, if we occupy the Philippines, it will be easier, from the Navy's point of view, to carry on the war.

I believe that our defenses in the South Sea Islands are strong and that we can put up a good fight there.

Punctuating the rising tide came an incident on July 29, a virtual repeat of the *Panay* affair, in which Imperial Navy bombers mistakenly hit the American gunboat *Tutuila* on the Yangtze. This time Nagano had no tears.

On July 31 Emperor Hirohito received his Navy chief for a private audience. Admiral Nagano expressed strong opposition to the Tripartite Pact and remarked that he felt there could be no settlement with the United States so long as Japan continued that alliance. At the same time, Nagano warned, the loss of oil sources would force Japan to sally forth. Hirohito regarded Nagano's opinion as identical to that of Prince Fushimi, both favoring efforts to avoid war if possible. Hirohito asked Nagano about prospects in war, he later told Marquis Kido Koichi, keeper of the privy seal. "He is of the opinion," Kido recorded in a diary, "that we would gain a victory, even if it was not the sweeping victory we secured in the Russo-Japanese War. But Admiral Nagano's overall outlook on a war is quite pessimistic."

In the days that followed, Naval General Staff officers worked with the Army staff to clarify the situation. Captain Ono Takeji, a former chief of operations now directly attached to the head of the NGS First Bureau, made special efforts on the Russian question. Ono held an amorphous job that included formulation of Navy propaganda policy as well as troubleshooting on sensitive matters, and he got the Army to concede that it was not attempting to push the Imperial Navy into war with Russia, but forging unity behind a policy of fighting should the *Russians* attack. The relegation of the strike north option to the status of precautionary contingency opened the way to southern operations. Ono's reward would be command of the light cruiser *Kiso.*

War preparations began to move into high gear. According to NGS operations staffers meeting with the Army on August 16, the Navy began the week before to requisition its first 300,000 tons of commercial shipping. An initial increment of three battalions of the SNLF would be brought back from China in early September, more shipping would be diverted as of the middle of that month, and all preparations would be complete before mid-December. Commander Onoda Sutejiro also presented a Navy position paper on overall policy, one compiled by the highest circles of the Navy command, which provided that war preparations would be made without any decision, for the moment, upon whether to go to war. Negotiations could be carried out until late October. If no favorable outcome emerged, the decision on force could be made at that point. This Navy plan became the focus of Japanese policymaking.

When this paper went officially before a liaison conference on September 3, Admiral Nagano reiterated the position he had taken in July. "We are getting weaker," Nagano said. "By contrast, the enemy is getting stronger. . . . We will endure what can be endured in carrying on diplomacy, but at the opportune moment we must make some estimates. Ultimately, when there is no hope for diplomacy, and when war cannot be avoided, it is essential that we make up our minds quickly."

Admiral Nagano did not shrink from giving the group his actual estimate of the military prospects. The Navy, he declared, thought in terms of both a short war and a long one. "We hope that the enemy will come out for a quick showdown; in that event there will be a Decisive Battle in waters near us, and I anticipate that our chances of victory would be quite good. But I do not believe the war would end with that. It would be a long war. . . . I think it would be good to take advantage of the fruits of [an initial] victory to cope with a long war. If, on the contrary, we get into a long war without a Decisive Battle, we will be in difficulty, . . . since our supply of resources will become depleted."

The liaison conference went on to approve the Navy proposal.

On September 6, at a follow-up meeting, Nagano returned to the same themes. In this instance his military analysis happens to have been especially clear:

> By the latter half of next year America's military preparedness will have made great progress, and it will be difficult to cope with her. Therefore it must be said that it would be very dangerous for our Empire to remain idle and let the days go by. . . .
>
> As to our predictions of the way military operations are likely to go, the probability is very high that they will from the outset plan on a prolonged war. Therefore, it will be necessary for us to be reconciled to this and to be prepared militarily for a long war. If they should aim for a quick war leading to an early decision, send their principal naval units, and challenge us to an immediate decisive battle, this would be the very thing we hope for.

. . . However, even if our Empire should win a decisive naval victory, we will not thereby be able to bring the war to a conclusion. We can anticipate that America will attempt to prolong the war, utilizing her impregnable position, her superior industrial power, and her abundant resources.

Our Empire does not have the means to take the offensive, overcome the enemy, and make them give up their will to fight. Moreover, we are very short of resources at home, so we would very much like to avert a prolonged war.

The main chance, Nagano related, would come if Japan's first stage of operations was successful, in which case the Empire would have seized important resources in the Southern Area enabling the nation to have the best chance in a long war.

> The essential conditions that give a chance of success in the first stage of operations are, first, to decide quickly to commence hostilities in view of the realities of our fighting capacity and theirs; second, to take the initiative rather than allowing them to do so; third, to consider the meteorological conditions in the operational areas in order to make operations easier.

In a peroration evoking the old Nagano, the chief of staff urged, "We must spare no efforts in seeking a way to settle the present difficult situation peacefully." Navy Minister Oikawa repeated that sentiment, saying "We will carry diplomatic negotiations as far as possible." The problem remained, as before, that what Tokyo regarded as a minimum acceptable settlement, Washington felt would be a sell-out of its Far Eastern interests.

Emperor Hirohito knew what was coming at this Imperial Conference (the name given a liaison conference when it sat in the presence of the Emperor). As noted, he had talked privately with Nagano earlier, and he had spoken again to the admiral the day before the meeting. On that occasion Hirohito had been with Prince Konoye Fumimaro, then prime minister, and made inquiries Konoye felt could not be answered without senior military authorities. Nagano and Sugiyama had been summoned. Admiral Nagano had sounded almost desperate: "To his mind Japan was like a patient suffering from a serious illness . . . the patient's case was so critical that the question of whether or not to operate had to be determined without delay." Hirohito answered indirectly the next day at the Imperial Conference, reciting a poem by his grandfather the Emperor Meiji:

> All the seas, everywhere
> are brothers to one another
> Why then do the winds and waves of strife
> rage so violently through the world?

Participants at the September 6 session professed their determination to press negotiations, but approved the Navy policy of simultaneous war preparations. They also understood Admiral Nagano's repeated assertion of the need for an urgent war decision when the time came.

There is one point important to make about the Naval General Staff planning that lay behind Nagano's statements at the liaison conferences. The chief of staff spoke, not once but repeatedly, of the probability that any conflict with America would be a long war. Yet Navy doctrine and training had prepared Japanese for a *short* campaign leading to Decisive Battle. This mismatch between war plans and tactical preparations would be a serious problem and had much to do with the outcome of the war.

War planning came directly to the fore with the passage of autumn. War games indicated desirable changes in the plans, as will be seen presently. With close coordination between NGS and the staff of the Combined Fleet came closer contact between Nagano and Admiral Yamamoto Isoroku. Nagano had full and implicit confidence in Yamamoto, who has been quoted as thinking Nagano less brilliant than his reputation, but the two held similar views on war with America. Yamamoto wrote the NGS chief in a September 29 letter:

> If I may express my opinion as an impartial observer, it is obvious that the Japan-American war will be a protracted one. As long as Japan remains in a favorable position, the United States would never stop fighting. As a consequence, the war would continue for several years, our supplies would be exhausted, our ships and arms would be damaged, and ultimately we would not be able to escape defeat. Not only that, as a result of the war, people of this nation would be reduced to abject poverty.

That such perceptions did not turn Japanese leaders away from their press for war is a remarkable comment on the fatalism of the Japanese.

At the beginning of October, with Nomura reporting Washington talks deadlocked, Admiral Nagano again took up his refrain. "There is no longer time for discussion," he told an October 4 meeting; "we want quick action." A few days later, Nagano and General Sugiyama resolved all remaining questions concerning war plans. At a liaison conference on October 9 Navy Minister Oikawa kept Nagano from speaking out again, but the chief of staff simply awaited the end of the meeting, then handed his strong statement to the foreign minister. Oikawa failed to take an open stand against war himself, even when Prince Konoye held a private meeting of key cabinet ministers having been told by a senior Navy Ministry aide that that service wished to avoid war and so opposed any rupture of negotiations. Admiral Oikawa talked of leaving the decision entirely to the prime minister, in effect avoiding responsibility, but advising a course that could not be carried out if opposed by the military chiefs of staff.

Konoye Fumimaro concluded that his effectiveness had evaporated and resigned a few days later. On October 17 a new government took office under former war minister General Tojo Hideki. The real issue in this change, perhaps not well appreciated at the time, concerned settlement of the Far Eastern crisis: Tojo pledged to continue talks while Konoye, not a military man, could no longer restrain the military leaders. The new cabinet ushered in a new Navy minister, Admiral Shimada Shigetaro, soon to fall under Tojo's spell but initially not prepared to hold back Nagano. Thus even with Tojo in power, Nagano complained about Navy fuel consumption to prod the government. Both he and Sugiyama objected to delays in the decision for war.

"We were to have reached a decision in October, and yet here we are," Admiral Nagano fretted on October 23. Tojo had been in office less than a week.

The next day Nagano's vice chief, Admiral Ito Seiichi, officially reported the Navy estimate that six to eight months would be needed to complete the first stage of operations. Shimada warned against overestimating the construction rate for new merchant ships. The Navy's official position on war prospects, in answer to a cabinet questionnaire, was that "we will be all right in the beginning; but if the war is prolonged, our chances will depend on the international situation and the determination of the people." Again the long-war question had been raised.

Admiral Nagano suggested at one session toward the end of October that Japan might offer, in effect, to accept America's Open Door policy in order to reach agreement, but at the key liaison conference of November 1 the chief of staff spoke in favor of war now rather than later. Nagano declared that nobody knew what Japan's chances might be three years in the future. "I think it would be easier to engage in a war now," Nagano said. "The reason is that now we have the necessary foundation for it."

A little later, Finance Minister Kaya Okinori returned to the question of timing and asked, "Well, then, when can we go to war and win?"

"Now!" Admiral Nagano thundered. "The time for war will not come later!"

The Navy agreed to permit negotiations until November 20, but both Nagano and Sugiyama held that it would infringe on their right of supreme command if the government wished to call off the war at the very last moment. When the deadline for negotiations was set five days before the deadline for war, the latter was moved back to December 5. The group discussed and approved final diplomatic proposals, respectively "A" and "B," the former providing a sweeping settlement, the latter a limited compromise. Nagano advocated standing with the "A" proposal, in effect offering a choice between a full settlement or war. A senior Army official perceived his stand exactly that way: "Nagano . . . is clearly determined that we go to war now." As for Admiral Shimada, he had said the prospects were not clear but he "appears to think, like Nagano, that there is no alternative but to go to war now."

The new deadline cast the die for war. As Admiral Nagano put it in his next statement before the liaison conference on November 5, "Hereafter we will go forward steadily with our war preparations, expecting the opening of hostilities in the early part of December." As he emphasized, "Success or failure in the initial phases of our operations will greatly affect . . . the entire war. . . . Consequently, the concealment of our war plans has an important bearing on the outcome of the war."

As before, the Imperial Navy remained mindful of relative forces, as Nagano explained in answer to inquiries during the November 5 meeting. He discussed the strength of the U.S. fleet in specific detail, put the ratio existing in the Pacific at that moment at 7.5:10, and estimated the force the British would be able to send to the Far East at only a single battleship, ten or more cruisers, and some aircraft. In conclusion Nagano stated: "We are, therefore, confident of victory. We can destroy their fleet if they want a Decisive Battle. Even if we destroy it, however, the war will continue long after the Southern Operation."

With preparations moving to completion there ensued a final flurry of diplomatic activity. Japan sent a special envoy, Kurusu Saburo, to join Nomura for the last talks, and they presented the "B" proposal. The Americans replied after what Cordell Hull called "minute study" by himself and his "associates," in which they assembled a modus vivendi proposal that was "clutching at straws to save the situation." In fact Hull told a White House meeting with President Roosevelt on November 25 that virtually no chance remained to avoid war, and his reply to the Japanese, tendered the next day, contained ten stiff conditions. Among them were demands that Japan accede to the Open Door and withdraw all troops from both Indochina and China, all to gain an extra three months (FDR had suggested a duration of six). These conditions would plainly be unacceptable in Tokyo. To paraphrase one of the cables Tokyo sent Nomura and Kurusu, things were going to begin to happen automatically.

During the interim, however, Japan had still to make some reply to Hull's note of November 26, and there were those who favored a last-minute effort to settle short of war. On the American side, some even talked about a summit conference between Roosevelt and Hirohito. Tokyo had set December 1 as the date for an Imperial Conference that would ratify the decision to open hostilities. On Saturday, November 29, occurred a liaison conference to confirm the agenda for the larger meeting and review late diplomatic developments. Foreign Minister Togo Shigenori, who expected a cabinet meeting on the note the next day, wished to clarify just how much time remained for negotiations.

"We do have enough time," Admiral Nagano replied.

That was not sufficient for Togo. "Tell me what the zero hour is," Togo shot back. "Otherwise I can't carry on diplomacy."

"Well, then, I will tell you," retorted Nagano. "The zero hour is"—Nagano's voice fell practically to a whisper—"December eighth."

The Navy chief of staff went on to warn that what was needed was "the kind of diplomacy that will be helpful in winning the war." In fact Nagano urged, in unison with Admiral Shimada and Rear Admiral Oka, that diplomacy be "sacrificed" to win the war. Togo asked if embassy staff in Washington could be told how long they had left. Nagano replied that the Navy had not even told its own attaché; there could be no question of revealing this information to Foreign Ministry people.

On December 1 the Imperial Navy and Army chose to deliver a joint statement before the Imperial Conference, which this time included elder statesmen in addition to regular participants. It was Admiral Nagano who rose to make the declaration. Again he argued that time was not on Japan's side; thus an immediate war was preferable to one in the future. Nagano also termed the situation the "most serious crisis since the founding of our country." Nagano's last word came at a liaison conference on December 4, when in discussing the contents of the final message Japan would send to the United States upon the declaration of war, someone suggested wording that would leave open the possibility of holding further negotiations. Admiral Nagano rasped, "There is no time for that."

With the decision for war made and the troops and ships and planes in their allotted places, the things that would happen automatically, offensive thrusts in a Pacific-wide surprise attack, were in train. What would follow was the war of the Combined Fleet, Yamamoto's war; yet the first part of that war, and the decision for it, had more to do with Nagano. This might be Yamamoto's war, but it had been Nagano Osami who had the featured role in the first act.

# "So Long as I'm CinC We Shall Go Ahead"

J APAN HAD RECOGNIZED A STATE OF WAR AS EARLY AS NOVEMBER 1937, WHEN EMPEROR Hirohito sanctioned reactivation of the Imperial General Headquarters, a high-command organization intended to be used only in time of war. Activation of IGHQ solidified the power of the chiefs of staff by endowing armed-services staffs with additional autonomy, increasing their independence from the service ministries, bringing the staffs into a direct relationship to the Emperor. The chiefs of staff had long had the right of direct access to the Emperor, but IGHQ formalized the relationship. The main beneficiary in the Imperial Navy was the chief of the Naval General Staff (*gunreibu*), anointed in the Emperor's name to function as supreme commander. Admiral Nagano Osami enjoyed these powers in the months leading up to the Pacific war.

The effective power of the Navy General Staff and its chief can be seen to advantage in the process of contingency planning in the Imperial Navy. As in armed services the world over, the Japanese constructed hypothetical plans for war, even in peacetime. The United States had for a long time been held as the main hypothetical enemy, but plans were also drawn up against Russia and Great Britain. The annual plans were a budgetary device, completed by the beginning of the Japanese fiscal year in April. The plans enabled NGS to judge adequacy of the Navy's warship and aircraft inventories. Where forces appeared insufficient the chief of staff would then present requirements for additions to the Navy Ministry. The ministry's role was to juggle resources to fit requirements set elsewhere. Since one major mechanism for asserting political control over armed forces is to hold decision power over force levels, it can be seen that such control in the Japanese case was limited at best.

Comprising a number of functional bureaus (*bu*), the Naval General Staff could truly be considered the brain of the Imperial Navy. The First Bureau of NGS handled the critically important matters of operations, the Second the details of mobilization and armament. The Third Bureau, already discussed at some length, was the Navy's intelligence service. The Fourth Bureau, previously briefly mentioned as well, was sometimes called the Naval Communications Bureau and had the additional function of serving at the head of Japanese naval radio intelligence. The chief of staff presided over NGS with the help of a vice chief. Fewer than a hundred officers on NGS and in coordinate related offices of the Navy Ministry in effect ran the Imperial Navy.

Admiral Nagano Osami arrived to take up the reins of chief of staff in April 1941. His vice chief until that September, during most of the period of war planning, was a man ten years younger, Vice Admiral Kondo Nobutake. This officer embodied almost all the attributes considered important in an Imperial Navy staff man. Kondo had graduated first in his class at Etajima; he had been naval aide to Hirohito and naval attaché in Germany, had served twice on the staff of the Combined Fleet, and twice again had done tours with NGS, both times with the operations section. Kondo had headed the First Bureau. Just prior to that he had been Combined Fleet chief of staff, and was considered to have done an excellent job of it. He had held commands in southern China, most prominently that of the fleet that carried out the invasion of Hainan in February 1939. Ten months afterward Admiral Kondo received an appointment as vice chief of NGS. He spoke fair English and German and was considered pro-American but anti-British.

Next to its chief and vice chief, the key figure on the Naval General Staff had to be the chief of its First Bureau, the operations bureau. When Nagano took over, that was Rear Admiral Ugaki Matome, who soon traded places with Rear Admiral Fukudome Shigeru, chief of staff of the Combined Fleet. The chief of the First Bureau controlled two staff sections, respectively for operations and for defenses. With six operations staff planners, the First Section of the First Bureau lay at the heart of NGS. The Second Section, the defensive one, handled everything from antisubmarine warfare and convoy policy to harbor defenses. For present purposes the First Section is the more important.

Until the advent of the Tripartite Pact—which, like Ugaki, he opposed—Captain Nakazawa Tasuku had been chief of the First Section. From October 1940 on, the senior operations staffer would be Captain Baron Tomioka Sadatoshi. The forty-four-year-old Tomioka was third-generation Imperial Navy, his father having been an admiral during the Russo-Japanese War. Tomioka had been Imperial Navy delegate at Geneva for League of Nations disarmament negotiations between 1930 and 1933, had subsequently taught strategy at the Naval War College (where he expressed optimistic views on Japan's chances in war with the British and Americans), and had been skipper of a destroyer in China waters.

Under Captain Tomioka a half-dozen operations-staff officers drafted the plans that drove the Navy's ships and planes. From about 1937 to 1940 these plans remained purely theoretical. Arthur Marder notes, for example, that the Imperial Navy had no actual war plan against Great Britain during this period, merely a set of general principles laid down in 1936. Under these, in the first phase of a war the Japanese would smash forward British naval forces and occupy key points in British Borneo and Malaya along with Hong Kong and Singapore. When Lieutenant Commander Miyo Tatsukichi joined the NGS operations section in November 1939, the British war-plan file contained just a few pieces of paper covered with penciled notations describing an amphibious landing on the east coast of Malaya, to be carried out by the Japanese Army with Imperial Navy cooperation.

At the time, the war plans had been of the traditional sort, underpinning the Fourth Replenishment Program just adopted. Commander Miyo watched as the 1940 war plans were used to compile requirements for a new naval building program, the Fifth Replenishment Program, considered by a high-level Navy conference in January 1941, originally intended to cover naval procurement over the period from 1942 to 1946. Among other items, the program provided for three more *Yamato*-class battleships, two battle cruisers, three aircraft carriers, and sixty-seven squadrons of combat aircraft. These would be substantial additions but conventional ones. The senior aviation officer of the Navy Ministry was then–Vice Admiral Inoue Shigeyoshi, chief of the Bureau of Aeronautics, and Inoue objected to the orthodox character of the scheme, commenting that NGS ought to withdraw the proposal and rethink its approach.

Admiral Inoue subsequently prepared a paper he sent to the navy minister predicting that in a U.S. war American submarines and airpower would be the key dangers. In particular, Inoue wrote, "it is quite unlikely a Decisive Battle involving battleships will take place unless the commander-in-chief of the U.S. fleet is very ignorant and reckless." Inoue prescribed preparations to secure the sea-lanes against U.S. submarines plus dominant airpower, with only those fleet forces required to capture necessary bases in the Southern Area, the name the Japanese used for the countries of Southeast Asia they felt could supply raw materials. The navy minister received the Inoue proposal in August 1941 and quashed it, making no reply and going ahead with the Fifth Replenishment Program.

Within the Naval General Staff, however, Commander Miyo rose to the challenge. Miyo happened to be the operations staff officer for aviation at NGS and had been a major player in assembling the Fifth Replenishment

Program proposal, delayed because the Japanese Army went slowly on its corresponding plan. Miyo harbored doubts about war with the United States and spoke out against the Tripartite Pact, so strongly that Admiral Ugaki had called his boss, Captain Nakazawa, to the office for a private consultation. In any case, Miyo knew from a previous survey trip to the Mandates that in a war with America the Imperial Navy would have base problems— there had been plentiful sites suitable for seaplane bases, but few for airfields. For this reason Miyo supported development of large seaplane bombers but held down JNAF force levels in the Fifth Replenishment Program. Admiral Ugaki asked Miyo for a paper detailing what air forces would be necessary to fight the United States. Commander Miyo delivered in January 1941 a requirement so impossible to fulfill that he thought it would help dissuade his superiors from war. Miyo underestimated the desperation of Japan's top leaders.

From early 1941 demands were made of the *gunreibu* for concrete operations plans that could actually be executed. Prince Kacho Hironobu, a son of Fushimi who joined NGS toward the end of 1940, was assigned to update the plan against the British. Commander Miyo arranged for seaplanes to reconnoiter parts of the Malayan coast, and from September on several such aircraft were allotted to a more systematic photographic reconnaissance effort. Maneuvers in March and April involved the movement of an invasion force from the Yangtze, the repulse of adversary naval and air forces, a landing on Kyushu, and overland advance to Sasebo Navy Base. This scenario appears very similar to the sequence of operations necessary to capture Malaya and Singapore. Intelligence of vital importance for such a plan came from the Germans, who seized secret correspondence regarding Singapore's defenses from the British steamer *Automedon*, captured by a German surface raider in November 1940.

A key question pertaining to any war plan to seize the Southern Area was what would be the combination of adversaries. During the summer of 1940 Japan tried dealing with the Dutch, in the Netherlands East Indies, and the British independently of the Americans. The Japanese pursued trade negotiations with the Dutch, hoping to secure sure access to a sufficient share of Netherlands East Indies oil production to meet the nation's needs. The Dutch took their general cues from Washington, drawing out talks and finally denying the Japanese demands outright. A conference among Dutch, British, and American military authorities in the spring of 1941 produced some joint plans, while an Anglo-American united front would be cemented by the Churchill-Roosevelt summit at Placentia Bay that August. By then the Americans had frozen Japanese assets in the wake of the southern Indochina move.

As a consequence of these international developments, as 1941 wore on it became obvious to the Naval General Staff that such war plans as were drawn up would have to provide for simultaneous hostilities against the British and Dutch as well as the United States. According to a postwar statement by Admiral Oikawa, this was the first time the Navy had ever compiled a plan for such simultaneous combat actions. In substance, the NGS design conceptualized the first stage of the conflict as parallel campaigns: enabling the Japanese Army to invade Malaya, naval forces would switch to supporting an invasion of the Philippines, then support a series of successive amphibious landings to overcome the Netherlands East Indies. In conformity with Imperial Navy doctrine the main battle fleet would be withheld for a Decisive Battle while forces allocated to local operations would be just sufficient to counter local resistance. The plan provided economy of force and preparation for the Decisive Battle; it was exactly what one would have expected from an operations staff steeped in Imperial Navy doctrine. Besides Baron Tomioka and Commander Miyo, the plan's authors included seven other officers, all commanders or lieutenant commanders: Prince Takamatsu Nobuhito; Marquis Kacho Hironobu; Kami Shigenori; Nakano Nasatomo; Uchida Shigeshi; Sanagi Sadamu; and Yamamoto Yuji. The Japanese would seize their objectives, convert resources to the use of the Empire, await the counterattack from their defensive perimeter, then fight the Decisive Battle. For attrition operations, in the South Seas region the Imperial Navy would complete its perimeter by capturing an assortment of American, British, Australian, and other island possessions. It expected that these could be scooped up by Fourth Fleet forces with support from a single division of heavy cruisers assigned by the Combined Fleet. The only defect of the *gunreibu* plan was, in fact, with regard to the Combined Fleet itself: The plan did not meet the expectations of the fleet's commander in chief, Admiral Yamamoto Isoroku.

AMID ENMITY AND CONFLICT, CONTEMPORARY POPULAR PORTRAITS AMERICANS DREW OF THE Japanese fleet commander were hardly flattering. One author noted that "no Western commentator . . . fails to notice the implacable hatred [Yamamoto] entertains for the Western powers, particularly the United States." Another commentary is that of Willard Price, whom we have encountered already in these pages. "I met . . . Yamamoto long before he had become an admiral," Price wrote in an article published in April 1942. "He was already hating, icily." According to one author, Yamamoto was a determined expansionist and big-navy man, a stern disciplinarian with a modest personal life, although he ate, drank and smoked unsparingly. Willard Price has Yamamoto answering questions brutally, as when he is quoted as saying, in response to a query on why he chose to join the Imperial Navy, "I wanted to return Commodore Perry's visit." Price, too, recorded that Yamamoto's smoking, drinking, and eating "are all on quite a grand scale." He pictured Admiral Yamamoto as a man of enormous conceit, with a "conquest complex," and the brains and stomach to back his bluster.

The Yamamoto of history, the man who has emerged in biographies penned since World War II, is in total contrast to these caricatures in many respects. Far from being a big-navy man, Yamamoto Isoroku came down on the side of the treaty faction. In fact, Admiral Yamamoto's appointment to command the Combined Fleet originated as a measure to get him away from the rarefied political atmosphere of Tokyo where right-wing (big-navy) activists posed a threat to his life—not an idle threat, in Japan's "government by assassination" of the 1930s.

Unlike the Yamamoto pictured by wartime adversaries, the Yamamoto of history was never an America-hater. We do not have the evidence to conclude that Yamamoto *loved* the United States, but he had traveled throughout North America, spent perhaps four years here, and remained a sympathetic observer of the American scene. As fleet commander he still subscribed to *Life* magazine. A language officer at Harvard ten years after first visiting America on a 1910 training cruise, Yamamoto returned as a captain in 1925 and spent two years in Washington as naval attaché. One summer he spent touring oil fields in Mexico, staying at cheap hotels; another trip took him to the automobile assembly lines of Detroit. Though Yamamoto's speeches sometimes contained language critical of treaty ratios or supportive of planned naval construction, he often remarked on the folly of Japan's becoming involved in any naval race with the United States. When the question descended to whether there should be a war against America, Yamamoto, as shall be seen shortly, opposed it. Not hatred of America, not necessarily love either, Yamamoto's attitude can be most accurately described as one of realism.

Yet another aspect the wartime American writers got wrong was the personal one. Where the Japanese admiral was presented as a big drinker and eater, Yamamoto Isoroku in actuality appears to have been quite abstemious. Legend has it Yamamoto became quite drunk once at Etajima with his comrades and thereafter forever forswore alcohol. He might bet with subordinates, offering liquor as the stake, and often paid a share of the liquor bill when out for entertainment with fellow officers, but Yamamoto himself was not a lush or even a social drinker. At about five feet three inches and perhaps 130 pounds, Isoroku also happened to be small for a Japanese—which says something about his consumption of food as well, though his Imperial Navy orderlies recall that his appetite usually seemed good.

As for the admiral having a quiet home life, once more the wartime writers got it wrong. Yamamoto married in his thirties, late for a Japanese naval officer, but while the impression is often that this was due to total focus upon career, the fact is Isoroku cut a wide swath in both geisha and gaming circles. There were at least three geisha whom the admiral knew very well, including one first met when she was just twelve, a child apprentice. An avid game player who became skilled at *shogi*, chess, bridge, and poker, Yamamoto made himself a second income on these games, supporting the geisha he frequented, living beyond the means of an Imperial Navy officer. Between these two after-hours avocations Isoroku really spent very little quiet time at home. In fact, it is recorded that on one occasion when he *did* go home for the night, right after hosting a naval review for the Emperor, Yamamoto's visit proved so unexpected that the house was closed to him and he had to get in by climbing over the garden wall.

Isoroku reached quite an exalted station for a poor boy with no ties at all to Satsuma. He was from northern Japan, Nagaoka in Niigata prefecture, where he was born on April 4, 1884, the sixth son of Takano Sadakichi, schoolmaster of the village of Kushigun Sonshomura. The baby did not even have a name for several weeks, until his mother insisted on one and Takano named him for his age at the time of the boy's birth—"Isoroku" means "fifty-six." With a daughter and six sons to take care of on a teacher's meager wages, there was not much for Isoroku, and life would be hard at Nagaoka. His mother wove and dyed the material for the clothing the family used. Winters were especially difficult; the village was far enough north that snowfall literally covered the houses. Overhanging roofs edged in by boards created interior passageways, tunnels along which villagers shared virtually subterranean lives.

Nagaoka happened to be oil country, the most productive in a land almost barren of oil reserves, at one time producing 94 percent of the Empire's home-pumped oil. Perhaps this helped account for Isoroku's interest in oil, which stood him in good stead since in his younger decades Japan entered the machine age and the Imperial Navy shifted from coal to oil for its main fuel source. Oil ran machinery, which brought technological progress, which wrought changes in the very fabric of life. Nagaoka helped instill in Yamamoto a sensitivity to technological development that eventually made him one of the leading innovators in the Imperial Navy.

Isoroku's turn toward a naval career was not that far out of line with family tradition. His father had originally been a samurai, and both the father and two eldest brothers had fought in the Bosshin War (1868–1877), the last of the Japanese civil wars, which had rung in the Meiji Restoration and eliminated the samurai class of society. With a bit of military tradition from his family, and a little seafaring tradition from Nagaoka's history, Isoroku also received early exposure to a foreign language, specifically English, at the hands of an American missionary teacher in the local school. Again this contradicts wartime writer Willard Price, who claims that Isoroku met no foreigners for many years and was turned against them by tales by his father, allegedly of "hairy barbarians . . . with an animal odor." Actually the combination of exposure to foreign influence plus family and local traditions are probably the very things that led Isoroku to choose the Imperial Navy.

The boy took national competitive tests for Etajima and won appointment to the naval academy in 1901. He graduated eleventh in a class of 191 in 1904, just in time to participate in the Russo-Japanese War. During the famous battle of Tsushima Isoroku sailed as an ensign aboard the armored cruiser *Nisshin*. He lost the middle and index fingers of his left hand in the battle. It has usually been recorded, even in writings by Yamamoto himself, that this injury was caused by shrapnel from a Russian shell, but biographer Agawa Hiroyuki believes the young officer was in effect a victim of friendly fire: One of *Nisshin*'s heavy guns overheated during the battle and burst too close to Isoroku's duty station.

Loss of fingers did not stifle Isoroku's enthusiasm for another of his great passions, gymnastics. In school he had excelled in this sport, and as a Navy officer he acquired a reputation as quite a daredevil, ready to perform feats at the drop of a hat. One story told of the man is that he broke the ice between Japanese and American passengers aboard a liner bound for the United States by standing on his head while balancing plates on a table. For a bet or just for a lark, more than once he did handstands on the railings of Imperial Navy vessels.

Isoroku became Yamamoto at the age of thirty-two in 1916, after finishing the course at the Naval War College. Yamamoto Gombei had been chief of staff of the fleet at Tsushima. One of the more prominent Nagaoka families, whose patriarch had been beheaded after losing a battle in the Bosshin War, asked Isoroku to take the name and carry on the family tradition. This assumption of a name by ascription, not uncommon in Japan then, made him Commander Yamamoto Isoroku. As Yamamoto he married in 1918, siring three daughters and a son between then and 1932. As Yamamoto he became known to history.

Yamamoto's predilection for games of skill and risk had many facets, including a social aspect. He used this to advantage during his years in Washington as naval attaché and later in London as arms negotiator. When Yamamoto served in Washington the Office of Naval Intelligence noted that Japanese interest seemed to have shifted from technical intelligence matters to ones of strategy, and eventually concluded that this resulted from then-Captain Yamamoto's own interests. To keep tabs on Yamamoto, ONI language officer Ellis Zacharias was soon seeing him socially, and was surprised at the way the Japanese officer mixed work with pleasure:

> When I entered his apartment, I encountered the same stocky, black-browed man of years before. . . . He smiled broadly but in a rather conde-

scending manner, his aggressive nature unconcealed. . . . Almost immediately cocktails were served and then dinner, a mixture of Japanese and foreign dishes. It was obvious that he loved his game, this combination of intelligence and cards, since the dinner was hardly over when the table was cleared and set up for poker, he inviting us to indulge in a game. He was soon interspersing his bids and bluffs with slightly concealed inquiries of a distinctly naval character.

In our subsequent meetings, too, he tried to combine his two favorite pastimes, and it needed considerable effort to beat him at both games. Yamamoto had only three fingers on his right [*sic*] hand. . . . I found it distracting to watch him manipulate his cards with unusual dexterity with those three remaining fingers. I felt he was aware of this trick and emphasized it by using his three fingers in a wizardly manner, laughing out loud whenever we complimented him on his skill.

In Washington and London Yamamoto managed to play poker or bridge with many American and British officials, including senior British diplomats and the U.S. chief of naval operations.

Intelligence, perhaps better described simply as learning, was always a two-way street, however. Zacharias is convinced that he learned much about the Imperial Navy from his sessions with Yamamoto Isoroku, including important hints on the basic direction of Japanese naval development. It was during this time that Zacharias recognized Yamamoto's obsession with the combination of seapower and airpower. In fact, Yamamoto has been quoted as saying as early as 1915 that "the most important ship of the future will be a ship to carry aeroplanes." Captain Yamamoto commanded the naval air station at Kasumigaura before his service in the United States, and skippered the aircraft carrier *Akagi* afterward. Before disarmament negotiations and the Navy Ministry he also commanded the Navy's Carrier Division 1, the heart of JNAF strength. Admiral Yamamoto's achievements at the Bureau of Aeronautics in the 1930s have already been noted. In short, Yamamoto Isoroku was acutely aviation-conscious. He would remain true to his convictions as commander in chief of the Combined Fleet.

A typical formulation of Yamamoto's thinking after he had become a senior commander is this comment on the tactics he anticipated in a future Pacific war: "As I see it, naval operations of the future will consist of capturing an island, then building an airfield in as short a time as possible—within a week or so—moving up air units and using them to gain air and surface control over the next stretch of ocean." On another occasion he warned an aide that war would mean large-scale air raids against Japanese cities—which, built of wood, would burn very easily. As for the battleship, traditional staple of seapower, Yamamoto told friends, "these ships are like elaborate religious scrolls which old people hang up in their homes." On a more public occasion he declared: "These battleships will be as useful to Japan in modern warfare as a samurai sword."

Admiral Yamamoto declared quite frankly that he did not believe Japan could win a war against the United States, even while he recognized that that war was coming. Operations chief Fukudome Shigeru later observed:

> Admiral Yamamoto maintained that while civil war would not be fatal to the nation, an external war that had no chance of success would spell disaster. Accordingly, he was vigorously opposed to the idea of going to war. At the same time he said that as a result of the domestic situation, the evolution toward war was inevitable.

Though Yamamoto criticized Nagano Osami, in this at least, the two were similar. Fukudome quotes Admiral Nagano thus:

> It is agreed that if we do not fight now, our nation will perish. But it may well perish even if we do fight. It must be understood that national ruin without resistance would be ignominy.
>
> In this hopeless situation, survival can be accomplished only by fighting to the last man. Then, even if we lose, posterity will have the heritage of our loyal spirit to inspire them.

Yamamoto, too, spoke of sacrifice, as in this comment recorded by his friend Baron Harada Kumao from their dinner conversation of October 14, 1940, two weeks after finalization of the Tripartite Pact:

> Personally, I feel that if we're going to war with America we must accept the idea that we're taking on almost the whole rest of the world. . . . Now that things have come to this pass I'll throw everything I have into the fight. I expect to die in battle aboard the [flagship] *Nagato*. By that time, I imagine, Tokyo will have been set on fire at least three times and Japan reduced to a pitiful state. . . . I don't like it, but there's no going back now.

In the period of the war decision, Prince Konoye Fumimaro wanted Yamamoto's considered opinion and asked him by. Yamamoto resisted but was prevailed upon to visit. At their meeting Yamamoto made a celebrated statement: "I can raise havoc with them [the Americans] for one year or at most eighteen months. After that I can give no one any guarantees." In a more formal statement in 1941, Yamamoto repeated the essence of this judgment but even cut back his estimate of the time span:

> If it is necessary to fight, in the first six months to a year of war against the United States and England I will run wild. I will show you an uninter-

rupted succession of victories. But I must also tell you that if the war be prolonged for two or three years I have no confidence in our ultimate victory.

Similarly, again, Yamamoto warned ultranationalist leader Sasakawa Ryoichi in a January 1941 letter:

> Should hostilities once break out between Japan and the United States, it is not enough that we take Guam and the Philippines, nor even Hawaii and San Francisco. We would have to march into Washington and sign the treaty in the White House. I wonder if our politicians (who speak so lightly of a Japanese-American war) have confidence as to the outcome and are prepared to make the necessary sacrifices?

Shorn of its key qualifying language, the part of this letter referring to a treaty, as it were, dictated in the White House, was later broadcast as propaganda. This played an important role in creating the image of the arrogant, hateful Yamamoto presented at the head of this section.

Two final Yamamoto statements perhaps serve to round out the profile of this sensitive officer trapped in the slide toward war. One is a comment Yamamoto made at a reunion of Nagaoka schoolmates held in September 1941:

> It is a mistake to regard Americans as luxury-loving and weak. I can tell you that they are full of spirit, adventure, fight, and justice. Their thinking is scientific and well advanced. Lindbergh's solo flight across the Atlantic was an act characteristic of Americans—adventuresome but scientifically based. Remember that American industry is much more developed than ours, and—unlike us—they have all the oil they want. Japan cannot vanquish the United States. Therefore we should not fight the United States.

Finally, there is the letter Yamamoto Isoroku sent his Navy friend (and banished treaty faction colleague) Horie Teikichi on November 11, barely a month before the war finally began: "What a strange position I find myself in now—having to make a decision diametrically opposed to my own personal opinion with no choice but to push full-speed. . . . Is that, too, fate?"

Yamamoto liked to write poetry in fine calligraphy. His poems of this period progressively acquire a more tragic tone.

Thus we have Admiral Yamamoto at the brink of war, commander in chief of a fleet with a very ambitious plan. Several things in Yamamoto's background made classic Imperial Navy doctrine seem questionable: An air-oriented officer, Yamamoto could see the plans made poor use of available aircraft carrier forces; an intelligence officer, Yamamoto could see that the plan, even if fully executed, left the U.S. fleet at full strength, perfectly poised to interfere with the contemplated southern operations. If Yamamoto were truly going to run wild, he could not permit that situation to obtain. That undoubtedly lay behind a remark Yamamoto made in early 1941 to his chief of staff, Rear Admiral Fukudome Shigeru: "We have no hope of winning a war against America unless the United States fleet in Hawaiian waters can be destroyed."

ADMIRAL FUKUDOME RECALLED THE MOMENT VERY WELL. IT HAD BEEN IN APRIL OR MAY OF 1940, during fleet maneuvers. At the time Fukudome happened to be Yamamoto's chief of staff at Combined Fleet headquarters. The two men stood on the flag bridge of battleship *Nagato* watching the evolutions of the fleet all around them. In this instance the ships had been divided into "Blue" and "White" forces. Fukudome Shigeru and his boss were with the White Force, the battleship force, with the mission of defending Tokyo against a Blue Force of aircraft carriers coming up from Taiwan. It was the first time the Imperial Navy had permitted carriers to function in this kind of strategic role, with an independent mission, and was certainly due to Yamamoto's efforts.

The results must have been highly gratifying. Although White Force battleships successfully evaded the exercise torpedoes and bombs of the first two waves of attacking aircraft, the third wave of torpedo bombers split into two groups and came in from both sides of the fleet. They scored impressively. Umpires ruled that the combat power of the White Force had been reduced by half.

On the bridge of the *Nagato* Fukudome turned to Yamamoto. "There is no means for a surface fleet to elude aerial torpedoes simultaneously launched from both sides," Fukudome observed. "It seems to me that the time is now ripe for a decisive fleet engagement with aerial torpedo attacks as the main striking power."

Yamamoto was not then willing to go quite so far. "Well," replied the commander in chief, "it appears that a crushing blow could be struck on an enemy surface force by mass aerial torpedo attacks executed jointly with shore-based air forces."

A few months later—on November 11, 1940, to be exact—British carrier-borne torpedo planes executed a daring night raid against the Italian fleet in base at Taranto, sinking or heavily damaging three of five battleships moored in the harbor. The attack, which had involved a heavily defended base under wartime alert conditions, including barrage balloons and (incomplete) torpedo nets surrounding the target ships, inevitably aroused considerable interest in the Japanese Navy. Lieutenant Commander Naito

Takeshi, a member of a naval mission that visited Germany, flew to Taranto for a personal inspection from the Italian side. Naito found several things the British had done that improved their capability to attack in shallow water as at Taranto.

It was at about this time that Admiral Fukudome heard his commander in chief muttering, wondering if it might be feasible to have aircraft attack Pearl Harbor. Fukudome in 1950 recalled his own reply: "It's better to have a Decisive Battle once and for all with our entire fleet at sea near Hawaii; then we can launch an air attack there."

Longtime ONI officer Ellis Zacharias later wrote that Yamamoto must have gotten his idea for an attack on Pearl Harbor during the years he was assigned in the United States. In *The Rising Sun*, a fine study of Japan at war published in 1970, historian John Toland speculated that the idea could have originated with Hector C. Bywater, a naval writer of the interwar era. Bywater had published a novel, *The Great Pacific War*, which received prominent critical attention when it appeared in 1925, a time Yamamoto was just beginning his tour as attaché in Washington. Bywater's previous work, *Seapower in the Pacific*, a 1921 survey of naval affairs in that region, had been translated for circulation among senior Japanese officers at the behest of NGS. The novel would be adopted for the reading list at the Naval War College. More recently Toland's speculation has been raised to the level of a formal claim by writer William Honan in *Visions of Infamy*. Honan presents evidence that Yamamoto met Bywater while working as attaché and diplomat, and that Bywater visited Japan to lecture on his own ideas.

There are other claimants to intellectual authorship of the Pearl Harbor attack as well. In 1927–1928 a young officer just out of the war college wrote up a Pearl Harbor attack plan as part of an indoctrination course on aviation presented to senior officers in a special session at Kasumigaura. This proved to be highly ironic since the aviator, Kusaka Ryunosuke, as shall be seen, would oppose the Pearl Harbor attack plan of 1941. Another 1941 opponent, Nagano Osami, numbered among Kusaka's auditors at Kasumigaura. In 1933 came a public discussion of the possibility when Hirata Shinsaku published *When We Fight*, which considered a raid on Pearl Harbor by two *Akagi*-class aircraft carriers. Practical demonstrations of the possibility occurred in the 1930s when *American* sailors in naval maneuvers made air strikes on Pearl Harbor. There was also a 1936 study done at the Naval War College, titled "Strategy and Tactics Against the United States," which included the option of an attack on Pearl Harbor.

Victory has a hundred fathers, while defeat is an orphan.

The specific attack plan the Combined Fleet developed in 1941 began with Admiral Yamamoto. Early that January the commander in chief prepared a paper he called "Views on Preparations for War," sent to the navy minister on January 7. Yamamoto left a second copy of the document with his friend and former colleague Horie Teikichi, who had the envelope kept in a Navy Ministry safe through the war but eventually made it public in 1949. Horie explained that in the immediate postwar period he had wanted to avoid any move that might have contributed to an effort to portray Yamamoto as a leading Japanese jingoist.

Admiral Yamamoto's paper was nothing if not explicit. He referred to the Russo-Japanese War as conveying the lesson that Japan needed to get in the first blow. He asserted that Imperial Navy war games showed Japan had never won a scenario that required the fleet to adopt wait-and-react tactics in the western Pacific. Yamamoto maintained that Japan could ensure victory by making a daring attack on the first day of war. Under this concept the Imperial Navy should hit Pearl Harbor, primarily with air forces, and follow that with a submarine blockade. The commander in chief envisioned using the Navy's first-line carrier force for the attack and volunteered to give up his own post to take charge of that attack force. Yamamoto recommended he be succeeded in command of the Combined Fleet by Admiral Yonai Mitsumasa. In translation a key passage of the document read: "We will make a storming assault (or a surprising attack) against the enemy in the moonlight or dawn."

Yamamoto told Fukudome he wished the project studied by an aviator not wedded to traditional ways of thinking; this criterion must have been a covert reference to the conventional doctrine of Decisive Battle.

Selected to study the feasibility of Yamamoto's plan would be Rear Admiral Onishi Takijiro, an officer unconventional indeed. Onishi, a practical flier where Yamamoto had been an administrator, shared the chief's passion for contests of skill and risk. He had known Yamamoto since stationed at Kasumigaura in 1924, when Isoroku arrived there to be executive officer. Onishi had flown every type of plane and had taken the training course for paratroopers. Some thought him impulsive and headstrong; others saw him as a man of action who nevertheless looked carefully before he leaped. Like Yamamoto, he was a skilled player of bridge, poker, and mah-jongg; he had once won a national mah-jongg competition he entered under an assumed name. Onishi rose to high rank despite never having attended war college (he failed the entrance examinations), and had even lectured at that exalted academy. He led the first air group to fly Zero fighters in combat in China, felt the huge *Yamato*-class battleships a waste of resources, and had been working at the Bureau of Aeronautics when tapped for Yamamoto's special assignment. An Etajima classmate of chief of staff Fukudome, Onishi may have been controversial in the Imperial Navy, but he had the full confidence of the Combined Fleet leadership.

To assist in assessing the complex Pearl Harbor project, Admiral Onishi selected Commander Genda Minoru, the thirty-five-year-old Imperial Navy aviation pioneer. Onishi and Genda had first served together at Yokosuka in

1934. Four years later these comrades created a private discussion group they called the Society for the Study of Aerial Might. Genda had just returned from Great Britain, where he had observed at close hand the battle of Britain, and he had been posted as air staff officer for Carrier Division 1, where he had access to the latest data on the capabilities of Japanese carriers and their aircraft. In earlier years he had himself flown from carriers *Akagi* and *Ryujo* and knew Admiral Yamamoto from those days. The fleet commander told Onishi he had no objection to bringing Genda in on the project.

In postwar interrogations and in his deposition for the Tokyo war-crimes trials, Genda Minoru gave several slightly different versions, not necessarily inconsistent except in fine detail, of how he was asked to assess the feasibility of a Pearl Harbor attack. One version is that the idea arose in a conversation with Onishi on February 1, another that it came from an unofficial letter Yamamoto sent Onishi, variously dated January 27, February 1, or February 10. Whatever its provenance, the request for a feasibility study of a Pearl Harbor attack interested Genda, who liked nothing better than to let his fertile mind range over novel aviation problems. In about ten days Genda went back to Onishi with his judgment that the operation would be risky and difficult to mount but offered a reasonable chance of success.

One key problem, in Genda's view, concerned relative strength of attacker and defender. Pearl Harbor had become such a major center of U.S. strength that a few planes from a carrier, or even a carrier division, would not do the job. The challenge of a Pearl Harbor attack became a concrete application of the general problem of concentration of carrier airpower with which Genda had been wrestling for some time. One day at a downtown Tokyo theater Genda saw a newsreel of four American aircraft carriers steaming together in a column formation, in much the same fashion as fleet battle lines were often exhibited. Genda watched the film and thought about how strange it was that four carriers should have been together like that. Days later as he stepped off a streetcar sudden inspiration came to him: Concentration of carriers meant concentrated airpower. When he evaluated the Pearl Harbor attack project Commander Genda recommended that the Imperial Navy use all its large aircraft carriers in one attack force.

At the time there were four of these fleet carriers: *Akagi, Kaga, Hiryu*, and *Soryu*. However, two more large carriers—*Zuikaku* and *Shokaku*—were scheduled to join the fleet within months, and Onishi advised adding them, too, when in early April he went back to Admiral Yamamoto with his own conclusions. Genda agreed as well. On the basis of observations by one of his own subordinates, Eleventh Air Fleet staff officer and torpedo expert Commander Maeda Kosei, Onishi also advised on the method of attack. Yamamoto had originally been thinking in terms of an aerial torpedo attack. Maeda warned that torpedoes dropped in the shallow waters of Pearl

Harbor would almost certainly sink to the bottom and embed themselves there. Onishi reacted by advocating dive-bombing as offering the best accuracy potential, but joined with Genda in an April feasibility study to argue that all types of attack ought to be used, including not only torpedo bombing and dive-bombing but level bombing as well. Onishi and Genda combined to turn aside Yamamoto's initial notion that attacking carriers would launch their aircraft on one-way missions and then immediately turn to escape. Genda objected to the loss of planes and highly trained aircrews in such a case, and also held out for repeat strikes on the target if necessary. Onishi seconded him.

Admiral Yamamoto received the results of the feasibility study and digested them. Gordon Prange and his co-authors put the date on or about March 10, but Admiral Fukudome has written that it was in April, toward the end of April at that, and provides the additional fact that Onishi visited him at the Naval General Staff to explain the plan. Since Fukudome transferred to NGS to head the operations bureau there only in April, being replaced as Combined Fleet chief of staff by Rear Admiral Ugaki Matome, this provides some indication of the relevant date. Prange also writes that Yamamoto put his own staff to work on aspects of the plan no later than January. Captain Kuroshima Kameto, senior staff officer, had had several talks with the fleet commander during 1940 on the strategy to be followed in the event of war with the United States, and now got marching orders to draw up actual plans. Kuroshima called in Commander Sasaki Akira to examine several alternatives. Sasaki, the air staff officer, was to plan one-way missions for a long-range air attack (assuming the Americans were warned) or a short-range assault with all aircraft.

More of the Combined Fleet staff would be drawn in after Yamamoto had his feasibility study in hand. Kuroshima broke down the planning task into four parts and created clusters of officers to focus on each. Kuroshima and staff gunnery officer Commander Watanabe Yasuji concentrated on operations and logistics; beyond that there were plans and studies of air and submarine attack, navigation, and communications. Sasaki and torpedo staff officer Commander Arima Takayasu did the air and submarine plan, Commander Nagata Shigeru and meteorologist Commander Ota Kanai assembled navigation and weather data, and Commander Wada Yushiro studied communications aspects.

It is not often realized how closely knit was Admiral Yamamoto's official family. Except for Kuroshima, who graduated from Etajima in 1916, almost all the staffers had overlapped at the academy; in fact Watanabe, Sasaki, Nagata, and Wada were all classmates from the fifty-first class, the class of 1923. This was a post–Washington Naval Treaty class that had fallen to just thirty-seven graduates, a sixth the usual Etajima class size. The same four officers held places very close to one another on the 1940 Navy List.

Staffer Sugi Toma happened to be a little ahead of them, graduating from Etajima in 1922, while torpedo officer Arima had been a class behind, in 1924. Because Etajima classes joined in sports activities with classes ahead and behind them, most of the 1941 Combined Fleet staff had known each other ever since naval academy.

Arima Takayasu, like Yamamoto, enjoyed writing poetry, especially the thirty-one-syllable *waka* form. The youngest staffer, Arima became the butt of many practical jokes but had no enemies among his mates. During staff meetings he often sat back, folded his arms, and closed his eyes, never betraying a reaction by facial expression. He had been a language officer in the United States (Yale and Johns Hopkins) and was a destroyerman known for his enthusiasm for high-speed night torpedo action. Arima protested when he first learned of the projected Pearl Harbor air attack, but he later buckled down. According to Yamamoto's yeoman, it was as a result of Arima's pleading that the commander in chief agreed to include midget submarines in the attack plan.

Another staffer with experience in America was air officer Sasaki Akira, who had been an assistant naval attaché in the early 1930s. Regarded as a brilliant officer and aviator, Sasaki went on to become air staff officer in the operations section of the Naval General Staff and then held the same position on the staff of the China Area Fleet. On Yamamoto's staff Sasaki was actually on his third tour of duty as an air operations officer. He could only be regarded as well prepared for the task.

One of Sasaki's comrades on the China Fleet staff moved up to the Combined Fleet staff just as he did, and also to handle the same job as previously. That was Wada Yushiro, the staff communications officer. Where Sasaki seemed smooth and amiable, though, Wada became known for a temper that often got the better of him. Commander Wada had good knowledge of both the United States and Germany even though he had never been abroad—he read books. He acquired the nickname "the Fox" for both his looks and his character. He continually emphasized the need for there to be *no* communication by radio—that is, to minimize enemy opportunities to acquire radio intelligence. It was at Wada's initiative that the Combined Fleet set up a special airmail service to move documents and messages, again limiting the use of radio. Wada had always been interested in propaganda and intelligence. The Imperial Navy's entire early war communications network was planned by Commander Wada.

Perhaps Yamamoto's favorite, certainly his most frequent partner at chess or *shogi*, was Watanabe Yasuji, an impressive and expressive gunnery expert of sunny disposition. The tall, robust Watanabe, son of a steamship captain and grandson of a tall-ship skipper, traced his family line back a millennium to the feudal Heike who had lost in epic battle to the Genji family at a crucial juncture for the development of the Japanese state. Watanabe had taught gunnery at the school in Yokosuka, then been gunnery officer successively on the staffs of Cruiser Division 7 and the Second Fleet. He joined Yamamoto's staff in 1940, an up-and-coming thirty-seven-year-old lieutenant commander who held a very junior place on the Navy List (the Imperial Navy then had only one officer in this rank below Watanabe).

These men refined the plan for a Pearl Harbor strike, which eventually acquired the code designation "Operation AMO." Captain Kuroshima became the interface between Combined Fleet and NGS on the plan, and also conceived some of its more important ingredients. Watanabe planned the logistics necessary to make the scheme work, starting from Admiral Onishi's observation that refueling at sea would be necessary. Sasaki and Arima supervised fleet-training programs for air and submarine forces. The latter confronted a flap in mid-October when submarines *I-7* and *I-66* collided while exercising with the fleet (both sustained significant damage). The incident epitomized the realities of war. More such things would occur as Yamamoto's plan moved from conception to implementation, but the chief insisted, since he felt something *had* to be done about the U.S. fleet at Pearl Harbor. Years later, Watanabe Yasuji well expressed the core concept of Yamamoto's position: "In Japanese tactics we are told that when we have two enemies, one in front and one in the back, first we must cut in front by sword. Only cut and not kill but make it hard. Then we attack the back enemy and kill him. Then we come back to the front enemy." It was a classic application of the methods of kendo, a Japanese sword-fighting art.

In implementation, however, Yamamoto discovered that his key opponents were not American but Japanese. One center of opposition would arise in the Naval General Staff, another among the actual forces slated to carry out Operation AMO.

As spring blossomed in 1941 the imperial navy's high command stood in the midst of transformation. Not only did Fukudome Shigeru come to the Naval General Staff as director of operations, but Admiral Nagano Osami was taking over as chief of staff. It was Nagano, not the navy minister or the commander in chief of the Combined Fleet, who exercised the prerogative of command in the name of the Emperor. Thus it was Nagano and his staff who had to be convinced that the Pearl Harbor plan should be approved. Interestingly enough, though Fukudome worked for Nagano and came in with him, and though the operations chief received his first exposition of the plan from Onishi while at NGS, he did not bring it to Nagano's attention. The chief of staff told postwar interrogators that he was not informed of the Pearl Harbor project in April when he took over, that he did not even learn of its existence unofficially until sometime that summer, probably July. By then the fleet had begun training that Yamamoto specifically intended to enable it to carry out the plan.

Prior to that, Nagano recalled, war plans had been based on single adversaries; when in 1941 it became clear there would be allies ranged against Japan, it was a clear problem. Everyone knew, perhaps Nagano best of all, that America alone would be a more than formidable opponent. Long afterward Fukudome told reporters that the Navy had felt there was a 90 percent possibility of "national death," but that also meant a 10 percent chance of life. The question had been which combat actions offered the best shot at falling inside the 10 percent range.

Admiral Nagano, of course, had been steeped in the traditional concept of Decisive Battle which Yamamoto wanted to obviate with his plan. Moreover, when Nagano did learn of the project he was not especially impressed. As a young officer in the Russo-Japanese War, Nagano had gone ashore with a working party at Port Arthur with the task of refloating warships sunk in the harbor of that Russian naval base. The job took only three or four months, after which the salvaged ships were refurbished in Japanese dockyards and added to the Imperial Navy. On that basis Nagano judged that even a successful Pearl Harbor attack would gain Japan only equivalent time, and that the United States would be able to reconstitute its task forces in about ten months. Admiral Nagano's view of the Yamamoto plan was lukewarm at best.

Operations bureau chief Fukudome also took a dim view of the project. Even from their early canvass of the plan after he moved to NGS, Fukudome remembers that he rated the operational difficulties higher than did Onishi Takijiro, and where Onishi put the chance of success at 60 percent, Fukudome found himself willing to accord AMO only a 40 percent chance. "Opposition to the operation that was later expressed by the Naval General Staff," he wrote, "arose mainly from my opinion. Had I from the very beginning been entrusted with the study of the idea instead of Onishi, I would certainly have recommended to . . . Yamamoto that the Hawaii Operation be abandoned."

Yet a third source of opposition turned up as well: the operations section that worked for bureau chief Fukudome. Baron Tomioka Sadatoshi, chief of the section, gave tentative approval on the supposition that the Pearl Harbor attack would involve only three or four of the Japanese fleet carriers, leaving at least two for the offensive into the Southern Area. When it later turned out that Yamamoto wanted all six big carriers for his AMO plan, Captain Tomioka faced the necessity of going to the Japanese Army to ask for air assets that could replace carriers. That turned Tomioka's head and he, too, began to oppose the Pearl Harbor plan. Had there been no aircraft carriers Yamamoto would not have been tempted into this dangerous obsession, Tomioka later reasoned, and certainly what American aircraft carriers did to Japan as war progressed would also have been avoided. "If only the development of the aircraft carrier had been delayed ten years," Tomioka told American historian Stephen Pelz, "we could have beaten you."

Baron Tomioka spoke the truth, at least in regard to the temptation of Yamamoto, but there was no turning back the clock on aircraft carriers. Commander Genda stood at the cutting edge of thinking in that respect, with his theories on the concentration of airpower at sea. The Imperial Navy recognized this rise of the aircraft carrier officially and unmistakably on April 10, 1941, when it created a new fleet, the First Air Fleet, comprising the Navy's carrier force. Henceforth the carriers would be distinct from land-based airpower of the Japanese naval air force, which remained grouped into the Eleventh Air Fleet. Given the nature of Japanese offensive plans in 1941, both air fleets would fight major battles, and both would score major successes, but because of the Pearl Harbor plan it would be the First Air Fleet that stood at the center of controversy in the final prewar months.

Although the Navy progressed organizationally, the First Air Fleet suffered from weak leadership. The officer selected to head the Japanese Navy's carrier task force had no aviation training or experience. In the opinion of Etajima classmate Tsukahara Nizhizo, who *was* an aviator and commanded the Eleventh Air Fleet at the same time, the carrier commander was not suited by either temperament or interest for his post. Vice Admiral Nagumo Chuichi became carrier commander despite his shortcomings. A member of the delegation at the Washington Naval Conference, Nagumo later became a solid adherent of the fleet faction, allied to officers who forced the purge of Horie Teikichi and others. That put Nagumo in a bad light for Admiral Yamamoto, now his direct superior. Though Nagumo was known to indulge his hot temper—at one of Prince Fushimi's garden parties he had gone up to colleague Inoue Shigeyoshi to say how easy it would be to put a knife up between his ribs—his leadership of the carrier fleet would be oddly passive and tentative.

Technically Nagumo Chuichi had specialized in navigation. Most likely he had seemed attractive to the personnel bureau because he had not been a big-gun man, but that nevertheless was where his experience lay. As a captain and later, Nagumo had skippered the light cruiser *Naka*, the heavy cruiser *Takao*, and the battleship *Yamashiro*. He had led Destroyer Division 11, 1st Destroyer Flotilla, and had befriended torpedo specialists like Hara Tameichi. Ashore, Nagumo, an admiral in 1935, had been NGS chief of operations during the Pakhoi incident, the moment, a year later, that the Imperial Navy took a long step toward war with China. When war indeed came, operations chief Nagumo was not adverse to escalation in China, then he went to sea off Shanghai in command of Cruiser Division 8, promising the Chinese a whiff of grapeshot. It was a matter of wonderment that the aggressive Nagumo proved squeamish when it came to Yamamoto Isoroku's aggressive Pearl Harbor plan.

It was in late July 1941 that the commander in chief brought Nagumo directly into the picture. The occasion was a meeting Yamamoto held for the commanders of carrier and submarine forces, the main units that would execute Operation AMO. In addition to Nagumo, the other senior officer present was Vice Admiral Shimizu Mitsumi, who led the Sixth Fleet. Much as Nagumo was a carrier commander without experience in aviation, Shimizu was a submarine leader who knew nothing of submarines. Rather, almost all Shimizu's assignments at sea had been to cruisers or battleships. His immediately preceding billet, in command of the 3rd China Expeditionary Fleet, also had not prepared Shimizu for the top submarine post. Though many acknowledged Admiral Shimizu's brilliance (he had achieved the rare distinction of graduating from the war college with honors), the AMO plan absolutely relied on the Sixth Fleet's subs for poststrike blockade of Hawaii, infliction of losses on U.S. ships steaming out of Pearl Harbor, and recovery of downed pilots. Much depended upon whether and how quickly Shimizu Mitsumi could step into the shoes of a submariner.

At the July conference both subordinates promised their best efforts, but both harbored silent doubts. It was a pattern characteristic of command relationships in the Imperial Navy, more pronounced as the odds lengthened and the war progressed but present already before war ever began. Part of the difficulty certainly had to do with the ingrained vision of a Decisive Battle, from which the Pearl Harbor plan represented an important break. Part of the problem also arose from the plan's dependence on novel forms of warfare—not so much submarine operations, for which the Japanese had long prepared, but air attack, in particular air attack from the sea. Soon a further novelty, midget submarine intruders, would be added to an already freighted scheme.

Captain Oi Atsushi spent part of this period attached to the NGS and retained vivid recollections of how the Navy ended up in this war: Chief of Staff Nagano was too clever, too afraid of losing face; a Yamamoto or a Yonai might have stood up, clearly stated the Navy's opposition, and turned the course of the nation. The Japanese method, however, was the Nagano method. Senior officers confined themselves to generalities while *staffs* did the infighting, engaging in bureaucratic warfare, structuring situations for chiefs. Just as Admiral Nagano did on overall questions of national policy, so did Admiral Yamamoto with his Pearl Harbor plan. So, too, did others who opposed the AMO operation, in particular Nagumo, who let his own chief of staff become a focal point of resistance to the mission.

Catalyst for the continuing opposition, the planning process moved forward through summer and into the fall. At NGS the operations staff completed tentative plans for the Southern Area on August 15. Yamamoto's senior staff officer, Captain Kuroshima, then visited NGS to help arrange war games to test the plans, including the Pearl Harbor plan, about which Kuroshima and Tomioka of the NGS reached a preliminary understanding. Kuroshima asked for a special secret room to be set aside at the Naval War College, where the games were to be held, for the simulation of Operation AMO. Yamamoto and Nagano jointly issued invitations for the war games on August 28.

In this matter of the war games, as in much else concerning Pearl Harbor planning, there are important differences in chronology among available sources; the differences are probably not unrelated to the controversy that still surrounds the attack. For this reason the present narrative takes the dates given by Noda Mitsuharu, a yeoman serving the Combined Fleet staff who was captured during the war and gave his account at a time when he could not have known how controversial Pearl Harbor was becoming to Americans. Noda stated that he and other participants from the Combined Fleet traveled up to Tokyo from Hashirajima, where the flagship *Nagato* was then anchored, on September 2. Security was poor at the Naval War College, Noda recalls, with regular classes in session: "Any man with a half-official air could easily have walked in."

The map exercises opened with an introductory talk laying down the general aims of operations. Nagano and Fukudome, together with staffers from the NGS operations section and Navy Ministry, acted as umpires. Yamamoto and his Combined Fleet staff played the Japanese side, with subordinate teams for key units, including Admiral Nagumo and his First Air Fleet staff. An E team represented the British, under Vice Admiral Kondo Nobutake; for the Americans there was an A team, headed by Vice Admiral Takahashi Ibo. On the second day officers studied documents outlining the scenario and Japan's objectives; Commander Watanabe handed Yeoman Noda fifty copies of the material to distribute. To Noda the outline looked as if it reflected extensive prior planning work.

Friday, September 5, found Noda assigned to Combined Fleet air staff officer Sasaki Akira in the secret room. That day the Pearl Harbor simulation kicked off with an exposition by Watanabe of the main points of the plan. When Noda entered he found the room filled with smoke and was surprised to hear officers present talking about having lost two aircraft carriers in the game—the *Akagi* and a *Soryu*-class carrier were judged sunk. What happened was that the team playing the American defenders of Pearl Harbor, headed by the *joho kyoku*'s Captain Ogawa Kanji, the Navy's top intelligence expert on the United States, had mounted vigorous air searches from Pearl, found Nagumo's carriers, and warned of an impending attack, so the

Japanese air strike had had to proceed against alerted defenses. To top all this off, Ogawa's bombers followed the Japanese planes back to their carriers to sink the ships judged lost.

Over the next two days officers debated how to avoid such an outcome. Noda attended both days because he happened to be handy with an abacus, and the planners wanted calculations of fuel consumption by the carrier task force under various options. In the initial game, First Air Fleet approached Hawaii from the Mandates. Genda Minoru objected—using a route across the northern Pacific was slightly shorter and used an area hardly frequented by ships; it seemed the best chance for surprise. Support for Genda's view came from Commander Sasaki and from the leader of Carrier Division 2, Rear Admiral Yamaguchi Tamon. Nagumo preferred the southerly route but gradually changed his mind. In a second iteration of the war game the task force was judged to have sunk two American aircraft carriers and four battleships, to have damaged one of each, and inflicted other damage as well, in exchange for loss of a single aircraft carrier.

Thus the war games confirmed that surprise would be crucial to the success of the Pearl Harbor plan.

There was another issue that reasserted itself as a result of the war games, however, and that was proper disposition of available forces. In the larger simulation of the offensive into the Southern Area, Eleventh Air Fleet players found themselves hard-pressed to meet their many commitments with the limited land-based airpower available. Rear Admiral Onishi Takijiro, air fleet chief of staff, pleaded for more resources in his summation at the conclusion of the games. Since he was in Tokyo for the games, but would be leaving for Eleventh Air Fleet headquarters on Taiwan, Onishi also stopped in at NGS to confer with his Etajima classmate Fukudome Shigeru. This time Onishi told Fukudome that he had turned against the Pearl Harbor plan: It was just too risky.

Another officer keenly aware of the risks was Rear Admiral Kusaka Ryunosuke, Nagumo's chief of staff. Kusaka had learned of the Pearl Harbor plan in May, when Fukudome summoned him to NGS and handed over a copy of Onishi's original feasibility study. He was not impressed with the paper, which seemed primarily a compilation of intelligence information, and objected that he could draft no operations plan based on it. Obviously he had, since First Air Fleet's plans had just been tested in the games, but Kusaka had gone on to beard Onishi directly in a series of conversations that triggered the latter's change of heart. Toward the end of September there came an official conference of JNAF commanders at Kanoya Naval Air Station, as a result of which the two chiefs of staff got the signatures of their respective bosses on a memorandum asking that the Hawaii plan be abandoned.

The most direct result of the JNAF memorandum would be an invitation to both Onishi and Kusaka to visit aboard the flagship. The commander in chief listened to the full catalogue of objections marshaled by the two admirals. As he had at the Naval War College in Meguro, Onishi emphasized the difficulties and importance of the Southern Area offensive. Admiral Yamamoto called on air officer Sasaki to counter with an analysis of the state of American air units in the Philippines. Kusaka Ryunosuke objected to the tremendous gamble, the risks inherent in Operation AMO, going so far as to assert the concept amounted to the notion of an amateur strategist. One can imagine the silence which greeted that remark. Yamamoto talked about the Americans, how if nothing were done about Pearl Harbor they might advance across the Pacific and attack Japan while the Imperial Navy's forces were tied up in the south.

Yamamoto built to a climax as he spoke. "Are you suggesting that it's all right for Tokyo and Osaka to be burned to the ground so long as we get hold of oil?"

The admiral had a ready bottom line as well. "So long as I'm CinC," Yamamoto said, "we shall go ahead with the Hawaiian raid. . . . I'm asking you to proceed with preparations on the positive assumption that the raid is on."

Directing his next remark at Kusaka—who, unlike Yamamoto and Onishi, had no taste for games of chance—the fleet commander teased, "I may be fond of bridge and poker, but I wish to hell you'd stop calling it a gamble!"

Yamamoto insisted—Pearl Harbor had become an "article of faith" for him. The confrontation ended on that note; Onishi stayed into the evening to play chess. Kusaka preferred to leave. Admiral Yamamoto walked him to the gangway of the *Mutsu* (*Nagato*, the usual fleet flagship, happened to be in dry dock) and asked Kusaka's personal help making the operation work. In exchange Yamamoto promised assistance in overcoming any obstacle.

This October 3 session in the flag quarters of *Mutsu* became the latest round in a quite political struggle to build a consensus behind the Yamamoto plan, involving even officers who knew nothing of the top-secret details. *Nagato* had come out of dock in time for the next move, a reception Yamamoto held aboard the battleship in Hiroshima Bay on October 9 for the skippers of some 200 Imperial Navy warships.

"We are undoubtedly in the most serious crisis of our history," Admiral Yamamoto declared. "Once the nation decides on war with the Allies, it is the duty of the Combined Fleet to defend our nation. . . . I expect each of you to do his duty along with me, so that we can fulfill our destiny."

Ugaki Matome also spoke to the group. "It may be that this meeting of all Combined Fleet officers . . ." The chief of staff's voice broke, but he picked up his thread: "This may be the last meeting of its kind. We may not be able to see each other again in this fashion."

Rear Admiral Ugaki was right. There would never again be another such gathering of the fleet.

On the evening of Saturday, October 11, *Nagato's* wardroom was host to a crowd of senior Combined Fleet officers who were invited to dinner after the first of a new series of war games. In a replay of the session with Onishi and Kusaka, after the dishes were cleared those present were told the meeting would be off the record and they were invited to voice objections to the plans for war. There were various complaints, all familiar; finally Yamamoto got up and said his Pearl Harbor attack was essential for Imperial Navy strategy and it would go ahead as long as he remained fleet commander.

Meanwhile the NGS operations staff had been using the results of the September war games for an elaborate directive. The forty-page document, eventually mimeographed, laid out a panorama of tasks the Combined Fleet would be expected to accomplish. About a hundred copies were bound into four bundles to be sent to Yamamoto's flagship, and Yeoman Noda went to Tokyo with another sailor to bring them back. A quick glance showed that the documents were concrete orders pertaining to a war with the United States, Great Britain, and Holland. Noda and his companion took a third-class sleeper compartment in the train back. During the trip the yeoman overheard other travelers arguing over the major topic of the day: whether there was going to be a war. Noda contemplated his bundles of orders, recognizing the irony of having in his hands the  answer to the most-discussed question of the day. That brought a brief reverie during which Noda speculated how much the press might pay for these secrets, but then it was time for the launch ride out to the *Nagato,* two hours of bobbing in harbor waters since the ship had been moored fairly far out.

Once the fleet saw the Naval General Staff document a near panic ensued among the select circle privy to Operation AMO. The list of forces slated for the offensive into the Southern Area included Carrier Division 2, Admiral Yamaguchi's unit, with the vessels *Hiryu* and *Soryu.* This appalled Yamaguchi, who had been one of the staunch supporters of the Pearl Harbor plan. Yamaguchi insisted that his ships were needed for the Hawaii mission and begged to be included. A jarring scene followed in Admiral Nagumo's cabin aboard *Akagi,* where Yamaguchi appeared, drunk, and—so insistent was he on participating—began to wrestle with his boss. Yamaguchi got a headlock on Nagumo, who overconfidently expected to be able to best the taller, younger man, then could not. The incipient fight was broken up by Rear Admiral Kusaka, who happened into the office at that moment. To placate Yamaguchi there was talk of permitting his crews to man the new carriers *Shokaku* and *Zuikaku,* which were going on the mission, but that left Yamaguchi himself behind and was clearly a silly idea— there was no way the Carrier Division 2 sailors could learn new ships in time to be of any use at Pearl Harbor.

Kusaka Ryunosuke calmed Yamaguchi, but he knew as well as the carrier division commander that Yamaguchi's ships would be necessary to make the Pearl Harbor attack work. Admiral Kusaka paid a visit of his own to the Naval General Staff to get the ships restored to Nagumo's task force. Officers at NGS refused, some hinting that they might resign before taking such a step. Kusaka stepped out of channels and fired off a missive direct to Yamamoto: The commander in chief had promised his help; where was it now?

Yamamoto saw and heard. His own staff was in an uproar as a result of the reduction in carriers allotted for Operation AMO. Yamamoto sent senior staff officer Kuroshima to see Baron Tomioka, and was confronted, for the first time, by a set of formal operations-staff objections. The NGS argued that surprise could not be maintained because the attack force would have to assemble before the mission; that the United States would not advance so rapidly across the Pacific that the fleet at Pearl Harbor would pose a threat; that the technical aspects of the refueling problem were insoluble; that there was too much danger of the task force being discovered by U.S. air searches; and that any leak of the Japanese plans would ruin negotiations with Washington. At about the same time, with the Combined Fleet operations order intended to govern the first stage of the war in its final draft, the *Nagato* received a message asking the fleet command to specify just how much time negotiations could be permitted to continue before hostilities *had* to be initiated. Ugaki answered for the fleet that December 8 (December 7 in Hawaii) would be ideal, and that in the worst case talks could be allowed until June 1942. As for the NGS objections to the Pearl Harbor plan, Captain Kuroshima took the fleet staff's best answers with him when he carried a copy of the draft operations order to Tokyo on November 3.

Baron Tomioka professed not to be moved by the Combined Fleet responses to his objections. Yamamoto's senior staff officer then went into another room to place a phone call to the flagship, lying at Hashirajima. When Kuroshima came back he produced a letter from Admiral Yamamoto, one final display of command authority. The American fleet at Pearl Harbor was a dagger pointed at the heart of Japan; if it were not neutralized, Yamamoto did not feel he could fulfill his responsibilities in the Southern Area offensive. If the General Staff did not accept Yamamoto's plan, Kuroshima warned, the commander in chief would resign and the entire Combined Fleet staff with him.

Existing accounts pass over Yamamoto's threatened resignation with little analysis. The fact is that the Naval General Staff, not Yamamoto, held the prerogative of command. Why, then, the threat, and how could it be effective?

Yamamoto's threat succeeded because it was palpable and political, not some narrow dispute over naval strategy. Nagano Osami happened to be an overage, retread admiral called back to the high command. Resignation of a popular Combined Fleet commander with his entire staff would have ignited a scandal with echoes of the *Tomodzuru* affair—the safety of the fleet endangered by callous leadership (see page 61). Decisive Battle orthodoxy would not have saved Nagano in such a circumstance. The scandal could not have been hushed up and it might have threatened Shimada and the Tojo cabinet as well, with secret details of the war plans becoming public as a result of political controversy. The better part of valor was for Nagano to accept Yamamoto's plan.

Admiral Nagano actually described these events laconically when questioned about them in March 1946: "I originally agreed with the Naval Operations Department . . . as that [plan] seemed to be the more logical, but not to have the Commander of the Fleets resign, as he would have, if his plan did not go through, I thought the best thing to do was to approve."

So this challenge settled the question of whether Japan would go ahead with Pearl Harbor. Final preparations moved with alacrity. Prince Takamatsu, Hirohito's brother, conferred with him on November 30; and some believe that the NGS officer told the Emperor that morning of the fears regarding the plan. In any case, on Tuesday, December 2, Admiral Nagano and General Sugiyama had an audience with the Emperor to apprise him of last details, and the NGS chief had key exchanges with Hirohito showing that the Emperor knew both the reason for the date selected and the fact of the Pearl Harbor plan.

"On what day does the Navy intend to move?" Hirohito asked.

"The eighth," Nagano answered, "according to our schedule."

"That is a Monday, is it not?"

Nagano had replied, "We thought the day after a holiday, when they were all tired, would be best."

The admiral did not in this remark call attention to the fact that it would be Sunday in Hawaii, but he said so explicitly in a paper submitted to Hirohito at the same time: "We also consider that it would be advantageous to carry out the Hawaii raid by the naval task force on a Sunday, when the number of ships at anchor in Pearl Harbor would be relatively large. . . . We have given prior importance to the raid by the task force in our choice of day."

Hirohito, in an oral history recorded by an aide in 1946, maintained that he had been reluctant to go to war but had no choice. The oil embargo and economic blockade created a crisis for the Empire—"cornered Japan," as the Emperor put it.

> Once the situation had come to this point, it was natural that advocacy for going to war became predominant. If at that time I suppressed opinions in favor of war, public opinion would have certainly surged, with people asking questions about why Japan should surrender so easily when it had a highly efficient army and navy, well trained over the years.

Hirohito felt he had had very little choice: "It was unavoidable for me as a constitutional monarch . . . to do anything but give approval to the Tojo Cabinet on the decision to start the war." Otherwise, the Emperor said, "it would have led to a coup d'état."

So the die had been cast for Pearl Harbor. At that point the implementation of the plan and its success began to depend on the effectiveness of Japanese intelligence and the Imperial Navy's material preparations. Those had been very good indeed.

Japan's foremost Pearl Harbor spy was an odd sort of Imperial Navy officer. A leading student in his class at Etajima, Yoshikawa Takeo did not study. While friends boned up for exams, Yoshikawa read Zen philosophy. His father had been a soldier in the Russo-Japanese War, later a police officer, then a businessman, but Takeo gravitated to the Navy. Zen was a useful corrective for his hot temper, which Yoshikawa also sublimated into a fourth-level rank at kendo sword-fighting. After outstanding work on his training cruise aboard battleship *Asama*, Yoshikawa became code officer on a cruiser. He liked surface ships more than submarines and aircraft, to which he had also been introduced during the Etajima years. Too much drinking brought a serious stomach ailment, however, and the twenty-two-year-old ensign resigned his commission. Yoshikawa admitted later that he had considered suicide before choosing this other drastic step instead.

In time Yoshikawa's ailment redounded to his advantage, for he received an offer to join Imperial Navy intelligence with a reserve commission. This he did in 1934, serving first in the 8th Section dealing with British intelligence, later with the American specialists in the 5th Section. Ensign Yoshikawa loved ships and became an avid reader of *Jane's Fighting Ships* and other standard sources, which made him more or less expert at ship characteristics and recognition. This skill, somewhat unusual in the Japanese Navy, made Yoshikawa a natural for assignment to a forward post like Pearl Harbor as a naval observer. In spring 1940, before there ever was a Pearl Harbor plan, section chief Takeuchi Kaoru asked Yoshikawa if he would volunteer for Hawaii.

Yoshikawa took the Foreign Ministry language examination for English and passed, then awaited his travel orders. He received no special training either as diplomat or spy. Nevertheless Yoshikawa proceeded under diplomatic cover as assistant consul in Honolulu, close to Pearl Harbor. When the time came, posing as "Morimura Tadashi," Yoshikawa booked first-class passage to Honolulu aboard the liner *Nitta Maru*. (The ticket cost ten times his supposed earnings as a junior civil servant.) Yoshikawa's great adventure began in March 1941, when the *Nitta Maru* docked at Pier 8 in

Honolulu. Under instructions received at sea, he remained in his cabin until called for.

Following the movements of the Pacific Fleet turned out to be no more difficult than going out to dinner. Literally. The Shunchu-ro Restaurant, a Japanese place where Consul General Kita Nagao took Yoshikawa to celebrate his arrival, happened to be located halfway up a hill overlooking Pearl Harbor and had its own telescopes to boot. The restaurateur, a woman from Yoshikawa's own home prefecture, employed five geisha at her establishment. Yoshikawa had extra money for expenses. It was a perfect setup. "My favorite viewing place," Yoshikawa later remembered, "was a lovely Japanese teahouse overlooking the harbor. I knew what ships were in, how heavily they were loaded, who their officers were and what supplies were on board. The trusting young officers who visited the teahouse told the girls there everything. And anything they didn't reveal I found out by giving rides to hitchhiking American sailors."

The Japanese spy first surveyed his area of activity, touring the Hawaiian Islands, motoring a couple of times around Oahu, hiring a private plane to fly him over Pearl Harbor for an aerial view. Yoshikawa even visited the base to take the tourist-launch junket offered by the U.S. Navy. Convinced that Oahu had become the primary U.S. base, Yoshikawa focused his efforts there, not only at Pearl Harbor but at nearby Army and Marine installations. An expert swimmer, Yoshikawa did some offshore work as well. He never used a camera or notebook, instead memorizing facts and impressions and making whatever notes he needed back at the consulate. Only once, when a U.S. Navy guard saw him near an electrified fence and fired a rifle at him, was Yoshikawa in any danger.

There was precious little help from Oahu's Japanese immigrants or residents descended from Japanese, the vast majority of whom considered themselves patriotic Americans. A few residents did help though, perhaps most usefully just in getting Yoshikawa to where he wanted to go. One was taxi driver John Yoshige Mikami, who worked from a stand on Vineyard Street. Mikami did errands for the consulate and was familiar there, so Yoshikawa hired him for his initial trip around Oahu. That episode led to much additional work from the naval observer. Another helper was Richard Kotoshirodo, a nisei clerk at the consulate, who also provided transportation. For the most part, however, Yoshikawa needed no help, because his task on Oahu was basically very simple.

Ensign (for he had never been promoted) Yoshikawa would be the chief asset of the "inside" network of Japanese who did their spying under diplomatic cover. According to writer Ladislas Farago, formerly of ONI, there would also be an "outside" network of agents directly infiltrated from Japan. Farago names no names, but he gives a figure of "almost a dozen" true spies including a grocer who kept boarding visiting Japanese warships, a café owner alleged to be an Imperial Navy officer, and the chemist of a local sake brewery, who reportedly bragged he was the son-in-law of senior Japanese admiral Hyakutake Gengo. Titillating as these stories may be, there is no independent evidence for the existence of Farago's "outside" network. The FBI and Navy counterintelligence, who can hardly be accused of reluctance to perceive Japanese as spies, prosecuted just one (German) person for espionage on Oahu after Pearl Harbor. Zealous ONI and FBI minions quietly eavesdropped on Japanese consulate activities in Honolulu for eighteen months without uncovering such a net, or, for that matter, any evidence of special interest in Pearl Harbor. Japanese espionage there was, but it was centered on the U.S. West Coast, and the fleet had permanently come to Pearl only quite recently.

On the mainland the Japanese spies were having their own difficulties. A May 1941 report, intercepted by U.S. authorities when Japanese embassy second secretary Terasaki Taro visited New York, asserted that the United States was so vital a target that Tokyo ought to have available "at least one third of the personnel that they have in Shanghai for intelligence." The document also discussed several agent sources, liaison between the embassy and the New York office, and budget questions. Here too the spies complained—of their $30,000 annual general budget for U.S. activity, only about $3,900 could be used to procure actual information and another $1,800 on entertainment and receptions, where prospects could be evaluated and frequently information gleaned most easily. Terasaki, held to be the head of Japanese intelligence in the United States, wanted to take up a post in New York and unify the Washington and New York networks. The report requested an additional half million yen during calendar year 1941 "for the development of intelligence."

A clear setback would be the Tachibana affair, in which one of the *joho kyoku*'s most active agents, supposed "language officer" Lieutenant Commander Tachibana Itaru, was exposed and expelled from the United States. Tachibana, who operated out of Los Angeles using the alias Yamato, ran a string of nightclubs and brothels as his cover. He ranged up and down the West Coast, with interests in San Francisco, Portland, and Seattle in addition to L.A. He employed a driver, one Kono Toraichi, who had once been chauffeur to Charlie Chaplin. Kono encountered an old acquaintance one day who went to the FBI and ONI to report the interest Kono and "Yamato" took in information about the Navy. The acquaintance, Al D. Blake, better known as Keeno, King of the Robots, for a world record he had set for standing motionless, had met Kono in 1917 when playing a bit part in the Chaplin film *Shoulder Arms*. Now American counterintelligence set up Blake as a double agent in a gambit to catch Kono and Tachibana. The ploy ended in Honolulu, where Blake talked too much to an old girlfriend from vaudeville, but not before Tachibana was tracked to the Japanese embassy in Washington, carrying a briefcase full of doctored intelligence from Blake. Tachibana and another language student were arrested and left the United States aboard the *Nitta Maru* in June 1941.

Unlike such outside espionage, good old (or perhaps "newfangled" would be a better word) technical intelligence collection offered better opportunities for gathering information on the U.S. fleet. American counterintelligence officers were convinced that Japanese official vessels visiting U.S. waters were collecting intelligence. Such claims were made, for example, in connection with the August 1940 visits to Hawaii and Kauai by the Japanese merchant marine training ship *Taisei Maru*, the Honolulu visit that same month by naval tanker *Shiriya**, the San Francisco visit in October 1940 by naval tanker *Naruto*, and the Honolulu visit two months later of the Japanese freighter *Sagami Maru*. That December, during a port call by freighter *Durban Maru*, charts of military objectives in Hawaii were reported to have been seen aboard the vessel.

Radio intelligence picked up by Japanese special duty groups also figured in a quite major way in *joho kyoku* knowledge. The Japanese set up a forward listening post in Mexico City, the so-called L *kikan*, or L Section, in early 1940 under Commander Wachi Tsunezo. Disingenuously telling U.S. interrogators in 1945 that his concern in Mexico (with the cover duty of assistant naval attaché) had been the entertainment of senior Mexican officials—"We devoted much *sake* and *sukiyaki* to that end"—L Section actually concentrated on the interception of U.S. naval communications, especially from the Atlantic. The forty-year-old Commander Wachi was well suited to his task, having spent ten years as a communications specialist, including with the special-duty group in Shanghai (his cover there had been with the resident naval officer), with the Navy Ministry communications station, and with the NGS/IGHQ communications section. Wachi also had seagoing experience on the battleship *Mutsu*, the light cruiser *Naka*, a destroyer, and a tanker.

Living his cover as attaché, Commander Wachi moonlighted with conventional espionage alongside his more esoteric duty. He sent Tokyo reports every two or three months that excerpted American open-source publications, and he made at least one visit to Bogotá, Colombia, to keep up the pretense that he monitored naval matters in the entire mid-American region. Under attachés Captain Sato Katsunori and Captain Hamanaka Kyoho the main job supposedly had been to assure Mexico's neutrality. To this end much attention went to massaging Mexicans' psyches. "There was some rivalry between our staff and the U.S. embassy in entertaining the Mexican

---

*It is suggestive, though hardly conclusive, that the skipper of the *Shiriya* in 1940 was Captain Sato Shiro, who happened to be an Etajima classmate of the *joho kyoku*'s Ogawa Kanji.

generals," Wachi later recounted. "We thought of the Mexicans as a somewhat low-class people who could best be appealed to through entertainment." There was also attention given to the 2,000 or so Japanese residents in the country. Wachi never made it to Baja California, though he did see Manzanillo, a favorite port for Japanese fishing ships, which the Americans feared to be intelligence collectors. "I think the American emphasis on our fishing industry as a source of information is comical," Wachi said.

Entertainment for Mexicans was more than sake and sukiyaki, however. Thousands of dollars in bribes went to officials, particularly once it became necessary to avert the consequences when a bottle of contraband mercury Wachi had surreptitiously procured broke while being loaded for shipment. Also on Commander Wachi's paylist was "Sutton," a disgruntled U.S. Army officer who provided Tokyo with details of the Arcadia secret meetings between Churchill and Roosevelt at Washington, along with other intelligence tidbits.

Commander Wachi told interrogators that he read *The New York Times, Life,* and *Time.* "Research was important but we had little time for it," he said. In fact, Wachi had been the first Imperial Navy officer to conduct systematic research into British codes, and he did the same with American ones while in Mexico. The L Section under him had a petty officer and four intercept operators at a facility on Calle Orizaba. Among the intelligence they gathered figured news of ship movements through the Panama Canal (some of this information was supplemented by "Sutton"), on the first U.S. Navy convoys of war matériel to Europe, even (again from "Sutton") material on the design of a new very heavy bomber (the B-29) and on changes in U.S. war plans.

American counterintelligence inevitably became aware of nefarious activities in Mexico City. In June 1941, asked to suggest a policy to counter Japanese espionage in the United States, the Far East Division of ONI noted the Japanese legation in Mexico City had been designated communications headquarters for activities in the United States. Commander Wachi himself saw, about the same time, individuals he took to be FBI agents trying to follow him. Wachi discovered that the shadowers concentrated on tailing his car, so he drove to some restaurant or theater, parked there, then hailed taxis to his real destinations. That the Naval General Staff much appreciated Commander Wachi's work would be shown once he returned to Japan: He was made chief of staff of the Imperial Navy's radio intelligence service.

Not only did ONI know about Wachi's L Section in Mexico, it knew about Imperial Navy designs for an improved espionage system. "There is also a plan on the part of the Japanese," the Far East Division noted in June 1941, "to introduce into each Consulate a naval officer under the guise of a civilian employee who would specialize in directing espionage activities concerned with the obtaining of naval information." This was Ensign

Yoshikawa at Pearl Harbor, if not by name at least by function, and the extent of this U.S. knowledge is remarkable. The existence of this *joho kyoku* plan also explains why Yoshikawa had been asked to volunteer for a Hawaii mission at a time when there was no plan to attack Pearl Harbor. Yoshikawa's mission, therefore, should not be linked to any specific offensive intent against Hawaii.

As Yoshikawa's espionage continued, his information contributed to the plan that did emerge. The Japanese made other efforts as well, apparently including one through the Germans, who were asked to have one of their agents procure information regarding Pearl Harbor. That agent, one Dusko Popov, happened to be a double agent working for the British, and for the FBI during the time he was in the United States. Popov received a shopping list of information wanted in Berlin, in the form of tiny photographs called "microdots" attached to an innocuous letter. When developed the microdots requested information on munitions depots in Hawaii and airfields on Oahu, as well as exact details (including sketches) of shipyards at Pearl Harbor, the submarine base there, pier layout, mooring berths, and so forth. There was also a special assignment to find out about anti-torpedo nets introduced into American and British navies. These questions sent to Popov in the summer of 1941 arguably represent a selection that would be of great value to planners contemplating an attack on Pearl Harbor.

Dusko Popov happened to be in Lisbon at that time, and any information he might have turned up would have to go through Berlin. Right in place at Pearl Harbor was Ensign Yoshikawa, who had direct communications with Tokyo. There was also a sleeper spy in Hawaii, the German Bernard Julius Otto Kuehn, who was supposed to remain inactive until war actually began but who could have been mobilized in a pinch. Interestingly, neither of these agents in place seem to have been asked for the same data as Popov. Japanese war-gaming of the Pearl Harbor attack plan in early September also indicates that by that point the operational plans had largely been completed. On September 24 Yoshikawa even received a cable that went beyond a search for basic intelligence data: He was asked to report U.S. fleet movement in precise detail and by area of the harbor. This so-called "bomb plot" message apparently forms Yoshikawa's basis for his later assertions that he knew Pearl Harbor would be attacked, although he was never made privy to any such intention.

The man who sent that dispatch to Yoshikawa was *joho kyoku*'s Captain Ogawa Kanji, who in fact was the Naval General Staff's first focal point for Pearl Harbor matters, drawn in long before the operations staff became enmeshed in argument with the Combined Fleet over whether the project could work. Different accounts time Ogawa's first contacts with Admiral Yamamoto on the subject either in January 1941 or early in February. At that time the NGS Third Bureau already possessed a mountain of information on Hawaii, so much that it had on file a monograph, described as a 500-page mimeographed tome, regarding Hawaiian defenses and the routine patterns of U.S. fleet operations in that area. Naturally a certain amount of Third Bureau intelligence was out of date, and another proportion represented speculation, but there is no reason to suppose that *joho kyoku* was fundamentally misinformed. In fact, Ogawa Kanji's performance at the secret war games, in which he initially defeated the hypothetical Japanese task force, suggests his information was very good indeed.

Nevertheless there was great demand for precise intelligence, and Captain Ogawa did his best to obtain it. The Popov questionnaire suggests that the Japanese went so far as to pump the Germans for relevant knowledge. The "bomb plot" message shows the Third Bureau demanding detailed tactical reporting long before the planned operation. A most ambitious final effort would be the compilation within *joho kyoku* of a set of ninety-seven questions pertaining to Hawaiian defenses. Either Captain Ogawa or his superiors considered the list too sensitive to commit to the airwaves or cable traffic. Instead it was hand-carried to Honolulu. That was apparently done by Lieutenant Commander Nakajima Minato (or perhaps another officer, Fukushima) who handed Consul General Kita a sealed envelope, plus money and instructions for the sleeper agent Kuehn, when the *Tatuta Maru* passed through Honolulu in late October.*

Meanwhile, the Japanese prepared a dress rehearsal of the Pearl Harbor mission using another liner. Summoned to participate, Lieutenant Commander Suzuki Suguru, a seaplane pilot, air staff officer of the China Area Fleet, and at the time the youngest officer (Etajima, 1927) in his grade in the fleet, sailed on board. Suzuki balked when brought back from China that July, objecting to being used as a spy, but he calmed down and later

---

*An exceedingly thorny question, this Japanese list continues to be a point of confusion among historians. Apparently working from an interview given CBS Television by former Japanese officer Suzuki Suguru, Ladislas Farago in his 1967 account notes that the list was on a sheet of rice paper crumpled into a ball, and that Commander Suzuki gave it to Consul Kita during a November 2, 1941, meeting at the Honolulu consulate. John Toland's 1970 version is that Suzuki concocted the list of ninety-seven precise intelligence questions as his ship, the liner *Taiyo Maru*, lay in Honolulu, but fudges the matter of where and how the list reached Yoshikawa, except to imply that it was during *Taiyo Maru*'s port call. Toland based this account on a 1966 interview with Suzuki, but in the notes to that interview Commander Suzuki remarks that he never went ashore while in Honolulu, and he makes no mention whatever of any list, simply speaking of the intelligence he received. To complicate matters further, Suzuki provided a statement for Walter Lord in 1956 asserting that he *did* leave the ship, twice, but again without mention of any list.

Gordon Prange and his co-authors write that the list was drafted by the Third Bureau, not Suzuki, which makes sense since it seems improbable that Commander Suzuki could have concocted such a long list of precise questions off the top of his head. It also fits

participated in the Naval War College secret war games, playing the role of a U.S. staff officer. Now Suzuki put his knowledge to work monitoring sea and air conditions along the northern Pacific route, watching for other ships on the way, gathering information in Hawaii when he arrived. With Suzuki to take care of air matters, another officer, Commander Maejima Toshihide, went to examine submarine issues together with a junior partner.

Among the passengers when *Taiyo Maru* weighed anchor at Yokohama on October 22 were American teacher Carl S. Sipple, his wife, and their two children. They liked the *Taiyo Maru*, a Nippon Yusen Kaisha (NYK) liner, because it was roomy and comfortable, a fruit of German war reparations after 1918, but they hated the route the ship took for their voyage. During virtually the entire trip Sipple and his family were tense and uneasy, seeing no other vessels and disturbed by the fact that the ship's position was never posted for the public, as was customary. Stormy weather did not help either, and from the position of the sun they could tell the ship had sailed north of the usual sea-lanes. Wanting to message friends in Honolulu to help find a place to stay, Sipple was refused permission to dispatch anything. *Taiyo Maru* maintained radio silence.

That was fine for Commander Suzuki and his companions, who had first-class cabins and were busy compiling a daily record of weather and sea conditions. Suzuki posed as the ship's assistant purser, Maejima as a doctor. They were surprised, however, to encounter American planes as the ship neared Hawaii. In battle exercises the planes made mock attacks on the ship,

---

what we know from recent scholarship about Japanese-German intelligence cooperation. Prange et al. also assert that Suzuki and his companions resolved to put nothing on paper until after departing Honolulu, to minimize the chance of compromise in case of any search of the ship. If true, this makes it even less likely that Suzuki would have been carrying any such list.

Aside from Commander Suzuki's varying recollections, the difficulty with all these versions is one of time. Unless the ninety-seven questions were very simple indeed, Ensign Yoshikawa would have had little chance to collect the necessary information during the *Taiyo Maru*'s stay at Honolulu. Yoshikawa himself mentions the list, but never clarified how it came to him.

We know that Yoshikawa took aerial photos of Pearl Harbor from a tourist plane on October 20 or 21, undoubtedly under instructions, and before the arrival of Suzuki's ship. In addition we know that the liner *Tatuta Maru* passed through Honolulu at this earlier time, that it *was* carrying other documents (money and instructions for sleeper agent Otto Kuehn, plus orders for the "outside" network to close down), and that it had aboard another officer of *joho kyoku*'s American section, Lieutenant Commander Nakajima Minato. Unfortunately Nakajima died in August 1943 and left no record regarding Pearl Harbor.

My conjecture from all this is that the list originated in the Third Bureau and was carried aboard the earlier ship, *Tatuta Maru*.

flying so close that passengers waved to the airmen. Outside harbor, pilots, American naval officers, and a detachment of marines or military police came aboard, not only to guide the ship into Honolulu, but also, some believed, to prevent any attempt to stall the ship or otherwise block the entrance to Pearl Harbor. Nevertheless the pier assigned the liner had a good view of the naval-base entrance, so Suzuki was able to get photographs with his Leica camera.

Kita Nagao went aboard the *Taiyo Maru* the first day and was told that the naval officers wanted information about U.S. military facilities. Suzuki never went ashore, and put nothing on paper before leaving. Some answers to the questionnaire, as well as aerial photos taken from a tourist flight in late October, were smuggled aboard. Suzuki, who knew Yoshikawa, avoided any contact with him, and Yoshikawa was kept away from any association with the liner. When the *Taiyo Maru* left on November 5 it carried a special diplomatic pouch (its approximate dimensions were a foot by a foot and a half) that Suzuki had been told contained material for the Navy.

Commander Suzuki verified details of American naval routine during the visit, confirming that the anchorage at Lahaina was not in use, discovering the thickness of the concrete roofs of hangars at Hickam Field, and learning that seaplane scouts could be launched from the sea prior to the attack. Suzuki calculated bomb requirements to hit the airfields, and the quantity of bombs and torpedoes needed to assure sinking the American battleships at Pearl Harbor. It was a useful mission.

Naval headquarters very much agreed that Commander Suzuki's information was of vital import. When *Taiyo Maru* reached Yokohama on November 17 Suzuki went immediately to a Navy launch that carried him across to battleship *Hiei* off Kisarazu. The *Hiei* happened to be one of the war-ships assigned to the task force, and it conveyed him to Hitokappu Bay (also called Tankan Bay), where Admiral Nagumo's force assembled for the Pearl Harbor attack. Suzuki arrived there on November 21. On the evening of the twenty-third he met in conference aboard flagship *Akagi* with Nagumo, Genda, and various other officers. A friend of Genda's, Suzuki remained aboard until the task force sailed. He and Commander Kanamoto Yoshihira, a *joho kyoku* expert who flew up from Tokyo and then shuttled on a boat from Ominato, briefed the flight leaders that night. Suzuki recalled Commander Fuchida Mitsuo taking copious notes. Fuchida, top flight leader, who would lead the first-wave air attack, needed all the intelligence he could get.

The task force sortied on November 26. On the eve of its departure Admiral Nagumo called in Suzuki at about two in the morning to check once more whether the Americans had really stopped using Lahaina. In his sleeping kimono Nagumo apologized for awakening the officer but was perfectly serious about his question. On the very eve of departure the admiral remained nervous indeed. With morning the warships raised steam and left the harbor.

Japan's Pearl Harbor attack had begun. Commander Suzuki stayed behind, aboard patrol vessel *Kunashiri,* which would return him to the mainland. Ironically, Suzuki had been the subject of several Japanese radio messages the Americans intercepted between November 17 and 20, messages that were ignored amid the press of business and only decrypted in 1945, after the war had ended. Historian Frederick D. Parker argues that had these and other messages associating the First Air Fleet with northern Japanese waters been decoded at the time, the United States could have been tipped off that the *eastern* Pacific was about to become a target for Japanese carrier attacks. Of course, the most worthwhile objective in that sea area happened to be Pearl Harbor.

ADMIRAL NAGUMO CHUICHI MUST HAVE PROMULGATED HIS FIRST AIR FLEET TRAINING PLAN shortly after learning about the Pearl Harbor project. The plan provided that the air units of his carriers would train up to full proficiency by July, and attain battle-ready status toward the end of August. This training took place mainly on Kyushu in the Home Islands, where fighter, torpedo-bomber, and dive-bomber units were farmed out to various shore bases for their exercise programs. In a departure from Navy doctrine, which made ship captains responsible for their air groups, the overall program was supervised by First Air Fleet staff officer Genda Minoru.

In fact Genda was the prime mover for much of the preparation that took place. He was everywhere—helping plan detailed training routines with air squadron commanders, contributing to the operation plans, monitoring progress, solving technical problems. There were three major technical difficulties with the raid plan, and Genda helped with two of them. One was the lack of a shallow-water torpedo. Genda contrived new low-altitude release tactics to reduce the bottom-out depth for air-dropped torpedoes, and when that proved insufficient he needled experts at the Yokosuka Torpedo School to come up with a hardware solution. Actually, experiments were already under way at Yokosuka, and by February 1940 had succeeded in reducing plunge depth to some sixty feet. A forty-foot requirement had to be met, however, and this took considerably longer, though British success at Taranto constituted evidence that a solution existed. The problem would be solved with a special added fin on aerial torpedoes, a solution found in September–October 1941. Then the problem became getting enough torpedoes: Only thirty would be ready by mid-October, with another fifty at the end of the month, but the next hundred would not become available until the end of November. Among messages intercepted by American radio intelligence but not decoded until after the war was one on October 28 stating that the First Air Fleet would pick up the torpedoes at Sasebo and hold classes on using them at Kanoya. Somehow the fleet got enough to drop forty torpedoes at Pearl Harbor.

Another of Genda's focuses became bombs. Standard Japanese bombs in 110-, 220-, and 550-pound sizes were just not powerful enough to penetrate the deck armor of battleships. Experiments showed that a 1,760-pound bomb would work for battleships and a 1,200-pound bomb for aircraft carriers. With strict limits on steel available for casings, another expedient proved necessary. This time the Japanese adapted 16-inch shells used by *Nagato*-class ships, which proved quite suitable with a few modifications and the addition of stabilizers.

Air training and leadership also featured among Commander Genda's concerns. He insisted upon the best men, and also insisted there had to be a single overall air commander, another departure from Imperial Navy doctrine. Attaining agreement on this, Genda handpicked Lieutenant Commander Fuchida Mitsuo for the job. Fuchida, serving in a staff capacity with Carrier Division 3, suddenly found himself reassigned to *Akagi* in September 1941. It was a job he had held just a year before and Fuchida was mystified until Genda told him that he would be given additional duty as commander of all air groups in the carrier fleet.

"Now don't be alarmed, Fuchida," Genda said, "but we want you to lead our air force in the event that we attack Pearl Harbor!"

Fuchida remembers that the idea almost took his breath away, and the more he heard about it the more astonishing it seemed. Almost immediately the two officers left the flight line at Kagoshima base to board a launch out to the *Akagi*, where they went to meet with Vice Admiral Nagumo and his chief of staff, Rear Admiral Kusaka Ryunosuke. There Fuchida first saw a detailed model of Oahu and was told the fine points of the plan.

If Genda Minoru was the troubleshooter and front man, Kusaka Ryunosuke played the power behind the throne. Though not himself a pilot, Kusaka had held aviation assignments ever since completing Naval War College, and considered himself an aviation manager, perhaps emulating his father, who had been a businessman. Kusaka had two sons, one of whom was approaching military age, and four daughters, the youngest six years old in 1941. He did not want war; there had been too much fighting already (Kusaka had skippered carrier *Hosho* off Shanghai at the time of the outbreak of the China Incident, and then became naval chief of staff in those waters, the job he held at the time of the sinking of the American gunboat *Panay*). The passion of the warrior went against the grain of his deeply felt Zen Buddhism.

On the other hand, Zen gave Kusaka calmness to meet the constant crises flowing from war preparations, and he also knew his men. Fuchida and

Kusaka had overlapped for a time in 1940, when the latter captained the *Akagi* and the other her air group. Kusaka had known Genda at least since China days. His senior staff officer, Commander Oishi Tamotsu, Kusaka appreciated as a good organizer. It was Oishi whom Kusaka assigned to come up with the nonaviation portion of the task force plan.

Thus it was Commander Oishi, not Genda, who faced the third big headache in getting ready for Pearl Harbor. That was fuel. Most of the Japanese ships would have to fuel at least once during the voyage. Refueling at sea would be a novel technique for the Japanese and, in addition, there were only a few days each month when the sea in the North Pacific would be calm enough for this. Fortunately Oishi's nautical specialty was navigation. He rose to the challenge.

Eight tankers were assigned to support the task force. In addition, the warships, especially the carriers and other heavy ships, were to carry drums of extra fuel oil in every available space. Such action was prohibited by Japanese naval regulations, however, so Commander Oishi had to resort to the manager. Admiral Kusaka found the Navy Ministry reluctant to waive the regulations on fuel loading. Kusaka's attitude was that since Japan had determined to cross the Rubicon everything necessary should be done to make the mission a success. Kusaka enlisted Yamamoto to put additional pressure on the ministry, which caved in early in November. The regulations were waived to the extent that drums of fuel "absolutely necessary for operational reasons"—a total of 1,400 tons in all—could be loaded aboard *Akagi*, *Hiryu*, and *Soryu*, following instructions on weight distribution the ministry furnished.

Messages referring to the drummed fuel loads, weight distribution, and tanker practice in refueling at sea with aircraft carriers were among those intercepted by American radio intelligence but not decoded until after the war. The Americans would also intercept a message from the naval tanker *Shiriya*, which had been delayed by repairs and wished to provide data on its future positions. This message showed that in early December the ship would be at a latitude north of Midway Island, and proceeding east. Earlier, *Shiriya* had been suspected of gathering intelligence for the Japanese around Hawaii; it is ironic that her messages might have provided the Americans with clues to the Pearl Harbor attack.

Another problem concerned clothes and equipment usable in the cold of the far north. Requisitions for cold-weather gear raised eyebrows at Navy supply depots when most of the fleet was preparing for war in the tropics. Kusaka's supply officer ordered both kinds and sent the equipment to Hitokappu Bay.

By then the forces were beginning to concentrate at that very place. The warships did not come in big formations whose departure from home bases might be noted; they slipped away by ones and twos, some coming in almost late. Admiral Nagumo assembled a formidable task force, including Japan's six largest aircraft carriers, two battleships, two heavy cruisers, a light cruiser, and eight destroyers. There was also a special unit of two destroyers to bombard Midway Island, and another of three submarines to scout in advance of the task force. The First Air Fleet, called the Nagumo Force, in Japanese parlance acquired the tactical designation Striking Force, or Kido Butai. An Advance Force with twenty-four submarines of Japan's Sixth Fleet would simultaneously assemble around Hawaii to institute an underwater blockade. Five of the subs would carry two-man midget submarines that would try to penetrate Pearl Harbor.

The ships arrived at Hitokappu Bay in staggered fashion. Aircraft carrier *Kaga* left Sasebo on November 7 and reached the assembly port on the fifteenth. Seaman Yokota Shigeki found that no liberty or contact with the shore was allowed, nor was any rubbish to be thrown overboard. All garbage would be collected and burned by a working party near the pier. Yokota went with the detail. They saw several fishermen from nearby houses, but no one spoke to them. The *Hoko Maru*, carrying the task force's cold-weather gear, arrived on November 16, as did three oilers and the carrier *Soryu*. Other ships arrived one by one.

Admiral Yamamoto sent Nagumo orders on November 25 to leave port the next day. Kido Butai was to make every effort to conceal its movement, advance to a holding point, and refuel pending final go-ahead for the attack. Nagumo's force began to weigh anchor at about 6:00 A.M. It was a dark, cloudy morning. On *Akagi*'s bridge the ship's navigator, Miura Gishiro, was so tense he had abandoned his usual slippers for shoes and lost his typical easygoing temperament. Fuchida Mitsuo sat in the flight-deck control post beneath the bridge watching the mountains of the Kurile Islands recede. Patrol vessel *Kunashiri* signaled "Good luck on your mission." Ashore, ten-year-old Sakurai Kazuko, the postmaster's daughter, looked to the bay and saw it empty. Like apparitions, the warships had vanished as silently as they had come.

"May God help us," Genda Minoru wrote in his diary, "for this time we are advancing on Pearl Harbor not in a dream, but in reality."

# Who Slept at Dawn?

EVER SINCE PEARL HARBOR, AMERICAN HISTORY HAS REVERBERATED WITH THE CHARGES and countercharges of those who would assign the blame for what became a major military disaster. Tons of ink, mountains of paper produced no definitive answer on whether disaster was avoidable or not, whether the surprise the Japanese attained was inevitable or not, who was culpable or not. Such questions cannot be resolved in the relatively tiny space available here. What I will do is summarize the evidence from various intelligence channels and then move on to the tragic events of the attack itself. To be plain about the standpoint taken, I will say that it is impossible to tell whether there was a conspiracy to suppress warnings of a threat to Pearl Harbor. There was, however, a rush to judgment after the battle, and a perhaps natural desire to find scapegoats. Too many of the resulting theories require contrived explanations. Awkward as it may seem, the simple fact is that the Japanese strike mission, as we have related at some length, was a secret operation secretly planned and executed. It should be no wonder that the Imperial Navy managed to achieve a measure of surprise. Americans at all levels did their jobs as well as they could, but the Japanese had left nothing to chance. Americans were skillful and clever, but on that day, Pearl Harbor day, it would be Yamamoto's war.

"OUR TASK FORCE HAS ENTERED WESTERN LONGITUDE," WROTE COMBINED FLEET CHIEF OF staff Ugaki in his diary. "A high atmospheric pressure luckily happens to be just behind them, following them eastward; they'll be able to refuel, I'm sure." That day, December 2, Admiral Yamamoto appeared before Emperor Hirohito to receive the imperial rescript authorizing war. On the *Nagato*, in anticipation of the rescript, and already under Naval General Staff orders to open hostilities as planned, Ugaki Matome and fleet staff concentrated on composing a suitably encouraging message to the men under Yamamoto's command. Ugaki drafted language similar to Lord Horatio Nelson's exhortation before the battle of Trafalgar and Togo's before Tsushima. Ugaki gave the proposed message to Commander Watanabe Yasuji to show the other staff officers. Watanabe returned to suggest just two words be changed. Later Admiral Ugaki received an NGS order setting the time for beginning war at midnight, December 8 (December 7 east longitude date). He informed the fleet using a phrase previously selected for this purpose: "Climb Mount Niitaka 1208."

As Nagumo's task force steamed steadily east, at a constant rate of about 13 knots without zigzagging, a few more deceptive actions were taken. The commandant of the Yokosuka Naval District got orders to permit as many of his men as possible to go ashore, and give leave to sailors in the barracks, so that an impression of normality could be created by the large number of sailors on liberty in Tokyo and Yokohama. The NYK passenger liner *Tatsuta Maru* also cleared Yokohama at this time for the last of three voyages to repatriate Japanese citizens in the U.S. Finally, the commander of the 1st Combined Communications Unit, beginning on Y-Day (November 23), was to "send false messages to give the impression that the main strength of the fleet is in the western part of the Inland Sea." This last, a touch inserted in the planning at the insistence of Commander Wada, proved to be a real contributor to American confusion.

In deception as in so much else, the simplest is often what works best, and the best thing for the Japanese in 1941 was that the Americans were working from a knowledge of the Imperial Navy's traditional concept of Decisive Battle. The Japanese prepared for an offensive into the Southern Area. In all the years of prewar hypothesizing such an offensive had always formed the prelude to the Japanese sitting back to await the American or British counterattack. Japanese preparations to invade the Philippines and Malaya, their final concentrations of force, their assembly and launch of troop convoys were all to some extent detected by the Allies. Those moves formed part of an expected strategy. To attack Pearl Harbor would be unexpected. That, too, contributed to American confusion.

Finally, the Japanese attained surprise because they kept the Pearl Harbor attack mission secret. Some years after the war, Admiral Fukudome estimated that only seven senior naval officers, five Army officers, and Prime Minister Tojo knew about the plans. Fukudome exaggerated the degree of secrecy, and one may dispute exactly how widely knowledge ran, but however wide one draws the circle, not that many knew. Postwar reconstruction by U.S. interrogators and Allied war-crimes investigators established that the ring of knowledge included Admiral Nagano; his vice chief, Ito Seiichi; operations chief Tomioka and members of the operations section; Admiral Fukudome, who went from Combined Fleet to the NGS as chief of the operations bureau; Yamamoto and his staff; Nagumo and his staff. Those with partial knowledge included the navy minister and his vice minister; the chiefs of his naval affairs bureau and of two sections of that bureau; the chiefs of section in the Naval General Staff other than the operations section; and the commanders and chiefs of staff of the various fleets within the Combined Fleet plus selected members of their staffs. Even allowing that other officers, primarily specialists, learned of part or all of the plan through their technical duties, the total hardly passes a hundred, and most of those were at sea. Possibilities for a leak were small, especially in the heated Tokyo atmosphere of 1941.

It is a tribute to the proficiency of the Japanese Navy that an operation of the scope of the Pearl Harbor mission, including even concomitant technological developments, could be carried out within such a small circle of knowledge.

Of course such procedures had drawbacks in addition to their advantages. Thus, for example, pilots and aircrews trained for a generalized mission, not the specific strike on Pearl Harbor. Commander Fuchida, who would lead the strike, always believed the men would have trained even harder had they known the real object of their efforts, but that had been considered too risky. So the group commander did the best he could. Actually Fuchida himself proved not above a little dissimulation—after the war, when it looked as if the surprise attack might become a subject for criminal prosecution, the Pearl Harbor air leader told American interrogators (incredibly) that when the task force left port he had thought they were en route to Singapore.

In a more accurate rendition Fuchida provided interrogators in late November 1945, he admitted he had been in charge of preparing the flight personnel, at least aboard *Akagi,* and he characterized a December 3 (east longitude date) briefing (previously alleged to be the time he first learned of the mission) as a practice session. Unit leaders had learned of the operation from the meeting held with Commander Suzuki at Hitokappu Bay. Fuchida held discussions and war games with them during the initial days out of port. It was pilots and crewmen who learned on December 3, when Fuchida brought out maps and charts, not only of the Hawaiian Islands, but of Oahu and finally of Pearl Harbor itself. The men drilled all day to hone their knowledge of local conditions and recognition of U.S. warships. Fuchida briefed the intelligence, unusual because in Japanese practice the carrier captain usually handled these aspects of pre-mission preparation. Having been in Hawaii only once, during his 1924 midshipman training cruise, Fuchida found that there were many questions he could not answer. "I was never really satisfied with the information," he recalled, "until I was over the target."

Meanwhile the task force advanced eastward across the Pacific. Fortune smiled upon the brave, and a high-pressure weather front settled in behind Kido Butai and more or less followed it. Although Nagumo's force encountered fairly rough seas along portions of its route, the weather ensured that his ships were able to refuel when necessary. Final orders to proceed with the attack led to a further refueling of the carriers and destroyers just before Admiral Nagumo turned his ships southeast to begin his final run in.

The orders also led to thoughtful circumspection, at least in some quarters. Admiral Hara Chuichi, who commanded Carrier Division 5 with the spanking-new fleet carriers *Zuikaku* and *Shokaku*, felt troubled when he learned that the attack mission had been confirmed. "There were those among us who thought as I did when we attacked Pearl Harbor," Hara said. "After the attack was definitely ordered, I thought 'what can be the reason' for I never doubted the righteousness of the Emperor, though I was extremely concerned because the order did not fit any thinking that I knew to be right." And of course there were those doubters Nagumo and Kusaka, of central importance to the entire enterprise, who stood on the flag bridge of the *Akagi*.

Admiral Nagumo had brought with him a special flag he raised to inspire his sailors—the "Z" signal flag made famous by an earlier Japanese naval hero, Togo Heihachiro at Tsushima, who had used it to send a message in the tradition of Lord Nelson. As the carriers of his task force turned south on the night of December 6 to race toward the designated attack position, Nagumo ordered the "Z" flag brought out. The Japanese pilots were starting to man their planes. It was the end of an era in Pacific relations.

How could Pearl Harbor have been warned? How could the Pacific fleet have avoided being taken by surprise on the morning of December 7, 1941? The short answer is, by intelligence on Japanese activities. Unfortunately the short answer is not satisfactory. In the years since that fateful day, participants, historians, and analysts of many hues have never ceased claiming that the approach of Admiral Nagumo's carriers was known but suppressed by a conspiracy, or that the intelligence was available but was obscured by the mass of facts in the system, or that the fleet could have been warned but for key players' inability to agree in Washington, or that any of several other interpretations is correct. A review of potential intelligence indicators shows this to be a thorny matter indeed—it is more difficult to come to any firm conclusion than the plethora of theories suggests. This in itself may account for the persistant controversy over the surprise at Pearl Harbor.

A good place to begin is with the U.S. embassy in Tokyo, and Ambassador

Joseph C. Grew, naval attaché Commander Henri Smith-Hutton, and their language officers. Despite the difficulties of intelligence work in Japan, the embassy became the source of the first specific information indicating that Japan might attack Pearl Harbor in a surprise mass attack. Grew's first secretary, Edward S. Croker, heard it from a friend, senior Peruvian diplomat Dr. Ricardo Rivera-Schreiber. The claim's origin has been variously attributed to a remark dropped during a Peruvian diplomatic reception by a translator for Prince Konoye or to the minister's own Japanese cook. Rivera-Schreiber considered it fanciful but so serious he had to pass it along.

Ambassador Grew discussed the report with attaché Smith-Hutton. The Japanese were capable of acting quickly, Smith-Hutton explained, and surprise had been a favorite method, as everyone knew. The attaché noted that it would be logical for the Imperial Navy to strike at the U.S. fleet no matter where located. Nevertheless Commander Smith-Hutton thought the rumor just that; he had heard similar rumors before, and it was highly unlikely that Imperial Navy planners would permit their real intentions to become known. Grew cabled the report to Washington on January 27, 1941. Smith-Hutton did not think it warranted any separate follow-up through Navy channels, and at ONI an inquiry by the Far East Division concluded the report to be without merit.

It would have been an intelligence coup for the American embassy and attaché, so isolated in Japan, to have stumbled upon the secret of the Pearl Harbor attack. As far as we know, however, at this time the notion of such an attack existed only in the mind of Yamamoto and his chief of staff, while preliminary intelligence gathering was under way at the Third Bureau of the Naval General Staff. It requires excessive credulity to believe that Japanese plans leaked at this stage in their evolution.

Logically, of course, it is possible to proceed from incorrect premises to an accurate conclusion, and it is significant that in February 1941 Washington showed sudden interest in the anti-aircraft and anti-torpedo defenses of Pearl Harbor. Still, before long the flurry died down. A report jointly compiled by the Army and Navy air commanders in Hawaii, pointing the way toward greater preparedness against air attack, would be shelved because requirements for effective air defense were seen as impossible to achieve.

Despite almost total isolation, Commander Smith-Hutton and his assistants actually managed to come up with several indications of true Japanese activities, though all of them pointed to the traditional concept of Japan's strategy. In February the attaché reported Japanese forces gradually closing in upon Singapore, though the document carefully noted that there was no sign as yet of any attack on the British or Dutch. In April the embassy reported rumors current in Tokyo of impending attack on Singapore. This was additionally alarming in the light of a March 12 attaché report of a recent speech by former Combined Fleet commander Admiral Takahashi

Sankichi predicting that a "problem" between Japan and the United States would arise, at the latest, once the Americans took charge of British interests, after German U-boats defeated that nation. "Japan's navy . . . is fully prepared for any eventuality," Takahashi intoned, "Our navy is convinced it cannot be defeated by a navy of any other nation." A couple of weeks later an attaché report quoted another former admiral to the effect that naval action in a U.S. war would "culminate" in attacks on the Philippines, Hawaii, San Francisco, and Panama. Though it represented mere whistling in the wind, this was suggestive. Even more alarming, given what we know in retrospect about where and how the Japanese trained their air groups in the summer of 1941, was a July 10 dispatch in which Smith-Hutton noted that the Imperial Navy would begin maneuvers in the Ariake Bay area in August featuring destroyer and aircraft torpedo attacks against capital ships. Through the fall there were attaché reports of the naval buildup in the Mandates, and in November a series of dispatches warned of a Japanese invasion of Thailand, with a move against the Philippines if the United States intervened. Japan might also risk war, the dispatch specified, if negotiations with Washington faltered.

"In this event attack southward may develop suddenly with little or no advance notice possible from this office, since preparations have been underway since July and are undoubtedly complete."

That Tokyo attaché dispatch carried a November 17 dateline. American attachés in Japan clearly did a far better job than they have ever been given credit for.

The Americans' closest source, far more intimate than our naval attaché was with secret Japanese deliberations, remained codebreaking. Not the breaking of naval codes, this time, though they shall be discussed in due course, but that of Japanese diplomatic codes. Americans had long worked to break the encipherment systems used by Japan's Foreign Ministry, and there came a time when OP-20-G's Lieutenant Jack Holtwick succeeded in devising a machine that could strip the ciphers off messages the Japanese sent using their first mechanism of this type, the so-called A Machine, which Americans knew as Red. In 1939 the Japanese switched most of their diplomatic cable traffic to a new system designed by the same expert, even more complex, which they called the B Machine, and which the Americans called Purple. In a remarkable codebreaking success Washington managed to solve the Purple system, constructing analogue machines that could be used to decipher the messages Tokyo sent using this mechanism. Ever since then historians have debated whether Washington should have known about Pearl Harbor because it was reading the Japanese diplomatic messages.

A word on the achievement is appropriate before we press ahead. The break into Purple is especially remarkable both because the B Machine was highly sophisticated—much more sophisticated than the Germans'

Enigma—and because the code was solved entirely by mathematical analysis. The B Machine used six-level, twenty-five-point stepping switches, of a type then common in telephone exchanges, where the Enigma utilized rotors. The electrical principles upon which the Japanese relied were inherently more flexible than the mechanical ones in Enigma. Moreover, the British analysts who solved Enigma had the benefit of previous important breakthroughs by French and Polish experts and could even examine early versions of the machine, commercially available. Americans solved Purple all by themselves.

This is not to say the solution occurred in a vacuum, however. It was OP-20-G that had solved Red, predecessor to the new diplomatic system, and Commander Safford recognized that his organization needed outside help on Purple. He went to his Army counterpart, the Signal Intelligence Service (SIS), which formed part of the Signal Corps; there, senior cryptanalyst William F. Friedman was an expert on machine-based encipherment systems. Under Friedman, chief of the team attacking the B Machine would be Frank B. Rowlett. Other SIS cryptanalysts, an electronics engineer, accounting-machine experts, and Japanese linguists formed the rest of the group. Friedman, too often given credit as the man who "broke" Purple, made only sporadic contributions amid other duties. His main role came in selecting members of Rowlett's team, with an assist on diagnosis and analysis of the system. Robert O. Ferner was Rowlett's second, with cryptanalysts Genevieve Grotjan, Albert W. Small, and Samuel S. Snyder plus cryptographic specialists Glenn S. Landig, Kenneth D. Miller, and Cyrus C. Sturgis, Jr. The top Japanese linguist was John B. Hurt, a Virginian like Rowlett himself.

Work proceeded over a period of about eighteen months. The SIS effort received support from the Army's chief signal officer, General Joseph O. Mauborgne, who liked to call the cryptanalysts his "magicians" and eventually called their product Magic. However, the Army lacked funds and resources for the attack on Purple, so at Safford's initiative the Navy underwrote the cost, OP-20-G absorbed some routine SIS work to free Rowlett's team for the main task, and the Army was also provided interception services along with a copy of the Red machine as reconstructed by Lieutenant Holtwick, which helped reveal the methods of its Japanese inventor, Imperial Navy Captain Ito Jinsaburo.

The B Machine's operating principles had to be reconstructed entirely by brainpower. In the popular literature, junior cryptanalyst Harry L. Clark is seen as the first to suggest the Purple machine might use electrical switches rather than rotors, but it was Genevieve Grotjan who made the first of a series of mathematical associations which demonstrated that this was the case. The team gathered around, found another proof, then celebrated: Rowlett ordered Cokes for everyone!

After that, breaking Purple became a process of trial and error, but one that proceeded along well-understood lines in a group of about eight offices clustered around Room 3416 of the Munitions Building, Rowlett's office. Recent recruit Leo Rosten built the machine and first hit on the idea of using stepping switches. Total cost came to $684.85, even after ransacking Washington hardware and electrical-supply stores for dozens of the stepping switches. Later copies of the Purple analogue machine were manufactured under supervision of Commander D. W. Seiler at the Naval Code and Signal Laboratory in the Washington Navy Yard. Like the initial break-in, construction would be funded by the Navy's Bureau of Ships. At OP-20-G young Lieutenant Francis A. Raven made another vital contribution by recognizing the method the Japanese used to compile the daily key used with the machine. Subsequent recovery of keys became much easier, and soon Washington was handling fifty to seventy-five Japanese messages a day in the Purple cipher. Of course Washington continued to read messages in the Red cipher and in certain other minor Japanese systems like the PA Code. Many thousands of these messages would be decoded before December 7, 1941, with Purple decrypts beginning to flow in September 1940. To handle the volume, the Army and Navy alternated days when each would be responsible for decryption, translation, and circulation of the day's messages to a restricted list of key officials.

With the privilege of reading Tokyo's mail, as it were, should not Washington have known about Pearl Harbor? The simple answer has to be no. The Japanese diplomats did not know their own military plans. Some Japanese messages—for example, one that required Ambassadors Nomura and Kurusu to deliver the final ultimatum at a certain precise time—contained hints of military action, but only if successfully interpreted. The threat to Pearl Harbor was submerged within much more obvious signs of Japan on the march across the Pacific as a whole, particularly Southeast Asia.

Although we do not intend any extended discussion of the diplomatic cables, a few require special comment. One is the so-called "bomb plot" cable, in the minor PA Code, sent to Honolulu for Ensign Yoshikawa in late September. The cable was actually an instruction from *joho kyoku* to report U.S. ships at Pearl Harbor by their specific anchorages. In consequence, Yoshikawa created a grid system which he then used as the basis for periodic ship-movement reports. Critics have charged that Washington slept in failing to appreciate that the cable portended a specific threat of attack. In fact, the cable was intercepted but not completely deciphered and translated until eight days later, about the average for this minor code which (paradoxically) put more strain on limited American cryptanalytic resources than the machine-based Purple. When finally broken out, the messages had no special impact in Washington, but Pacific Fleet intelligence officer Edwin

T. Layton believes they would have rung alarm bells on Oahu, especially in conjunction with others linking Hawaii and Captain Ogawa, who desired a special courier mission to that place.

The basic problem remained policy, however, not intelligence. It is hardly surprising that, given limited resources, senior officials gave priority to the high-level diplomatic cables. A corollary intelligence policy, however, assigned the radio intelligence unit at Pearl Harbor to work exclusively on the Imperial Navy's Admirals' Code rather than have any role in deciphering diplomatic codes or the more widely used JN-25. Layton's logical solution would have employed the Pearl Harbor unit on at least some of the relevant traffic, like that to the consul at Honolulu. But such decentralization, however desirable in theory, would have been no guarantee of superior performance. For example, had the bomb-plot messages been deciphered in Pearl Harbor and not Washington, the Pacific command might have found it difficult to get the capital, preoccupied with supposedly larger concerns, to take the local intelligence seriously.

According to postwar testimony the chiefs of ONI—including its boss, Rear Admiral Alan G. Kirk; its chief of foreign intelligence, Captain Howard D. Bode; and OP-20-G's Commander Safford—all wanted to tell Pearl Harbor about the bomb-plot cables. Safford even drafted a message to that effect, instructing the Pacific fleet radio unit to begin decrypting local consular traffic. The move was quashed by Rear Admiral Leigh Noyes, the director of naval communications, who held top responsibility for radio intelligence, on the grounds that he did not want to tell area commanders how to do their jobs. At this point Admiral Kirk was replaced as chief of ONI by Rear Admiral Theodore S. Wilkinson, who became the third director of naval intelligence in that one year.

"Ping" Wilkinson had been chief of staff to the Hawaiian command before the fleet moved there, then captain of battleship *Mississippi*, but he had no particular intelligence experience. Wilkinson let ride Noyes's decision to make no bomb-plot warning. A brilliant officer—first in his graduating class at Annapolis in 1909—Ping was at least sensitive to Washington's reluctance to provide Pacific commander Kimmel with proper intelligence support. When the Japanese began transmission of the infamous fourteen-part message that became their de facto declaration of war, Wilkinson urged the chief of naval operations to telephone a warning to Pearl Harbor. The CNO refused. A cable warning sent later by the Army was delayed by fate, delayed further in decoding by lack of any priority precedence, and would be passed on to naval authorities only many hours after the attack.

Messages concerning destruction of Japanese codes and related equipment (such as their Red and Purple machines) also deserve comment. It was the instruction to destroy the last set of equipment that furnished the formal basis for the Army warning dispatch just mentioned. Actually the Japanese had sent preliminary orders regarding codes as early as December 1, when Washington learned that the London embassy and the consulates at Manila, Singapore, and Hong Kong had been told to destroy their cipher machines. The next day the Japanese embassy in Washington would be directed to burn all codes but two, destroy other secret papers at discretion, and preserve just one cipher machine until further notice. These actions to preserve the security of secret communications were a clear indication that Japan anticipated imminent hostilities.

At least some in Washington appreciated this indication for the war warning it was. Commander Safford and Commander McCollum each drafted messages informing Philippine commanders of the Japanese actions. Both messages were sent within five minutes of each other in the evening of December 3. Safford also ordered the radio intelligence monitoring station on Guam to destroy all but currently essential materials. That order would be cleared through the assistant chief of naval operations late on December 4. At the Army's SIS, Frank Rowlett always remembered the scene when the Japanese message about destruction of codes was translated that Wednesday. Working on the cable had been the Army's job since SIS had the responsibility on its date of origin. Colonel Otis K. Sadtler, chief of the operations branch of the Signal Corps, who acted as supervisor over SIS, immediately went to their offices to discuss the message with Friedman, whom he could not find, so he talked to Rowlett. The latter had just come back from meeting with OP-20-G cryptanalysts and was in the middle of reading the cable when Sadtler burst in and wanted to know what it meant. Sadtler seemed desperate, waving his copy in the air, but Rowlett waved his own copy back and said he had just been reading the thing for the first time. Sadtler asked if the Japanese had ever done anything like this in the past. Rowlett knew they had not, and explained Tokyo's usual procedures for introducing codes: in an orderly fashion, usually on the first day of the month, never ordering mass destruction like this. Sadtler's eyes flashed and he straightened to his full height. He was last seen literally running down the hall toward the offices of Army G-2 intelligence chief General Sherman Miles. The Army's War Plans Department, however, considered warning messages it had already sent Hawaii sufficient and did nothing further. Unfortunately those November warnings had been interpreted as instructions to guard against sabotage rather than direct attack.

Another controversy would later erupt regarding the so-called Winds code, which also concerned Japanese instructions to destroy codes and ciphers. The Winds code is an example of what is termed an open code—a prearranged signal (whether by words or any other sign) that conveys specific meaning unknown to all but those privy to it. Thus an open-code message can be sent without any special protection or enciphering. The Winds code was designed precisely this way: Innocuous phrases were to be inserted

into regular weather reports sent by Radio Tokyo indicating whether diplomatic relations were in danger. The Winds code provided for problems not
only with the United States, but also with England or Russia. Two Tokyo
cables on November 19, the so-called Winds setup messages, established
that such signals might be sent and the phrases of the open code. These were
*higashi no kaze ame* ("east wind, rain"), meaning "danger in Japan-U.S. relations"; *kita no kaze kumori* ("north wind, cloudy"), meaning "Japan-Russia
relations in danger"; and *nishi no kaze hare* ("west wind, clear"), meaning
"Japan-Britain relations in danger." Upon receiving one of these messages,
embassies and consulates affected were to burn documents and destroy
their last codes and cipher equipment.

So far, so good, but the controversy lies in whether any of the enumerated
phrases was ever broadcast and if so, which one or ones. Such a broadcast
would have been the "Winds Execute." During some of the early Pearl
Harbor investigations Commander Safford professed not to remember anything about a Winds Execute, but reversed himself before a joint congres-
sional committee sitting in 1945–1946, maintaining ever after that Tokyo
had sent such a message on December 4 and that it had been intercepted by
the OP-20-G radio monitoring station at Cheltenham, Maryland. Safford
also reported that he had seen the message and discussed it with translation
section chief Alwyn D. Kramer. He noted much the same information in
1943, when he wrote a history of radio intelligence, and in several 1945
memoranda for Pearl Harbor investigators.

Commander Kramer did not recall any Winds Execute message pertinent
to the United States, though he did remember one pertaining to the British
and a false alarm from another Tokyo broadcast. Ralph T. Briggs, then a
chief watch supervisor at OP-20-G's Cheltenham listening post, recalled in
a 1977 oral history that he himself had been the one who recorded the
Winds Execute. Expecting word of a diplomatic break with Great Britain
("west wind, clear"), Briggs found he had received "east wind, rain." It was
late on December 4 when he logged the message and got instructions to put
it on the teleprinter line to OP-20-G head offices at the Navy Department. As
was his custom, Briggs signed the log "RT," which stood for "Right Tender"
or "Rough and Tough" (take your pick, says Briggs), added the frequency of
reception, the key words of the message, the time, and a notation that the
entry referred to Winds Execute.

From there on out the trail becomes very rocky indeed. Lieutenant (junior
grade) George W. Linn, assistant to Safford in Washington, remembers
reception on December 4 of a *false* Winds Execute, not a real one. No original or any of the copies of the alleged Winds Execute for December 4 could
be found, and other testimony was hearsay. For example, William F.
Friedman testified that he had heard Colonel Sadtler speak of a Winds
Execute received on December 4 or 5 but never saw the message, and SIS

proved unable to get any formal confirmation from the director of naval communications.

In addition to Ralph Briggs, several On-the-Roof Gang radio operators from OP-20-G's tightly knit prewar organization have commented on their own experience at Cheltenham or the "east wind, rain" controversy. Kenneth A. Mann, an operator at Cheltenham until August 1942, says, "The only thing I know was there [was] something said about a message sent from Cheltenham to the Navy Department." But Mann heard that the message merely concerned orders to merchant vessels to head for neutral waters. Robert L. Dormer worked at Cheltenham until June 1942; his interview passed over this critical period. Jacob J. Mandel knew Briggs but worked other circuits and never had much to do with him. As for "east wind, rain," "there was something way over my head." On the other hand, a rumor current at Cheltenham was that after receipt of the infamous (alleged) message, Commander Safford came out to the station to present a bouquet of roses.

Another possible path to confirmation lies through the Netherlands East Indies. In Batavia, the Dutch had a radio intercept unit called "Kamer 14," a decoding operation much like OP-20-G. On December 4 Dutch general Hein ter Poorten passed to his American liaison officer, Colonel Elliott R. Thorpe, the gist of a message the Dutch had broken in a minor code Washington knew as J-19. This message *set up* an open code using the Winds phrases that would signal the moment to begin hostilities in the Far East. Thorpe and the local U.S. naval attaché had to pound at the door of the central post office late at night to get someone to transmit their cable to Washington. Consul General Walter Foote sent the State Department the same information in his Batavia Message Number 220. Commander Safford notes that these warnings corresponded to the Winds system OP-20-G had discovered in late November intercepts. The Dutch did not claim to have received any Winds Execute message, however. Significantly, the *only* Winds Execute that several observers agree on, *and* the only one the Japanese admit to having sent, was "west wind, clear," and it coincided with the Pearl Harbor attack on December 7—a form that corresponds to the notion of using the Winds as a signal for hostile action.*

British codebreakers were also active in the Far East, and they too had an inkling of what portended, also apparently based on the "Winds setup" mes-

---

*Although no Japanese authority officially admits *sending* "east wind, rain," attaché Sanematsu Yuzuru has written that he *received* that message. In a book about his service as assistant naval attaché in Washington in the last year before the war, Commander Sanematsu noted that on the afternoon of December 4 his chief radioman entered the office shouting "The Wind blew!" Sanematsu and the petty officer went into the radio room in time to hear, several times, "Higashi no kaze ame." In August 1982 John

sages. The British apparatus, at this time based at Singapore, was known as the Far East Combined Bureau (FECB), an offshoot of the innocuous-sounding Government Code and Communications School, to whose Far East desk FECB reported. Admittedly the British codebreakers focused most closely on the threats closest to home, the Germans and Italians, but they had long been interested in Japan too. The British Army led in this respect, training some 130 Japanese-language officers between 1903 and 1937. The Royal Navy, though it had had an active alliance with Japan, proved much less active, with certain admirals arguing that language training ruined their officers and that the Japanese would learn to speak English. In the 1920s there were barely a dozen British naval officers fluent in Japanese. The Japanese section at the Government Code and Communications School had just two linguists plus a naval liaison officer.

As tensions rose in the Far East, the Government Code and Communications School made some effort to improve capabilities in this area. Experienced linguist-cryptanalysts were seconded from Dominion navies—Lieutenant Eric Nave, for instance, came from the Australian. At home the codebreaking unit hired four Japanese linguists, three of whom were former British Army language officers. One of them, Captain Malcolm Kennedy, had already written extensively on Japan, including two books on the Japanese Army, acquiring a reputation as a Japanese expert. British ability to intercept Japanese communications rested upon monitoring stations at Singapore and, after 1936, in Hong Kong as well.

The British continued plugging away, becoming more intimate with American codebreakers as the Western democracies grew closer in the face of the dictators. Working out of Hong Kong from 1935 on, the FECB had an ideal vantage point to view Japanese activities in China. Even later, when the British codebreakers moved their center to Singapore, radio monitoring from Hong Kong continued to be important. In 1940, with the British fighting desperately in Europe, Prime Minister Winston Churchill arranged with FDR to trade bases in the Western Hemisphere for old American destroyers. That fall planning for cooperation extended to intelligence matters. An October 25 memorandum within OP-20-G designated an extensive list of restricted publications for immediate transfer to some (deleted) entity which most probably was the FECB. The list included information on Japanese communications and naval ciphers along with copies of the Japanese mer-

---

Toland interviewed Sanematsu concerning this assertion, and the former Imperial Navy officer confirmed it. Questioned about the discrepancy between Ralph Briggs's recollection of receiving the broadcast in the morning, and his own claim of an afternoon time, Sanematsu speculated that Tokyo might have broadcast such an important message several times. Toland reports this material in the postscript to the paperback edition of his book *Infamy* (pp. 346–47).

chant ship and Blue naval codes and a partial solution for the administrative cipher. The British at Singapore and the Americans in the Philippines exchanged liaison officers, and the countries increasingly shared code information as well. In early 1941, the United States sent Britain a Purple decrypting device while the British reciprocated with one of their versions of the German Enigma machine.

In sum, by 1941 the British as well as the Americans were at work on the Japanese diplomatic codes, which is relevant to the Winds mystery. Like Washington, the British received and broke the Winds setup messages. In addition, Commander W. W. Mortimer of FECB assembled a global picture of Japanese merchant shipping moves which showed these vessels returning to Empire waters at a rapid rate. Captain Malcolm Burnett, chief of the Code and Communications School's Far East section, reportedly put together some kind of warning he was sure would get through to Washington, and after Pearl Harbor was furious because the Americans had been surprised anyway. On the other hand, later in the war Burnett worked in Pearl Harbor with American code expert Thomas Dyer and never made the least claim to have known about the attack in advance. Similarly, on the day of the attack itself, Malcolm Kennedy, the senior Japanese linguist at the Government Code and Communications School, scribbled in his diary: "The news on the 9 p.m. wireless that Japan had opened hostilities with an air raid on Pearl Harbor . . . came as a complete surprise."

By this time Eric Nave, the Australian officer who had long figured among the school's Japan experts, was back home helping create an Australian radio intelligence organization. He recalls that the Australians decrypted the Winds setup cables *and* received the open code phrase "east wind, rain." The authors additionally claim that the British and Australians were reading the new JN-25(b) and had specific evidence that the Nagumo force was bound for Pearl Harbor with the mission of attacking that place.

This seems fanciful. The claim apparently confuses the initial and "b" versions of JN-25, while Nave was no longer engaged in naval cryptanalysis at this time. Moreover, the Japanese directive cited as specific evidence was hand-carried to Nagumo while messages said to be relevant intercepts are no more than general broadcast dispatches from the Combined Fleet. Kido Butai appears as an addressee in only some of the messages; this is not tantamount to the Nagumo force itself *breaking* radio silence, which the Japanese have always maintained it did not do.

One further indication lies in a 1945 internal study of British naval intelligence, recently released in British archives and found by historian Anthony Best. The study agrees almost precisely with U.S. radio traffic analysis data that, as of December 1, four of the Japanese aircraft carriers were in Taiwan, four more in Empire waters, and the last two in the Mandates.

Like the Americans, the British focused on the threat they understood: the threat to Singapore. They detected assembly of invasion convoys, even sighting these at sea. Gerald Wilkinson, British liaison in Manila, as early as December 2 warned the Philippine command (and cabled Hawaii) concerning Japanese forces moving from Indochina. In Washington, OP-20-G was following the same movements.

RADIO—ANY RADIO USE—WOULD INDEED HAVE BEEN A KEY TIPOFF IF TRANSMISSIONS FROM Admiral Nagumo's task force had been intercepted as it approached Pearl Harbor. Chief of staff Kusaka noted that the radios of ships in the task force had been sealed and sailors ordered to stay away from the equipment. An official Japanese appreciation of the operation later reported that measures had gone as far as the removal of fuses from the transmitter circuits or the detaching and storing of keying equipment. Other sources report placing paper slips in keying mechanisms to prevent the electrical contacts used to generate Morse code signals. Pilots agreed not to break radio silence even to report emergencies with their aircraft, according to Genda. Fuchida sums up: "The fleet observed strict radio silence, but concentrated on listening for broadcasts from Tokyo or Honolulu."

Despite such disclaimers from the Japanese, there were Americans convinced they had observed something out there in the Pacific, perhaps the Kido Butai. Possibly the most controversial of these claims would be reported by John Toland for the first time in 1982, when he published his study *Infamy: Pearl Harbor and Its Aftermath*. Toland uncovered a "Seaman Z" who had worked for ONI's district intelligence officer in San Francisco and had plotted signals north of Hawaii beginning December 2, 1941. This individual, later identified as Robert G. Ogg, was an electrical engineer who had left school earlier that year after volunteering to work with the Navy. His main job was to support ONI counterintelligence operations in the San Francisco area, installing wiretaps and arranging for other types of monitoring. He was brought into the Pearl Harbor business by his immediate superior, who knew Ogg to be an experienced navigator and who had received from RCA and other communication companies news of strange, unexpected signals. Ogg plotted them and found their initial position in the northern Pacific just east of the international date line. Ogg recalls that the bearings he plotted were strictly from commercial receivers, one in San Francisco, the other somewhere further south in California. He remembers receiving four different sets of bearings, usually one a day but perhaps two on one day. There were no indications of the validity or quality of the signals recorded. Ogg had no specific knowledge that the signals emanated from Japanese warships.

John Toland also noted a second source, the Matson Lines steamship

*Lurline,* that claimed to have plotted bearings on radio transmissions in the northern Pacific. This report, first cited in a 1969 account by British historian A. J. Barker, then repeated in a 1981 history of Matson Lines, was supplemented by Toland, who quoted the diary of *Lurline*'s communications officer, Leslie E. Grogan. In all his thirty years at sea, Grogan recorded, he had never seen such a transmission pattern, and opined that it must have been Japan's mobilization order. *Lurline* tracked a low-power retransmission of a Yokohama signal for several days, plotting the bearings as to the north and west of their own position on the sea-lanes. Coast Guard authorities (*not,* as previously reported, naval ones) impounded *Lurline*'s logs for this period when she docked at San Francisco on December 10.

Finally Toland reports a note made on December 6 by Robert E. Israel, an infantry company commander at Dutch Harbor, where OP-20-G had one of its radio direction-finding stations. Israel noted that at 1:05 A.M. that day the Navy placed Japanese ships at a point 270 miles southeast of Dutch Harbor. Toland was not able to secure any other confirmation of this report. Plotting a 270-mile-radius circle around Dutch Harbor shows no Japanese task force within the area; in fact, distance measurements from the Nagumo force to Dutch Harbor show the Japanese positions on December 2 and 3 each to be a little more than 700 nautical miles. By December 6 the distance had lengthened appreciably.

It is nevertheless correct that there *was* an OP-20-G station at Dutch Harbor whose personnel were hard at work during this period. We have recollections from several of the On-the-Roof Gang operators stationed there in December 1941. About two weeks before Pearl Harbor, Thomas A. Gilmore remembers, the station received a dispatch from its network control center in Hawaii which set priorities for the Combined Fleet frequencies it was to guard. Carriers were a high priority. Gilmore would always recall this message because of the inauspicious words at the front and back of the text, meaningless words called "fillers" and used to confuse potential adversary codebreakers, which Pearl Harbor selected for this dispatch. They were "conquest" and "insidious." Tom Gilmore says quite frankly: "During that two-week period . . . not one of us ever heard a word on those carrier frequencies."

Frank W. Hess also remembers the disturbing fillers Pearl Harbor used on its assignment order. He recalls that most of the bearings received at Dutch Harbor during these last weeks before the war were on the western side of Hawaii. Once hostilities commenced they tracked Japanese submarines between Alaska and the U.S. West Coast, but "it was quite slack just before the war."

Still, everyone knew what was coming. "We were aware from the assignments we got and the political situation at the time," Tom Gilmore says, "that we were close to something that was going to happen."

There was another Navy direction-finding station in Alaska as well. That was at Sitka, near Juneau. Elmer H. Frantz was one of the radiomen there, and he felt something *should* have been intercepted: "All my experience with Orange [Japanese] communications . . . would lead me to believe that while their security was good, there was a preponderance of evidence to show that it was never that tight. It is inconceivable to me that a force represented by the *Kido Butai* with 33 ships involved of all different types . . . and no radio communications, communications black out on orders—I just don't believe it!" But Sitka's assignment was to monitor Japanese merchant ship traffic, and although it had a low-frequency direction-finder, that equipment was rarely used except for training routines. This, Frantz believed, was unfortunate, because radio-wave propagation from south to north seemed especially good, leaving Sitka well positioned for interception: "That area up there had its own environment as far as reception was concerned. There were times during the night when, I think, if anybody rubbed two pieces of wire together out there in the middle of the Pacific we would hear it."

Frantz had had the late evening–early morning watch the night before the Pearl Harbor attack. He had come off watch, had breakfast, and settled down to sleep. Suddenly someone shook him awake.

"Get awake, they have just hit Pearl Harbor!"

"Hit Pearl Harbor?" Frantz sputtered. "They couldn't, I had the mid-watch!"

ORDERS FOR AMERICAN RADIO MONITORING POSTS IN THE MID-PACIFIC WERE COMING FROM the very place that had been the object of so much attention, Pearl Harbor. There was located Station Hypo, in the basement of the 14th Naval District headquarters building. Station Hypo functioned as a major provider of intelligence information to Admiral Kimmel and his fleet intelligence officer, Edwin T. Layton. Actually Hypo evolved from a much different operation— a simple direction-finding unit that existed at Heiia. Then-Lieutenant Thomas H. Dyer added a codebreaking capability to Hypo while stationed at Pearl Harbor with the Hawaiian detachment of the U.S. Fleet. At the beginning Dyer alone *was* Hypo; it had none of the omniscience attributed to it later. That began in 1936. By 1938 Dyer had branched off from Heiia to found a processing office at Pearl, with both intercept and direction-finding stations, at Heiia and Wahiawa. Nominally part of the 14th Naval District command, Station Hypo actually functioned under orders from OP-20-G, which established the division of labor for U.S. communication intelligence units worldwide.

While the dedicated Dyer struggled with his infant, the future dynamo of Station Hypo, Commander Joseph J. Rochefort, had been away from communications intelligence duty, serving with the fleet. Becoming a Japanese-language officer between 1929 and 1932, and then serving with OP-20-G for just a few months before being ordered to the staff of the battle force, U.S. Fleet aboard the battleship *California*, Rochefort then did a tour on the staff of the commander, U.S. Fleet, and one as district intelligence officer in San Diego. In each of these billets he had intelligence duties but not in his primary specialty. From 1937 to the fall of 1939 Rochefort would be assigned as navigator of the treaty cruiser *New Orleans*. After that he went to the cruiser *Indianapolis* on the staff of the commander, scouting force, U.S. Fleet, who also commanded the Hawaiian Detachment, a unit of two aircraft carriers, perhaps a dozen heavy cruisers, and appropriate escort vessels. The forty-three-year-old Ohioan, who had made officer through the Navy's enlisted ranks just after World War I, heard in April 1941 that he would be transferred to head Station Hypo.

In the meantime Tom Dyer labored on at Hypo, where he had been superseded in command by Lieutenant Commander Thomas B. Birtley, Jr., a former head of OP-20-G's translation section. Birtley and Lieutenant Ransom Fullinwider were at that time the only Japanese-language officers with the combat intelligence unit. This proved especially vexing since OP-20-G had adopted a policy of assigning major work on the Imperial Navy's Admirals' Code to Hypo, while Station Cast at Cavite along with OP-20-G itself led the attack on JN-25(b). Pearl Harbor had jurisdiction over the Japanese administrative code, while Washington led on solutions for Imperial Navy merchant ship, materials, and intelligence codes. Although Pearl Harbor's share in the breaking of the Japanese ciphers had been restricted, its need for the intelligence they contained continued to be enormous. Eddie Layton firmly believed that Kimmel's Pacific Fleet command had been short-changed on the intelligence it received, and many would agree with him. At the same time, the Japanese themselves were having trouble with the cumbersome Admirals' cipher, which their own radiomen found difficult to use, and increasingly made sole use of JN-25(b), a novel form of the original JN-25 which the Imperial Navy had put into effect in December 1940, obviating previous OP-20-G success with that code. In 1941 the JN-25(b) cipher continued to resist efforts to break into it. Station Hypo's assistance could have been useful had it been brought into the attack. It was not.

Commander Rochefort took over a station that had twenty-nine intercept operators and perhaps twenty direction-finding specialists. One of his first actions was to change the organization's formal name to "Combat Intelligence Unit" (CIU). As it expanded the CIU moved to air-conditioned offices in the basement at the Diamond Head (southeast) end of the 14th Naval District headquarters building. By June the CIU had just under eighty persons involved in interception or direction finding and about twenty in its processing and codebreaking element. Rochefort transferred Hypo from a peacetime routine to an eight-day week in which his people would each work six days, then have two off. With eight shifts, Hypo began to run around the clock, being completely closed only on July 4, Labor Day, and Thanksgiving. On September 4 the Navy increased enlisted billets provided for the CIU to a hundred yeomen at Pearl Harbor plus ninety-two radiomen and two yeomen for intercept and other activities.

As Rochefort took over Hypo, Commander Safford gave him to understand he could have anyone he wanted. He made sure Tom Dyer stayed on, and supplemented him with Lieutenant Wesley A. (Ham) Wright. His language officers were good, but Rochefort pressed for more, though he did not get them just yet. Materials were also slow in arriving, due to the growing demands of Lend-Lease for Europe. Intercepts still had to be physically carried by bicycle, motorcycle, or jeep from the outstations down to the district office, rather than flashed by teletype. "This was just lousy," Rochefort observed. "It's like having a million-dollar organization with a ten-cent-store communication system."

Without access to JN-25 data, the best Station Hypo could do was with the "externals" of messages—addresses and call signs and the like—and with direction finding. Here the Japanese outfoxed the Americans with radio silence, and by changing all their call signs on December 1. The 14th Naval District daily reports on Japanese fleet movements show a pattern of increasing inaccuracy as Japan deployed for war. For example, the Japanese carriers staged at Hitokappu Bay; various heavy cruisers moved to Palau or Taiwan; and two battleships and other heavy cruisers sailed to support the Malaya invasion and Philippines expeditionary forces. Yet during early November summaries placed the Japanese aircraft carriers in southern Kyushu, and by November 24 the summary reported no definite information on the carriers at all. This situation continued, although apparently the presence of an Imperial Navy destroyer unit usually associated with one of the carrier divisions led to statements that at least one of the Japanese carrier units had been located in the Mandates.

Station Hypo did rather better on other Japanese fleet units, reporting on November 24 that the big task force the Japanese were forming under Admiral Kondo Nobutake had been linked in messages with Taiwan and French Indochina, as well as south China. Subsequent reports referred to these concentrations as well as to assembly and movement of a large convoy from Shanghai to Camranh Bay and then to sea, where British aircraft from Malaya spotted it on December 5. These reports mirrored ONI's daily summaries.

Meanwhile no one knew about the Japanese aircraft carriers. The 14th District logs contained references to carrier units or the carrier force commander on November 25, 27, and 30, but then Heiia chronologies admit not knowing about the carriers on December 2, and speculating about them still being in Empire waters that day and the next. No doubt the actual presence of one Japanese carrier, *Ryujo*, at Palau helped confuse American monitors. So deep was the mystery that it bothered everyone in the Pacific Fleet command, not least fleet intelligence officer Commander Layton and commander in chief Admiral Husband E. Kimmel.

"Do you mean to say," Kimmel asked Layton on December 2, "they could be rounding Diamond Head and you wouldn't know it?"

"I hope they would have been spotted before now," Layton lamely answered.

At Station Hypo Rochefort's best traffic analysts disputed the meaning of the lack of information. Lieutenant Thomas A. Huckins agreed with Rochefort and Layton that the disappearance of the carrier call signs meant the ships were tied up in Japanese ports awaiting orders. Lieutenant John A. Williams argued that the lack of traffic meant the Japanese had adopted radio silence and something was up. It was certainly true that that summer, when Japan had moved into southern Indochina, a lack of carrier call signs had indeed meant those warships were operating under radio silence. They had subsequently turned up in Indochinese waters. No one could tell in December, unless perhaps the Japanese carriers turned up off Diamond Head, as indeed they were practically to do.

One officer who was sure was a Marine language officer, Bankston T. Holcomb, then at Pearl Harbor after many years in Japan and China. Holcomb had seen the Japanese at their air-raid drills, virtually every day; he had seen them rationing gasoline; he was certain the Japanese were coming—and, he told friends, "it wouldn't be a surprise to me if they attacked us." Holcomb's friends just laughed at him. Early on the morning of December 7, the Japanese came. "I think I was the only one who had a smile on his face that Sunday morning," Holcomb recalls.

At Station Hypo, Lieutenant Ham Wright had the morning watch, seconded by Williams, the traffic expert who had been sure the Imperial Navy was up to something. Suddenly pandemonium outside interrupted the careful concentration of the men in the combat intelligence unit. Ham Wright sent John Williams upstairs to see what was happening. Williams returned. There was no smile on his face. He flatly declared, "They're Japanese aircraft and they're attacking Pearl Harbor."

# Air Raid, Pearl Harbor

Seaman Kuramoto Iki thought ten years' arduous training and many hardships were coming down to one day. A lookout aboard *Akagi*, Kuramoto had learned from Lieutenant Commander Yano, the ship's assistant navigator, that the carrier was to make a surprise attack on Hawaii. Kuramoto felt buoyed by the idea that the task force would strike the first blow in the greatest of all wars, but still there were rough days—the ship's flag had been carried away and men blown overboard. Kuramoto thought himself and everyone around him exhausted by continuous watches, night and day battle practice, and "the silent struggle with nature." Raging seas and gales on the way out from Japan alternated with calm days when the ships refueled. Captain Hasegawa Kiichi spoke to the crew over the loudspeaker system a few days before the secret "X-Day," and announced that Admiral Yamamoto had been summoned by the Emperor to be told war would have to be declared against America. Hasegawa made it official: *Akagi* would attack Pearl Harbor.

"Behind us there were a hundred million people," Kuramoto wrote, "who had limitless faith in us. Imagine the joy of those people when we should successfully carry out this operation."

On December 5 Japanese oilers gave Nagumo's screen ships one last refueling. The task force then went to battle speed, 24 knots. A submarine reconnaissance message on December 6 confirmed American ships were not using the alternate anchorage at Lahaina Roads. That evening the staff had a final conference to go over the plan and the latest intelligence reports with Commander Fuchida. Ensign Yoshikawa's last reports came through that night, repeated by *joho kyoku*, and the pilots would find the intelligence posted on blackboards when they reported for preflight briefings the next morning. There were differences over whether to expect U.S. aircraft carriers to be in harbor. Admiral Kusaka thought not, and he turned out to be right. Air staff officer Genda hoped there would be some, but he would be disappointed. Senior staff officer Oishi was willing to settle for battleships. Lieutenant Commander Ono Kenjiro restricted himself to outlining American operating routines. Admiral Nagumo Chuichi made the final decision to proceed.

Already, shortly before noontime that day (Hawaii time), the Kido Butai had come around to a due south heading and increased to their full speed of 26 knots. On the carriers' flight decks, Japanese aircraft were lined up and mechanics were giving them thorough checks. The pilots, each in his own way, had begun preparing for their first combat mission against America. Some meditated, some visited Shinto shrines aboard the ships, others drank beer or sake. Slowly they gravitated toward the ready rooms. Aboard *Akagi* the ship's air officer, Commander Masuda Shogo, checked with Fuchida about postponing the takeoff time since seas were heavy and the flight decks were rolling and pitching. Fuchida, judging that takeoffs could be timed to coincide with the pitch, refused any postponement; this was not training anymore.

The pilots began to man their planes. A mechanic handed Commander Fuchida a *hachimaki*, a good-luck talisman in the form of a headband. He tied it around his flight cap as he stepped up to his attack plane. In the dark a green lamp waved in a circle, the signal from the flight deck officer to take off. Planes began to roll. The scene was repeated on each of the other carriers as, within fifteen minutes, 183 fighters, bombers, and torpedo planes launched for the first wave.

Deckbound sailors were thrilled at the spectacle of the aerial armada forming up overhead. Stoker Omata Sadao, aboard *Soryu*, was a farmer's son and had never expected to be in such a place. Omata thought his ship "the treasure of the Japanese navy," and felt at that moment his country had to be invincible. He could hear the shouts of "Banzai!" through the blowers as the deck crew cheered each plane. On *Akagi*, Captain Hasegawa Kiichi had put it quite simply to the pilots: "All right, all the plans are made, let's get going!" On *Kaga*, Seaman Yokota felt "a little fright" when, simultaneously with the takeoffs, the men were informed of the imperial rescript declaring war, but "as a Japanese," Yokota "took war for granted." On *Akagi*, Seaman Kuramoto felt inspired: "Our sea eagles, with the drone of their engines resounding across the heavens like a triumphal song, turned their course toward Pearl Harbor on the island of Oahu and set forth on their splendid enterprise."

By then it was 6:15 A.M. Commander Fuchida had forty-nine level bombers under his direct commend. Below, to his right, were forty torpedo planes under Lieutenant Commander Murata Shigeharu; above, to Fuchida's right, were fifty-one dive-bombers under Lieutenant Commander Takahashi Kakuichi. Overhead and flying cover were forty-three of the agile Zero fighters under Lieutenant Commander Itaya Shigeru. Fuchida had a radio direction finder in his plane and tuned in to one of the Honolulu radio stations; it provided light music, and he could follow its beam right in. At 7:00 A.M. the strike leader estimated they were less than an hour from the target.

Lieutenant Matsumura Hirata flew from the *Hiryu.* Matsumura had fond memories of visiting Baltimore and Annapolis on his student cruise after graduating from Etajima in 1936. Now he carried one of the new lethal shallow-water torpedoes back to the Americas on his Nakajima Type 97, soon to become known to U.S. intelligence as a Kate. Matsumura had cut a lock of his hair and snippets of his fingernails for his wife, sure he would never be coming back. It was black night when he got up, but sunrise once he took off looked spectacular, the way it did over Mount Fuji, better, a fine omen for the mission. "All the way we were flying above a thick blanket of clouds," says Matsumura, who led the *Hiryu* torpedo attack unit. "But just when we were crossing over the coastline of Oahu Island the clouds below us split. It was like a white sheet had been pulled back."

Lieutenant Ohtawa Tatsuya, also flying a Kate but from the *Soryu,* saw fields of sugar cane glinting like emeralds in the sun. "It was lovely," Ohtawa recalled, and he loved flying, so much that he would go on to establish an aerial navigation school after the war. That day he felt he was about to bear fruit, to be a man; there was a tremendous rush of excitement when he first saw Kahuku Point, the northern tip of Oahu. Of Pearl Harbor Ohtawa said, "We were about to change an island of dreams into a living hell."

I̲N THE BEFORE DAYS IT HAD BEEN CALLED WAI MOMI, "RIVER OF PEARLS." A BACKWATER BAY, sheltered from the sea by sandbars and a reef, the place had been known for *puuloa,* the pearl oysters for which Hawaiians dove. In local lore Kaaupahau, the benevolent queen of the shark gods, dwelt in a cavern in the bay with her family and chased away fierce sharks that might have attacked Hawaiians. There was no keeping away the outside world, however, which began to encroach upon the strong indigenous culture after 1778, when British explorer Captain James Cook made an unexpected landfall at Kauai. The place became a natural stopping point for transpacific ships, including American ones, and Americans forged increasingly close links of religion and commerce with friendly Hawaiians. Naval officers had their eyes on the beckoning entrance of Wai Momi as early as 1840. The king of Hawaii gave the United States the exclusive right to enter this river and make use of the bay in 1887, an arrangement that predated the 1898 U.S. annexation of Hawaii.

Creation of a naval base at Pearl Harbor came slowly, set back repeatedly by difficulties dredging the mouth and problems consequent to collapse of the dry dock Americans began building in 1909. Once cofferdams had been erected and the wreckage of the first attempt dug up, engineers discovered the skeleton of a fifteen-foot shark embedded in the foundation. Hawaiians were not surprised; the dock had been sited at a point believed to lie directly above the cave of Kaaupahau's son. A redesigned dry dock was completed only in 1919.

By then Pearl Harbor was really a harbor. The gunboat *Peterel* had been the first American warship to enter the place, in January 1905. The first major warship would be the (pre–World War I) armored cruiser *California*. The first concentration of a large fleet at Pearl came in 1925 when 137 vessels massed for a big naval review. By this time Pearl Harbor had acquired a standard role in U.S. war plans against Japan—the Orange plans—as the point of concentration for a fleet to counterattack across the Pacific. In the 1930s the Hawaiian Detachment of the U.S. Fleet, essentially comprising that fleet's scouting force, became the largest naval unit yet permanently based at Pearl Harbor. It was surpassed, of course, when FDR ordered the fleet to stay at Pearl after 1940 maneuvers there. The reunited fleet became the Pacific Fleet in early 1941, and it was that force, unsuspecting, which now faced a threat that left nothing to chance.

Admiral Kimmel's Pacific Fleet got one last opportunity to avoid being taken completely by surprise—not a strategic or long-term warning that would have permitted the fleet to disperse and dispose itself for war, but a tactical kind of warning, enough to alert the ships and get the guns manned. In the final analysis it was Admiral Yamamoto who gave Kimmel this opportunity, by his October decision that there should be a simultaneous attack on Pearl Harbor by two-man midget submarines the Japanese had developed. Ironically, the Combined Fleet commander, though he at first liked the idea, had then rejected it because a submarine detection might alert the Americans (and because the Japanese crews would probably not be recoverable). Yamamoto had been brought around by repeated arguments from staff officers, not least Commander Arima Takayasu, his own torpedo staff officer. In the early-morning hours of December 7 that decision almost cost Japan the surprise at Pearl Harbor.

Five midget submarines were involved in the attack. They had been carried by fleet subs of the Sasaki Group, named for Captain Sasaki Hanku, commander of Submarine Division 3 of Admiral Sato Tsutomo's Submarine Squadron 1. Sato had picked five boats to work under Sasaki on the mission, and these had been modified at Kure for "special fittings," the euphemism for the two-man midgets. Then Sasaki's boats, *I-16*, *I-20*, *I-24*, *I-22*, and *I-18*, had been assigned to patrol closest inshore to Oahu and, incidentally, have suitable release points for the midgets. Captain Sasaki sailed in *I-22*, whose midget would be piloted by Lieutenant Iwasa Naoji, pioneer of the development program. The plan was for the midget submarines to somehow penetrate the boom protecting the harbor entrance, then attack between the first and second waves of aircraft.

The midgets were released from their mother submarines at distances ranging from seven to about thirteen miles off the harbor mouth. Lieutenant Iwasa seems to have been first off, at about 1:16 A.M. on December 7. Last would be Ensign Sakamaki Kazuo, who launched at 3:33 A.M. Sakamaki's boat had a defective gyrocompass and trim problems; it would be put out of action after several attempts at getting into Pearl Harbor. Sakamaki's boat ended up drifting east, then north, past Honolulu and Makapuu Point, to run aground in Waimanalo Bay. Ensign Sakamaki was captured, his shipmate drowned. Sakamaki was the sole survivor among the submariners.

It turned out to be inauspicious that the Japanese had adopted the code name "Target A" for the midget submarines. They indeed became priority targets for the Americans, beginning at 3:42 A.M., when minesweeper *Condor* sighted the wake of a periscope approaching the harbor entrance. *Condor* summoned destroyer *Ward*, which had antisubmarine duty off the channel that night, and *Ward* barreled down on the sighting point. The World War I–vintage destroyer made some depth-charge attacks without apparent result. The ship continued nosing around on inshore patrol until about 6:30, when supply ship *Antares* spotted another suspicious object in the water. Just ten minutes later a PBY Catalina flying boat of Patrol Squadron 14 positively identified a submarine off the harbor. By then *Ward* had seen the sub, too, with its conning tower above the surface; *Ward* opened fire and turned for a depth-charge run. At 6:51 and again two minutes later the destroyer reported its actions to 14th District. There followed a third submarine contact at 7:03, which *Ward* attacked and was convinced she had sunk. It is doubtful whether any destroyer skipper on his first patrol with his first command, as was Lieutenant William W. Outerbridge of *Ward*, had ever sunk as many submarines in so short a time.

Meanwhile messages *Ward* had sent gave Pearl Harbor its last chance. Unfortunately they were in code and it was 7:12 before the duty officer, Lieutenant Commander Harold Kaminski, saw the report. He called the admiral's aide, was unable to get him, and then the chief of staff. That officer, Captain John B. Earle, seemed incredulous but was quickly on the phone to the district commander, Admiral Claude C. Bloch. These two officers tried to decide if the submarine report was valid while various others were being brought into the picture. Admiral Kimmel's duty officer got his first news about 7:20, and twenty minutes later the commander in chief himself heard the report for the first time. By then Patrol Wing 2 on Ford Island was reporting that Ensign Tanner, flying one of its PBYs, had also attacked a sub.

At about 7:51 the ready duty destroyer *Monaghan* had been ordered to get under way immediately to supplement *Ward.* A submarine emergency was serious, but it was not treated as a general attack. No one knew, at that moment, that Commander Fuchida's air assault was already over Oahu and just four minutes away.

EVEN AFTER ALL THE OTHER LAPSES AND MISHAPS, THE TECHNOLOGY OF WARFARE FURNISHED the Pacific Fleet with one final chance to appreciate danger. This came as a result of radar, then a novelty. Radio waves bounced off an object and reflected back to the mechanism can be used to disclose an object's distance, direction, and altitude, as well as other data about it. The primitive radars available on Oahu on December 7, 1941, were not so capable, but could still tell position, and one of these new radar sets stood at Opana at the northern tip of the island.

Two vans housed the 270-B radar unit at Opana, and standing orders for the Army soldiers who ran it were to work the equipment from 4:00 to 7:00 each morning. Privates George E. Elliott and Joseph L. Lockard had the duty that Sunday morning. Lockard was watching the oscilloscope at 6:45 when a contact appeared north of Oahu. A minute later the 270-B mobile unit at Kaaawa (there were five on Oahu) also saw the contact. These data were telephoned to an information center at Fort Shafter, where the sighting was presumed routine. At 7:00, in accordance with instructions, the plotters and other personnel at the information center and at the radar units other than Opana closed down and went to breakfast.

At that point two men were left at the center in Fort Shafter. One, Lieutenant Kermit A. Tyler, the executive officer of a fighter squadron, had been assigned to the center to familiarize himself with it. The other, Private Joseph McDonald, was the administrative switchboard operator. For some reason Tyler had orders to remain on duty until eight o'clock, while apparently no one told McDonald (who had been working since Saturday evening) that he could leave. At any rate, there they were when the telephone from Opana rang.

The two Army privates on the radar at Opana had decided to stick around after hours to get a little extra practice. Shortly after 7:00 A.M. a huge blip appeared north of Kahuku Point. The indicator was so unusual the operators checked the 270-B set to see if it had malfunctioned. Lockard, more experienced, estimated the range to the target at 136 miles, again unusual since the 270-B had a theoretical range of 130 miles. At 7:02 Private Elliott called the information in to Fort Shafter.

The Opana operators got no one on their tactical telephone line, but on the administrative one they connected with Private McDonald, who then ran into Tyler as he went to check the clock in the operations room. Tyler got on the phone to learn that a large flight of planes was headed for Oahu; the largest sighting Lockard had ever seen on the 270-B. Lieutenant Tyler knew a flight of B-17 bombers was due in from the mainland that morning, en route to the Philippines, and told the Opana radarmen not to worry; then he hung up.

At Opana the two privates actually continued to use their radar until they lost the contact amid false returns caused by Oahu's mountains. At 7:15 the contact was at 88 miles, by 7:30 at 45; when Opana lost contact at 7:39 the distance had shrunk to 20 miles. The Japanese air strike force had arrived over Hawaii.

In the mid-1960s Kermit Tyler, risen to colonel, was a senior officer at the North American Air Defense Command, the force charged with ascertaining if the United States was being subjected to nuclear missile attack.

IN THE COCKPIT OF HIS ATTACK PLANE, FUCHIDA MITSUO WAS TROUBLED AT HAVING HEARD nothing from the floatplanes sent ahead of the strike force to get one last look at the target. This final report was supposed to give Fuchida the picture he needed to decide whether to assume they were going to achieve surprise, or deploy for an opposed attack. It made a difference, in particular for Commander Murata's torpedo bombers, which were to attack first if there was surprise, in order to have the best possible conditions for laying down torpedoes. If the attack were opposed Fuchida planned to lead with Commander Takahashi's dive-bombers to suppress the American airfields.

Without word, but listening to Honolulu radio, Fuchida began to believe that everything seemed so normal the Americans could not possibly suspect anything. He determined to have Murata lead off and assume there would be surprise. At 7:40 A.M. Commander Fuchida made the signal for this disposition, firing a single flare just as his planes came up on Oahu's coast. Fuchida also decided, on the basis of a weather report from local radio, to have his force come down the west side of Oahu to its attack positions.

One of the few errors to mar Japanese conduct of the Pearl Harbor attack occurred at just this point: The covering fighter group did not seem to notice the surprise signal. Appreciating this, Fuchida fired a second flare, but two flares happened to be the prearranged signal for deployment assuming an opposed attack, and Takahashi's bombers now assumed this to be the decision. The dive-bombers put on speed and split into two units; Takahashi would attack Ford Island and Hickam Field with one, Lieutenant Sakamoto Akira led the second, against Wheeler Field. Fuchida had his radioman tap out a signal at 7:49:

TO, TO, TO, TO . . .

It was the order to go in for attack. Shortly thereafter, before the first bomb had actually fallen, the air group commander ordered a second message:

TORA . . . TORA . . . TORA

That signal informed Admiral Nagumo that surprise had been achieved and the attack begun. Due to favorable atmospheric conditions, the signal was also received aboard Admiral Yamamoto's own flagship, *Nagato*, at Hashirajima in Empire waters.

Meanwhile, seeing the dive-bombers peel off for their attacks and fearing that smoke from their bombs would obstruct the approach of his torpedo planes, Commander Murata increased the speed of his own formation. As a result the first torpedo attacks were made approximately five minutes ahead of schedule, while the first bombs fell at about 7:55 A.M. Lieutenant Goto Inichi loosed the first torpedo, which squarely struck battleship *Oklahoma*. More followed. Fuchida led his own level bombers with their 1,760-pound modified cannon shells against the American ships moored alongside Ford Island at 8:05. The Japanese attack proceeded with clockwork precision.

Below all was chaos. Some confused the attackers with American planes; more than one officer wanted to report these pilots for improper barnstorming antics. Once flames and explosions began to erupt everywhere, and people began to see the rising-sun insignia painted on the aircraft, awareness dawned among the victims. Americans struggled to bring anti-aircraft batteries into action, to get their ships under way, their planes into the air. In too many cases the effort proved futile. Within fifteen minutes crucial hits had been inflicted on many warships. The battleships *Arizona* and *Oklahoma* were sunk, the *West Virginia* and *California* damaged. The cruiser *Raleigh*, also hit by a torpedo and only miraculously afloat, brought her guns into action at 8:01, becoming one of the first warships to do so.

The *West Virginia* action provides a good microcosm of the horror of that day, the instant transition from peace to war. This was the ship attacked by the nine-plane torpedo unit from *Hiryu* led by Lieutenant Matsumura Hirata. Under instructions from Murata, the planes had swung past Oahu and come back in from the sea, climbing a little to clear the dockyard area, then right on the deck. "We had to avoid smoke and pick a target," Matsumura recalled. "I flanked out to the right. . . . I didn't know which ship it was. . . . I was running straight in toward that ship, and I was bent over looking down through my bombsight. A few seconds ahead of the target my navigator and I both pulled our firing levers." Matsumura worried that his torpedo would not run, or that it would sink to the harbor bottom. "That would be awful, after we had come that close," but after a few seconds the navigator began shouting "Hashite iru! Hashite iru!" ("It's running!") In fact the *West Virginia* would be hit in minutes by seven deadly torpedoes.

In his cabin belowdecks near the stern of the ship was Commander Roscoe Hillenkoetter, the *West Virginia*'s executive officer. As soon as the attack began Hillenkoetter began making his way to the bridge, yet such was the ferocity of the strike, and the enormity of damage, that he had to stop to order counterflooding to keep the ship from capsizing. Before Hillenkoetter arrived at the bridge his ship was settling to the harbor bottom, and to add further injury she would be hit by two big bombs from Fuchida's unit. Captain Mervyn Bennion, who also ordered counterflooding to correct an increasing list to port, would be mortally wounded; 104 others also died. The damage control officer, Lieutenant Commander John Harper, did the right things as quickly as he could, but the truth was it was already too late.

Mori Juzo flew a torpedo bomber from the *Soryu* that morning. He, too, figured among the group that swung out over the sea to come back in against Battleship Row. From the mission briefings, Mori recognized his target as the *California*, nestled by herself against Ford Island, as appropriate for the battle force flagship. Mori flew so low that his propeller tips nearly touched the water. "Nobody returned fire," Mori recalled. "I saw many officers and men looking up in confusion. They looked like they couldn't believe what was happening. There were huge spouts of water . . . and fires breaking out all over." As Mori banked right, above the deck of another battleship, he noticed a curtain of machine-gun fire. "I knew then that we were at war."

The *California* was hardly prepared for war that Sunday morning. Many of the crew had been out late the night before, some of them rooting for the ship's band in a big band competition. The ship itself was prepared for maintenance, with five manhole covers opened and a good dozen watertight compartments compromised. There would have been no way to restore watertight integrity even if the fleet had had warning. Warren Harding, one of the musicians from the *California*'s band, had seen an omen in the night— a sparkling meteor shower. His grandfather had once told him that seeing a meteor meant someone you knew was about to die. Harding wondered how many deaths the shower meant. In fact, ninety-eight of the *California*'s men were missing or dead, sixty-one others wounded.

So many men, so many stories, so much misery, heroism, ingenuity; this was a day to remember, and virtually every American then alive remembers what happened to them at Pearl Harbor, or, if not there, what they were doing when they heard the news. Most knew soon, at least in the Navy, as a result of the message sent from 14th Naval District headquarters. The radio shack, perched on the very shore, partly on piers above the water, was fortunate to be still in action; sailors saw at least one Zero make a run right down the shoreline. But the plane did not strafe; it must have been looking for something, or else out of ammunition.

In the radio shack was Buzz Boyer, a landlubber who ended up in the Navy and so got himself into communications. Boyer was operator of the automatic keying equipment at Navy Station NPM, six miles east of Pearl Harbor, which communicated with the mainland. He was at the 14th District shack that morning to stand in for a friend. Suddenly the Marines were reporting from Ewa Field that they were being bombed and strafed. Boyer thought someone must be drunk, but Ewa insisted it was the real thing. A superior told him to get it on the air immediately. Boyer sent

AIR RAID, PEARL HARBOR—THIS IS NO DRILL

More than three decades later, by then parts manager for a Ford Motor Company tractor plant in Greenville, Ohio, Boyer wondered what had happened to his buddies from the 14th District.

Joe Rochefort the radio intelligence expert was all set to go on a picnic that Sunday morning. He had loaded steaks and barbecue stuff in the car, but kept puttering around the house instead of leaving. Suddenly the phone rang and Tommy Dyer was on the other end telling him Pearl Harbor was under attack. Rochefort took a little convincing, but then rushed down to Station Hypo, hardly to leave the place again. Soon Rochefort would be asked if he had a use for the band from the U.S.S. *California*, who by then were without jobs or even musical instruments.

Lieutenant Commander Dyer himself was hardly expecting Pearl Harbor when he went on as duty officer the evening of December 6. Actually Dyer was not supposed to be there at all, but his son was having a first piano recital the night of the fifth, when he was scheduled for duty. Dyer traded with the officer scheduled for the fourth, then found himself invited to a party that night. Dyer traded again and took the duty for the sixth. The night shift was himself and one enlisted man, Radioman 2nd Class Tony Ethier. Dyer spent the night working on the special cipher the Japanese were using in the Mandates. He received one of the *Ward* messages about a submarine and called the district communication office, because he knew a fresh reservist had the duty there, to make sure the message had been passed up the line. About 7:00 A.M. Commander Dyer knocked off for breakfast at a little Greek restaurant, returning a half hour later to clean up his desk before going home, as scheduled, at eight o'clock. Then he heard noises outside the relatively soundproof basement offices of Hypo. At first he thought they were anti-aircraft guns, but Tommy Dyer could not understand why the Army should be firing anti-aircraft guns. Then he heard a louder explosion, which sounded like one of the Army's 14-inch coast-defense guns from Fort Kamehameha. Instead, Chief Radioman Farnsley C. Woodward came downstairs to say planes were flying around dropping things. Dyer went up to see for himself.

"About three hundred yards away," Tommy Dyer recalls, "was a torpedo plane in a tight bank, a tight turn, and the rising suns were shining right at me. I caught on fast."

That was when Dyer went to call Commander Rochefort.

Another Hypo man to be surprised was Jasper Holmes, actually Commander Wilfred J. Holmes, a former submarine skipper who went by his initials and wrote short stories under the pen name Alec Hudson. Holmes had been invalided out of the service for a bad back but had returned as an intelligence officer, indexing and finding other systems for recording the information gained by Hypo's codebreaking. Holmes was in bed; his son told him the Sunday paper had not come, there was no coffee, and the neighbor was saying the Japanese were attacking. Holmes explained patiently that they were off somewhere in the Netherlands East Indies. When his telephone rang it was the duty officer at the district intelligence office with a simple "General quarters!"

An hour behind the Japanese first wave followed a second, under Lieutenant Commander Shimazaki Shigekazu, with fifty-four Kate attack planes, eighty-one of the dive-bombers the Japanese called the D3A1 (soon to be "Vals"), and thirty-six Mitsubishi A6M2 Zero fighters, for a total of 181 planes, of which one aborted the mission. Commander Fuchida circled over Pearl Harbor to supervise the second wave, which added to damage at the naval base and surrounding airfields. Shimazaki arrived over Kahuku Point at 8:40 A.M. and immediately began his attack. In an hour it was all over. Fuchida circled again to observe results and take photographs, then headed back to Kido Butai.

The single largest disaster among the many to befall Americans that day was the destruction of the battleship *Arizona*. She had been moored at the northeast tip of Ford Island, inboard of repair ship *Vestal*. In the event, *Vestal* proved little protection, for this time the agent would be bombs. Historian Thomas C. Hone, who has made the most detailed examination of the devastation of the vessels on Battleship Row, points out that although the bombs converted from 16-inch shells had a very small bursting charge (66.5 pounds), and although the torpedo planes achieved better accuracy than the high level bombers (40 percent against about 16 percent), the ship sunk by bombs stayed sunk while those torpedoed were raised and repaired, except for *Oklahoma*. This may be true, but the comparison is limited, since only *Arizona* was entirely a victim of bombs.

Be this as it may, *Arizona* began to suffer as soon as Fuchida's first wave started dropping, and the crucial damage occurred at about 8:12 A.M. One of the huge shell-bombs apparently fell right down the ship's stack and into her vitals. It is disputed whether this particular bomb caused the critical damage, but most agree that the factor which led to destruction of the battleship was explosion of its forward magazine, powerful enough to blow a heavy gun turret right off the ship and send a column of smoke over a thousand feet into the air. Some 1,177 sailors (or 1,103, depending on the count accepted) perished. Like *West Virginia*, *Arizona* settled to the bottom and was there to be a target when the Japanese second wave arrived. Lieutenant Abe Zenji, a dive-bomber squadron commander from the *Akagi*, attacked her with 550-pound bombs when the second wave arrived. The damage-control officer, Lieutenant Commander Samuel Fuqua, did not actually order the ship abandoned until about 9:00 A.M. Still, after the Japanese first wave Fuqua's efforts aimed more at rescue than at saving the *Arizona*.

So that was Pearl. Ship after ship hit; many damaged or sunk. The *Arizona* and *Oklahoma* were lost forever; battleships *West Virginia* and *California* settled or capsized but were later refloated and repaired. The *Nevada*, the only battleship able to get under way that morning, made a heroic dash for the harbor mouth, received damage from bombs and a torpedo, and picked up some of the *Arizona*'s fires as she sprinted past that doomed battleship. *Nevada* had to beach in order to avoid blocking the ship channel. Less severely damaged were *Pennsylvania*, *Maryland*, and *Tennessee*, and the cruisers *Helena*, *Honolulu*, and *New Orleans*. The cruiser *Raleigh* suffered extensive torpedo damage, the target ship *Utah* was sunk, and repair ship *Vestal* also incurred major damage. Some 2,403 Americans died and another 1,178 were wounded or injured. On Oahu's airfields, 96 Army and 92 Navy or Marine aircraft were destroyed, and 159 more from all services were damaged.

The attack had barely ended when Station Hypo was beginning to make possible American countermeasures. An overzealous bid to prevent communications among presumed Japanese spies led to cutting off electric service to Oahu's telephone system, complicating liaison among Commander Rochefort's outstations, completely isolating the sophisticated radio direction finder at Lualualei. Hypo therefore relied on Heeia. At 10:30 A.M., about the time Shimazaki's second-wave airplanes would be nearing their carriers, Heeia intercepted traffic showing "commander, carrier divisions" to be in charge of the Japanese force. Just ten minutes later the *Akagi* would be identified. Lualualei came back into action by getting a bearing on some of these transmissions, at almost due north (357°), but since there was no cross-bearing to pinpoint the source, it could also have been south of Oahu. Commander in chief Pacific (CINCPAC) would be the first to pick up this report, which it then relayed to Hypo. When CINCPAC sent out an action order, however, it noted both possible locations, and since the southernmost possibility concorded with an Imperial Navy offensive out of the Mandates, many officers focused upon that threat.

The two available American carrier task forces were that day at sea. The *Enterprise* task force, under Vice Admiral William F. Halsey, was returning from delivering a squadron of Marine fighter planes to Wake Island. It was northwest of Pearl Harbor and in the best position to respond to Kido Butai, but the carrier's scout planes had flown off to precede her to Pearl Harbor and, in fact, arrived between the Japanese attacks. Halsey brought his task force back to Pearl, picked up his planes, and left again, but then it was far too late.

A task force with carrier *Lexington* was the other strong arm of America. This group was almost due west of Oahu, under the temporary command of Rear Admiral J. H. Newton. They turned to a southeast course and increased speed, scouting ahead, once more reflecting an assumption that the Japanese had come from the Mandates and were south of Pearl Harbor. Not surprisingly, the *Lexington,* too, found nothing.

During those initial hours of war American confusion thus continued to flow from preconceptions founded in the prewar years. Symptomatic of this is a report from Station Cast, the radio intelligence unit at Corregidor, sent the second day of the war. It dwelt in part on the *Akagi,* in actuality Admiral Nagumo's flagship, which Hypo identified among the Pearl Harbor attackers:

RADIO BEARINGS INDICATE THAT AKAGI IS MOVING SOUTH FROM EMPIRE AND IS NOW IN NANSEI ISLANDS AREA.

The Nansei Shoto was the region of Okinawa, not of Pearl Harbor.


THE FINAL DAY OF PEACE FOUND ADMIRAL YAMAMOTO ISOROKU BACK ABOARD HIS FLAGSHIP, *Nagato,* having returned from Tokyo, where Emperor Hirohito had graced him with an audience to receive the orders for war. At Hashirajima, the battleships of the First Fleet, Combined Fleet, were at four hours' notice for sea. A succession of senior officers visited, beginning with Vice Admiral Takasu Shiro early in the morning. The *Nagato* completed loading ammunition for her 16-inch guns, cut her telephone lines and other connections with the land, and became an enclosed world. The next morning, December 8, the ship slipped her mooring lines. Captain Yano Hideo turned her prow toward the ocean. All around, other First Fleet ships did the same. Dawn passed without incident.

Once at sea, First Fleet commander Admiral Takasu set a course toward the southeast. *Nagato* led a column of six battleships steaming in single file, with light cruisers out on both sides and 4,000 meters between her and the second ship, the *Mutsu*. Admiral Takasu flew his flag on *Ise*, third ship in column, while the tail-end Charlie, battleship *Yamashiro* at 20,000 meters, was so far away only her upperworks were visible above the horizon. Destroyers fanned out ahead and to the flanks of the fleet formation. The eye beheld a scene of majesty and power as darkness fell.

The nerve center of the Imperial Navy went to sea with Admiral Takasu's fleet that day. "Admiral's country" on the *Nagato* housed the staff and commander of the Combined Fleet. Toward the stern, a series of compartments along the ship's port side, plus a large conference room and mess that extended the width of the ship, were the places Admiral Yamamoto was likely to be found. Even though *Nagato* was his flagship, Yamamoto quietly went about fleet business and rarely roamed the ship. Most sailors aboard, seamen like Kurosawa Saburo, hardly saw Yamamoto at all, unless they happened to have deck duty and the admiral was leaving the ship or being piped aboard. One opportune moment had been on November 3, a memorial day honoring Emperor Meiji. On that and other national holidays the Emperor's portrait, housed in a recessed compartment in the big conference room, was opened for all the crew to pay their respects. If he was aboard ship, Yamamoto sometimes met ordinary seamen on such occasions.

Admiral Yamamoto's office was just forward of the conference room. It opened onto the passageway and also directly into the conference room. Forward of that was Yamamoto's cabin, and opening off it a bathroom, whose main distinguishing feature was a Western-style tub. Yamamoto's rooms were plain, with no wall hangings and with linoleum floors except in the office, which was carpeted. Even the conference room was plain save for a beautiful painting of Mount Fuji, and the doors shielding the Emperor's portrait.

Admiral Ugaki Matome, the Combined Fleet's chief of staff, lived in the cabin next door to Yamamoto's, and the compartment forward of that housed the operations room, with desks and tables for the staff. An administrative office occupied the next room forward, where Yeoman Noda and perhaps fourteen others kept track of routine business. Admiral Yamamoto typically conferred with staff in the operations room, and sometimes worked in his private office. The big conference room was used mostly on formal occasions or for the staff luncheons the admiral hosted daily. Then the *Nagato*'s forty-man band would play during the time it took the admiral to go out into the passageway and enter the conference room. Lunch could be fish, beef, pork, or chicken, and there was usually a soup, bread, fruit or cake, and coffee. The admiral's steward, Petty Officer Omi Heijiro, often arranged with the band leader to play folk songs from Yamamoto's home province or popular tunes he liked such as "China Nights."

For the big day of the Pearl Harbor attack the commander in chief dispensed with ceremony. Tea and cakes were provided in the operations room as staff huddled over the charts. Yamamoto retired early, and Ugaki also went to bed. Aircraft launch from Nagumo's force was about 1:30 A.M. Japanese time, December 8, and no news was expected for hours after that. Full of anticipation, chief of staff Ugaki, for one, woke up about 3:00. He had just risen and was having a smoke when air staff Sasaki Akira hurried in, reporting that *Nagato* herself had picked up Commander Fuchida's attack signal, very surprising considering the low-power radio in Fuchida's Kate.

There were exceptional conditions for radio reception that night, and the news continued, with *Nagato* receiving snippets of radio chatter among senior pilots in the attack. (Limited production of aircraft radios forced the JNAF to restrict radio installation to topmost pilots.) The *Nagato* also intercepted certain American transmissions, including CINCPAC's order for all ships to sortie from Pearl Harbor, an order to sweep mines south of Ford Island, and an order to the Asiatic Fleet to activate a certain war plan. Ugaki supposed that the order to sweep mines resulted from a mistake, the Americans erroneously thinking that damage inflicted by the midget submarines had been from mines. Not until much later would the Japanese learn their "Target A" midgets had been completely ineffective. Ugaki summarized available reports from Kido Butai and other war fronts for senior officers before the First Fleet, whose tactical designation was Main Body, weighed anchor at about 8:30 A.M.

As the Main Body sailed, the Japanese planes were arriving back aboard their carriers. That was when Admiral Nagumo broke radio silence to send a brief dispatch estimating results of the attack. (It was most likely this message from which the Americans got a radio bearing and identified the *Akagi*.) Without waiting to complete decoding of the dispatch, codes officer Lieutenant Takahashi Yoshio spoke up over the voice tube to inform the staff on the flag bridge that the Nagumo force had succeeded in achieving surprise. There was great joy.

Petty Officer Omi judged the moment propitious to serve sake along with *ozeki* and *surume*, traditional dishes for happy occasions. This was much more difficult than regular meal service, since the galley cooked food in the bowels of the ship while the flag bridge was located many decks above, in the *Nagato*'s superstructure. Still, Omi, whose previous assignment had been running the canteen and managing supply for the entire crew of more than 1,300 men, was nothing if not resourceful. The staff officers toasted torpedo expert Commander Arima, who had had a major part in the innovation of the shallow-water torpedoes. Arima had been confident that the expedient would work, but very nervous about the attack.

Nagumo's initial report conservatively estimated damage as one battleship sunk and two badly damaged. Aboard the Combined Fleet flagship this instantly triggered the twin questions of whether the damage had not in fact been greater, and what should be done to maximize the impact of the attack.

Those same questions became key features of discussion on Admiral Nagumo's own flagship, carrier *Akagi.* There the task force chief of staff, Rear Admiral Kusaka, met Fuchida's plane as it settled on the flight deck and rolled to a stop. Kusaka conducted Fuchida to the bridge, where Nagumo was listening to the staff. Fuchida could tell the discussion had been heated. He was asked to estimate the damage at Pearl Harbor, and put it at four battleships definitely sunk.

That seemed to please the commander in chief.

"We may then conclude that anticipated results have been achieved," Nagumo said.

Fuchida was horrified. "All things considered," the air group leader replied, "we have achieved a great amount of destruction, but it would be unwise to assume we have destroyed everything. There are still many targets remaining which should be hit. Therefore I recommend that another attack be launched."

At that moment, in fact, mechanics were spotting rearmed aircraft on the flight deck for takeoff in a further attack wave.

Genda also favored a further attack. From the *Soryu* came support from Admiral Yamaguchi, who reported his Carrier Division 2 ships ready to launch. Captain Okada Jisaku of the *Kaga* specifically signaled a recommendation to strike the fuel tanks and installations at Pearl Harbor.

Admiral Kusaka differed. Any further attack would find the Americans alerted. There would be much more opposition and the task force itself could be endangered. The Japanese had been lucky so far, Kusaka reasoned, but no logic promised that luck would hold. The American carriers had not been at Pearl Harbor; at any moment they might pop up to threaten Kido Butai.

"We should retire as planned," Kusaka advised Nagumo.

Someone suggested that they ought to deliberately seek out the U.S. carriers and sink them.

Opinion was divided. Kusaka had no hesitation recommending a withdrawal, however, and Nagumo none in accepting that course. Here was revealed a key weakness in Yamamoto's plan: The men responsible for carrying it out had no faith in the project. Since the rationale for attack was to permit unimpeded advance into the Southern Area, results already seemed satisfactory to both Nagumo and Kusaka. The Japanese at that moment had the unparalleled opportunity to mount punishing strikes on the submarine base and the oil storage facilities at Pearl, both of which could have had greater long-term impact upon the U.S. war effort in the Pacific than even the sinking of the battleships. Queasy about the whole Hawaii operation in the first place, Nagumo and Kusaka were happy to forgo the possibility. The latter went so far as to denigrate, in a postwar memoir, those who concerned themselves with the fuel and submarine base as small men.

"We will have no more attacks of any kind," said Kusaka. "We will withdraw."

Admiral Kusaka's declaration might have ended talk on the bridge of the *Akagi*, but it started tongues wagging on the Combined Fleet flagship, which that night received Nagumo's dispatch reporting that not only was the task force returning without further attempts to attack, but it was also abandoning a subsidiary air strike on Midway. The discussion on the *Nagato* would be as heated as that among Nagumo's staff. Chief of fleet staff Ugaki held that Kido Butai ought to be summarily ordered back into action, but there were objections. Senior staff officer Kuroshima Kameto, who favored invasion of Hawaii as a longer-term option, opposed extension of the Pearl Harbor attack at this moment. Obviously the Americans would now be alert, and there was the chance of a carrier attack from the flank; the plan for renewed attack would be improvised, with little preparation; it would affect morale to force reluctant local commanders into renewed effort. Kuroshima won the day, to the extent that Admiral Yamamoto ordered preparation of a plan for an invasion of Hawaii. Petty Officer Omi, who sat listening in the adjacent orderly room, believed long after the war that the decisions made at that meeting swayed the whole future of the Imperial Navy.

Ugaki Matome bared his own frustrations in his diary, objecting that Nagumo's precipitous return was open to criticism as "sneak-thievery and contentment with a humble lot in life." There was some introspection as well. "If I were the commander of the task force," Admiral Ugaki penned in a more extended comment, "I would be prepared to expand the war result to the extent of completely destroying Pearl Harbor, by encouraging my subordinates at this critical time. But I should not measure others by my standard."

It was fortunate indeed for the United States that Nagumo proved unwilling to accept greater risks for the promise of greater results, and that Yamamoto proved reluctant to intervene in this operational decision by his tactical commander.

The withdrawal of the Nagumo force meant that any follow-up would have to come from Japanese submarines around Hawaii. In addition to the Sasaki Group, which had carried the midget submarines, there were seven boats of Rear Admiral Yamazaki Shigeteru's 2nd Submarine Squadron between Oahu and Molokai, and nine boats of Rear Admiral Miwa Shigeyoshi's 3rd Squadron south of Oahu. Miwa's submarine *I-72* had already contributed to success by furnishing last-minute notice that no American ships were at Lahaina anchorage off the island of Maui. Captain Sasaki's submarines had contributed by loosing the midgets. These had increased American confusion, though they had no practical effect at Pearl

Harbor. On the contrary, American capture of Ensign Sakamaki Kazuo provided intelligence interrogators with their first inside peek at Japanese submarine doctrine and practices. When Yamamoto learned months afterward that the Americans had captured Sakamaki he delivered a severe dressing-down to Combined Fleet torpedo staff officer Commander Arima, who had convinced him to include the midget attack in his plan.

The submarine blockade of Hawaii continued until December 23, when the boats were ordered either to patrol off the American West Coast, or back to Sixth Fleet's base at Kwajalein. During that interval the subs sank five merchant ships in Hawaiian waters. Submarine fleet commander Shimizu, learning the submarine trade on the job, got only one chance for a significant war result. That began early on December 10 off Kauai, when the *I-6* sighted an aircraft carrier she took for the *Lexington* (actually it was Halsey's *Enterprise*). Shimizu ordered the 2nd Submarine Squadron to pursue and destroy. Several I-boats participated in a two-day chase and actually made torpedo attacks, with no success. The *Enterprise* sent up planes which found three Japanese submarines. One escaped, one was thought to have been hit, the third tried to fight on the surface as Lieutenant Clarence E. Dickenson attacked in a dive-bomber. Samuel Eliot Morison's postwar, official history concludes the last two contacts were both with the same submarine, Commander Sano Takashi's *I-70*, which Morison thinks was damaged so heavily she could not submerge when hit later that day. In any case the *I-70* went down on an even keel amid a widening oil slick, never to be heard from again. Carrier *Enterprise* would be credited with the first warship sunk by American vessels in the conflict.

Bombing the *I-70* drove to a conclusion a submarine battle for the first time, but there had already been several desultory contacts. The Japanese, who had rushed war preparations to such a degree that four boats in the blockade lines had joined the fleet just weeks before, were on station in time for *I-10* to sight an American cruiser near the equator. The submarine's skipper had good attack position but refrained since hostilities had yet to begin. On the other side, Lieutenant James Cobb, flying a PBY Catalina from Ford Island, saw a surfaced submarine just two miles off Diamond Head on December 6. That happened to be the patrol area of Lieutenant Commander Otani Kiyonori's *I-18*. Like the Japanese skipper, the American pilot had been in a good position to attack but did not do so.

Former Imperial Navy submarine officer Orita Zenji believes the most harrowing experience among those who returned from the Pearl Harbor operation was that of the crew of *I-24*, one of the brand-new boats. Commander Hanabusa Hiroshi, the skipper, ordered a routine dive only to find that pressure valves for the forward ballast tanks were stuck. The boat, carrying Ensign Sakamaki's ill-fated midget submarine, was deeper than her test depth when Lieutenant Hashimoto Mochitsura managed to free the valve and get air pressure in to blow out the tank, finally righting the submarine.

Lieutenant Commander Watanabe Katsuji's *I-69* must also be considered for the dubious distinction of most harrowing experience. On the day Nagumo attacked Pearl Harbor, Watanabe was about seventeen miles southwest of Pearl Harbor, patrolling his assigned sector. He surfaced at night to recharge batteries but was forced under by a group of five American destroyers. Knowing he would need the battery power the next day, Watanabe took the *I-69* off toward Barber's Point for a quieter area where he might be able to surface again. The submarine began its task, with Watanabe observing Oahu as the boat recharged: "Pearl Harbor shone red in the sky, like a thing afire." But Barber's Point proved not so quiet after all: Another destroyer attacked the *I-69*, which submerged again, her batteries only 73 percent replenished. The submarine was running at a shallow depth when she felt a strange vibration thought to be an antisubmarine net. Watanabe was stuck among obstructions, and forced to drop to the ocean floor where he had to await the next night to surface. Leaks sprang in several places, and *I-69* shipped an estimated fifty tons of water before she was able to surface, thirty-eight hours later. The crew were gasping; many had headaches from carbon dioxide accumulation in their air. The situation seemed so bad that all secret documents were destroyed before *I-69* attempted to surface, three hours after sunset on December 8. This time all was normal and the *I-69* left the area. Unknown to the Japanese, *I-69* had blundered into a mine field laid off Barber's Point several months before the war began. Moored training mines were connected by a common chain that would have pulled many different mines toward the submarine. When this field was later swept, five of its mines were inexplicably found severed from the chain.

In all, Japanese submarines proved incapable of expanding the results Imperial Navy aircraft carriers had achieved. So ended Admiral Yamamoto's very ambitious Hawaii operation. The Combined Fleet commander was especially upset once he discovered that, due to delays in the decoding and typing of Japan's final fourteen-part message, the presumptive declaration of war had not actually been handed to Secretary of State Cordell Hull until about a half hour after Fuchida's planes began to attack. President Roosevelt termed December 7 a "date which will live in infamy," and Americans were particularly provoked by the notion that the Japanese had set out deliberately to mount a sneak attack. The provocation united Americans to a degree that probably would not have obtained had the Japanese merely attacked in Southeast Asia, or had the attack been preceded by some initial period of hostilities. The Japanese were at least somewhat aware of these considerations, albeit from the standpoint of honor: In their view, it would dishonor the Imperial Navy to attack before the instrument declaring war had been handed over. Yamamoto himself has been quoted to this effect. Commander Fujii Shigeru, who joined Combined Fleet staff as a political officer about the time of Pearl Harbor, was assigned to investigate the matter of timing in detail. The truth became obvious during the summer of 1942 when the sides exchanged diplomatic personnel using the liner *Gripsholm*. Then Nomura and Kurusu could tell their story directly.

"One can search military history in vain for an operation more fatal to the aggressor," writes Morison, who insists that, far from Yamamoto's vision of a strategic necessity, attacking Pearl Harbor was "strategic imbecility." That was not merely a judgment made in retrospect, or some impression common only to Americans. Commander Fuchida wrote that despite the success of the attack, Pearl Harbor brought upon Japan disgrace that persisted even after the war. When Fuchida returned to Hawaii to lay a wreath on the wreck of the *Arizona*, in 1953, there was an uproar in the Honolulu press; the U.S. Navy barred him from entering Pearl Harbor.

"We won a great tactical victory at Pearl Harbor and thereby lost the war," said Admiral Hara Chuichi in 1945. Hara, the commander of Carrier Division 5, had had misgivings on the voyage out. He recounted: "I thought this at the time but told no one. I understood the United States and believed that the fighting spirit of an individual in a democracy where each person has a part in the government would rise in anger to build up a strong fighting force."

Admiral Yamamoto achieved a measure of what he wanted from the bold plan to attack Pearl Harbor; but, as Hara's comment suggests, the very concept reflected a certain misjudgment of Americans. This, too, was a contemporary conclusion, not one drawn (by Admiral Hara or anyone else) after the fact. The argument was put very well by *New York Times* reporter Hugh Byas in 1942:

> The Japanese Naval General Staff has checked and re-checked all its calculations of the military problems. Every detail that could be foreseen, every development that could be imagined, have [*sic*] been provided for. Their plans are as complete as plans can be. But wars are not won by plans alone. In the end it is mind against mind, will against will. The ultimate blunders in any situation are psychological. The Japanese military mind, now dominant in Japan, does not understand the American.

As a result Japan failed to appreciate the forces set in motion by Pearl Harbor. Hugh Byas had it exactly right: Yamamoto Isoroku was going to run wild, but he had stirred up a nest of rather ingenious hornets.

# Wings Across the Water

ONE JAPANESE HOUSEHOLD TRANSFORMED BY THE NEWS FROM HAWAII WAS THAT OF General Tojo Hideki, the prime minister. As recently as the previous night the general's wife, Katsuko, had been in fear of ultranationalist plots, reported on the radio, in retribution for Tojo's (supposed) inability to make any decision for war. That night Hideki and Katsuko slept in bedrooms in different parts of the prime minister's residence. The general awakened to an early-morning telephone call—news he expected and considered good. General Tojo convened an immediate meeting of the cabinet.

Hoshino Naoki, too, was awakened by the ringing, insistent timbre of the phone, at about 3:00 A.M. Hoshino was General Tojo's cabinet secretary and considered himself an excellent aide. He had devoted a lifetime to making things happen in accordance with the wishes of bosses. Hoshino dressed quickly, made the three-minute drive to General Tojo's residence, and began summoning cabinet members by phone. The group assembled by 5:00. Tojo opened the impromptu meeting by declaring it an important one, then gave the floor to Admiral Shimada, the navy minister. Shimada revealed the Imperial Navy had just bombed Pearl Harbor and that initial reports indicated good results, but cautioned that pilots tend to exaggerate their exploits. The navy minister seemed calm. One attendee actually asked, "Where is Pearl Harbor?"

General Tojo had also arranged to report to the throne. Following the cabinet session he mounted his official car—a Buick—for the drive to the Imperial Palace. Karasawa Yoshisaburo, Tojo's chauffeur, recalled later how he felt an elbow poking him in the ribs, and the bodyguard sitting next to him whispered, "Look at the face of the old man." Karasawa glanced up at his rearview mirror. "He looked really awful, mean, anguished," Karasawa said of Tojo. "But I could understand that. After all, he began that kind of big war."

By 7:30 Tojo had joined Admiral Nagano of NGS and General Sugiyama of the Army to give the Emperor an official briefing, which they presented to Marquis Kido, lord of the privy seal. Kido, inspired as he saw the sun rise over the hill on which the palace stood, noted that he heard "great news of our successful attack upon Hawaii." The marquis met with Hirohito to convey the news at 11:40, and stayed with the Emperor for twenty minutes. It was apparently only on this latter occasion that Hirohito actually signed the imperial rescript declaring war on the United States and Great Britain.

One minister absent from the early-morning cabinet session had been Foreign Minister Togo Shigenori. It was Togo who had gotten Kido up to see the dawn, consulting with him on the reply to a last message from President Roosevelt. When morning came, Togo was closeted with American ambassador Joseph Grew and British emissary Sir Robert Craigie to, as he put it, "express personally my appreciation for their past efforts." Togo gave the ambassadors copies of the imperial rescript, solely for their information since notice was officially transmitted by Japan's fourteen-point cable handed over in Washington. In yet another mishap for Japanese diplomatic timing that day, both ambassadors arrived late because Tokyo police had already cut telephone service to the embassies when Togo's secretary began trying to get them.

Of course, cutting telephone service was the least of it. Police actually apprehended the diplomats, their families, and such foreign nationals as reporters and correspondents. At the American embassy it was simply a question of putting a guard on the gate and locking everyone up inside. Naval attaché Henri Smith-Hutton had the defining experience: He'd heard Japanese ships had been sighted along the coast of Malaya, moving south, and of FDR's message for the Emperor. He and his wife, Mary, decided to keep their daughter out of school that day. In the morning he found he could not tune in San Francisco radio but could get Shanghai, which was advising Americans to keep calm but stay off the street. Smith-Hutton went to the embassy to see what he could learn; in an assistant's office stood a crowd of people, listening to station KGII from San Francisco, which had announced the bombing of Pearl Harbor. Smith-Hutton called the news up to Joseph Grew, who was surprised and reported that he had left the Japanese Foreign Ministry just fifteen minutes before and Togo had said nothing of it. Grew asked Smith-Hutton to verify the news through Navy channels.

The attaché ordered his car for the drive to the Navy Ministry—only a few blocks away, but these days foreigners were much safer inside cars—and arrived there in about three minutes. He asked to see Captain Nakamura Katsuhira, a senior aide to Shimada whom he had known for several years. Smith-Hutton recounts:

> I told him that my ambassador had sent me. I asked about an attack on Pearl Harbor, whether there was truth in the report and if so, when we could expect to get a notice of the declaration of war. He looked rather sad, because I think he was really a friend of the United States. He said, yes the report was true. He had just learned about it himself, and could verify it. As to the declaration of war, he couldn't say, because that would have to come from the Foreign [Ministry] and was not a Navy Department matter. . . . He said I could report to the ambassador that the attack had taken place, and that he personally was not happy about it. I told him I wasn't either, and I said that this might be the last time I would see him. I hoped he would survive the war. He said he hoped the same for me.

Nakamura usually bade farewell in his office, but this time he saw Smith-Hutton down the ministry's grand staircase and to his car. Shortly after the attaché returned to the U.S. embassy, the electricity there was cut off and police arrived to confiscate radios. Thus began an internment that would endure until the summer 1942 exchange on the liner *Gripsholm*.

In the meantime Captain Nakamura had a further appointment that day, with the *German* naval attaché. A state of war with the Allies meant that the Japanese and Germans had become allies too, in fact rather than theory. Vice Admiral Paul Wennecker, German attaché, had long been receiving a modicum of cooperation from the Imperial Navy on such things as acquisition of commodities for import to Germany, organizing voyages by blockade runners, limited technological exchanges, exchange of intelligence information, and supplies for German merchant raiders. But the Japanese had always been reticent about sharing anything regarding Imperial Navy operations. On the afternoon of December 8, according to Wennecker's diary, Nakamura "emphasized in solemn terms that as from today Japan has entered the greatest epoch in the whole of its history. He thanked me warmly for past cooperation and he asked me for my continued support. He spoke at length about cooperation between our two nations as the urgent priority of the moment."

Captain Maeda Tadashi, chief of the *joho kyoku*'s German desk, was appointed special liaison with the Germans. Wennecker had already met Maeda that day. Among the operational details the Japanese disclosed were locations of air attacks, the landing of Japanese troops at Singora on the Kra Isthmus, the fact that I-boats were off San Francisco, and Tokyo's decision to make no attack upon the Russians. Interestingly, the Japanese specifically told the Germans that damage at Pearl Harbor had included "numerous major units *and storage tanks*" (my italics). Later that day the Imperial Navy informed the Germans that the British battleship *Prince of Wales* had left Singapore, presumably to attack the invasion forces, and that no U.S. aircraft carriers had been at Pearl Harbor when it was attacked. Captain Nakamura told Wennecker that American embassy staff would likely be handed over to the Portuguese at Macao. This latter apparently reflected a preliminary intention never carried out. Nakamura also referred to the "farewell visit" of attaché Smith-Hutton, whom Wennecker had known well for a number of years from the old Attachés' Club.

The German Wennecker and any number of others say that the Navy Ministry put out its first communiqué, noting the existence of a state of war, at 6:00 A.M. There were quickly special editions of the biggest Japanese newspapers, including *Yomiuri, Nichi Nichi,* and *Mainichi Shimbun.* So quick were the Japanese that the first memory of that day on the part of French reporter Robert Guillain was of newsboys hawking the extra editions. Guillain remained free and was not molested because the Vichy government of France, officially cooperating with the Japanese in Indochina, remained at peace with the Empire. Guillain went to a 9:00 A.M. press conference called by the Foreign Ministry and looked in vain for friends and colleagues like Otto Tolischus of *The New York Times,* Bob Bellaire of the United Press International, and Max Hill from Associated Press. Unknown to Guillain, the Japanese police had already sequestered them.

At the press conference and afterward, Guillain found troubling anomalies in Tokyo's account of the inception of the war. Guillain asked the Foreign Ministry spokesman whether the mimeographed documents they had been handed, including an imperial proclamation announcing war, were copies of the declaration of war delivered in Washington. The reporter wrote: "The only answer I got was a scowl and a look of repressed fury." Guillain later discovered that the proclamation he held at 9:00 A.M. was not actually signed by Hirohito until 11:45 (probably during the audience with Kido), that a "declaration" of war was first mentioned on the radio at exactly that time, but that Japanese were informed at 11:20 that there had been an attack on the American fleet in Hawaii, and had known since 6:00 A.M. that fighting had broken out across the Pacific.

Meanwhile the whereabouts of reporter Otto Tolischus had also been of concern to Ofusa Junnosuke, his Japanese assistant. Ofusa had gone to the *New York Times* office, near the U.S. embassy, upon hearing the news of war from his wife, who had gotten it from the radio. Tolischus was nowhere to be found. Ofusa talked to local police detectives, who confirmed he had been arrested and taken to the Akasaka station. The most Ofusa could do was arrange for some breakfast to be taken to Tolischus. He and other American reporters would eventually be repatriated aboard the *Gripsholm.*

Reporters Tolischus and Ofusa found December 8 especially trying because they had been up late the night before preparing to cover a speech General Tojo had scheduled in Hibiya Park. With the start of the war, in fact, Tojo had a wild day. Thousands turned up for the speech, making the occasion, impromptu, even more a patriotic rally than intended by its organizers. Tojo drank in the excitement of the crowd; later he paid his respects at the Yasukuni Shrine and the grave of his own father, who had also been a general in the Imperial Army. Tojo capped his day with a speech over Radio Tokyo:

"Japan has done her utmost to prevent this war," the prime minister declared, "but in self-preservation and for self-existence, we could not help declaring war."

So began the heady days of the first stage of the war, Japan's wild celebration of victory upon victory; there were so many victories that acute observers began to caution against "victory disease." Like Pearl Harbor, many of the early victories would be products of airpower, of wings across the water, of the Japanese Naval Air Force striking across the sea.

THE VICTORY TOKYO HAD THE LEAST RIGHT TO EXPECT WAS THE ONE IT GAINED IN THE SKY over the Philippines. As a means of protecting Philippine invasion forces the Japanese hoped to gain supremacy in the air over those islands. Unfortunately for the Japanese, an insuperable obstacle barred their way to any easy assertion of air control over the Philippines. IGHQ had determined to give preference in timing to the Navy's Pearl Harbor attack, and the separation in distance (and time zones) between there and the Philippines was so great that the necessary early-morning attack on Hawaii would occur during the middle of the night, Philippine time. The state of aeronautical science, navigation, crew training, and aircraft technology (avionics) in 1941 was such as to make an extended range night flight to target over water by a bomber formation next to impossible. Thus the American command in the Philippines would inevitably know that war had begun. There was no possibility of taking the Philippines by surprise. As a matter of fact, a transpacific telephone call at 3:40 A.M. on December 8 alerted Philippine commander General Douglas MacArthur that Pearl Harbor was under attack.

A second obstacle in the way of any Japanese assertion of air control would be the strength of the American and Filipino air units there. Some of these planes, in particular those of the Filipinos, were obsolescent to be sure, but then so were some Japanese aircraft. Moreover, a large fraction of the air strength the Japanese had assembled in Taiwan, formations of the Imperial Army's 5th Air Division, could be counted out almost entirely because the crews lacked skills for over-water navigation and the planes could barely fly far enough to reach the tip of Luzon, the northernmost major Philippine island. American air bases ringed Manila, in central Luzon a hundred miles or so farther south. The round-trip distance from there to Japanese bases on Taiwan was on the order of 1,100 miles, and there was not a fighter plane in the world in 1941, including the vaunted Zero, that could make a flight that long and fight a battle in the middle of it. Against unescorted bombers the Americans had 175 fighter planes in the Philippines, some 107 of them relatively modern P-40 Warhawks.

The number of American fighter planes suggests the dimension of the final difficulty for any adversary that wished to gain air superiority over the Philippines—that is, the sheer size of the Philippine-American force. Including obsolescent and miscellaneous aircraft, the count in the U.S. Army's official history of this campaign comes to 277 planes. One may discount ten squadrons of the Philippine air force with the oldest and slowest aircraft, but between P-40 fighters, Boeing B-17 "Flying Fortress" bombers, and U.S. Navy PBY Catalinas there were about 175 or so modern aircraft. Japanese operations staff officer Captain Tomioka Sadatoshi has been quoted in a history by MacArthur's postwar command to the effect that experience in China suggested a three-to-one margin in aircraft was necessary to ensure success. The Japanese on Taiwan did not meet that benchmark, even counting unusable Army aircraft. If the American air forces in the Philippines had grown much more than they did, the Japanese air offensive that ensued might have proved altogether impossible.

In terms of actual strength, the Japanese Naval Air Force assembled on Taiwan some 108 Zero fighters, plus spares and reserve planes—almost 250 fighters; 81 G4M ("Betty") medium bombers, 36 older G3M ("Nell") medium bombers, 15 reconnaissance planes, and 27 transports. Together the air armada (not counting reserves) amounted to 267 aircraft. Even with 13 older A5M fighters and 24 flying boats the JNAF had in the Mandates, centered on Palau, this did not measure up to Baron Tomioka's margin of advantage. To these numbers the Japanese Army Air Force could add 72 fighters, 27 medium bombers, 54 light bombers, 27 reconnaissance planes, and 12 liaison planes in its 5th Air Division. As noted, these aircraft were of extremely limited operational utility, and about all the JNAF's Eleventh Air Fleet expected from the Army planes was the necessary air support for the Japanese Army troops once they had landed in the Philippines.

Complicating other Japanese difficulties, the Far East strategic situation hardly remained static. There were important developments during the last prewar months. This was not a matter of mobilization of indigenous forces, although that was under way in the Philippines, the Netherlands East Indies, and Malaya too, but of a new strategic initiative from Washington. President Roosevelt and Army chief of staff General George Marshall appear to have concluded that Japan might be deterred if the Philippines could be built into an air bastion threatening offensive action against Taiwan and Japan itself. It was to this end that B-17 four-engine heavy bombers suddenly joined the Americans' Far East Air Force; and the planes present on December 8 represented about half the complement the United States expected to reach by early 1942. Additional artillery and anti-aircraft units, plus specialized troops, were also en route to the Philippines as part of this buildup. The onset of war halted the effort. The Japanese, who mounted ventures during the last months of peace to gather data on Philippine air assets, perforce became aware of the forces' augmentation.

Given Japan's plans for invasion of the Philippines it was necessary to neutralize the American airpower, but the attempt was going to be dicey precisely because Baron Tomioka's formula remained unattainable. That put a premium on cooperation between bombers and fighters, but led the Japanese directly back to the limitations of their available fighters.

One possibility was to utilize aircraft carriers to bring fighters into Philippine waters, launching them from there to cover bomber flights. In October the Navy sent to Taiwan Rear Admiral Kakuta Kakuji's Carrier Division 4, with two light carriers and a converted ship, but the combined capacity of these aviation vessels amounted to just over seventy aircraft and that was hardly enough. While sources usually focus on this factor, there would have been an added difficulty in coordinating actions between fighters and bombers flying from different points and responding to different chains of command. This is especially true in view of the JNAF's limited radio equipment.

There were a number of good problem solvers among the Eleventh Air Fleet and its staff, not least chief of staff Admiral Onishi, previously seen aiding the inception of the Pearl Harbor plan. Others included his Etajima classmate Rear Admiral Tada Takeo, who commanded the 21st Air Flotilla; Captain Kamei Yoshio, of the 3rd Air Group, who had pioneered the systematic study of air battle tactics in the JNAF; Commander Okamura Motoharu, formerly a daredevil aviator of Genda's Flying Circus; and Lieutenant Shingo Hideki, brilliant leader of Zero fighters and currently top pilot and director of training for the Tainan Air Group. Practically all the senior officers of the air fleet had experience in China and many of them, in particular Shingo, knew that the JNAF had set distance records in fighter escort of bombers, most recently in attacks against Chungking from Hankow. Someone suggested boosting the Zero's endurance to execute the Philippine missions directly from Taiwan. Admiral Onishi was not adverse to this solution, which also garnered support from air fleet senior staff officer Commander Ikegami Tsuguo.

The nucleus of the JNAF air units on Taiwan, at least the fighter arm, consisted of veteran pilots from China whom Lieutenant Yokoyama Tamotsu had brought with him that summer, when the Japanese broke up their old land-based air units to man the fleet. Many veterans were assigned to Captain Kamei's 3rd Air Group, a JNAF experiment with a large all-fighter unit. Kamei's group proved so efficient that the JNAF quickly added the Tainan Air Group commanded by Captain Saito Masahisa. Both captains began to emphasize long-distance flying in their unit training. According to Petty Officer Sakai Saburo of Tainan Air Group, some 150 fighter pilots plus an equal number of bomber crews made the move to Taiwan in September. "All the men were restricted to their home fields," Sakai writes. "From day-break until late at night, seven days a week, in all kinds of weather, we were engaged in training flights to learn the finer points of escort missions, mass formation flying, strafing runs, and so forth."

Commander Okumiya Masatake, an Eleventh Air Fleet staff officer, con-firms that Kamei and Saito were tough trainers of men. Under their leader-ship the Zero pilots accomplished feats of air endurance. By cruising at a slower speed (115 knots) at medium altitude (12,000 feet), reducing pro-peller pitch, and using the leanest possible mixtures of aviation gasoline with air, the Japanese pilots cut average gas consumption from thirty-five gallons per hour to eighteen. Sakai Saburo himself set the record, less than seventeen gallons per hour. The Zeros became capable of flights of ten to twelve hours, and suddenly acquired the range to strike the Philippines and return.

In early November, Eleventh Air Fleet held a critical staff conference to finalize arrangements for the anticipated offensive. Vice Admiral Tsukahara Nizhizo, the commander, had to make a final choice between land-based air operations or the ships of Carrier Division 4. Tsukahara's staff had been con-ferring constantly with the air groups and also consulting aeronautical engineers from Japanese industry. Some officers pointed out additional drawbacks in the carrier option: It would divide the fleet's limited number of mechanics between shore and ship bases; the small carriers would have to fly off their fighters a few at a time because of deck capacity; some fighters would have to be kept behind to protect the ships; and moving the carriers close to the Philippines risked warning Americans of the coming attack. Admiral Tsukahara unhesitatingly chose the land-based option. Light car-rier *Ryujo* moved south to Palau to attack the southern Philippines, while the other two ships returned to Empire waters.

Now there was only the countdown for war. Tsukahara sent reconnais-sance planes over the Philippines on December 2, and on the fourth and fifth they returned for aerial photographs of the American air bases at Clark and Iba fields from just 20,000 feet. The pictures showed thirty-two B-17 bombers, three medium-size aircraft, and seventy-one small planes. The Imperial Navy estimate of U.S. aircraft on Luzon increased to 300 planes. Japanese pilots braced for a rough fight.

The Americans, too, had reconnaissance tentacles out, primarily the PBY

Catalinas of Patrol Wing 10. These planes scouted Taiwan on cloudy days, flying as low as 1,500 feet and slowly to boot. The JNAF repeatedly tried to intercept and bring them down, sometimes scrambling fighters by the dozen. "The American pilots were amazing," recalls Sakai. "With their lumbering, slow planes, they should have proved easy prey, but we failed ever to intercept a single PBY . . . invariably the Catalinas slipped into the heavy cloud cover and escaped unscathed. Their pictures, taken at such low altitude, must have told the Americans everything they wanted to know about our air units."

This comment brings the discussion back to Pearl Harbor Day, December 8 in the Philippines. The Far East Air Forces had B-17 bombers in place at Clark Field (with fighters at Iba and Nichols fields), evident knowledge of Japanese dispositions, an emerging shift in war planning to assume an offensive stance, and warning of the Pearl Harbor attack at such an early hour that no JNAF attack forces could yet take to the air. What happened?

Major General Lewis Brereton, in charge of the Far East Air Forces, went to General Douglas MacArthur's headquarters in Manila to get permission to send the Flying Fortresses on an offensive mission against Taiwan. Brereton arrived about 5:00 A.M., only to find that MacArthur was already closeted with senior subordinates. Brereton could get no further than chief of staff and éminence grise General Richard K. Sutherland. The two officers gave contradictory accounts of what then transpired. Sutherland claimed that Brereton wanted to mount a strike but did not know what was in Taiwan and needed reconnaissance first, and that he himself approved the idea for MacArthur. Brereton's account was that he announced he was going to attack, in two waves, starting with his B-17s at Clark Field and following with the rest, previously relocated to Del Monte Field on Mindanao. Brereton had Sutherland telling him to go ahead and make preliminary preparations but do nothing until MacArthur's approval. MacArthur himself recounted that no request for such an attack was ever made, and that he first learned of it from a newspaper article months later.

There is no way to make sense of the conflicting accounts. Some authors are inclined to excuse the general and blame Sutherland for acting (or not acting) in his name. Dwight D. Eisenhower, who had served under MacArthur until 1939, later told journalist Cyrus L. Sulzberger that MacArthur had had some notion the Japanese would not attack the Philippines. If so, the idea was out of step both with longstanding American expectations for Japanese strategy and with the obvious JNAF buildup on Taiwan. Commander (later admiral) John Bulkeley, who skippered the PT boat unit that successfully evacuated MacArthur and his family to the southern Philippines, where they were flown out to Australia, had another version in which Philippine president Manuel L. Quezon asked MacArthur to refrain from offensive action. As quoted by his later intelligence chief,

Courtney Whitney, the American general said in his own defense: "My orders were explicit not to initiate hostilities against the Japanese." Whose orders those might have been, MacArthur left unsaid. If Washington's, presumably in accord with the policy of late November, these were canceled by instructions on the morning of Pearl Harbor to execute existing war plans. If Quezon's orders were being referred to, there is as much evidence of them (none) as MacArthur wrote there was of Brereton's request to attack Taiwan. Even MacArthur's biographer D. Clayton James concedes that the general inevitably bore a share of the responsibility.

Despite American confusion, things might still have turned out all right. The Japanese had their own difficulties in those first hours of war. For an air strike at daybreak (6:12 A.M.) JNAF commanders planned to launch their planes at about 4:00. Petty Officer Sakai remembers being awoken by an orderly around 2:00. Sakai recalls fog shrouding his field at Tainan an hour later. Other Japanese accounts maintain that fog had already closed in all over Taiwan, very unusual for this subtropical climate, and persisted until after 9:00 A.M. The predawn takeoff for the air strike had to be postponed, and launch occurred only shortly before the fog dissipated.

A further mystery regarding the Philippine air battle concerns feint attacks. Japanese accounts state that the Eleventh Air Fleet planned a diversionary effort to exhaust American fighter potential before arrival of the main strike waves. But once weather had set the Japanese back more than six hours, they maintain, Admiral Tsukahara canceled the fancy feints. Americans, however, believe they detected precursor raids (perhaps these were diversions) and responded to them. Between 8:00 and 8:15 A.M. Iba Field's radar station, the only one in the Philippines, picked up Japanese aircraft, and P-40 fighters scrambled to intercept them. The seventeen B-17 bombers from Clark Field took off to avoid being caught on the ground by an air attack. There was nothing to intercept, though, for the only Japanese planes aloft at that time were JAAF groups bound for northern Luzon and a couple of single JNAF aircraft sent to check the weather.

Eventually the P-40s had to return to Iba to refuel, and the B-17s were recalled to Clark to be loaded in anticipation of orders to fly against Taiwan. Their crews went to lunch. About 11:45 A.M. the Iba radar again sighted a formation of planes over the South China Sea. Warnings went to Clark by radio, teletype, and phone. The message over the Far East Air Forces radio net may have been blocked by JNAF interference, but it has also been stated that the responsible radio operator at Clark had left his post for lunch. At headquarters someone recorded the teletype message being composed, sent, and acknowledged, but no one at Clark Field remembers it. Finally, an air warning by phone was received by an unidentified junior officer at Clark who promised to tell the base commander or his staff, but there is no record of his doing so.

At Nielson Field communications were better, and a squadron of interceptors was dispatched to cover Manila, another Bataan, and the 34th Pursuit Squadron from Del Carmen was ordered to cover Clark. Unfortunately a dust storm precluded takeoffs from Del Carmen. By 12:15 P.M. the 20th Pursuit right at Clark had been rearmed and was ready to take off, but it got no warning or any orders to patrol over the field. Very shortly thereafter the first Japanese planes appeared overhead.

Japanese air planners programmed an initial attack by medium bombers flying at altitude. There were twenty-seven of these planes in the formation that hit Clark Field, laying down strings of bombs that walked the length of the base. The Zero fighters continued to escort for the first ten minutes of the bombers' return flight, to block any last-minute counterattacks, then swung back to strafe Clark in low-level runs. It would be the same at Nicolson and several satellite fields. Wrote Petty Officer Sakai, "We still could not believe that the Americans did not have fighters in the air waiting for us." Similarly, Commander Shimada Koichi, who began the day aboard one of the JNAF weather planes and ended it greeting returning fliers on behalf of air fleet staff, witnessed repeated expressions of bewilderment from crews puzzled at the absence of opposition.

In terms of statistics, the Eleventh Air Fleet sent 53 medium bombers and 53 fighters against Iba Field, plus another strike group of 54 bombers escorted by 36 fighters against Clark. American and Filipino losses included 53 P-40s, 3 P-35s, and 16 B-17s destroyed along with 20 to 30 older aircraft. Many other planes were heavily damaged, along with facilities and runways. Casualties amounted to 80 killed and 150 wounded. The JNAF losses were 7 Zero fighters. Some began to call the Philippine air disaster a little Pearl Harbor, but in contrast to the Hawaiian debacle, which resulted in the immediate replacement of Admiral Husband Kimmel, in the Philippines General MacArthur retained command.

Also in contrast to the Japanese at Pearl Harbor, from Taiwan Admiral Tsukahara's fliers systematically exploited initial success. On December 9 the JNAF shifted target to the fighter base at Nichols Field and its satellites, programming a night bombardment to be followed by a big daylight attack. The night bombing by seven planes (two bombers of the nine-plane squadron had had to abort the mission) went according to plan, but fog over Taiwan this time forced cancellation of all daytime activity. On December 10, spurred by predictions of clearing weather, the JNAF sent twenty-seven bombers and thirty-six fighters against the Nichols complex, eighteen Zero fighters to Del Carmen, and another eighteen Zeros to provide cover for invasion convoys bound for the small northern Luzon ports of Vigan and Aparri. The main strike of fifty-four bombers, however, was aimed at the Cavite Naval Base, along Manila Bay.

At Cavite, pandemonium soon reigned. Over the two previous days the

Americans had tried to move such supplies of ammunition, torpedoes, and spare parts as they could, and to prepare the base for attack. Most of the Asiatic Fleet had already dispersed, to act in concert with the British in Malaya and the Dutch in the Netherlands East Indies to defend the chain of islands strategists had begun calling the Malay Barrier. Destroyer *Peary*, virtually the only major surface combatant at Cavite that day, would be hit by a 220-pound bomb. Submarines, submarine tenders, PT boats, and fleet auxiliaries were also present; several were hit. But the worst damage was to the base itself, where the power station was hit, crippling water pumps needed to fight fire, and then the torpedo works were set ablaze. For the rest of that day and night Cavite would be rocked by explosions, seared by fires. The flames lit the night sky for Manila across the bay. Much of the base was burned to cinders.

Thus early operations by the Eleventh Air Fleet crippled MacArthur's defense. The Philippine campaign was just beginning, and the main Japanese armies had yet to set foot on Luzon, but already Americans were laboring under very adverse conditions, at least on the ground. At sea and in the air, subsequent attempts at defense amounted to little: fugitive PT boats furtively working out of coves on Bataan; submarines making war patrols until their tenders were driven away, then relocating to Australia; PBY Catalinas of Patrol Wing 10 leaving to join the Dutch. On December 31 the *Mactan*, an ancient interisland steamer suddenly transformed into a hospital ship and crammed with 134 American and 90 Filipino wounded, became the last vessel (other than blockade runners) to escape from Luzon.

Naval shore personnel, except for OP-20-G's codebreakers, were reorganized as infantry to help defend Bataan. On January 9, 1942, was created the Provisional Naval Battalion, which consisted of 150 ground crewmen from Patrol Wing 10; 80 sailors from the Cavite ammunition depot; 120 sailors from various shore installations at Cavite, Mariveles, and Olongapo; and 130 sailors from submarine tender *Canopus*. The battalion would be led by the senior remaining aviator from Patrol Wing 10, Commander Francis J. Bridget, whom we first encountered as an assistant naval attaché in Tokyo. Here was Bridget, still in the Philippines, still doing penance for running afoul of his Tokyo boss. Bridget's unit fought in key battles in Bataan in late January, absorbed losses, and finally had to be broken up. Bridget himself, with 300 men, ended up defending Fort Hughes, in Manila Bay just off Corregidor. They would be lost when that island fort surrendered to end American-Filipino resistance on Luzon.

The whole saga of "little Pearl Harbor" and the way MacArthur's command was taken by surprise as the war began is especially distressing in view of the fact that Luzon happened to be a major center of the secret intelligence war against Japan. There the 16th Naval District's Station Cast was actively involved in the OP-20-G codebreaking effort. Unlike Pearl Harbor,

Station Cast had not been denied intelligence; it was the location of one of the very precious American analogue machines capable of deciphering Purple message traffic. Again unlike Pearl Harbor, Station Cast was directly engaged in the effort to break the JN-25 fleet codes. Thus MacArthur not only received warnings from Washington but had access to his own code-breakers. The story of Station Cast has never appeared in public print.

IN IMPORTANT WAYS THE RISE AND FALL OF THE PHILIPPINE STATION OF OP-20-G MIRRORED that of the treaty system that was supposed to ensure peace. Always an important link in the chain of American radio intelligence, the Philippines became progressively more vital as the Far Eastern crisis grew. Its radio monitors supplemented those at Shanghai and Guam; along with the latter, also, the Philippines became the first of the mid-Pacific network of radio direction-finding stations. Its importance waxed even greater when, in 1940–1941, as a result of worsening tensions in China, the 4th Marines were withdrawn from Shanghai along with OP-20-G's erstwhile Station A. Henceforth Far Eastern monitoring resources were concentrated in the Philippines, which also offered the best cryptanalytical capability west of Pearl Harbor.

Perversely in a way, as the importance of the Philippines grew, capability for radio interception shrank. This was partly because Station A had been an ideal interception site given the presence of major Japanese radio facilities in the same city. That listening post could not be matched by the Philippines, located miles from the nearest Japanese radios. But another factor in the loss of capability would be the realignment of the facilities in the Philippines themselves, an action expressly intended to improve their defensibility in time of war.

What has been called the Philippine station here actually consisted of several facilities, including at times (after 1929) units at Olongapo and Mariveles in Bataan, at Sangley Point, and at Cavite Naval Base. The outstations were direction-finding or interception units; Cavite had both a radio unit and Station C's cryptanalytical and administrative staffs. The Cavite facility was housed with the base brig. Enlisted men's quarters were located above the commissary in the old Spanish fort. An interception unit worked at Cavite from 1936 on.

As the treaty system broke down, however, Washington began considering fortification of Pacific islands, as had been prohibited by the arms-control regime. The question of fortifying Guam received much attention at the time, and efforts at Midway and Wake have attracted interest since the war, but little has been said about the island of Corregidor in Manila Bay. The Navy resolved to build a new facility for Station C on that island located in an underground (therefore bombproof) tunnel and defended by Corregidor's extensive fortifications. The U.S. Army provided a site and approved construction in November 1938, an effort partly utilizing convict labor from local prisons. The Navy's Bureaus of Docks and of Engineering each initially provided $10,000 for the project, with the bulk of money included in the fiscal year 1940 defense budget under the innocuous title "improvement of radio facilities." Eventually $39,000 was spent to build the tunnel itself and $53,000 for quarters, services, and equipment.

During 1939 an advance party of four radiomen plus Chief Radioman O. C. Coonce went to the site to test reception conditions there. The new Station C would be at Monkey Point on Corregidor, so called because a colony of monkeys inhabited the place, on the south shore of the island. The sailors more or less uneasily coexisted with the curious monkeys, who climbed over everything. The monkeys were frightened, however, when blasting began for the tunnel, which began as a pit more than 130 feet long, 70 feet wide, and 30 feet deep. Essential facilities were built, the whole thing was backfilled, and then barracks, officers' quarters, and a tennis court were constructed aboveground, about a hundred yards from the tunnel entrance. Station C moved in toward the end of summer 1940.

Life during the earliest months was about as sweet as it got in the Philippines. The heat and humidity were grueling except during the rainy seasons, of which there were two—a precursor phase of late-afternoon tropical showers, then a monsoon period with sheets of water falling from the sky. The misery of the rain was offset by the tendency of the air to cool after a few days of showers. Quarters at Monkey Point were simple but adequate, and the men had Filipino house servants. Life was most pleasant until December 1940, when the Navy sent all families and dependents home. Only the wife of Station C's commander, Lieutenant Rudolph J. Fabian, stayed on, with their son. She had a broken leg at the time and was unfit to travel. Mrs. Fabian left about a month afterward.

None of the various figures on the complement of Station C agree. There was steady growth, however. In fiscal year 1939 the Asiatic Fleet had been authorized three Navy officers and a Marine officer, five cryptanalytic clerks, and thirty-eight radiomen. By the late summer of 1941 there were fifty-five or sixty personnel, including about ten cryptanalytic people and perhaps six officers, both cryptanalysts and language officers. Lieutenant Fabian still commanded and his planned relief, Lieutenant John M. Lietwiler, who had just completed cryptanalytical training, worked under him. Later they reversed roles. Language officers included Allyn Cole, very shortly sent back to Pearl Harbor; Rufus L. Taylor, and Thomas Mackie, both of whom were among Smith-Hutton's last crop in Tokyo, men he rushed out of Japan to prevent their being caught there by the onset of war.

The men of the "Naval Radio Laboratory," as Station C was once innocu-

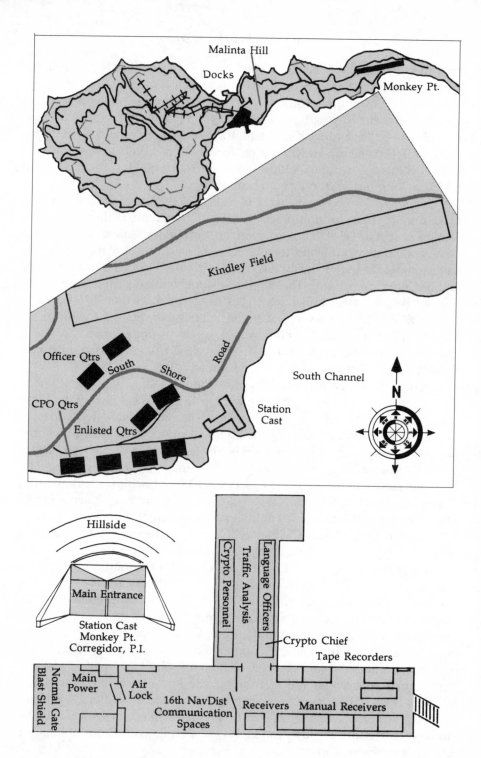

II. Station Cast (Philippine Islands)

ously called, kept very busy after families left. It seemed everyone had a pet project. A draft of seven additional yeomen was added in early 1941 to augment the unit's cryptanalytical capabilities. One of them, Yeoman Robert E. Dowd, had been typing up ship's logs aboard the Asiatic Fleet destroyer *John D. Ford* until called one day to the destroyer tender *Blackhawk* for an interview with fleet intelligence officer Redfield Mason. The officer asked if he drank or smoked and that was about the extent of the examination of his qualifications.

Dowd, who had led a peripatetic life, beginning with his effort to become a newspaper cartoonist, was immediately put to work on the Imperial Navy's five-digit numerical code, the infamous JN-25, by this time in its "b" version. "I didn't know that ships communicated except by flag, by semaphore, and by signal," Dowd recalled. "I was a cryptographer?" When he did not do too well with JN-25, he was put to work in the tunnel's vault, which housed the station's analogue machine for deciphering the Japanese diplomatic Red Code. In the spring of 1941 a Purple machine arrived, giving Corregidor both capabilities. Dowd became proficient on the machines. The station also had IBM card-sorting equipment, run under the careful supervision of Chief Yeoman Jerry Knutsen, which was critical for finding solutions to groups in JN-25(b), a cipher that Cast actively attacked, but that only slowly yielded its secrets.

Supporting the officer cryptanalysts by preparing forms used to find comparisons among code groups, at least until mid-1941 when he returned to the States, was Chief Arnold Conant. Actually Conant had been a pharmacist and ended up in radio intelligence, like many others, only by indirection. He had been on Guam dispensing medicine and began fooling around with a cryptanalysis correspondence course OP-20-G offered. He'd given up, but a buddy of his had tried the same thing and kept asking Conant for help. Cryptanalyst Joe Wenger examined the man's assignments and asked who had been helping him. The next thing Conant knew, OP-20-G had asked him to join. Conant made an arrangement that would not set him back on promotions; then he transferred.

There were as many stories as there were men. Edward Otte, one of the Corregidor intercept operators, grew up in Sheboygan, Wisconsin. He and his friends liked to pass the time in a downtown soda fountain where they were served by a fellow named Tack Walford. The soda jerk enlisted in the Navy, and Otte saw him on home leave once. He himself got ideas about enlisting and became a radioman, then an intercept expert. Posted to Cavite, Otte was walking down the street when who should he meet but Tack himself, who it turned out had become a radioman too and was even with the same unit.

The intelligence product from Station C, Cast, provided an extra window on the Japanese. Radio direction finding and traffic analysis, both important

at Cast, provided some of the earliest indications of Japan's war preparations. One report on Imperial Navy fleet organization done from traffic
analysis and completed in October 1941 received Redfield Mason's endorse-
ment: "The conclusion that must be drawn from the organization presented
here is that the Japanese are on a wartime disposition." This paper went to
Washington and nothing more was heard of it. Station Cast also reported
the assembly of Japanese forces and shipping for the Southern Area invasions. At first there was an inclination to disbelief here too. Duane L.
Whitlock, one of Cast's traffic analysts, recalls that Corregidor once reported
the concentration of Japanese shipping for the invasions reached something
like 200 bottoms. They heard nothing for days; then Washington simply
asked whether Corregidor could confirm the figure for the number of ships.
According to Whitlock, by that time Cast analysts had associated about 250
ships with the invasion forces, and they sent the new number. As has
already been seen, by mid- to late November Washington had begun to follow the invasion convoys closely.

Station Cast also had its contribution to make on the "Winds" controversy.
Radioman Edward Otte remembers being asked to listen for such messages
but not anything that happened afterward. Language officer Tom Mackie
would later maintain he *had* received the infamous "east wind, rain" phrase,
but that no one believed him because of the characters used in the kana
message. Yeoman Bob Dowd was working at the next desk on December 4
when Mackie and another officer, named Carlton, were laboring on the
day's intercepts. Dowd remembers they "sat there hour after hour looking
and reviewing and waiting . . . one time they got excited and they didn't say
anything, they jumped and ran." Dowd does not know for certain if this was
the Winds message, but he believes Station Cast did receive it.

Duane Whitlock got his introduction to drawing intelligence conclusions
from radio traffic one day when Lieutenant J. R. Dennis was at Cast.
Whitlock decided that some messages to Japanese destroyers showed they
were about to sail from Taiwan to Palau and he showed the intercepts to
Dennis. The officer took the wind out of his sails, observing that ships bound
for Palau usually went by way of Saipan or Truk. Several days later a Patrol
Wing 10 PBY sighted the Japanese destroyers in the Philippine Sea on their
way to Palau. Dennis began to use Whitlock on analysis after that, and
looked out for his career, too; Whitlock, who had been a radioman second
class when he came to the Philippines, would retire from the Navy a captain.

Japanese aviation was a natural intelligence target for the traffic analysts
and the direction-finding crew. The analysts discovered repeated references
to JNAF units much larger than squadrons, a level of organization not found
in the U.S. Navy. Charlie Johns, a chief petty officer among the traffic analysts, suggested that the units be called air flotillas. More than a year later,
when the United States captured an actual Japanese codebook, radio intelli-

gence discovered that this was the nomenclature the Imperial Navy in fact used.

Direction finding also offered potential for early warning of air raids. Taiwan was almost directly north of the Philippines, and Cast could pick up JNAF transmissions as soon as the planes took to the air. As a JNAF formation flew south and took a route either east or west of Luzon, the bearing would change. Plotting successive bearings could reveal speed, and when the bearings switched to a more direct line one could infer that the planes were swinging in on their final approach. About an hour of warning could be had in this fashion.

Station Cast's official customer was Admiral Hart, commander in chief of the Asiatic Fleet, but the station also had a direct line to the G-2 office of MacArthur's command. There is no evidence whether Cast picked up JNAF traffic, or issued any warnings, on the morning of the debacle at Clark Field. The question was already mostly moot for Hart, most of whose fleet had dispersed to the Malay Barrier. As for MacArthur, a recurrent complaint heard from Navy radiomen at Corregidor would be that G-2 seemed to have no idea what to do with their intelligence, how to draw a substantive conclusion from a report or how to act on it. Most likely, therefore, a Station Cast warning, even had there been one, could not have averted the "little Pearl Harbor" of December 8.

Whatever else happened, Station Cast, at least, began the war with confidence. Ed Otte put it well when he recalled that at first war "was very hard to believe but we thought, 'So what, we can whip the Japanese easily.' We were so propagandized with the fact that the United States is the strongest military nation in the world. We didn't worry about anything, until the next day when these big bombers came." That was the day of Cavite, and the sailors went outside the tunnel to see the JNAF bombers, silver streaks against an azure sky, flash over them and on to the other side of Manila Bay. Soon they could see columns of smoke against the shoreline.

The Cavite bombing punctuated what might otherwise have been a very celebratory mood for, as it turns out, Station Cast had just produced the first meaningful decrypt from JN-25(b), the Japanese naval code. Unfortunately it was too late for Pearl Harbor and also for the British, who had a battleship unit at Singapore they called Force Z. Like Clark Field, no British or American intelligence warning could have saved them. The ill-fated warships had left on a death ride up the Malay coast.

GIVEN JAPAN'S DESPERATE NEED FOR RESOURCES FROM THE SOUTHERN AREA, A CONSIDERAtion that had led Tokyo to war in the first place, it is hardly surprising that the Japanese acted to seize those objectives from the very first day. In actuality Tokyo planned to invade Malaya at the outset, and assembly of the invasion convoys for this operation, for most of the forces involved were destined to come by sea, was utilized to cloak the secret mission to Pearl Harbor. A corollary would be that the Japanese expected their Malay invasion forces to be discovered en route, with the British making their best effort to repel them.

Under Imperial Navy plans, Vice Admiral Kondo's Southern Expeditionary Fleet was responsible for all invasion operations, not only the Malayan effort but also attempts to conquer the Philippines and Netherlands East Indies. But Kondo himself merely provided general cover for the initial wave of invasion convoys, with a main body built around the battleships *Kongo* and *Haruna*. The admiral assigned the tricky business of shepherding the invasion convoys to their landing points would be Ozawa Jisaburo, commanding the so-called Malay Force.

At IGHQ the Army and Navy negotiated a central agreement concerning southern operations, but details were left up to the field commanders of both services. Key features were settled at a conference among staffs at Saigon on November 15. Army operations staff officer Colonel Tsuji Masanobu, who had had much to do with Japanese Army intelligence collection in Malaya, saw Ozawa here for the first time. The operations staff officer thought the admiral had thick, heavy lips, a not uncommon reaction. (Ozawa, Nagano, and Nagumo were regarded as the ugliest admirals in the fleet.) Tsuji nonetheless admired Ozawa as one of the bravest of naval officers. On this occasion, too, Ozawa came through.

"I shall do everything possible that is desired by the military forces," the admiral declared. "I will be responsible for protection of the convoy of ships and of the disembarkation."

Silence prevailed in the crowded room as the officers present pondered Ozawa's words. Tsuji thought it "a tragic and grim resolution," and later wrote that cooperation between the Army and Navy for the Malayan campaign was "unparalleled."

Though Japanese Army officers present had some notion of the import of Ozawa's words and the difficulties of the task assumed, Navy men had a rather better idea. The obvious threat came from British aircraft based in Malaya, for the invasion convoy would be within their striking distance for two days or so. Japanese prewar estimates were that the British had about 350 aircraft in Malaya, a formidable force. (In reality British defenses were in a woeful state; unknown to the Japanese, the number of British planes available was just 158, mostly obsolescent or worse. British officers nonetheless made extravagant claims for their capabilities—for example, at a summer 1941 meeting a Royal Air Force staffer asserted that airpower would sink 70 percent of any invasion force.)

More formidable was the threat posed by two British capital ships at

Singapore under Admiral Sir Tom Phillips ("Tom Thumb" to British seamen for his short stature). Force Z contained the battleship *Prince of Wales,* known for her role in the destruction of the German superdreadnought *Bismarck,* and battle cruiser *Repulse,* along with four destroyers; it had been sent at the behest of Prime Minister Winston Churchill in late October. London wanted these heavy ships to deter Japan from starting war. Accordingly substantial publicity was given to arrival of the *Prince of Wales* at Cape Town on November 16 and Colombo on the twenty-eighth. The Japanese had the east coast of Africa well planted with agents, including at Lourenço Marques in Mozambique, immediately north of South Africa, and could not miss these events. By the time the battleship made Colombo it was obvious that she was headed for the Far East, and Force Z turned up at Singapore, again to loud fanfare, on December 2.

The presence of British capital ships at Singapore greatly complicated Admiral Ozawa's problem escorting the Malay invasion force. Nevertheless, Force Z represented British weakness and not strength. For many years British Far Eastern defense policy had been based on dispatch of the full battle fleet to Singapore—"Main Fleet to Singapore" had been the slogan—and the Malayan military contingent was intended simply to defend the Kra Isthmus and Singapore naval base for the length of time necessary to deploy the fleet. Force Z was no more than a detachment, a sliver drawn away from important naval tasks in the Mediterranean and North Atlantic. British Commonwealth nations like India, Australia, and New Zealand wondered what had become of the "Main Fleet" policy, and Churchill's insistence on sending Force Z may well have had a political purpose in addition to its avowed military function. Be that as it might, at 6:00 A.M. on December 4, when the Malay invasion convoy left Samah port on Hainan, there were British heavy ships in the Far East, and Vice Admiral Ozawa might well have to face them.

A student of naval history sent to the fleet from the presidency of the torpedo school, and a brief stay at Etajima, Ozawa knew that battleships were traditionally considered to possess special advantages. As a young officer after World War I he had made a detailed study of the battle of Jutland, the biggest battleship engagement of that conflict. Interviews with German officers had convinced Ozawa, however, that well-led scouting forces could elude heavy ships. Command of battleship *Haruna,* and later of the Imperial Navy's Battleship Division 3, also gave Ozawa a close understanding of both the potential and limitations of these heavy ships. Ozawa's maneuvers with the Malay Force during the sortie of Force Z show his intention to lead the British battleships back toward Admiral Kondo's covering force.

Flying his flag in the cruiser *Chokai,* Ozawa had under him the four ships of Rear Admiral Kurita Takeo's Cruiser Division 7. These were the *Mogami-*class heavy cruisers, which had confused foreign naval observers when they were first completed with smaller guns and classed as "light" cruisers. There were also a light cruiser and fourteen destroyers of Rear Admiral Hashimoto Shintaro's 3rd Destroyer Flotilla. The British Force Z, with Sir Tom Phillips in the *Prince of Wales,* also included *Repulse,* which, sent on a cruise to Australia, had had to be recalled, and almost missed the sortie. Phillips left Singapore late in the afternoon of December 8. "We are off to look for trouble," he said.

At one point after nightfall on the ninth, only about twenty miles separated Force Z from Ozawa's Malay Force.

Anyone who anticipated a sea battle would be disappointed, however. As at Pearl Harbor, airpower made all the difference in the South China Sea. Specifically, the power of the JNAF's 22nd Air Flotilla, based in French Indochina, carried the day. Under Rear Admiral Matsunaga Sadaichi, an Etajima classmate of Ozawa's destroyer commander Hashimoto, the 22nd Flotilla, a component of the Eleventh Air Fleet, transferred from Taiwan to southern Indochina precisely in order to support the Malaya invasion. The air strength included the Genzan Air Group at Saigon, with thirty-six G3M "Nell" medium bombers and twelve A5M "Claude" fighters; the Mihoro Air Group and Kanoya Air Group at Thu Dau Mot, with thirty-six Nells and twenty-seven G4M "Betty" bombers; and, at Soc Trang, the Yamada unit with twenty-five Zeros and six reconnaissance planes. In all there were about a hundred bombers. These attack planes had the range to strike Force Z anywhere in the South China Sea. Moreover, the Kanoya Group had had long practice in aerial torpedo attack on ships under way.

Okumiya Masatake, Eleventh Air Fleet staff officer, recounts that the JNAF knew from late-November intelligence that Force Z was steaming through the Indian Ocean toward Singapore, and also learned quickly of the ships' arrival there. The threat to Japanese invasion plans was as palpable to Matsunaga as to Ozawa. He had crews scouting the sea up to a hundred miles south of Singapore from December 6 on. "Patrol duty was an unpleasant experience," said Lieutenant Takai Sadao of Genzan Air Group. "We were a single lonely plane flying through the cloudless skies over the southern seas."

To judge from the commentaries in his diary, Admiral Ugaki's Combined Fleet staff worried more about what was happening off Indochina than about the Pearl Harbor mission. Perhaps it was merely that the Nagumo task force operated under total communications blackout, while fleet radio links to the Southern Area stayed open. In any case, on December 5 Ugaki recorded two submarines sighted near Poulo Condore, an island off the Indochina coast that the Malay Force would have to pass. "What is most worrisome is what may happen at Siam Bay tomorrow," Ugaki wrote on December 6, when the Japanese knew they had been seen by British aircraft. But no special dispatches came from Ozawa or Kondo reporting the feared clash, and Ugaki worried instead that rain must have held up the convoy. A JAAF plane flying escort as the convoy passed Point Camau, the southern point of Indochina, actually shot down a British scout aircraft that day. Later the convoy split into smaller units and proceeded to planned landing points at Singora, Patani, and Kota Bharu. Colonel Tsuji, with 25th Army headquarters in *Ryujo Maru*, noted that the actual time of landing, 12:30 A.M. local time, December 8, was a little over an hour *before* Japanese bombs began to fall on Pearl Harbor.

At that moment Force Z remained snugly ensconced in Singapore. Admiral Phillips did not sail with the fleet until 5:35 that afternoon. He could hardly know it was already too late—the major part of the landing activities was completed on the night of the ninth. Phillips bravely steamed north, however. Premonitions of disaster are recorded, from Phillips and many other sailors with the doomed fleet.

The pace of the Japanese landing was not the only matter of which Admiral Phillips remained ignorant. In this respect there seems to have been a disconnection between Force Z and the Far East Combined Bureau (FECB). Captain L. K. Harkness, the FECB chief through 1942, was a gunnery specialist with no previous intelligence experience. He had commanded a destroyer during the early days of the European war. Still, the naval section of FECB was its largest and the boss, Malcolm Burnett, did have such experience. The order-of-battle experts at FECB knew there had been a huge buildup in Japanese air strength in Indochina (from an estimated 74 planes to 245 during November) but failed to appreciate the true extent of the increase (actual numbers of Japanese aircraft were 459 Army and 142 Navy). The British were also aware of the appearance of the JNAF 22nd Air Flotilla in Indochina, the movement of the *Mogami*-class cruisers, and the deployment of the amphibious-trained 5th Infantry Division of the Japanese Army.

Captain Harkness, as senior intelligence officer (in British parlance, chief of intelligence staff, or COIS), had responsibility for passing such information on. But Admiral Phillips was away from Singapore (to confer with American admiral Hart in the Philippines) from December 4 to 7. Phillips's senior planning staff officer, Commander Michael Goodenough, himself handled dealings with FECB, cutting the fleet intelligence officer out of the loop. Goodenough did meet Harkness, but there is no record of anything that passed between them. The FECB and British naval attaché in Tokyo were both reportedly unaware of Japanese prowess at aerial torpedo attack, considering bombing the greater threat. Either way, Tom Phillips never requested any FECB briefing.

Now, Phillips had been deputy chief of naval staff for the Royal Navy during 1939–1941, so he was certainly aware of the growing power of aircraft, whether or not he had specific intelligence from FECB. But the British put

Japanese airmen on a par with Italian, and underestimated Imperial Navy surface forces as well. Under these circumstances the sortie into the South China Sea seemed risky but it was a calculated risk.

The rest is practically anti-climactic. Admiral Phillips had misgivings but took Force Z to sea anyway. Phillips requested air cover, but this was denied. The chief of FECB's air section, asked to estimate the scale of attack Force Z might anticipate, put it at at least a hundred aircraft and possibly more. At sea Phillips was informed by the air commander in Malaya that attack might follow sighting by five hours and could be by fifty to sixty bombers. In mid-stride, with the prospect of a gunnery action at dawn off Kota Bharu as he had planned, Tom Phillips was then told of a landing at Kuantan, farther south on the Malayan coast. This report was entirely erroneous. Phillips determined to strike Kuantan and altered course accordingly. Then the Force Z commander failed to tell Singapore of his change in plans or ask for fighter cover off Kuantan. To take a phrase from a fine account of the full Malay campaign, it was truly a "chain of disaster."

On the Japanese side first notice came from submarine *I-65* (Lieutenant Commander Harada Hakue), which saw Force Z from about twelve miles' distance in the early afternoon of December 9, and reported two *Repulse*-class battleships headed north-northwest. From Saigon, Admiral Matsunaga sent torpedo bombers to try for an evening or even night attack. They missed Force Z, however, and instead found Ozawa's Malay Force. A plane of the Mihoro Air Group dropped a flare over the ship it saw below only to discover the vessel was the heavy cruiser *Chokai,* Ozawa's flagship. Fearful of mistakes in the darkness, Matsunaga recalled his planes to base. Ozawa, meanwhile, had orders from Kondo not to seek a night surface action, but to try to draw the British north, where battleships *Kongo* and *Haruna* could fight them after dawn. Judging Force Z's position with reports from *I-65* and his cruiser floatplanes, Ozawa tried to use shipboard radio traffic to attract British attention. Shortly after that the aircraft flare incident occurred, horrifying the sailors on the surface ships. Force Z was lost.

This remained the situation until a little after 2:00 A.M., December 10, when lookouts under Lieutenant Commander Kitamura Soshichi of *I-58* spotted the two big British ships speeding south, practically on top of him. The sub dived immediately, though it had a problem with a stuck hatch, and remained undetected by sound gear aboard the British destroyers. Kitamura got off a salvo of five torpedoes and missed, but his sighting report enabled Admiral Matsunaga to plan ideal distribution for his morning search; eleven planes from Saigon and Soc Trang at 4:55 A.M. Without awaiting scout reports, Matsunaga then sent out three strike groups totaling 85 planes between 6:25 and 6:50. The aircraft flew toward an estimated position calculated from assumptions as to British course and speed; it proved inaccurate. One squadron encountered British destroyer *Tenedos* and bombed her without result. The others reversed course and were headed home when a new sighting of Force Z sent them after the quarry.

The plane that found Force Z was a Nell from the Genzan Air Group piloted by a reserve ensign, Hoashi Masane. He had flown to a point eighty miles from Singapore and found nothing, then turned north up the Malayan coast, where he saw *Prince of Wales* and *Repulse* off Kuantan. Hoashi sent several reports between 10:15 and 10:45 A.M. Some were received directly by other Genzan and Mihoro Air Group planes. The torpedo experts of the Kanoya unit, however, continued toward base until an 11:30 clarification from Matsunaga put them on the right track.

Japanese bombers began arriving on the scene soon after 11:00. First on the scene were eight planes of Lieutenant Shirai Yoshimi's squadron of the Mihoro Air Group. Their bombs dropped in tight patterns around *Repulse* but there was only one hit, a minor one on the port hangar. A torpedo attack on the *Prince of Wales* between 11:44 and 11:46, in which Genzan Air Group pilots struck from both sides of the ship, inflicted two hits that buckled a propeller shaft, flooded machinery spaces, and opened up watertight compartments. The British flagship's speed fell to 15 knots; she quickly developed a port-side list. Never again would the battleship be under full control, and at 12:10 Captain John C. Leach was forced to hoist a signal admitting his ship out of control. At that moment the *Repulse* (Captain W. G. Tennant) remained fully capable and had even moved near the flagship to offer assistance.

The final and decisive attack against Force Z was that of the Kanoya Air Group. Some twenty-six aircraft of this group reached the estimated British position but found nothing there, and were within minutes of the limit of their radius when the ships came into view. Six planes closed on *Prince of Wales* to make four hits (Japanese accounts say five), and the remaining aircraft launched torpedoes at the *Repulse* from all points of the compass. She was hit by five torpedoes (Japanese accounts maintain seven). Both ships were left in a sinking condition, although there were two further attacks and a few additional bomb hits. Of the 1,309 crewmen on the *Prince of Wales* some 513 were lost, as were 327 officers and men of the 1,612 on *Repulse*. Among those lost were Admiral Phillips and Captain Leach.

Aboard Combined Fleet's flagship, *Nagato*, where the atmosphere had gotten very tense beginning with reception of the *I-65*'s initial sighting report, there was continual speculation about the fragmentary information available. On the first day, the staff wondered whether there would be enough daylight left for a surface engagement and whether planes would be able to reach the scene. On the second morning, everyone was smiling when *Nagato* learned that contact had been reestablished. Relief followed elation when the Combined Fleet discovered that friendly losses were only three planes shot down and a few damaged. Commander Miwa Yoshitake, air staff officer, had had a bet going with Admiral Yamamoto that the JNAF could get both British battleships (the commander in chief would have been content to sink one and damage the other). Now he stood to collect ten dozen bottles of beer. When Miwa reminded Yamamoto, the latter replied he did not care if the staff got *fifty* dozen.

It would not be quite so easy in all of the Combined Fleet's battles. One of the tougher ones was in progress at just that moment, in the South Seas.

# Islands in the Sun

T HERE WERE SEVERAL POTENTIAL POCKETS OF RESISTANCE, ISLANDS, IN THE WAY OF Japan's domination over East Asia and the Pacific. Most would be assaulted in short order. Most would fall as quickly. Some of the pockets were actual islands, specifically Guam and Wake; some were merely figurative, like Hong Kong and Shanghai. In a certain sense, Japan's sweeping away of these obstacles denoted the end of European-style colonialism, at least in China. In another sense, the offensive eliminated the final ambiguities of peace and cleared the board for a cataclysmic struggle that could end only in humiliating defeat for one side or the other. In the short term Japan seemed all-powerful, however. There was but a single island where the Imperial Navy sustained any setback, one of the real ones in the Pacific. This is the story of the islands.

THE FIRST DAY OF WAR FOUND THE CHINA AREA FLEET FLAGSHIP, ARMORED CRUISER *IDZUMO*, anchored in the Whangpoo River at Shanghai, as it had been for many years. Along the Bund behind her, as the river makes a loop, were several Japanese gunboats. Anchored beyond them in midstream were the U.S. gunboat *Wake* (Lieutenant Commander Columbus D. Smith) and the British gunboat *Peterel* (Lieutenant Stephen Polkinghorn, RNR). The ships were the last Western forces at Shanghai, the only Japanese opponents on the China coast other than the British garrison at Hong Kong. *Wake* had been in Shanghai for little more than a week; lacking the size and freeboard for an ocean voyage, she was left behind as station ship when Rear Admiral William A. Glassford pulled out for the Philippines with two larger gunboats and the 4th Marine Regiment. The Yangtze patrol had had no need of fancy decrypts of diplomatic messages to tell that war portended. *Wake* had been wired for demolition and left with only fourteen crewmen, eight of them radiomen, and half of that group actually manning radios at the American consulate ashore. In the event of war, Commander Smith's main job would be to sink his ship, not fight it. Smith, who held the Navy Cross from action in World War I, could be trusted to do that. A reservist, Smith was recalled to active duty, and had held command of the *Wake* for just a week before war broke out.

During the night of December 8 the Japanese warships nearby trained their guns on the British and American gunboats. *Peterel* seems to have been the first to notice, but took the act in stride, for there had been many like instances as the powers jockeyed for position in China. This time, however, the Japanese assembled a unit of Special Naval Landing Force (SNLF) troops to assault the gunboats. Commander Smith was ashore sleeping in an apartment when awakened by a phone call from his quartermaster. By that time the SNLF had already taken over the *Wake* and herded her crew together as prisoners.

Having some warning, the *Peterel* did a little better, avoiding any easy takeover by the SNLF and turning back an Imperial Navy emissary, Captain Ikushima. The spurned intermediary fired off a red flare; then Japanese guns began a brief bombardment, which killed six sailors and wounded all the other twelve aboard the ship. Lieutenant Polkingham denied the Japanese any satisfaction by detonating demolition charges already set in the hull of his gunboat. The *Peterel* turned turtle and sank.

Commander Smith meanwhile made no effort to go out to the *Wake* once she had been occupied, instead getting in a taxi and making for the American consulate, where he supervised destruction of radio equipment and codebooks. Two *Wake* sailors overpowered their guards and escaped to the Philippines aboard a Dutch vessel, where they were assigned to destroyer *Peary* just before she left Cavite. The Japanese gave language officer Lieutenant (j.g.) Alfred D. Kilmartin attaché status, and he would be repatriated aboard the *Gripsholm*. British radioman Jim Cuming eluded the Japanese altogether and lived in Shanghai throughout the war. Commander Smith, a British officer, and another marine later escaped captivity, made their way across China, and rejoined Allied forces.

Throughout China, beginning at 7:30 A.M. on December 8, the Japanese seized British and American property. At Hankow, for example, the First China Expeditionary Fleet records that it took over six vessels of 2,500 tons or more, plus thirty smaller ones. The Hankow Area Special Base Force also seized petroleum storage tanks of Standard Oil and Asia Oil in the area. The ships were sent to Shanghai to be used in the war. Small businesses owned by expatriates got a few final moments of freedom—they were not taken over until after inventory.

Hong Kong was the last continental "island." There the garrison was real, slightly over 10,000 officers and men including two Canadian battalions arrived just weeks before; these were, however, no match for the Japanese forces arrayed against them. The British defenses centered on the so-called Gin Drinkers' Line above Kowloon. This battle offered only a foregone conclusion, reached on Christmas Day when the defenders simply could not go on any longer, with the forces fracturing under attack, losing contact with each other, and being defeated in detail. The Imperial Navy's role in the action was minimal and handled by local forces of the China Area Fleet.

"THE PRESENT SITUATION IS CERTAINLY NEARING ITS CLIMAX," DECLARED CAPTAIN Takahashi Yuji of the heavy cruiser *Kako*, tied up to the number fourteen buoy at Kure. Standing to address freshly commissioned ensigns joining his ship for the coming campaign, Takahashi described the crisis as "in its most pregnant stage." The young officers had trained diligently for three years; now "your emotions have been heightened, as you sense impending action." No doubt there would be action. "This is no training squadron," the captain exhorted; "you have been assigned directly to the front. . . . I earnestly desire from you an uncommon amount of determination and effort."

Well might Takahashi ask for extraordinary efforts. The fact was that the *Kako*, one of four ships of Rear Admiral Goto Aritomo's Cruiser Division 6, had been slated to provide a cover force for an invasion convoy carrying the South Seas Detachment to land on the island of Guam. Built around the 144th Infantry Regiment plus an engineer company and the 1st Battalion/55th Mountain Artillery, the unit was led by Major General Horii Tomitaro, the group commander of infantry for the 55th Division, which remained in Shikoku. Horii's staff estimated the opposition on Guam at 300 U.S. Marines and 1,500 native infantry along with anti-aircraft guns and heavy coast-defense guns emplaced in the interior. Such defenses seemed to call for an assault force the size of the Horii detachment with support from Admiral Goto's cruisers. On November 6, IGHQ laid down the plans in a secret directive. The convoy departed from Sakaide harbor, Shikoku, and rendezvoused at Haha Jima in the Bonins with Goto's warships on December 2. After two days of last-minute preparations the convoy headed for Guam, about 800 miles away.

If Guam was supposed to be some kind of island fortress, that would have been news to Captain G. J. McMillin, the senior officer present. It is true there had been talk in the press of big expenditures to fortify Guam, and occasional speculation within the Navy of the desirability of doing so, but nothing had ever been done about these ruminations. In December 1941 Guam had 153 marines (officers and men) and an Insular Force of 245—in all, about 400 troops, a quarter of what the Japanese expected. There were three patrol craft at the naval base, plus an old harbor oiler; naval personnel included thirty officers, six warrant officers, five nurses, and 230 sailors. Not only were there no heavy coast guns, there was no weapon on the island larger than a .30-caliber machine gun.

What Guam did have that was less defensible than coastal artillery but probably far more valuable was Station B of the radio intelligence network. Originally located in Agana in a building of the naval base there, Station B moved to an abandoned tuberculosis hospital on a hill outside town sometime in 1933 or 1934. In October of the latter year the Asiatic Fleet commander had recommended that the intercept facility be moved again, to Libugon, four miles from Agana. Libugon had been used since 1917 as a remote transmission and receiving site, but was deactivated in a 1932 budget cutback. Thus it remained until the Japanese came.

Guam operated cast-off equipment, no longer wanted or needed elsewhere, but it made do. In December 1936 Station B got its first three RIP-5 kana typewriters; in March 1938 it received recording equipment to help transcribing messages; in July 1937 a high-frequency direction-finding system was added, with modern equipment progressively supplementing older stuff, but personnel constraints prevented much more than sporadic use in 1941. Guam had ten sailors running Station B, and a request had been made (and denied) for an increase to fourteen. In December 1941 eight enlisted sailors under Chief Radioman D. W. Barnum were the entire complement of Station B.

The island would not be forgotten in the descent to war. On December 4 Commander Safford at Op-20-G drafted, and the Chief of Naval Operations sent, the following dispatch:

GUAM DESTROY ALL SECRET AND CONFIDENTIAL PUBLICATIONS AND OTHER CLASSIFIED MATTER EXCEPT THAT ESSENTIAL FOR CURRENT PURPOSES AND SPECIAL INTELLIGENCE RETAINING MINIMUM CRYPTOGRAPHIC CHANNELS NECESSARY FOR ESSENTIAL COMMUNI-CATIONS. . . . BE PREPARED TO DESTROY INSTANTLY IN EVENT OF EMERGENCY ALL CLAS-SIFIED MATTER YOU RETAIN. REPORT CRYPTO CHANNELS RETAINED.

Libugon complied, immediately burning all records prior to the last week or so. At least one operator wondered whether it would not have been more useful to take the risk of hanging on to the equipment a bit longer, to have it working for a few more days' intercepts.

Radioman Second Class Stewart T. Faulkner was in bed the first morning of the war. He and the other Station B operators had been following the progress of the Malayan convoy, a huge thing of ninety ships or more, tirelessly, with no thought for themselves. It was about ten after six when the phone rang; Faulkner had to answer it since he had the day watch.

"Oh, this is Radio Agana," Faulkner said.

"Hostilities have begun," a voice said without preliminaries. "I say again, over, hostilities have begun."

"Well thanks," Faulkner replied. "I'm welcome."

The radioman got back into bed. He lay there ten minutes or so, then jumped up, his mind racing with expectations, with wonder. The telephone rang again. Honolulu had been bombed. The war was serious now. Chief Barnum carried out their last-ditch instructions, even though Eddie Dullard, the radioman on duty, had been intercepting the most fascinating messages imaginable: Japanese kana interspersed with good old American names like "Oklahoma," "Tennessee," "California," names that belonged to U.S. Navy battleships. Only about an hour later Japanese bombers arrived over Guam to soften it up for invasion.

Markle T. Smith, a radioman first class whose promotion to chief was in the mail but would not reach him before he went into captivity, remembers destroying the last equipment right after the initial JNAF raids. He felt pangs of regret for, until Thanksgiving, Smith and men at Station Cast had been made enthusiastic by the excitement of the chase—tracking Japanese aircraft carriers, evidently Carrier Division 4, following them by getting cross-bearings. From here on out there would be nothing.

Chief Barnum's men destroyed the RIP-5 typewriters, taking the caps off with a blowtorch. Markle Smith personally carried these to a brook and buried them underwater. Cables to the antennae were cut, the generator block broken to incapacitate it, and the cryptographic equipment smashed. To make sure, the sailors rolled a couple of fifty-five-gallon drums of gasoline into the station house, strung a fuse, and set them off. The resulting fire melted the radios right down to pools of aluminum.

The Japanese continued air raids, using Fourth Fleet air from Truk plus the floatplane unit of the tender *Kiyokawa Maru*. Admiral Goto's invasion convoy reached Guam shortly after midnight on the morning of December 10. The landing forces hit the beach from 2:30 to 5:00 A.M., including a detachment of Yokosuka SNLF under Commander Hayashi Shojiro, which rapidly advanced to Agana. On the plaza they met the Insular Guard backed by a few marines and policemen. The defenders drove off two assaults and suffered seventeen dead (twelve of them marines), but at about 5:45, as Captain McMillin learned of Japanese landings at other points on Guam, he decided further resistance was useless. McMillin blew a car horn to sound the cease-fire.

The Japanese made careful note of assets captured on Guam: facilities for a naval station; an airstrip; a seaplane base (converted from a Pan American flying boat facility); 6,000 tons of coal; six oil storage tanks of unknown capacity. What the Japanese did not find was the men of Station B, and they were looking. The Libugon radiomen holed up on a hill; not until about the third day did a Japanese patrol reach them. Markle Smith remembers the Japanese as SNLF troops and "sharp operators," who were definitely on the lookout for the American radio intelligence personnel. The Yokosuka SNLF held the Americans for days before turning them over to the Army, questioning them all the while. Smith and the others tried to make themselves as scarce as possible while sending forward other Americans to be interrogated. One, a chief named Myers of Radio Agana, had the Japanese thinking they had found the codebreakers because he tried to stay out in the bush after most others surrendered. Japanese experts put earphones on Myers's head, then sent their Morse to him, but he proved completely ignorant. Both Smith and Stewart Faulkner attest that the Japanese never found the real Station B operators. After about a month in captivity on Guam the American prisoners were put on the *Argentina Maru* and sent to a prison camp in the Home Islands. They endured the rest of the war building terraces for hillside farming or working as stevedores.

JAPAN'S ONSLAUGHT FOUND ANOTHER AMERICAN ISLAND POST RATHER BETTER PREPARED. That was Wake island, just reinforced by Major Paul Putnam's Marine fighter squadron VMF-211, the deployment that had kept Bill Halsey's *Enterprise* away from Pearl Harbor on December 7. In addition to the dozen F4F-3 Wildcat fighter planes, Wake had 5-inch coast-defense guns, 3-inch anti-aircraft guns, .50- and .30-caliber machine guns, and a U.S. Marine garrison of 388 men. This was far from an island bastion, and plans to build up defenses on Wake were still in their infancy; a civilian contractor group of 1,146 men constructing installations actually made up the bulk of manpower. The marines and their guns belonged to Major James P. S. Devereux's 1st Defense Battalion. Head of the naval air station and island commander by virtue of seniority was Commander Winfield Scott Cunningham, U.S.N.

Like other stations in the Pacific, Wake received the famous "This is no drill" message, thus learning of the start of war. A radioman brought Devereux the news that morning while he was shaving. The Marine ground commander had time to confer with Commander Cunningham; the island went on alert. Cunningham ordered patrols of four Wildcat fighters to screen Wake from Japanese air attack. Thus Wake was not taken by surprise, but it was nevertheless hard hit around noon by a strike group of thirty-six JNAF medium bombers flying from Kwajalein.

Captain Henry Elrod led a four-plane flight of fighters up to relieve the first patrol. According to Japanese war correspondent Tsuji Norio, who (in an account released by IGHQ press censors) implied that he witnessed these events, the incoming strike group actually saw the Marine fighters climbing in the distance as they approached the island. "They did not even notice our large formation," Tsuji wrote, "and climbed higher and higher into the skies and finally disappeared." The JNAF force split into two units and swept in from the sea, dropping down through clouds that shielded them from view of Elrod's fighters. The Japanese planes broke through the clouds just as they crossed Wake's coastline, bomb bays already open. Marines on the ground had no more warning than those in the air.

Bombs left a swath of destruction behind. Wake lost its major gasoline supply when a 25,000-gallon tank began to burn; a number of drums were also set ablaze. Seven of eight Wildcat fighters on the airstrip were smashed, and the other was left with unrepairable damage in its auxiliary gas tank. The Pan American seaplane station was destroyed, its hotel badly damaged, and ten Chamorro employees from Guam killed. Thirty-four marines were dead or wounded at the airfield. To add insult to injury, when the Marine fighters aloft returned to base, one of the planes caught its propeller as it landed on the badly holed airstrip.

Japanese pilots worried that Marine fighters might catch them on departure, but that did not occur either. The Japanese flew home through heavy clouds, but once they landed they heard that terrific storms had swept down upon Kwajalein that morning soon after their takeoff. If the JNAF strike group had not taken off when it did, the mission would have had to be canceled. The luck had all gone one way that day, the way of Rear Admiral Goto Eiji's 24th Air Flotilla.

Two days later the luck would be equally one-sided, but the lady favored Americans. Major Devereux slept in his command post when the phone rang and a lookout reported "movement," what kind he could not say, plus possible lights offshore to the south. A second report came from Wilkes islet; then Devereux saw ships himself through night binoculars. A ringing telephone awakened Commander Cunningham, who stumbled into the hallway to learn of ships on the horizon. Wake went on alert but held its fire, hoping the Japanese would move in close enough for Marine 5-inch guns to take a toll of the attackers.

Those ships on the horizon were actually a Japanese invasion fleet under Rear Admiral Kajioka Sadamichi, commanding the 6th Destroyer Flotilla. Kajioka was aboard light cruiser *Yubari* and had six destroyers, two converted destroyer-transports carrying 225 SNLF troops each, and a covering force with light cruisers *Tenryu* and *Tatsuta* of Cruiser Division 18. At about 5:30 A.M., Kajioka led his column onto a northwest course and began to shell Wake. Two transports stayed on the opposite side of the Japanese column. The bombardment did little except set fire to some oil tanks. Kajioka turned to starboard and settled onto a southeast course for a second firing run, then to port for a third. By that time his lead ship, flagship *Yubari,* was just 4,500 yards offshore.

Admiral Kajioka began his third run at about 6:10. Major Devereux now ordered Marine batteries to reply. At the tip of Wake, Peacock Point, First Lieutenant Clarence A. Barninger's Battery A hit *Yubari* with its second salvo, and then twice more to boot. The Japanese cruiser turned away behind a smoke screen. Battery A went on to hit one of the destroyer-transports. From Wilkes, Second Lieutenant John A. McAlister's Battery L targeted Kajioka's destroyers. Though the battery's range finder had previously been destroyed, their shooting proved so good that destroyer *Hayate* was holed and had to beach. Meanwhile Major Putnam's Wildcats, with jury-rigged bombs, got off Wake's airfield and made for the Japanese ships. They dropped bombs and strafed in repeated passes giving Kajioka's sailors no respite. Captain Elrod made up for his gaffe the first day of the war by dropping a bomb on the destroyer *Kisaragi.* From the *Yubari* Captain Koyama Tadashi, Kajioka's chief of staff, could see a tremendous explosion. There were no survivors among the *Kisaragi's* 150 crewmen. Koyama thought that as many as seven American planes were shot down. In fact only one of the four planes that flew that morning, Elrod's, would be so badly damaged as to be of no further use.

By this time the Japanese were in a serious predicament. Two destroyers had been lost and two, the *Yayoi* and the *Oite,* damaged by planes or guns. Transport *Kongo Maru* was bombed and set afire. Hits also knocked out the torpedo battery on *Tenryu* and radio shack on *Tatsuta.* Despite this damage, the primary mission appeared no closer to accomplishment. According to Captain Koyama there had already been attempts to launch landing boats; these had immediately been swamped in rough seas. The marines ashore were certainly ready to fight. Admiral Kajioka made the decision to retire to Kwajalein and try again.

To crown their glory, later two Marine F4Fs intercepted a raid of Nell bombers and shot down two of them. Eleven other JNAF bombers were damaged by anti-aircraft fire.

One further report that day, that Lieutenant David D. Kliewer had sunk a Japanese submarine, proved apocryphal. Two submarines indeed were scouting Wake in advance of Kajioka's invasion force, and were ordered home after its defeat. One would be lost, but not from an aircraft bomb: The *Ro-66,* late because she failed to receive the recall order, collided on the night of December 17 with the *Ro-62* and sank immediately. All hands were rescued. She was the only submarine lost in the Wake operation.

The news for the Japanese was bad enough, with substantial losses and no results. Preliminary reports reaching Combined Fleet flagship *Nagato* induced Admiral Ugaki to speculate that Wake was considerably stronger than estimated by Japanese intelligence. The day after the failure, Fourth Fleet chief of staff Captain Yano Shikazo asked Combined Fleet for at least one aircraft carrier. The request crystallized questions about employment of Nagumo's carrier task force, as will be seen momentarily. Fourth Fleet commander Admiral Inoue, invasion force commander Kajioka, and their staffs also huddled to rethink their plan. Both considered that any element of surprise had been lost. The possibility arose that a further attempt against Wake would bring an engagement with the U.S. fleet. Inoue strengthened Kajioka's force, adding the heavy cruisers of Admiral Goto Aritomo's division as a covering force with some of the destroyers that had escorted Goto at Guam to replace losses. More troops were added for ground combat. The Kajioka and Goto forces would proceed jointly until a point south of Wake, whereupon Goto's cruisers would split off to run interference, proceeding to a point fifty miles east of Wake, then acting as the situation warranted.

As for the Kido Butai, controversy began to swirl around Admiral Nagumo almost the instant his second-wave planes left Pearl Harbor. Nagumo had orders to raid Midway Island during his return voyage. The order displeased Nagumo and others of his staff, not least air officer Genda and chief of staff Kusaka, and the task force leaders simply decided to ignore it. On the *Nagato*, Admiral Ugaki was left to wonder whether fuel problems were hampering Nagumo and complain how dangerous it was to use radio messages to find out.

Interesting light on Nagumo's frame of mind is cast by an incident aboard the *Akagi* about this time. Abe Zenji, one of the aircraft squadron commanders on Nagumo's flagship, had just heard on a radio broadcast that the hapless American Pacific Fleet commander, Husband Kimmel, had been replaced as a result of the Pearl Harbor debacle. Then Abe encountered Admiral Nagumo himself in one of the ship's passageways, and recounted what he had heard. Abe recalled that Nagumo's face fell and he answered with a deep sigh.

"I feel I have done a very sorry thing to him," Nagumo had said.

It seemed as if Nagumo wanted to have nothing more to do with the Americans.

Kido Butai's passivity enraged Ugaki and others, but Nagumo had defenders as well. Some wished to dispatch direct orders for Nagumo to hit Midway. Defenders claimed that it was a waste. Among the latter, Yoshida Toshio of the *joho kyoku* argued that the Midway orders simply outraged Nagumo: "It's like asking a junior sumo wrestler who's just beaten a grand champion if he'd mind buying some vegetables for dinner on the way home."

The Wake Island setback brought argument full circle because here was a situation that demanded carrier action. Carriers no longer seemed desirable, as at Midway, but necessary. When ordered to support the Wake attack, however, Nagumo responded by detaching only part of his force—Rear Admiral Yamaguchi Tamon's Carrier Division 2, with carriers *Soryu* and *Hiryu* plus escorts.

Imperial Navy officers were not wrong to prepare for naval battle over Wake. That island had been at the center of Husband Kimmel's thinking at least since April 1941, when he wrote Washington to warn that it was very likely one of Japan's initial operations in time of war would be an effort to seize Wake. Admiral Kimmel planned in detail to counter such a move, as shown by historian Edward S. Miller in his account of Plan Orange, America's prewar scheme for conflict with Japan. Pearl Harbor made moot Kimmel's hypothetical plans for the use of battleships, but American carrier strength remained untouched and sending out the carriers seemed a good way to startle the Japanese. Though Admiral Kimmel set these moves afoot, he was replaced before much could be accomplished. Admiral Chester W. Nimitz, appointed to succeed him, had been serving as chief of naval personnel; he had to come from Washington and did not reach Hawaii until Christmas. The Wake Island naval maneuvers would therefore have to be conducted by an interim leader, Vice Admiral William S. Pye, an erstwhile battleship commander now unemployed as a result of the December 7 attack. With advice from naval district commander Claude Bloch, Pye ordered American fleets into harm's way.

While Pearl Harbor deliberated, Vice Admiral Inoue's Fourth Fleet occupied points in the Marshalls and Gilberts. The airfield and communications facility on Howland Island were judged destroyed by JNAF raids on December 9. Rear Admiral Shima Kiyohide's 19th Minesweeper Division, escorted by a couple of destroyers, occupied Tarawa and Makin in the Gilberts. *Nagata Maru* carried men and equipment to Makin. At Howland on December 11, boats of the 33rd Submarine Division scouted and shelled remaining installations.

From Pearl Harbor it looked as if Japan was on the move everywhere, and uncertainties regarding Imperial Navy strength played a key role in the fleet support to Wake island. Radio traffic analysis established the arrival on Makin of wherewithal for a seaplane base. Station Hypo also identified Jaluit as the location of the Japanese submarine fleet commander, and from the Gilberts came exaggerated reports of the strength of the Yokohama Air Group. Fleet intelligence officer Layton told senior commanders that the JNAF might have anywhere from twenty to two hundred aircraft.

At the time Admiral Pye had sent Wilson Brown to hit Jaluit with his task force built around the *Lexington,* while Vice Admiral Frank Jack Fletcher maneuvered toward Wake with the *Saratoga.* The latter carried another Marine fighter squadron (VMF-221) to reinforce the depleted air unit on

Wake. Captain Clifton Sprague's seaplane tender, *Tangier,* carried reinforcements and new gear for Wake, including radar and fire-direction equipment for the Marine gun batteries there.

Rear Admiral Fletcher made for Wake as soon as the *Saratoga* reached Pearl (she had been coming from the West Coast). Fletcher started out smartly but then marked time as Wake reeled under JNAF bombs. On December 17 radio traffic analysis associated the Japanese Carrier Division 2 with their 24th Air Flotilla. This was a deadly accurate report, as it was Admiral Yamaguchi's *Soryu* and *Hiryu* that Nagumo had detached to support Wake operations. The carriers were accompanied by two heavy cruisers and two destroyers. Most likely the messages detected on the seventeenth were Yamaguchi checking in with Fourth Fleet commanders to receive his assignment.

If ever there was a time for urgency, this was it. But Frank Jack Fletcher did not rise to the occasion. Fletcher's task force caught up to the oiler *Neches* that same day and he elected to proceed in company with her. This meant imposing stringent limits on his speed, since *Neches*'s maximum was no more than 15.3 knots and a practical speed for her little better than 12. Fletcher's later action in refueling his destroyers from the *Neches* even though they did not need refueling has attracted the most criticism, but Fletcher apparently had orders to refuel as a means of enabling the *Lexington* to catch up with him. However, it is his earlier decision to proceed with *Neches,* slowly, that should be opened up to scrutiny. During four days, from December 17 to December 21, Fletcher had ample time to close to within adequate supporting distance of Wake, and he was not constrained at that time by orders to wait for Admiral Brown's *Lexington* group.

At Pearl Harbor the operation was rethought as a result of the exaggerated impression of Japanese strength. Wilson Brown's contemplated attack on Jaluit was called off, averting the danger that he might be trapped by Japanese submarines. Brown was ordered north to assist Fletcher. Admiral Pye felt that Brown had lost any possibility of surprise and that *Lexington*'s own need to refuel would give the Japanese more time to prepare a hot reception. Pye was also driven by the impression that losses to Admiral Brown's Task Force 11 would have depressing morale effects and endanger the defense of Hawaii. The commander in chief, Pacific, reported his conclusions to Washington by dispatch:

IN VIEW INDICATED INCREASED AIR ACTIVITY MARSHALLS WITH ASSURANCE ONE AND POSSIBLY TWO [Japanese] CARRIER GROUPS AND EVIDENCE OF EXTENSIVE OFFSHORE LOOKOUT AND PATROL NOW CONSIDER SURPRISE ATTACK IMPROBABLE. I HAVE RELUCTANTLY ABANDONED PROPOSED CARRIER ATTACK ON MARSHALLS. WAKE BOMBED BY CARRIER PLANES TODAY. OPERATIONS RELIEF OF WAKE CONTINUE BUT CARRIER NOT TO APPROACH CLOSER THAN TWO HUNDRED MILES.

Pye's reference to the possibility of two Japanese carrier groups was due to a radio message linking Carrier Division 5 with the Mandates, but this turned out to be spurious. The real threat, though, was closing in quite rapidly. The report of a carrier plane attack was accurate; on December 21, from about 200 miles northwest of Wake, the Japanese sent eighteen dive-bombers with an escort of eighteen Zero fighters to strike the island. From Kwajalein Admiral Kajioka set sail with his augmented invasion force plus Admiral Goto's covering force of heavy cruisers. Time was running out for the Americans.

By now Fletcher's Task Force 14 wallowed in high seas in an annoying attempt at refueling his destroyers. Concern bristled up and down the U.S. chain of command. Washington informed Pearl Harbor that the new chief of naval operations, Admiral Ernest J. King, considered Wake a liability to American dispositions in the eastern Pacific. Submarines *Triton* and *Tambor*, which had helped defend Wake against the previous invasion attempt, were now back at Pearl or on the way there. Reinforcement was no longer possible. Fletcher's task force that evening was still 625 miles away from Wake.

December 22 brought another strike by Yamaguchi's carrier planes, this time eighteen level bombers under Lieutenant Abe Heijiro along with eighteen Zeros under Lieutenant Suganami Masaharu. A Marine F4F attacked out of the clouds and downed two of Abe's Kates, but Zeros then shot down the American. Besides the carrier planes, land-based aircraft of the 24th Air Flotilla had been hitting Wake daily with an average of eighteen medium bombers in the daytime and four patrol bombers at dusk. With additional carrier strikes, the JNAF mounted close to 300 sorties in its effort to soften up the Marine garrison. Over the course of the campaign, according to documents captured later, fifty-eight JNAF planes were damaged and six more shot down.

Meanwhile Admiral Kajioka's invasion fleet neared Wake from the south. Submarines guided the last leg of the voyage. The fleet reached positions off Wake at about midnight on December 23. Kajioka ordered the landing force ashore, more than 2,000 tough troopers of the 2nd Maizuru SNLF. A number of the soldiers wore white sashes. This time Kajioka eschewed any bombardment that might alert the Americans to his arrival. First reports to Major Devereux and Commander Cunningham were of lights on the sea, boats in the water, and a landing on Toki Point. The last report was premature, but soon enough there were landings at several places. Wake sent Pearl Harbor a message that acquired a certain fame: ENEMY ON ISLAND—ISSUE IN DOUBT. Major Devereux lost communication with his subordinate units, and some were even on the offensive at the moment he told Cunningham what dire straits they were in. But the outcome appeared inevitable and any Japanese setbacks temporary. The disparity in force was simply too great. Some 400 marines went into captivity.

Having taken Wake, Admiral Inoue of the Fourth Fleet turned his attention to the Solomon Islands and the Bismarck Archipelago, the chains of large and small islands that stood between the Mandates and the coast of Australia. Here were the southernmost reaches of the "South Seas," the outer fringe of the *nanyo* of tradition, a necessary anchor for the planned defensive perimeter, and a vital point of departure if someday there were to be any operations against the continent down under.

At this early stage, in this theater of war, the enemy was the Australians. Only the merest trickle of Americans had arrived in the South Pacific at that time, and none had been committed to local defense. The British, to whose Commonwealth Australia belonged, and upon whom Australia had long counted for defense when the chips came down, were preoccupied with Malaya, Burma, and India, with nothing to spare for the South Pacific. Australians themselves were spread very thinly, having sent the bulk of their trained ground forces to fight with the British Eighth Army in North Africa. Most of the rest—two brigades of the 8th Australian Division—were embroiled in Malaya. A single brigade, three infantry battalions, was left for the islands and even there Australia generously allotted two thirds of the force to help the Dutch defend Ambon and Timor in the Netherlands East Indies. The only force that could be spared for the Bismarck Archipelago was a single battalion, the 2/22nd Australian Infantry Force, and it went to Rabaul in New Britain.

The Australian disposition may have been weak, but it was logical. Even then Rabaul constituted the sole settlement of any size in the islands, which for the most part contained only small villages or plantations. While not exactly urban or metropolitan, Rabaul had a downtown section, more than a single dusty street, and a built-up area of perhaps twenty blocks. The town contained about 4,000 settlers, of whom perhaps 1,000 were white, 1,200 Chinese, and a couple of dozen Japanese. With outlying villages the whole nearby population amounted to perhaps 12,500. The administrative center of the islands, Rabaul had a fine anchorage, called Simpson Harbor, and two airfields nearby, Vunakanau and Lakunai. There were a couple of 6-inch coast-defense guns covering the harbor entrance, including a German emplacement of 1914 vintage which the Australians were refurbishing, and a squadron of obsolete Wirraway aircraft to contest the sky. Total Australian troop strength at the moment of the ensuing battle was 76 officers, 1,314 men, and 6 nurses.

There was another Australian resource, an intelligence resource, of some import then but considerable importance later. This was a network called Ferdinand—its name taken from the children's story *Ferdinand the Bull*—set up by Australian naval reservist Eric A. Feldt. A veteran of the British Grand Fleet in World War I, Feldt was assigned to naval intelligence when mobilized and discovered that his good friend and erstwhile classmate, Commander R.B.M. Long, had risen to director of naval intelligence. Long sent Feldt to Port Moresby as staff officer (intelligence) and Feldt, until recently one of the government's local affairs administrators on New Guinea, conceived the idea of enrolling plantation managers, government administrators, missionaries, anyone who wanted to serve, as watchmen who could inform naval intelligence of enemy movements and actions. From this came Ferdinand, the network of radio-equipped observers soon christened coastwatchers. By December 1939 Lieutenant Commander Feldt had enrolled as many as 800 in the Ferdinand organization, with coast-watcher posts everywhere in New Guinea, the Bismarcks and Solomons, and chief observers trained to communicate by radio.

Ferdinand demonstrated its usefulness at the outset of the Japanese thrust into the Solomons, for Fourth Fleet inaugurated its campaign with a series of air attacks. The first of these, in late December, involved eighteen H6K "Mavis" flying boats winging south from Truk. Beginning on January 4 there were a series of strikes by land-based bombers, twenty-two Nells in the first of them. These air formations usually made a landfall at Tabar Island, a little over eighty miles almost due north of Rabaul, where there was a Ferdinand coastwatcher named Cornelius L. Page. The Japanese formations were duly reported. Had the Australians had some real air assets at Rabaul, the JNAF might well have suffered substantial losses. As it was the old Wirraways and the two 3-inch anti-aircraft guns were just not enough. Australian A-20 twin-engine bombers, which had used Vunakanau, were forced to withdraw. Before they did, the Australians mounted a reconnaissance flight to Truk on January 8, which reported a large warship plus a dozen cruisers or destroyers at anchor, along with twenty-seven JNAF bombers.

Unknown to the Australians, the Japanese were already concentrating to attack Rabaul. Admiral Inoue's staff anticipated a fight at least as tough as at Wake. Estimates were that the Australians might assemble up to fifty aircraft and that there might be as many more American Catalinas; also, the Australian fleet had two heavy and three light cruisers whose whereabouts were not known. In addition the Japanese estimated that British or American (primarily the former) fleet forces could be brought to bear and might total as many as five battleships, four heavy cruisers, and two aircraft carriers. These estimates turned out to be greatly exaggerated, but the Japanese could not have known of British fixation on their own problems. Before the fact the estimates must have seemed prudent ones.

Fourth Fleet again asked the Combined Fleet for heavy support forces, and Yamamoto assigned Admiral Nagumo's Kido Butai to back the Rabaul invasion. Nagumo detached Carrier Division 2, but with the remainder of his task force sailed for Truk on January 5. Since, due to intercepted radio traffic, the Japanese suspected that the American fleet was on the move some-where in the northeast Pacific, Nagumo left with orders to search the sea around Marcus Island on his way. Finding nothing, the Kido Butai arrived at Truk on January 12.

For seaman Kuramoto Iki the voyage was the fulfillment of childhood dreams of the *nanyo*. Kuramoto's vision was a common one among the 11,000 sailors in Nagumo's force and the 65,000 more who manned ships and units of the Fourth Fleet. By the same token, Kuramoto must not have been the only sailor whose visions of naked natives dancing in the shade of coconut trees were to be shattered by the realities of the Tropical Zone, as the Japanese were soon calling this war theater. Truk became the "land of eternal summer," where sailors changed to tropical uniform. "The bright sun sent out blazing rays and it was steaming hot inside the ship," Kuramoto recorded. "This completely dissipated my cherished illusions about the tropics." Night brought vague feelings of longing for home. Only the evening breeze, and the cool wind that accompanied squalls, relieved the relentless heat. Kuramoto would be happy when Nagumo's task force completed its resupply and sortied toward Rabaul.

As had been the case for the Wake operation, the Japanese sent several task groups to sea. The invasion force included more than forty transports and cargo ships escorted by Fourth Fleet units. Admiral Goto's four heavy cruisers again made up the cover force. Given his rank and seniority, the Japanese arranged that in case a naval battle developed Nagumo would take command of the various task groups. There would be no British intervention, however, and the Australians did not contest the Rabaul operation with their own slender naval resources. Consequently Nagumo merely maneuvered around the equator, mounting a series of powerful air strikes by eighty to ninety planes against Rabaul on New Britain, Kavieng on New Ireland, and Lae and Salamaua on the northern coast of New Guinea.

The detailed invasion plan was agreed at a conference aboard light cruiser *Katori* in Truk on January 3. Admiral Inoue agreed to provide escort for the convoy that left Guam on January 14 bearing General Horii's South Seas Detachment. Rear Admiral Shima Kiyohide commanded the close escort. Troops simultaneously landed at Rabaul and at Kavieng on January 23. The main landing took place at night. By the next night Japanese troops had control of Lakunai airfield and Rabaul town and had driven off the 2/22nd Australian Infantry Force. Japanese losses were sixteen dead and fifteen wounded; the Australians lost two officers and twenty-six men. About 400 Australian troops escaped, many of them aboard a leaky old vessel that barely made it to New Guinea. Two large groups surrendered, and Japanese soldiers in pursuit massacred some 160 Australians from a group at Tol in early February. By then Japanese troops were occupying further points in the Bismarcks. Aircraft losses from Nagumo's carriers amounted to one fighter and one attack plane.

Following his strikes in the Rabaul vicinity, Admiral Nagumo returned to Truk for upkeep. As he did, the Americans were secretly deploying carrier task forces farther east, for strikes against Japanese bases in the Marshalls. One prong of the effort was inadvertently turned back by submariner Togami Ichiro, of prewar espionage fame, who commanded the *I-72* and sank the U.S. oiler *Neches* on January 23. The oiler had been moving into position to refuel Admiral Wilson Brown's *Lexington* task force after a planned strike on Wake, and *Neches*'s sinking forced cancellation of that event. Admiral Halsey persisted, however, as did Admiral Fletcher with a task force built around the carrier *Yorktown,* just arrived from the Atlantic.

On February 1 *Yorktown* planes struck Jaluit, *Enterprise* ones Kwajalein, and cruisers and destroyers Halsey detached bombarded Wotje and Taroa. Nagumo's aircraft carriers, scheduled to leave Truk that day for further South Seas operations, diverted to the east in a high-speed chase. The Fourth Fleet also sent Admiral Goto's heavy cruisers to sea, and it ordered the new light carrier *Shoho*, which had just been assigned to the fleet, to join him. Recognizing that there was virtually no chance of catching up to the American raiders, the Japanese broke off after a day or so.

These February raids nonplussed the Japanese defenders. "After experiencing defensive weakness ourselves," Combined Fleet chief of staff Ugaki wrote that night, "we cannot laugh at the enemy's confusion at the time of the surprise attack on Pearl Harbor." Japanese defenders reported an inaccurate position for the Americans, misidentified the ships they saw, and made mistakes encoding messages. Aircraft from Truk flew to Kwajalein, but the only attacks were from planes already on the forward bases. Lieutenant Nakai Kazuo led a morning attack that slightly damaged cruiser *Chester.* That afternoon Nakai, a veteran of fifty missions in China, was back with two more planes to go directly against the *Enterprise.* Hit by antiaircraft fire, he tried a crash-dive on the carrier. An emergency turn by the ship, and a brave crewman who bolted across the flight deck to take the machine guns in the back of a deck-spotted dive-bomber for a last shot at Nakai made the difference between solid hit and glancing blow. Seven submarines sailed from Kwajalein but, like the ships from Truk, could not catch the Americans.

As was not unusual for that time early in the war, Americans had an exaggerated notion of the damage they had inflicted. Halsey reported sinking a light carrier, a light cruiser, two submarines, and many auxiliaries, plus damaging more ships and wiping out eighteen aircraft. The Japanese actually suffered damage to Sixth Fleet submarine *I-23*, light cruiser *Katori*, and the old cruiser *Tokiwa*, serving as a minelayer. Submarine fleet commander Admiral Shimizu was wounded and the rear admiral commanding the local base force killed. Still, the primary effect was psychological.

Admiral Ugaki noted that "our carelessness in being ignorant of the enemy approach until he was so close was extremely regrettable." Upon investigation, it even turned out that the Imperial Navy's 6th Communications Unit *had* warned that the Americans were planning some offensive move, but the message arrived only when attacks were already in progress.

In the meantime the Fourth Fleet further increased the scope of its activities. In early January, simultaneous with the Rabaul planning, the command proposed operations against eastern New Guinea. A message to the Naval General Staff warned that, unless followed by occupation of New Guinea, the mere conquest of Rabaul and Kavieng would not improve the situation on the southeastern front. At NGS, Commander Mikami Sakuo agreed with these observations. On January 29, after reaching an accord with Army authorities, Admiral Nagano signed Navy Directive Number 47, providing for control of waters north and east of Australia by means of taking over key areas of New Guinea and the Solomons, including Lae, Salamaua, and Tulagi. Though no one knew it yet, Directive Number 47 had just laid the cornerstone for what became the bloodiest campaign of the Imperial Navy's war.

While Japan fleshed out these new plans, Nagumo's carriers intervened further west, mounting a raid on Port Darwin in northern Australia after a brief stopover in Palau. On February 19 Commander Fuchida led 188 planes against Darwin, destroying Government House, starting fires that wrecked many buildings, and leaving 243 dead and over 300 wounded. In forty minutes the JNAF attackers destroyed all eighteen defending planes and sank half the ships in the harbor, nine in all, including American destroyer *Peary*—which had been considered lucky to have survived the Cavite bombing in December—and two Australian corvettes. Ironically, the U.S. cruiser *Houston* had been at Darwin the day before and could easily have been caught in this raid. Doubly ironic, while the Japanese fliers were off raiding Darwin, the *Lexington*, one of the U.S. carriers they so ardently wished to catch, was about to strike Rabaul, off which some of Nagumo's ships had lurked just a few short weeks before.

Actually the American raid at Rabaul did not come off quite as planned. Instead the unit, Task Force 11 under Wilson Brown, was discovered by a JNAF search plane just as it was nearing its launch point. Combat air patrol (CAP) fighters shot down the intruder, but another came up fairly quickly. Again the CAP reacted, but Admiral Brown judged the risk too great and instructed Captain Frederick C. Sherman, skipper of the *Lexington*, to turn to a southwesterly course. It was midafternoon when radar warned of a large group of Japanese planes approaching from the direction of Rabaul and about eighty miles away. Lieutenant Commander John S. Thach was one of the few pilots to get off the ship to reinforce Lieutenant Noel S. Gayler's combat air patrol.

Lieutenant Gayler, who would go on to achieve high position in the U.S.

Navy, would have died that day but for the failure of a Japanese bullet to penetrate the windshield of his F4F Wildcat. Gayler's fighter defense shot down four JNAF bombers. That morning, Lieutenant Commander Thach had led the CAP which had downed the Japanese scout planes; he would conceive the "Thach weave," an air tactic enabling slower Wildcats to fight Japanese Zeros, but his moment had not yet come that February 20. Lieutenant Edward H. (Butch) O'Hare's had: Butch shot down five Betty bombers in as many minutes.* He received a double promotion and a Medal of Honor. Of two JNAF flights with nine planes each, American CAP or anti-aircraft (mainly the former) downed thirteen bombers and two more crash-landed (some accounts put losses as high as seventeen aircraft). Fewer than half the Japanese planes even released bombs, and none of those fell any-where near American ships. The *Lexington* lost two F4F Wildcats and one pilot.

As had been the case with the Marshall Islands raids, Japanese reaction would be larger than the immediate attack from Rabaul. The Fourth Fleet apparently judged that Brown's Task Force 11 intended to strike the Marshalls from the rear, so to speak, and various precautionary measures were ordered. The Combined Fleet sent aircraft to Truk from as far afield as the Netherlands East Indies. Light carrier *Shoho* with an escorting destroyer, ferrying aircraft to Palau, was ordered back south, and Goto's heavy cruis-ers went to sea from Truk with orders for a night surface attack. Other war-ships also sortied from both Truk and Rabaul, but a communications error gave an inaccurate course for the Americans and no contact was ever made. Admiral Ugaki grumbled about the poor information available to the Combined Fleet, observing that such data made proper decisions impossible.

In the meantime Admiral Inoue of the Fourth Fleet hurried his prepara-tions for Operation SR, the planned occupation of the north coast of New Guinea. By March 3 invasion forces had assembled at Rabaul; two days later they set sail. Heavy cover was provided by Rear Admiral Goto with the four ships of his own Cruiser Division 6 and two light cruisers of Cruiser Division 18. Commanding the invasion force was Rear Admiral Kajioka, the hapless veteran of the Wake fiasco. Kajioka's escort was made up of his own 6th Destroyer Flotilla, a couple of minelayers, and a converted gunboat. He had three big transports carrying a battalion of the South Seas Detachment to be landed at Lae, and an SNLF unit for Salamaua.

Unknown to the Japanese, the American carrier that had been off Rabaul had by no means gone away. In fact, Admiral Brown had been reinforced by Admiral Frank Fletcher's *Yorktown* task force, with Fletcher taking overall

---

*Recent detailed analysis by historian John Lundstrom (*The First Team* [Annapolis, Md.: Naval Institute Press, 1984], pp. 124–31) revises O'Hare's claim to three planes shot down plus two more damaged.

command. Fletcher had orders straight from Washington, from Admiral Ernest J. King, now the fleet commander in chief and chief of naval operations rolled into one, to make attacks in the New Britain–Solomons area. With two carriers Fletcher had the most powerful force yet fielded by the U.S. Navy.

It was not long before Admiral Fletcher had intelligence reports of the Japanese movements. In the late afternoon of March 7, the day after the American carriers rendezvoused, an Australian Air Force A-20 Hudson, on the return leg of its search flight, reported a Japanese light cruiser, four destroyers, and six transports (some minelayers and auxiliaries were misidentified) headed slowly southwest. At the same time, reconnaissance of Rabaul that morning showed several cruisers and other vessels in harbor, while radio intelligence reported the Rabaul area quiet. Kajioka's SR invasion force made its final run that night to begin landing at Salamaua about 1:00 A.M., with Lae following at 2:30. In less than two hours the airfield and radio station at Lae had been occupied, and by dawn both towns were in Japanese hands. Allied intelligence immediately reported the Japanese in both places. On March 9 air reconnaissance showed no warships in Rabaul, with a further convoy off Gasmata (on New Britain's southern coast) headed toward New Guinea. By then the Japanese were far along repairing demolition damage at Lae airfield. Planes at Rabaul awaited orders to move in.

As this intelligence rolled in, Fletcher's task force was steaming through the Coral Sea aiming to strike Rabaul and Gasmata. When he learned of the Lae and Salamaua landings it seemed a perfect opportunity to hit the Japanese before they could bring new bases into operation. A strike from the Solomon Sea, however, where Fletcher had been headed, left open the possibility of air counterattacks from Rabaul and Gasmata. Fletcher therefore resolved to strike from the sea south of New Guinea, with planes to fly over the Owen Stanley Mountains before hitting Kajioka's invasion force anchored in Huon Gulf.

What followed on the morning of March 10 was the first coordinated air strike mounted from different American aircraft carriers during the war, and the only carrier strike ever across a mountain range. In all there were 104 aircraft, in equal portions from each carrier, led by Commander William B. Ault, air group boss of the *Lexington*. In an attack lasting a little over one hour the Americans sank the converted gunboat *Kongo Maru*, a transport, and a minesweeper. Another cargo ship was forced to beach. Admiral Kajioka's flagship, light cruiser *Yubari*, endured strafing and five near misses; nine sailors were killed and fifty wounded aboard her. Destroyers *Asanagi* and *Yunagi* each took a direct hit. Various other damage was reported, with total casualties 102 killed and 125 wounded.

The air battle at Lae and Salamaua was the clearest reverse yet suffered by the Imperial Navy. Immediately afterward the 25th Air Flotilla sent fighters forward to Lae airfield, but the barn door was being closed too late. That afternoon a Yokohama Air Group search plane spotted the *Lexington* task force (reporting her as the *Saratoga*), but there was no effective counterattack. The Americans lost but a single plane shot down. Solid intelligence reporting provided the basis for this success. In view of the recent popularity of radio intelligence, it is instructive that in the Lae-Salamaua raid standard air search proved of greater value. The beginning of wisdom about intelligence in the Pacific is that a synergism existed between different kinds of intelligence reporting, and that a multidimensional intelligence effort would be greater than the sum of its parts. If only the Allies had learned this lesson sooner they might have avoided some of the great tragedies that befell them in the struggle to defend the Malay Barrier.

# TWELVE

# "Great Speed, Grim Determination, and Taking All Risks Is Necessary"

CAPTAIN KATO TADAO PROBABLY FELT HE HAD BEEN SHUNTED AROUND IN THE LAST months before the war. Kato happened to be captain of the light carrier *Ryujo*, sent to Taiwan to supply fighter cover for the Philippine air attacks, a mission that was canceled once JNAF experts determined that land-based cover would be preferable. The *Ryujo* next went to Palau, to which Captain Kato was no stranger. As an official of the Naval Aeronautical Bureau in the mid-1930s, Kato had worried about the paucity of air bases in the Mandates. At the time he had heard many officers opine that Palau should be a primary candidate for such a base. By 1941, when *Ryujo* arrived, there was an airstrip at Palau, and some seaplanes at the seaplane base, but the light carrier's own aircraft made up the air strength on the island. Those planes soon left, for officers at the Naval General Staff, whose Baron Tomioka was an Etajima classmate of Kato's, had given *Ryujo* the new mission of making air attacks on Mindanao, supposedly the soft underbelly of the Philippines.

Kato's *Ryujo* left Palau in company with two heavy cruisers and a couple of destroyers. At sea they joined the 2nd Destroyer Flotilla, which formed the escort. Here again were a pair of instances in which Japanese actions could have warned Washington; days before, one of the destroyers had had a submarine contact and almost made a depth-charge attack. Such action would undoubtedly have alerted the Americans. Even more direct a warning, at least for American air units in the Philippines, was the actual air attack *Ryujo* made on Davao harbor at dawn December 8, still hours before the Clark Field debacle. The Japanese planes found virtually no targets at

Davao. Fortunately for the Americans, Japanese intelligence had overlooked Del Monte Field on Mindanao, where were located B-17 bombers recently redeployed from Luzon. A strike there would have made the Philippine air disaster absolute.

In conjunction with the *Ryujo*'s air strike, the 2nd Destroyer Flotilla sent four ships into Davao Gulf to mop up American vessels attempting to escape. Nothing was found.

It was not by luck that the Americans evaded these Japanese initiatives. Rather, the Asiatic Fleet quite deliberately had dispersed according to its war plan. There had been a seaplane tender at Davao, but it had gone. Most of the Asiatic Fleet was en route to the Netherlands East Indies, where British, Australian, and Dutch naval forces hoped to combine with Americans to defend the Malay Barrier. Sir Tom Phillips, the British admiral commanding Force Z, had appealed for destroyers to help escort his heavy ships, and a division of Hart's destroyers was making its way to Singapore when the war began. Phillips had not waited, however, and had instead sailed to his destruction.

In another incident connected with the Asiatic Fleet's redeployment, it was Japanese ships that might have been destroyed. On the evening of December 10 an American convoy was proceeding southwest from the Philippines when a Japanese cruiser and a destroyer were seen at 28,000 yards, silhouetted against the setting sun. This group contained a good deal of the strength of the Asiatic Fleet, including its flagship, heavy cruiser *Houston;* the modern light cruiser *Boise;* four destroyers; the aircraft tender *Langley;* and a couple of oilers. The American crews cleared for battle, but Rear Admiral William A. Glassford, formerly of the Yangtze Patrol but now commanding Task Force 5, the main body of the Asiatic Fleet, gave no attack orders. Darkness came and the Japanese were lost to view.

Admiral Glassford has been criticized, notably by former members of the *Houston*'s crew, for letting slip this opportunity. It has never been noted that the distance was beyond the effective range of the American ships or that a chase would have led to a night surface engagement, a notoriously confusing situation in which, at that point in the war, the Japanese had certain advantages.

There is also the question of the veracity of this sighting. Glassford's ships had left Iloilo on Panay and were steaming through the Sulu Sea. No Japanese warships are known to have been in that area at that time. The only vessels anywhere nearby were the light cruiser *Jintsu* and two destroyers of the 2nd Flotilla accompanying a minelayer into Surigao Strait. These ships were approaching from the *east,* however, not through the Sulu Sea. Rear Admiral Tanaka Raizo scouted the strait on December 11, and a field of 450 mines was laid there. If it was Tanaka's warships that were somehow seen, that admiral was no slouch and would probably have welcomed a night action. He would also have summoned help, and that would have brought air attacks from Kato's *Ryujo*. American sailors were understandably excited at the prospect of battle, but Admiral Glassford may have been wiser than they thought.

As it was, American ships safely reached the Netherlands East Indies. The only vessels that remained in Philippine waters were submarines and torpedo boats, the fast new craft known as patrol torpedo, or PT, boats.

Imperial Navy units conveyed invasion forces to Luzon and Mindanao. The Luzon troops made their major landing at Lingayen Gulf with an ancillary one at Lamon Bay, in effect two pincers threatening Manila. By the end of December there was no question of defending that place. General MacArthur declared Manila an open, or undefended, city while American-Filipino forces under General Jonathan M. Wainwright withdrew to the Bataan Peninsula northwest of the city. The Japanese 14th Army prepared to attack Bataan, beginning a siege that would endure through the first months of 1942.

Behind Bataan were the island forts of Manila Bay, principal among them Corregidor, which became the nerve center of the U.S. command. As far as the Navy was concerned, continued operations from Manila Bay became increasingly foolhardy. With the Japanese bombings of Cavite, then the Manila waterfront, the end was in sight. Fuel supplies became dangerously low, many torpedoes had been destroyed at Cavite, and the only machine tools left for maintenance work were those aboard the tender *Canopus*, which hardly sufficed. On New Year's Eve the submarine commander ordered remaining boats south to Surabaya in the Netherlands East Indies. That ended the submarine battle for the Philippines, which had reached its high point at Lingayen Gulf. There six American submarines had been ordered to hit Japanese invasion shipping. One transport sunk by the *S-38* became the sole casualty. In all, Asiatic Fleet submarines made forty-five separate attacks during December 1941 and claimed eleven ships sunk, including two destroyers. Postwar research confirmed only three sinkings, none of them warships.

With no Asiatic Fleet, nor even a submarine force, for which to provide radio intelligence, much of the raison d'être for Station Cast on Corregidor evaporated. Lieutenants Fabian and Lietwiler and their operators, analysts, and translators continued to work hard but were being exposed to increasing risks for little return. Japanese aircraft bombed Corregidor repeatedly, among other things destroying the tennis courts and many of the billets Cast's men had used before the war. In mid-January a Japanese destroyer impudently sailed right into Manila Bay and made a circuit, bombarding Corregidor and Bataan as she passed. When the British pulled their Far East Combined Bureau out of Singapore that month, Washington could hardly avoid considering the exposed position of its own Philippine codebreakers.

Looked at another way, the seventy-odd personnel of Station Cast amounted to a significant fraction of the U.S. Navy's accumulated expertise in and knowledge of both Japanese codes and the Japanese language. The skills of Cast personnel were going to be necessary and difficult to replicate. Their experience was irreplaceable. On February 1 a dispatch from the naval commander in chief in Washington suggested partial evacuation from Corregidor of some Cast people and equipment, to set up a similar fleet radio unit at a Dutch or Australian base. There were concomitant exchanges between Washington and the Asiatic Fleet submarine force regarding the evacuation.

Lieutenant Rudolph Fabian headed the first Cast group taken off Corregidor. With him went sixteen others and fifteen boxes of equipment, amounting to one and a half tons, which included direction-finding gear, kana typewriters, and the top-secret Red and Purple machines. The men's hopes soared on February 2, when submarine *Trout* appeared, but that boat had orders merely to transport the Philippine government's gold reserves. On February 4, however, Commander Pete Ferrell arrived with the *Seadragon* for the codebreakers. Chief Radioman Charlie Johns remembered it was late afternoon when the evacuation party began to move gear from Monkey Point, and late night before everything was stowed. Rather than leave with morning coming, Ferrell simply submerged in the middle of Manila Bay, slept through the day, and left on the night of February 5. In addition to codebreakers, *Seadragon* carried submarine spare parts, torpedoes no longer needed in Manila, and three other officers, two Navy and one Army.

The submarine itself proved more dangerous than the Japanese, who never interfered with *Seadragon*'s voyage. The boat had been damaged in the Cavite bombing and had had only makeshift repairs. It was supposed to be safe to a depth of sixty feet. "But I don't believe the submariners believed it," Charlie Johns observes. "They didn't trust it." In addition, the *Seadragon*'s evaporators had not been repaired; only one was producing water to drink. This meant that water to wash one's face or brush one's teeth was condensation drippings from inner hull walls. *Seadragon* was so overcrowded the passengers slept in passageways. Johns: "If you had to go forward, you just walked and hoped you didn't hurt somebody too." Still, the radiomen thought submariners were living high off the hog—they could take water from the one good evaporator and make a cup of coffee or cocoa that was not salty! It was not like life on Corregidor.

Fabian's codebreakers arrived at Surabaya about February 11. They spent the night at a Dutch barracks with their crates of equipment, over which an armed guard had to be posted at all times. The next day they were joined by Lieutenant Commander Raymond S. Lamb, a former Asiatic Fleet communications intelligence officer whose current submarine command,

*Stingray,* was in Surabaya for repairs. The group proceeded by train to Bandung, then to a village where the Dutch were building a camouflaged radio intelligence station. Charlie Johns thought the operation could not last long, because there were too many people all around. His feeling proved correct, though for rather different reasons.

In fact, Lieutenant Fabian's men had moved to a place where an independent Dutch radio intelligence organization was well established and quite active. The Dutch Army cryptanalytic unit, known as Kamer 14, was at Bandung Technical College. Its master cryptanalysts were its chief, Lieutenant Colonel J. A. Verkuyl, and his wife, plus Verkuyl's deputy and successor, Captain J. W. Henning. They had been following Japanese ciphers at least since 1932, with emphasis on the diplomatic codes, the first of which had been broken by Army captain W. A. van der Beek. In 1934 and again in 1941, Kamer 14 provided Dutch negotiators with details of Japanese instructions pertaining to trade talks.

The Dutch Navy had had a radio monitoring station working from Batavia against the Japanese since March 1933. An intelligence section on the naval staff at Batavia, Afdeling I, had existed since 1934, initially headed by Lieutenant J.F.W. Nuboer, cryptographer and author of the Dutch manual on Enigma cipher machines, which the Dutch had used beginning in 1931.

Robert D. Haslach, the leading authority on Dutch codebreaking in the East Indies, believes that the Dutch were not reading the code Washington knew as JN-25(b). Nevertheless, Kamer 14 worked hard, had help from a draft of fifty engineering and math students from Bandung College, and was adept at the arts of radio direction finding and traffic analysis. Dutch Army general Hein ter Poorten is on record as claiming that Kamer 14 informed him of Japanese aircraft carriers concentrating in the Kurile Islands. Similarly, as early as the third week of November 1941, Dutch liaison told Americans the Japanese were concentrating some of their fleet at Palau, which they did in fact do. Dutch liaison in Australia kept the Aussies up-to-date on movements of the Japanese convoy bound for Malaya. Once war began, radio intelligence provided warning of such moves as the mid-February Japanese invasion of Sumatra, and at least some of the convoys sent against Java.

Americans of the On-the-Roof Gang were surprised at the level of experience exhibited by Indonesian senior NCOs the Dutch seconded to help them. Except for their own encoding equipment, Fabian's men hardly needed any of their gear. Dutch radios sufficed for most needs. The Indonesians had just a smattering of English, but they could use Dutch, Indonesian, German, and two or three other languages to figure out how to put something together. Charlie Johns, for one, was impressed: "These fellows amazed me with how well they could go from one language to another." Johns was also amazed at the difference from the American standard of need-to-know and the social practices of the Dutch: "We had a Dutch intercept operator. He was sitting there copying Japanese. His family was there with him. I guess they'd make up his message blanks and things like that. Papa was looking over his shoulder." Lieutenant Fabian kept the Dutch and Indonesians away from American encryption materials, but he appreciated their help.

Neither Fabian nor the other Americans could know how long their joint effort would last. As a matter of fact it did not continue very long—even the best intelligence is useless if friendly forces are not sufficient or capable of utilizing it. On February 20 at Lembang, fleet intelligence officer Redfield Mason agreed to pull out the Fabian unit and send it on to Australia. Presently he received instructions from Admiral Glassford to move to Tjilatjap harbor, on the south coast of Java, where submarine *Snapper* evacuated them. When Fabian made the move, on February 21, 1942, the Malay Barrier had but a few days left.

ALTHOUGH THE DUTCH FOUGHT ALONGSIDE THE BRITISH AND AMERICANS FROM THE BEGINning, and indeed their submarine *K-16* sank the Imperial Navy destroyer *Sagiri* on Christmas Eve, Japan did not declare war on the Netherlands until January 10, 1942, and at first made no move to invade the East Indies. Initial Japanese actions were against British possessions—Kuching and Miri in northwestern Borneo—or American ones, like Jolo, a part of the Philippine archipelago. The moves were essentially preparatory: Kuching had a harbor useful for further thrusts into the Netherlands East Indies, Miri had an airfield. Right away the pattern of Japanese operations was revealed; at Miri, for example, initial landings were on December 16, then on the twenty-second eighteen JNAF fighter planes advanced to use the airfield. It was the same with Jolo. In that case Admiral Tanaka's 2nd Destroyer Flotilla escorted an invasion force to Davao, then immediately left for Jolo, where troops made a night landing and occupied the airfield early on Christmas morning. On December 30 twenty-seven JNAF fighter planes flew from Taiwan to the new base.

In each case amphibious forces seized airfields; air units advanced rapidly to the bases, extending their radius of air cover over the next set of objectives. It happened that in the years before the war the Dutch in the East Indies had debated use of seaplane bases versus air bases as mechanisms for applying airpower to island defense. The Dutch Army, which operated Holland's land-based aircraft, had advocated air bases and won the debate. Now the extensive Dutch base network gave the Japanese focal points for their advance. At the same time the Dutch air force had fewer than 150 obsolescent aircraft, including twenty-four Curtiss 21-B fighters, nineteen

Curtiss P-36 fighters, and ninety Brewster Buffaloes. The Dutch Navy also had ten Fokker twin-engine bombers (T-IV-W) and fifty-six single-engine trainers. These forces were insufficient to deny the network to the Japanese or even make full use of it themselves. With an additional thirty-nine Dorniers, thirty PBY Catalinas, and thirteen single-engine seaplanes, the Dutch Navy operated the bulk of offensive airpower in the East Indies without using the bases at all. In the end it was the Japanese who benefited most from the base network.

America's final aircraft exports to the Netherlands before war began, twenty-nine Lockheed A-20 twin-engine bombers, did little to alter the existing disparity of forces.

At sea the Dutch Navy provided a homogeneous if small force whose most important elements were light cruisers, destroyers, and submarines. Dutch naval forces at the time were regarded highly in the professional media—for example, the *U.S. Naval Institute Proceedings.* In March 1938 this source quoted Italian reports that the Dutch had "taken special care with the systematizing of defense plans of their East Indian possessions." A few months later *Proceedings'* own commentator noted it was an "open secret" that the Dutch had initiated a naval buildup. Where in 1938 the analysis was that even when their buildup was complete the Dutch would "make but a poor showing against the seapower of Japan," in a report published in December 1941, the conclusion was that "the Dutch . . . have prepared a navy of small, fast ships of an offensive nature. . . . This is a fleet with a 'sting.' It is little publicized, but anyone who has seen it in operation . . . knows its striking power far exceeds the size of the ships."

At the outset of hostilities the Dutch fleet in the East Indies consisted of light cruisers *De Ruyter, Java,* and *Tromp;* six destroyers; and eleven submarines. Naval headquarters was at Batavia on the island of Java, and the fleet was under Vice Admiral Conrad E. L. Helfrich. An exact contemporary, at age fifty-five, of his Japanese opponent, Admiral Kondo Nobutake, Helfrich knew the Indies well, having been born in Java, son of a Dutch doctor who lived near Surabaya. A number of his ship commands had been in the Netherlands East Indies, where he had led a destroyer division, and then the seagoing fleet, before becoming naval commander in chief in January 1940. When war began Helfrich's current service in the Indies had extended over more than four years. He had become a recognized expert on the hydrography of the region.

When it came to Allied cooperation, however, the Dutch commander would be passed by. Instead, in mid-January, the Allies created a new international command structure called the American-British-Dutch-Australian Command, or ABDACOM. To head it the British nominated, and the Allies accepted, General Sir Archibald P. Wavell. Under Wavell there were senior commanders for ground, naval, and air forces. The naval command went to

American admiral Thomas C. Hart, who had a British admiral as chief of staff. Dutch fleet elements attached to ABDACOM were under Rear Admiral Karel W.F.M. Doorman. Similarly, Admiral Glassford led the U.S. contingent, and a British officer such Royal Navy ships as were in the combined ABDA striking force.

In many ways the ABDA arrangement was more than awkward, it was a mess. The British were mostly concerned with reinforcement convoys to Singapore, and later Rangoon in Burma. British warships for the most part merely shuttled through the area. When Singapore fell on February 15 most British ships withdrew into the Indian Ocean. Such vessels as the British assigned to work with ABDACOM had never so much as steamed with Dutch or American warships, much less exercised or fought alongside them. The same was true of American ships, though at least there the Asiatic Fleet focused on the fight for the East Indies and made no attempt to flee until the very end. The joint force lacked up-to-date maps of East Indian waters, full of shallow or dangerous passages, small islands and reefs, even barely charted coral outcroppings. Logistics were a further headache since there were myriad differences in the three navies' diets, ammunition types, other supplies, and their standard operating procedures.

Exercising command had to be the biggest headache of all. Here the three navies spoke two languages, and even British and Americans were not entirely compatible despite common use of English, since naval terminologies were different and signaling practices distinct. The best that could be done was to keep the national groups together wherever possible, with national flagships to relay orders. Aboard the overall flagship there would be signalers and language officers to translate and interpret the orders and pass them to national contingents. The need for immediate operations to oppose the Japanese advance left no time for niceties like a common signal manual or communication system. Thus extra filters were put in place, adversely affecting the responsiveness and tactical cohesion of the ABDA striking force.

As the Allies rushed to establish ABDACOM, the Japanese geared up for their next advances. At Davao Imperial Navy officers organized an invasion force to sail for Menado on the Celebes, plus another to take Tarakan, a vital island oil port on the northeast coast of Borneo. Dutch infantry defended Tarakan for a few hours; virtually all resistance at Menado came from a couple of strikes by Dutch A-20 Hudsons. Light cruiser *Jintsu's* floatplane actually claimed to have downed a Hudson on January 17 but soon afterward was shot down in its turn. The Menadc garrison of about 1,500 was overwhelmed by invaders who included 334 paratroops of the 1st Yokosuka SNLF, making Japan's first combat parachute assault. Some JNAF aircraft immediately began using Menado, while others advanced to Tarakan. Petty Officer Sakai Saburo, among the Zero fighter pilots who flew to Tarakan, recalls that airfield as one of the worst in the East Indies, almost always treacherous with slippery mud.

While the Japanese rushed ahead, General Wavell wrestled with ABDACOM's command framework. It was January 15 before this was sufficiently ironed out that Wavell activated the system and began directing operations. Even then, arguing that he was not informed of local conditions, Wavell proposed to exclude the Philippines, asking for an expression of Allied strategic interests in that area. The answer came in the form of a cable from Admiral King through Asiatic Fleet commander Hart. This expressed the ABDA governments' approval of President Roosevelt's initial insistence that the Philippines indeed belonged in the ABDACOM sphere. The Combined Chiefs of Staff—that is, the British and American senior leaders acting in unison—understood that operations to relieve the Philippines were not feasible but saw a larger purpose served by their inclusion in Wavell's command:

AN IMPORTANT REASON FOR THE ESTABLISHMENT OF UNITY OF COMMAND IN THE ABDA AREA WAS THE REALIZATION THAT UNCOORDINATED ALLIED EFFORT IN THAT REGION COULD NEITHER SAVE THE PHILIPPINES NOR BLOCK THE JAPANESE ADVANCES THAT THREATEN THE SECURITY OF THE MALAY BARRIER.

In consequence Wavell expended some of his scant minutes and hours working through requests, reports, and appeals from General MacArthur about which he could do very little. Hours and days passed in visits to far-flung frontline positions in the theater, ranging from Burma to Malaya, to Sumatra. In the middle of it all came the sustained trauma of the disintegration of Britain's defense of Malaya and Singapore, the fortress that never was. As commander of ABDACOM, General Wavell experienced political pressures from many directions; his biographer John Connolly concludes that these were worse than the ones Wavell faced as Middle East commander answering to Winston Churchill alone. As students of the North Africa campaign must be aware, *those* political pressures had been enormous.

The Japanese had no time for Allied political headaches. With single-minded tenacity they forged ahead, executing one invasion after another, quite frequently using the same troops. The Sakaguchi detachment, for example, built around the Army's 56th Infantry Regiment and the Navy's 2nd Kure SNLF, captured Tarakan, then jumped ahead to another Borneo oil port, Balikpapan, a couple of weeks later. So well organized were they that groups of oil technicians and engineers, along with pumps and equipment to replace those demolished by the Dutch, landed right behind the assault units at Brunei (January 5) and Balikpapan (January 23).

Off Balikpapan a Dutch submarine sank one transport and damaged another. The invasion force bound for Balikpapan had been spotted by a

Patrol Wing 10 Catalina, which led to the first surface naval battle of the Pacific war. At that moment American warships were in harbor at Kupang on the southwestern end of Timor. The *Houston* and various destroyers had been detached for convoy escorts while other ships were under repair. When he received orders to attack in the Makassar Strait, Admiral Glassford had only light cruisers *Boise* and *Marblehead* and six destroyers. The *Boise* ran onto a rock as the small fleet steamed away from Timor, slashing open her hull, and had to be sent away for repairs. Within hours the *Marblehead* burned out a turbine, cutting her speed in half. As a result she was relegated to a covering role. A fairly strong striking force would thus be reduced to just four destroyers, the *John D. Ford, Pope, Parrott,* and *Paul Jones* of Destroyer Division 59 under Commander Paul H. Talbot. All were old, small, World War I–vintage destroyers, so-called four-stackers or "flush deck" ships, each armed with four 4-inch guns and twelve 21-inch torpedo tubes.

Commander Talbot sailed aboard the *Ford.* Due to the basic weakness of his force he had little reason to expect success. The Japanese unit at Balikpapan included four minesweepers, three submarine-chasers, and three old destroyers converted to patrol craft/transports. The big stick, though, was Rear Admiral Nishimura Shoji's 4th Destroyer Flotilla, his flag in the light cruiser *Naka,* with ten other destroyers. Thus Commander Talbot was outnumbered about three to one, while the Japanese destroyers were newer, bigger ships, armed for the most part with five or six 5-inch guns and deadly oxygen-powered 24-inch torpedoes. The Imperial Navy commander, Nishimura, was a torpedo specialist and experienced seagoing officer.

Despite Nishimura's advantages, luck was not with him the night of January 23–24. Midway through their amphibious landing, the Japanese transports were anchored, ready to resume unloading in the morning. They were completely unmaneuverable. The Dutch, of course, were perfectly familiar with Balikpapan, where oil storage tanks had towered over palm-roofed huts since as early as 1900, and used their knowledge to bomb key oil installations and one of the Japanese ships. Fires from those actions lit the shoreline and provided a backdrop against which the American destroyers saw their quarry. Finally, the Dutch submarine *K-17* (Lieutenant Commander van Well Groeneveld) torpedoed transport *Tsuruga Maru* after missing the *Naka.* This resulted in Nishimura's destroyers dashing off on a submarine hunt just before the American warships arrived on the scene.

A Japanese destroyer challenged Commander Talbot's ships as they entered the anchorage, but the Americans made no reply, went to high speed and commenced torpedo attacks. Talbot's four ships launched forty-eight torpedoes, which sank three Japanese transports plus the converted destroyer *P-37.* It was an impressive hour's work. The *Ford* suffered one significant hit; the other warships came off undamaged. If every battle could be like Makassar Strait, the Japanese would never break the Malay Barrier.

The Japanese had no intention of being turned back, however. They next struck the island of Ambon at the eastern fringe of the Netherlands East Indies. Admiral Tanaka's 2nd Destroyer Flotilla provided close escort. He gave orders that to preserve the element of surprise, there be no prelanding bombardment, but the Dutch and Australians were ready for the invaders. Commander Ieki Konnosuke of the 1st Kure SNLF found his naval troops pinned down; he would be killed the first day of the battle. Dutch troops surrendered that night, but the Japanese could not take Laha until February 2. The entire island was under Japanese control by February 4.

There was one other Australian infantry battalion in the region, the 2/40th Australian Infantry Force, also called Sparrow Force. Along with Dutch troops, that unit helped garrison Timor, divided into Dutch and Portuguese sections. The Allies took over Portuguese Timor, arguing that the Portuguese lacked capability to defend it themselves. The Allies promised to withdraw from Portuguese Timor once that European power had sent troops to defend it, but in the meantime planned further reinforcements. Roughly 600 Dutch troops under Colonel van Straaten completed the garrison. Of these, an Australian independent company plus 270 Dutch held the Portuguese section of the island, the Dutch were scattered about, and the main body of Sparrow Force was stationed at Kupang, where the airfield was a critical link for the Allies, who could use it to stage aircraft from Australia to the Netherlands East Indies.

Timor's value was not lost on the Japanese, though the Portuguese half of it occasioned pause in Tokyo. Landings had been planned for the Dutch portion, but now the Naval General Staff wanted to occupy the Portuguese half as well. A January 28 liaison conference on the plan erupted into bitter argument between Admiral Nagano and Prime Minister Tojo plus Foreign Minister Togo. Nagano insisted on the occupation, Tojo and Togo countered that Japan hardly needed to make any more enemies and should preserve its amicable relations with Portugal. No one else said a word. A further meeting followed on February 2. The Navy insisted on access to Portuguese Timor to establish a base to bomb Darwin in Australia. Through the services' military affairs bureau chiefs, the Navy agreed that efforts to reach diplomatic understanding with Portugal would precede invasion of the Portuguese side of Timor, and that Army troops would withdraw once the air base was in place. Afterward General Tojo went to the Imperial Palace and told Lord Kido that the Timor problem had been solved. Senior Army officers observed that Tojo and Nagano stopped talking to each other after this incident. Ironically the Navy's attaché in Portugal turned out to be one of the Naval General Staff's best wartime sources for intelligence.

An Allied convoy bound for Timor with reinforcements turned back after aircraft attacks from Captain Kato's *Ryujo*. They would be trapped at Darwin on February 19 by strikes from Nagumo's Kido Butai, followed by medium bombers flying from Kendari on Celebes. That night the Japanese landed on Timor spearheaded by SNLF troops who secured the invasion beaches according to classic Japanese amphibious doctrine. Naval troops were followed by the Army's 228th Regiment, victors of Hong Kong, to begin a tough battle against the Australians. Several hundred paratroopers of the 3rd Yokosuka SNLF from Kendari dropped behind Allied lines after dawn, disrupting defenses and forcing some withdrawals. Many were mopped up by an Australian company the next day, but a second paratroop drop sustained the SNLF while Japanese Army forces captured Kupang and its airfield. The SNLF paratroops distracted the Allies long enough for other Japanese troops to envelop both flanks.

Erroneously thinking themselves surrounded, elements of Sparrow Force surrendered on February 23. Remaining Australians joined Dutch troops in Portuguese Timor. The Japanese did not immediately follow, since they were carrying on diplomacy with Lisbon. A kind of guerrilla war continued on Timor through January 1943, with Dutch and Australians making repeated forays against Japanese. The Japanese air campaign against Darwin began from Kendari, continued from Kupang, and used Portuguese Timor only toward its end in 1943. There were fifty-eight JNAF raids against Darwin or other bases along Australia's northern coast, the last on November 12, 1943.

In the meantime Allied flags came down all along the Malay Barrier. Singapore fell on February 15, 1942, the day after the Japanese invaded Sumatra, again combining amphibious operations with a parachute drop. With intelligence of the operation, ABDACOM nevertheless proved unable to interfere, as a naval force was bombed and withdrew before contact. Barely touching port at Batavia, Admiral Karel Doorman, who had been made commander of the combined ABDA surface fleet, resolved to hit Japanese invaders about to wade ashore at Bali, a twin operation to the invasion of Timor. Again ABDA had warning—in fact, just as the Japanese left harbor—which must have come from radio intelligence.

Admiral Doorman faced serious problems, with competing demands for scarce surface ships, which for weeks had been melting away under strong attacks. In the Makassar Strait on February 4 bombers of the Kanoya and Takao air groups had caught Doorman's ships with especially telling effect, crippling *Marblehead* by disabling her rudder and causing other damage and casualties. Among the latter was Commander William B. Goggins, her executive officer, burned and suffering a head wound. (Goggins would be put ashore on Java, make a miraculous escape by sea, and join the codebreakers at Pearl Harbor after a lengthy convalescence.) Heavy cruiser *Houston* took a bomb hit aft that knocked out her rear 8-inch turret, a third of her heavy armament. The Dutch destroyer *Van Ghent* was lost running aground in the Bangka Strait on February 15, while the *Van Nes* sank after JNAF bombing.

Several British ships left to escort the last convoys out of Singapore. Thus, when it came to opposing the Japanese at Bali, Doorman could assemble only a scratch force.

Doorman's hurry to get at Bali stands in marked contrast to the caution Samuel Eliot Morison attributes to him in his history of U.S. naval operations in World War II. Though Morison tempered this judgment somewhat in a later condensation, calling Doorman "a fine type of fighting sailor," negative remarks in his semi-official history have carried great weight among historians and should be directly confronted. Doorman is criticized, for example, for ordering the fleet south of Java to refuel at sea. Morison does not note that American commander Admiral Glassford ordered an exactly parallel retirement at one point to refuel in the Indian Ocean—farther than the Dutch ever retreated. Morison's history also contains oblique criticism that "some Dutch naval commanders" had not learned that defense is impossible without a tactically offensive posture. If Doorman had a weakness it was rather the opposite—he remained aggressive to the point of recklessness, time and again driving his ships to sea on some attack mission. His schemes were foiled more often than not by logistics, air opposition, navigational problems, and the difficulties of working with a multinational force. The defense of the Malay Barrier might have done better had Doorman spent less time attacking and more arranging common fleet signals or exercising ships together.

A native of Utrecht, Karel Doorman had been a naval officer since 1910 and a pilot since 1915. He became one of the first flying instructors in the Dutch naval air service, and rose to command that air arm in 1938. Promoted rear admiral in May 1940, he then commanded, under Helfrich, the fleet forces in the East Indies. Approaching his fifty-third birthday, Admiral Doorman could hardly be regarded as inexperienced and ought not to be seen as overcautious. One of Doorman's destroyer skippers in 1940–1941 later told Morison that his boss had been a clever man and experienced sailor and his views on strategic and tactical problems had always been logical and sound. As is apparent from Doorman's background, he also could not be accused of failure to appreciate the importance of airpower. This is important given what happened off Bali and soon afterward in the Java Sea.

The sea fight off Bali on February 19–20 has come down to history as the battle of the Badung Strait. In it, the Allies suffered the consequences of their scramble to put a striking force to sea. Admiral Doorman had sent his ships out in packets. As a result he did not have a fleet but rather three "waves" of attack ships. Doorman led the first wave himself from the light cruiser *De Ruyter;* he had another Dutch light cruiser, *Java,* plus two Dutch and two American destroyers. All had sailed from Tjilatjap on the south coast of Java. The second wave came from Surabaya under Captain J. B. de Meester of the Dutch light cruiser *Tromp*. He had four more of the American flush-deck destroyers. The final wave consisted of five Dutch motor torpedo boats. This use of waves of attackers dissipated Doorman's numerical superiority. The necessity of a night attack further reduced Allied advantages. In what might almost have been comedy were it not so tragic, Dutch destroyer *Kortenaer* ran aground; then another Dutch destroyer, *Piet Hein*, zigzagged and began to make smoke, obscuring the range for the American destroyers following her. Where Morison records that the purpose of this action simply mystified the Americans, a Dutch officer notes apparent error: The make-smoke button was located on the wall at the back of the bridge and was uncovered; as the ship heeled into her battle turn someone lost his balance and fell onto the wall, hitting the button with his back. The second wave failed to make contact with the first. They fought a pitched battle with Japanese destroyers, and the American *Parrott* briefly ran aground before getting off. The torpedo boats claim to have traveled the Badung Strait from one end to the other without seeing anything at all. The final result was Dutch *Piet Hein* sunk as against Japanese destroyer *Michishio* damaged.

Misfortune at Badung Strait seemed normal for Allied luck as the Malay Barrier campaign went into its endgame. Fuel for warships became a problem amid the plenty of this oil-producing land. Vice Admiral Glassford, who was promoted and succeeded Admiral Hart, found himself sending tankers to Australia, Ceylon, even the Persian Gulf to find what ought to have been available just where he was. Ship services of all kinds, anti-aircraft ammunition, and repairs became urgent needs.

A major factor in the steady attrition of the ABDA fleet was lack of aircraft. The Japanese scored big as early as February 3, when bombers and fighters from Kendari struck around Surabaya and recorded as many as sixty-two planes burned on the ground. Some Allied sources give even higher figures. Efforts to strengthen Allied airpower included shipment of more than 120 P-40 fighters from Australia, and a fly-off of fifty British Hurricanes from carrier *Indomitable*. Repeat performances by the U.S. aircraft transport *Langley* and the British *Indomitable* both came to naught—the *Langley* sunk on the Darwin–Java route, while the British carrier's mission was canceled when it became obvious that the end had come in Java. Aircraft wastage in the Netherlands East Indies remained high, climaxing on February 18 and 19 when both sides mixed it up over Surabaya, as JNAF Zeros escorted attack planes to that place. Japanese sources claim twenty-six planes shot down and six probables in these air battles. Statistically, Allied bomber strength at the beginning of March stayed near what it had been a month earlier while fighter strength had dropped 40 percent—which sounds good until one considers that these results followed reinforcement by over 200 aircraft!

The drumbeat of Allied disaster continued virtually without interruption.

Dutch submarines provided one of the few moments of relief with their successes: three transports sunk and four damaged in the South China Sea, and two more sunk and two damaged off Borneo. The cost, however, was three Dutch submarines sent to the bottom. General Wavell grew increasingly pessimistic about ABDACOM's prospects. On February 19 he reported that how long Java's fighter defense lasted would define the potential for resistance, since once it was gone neither bombers nor naval bases could be protected any longer, and fighter defenses had no more than two weeks left to them. *That* was *before* the big air battles over Surabaya. On February 21 Wavell sent decidedly bad news:

THERE ARE SIGNS THAT JAPANESE ARE COMPLETING PREPARATIONS FOR INVASION OF JAVA WHICH OBVIOUSLY WE CAN DO LITTLE TO PREVENT. . . . I AM HAVING STOCK TAKEN OF SHIPPING AVAILABLE IN ISLAND SHOULD EVACUATION . . . BE ORDERED BY YOU.

The ABDA commander had already reported Helfrich's conclusion that it would be impossible to defend Java with the naval forces available, and on February 21 Wavell remarked, "I am afraid that the defense of the ABDA area has broken down." General Wavell left for Colombo, Ceylon, on Wednesday, February 25.

Only the Dutch still believed in the Malay Barrier. Admiral Conrad Helfrich, Dutch naval commander in chief, told his government on February 24 that the British and American view seemed too gloomy:

I AM CONCENTRATING EVERYTHING IN JAVA SEA AND VICINITY AND AM TRYING TO IMBUE AMERICAN SUBMARINES WITH GREATEST OFFENSIVE SPIRIT. IT IS STILL NOT TOO LATE BUT GREAT SPEED, GRIM DETERMINATION, AND TAKING ALL RISKS IS NECESSARY.

As Helfrich well knew, Karel Doorman was just the sailor to take extreme risks for Java.

ADMIRAL KAREL DOORMAN HELD HIS FINAL COMMAND CONFERENCE AT SURABAYA ON February 26. It lasted somewhat over an hour. Beyond the inevitable exhortation to his captains to fight hard, Doorman's main subject was intelligence. All through the campaign intelligence had served the Allies well. It is true that there had been difficulties with photographic intelligence—in mid-February there were no suitable aircraft and no photographic supplies in the theater—but radio intelligence made up the slack. The British reported within days the sailing of Nagumo's Kido Butai, and there had been advance word of the Japanese operations against Balikpapan, Sumatra, Bali, and others. The Admiralty and Far East Combined Bureau, then being reestab-

lished at Colombo and Kilindini (in East Africa), were feeding a constant supply of Imperial Navy radio call signs and traffic indicators. The
Dutch knew that messages for Admiral Kondo's Southern Expeditionary Fleet, Nagumo's carriers, and Admiral Tsukahara's Eleventh Air Fleet
were all being routed through Palau. The Dutch also supplied location
reports for such Japanese units as light carrier *Ryujo*, cruiser *Natori*, and the
Kanoya Air Group. Radio intelligence was undoubtedly the source for
ABDACOM's report to London on February 24 that a new Japanese convoy
was scheduled to arrive at Bali the next morning. And there were various
reports, both radio and air reconnaissance, of the disposition of JNAF
bomber squadrons.

The intelligence may have been scary, but the bulk of it had been quite
accurate. Doorman was thus predisposed to believe when the prediction
came that Java would be the next target. Air scouts reported transports in
the Makassar Strait on February 25, and radio intelligence noted convoys
on both sides of Borneo the next day. Among call signs identified by the
British as addresses for communications they intercepted was Rear Admiral
Nishimura's 4th Destroyer Flotilla, which was indeed escorting one of the
Japanese invasion convoys toward Java. On February 26 there were seven
naval sightings reported by the intelligence center at Bandung. At his meeting Doorman was confident the Japanese were on the move. He intended to
intercept the forces steaming down the east side of Borneo. There would be
no immediate interception for the western invasion convoy, since Admiral
Helfrich had ordered British and Australian ships at Batavia to Tjilatjap on
Java's south coast to fuel.

On the Japanese side much also happened. The Combined Fleet ordered
Kido Butai, temporarily including both Nagumo's aircraft carriers and
Kondo's battleships, to continue west into the Indian Ocean, raiding
Christmas Island and picking off ships attempting to flee Java. With Kondo
Nobutake in tactical command, the task force left Celebes on February 25.
"Ripple free as floating oil," the water reminded Seaman Kuramoto Iki of the
Inland Sea. Kuramoto saw wild ducks flocking together, a great school of
dolphins sailing in company with the ships; "words at such a time fail to
express what I feel," he recorded. "Could it be that a bloody war is being
fought on such a sea?"

Also in motion were the direct instruments of Java's demise. To the west
of Borneo, Admiral Ozawa Jisaburo commanded the support force for a convoy of fifty-six transports; to the east, Vice Admiral Takagi Takeo led the
covering force for a forty-one-transport convoy. Aside from the usual close
escort, the destroyer flotillas of Admirals Nishimura and Tanaka protected
Takagi's convoy. It was their force that Karel Doorman decided to attack, in
the Java Sea north of Surabaya, which became the scene of the biggest surface naval battle to date, a battle that spelled doom for the Malay Barrier. At

his council of war in the wardroom of the *De Ruyter,* Doorman had no illusions: The fleet should risk everything to prevent a landing on Java; the destroyers should lead with torpedoes, closing right in to mix with the Japanese transports and sink them with gunfire afterward, withdrawing to Tanjung Priok, the port of Batavia at the west end of Java. Speaking in English, Doorman mentioned the possibility of friendly fighter cover, but the officers present had heard that so often it was regarded as a joke. They laughed.

Admiral Doorman's ships weighed anchor as the sun set behind the mountains west of Surabaya on the evening of February 26. It was 6:30 P.M. The ships had already endured three air raids that day, fortunately without damage. During the afternoon they were joined for the first time by some British ships: heavy cruiser *Exeter* (Captain Oliver Gordon), Australian light cruiser *Perth* (Captain Hector Waller), and three destroyers. The sailors were itching to get at the Japanese.

Doorman apparently thought the Japanese had timed their invasion force to arrive off the Java coast that night. He sailed west to the tip of Madura, the island off the Javanese coast that shields Surabaya, then doubled back east toward Bali. By noon of February 27, having made no contact, Doorman turned back. His sailors were exhausted. It was two days since he had reported the collapse of morale in the fleet, and now the men had been keyed up for battle but found nothing. Aboard the *Houston,* for example, the crew had spent twelve hours at battle stations, and that was the *second* consecutive night they had stood such a hard watch. Doorman saw little alternative but to rest the men.

Just as the fleet entered the channel into Surabaya, however, air reconnaissance reported the Japanese to the north, only about fifty miles away. Admiral Doorman ordered the fleet to follow him and laid a course for the location. "Suddenly," noted Walter Winslow, a floatplane pilot on the *Houston,* "men were no longer tired." With the cruisers in line-ahead battle formation the fleet headed north-northwest at 25 knots.

Available accounts from the Japanese side reflect concern as much as excitement. Imperial Navy officers were well aware that the Allies had a fleet to contest the Java approaches. The invasion convoy had been bombed repeatedly, twice that very day (without result). About noon the force feinted by following a westerly course into the Java Sea. Commander Hara Tameichi, skipper of destroyer *Amatsukaze* in Tanaka's 2nd Destroyer Flotilla, wrote that the convoy's heavy covering unit, Cruiser Division 5, "followed haughtily behind the convoy," or again that the two ships of this unit were "following us far to the rear." Hara recorded their distance as 200, then 150 miles, but the first contact report with the Allied force came from a plane based at Balikpapan as early as 10:25 A.M. (according to 4th Destroyer Flotilla records). This gave Admiral Takagi hours to catch up; his heavy cruisers, incidentally, launched their own scout planes to continue reporting the ABDA fleet.

Admiral Nishimura's 4th Flotilla sighted the mast of Tanaka's destroyer leader, the light cruiser *Jintsu*, at 1:15 P.M. Just fifteen minutes later Takagi's heavy cruisers first appeared to the northwest. The convoy had been ordered to make speed to the north, away from the approaching Allied warships. Nishimura's flotilla had an alarm at 3:50, but that turned out to be a Japanese ship. Soon thereafter the enemy hove in sight. *Naka*, Nishimura's flagship, spotted Doorman's fleet at 4:14. Destroyers *Hatsukaze* and *Tokitsukaze* of Tanaka's flotilla both saw the Allied ships at 4:12, while the earliest reported sighting, at 4:11, was by Captain Kiyota Takahiko's heavy cruiser *Nachi*, Takagi's flagship. On the Allied side, accounts agree that the British destroyer *Electra* made the initial sighting of Japanese at 4:12 P.M. According to *Amatsukaze*'s Captain Hara, at the moment of sighting Admiral Takagi's heavy cruisers had not yet arrived to support the flotillas, though if that is true those vessels must have been just below the horizon. Hara worried that if the ABDA fleet merely increased speed to 30 knots the convoy would be caught unsupported. No Japanese knew that Admiral Doorman had restricted speed to 27 knots to accommodate Dutch destroyer *Kortenaer*, with propulsion problems as a result of the Badung Strait action. Hara thought he saw another mistake as well: Doorman altered to a westerly course, which gave Vice Admiral Takagi more time to bring up cruisers *Nachi* and *Haguro*. Had Doorman maintained his original heading, Hara believes, the ABDA fleet would have had favorable gunnery positions while minimizing exposure to Japanese gunfire. Doorman would also have brought his three light cruisers, with their smaller 6-inch guns, into effective gun range. Maintaining course, however, would have afforded the Japanese an opportunity to get ahead of the ABDA fleet and, on their converging course, "cross the T," bringing their broadside to bear on the limited forward firepower of the Allied ships. The *Kortenaer*'s speed may well have been the determinant for Doorman, since once he let the Japanese get ahead there would be no catching them—Takagi's *slowest* ships, his cruisers, were capable of 33 knots.

On the bridge of Japanese flagship *Nachi* a key decision had to be made on when to open fire. It is sometimes said of Karel Doorman that he had never been in battle before, but this was equally true of his opponent, Takagi Takeo, as well as the latter's senior staff officer, Commander Nagasawa Ko. The closest Takagi and Nagasawa had previously come to combat had been at Davao in early January, when their flagship of that time, heavy cruiser *Myoko*, had been bombed at anchor. Takagi subsequently commanded a number of the Netherlands East Indies invasions, but had never faced combat. Commander Nagasawa recalls that Allied warships began shooting before he recommended to Takagi that the Japanese do the same. Action records for both *Nachi* and *Haguro* show these ships using their 8-inch main batteries from 4:17 P.M. Records of the 4th Destroyer Flotilla have the *Jintsu* opening fire at 4:15 and the flotilla's own light cruiser, *Naka*, starting a half-minute later.

Allied observers report that the ABDA fleet held fire until the Japanese opened up. The exact moment *Houston* and *Exeter* first fired their 8-inch guns seems to have gone unrecorded, but Nishimura's battle report puts it at 4:17 P.M.—that is, at exactly the same instant as *Nachi* and *Haguro*. Observers on both sides believe their first salvos fell short of the targets. In a word, both fleets commenced fire at excessive range. Doorman's light cruisers seem to have recognized this and initially remained silent. The Japanese light cruisers did not, and accomplished nothing.

The cannonade went on for almost an hour before there was any appreciable result, again contrary to claims on both sides. Lieutenant Commander Arthur L. Maher (*Houston*'s gunnery officer) and some of her turret officers thought they saw hits on about the tenth salvo. Walter Winslow, standing on *Houston*'s signal bridge, writes of a straddle on the sixth salvo and effective hits beginning with the tenth, and says that by 4:30 the Japanese cruiser that was their target was on fire both forward and amidships, and turned away. Neither of the Imperial Navy heavy cruisers reported *any* damage, however. Moreover, in postwar interviews neither Commander Nagasawa Ko nor Midshipman Kimura Hachiro, both of whom were on *Nachi*'s bridge, note any damage to the Japanese heavy ships. Kimura, who spoke of how Nagasawa seemed to grip the ship's compass with tension each time a salvo fell close, surely would have noted any actual hit. Nagasawa, who acknowledges that Admiral Takagi and his staff felt uneasy in this, their first battle, would have mentioned damage in exculpation of charges that Takagi handled the fleet poorly in the engagement. Neither did.

As for the Japanese, *Nachi*'s action record reports sinking two cruisers, heavily damaging one, and sinking three or four destroyers. This is wild exaggeration. Observers agree that the Japanese shells fell in tight, well-aimed patterns; they were trained in long-range firing without benefit of ranging salvos. Winslow wrote: "Japanese gunnery appeared to be extremely accurate . . . after the first few salvoes our lead ships were being dangerously straddled." Nevertheless damage was nothing like what was reported. *De Ruyter* was hit by two shells, which failed to explode, *Houston* by one. These did minimal damage. The Japanese light cruisers hit nothing.

Technical factors account for a proportion of fleet ineffectiveness. Commander Maher maintained later that *Houston*'s fire-control equipment for her big guns was obsolete before the war began. More practically, on the fifth salvo a fuse box failed in *Houston*'s A turret, incapacitating the mechanism for ramming the shells and powder bags into the gun barrels. Doing

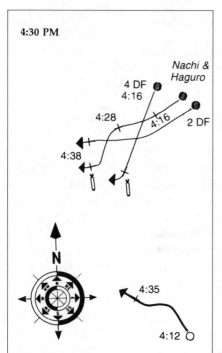

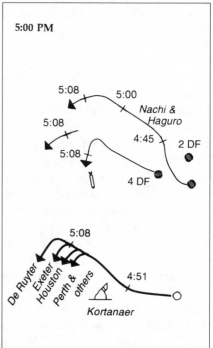

Abbreviations are identified in the general list of abbreviations for this book.
Map symbol key can be found following the list of abbreviations.

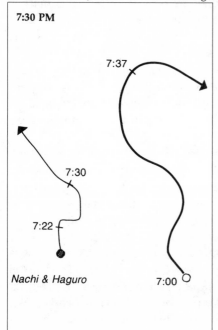

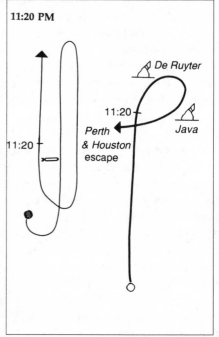

III. Battle of the Java Sea (February 27–28, 1942)

this work by muscle power, regarded as virtually impossible before the war, was certainly extremely difficult and reduced the ship's gunnery efficiency. On the *De Ruyter* the concussion of guns firing broke the flagship's signal lamps, further complicating already atrocious command control. Allied liaison officers were reduced to radio, for which encoding and decoding delays made battle direction almost impossible. Doorman could pass flag signals in Dutch to his liaison officer aboard *Houston,* who translated the commands and passed them to other English-speaking ships, but this extra layer in the command net proved extremely cumbersome. To complete the headache, the British ships also passed signals among themselves using Royal Navy flag code, which none could read save Englishmen.

Meanwhile, aboard *Nachi,* staff officer Nagasawa turned to Admiral Takagi and said that since Doorman was not letting them get much closer, it must be time to attack with torpedoes. Takagi approved. A torpedo expert professionally, Nakasawa held that post on Takagi's staff as well as being senior staff officer, so it fell to him to pass the admiral's order. Admiral Nishimura responded immediately with his 4th Flotilla, but Tanaka's 2nd, in view of the great distance to the Allied fleet, held its fire. Between 4:33 and 4:45 Nishimura's warships launched forty-three Long Lance torpedoes. At 4:52 Captain Mori Tomoichi's heavy cruiser *Haguro* followed suit with eight torpedoes of her own. Ironically, *Nachi,* the flagship, launched no torpedoes because the stop valve for the compressed-oxygen system had accidentally been left open too long.

Despite difficulties Karel Doorman was trying to bring his firepower into play. He made two course alterations to put ships closer, bringing the 6-inch guns of his light cruisers into effective range for the first time. No existing account notes any reaction by the Allies either to Nishimura's torpedo launch or the premature detonation of a number of those torpedoes after just a few thousand yards. On the other hand, "Windy" Winslow wrote of the Allies scoring even more direct hits, which forced a Japanese light cruiser to leave the action smoking and on fire. One wonders if this was Nishimura's *Naka* turning away after her torpedo run.

In any case, the first Allied knowledge of the Japanese torpedoes appears to have been when sailors began to see them in the water. All of a sudden there was pandemonium as everything happened at once. *Haguro* scored a telling blow at 5:07 when she put an 8-inch shell into *Exeter,* impacting at a port-side secondary gun, then penetrating to explode in a boiler room. Steam pressure dropped precipitately, along with *Exeter's* speed, as six of eight boilers went off-line. Electric power to the main armament failed temporarily. Captain Gordon took his ship out of the battle.

Aboard *Houston,* Captain Albert H. Rooks turned to port when he saw the *Exeter's* maneuver, in order to avoid a collision. At that point the cruisers following Rooks, expecting an order to evade, assumed *Houston* was acting on such and followed. Admiral Doorman in the *De Ruyter*, unaware of what had happened behind his ship, steamed blissfully ahead until someone noticed the fleet disappearing, whereupon *De Ruyter* turned to conform with the rest. Australian cruiser *Perth*, realizing what had happened to *Exeter*, circled her to lay a protective shield of smoke. Commander A. Kroese's Dutch destroyer *Kortenaer* was then hit by one of the Long Lance torpedoes. She broke in two and sank, leaving her skipper and many of his crew in the water. By now fog and smoke obscured the battle area and there was little possibility of regrouping, so Doorman retired at 5:20. The maneuver mystified some Japanese. Petty Officer Kawabata Shigeo, aboard the *Kawakaze*, one of the vessels of the 2nd Destroyer Flotilla, recalled that "a sudden squall came up during which the Allied force scattered and was lost."

In fact Kawabata had had a good vantage point, because at that moment Admiral Tanaka's 2nd Flotilla happened to be the force closest to the ABDA fleet. That was because Tanaka had ordered execution of the torpedo attack previously directed by fleet commander Takagi. Eight destroyers dashed in. Commander Hara on the *Amatsuzake* specifically credits the confusion in the Allied line with enabling the destroyers to close. Captain Sato Torajiro of the *Jintsu* covered with 5.5-inch shell fire. For the *Kawakaze* there was an element of satisfaction: These American destroyers she now faced had been arrayed against her in various international incidents on the Yangtze when she was assigned there in 1938. The *Jintsu* launched eight torpedoes at 5:27, with the destroyers following as their skippers judged the moment ripe. One ship signaled Commander Toyama Yasumi, Tanaka's senior staff officer, "It is simple. Exactly like a maneuver!" Of seventy-two torpedoes, however, there would not be a single hit! Worse, Allied ships scored shell hits on destroyers *Tokitsukaze* and *Asagumo*.

Admiral Doorman countered by sending his three British destroyers on a torpedo run against the Japanese. *Electra* (Commander C. W. May) was stopped and eventually sunk by gunfire, one of her main persecutors being Sato's *Jintsu*. *Encounter* and *Jupiter* made independent attacks before teaming up with Dutch destroyer *Witte de With* to escort *Exeter* out of the battle area. The British destroyers rejoined Doorman as he got his remaining four cruisers and six destroyers in column for a renewed thrust north. About 5:45 P.M. the column emerged from haze to find the Japanese ships arrayed in front of them. Gunfire predominated, though Nishimura and Takagi made some torpedo attacks. At one point Nishimura ordered flotilla-wide preparations to counter gas attack. Several hits were claimed, including, in one account, the sinking of a submarine by the *Jupiter* with a torpedo. (But no Japanese submarines have been recorded as lost on this date.) Sunset came at 6:21, at which time Admiral Takagi deployed to protect the invasion convoy and recover observation planes.

Commander Nagasawa, on the bridge of the *Nachi*, recalled that the staff were all very nervous. Torpedo detonations had been taken for mine explosions; sunset had come and gone, and night battle always offered opportunity for confusion. According to Japanese naval historian Chihaya Masataka, Admiral Takagi's considerations in calling off pursuit of Doorman's fleet were that he wanted to avoid blundering into any mine field in the dark; he had observed the Surabaya lighthouse in the distance (again making him fear mines); and he was worried about Allied submarines in the area.

The decision was taken out of Takagi's hands. As the *Nachi* worked to ship the last of five floatplanes, about 7:30, masts were seen in the darkness. Lieutenant Commander Ishikawa Kotaro, intelligence staff officer, identified them as Allied. Lookouts mistook the vessels for Japanese *Kongo*-class fast battleships. There were tense moments as the Japanese cruisers, stopped, lay vulnerable to Allied gunfire. The *Nachi* opened fire at 7:37 but seven minutes later Doorman reversed course and turned south, ending the engagement.

There would be one more iteration when Doorman turned north and made another sally later that night. With a signal error he lost his four American destroyers, and soon afterward the British *Jupiter* (Lieutenant Commander N.V.J.T. Thew) blundered into an actual Dutch mine field and sank. When the force came upon survivors of the *Kortenaer* in the water, *Electra* was detached to pick them up, leaving Doorman without any destroyers at all. Shortly after 11:00 P.M. the Japanese again glimpsed Allied ships in the darkness. *Nachi* went to action stations three minutes later and ordered preparations for torpedo action. Aboard *Naka*, destroyer leader Nishimura saw star shells, and gunfire lit the horizon, when Admiral Takagi engaged Doorman at 11:21. Two minutes later the Japanese cruisers launched twelve more torpedoes.

This time the Japanese torpedoes ran hot and true. At 11:36 Dutch cruiser *Java* (Captain P.B.M. van Staelen) and four minutes later the *De Ruyter* (Captain E.E.B. Lacomblé) were struck. Far away to the northwest, torpedo expert Hara on his *Amatsuzake* saw a tremendous pyrotechnic display as the Dutch ships exploded and caught fire. Karel Doorman chose to go down with his flagship. Some 344 Dutch sailors went with him.

Doorman's demise left remnants of the ABDA fleet to shift for themselves. The British destroyer *Encounter* stopped at Surabaya, then continued in company with cruiser *Exeter* and American destroyer *Pope*. On March 1 these ships were caught between Takagi's heavy cruisers and another Japanese force under Vice Admiral Takahashi Ibo. All were sunk, though the Japanese recovered some survivors. The *Kawakaze* picked up thirty-five, including four or five officers, who were kept under a canvas awning on deck. Though treatment of Java Sea survivors later became an issue for war-crimes investigation, *Kawakaze* petty officer Tokugawa Yoshio reported that these men were not ill treated or interrogated while on his ship, and were given medical treatment.

Commander Thomas H. Binford's four American destroyers—*Jones, John D. Edwards, Ford,* and *Alden*—stopped at Surabaya. Binford heard there were Japanese in the Bali Strait and set out to attack them. Finding nothing, the ships continued to safety. Another destroyer, *Pillsbury,* was sent to Tjilatjap, known to Americans as "Slapjack," to escort vessels now attempting to flee Java. She disappeared, apparently the victim of Japanese heavy cruisers. Admiral Kondo's battleships teamed up with *Soryu* aircraft to finish off destroyer *Edsall.* Aircraft tender *Langley* succumbed to carrier dive-bombers.

The most famous post–Java Sea adventures were those of the Galloping Ghost—*Houston*—and the Australian *Perth.* These cruisers, led by Captain Waller of *Perth,* attempted to disrupt the Japanese western invasion convoy in its landing site at Banten Bay. *Houston* had expended all ammunition for her forward 8-inch turrets and had to replace it by trundling shells from the aft magazine through the bowels of the ship. In the night action, which recent scholarship argues was fought off the mouth of, and not inside, Banten Bay, the gun flashes of Japanese ships were like lights blinking along the horizon. Japanese vessels included heavy cruisers *Mogami* and *Mikuma* and the 5th Destroyer Flotilla. Again the Imperial Navy used torpedoes, which probably sank some of its own transports. Among the losses was *Ryujo Maru,* amphibious command ship, from which 16th Army commander General Imamura Hitoshi was unceremoniously dumped into the water. When he reached land after an arduous swim, one of his staff joked that at least there would be no more delays getting ashore.

The Banten Bay battle was so desperate that Captain Rooks of *Houston* considered beaching his ship at the end and then moving surviving men ashore to fight alongside the Dutch. A sailor actually used the rifle he was issued to shoot out the searchlight of an opposing destroyer. In little more than an hour the *Perth* lost 352 of her 686 crew (116 more would die as Japanese prisoners) while *Houston* casualties amounted to 738 out of 1,008 officers and men (104 died in captivity). This action, known as the battle of the Sunda Strait, amounted to the heaviest resistance there would be to the Japanese invasion.

Once the Imperial Army forces reached shore on Java, events moved inexorably to the conclusion predicted by ABDA commander Wavell. Dutch ground forces and such Australian and American troops as remained were overwhelmed. Thus came the end of the Malay Barrier.

THE DEMISE OF THE MALAY BARRIER LEFT ONLY THE PHILIPPINES STILL RESISTING IN THE FAR East. The end there was predictable too. At one point in January, MacArthur appealed to General Wavell for blockade runners. Efforts were made, starting with the submarines *Trout, Sargo,* and *Seadragon.* On February 19 submarine *Swordfish* stopped at Manila and picked up President Manuel Quezon and his party. Some blockade running was also attempted by Filipino inter-island steamers including the *Legaspi,* which completed two trips but was sunk on her third try; *Princesa,* arrived from Cebu on February 21; and *Elcano,* entering Manila Bay from Mindanao at the end of February. By then the Filipino-American defenders of Bataan had undergone their first Japanese offensives, and both Bataan and Corregidor were on short rations. General MacArthur left Manila on March 10, traveling by PT boat to the southern Philippines, then by aircraft to Australia, where he promised he would return.

Still in the Monkey Point tunnel on Corregidor were the remaining code-breakers of Station Cast. The question of evacuating them sharpened after the fall of the Netherlands East Indies. The first party had gone on to Melbourne, Australia, after arrival from Java on March 3. The group, now augmented to five officers and twenty-two men, was initially supervised by Commander Redfield Mason. A small additional contingent had been en route to Cast but were stranded in Australia by the start of the war; these men became part of the new unit. With equipment from Manila, including the Red and Purple machines, Red Mason and Rudy Fabian had radio intelligence capability. In Melbourne the Americans joined up with a Royal Australian Navy (RAN) radio unit under Lieutenant Commander Jack Newman at Victoria Barracks, as well as a small British radio intelligence staff. Already foreseeing the need for expansion, the Australians procured a block of flats called the Monterrey. In keeping with the Allied nature of the new unit, Commander Newman, RAN, became deputy chief.

Establishment of a radio group in Melbourne made superfluous Lieutenant Lietwiler's unit at Monkey Point. Even worse, the Corregidor unit had become a security risk, a leak just awaiting some clever Japanese interrogator who could uncork it. In addition, the Australian unit had need of the skilled radio operators, cipher clerks, and language people stuck in the Philippines. From Washington on March 5, COMINCH ordered the Philippine Naval District to get Lietwiler's men out of there, by submarine if possible, by *any* means if necessary, at least as far as the southern Philippines. Admiral King also ordered precautions to prevent loss of any radio intelligence personnel.

It was easy enough for Washington to order something like this, much harder for a hard-pressed local command to carry it out. Almost the last boats available were those MacArthur used to escape five days later. Submarine *Permit,* under Lieutenant Wreford Goss ("Moon") Chapple, got orders for Manila to remove MacArthur, but arrived to discover that the general had already left. The naval district command told Chapple to evacuate Station Cast. In turn Moon Chapple gave the senior naval officer, Captain Kenneth M. Hoeffel, a problem of his own. Coming up to Corregidor the *Permit* had run into one of the PT boats used for the MacArthur mission, which had broken down and been left behind, its gasoline siphoned off. Chapple destroyed the marooned boat and took off her crew. At Manila, according to a Cast codebreaker, the PT boat skipper told Captain Hoeffel that his crew should join the naval battalion on Bataan but he himself ought to rejoin his unit. That meant getting out of the islands, since PT commander John D. Bulkeley had gone to Australia on the planes that evacuated MacArthur.

Moon Chapple had a different idea, again according to the former Navy codebreaker. By any measure a brave submariner, in fact the only one to have penetrated Lingayen Gulf during the Japanese invasion and sunk a ship there, Chapple took the position that the PT men had fought their battle and he was going to get them out. At Monkey Point, meanwhile, *Permit*'s arrival caused Lieutenant Lietwiler to select the evacuation party. Eighteen would go. A truck drove up about dusk to move the men down to the base, where they boarded the *Permit.* Then Moon shoved off, carrying the PT crew but leaving their officer behind. The officer went to Captain Hoeffel, who was furious that the *Permit* had ignored orders to put the PT men ashore. He directed the submarine to return and disgorge these passengers, but gave no order regarding the PT officer himself.

The sudden return of the *Permit* reactivated the procedure for getting Station Cast personnel out of the Philippines. Instantly there was a scene at Monkey Point. Depressed that he was not among those taken off, for example, Duane Whitlock quit work early that night, March 16–17, and spread his sleeping gear on the grass outside the tunnel. All of a sudden he woke up to see a chief petty officer named Novack running toward the entrance while trying to put on his pants and buckle his ammunition belt at the same time. Whitlock thought the Japanese had landed and, since he had been detailed as one of the team to destroy classified equipment when the last battle began, ran to the tunnel himself. There Whitlock saw Rufus Taylor, whom he regarded as a brave fellow, telling Lietwiler that *he,* for one, volunteered to stay in the tunnel. That jarred Whitlock; it was so out of character for Taylor. Then the yeoman realized that the officers were talking of another evacuation and that Rufe Taylor was volunteering to stay behind. This proved to be the case.

Whitlock was among the new evacuation party, who made a wild run down past Malinta Tunnel to the north dock, where a launch awaited them. The boat took the party to Mariveles where the submarine was supposed to be, only to be told she had left. The launch headed back into the bay and found *Permit* on the surface, where she had remained to negotiate American mine fields. Moon Chapple stopped when hailed. One of the codebreakers heard the skipper say he only had room for fighting men, and a heated discussion followed. Finally the codebreakers were told to board *Permit* but stay on deck. The officer from the launch went below and began to come back with other sailors, one or two at a time, whom he put on the launch. With dawn approaching, Chapple said he had to dive, telling everyone on deck to lay below, leaving their gear behind.

On board the submarine Whitlock and the new group found the previous evacuation party. It was the first time they realized that all were on the same submarine. Months later one of the *Permit* group ran into a sailor on guard duty at Monterrey Flats who had been one of the PT crewmen Chapple had not had time to get off his boat.

Meanwhile, the boarding incident framed the beginning of an eventful voyage for the *Permit*. Moon Chapple now had 111 persons aboard his submarine, including the Station Cast group of thirty-six under language officer Thomas R. Mackie. The trip immediately illustrated the problems of security in combat intelligence. As a result of their work at Monkey Point, some of Mackie's men knew that a Japanese destroyer division was operating south of Manila in hopes of picking off blockade runners. Now they learned that these were precisely the waters Commander Chapple intended to transit. The codebreakers held a quiet conference to resolve whether to tell the submarine skipper of this threat. They decided not to. Sure enough, the next night Chapple saw three Imperial Navy destroyers in column coming up astern. He fired two torpedoes without result; then the Japanese counterattacked. A dozen depth charges exploded nearby as *Permit* went deep, and there were two near misses later. The destroyers attacked again and again for twenty-two and a half hours, forcing Chapple to resort to bottled oxygen to freshen the air. There was minor damage, but all in all the *Permit* was extremely lucky. Her luck held on April 3 west of the Australian coast, when the submarine was attacked again, this time by an Allied patrol plane.

Everyone aboard was no doubt very happy when *Permit* arrived at Fremantle on April 7. Lieutenant Mackie and his codebreakers went to Melbourne, arriving on April 19. Instead of commending the submariner for his successful evacuation of key personnel from Manila, the U.S. submarine command, ignorant of the value of Moon Chapple's cargo, censured him for not protesting the large number of passengers he had been ordered to carry.

Back at Monkey Point the outlook inevitably seemed grimmer. Lieutenant Lietwiler had already set up a roster for beach defense; now most of the sailors on it were gone. Only a crippled defense was possible, and some worried about what the Japanese would find out from the codebreakers. One sailor saw Rufe Taylor cleaning a pistol one day and joked with the officer, only to be told quite seriously that one of the bullets was for him—the gun was going to keep codebreakers from falling into Japanese hands.

Salvation took the form of submarine *Seadragon* (Lieutenant Commander

William E. [Pete] Ferrall), on patrol off French Indochina and ordered to Cebu to pick up food for Corregidor. Ferrall did as asked, off-loading torpe-does and ammunition to carry thirty-four tons of food. *Seadragon* arrived off Corregidor on April 6 and was met by a lighter. By then Captain Hoeffel deemed the situation critical; Bataan was about to fall and the Japanese might attack Corregidor at any time. Hoeffel ordered the submarine to cease transshipping supplies and instead take the Station Cast codebreakers.

At Monkey Point, meanwhile, everyone expected the worst. In Lietwiler's phrase, the men ate their meals "with one eye for food and one for planes, but both ears cocked for shells." Corregidor's electric power and water sup-ply had been knocked out on March 24, and the radio intelligence tunnel was using its own diesel generator, the fumes greatly worsening already marginal working conditions. Water tanker trucks came daily, enabling Lietwiler to reserve the tunnel's own 5,000-gallon tank, except for a couple of days when the tanker could not get past Malinta Tunnel due to shell fire. Manila was expecting another submarine, the U.S.S. *Snapper*, and Captain Hoeffel's original idea had been to store Cast's remaining equipment preparatory to sending out the men aboard her. A truck to do that was expected at Monkey Point the evening of April 8. Instead, Lietwiler's tele-phone rang. Hoeffel told the codebreaker to have his men ready to leave in just fifteen minutes with no baggage at all. The last codebreakers left Corregidor without even a toothbrush, although they did take a cipher machine and two small boxes of classified publications. The group included Lieutenants Lietwiler and Taylor and nineteen others. They would eventu-ally be recommended for an Army citation ribbon.

The codebreakers boarded the *Seadragon*, which left with orders to resume her combat patrol despite the passengers on board. The next day skipper "Pete" Ferrall spotted a Japanese destroyer off Manila Bay and took a shot at her, unsuccessfully. Next the boat was shaken by an earthquake. She con-tinued on to Fremantle, and the intelligence specialists eventually reported to Melbourne on May 6. That happened to be the dawn after the Japanese landed on Corregidor, kicking off the final fight for the island fortress. Only one Station Cast man had been left behind—the cook, a seaman first class named Thompson who knew nothing about codebreaking. Thompson sur-vived the war and encountered Rudy Fabian afterward at a bar in Hong Kong. He recounted that the Japanese had lined up everyone who had taken refuge in the Monkey Point tunnel and questioned men at random as to who were the codebreakers. Someone told them the people they wanted had left more than a month before. The Japanese did not believe this; for over a week they kept up the random questioning, then finally gave up.

Well might Japan be disappointed. The silent adversaries, the specialists some refused to think of as fighting men, were already striking damaging blows. One came in waters north of Australia even as Corregidor fell.

Another, a kind of denial, came to the west, in the Indian Ocean, where warning from codebreakers prevented what could have been a major British defeat. All this contributed to a huge dilemma for Admiral Yamamoto and his Combined Fleet, for with the fall of the Malay Barrier the Japanese had completed the sequence of operations which they had long planned and rehearsed. Now the question became what to do next—and that, Yamamoto knew, was unfamiliar water.

# West, South, or East?

O NE COULD NOT HAVE TOLD FROM THE INTELLIGENCE THAT ANY STRATEGIC DILEMMA BESET the Japanese fleet command. Instead the Allies saw single-minded pursuit of British and Allied forces right out of the ABDA area and into the Indian Ocean. Some of the best works on the Royal Navy in the Pacific war attribute British ability to avoid Japanese pursuit to an intelligence coup—decryption or partial decryption by the Far East Combined Bureau of an Imperial Navy message on March 28, 1942. The message furnished clear evidence the Japanese intended to raid the Indian Ocean, and it enabled the British to get out of their way.

In fact intelligence *was* a key feature determining British strategy at this point, for the fleet forces themselves were too weak to face the Japanese. In the East Indies, indeed, the fleet proved unable to halt the Imperial Navy's advance even *with* intelligence on its side. Admiral Sir James Somerville, who became commander in chief of the Eastern Fleet on March 26, had a keen awareness of just how weak his forces were, not only numerically but also in terms of training and preparedness. Somerville had already opined that a major aim should be to *avoid* operations "which entail considerable risk." From London the Admiralty effectively sanctioned this policy on March 18 when they instructed commanders to sacrifice Ceylon if that were necessary to save the Eastern Fleet.

Royal Navy operations in the Indian Ocean, in particular avoidance operations, were facilitated by the plethora of possibilities available. Somerville's fleet could be in Ceylon, or it might be sailing from Calcutta or Bombay, big ports on the east and west coast of India proper. For that matter the fleet might be on the west coast of Africa—hopelessly beyond Japan's range, given that the Imperial Navy had yet to make good the demolitions the British had accomplished at the Singapore Navy Base. The Eastern Fleet even had a wholly *secret* base available—at Addu Atoll in the Maldive Islands. With the Maldives a British protectorate since 1887, the Admiralty had selected Addu before the war as an emergency anchorage and equipped it with store ships, tankers, and a hospital ship. There were no defenses to speak of—only searchlights to spot planes, nothing to shoot at them, no antisubmarine defenses—but since the anchorage was secret this might not matter. In any case, finding the Eastern Fleet on the broad expanse of the Indian Ocean became a primary problem for Japanese raiding forces.

The British had a much better idea of the activities of their adversaries, and not just because of some partial decrypt toward the end of March. A constant stream of intelligence informed Admiral Somerville and his predecessor, Sir Geoffrey Layton, of Japanese actions antecedent to their Indian Ocean raid. As early as March 3 intelligence warned that five or more I-boats would shortly begin operating in the Indian Ocean and that they would probably base at Penang. To convey some notion of the degree of warning involved here, it should be noted that the Imperial Navy formed its Submarine Squadron 8 of precisely five I-boats and based this unit at Penang under Rear Admiral Ishizaki Noboru. Its submarines began to leave on operational missions only toward the end of April.

In their monumental history of American submarines in the Pacific, Clay and Joan Blair write that codebreakers followed movements of the Nagumo force aircraft carriers right through the Netherlands East Indies campaign and then anticipated a Japanese offensive against Australia. The combat intelligence unit at Pearl Harbor (Station Hypo) did warn of a move against the Australia–New Zealand area in some unspecified future, but the March 4 bulletin containing this observation restricted the force concerned to Admiral Yamaguchi Tamon's Carrier Division 2—that is, carriers *Soryu* and *Hiryu*. On March 10 intelligence placed Yamaguchi's aircraft carriers still in the Java area together with all escort elements previously associated with the Nagumo force. On the fourteenth, another bulletin put the *Akagi* with that force, noting the *Kaga* as returning to Japan and Carrier Division 5 as in the Bonin Islands. The same bulletin noted "increased activity in Singapore and Penang area both air and submarine," with Vice Admiral Ozawa's Cruiser Division 7 expected at Penang. As a matter of fact the Japanese planned for Ozawa's heavy cruisers to cover an invasion of the Andaman Islands, north of Sumatra, touching Penang and Mergui before raiding into the Indian Ocean.

Intelligence furnished warning of the Andamans operation too. As early as March 7, the Admiralty reported a message containing a timetable for an operation against a target labeled ZL in the Japanese geographic designator system. The schedule reported correlates precisely with Japanese progress in the actual Andamans mission, which the Imperial Navy code-named

Operation D. The British report specifically speculated that "ZL" could be the designator for the Andamans. The report also noted preparations for setting up air activity of some sort at ZL; Japan did in fact make the Andamans a base for seaplanes.

Beginning with mid-March, intelligence indicators fell into place with disturbing speed. On March 15 Pearl Harbor noted Carrier Division 5 en route to Staring Bay (Kendari), at Celebes Island, where the remainder of the Nagumo force, along with Admiral Kondo's battleship force, was already located. This report also placed light carrier *Ryujo* in Malaya (in fact she was operating with Ozawa's heavy-cruiser unit). "Movement west from Malaya . . . in progress by naval units" was the news on March 16; on the nineteenth, "increasing indications of offensive operations from Malay peninsula" would be the most significant notation. On March 21 the Far East Combined Bureau reported that "an air unit or units" had left Staring Bay that very day for an attack on "DG" on or after April 1. This report speculated that the "D" prefix might refer to India, Ceylon, or Australia, but explicitly noted that the Japanese designator "A" had previously been thought to indicate Australia.

In fact the Nagumo force left Staring Bay on March 26, with Kondo's fast battleships in company—in all, five aircraft carriers and four battleships. Following Imperial Navy doctrine, Admiral Kondo exercised command of the joint force. Aboard the *Akagi*, lookout Kuramoto again saw dolphins as the fleet passed into the Indian Ocean. Seaman Kuramoto also kept watch as the ships refueled at sea. Admiral Kusaka noted with satisfaction that Nagumo's vessels had now performed this task so often they were able to accomplish it easily despite high waves. Watching the other ships made Seaman Kuramoto think back to the German commerce raiders that had plied these seas in World War I. "In the Indian Ocean," Kuramoto wrote, "where once the German ship *Emden* played a spectacular part in the destruction of trade, there is now not a shadow of the enemy, and an uncanny silence pervades the surface of the sea."

The intelligence was transparent enough that on March 26 Admiral Nimitz at Pearl Harbor felt obliged to cable warning direct to incoming commander in chief Somerville: "Indications remain strong that Orange intend offensive action Indian Ocean area." The CINCPAC message paraphrased the eleventh bulletin from Station Hypo's combat intelligence unit, which stated that there were "continued indications of offensive action by enemy in Indian Ocean area." The codebreakers also noted that Admiral Kondo was in command and that the Japanese expected reinforcement by additional cruisers and destroyers. These warnings originated prior to or simultaneously with the British decrypt previous historians have cited as the rationale for Somerville's orders to his fleet to sail to the secret Maldives base.

Meanwhile the Japanese used their developing raid into the Indian Ocean as strategic cover for other actions. Most important, a pair of convoys moving north from Singapore made a landing at, then greatly reinforced Rangoon, marking the beginning of intense fighting in Burma. In a minor flanking operation south of the Netherlands East Indies, the Japanese made an unopposed landing at Christmas Island. American submarine *Seawolf* (Lieutenant Commander Fred Warder) intervened and put a torpedo into light cruiser *Naka*, flagship of Nishimura's 4th Destroyer Flotilla, flooding two boiler rooms, shorting out electric power, and causing damage that kept this ship out of action for nearly a year. It was a further stiff blow for the unfortunate Rear Admiral Nishimura. The damage to *Naka* was the worst blow inflicted on the Japanese throughout this phase of the Indian Ocean campaign, however.

Admiral Somerville concentrated to the south of Ceylon, entertaining thoughts of engaging Japanese raiders, but found nothing and returned to the Addu base. This was just as well, since his Eastern Fleet at that time merely comprised a collection of ships, not very powerful ones at that. On paper Somerville had three carriers, five battleships, eight cruisers, and fifteen destroyers. But four of Somerville's battleships were of the 1914–1916 vintage *Royal Sovereign*, or "R," class, old and slow, with worn-out boilers and other machinery problems. The other capital ship, *Warspite*, though launched as early as 1913, was faster and had at least been modernized. There were two 23,000-ton fleet carriers, *Indomitable* and *Formidable*, plus the 15,000-ton light carrier *Hermes*, but together the three ships had about the same number of planes as a single one of Nagumo's five Japanese carriers, so the whole force was no match for JNAF airpower. The Eastern Fleet's cruisers and destroyers were a grab bag of what was available, including older, slower, and undergunned ships that had been relegated to convoy duty because they were not considered capable of fleet work. Dutch cruisers *Tromp* and *Heemskerck* were among the pack, with the communication difficulties already apparent in the East Indies. The practical effect of the engineering defects in the Royal Navy ships is seen in the R-class battleships: Condensers for the boilers of some of these were so poor they could furnish water for just a few days at sea. Somerville was told that the R class would have to be in port by April 5 or risk using salt water in their boilers, which would force dockyard refits.

Ironically, the officer commanding the R-class ships believed that if water shortage had not forced his return to Addu, the Japanese would have sighted his ships the next day, which would have forced a fleet action highly disadvantageous to the British. Had such a fleet action occurred it would have been the first carrier-versus-carrier battle in history, displacing claims to that distinction by the later battle of the Coral Sea. The Japanese would have been afforded an opportunity to learn carrier tactics against opponents much more weakly armed than their eventual American adversaries.

As it was, a British plane saw the Japanese first, on April 4 when the R-class ships were already on their way to Addu, and there was another sighting early the next morning, directly south of Ceylon. By then the Japanese had already launched an air strike—180 planes against Colombo, a major Ceylonese port and location of the British radio intercept unit. Once again the attackers were under the redoubtable Fuchida, who saw British Swordfish torpedo bombers he thought were headed for his own fleet as he neared the port, assumed British fighters would be awaiting him, and therefore led the entire force around to the north to hit Colombo from the opposite direction. "Still wet from a recent rain squall," Fuchida writes, "the city lay glistening in the sun. No airborne fighters were visible as we came over, and the big airfield southeast of the city was also empty of planes." British Hurricane and Fulmar interceptors eventually opposed the attackers, downing seven JNAF aircraft in addition to two lost to anti-aircraft fire. But twenty-five British fighters and all six Swordfish were also lost.

Japanese search planes that morning spotted British heavy cruisers *Cornwall* and *Dorsetshire,* which had just left Colombo to join Somerville's main body. A second wave of eighty JNAF planes immediately attacked them, sinking both ships. The bombers tallied a very high percentage accuracy. A destroyer, other auxiliaries, and merchant ships were sunk at Colombo. Unknown to the Japanese, their own fleet had also been sighted (though shadowers failed to report any aircraft carriers). Admiral Somerville was within range with his carriers but made no attack. Impressed by the efficiency with which the Imperial Navy had dispatched his two heavy cruisers, Somerville suddenly realized just how overmatched he was. After rendezvous with the R-class ships and a search for survivors of the sunken cruisers, Somerville detached his oldest vessels to the African coast. The remainder of the Eastern Fleet continued to function as a mobile force but did not attempt to seek battle with the Japanese.

Admiral Kondo, having encountered no opposition to the Colombo carrier raid, resolved to attack Ceylon at Trincomalee, a port on its east coast. Fuchida commanded as ninety-one dive-bombers with an escort of forty-one Zeros flew in the first wave on April 9. Trincomalee radar provided warning and the British got twenty-three fighters of their own into good interception positions. This time the Japanese lost fifteen planes to fighters and nine to anti-aircraft, a toll almost as high as in the great raid on Pearl Harbor; British losses were eight Hurricanes and three Fulmars.

For the first time also there was an aerial counterattack. Nine Royal Air Force Blenheim bombers from Number 11 Squadron hit Kondo's fleet at midmorning, catching Nagumo's carriers from the rear. This was much more significant than anyone realized at the time, for one Japanese carrier had recently been equipped with "search installations," experimental radars. *Hiryu,* Admiral Yamaguchi's Carrier Division 2 flagship, observed in its battle report for the Indian Ocean raid, intended to draw combat experience, that the radar could not detect "an enemy bomber unit that breaks into the center of the cruising disposition from the rear. . . . On *Akagi* there have been many times when the first warning was the splash of the bombs."* Despite fighter cover over the Japanese ships the Blenheims were able to attack undisturbed; only afterward did Zeros catch up and massacre five British bombers. Half a dozen bombs fell close aboard the *Akagi*. Admiral Nagumo's luck held that day, but the event would shortly have strong reverberations at Midway on the other side of the Pacific. Seaman Kuramoto shrugged off the incident, observing that the bombs "did no more harm than startling the fish in the sea."

Next act in this British tragedy was the demise of light carrier *Hermes*. With so few planes that she was no asset to Somerville's task force, the *Hermes* had been sent to Ceylon for exercises, later to add her fighters to the Trincomalee defenses. A Japanese scout plane found the *Hermes* under way on the morning of the ninth, steaming toward Colombo. Nagumo used his second wave attack to hit this light carrier, whose sole escort was the destroyer *Vampire*. In the early afternoon the ships were attacked by a force of eighty-five dive-bombers. By this time the Japanese were running short of naval ordnance, so the first three planes of each strike unit were armed with 550-pound land-type bombs instead. *Hiryu*'s battle report noted that these weapons seemed especially effective in neutralizing anti-aircraft fire, since resistance diminished noticeably after attacks by planes armed in this fashion. The *Hermes* alone suffered thirty-seven bomb hits, with plenty more on the *Vampire*, a nearby corvette, and two merchantmen unlucky enough to be in the area. Returning Japanese planes recognized a British hospital ship and directed her to the battle area, where she rescued 600 survivors. At this point Admiral Kondo judged the carrier force had achieved sufficient results and terminated the raid, with Kido Butai back in the vicinity of Singapore by April 11.

The denouement was the true raid, a commerce raid in the classic fashion like that of the *Emden* of which Seaman Kuramoto dreamed. This raid was carried out by Admiral Ozawa's old Malaya Force, built around Kurita

---

*In view of the novelty of this claim I note here the source for the quotation beginning "an enemy bomber unit": Carrier *Hiryu*, Detailed Battle Report No. 5 (March 26, 1942–April 22, 1942), which can be found in the Naval Operational Archives (NHC:RJN:Washington Document Center Series, b.37, folder "WDC 160647"). Although *Hiryu*'s report does not utilize the term "radar," actually an acronym of American origin, it is clear from the source document that *Hiryu* carried an electronic detection mechanism with a blind spot to the rear, very probably a radar device with a blind spot attributable to a fixed antenna, a weakness replicated in early radar installations in both the U.S. and British navies. Until now it has been accepted that no Imperial Navy warship carried radar prior to the summer of 1942.

Takeo's heavy cruiser division and Kakuta Kakuji's Carrier Division 4, with but a single light carrier, *Ryujo*. Unlike the British, who had sent their light carrier away, the Japanese had no hesitation in committing *Ryujo*, which mounted a series of two-plane scout bomber flights, attacking shipping along India's east coast. Captain Kato Tadao also briefed his air group for several larger strikes, putting twenty sorties against a couple of minor Indian ports. There were another eighteen fighter sorties flown as cover for *Ryujo* or others of Ozawa's ships. *Ryujo* claimed two ships sunk and seven damaged. Surface ships accounted for twenty merchantmen sunk or damaged, almost half by Rear Admiral Kurita's Cruiser Division 7. In all Ozawa's raid sank twenty-three ships of 112,312 tons and damaged others, for a total of about 185,000 tons.

Ozawa, too, returned to Singapore on April 11, leaving only submarines in the Indian Ocean. Nine merchantmen succumbed to I-boats in early April, making an impressive start for the Japanese campaign in the Indian Ocean. Surprisingly, despite this auspicious beginning, for the most part the Imperial Navy had just left the Indian Ocean for good. There would be submarines to be sure, and a spectacular midget submarine raid at Diégo-Suarez, Madagascar, at the end of May, plus some commerce raiding by auxiliary cruisers, but the big ships were gone. As the days passed the British were able to relax. To a considerable degree, it was a recasting of Japanese strategy that made it possible for Admiral Somerville and other British commanders to breathe easier.

The INDIAN OCEAN RAID THE JAPANESE ACTUALLY CONDUCTED WAS NOT THE LEADING edge, but rather the remnant, of much more ambitious plans worked through IGHQ and the Navy command. This was truly a lowest-common-denominator policy. Japan had an alliance with Germany, and the sides reached a formal agreement on war cooperation on January 18, 1942, with the Indian Ocean the obvious point at which any junction of forces would be made. Hitler's Germany wished to avoid explicit commitments as to military operations, however, and simply pressed for a line of demarcation to *separate* the respective allies. This was set at the seventieth meridian of east longitude. The Japanese Army, though aware of German desires that Tokyo attack Russia, was intensely conscious that it lacked the capability to wage war simultaneously in the Pacific, in China, and against the Soviet Union. The Army therefore agreed to eschew explicit undertakings as to strategy, and carefully informed Russia that Tokyo had no aggressive intentions. The Imperial Navy simply went along with the senior service.

If the Naval General Staff had any notion that improved cooperation with the Army would follow acquiescence, it was destined for disappointment.

The NGS had its own ideas for strategy in the second stage of the war, and these proved completely unacceptable to the Army. Captain Tomioka of the operations bureau favored invasion of Australia to prevent that land becoming the base for Allied counteroffensives into the Southern Area. Baron Tomioka worried most about Australia because NGS believed the Central Pacific islands lacked the land mass necessary to concentrate and fully develop airpower. Combined Fleet staffer Commander Miwa Yoshitake remarked on the urgency of a decision as early as January 6, noting that the United States had already begun reinforcing Australia and outlying island positions on Fiji and Samoa. Calculations by NGS foresaw that only key points need be occupied and that a force of just three divisions, or between 45,000 and 60,000 troops, would suffice.

The Army rejected this approach. Far from being an easy objective, Australia would be bitterly defended, capable of holding off quite large forces. Army studies concluded that almost all of Australia, not merely important points, would have to be occupied, and the task would require ten divisions (150,000 to 200,000 soldiers), the bulk of the Combined Fleet, and 1.5 million tons of shipping. At a minimum this meant that thousands of tons of shipping requisitioned for the first-stage operations, scheduled to revert to civilian control, to import materials for war production, would have to be retained. The whole war effort would be set back thereby. Moreover, the necessary troop levels could not be attained without either stopping the China Incident or abandoning Manchuria, neither of which was acceptable to the Army.

Far preferable from the Army standpoint was an option that could be carried out without further commitment of troops whatever, the so-called FS Operation. This would not conquer Australia but isolate it by occupying key islands on its shipping routes to the United States, building air bases to further extend the controlled area. This FS plan was tentatively agreed upon at a liaison conference on January 10, and a few days later formed an underlying basis for an Army-Navy accord making the former responsible for operations against India and the latter for those pertaining to Australia. The Navy nevertheless introduced its plan for a limited invasion of Australia at a joint services conference on February 6, and the following day the Navy Ministry's Captain Ishikawa Shingo went so far as to declare, "There will be no security . . . unless we make Australia the main target in stage two of our basic war plan and annihilate it as a base for the American counteroffensive." On February 11 at the Army-Navy Club, NGS operations bureau staffer Commander Yamamoto Yuji, probably reflecting pressures from the Combined Fleet, expanded the Navy scenario to include both invasion of Australia and attacks on Hawaii.

Indeed, Imperial Navy strategy could not be determined by NGS alone. The Combined Fleet had a say, too. Admiral Yamamoto's success in forcing the NGS to accept his Pearl Harbor plan established a precedent that could not be ignored. The triumph of the attack and the Combined Fleet's highly successful conduct of first-stage operations ensured its staff a role in elaborating future strategy. During Pearl Harbor planning, the fleet's senior staff officer, Captain Kuroshima, had espoused going beyond a simple raid to invade Hawaii. Chief of Staff Ugaki also came around to this view at the moment Admiral Nagumo failed to press his advantage from surprise. Ugaki went full circle from doubting that Hawaii could be held if captured (in late November discussing the intelligence with Commander Suzuki, then just returned from Honolulu) to assuming personal responsibility in late December for accelerated planning of what came to be called the Eastern Operation.

The first NGS learned of the Eastern Operation was on December 16, when Captain Tomioka visited the *Nagato* in company with Commander Uchida Shigeshi to discuss upcoming options. Kuroshima briefed them on a proposed seizure of Palmyra Island, a Central Pacific outpost for Hawaii, and Tomioka in turn outlined the southern strategy, invasion of Australia. Even then the FS plan was being bruited about, and Tomioka apparently supposed that the Combined Fleet would support it. The Army did not, and after hearing what Tomioka had to say about opinion among Combined Fleet staff, Tomioka's Army opposite number feared that a Hawaii operation could threaten the consensus underpinning Japanese war leadership. When Army staff openly made this argument, Tomioka was troubled. Four days later, on December 27, Combined Fleet staffer Miwa Yoshitake came to Tokyo to inform NGS of the latest fleet thinking on the Eastern Operation. Baron Tomioka now realized that a full assault on Hawaii, not some outlying position, was at issue.

At this juncture Tomioka called in Commander Kami Shigenori. A key member of the operations section, whom Tomioka trusted implicitly despite the great emotionalism with which he argued every issue, Commander Kami was a communications specialist with extensive staff experience. A former assistant naval attaché in Berlin, Kami was considered pro-German in the Imperial Navy and had been an outspoken proponent of the Tripartite Pact. He was also a surface-ship fan, and as such, was now asked by Baron Tomioka to study whether Hawaii could be taken and, if so, what would be needed to hold it. Tomioka may have thought a staff study by Kami might be more acceptable since he was an Etajima classmate of some Combined Fleet staff officers (Miwa) and the contemporary of others (Nagata, Sanagi, Sasaki, Sugi, Wada, Watanabe). Kami's conclusions, presented on January 11, were similar to what Ugaki had thought when the Eastern Operation was first suggested to him: Hawaii could be taken but not held. Commander Kami calculated that, given population and the proportion of food imported, Hawaii would require perhaps twenty-five ships a month just for sustenance, plus another thirty with military matériel, for a total flow of 3 million tons a year. Japan could not afford to tie up this much shipping.

In Tokyo the maneuvering led to agreement between Admiral Nagano and General Sugiyama, at a liaison conference on January 10, that the FS Operation should be carried out but any Hawaii initiative avoided. Thus when Combined Fleet air officer Sasaki Akira arrived three days later with the preliminary plan for the Eastern Operation, he found Tokyo united against it. At Hashirajima on January 14, Admiral Ugaki noted for his diary the main points of the Eastern Operation plan and gave six reasons it should be carried out. Time was not on Japan's side. In spite of his preferences, he was now obliged to work on plans for the FS option, for Australia and Burma, or for an assault on Ceylon. Once the Army refused to allocate troops to the latter option, it had perforce to be scaled back to a naval raid, the raid carried out that April.

By February 20 Admiral Ugaki had prepared a series of war games aboard *Yamato*, the new Combined Fleet flagship, to test the second-stage plans. A Ceylon invasion was war-gamed unsuccessfully—the hypothetical British fleet escaped and their airpower proved resilient. The other options seem to have been gamed inconclusively. Admiral Yamaguchi Tamon, meanwhile, distributed copies of a plan he had developed after Nagumo's failure to follow up at Pearl Harbor; this provided for a Hawaii offensive beginning in early 1943. Ugaki's own plan foresaw Hawaii operations in the summer and fall of 1942. Admiral Fukudome and Baron Tomioka, who attended the war games, were no doubt lukewarm to both proposals. When NGS and the Army held further discussions in early March, both eastern and western options dropped out of their picture altogether. Admiral Yamamoto's March 9 orders to prepare an Indian Ocean naval raid were thus unilateral ones, not responsive to any IGHQ directives. The Army and Navy affirmed the FS Operation and the occupation of points in New Guinea, north of Australia, agreed upon in late January. It was at this point that American activities intruded upon Tokyo planners. There was not going to be any quiet, dispassionate planning process. Tokyo's plans would be made, but they would respond to Japan's own fears, magnified by some judicious pinpricks.

THERE WAS AT LEAST ONE PINPRICK THAT WAS JAPANESE. THIS CONCERNED PEARL HARBOR. Submarines were the key; not only could undersea vessels snoop around the islands but also the largest classes of I-boats were equipped to carry small floatplanes that could be used for aerial reconnaissance. In the weeks after the December 7 attack Japanese submarines were enough of a presence to (mistakenly) claim sinking two aircraft carriers and a heavy cruiser.

Submarine aircraft overflew Pearl Harbor on December 19, 1941, and again on January 4, 1942. In this fashion the *joho kyoku* learned the Americans were working diligently, even at night under floodlights, to repair damage at Pearl Harbor and refloat ships sunk there.

The Naval General Staff did not oppose spoiling operations in the Pearl Harbor vicinity; these were the kind of pinpricks that could be positively useful. Some NGS officers—such as Commander Miyo Tatsukichi, who had advocated the development of long-range flying-boat bombers precisely in order to have a weapon capable of attacks from a distance—engaged more actively in such thinking. Miyo dreamed of Pearl Harbor strikes by these patrol bombers; now, in the spring of 1942, he was to have his chance. Commander Suzuki Suguru, the last Navy officer to visit Pearl Harbor, did the detailed planning. During the planning phase one more night overflight of Pearl Harbor occurred, from the submarine *I-9* on February 24.

In actuality the Imperial Navy went to great trouble to get just eight 550-pound bombs over Hawaii (that was the combined load of two H8K "Emily" patrol bombers used on this mission). The Emily had just become available and enough planes had reached the fleet so that Fourth Fleet's Yokohama Air Group had some. Rear Admiral Goto Eiji, commanding the air group's parent 24th Air Flotilla, arranged with Sixth Fleet to send several submarines (*I-15, I-19, I-23*) loaded with aviation gas to an uninhabited atoll west of Midway called French Frigate Shoal. American intelligence officer Edwin Layton believes that refueling the Emilys was necessary because the planes had not met their performance goals, but aircraft data show the H8K to have almost exactly the range required for the 3,796-mile round trip from Wotje to Pearl Harbor and back. In addition, the JNAF planes were given half-size loads for this, their first combat mission. More likely refueling seemed appropriate to give the planes an extra safety margin against navigational errors over the long trip. Sixth Fleet also sent several other I-boats on the mission, including *I-9* to serve as a radio beacon, and *I-23* to provide weather reports near Oahu and for air-sea rescue.

Such extensive cooperation between the JNAF and submarine force required a good deal of radio communication. This provided entree for U.S. radio intelligence. Layton writes that Station Hypo did not do well on this occasion, but wartime records suggest any failure to be one of analysis more than of interception. Direction finding placed two submarines east of Midway, the *I-9* and Commander Shibata Genichi's *I-23*, which apparently foundered late in February. On the morning of March 2, Joe Rochefort's people decrypted a message indicating that the K Operation, which is how the Japanese knew this project, would begin March 5 (the fourth at Pearl Harbor), and on that date Station Cast wired from Corregidor to say that a message it had intercepted provided "further indication of impending sub and air attack probably for tomorrow."

Of course weather would be a vital question for JNAF pilots approaching Pearl Harbor, and once *I-23* disappeared there was no unit to make direct reports from the Hawaiian area. Some writers state that NGS expected to rely on *American* weather reports, then comment that the U.S. weather code fortuituously changed on March 1. However, Station Hypo's radio intelligence bulletin of March 4 specifically notes that Tokyo furnished Fourth Fleet that day with Hawaiian-area weather forecasts for March 4 and 5.

The K Operation went into effect before dawn on March 4, when the two H8K1 patrol bombers took off from Wotje, piloted by Lieutenant Hashizumi Toshio, the flight leader, and Ensign Tomano. A little over thirteen hours later they put down at the refueling point, where 3,000 gallons of gas were pumped in three hours and ten minutes before the planes took to the air again. Heavy cloud over Oahu frustrated the pilots, but not so badly as all that—the mission brought back a photograph and three sketches of Pearl Harbor. As far as bombing accuracy was concerned the weather proved determinant; one of the Emilys apparently loosed her bombs over the sea, the other on the slopes of a mountain. Later the 24th Air Flotilla reported that the target had been Pearl Harbor's machine shops.

Ensign Tomano flew directly to Wotje, while Lieutenant Hashizumi went to Jaluit, where repair facilities could fix damage his plane had sustained on her original takeoff. Over the next few days K operations continued, with patrol bombers reconnoitering Johnston Atoll and Midway. The latter flight also refueled at sea from a submarine.

At Pearl Harbor the incoming raiders were detected by radar over 200 miles away. Fighters scrambled but, without radar themselves, found nothing in the night; PBY Catalinas were dispatched to find the Japanese carriers supposed to be the source for these blips on the radar screens. Honolulu was eventually startled to hear air-raid sirens in the middle of the night. At Midway the JNAF flying boats were also seen by radar, though with a different result. Four fighters intercepted one of the Emilys still forty-five miles away and shot it down; one pilot was wounded and his fighter plane damaged, but he managed to land all right. The other radar target on Midway's screens was never found by the interceptors. Japanese reports suggest that perhaps only one plane went on this flight. The lost plane had departed from Wotje, never made its refueling point, and was last heard from fourteen hours into the mission.

Admiral Goto's report notes that the K Operation took five submarines and two important aircraft away from other duties, not once but twice—in January when the operation was rehearsed, and again when it was carried out. In all, these assets were diverted for several weeks at a key time in the war. Both submarine and air officers were said to regard the project as a failure. On the other hand, submarine skipper Orita Zenji thought of it as symptomatic of the spirit among Japanese leaders at the time: "very confident, and willing to try anything that would keep the enemy off-balance and worried."

Americans were just about willing to believe that too. According to Commander Layton, Joe Rochefort suspected the Japanese were about to make a wild seaplane attack on Pearl Harbor using some of their well-equipped tenders. Other Americans were a lot more skeptical. Hypo code-breaker Thomas Dyer was home the night of the K Operation air attack, and the Japanese bombs actually fell in a valley just a mile away from his house. The noise instantly awoke both Dyer and his wife.

"That sounds like the real thing," said Edith Dyer.

"Never mind," Tom replied, "we'll go on back to sleep."

So ended the last Japanese attack on Pearl Harbor.


AMERICAN PINPRICKS IN THE CENTRAL PACIFIC PROVED FAR MORE FATEFUL THAN THEIR MILI-tary importance suggests. In essence this was because the Japanese Empire had a long open flank facing the Pacific. This flank could not be defended by land forces, and even airpower was stymied by the scarcity of islands for bases in the North Pacific. Only the very same factors of time and space (fuel) that had been obstacles for the Pearl Harbor attack protected the Empire's open flank. The raid itself had been an effort to eliminate the threat from that quarter, but Nagumo sailed away without accounting for the American aircraft carriers—the very vessels capable of projecting power ashore, as they soon showed in the Marshalls, and at Rabaul and Salamaua. The energetic but ineffectual Japanese responses to these carrier raids showed how sensitive they were. Such Imperial Navy operations provided opportunities for American naval intelligence to eavesdrop. In an important way U.S. intelligence reached full stride in the raiding operations that now took place.

Ironically for the Japanese, their difficulties began at Wake Island, where they had been frustrated before and where an American carrier riposte had also miscarried. In late February, Vice Admiral William Halsey returned to Wake with Task Force 16, built around the *Enterprise*. American aircraft attacked on February 24. As he retired northwestward after the raid, Bull Halsey got a message from Admiral Nimitz instructing him, if possible, to extend his cruise long enough to launch a further raid on Marcus Island. Halsey was unable to refuel any ships save the *Enterprise* and two cruisers. Perhaps remembering Frank Fletcher at Wake, who had been critically delayed by waiting to refuel destroyers, Bull Halsey left his destroyer screen behind and dashed off to execute the raid with only the *Enterprise* and her cruisers. American aircraft hit the place with such stealth that Japanese facilities were demolished even before their radio could warn Tokyo. Only the chance arrival of a supply ship provided the local Japanese commander with a working radio with which to report the mishap.

Admirals Yamamoto and Ugaki, with their standard ceremony, had just sat down to a sukiyaki dinner with visiting staff officers from the Navy Ministry and NGS, including operations section member Sanagi Sadamu, when word arrived of the Marcus raid. There was nothing between Marcus and the Japanese mainland, and Halsey's carrier force could just as easily have gone on to strike directly in Empire waters. Yamamoto had explicitly used the specter of air attack on the Empire to help force through his Pearl Harbor plan, and one can imagine his thoughts this night.

Japanese concern became explicit a week later. Chief of Staff Ugaki and subordinate intelligence officers had noted Pearl Harbor going on alert (coincident with the K Operation), an alert continued since that day. The Japanese also noted intensified U.S. submarine activity in Empire waters. By March 11 the Combined Fleet had decided that all this presaged some big American operation and ordered out the First Fleet, the Navy's big battleship force, along with the fleet carriers of Carrier Division 5.

Except for those ships supporting Nagumo or Kondo, the Japanese battleships had been at anchor virtually since the first day of the war. Occasionally moved from one port to another, or out for gunnery practice, the ships had had no real operations. The diary of one seaman aboard the battleship *Hyuga* furnishes a fine illustration of the prevalent mood. At Hashirajima on January 3: "I wonder how much longer we will stay anchored here. Things are dull without shore leaves." On January 28: "Training every day is by no means pleasant." Late in February the command changed; incoming skipper was Captain Matsuda Chiaki, a former head of the American section of Japanese naval intelligence. Matsuda told the crew they must display aggressiveness to obtain victory. *Hyuga* seamen settled down somewhat. On March 6 our diarist noted: "The reason why Great Britain and the United States cannot approach Japan is because of the position our capital ships are maintaining in full readiness."

The Combined Fleet thought differently on March 11 when the battleships were ordered out—Matsuda's *Hyuga* along with sister ship *Ise*, the carriers *Shokaku* and *Zuikaku*, two cruisers, and five destroyers, all under Vice Admiral Takasu Shiro. Having spent so much time in port, and so anxious to secure success, the Japanese now experienced a comedy of errors: One of Takasu's scout planes reported an enemy fleet, creating an uproar. The "enemy" was identified as two or three carriers, ten cruisers, and nine destroyers. Later it transpired that the erroneous report was just a practice message. In the meantime the JNAF had recalled its 21st Air Flotilla to Kisarazu and launched massive air searches to the east, and the Sixth Fleet had ordered submarines to these waters. American codebreakers followed all this action, from the Takasu sortie right through to a reinforcement of Wake by planes of the Chitose Air Group.

There can be little doubt that the possibility of air raids greatly exercised the Japanese. Before the war, drills against air attack had been a recurrent feature of life noted by American naval attachés. Yamamoto's fears were common ones. A round-table discussion between journalists and Japanese naval aviators (reported in March 1941) had a Commander Miura remarking that "to a certain extent" Japan would indeed be subjected to air raids in any future war, while another commander, Inoue, declared, *"Being air-raided to a certain extent will be unavoidable"* (italics in the original). The hint was taken by some official organizations, such as the Army Ministry and general staff, which moved to concrete buildings on Ichigaya heights with the coming of war. On the occasion of the March 1942 Takasu fleet sortie, an alert against air attack was again called for Tokyo. No one knew how soon the threat would become a real one.

At Pearl Harbor the American plan was to do just what the Japanese feared. In a demonstration of interservice cooperation that contrasts with Japanese practice, the U.S. Army agreed to prepare crews to fly twin-engine B-25 medium bombers off a carrier flight deck. Sixteen planes from the Army's 17th Bombardment Group were drafted for the assignment, with volunteer air crews trained by aviation pioneer Lieutenant Colonel James H. Doolittle at Elgin Field in Florida. The B-25s then flew to California, to Alameda Naval Air Station, where they were loaded onto the deck of the carrier *Hornet*, a brand-new ship on her maiden voyage. Too large to be taken belowdecks, the B-25s were lashed down to secure them right on the flight deck from which they would take off. Each of the planes could carry 3,000 pounds of bombs with which to hit Japan.

The Doolittle mission owed much to the thinking of COMINCH, Admiral Ernest J. King, who had looked for a way to make a spectacular diversion to draw the Japanese away from the Southern Area. A raid on the Empire might do that. Army bombers were necessary because no one believed that aircraft carriers could get near enough to the Japanese coast to use their own planes. Preparations were made in great secrecy; even the skipper of the *Hornet*, Captain Marc A. Mitscher, knew nothing until a few days before the B-25s were hoisted aboard his ship, though apparently his air intelligence officer was consulted by mission planners at an earlier stage.* The *Hornet* sailed from San Francisco on April 2 with her bombers plus seventy officers and 130 men the Army sent to service and fly them. The plan was to rendezvous at sea with Bull Halsey, who commanded the actual operation.

In a significant way the Doolittle raid was a blow American intelligence inflicted upon the Japanese. The targets selected were based upon the pre-

---

*Morison's history (*Rising Sun in the Pacific*, p. 390) asserts that Captain Mitscher knew nothing of the operation until a few days before Doolittle's bombers were hoisted aboard his ship. However, Theodore Taylor's biography of Admiral Mitscher (*The Magnificent Mitscher* [New York: W. W. Norton, 1954]) notes that there were B-25 takeoff tests from the *Hornet* in early February, followed by speculation among the crew. While Taylor agrees that Mitscher did not know of the raid plan, Stephen Jurika, then the ship's air

war attaché reports. In fact, the raid represented a symbolic return engagement by ONI, since *Hornet*'s air intelligence officer happened to be former air attaché Stephen Jurika, assigned after his return from Japan to help commission the carrier. Jurika recalls that he and *Hornet* shipmates saw the Doolittle fliers as a scruffy lot, casual, with short attention spans and not that much contact with Doolittle, who never addressed them at any of the formal briefings. Jurika himself lectured on Japanese anti-aircraft defense methods, and told those Army fliers willing to listen what he could about the Japanese and their attitudes toward prisoners, and what the fliers' chances might be in a situation like this (not good, Jurika thought, and turned out to be right when crewmen the Japanese did capture were executed).

Another officer symbolically returning to Japan was Lieutenant Gilven M. Slonim, one of the language officers studying in Tokyo until sent home by Henri Smith-Hutton in the summer of 1941. At Pearl Harbor, Slonim had been put to work for Station Hypo, then sent to sea as intelligence officer aboard *Enterprise*. There a detachment of four radio intercept operators joined him; the five became a mobile radio unit to advise Halsey of Japanese communications overheard. The duty was constant on these fleet mobile units, says Raymond A. Rundle, one of Slonim's operators, but he preferred it because they got away from Wahiawa and escaped routine base details. Volunteers only were accepted, and Rundle volunteered every chance he got.

The mobile radio unit became critically important on April 18, the day Halsey expected to reach the launching point for the Doolittle mission. Already Admiral Halsey's screen had been reduced because, as on the Marcus raid, he chose to dash ahead with cruisers and carriers alone, leaving destroyers behind—which simplified fuel considerations but made the task force more vulnerable. Dawn of April 18 revealed a Japanese fishing boat on picket duty just a few miles from cruiser *Nashville* and in easy visual range of *Hornet* and *Enterprise*. Another picket boat was visible on the horizon. These Japanese scouts were destroyed, but the crucial question became whether Tokyo had been warned. Slonim's radio unit confirmed that it had. With the fleet still several hours from the planned launch point, Halsey decided it would be unwise to give the Japanese that warning time to organize a counterattack. He ordered Doolittle's B-25s into the air. Aboard *Hornet* Lieutenant Jurika worked as flight-deck officer to help launch the planes. At Doolittle's suggestion, Jurika provided a Japanese medal he had been awarded to be affixed to one of the bombs the Army flier was taking to

---

intelligence officer, recalls that Captain Mitscher mentioned the raid to him at least a week *before* the *Hornet* arrived at San Francisco to load Doolittle's planes (USNI Oral History, p. 576). Jurika also confirms Taylor's account that COMINCH planners had discussed with Mitscher (and the intelligence officer, too) the possibility of flying the big bombers off a carrier deck.

Tokyo. President Roosevelt would tell the American people the bombers had flown from a mythical place, the kingdom of Shangri-la.

Among Japanese the crisis began early that morning with the picket-boat report. Combined Fleet staff had just finished breakfast when a telephone call from NGS informed them of the contact report, which mentioned three aircraft carriers. Admiral Kondo in the *Atago* had returned to Yokosuka from the Indian Ocean raid just the previous day, and Combined Fleet put him in temporary charge of the response. Picket boats saw Doolittle's planes but not Halsey's carriers, while aircraft from the 26th Air Flotilla also failed to make contact. Tokyo flashed general warnings to the fleet, and soon had to report it had been bombed, along with Yokohama, Yokosuka, Nagoya, Wakayama, and Kobe. Submarine tender *Taigei* was damaged in dry dock. Admiral Yamamoto pulled every available string to catch the Halsey task force.

American intelligence observed the resulting Japanese activity with growing awareness. Aboard the *Enterprise*, Radioman Rundle copied an Imperial Navy message sent to, among others, the Nagumo force. That was a clear indication that Kido Butai had returned from the Indian Ocean (in fact, except for elements sent to Truk, it was at that moment off Taiwan). Americans detected assembly of an eighty-bomber strike force at Yokosuka, and the concentration of aircraft from the Mandates on Wake, from which they hoped to take Halsey from the flank. The employment of Admiral Kondo was also detected and reported. Then there was Baron Tomioka's NGS dispatch of April 19, citing U.S. strength of three carriers and admitting confusion in the patrol lines, but accurately identifying the attack planes as B-25s. The next day radio intelligence noted Japanese air and surface units beginning to return to normal duties. The 24th Air Flotilla reported submarine sightings from Wake aircraft on April 21 and 22, and patrol bombers were sent to scout Howland and Baker.

At home, pandemonium ruled. French reporter Robert Guillain was a direct observer of Doolittle's impact. He heard a string of explosions followed by belated anti-aircraft fire. Guillain left his home for the Ginza and the area of the ministries in downtown Tokyo. The bombs brought everyone else out too, instead of eating lunch at their desks. Ministry typists babbled away like sparrows after the Tokyo earthquake. Rumors washed over the city for hours before the Tojo government got out an official statement. As recently as the day before, the populace had been assured they were safe from *American* planes, so one rumor was that the attackers had been Soviets. A statement from the Domei agency said nothing of nationality and asserted that the Emperor and palace were undamaged. This permitted rumor to flourish as Japanese wondered if that meant the rest of Tokyo lay in ruins. Guillain remembered the U.S. raid on Marcus in March, when officials had said that the carrier raid was evidence of American strategic disarray, while Tokyo police imposed a complete blackout on the city. If the Americans were merely waging a war of nerves, as the Tojo government liked to say, perhaps they were really winning it!

Senior officers with responsibility, men like Yamamoto, were if anything more affected than the general public. The Combined Fleet commander had been saying, in letters to colleagues, girlfriends, and assorted Japanese, that the threat had been turned away. The Doolittle raid furnished evidence to the contrary.

A denouement of sorts came on April 24, when *joho kyoku*'s Rear Admiral Maeda Minoru issued a six-paragraph report summarizing what the Japanese then knew about Doolittle's airplanes. Unlike the public at large, Yamamoto and other senior officers could appreciate that the raid would have been quite impossible had not the American carriers survived Pearl Harbor. The realization must have steeled Yamamoto's determination to get at the carriers. Given Imperial Navy tradition and doctrine, the way to do that was plainly to seek a Decisive Battle with the U.S. fleet, though this represented a reversal of the classic vision of that doctrine, in which Japan would enjoy the advantages of being on the defense. To Yamamoto such an offensive battle seemed the sole solution.

PETTY OFFICER OMI HEIJIRO COULD NOT MISS THE EFFECT THE DOOLITTLE RAID HAD UPON Admiral Yamamoto. Suddenly this Combined Fleet commander who so liked answering letters sent by small children had no time for them. Yamamoto shut himself up in his cabin for a full day. Responsible for the care and feeding of the fleet commander, Omi had never seen Yamamoto look so pale or seem so downhearted. Nor was the fleet commander the only senior officer so affected. Premier Tojo himself was shaken—literally—when his plane, returning from a routine inspection, had to dodge one of the fast American bombers. Baron Tomioka, the NGS operations bureau chief, happened to be at the Army-Navy Club with Army operations chief Colonel Hattori when the raid hit Tokyo. The officers were discussing Combined Fleet's latest version of its Eastern Operation, which stopped short of an invasion of Hawaii but still provided for attack on the American outpost Midway Island. Both opposed the option. Tomioka is reported to have welcomed the air raid at first, apparently thinking it had been mounted by carrier aircraft and therefore constituted a real opportunity to get at the American carriers and sink them without offering battle in the eastern Pacific. Over succeeding days Tomioka's feelings changed as he saw the Doolittle raid turned into an argument for Yamamoto's offensive.

Fleet chief of staff Ugaki had already made the general strategies of west or south versus east the subject of war games aboard the *Yamato* in late February. This resulted in a plan for an offensive toward India which, however, had been rejected by the Army. Ugaki's staff felt free to explore their own preferences and at the end of March assembled the preliminary plan for an operation to capture Midway. Discussions between Combined Fleet and NGS staffers followed in the first week of April. Captain Tomioka opposed the scheme, using the arguments that NGS had developed against a Hawaii option—the place might be captured but could never be held. Miyo, the NGS air staff officer, who also opposed Midway, wondered whether fleet staff had considered how ineffective air searches from a Midway base toward Pearl Harbor would be.

Yamamoto's representatives in these discussions were senior staff officer Captain Kuroshima along with Commander Watanabe. When Baron Tomioka refused to yield, Kuroshima put a telephone call through to Yamamoto and came back to say that the fleet commander would resign. Tomioka retorted that they were discussing strategy, not personnel matters, and that Yamamoto's resignation had nothing to do with it. The discussion was, however, taking place before Admiral Fukudome, chief of the operations division, and Admiral Ito, vice chief of NGS, and neither went along with Tomioka's objections. Fukudome, of course, had served under Yamamoto as fleet chief of staff, and Ito Seiichi had been under him as an assistant naval attaché in Washington in the twenties. Now Yamamoto was the mastermind behind the Pearl Harbor victory. His Midway plan would not be stopped. The NGS option for the southern operation, beginning with Fiji and Samoa, would be rescheduled to follow the Midway offensive.

Baron Tomioka's objections did result in a diversionary aspect being added to the Midway plan—the occupation of certain points in the Aleutian Island chain off the Alaskan coast. There may also have been an understanding, though this is not clear from available sources, that carriers *Zuikaku* and *Shokaku*, then detached to support an attempt to capture Port Moresby in New Guinea, would be withheld from Kido Butai regardless of the result of their operation. American historian Michael Barnhart argues that this was the case and also that it represented a classic application of bureaucratic politics: Over NGS, Yamamoto had gotten all the fleet carriers included on the Pearl Harbor sortie; now NGS was striking back. Be this as it may, on April 16 IGHQ Directive Number 86 formalized acceptance of the objective, providing for occupation of Port Moresby in May, Midway and the Aleutians in June, Fiji and Samoa in July. The die had been cast.

Yamamoto Isoroku had accomplished precisely what he had set out to do: For six months he had run wild in the Pacific. Now that period was fast drawing to a close. Yamamoto's war was ending. The shadow war of intelligence was about to reach its height.

# PART III

---

## HIGH

---

## TIDE

---

## OF THE

---

## SHADOW

---

## WAR

---

**J**APAN HAD OVERTHROWN THE WHITE COLONIAL EMPIRES IN THE FAR EAST AND HAD SET up her defensive perimeter only to be stung by American attacks at the heart of the Empire. After the war ended the execution of Doolittle-raid fliers became a subject of war-crimes prosecutions, but the immediate impact on the Japanese strategic debate had now led Japan to abandon long-prepared plans. Midway was selected as the venue for a Decisive Battle because Yamamoto felt the objective important enough to bring out the American fleet in defense of it.

Many Western and Japanese historians write of "victory disease" as the reason the Imperial Navy stepped beyond its plans to bid for Midway. This malady, to which the Japanese succumbed as they ran wild, in Yamamoto's phrase, so successfully, revolved around the delusion that Japanese could accomplish anything. But this explanation is commonly stretched too far. Although overconfidence undoubtedly played its role in bringing down Japan, psychological and even political factors contributed to the Midway plan, which became Tokyo's key false step. Moreover, "victory disease" does not explain the specific timing or content of the attempt to go beyond the defense perimeter. Conversely, victory-disease theories also do not explain why the Japanese *limited* their plans rather than seeking more grandiose objectives. If IGHQ was so deluded, why not invade Australia instead of Port Moresby and Fiji-Samoa? Why not India instead of just Burma? Why Midway rather than Hawaii directly? Why not do *all* these things?

The Imperial Navy followed a real planning process to arrive at the strategy it pursued. Tokyo tried to limit its goals. But the effect of the Marcus and

Doolittle raids was to jar the planners off their conservative timetables, to make them rush ahead in their desire to obliterate the threat emanating from the east. Tactical overconfidence led to the temptation to divide available forces too much. The new plan also required more communications with forward forces to prepare them to move beyond the perimeter. Thus Doolittle's raid triggered developments that played into the hands of Allied intelligence. In addition, *Japanese* intelligence failed to meet the needs of the Imperial Navy.

This period, which began in the aftermath of the Doolittle raid and continued roughly through the end of 1943, became the key phase of the war. The battles fought reversed the course of the conflict, then accelerated the pace at which it raced toward a conclusion. A shadow war between intelligence on both sides underlay the clashes of fleets and air flotillas. This shadow conflict had everything to do with the outcomes of the naval and air battles, and yet, with the obvious exceptions of Coral Sea and Midway, the intelligence war has hardly been touched by historians. It was a result of the intelligence battle that the skill of the Imperial Navy would be frustrated and its power blunted.

# Incredible Victories?

"**I** MADE ONLY A FEW IMPORTANT REPORTS," SAYS CAPTAIN SHIGEHIRO ATSUO, THE Japanese naval attaché in Argentina and Brazil through mid-1942. Shigehiro was supposed to send reports monthly on items of interest; he simply neglected to make them. When the Naval General Staff reminded him of the requirement, Captain Shigehiro responded with one report detailing U.S. fleet movements from Atlantic to Pacific, then lapsed into his customary silence, broken only when he thought there was something vital to say. Captain Shigehiro told Tokyo about the Argentine declaration of neutrality, Brazil's severing of relations with Japan, and American occupation of the Galápagos Islands. Shigehiro considered one of his more important contributions to have been the report he assembled from items in the American press on "the problem of movement of convoys across the Atlantic and whether escort units of the Pacific Fleet should be moved to the Atlantic."

Like colleagues such as Commander Wachi in Mexico, Shigehiro made it seem that his was but a sleepy backwater post where nothing much happened. As with Wachi in Mexico, there was more than met the eye. There were meetings, many meetings, with local Japanese residents or with Argentines. Shigehiro had just one assistant, and in the entire embassy there were only nine more persons including the ambassador. The press of engagements could be significant, especially since the attaché was to collect data on the Argentine Navy and assist the ambassador in lending prestige to the embassy and, by extension, to Japan. Shigehiro maintained that the United States was not his intelligence target.

Naturally, much of this pretense, a certain delicate dance already referred to, was transparent to Americans. Japanese pretended that their activities were wholly innocuous and American interrogators that their questions were completely innocent. Those with access to the codebreakers' product saw a different picture of Japanese actions in Latin America. They knew, for example, that in the fall of 1941 the vessel *Tao Maru* had carried to Argentina nine crates of radio equipment and parts, which Captain Shigehiro had then sent on to Rio de Janeiro. When Brazilian police later moved against the supposed Japanese spy nets in their country, among their seizures were six complete radio outfits, including one with a transmission range of over 12,000 miles. Those arrested included an Imperial Navy admiral, posing as a farmer, who had allegedly directed the activities of a fleet of fishing boats in Atlantic waters. Other internees numbered several hundred and included individuals reputed to be Japanese agents whose countries of origin—Sweden and Hungary—had nothing to do with the Japanese war. In the summer of 1942, after German U-boats had sunk over a dozen of its merchant ships, Brazil entered the war on the Allied side, and would eventually contribute an infantry division to the Allied forces in the Mediterranean theater. Captain Shigehiro's reporting of Brazilian events was not simply diplomatic.

Communication posed an increasing difficulty for naval attachés in Latin America as well. Argentina soon prohibited Axis embassies from sending coded communications, an instruction renewed in 1943. Captain Shigehiro and his successor, Rear Admiral Yukishita Katsumi, who would be briefly held under house arrest in the spring of 1944, labored on as best they could. One naval attaché in Mexico, Captain Hamanaka Kyoho, solved the communication problem by using German espionage channels to transmit his reports with microdots, a technique that used photographic processes to shrink a report to tiny proportions. Because the U.S. Federal Bureau of Investigation was working closely with the Mexicans and had solved the microdot method, some Japanese intelligence reports later turned up in FBI files.

Despite his claims that the United States was not an intelligence target, the reports Captain Shigehiro remembers sending mostly bear on America. His major sources were the U.S. press, especially *The New York Times*, *Newsweek*, *Time*, and the *Army-Navy Journal*, from which Shigehiro claims he did not get good information. Postwar investigation established that the press had indeed been a major source for the Japanese intelligence system, and that the attaché offices in neutral countries, like Shigehiro's, were the main conduit for these materials, often through locals who held the subscriptions in their own names. Once the war began, naval attachés could procure items totally inaccessible in Japan.

For many years the Imperial Navy had included special "secret funds" (*kimitsu hi*) in its budget to cover costs both of this open-source procurement and of espionage. There were ordinary secret funds used for embassy entertainment and what might be termed the publication program, and emergency secret funds, covering more nefarious needs. Until the China Incident began, secret funds had been strictly limited—the Navy-wide total in 1937 was apparently only about ¥80,000—but as hostilities neared the fund swelled to as much as ¥500,000. Japanese officers report that the Army had far greater secret funds, and the Foreign Ministry also had a small but useful secret fund. The Navy fund became relatively large, but when one considers the comment of a former resident naval officer in China, who estimates typical annual payments to maintain top-level Chinese sources at ¥10,000–¥20,000 per spy, at a global level the Japanese were virtually restricted to the publications program.

It was the secret fund and its administration that clued in the Allies to what was going on with Japanese intelligence. Australian and American codebreakers decrypted a number of communications in 1941–1942 regarding cash transfers from Japanese accounts in various South American countries. Argentina seems to have been one major center of this activity, with Chile and Peru also involved. Some cash transfers covered expenses of pro-German or pro-Italian initiatives in South American lands; these were reimbursed in Europe by Axis partners. In other nations—for example, Argentina, where the Japanese transferred some funds into Buenos Aires through Italian authorities—the situation was reversed.

The general dimensions of the effort are suggested by a March 1942 message through the Japanese minister in Santiago, Chile, proposing to spend U.S. $28,200 on secret services for the coming year (the Japanese fiscal year ran from April 1 to March 31). This sum included payments to individuals, publications, propaganda projects both to influence local Japanese and in behalf of the Italians, and intelligence against the U.S. target. As the 1942 fiscal year progressed, messages discussed specific spy projects to collect intelligence from merchant seamen at Valparaiso and Santiago, even to infiltrate an agent into the United States.

South American schemes conformed to a six-point menu of intelligence regarding the United States that circulated in the Japanese embassy in Madrid. Americans gained access to this list of key intelligence questions and quietly warned Washington officials in February 1942. The Japanese wanted information on movements of U.S. shipping, including both numbers of ships and manner of dispatch; on political or economic problems that might weaken the Roosevelt administration; on racial questions, which could lead to disunity; on American aid to South America; on the movement of aid to England, China, and Russia; and on social problems or ones related to inflation. A later priority list from the naval attaché's office in Italy specified intelligence on Allied intentions, warship movements to the Pacific, and arms and armaments. Such requirements stood at the heart of Japanese foreign-intelligence efforts throughout the war.

Espionage was far more sophisticated than suggested by references to mere reading of the American press. Radio intelligence reports from Mexico have been discussed previously. Spy reports were also sent by the Japanese using microdots (a German technology) through Swedish accommodation addresses. Among these were reports from Japanese agent "Q" in the United States (possibly the American Major "Sutton") on strategy, lists of warships lost at Pearl Harbor, and reports of warship transits of the Panama Canal between December 13 and 22, 1941, including battleships *North Carolina* and *Washington*, aircraft carriers *Yorktown* and *Wasp*, British carriers *Formidable* and *Furious*, and others.* Tokyo was further put on notice that transports were leaving San Diego or San Pedro for the Pacific at a rate of three or four a night. Reports from Argentina were generally based on enumeration of ships calling at Buenos Aires en route around South America, a pattern that continued after mid-1942, when Rear Admiral Yukishita Katsumi with a new assistant attaché replaced Captain Shigehiro, who returned to Japan to head the personnel office at Yokosuka Naval District.

American codebreakers encountered evidence that the Japanese were garnering intelligence by more immediate methods as well. On several occasions in February 1942 Station Cast analysts (then still at Corregidor) reported Japanese radio intelligence listing call signs of U.S. warships. By late February the Owada Communications Unit was reporting new American call signs within fourteen or fifteen hours of their first use by the Allies. Americans initially believed that this Japanese knowledge flowed from documents seized on Wake Island. On March 13 the Third Bureau informed major commands of U.S. fleet strength and building programs, data based upon a document captured at Singapore. On March 22 *joho kyoku* reported details of an American convoy carrying trucks, bombs, gasoline, and 2,800 aviation personnel in twenty or more ships. Observers (in late 1942) concluded that the Japanese had a copy of the Allied merchant ship code taken from a vessel captured in the Indian Ocean.

Information from all sources flowed into *joho kyoku*, where it was analyzed and filed. The Third Bureau circulated intelligence reports, like those cited above, on information seen to have immediate value. Beyond that the intelligence bureau responded to specific queries, replying orally or producing monographs as necessary. Under Rear Admiral Ogawa Kanji, the intelligence specialist, the American experts of the 5th Section were now headed by Captain Yamaguchi Bunjiro, a naval academy classmate of the Argentine attaché Shigehiro. Yamaguchi had some background in espi-

---

*The reports Tokyo received were by no means entirely accurate. For example, *Washington* and *Wasp* fought in the Atlantic throughout the first half of 1942, entering the Pacific only toward the end of August.

onage, and had spent a month in the United States as recently as April 1941, when he already headed the 5th Section. Certainly aware of America's huge production base, which he had seen as an attaché in the 1930s, Yamaguchi had no illusions; nor did Ogawa, but they were not the operations bureau. Admiral Fukudome and Baron Tomioka were. The chiefs of the operations bureau, indeed all the top NGS planners, met daily with *joho kyoku* chief Ogawa at staff conferences presided over by Admiral Nagano. Each day a duty officer reviewed the war situation, briefing the latest dispatches from the front. Admiral Ogawa was listened to, but not very seriously. At the moment Japan was strong, but adversaries were growing mightier by the day, and Nagano, Fukudome, Tomioka, and their cohorts were consumed by the desire to forestall the impending counteroffensive by isolating Australia.

The Third Bureau's intelligence regarding Australia was thin, essentially leaving the operations chiefs to their own devices. There were no data about any American carrier force, but since carriers had already appeared twice in the theater, "there is a great possibility that the Allies are becoming stronger in this area." First-line aircraft were estimated at 200, concentrated in the Townsville and Darwin areas. A "British" naval force of a battleship with two or three cruisers plus destroyer escort was thought to be the main naval strength present. Submarines were in the theater but NGS had no indication of numbers or activities.

In reality there was an Australian, not British, naval force, a strong American submarine force, and a real garrison at Port Moresby, New Guinea, the immediate target of the operation the Japanese code-named MO. There was no Allied battleship, but on the other hand there was a strong task force under Admiral Frank Fletcher with carriers *Lexington* and *Yorktown*. The *joho kyoku* estimate of Allied aircraft was fairly close (actually there were 225 bombers and fighters) but these were heavily concentrated in the sector the Japanese intended to assail, not scattered as the Third Bureau anticipated. On the whole, Japanese intelligence for the MO Operation has to be rated marginal.

There was still radio intelligence. It might yet warn the Imperial Navy of the danger impending. Both the 4th and 8th communications units, the latter a new detachment centered around Rabaul, were in position to intercept Allied transmissions. Much now rode upon their success. The Australians and Americans, on the other hand, had fewer forces but, as will be seen, far better intelligence.

IN TRUTH THE ALLIED INTELLIGENCE SITUATION WAS THE OPPOSITE OF THE JAPANESE—AN embarrassment of riches, a wealth of intelligence so good that the main danger became differing interpretations, argument over which might preoccupy Pearl Harbor and other command centers while the Japanese went about their business. Indications of a Japanese effort against Port Moresby emerged as early as March 25, when a message instructed certain Imperial Navy air commanders in the *nanyo* as to their tasks in attacking "RZP." Other Japanese geographical designators also appeared very quickly in the traffic, including "RZQ" and the code name "MO." The question was what they meant.

Washington had its own vision of the war in the Pacific, and OP-20-G increasingly saw events differently than either Station Hypo or Belconnen, the name given the newly constituted Australian-American codebreaking unit at Melbourne. The situation was of special delicacy since the Washington unit both controlled the field stations and served directly with Navy commander in chief Admiral Ernest J. King. With direct access to King, the Washington codebreakers had myriad opportunities to build his regard for them. This might not have mattered if Laurence Safford had remained in charge of OP-20-G, but the Pearl Harbor debacle had resulted in Safford's being shunted aside, into technical and training jobs. Safford was destined to play a key role in efforts to maintain the integrity of U.S. codes, but the positive intelligence force he had created would fight the war without him.

The new director of OP-20-G was Captain John R. Redman, a communications specialist but no codebreaker. One of the Annapolis class of 1919, graduated early for war service in World War I, Redman had served in battleships, cruisers, and destroyers. He had played football and lacrosse at the naval academy and had been captain of the wrestling team, which may not have given Redman his instinct for the jugular but is indicative of his competitiveness. Redman honed his instincts in many staff communications billets, and his wrestling skills at the 1920 Olympics, in Antwerp, where he took fourth place in the light heavyweight category. When the war began Redman had been in a liaison job in the CNO's office, and was sent to OP-20-G in place of Safford in February 1942. His best attribute happened to be his brother, Rear Admiral Joseph R. Redman, who became director of naval communications at about the same time. The Redman team was tight and ambitious, and it struck sparks throughout the naval radio intelligence organization.

Deputy to the new boss would be Joseph Numa Wenger, a forty-year-old commander who had returned to the Navy Department after a tour as navigator aboard the light cruiser *Honolulu*. Although some officers in the Pacific considered Wenger an opportunist, throwing in with the Redmans, he was at least among the originals in the radio intelligence business. Like Redman, he had gone into communications, but took cryptographic training from 1929 to 1931 under Aggie Driscoll's tutelage. Toward the end of this period Wenger played a role in the introduction of sorting machines in OP-20-G decoding work. In 1932 he went on a mission to survey European code machinery and subsequently joined the Asiatic Fleet staff as top man for radio intelligence. In Far Eastern service he became a close friend of language officer Henri Smith-Hutton. Following a year at sea, Wenger returned to Washington as chief of the codebreaking section of OP-20-G, a post he held until the summer of 1938. His subsequent command of a destroyer and work aboard the *Honolulu* conformed to the Navy's policy of alternate shore and sea duty.

In any case, with John Redman and Joe Wenger at the helm, OP-20-G, called Negat as a cable addressee, sidled ever closer to Ernie King. Pacific Fleet intelligence officer Edwin Layton seems to have convinced himself that OP-20-G was unduly alarmist, continually running to King with apocalyptic fears of Japanese master coups. Layton preferred the more considered approach of Hypo and Joe Rochefort, who had been both intelligence and operations officer on a fleet staff, and therefore had some idea of the effects of running off with half-baked information. In the case of the run-up to the naval battle off Port Moresby, Washington's vision was that Tokyo intended to move instead in the North Pacific, perhaps the Aleutians, the Japanese geographic designators for which had first been recovered in January.

But Japanese interest in the Port Moresby–Solomons area could not be ignored. Indications appeared ever more frequently in the message traffic as the Imperial Navy deployed for its MO Operation. Many were first reported by Hypo, although Melbourne, Washington, and the British all had a share of key firsts. The reinforcement and reorganization of air units in the Solomons, Hypo commented on April 3, was among "numerous indications *which point to impending offensive from Rabaul base*" (Hypo's italics). On April 7 OP-20-G informed Admiral King that a new extension of Japanese air search patterns clearly indicated interest in the Coral Sea. On April 14 Hypo reported the new Japanese light carrier *Shoho* (mistakenly known as *Ryukaku*) about to leave for Truk and expected to arrive there on the twenty-fifth. That same day came a British dispatch from Colombo:

PART OR WHOLE OF FIRST AIR FLEET APPEARS TO BE CONNECTED WITH AN OPERATION AGAINST RZP (IDENTIFIED AS PORT MORESBY). DATE AND DETAILS UNCERTAIN.

The next day the British followed up with news that Japanese fleet carriers *Shokaku* and *Zuikaku* (Carrier Division 5) had in fact been detached from Nagumo's First Air Fleet and were expected at Truk about April 28.

"Japanese Naval Activities," the official daily report by the Office of Naval Intelligence, assembled by Japan Desk personnel in consultation with OP-20-G experts, supplied a constant stream of running commentary. On April 16 the ONI report, signed by Japan Desk chief Lieutenant Colonel Ronald A.

Boone, USMC, observed that the withdrawal of Japanese aircraft carriers from the Indian Ocean, at first thought to be for the purpose of replacing lost aircraft and crews, was now believed to be for fresh operations. Boone's report for April 17 specifically noted: "Already the new focal point of concentration is shifting down to the Truk area, an indication that future offensive action may be directed against the Australian sphere."

Thus, the day *before* Doolittle's raiders hit Japan, American intelligence had evidence of Japan's intention to mount an operation into the Coral Sea.

At Pearl Harbor the emerging intelligence picture appeared vital to Admiral Nimitz, who needed to optimize deployment of his very limited forces. Nimitz had built a modicum of confidence in his codebreakers and paid them very serious attention. Commander Rochefort was already predicting a Japanese offensive in the New Guinea area but, Jasper Holmes writes, the evidence was still thin, consisting primarily of the ruminations of language officer Joe Finnegan, who was the man to report the *Shoho*'s impending deployment. On April 9 Admiral Nimitz showed special interest in Commander Layton's briefing of the latest radio intelligence. On April 17, coincident with the solidifying intelligence picture, Admiral King gave Nimitz command of the Coral Sea area, and CINCPAC held a detailed review of available data. Nimitz rejected a Melbourne prediction that the Japanese might move as soon as April 21, agreeing that the Imperial Navy could not assemble its forces much before the beginning of May. On this basis Nimitz ordered Frank Fletcher to rendezvous the *Lexington* and *Yorktown* and have them ready for a fleet action in the Coral Sea in early May. Fletcher did just that.

From Washington, Admiral Ernest King also took a hand in checking the radio intelligence. Uncomfortable with differences between OP-20-G and Station Hypo, King reached down the chain of command to ask Joe Rochefort directly for Hypo's analysis of the intelligence. Rochefort's reply, drafted and sent in just six hours, conjectured that the Imperial Navy had completed Indian Ocean operations, that two other offensives were now planned in New Guinea and the Coral Sea, that there was no evidence that the Japanese intended to invade Australia, and that an even larger operation for the Central Pacific was being prepared. This latter shows the strong conceptual link the American codebreakers had already made between the Coral Sea campaign and what became the Midway operation.

Finally, toward the end of April the Australian-American codebreakers in Melbourne made a supreme contribution to intelligence preparations for the coming battle by deciphering messages that detailed the organization of the Japanese forces. Although Jasper Holmes attributes this discovery to Lieutenant Finnegan, he mentions only the MO Covering Force, MO Occupation Force, and a second occupation force seemingly connected with the Solomons. Other sources trace key discoveries to Rudolph Fabian and

Rufus Taylor at Melbourne, including details of a striking force which contained the big Japanese fleet carriers. The Americans were fast girding for battle.

CARRIER DIVISION 5 STEAMED INTO TRUK PRECISELY ON SCHEDULE. REAR ADMIRAL HARA Chuichi had the two newest fleet carriers in the Imperial Navy. At Truk he found the *Shoho*, even newer though a light carrier, and the heavy cruisers of his support group, *Myoko* and *Haguro*. Wearing his flag on the *Myoko* was Vice Admiral Takagi Takeo, victor in the Java Sea, now destined to be force commander for the carrier group allotted to the MO Operation. Along with Takagi the other Japanese tactical commanders were of a familiar stripe, all flag officers who had worked under the *nanyo* skies, Fourth Fleet stalwarts. There would be several conferences among senior officers, but the most important, given the carriers' roles, would be those between Takagi and Admiral Hara.

As a torpedoman Takagi knew precious little about carriers, but he had gained appreciation for airpower in the Netherlands East Indies campaign, and he and Hara Chuichi were fellow members of Etajima's thirty-ninth class, graduated in 1911. Close friends, Takagi and Hara were disposed to cooperate; they found at Truk that they agreed on most aspects of the MO plan. Equally important was collaboration between the admirals' respective senior staff officers, and there too the Japanese were fortunate in that Commander Yamaoka Mineo, Hara's top staffer, and Commander Nagasawa Ko, Takagi's man, also happened to be Etajima classmates and friends. Yamaoka was not a pilot but an aviation management type in the tradition of Yamamoto Isoroku; he had worked off and on at the Naval Aviation Bureau and been executive officer of carrier *Hiryu* at Pearl Harbor, transferred to Admiral Hara's command in February 1942.

Thinking about the operation, Nagasawa Ko reasoned that the Coral Sea had become so important to the U.S. Navy that it would surely be defended. Regardless of the intelligence, therefore, Nagasawa expected to find a U.S. carrier unit facing them. Admiral Takagi agreed with that view, even expecting a big U.S. force. Yamaoka and Nagasawa, who had also been at staff college together, focused on the real possibility that Coral Sea could become the first battle in naval history fought entirely between aircraft. They agreed the task force would have to be very careful, should conduct the widest possible air searches, and would concentrate on disabling U.S. carriers.

All this sounded good to Admiral Hara. No airman himself—the Imperial Navy never had a carrier admiral who was a pilot—Hara was of flexible mind and had enough time commanding carriers to have become aware of their special features. Almost three years older than Takagi, Hara was also a torpedo specialist, a man who had received awards in earlier years for making technical and equipment innovations. His career may have been held back by the technical work—always less appreciated than sea duty in the Imperial Navy—or by his opposition to escalation while serving with the China Area Fleet in the period 1938–1940. Perhaps what slowed his rise had been some of the other incidents, like the time in 1932 when, as a ship captain off Shanghai, he had denied Army officers the use of his communications gear to send inflammatory dispatches; or the time, again at Shanghai, when he got so drunk he pulled a British officer around by his whiskers (Hara had apologized, claiming that the man's whiskers were so praiseworthy he had wanted to feel them out of envy). An international incident had been averted on that occasion, but it suggests that Hara's nickname, "King Kong," was not solely due to his heavy build. In any case, Takagi had beat Hara to vice admiral and now would lead the carrier force into the Coral Sea.

The others in the Japanese lineup were well known from Fourth Fleet operations in the Mandates and Central Pacific. Admiral Inoue moved his headquarters temporarily from Truk to Rabaul to exercise overall control. An invasion convoy of six slow (6.5 knots in formation) transports would carry the South Seas Detachment to Port Moresby under close escort by Rear Admiral Kajioka Sadamichi and his 6th Destroyer Flotilla. A separate invasion group would head for Tulagi Island in the Solomons under Rear Admiral Shima Kiyohide. A third occupation group accompanied by two light cruisers under Rear Admiral Marushige Kuninori would take Deboyne Island, between the Solomons and New Guinea, to set up a base there for floatplanes from the *Kamikawa Maru*. The heavy support would be Cruiser Division 6 under Admiral Goto, with air cover from light carrier *Shoho* and the 25th Air Flotilla at Rabaul and on Shortland Island.

The last provision of the Japanese plan led to problems as the MO Operation moved to its execution phase. A requirement for land-based fighter cover was logical, since the *Shoho* had only a small air group (nine Zero and three Claude fighters, plus nine Kate torpedo planes). Several vital Japanese task groups would be sailing in company for most of their voyage, and that was too many eggs for the basket the *Shoho* could cover by herself. However, Rear Admiral Yamada Sadayoshi's 25th Air Flotilla had difficulties of its own, including the fact that over the month of April it had lost six Zero fighters and had its strength reduced by six more under repair, both from crashes and the fighter battles being fought almost daily over Port Moresby. Yamada therefore needed reinforcements to cover the MO task groups.

Admiral Hara's fleet carriers ended up with the task of making good Yamada's losses, among the other ancillary missions with which they were saddled. One other mission—mounting strikes to neutralize Allied airpower in northern Australia—was canceled due to the danger of exposing the carriers to powerful aerial counterattacks. The Rabaul fighter ferry mission was left on the boards, however, and the planes themselves had to be flown by Carrier Division 5 pilots who would then return on other carrier planes sent to retrieve them. In the event, the ferry mission cost Takagi a day, because on the first attempt weather prevented planes from getting to Rabaul. The setback not only gave the Allies an additional day to concentrate but also gave Allied codebreakers another twenty-four hours to work. The delay proved a useful assist in view of the fact that Fletcher's *Yorktown* and Rear Admiral Aubrey Fitch's *Lexington* rendezvoused only on May 1, at a sea position Nimitz had jauntily named Point Buttercup.

Jasper Holmes, a leading figure at Station Hypo and the Combat Intelligence Unit formed to integrate its product, makes a point of noting that just one in ten of the messages in JN-25 variants at this time was being read well enough to obtain useful intelligence, and that this made for a huge element of chance. This tells just a little of the story, however, obscuring the fact that a great deal of information flowed from traffic analysis of messages not broken. Difficulties of individual codebreakers working on specific messages were also mitigated by the fact that not only Pearl Harbor, but also Melbourne and Washington, were working the traffic. Finally, simply in percentage terms, though 10 percent might seem a small proportion, at this time there were more than a thousand messages in JN-25 being intercepted each day, and the ones to be worked on were selected after screening out those that seemed routine, surely the bulk of the Imperial Navy message traffic.

Make no mistake: The codebreakers had the goods on the MO Operation. For example, Americans decrypted the Fourth Fleet message informing subordinates of the delayed ferry mission from the Japanese carriers to Rabaul; that message was circulated the day it was sent (and just a day after Hypo warned that the MO Operation was "now underway"), together with a résumé of involved forces. This was only the beginning. On May 3 Hypo circulated the gist of Fourth Fleet's general orders to Admiral Takagi's force, and on May 4 a status report giving strength, aircraft lost in April, and crews required for each plane type in the land-based 25th Air Flotilla. On May 5 and 6 there were repeated messages from Admiral Kajioka's MO Occupation Force giving his position and plans for sailing south on May 7, when American search planes very conveniently found him, initiating the sequence of air strikes that became the main action in the Coral Sea battle.

Even negative intelligence was available to the Americans. Combined Fleet orders on May 3 to carry out radio deception measures were reported by Hypo the same day, and on the sixth Hypo reported details of some of the Japanese tricks. Among them was the use of other vessels' call signs by warships sending messages. The codebreakers duly observed that carrier *Sho-kaku* was using the call sign of Truk radio station. About the only obvious error in U.S. radio intelligence reporting was the information on May 3 that a battleship, probably *Hiei* or *Kongo,* was operating out of Rabaul or in the Mandates. This was likely a case of Japanese deception by use of extraneous call signs.

Admiral Frank Fletcher was undoubtedly gratified to learn from radio intelligence on May 5 that Takagi's MO striking force would be in position by 10 A.M. that day (in fact Takagi was just then passing south of San Cristobal Island in the Solomons). This gave Fletcher ample time to get his own task force out of the way after the air strike they had made the previous morning on Japanese invaders of Tulagi. On May 6 Pearl Harbor followed up with its analysis that the Japanese were now aware that their campaign would no longer come as any surprise to the Allies.

The Imperial Navy could only wish for equivalent performance from its own radio component. According to Japanese sources, their 4th and 8th communications units intercepted Allied messages but the reporting was delayed and therefore of little value.

Of course, in naval affairs as in any others, skill and good fortune are never enough; personal chemistry also becomes a factor. Here the Japanese had an advantage, with the seasoned operators of Fourth Fleet working alongside Takagi's task force: The senior leadership benefited from long ties of personal friendship. In contrast the prickly Fletcher had no relations to speak of with his Australian counterpart, Admiral Sir John Crace, and somewhat delicate ones with his American colleague Rear Admiral Aubrey W. Fitch. Fletcher also got his back up in a dispute with his personal codebreakers, the mobile radio unit assigned to *Yorktown* and led by Lieutenant Forrest R. Baird. Invited by the admiral to describe before an entire wardroom full of officers just what his radio intelligence unit did, Baird refused, no doubt conscious that most of those present were not cleared for knowledge of codebreaking material. Baird incurred Fletcher's wrath, which he deepened a few days later when his radio unit was unable to confirm whether a Japanese submarine depth-charged nearby had sent a contact report. Lieutenant Commander Ransom Fullinwider, who had a mobile radio unit aboard the *Lexington,* reported that it had.

The skills of the radio officers did not come into play on May 4, the day Fletcher took *Yorktown* within fifty miles of Tulagi to make several air strikes on the Japanese force under Admiral Shima there, but they might have. Edwin Layton makes the point that *Shokaku* and *Zuikaku* were out of range only because they delayed a day for the aircraft ferry mission to Rabaul. Even so, at midnight that night only about 350 miles separated the two admirals' carriers. That distance would not prevent some Japanese admirals in later Pacific battles from launching strikes anyway.

On May 5 a Japanese patrol bomber of the Yokosuka Air Group was fired upon by a carrier interceptor, but the day was overcast, the plane had no accurate navigational fix, and the 25th Air Flotilla was unable either to mount saturation air searches or any strikes. Nevertheless, Kenneth A. McIntosh, a *Yorktown* seaman, recalls that that evening the fleet loosed an impressively pyrotechnic anti-aircraft barrage upon discovering four unidentified aircraft in the landing pattern. McIntosh also remembers a searchlight showing for a few seconds on the horizon, presumably from the unidentified planes' true home.* Movement plots, however, place the sides' aircraft carriers about 250 miles apart at this time. The account by Captain Frederick C. Sherman, *Lexington*'s skipper, makes no mention of the searchlight incident.

One more radio intelligence issue needs to be raised here, the matter of the actual position of Takagi's carriers. Layton and his co-authors write as if Fletcher believed all the Japanese carriers were together, all essentially with the MO group of forces. One Station Hypo dispatch, enumerating Imperial Navy carriers in the MO order of battle, mentions the *Shokaku, Zuikaku,* and *Shoho* all together, while an error in translation gave the impression that Takagi would pass through rather than proceed east of the Solomons. On the other hand, Hypo explicitly warned that it lacked information on the position of the Japanese carriers. Any error Fletcher made regarding Japanese dispositions can equally well be charged to aerial reconnaissance, specifically communications, for the search plane that found the Japanese on the morning of May 7 saw two cruisers and two destroyers but sent a message improperly coded to read two *carriers* and four *heavy* cruisers. Even worse, investigation eventually showed that this sighting, by a *Yorktown* plane, had actually been of a minor Japanese group of two elderly cruisers and three gunboats!

In any case the Americans responded with alacrity. *Lexington* began to launch her strike group at 9:26 A.M., *Yorktown* somewhat later, and by 10:30 there were ninety-three planes winging toward the reported position. Shortly after 11:00 one saw *Shoho* with Goto's accompanying cruisers. Within ten minutes the planes reached attack positions; in the next fifteen destruction of the hapless *Shoho* was accomplished. She was the victim of seven torpedoes and at least thirteen bombs. One of the Americans radioed his ship, "Scratch one flattop!"

Captain Izawa Ishinosuke ordered *Shoho*'s crew to abandon ship at 11:31, and five minutes later the carrier disappeared beneath the waves. She was the first major Japanese warship lost in the war, and her loss must have caused at least momentary concern at Fourth Fleet headquarters, for the fleet chief of staff, Yano Shikazo, had been a comrade of Izawa's at the naval

---

*An incident like this did in fact take place, but on May 7, not May 5.

academy. But Captain Izawa survived the *Shoho*'s demise, to be picked up hours later by destroyer *Sazanami*, together with 131 other officers and men and another 72 wounded. Some 631 sailors went down with the ship. Of six *Shoho* aircraft in the air at the time of the attack, three made forced landings on Deboyne Island, and three fighters were claimed shot down by Americans.

At the moment *Shoho* sank, the Japanese were hustling to prepare their own attacks, for scout planes from Goto's Cruiser Division 6 found Admiral Crace's Australian cruiser force, which they took to be a detachment of a carrier unit. *Shoho*'s strike on this target was aborted by her ordeal, but Yamada's 25th Air Flotilla came through with attacks on the naval force, which had in fact been part of Fletcher's task force but was sent ahead for a surface attack on any Japanese ships that tried to round the tip of New Guinea. A formation of Motoyama Air Group planes flying toward Port Moresby diverted to the new target with a torpedo unit sent directly from Rabaul. They encountered Crace's ships in early afternoon, achieving nothing better than near misses, but claiming to have inflicted extensive damage on a *Warspite*-class battleship and sunk a *California*-class battleship plus a heavy cruiser. None of the ships cited was even present in the Australian theater, much less hit that day. Four JNAF planes went down, one made a crash landing, and eight others suffered varying degrees of damage.

Events on May 7 clearly demonstrate a key weakness in Japanese intelligence: reconnaissance. The flaw was due primarily to inadequate preparation of pilots for identification of ships at sea. Only one of the three cruisers with Admiral Crace was correctly identified, the American warship *Chicago*. Even worse would be the performance of the dawn search from Hara's Carrier Division 5. Planes from *Shokaku* reported a carrier and three destroyers when they had really seen the oiler *Neosho* and a single destroyer, *Sims*. Following dictums laid down at Truk before the mission, Admiral Takagi immediately ordered, and Hara complied with, a full-strength strike on the supposed carrier. After the attack planes, led by Commander Takahashi Kakuichi, had taken off, Takagi received another sighting report from a floatplane off cruiser *Kinugasa* of Goto's group. This plane gave Fletcher's correct position, though it too misidentified strength, putting the Americans at one carrier and ten destroyers when Fletcher's true strength stood at two aircraft carriers, five cruisers, and eight destroyers.

Rear Admiral Hara must have rolled his eyes when he saw the *Kinugasa* sighting report. Had the Japanese been highly technological and well equipped with aircraft radios (as were Americans at the time), Takahashi's attack unit could simply have been sent on to the second target. But radio equipment was in short supply in the Japan of that era and there was no assurance that Carrier Division 5 could get through to Commander Takahashi or that Takahashi would be able to get the airplanes with him to understand new target orders. The episode must have been one of special chagrin for Lieutenant Commander Ishikawa Kotaro, Admiral Takagi's communications and intelligence officer and an Etajima classmate of Takahashi, who had a fine appreciation for both the ironies in the sequence of sighting reports and the inability to communicate this intelligence to the attack forces.

In the event, Commander Takahashi flew to the reported position of the carrier but found only the *Neosho*. He searched for a time for the reported target, but finally released his planes to attack. *Sims* was quickly sunk and *Neosho* left in a sinking condition, though she drifted for several days before succumbing to the sea.

On board flagship *Zuikaku*, Admiral Hara huddled with his staff. Obliged to follow through on the attack that sank the *Neosho*, Hara told his officers, "We will join battle with the enemy in the west after we have attacked to the south." Now everything depended upon how quickly the air groups could be recycled and prepared for another strike. Hara ordered *Zuikaku* to broadcast homing signals Takahashi could use to guide his planes back to the ships. This act left an opening for American radio intelligence, for the *Zuikaku* transmissions were intercepted by the radio units on both American carriers. The signals gave both course and speed of the Japanese task force. It was a priceless gift to Frank Fletcher, who did not know where the Japanese carriers were, and had been scared silly to learn from the *Neosho* attack that Imperial Navy strike forces were behind him as well as in front. But now Fletcher became the victim of his own animosity toward his radio intelligence officer, Lieutenant Baird. When Baird came up to tell the admiral what had been learned from the Japanese transmissions, Fletcher queried Lieutenant Commander Fullinwider aboard *Lexington*, who had mistranslated the signal as a report on *American* course and speed. Fletcher believed Fullinwider, letting slip an opportunity to hit Hara's carriers while they were servicing aircraft and most vulnerable. Baird's data on the Japanese position, which resulted from direction finding and plotting the coordinates of *Zuikaku*'s broadcasts until her planes landed at about 2:00 P.M., went completely to waste. Choosing to disbelieve Baird, Fletcher had not a clue as to Admiral Takagi's whereabouts.

Senior staff officer Nagasawa Ko, on board *Myoko*, was one Japanese who wondered why Fletcher made no attack on the MO striking force. Nagasawa and his boss, Admiral Takagi, conferred at length on tactics, and had some exchanges by signal lamp with Hara on *Zuikaku*. Wanting to launch another attack wave themselves, the Japanese were hampered in that they had had to run directly east, away from Fletcher, in order to recover planes from the morning strike. By midafternoon, when Takagi ordered full speed on a westerly course, it was evident that any strike on the Americans would involve a dusk attack and a difficult nighttime aircraft recovery. Hara was asked if this was feasible and replied that some of his pilots were good enough to do that. Late that afternoon Takahashi led a second group of twelve dive-bombers and fifteen torpedo planes in a bid to engage the U.S. carriers.

Takahashi's planes found nothing but bad weather. At the reported location of the American warships the sea was empty. Searching for the second time that day, again without result, the JNAF planes finally jettisoned their bomb loads into the sea and turned for home, only to fly almost directly over Fletcher's task force. With radar to see enemy planes, Fletcher was hardly so blind as Takahashi, and air controllers on *Yorktown* and *Lexington* vectored fighters to stop the Japanese, who lost a dive-bomber and eight attack planes. Some pilots were so confused they lined up to land on the American carriers, thinking themselves at home.

In actuality Admiral Takagi had ordered his fleet to assume a novel formation, all ships on a north–south line with searchlights crisscrossing in the sky to attract the attention of their wayward airplanes. The Japanese planes straggled to roost as well as they could.

Everyone's attention was now focused on the air battle that promised for the morning of May 8. At Rabaul, Admiral Inoue gave in momentarily to the temptation to order a night surface engagement, getting Goto's cruisers and Kajioka's destroyer flotilla to leave the MO convoys and speed ahead, but the Fourth Fleet commander changed his mind. Inoue finally sent two of Goto's heavy cruisers to join Takagi and had all the rest escort the original invasion convoy, now heading north to evade the air threat. The planned Port Moresby landing was postponed two days, and would eventually be canceled.

Both sides were quick off the mark in the morning, with Hara launching a very ample search followed an hour later by Takahashi's strike group—thirty-three dive-bombers, eighteen torpedo planes, and eighteen fighters. This time the planes were briefed not for a particular target but rather to follow Takahashi wherever he went. The sighting came from Warrant Officer Kanno Kenzo, flying a Kate; he got word to Hara barely ten minutes after the strike group left the carriers, and used up the last of his fuel to join Takahashi and guide him directly to Fletcher's ships.

Meanwhile the Americans, too, had launched a dawn search from the *Lexington,* and first sighting was made by Lieutenant Joseph G. Smith, within minutes of the Japanese contact. Admiral Fletcher immediately ordered a full attack, and a total of eighty-two planes took to the air, including forty-six dive-bombers and twenty-one torpedo planes. *Yorktown* planes attacked first, later the *Lexington*'s, and despite resistance from a combat air patrol (CAP) of six Zeros plus seven more launched during the air battle, the Americans pressed their attacks home. Captain Jojima Takatsugu's *Shokaku* absorbed two bomb hits in the first attack and another in the second, with additional near misses. There was flight-deck and topside damage, but the ship's maneuverability remained unimpaired. Captain Yokokawa Ichibei's *Zuikaku* happened to be under a squall at the critical moment and escaped without even being attacked.

The Japanese air strike arrived late over the American task force because of the scouting it had done along the way. On the other hand, the *Lexington*'s air controller muffed interception of the incoming strike because he could not accurately determine the altitude of the JNAF planes and failed to get his fighters high enough. Only about half the American interceptors could even engage, and many of those did so too close to the task force, where their own anti-aircraft fire proved as much a danger as the Japanese. Determined, the Imperial Navy sea eagles bored in. Takahashi's plane went down. Scout Kanno, the man who had no more fuel, approached the Americans as if he were making a real attack, so as to divert the anti-aircraft gunners. Lieutenant Commander Shimazaki Shigekazu, Pearl Harbor veteran and Carrier Division 5 senior pilot, said a few weeks later there had been a virtual wall of anti-aircraft fire. "Never in all my years have I even imagined a battle like that!"

Captain Ted Sherman stood on the bridge of the *Lexington* calmly ordering evasive maneuvers and thus avoided some torpedoes, but three hit his ship between 11:18 and 11:20, and there may have been two other hits as well. Captain Elliott Buckmaster of the *Yorktown*, whose vessel could turn in half the radius of her older sister, evaded all torpedoes. But Buckmaster could not escape the dive-bombers, and *Yorktown* rocked as an astounding eleven or twelve bombs barely missed her. With such accuracy there had to come a hit, and it did, at 11:27: A bomb passed through the flight and hangar decks to explode just above a fireroom. Two or three more bombs hit *Lexington*. The Japanese pilots returning to their ships exulted that they had sunk one of the U.S. carriers and left the other heavily damaged, expected to sink.

In fact the *Yorktown* survived to play a key role in an even bigger battle coming at Midway. The *Lexington*, which at first seemed repairable, succumbed later in the day to massive fires and internal explosions triggered by sparks from an electric motor. On the Japanese side, Admiral Takagi detached the *Shokaku* to Japan for repairs, prancing past U.S. submarines warned to keep lookout for her. Admiral Yamamoto wanted to seize the opportunity to pursue the chimera of Decisive Battle, and ordered the rest of Takagi's task force back into the Coral Sea, even though Carrier Division 5's air strength had been reduced to just nine bombers and six torpedo planes plus twenty-four fighters.

From Combined Fleet headquarters Admiral Ugaki observed these events and recorded, "A dream of great success has been shattered. There is an opponent in a war, so one cannot progress just as one wishes." More prosaic, but quite to the point, was the opinion Fourth Fleet furnished the day after the big carrier battle: Without high-speed transports and support by power-ful carrier forces, there could not be another attempt at seaborne invasion of Port Moresby. This disheartening realization did not preclude Emperor Hirohito from issuing a rescript congratulating the fleet, or IGHQ from releasing another bombastic communiqué claiming to have sunk two carri-ers and two battleships. The Japanese would be surprised indeed when one of those carriers ambushed them off Midway.

As IMPERIAL NAVY DETACHMENTS FOUGHT TO A STALEMATE AT CORAL SEA, A BATTLE THAT may have been a tactical victory but amounted to strategic defeat, in Empire waters final preparations were under way for the great Midway foray. Air officer Genda of Kido Butai worried that the effort seemed superficial—far less thorough than preparations for the Pearl Harbor mission. This time there were no detailed models, drills on identifying ships, or rehearsals. Flying practice was simplified to meet the operations schedule, and training for air combat never went beyond basic one-on-one encounters. Bombers worked out of Iwakuni and used the target ship *Settsu*, but the old ship was restricted to the Inland Sea, forcing dive-bombers to make long approach and return flights, limiting them to a single bombing practice a day. Even that rate could hardly be maintained since crews were also busy with air-craft maintenance work. Torpedo-bombing practice results were so bad, wags cracked that the Coral Sea results were impossible ones. On May 18, 1942, when the attack planes launched practice torpedoes against cruisers *Tone* and *Chikuma*, results remained exceedingly poor and about a third of the torpedoes were lost. Genda tended to agree with Admiral Kusaka Ryunosuke, who argued that the Nagumo Force needed extended recuper-ation and retraining after its exertions. Kusaka himself, however, was car-ried away by the exuberance of the fleet staff, and went along with Yamamoto's grand scheme.

Material deficiencies were as serious as training shortcomings. Carrier *Kaga* wore the flag of First Air Fleet commander Nagumo from May 4 to May 18 while *Akagi* went into dry dock. During that time *Kaga* was the only ship in condition for planes to practice carrier landings and takeoffs, again restricting the amount of practice possible for each aircrew. The *Kaga* had already had her bottom scraped, missing the Indian Ocean sortie for that reason; now the other fleet carriers had their turn. *Hiryu* returned from dry dock on May 8 to become temporary flagship of Carrier Division 2, an assignment soon made permanent. *Soryu* took longer in dockyard hands. Of Nagumo Force escorts, battleship *Kirishima* and heavy cruiser *Chikuma* also needed spells in dry dock. The 10th Destroyer Flotilla, newly formed and designated to accompany the task force, comprised ships which had focused on anti-aircraft training and others that had concentrated on antisubmarine practice; it had never had much chance for combined training.

As the carrier fleet, so the rest. Ships going through dry dock in late April or May included battleship *Kongo* and the heavy cruisers *Chokai, Kumano, Mikuma,* and *Mogami*. Returning from the South Seas, the *Aoba* went into dry dock too, though at least she was not slated for Midway. Floatplanes, used for scouting by both the carrier force and the battleship fleet, did not begin training until May 6 at Kagoshima. Only on May 25, a few days before sailing, was installation of radar sets completed aboard the *Ise* and *Hyuga;* fleet chief of staff Ugaki hoped the result would justify the long wait.* Both battleships suffered misfortunes of their own. Aboard the *Hyuga* a breech block blew out of one of her big guns during firing practice on May 5, igniting propellant charges for two rounds and forcing the flooding of both after powder magazines. The accident left fifty dead and eleven injured. Tragedy struck the *Ise* on May 11 when valves whose maintenance had been neglected stuck and her number two engine room flooded. That same day Battleship Division 1 furnished live targets for JNAF air attack exercises while the ships themselves practiced gunnery against the islet of Iyo Nada. On May 19 the big ships sailed from Kure for four days of exercises. Leaving harbor, light carrier *Junyo* almost sideswiped *Yamato;* sailors were breathless aboard both warships. It was a poor omen for the fight ahead.

Admiral Yamamoto finished his own plans for the battle with detailed war games aboard *Yamato* during the first days of May. This was the occasion of the celebrated incident in which chief of staff Ugaki intervened to change game results, injecting a notable element of unrealistic play into fleet planning. Much as had happened war-gaming Pearl Harbor, during one simulation the American team struck very effectively, putting carriers on the flank of Kido Butai as it closed to attack Midway and catching the Imperial Navy carriers as their air groups were hitting the island. The umpire officiating happened to be Commander Okumiya Masatake, metamorphosed from the young JNAF pilot of *Panay* fame (or infamy) to an experienced air staff officer, now with Carrier Division 4, scheduled to strike the Aleutians. Okumiya ruled that the Nagumo Force would lose two carriers sunk and a third damaged. Admiral Ugaki reduced the nine hits generated by the game rules to just three, which cut losses to just a single carrier sunk

---

*Sources maintain the installations on the *Ise* and *Hyuga* were the first two radar sets in the Imperial Navy. But to judge from the *Hiryu* battle lessons report previously quoted, that carrier may have had radar also. The discrepancy may be between experimental installations versus field equipment. Air officer Amagai Takahisa of the *Kaga,* explaining Kido Butai's methods of fighter defense to interrogators after the war, also spoke of radar, though he added his own ship lacked such equipment.

plus one damaged. The hypothetically sunken carrier then rematerialized to participate in the next phase of the war game.

On May 5, just after the games climaxed with a hypothetical invasion of Hawaii, the Naval General Staff issued Order Number 18 providing for the sequence of operations from Midway to the Aleutians. Even now there was disquiet in the fleet. Vice Admiral Kondo, for example, who had not seen Yamamoto since the beginning of the war and had now returned to participate in the Midway war games, objected to several features of the plan, voicing some of the same complaints as NGS had previously. Yamamoto and Ugaki visited aboard the damaged carrier *Shokaku* once she arrived at Kure on May 17. The ship, which could not even moor due to her damage, and whose horribly burned wounded the admirals consoled, furnished a cautionary note, reinforced two days later when King Kong Hara came aboard *Yamato* himself to report on the Coral Sea battle. In addition to Hara, during the last two days before fleet exercises Yamamoto received visits from Colonel Ichiki, commanding the Army unit slated for Midway; Admirals Nagumo and Kusaka; and Commander Uchida of NGS, bearing the written text of the IGHQ orders for the contemplated Fiji-Samoa follow-up operation. After the maneuvers, on May 25, officers met on the *Yamato* for a final limited tabletop war game, a briefing on second-stage operations, and a talk by Admiral Takagi Takeo on experiences in the battle of the Coral Sea.

This day finished with a reception on the flagship for more than 200 officers of the fleet—from ship captains right down to destroyer skippers. Petty Officer Omi Heijiro served sake sent by Emperor Hirohito. While the toasts may have been a success, Omi would be denounced by Yamamoto's flag lieutenant for the food—sea bream cooked whole, a dish that was traditional on birthdays, at weddings, on occasions marking the completion of something. However, Omi missed the error when the cook broiled the fish, or *tai*, in bean paste (miso), thereby robbing the dish of its happy connotation. To "put miso on food" was to botch things up. That was the memory sailors took with them when Rear Admiral Kakuta Kakuji's Aleutians striking force weighed anchor the next day. Nagumo's task force sailed on May 27. Kondo went to sea from Saipan. Yamamoto himself left Hashirajima on May 29. The Imperial Navy was out looking for trouble.

THE DISCOVERY OF IMPERIAL NAVY PLANS TO ATTACK MIDWAY IS VERY LIKELY THE BEST-known accomplishment of naval intelligence in the war with Japan. We shall encounter achievements of equal magnitude, and perhaps greater scope, but more has been said and written about Midway than any Pacific war event other than Pearl Harbor. Even so, and even at this late date, some aspects of the achievement at Midway remain poorly understood. The value of knowledge of the Japanese plans has been equated to the strength of an additional carrier group on the American side—in other words, it was enough to equalize the balance. Such a valuable increment to the slender forces available to Admiral Chester Nimitz proved decisive. It is worth reviewing the intelligence breakthrough at Midway, in particular because a number of retellings make the achievement seem much easier, less of a near thing, than in fact it was. Existing accounts overemphasize individual units' contributions, ignoring other efforts.

Let there be no doubt that Station Hypo did yeoman work breaking into the Japanese plans, however. Commander Joseph Rochefort, padding around the basement offices in his slippers and smoking jacket, was saying even before the Coral Sea engagement that the Japanese intended a major effort in the Central Pacific. Rochefort recalls the enormous personal efforts made by his Hypo people—it was unusual for them to work less than twenty hours a day during this period—but attributes Hypo's success to the fact that he was given the pick of naval communications personnel arriving in Hawaii. With Ham Wright and Tommy Dyer spearheading the attack on the JN-25 code groups, Jack Holtwick playing the IBM machinery like a skilled pianist, and Alva Lasswell and Joe Finnegan as lead translators, the Pacific commander in chief had an excellent communications intelligence organization.

At the time, the mid-Pacific radio net was intercepting about 60 percent of Imperial Navy message traffic. Fleet intelligence officer Layton estimates that only about 40 percent of that was actually being read. He likens the effort to assemble a picture of Yamamoto's plan to trying to put together a jigsaw puzzle missing many pieces. Nevertheless Rochefort had some key advantages; for one thing, he had already recovered the meanings the Japanese attached to a number of their geographical designators for the Central Pacific, including values for Pearl Harbor, points in the Aleutians, and "AF," which was held to be Midway. Another advantage was knowledge of Japanese activity levels in the Mandates developed during the K Operation. It was soon clear that forces concentrating at Saipan were far greater than any previous effort in this area.

Japanese preparations played into American hands in a number of respects. For example, Vice Admiral Kondo had worried precisely about the force concentration at Saipan and had held out for the assembly point to be changed to Truk. Yamamoto refused to countenance any modification, yet such a change would have helped disguise preparations by embedding them within the larger pattern of Fourth Fleet activities in the Mandates. Another problem was failure to maintain operational security. The temptation to show that something was being done to ensure against repetition of Doolittle-type raids seems to have been too much, and plans for a Central Pacific operation became something of an open secret in Japan. Commander

Genda at one point was confronted by a worried *Akagi* aircraft squadron commander who revealed that a friend as far away as China had written him a letter wishing him good luck on the forthcoming operation against "M." The worst single error was the delay in shifting to a new version of the fleet code (JN-25, which the Japanese called the D Code), activated only in late May. That gave the Allies time to dig out the main features of the Midway plans.

Though by no means the result of error, the very occurrence of the Coral Sea battle further improved American intelligence by forcing the Japanese into high-volume communications traffic, thereby furnishing U.S. code-breakers additional opportunities to break down JN-25 number groups.

As early as May 2 Americans intercepted a message from Admiral Kondo's command noting that the striking force plus some unidentified additional force would be in Truk for a couple of weeks beginning in late June. This left unanswered the question of what these forces would do before arriving at Truk, but just two days later a message to Combined Fleet from battleship *Kirishima* expressed regret that she would be in dock for repairs during the coming campaign. On May 5 the Combined Fleet asked the Navy Ministry to expedite delivery of fueling hoses, suggesting a need to refuel at sea, while the next day a First Air Fleet dispatch again referred to an upcoming campaign. A Central Pacific focus was suggested by several intercepted messages concerning a renewed K Operation (Pearl Harbor reconnaissance). The Central Pacific focus was confirmed by another Kondo dispatch, Second Fleet Operations Order Number 22 on May 11, which directed concentration of an "occupation force" for the forthcoming campaign at Saipan. Two days later the code designator "MI" was used in connection with the occupation force. The gist of Nagumo's carrier operations plan was in a May 16 message reporting his intention to stage air attacks beginning two days before the invasion and starting from a point fifty miles northwest of "MI." In a May 22 message from Combined Fleet, MI was revealed as a code name for AF (Midway) Island.

Here for the decrypting, and the necessary deduction and reconstruction, lay the heart of Admiral Yamamoto's Midway plan. Rochefort's stalwarts rose to the occasion. One by one the various Japanese messages yielded their secrets. Among the first to fall were those related to the new K Operation. Rochefort passed the intelligence to Eddie Layton, who told Nimitz. The latter had already taken action to preclude JNAF patrol bomber missions to Hawaii, for an observation detachment consisting of a Marine warrant officer, seven enlisted men, and four sailors equipped with a radio set and a 3-inch gun were put ashore on the eastern islet of French Frigate Shoal on April 14. Either the unit withdrew or Nimitz now judged it inadequate, for he sent seaplane tenders *Thornton* and *Ballard* to French Frigate Shoal to set up an advanced patrol base. When Japanese submarines arrived to await the Emily seaplanes, they thus found U.S. warships already there. The lead submarine, *I-123*, chose to abort its refueling mission. That effectively scotched the K Operation.

By May 15 Hypo was developing an increasingly detailed picture of Japanese forces involved even though the codebreakers had yet to decrypt or translate some key dispatches. That day U.S. intelligence commented on a routine Japanese cable by observing evidence of links between Admiral Kondo's command and the key elements of Nagumo's task force, Carrier Divisions 1 and 2 and Battleship Division 3, noting these units might become a striking force aimed southward or toward Hawaii. Meanwhile, on May 18 the message indicating Nagumo's planned position and timing for attacking Midway was translated, and two days later the dispatch revealing the scheduled time of departure from Saipan of the Midway occupation force.

This may sound as if U.S. intelligence had the Japanese plans down cold, but the reality is that there were important differences between codebreakers in the field and those at OP-20-G. Washington entertained a succession of versions of the Japanese plan that fell wide of the mark and owed much to preconceived notions of Imperial Navy strategy. For example, the day Doolittle's bombers raided Tokyo, ONI's Japanese naval-activities summary speculated regarding revenge raids against Hawaii or even the U.S. West Coast. This became OP-20-G's initial prediction, ridiculed by Rochefort and others who rightly insisted that the Imperial Navy lacked sufficient support forces to make any West Coast raid. Hawaii, now on alert, also was not the easy prospect it had been. Later OP-20-G's prediction changed to expect renewed effort against Port Moresby, then the Aleutians, and finally to a major offensive toward Samoa. Layton credits neophyte codebreaker Jack Redman and his deputy Joe Wenger with pushing these versions of the Japanese threat. However, other centers in Washington, including the Joint Intelligence Committee, also predicted Japanese action in the Aleutians rather than against Midway. The extent to which JIC and ONI reporting may have been influenced by OP-20-G is unknown but probably significant.

Perhaps as a result of its own pessimistic assessments, perhaps because of OP-20-G's, or perhaps because it presumed a Japanese fixation on the South Pacific, COMINCH had markedly different views than Pearl Harbor as to Pacific strategy in the days after the Coral Sea fight. Admiral King wanted to keep Bill Halsey down south with the carriers *Enterprise* and *Hornet*, further reinforcing the area by landing the air group of the damaged *Yorktown* and such aircraft as survived from the *Lexington*. That would have been fine had the Japanese intended a replay of Coral Sea, but it would be useless against a Central Pacific offensive.

At this point the codebreakers in Melbourne played a critical role in changing American strategy, a contribution to the Midway battle hardly noted which deserves recording. Laurence Safford once rated Rudy Fabian the Navy's third-best codebreaker (after Rochefort and Ham Wright) and Tom Mackie as fourth. Now they showed their stuff, along with language officer Rufe Taylor. Melbourne's first key contribution was a decrypt showing that the Japanese had abandoned the plan for amphibious landing at Port Moresby in favor of an offensive across the Owen Stanley Mountains. This made Halsey's carriers superfluous in the South Pacific and enabled Nimitz to justify recalling them. CINCPAC deceived the Japanese, ordering Halsey to make sure he was seen before returning, and Halsey turned back a Fourth Fleet move against Ocean and Nauru islands by being spotted by a search plane flying from the Solomons base Tulagi.

Another Radio Melbourne coup was decryption of a First Air Fleet order that showed when Nagumo intended to leave his training bases and marshal forces for the operation. Rufus Taylor, it is said, became the first to unravel the planned date for the Japanese attack on Midway when he spotted a second occurrence of a certain time-date group in a Japanese message. Traffic analysis performed at Melbourne identified every ship in the Japanese order of battle, reportedly missing just one transport. Melbourne watched the Japanese buildup and knew from it that the operation would be either against Midway or Hawaii. At one point, one Melbourne codebreaker remembers, either Fabian or Rufe Taylor came into the room and said, "Now you guys be sure of what you're writing because they're moving aircraft carriers on the basis of what you guys are saying."

Melbourne's intelligence confirmed Rochefort's at Pearl Harbor. That satisfied Ernie King, who cabled Nimitz on May 17 his full agreement with the latter's belief that the Japanese were about to attack Midway. Laurence Safford observed after the war that if Melbourne and Hypo had not agreed, OP-20-G's diffuse fears for Alaska might have held sway. As it was OP-20-G was not convinced of the Midway objective despite its agreement, months before, that the designator AF now appearing in traffic stood for Midway. Nimitz's staff concocted a celebrated test which induced the Japanese themselves to confirm the identity of the objective. There are various versions of the idea for this ruse. Jasper Holmes claims credit for suggesting to Rochefort that fresh-water supplies were a constant concern on Midway, and a supposed problem with them would surely attract Japanese attention. Rochefort himself did not recall exactly who came up with the idea, but attributes it possibly to Layton, to himself, or to someone else at Hypo. Layton attributes the inspiration to Holmes. Nimitz approved the ruse, and a message went to Midway that it was to report back in an uncoded dispatch that there were problems with the fresh-water evaporator.

Midway's message was duly intercepted by the Imperial Navy special-duty group on Wake, where Nakamuta Kenichi had recently arrived as a young language student. Knowing nothing of the massive operation planned against Midway, Nakamuta was surprised that his colleagues were so interested in this seemingly incidental information pertaining to the American island. Wake sent out an immediate report of the water problem on AF, and Tokyo quickly informed fleet units that MI was short of fresh water. This dispatch was intercepted and broken by Melbourne. For added confirmation, the U.S. intercepted a Combined Fleet message listing new geographic designators that were to be used temporarily; AF was listed as MI.

There can be little doubt that the radio intelligence units in the field played the lead role divining the Japanese plans for Midway. Yet the achievement received faint praise from OP-20-G. The Midway segment of the secret history "The Role of Radio Intelligence in the American-Japanese Naval War," compiled in September 1942, treats in detail intelligence on the Aleutians (in which OP-20-G was interested) but begins its account of Midway only on the day of battle. Although the traffic discussions portion of the study contains the messages noted in this narrative, they are not highlighted in any way or featured in any summary, as is the Aleutian material. Similarly, in a 1946 lecture to trainees, designed to demonstrate the accomplishments of radio intelligence, then–Rear Admiral Joseph Wenger left out Midway altogether, proceeding directly from the Coral Sea battle to events later in the war. These were not odd lapses but tokens of competition between OP-20-G and units in the field.

In the meantime the capstone on the intelligence achievement at Midway was put in place by Hypo. This resulted from a long message from Yamamoto on May 20, his final operations order for the offensive. The American radio net picked up the transmission and the denizens of the basement of 14th Naval District headquarters got busy. Language officer Joe Finnegan, at the end of a twelve-hour shift, enlisted Ham Wright to solve the time-date groups in Yamamoto's order, and they worked on through the night. Joe Rochefort was also drawn into the effort. Though Jasper Holmes writes that Tommy Dyer participated as well, Dyer himself says he did not. Dyer also recalls that this internal time-date code had only appeared three times in Japanese messages, making Finnegan's and Wright's solution of it "a brilliant piece of work." Marine major Alva B. Lasswell, the cigar-chomping senior language officer, for whom Finnegan was "my strong right arm during World War II," also worked through that night translating the operations order.

"All I knew was I detected something important that night," Lasswell remembers. "I spent the whole night on it. . . . There were several problems involved, such as the area codes and grid. . . . I was sure of myself, but others thought I was wrong. . . . I don't think that Rochefort even knew I was working on this thing till the next day." Lasswell remembers the Midway break as his greatest wartime achievement.

Commander Rochefort had to go to bat for Station Hypo the morning of May 27, when Admiral Nimitz called him to Pacific naval headquarters for a personal briefing on the intelligence, still regarded dubiously by some on Nimitz's staff. Rochefort arrived a half hour late, having waited to get the final results of translation.

These were the last data there were going to be, for at midnight May 25 the Japanese had implemented their long-delayed code change, making JN-25(b) into JN-25(c) and denying the Allies further communications intelligence until the new code could be worked out. At the CINCPAC meeting Rochefort found Nimitz and members of his staff, including fleet intelligence officer Layton and James M. Steele, keeper of the CINCPAC war diary, who had been instructed to become a kind of devil's advocate regarding intelligence.

Rochefort proceeded to lay out an exposition of the Japanese plan, predicting that the Imperial Navy would commence operations in the Aleutians on June 3 and those against Midway the following day. He described the general features of the MI plan, including Yamamoto's disposition of forces. CINCPAC staff officers were slightly incredulous. Questions revolved around the room. Hypo chief Rochefort, who much preferred to be back in his lair, did not retain any clear recollection of the meeting. Nimitz's biographer E. B. Potter supplies additional details: Staff officers objected that such key orders were not usually sent by radio. They speculated that the orders might be fakes designed to draw out the Pacific Fleet, and questioned why virtually the entire Combined Fleet would be committed to battle for a small island in the Central Pacific and a minor adjunct operation in the forsaken Aleutians.

Commander Layton knew Nimitz had confidence in his codebreakers, and sure enough, the admiral now came to their rescue. The fleet commander argued the Imperial Navy might be moving in force precisely because it hoped to draw out the U.S. Navy and fight it. Nimitz observed that no one had any better information, then instructed his plotting-room people to begin tracking on the basis of the intelligence, keeping a constant check against all other sources. Nimitz gave Layton the same instructions; later he asked his fleet intelligence officer for more precise predictions.

"I have a difficult time being specific," Layton responded.

Nimitz fixed his glare on the intelligence officer.

"I want you to be specific," the admiral insisted. "After all, that is the job I have given you—to be the admiral commanding the Japanese forces and tell us what you're going to do."

"All right then, Admiral," Commander Layton essayed. "I've previously given you the intelligence that the carriers will probably attack Midway on the morning of the fourth of June, so we'll pick the fourth of June for the day. They'll come in from the northwest on bearing 325 degrees and they will be

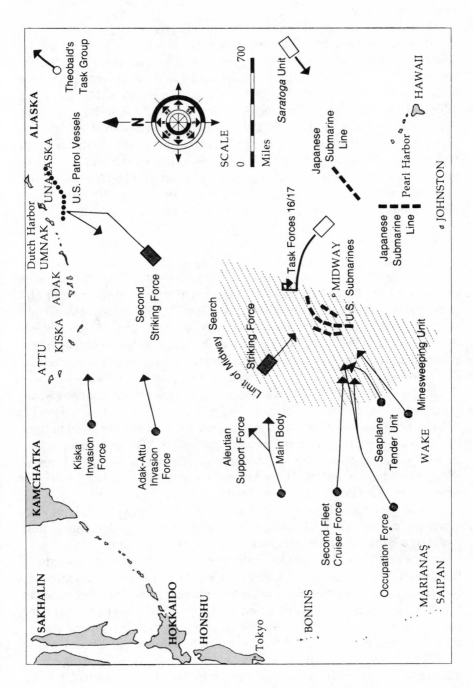

IV. Battle of Midway (Midnight, June 3, 1942)

sighted at about 175 miles from Midway, and the time will be about [6:00 A.M.] Midway time."

On the basis of his intelligence, Nimitz ordered the *Enterprise-Hornet* task force to a position northeast of Midway he called Point Luck. Bull Halsey had developed some kind of skin disease and had to be put in the hospital. In Halsey's place sailed Rear Admiral Raymond A. Spruance, erstwhile commander of screening forces. The task force returned to Pearl Harbor under full radio silence to prevent the Japanese from learning that the ships were not still in the South Pacific. At Point Luck they were joined by Admiral Frank Fletcher with the *Yorktown*, given temporary repairs from her Coral Sea wounds by swarms of Pearl Harbor dockyard workers in a burst of intense effort to get the ship out. *Yorktown* may have had bulkheads shored up with wooden braces, and elevators wired in place, but she could fly off planes, and that was the only thing that was going to matter at Midway.

*Y*ORKTOWN SAILORS HEARD PLENTY DURING THE DAYS JUST BEFORE MIDWAY. THEY HAD BEEN pressed into service to help the 1,400 workmen who tried to patch up the ship, and they had been worked ragged to load her for sailing. Her supply chief signed a requisition for seventy-five days of provisions. Steaming west, well at sea, Captain Elliott Buckmaster addressed the ship's company, just emerged from one bloody battle, to tell them the *Yorktown* was going to fight one more. The words were more prophetic than Buckmaster knew. He was thinking of taking the ship back to the States and giving the crew some leave. He did not know the *Yorktown* had just a few days of life left to her.

Lieutenant Commander John C. Waldron did not know either, but he, too, talked to his men, the pilots of Torpedo Squadron 8. "The approaching battle will be the biggest of the war and may well be the turning point also," Waldron told his pilots. "It is to be known as the battle of Midway. It will be a historical and, I hope, a glorious event."

Someone who knew a little more was Ransom Fullinwider. Having survived the demise of the *Lexington*, Commander Fullinwider plus a new mobile radio unit had been put aboard *Yorktown* to help Frank Fletcher, who remained task force commander. Fullinwider's team comprised volunteers from the Hawaiian intercept stations, among them Radioman Raymond A. Rundle, off on another jaunt to escape routine duty. The operators tuned to Imperial Navy frequencies and got an earful: The *Yorktown* happened to be traversing seas between Pearl Harbor and Midway that the Japanese were trying to interdict with submarines, thirteen I-boats of Squadrons 3 and 5. The Americans proved lucky—some of the Japanese submarines were delayed by a typographical error in their orders that started them off toward the wrong place, while others were older boats of a unit that staff had recommended be left behind. The upshot was that the first arrow in the Japanese quiver proved useless.

Meanwhile, Admiral Raymond Spruance refueled his Task Force 16 from an oiler on the last day of May, then proceeded to Point Luck, roughly 325 miles northeast of Midway. On June 1 Spruance sent all his ships a warning of battle, remarking that Midway would be attacked by four or five Japanese carriers, expecting a tough battle in which victory would be of great value to the United States. Fletcher and the *Yorktown* joined on June 2, and the next day the warships spent making final preparations. A Catalina flying from Midway that day discovered the Imperial Navy's MI Occupation Force, the amphibious group en route from Saipan. It was still 700 miles west of Midway. Admirals Fletcher and Spruance, with the former in overall command due to seniority, knew Nagumo's Kido Butai had to be near, probably under a bad-weather front north of the island.

Dramatic though it turned out to be, the battle of Midway unfolded for the Japanese with all the inevitability of a Greek tragedy. Harbingers of defeat came on June 3, when B-17 bombers attacked the MI Occupation Force without result. The Americans were definitely alerted. In the north, where Rear Admiral Kakuta Kakuji was to fling his carrier aircraft against U.S. Aleutian bases to deceive the Americans, dawn came blanketed by fog, delaying takeoffs. Captain Kato Tadao anxiously paced the bridge of his light carrier *Ryujo*, flagship of the force. Kakuta turned to his air officer, Lieutenant Commander Okumiya, who advised waiting until there was at least enough light to make visible the ships around them. The raid was launched late and accomplished little. In the south harbingers took the form of false alarms, fanciful sightings of American planes, until just before dawn of the fourth, when the sighting from *Akagi* appears to have been real. At this crucial moment the Japanese suffered because Commander Genda was down with a high fever and Commander Fuchida was recuperating from appendicitis. Nagumo simultaneously lost the services of the fleet's best air planner and flight leader.

Admiral Nagumo pressed on to his preplanned launch point for the air attack on Midway. There were 108 planes in all, led by Lieutenant Tomonaga Joichi, air group commander of the *Hiryu*. Tomonaga's strike group was seen by an American search plane on its way to Midway, then by radar as it closed in on the island. Navy and Marine fighters had the chance to reach good intercept positions, and they shot down two Kates and a Zero as Tomonaga's planes approached, damaging many others. Only hopelessly outclassed technology in the American fighters—twenty F2A-3 Buffaloes and just five F4F-3 Wildcats—spared the JNAF much higher losses. Two more Kates, a Val, and a Zero went down under anti-aircraft fire. The Zero escort, on the other hand, blew away nineteen intercepting fighters. The Midway raid did a certain amount of damage to American ground installations, but it was not enough. Lieutenant Tomonaga reported that another attack would be necessary.

While the raiders were off at Midway there were developments critical to the future of Kido Butai. The first sighting of Nagumo's carriers, reported without necessary details, was received aboard the *Enterprise* at 5:34 A.M.* A report with requisite detail came from a PBY at 6:03. This reported position was inaccurate by about forty miles, and mentioned only two of four Kido Butai carriers, but it furnished the target coordinates so vital to plotting flight routes. At 6:07 Admiral Fletcher ordered Spruance to attack as soon as Nagumo's carriers were definitely located.

When the initial sighting reports arrived at CINCPAC headquarters, sent in the clear but on Midway's undersea cable to Pearl Harbor, Admiral Nimitz immediately went into his operations plot room to find the location on the maps. Once Nimitz saw where it was, he turned to intelligence officer Layton.

"Well," Nimitz said, "you were only five miles, five degrees, and five minutes off."

LIKE THE AMERICAN CARRIERS, MIDWAY ITSELF LAUNCHED ALL AVAILABLE PLANES. FOR MORE than an hour beginning at 7:07 A.M., Nagumo faced recurrent air attacks from American planes, heavy bombers, torpedo planes, dive-bombers, even some fighters strafing. The ragtag armada arrived in groups of three, or four, or nine, or even alone, just as they went out, without waiting to form fancy formations. Japanese sailors were proud that their combat air patrol fighters intercepted most of these attack waves and their ships evaded every bomb dropped and torpedo launched during this phase of the action.

At about 7:30, while Tomonaga's planes were still winging back to the carriers, a floatplane from heavy cruiser *Tone*, one of those on the dawn search, suddenly reported American ships northeast of Midway. Like the initial American contact report, the first Japanese one lacked necessary detail as to ship types; this scout sent four successive reports, on things as far removed as the weather, before, prodded by the flagship, the scout replied, "The enemy is accompanied by what appears to be a carrier."

There ensued consternation on the bridge of *Akagi*. The report crystallized

---

*American messages must necessarily be cited from *Enterprise* dispatch files since flagship *Yorktown* did not survive the battle. They are as reported by Morison in his *Coral Sea, Midway, and Submarine Actions, May 1942–August 1942* (vol. 4). Japanese dispatches, unless otherwise noted, are taken from Admiral Nagumo's after-action report, translated and published by the Office of Naval Intelligence as *The Japanese Story of the Battle of Midway* (OPNAV P32-1002, June 1947).

everyone's worst fears. Chief of staff Kusaka, who had raised the question during final pre-mission conferences of what to do if U.S. carriers were met during the invasion, seems to have received no clear guidance despite the fact that the primary intention of the operation was to seek a Decisive Battle. Commander Ono Kenjiro, who had prematurely expressed his belief that there were no American carriers present, must have been mortified when the *Tone* plane updated its report. As Nagumo's intelligence officer, Ono should have made it his business to avoid such wishful thinking. Senior staff officer Oishi, consulted by Nagumo, failed to clarify his chief's thinking, observing the day before the battle that while the U.S. fleet continued to be the main object, failure to neutralize Midway would block the occupation operation. Admiral Nagumo was left to think he must do everything at once, and, on the morning of June 4, that was too much.

Upon initial reports, air officers on the Japanese carriers rearmed their second-wave aircraft. These had initially been prepared for antishipping operations, in case the U.S. fleet appeared, but when Lieutenant Tomonaga advised further attacks on Midway, the planes began to be reloaded for that mission. Everything was slowed down by the succession of strikes coming from Midway itself; ineffective though these might otherwise have been, the Midway attacks had the effect of increasing Japanese vulnerability at a key moment and slowing their own battle preparations. Nagumo ordered rearming suspended at 7:45, but then attack planes were increasingly shoved out of the way to launch fighters to defend the task force. When positive identification of an American carrier finally arrived, Kido Butai had already launched all the fighter aircraft assigned to the second-wave attack force.

These intercepting fighters joining the CAP achieved significant results against the early American attacks, especially beginning about 9:30, shortly after Nagumo turned to a northeasterly heading. As that turn was executed, the *Chikuma* sighted planes approaching from east-southeast, planes that turned out to be Torpedo Squadron 8 from the *Hornet*. The CAP interceptors accomplished fearful destruction of the American torpedo planes, obsolescent TBD Devastators that lacked speed, range, maneuverability, and defensive firepower. Every one of the fifteen planes was shot down, and only Ensign George H. Gay, floating on a life raft with the Japanese fleet all around him, then rescued by a Catalina the next afternoon, survived the ordeal.

Next after Torpedo 8 came Torpedo 6 from the *Enterprise*. Again CAP and anti-aircraft fire accounted for ten of its fourteen TBDs. Squadron skipper Lieutenant Commander Eugene E. Lindsey was not among those who came back. There were no hits. Finally attacked Lieutenant Commander Lance E. Massey's Torpedo 3 from *Yorktown*. Once more interceptors roared down on them, though at least the Japanese pilots had to fight their way through

Lieutenant Commander John S. Thach's escort. His Wildcats employed for the first time the maneuver that became known as the Thach weave. Torpedo 3, however, was nonetheless slaughtered—just two of thirteen TBDs returned to a carrier—and again there were no hits.

Despite all this the torpedo planes provided a huge boost to the chances of the dive-bombing units, diverting Nagumo's fighter defenses. When the torpedo plane engagement ended, dive-bombers were nearing Kido Butai and closing fast. The Japanese had no chance to regain altitude or position to intercept these new attacks. Moreover, due to imprecise initial position fixes on the Japanese, most dive-bombers had flown beyond the Nagumo Force, then turned back before they picked up the scent. This meant that they finally approached from the rear, precisely that quadrant of invisibility the *Hiryu* had identified in her Indian Ocean report. The dive-bombers burst upon the Japanese like a typhoon out of nowhere. Lieutenant Commander Clarence Wade McClusky with thirty-seven planes of Bombing 6 and Scouting 6 smashed *Akagi* and *Kaga*. The former was left drifting, engulfed in flames just three minutes after evading the last torpedoes launched against her. With forty planes on her flight deck being serviced, *Akagi*'s vulnerability to secondary explosions and fires proved vastly increased. Meanwhile, seventeen SBD Dauntless dive-bombers of Lieutenant Commander Max Leslie's Bombing 3 struck the *Soryu* and left her, too, in flames.

Ironically, it was the *Hiryu*, temporarily hidden under clouds to the north of the other ships, that survived the devastating bomber attack. She became the single battleworthy carrier left to Nagumo.

The *Hornet*'s dive-bombers, so low on fuel they had to fly to Midway after trying in vain to find the Japanese, were not even needed to accomplish the destruction of the Nagumo Force.

Commander Fuchida provides a graphic description of the situation aboard *Akagi* at this point:

> Unable to help I staggered down a ladder and into the ready room. It was already jammed with badly burned victims from the hangar deck. A new explosion was followed quickly by several more, each causing the bridge structure to tremble. Smoke from the burning hangar gushed through passageways and into the bridge and ready room, forcing us to seek other refuge. Climbing back to the bridge I could see that *Kaga* and *Soryu* had also been hit and were giving off heavy columns of black smoke.

Fuchida felt crushed. "The scene was horrible to behold," he wrote. Then the expert flier encountered Commander Genda. "We goofed!" the air planner simply said. The scene seemed beyond mere words.

Command of Kido Butai temporarily devolved on Rear Admiral Abe Hiroaki, next senior officer, while a poignant scene took place on the *Akagi*.

It was quickly obvious that Admiral Nagumo could not control the task force from the crippled *Akagi*, and Captain Aoki Taijiro, an Etajima class-mate of chief of staff Kusaka, promptly told his comrade that the air fleet commander and his staff should transfer to another vessel. Kusaka agreed but Nagumo insisted and refused to descend from the bridge. At first no one dared challenge the extremely hot-tempered Nagumo, and in the meantime flames crept closer to the island superstructure, until finally climbing down a rope became the only way to escape. Kusaka got staff officers to manhan-dle Nagumo down. Kusaka went down the rope himself, landing so hard he sprained an ankle, an injury to add to burns on his hands and feet. At 11:30 Nagumo's flag was raised aboard the light cruiser *Nagara*. As Admiral Kusaka later told interrogators, "That is the way we abandoned the *Akagi*—*helter-skelter, no order of any kind.*" (The italics are Kusaka's.)

Rear Admiral Yamaguchi Tamon on the *Hiryu* now held all Japanese hopes in his hands. Yamaguchi had long railed against Nagumo's indeci-siveness, and with his modernist outlook had just recently been pressing for a fleet reorganization that would have greatly increased the anti-aircraft firepower of the task force. But there was little satisfaction in the confirma-tion that he had been right, only great need for immediate action, and now Yamaguchi discovered that precious few resources for action were left to him. Airborne at 10:40 A.M., Yamaguchi's first strike against the Americans consisted of just eighteen dive-bombers, escorted by six fighters led by Lieutenant Kobayashi Michio.

Now American forces were in for much the same as had befallen the Japanese. Unlike their adversaries, however, Admirals Fletcher and Spruance knew the score. Aboard *Enterprise*, Lieutenant Gilven M. Slonim's radio intel-ligence unit overheard the original sighting reports from Japanese search planes. Slonim's boys could not understand all the follow-up reports, but did intercept one containing the word *kokubokan*, Japanese for "mother ship of aircraft"—that is, aircraft carrier. Since the word was the same singular as plural, Slonim could not tell if all the U.S. ships had been sighted, but the admirals heard enough to anticipate attack. That came at 11:40 A.M., and it went against *Yorktown*. Kobayashi's pilots scored at least three hits; sud-denly *Yorktown* was dead in the water and on fire.

The damage to the *Yorktown* was brought under control within just a couple of hours. The ship even got under way again. But Captain Buckmaster reckoned without Yamaguchi, and even as American sailors were thanking their lucky stars, a new Japanese strike was in the air. Yamaguchi's second wave was weaker than his first—just ten torpedo planes with six fighters to cover them—but they broke through all defenses and put two torpedoes into the *Yorktown*'s port side. "Abandon ship!" was soon ordered.

Naturally the crippling of his flagship brought the same sort of dilemma for Frank Jack Fletcher as it had for Nagumo before him. It also meant tribulation for Ransom Fullinwider's top-secret radio intelligence unit. Ray Rundle and his buddies were on the radios and, with all the noise, did not even realize the ship had been hit. They persisted in the face of hellish conditions, for the *Hiryu* bombing attack had put one bomb into the *Yorktown* right near the superstructure, where it penetrated the ship and ruptured the stack leads. This sent noxious stack fumes right into the radio intelligence compartment. First there was the smell of the exhaust gases; then little globules of soot and oil seemed to come right through the bulkheads. Before they knew it, the radiomen and their equipment were covered. Then the ship's vibrations ceased. Ray Rundle realized the *Yorktown* was without power or steerage way. Then Fullinwider arrived to make sure everyone had evacuated, because nearly everyone in *Yorktown*'s superstructure had already gone; now he found his radiomen still in place.

Admiral Fletcher made his own decision to leave the flagship. Commander Fullinwider helped here, too. He had been on the *Lexington* with another radio unit when she sank at Coral Sea. Now Fullie, as he was called, had perhaps more experience in this situation than anyone else around. Fullie stood on the flag bridge with Fletcher, watching sailors go over the side. Fletcher did not seem to know what to do.

"Admiral, follow me," Fullie said. "I've been here before."

A boat from cruiser *Astoria* was summoned for Fletcher and his staff, including the radio people. Their immediate thoughts were for the security of their intercepts and the RIP-5 Japanese kana typewriters, of which there were two. Rather than abandoning ship immediately, the radiomen stayed around to destroy documents. They dropped one RIP-5 into the ocean and lugged one to the *Astoria* whaleboat to continue their work. Radioman Tack Walford brought the last documents out of the radio shack.

By now the Japanese knew they were facing three American carriers, not one, and, because *Yorktown* had looked undamaged when the second attack wave hit her, convinced themselves there was just one carrier left. Yamaguchi determined to field a third wave to find it. Before he could, at 5:01 P.M. cruiser *Chikuma* saw more planes approaching, an assortment of twenty-four dive-bombers from *Enterprise* which wrecked *Hiryu*'s flight deck and left her afire. Yamaguchi and Captain Kaku Tomeo plus 416 other sailors would eventually be lost with the ship. One group of thirty-four engine-room people in a lifeboat were made prisoner. Interrogation of these prisoners provided Americans with inside information on the Japanese at Midway.

The Japanese were doing some interrogating of their own, and important intelligence was embodied in a 1:30 P.M. dispatch from Captain Ariga Kosaku, commander of Destroyer Division 4 on the *Arashi*. The destroyer fished a Torpedo 3 pilot out of the water as she was hunting for U.S. submarine *Nautilus,* which had been detected following an ineffective torpedo attack. This interrogation yielded the identities of the three U.S. carriers and details of *Yorktown*'s task force and of her voyage from Pearl Harbor. The prisoner who had divulged this information was apparently executed on the *Arashi*'s fantail later that day. (War-crimes investigators later discovered that all principals in this macabre drama were dead.) In a second similar instance, Commander Fujita Isamu's destroyer *Makigumo* got orders that afternoon to check on a mysterious red object in the water, seen from flagship *Nagara,* and ended up rescuing two *Enterprise* aviators. This interrogation yielded details of strength and installations on Midway itself. Again the prisoners perished, though at a time and by means that have never been established. After the war ONI investigators were unable to establish any details or trace responsibility, though they did uncover indications that skipper Fujita received some sort of reprimand for the disappearance of the Americans.*

That the Imperial Navy needed to pick up key data from prisoners in the midst of battle is a measure of the paucity of its intelligence going into Midway. Intelligence support turned out poor at best. Yamamoto's May 20 operation order contained a reasonable estimate of American strength at Midway and Hawaii *if* one considered the two places as a single objective area. In fact, the air strength at Midway was far greater than foreseen, while the Japanese were never sure whether Halsey's carrier task force (the one Spruance led at Midway) was not still in the South Pacific. Japanese special-duty groups, their radio intelligence organs, actually overheard aircraft messages indicating a carrier unit leaving Pearl Harbor, but they were unable to tell its destination, and Nimitz brilliantly carried through on the South Pacific ruse by having a cruiser in that theater begin to make heavy use of radio frequencies the Americans usually reserved for aircraft carriers.

One coup the special-duty groups did achieve was interception of a long submarine transmission the day the Nagumo Force left Empire waters. The transmission was interpreted to mean that the Midway attack would not be a surprise, but the realization appears to have made no practical difference to Nagumo, who failed to capitalize on the knowledge. Another Japanese gain was data indicating that the Americans had learned of the occupation force en route from Saipan. Once more the Imperial Navy took no advantage of the knowledge. The *Akagi* intercepted American transmissions and conducted simultaneous jamming, but that did not prevent her being turned into a burnt-out hulk.

Going into Midway, Admiral Yamamoto and his communications ace,

---

*In contrast, three American aviators were picked up in Aleutian waters by cruiser *Takao,* and nothing was done to them despite their steadfast refusal to divulge anything under interrogation.

Commander Wada, had concocted a radio deception plan under which the 1st Combined Communications Unit and the Kure Naval District commandant were to create the false impression that most of the Combined Fleet was training off southern Kyushu or in the western Inland Sea. But, given American intelligence on the Japanese plans, the scheme never had a chance.

That left Yamamoto, the top field commander, with rather poor intelligence in the face of the most serious crisis the Imperial Navy had faced in the war. The commander in chief sailed in the *Yamato*, roughly 600 miles behind Kido Butai, in the role of main body. His voyage began pleasantly enough. "White clouds drifted lazily across the sky," recounted Yeoman Noda. "The thin smoke which poured out of the stacks hung in the air like summer clouds over a field in May." It was perfect sailing weather, and many sang war songs at the top of their lungs. Even when the main body entered the weather front spirits stayed up, though tension grew, amid the ceaseless bellowing of foghorns.

The Combined Fleet staff followed a particular routine. The commander in chief, rising early, checked the weather and made for the elevator to *Yamato*'s bridge, six decks up in the conning tower. At breakfast time he was spelled by Ugaki. The meal would be served on the flag bridge (not the compass bridge) by Petty Officer Omi. It was quite difficult to move the hot food up into the place without disrupting other activities. Breakfast might be boiled rice, miso soup, egg, dried fish, and trimmings. After the food, staff usually stayed to discuss matters of concern, and chief of staff Ugaki would join in, his watching brief on the compass bridge taken up by Captain Kuroshima. Shorter staff discussions followed lunch and dinner, to review events of the day. The latter meal would be served more formally, in the staff mess, as on the *Nagato* but on the starboard side of the ship.

The day of battle began like the others save perhaps that officers arrived on the flag bridge earlier than usual. They knew this day would be crucial, not only because of planned attacks but due to indications the Americans might have something up their sleeves. On June 3, fully 72 of 180 messages detected as originating at Pearl Harbor had been urgent or of high precedence, very unusual traffic that hinted at trials to come. Yeoman Noda recalls Yamamoto as having had stomach problems for several days before the battle, but Omi Heijiro believes he was in fine health and had a normal appetite that day. Notice of Nagumo's attack came just as the main body itself set an alert for battle. To Noda the commander in chief seemed in low spirits. "The members of the staff were feeling very tense, thinking, 'Well, this is it!' "

As new messages arrived the picture they gave was the reverse of what the staff had hoped for. A dispatch reported Kido Butai under very serious attack. "Yamamoto and his staff bent their heads together in confusion and apprehension in the tiny bridge operations room," Noda recalled. More messages described the swiftly mounting toll: *Akagi* hit—*Soryu* afire—no possibility of putting out the fires raging on *Akagi*—*Kaga* hopelessly aflame—flag moved to *Nagara*—*Hiryu* hit by three bombs. "The members of the staff, their mouths shut tight, looked at one another," Noda said later. "The indescribable emptiness, cheerlessness and chagrin did not bring forth any tears."

Admiral Yamamoto made some effort to command the fleet. As he sat impassive, senior staffer Kuroshima proposed gambits to save the day. One lay at the foundation of the order the chief sent at 12:20 directing the Kakuta force of carriers in Aleutian waters to join Nagumo's remnants while the invasion convoy held back from the arena of battle. About an hour later, Yamamoto ordered all elements to concentrate and annihilate the U.S. fleet. The latter was tantamount to an order for surface engagement. Yamamoto also ordered submarines to the cordon line nearest the battle area. There was hope with news that *Hiryu* was striking the enemy, but despite the wishes for her protection that Commander Watanabe remembers being uttered in *Yamato*'s staff spaces, word of the last carrier hit and aflame came with a certain inevitability.

By midafternoon Yamamoto had received a situation report from Kakuta in the Aleutians. It was clear from his position plot that he could not reach Midway for days, and would have to refuel along the way. With no help there, the Combined Fleet still hoped to force a night surface battle, ordering Nagumo and Kondo forward with their forces, and reiterating the order to Nagumo when he persisted in withdrawal. Captain Kuroshima suggested a further wild scheme requiring the Japanese battleships to close in on Midway in broad daylight and shell it. Ugaki rejected the notion as foolhardy. Commander Sasaki suggested a go-for-broke air attack on the U.S. carriers with a force cobbled together from the light carriers *Zuiho* and *Hosho*, which were escorting Kondo and Yamamoto, plus battleship and cruiser floatplanes. That was simply not a serious option.

Far to the north there was a second main body, a battleship force supporting the Aleutians strike commanded by Vice Admiral Takasu Shiro in the *Hyuga*. There had been a panic of sorts the day before when someone saw an object that resembled a submarine; now the ships prepared for high speed to join the forces off Midway. It was the eighth day of sweltering work for the engine-room gang, toiling in a place where the temperature averaged 96 degrees even though they were in the cold North Pacific. A *Hyuga* diarist recorded:

> We, the engineer crew, who are the motive power of this ship, are watching the revolving engines day and night without an unguarded moment, and the countenance of each man on duty is flushed and tense.

. . . Sweat is pouring down from our faces and bodies; yet among these faces, there are some who are smiling.

Admiral Takasu probably was not smiling. Vice Admiral Hosogaya Boshiro, senior commander of the Northern Force, ruled that the Aleutian operations would proceed on schedule *except* for the recall of Kakuta's carriers. Though Takasu was under Yamamoto's direct command, his departure from the scene would rob Northern Force operations of any support whatever. Takasu had to remain in place; there would be no Decisive Battle for him.

In the end there would be no Decisive Battle for Yamamoto either—or rather, the battle was decisive but the decision ran against him. The *Soryu* sank of her own damages in the evening. American submarine *Nautilus*, thinking she was attacking *Soryu*, fired torpedoes at the derelict *Kaga*, but these are now thought to have been ineffective. *Kaga* nevertheless foundered, and the American submarine was credited with sinking *Soryu*. Ships were still standing by *Akagi* and *Hiryu* in hopes of quenching fires and taking the hulks in tow, but every minute added to the danger that an American air strike or submarine, like the *Nautilus*, would catch the rescuers and add to the toll.

The locus of decision was the *Yamato*, where Admiral Yamamoto barely moved his lips when speaking, and spent much time staring through binoculars at the horizon to the west. Yeoman Noda felt strangely distressed by "the sound of the wind howling incessantly in the rigging." The wind grew stronger toward evening, breaking the heavy silence that had settled in the operations room, where the only sound was the crimson curtain flapping over the porthole. After dark there was the usual chess match pitting Yamamoto against Watanabe and, indeed, some of the commander in chief's orders were rasped out as he huddled over the board. With time, heads became a little cooler, and Yamamoto realized how rash had been the order for a headlong chase against Americans with aircraft carriers plus the island defenses of Midway. He canceled the assault orders.

That decision crystallized the question of the derelict Japanese ships. *Hiryu's* problem became moot when Yamaguchi Tamon ordered destroyers to torpedo her. Yamamoto, who had once commanded the *Akagi*, was left to order her scuttling. Admiral Ugaki was overheard to say, "There is nothing else we can do, is there?"

Senior staff officer Kuroshima, according to Watanabe, voiced the ultimate objection: "We cannot sink the Emperor's warships by the Emperor's own torpedoes!"

The commander in chief made clear his heartfelt regret and said he would apologize to the Emperor for using Japanese torpedoes to sink Imperial Navy ships. This exchange or one like it is probably the one meant by Fuchida when he quoted staff officers as asking how the defeat could be explained to the Emperor. Yamamoto's reply is usually rendered, "I am the only one who must apologize to His Majesty."

*Akagi* sank toward morning after her captain, Aoki Taijiro, who had lashed himself to the anchor chain, was ordered off the ship by a more senior officer. He had no need to perish if it was Japanese torpedoes that were going to sink her.

Meanwhile, tragedy of a different sort was played out by an element of Kondo's occupation force. Rear Admiral Kurita Takeo's Cruiser Division 7 had been given the very dangerous task to close in and bombard Midway Island. Kurita had raced ahead at battle speed and, when Combined Fleet called off the operation, was too far advanced to get out of American aircraft range in time. Even worse, as Cruiser Division 7 turned away, heavy cruiser *Mogami* did not receive the order in time, and collided with sister ship *Mikuma*. *Mogami* lost her bow forward of the number one turret. *Mikuma*, though not impaired, was detailed to stay behind to accompany the stricken cruiser. During the day on June 5 American planes from both Midway and the carriers had a field day attacking this hapless unit, sending *Mikuma* to the bottom of the sea. Equally significant, photo reconnaissance planes snapped excellent pictures of the Japanese heavy cruisers, and these pictures settled beyond question the long-standing doubts at ONI over whether this class of Imperial Navy cruisers had been rearmed with 8-inch guns (they had) or retained their original 6-inch armament. Surviving prisoners gave the Americans even more intelligence.

The Japanese got in their last licks of the Midway battle on June 6, when Lieutenant Commander Tanabe Yahachi's submarine *I-168* fell in with the *Yorktown*, incredibly still afloat after all her travails. Tanabe sank the American carrier, firing four torpedoes, two of which struck her and another the destroyer *Hammann*, which succumbed to damage.

This final blow, nevertheless, did not equalize the results of Midway, and those results were further unbalanced by an event in the Aleutians, one that seemed inconsequential at the time but would have untold implications for the Japanese Naval Air Force. This resulted from Admiral Kakuta's second air strike on Dutch Harbor, which he carried out on June 4 before steaming south. Lieutenant Abe Zenji led the bombers on the strike, which included eleven Vals, nine Kates, and an escort of eleven Zeros. Over Dutch Harbor, or perhaps while shooting up an American Catalina that was downed that day, one of the Zeros sustained critical damage—a parted oil feed line—which made it impossible to regain her ship. The plane, *Ryujo*'s Zero Number 4593 piloted by nineteen-year-old Koga Tadayoshi, made a crash landing on Akutan Island, near which an I-boat had been stationed to rescue downed aviators. The plane flipped over on touching the ground, however, and Petty Officer Koga died in the crash. His wingmen, who had orders to destroy any Zero that had to land, could not bring themselves to fire at Koga's plane since they were not sure whether he had survived. They left the wreck intact, and it was discovered in July 1942 by Americans, who salvaged the Zero and found it still flyable.

By August the captured Zero was at San Diego, behind a stockade guarded by marines, and being rebuilt around the clock by shifts of workmen. Number 4592 was ready to fly again in late September and made many flights in U.S. service. This was no mere curiosity, but rather a gold mine of technical intelligence for American aircraft designers, who were able to develop planes superior to the Zero, and for combat pilots, who innovated tactics to counter it. The intelligence came in time to confirm hopes Americans had for the Grumman F6F Hellcat, the prototype of which flew for the first time on June 26, 1942. Production models and later versions benefited directly from knowledge gained from the captured Zero. Of 6,477 adversary aircraft destroyed by carrier-based planes during World War II, according to U.S. Navy records, 4,947 were shot down by Hellcats. Next to lost carriers, capture of a Zero may well have been the Midway result most detrimental to Japan.

Myriad are the reasons for the outcomes at Coral Sea and Midway. Allied advantages in radio intelligence stand high among them. Prescient knowledge went a long way toward offsetting Imperial Navy margins of strength. But intelligence is not the whole story. Already the Malay Barrier campaign had shown that even intelligence was of little use without real capability and the imagination necessary to use it most effectively. The often cited factor of victory disease is also inadequate, in my opinion, to explain these outcomes. Too facile by far, the notion that the Japanese were simply overconfident obscures as much as it explains. Other factors contributing to the outcomes include the Japanese shift from well-rehearsed (first-stage) to novel (second-stage) operations; the effort to apply a familiar doctrine of Decisive Battle to a completely alien and remote geographic region; the bifurcation of their own effort between Central and North Pacific foci; and the desire to save face, which resulted in clinging too long to a rash assault plan. Victory disease helps explain why the Japanese carried on despite a succession of oversights and weaknesses in their plan and individual errors of implementation, but surely one must turn to factors like service politics to explain why rigid commanders like Nagumo were kept in command, or why a Yamamoto could override the wishes of IGHQ. Moreover, there is nothing in the conventional explanations to show us, for example, that Japanese task force commanders were typically more tired than American counterparts because, in addition to their overall responsibilities, they were also the commanders of individual administrative units like carrier divisions or cruiser units. The extra workload hardly helped them concentrate on their strategic roles.

In view of the accumulation of small failures and myriad errors that grew into the setbacks at Coral Sea and Midway, there is a good case to be made that these Allied victories were not incredible but inevitable.

In the meantime the Combined Fleet began to head home from its ambitious adventure. The atmosphere was glum aboard flagship *Yamato*. Air officer Sasaki sat, seemingly in a daze, at the back of the operations room. "He looked as if he felt he was personally responsible for the defeat," noted Noda, "showing it in his growth of beard, his sunken eyes, his unhappy, weary face." Yamamoto looked ashen, his eyes strangely glittering. The admiral disappeared into his cabin for several days and ate little, until he appeared on the compass bridge sipping rice gruel.

"Is Genda all right?" That had been Yamamoto's question at the height of the battle. Noda puts it well: "Yamamoto in the midst of all the terrible blows . . . was all the more worried about the safety of Genda. . . . Genda alone could not be killed. He was a person essential to any revival."

Three days after the end of the Midway battle, with Yamamoto's Main Body still at sea and headed for Empire waters, there was a rendezvous with the remnants of the Nagumo Force. The engines of the *Yamato* suddenly cut out. The huge battleship coasted to a stop. Light cruiser *Nagara* came alongside. The *Yamato* quickly lowered a boat. After about a half hour dark figures mounted the side. One of them was Commander Genda.

# "The Most Imperative Problem at Present"

**T**HE DARK FIGURES MOUNTING THE DECK OF THE FLAGSHIP WERE NONE OTHER THAN KEY officers of Nagumo's staff arriving to give their story of the Midway action gone awry. In addition to Genda, the group included Admiral Kusaka, Commander Oishi, and First Air Fleet's flag secretary. Kusaka, rolled up in a mat to be lowered from *Nagara*, hated being handled like a package. Perhaps the handling was symbolic of the feelings that ran in the fleet at that moment. Admiral Ugaki went to some effort to make Kusaka feel that the Combined Fleet continued to hold him and his commander in high esteem, pressing yen into his hands and giving him gifts and explanations, but Kusaka could hardly remain unaffected by the loss of every one of the carriers with Kido Butai. At that moment the more important explanations were Kusaka's own—his descriptions of how the ships had been sunk, details of battle to flesh out sparse dispatches sent in the heat of action and the laconic battle report rendered toward the end of that terrible day.

Nevertheless the problem had already passed beyond the details of Midway, the concern now was getting on with the war. Chief of staff Kusaka appealed to Yamamoto, with tears in his eyes, to give Nagumo another chance, an opportunity to avenge the Midway losses. To Kusaka the commander in chief's eyes also seemed a little misty as he replied that they could have such a chance.

To have any chance at all required reconstitution of the carrier air arm of the Japanese Naval Air Force. It was, as Admiral Ugaki put it, "the most imperative problem at present." That was where Commander Genda Minoru came in, for having played a formative role in creation of the JNAF,

Genda was well placed to put the air arm back on its feet. He also had the combat experience to mold the reorganization along the lines modern warfare required. To begin work as speedily as possible, Admiral Yamamoto ordered that Genda be flown to Japan in a seaplane. Genda was about the only naval officer to return from Midway aboard an aircraft.*

The first bottleneck would be personnel. Most historians writing about Midway emphasize the Japanese loss of skilled pilots resulting from the carriers sunk, saying the JNAF never recovered from the loss. However, a substantial majority of Imperial Navy aviation experts interrogated after the war maintained that the JNAF was able to preserve the high quality of its pilot cadre right through the fall of 1942; there are differing opinions as to when the precipitous dropoff really began, but no one dates it from the Midway debacle. Genda himself, who managed the reorganization of the air groups, insists that fully two thirds of JNAF pilots with Kido Butai survived Midway, with the hundred or so lost concentrated in the attack squadrons.

A parallel issue rarely discussed is the loss of skilled *maintenance personnel* aboard the carriers. If anything the cadre of maintenance personnel was an even more crucial bottleneck than numbers of pilots, because maintenance men kept the planes flying. High serviceability rates meant more combat sorties and also helped preserve pilot cadres, since good maintenance reduced accidental losses. The JNAF rule of thumb was that eight ground-crew men were necessary for each single-engine aircraft and sixteen for each large one. Although exact data are lacking, by this standard air unit ground crews may account for as many as 2,600 of 6,200 sailors on the carriers at Midway. The number of ground personnel trained by the Imperial Navy establishment throughout 1942 amounted to roughly 6,100. Thus, even though some maintenance men, like many pilots, returned from Midway, losses amounted to a substantial fraction of the *total* replacement rate. Japan could not afford too many battles like Midway.

From the aircraft standpoint, losses were serious but not that bad. The Nagumo Force had had extraordinarily good luck in the months before Midway, losing only fifty or sixty planes in combat and twenty or thirty to other causes. Even though the entire plane complement of the carriers was then expended in this battle, wastage measured over the full period did not seem out of line. The JNAF lost 462 aircraft in the main combat categories

---

*Gordon Prange and his co-authors imply (*Miracle at Midway*, p. 361) that Genda returned to Kure aboard the *Nagara*. The Ugaki Diary, from which they appear to have been working, simply says that Admiral Nagumo's flagship was permitted to return ahead of other vessels. It contains no direct evidence on Genda. However, Genda himself told interrogators (USSBS No. 479) that he returned to Japan in an aircraft upon Yamamoto's order. Yeoman Noda also remembers Genda in a seaplane, though Noda recalls Genda as arriving, not leaving, in it.

from all causes in June 1942, but in all the period since December 1941 overall losses were 1,641, for a monthly average of 234. In February, at the height of the Malay Barrier campaign, monthly losses ran at 209; in May, with Coral Sea, the loss was 292. New production outpaced aircraft losses in every category save carrier-based attack and dive-bombers.

Therein lay the rub. In fact, pilot losses at Midway were also concentrated disproportionately in the attack and dive-bomber squadrons, precisely the units that had to brave all defenses to press home their attacks. Commander Genda saw a need to increase the number of fighters aboard each carrier as a result of war experience, but to a degree the Japanese also responded to necessity. To a significant degree Coral Sea and Midway set back the carrier attack units. In May and June, losses among *these* aircraft types amounted to 300 planes (out of 475 for the full period since Pearl Harbor), against production since December 1941 of fewer than 250. *Because of the loss of carriers*, there were fewer air groups to maintain at strength, and for the short run Genda and other JNAF authorities could preserve the force by reassigning personnel, but the long-run trend was definitely worrisome.

Reorganization became the rule throughout the carrier force. Carriers *Shokaku* and *Zuikaku*, now the big bruisers of the fleet, were reconstituted as Carrier Division 1 under direct command of Admiral Nagumo. The vessels that had gone to the Aleutians with Kakuta became Carrier Division 2, with light carrier *Hiyo* added to beef up the unit. Naval construction plans were modified to emphasize aircraft carriers with an order for a number of *Hiryu*-class ships under the 1941 program increased and a rush to convert seaplane tenders and liners into additional light carriers. The First Air Fleet and Carrier Division 5 were both deactivated.

The experience of Midway also induced the Japanese to pay greater attention to damage control. Only as recently as 1941 had the Imperial Navy, according to Commander Smith-Hutton's attaché reports, bothered to establish a school for damage control, but postwar investigation suggests that the "school" consisted of no more than courses established at the gunnery school in Yokosuka, the navigation school, the workshop and repair school, and the engineering school. Officers took a six-month course (double that in peacetime), enlisted men a four-month ordinary or five-month higher course. Trainees spent two weeks on temporary duty in each of the other schools to become familiar with their different approaches to damage control. The navigation school taught firefighting, counterflooding, and dealing with casualties; the workshop school course dealt with repairs and water-pumping techniques; the engineering course covered repair of machinery and equipment. The executive officer of each warship held responsibility as its chief for damage control.

Specialists staged demonstration fires using four old ships moored at

Yokosuka. Gasoline fires would be extinguished using foam. Another method was to shut up a compartment aflame and let the fire burn out from lack of oxygen, while cooling exterior walls with water. Either method would have been very useful at Midway, where three of the four carriers that sank were victims of fierce blazes, precisely from gasoline (and munitions), which had been brought out to service aircraft. As a result of Midway the Imperial Navy adopted new practices for aircraft carriers: Before battle all fuel lines would be drained, and refilled with inert gas to prevent fires. Munitions would be stored. Damage-control teams would be marshaled before fires started.

Another aspect of reorganization had to do with pilot training. The Japanese had expanded pilot training in 1941, not (initially) by watering down entrance qualifications or by increasing the number of training centers and groups (the first new training air group formed only in late 1942, though the number would balloon from fifteen to forty-eight during 1943–1944) but by increasing class size and easing graduation requirements. Ace Sakai Saburo in 1937 had been selected from among 1,500 applicants for a class of seventy students of whom just twenty-five graduated. That failure rate of 64 percent decreased to about 40 percent under revised practices. Koga Tadayoshi, the Zero pilot whose plane was captured in the Aleutians, had gone through the flying program in 1940 as one of a class of 260 students.

Part of easing selectivity, unfortunately for the Japanese, was paring back the number of flying hours student pilots received in training. Lieutenant Commander Shigeki Takeda, who went through flight training in 1939–1940, received about 330 flight hours, half of it in combat-type aircraft. A Luftwaffe pilot in 1939 averaged 260 flying hours (100 in combat types) and one in the Royal Air Force just 200 (65 in combat aircraft). Until December 1940 the JNAF distinguished between elementary, intermediate, advanced, and operational unit training, with flying hours allocated to each level. First the number of hours was cut back to less than 200; then elementary and intermediate flight training were combined, with progressive reductions in flying hours, until by 1944–1945, pilots were graduating with just 100 or 120 hours in the air, no firing practice, and only basic air tactics. By that time U.S. pilots were graduating with 400 flying hours, half in combat aircraft. The differences became obvious in combat.

In any case, before that nadir, in the heady days of 1941 the JNAF had massaged its programs enough to graduate 2,000 new pilots plus 2,500 air crewmen. In 1942 there were another 2,300 pilots trained. Commander Genda got bodies to replace fliers lost at Midway and in other operations. Inevitably, however, their experience levels fell, because they had both less training and less time in service. A typical formation leader in 1941 had logged about 1,500 hours in the air; a carrier-qualified pilot had

800–1,000; a land-based pilot averaged 600, an air staff officer 2,000. There were between 1,000 and 1,500 JNAF pilots who were carrier-qualified according to Genda. The Midway and Coral Sea losses, whatever they were, could be replaced. It was the future that would be a problem, for Midway ushered in a period of attrition warfare that never ceased.

One aspect of JNAF activity that could have stood some shaking up after Midway was the Bureau of Aeronautics' plans for aircraft development. Excepting the redoubtable A6M Zero, which would have many modifications, the Japanese carrier aircraft going into the war were old designs approaching obsolescence. The JNAF remained complacent, however, because a new generation of combat aircraft was already on the way, responding to specifications issued between 1938 and 1940. However, war experience taught lessons about the need for firepower, self-sealing fuel tanks, and armor on aircraft that could have been embodied in a new series of planes. Instead, very little was done until late in the war. Tinkering with existing aircraft consumed up to 40 percent of Japanese design manhours in 1943 and 60 percent the following year, only dropping in 1945 when the production of novel designs had become practically impossible. The supposedly advanced JNAF planes of the late war, aircraft like the Raiden (Jack), Shiden (George), Tenzan (Jill), Suisei (Judy), and others all originated before war experiences were available to improve design. In fact, a couple of pre-production Judy aircraft sailed to Midway aboard the *Soryu* to be used as scout planes in the battle.

The final Japanese failure flowed from the rhetorical stance Imperial General Headquarters chose to assume regarding the battle, playing it down. A June 10 IGHQ communiqué admitted the loss of just one aircraft carrier and only thirty planes. Within the Navy the single sunken ship was said to be the *Kaga*, and damage to the *Soryu* and *Mikuma* was admitted, but that was all. The Americans were said to have lost the *Yorktown*, a *San Francisco*–class cruiser, a submarine, and 150 planes. The *Enterprise* was said to be badly damaged, as in this account rendered later during the war: "Our fliers flew directly to the *Enterprise* and, striking her, met heroic deaths. All told the *Enterprise* took a total of six vital injuries, one after another, and the whole ship was wrapped in flames. Barely keeping afloat, she fled." According to this the United States spent $10 million turning Midway into a fortress *after* the beginning of the war and still barely managed to defend it.

Keeping the lid on the truth preserved the propaganda, but made it much more difficult for the Imperial Navy to learn from the Midway debacle. Sailors remained exhausted because no leave was given after the battle; wounded were spirited off their ships in the dead of night, their faces covered, and were put in isolation wards with no contact permitted—even doctors and nurses were barely allowed. The Yokosuka Torpedo School finally commissioned a major battle-lessons study, but to a considerable degree its conclusions were suppressed. After all, if Midway had been a success, who needed to learn from it? The experience brought great frustration to Commander Fuchida Mitsuo, study participant, who invested much in advocating a new naval doctrine. In the meanwhile the war marched on. Barely had the Japanese reorganized the carrier forces when new challenges arose in the *nanyo*.

THE AMERICANS TOO HAD AN IMPERATIVE AFTER MIDWAY, ONE THAT CAME PRECISELY FROM fear that their success with the Japanese codes had been compromised. It began with the Sunday edition of the *Chicago Tribune* on June 7, which contained a front-page story asserting that the United States had known the details of Japan's plans to attack Midway. There followed consternation at the Navy Department, where Ernie King was furious at the breach of security and ready to crucify the officer who had leaked this information. The *Tribune* story carried a Washington dateline and its gist was repeated in the Washington *Times-Herald* and other papers (though, significantly, *not* in *The New York Times*). When Commander Arthur H. McCollum, ONI Far East intelligence maven, arrived at his office that morning he encountered the flap in full progress. "The place was shaking," he recalled, and was told that Admiral Charles M. Cooke, Jr., wanted to see him immediately. Wondering how these emergencies all came on Sundays, McCollum went to see "Savvy" Cooke, a senior aide to naval commander in chief King, who practically accused him of giving the story to the *Tribune*. The two argued until McCollum heatedly asked for a chance to compare the news story with data in ONI files. Cooke allowed him to do so.

Commander McCollum went back to the Far East Division and got out his files, which contained notes copied from Nimitz's warning to his admirals of Japanese plans and strength before Midway. McCollum immediately noticed that the *Tribune* story not only had the same information as the Nimitz dispatch, but also identical errors and communications garblings. McCollum went up the hall to Rear Admiral Wilkinson, director of naval intelligence, and showed him what he had found. Ping Wilkinson marched straight toward Ernie King's office, with McCollum chasing him to beg that he *not* show the Nimitz dispatch to King, since it was contrary to communications regulations for ONI to have material from operational dispatches. Wilkinson, a little deaf anyway, paid no attention. Admiral King predictably exploded, but his own communications officer, Carl Holden, was able to show that all five formal copies of Nimitz's dispatch were properly accounted for. No one at the Navy Department had talked to any *Chicago Tribune* reporters either. The leak had occurred elsewhere.

That afternoon Admiral King gave a news conference in Washington at which he supplied a different version for why American carriers had been off Midway awaiting the Japanese. Then King went off the record to complain of the compromised secrets. The newspaper, its publisher (a vocal opponent of the Roosevelt administration), and the author of the report were threatened with legal action. Navy Secretary Frank Knox gave the case to Attorney General Francis Biddle, who announced on August 7 that a grand jury would convene to study treason charges against the newspaper. There were five days of hearings as the panel listened to editors and journalists but no naval officers.

There were no naval officers because in the meantime the Navy had traced the leak to the transport *Barnett*, plying the Pacific with survivors of the *Lexington* aboard, including *Chicago Tribune* reporter Stanley Johnston. Among the survivors was Johnston's good friend Commander Morton T. Seligman, former executive officer of the *Lexington*, who shared a cabin with the reporter and permitted him to see classified dispatches. One of these was Nimitz's Midway warning, which had been recirculated in a lower-grade code by the South Pacific command. Johnston took notes on the message, and later left the ship to fly to Chicago. He alighted the day before the Midway battle with time to write. Because Johnston had never sought war-correspondent credentials, he had signed nothing obliging him to submit his material to censorship. Commander Seligman was denied further promotion and left the Navy under a cloud, but the legal case against reporter Johnston was not strong, especially once ONI expert McCollum got Wilkinson to recognize that no prosecution could be successful without divulging details of OP-20-G's codebreaking success. McCollum made the same argument to Savvy Cooke. Plans for prosecution evaporated.

The *Chicago Tribune* affair continued to reverberate down the corridors of power long after the events of Midway. It was a factor in 1944, when secret emissaries went to Republican presidential contender Governor Thomas E. Dewey with a letter from General George Marshall to dissuade the politician from making any use of what he knew about codebreaking at Pearl Harbor. The Marshall-Dewey correspondence referred explicitly to both Coral Sea and Midway and argued that the United States still used knowledge of Japanese activities gained from codebreaking. Inside the Navy, a portion of the secret history (completed in April 1943) of codebreaking in the American-Japanese naval war argued that the Japanese changed *all* their codes after Midway as a consequence of the *Chicago Tribune* affair.

As with many aspects of the history of Pacific intelligence, truth is not obvious and the case is far less compelling than conventional wisdom would have it. The Japanese had no easy means of ascertaining what had been written in the *Chicago Tribune*. There were no known agents in the United States. The diplomatic corps, including naval attachés, was sequestered at a resort in Hot Springs, West Virginia, and had all the American news sources they wanted, but at this precise moment they were beginning to move to New York for repatriation and access was cut off during the period of transit. Publications programs run by embassies in South America were curtailed because Japanese in a number of those countries were also being sequestered and repatriated, while at the same time, the *Chicago Tribune* was not *The New York Times* and was not watched assiduously for intelligence.

The Japanese *did* change some codes and communications practices to a significant degree after Midway, but one must question whether this action was not part of a *general* tightening of security. The one key code implicated in the Midway disaster, the fleet code (JN-25), the Japanese initially *left untouched.* They had changed this system just before Midway and would do so again later, but in a way that suggests routine rather than emergency. This does not accord with the arguments of those who believe that the Japanese *knew* their main code had been broken.

This is the place to dispose also of the *Nankin* affair. The *Nankin* was an Australian steamer outbound from Fremantle that was captured in the Indian Ocean on May 10, 1942, by the German raider *Thor.* Mail carried by the ship, like that taken by another German raider from the *Automedon* before Pearl Harbor, included secret documents, in this case four issues of a New Zealand weekly intelligence summary on their way to the British Eastern Fleet commander. James Rusbridger wrote in a 1985 article that the summaries showed increasing Allied knowledge of Imperial Navy dispositions before Midway, ergo the conclusion the Japanese must have been able to tell that JN-25 had been compromised. *Thor* handed over these summaries to her supply ship *Regensburg,* which delivered them to the German embassy in Tokyo upon docking at Yokohama. Attaché Admiral Paul Wennecker cabled the gist of the material to Berlin, which gave him permission to pass the documents to the Japanese, a task Wennecker accomplished at the end of August. Rusbridger writes that fears for the secrecy of communications led Japan and Germany to conclude a special agreement on September 11 under which the Germans gave Japan some five hundred Emigma machines during 1943. Meanwhile, according to Rusbridger, Japanese security improvements denied the U.S. intelligence from codes well into 1943, blinding them during key battles of the Guadalcanal campaign.

There are a number of problems with this thesis, starting from the fact that it is not clear the New Zealand reports contained U.S. radio intelligence material. Even if classified "Most Secret"—the slug the British usually gave to documents containing code material, it is not possible to infer that Ultra was involved. Other kinds of intelligence also received that classification, New Zealand's security practices did not necessarily correspond to British, and anyway neither the Germans nor the Japanese had any inkling of the use of "Most Secret" in connection with code material. Moreover, it was common practice for intelligence organizations to estimate Japanese fleet dispositions and movements based on material other than Ultra—for the United States both ONI and Pearl Harbor's area command (14th Naval District) did this weekly or monthly. Next, as will be seen presently, certain U.S. radio intelligence units received secret commendations for some of the same battles in which Rusbridger maintains the U.S. suffered unexpectedly severe losses due to the alleged intelligence blackout. Finally, it is true that the Germans gave the Imperial Navy five hundred sets of the Enigma "T" machine—a specially wired version of the commercial machine—but Germany also supplied special "G" model commercial Enigmas to Italy and her Eastern European minor allies. Clearly the intent must have been to secure joint communications, not to shore up ailing Japanese code security.

The Imperial Navy was perfectly able to improve security all by itself, but the actions the Japanese took in the summer of 1942 suggest a general focus more than a crisis response. In July they introduced a low-level code for Army-Navy liaison in the Solomons, and a patrol-vessel cipher. There were major changes in August (*before* receipt of the *Nankin* material): termination of an operational and communications intelligence code used since November 1941; modification of one submarine code and discontinuation of another; introduction of a code for communication with German merchant vessels. Message serial numbers wholly disappeared from Imperial Navy radio traffic. The fleet changed radio call signs in mid-August, began using a special code to report Allied activities, and in September introduced new codebooks for merchant-ship messages and for the administrative traffic of posts in the *nanyo*.

In August (some sources say December) the Japanese began use of a new general-purpose, high-grade fleet cipher, a machine-based system the Allies called Jade (Japanese called the machine the 97 Siki Inziki—1, 2 Gata), which used twenty selectors (electrical pathways) instead of the sixteen in the Purple machine. Jade at first carried a lot of traffic, but then its use tapered off until Jade virtually disappeared by August 1944. Only a certain number of Jade machines were built and their use was restricted to bases on land. One expert speculates the Japanese curtailed Jade to conserve scarce metals for war production. Another American, one of the codebreakers who had worked on Purple, offers the opinion that the machine was weakened by a draftsman's error in drawing its blueprints and thus Jade did not stand up to field use. The system's unpopularity also stemmed from Japanese preference for documents over typescript dispatches (Jade could not handle kanji characters). American codebreakers broke into Jade relatively quickly, and by August 1943 had recovered their first data from messages sent in Jade.

In any case the 1942 period saw important changes in standard procedures for communications. Beginning in April the Japanese started using a new series of call-sign books and switched call lists every seventeen days. After Midway they increased the frequency of list changes and began use of a new set of books on September 1, a date that had to be pushed back a month due to distribution problems. At that time the Imperial Navy further strengthened communications security by providing each station two call signs, one for normal use, the other for use only when supreme security was required. Such secure call signs would be changed daily. Moreover, in July 1942 the Japanese began to utilize a procedure standard in the U.S. Navy whereby operating units used a single, general call sign and their messages were repeated by land stations to the addressees, thus disguising the originators of messages. At first such procedures could be countered by making time studies of the sequence of rebroadcasts, thus identifying the general area of origination, but later this, too, became more difficult.

These changes very much seem parts of a program rather than responses to a specific security breach, and failure to modify JN-25 is the dog which did not bark in the night. At the same time, we know from the Japanese postwar monograph on communications that there were fears after Midway that some codebooks had been lost and seized by the Americans. Certainly simple aircraft codes and geographic grid material could have been lost on the aircraft shot down over Midway and in the Aleutians. Combined Fleet staff took the position that any compromise of codes posed no immediate danger. The Central Agency, that unit of the Navy Ministry responsible for creating codes, agreed. A new codebook, called the RO Book to distinguish it from the D Code, began to be distributed by the Navy library. Destroyers and aircraft completed delivery to most Combined Fleet units by early September. Distribution throughout the China Area Fleet required another month or two, and the code was put into effect only toward the end of 1942. Thereafter the Imperial Navy made plans to change major codebooks every six or twelve months, additive tables within one to six months (rather than every six to twelve months, as before), tactical codes every month, and call signs once a month, with modifiers applied every day or once a week.

In view of the fact that it had taken almost two months to circulate a revised codebook just to the most important elements of the Combined Fleet, even with full cooperation of that fleet plus a sense of urgency, further security measures seemed necessary. In December 1942 the Japanese created a Communications Defense Countermeasures Committee chaired by the Navy's chief of communications, initially Rear Admiral Kaneko Shigeharu, and including members from the Naval General Staff, the communications school, the Bureau of Aeronautics, the Yokosuka Air Group, and the Navy Ministry, plus technical research experts. The timing of the committee's creation, and its broad study of security, again suggest that the Japanese were coping with a generic problem rather than a specific breach. Furthermore, the fact that at this late date, when a communications security group *was* established, it received no *specific* mandate to counter a code breach indicates the Japanese lacked any knowledge of the revelations by Stanley Johnston and the *Chicago Tribune*. The codebreaking secret was safe even as both sides went on to new intelligence breakthroughs.

ALTHOUGH RECENT SCHOLARSHIP HAS BEEN DELVING EVER MORE DEEPLY INTO THE SAVAGERY and racial biases of the Pacific war, it is a measure of the careful diplomacy on both sides that they proceeded to exchange diplomats. Despite the surprise attack on Pearl Harbor, which so many considered an act of treachery, it was the United States that made the initial proposal for repatriation of diplomatic staffs, on December 13, 1941. Moreover, despite bitter and desperate hostilities, the sides were willing to ensure safe passage through vast war zones of Japanese and Swedish liners, the ships to meet at the Portuguese African port Lourenço Marques. The result of the exchange would be an intelligence windfall for both sides.

This is not to say that Tokyo, Washington, London, and other interested parties did no haggling over these exchanges. Such differences consumed months following Tokyo's January 5, 1942, acceptance of Lourenço Marques as the site of exchange. Nevertheless, the process was essentially straightforward and the end was never in doubt. In the meantime Japanese diplomatic and consular staffs spent their time at the Greenbrier, a luxury resort owned by the Chesapeake and Ohio Railroad and set amid the Allegheny Mountains in West Virginia. The Japanese enjoyed continued access to American media—newspaper, magazines, and radio—and were free to compare notes with German and Italian diplomats who were also housed at this hotel. Details of the exchange more or less settled, at about the time of Midway the Japanese were moved to New York and put aboard the Swedish liner *Gripsholm* for their voyage. Official Japanese were all aboard by June 11. Following last-minute disputes over who else would be included, the *Gripsholm* sailed on June 17. She stopped in South America to pick up additional Japanese, then crossed the Atlantic to round the Cape of Good Hope and make for Portuguese East Africa.

The Americans (and British) repatriated represented but a small fraction of the 24,400-plus who had been in the Far East in the spring of 1941. A number of those returned of their own accord before the war; others had made for Nationalist-controlled parts of China. The ones now being exchanged included such key persons as military and naval attachés and journalists. The Americans had been interned in their own embassy compound. They, too, were allowed to read the national press, including the

English-language *Japan Times and Advertiser,* and were permitted one small radio to listen to the news, but the level of information was so poor that on the day of the Doolittle raid people in the American embassy could not tell whether there had been a real air raid or not. Food was scarce, as was fuel in the face of an especially harsh winter, and embassy wives made clothes out of the drapes. There were bridge and poker every day, and an assistant attaché figured out how to lay a nine-hole golf course around the apartments and swimming pool. Some played badminton, others just waited.

On June 17 Japanese police took the Americans from their compound, through Tokyo streets cleared of passersby, to the train station. Rear Admiral Nakamura showed up to bid farewell to attaché Henri Smith-Hutton. The Americans trained to Yokohama, where they boarded the liner *Asama Maru,* which moved into the harbor, but then sat until June 25 or so awaiting final route changes and clearances. The *Asama Maru* picked up additional passengers at Hong Kong, Saigon, and Singapore. The Italian liner *Conte Verdi* carried Americans from places in China. In all some 2,768 Westerners were included in this exchange against an equal number of Japanese.* There was a shipboard romance on the *Asama Maru,* as well as other minor diversions. As the ship negotiated the Sunda Strait, Commander Smith-Hutton looked out for wreckage left from the battle in which the *Houston* came to her end. The Chileans, Canadians, and Brazilians aboard the ship gave the contingent an international flavor.

When the *Asama Maru* reached Lourenço Marques on July 23, the *Gripsholm* had not yet made her entrance; the *Conte Verdi* followed in about two hours, and the *Gripsholm* late that afternoon. Exchange of passengers commenced the next morning. Lieutenant Commander Ethelbert Watts of ONI checked that every listed passenger was in fact transferred. Relieved to have escaped from the cooks on the *Asama Maru,* who managed to turn good basic ingredients into tasteless meals, Smith-Hutton found a fine smorgasbord laid out on the Swedish liner. All the new passengers delighted in it. On the trip back Smith-Hutton and Major Gregon Williams, the erstwhile Shanghai spy, got orders to use any means necessary to get a roll of Japanese film that was being carried by a certain Chilean journalist, film showing scenes of Japanese victory in the first stage of the war and clearly meant for Japanese propagandists in South America. The Tokyo attaché and the Marine spy broke into the journalist's compartment, ransacking luggage until they found the film hidden in a shaving-soap container. Washington's orders for this mission evidently resulted from an intercepted Japanese diplomatic message.

---

*Some sources put the figure at just 1,400. The discrepancy may lie in the difference between total numbers exchanged and the figure for Americans aboard the exchange vessels.

Commander Smith-Hutton also brought back intelligence of his own. This included complete sets of the *Japan Times* and the Tokyo *Nichi Nichi* through his day of departure, bulky collections concealed among his wife's numerous trunks, which the harried Japanese neglected to inspect. Even more important were several shipping yearbooks with basic data on Japanese merchant vessels, and Smith-Hutton's card-index file, with biographical details and personality notes on every Imperial Navy officer in the rank of commander and above. On his own person Smith-Hutton carried a journal with details of events and observations during internment.

When the *Gripsholm* reached Rio de Janeiro on her return voyage, Smith-Hutton and his assistant received orders to fly back to Washington. The urgency of intelligence work cut short the trip.

The Japanese got an intelligence boost of their own from the returnees, some 1,400 of whom arrived at Yokohama on August 20. Among them was Admiral Nomura, but certain other naval officers were gone. Just like the Americans, the Naval General Staff ordered key intelligence people off the *Asama Maru* when she touched port at Singapore. Washington attaché Yokoyama Ichiro; his assistant, Sanematsu Yuzuru; air attaché Terai Yoshimori, and radio intelligence expert Wachi Tsuneo all arrived in Japan by plane. Without skipping a beat the NGS sent them to the Naval War College to war-game the Japanese-Allied conflict. The simulations went on right through October, using one big room at the school, under top-secret conditions. The returnees played the Americans, with NGS operations staffers in the Japanese role, relying upon the best intelligence available from the *joho kyoku*, and the best economic data assembled by experts from the Total War Research Institute. Fewer than ten officers participated on the respective teams, which submitted one turn plan per week to the umpires. Starting from Australia, Admiral Yokoyama's "American" team advanced step-by-step through the islands, capturing Guadalcanal and New Guinea, and driving right to the Philippines, where they planned an invasion at Lingayen Gulf on Luzon in late 1944, game time. The simulation bore an uncanny resemblance to the actual evolution of the war, but the NGS did not yet know that when, having had too much, it halted the proceedings. The Navy made little apparent effort to capitalize on the synthetic experience provided by this secret war game.

Nevertheless the Imperial Navy made good use of personnel from the diplomatic exchange. Captain Yokoyama was sent to sea for a year as skipper of the light cruiser *Kuma*, but after that he became a top aide to the navy minister. Commander Sanematsu immediately found himself drafted into the American section of *joho kyoku*. There Sanematsu, later a captain, worked through the rest of the war as "Staff Officer A," the man in charge of projecting total U.S. strength and predicting American intentions. Commander Terai became an NGS operations staff officer. As for Tsuneo

Wachi, also promoted to captain, he became chief of staff of the Owada Communications Unit, the Imperial Navy's radio intelligence organ.

As the Navy's top American expert, Captain Sanematsu found himself repeatedly lecturing on the United States to students at the Naval War College. Serving officers the first year refused to credit his account of the strength of American shipbuilding or his prediction that German U-boat successes would begin to go flat. They talked of Sanematsu behind his back as an America-lover. The following year the student officers sat with rapt attention as Sanematsu rendered his judgments on American prowess. By 1944 the officers, returned to war college from the front, were telling Sanematsu that his lectures *underestimated* the Americans.

The Japanese plainly found their personnel exchanges useful even in the midst of war. The Americans did, too. After the first one the State Department still had a list of 7,050 American nationals whose repatriation it deemed desirable. They ranged from business figures to family members of combatants, people like language officer Stephen Jurika's mother. She had been offered the opportunity to get out on the *Asama Maru* after Jurika learned of the exchange program, but she had no desire to leave the islands in which she had passed most of her life. Jurika understood, and anyway he was preoccupied in the days before Midway with informing *Hornet* fighter pilots of the fine points of the Zero fighter. In any case, one dispute after another delayed a second exchange; it began only on September 2, 1943, when the *Gripsholm* sailed with another 1,340 Japanese aboard, many of whom had been interned in South American lands. American returnees this time were primarily from Japan. Washington worried that returnees would furnish aid to the Japanese war effort, though little of that had been found (exclusive of the military and naval personnel) on the first exchange: One Japanese returnee had been captured on Guadalcanal; a second managed an English-language newspaper in Singapore; one other was making propaganda radio broadcasts. For the second exchange there were worries regarding former Japanese residents of Hawaii, and various other categories of individuals whose release might prove detrimental to American national security. More than the first round, when diplomatic personnel were at stake on both sides, the second exchange proved an exercise in finding common ground. There never would be another.

IT IS VIRTUALLY IMPOSSIBLE TO SAY ENOUGH ABOUT THE CONTRIBUTIONS OF PREWAR INTELLI-gence pioneers like Henri Smith-Hutton, Arthur McCollum, and the others. Without their language experience and intelligence savvy the Pacific war would have gone on longer and been a great deal bloodier even than it was. Smith-Hutton, in particular, did much to help equip the United States for conflict with a nation whose language hardly anyone here could even speak. Aside from shepherding young language officers through their time in Tokyo, Smith-Hutton's procurement of Japanese textbooks and grammars furnished raw material for a wartime language-training effort that was clearly going to be necessary.

But Smith-Hutton was not alone as a visionary among ONI officers. Others, too, helped create resources for teaching Japanese linguists. One key figure was Albert E. Hindmarsh, then a lieutenant, later a captain, who went to Art McCollum at the end of 1940 to propose a survey of Japanese-language capability in the United States. To understand just how visionary this was, one need only know that OP-16-FE, the Far East section of ONI, at the time comprised a *total* of six substantive experts plus one clerical worker; war with Japan loomed but was by no means a certainty. McCollum got behind the idea and took it to the director of naval intelligence, who forwarded it to the chief of naval operations, then Admiral Harold Stark. The survey would be approved in February 1941 and Lieutenant Hindmarsh became the primary action officer conducting it.

What the Navy discovered was hardly reassuring, though it was not as bad as *Life* magazine later made out, claiming that there were only about a hundred Americans qualified in Japanese. In fact the Navy was able to identify 650 Caucasian Americans fluent in the language, though that was few enough, and there were just five or six universities offering courses in Japanese. Completed in August 1941, the Navy survey indicated that a mere sixty Caucasian students were at that time enrolled in existing Japanese-language programs. Within the Navy itself just a dozen of the language officers were rated as capable of everything from translation to interpreting in a technical and dynamic context; the two dozen or so others were assessed as translators only. In terms of Japanese-language skills the picture could only be termed a crisis.

Al Hindmarsh took the lead, planning for, then actually organizing, a new Japanese-language program tailored to Navy needs. The program was designed to give students enough of the language to become translators in about fourteen months of study. There were two shortcuts that could be tried to jump-start the effort; the Navy took them both. One was to find Americans of Japanese ancestry; the other was to search for Caucasians who already had some Japanese. In both cases the Navy would simply have to furnish technical knowledge and matching vocabulary to make its initial crop of fresh Japanese linguists effective. Some of them could then train others.

Hindmarsh, professorial and seemingly humorless, a stocky fellow of medium build, attended a conference of Japanese teachers and networked among them. He found a home for the new Navy language program on each coast—at Harvard in the East, and at the University of California, Berkeley, for the West. From the 650-name list the Navy found fifty-six persons willing to sign on, and split them in two groups for the training.

Edward Van Der Rhoer became one recruit to the language program. A New York boy, studying Japanese with a Buddhist priest who had a church near Columbia University, holding down a liquor-store job in Washington Heights, Van Der Rhoer tried to enlist only to be rejected for poor vision. Writing direct to ONI, he wound up being interviewed in Al Hindmarsh's office. The next thing Van Der Rhoer knew he was at Harvard, thrown together with such characters as a New York taxi driver, a poet who had learned ideographs to read Chinese verse, an engineer born in China, a Denver dry-cleaner, and a businessman who had worked in Japan. One student was the son of a missionary and had grown up in Japan, then come out before the Far East boiled over and the *Gripsholm* became the last route to freedom.

Professor Serge Elisséeff headed the Harvard-Yenching Institute, which conducted the East Coast program. Before the Navy arrived, Elisséeff had had Japan scholar Edwin O. Reischauer as an associate, three good junior instructors, and twenty students. Suddenly the Navy more than doubled the latter figure with their group of twenty-five. With the war come, Elisséeff and Reischauer decided to start an intensive course in elementary Japanese in February for the spring semester rather than awaiting the fall as was the usual practice. Instead of the usual five or ten new students, or even the "somewhat" larger group they had expected, they found a hundred prospective linguists in the lecture hall. The two professors used a Rockefeller Foundation grant to collaborate on a reprint edition of a Japanese-English dictionary brought over from Tokyo.

Scion of a prominent St. Petersburg family, Elisséeff had learned his Japanese as a boy living in Tokyo. A later refugee from Soviet communism, he was distinctive in America as one of the few Western graduates of Tokyo Imperial University, and at Harvard would for a long time be thought of as the leading American scholar on Japan. Probably because of this, Elisséeff was not prepared to teach in the fashion the Navy wanted, or use the materials it provided, as Lieutenant Commander Hindmarsh discovered during a February 1942 inspection. He took steps to terminate the language program at Harvard. Van Der Rhoer's class with its various characters would be the last. The Harvard-Yenching Institute began to work with the Army, and Edwin Reischauer would end up in Washington teaching classes of Army codebreakers.

Meanwhile the Berkeley program, superficially more disrupted than the Harvard one due to the exclusion from the West Coast of Japanese citizens and of nisei, in the long run did better. The exclusion, a travesty based upon misguided fears that Japanese-Americans posed some kind of security threat, resulted in virtual incarceration for more than 120,000 U.S. citizens and gave many others the worst kind of excuse to discriminate against fellow Americans. Issued by General John L. De Witt after an executive order FDR signed on his recommendation, the exclusion prohibited Japanese or nisei from residing within 700 miles of the Pacific coast. It was issued at a time of hysteria, when a few Japanese submarines were loose in the eastern Pacific, shelling a couple of places in California, starting forest fires in Oregon from floatplane sorties, but accomplishing nothing truly serious. De Witt's order proved far more deleterious to American security than anything it prevented—resettlement slowed the war effort, while nisei resentment robbed the United States of the services of many of America's best Japanese linguists. Those nisei who served despite the obstacles and racism they encountered rendered a great service and should be considered doubly patriotic. This goes for the nisei infantry of the 442nd Regiment, which fought in Italy, those of the 25th Division's original regiments in Hawaii, and those who are our concern here, the Japanese linguists.

Apart from anything else the exclusion order made recruitment of nisei linguists far more difficult. The Marines, for example, with even fewer language officers than the Navy, began right away to seek linguists. The most natural recruiting grounds were right in California and Hawaii, where many nisei resided. Major Alva Lasswell was sent several times to San Francisco on temporary duty to interview prospective linguists who were brought to brush up their Japanese and learn technical terminology in a class at the University of Hawaii. After the exclusion order, the Marines could no longer recruit on the West Coast.

Both the Navy and the Army had language classes in the San Francisco area. The Army's, at the Presidio, was forced to displace to Minnesota. The Navy's program at Berkeley moved to Boulder, Colorado (and later to Minnesota as well). Miss Florence Walne, who had directed the Navy effort, continued in charge, while all employees were paid by and materials furnished through the University of Colorado. Beginning in June 1942 nisei and Caucasians worked elbow to elbow in the mountain air. The Navy program proved so successful that in early 1944 it added courses in Russian, Chinese, and Malay, becoming a school of Asian languages. By then a number of universities had begun elementary-Japanese programs that served as feeders to the Navy effort, which itself graduated or had in training over 800 Japanese linguists. The program trained linguists for the Marines, for naval intelligence, even ten Japanese speakers for the Royal Navy. At last there was significant Japanese-language capability to fuel the intelligence effort.

MANY FRESH JAPANESE LINGUISTS—INITIALLY, PERHAPS ALL WHO WERE NOT TAKEN INTO OP-20-G or ONI—found their way into the so-called advanced intelligence centers that sprang up at Pearl Harbor, in the South Pacific, and in Australia. The idea evolved from application in Washington of a British concept, which was to have a place where data regarding friendly and enemy forces could be pooled and put in focus for commanders to make operational decisions. In simple terms one can think of the notion as a fusion of information; at the intelligence level such fusion meant combining inputs from all the many sources available, and displaying the result to those making the decisions.

The Royal Navy called its concrete application of this fusion concept an operational intelligence center. This unit at the Admiralty proved quite important in turning back the U-boat challenge, and figured in such naval actions as pursuit and sinking of the German battleship *Bismarck*. America's application of the fusion concept was not exact, but the widening use to which it was put places the concept at the forefront of techniques that helped the United States regain the balance in the Pacific even before the fruits of superior productive capacity began to be felt. Fusion began right at the top, with the President's Map Room, and extended down, ultimately, to every major warship, where fusion took the form of the combat information center.

This development started in the Navy while Admiral Harold Stark was still the chief of naval operations. In early 1941 the CNO created a Combined Operations and Intelligence Center in straightforward imitation of the British, putting it under an admiral who didn't understand fusion or really want the job. When Ernest King became CNO and COMINCH, he asked his flag secretary, Commander George C. Dyer, to relieve the ineffective chief, who in fact had two captains subordinate to him. Not wanting to ruffle the feathers of so many superior officers, Dyer objected. Admiral King promoted Dyer (no relation to Thomas) to captain on the spot and transferred the captains away to smooth the path. In January 1942 King signed a directive transforming this war room, and also setting up a fleet intelligence branch within ONI. Virtually simultaneously Captain John L. McCrea went to the White House and set up the President's Map Room, starting with just a desk and two file cabinets. Copies of operational and intelligence messages went to these war rooms, where results were displayed for commanders.

Arthur McCollum's division at ONI provided support for the fleet intelligence branch that sustained the situation room at the Navy Department. Though changes expanded his own unit to the unheard-of size of twenty-five people, McCollum looked askance at the proliferation of war-room-type facilities all over Washington. To place this kind of activity on a firmer basis McCollum and others advocated full-scale operational intelligence centers. Admiral King approved this idea in June 1942, and subordinates planned advanced intelligence centers, the prototype of which would be set up at Pearl Harbor. The Washington unit was restyled the Combat Intelligence Branch and its previous role in dissemination of reports was eliminated, though it continued responsible for merchant shipping notices and a display center. The frontline units, advanced intelligence centers, would become true focal points for fusion of all-source intelligence data.

In the meantime Captain George Dyer had a mind to get back to the fleet.

The Combat Intelligence Branch job had been an important function, but it was not a command or a good post on a fleet staff. Dyer eventually wangled a billet on the staff of a newly forming amphibious force. By then it was high summer 1942 and the *Gripsholm* transfer had been accomplished. Arthur McCollum suggested Commander Henri Smith-Hutton as a suitable replacement for Dyer, and that became the former Tokyo attaché's assignment. At the same time, however, the staff supporting the Combat Intelligence Branch was taken out of ONI and located within OP-20-G. This became the first in a series of moves in which radio intelligence organizations effectively shut the Office of Naval Intelligence out of the business of current operational information. Eventually OP-20-G developed a virtual lock on naval operational intelligence, at least at the Washington level, while ONI functioned primarily as a producer of basic and static intelligence such as ship and aircraft characteristics or geographic area studies.

Ambiguities remained on the administrative side, however, in that the Office of Naval Intelligence retained formal responsibility for manning the situation room, displaying intelligence from OP-20-G. In March 1943 the situation room's ONI title was changed to OP-16-FP, with the final letters meaning "foreign plot." The room itself was rebuilt to incorporate the latest display technology, and it became the locale for the critical morning staff meeting held daily by the secretary of the Navy. In attendance would be the assistant and undersecretaries, the Navy commander in chief, his deputy, his chief of staff, the vice chief of naval operations, the commandant of the Marine Corps, the commandant of the U.S. Coast Guard, and staff division chiefs and bureau heads as necessary. Shortly after the D-Day invasion of France a new arrangement was adopted whereby Secretary of the Navy James Forrestal's 9:30 A.M. staff meetings were followed at 11:00 by ONI's own daily staff conferences.

An indirect but nonetheless telling indication of the growth in importance of the situation room lies in the fact that its director, Captain A.V.S. Pickhardt, went on to be deputy director of naval intelligence, replacing the long-suffering Ellis Zacharias.

There is quite an important story in the creation and growth of the field fusion units, the so-called advanced intelligence centers, a story that includes the final struggle between OP-20-G's Washington wizards and poor Joe Rochefort at Pearl Harbor, but before that happened there were explosive naval developments in the South Pacific. These need to be related before the intelligence story can be further advanced.

# Chrysanthemum and Cactus

FRANKLIN ROOSEVELT'S STRATEGIC DECISION, MADE LONG BEFORE THE BATTLE OF MIDWAY, in fact before the war ever began for the United States, was to focus on Europe first. Sanctified in conferences with the British at Placentia Bay in the summer of 1941, then with Winston Churchill in Washington immediately after Pearl Harbor, the Europe-first strategy acquired the aura of dogma. The Pacific war was to be a simple holding operation. More than anyone else, Ernest J. King became the man who made that dogma change. Admiral King argued that the United States could not afford to play a merely passive role in the Pacific; he fought for sufficient reinforcements to permit counteroffensive activities. The Navy chief won his point, convincing other members of the Joint Chiefs of Staff to support a limited offensive. In the aftermath of Midway a counterattack seemed even more logical. Americans were still unsure of the degree of their success—several of the Japanese warships sunk at Midway continued to be carried on ONI's order of battle for the Imperial Navy for some weeks—but victory was palpable and certainly merited follow-up.

Given a desire for offensive operations, the question became where. The prewar Orange plans, of course, provided for operations in the Central Pacific, capturing islands in the Mandates or perhaps the Marshalls and Gilberts. But Japan's southward advance drew American eyes to the need to preserve sea-lanes to Australia. The Japanese arrival at Rabaul in January 1942 made the threat concrete, a threat unmistakably demonstrated in the Coral Sea. When President Roosevelt held a meeting to discuss Pacific strategy with the Joint Chiefs in early March, Admiral King spoke in favor of putting bases south of the Solomons, perhaps in the New Hebrides and New Caledonia, then driving up into the Bismarcks. In mid-April, planner Admiral Richmond Kelly Turner put flesh on the notion with a paper defining a four-stage plan to include halting the Japanese, then an offensive through the Solomons and New Guinea to capture the Bismarck Archipelago. Turner was soon sent out to form a South Pacific amphibious force while Admiral Nimitz raised the possibility of hitting Tulagi. In late May, the South Pacific command was carved out of Nimitz's and MacArthur's respective areas and put under Vice Admiral Robert L. Ghormley, formerly chief of the U.S. naval mission in England.

As American attention fastened upon the southern Solomons, Japanese activities there further increased the importance of the area. Parties of Japanese sailors from Tulagi began to circulate throughout the surrounding islands, including the big one across the bay, the island known as Guadalcanal. At first the Japanese merely traded for fruit and fish, but before long aviators began to search out a site for an airfield. They found one at Lunga Point on Guadalcanal. First Yokohama Air Group commander Captain Miyazaki Shigetoshi reported the find; then a survey team from Rabaul came down to confirm his opinion. The Midway defeat just a week later forced the Japanese to begin considering means of defense, not least island airfields to replace sunken aircraft carriers. On June 13 the Naval General Staff decided to put an airfield on Guadalcanal, and engineering teams twice visited the Lunga Point site. On June 19 a team accompanied Vice Admiral Inoue Shigeyoshi, Fourth Fleet commander, on the first inspection of Guadalcanal by a senior naval officer. In Tokyo the Navy reached agreement with the Imperial Army on a defense strategy for the Solomons and adjoining regions, consecrated by IGHQ Navy Directive Number 109 and called the SN Operation.

By then the Japanese were a going concern on Guadalcanal, actual detachments having arrived June 8. Airfield site preparations began on the twentieth, and on July 6 a twelve-ship convoy delivered heavy equipment along with 2,600 men of the 11th and 13th construction units. The Japanese burned off the vegetation, installed a rail track for carts to haul fill, and laid out a single-runway airstrip, which they began to clear and grade. In early August the strip was so advanced that the naval command accepted the latest of several proposals to send aircraft to Guadalcanal.

Unknown to the Japanese their chance to use the airfield was already almost gone. On June 24, with the strip still in early stages of construction, Ernest King ordered Chester Nimitz to prepare to seize Japanese facilities in the Tulagi area. A Joint Chiefs of Staff directive governing the planned invasion, christened Operation Watchtower, appeared on July 2. At that time Major General Alexander A. Vandegrift arrived in New Zealand with his 1st Marine Division, chosen to be the combat force. Vandegrift had quite a time

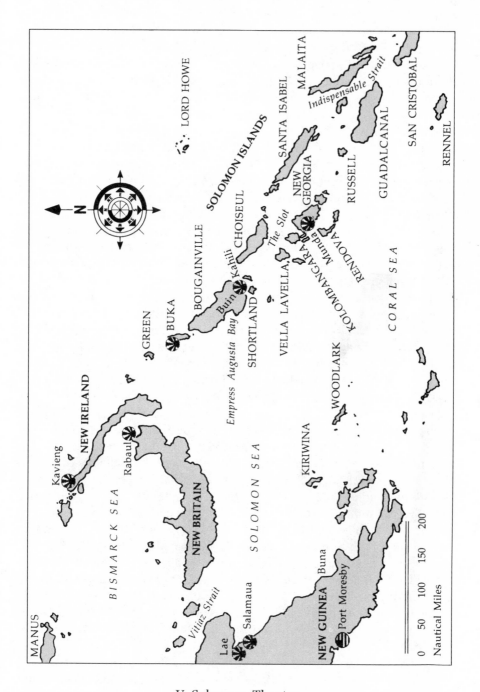

V. Solomons Theater

pulling together the disparate elements of his division, scattered across the South Pacific from Samoa to Wellington, and a mix of cadre left after forming new units with completely green recruits. This force had been slated for a major landing little more than a month away.

Not the least of Vandegrift's problems was intelligence. Coastwatchers of the redoubtable Ferdinand organization, which had headquarters in the northern Australian settlement of Townsville, reported the Japanese arrivals and correctly analyzed Imperial Navy activity as preparation of an airfield. There were four key coastwatchers in the Guadalcanal vicinity. On Florida Island, overshadowing Tulagi and across the strait from Guadalcanal, was Donald S. MacFarlan, who had broken a bone in his foot while snooping around near Lunga Point in July. Actually stationed near there was Lieutenant Commander Hugh MacKenzie, Ferdinand chief for Guadalcanal, earlier instrumental in helping beleaguered Australians escape from Rabaul and New Britain when the Japanese took it over. At the western end of Guadalcanal was F. Ashton (Snowy) Rhoades, joined by an older man, a Norwegian former trader named Leif Schroeder who had come across from Savo Island after the Japanese visited there looking for him. At Aola Bay, to the east of Lunga, was Martin Clemens, a young fellow with the colonial service who volunteered after Pearl Harbor. Clemens's boss, Donald Kennedy, had been district officer on Tulagi until the Japanese occupied it, then made his way to Malaita, then to New Georgia, where he became another key coastwatcher. Finally on Bougainville, almost overlooking the Japanese forward naval anchorage at Shortland Island, was Paul Mason, a plantation manager and radio expert with twenty-five years' experience in the islands.

The coastwatchers reported Japanese movements well enough, but General Vandegrift lacked all kinds of basic intelligence he needed to plan an invasion; things like the gradient and firmness of the beaches, the depth of streams, the extent of Japanese fortifications, were all unknowns. Lieutenant Colonel Frank B. Goettge did his best to solve every intelligence mystery. As 1st Marine Division D-2, or intelligence officer, Goettge seemed a little out of place. A football star at Ohio State, he was a man of action, hardly the cerebral sort. Nevertheless Goettge dealt effectively with MacArthur's headquarters for information available in Australia, and he canvassed Wellington for every scrap of knowledge regarding Guadalcanal and its environs. The objective soon acquired a code name: Cactus. Tulagi became Ringbolt. Friendly bases acquired code names too: New Zealand was Spooner, Espíritu Santo was Button, and Efate was Roses; the code for Midway was Balsa.

Colonel Goettge brought eight former Guadalcanal residents to meet Marine planners in New Zealand, pumping them for information. Memories, old pictures, sketches, everything was plumbed for intelligence value.

General Vandegrift recalled getting information on streams near Lunga Point that turned out to be dead wrong. MacArthur's intelligence officer, then-Colonel Willoughby, promised aerial photography of the objectives, and apparently the Southwest Pacific Command actually assembled mosaic pictures of Cactus and Ringbolt. But the photos were forwarded to the wrong address and the 1st Marine Division never got them.

Vice Admiral Ghormley has generally received short shrift from historians but deserves good marks on the matter of aerial photography at least. It was a result of Ghormley's effort that the U.S. Navy began to take a serious interest in the technique, after he observed its use by the British in the European war. From London in the spring of 1941 Ghormley got the Navy to send a delegation to see what he saw, and the Navy sent Captain Gooderham McCormick and Lieutenant Commander Robert S. Quackenbush, Jr. The Marines dispatched Captain Charles Cox. The group spent three months with the British and returned with many training materials. It took Ghormley just a few weeks to convince the Navy to start a school for photographic interpreters. Located in the Washington district called Anacostia, the school had as its first instructor Commander Quackenbush, affectionately called Q-bush, who became one of the Navy's premier photo spotters. When Admiral Ghormley went to the South Pacific he demanded a photo interpretation unit with Quackenbush in charge.

Commander Quackenbush found himself summoned to the office of the assistant chief of naval operations for air, who asked how many sailors would be needed for a field unit. Quackenbush asked for fifty, but the admiral snorted and seemed concerned that the men wouldn't have enough work to keep them busy.

"In the Fire Department," Q-bush shot back, "the men have nothing to do for days on end, and they sit around playing cards and loafing. But when there's a fire you're glad they're there."

Quackenbush got his interpreters, and the Watchtower forces got at least some of the photography they needed. Forrest Sherman, commanding the carrier *Wasp* during the Guadalcanal operation, noted in his after-action report that an aerial photo mission flown on August 2 plus radio intelligence had given his pilots all they needed for their invasion support mission.

Standing before his admiral's door, message flimsy in hand, Commander Ohmae Toshikazu realized he had been thrown among extraordinary events. The forty-year-old commander had arrived in Rabaul just three weeks before, relieved to be with the fleet again after five years in shoreside billets. The message in Ohmae's hand reported American troops landing at Tulagi, proof positive that Ohmae's new post as operations officer on the staff of the newly created Eighth Fleet was not going to be the backwater garrison job he might have feared. Not since Shanghai, when Ohmae as a young destroyer skipper had skippered the lead ship into the maelstrom of the Woosung landing, had there been a moment of such danger.

Of moments of delicacy there had been plenty. It had been Ohmae who, as an officer in the Military Affairs Bureau of the Navy Ministry just before Pearl Harbor, conveyed sealed orders to the captain of the liner *Tatsuta Maru* instructing him to terminate his voyage to the United States on the first day of hostilities and return to Yokohama. That time a loaded pistol went with the orders, whether to help the captain enforce them or greet his ancestors not specified. There had been other delicate moments in the mid-1930s, when Ohmae was assigned to U.S. duty as an Imperial Navy language officer. It was among the celebrated prewar exploits of American intelligence that Ohmae had been distracted in Davenport, Iowa, by the favors of a young lady for long enough to enable Americans to photograph the code materials he carried with him. Later ONI watched Ohmae as he allegedly serviced Japanese networks on the U.S. West Coast.

More than some ordinary spy, however, Ohmae was a well-rounded naval officer ideally suited for an operations staff. A torpedo specialist, one of a group with a sort of cowboy reputation in the Imperial Navy, he had nevertheless earned high marks at Naval War College. Ohmae also had a solid reputation from the Navy Ministry, where he served in one of the most difficult sections. In short, Ohmae had wide background and great insight into naval operations and planning. At Truk, where the newly established Eighth Fleet staff conferred in late July 1942 with Fourth Fleet officers, Ohmae confirmed his reputation for his new boss, Vice Admiral Mikawa Gunichi. The operations staffer made cogent points while Admiral Inoue's Fourth Fleet officers professed a total lack of concern for matters in the Solomons. Ohmae and Mikawa found Japanese Army eyes focused upon New Guinea, where the Army planned an effort to get at Port Moresby by an overland route. Meanwhile naval officers, unaware of the truth of the Midway outcome, had no reason to think the Americans were itching to conduct an offensive.

Japanese radio intelligence, the vaunted special-duty group, identified a new American headquarters in the South Pacific from the pattern and volume of U.S. message traffic. From Tokyo the Owada group suggested on August 5 that Allied traffic patterns indicated happenings in the *nanyo*. The fleet's own 8th Communications Unit detected changes in Allied messages as South Pacific forces marshalled for Watchtower. One staffer later claimed that he deduced from the pattern the objective might be Guadalcanal.

These signs were straws in the wind. At Rabaul the principal concern had been finding planes to advance to Guadalcanal, and the transfer had finally been scheduled when, on the morning of August 7, Admiral Richmond

Kelly Turner and General Vandegrift appeared off that island and began landing 13,500 Marines.

Now Commander Ohmae stood at Admiral Mikawa's door, holding a report of the invasion. Mikawa answered the knock quickly, then ordered a preliminary concentration of forces. By the time he had dressed and walked the block's distance to headquarters there were reports confirming landings on both Tulagi and Guadalcanal. Captain Kami Shigenori, fleet senior staff officer, seconded to Rabaul from NGS, recommended a night surface attack. The hyperaggressive Kami was a known hothead—in Tokyo he had astonished even Baron Tomioka by pressing for an attack on the Panama Canal—but at least he had a concrete idea of what to do. Kami was also well connected, being an academy classmate of Combined Fleet staff officer Miwa Yoshitake, not to mention Kato Kenkichi, executive officer of Mikawa's own flagship, the *Chokai*. Though a poll of Combined Fleet staff showed a majority opposed to an attack, Admiral Yamamoto, who happened to be close to Miwa, gave the go-ahead. Eighth Fleet headquarters, at the former Rabaul Club on Court Street, then became the scene of more heated discussions.

Admiral Mikawa was especially concerned that his available warships had never worked together, except for the cruisers of Goto's Cruiser Division 6. He knew also that carrier aircraft were active around Guadalcanal. Mikawa, who had commanded the screen forces of Kido Butai until shortly before Midway, could not miss the significance of that fact. And he knew from intelligence that a U.S. task force that could augment the Allies had steamed out of Pearl Harbor on August 2 (actually this force had left Fiji a day earlier and thus was even nearer than feared). It is a measure of Mikawa's fighting spirit that he went ahead to order the attack Kami recommended.

Eighth Fleet included Goto Aritomo's four heavy cruisers, two old light cruisers of Cruiser Division 18, and a destroyer division of which in reality just a single ship, the *Yunagi*, was present. The fleet flagship, Captain Hayakawa Mikio's heavy cruiser *Chokai*, was herself en route to Manus and had to return to Rabaul to pick up Mikawa. Goto's ships, which had been scheduled to revert to command of Fourth Fleet, had been a bone of contention at recent Truk staff conferences, and Mikawa had appealed for their support of his small force. Based at Kavieng, the cruisers were at this instant dispersed, half at that port and half with *Chokai*, and all had to join to make an attack.

According to an estimate of the situation made that day, Mikawa believed it possible to defeat the Allied fleet regardless of strength by decoying it within range of JNAF strike aircraft. By noon Mikawa and staff had completed a preliminary plan and radioed it to Tokyo. At NGS, Admiral Nagano, considering the idea reckless, initially ordered the plan quashed but reversed himself after talking to Baron Tomioka's planners. At about 2:00 P.M. the *Chokai* entered Simpson Harbor, Rabaul's fine port, and a half hour later Mikawa's flag, a Rising Sun ensign topped by the broad red stripe of a vice admiral, flew on her mast. Captain Hayakawa immediately got his vessel under way to rejoin Goto's cruiser division. Unknown to the Japanese, the Allies had six heavy and two light cruisers off Guadalcanal, and south of that island Admiral Frank Fletcher had three aircraft carriers backed by a battleship and six more cruisers. If the battle had not turned out as it did, Admiral Mikawa's bravery would have seemed foolhardy.

Indeed, what followed was a battle of many ironies. Not only might Japanese have avoided such an engagement, right-thinking Allied officers might have anticipated it. The 14th Naval District's Combat Intelligence Unit had repeatedly reported Japanese cruisers at sea in the Rabaul area. While the Imperial Navy ships were actually engaged in transport and escort missions among the Bismarcks, the mere fact that they were operating could have indicated to Allied commanders a high probability of a surface attack. At least one of the American captains, Howard D. Bode of the heavy cruiser *Chicago*, the former chief of foreign intelligence at ONI, was well equipped to interpret such indications. Allied intelligence also had a good count on the actual strength of Japanese naval forces in the Solomons, with the single exception of crediting them also with having present the heavy cruiser *Suzuya* (actually running convoys into Mergui at this time). In fact, Goto's ships were seen at Kavieng by a photo mission on August 2. A further reconnaissance mission over Rabaul the day before the invasion placed eight cruisers and destroyers at anchor there. Mikawa actually came down The Slot, as the waters between the Solomon Islands soon became known, with five heavy and two light cruisers plus a single destroyer, eight warships in all. Richmond Kelly Turner, amphibious force commander, actually asked for supplementary air searches for August 8 over the very waters Mikawa traveled through. They were not carried out. On the other hand, Mikawa actually was spotted and shadowed by an Australian search plane, but the contact reports reached the fleet off Guadalcanal just hours before the Japanese attack.

In the ultimate irony, American radio intelligence intercepted Mikawa's dispatch to NGS reporting his plan to leave in the *Chokai*, join Cruiser Division 6, and proceed to Guadalcanal, thereafter operating against the Allied convoy depending upon reconnaissance results. The dispatch gave time of departure, from which progress could be charted, as well as identifying the major Japanese units involved. Unfortunately codebreakers did not succeed in breaking out this message until August 23, weeks after the battle of Savo Island.

The battle, on the night of August 8–9, took its name from the island off the northwestern tip of Guadalcanal, land that quite naturally split The Slot into two, effectively providing two approaches to the anchorage in which the Allied invasion transports lay. To block both, Australian admiral Sir Victor Crutchley divided his ships into two groups, each with three cruisers and a couple of destroyers. Crutchley himself was in the heavy cruiser *Australia* with the southern group, but Turner summoned him to the transport anchorage for a meeting, so Crutchley missed the actual battle. The ships from his group had been with Crutchley's Task Force 44 since before the Coral Sea battle and were familiar; he kept them together. The other three cruisers Crutchley had never seen before, but at least they were all U.S. Navy and so had common methods and doctrine. Admiral Mikawa's Japanese ships cleared for action in the evening and assumed line-ahead battle formation before dark.

It was the southern group that Mikawa's ships saw first, with Captain Bode on the *Chicago* the officer in tactical command. Destroyer *Blue*, which had picket duty to warn the other ships, never saw the Japanese, either visually or on radar. *Canberra* also missed them on her radar, but, without radar, the Japanese saw the Allies, even against the dark background of Guadalcanal. Mikawa ordered a torpedo attack and independent firing before the Allies saw anything at all. When they did, disaster was already about to strike. In just minutes the *Canberra* sank and *Chicago* lost her bow. Amid the press of emergencies Captain Bode neglected to send any warning to the northern group of cruisers, which Mikawa engaged only five minutes after hitting the others. All three of those ships—*Astoria, Vincennes,* and *Quincy*—were sunk within about three quarters of an hour. By 2:30 A.M., August 9, Admiral Mikawa had a decisive victory against the forces protecting U.S. amphibious shipping off Guadalcanal.

What next? Kelly Turner's amphibious ships were about everything the United States had to move troops and supplies in the South Pacific. The JNAF had already failed to sink them in two days of expensive strikes—warned by Commander Eric Feldt's coastwatchers, so well placed along the flight route between Rabaul and Guadalcanal, Turner's ships were ready for every attack. Only one transport had been damaged enough to be forced onto the beach of Florida Island. If Mikawa could now hit the transports he would cripple Allied amphibious capability, strand the Marines ashore, deny them the supplies yet to be landed, and lay the foundation for a crippling defeat of the first Allied counteroffensive.

Instead Mikawa returned to Rabaul. According to Ohmae, the admiral reasoned that his ships had become scattered during the battle and it would take too long to re-form for a venture into the anchorage. They had consumed much ammunition and many torpedoes (roughly a quarter to a third of main battery ammunition and half the available torpedoes). Most important, if Mikawa tarried, dawn would find him in position to be hit by American carrier planes. Beyond these reasons, however, lay the cult of the Decisive Battle. Mikawa had engaged the warships and sunk them. That

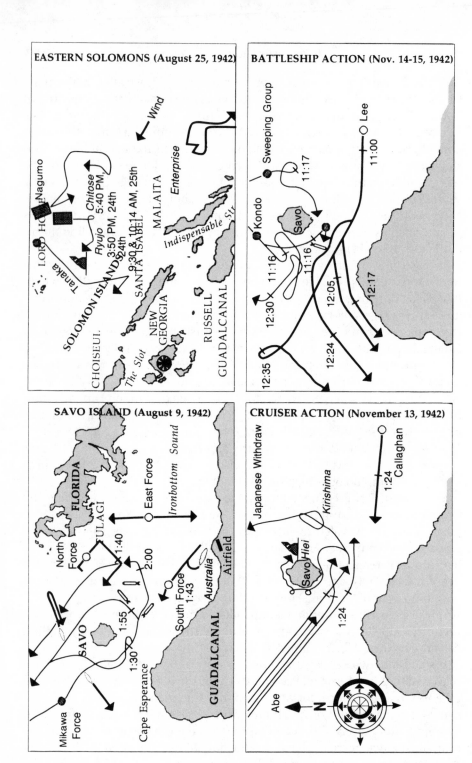

VI. Key Battles off Guadalcanal

was the function of a fleet. What did it matter that transports had been left behind? Both Kami and Ohmae supported the decision. As the Japanese would presently learn, being compelled to face invasion after invasion, it mattered a very great deal that the Allied amphibious forces survived the Savo debacle.

One man who did not survive was the former intelligence chief Howard Bode. Facing the inevitable court of inquiry, having had his ship shot out from under him, and bearing a measure of responsibility for the surprise defeat, Bode took his own life.

THOSE SHIPS SUNK DURING THE SAVO BATTLE BECAME THE FIRST OF MANY, SO MANY THAT THE body of water delimited by the islands Guadalcanal, Tulagi, and Florida soon became known as Ironbottom Sound. The battles that inflicted such losses were necessary efforts to command the sea off Guadalcanal, and this in turn would be vital to both sides' efforts to land supplies and reinforcements on the big island. Japanese counterlandings were so frequent that Americans began calling any naval force headed southward down The Slot a Tokyo Express. American efforts to bring up additional troops and supplies were also critical right from the beginning, since the dangers of remaining were such as to make Admiral Turner sail away before General Vandegrift's supplies had all been unloaded.

Air operations from Guadalcanal became a factor whose importance would be central to the entire Solomons campaign. Here the advantage went squarely to the Americans, who occupied Guadalcanal airfield before the JNAF could make it work. Ironically, the engineering equipment necessary for Americans to complete the job sailed away on Turner's cargo ships, so *Japanese* equipment made the difference in finishing the field. Six trucks, two narrow-gauge locomotives, fifty hauling carts for the tracks, six steam-rollers, four generators, shovels, and explosives, all abandoned the day of the invasion as the Japanese fled inland, enabled Americans to grade and fill in the last gap in the center of the runway. On August 12 the Cactus runway was named Henderson Field in honor of Lofton Henderson, a Marine fighter leader killed at Midway. Six days later the field reached full length at 3,778 by 150 feet. The first American aircraft, nineteen F4Fs and twelve SBD Dauntless dive-bombers of Marine Air Group 23, arrived on August 20, conveyed from Button by the new small escort carrier *Long Island.* From that day forward Henderson Field became a hornet's nest.

Many obstacles stood in the way of Japanese air operations against Guadalcanal. The JNAF had not planned for a campaign in the Solomons, and its 25th Air Flotilla was counting the days until pending relief by the 26th. The Japanese airfields were at Rabaul—the former Australian fields

Vunakanau and Lakunai—and that was a very long way from Guadalcanal. Map measurement shows a distance of 572 miles from Rabaul to Henderson Field. At that range Zero fighters were at the edge of their envelope, while damaged aircraft would have a very dicey time making it back to base. True, the Japanese had carried out missions to this range during the Philippine attacks, but it was one thing to mount special efforts for key targets and another to operate at this distance on a daily basis for an extended campaign.

The essential difficulty is well mirrored in the experience of Petty Officer Sakai Saburo, fighter ace, recalled from Lae to Rabaul just days before Watchtower. Admiral Mikawa's orders for air strikes occasioned argument with his air wing leader, who wished to use only his best pilots. Mikawa insisted on a maximum-effort strike. The two compromised on a plan for eighteen Zeros plus bombers. The fighters took off to face sustained opposition over Guadalcanal. Sakai downed one F4F and an SBD dive-bomber, but his plane was crippled by fire from TBF Avenger torpedo bombers. Almost paralyzed on his left side, blinded in his right eye, Sakai gained Rabaul only through a supreme effort of will. Petty Officer Sakai was one of the best; ordinary JNAF pilots had correspondingly less chance to survive.

What applied to the air force proved equally if not more true of sea forces. Once American fliers garrisoned Cactus no Japanese ship was safe in daylight hours within 150 miles of that place. Tokyo Express commanders were forced to adopt a pattern of operations featuring nighttime arrival off Guadalcanal, rapid unloading, then a high-speed dash to escape Henderson Field's reach before daylight. As much as anything else these tactics were dictated by inevitable time and space factors.

Japanese development of a base network in the central and northern Solomons was driven by operational problems of fighting at Guadalcanal, which place many began calling "Isle of Death." An airfield at Buka, off northern Bougainville, started as a place for damaged planes to recover without having to make the full distance to Rabaul. The anchorage at Faisi on Shortland Island gave ships more chance to reach Guadalcanal in a single jump. Supporting airfields at Kieta, Buin, and Ballale completed the Bougainville complex, but all these were far to the north, 300 to 400 miles from Henderson Field. Within weeks of the Watchtower invasion the Japanese had come to the decision to build an airfield on New Georgia, the next island up the Solomon chain. Scarce construction resources and site problems delayed the field at Munda, about 180 miles northwest of Henderson; it was not completed until almost Christmas of 1942.

Meanwhile, the fight for Cactus intensified. Imperial General Headquarters had predicted even before Watchtower that the first Allied landings would be reconnaissance missions, and they were disposed to believe this when marines actually invaded Guadalcanal and environs. A cable from a

Japanese attaché in Moscow strengthened that belief with bogus intelligence supposedly gleaned from the Soviets. Japanese construction workers on Guadalcanal took to the bush, and the 400 or so SNLF troops present had little alternative except to join them. When Mikawa made his dash to Savo, a few hundred more SNLF were run in on Navy ships. The first real unit sent, however, was Colonel Ichiki Kiyonao's 28th Infantry Regiment, originally slated for Midway but now seconded to the 17th Army, a Japanese Army command that at this time covered both the Solomons and New Guinea. Ichiki, too, believed the Marine landing a mere reconnaissance; convinced of the superiority of Imperial Army troops, he insisted upon going ahead with the landing of an advance echelon of his unit without awaiting the rest. Once on Guadalcanal, Colonel Ichiki decided to attack right away, again with only his advance detachment, less than a thousand men. The Ichiki detachment was slaughtered when it tried to overrun Marine positions along the Tenaru River.

General Vandegrift's Marines were themselves not immune to headstrong stupidity. In their case the difficulty was with the intelligence officer Lieutenant Colonel Goettge. For several days after the landings, Goettge benefited from a trickle of prisoners willing to be interrogated. These were mostly Korean or Taiwanese laborers who had given up trying to survive in the jungle. One Japanese sailor, however, hinted that there were others like him, Japanese who might also give up. Excited at the prospect, Colonel Goettge joined a patrol sent to investigate, along with medical personnel and other members of the Marine intelligence staffs. The patrol never came back. Worst of all, a Japanese interpreter for the 5th Marine Regiment, one Lieutenant Ralph Corry, who was among those missing on the Goettge patrol, had come to the division after working on Japanese codes in Washington. This amounted to a potential security breach of breathtaking dimensions. Fortunately for the codebreakers, the Japanese appear to have made no effort to take prisoners from the Goettge patrol.

Following the defeat of the Ichiki detachment IGHQ began to take the Guadalcanal problem more seriously. This time the Japanese planned to send a full brigade to drive the Americans into the sea. This was still a smaller force than that which Vandegrift himself disposed, and the Imperial Army also lacked American firepower, but IGHQ did not know that at the time and remained overconfident. General Kawaguchi Kiyotake, who commanded the unit, the 35th Brigade, demanded he be delivered to Guadalcanal with all equipment and supplies. Kawaguchi's demand was wise in view of what had happened to Ichiki, but imposed additional burdens on the Imperial Navy, which was to provide transportation. In effect, Kawaguchi's transport requirements involved the full Combined Fleet in the Guadalcanal campaign for the first time.

On the eve of a major fleet action the Americans did one more thing that momentarily gave pause. Out of nowhere there was an attack against the Japanese outpost on Makin Atoll in the Gilberts. Sometimes characterized as a diversion, sometimes as a real but light punch, the Makin attack was carried out by 220 men under Lieutenant Colonel Evans F. Carlson. Carlson's 2nd Marine Raider Battalion had been formed after experience as a language officer in China led Carlson to believe in special commando-type units. The Raiders were transported secretly to the Gilberts by submarines *Nautilus* and *Argonaut*. To plan the raid, Marine intelligence officer Lieutenant Jerry Holtom traveled to Palmyra and Christmas islands to gather information about Makin and speak to fishermen picked up off its shores.

During the night of August 17–18 the Raiders went ashore from the submarines using inflatable boats in a rough sea and heavy rain. Once on land the Marine Raiders slogged across Makin, encountering its Japanese defenders before dawn. There were no more than a platoon or two of the 62nd Guard Unit, fewer than fifty men in all, and by morning they had been pressed up against the shore in a last-ditch defense. A couple of flying boats came to reinforce the hard-pressed Japanese, but the Raiders shot up one and the other did not land. A scout plane alerted Truk to the situation, and Admiral Ugaki's diary shows that even the *Yamato* at Hashirajima in Empire waters was well informed as to the tactical situation. Still, the Japanese had no chance and expired in a hopelessly suicidal attack, of the type that became known as banzai attacks in the Pacific. After less than twenty-four hours Colonel Carlson took his men back to the submarines for a return to Hawaii. In the confusion of the withdrawal a dozen marines were left behind; nine of them survived, only to be executed by the Japanese as spies.

Contrary to claims in Marine monographs and other histories of Marine Raiders, there were no diversions of Japanese cruisers or destroyers to Makin. Japanese records indicate that a relief expedition arrived partly by air and partly in a transport some days later, escorted by three sub chasers and the minelayer *Tokiwa*. The only major warships in the area on August 25 were destroyers *Shigure* and *Shiratsuyu*, and they were between Kwajalein and Jaluit. No CINCPAC fleet intelligence summaries or 14th Naval District communications summaries indicate sorties toward Makin, nor do Japanese major ship movement records.

The Makin raid is sometimes faulted for alerting Tokyo to the threat against its Central Pacific defenses. No real invasion would occur for more than a year. This criticism is too facile, however, since the threat to the Mandates was obvious and the Japanese had many years of prewar analyses to guide them. There was a general thickening of Central Pacific defenses during 1942–1943, not necessarily attributable to the raid. "We didn't attach much importance" to the Makin raid, NGS operations bureau chief

Fukudome Shigeru told inquisitors, "because it wasn't very significant, merely an attempt from submarines to destroy land equipment."

On the other hand, there was a worthwhile development from the raid for CINCPAC. The officer commanding the submarines went to Jasper Holmes of the Combat Intelligence Unit, looking for good inshore charts and hydrographic data—the same type of material that had been a problem for Watchtower. Holmes discovered that his files contained practically nothing, although British suzerainty over the Gilberts dated from 1892. The same lack of material applied to the Aleutians, and that would become a special thorn when CINCPAC officers tried to compile a set of sailing directions later in 1942 for *Allied* bases. These discoveries led directly to the creation at the CIU of a desk, later an entire section, dedicated to collecting topographic material. At Pearl Harbor, this unit became the main center for photographic interpretation.

While these developments would be of great importance, in the meantime the South Pacific boiled over. On August 17, coincident with the Makin raid, the Imperial Navy again changed its radio call signs. This act led Allied intelligence officers to fear that the Japanese had begun a big push. The Japanese were indeed on the move, and their actions led to a fierce battle in the air and on the sea.


THE DIE WAS CAST FOR A FLEET ENGAGEMENT IMMEDIATELY AFTER THE SAVO ISLAND BATTLE. Admiral Yamamoto talked the situation over with his staff; he wanted to exploit the success Mikawa had won off Guadalcanal. As early as August 10 Yamamoto brought together carrier commander Nagumo and his senior people, surface fleet leader Kondo and his staff, plus top Combined Fleet officers in the commander in chief's own cabin aboard *Yamato*. Yamamoto resolved to pounce upon any Allied warships that interfered with the fast convoy he would send bearing General Kawaguchi's Army brigade. Simultaneously the Japanese saw this as an opportunity to neutralize Marine aircraft recently arrived at Henderson Field. Admiral Nagumo went to sea with a reorganized Kido Butai on August 16. This time Nagumo's personal command, Carrier Division 1, had the *Shokaku* and *Zuikaku*. King Kong Hara, former commander of those carriers, now had a detached mission with the single light carrier *Ryujo*. Admiral Kondo would bring separate surface forces to bear on any U.S. fleet inept enough to come within reach.

Inklings of Japanese intentions came to American intelligence, though this time there was to be nothing like the breakthroughs before Coral Sea or Midway. Still, uncertainty gradually hardened to conviction, as is illustrated by reporting on the disposition of Imperial Navy carriers, obviously key elements in Yamamoto's attack plans.

Commander Layton's daily fleet intelligence summary for August 6, just before Watchtower, forthrightly noted the Kido Butai in Empire waters but able to sail at any time; Layton thought a Malay–Indian Ocean mission "slightly the favorite to date." Six days later Layton reported creation of a task force of First Air Fleet plus heavy units, but no departures from Japan. On August 14 the task force mission was given as repelling a Doolittle-style raid on Japan (Admiral Ugaki's diary confirms sightings of alleged American scout planes and fears of attack on Japan at this time). The next day the carriers were still reported in Japan, but departure of heavy units was seen as imminent and Admiral Kondo was placed near Saipan on his way south. August 16 brought a notation that several light carriers might be at sea near Marcus but that Kido Butai could be in southern Japan or on its way south.

So far, so good, but Nagumo sailed with his carrier force on August 16, and for the next five days CINCPAC summaries continued to carry Kido Butai in Empire waters, going so far as to comment (on August 21) that "unless ORANGE radio deception is remarkably efficient, this force remains in the homeland still." This same report speculated that the reason must be that the Japanese lacked information on the location of U.S. carriers. However, the very next day's intelligence summary began to show Nagumo in the *Shokaku*, either already at Truk or in its vicinity. Notations made by 14th Naval District's Combat Intelligence Unit generally confirm Layton's reporting. On August 19, Commander Wilfred J. Holmes's CIU noted all carriers in Empire waters, while on the twenty-second it held *Shokaku* and *Zuikaku* to be en route to Truk. In one notable divergence from reality, the August 22 entry placed light carrier *Ryujo* in dry dock when in fact she was soon to hit Guadalcanal. The fleet intelligence summary made good this prospective error on August 23, putting all three Japanese carriers in the Truk area.

A further corrective view is supplied by the CINCPAC war diary, kept by Nimitz aide Commander James Steele. The war diary on August 10 reveals that American light cruiser *Boise*, on a diversionary cruise into Japanese waters, had lost two floatplanes and broken radio silence trying to find them. Here indeed is the explanation for Japanese fears at this time of U.S. fleet operations in Empire waters. Steele also noted formation of a Japanese battleship-carrier task force, but rather than relating it to the *Boise* diversion he described its purpose as "employment in the Bismarck-Solomons area." On August 16 the war diary notes signs of a large Japanese effort to recapture Guadalcanal and estimates that if carriers were to be used the attack could not occur before August 25—right on the button. The notation on August 17 is that "it is not at all certain that the Jap [carriers] are still in home waters," but the following day this was put the other way—no evidence of the carriers' departure. Admiral Ghormley in the South Pacific at

Button reported himself preparing for attack between the twentieth and twenty-third. Again, while on August 20 the CINCPAC war diary notes no good evidence the Kido Butai had left Japan, the next day it clearly states: "It now seems most probable that two striking forces are at Truk en route to the Solomons area and that the suspected all out attempt to recapture positions in the Tulagi area [will start] as early as August 25."

A further vision of the coming battle is furnished by Admiral Ghormley's South Pacific command, which was sending out a steady stream of dispatches labeled "handle as ultra secret." On August 17 he warned of surface attacks led by Admiral Goto of Cruiser Division 6. The next day there were more warnings of Japanese surface forces. In one of these Ghormley remarked: "No positive info as to presence of carriers with hostile force however such presence considered highly likely." Beyond the cable-ese in which it was written, Ghormley's message was unmistakable. A further dispatch from the South Pacific Command chief direct to Admiral Fletcher, his carrier commander, on August 22, read in part:

INDICATIONS POINT STRONGLY TO ENEMY ATTACK IN FORCE ON CACTUS AREA 23–26 AUGUST. FROM AVAILABLE INTELLIGENCE . . . PRESENCE OF CARRIERS POSSIBLE BUT NOT CONFIRMED. . . . IMPORTANT FUELING BE CONDUCTED SOONEST POSSIBLE AND IF PRACTICABLE ONE CARRIER TASK FORCE AT A TIME RETIRING FOR THAT PURPOSE.

Apparently the Navy wished no repetition of the mixup that had ruined Fletcher's Wake Island expedition in December 1941.

This evidence demonstrates that the American commands had no doubts by August 22 at the latest that a major naval engagement impended.

Like some kind of macabre rerun in a different space and time, the antagonists in what would become known as the battle of the eastern Solomons were once again Nagumo for the Japanese and Fletcher for the Americans. This time Admiral Nagumo wore his flag in the *Shokaku* and Fletcher had his in *Saratoga*. The carriers maneuvered to the east of the Solomons with Nagumo acting in support of a fast transport convoy containing General Kawaguchi's Army brigade, sailing directly down The Slot. Distant cover and picket duty were provided by several detachments of Japanese warships, including a Vanguard Force (Rear Admiral Abe Hiroaki) south of the Kido Butai, an Advance Force (Vice Admiral Kondo Nobutake) to the east, and to the southwest a force to run interference between Nagumo and American planes at Henderson Field, the light carrier *Ryujo* (Captain Kato Tadao) and heavy cruiser *Tone* plus a couple of destroyers, led by Rear Admiral Hara Chuichi. American tactical organization comprised three groups, each built around a single carrier, all under Admiral Fletcher's general command in Task Force 61.

One American carrier, *Wasp*, missed the main action due to being sent south for refueling, leaving the bulk of the fight to *Enterprise* and *Saratoga* plus aircraft based at Henderson Field. The U.S. fleet, more specifically Rear Admiral Thomas C. Kinkaid commanding the *Enterprise* task group, benefited from the services of Lieutenant Gilven Slonim's mobile radio intelligence unit. For their part, the Japanese had radar aboard a carrier— *Shokaku*—though its installation was so recent that Imperial Navy technicians remained neophytes in its use (these early Japanese radar sets themselves were also quite primitive). Together the American carriers disposed of 68 dive-bombers, 29 torpedo bombers, and 59 fighters; ashore there were another 11 dive-bombers and 18 fighters at Henderson, plus 25 B-17s flying from Button. The Japanese had 54 dive-bombers, 45 torpedo bombers, and 78 Zero fighters aboard their carriers, and 114 aircraft of assorted types at shore bases.

As the battle played out, on August 24 the *Ryujo* got in first licks by a raid on Henderson Field which, duly warned by coastwatchers, decimated the attackers. The American search planes found Captain Kato's *Ryujo*, which had blazed a path from the Netherlands East Indies to the Aleutians, only to come to her end now off Guadalcanal, where she was finished off by strike groups from the *Saratoga*. While Fletcher's planes were off attacking *Ryujo*, however, the noon search from *Enterprise* saw Nagumo's main force. Now there was no strike unit to exploit the contact. The two SBD dive-bombers that had made the sighting tried an attack on their own but missed the *Shokaku*.

Lieutenant Slonim's radio unit advised that two JNAF planes shot down near the American task force had not been able to get out any sighting reports, but Fletcher assumed to the contrary, ordering maximum fighter cover, so that as many as fifty-three F4Fs were in the air when American radar identified an incoming Japanese strike from Nagumo's carriers. Difficulties tracking and directing defending fighters combined with poor radio discipline, however, to make it impossible to stop the attack. *Enterprise* received considerable damage. That night the American carrier retired, but she was effectively replaced by the *Wasp*, while Admiral Nagumo led his carriers north to a fueling rendezvous that suddenly seemed important. The *Ryujo* sank under the weight of damage she had absorbed. The next day, American carrier and land-based aircraft worked over the Japanese convoy in The Slot. Rear Admiral Tanaka Raizo, the convoy escort commander, found the aerial opposition so fierce he retired to Shortland Island. Several transports and a destroyer were sunk, others plus his flagship, light cruiser *Jintsu*, damaged. The eastern Solomons ended as a clear setback for the Japanese.

To get at least some Japanese ground troops onto Guadalcanal, Admiral Tanaka loaded them onto his destroyers and dashed down The Slot. Remaining troops would have to follow by barge, a slow process of percolating forward from island to island, in effect infiltration by sea. Increasingly the Japanese found themselves forced to resort to expedients as Allied air power on Cactus grew. Before long there were names for the methods: Destroyer transport missions began to be called rat runs, the barge operations ant activities. They would also be supplemented by destroyer and submarine missions to carry supplies in sealed drums that could be tossed into the sea and, one hoped, float ashore. Japanese ingenuity fashioned a submersible "sled," a refinement of the midget submarine, which enabled numbers of supply drums to be preloaded at base and loosed at one moment to navigate for shore. Americans, fearful or contemptuous by turns of the Tokyo Express, saw these tactics born of desperation as evidence of Japanese stubbornness.

In Japanese folklore the rat or mouse (*nezumi*) is a lucky animal, symbolizing prosperity since these animals are usually found where there is an abundance of grain. The *nezumi* may be lucky, but the Tokyo Express always remained difficult and dangerous. Any vessel damaged and forced to reduce speed was in mortal danger, along with any ship that stopped to succor it. This would be demonstrated as early as August 28, when destroyer *Asagiri* was sunk and two more damaged in such a circumstance. A steady stream of warships followed her to the bottom or sustained damage. Air attacks damaged the light cruiser *Yura* in September, then sank her on another mission exactly a month later. Other air attack victims that October while conducting rat operations included cruiser *Tenryu* and two destroyers damaged, and another two sunk. The Japanese managed to repair *Tenryu* from local resources at Rabaul, then sent her out again. Escorting a convoy to Madang, New Guinea, this light cruiser would be torpedoed and sunk by American submarine *Albacore* at her destination.

Codebreaking and aerial reconnaissance contributed greatly to the difficulties of the Tokyo Express. For one example, the American codebreakers furnished specific warning of the *Tenryu* convoy to Madang. Another typical example is this New Zealand decryption concerning a previous *Tenryu* voyage:

ON NIGHT OF 4TH AND 5TH SEPTEMBER *TENRYU* AND THREE SMALL CRAFT (200 REINFORCEMENTS) ON 6TH SEPTEMBER *TENRYU* AND *ARASHI* ON 7TH AND 8TH SEPTEMBER *TATSUTA* AND *HAMAKAZE* WILL ENTER PORT AND ANCHOR. . . . PREPARATIONS SHOULD BE MADE TO BE PICKED UP WHEN (CORRUPT—MAY EITHER BE *HAMAKAZE* OR "ON BEACH") MAKES CONTACT BY BURNING A ?SEARCHLIGHT. MEETING PLACE SHOULD BE INDICATED BY A WHITE LIGHT.

Though the text shows a couple of places where codebreakers were uncertain of the language in the original Japanese message, or where transmission errors corrupted portions of it, it remains clear that such a decrypt furnished sufficient data from which to prepare a hot reception for unsuspecting sailors. The message identified Imperial Navy ships involved, gave a prospective schedule, and even divulged planned recognition signals that might permit Allied warships to mimic the Japanese.

What was true for the Tokyo Express would also be true for more serious efforts to neutralize Cactus, especially its airfield. The Japanese knew full well that the main obstacle in their way was Henderson Field. If Allied airpower could be suppressed, the Imperial Navy could move troops and supplies with impunity. This in fact became the core of the Japanese plan once a Guadalcanal attack by the Kawaguchi Brigade had failed and the new option became massive reinforcement for a full-scale assault on the U.S. Marines.

The possible means for knocking out Cactus airpower were several but the Japanese had problems employing each. One means, ground fire, remained restricted by Japanese limitations in artillery ammunition, caliber, and numbers, a function of both the tenuous supply line and IGHQ failure to appreciate the importance of Guadalcanal. Lieutenant Tani Akio, who commanded one of several 105mm gun batteries on Guadalcanal under the 4th Artillery Regiment, recalled that his men reached the island with just 800 shells and never received any more. They could never afford to shoot more than ten rounds a day. Tani remembered also being hampered because his four guns were worn out from service in China and Manchuria, and because the Americans used steel mesh plates that he feared were impervious to the Japanese 105mm shells. Tani's situation was typical. The heaviest artillery the Imperial Army ever deployed to Guadalcanal was 150mm guns, and there were only a handful of those. Also, because the Japanese never really developed a good beachhead supply port or a high-volume overland transport system, capabilities of such forces as arrived on Guadalcanal remained severely restricted. Cactus airpower survived the Japanese Army.

From a World War II perspective especially, an obvious alternative means of neutralizing Cactus would be the Japanese Naval Air Force (JNAF). That the Japanese recognized this from an early date is demonstrated by the arrival at Rabaul on August 8 of Eleventh Air Fleet commander Vice Admiral Tsukahara Nizhizo. Within one day of the invasion the Imperial Navy sent down their top land-based air commander, this despite the fact that the Solomons air garrison, 25th Air Flotilla, happened to be worn out and scheduled for repatriation. Tsukahara became theater commander, heading something the Japanese called the Southeast Area Fleet, which comprised both Vice Admiral Mikawa's Eighth Fleet and Rear Admiral Yamada Sadayoshi's 25th Air Flotilla. As the JNAF built up strength around Rabaul, the mere air flotilla would be supplanted by the full Eleventh Air Fleet as the Japanese began to fly multiple air flotillas from the Rabaul complex.

The JNAF air effort against Henderson Field became the staple of Solomons operations for six months. At first Japanese forces would surge their sortie rates, then fall back on harassment flights as numbers of available aircraft dropped. This was the case with the invasion reaction raids and the eastern Solomons battle. Toward September the air effort became a sustained one, with an average twenty-nine or more sorties a day flown against the Cactus air force. Air strength diminished until JNAF reinforcements began to arrive. The average number of serviceable aircraft in the Eleventh Air Fleet fell between August and early September from over a hundred to fewer than fifty, before ballooning near the end of the month to over 200. Where August aircraft losses (for the entire JNAF) numbered 352, the September figure was only 236. The dangers of flying the Guadalcanal run are amply illustrated by the fact that in September planes lost for accidental and operational reasons outnumbered combat losses, in particular for fighters, a situation that had not obtained since the first-phase offensive, when the JNAF had similarly been mounting much of its effort at long range from poor bases. Actual sortie rates are available only for the *Zuikaku,* whose seventy-two planes flew 209 combat missions and 1,213 training sorties between August 1 and 31, an overall sortie rate of less than one per plane per day with combat sorties a small fraction (less than one tenth) of that.

Tactics were necessarily constrained by the long range to Guadalcanal. Fuel confined the Japanese to a few air routes, each featuring one or more of the ubiquitous coastwatchers. Zero fighters would be able to remain over Henderson Field for just a few minutes and liable to expend their available fuel in a mere few rounds of aerobatics. Mounting large fighter sweeps from Rabaul was difficult; those the Japanese attempted were ineffective due, as often as not, to coastwatcher warnings. More often fighter operations took the form of escorting bombers, which usually operated in a strength of several squadrons and flying in a V-of-Vs formation. The repetition of tactics was so obvious that reporter Richard Tregaskis, on Cactus with the Marines, noted the bomber formations in his reminiscence, *Guadalcanal Diary.* The Office of Naval Intelligence also did not miss the point, commenting on JNAF tactics in its Serial Report 144-42 before the end of the year. American fighter pilots knew the JNAF tactics best of all and used the Thach weave plus altitude advantages to counter them. Henderson Field survived the Japanese Naval Air Force.

A third string in the Japanese bow was surface naval bombardment. In some ways this was the Imperial Navy's forte, because big ships meant heavier and more concentrated firepower. The drawback, of course, was that the Japanese had to get their warships safely into Ironbottom Sound and then out again. They made a start with destroyer and destroyer flotilla forays, but these never seemed to put Henderson out of action. The Combined Fleet escalated, using heavy cruisers with their 8-inch guns and battleships with 14-inch armament. A battleship bombardment of Henderson Field had been considered and approved by Combined Fleet headquarters before the end of September, but at length the Southeast Area Fleet decided to lead with a cruiser bombardment. Rear Admiral Goto's division was selected, only to encounter a hornet's nest off Guadalcanal in what became known as the battle of Cape Esperance. Once again an American fleet plied the waters off Savo Island. Rear Admiral Norman Scott led a cruiser-destroyer force stronger than Goto's, which he was able to keep south of Guadalcanal, outside JNAF air range, for days while awaiting news a Tokyo Express was on its way. Various authorities attribute Scott's actual warning to CINCPAC intelligence or to Radio KEN, call sign for the station run by Guadalcanal coastwatchers, who had joined up with the Marines on Cactus. Since CINCPAC daily summaries and 14th Naval District reporting, not to mention the Combat Intelligence Unit war diary, all show no trace of knowledge of the Express run, one may credit Scott's warning to the coastwatchers.

On the night of October 11–12 Admiral Goto closed in on Henderson Field with three heavy cruisers and two destroyers. Scott's ships saw them on radar, then opened fire on the startled Japanese, just as Goto lined up to bombard Henderson. Scott's ships passed in front of the Japanese in the classic maneuver known as crossing the T and shelled them into insensibility. One American shell struck the bridge of Admiral Goto's flagship, *Aoba*, killing that officer and most staff, who died thinking themselves victims of friendly fire. The *Aoba* got off only seven shots of her own, the *Furutaka* twenty, and the *Kinugasa* sixty-one. The *Aoba* got some torpedoes into the water, and the *Kinugasa* fired very accurately at the U.S. light cruiser *Boise*, but *Furutaka* was sunk along with destroyer *Fubuki*. Only the confusion of the night engagement, in which Americans too feared they were firing on their own ships, prevented the damage from being even greater.

Petty Officer Saima Haruyoshi, an *Aoba* sailor assigned to a damage-control party, had a tough time that night. The *Aoba* absorbed more than forty hits. Saima's battle station was on the middle deck near the stern and that became a key location when a direct hit silenced the ship's C turret and started fires belowdecks. Saima and other sailors had to pick up the many wounded and push bodies out of the way just to get fire hoses into play. Captain Kijima Kikunori, the late Goto's senior staff officer, who afterward considered himself responsible for the defeat, took temporary command of the force and got the Japanese ships back to Shortland.

To cap this disaster for the Imperial Navy, the Americans managed to rescue 113 survivors from the *Furutaka* and *Fubuki* and, interrogating them, found a valuable storehouse of knowledge. Bit by bit battle results gained from the exploitation of tactical intelligence were providing new opportunities to fill in gaps in the Allies' basic picture of the Japanese Navy.

Thus the Cactus air force survived the first Japanese attempt at a major bombardment. By this time, however, there were plans for an even bigger push by both Army and Navy. Key Combined Fleet staff officers like Commander Watanabe and Admiral Ugaki had been down to Rabaul for discussions. Rabaul staffers Commander Ohmae of the Navy and Colonel Tsuji Masanobu of the Army had made the six-hour flight to Truk for vital talks. Any doubt regarding the importance Combined Fleet attributed to the planned offensive ought to have disappeared when Tokyo sent a fresh air-staff officer to Rabaul to oversee the aerial effort. The new face was that of Commander Genda Minoru. The Americans on Cactus faced their greatest challenge yet.

As OCTOBER BEGAN, GENERAL VANDEGRIFT'S MARINES ON GUADALCANAL WERE BEING REIN-forced, and even getting Army units from the Americal Division. Americans were arriving more reliably from Espíritu Santo than Japanese from Rabaul, a race whose outcome helped decide the campaign. Among the flow came a tiny contingent far more vital to Allied commanders than their numbers might suggest. The unit was a mobile detachment from radio intelligence.

The first radio intelligence people on Guadalcanal were a chief named Jim Perkins and one other sailor. They brought a high-frequency direction finder with them. Then came a full mobile detachment like the ones on carriers. It was selected in the usual way. Phillip H. Jacobsen, for example, a radioman at the intercept station in Hawaii, saw a notice on the bulletin board one day for volunteers to Guadalcanal. He put in and found himself with three other sailors and an ensign named Homer L. Kisner, but called Charlie, on a former Pan American Airways Clipper flying boat. With them went language officer Lieutenant Commander Daniel J. McCallum. They flew to Johnston Island, then Palmyra, then Fiji, then Espíritu Santo. Finally a Marine C-47 piloted by a staff sergeant carried them to Henderson Field. At the last stage the Marine plane could not haul all their 3,500 pounds of equipment, so they chose 2,000 to carry and left the rest to follow by boat about a month later.

The earlier arrival of Chief Radioman James J. Perkins with his direction-finding unit had been even more precarious. Perkins had been with the mobile radio unit on the *Enterprise* during its raids on the Marshalls, Wake, and Marcus, and was asked to go to Guadalcanal before the invasion. His assignment was characterized as a secret mission. He ended up on a mer-chant ship, which deposited him on Guadalcanal in mid-September. Unloading his own equipment, Perkins suffered his first strafing and bomb-ing. Amid the confusion some of the stuff was scattered, including one of his radios, which disappeared completely. Months later Perkins found the shell of that receiver on the beach—marines had been using it as an oven to cook with.

When Perkins tried to set up his equipment an officer asked what he was doing. Since the antenna and other items were all classified top secret the chief could hardly reply. He was told to move as the engineers were installing a new satellite fighter strip. Perkins ended up at one corner of Henderson Field—squarely on top of the bull's-eye. When the mobile radio unit came to Cactus it, too, ended up on a bull's-eye—at Lunga Point, right next to the new fighter strip.

The direction-finding unit became Station Button; most likely Able was local nomenclature for the mobile unit, formally attached to Naval Operating Base, Lunga. Ensign Kisner and Commander McCallum differed on what they ought to be doing; their opinions were pretty much based on what they knew how to do. Dan McCallum had been assistant naval attaché in Tokyo before the war, right through to the spring of 1941. A bridge player and easy reader of Japanese with good comprehension, McCallum wanted to do cryptanalysis on Guadalcanal. He understood the language and was senior officer but knew little of the radio aspects, on which Ensign Kisner, a former enlisted radioman, was expert. Ironically, Kisner's chain of command went directly back to Lieutenant Commander Thomas A. Huckins at Pearl Harbor, an Annapolis classmate of McCallum's. Kisner saw the unit focusing primarily on traffic analysis. Faced with such divergent interests among superiors the radiomen tried to divide their watches to produce some material for each of their bosses.

Chief Perkins got his direction finder working during the last week of September. Soon afterward Kisner's detachment arrived with several more radios, antennae made for installation on the coconut trees, an auxiliary generator, and RIP-5 typewriters. They had hardly gotten their gear unpacked when they were thrown, so to speak, into the intelligence breach.

As the Japanese increased their daily effort against Guadalcanal, the Cactus air force found itself hard pressed to respond, even though the Americans had the advantage of operating over their own base, and even with the coastwatchers. When to order fighters into the air became a daily dilemma of huge importance—too soon, and the planes used up their gas and had to land, leaving them sitting ducks for attack; too late and the interceptors would be unable to gain enough altitude to attain favorable positions. Radio intelligence made the difference because the JNAF usually used the same frequencies and set up a small net for their formation right after takeoff from Rabaul. All the radiomen had to do was listen for Japanese on the bomber frequencies and sound the warning. Even though radio receiving conditions were marginal in the Solomons and often varied considerably (the Japanese themselves frequently lost contact between Rabaul and Guadalcanal), Ensign Kisner's unit could usually count on detecting any incoming strike at least fifteen minutes before it showed up on radar.

Navy radiomen on Guadalcanal also brought in the first Japanese radio sets captured during the war, a boon for American technical intelligence. The unit monitored the general broadcast circuit from Rabaul, did direction finding for sea and air transmissions, and helped the Marines identify Japanese Army units on Guadalcanal itself.

Chief Perkins had a radioman who was too close to some Japanese bombs that exploded near their Henderson Field site. After that the radioman ran for a foxhole at the first sign of an attack and was also extremely nervous about doing night watches. Perkins finally went to Kisner and asked for help, after which Phil Jacobsen was seconded to the direction-finding unit. Soon after that came *the* bombardment, the night everyone on Guadalcanal remembers as *"The Night."*

Phil Jacobsen happened to be radioman on watch, trying his best to relax in a shelter the Seabees were building for the direction-finding unit but had not yet completed. Suddenly a star shell burst almost directly overhead. Jacobsen didn't like the look of that, and left to seek cover. All hell broke loose. Henderson was the target that night for battleships *Kongo* and *Haruna*, firing a mixture of high-explosive, armor-piercing, and special incendiary shells. This was the battleship bombardment Combined Fleet had been planning since September, made even more urgent by Admiral Goto's failure at Cape Esperance. Depending upon which count one accepts, the battleships fired either 873 or 918 shells, cratering the airfield, smashing some planes and leaving many more damaged, and damaging Chief Perkins's direction-finding equipment. After that, whenever it rained (which was frequently) reception deteriorated until the set could no longer take radio bearings at all. Perkins asked for replacement gear and was sent a new type, used until the direction-finding men left in the spring of 1943.

Yamamoto's October offensive, code-named the KA Operation, built in intensity and scope. The battleship mission was carried out under Vice Admiral Kurita Takeo, recently promoted to command a unit of this type. Kurita shrugged off a few PT boats that tried to oppose his battle wagons and went about his business. The morning after, Henderson Field had been holed, the Cactus air force had lost virtually its entire supply of aviation gasoline, and there were but seven dive-bombers and six fighters fit to fly. The night of October 14–15, Admiral Mikawa tried to extend Kurita's results with a cruiser bombardment using the *Chokai* and *Kinugasa*, which pumped 752 8-inch rounds into the Henderson Field area; the night after that, 926 more heavy-caliber shells came from treaty cruisers *Myoko* and *Maya*.

Having damned little to fight with, Cactus put on quite a show. After The Night, airmen spent the next day flying fuel up from Espíritu Santo to restore stocks at Henderson. Mechanics raced against time to repair damaged aircraft. The Japanese cruiser bombardments caused damage but were nowhere near as destructive as Kurita's battleships. Still, for a moment on the fifteenth, when Cactus discovered the Japanese to be running another high-speed convoy down The Slot (containing the bulk of the Army's 2nd Infantry Division) it looked as if there would be no U.S. attack planes at all. Then the Americans cobbled together a strike group with a jury-rigged torpedo-bearing PBY, a couple of SBDs, and an assortment of other planes, mostly fighters. On October 16 there were ten SBDs, including the half-dozen spares ferried up from Button. This tiny force, with the support of B-17s flying from rear bases, made up the slim margin of victory in the convoy battle, in which six Japanese fast transports were sent to the bottom. The few ships Rear Admiral Tanaka got all the way to Guadalcanal came under attack while unloading and sank offshore with much of the 2nd Division's heavy equipment and supplies.

It is not true, as claimed by some historians of carrier air warfare in the Pacific, that radio intelligence provided Nimitz with a précis of the Japanese plan, as it had at Midway. On the other hand, it is also inaccurate to say, as noted in a recent detailed history of the Guadalcanal campaign, that modifications in the Imperial Navy communications system, call signs, and codes introduced on October 1 reduced the United States to sheer speculation as to Japanese intentions. The truth lies somewhere in between. Commander Layton's October 1942 estimate of Japanese plans, made for Nimitz, specifically predicts an offensive in the Guadalcanal area, one involving efforts to neutralize the Cactus air force and break sea-lanes supplying Guadalcanal. Similarly, the relevant ONI combat narrative, published in December 1943, suggests a degree of foreknowledge. Most especially, knowledge before the fact seems indicated by Nimitz's treatment of the carrier *Enterprise.* She had been badly damaged at the eastern Solomons but, like the *Yorktown* before Midway, was rushed through repairs to get her back to the South Pacific in time.

Japanese communications security had been improving since Midway, as already seen, and the system changes in early October put Allied intelligence further away from detailed knowledge of Imperial Navy plans. Nevertheless Allied appreciation of the intricacies of the Japanese communication system showed growing sophistication that kept pace with Imperial Navy security measures. The war diary of the Combat Intelligence Unit at Pearl Harbor gives repeated indications of this. In late August Station Hypo made its first recoveries from recently activated Japanese codes. On August 26, with an entirely new system for weather data transmission working for the Japanese, Hypo made virtually instantaneous progress breaking into the new system. On September 2 the CIU recorded that the United States could read solidly a code in effect since mid-June.

Then the weather code became 85 percent transparent by September 29, when Pearl Harbor got access to captured codebooks, very possibly as a result of the Makin raid. On October 1 the substitution table for the code activated that very day was recovered, with the first code groups broken two days later. Throughout the period, further intelligence could be gleaned from traffic analysis.

That this is not a picture of intelligence merely speculating about the Japanese can be confirmed from a look at war-diary notations of CIU reports. On October 13 the Americans noted many Japanese sighting reports, more the next day, and by the fifteenth Pearl Harbor had established the call signs and radio frequencies used by two Japanese aircraft carriers, giving a position that differed by just one degree of longitude and one of latitude from the location given in a U.S. aircraft sighting report the same day. The CIU then predicted the second of the cruiser bombardments of Henderson Field some hours before it happened. On October 22 came a message from the Japanese submarine command at Jaluit, reported by CIU, informing the fleet that "Y-Day" had been postponed twenty-four hours. That Y-Day was the Imperial Navy's designation for the first day of its offensive would be confirmed by intercepts over the following days instructing naval units to attack the United States on that day, ordering operations against Henderson Field, and noting that Japanese Army units would also participate in the offensive.

In Washington the "Japanese Naval Activities" daily reports suggest that Imperial Navy intentions came into increasing focus before the new offensive. As early as October 13 the summary acknowledged growing Japanese interest, noting communications between Admiral Yamamoto and General Miyazaki Shuichi, chief of staff of the 17th Army at Rabaul. Yamamoto's Combined Fleet command would be listed repeatedly as an unusually frequent originator of message traffic. The summaries also note a heavy volume of Japanese operational messages (as opposed to administrative traffic), careful disposition of Japanese air search assets, and naval movements at Rabaul and elsewhere. By October 16 Washington concluded that Yamamoto was exercising direct tactical command. On October 19 came an ominous drop in high-precedence messages and other operational signal traffic, "indicating the possibility that the final period of adjustment and preparation for action on a major scale has been reached."

Veterans of Allied wartime intelligence often recall that Pearl Harbor and field commands generally had better information than the high command at Washington. While this conclusion does not emerge from the radio intelligence summaries just noted, it does get some confirmation from weekly Japanese-fleet-location reports assembled by ONI's order of battle (OP-16-F-2) section. These appeared on October 6, 13, 20, and 27—the latter, coincidentally, the day of what became the battle of Santa Cruz, named after a small island group southeast of the Solomons. Naturally Japanese carriers were key units for reporting; the ONI weeklies did a poor job on them. The OP-16-F-2 report of October 6 placed *Zuikaku* at Truk and *Shokaku* plus Carrier Division 2 in Empire waters. This remained unchanged a week later. The report of the twentieth put both big Japanese carriers in the Solomons area (correct), with light carrier *Zuiho* indefinite but probably at Truk, and no entry at all for the rest of Carrier Division 2. On the twenty-seventh the big ships were again listed in the Solomons, but Carrier Division 2, one of whose vessels was busily punishing the U.S. ships at Santa Cruz, was placed in Kyushu, southern Japan.

In actuality the light carriers *Junyo* and *Hiyo* of Carrier Division 2 left Japan on October 2, met the *Zuiho* of Carrier Division 1 at sea, and joined *Shokaku* and *Zuikaku* at Truk on October 9. These ships were among several task forces that steamed out of Truk on October 11 and maneuvered east and north of the Solomons. Captain Beppu Akitomo's *Hiyo* suffered an engine-room fire that restricted speed and forced her withdrawal from the scene. The *Hiyo* flew her air group to Buin Airfield on Bougainville, but this left Rear Admiral Kakuta Kakuji with just a single light carrier, the *Junyo*. As in the eastern Solomons battle, the Japanese were sailing in dispersed carrier groups with a unit of battleships for surface attack forward under Admiral Abe Hiroaki, another with Admiral Kondo and the big carriers that could detach at will. Vice Admiral Nagumo, sailing under Kondo's overall command, had better heavy-ship support than ever before.

The Imperial Navy task forces were first glimpsed at sea by Allied planes on October 13. Not only that, but search planes found four different forces, including a carrier group, a force of cruisers and destroyers scouting ahead of them, and the battleship force which that night subjected Henderson Field to its great bombardment. From the outset, therefore, aerial reconnaissance had already discovered the basic tactical disposition the Japanese would maintain right into the Santa Cruz battle. On the ground, Solomons coast-watchers did their usual fine job of monitoring Japanese convoy movements and the base on Shortland Island. Thus, where radio intelligence has recently been getting the most public attention and admiration, these other intelligence means were of equal value in the Santa Cruz campaign. In fact, there were further aircraft sightings of Japanese carriers on October 15, 22, and 24, and a searching PBY Catalina making a night bombing attack precipitating the actual battle on October 26.

When action came there was a new team of Americans in the South Pacific, for Ghormley had been judged wanting and Nimitz sent Bull Halsey in his place. Frank Fletcher also disappeared as carrier commander, replaced by Tom Kinkaid, whose Task Force 61 had groups built around carriers *Enterprise* and *Hornet*. They were the *only* carriers left to the Americans, for the *Saratoga* had been damaged by a torpedo *I-26* fired in August, while

Lieutenant Commander Kinashi Takaichi with the *I-19* had scored a (still unmatched) coup on September 15. With a single spread of torpedoes Kinashi inflicted fatal damage on the carrier *Wasp* and destroyer *O'Brien* plus lesser injury to the battleship *North Carolina*. Going into the Santa Cruz engagement also, Lieutenant Commander Tanabe Yahachi, who at Midway had inflicted the final fatal damage on the *Yorktown*, added to his score torpedo hits on heavy cruiser *Chester* such as to put her out of action for more than a year.

One of the first things Halsey did upon reaching Button was issue an exhortation to everyone to hit the Japanese even harder. Kinkaid also had orders from Nimitz to assume a position on the flank of the Japanese carrier forces, again like Midway, a strategy that was only possible due to intelligence, and one that the Pacific chief ordered days in advance of the actual battle.

Although the Americans were outnumbered in warships, combat tonnage, and aircraft, they possessed the important advantage of unsinkable airfields on Cactus, now not only Henderson Field but the satellite airstrip Fighter One. Further key advantages in intelligence have just been alluded to. Kinkaid had a final advantage in his mobile radio unit, embarked upon the *Enterprise*.

There is a little story here, along with a whiff of the danger the mobile radio units were exposed to, being sent into battle after battle. Gilven Slonim had headed the unit aboard *Enterprise* at the battle of the eastern Solomons, and of course the carrier had been damaged there. In fact, Kenneth E. Carmichael, leading radioman with the unit, had been leaning out the porthole to look at the action when near misses startled him. The mobile unit had two positions in continuous operation, with equipment including two or three receivers and two RIP-5 typewriters. With the ship damaged they were shifted to the *Saratoga*, but then *she* was torpedoed and headed east. They had only gotten as far as Tongatabu when the South Pacific Command ordered Slonim's unit back.* The men unloaded their gear, got a bus to the airport, and flew from Tonga to Fiji to New Caledonia and then Espíritu Santo. There they were put on a destroyer sent to rendezvous with carrier *Wasp*, and were preparing to tranship their equipment within sight of the carrier when the *I-19* torpedoed her. With yet another platform shot out from under them, the radio unit transferred instead to light cruiser *Helena* and eventually ended up at Espíritu Santo. There Slonim collected the classified gear and, with priority movement orders, returned to Pearl Harbor. The radiomen, however, could not get transport and could not practice their

---

*Ken Carmichael recalls being torpedoed aboard the *Enterprise* and leaving *her* at Tongatabu, but in fact no torpedo hit that carrier during the entire war. Conversely the *Saratoga was* torpedoed, in the Coral Sea, at just this time.

trade at Espíritu without a codebreaker–language officer. They cooled their heels until space could be found, as it happened, on one of the PBYs flying Admiral Nimitz and his staff back from an inspection of the South Pacific. Slonim's radio unit had moved its base or gear *twenty-six times* before getting back to Pearl Harbor.

A replacement unit manned the *Enterprise* at Santa Cruz. This became a moment of high tension for Marine Major Bankston T. Holcomb and his three radiomen, Elmer W. Disharoon, Stanley E. Gramblin, and Jack G. Kaye. The mobile unit suddenly gained extraordinary access to the contents of Japanese messages when Holcomb was handed a codebook recovered from a Japanese plane downed very early in the action. The codebook may have come from one of two JNAF planes that crashed aboard the *Hornet* while she maneuvered under attack.* One of those carried squadron commander markings and may have been the plane flown by strike leader Lieutenant Commander Seki Mamoru. Thereafter, notes a history of the mobile radio units, Holcomb provided very valuable intelligence throughout the battle.

Relatively less useful at Santa Cruz were radar and fighter interception. In this case the American strike and Japanese first wave flew identical courses in opposite directions, meaning that their returns on the radar screen merged and became indistinguishable for fighter-direction officers. Orders to fighters also went out too late, making it impossible for the American planes to gain sufficient altitude. The JNAF strikes came in with unstoppable power.

At Santa Cruz the Japanese also had absorbed some lessons of Midway (even though they had yet to admit the defeat). Although Americans were the first to radio a contact report, and though a deckload of planes had sat

---

*Enlisted aircrewman Tom Powell reports a different provenance for the codebook: Returning to Noumea to rejoin the *Enterprise* after a spell of flying from Henderson Field, Admiral Kinkaid gave the fliers a lift across the harbor in his barge. He invited officers to sit with him in the stern sheets. Because of a shortage of clothing, naval stores at Noumea had issued officers' khaki uniforms to Powell and other enlisted sailors. In the boat Powell listened in fascination as Admiral Kinkaid, seeking to reassure his officers after the losses at Santa Cruz, told the group that the Navy had recovered the current Japanese air code. The destroyer *Smith* had suffered heavy casualties when a JNAF plane crashed into her number two 5-inch mount, Kinkaid said, but the impact had thrown clear the bodies of both the pilot and crewman, and one of the bodies had had the codebook. Although this story rings true, the Japanese often did not install radios below the level of squadron commander, except for torpedo planes used as scouts. The *Smith* plane must have been configured this way. Richard B. Frank's recent history (*Guadalcanal*) reports the pilot who crashed aboard *Enterprise* to have been airgroup commander Murata Shigeharu. Older accounts such as Okumiya and Horikoshi (in their *Zero*) give Seki. John B. Lundstrom (in his *The First Team in the Guadalcanal Campaign*) writes that Seki crashed into the sea near *Enterprise*.

on the *Hornet*'s flight deck through the night awaiting news, the Japanese got two waves of planes up from Nagumo's carriers in the time it took Kinkaid to field a single strike. Since many of *Enterprise*'s strike aircraft were used that morning scouting, Kinkaid had little to follow up his first wave. Americans scored first nonetheless—one of the scout bombers put its ordnance on the flight deck of light carrier *Zuiho*—but the telling counterblow by JNAF left *Hornet* adrift and out of action. Before the Americans could get off any more strike aircraft, the Japanese second wave hit *Enterprise* and put her out of action, too.

The Japanese took their blows when *Hornet*'s strike group hit them, smashing *Shokaku* with four 1,000-pound bombs. This level of damage had been fatal to carriers at Midway, but this time ordnance was secure, gas lines had been drained, and fire hoses were ready. The *Shokaku*'s flight deck was disabled but her speed and flotation were unimpaired. She lost communications for a time but later restored them. Captain Arima Masafumi tried to stay in the battle line but was ordered to withdraw to preserve the ship. Admiral Nagumo was compelled to transfer to the *Zuikaku*, the third time in three battles he had had to shift his flag.

Exploiting initial success, other Japanese forces began to leap toward the American fleet. Rear Admiral Kakuta's force with the *Junyo* put up no less than three attack waves, while Nagumo's remaining *Zuikaku* sent another of her own. Surface action groups under Admirals Abe and Kondo raced toward the position of a crippled U.S. carrier reported by Japanese radio intelligence. Kinkaid meanwhile began to withdraw with the remnants of his task force, sending destroyers to scuttle the hapless *Hornet* with guns and torpedoes. The ship refused to sink until Japanese destroyers, having driven off the American ones, put four more torpedoes into the disabled vessel. Combined Fleet's Admiral Ugaki would have liked to tow *Hornet* to Japan as a symbol of success, but the carrier was simply too badly damaged to permit that.

The morning after Santa Cruz the Imperial Navy had carriers *Zuikaku* and *Junyo* at sea off the Solomons with 102 aircraft (perhaps 86 serviceable) and unmatched heavy support. On the Allied side there was not a single flight deck available in the South Pacific. Nagumo could have raided Cactus, done the same at Espíritu Santo, or interposed himself south of Guadalcanal and completely cut off the island's supply line. Americans recognized as much, sending every ship at Button to sea in a mad dash to get out of harm's way in case of a Japanese carrier raid. In fact Nagumo did none of these things, but merely returned to port after a day or so of milling about. The reason given is lack of fuel, yet Allied aerial reconnaissance the day of the battle identified an oiler at Shortland Island and three more at Rabaul. Admiral Nagumo was replaced immediately following the Santa Cruz battle.

The evidence suggests that the Japanese gave up in disappointment fol-

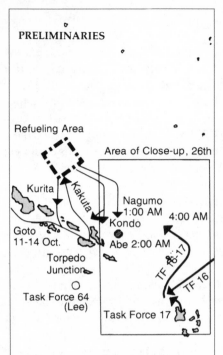

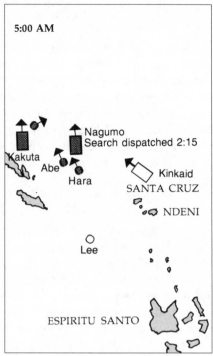

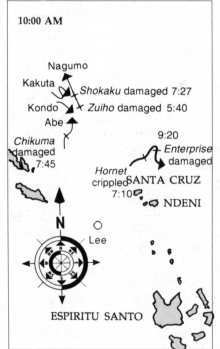

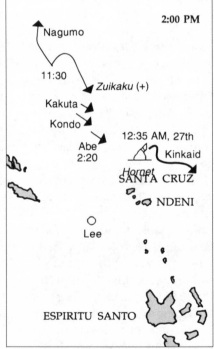

VII. Battle of Santa Cruz (October 26, 1942)

lowing failure of Imperial Army efforts to secure Henderson Field by ground attack. This failure ought not to mislead historians as to the outcome of the *naval* battle, however. Navy forces fought a pitched battle against an Allied fleet with several distinct advantages, and drove it from the field. The balance of losses was also unmistakable: American carrier *Hornet* and destroyer *Porter* sunk with *no* Japanese ships lost. True, cruiser *Chikuma* and carriers *Shokaku* and *Zuiho* had been damaged, but on the American side *Enterprise* had been badly damaged and battleship *South Dakota* lightly so. That American repairmen from the *Vulcan* performed superhuman feats in fixing up the *Enterprise* should not detract from the Japanese naval achievement, nor should the ineffectiveness of the Japanese on land. The *Enterprise* was patched up and thrown into the breach precisely because she happened to be the only flight deck left in the South Pacific, but only the most necessary work had been done; she would continue to operate at reduced efficiency. The Imperial Navy's victory at Santa Cruz was a real one.

HISTORIANS HAVE NEVER PAID MUCH ATTENTION TO JAPANESE INTELLIGENCE, AND SO READERS have not had much idea just how important this factor might have been either at Santa Cruz or in the Solomons campaign generally. In their efforts the Japanese brought to bear the same kinds of techniques as the Allies. Japanese intelligence efforts were never as successful as Allied, but then the Imperial Navy devoted fewer resources to them and had a different attitude concerning the utility of intelligence for combat.

Both sides in the war used aerial reconnaissance quite heavily, both tactically and for operational information. Air search methods were familiar to all, and the JNAF had established a regular pattern of search sectors that were covered daily from Rabaul or the seaplane base the Japanese set up at Rekata Bay, on the coast of Santa Isabel Island in the northeastern Solomons. Aircraft from task forces naturally also performed daily searches around the fleet itself. Much Japanese information came from this method, and not simply sightings of opposing task forces. Air search brought the Japanese intelligence about Allied fleet dispositions before the Savo Island battle, furnished data on movements between Guadalcanal and adjacent places like Tulagi, and supplied warnings of Allied naval activities. Poor searches or Allied countermeasures against Japanese searches contributed to the debacle at Cape Esperance. Positive intelligence in advance of Santa Cruz included sightings of U.S. carriers on October 13 and 16 and multiple reports mentioning other types of naval units, often battleships. The October 16 carrier report was confirmed beyond a doubt when U.S. carrier aircraft hit the seaplane base at Rekata later that day. The repeated identification of battleships among Allied naval forces, often in numbers greater than the two actually present in the South Pacific, injects a cautionary note: Poor warship identification by JNAF aircrews reduced the value of air searches.

Positive intelligence came from aerial reconnaissance when planes were used to gain information on troop or naval dispositions, ports, harbor defenses, and the like. This became a factor driving the increasing Allied reliance on photographic reconnaissance, but the Imperial Navy was slower to adopt that technique. At this stage JNAF planes mostly conducted visual reconnaissance, although they did occasionally use handheld cameras to obtain pictures. Alternatively, aircrew would sketch items of intelligence interest. In the Santa Cruz battle specifically, JNAF planes were sent to Guadalcanal to verify claims that Army troops had captured Henderson Field. Aerial reconnaissance demonstrated that the Japanese Army reports were inaccurate.

A related method was submarine reconnaissance. It was related since most such reconnaissance involved aircraft flying from large I-boats. The only records were extracts of reports the floatplanes sent on such missions, kept on file at the Naval General Staff. Submarine commanders simply assumed that all ports were defended with mines and antisubmarine nets, and tried to observe how Allied ships behaved as they approached the harbor entrance. Still, several scouting missions were conducted in conjunction with the October–November campaign for Guadalcanal. On October 13 a plane from submarine *I-7* made a dawn search of Espíritu Santo, while Nouméa was scouted from the *I-19* six days afterward. Commander Fujii Akiyoshi became the most diligent of the submarine skippers, using the floatplane of his boat *I-9* to scout Nouméa on October 30 and November 4, and Espíritu Santo a week later. A plane from the *I-8* made a midnight flight over Efate on November 2, and there were other scout flights over Nouméa and Fiji during the first fortnight of November. For the most part the submarines timed the aerial missions to arrive over targets at dawn, though there was an occasional night flight; Espíritu Santo was once scouted at dusk also. These recon missions were capable only of gathering the very ephemeral information of what ships were in harbor, leaving or entering at the time, and even that capability was limited by the pilot's skill at ship identification.

Coastwatchers were a resource for the Japanese in precisely the same manner as for the Allies. Unlike the Ferdinand organization, which was greatly assisted by the indigenous peoples of the Solomons, most Japanese coastwatchers were simply members of garrisons. There were a few prewar Japanese residents who were able to form bonds like those of the Australians, and in a few places the natives bowed to superior force, but for the most part this was not necessary. Japanese coastwatchers gained importance as Allied fleets moved farther north through the Solomons chain. For the Santa Cruz offensive, though, the Japanese landed a gunnery expert to serve as observer and liaison officer with a post atop Mount Austen. Lieutenant Funahashi Masatoshi of the *Yamato* enjoyed a panoramic view over U.S. positions and airfields, as well as Ironbottom Sound. American intelligence repeatedly noted the accuracy of his reports.

Finally, there was Japanese radio intelligence. At Rabaul the Navy had its 8th Communications Unit, while the 4th Communications Unit, in the Mandates, helped the fleet of that number. Both units had a collateral mission, intercepting Allied transmissions. More particularly there was the special-duty group, formally the 1st Combined Communications Unit, under Rear Admiral Kakimoto Gonichiro. The group was strongly represented at Rabaul, particularly after a frontline inspection in mid-September by naval communications chief Rear Admiral Kaneko Shigeharu.

Commander Ito Haruki was among a draft of about sixty officers and enlisted men sent to Rabaul to augment the special-duty group. The urgency of the move can be seen from the fact that they were flown into this forward base, not sent by ship. Ito thought Rabaul looked calm and beautiful from the air, and he found the intelligence unit in a grove of palms just west of the runway of Vunakanau base. There was a barracks, a small monitoring center, and two direction-finder huts. The local commander, a Lieutenant Ogimoto, had been in the radio intelligence business against the United States since before the war, when he was part of a secret monitoring unit within the Japanese embassy at Washington.

As early as October 12, the 14th Naval District Combat Intelligence Unit at Pearl Harbor was reporting interception of a Japanese message furnishing details of an American contact report. Intelligence summaries for the chief of naval operations in Washington noted on October 14 that traffic on Japanese Navy intelligence and direction-finding circuits had risen sharply after the Cape Esperance battle. This traffic continued at a high volume, especially from Rabaul. Two days later, as an example, Rabaul broadcast at least a dozen radio bearings on U.S. naval units. On October 22 Washington noted clear indications that the Japanese were recording U.S. radio call signs and attempting to track units. The next day the summary commented: "It is believed that the Japanese on Guadalcanal have now installed and are operating a high frequency direction finder." A note on October 24 informed recipients of the (accurate) suspicion that Combined Fleet staff maintained an intercept watch in coordination with Tokyo to facilitate rapid receipt of radio intelligence.

A specific contribution by the 1st Combined Communications Unit on October 20 was detection of growing numbers of U.S. submarines within direction-finding range. Kakimoto's unit warned the fleet. The special-duty group focused on U.S. submarine, patrol plane, and base transmissions until the onset of battle, then shifted to attack-plane and naval ship traffic. A postwar monograph on Japanese naval communications notes that "considerable success was attained in the collection of operational information."

The single most important development affecting U.S. strength at Santa Cruz would be arrival of the carrier *Enterprise* and her task group. The Japanese were aware of such movement—as early as October 4 (before the carrier actually sailed), Jaluit informed Tokyo of a task force at sea in the Hawaiian Islands. Later the Owada Group observed movement and a U.S. force under radio silence and broadcast: "A strong enemy task force sailed from Hawaii and is maintaining strict radio silence. Location and destination unknown." Of course strength was unknown, too, but it is worth saying that the term "task force" in Imperial Navy usage pertained to a naval unit that included aircraft carriers.

Japanese intelligence may not have been as advanced in breaking codes as OP-20-G and its field units, but the Imperial Navy got good support nevertheless. Still, Santa Cruz was only one battle. The next was about to begin.

BULL HALSEY WAS A DESPERATE MAN IN A SERIOUS SITUATION. THE CLEAREST SIGN OF HOW serious is what he did to get the *Enterprise* back to sea. Before the ship even made it to Nouméa—Poppy, in the coded argot of the South Pacific—Halsey called together the chiefs of his subordinate commands and told them to pool all their mechanics and repair specialists. All were to work on the damaged carrier or her planes, ship workers to be directed by personnel from the repair ship *Vulcan*. Specialists from that vessel went aboard the "Big E" as soon as she entered the harbor; their survey showed a necessity for about three weeks' work. They got eleven days. Another measure Halsey took was to move his headquarters ashore, freeing up command ship *Argonne* to be used more profitably. Then, grabbing his operations chief and an aide, Halsey flew a B-17 up to Cactus to see it for himself. Vandegrift—whose middle name, Archer, lent itself to his nickname, Archie—showed the admiral around, lent him his shack to sleep in, and was the picture of hospitality. Archie and Bull became great friends.

That Vandegrift's esteem for Bill Halsey endured may have had a good deal to do with U.S. intelligence. By November 4 Commander Layton's people were noting renewed indications of an upcoming Imperial Navy offensive, more ambitious than regular Tokyo Express runs, of which there had been plenty. Two days later the fleet intelligence summary commented: "All indications . . . point to continued preparations for offensive action," and on November 9 the CINCPAC summary furnished clear warning: "Predict an enemy all out attempt upon Guadalcanal soon." Lieutenant Robert Hudson, Layton's assistant, hazarded a guess on November 11 that the offensive would begin the next day or the one after. He also included an intelligence report that JNAF aircraft ground crews were already on Guadalcanal to bring Henderson Field into immediate operation under Japanese aegis once they captured it.

Predictions for the new offensive were entirely accurate. In fact, on November 9 the war diary of 14th Naval District's Combat Intelligence Unit included the gist of a Combined Fleet message sent late the previous day; it was Yamamoto's operations order for the new attack. Bill Halsey said in his own memoir that he was met on his return (from the visit to Cactus) by chief of staff Miles Browning "with news that another enemy offensive was brewing, one that would employ a vast number of ships and planes." The Japanese schedule was for heavy aircraft attacks, followed by naval bombardment of Henderson Field, then massive strikes from carriers, and finally new troop landings. The same gist was available on Cactus where Herbert C. Merillat, a Marine officer who functioned as liaison to the war correspondents and helped division intelligence on the side, noted it in his own diary entry for November 12. Merillat wrote that he expected a naval bombardment that same night.

Virtually the only item American intelligence got wrong on the November battle, which has become known as the Naval Battle of Guadalcanal, is the strength of Japanese carrier forces. On Cactus Major Merillat noted that intelligence expected five carriers. In actuality Rear Admiral Kakuta would command just one, the *Junyo*. Carrier Division 2's other ship, *Hiyo*, was at Truk repairing her condensers and fire damage. There, too, was *Zuiho*, repairing her flight deck. *Shokaku* had returned straight to Japan after Santa Cruz for dockyard repairs, while *Zuikaku* followed her on November 4, not for repairs but to begin training new carrier air groups.

In other respects American intelligence proved to be right on the money. Promptly on the night of November 12–13, a Japanese surface action group with battleships *Hiei* and *Kirishima* under Rear Admiral Abe Hiroaki arrived to repeat the big-gun bombardment that had been so successful a month before. This time, forewarned, Halsey interposed a cruiser-destroyer group led by Rear Admiral Daniel Callaghan, the victor of Cape Esperance. The brave Callaghan faced a superior force, but Abe played into his hands by waiting too long to shift to battle formation and by utilizing a cruising disposition much more complex than necessary. The American ships saw Abe first, hit hard, and kept hitting in a very confused night battle.

"We want the big ones," Callaghan signaled. "Get the big ones first!"

Admiral Callaghan himself was killed on the heavy cruiser *San Francisco*, while *Portland* was also heavily damaged, and four destroyers plus light cruiser *Atlanta* were sunk. Cruiser *Juneau* also emerged badly damaged, to be finished off next day by submarine *I-26*. For their part the Japanese lost destroyers *Yudachi* and *Akatsuki*, and Captain Nishida Masao's battleship,

*Hiei*, was so badly damaged that she was virtually marooned the following morning north of Savo.

Typical of experiences that night—it was Friday the thirteenth when the battle opened—was that of Commander Terauchi Masamichi, skipper of destroyer *Inazuma*, who approached Guadalcanal at high speed through terrific squalls. He could hardly see anything until, soon after they cleared the squalls, other ships reported sightings. The Americans looked huge in Terauchi's binoculars and soon rippled with gun flashes. *Akatsuki*, heading his column, crumpled under American gunfire. Terauchi sent his ship rushing toward the Americans without orders: It was his first battle and he was full of piss and vinegar. Then he read *Hiei*'s signal lamp. But Admiral Abe had no orders, just requests for information. The engagement quickly became a general one. Terauchi marveled at the tracers in the sky—red mostly, but blue and green too—thinking the battle seemed more like a fireworks display.

Commander Hara Tameichi aboard the *Amatsukaze* also noted the great confusion that night. He sailed on the opposite flank of the Japanese formation and believes his ship responsible for the initial torpedo hits on American cruiser *Juneau*. Hara remembers the fleet being handled hesitantly, with a stream of contradictory orders, use of radio where it could give away Japanese positions, and so on. There was also the critical moment when Admiral Abe had to decide whether to turn his battleships away while they changed ammunition, from the incendiaries they had been preparing to shoot at Guadalcanal to shells appropriate for a fleet engagement. Abe held his course; an Imperial Navy court of inquiry held that this decision resulted in the loss of *Hiei*.

By morning *Hiei* had been battered but not sunk, and had bare steerage way creeping north up The Slot. Both Pearl Harbor and Washington decrypted messages demonstrating that the crippled battleship remained afloat and was within striking distance of American aircraft. Planes from the *Enterprise* and the Cactus air force, flying from Henderson Field, sank the *Hiei* handily.

Meanwhile Vice Admiral Mikawa sortied from Shortland Island with a bombardment group, chugging down The Slot with heavy cruisers *Suzuya* and *Maya*, which that night dumped 990 rounds of 8-inch fire on Guadalcanal. Cactus answered the following morning, demonstrating just how ineffective bombardments could be; U.S. planes damaged Mikawa's flagship *Chokai*, the heavy cruiser *Maya*, the light cruiser *Isuzu*, and a destroyer. American planes sank the heavy cruiser *Kinugasa*. Planes also caught Rear Admiral Tanaka leading a convoy toward Guadalcanal, and eight transports sank beneath the waves.

One last arrow in the Japanese quiver was 2nd Fleet commander Kondo. Upon news of Abe's defeat, Vice Admiral Kondo steamed south with his own cruisers, picked up the *Kirishima* and the other undamaged vessels remaining from the Abe force, and tried to close Cactus again for a bombardment the night of November 14–15. Again radio intelligence warned the South Pacific Command with time to spare to get Rear Admiral Willis A. Lee's Task Force 64 into an interception position. Lee had the fast battleships *Washington* and *South Dakota* and engaged in the first surface battleship action of the Pacific war. All Lee's four destroyers would be sunk, but Kondo lost destroyer *Ayanami* and Captain Iwabuchi Sanji's battleship, *Kirishima*. Damage to the fast battleship *South Dakota* did not dampen American spirits.

The Naval Battle of Guadalcanal effectively ended another Japanese Solomons offensive. "This is far from my aim of destroying the enemy," Admiral Ugaki penned in his diary. Abe Hiroaki was held accountable for loss of the *Hiei* and put on the inactive list in early 1943. Captain Iwabuchi was sent ashore to posts with the Yokosuka and Maizuru districts, and later as base commander at Manila.

Americans were elated. Admiral Ernest King issued an official commendation to OP-20-G for its work at the end of October, which Nimitz passed along to the 14th Naval District, but after the naval battle the Pacific chief issued a commendation of his own: "Once again radio intelligence has enabled the fighting force of the Pacific and Southwest Pacific to know where and when to hit the enemy." In the cable forwarding the commendation to intelligence units in the South Pacific and Australia, Nimitz added, "My only regret is that our appreciation, which is unlimited, can only be extended to those who read this [code] system."

Japanese officers felt devastated after the mid-November battles. Nothing seemed to work against the Americans. Admiral Tanaka had even ordered four transports to rush ahead and deliberately run themselves aground in an effort to get some reinforcements through, and perhaps 2,500 men got ashore, but U.S. aircraft finished off the ships, and the troops landed without heavy equipment or much in the way of supplies. In fact, the Japanese soldiers on Guadalcanal were starving, desperate to eat, at a time when it had become apparent that little prospect remained of truly successful reinforcement. It was at this point the Japanese introduced the drum method of putting matériel ashore—highly inefficient because of the vagaries of wind and tide, but offering better chances of survival to the ships delivering supplies.

Rear Admiral Tanaka Raizo and his 2nd Destroyer Flotilla made the first cruise to Guadalcanal using the drum method. Tanaka loaded six ships with 200 to 240 drums each, and used destroyers *Naganami* and *Takanami* as escorts. He left Shortland Island during the evening of November 29. This time aerial reconnaissance warned the Allies of increased shipping at Shortland, and coastwatchers spotted Tanaka's sortie. Another U.S. cruiser-destroyer group moved to derail the Tokyo Express. The unit comprised four heavy cruisers, a light cruiser, and four destroyers. It moved through Ironbottom Sound toward the northwest coast of Guadalcanal just as Tanaka's destroyers arrived from the north for their drum drop. The transport destroyers were about to loose their loads when flares burst overhead and the American ships opened fire. Tanaka's escort destroyers replied with torpedoes, and others did, too, where they could. It would be the most successful Japanese torpedo attack of the war; all four American heavy cruisers were hit. The *New Orleans* and *Minneapolis* each lost her bow, the *Pensacola* was damaged, and the *Northampton* sank. The Imperial Navy lost only destroyer *Takanami*, smothered by shellfire in the first instant of combat. This battle of Tassafaronga was a marked Japanese success.

Far from resting on his laurels, Tanaka began planning immediately for another Tokyo Express mission once he regained Shortland Island. Indeed, this became the pattern, with a rat run required every two or three days just to get some food to the Japanese on Guadalcanal. Imperial General Headquarters could not stand the constant drain of the missions. Destroyer *Nowake* was damaged by air attack on December 8, and the *Teruzuki* was sunk off Guadalcanal by PT boats four days later. American aircraft sank the destroyer *Suzukaze* in The Slot on January 2, 1943; then a week later *Hatsukaze* was lightly damaged by the PTs; and planes struck again in mid-January, damaging four more destroyers within two days. Air operations proved equally expensive: 288 planes were lost in combat and 135 operationally during October; 202 in combat and 143 operationally in November; the December figures were 84 and 141; January cost 89 planes lost in combat and another 141 to accidents or malfunctions. This loss rate proved impossible to sustain.

There were only two basic strategic choices possible. One was to launch another major offensive against Cactus, the other to withdraw. Combined Fleet chief of staff Ugaki had begun speculating about withdrawal even before the end of November, but he refused to put forward such a suggestion for fear the Army would reduce even more its cooperation with the fleet if it felt it was being abandoned. By December, however, the New Guinea front was heating up perceptibly, with fierce fighting at Buna. Army staff officers themselves began to talk of withdrawal from Guadalcanal. Tokyo sanctioned such a plan with formal IGHQ meetings, including a liaison conference in the presence of Hirohito.

By January 1943 the Americans were on the offensive on Guadalcanal, with the 1st Marine Division replaced by a U.S. Army formation, the XIV Corps. As troops pushed west against opposition from Japanese who fought fiercely even while starving, U.S. intelligence began to detect some of the same signs previously always linked with an offensive: buildups of aircraft in the Rabaul complex; shipping; fleet preparations. Coastwatchers spotted the Japanese landing materials such as concrete at Munda on New Georgia for use on an air base there. More activity would be detected at Rekata Bay. By December 17 ONI considered Japanese moves preparation for increased air activity; by the thirty-first, in a report issued over the signature of old-timer Ellis Zacharias, plans for a major operation were said to be merely in a formative stage. Pacific Fleet daily summaries reported awareness of an impending operation by the last week of January; on the thirtieth this operation was called an offensive, and the summary of January 31 commented:

> A major action in this area is expected soon. This will probably consist of an attempt similar to the one on November 13–15 where transports attempted to land troops at Guadalcanal covered by fleet units. Whether or not carriers will be involved is unknown as yet. It is known though that a detached group of carrier aircraft is now operating shorebased in the Shortland area.

These intelligence reports in December and January amount to the most significant intelligence failure on the Allied side throughout the Guadalcanal campaign. The failure is understandable, however, because this time the traditional indicators had an opposite meaning.

In fact Combined Fleet sent large forces to sea in early February. Destroyer runs, rather than carrying reinforcements and supplies as the United States thought, were pulling out remaining Japanese personnel in what was called the KE Operation. Depending on the count one accepts, the Imperial Navy succeeded in evacuating between 10,652 and 12,805 Japanese from the Isle of Death. Destroyers on the runs each carried five or more rubber boats equipped with Johnson outboard motors, and anchored 500 to 600 yards from the beach. The Japanese waded out until the water reached their chests, climbed into the boats, then ascended rope ladders to destroyer decks. One naval officer observed that the starving evacuees asked for no food, only cigarettes. Only one ship was lost—destroyer *Akigumo*, during the third mission. Her skipper, Lieutenant Commander Soma Shohei, had had a premonition, and told others the ship would be sunk during the return voyage. Sure enough, American planes set the warship afire; her crew and passengers had to be transferred and the destroyer scuttled with a torpedo.

At Rabaul the special-duty group played a part in the evacuation, too. Lieutenant Ogimoto mimicked the communications of U.S. search planes to send misleading reports to base. Others cheered him on. Although a U.S. officer later found no basis to credit a specific claim for Ogimoto's success, there is no reason to believe Japanese radio intelligence would not have attempted this kind of deception measure in view of the serious evacuation effort.

For the Imperial Navy, whose Decisive Battle doctrine and combat tactics were always so aggressive, it is a final irony of the Guadalcanal campaign that one of their most successful endeavors should have been a retreat. The war would move right on up the Solomons, but Japanese efforts continued to be hampered by Allied intelligence. One of the most serious compromises of all, a security breach of the first order, was an incident during the final days of the Guadalcanal campaign. That breach set the tone for the campaign to isolate Rabaul—in American parlance, Operation Cartwheel.

# "You Don't Have to Be Crazy, but It Helps!"

I N JAPAN'S DESPERATE EFFORTS TO PUSH SUPPLIES DOWN THE SLOT TO FEED MEN ON Guadalcanal, it was not just destroyers which were pressed into service. Submarines, too, were increasingly diverted from their role as advance forces in fleet combat, as well as their other critical role interdicting sea-lanes. A dozen I-boats operated off the eastern coast of Australia during the year from mid-1942 onward; there was a celebrated midget-submarine attack inside Sydney harbor in May 1942, and a virtually unknown midget sortie into Ironbottom Sound that October. Considering that four I-boats had been off Australia at the moment the Guadalcanal battle was joined, and that the 7th Submarine Flotilla at Rabaul generally maintained a force level of eight or more I-boats, the dozen sorties to Australia represent a small proportion of the potential effort. Results proved commensurately small: nineteen ships sunk off northern or eastern Australia (roughly 80,000 tons) and another fifteen damaged, for a total of 605 fatalities, many in the months after the withdrawal from Guadalcanal. Diversion of the submarine effort into supply transport and other activities must be considered a key factor hindering war patrols by I-boats. The diversion of the submarines, not to say the destroyers, amounted to virtual attrition—a substantial reduction in Imperial Navy war-fighting capabilities, without actual sinking of ships. Such virtual attrition resulted in great part from intelligence, which made the Allies so successful intercepting conventional Japanese movement and resupply activity.

The saga of the *I-1* illustrates this metamorphosis in the war situation, a subtle but real harbinger of things to come. Not only was the *I-1* forced into unconventional supply work but, in the end, her demise served to further improve Allied intelligence knowledge, a true irony for Japan. Under her first skipper, Commander Ankyu Eitaro, *I-1* participated in the underwater blockade of Pearl Harbor, unsuccessfully attacking a tanker and a cargo vessel and shelling Hilo harbor. She would be involved in the futile pursuit of an American carrier which occupied several I-boats in the first days of 1942. Afterward, in the Netherlands East Indies, *I-1* first took blood, dispatching the 8,667-ton merchantman *Siantar* with guns and torpedoes. In port at Yokosuka the submarine used her anti-aircraft machine guns to fire on one of Doolittle's raiding bombers that April, and then *I-1* spent the summer on patrol in Aleutian waters.

This submarine's war patrols in the Aleutians ended, though, when she left for Truk in September. But the *I-1* happened to be a relatively old boat, built by the Kawasaki yard in Kobe and commissioned in 1926, equipped with diesel engines from Germany. The port-side engine had given the *I-1* trouble before, and in February 1942 a malfunction here had forced the boat to abort a mission following her first departure for the East Indies. Thus the *I-1* could not be regarded as among the most battleworthy submarines. On the other hand, she had easily completed a 25,000-mile test cruise, and had at one time held the Navy submersion record, for a 260-foot dive. So the *I-1* did seem capable of maneuvers of the sort deemed necessary for a transport mission. In the fall of 1942, when the Navy began to plan for so-called *mogura* (mole) transport runs by submarine, the *I-1* became the test bed for new submersible barges designed to move supplies ashore.

At Truk a forty-six-foot barge was fitted abaft the conning tower where a 5.5-inch gun had formerly been mounted. Vice Admiral Komatsu Teruhisa, Sixth Fleet commander, inspected Ankyu's boat with the new transport mechanism fitted to it on September 15. The barge was unloaded the next day and sent separately to Rabaul; the *I-1* picked it up for a test mission to the Admiralty Islands (Goodenough, in this case), where she landed rations and picked up sixty sick men who needed treatment at Rabaul. A second mission, again to Goodenough Island, was interrupted by an Allied patrol plane that swooped down in the middle of the night, forcing Commander Ankyu to jetison the barge. Days later Ankyu, who had a reputation as the hardest-drinking submarine skipper in the Navy, and two of his officers all came down with dengue fever. They would be replaced at Truk in early November, when Lieutenant Commander Sakamoto Eichi took over the *I-1*. On November 16 the Combined Fleet issued a directive establishing procedures for *mogura* operations. Commander Tanabe in the *I-176* made the first successful run to Guadalcanal and soon eleven boats were on mole runs to the Isle of Death. A route to Buna was soon set up for the same reasons— conventional shipping seemed too vulnerable to Allied airpower. Commander Ankyu went on to become the most successful *mogura* skipper, with sixteen successful missions in the *I-38*, most to New Guinea. His old boat, the *I-1*, and its skipper, Sakamoto, would not be so lucky.

First Sakamoto had to deal with the bane of this older submarine, a breakdown of the main starboard electric motor; *I-1* was obliged to return to Yokosuka, where she spent time in dockyard hands. Once she was back at Rabaul the 7th Submarine Flotilla slated Sakamoto for a mission to Guadalcanal, where one submarine could deliver enough food to keep Japanese troops eating for two or three days. At this time, late January 1943, with the Imperial Navy about to withdraw, it was vital for the troops to gather strength for the coming ordeal. The *I-1* departed Rabaul on January 24 and stopped at Buin on Bougainville to load supplies outside range of the Cactus air force. Then she sailed south, on the twenty-ninth reaching a point off Kamimbo Bay at the northwest corner of Guadalcanal, about ten miles from the leading spearheads of advancing U.S. Army XIV Corps units. When he brought the *I-1* to periscope depth at mid-evening, Sakamoto did not know that two New Zealand Navy antisubmarine corvettes, *Moa* and *Kiwi*, were steaming along right next to his position.

So far it has not been possible to discover whether Halsey's South Pacific Command had specific intelligence on the *I-1* mission, but in view of the repeated *mogura* runs over more than two months, the Allies cannot have been ignorant of the technique. There was enough general warning to suggest an antisubmarine patrol in waters off the remaining Japanese-occupied portions of Guadalcanal. The New Zealand ships' presence can be accounted for on that basis. Commander Sakamoto's failure to detect the corvettes before surfacing led directly to another nasty scrap.

*Kiwi* made the first contact with sonar at 9:05 P.M. Her skipper laid on full speed and, once he saw *I-1*'s wake, prepared to ram because the vessels were so close together (less than 150 yards). When engine-room crew questioned the order the skipper insisted, then quipped that the action might be good for leave time—at first a weekend in Auckland then, as the battle continued, a full week, even a fortnight. *Kiwi* opened fire, rammed the *I-1*, then backed off and fired some more. One of the first shots wiped out Sakamoto's primary gun crew and mortally wounded the commander himself. The submarine's navigator called for swords and replacement gunners; this would be the first warning to those belowdecks that an emergency had begun. The port engine was out of commission again—a popped clutch—reducing the boat's speed, and her steering gear broke down in the middle of the battle, as executive officer Lieutenant Koreda Sadayoshi tried to beach the boat on Guadalcanal.

The *Kiwi* rammed three times in all. As she did, the *I-1*'s navigator tried to board and fight it out with swords in the best swashbuckling tradition. A recent American account has overdramatized this episode, making out the Japanese officer to be a famous swordsman, but the Japanese narrative on which that is apparently based merely says the navigator was an expert with this weapon. Either way, his attempt to board *Kiwi* simply resulted in his being caught helplessly between the two ships, then hauled out of the water to become a prisoner of war. Meanwhile the *Kiwi* continued firing until her guns overheated, whereupon *Moa* took over, having raced to the scene of battle. Both corvettes stood by until dawn.

On the Japanese side Lieutenant Koreda became the senior surviving officer, with a crippled submarine incapable of submerging, and thirty dead sailors. He beached the *I-1* and got fifty survivors ashore. Koreda took some secret documents with him, including code material, and later told Orita Zenji, another submariner, that he had burned them. But other accounts, including that of submariner Hashimoto Mochitsura, aver the papers were merely buried. Moreover, Koreda had some inkling that secret materials had been inadequately treated: He sent working parties back to the ship in attempts to blow it up. These did not succeed, and the survivors evacuated to Rabaul amid the larger Japanese withdrawal. When Rabaul learned of the disaster, another submarine came down to try to torpedo the wreckage, while an air mission would be attempted on February 10. Torpedoes failed and the aircraft could not even find the wreck.

The Americans did, however, and began a very careful effort to salvage documents from the *I-1*. Submarine rescue vessel *Ortolan* did the work. Jasper Holmes, from intelligence at Pearl Harbor, notes that the papers recovered contained lists of call signs, old codebooks and charts, lists of the Imperial Navy's geographic designators, and so on. Holmes believes the current codebooks were taken ashore, but remarks that the *I-1* was also carrying copies of reserve codes scheduled to go into effect during future months, in effect a mass of material difficult to move. Orita Zenji insisted that the codes were burned; he wrote that the claim that valuable documents were captured is open to question. Let the question end here. Radioman Philip H. Jacobsen of the Guadalcanal communications intelligence unit handled these captured documents from the *I-1*. He comments:

> They brought the communication documents down to us. They were all salt water–logged. They were red-bound books with lead in them for destruction at sea. Four character Negori code books and nine character period code books, operational code books and we were drying them out to decide which ones would be sent to Pearl Harbor, I guess. We put them on top of a receiver to use the heat . . . to try to dry them out. We would take a page and put paper between each leaf and dried out every code book. They had maps, U.S. hydrographic maps from '41 with red corrections. . . . They had some strategic plans where they were going to go across the Indian Ocean into Diego Suarez into Madagascar. Their projections of overall planning. We got a lot of documents out of this Japanese

submarine. We kept them for about two days to get them in shape and box them. . . . We got them to our intercept site at Lunga Point. We made the decision on it because a lot of it wasn't of value. . . . We felt good about having a hand in getting this information and we handled it very carefully.

Commander Holmes agrees that the codes Pearl Harbor received were superseded by the time the captured documents arrived, but as always these kinds of materials furnished clues to the structure of Japanese systems plus a snapshot of codes recovered at a certain point in time. "It was very useful to have a complete code, fleet vocabulary," recalls Tommy Dyer, codebreaker extraordinaire. "It settled a number of arguments as to what word was used here or there."

In addition the *I-1* affair furnished intelligence of a more basic nature. For one thing, an engineer petty officer, Kuboaki Takeo, was rescued and interrogated after twenty-four hours in the water. Having been bitten by sharks in his right heel and left forearm before rescue, Kuboaki proved more than happy to talk about his nine years in the Imperial Navy. He gave a thumbnail sketch of the history of the *I-1;* tidbits on Japanese submarine forces; technical data on I-boats, both aircraft-equipped and otherwise; details of submarine losses and construction; and a description of air-raid warning signals current at Rabaul. Kuboaki also furnished the important operational intelligence that aircraft carrier *Shokaku* had still been repairing at Yokosuka in December, and he provided an accurate count of the number of guns in the main batteries of superbattleships *Yamato* and *Musashi.* Interrogated at Pearl Harbor later, directly by Commander Holmes, the Japanese *I-1* survivor confirmed that U.S. submarine torpedoes had detonation problems.

Documents that divers recovered from the *I-1* further provided a windfall for both South Pacific theater intelligence and ONI. Among those published by the former were notes on a conference of communications officers aboard the *Yamato* at Truk, held in November 1942, and a log of the *I-1*'s own career. Publications by ONI included details on *I-1* activities, Japanese documents detailing radio and sound equipment ranges; submersion time and endurance; battery life; cruising ranges surfaced and submerged; ship capacities; particulars of various classes of Japanese subs.

All of a sudden the United States had both an unparalleled view into the secret detail of Japanese submarine capabilities and a windfall of code and communications data.

The Imperial Navy would be more concerned about the compromise of code material than anything the United States discovered regarding Japanese submarines. The latter was regrettable but to be expected in war. But the code material, *that* involved compromise of 200,000 copies of assorted codes and ciphers. The semi-official monograph on Japanese naval communications confirms that the codebooks were buried, not burned, and at any rate (it further affirms) copies of other codes were left aboard ship. One feature of German-Japanese technical cooperation had been that the German Kriegsmarine gave the Imperial Navy details of its handy water-soluble inks, which would have made the codebooks in the *I-1* useless by erasing their secrets. Unfortunately very few of the materials aboard the hapless I-boat had actually been produced with this kind of ink. All the rest figured in the communications security failure.

Countermeasures were swift and went beyond the efforts to destroy the *I-1*'s wreck by torpedo and air attack. The Imperial Navy instantly changed the additive table used with JN-25, introduced revisions in encoding procedure, and began compilation of fresh codebooks. The Japanese did not, however, change their strategic code, and that would be a great boon to Allied intelligence.

It was no accident that the U.S. Navy could work so effectively recovering key materials from the wreck of the *I-1*. Navy salvage and repair crews had had specific experience rescuing sailors trapped when the submarine *Squalus* foundered in May 1939, later refloating the boat, recommissioned as *Sailfish*. The divers and others also got a great deal of knowledge, practice, and just plain determination to get back at the Japanese, from extensive work salvaging warships sunk at Pearl Harbor. Given existing salvage and repair capabilities, the Navy gave specific thought to how they could be used to advantage for intelligence purposes.

In March and again in May 1942 Admiral King issued instructions regarding recovery of information from enemy submarines. It is likely he was thinking mainly of U-boats at the time, but the technique was first used against the Japanese. King made this intelligence function a matter of standing orders, preferring to rely on naval personnel to minimize any chance the adversary could learn of a compromise through capture and introduce countermeasures.

Under the system introduced at that time, ONI was to be informed by immediate dispatch whenever materials were recovered from a submarine, or if there was any reasonable possibility of mounting an effort for salvage and recovery. Washington would then send an intelligence expert to advise the local naval command and accompany the salvage unit on a recovery project. Items of intelligence value were deemed to include all documents and any other materials and equipment, in fact *"everything of any nature whatsoever"* (italics in the original). Only Navy divers would be used to actually enter sunken vessels, and any entering divers would carry waterproof bags to retrieve papers and documents. All items recovered would be forwarded immediately for analysis.

Recognizing salvage crews' desire for tangible souvenirs showing projects they had worked on, the Navy Department undertook to return to the skipper of the original salvage vessel or vessels such artifacts as proved to have no intelligence value.

To further protect salvage operations from exposure to an adversary who would surely be greatly distressed to learn of them, suitable and plausible stories were prepared to account for diving operations. In addition, authorities were instructed to deny, automatically and always, that any documents or other materials had been recovered from any wrecks explored.

These procedures were used to recover documents for translation or equipment for technical intelligence analysis throughout the war. Perhaps the earliest instance of equipment recovery, of course, was that of the midget submarine beached on Oahu during the Pearl Harbor attack. Both the *I-1* and another midget sub would be examined at Guadalcanal in 1943. Intelligence from this source flowed into a system greatly changed from that of December 1941.

A HARBINGER OF CHANGE FOR INTELLIGENCE HAD BEEN THE SUDDEN SPROUTING OF WAR rooms all over Washington. As already seen, this effort to pool information from many different sources represented a departure from previous practice. Intelligence fusion became a powerful tool precisely because knowing the adversary was a matter of discovery and analysis, rather like fitting together pieces of a jigsaw puzzle, and different methods often supplied different pieces of the puzzle. Fusion seemed important enough in Washington, but in the theaters of war it was even more obviously vital. It was not long, only March 1942 in fact, before someone suggested operational intelligence centers in the field. In this case credit goes to the commandant of the Marine Corps, who first proposed a unit at Pearl Harbor manned from all services to provide intelligence to all commanders in the Pacific.

Although intelligence fusion might seem desirable in theory, there remained practical problems. The Marines, for example, calculated that a total of eighty-one officers and 121 enlisted personnel would be needed to operate the center they proposed at Pearl Harbor. To get the armed services to assign that many people would be one problem, while getting Admiral Nimitz to accept them would be another.

To test the waters for the fusion center, Washington sent a delegation to Hawaii to carry out preliminary discussions. Army representative on the mission would be Colonel Moses Pettigrew, deputy to Rufus Bratton of the Military Intelligence Division. There was an airman along, an older officer, and a Navy representative, the redoubtable Arthur H. McCollum. The group tried to fly out to Pearl but at that time there were just two clippers a week, the weather was terrible, and they finally left San Francisco on a transport, taking five days to reach port. McCollum knew most of the officers on CINCPAC's staff, though he had never met Admiral Nimitz. McCollum also hesitated to present the intelligence-center concept to Eddie Layton. Instead he talked with those officers with whom he was well acquainted and let the notion float to the top.

It was about the time of the Coral Sea battle when one day Chester Nimitz sent for McCollum. He sat the ONI man down, made some small talk, then came to the main topic.

"I've heard that you've been talking around about an Intelligence Center for the Pacific Ocean Area," Admiral Nimitz said. "Tell me about it."

McCollum explained the idea and a proposed organization that he had put together with ONI's senior planner, Captain Arthur D. Struble. Washington had a package and was simply awaiting CINCPAC's approval to put it in place.

"Sounds pretty good," Nimitz responded. "How many people is this going to take?"

"Well, Admiral," Commander McCollum replied, "we have tried to keep the original establishment down to a minimum. . . . We've figured and trimmed every corner, Admiral, and it takes about a hundred and twenty."

Nimitz roared with laughter, rocked back in his swivel chair, then retorted, "McCollum, how in the world am I ever going to get a hundred and twenty people of this kind of a thing on board my flagship, the *Pennsylvania?*"

The emissary from Washington delicately explained that the fusion center would be a shoreside unit, with perhaps just a few aboard the flagship. The Pacific chief admitted that that made better sense and asked McCollum to work out arrangements with several senior staff, talks that took about three days. Commander Layton opposed the intelligence center "rabidly," possibly because he saw it as a threat to his own position as fleet intelligence officer, and McCollum believes that Eddie Layton never did fully accept the center. However, Layton's job turned out to be secure—he remained with Nimitz through almost the entire war—and the fusion center eventually made Layton's work more valuable than ever. Before the war ended the intelligence center would swell to 1,767 officers and enlisted personnel, a number unthinkable in 1942, but Chester Nimitz never looked back. If asked, after the war, Admiral Nimitz would very likely have defended the Pacific intelligence center as worth the assignment of every person who worked with it.

On May 28 Admiral Nimitz sent Washington a memorandum officially endorsing an "Intelligence Center, Pacific Ocean Areas," outlining the sections the unit would have. He agreed to the creation of a similar joint unit in Australia, and a very small one at Dutch Harbor in the Aleutians, but insisted that the Pearl Harbor unit be the main one until it had been fully staffed and was up and running. On this basis, on June 12, Admiral Ernest King approved the establishment of these intelligence centers.

PEARL HARBOR AND WASHINGTON, D.C., WERE FOCAL POINTS FOR ALL INTELLIGENCE COLlected by equipment recovery, and for much else besides. Plenty of changes occurred after December 7, 1941, when Station Hypo had been under orders to ignore JN-25, a day when radiomen assembled at Wailupe had seen Japanese planes flying over them to attack Pearl Harbor, while others at Heiia had tried to burn stacks of IBM punch cards to keep intelligence data from supposed Japanese invaders. Among the biggest changes would be the move from plain radio intelligence to all-source materials.

At first the changes were in radio intelligence itself, which went from an important but tiny aspect of fleet activity to something truly central to naval operations. Radiomen did not see the changes immediately. One, arrived in the spring aboard the old ammunition ship *Nitro,* a vessel bearing a load of 8-inch shells for the ill-fated cruiser *Houston,* found himself caught up in petty work as the interception and the direction-finding units at Heiia were ordered to pack up everything, lock, stock, and barrel, and move to Wailupe. Tom Warren, who wanted to join radio and awaited an opening in a training class, happened to be cook at Wailupe when the CBI (combat intelligence) radiomen arrived, and spent off-duty hours with them (often playing poker); he decided CBI was the way to go. Just after the Japanese attack, another group of radiomen arrived on the transport *Henderson.* Either the Navy was desperate or it simply forgot about the radiomen, for they were sent to work at the Lualualei ammunition depot for several months.

Commander Joseph Rochefort had great need for more personnel, both for the CBI activities and for Station Hypo itself. The code breaks that made possible the Coral Sea, Midway, and Guadalcanal victories would not have been possible without a much enlarged organization. By about February 1942, Rochefort recalls, he had made an arrangement with the 14th Naval District personnel office that radio intelligence could have first pick of arriving drafts of sailors, who reached Hawaii with their personal records, ready to be selected. Chief Petty Officer Durwood G. Rorie would meet the incoming ships and look the men over. Rorie proved such a fine judge of talent for the arcane codebreaking business that he would be commissioned later in the war.

Joe Rochefort also picked up fifty to seventy-five sailors or officers already in Oahu for various reasons. Among them, immediately after Pearl Harbor, were the members of the *California* band led by Chief Petty Officer Lovine B. Luckenbach, "Red" Luckenbach, who would also be commissioned and ended up after the war as a senior executive with the IBM Corporation. About March, radio intelligence discovered and brought in the men from the Lualualei ammunition dump, including radiomen Albert M. Fishburn and Ralph Cox. Marine officer Alva Lasswell, once "father" of the Shanghai intercept station, was drafted from his assignment to set up a language-officer program, something else that was also sorely needed.

In the meantime the intercept and direction-finding stations moved again from Wailupe to a big building on a hill at Wahiawa. There new drafts learned to become katakana radio operators in classes on the second floor, taught by Harvey J. Howard, a tough bird by some accounts, and Elliott E. Okins, a much-respected officer. Radiomen first learned the Morse code for the Japanese characters, which they called chicken tracks, then how to copy them using sticks and ink, then how to use the RIP-5 character typewriters. Such was the demand for operators that the Wahiawa center had no formal classes or graduations but simply moved trainees out as soon as the men could handle about thirty words a minute.

Working conditions were by no means idyllic, though at first the radiomen were housed four to a unit in prewar duplex apartments that had been officers' quarters. Typically a radioman did a four-part week, starting with a work detail. This duty included making up message forms used to copy out intercepted transmissions, for which the station had an insatiable demand which merely grew as the war progressed; pulling guard duty for mail or dispatch runs down to Hypo; or doing assorted other things. The first radio watch would be an evening one, and before that the sailor would have to report in the afternoon for close-order drill. Sometimes there would be details to the rifle range for target practice. Few liked this kind of thing, save Major Lasswell, a crack shot who had led Marine rifle and pistol teams to championship trophies. Ordinary radiomen would follow an evening duty period with one that began at midnight (called a mid-watch), then would have a day watch followed by time off. Routines could be changed entirely by events; for instance, Al Fishburn was standing evening watch the night news came of the fall of Corregidor, a night there was great concern to listen for anything the Japanese might report finding from the former Station Cast.

Working conditions were not all that wonderful either. The Pearl Harbor raid triggered mandatory curfew rules—everyone had to be off the street by six o'clock (which made going into Honolulu no fun), and blackout rules were enforced stringently. Police initially had authority to shoot out any lights they found during blackout periods. The Wahiawa installation, combining a school with administrative offices plus as many as fifty radio positions that were manned constantly, was always crowded and odoriferous. At night, when every door and window had to be shut for the blackout, the place became hot and filled with stale cigarette smoke. Some thought it positively unhealthful. On at least one occasion an officer visiting from Hypo took it on his own responsibility to order all the doors and windows opened to air out the work space. Immediately the phones rang off their hooks with complaints that Wahiawa was showing lights. The officer stayed for a couple of hours fielding the calls and telling those who would not desist to talk to him at the Navy Yard. At length the Navy developed special louvers that admitted fresh air but showed no light, and these were installed in a new intercept facility built at Wahiawa in 1943, when the number of radio receiver positions increased to about eighty.

The blackout rules endured until after the battle of Midway. Authorities could not make up their minds that the threat had passed. Many objected that the blackout was wholly useless anyway, since throughout that period one could see Pearl Harbor from far away, clearly illuminated every night for the benefit of salvage and repair crews working to restore the damage of December 7. The blackout simply served to highlight the Navy Yard even more. During this period Kilauea volcano on Hawaii's Big Island also was in eruption, shooting molten rock and flames into the air as a beacon for anyone unable to view Pearl Harbor itself.

Work at the codebreaking facility down at the Navy Yard proved arduous, and not only for cryptanalysts like Commanders Dyer or Wright, who would work for stretches of thirty hours at a time. Ensign Elmer Dickey was at Wahiawa until the fall of 1942, sent there by Jack Holtwick, then running the IBM machine room at Hypo. Dickey, a former enlisted radio operator at Bainbridge, Shanghai, Cavite, and Heiia, was quite happy in direction-finding work until traffic-analysis boss Thomas Huckins discovered him at Wahiawa and wanted him down at the Navy Yard. Huckins called Dickey up one day and asked how he liked Wahiawa and what strings he had pulled to get there. Dickey replied he liked it fine and had no desire to leave, to which Huckins countered that that was too bad since he would be cutting new orders for the ensign right after the weekend. Dickey spent the rest of the war working on the radio traffic analysis summaries that were compiled every night to be read by Admiral Nimitz in the morning. It was like the city desk of a large newspaper, Dickey recalled: "Death was the only excuse" for not getting out the product, a five-to-seven-page summary. Preparation began at about 2:00 A.M. and the thing had to be ready to leave in a sealed envelope by 7:30. Nimitz read the reports himself; they then formed the basis for Commander Layton's fleet intelligence summaries.

Sacrifice was endemic among denizens of the radio intelligence vaults. Commander Jasper Holmes, whom Elmer Dickey admired as the senior officer most regularly interested in their traffic analysis findings (undoubtedly his interest was due to his role assembling data for the Combat Intelligence Unit), estimates that the ordinary clerks, typists, keypunch operators, and yeomen typically put in twelve-hour workdays, seven days a week. Alva Lasswell remembers many twenty-four-hour stints, and probably many were shared by another linguist, Joe Finnegan, since Lasswell and Finnegan most often worked as a team. Lasswell's family moved from the East Coast to Palo Alto to be closer to him, but he hardly ever got time off for leave. Once, to take advantage of a weekend pass, Lasswell hitched a ride in the tail gun turret of a B-24 bound for the States. Another time he was deliberately sent to Washington to rest, but once there got drafted to stand in for Redfield (Rosie) Mason instead. Ironically, Mason had gone to Pearl Harbor on temporary orders to fill in for Lasswell.

Tommy Dyer similarly got practically no breaks during the war. The most notable was an involuntary one at the direct instigation of Admiral Nimitz. The CINCPAC, it happened, had taught naval science on assignment before the war at the University of California, Berkeley, and one of Dyer's officers had been registrar there. Nimitz invited his friend, Tom Steele, to a beach bungalow he had on the north coast of Oahu and told him to bring two key people from the code unit with him. Steele brought Tommy Dyer and Ham Wright. Nimitz turned up with Admiral Raymond Spruance. When they got to the beach Nimitz declared he would favor his injured leg and just sit in the sun. Spruance took everyone else off on a swift walk of a mile or more, followed by a swim back. Dyer, who had spent the entire war in Hypo's underground offices, and who had very sensitive skin to begin with, was badly sunburned. In addition, the swimming trunks he had used, borrowed from the much bigger Wright, had chafed him badly. Dyer ended up in the hospital.

Still, even that day, there was work to do. Admiral Spruance, who had used the Midway intelligence so brilliantly, tried to understand better the periodic blackouts that occurred whenever the Japanese changed codes. Spruance thought there ought to be a way to have U.S. operations timed to go only when the codes were being read. Dyer and Wright educated the admiral as to how code changes were unpredictable.

It was perhaps not surprising that Tom Dyer exhibited a sign above his desk that read, "You don't have to be crazy to work here but it helps!"

The radio intelligence unit grew with deepening hostilities. By late May 1942, Joe Rochefort had 2 cryptanalysts, 3 traffic analysts, 9 language officers, 30 cryptographic clerks or assistants on that or traffic analysis, 56 kana intercept operators, and a clerical force of 70 persons. Plans for creation of the advanced intelligence centers provided that the director of naval communications assign as many as 500 people to Hypo. By August, Rochefort's complement had increased to 33 cryptanalysts or traffic experts, 21 language officers, 92 kana operators (with 46 more in training), and 137 yeomen or specialists. The vice chief of naval operations renewed orders to fill out the 500 billets, including 17 more cryptanalysts or traffic

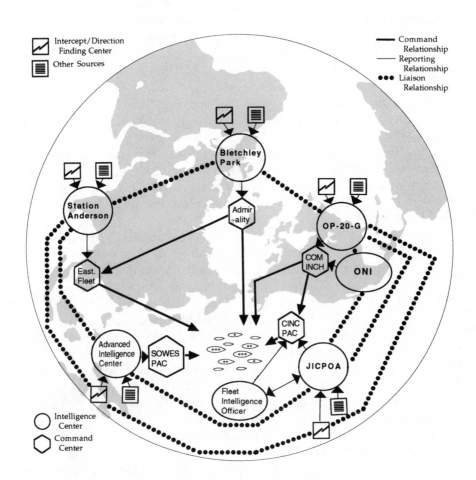

VIII. Pacific Radio Intelligence Network

people, 24 language officers, and 27 kana operators, plus specialists. Thus Hypo grew like Topsy.

Meanwhile the advanced intelligence center reared its own head. In July some 17 officers and 59 men were ordered to Pearl Harbor to create the Intelligence Center Pacific Ocean Areas (ICPOA); their number had been reduced considerably in view of Nimitz's opposition to large staff organizations, but the unit was nevertheless much more robust than anything previously. First officers to report were given desks among the Combat Intelligence Unit at Fleet Radio Unit Pacific (FRUPAC), the name given to Hypo in the new intelligence organization. These included Lieutenant Richard W. Emory, who became a leading expert on the JNAF, Marine Major Thornton M. Hinkle, who analyzed Japanese land forces, and Lieutenant George Leonard, who collected data on geographical matters. Each became the nucleus of an ICPOA section, while the combat intelligence unit itself would split off from Hypo to join the new fusion center. On September 25 ICPOA moved into offices totaling 6,000 square feet within the navy yard supply building. By then more than 80 officers and men were involved. Jasper Holmes moved with them to become a key figure in combined intelligence.

Joe Rochefort disappeared from Pearl Harbor in the fall of 1942. He left for temporary duty in Washington and never came back. The advanced intelligence center figured in his fall, which actually flowed mainly from Hypo's very success at Coral Sea and Midway. The issue was who should get the credit, and certain officers at the top of OP-20-G seem to have wanted it. Despite Washington's mistaken impression that Samoa was going to be the main Japanese target at that time, and its late appreciation of the threat in the Central Pacific, after victory the spoils were reserved for Washington. One found precious little credit given Pearl Harbor in the official account written later in 1942. By that time also, Jack Redman and Joe Wenger had escalated their little bureaucratic war against Hypo, extending efforts to micromanage Rochefort's domain.

Given Washington's poor track record, Joe Rochefort felt it had no business telling him what to do. Finally he put together a cable, for which he got approval from Chester Nimitz, that said that Hypo worked for Nimitz and King only. When ICPOA was established someone used it as a vehicle to get rid of Rochefort, who suddenly found himself appointed officer in charge of the fusion center. "I refused to accept that," Rochefort remembers, "I just flatly refused to have any part of it." Finally Washington relieved him of the extra duty, sending out Captain Roscoe H. Hillenkoetter, the unfortunate who had been executive officer of battleship *West Virginia* on the morning of the Pearl Harbor attack. Rochefort himself would be recalled. Before he left he gave Jasper Holmes a package of personal papers and the keys to his desk. Holmes somehow got the impression that Rochefort expected to be away longer than others at Hypo thought, and he looked worn-out, too, having lost weight and developed a bronchial cough. In fact, Holmes never saw Rochefort again during the war. Some weeks later a letter arrived from the former boss encouraging all to be as loyal to their new chief as to him. "The only probable explanation of what happened to Rochefort," wrote Holmes, "is that he became the victim of a Navy Department internal political coup."

Such was the mean-spiritedness of Rochefort's enemies that they went so far as to block the award to him of a Distinguished Service Medal for his work at Hypo, since such a decoration would have discredited their own claims to have won the battle of Midway in Washington. The original citation had been written by Holmes, proposed by the 14th Naval District, and endorsed by Admiral Nimitz; then nothing further was heard of it. In fact Admiral King was told it would be a breach of security to give the medal to Rochefort. A later award would be rejected on similar grounds. Joe Wenger and Rosie Mason were given that very medal at the end of the war, when it was again denied Rochefort, and Holmes himself, along with Tommy Dyer, also received it. Dyer comments that they were on the list only because it would have looked highly unusual otherwise. In 1958 Admiral Nimitz *again* recommended the medal be given to Rochefort but was told the time had passed for awarding medals for World War II service.

Returning to the fall of 1942, Rochefort not only did not return to Pearl Harbor, he was banished to Western Sea Frontier headquarters in San Francisco, and then to the Tiburon Peninsula in California, to the Floating Drydock Training Center. A greater waste of a first-rate intelligence expert can hardly be imagined. Rochefort fitted out and commanded the floating dry dock U.S.S. *ABSD No. 2* upon her commissioning on August 14, 1943. Fortunately he eventually returned to intelligence duty, in late 1944, when Ernest King wanted a special group to do extended reports and estimates, Joe Rochefort seemed the perfect man for the job. He finished out the war in Washington supplying COMINCH with some fine reporting.

In the meantime the Intelligence Center Pacific Ocean Area was under Roscoe Hillenkoetter, who had been a naval attaché for ONI but really preferred sea command, and stayed at ICPOA only a few months. His liaison with the Army, Lieutenant Colonel Joseph J. Twitty, who was a topographer by specialty and had been a Japanese-language officer as well, received a spot promotion to brigadier general and took over. In 1943 ICPOA became the Joint Intelligence Center Pacific Ocean Areas (JICPOA), the identity it retained through the rest of the war. Jasper Holmes became JICPOA's deputy officer in charge, replacing William B. Goggins, who moved over to head FRUPAC after Joe Rochefort's departure.

Bill Goggins, just recovered from bad wounds received in the Netherlands East Indies as executive officer of the cruiser *Marblehead*, was not an intelligence specialist, but he learned quickly. More important, he was no part of the Washington cabal and he proved willing to let FRUPAC experts take the lead. Goggins shared a house on Makalapa Hill with Jack Redman, however, who came out to Pearl Harbor in the fall of 1942 to become communications officer on Nimitz's staff. Goggins stayed until 1945, when he left FRUPAC to command the battleship *Alabama*. His replacement would be Lieutenant Commander John S. Harper, an old-timer at OP-20-G and another Pearl Harbor attack veteran (he had been damage-control officer aboard the *West Virginia*).

Makalapa Hill became a key place in the Pacific theater, much more so than the uninitiated could know. Not only was Nimitz's headquarters there but so were quarters for most of the vital officers. Less than a block from Goggins's cottage was that of Alva Lasswell. The Marine language officer shared the house with Tom Steele and, from time to time, Ham Wright. All loved to play chess and would while away their few spare moments over the game board with old-fashioneds clutched in their fists. This continued until late 1944, when Lasswell was ordered back to Washington to OP-23, the restyled combat intelligence center serving the naval chief. The Makalapa group house was right on the path Admiral Nimitz used every day when he walked down to headquarters, which he liked to do for exercise. Lasswell adopted the practice of accompanying the admiral for the last 400 yards or so of his daily walk.

Among the other dedicated "cryppies" at FRUPAC whose names ought to be recorded for history are Henry M. Anthony, the Coast Guard's gift to cryptanalysis, who specialized in the Japanese merchant shipping codes. When Jack Holtwick was reassigned out of FRUPAC his place in charge of the IBM machines would be taken by Lieutenant William S. Weedon, in civilian life a professor of philosophy at the University of Virginia. Tom Birtley, who had led a mobile radio unit early in the war and would be sent to Australia later, along with Don Miller, a professor of mathematics, led the effort to break the Imperial Navy's Jade machine code. Reserve officers Griffin Childs and Luther Dilley labored at FRUPAC through virtually the entire war. Tony Ethier, the chief who had had the enlisted night duty the evening before the Pearl Harbor attack, went on to become FRUPAC's expert on Japanese weather codes, which furnished much useful tactical information. Commander Linwood (Lin) S. Howeth played a leading role at FRUPAC until early 1945, when he led an advance detachment of codebreakers forward to a relocated CINCPAC headquarters.

Meanwhile, where radio intelligence had been almost the sole source for secret information in the early months, more sources developed to make fusion truly worthwhile. One of the most important, in the long run, would be photographic reconnaissance. Already noted briefly, the move of Commander Quackenbush to the South Pacific with an advance unit was merely the tip of the iceberg in the Navy photographic intelligence program.

Plans to train 150 photo interpreters mushroomed after Pearl Harbor, and ultimately 500 were trained, mostly in Washington at the school set up in Anacostia. Interpreters had to have a college degree, knowledge of architecture, geology, engineering, or a related field, and good eyesight; they had to meet security qualifications; and be between twenty-one and twenty-nine years old. The first class met on January 5, 1942, with nineteen Navy and eight Marine Corps officers. Ensign Clifton K. Mulinaux, a member of this class, recalls that the eight-week course included using stereoscopes and other technical aids to photo interpretation, determining scale from a photo, planning photo missions, making mosaics from photographs, map reading and mapmaking, cameras, models, and recognition of various kinds of installations and equipment. In January 1943 a postgraduate course would be added in model making.

The field unit at Pearl Harbor to deal in this area would be the Photographic Reconnaissance and Interpretation Section Intelligence Center (PRISIC). Formed on July 1, 1942, PRISIC began with twenty-three officers and four enlisted men. There were thirty more enlisted personnel at a photo laboratory nearby, plus eight officers assigned to aircraft carriers. The officers were in Quarters 49 on Ford Island, in prewar days the home of a petty officer, with two bedrooms, a living room, a bathroom and a small kitchen. A further group of fifteen officers arrived to augment PRISIC in August. Obviously it was already too big for its offices. The work schedule had to be stepped up to a two-shift sixteen-hour day, not because there was so much work but because there was no room for the workers.

In fact, at the time there was very little work for PRISIC. An Army photo sortie over Wake, and another flown in support of the Makin raid, were the only photographic missions carried out in the Pacific Ocean Area in all the summer of 1942. For the most part PRISIC kept busy drawing sketches to help South Pacific forces. As the organization continued expanding, it moved to downtown Honolulu and took over the second floor of the Kodak Hawaii building, then went back to the two-shift system in early 1943 as more trained officers arrived from stateside. At that point PRISIC began to cast plaster models of Aleutian objectives in support of operations in the North Pacific. Soon the organization resolved itself into an interpretation section, a multilith unit (which printed ICPOA/JICPOA's main intelligence bulletin), and the model section. In June 1944 PRISIC moved into a large building built expressly for JICPOA and became the photographic interpretation section of the larger organization.

In September 1943, when Nimitz prepared to assume the offensive in the Central Pacific, PRISIC had forty photography mates, responsible for such matters as repairing reconnaissance cameras or developing film, and seventy-five interpreters. The latter formed a pool assigned as necessary to aircraft carriers or amphibious-force staffs. Other PRISIC personnel worked for the geographic section of JICPOA, or to two actual interpretation "squadrons" the Navy formed. The number of interpreters at Pearl Harbor fluctuated depending upon operational conditions, from just fifteen to over ninety. At the end of the war, pool strength stood at thirty, all away from JICPOA on temporary duty, while 452 JICPOA personnel worked on aspects of photography, and 209 were in the Terrain Model Unit. Commander Harry P. Badger was chief photographic officer, while Commander Burt Benton headed the Terrain Model Unit. The volume of work grew to such proportions that in June 1945 the photographic unit handled 325,000 pictures; by the end of the war the Terrain Model Unit was producing seventy-five relief models a day.

Codebreaking and aerial reconnaissance both became most powerful tools in the hands of American intelligence. Prisoner interrogation was on its way, having come some distance from Midway, when Eddie Layton had had to send off his own deputy to question the first large party of Imperial Navy prisoners. Document translation and analysis really began in late 1942 and received impetus from the Guadalcanal and Makin operations, especially the recoveries from the beached *I-1*. This system proved very capable of learning significant things about a quite secretive adversary. If intelligence had had the relative value of an extra carrier group at Midway, its worth would grow even more as the war progressed.

One brief illustration of the value of intelligence can be had in the matter of mysteries regarding Japanese warships and their capabilities. Some writers have made much of how inexperienced translators incorrectly rendered the ideographs for the names of such Japanese aircraft carriers as the *Shoho* or *Junyo*, but these were really marginal issues. Unless the United States credited the Imperial Navy with carriers they did not possess, and it did not, exact transliteration mattered very little. Much more important, American observers at both the battle of Cape Esperance and the Naval Battle of Guadalcanal mistook smaller, older Japanese heavy cruisers of the *Aoba*-class for more powerful *Atago*-class vessels, or vice versa. Radio intelligence supplied true identities and cleared up the mystery. The corrections made added the equivalent (in 8-inch guns) of another *Aoba* to the estimated order of battle remaining to the Imperial Navy, since *Atago*-class ships carried ten guns to every six on an *Aoba*. These were the kinds of things that made a difference.

Similarly, intelligence caught a whiff of one of the most secret Imperial Navy developments of all—the conversion, begun in 1941, of a third super-battleship into the massive aircraft carrier *Shinano*. The information was included in a July 1943 report from ONI's OP-16-FE and came from interrogation of a Japanese airman. The report noted a sister ship to the *Yamato*, then explained that according to the Japanese she was being turned into a carrier with a length of 900 to 1,000 feet. Though ONI stuck to its prewar estimate of 50,000 tons for this class warship, and further compromised by speculating that the *Shinano* might be pared back to 30,000 tons or so, the key feature is that the United States had knowledge of the new aircraft carrier coming up.

Speaking of the *Yamato*, this class of warship had been a major intelligence mystery since prewar days too. Radio intercepts warned the U.S. fleet on the occasion when Yamamoto hoisted his flag aboard the *Yamato* and also when *Musashi* joined the Combined Fleet at Truk. A drawing captured on Tulagi was interpreted to furnish a crude schematic of the class, and an ONI report in October 1942 estimated size at 35,000 tons and armament as nine 16-inch guns. This misapprehension was strengthened because the Japanese, for security reasons, termed the ammunition for those guns "special type 40 cm" (15.738 inches) suggesting the 16-inch estimate was accurate, and this term was seen in an October 1943 Ultra message. On the other hand, CINCPAC intelligence in the spring of that year put out an item listing 17.7-inch guns; ONI ship-identification authorities, basing their work on interpretation of the first photos taken over Truk, estimated the *Yamato* to have 18-inch guns. They turned out to be correct.

Washington and Pearl Harbor may have had their differences, but enough advantage was inherent in the American intelligence system that despite drawbacks they ended up ahead of the Japanese. Some of the credit also ought to go down under—to those American, Australian, and New Zealand intelligence units supporting MacArthur in the Southwest Pacific and Halsey in the South Pacific.

An IMPORTANT COMPLEMENT TO THE INTELLIGENCE WORK CARRIED OUT AT PEARL HARBOR was that done in Australia. General MacArthur, when he left the Philippines, established his headquarters at Melbourne, one reason why the radio intelligence unit relocated there as well. The former Station Cast became Belconnen and, as we have seen, contributed importantly to Allied efforts at the battles of the Coral Sea and Midway. Later in 1942 MacArthur moved his Southwest Pacific (SOWESPAC) theater headquarters ahead to Brisbane, but the radio unit remained at Melbourne. When it did, certain fissures opened between intelligence and operations.

MacArthur's movement to Brisbane coincided with a metamorphosis and expansion in SOWESPAC intelligence efforts of all varieties supervised by Charles A. Willoughby, MacArthur's senior intelligence officer, or G-2, who enjoyed a meteoric rise from the rank of colonel to that of major general. Never easy to get along with, but supremely loyal to MacArthur, Willoughby was conservative, consumed by ethnic resentments, and intensely suspicious—not necessarily sterling qualities in an intelligence officer or manager either. Allison Ind, an associate thoughout the war, including the Philippines and the escape therefrom, called Willoughby part Prussian drillmaster, and he was right: The man had been born in Heidelberg to a Junker family, and only came to America at age eighteen. A graduate of Gettysburg College, the young Willoughby, commissioned in 1915, served under General John J. Pershing for the 1916–17 expedition chasing bandit Pancho Villa in Mexico. In the early 1920s Willoughby had visited Morocco, where the Spanish were fighting guerrillas in the Rif. There he met Francisco Franco, of whom he became a fervid admirer. Willoughby hitched his star to MacArthur before the Philippine invasion, and came out with the general in early 1942. In Australia he became a czar of a sort, supervising an increasingly ramified intelligence apparatus.

One key element of the burgeoning organization emerged as a result of a conference held in April 1942 among top intelligence officials. This was the Allied Intelligence Bureau (AIB), formed as an arm of SOWESPAC general headquarters. It was the brainchild of the Australian director of naval intelligence, Commander R.B.M. Long. The Allied Intelligence Bureau was to be an umbrella group supervising activities from information collection to guerrilla warfare; it was to be manned and financed by all the Allies, whose pooled resources made projects possible that might not have been otherwise. As an umbrella the AIB took over such existing units as Ferdinand, Commander Feldt's coastwatcher organization. It also included liaison with guerrilla fighters in the Philippines; Australian units that continued a guerrilla fight on Timor into early 1943; a Dutch special activities unit that mounted incursions into the Netherlands East Indies; and "Z Force," a unit that mounted daring commando raids, including one waterborne mission right into Singapore harbor in late 1943 that sank six cargo ships amounting to 46,000 tons. The AIB "controller," or director, was Colonel C. G. Roberts, civil engineer and son of a well-known artist, who was previously the Australian Army's intelligence chief. His deputy would be American major Allison Ind.

Before the war ended the AIB comprised more than 3,000 people and was officially credited with carrying out 264 missions, during which 164 men lost their lives and another 178 went missing (75 known to have been captured). Bureau operations accounted for over 7,000 Japanese dead and another 150 captured, plus 950 more who surrendered as a result of the propaganda produced by AIB's Far East Liaison Office. The Netherlands Foreign Intelligence Staff (NEFIS) not only mounted commando raids but produced useful intelligence on Japanese activities in the Netherlands East Indies, Burma, and New Guinea. The Australian coastwatchers, of course, had been vital during fighting on Guadalcanal, and would again play a key role in the final leap to Bougainville in the northern Solomons.

Another intelligence organ of the Southwest Pacific Command benefited coincidentally from Black Jack Pershing's expedition against Pancho Villa. That was where Charles Willoughby met Sidney Mashbir, a young officer with the 1st Arizona Infantry. Mashbir's maps of the border region and Sonora, Mexico, were an important aid to the expedition. Mashbir went on to became an Army language officer in Japan, one of those who helped the Japanese after the great earthquake of 1923. In the months after Pearl Harbor Mashbir found himself in charge of the Signal Corps reference library. A friend of Ellis Zacharias of ONI (they had been language officers in Tokyo together), Mashbir found himself being interviewed by Army Far East expert Rufus Bratton for a prospective assignment after Zach put in a good word for him. Colonel Mashbir ended up on a boat to Brisbane with orders to the Southwest Pacific Command. He left the United States on September 28, 1942.

In Australia, Mashbir found Willoughby ensconced comfortably as MacArthur's intelligence czar; he remembered Mashbir, was impressed with his ideas for translation work, and assigned him to replace Colonel Karl F. Baldwin, who headed something called the Allied Translator and Interpreter Section (ATIS). Located on an old, run-down estate called Indooroopilly, perhaps eight miles outside Brisbane, ATIS and Mashbir started with a single officer, Major David Swift, who was a capable linguist, eight nisei linguists (products of the U.S. Army training program), and three enlisted clerks. The day after his arrival a tray of blood-soaked documents appeared, taken after some tough patrol action on New Guinea. It was the beginning of a job that complemented the work of radio intelligence.

Japanese-Americans proved the salvation of SOWESPAC intelligence translation. The Army linguist program used nisei to a greater extent than the Navy (which used them only for teachers), not only for ATIS but for frontline work with the Counterintelligence Corps and unit intelligence sections. The heart of the program became Camp Savage in Colorado where, after false starts like the Navy's, the Army brought nisei for familiarization with military vocabulary. (One false start had been at the Presidio in San Francisco, which the program had to leave after General De Witt's exclusion of Japanese-Americans from the coast.) Not everyone went to Camp Savage. Dave Swift and eight nisei got on the boat to Australia. This rapid move to the front bothered Swift, who knew that his knowledge of written Japanese could have used work, particularly on military terminology. Instead, Swift spent weeks flat on his back in the hospital, a result of allergic reaction to the yellow-fever shot he had been given on the boat. The nisei with him, all enlisted men, had no say in their assignments and while Swift recuperated these Japanese linguists were put to work on a Dutch-Malayan dictionary. Only after September 19, 1942, when ATIS was officially established, did the men get to work on their own language. The first translation they performed was that of the diary of a Japanese officer recovered in New Guinea.

Colonel Mashbir's arrival at Indoroopilly signaled the beginning of a new phase in which translation became increasingly important. Mashbir quickly built his unit up to about twenty men—mostly, at first, Australian, Canadian, or British. Many had been businessmen in Tokyo, Yokohama, or Osaka, or diplomats and consular officials. One of the best translators, for example, was the Greek son of a former diplomat who had spent much of his life in Russia but was now in the Australian Army. In any case Caucasians were soon eclipsed by nisei translators, if only because these were the readiest source of talent. The ATIS staff expanded rapidly, to 767 by September 1944 (about 400 nisei translators) and almost 3,500 by the end of the war (1,957 of them in advance echelons or detachments).

The large concentration of nisei occasioned morale problems flowing from the attitude of racism that existed. Time after time, for example, decorations or awards would be given to Caucasians and not to nisei participants in the same or equivalent actions. Simple promotions were a problem as well. Most of the nisei in the Army deployed as corporals or sergeants. Once, when a contingent of ninety green Women's Army Corps volunteers arrived, nearly all of them outranked every single nisei, translators whom Mashbir saw as veterans of "ten campaigns." In fact, by late 1944 not one nisei had been promoted as much as a single rank. It is inspiring that in the face of such conditions, and of knowledge of how their friends and relatives were being treated back in the States, the nisei's enthusiasm for the work never flagged.

ATIS made a measurable contribution to Allied intelligence, not only in MacArthur's command but throughout the Pacific. Beginning with the translation of almost 500 pages of Japanese documents in September 1942, the pace of ATIS's work built gradually to 1,000 pages in January 1943, 2,500 that June, 4,000 in December, and 5,000 in January 1944; then, after a hiatus, a peak of nearly 6,000 pages was translated that April. By the end of the war the unit had translated a total of 20,598,051 pages of Japanese documents. These were digested and logged; important ones were reproduced in translated form for circulation to Allied units. In addition, ATIS produced vocabularies and lists of terms used throughout the Pacific, historical translations of documentary collections (such as items pertaining to the Japanese attack on Pearl Harbor, for example), and special studies built from translations, such as one in 1943 on sources the Japanese used for their own intelligence. The organization also participated in interrogations of Japanese prisoners and published summaries of those interviews. By late 1944 ATIS specialists had interrogated 690 Japanese prisoners and produced eighty-nine special studies.

It must be noted that the bulk of ATIS work supported ground combat operations, both because of the orientation of the unit and the sources of its raw material. Colonel Mashbir's Army linguists were naturally preoccupied with Army work, while land operations were the main form of combat in SOWESPAC. True, ATIS was divided into an overall staff under David Swift, an Allied Land Forces unit, an Allied Naval Forces unit, and an Allied Air Forces section, but the focus remained land operations. For example, in August 1944 the Land Forces section employed 263 persons as against 59 in the air unit and 55 in the naval one. John M. Wilson, the Australian who headed the naval section (he later became an officer) would be ably seconded by Sam Bartlett of the U.S. Navy Reserve, and temporarily assisted by one of the Navy's original language officers, Commander Albrecht, but none of them could change the sources of ATIS's material. That is, documents were captured primarily in a land campaign from locations where the Japanese Navy had no involvement or only a little. For example, by the summer of 1944 Lae had produced 1,562 documents; Hollandia was the source for 1,162; and from miscellaneous locations in New Guinea had come another 3,121. Solomons locations yielded less than a third as many captures, none from Imperial Navy base locations. Also, document volume varied a great deal depending upon the attention devoted to this by frontline units. During an early campaign one formation turned in 3,600 documents while the one in line next to it gave up just 35. That unit was put under a program of strict censorship, and document capture was emphasized; over the following eight months it gave ATIS no less than 8,000 documents, three quarters of which still had current intelligence value.

Yet another element of the Southwest Pacific apparatus was the Central Bureau, a specialized radio intelligence unit the Australians created to monitor Japanese activities, again primarily of ground forces, alongside the U.S. naval unit at Melbourne. The nucleus of the Central Bureau consisted of Number 4 Special Wireless Section, recently returned from service in the Middle East and Greece. There were also small naval and diplomatic code-breaking sections, both pioneered by Commander Eric Nave, a Royal Australian Air Force intercept section, and a fragment of the British Far East Combined Bureau consisting of an officer and a dozen men who escaped from Java to Australia. To begin with the British veterans taught the Australians the Japanese-style Morse kana. Accustomed to German and French practices, the Australians also had to learn Japanese code and communications techniques. Eric Nave took over to teach code methods and did so well, according to Central Bureau officer Geoffrey Ballard, that the new codebreakers quickly mastered JNAF codes and continued to break them right through the war.

Originally called the Australian Special Wireless Group, the new unit expanded into the Central Bureau in mid-1942, when an American contingent under then-Major Abraham Sinkov was added. Sinkov had participated in the very first exchange of code information between the United States and Great Britain, in which he had gone to Bletchley Park to be familiarized with the German Enigma, and he was to play a leading role at Central Bureau. Located near Brisbane, the Central Bureau expanded, putting out tentacles in the form of listening posts and forward detachments at Port Darwin, Port Moresby, Oro Bay, almost everywhere SOWESPAC troops could be found. Before the war's end the unit grew to more than 4,000 in strength and its main headquarters moved no less than five times.

By contrast, Station Belconnen, the former Corregidor naval codebreaker unit, never moved at all, though toward the end of the war it sent forward a detachment that eventually comprised almost all its American personnel, with Australian women volunteers taking over both the intercept and cryptanalysis work back at Melbourne. That, however, did not come until very late in the war. Belconnen (which apparently called itself Baker in internal documents), remained at Melbourne, with constantly increasing space difficulties. As has been mentioned, its offices were first set up at the Monterrey Flats apartment complex; bit by bit more of those apartments were taken over, amid complaints not only from the displaced residents but from radiomen who hated working from converted bathrooms and kitchens. With Belconnen projecting a requirement for over 300 personnel by mid-1943, and 203 of them already present for duty, space became critical.

There were several efforts to solve the space problem, simplified because Commander Jack B. Newman of the Australian Navy had replaced a U.S. officer in overall charge and he had much better understanding of Australian procedures and abilities, which focused on the Commonwealth Naval Board. This was responsible for space allocations, and it suggested a move into downtown Melbourne. When Lieutenant Commander Jack Holtwick came to Melbourne as temporary replacement for Rudy Fabian, he scouted out the proposed location, a furniture store at the corner of Flinders and Degraves streets. Then SOWESPAC's Seventh Fleet command rejected that site. The next idea was to build a new building near Victoria Barracks, but that, too, evaporated. Then hospital land was selected for a building site; it proved impossible to complete financial arrangements successfully. Finally, early in 1944 construction began on a two-story 242-foot-by-42-foot operations center; later, barracks buildings were built around it. The complex was at Albert Park. By that time, in keeping with the intelligence reorganization in the Pacific Ocean area, the unit had been redesignated Fleet Radio Unit Melbourne (FRUMEL).

To the south of Australia, Melbourne was invulnerable to attack, but by the same token was not the ideal intercept site. Although the bulk of FRUMEL intercept activity remained at Morrabin, over time the unit established certain forward detachments. Townsville had an intercept unit for almost a year, and Adelaide River for the duration—so long that eventually it was given a direct circuit to an advanced unit of FRUPAC that went with

Admiral Nimitz when he moved his headquarters forward in early 1945. North of Townsville a detachment worked out of Cooktown for a time; then finally the bulk of American personnel moved to a FRUMEL advanced echelon colocated with SOWESPAC headquarters at Hollandia on New Guinea, then eventually Manila.

The detachment at Exmouth Gulf on Australia's west coast proved FRUMEL's hard-luck unit. Exmouth Gulf became important as a refueling stop for submarines sailing from Perth, in Western Australia. An oil barge was anchored there and periodically supplanted by a fully laden replacement. At the time a total wilderness, the Exmouth Gulf fuel point was manned by convicts of courts-martial or others under discipline who volunteered for the duty in place of going to stockade. When FRUMEL set up a detachment for radio direction finding, its personnel were at first warned not to go among the ruffians. Later the entire unit moved ashore, and the British FECB sent a direction finder of their own to Exmouth, with the notion that the Royal Navy net would control its apparatus, and FRUMEL the existing one; both could combine for tracking multiple targets in the East Indies or Indian Ocean. While installation proceeded, however, a worker fell from the antenna platform, and although he survived without serious injury, parts of two dipole antennae were wrecked. Then FRUMEL and the British were forced to pool resources to keep a single direction finder in operation. The facility eventually came under full control by the Royal Australian Navy, just in time to be completely destroyed by a cyclone on February 3, 1945.

At the end of a lengthy supply line, radio intelligence work in Australia would continually be hampered by one lack or another. Tabulating and card-sorter equipment was short, but a more serious FRUMEL complaint in 1943 was that there was but one single repairman and he only partially qualified. Lieutenant Ralph Cook ran the machine room and somehow kept it going in the face of equipment breakdowns and a crucial drawback: short supply of cards for keypunching and sorting. The local British Tabulating Machine Company sold such cards to FRUMEL, produced locally from imported paper stock, but supply proved a bottleneck. Another problem, especially as FRUMEL sent out detachments, was RIP-5 kana typewriters. In fact the radio intelligence people found it almost impossible to find typewriters of any description in Australia. At one point they were reduced to begging Pearl Harbor to send them some typewriters *in disguised containers* so the machines would not be diverted along the way.

A number of changes occurred at FRUMEL as the organization expanded. These were in keeping with the U.S. Navy's creation of advanced intelligence centers. One was creation of an intelligence section, Melbourne's equivalent of Hypo's combat intelligence unit, headed at first by Corregidor veteran Commander Lietwiler. Lietwiler left for the United States on temporary assignment in mid-1944 but never returned. His place was taken by his deputy, Lieutenant Commander John S. Lehman. The latter's job in turn went to Lieutenant Commander Lester R. Schultz, who had come out from Washington after serving in Franklin Roosevelt's White House Map Room. The intelligence section grew from four officers to six, and there were seven enlisted men, working around the clock on a three-shift system. The intelligence-section watch officer doubled as FRUMEL duty officer.

Another change was the departure of Commander Fabian, more or less the father of the Corregidor survivors. When Captain Arthur H. McCollum arrived at Brisbane and found himself assigned as fleet intelligence officer for the Seventh Fleet, he drafted Rudy Fabian to help him create the advanced intelligence center that Admiral King wanted. They began with thirty sailors but the center, unlike JICPOA an integral part of the fleet intelligence officer's bailiwick, soon grew to 300. Before that Fabian had gone, sent on to Colombo. There he worked as U.S. Navy liaison to the British radio unit, which they called Station Anderson. There Fabian discovered that U.S. code materials forwarded from Washington to Pearl Harbor through FRUMEL to Anderson arrived faster than the same stuff sent through Bletchley Park.

Captain McCollum *knew* radio intelligence though he was not *of* it, but he labored under certain constraints working for the Southwest Pacific Command. One was the degree of centralization demanded by Willoughby and MacArthur. Decentralized, radio intelligence was used to instantly exchange solutions of code groups, messages, and whatnot on its own radio circuits. When JICPOA formed at Pearl Harbor, there was a tendency to send analyses and reports on the same free-floating basis, so requests arrived frequently at FRUMEL, ATIS, or the Central Bureau. Instead of being served, these were forwarded to Willoughby's headquarters and he decided which should be met. After some missteps all such requests were sent to McCollum, who gave them directly to Willoughby, eliminating extra delay.

On one occasion in late 1943, FRUPAC sent Melbourne an invitation for its commander, Jack Newman, to visit Pearl Harbor. Undoubtedly the Australian officer stood to gain from observing intelligence in action in Hawaii. Of course FRUMEL had to forward the request to SOWESPAC. Nothing more was ever heard of it. Officers at Melbourne advised that the only way to break the invitation loose would be for Admiral Frederick J. Horne, the vice chief of naval operations, to extend it directly to his counterpart in the Royal Australian Navy. No such action was taken. Commander Newman shortly afterward was taken ill and to the hospital. At bottom, the Southwest Pacific Command proved unwilling to recognize that anything could be learned from any other command or unit. The same absolutist attitude prevailed later in the war, when SOWESPAC rejected advice that it had breached security in its use of Ultra code material.

Etajima in the 1920s. The Japanese naval academy, first established with British help near Tokyo in 1898, moved to this island off Kure in 1873, and is still today Japan's school for future admirals. At the center, behind the wooded area, is the main classroom building. *(Naval Historical Center)*

The game room at the Japanese Naval War College as it appeared in the 1920s. Here generations of Imperial Navy senior officers were imbued with the doctrine of "Decisive Battle." In 1941 the game room was used to simulate the Japanese plan for the first stage of operations, and officers in a room off to the side wargamed the attack on Pearl Harbor. *(Naval Historical Center)*

Emperor Hirohito (right of center) on the afterdeck of Combined Fleet flagship *Nagato*, August 9, 1939. Behind him follow his brothers Prince Chichibu (in Army uniform) and Prince Takamatsu (extreme left), the latter wearing the aiguillette that went with assignment to the Naval General Staff. Takamatsu graduated with Etajima's 1924 class, which included spy and submariner Tachibana Itaru, code-breaker Ozawa Hideo, aviators Fuchida Mitsuo and Genda Minoru, as well as Kuroda Yoshio, gunnery officer of the *Yamato* on her final, fatal voyage. *(National Archives)*

Fierce fighting raged up the banks of the Yangtze, as suggested by this photograph of the Nanking waterfront, taken from the United States gunboat *Panay* on December 12, 1937. Hours later the *Panay* herself would be bombed and sunk by Japanese naval aircraft. Intercepted radio messages helped convince U.S. authorities of Japanese culpability. Later, former *Panay* radiomen proved a valuable addition to the personnel of the American radio intelligence unit stationed at Shanghai. *(Naval Historical Center)*

A tea party hosted by the Japanese Foreign Ministry and the Imperial Navy, one of a series of functions marking the special Yokohama visit in April 1939 of Captain Richmond Kelly Turner's cruiser *Astoria*, which returned to Japan the ashes of Ambassador Saito Hiroshi, who had died in Washington. Taking advantage of the port call, the United States secretly put a radio intelligence detachment aboard the *Astoria*, supplementing observations by naval attachés. Front row, from left to right: Captain Harold Bemis, U.S. naval attaché; unidentified; Captain Turner; and Admiral Yamamoto Isoroku, soon to be Combined Fleet commander and a prime target for U.S. intelligence.
*(Naval Historical Center)*

Navy Minister Yonai Mitsumasa (2) entertained visiting admiral Harry E. Yarnell (1) at a dinner on August 6, 1939. Americans present include Counsellor Eugene Dooman (3), and assistant naval attaché Henri Smith-Hutton (7) and his language officer aides Daniel McCallum (10) and Stephen Jurika (13), who would warn of the Zero fighter. Key Japanese commanders at this event include Koga Mineichi (4), future chief of the Combined Fleet, and Inoue Shigeyoshi (5), who would lead Imperial Navy forces in the Mandates. Also present are many Japanese intelligence officers, including Third Bureau chief Oka Takazumi (9), America experts Yokoyama Ichiro (12) and Sanematsu Yuzuru (11), Germany expert Maeda Tadashi (6), and Abe Katsuo (8), later to be the Imperial Navy's representative in wartime Berlin.
*(Naval Historical Center)*

A lunch given at Tokyo's Navy Club by Minister Yoshida Zengo (4) in May 1940 brought together many military officers of countries then warring with one another in Europe, which must have made for a tense atmosphere. This group includes the naval attachés of Italy (1), Germany (2), Russia (3), France (5), Britain (6), and the United States, in the person of Henri Smith-Hutton (7). The American attaché is seconded by assistants Daniel McCallum (16) and Stephen Jurika (15). Air attachés present, other than the American Jurika, include those of Germany (8), Rumania (9), Britain (10, and his assistant, 13), China (11), Thailand (12), and France (14). *(Naval Historical Center)*

This fragment of the Japanese Type B machine encryption device, which generated the code Americans called Purple, clearly shows three electrical selectors and their wiring. The fragment was found in 1945 in the ruins of the Japanese embassy in Berlin. It is the only known example of the Type B machine. *(National Security Agency)*

Captain Laurence F. Safford held together an infant U.S. Navy communications intelligence organization during the 1920s and 1930s, and brought it to the point at which the United States could gain significant information from reading Japanese naval message traffic. *(Author's collection)*

Captain Joseph J. Rochefort as a young codebreaker and language officer in 1934. Rochefort and Laurence Safford were the Navy's premier prewar cryptanalysts, and trained many of the individuals who would drive the codebreaking effort just before and during World War II. *(National Security Agency monograph)*

The Purple machine, constructed by a Navy mechanic from principles deduced by an Army codebreaking team led by Frank W. Rowlett, mimicked the operation of the Japanese Type B device. Using Purple, Washington produced its own copies of Japanese diplomatic messages, a variety of intelligence material called Magic. *(National Security Agency)*

Pearl Harbor the morning after. Heavy cruiser *Northampton* of William F. Halsey's *Enterprise* task force enters the base with her antiaircraft guns manned and ready. Erroneous radio bearings and general confusion the day of the attack had sent Halsey and the other carrier commanders everywhere *but* after the Japanese carrier force. *(National Archives)*

The battle of Midway resulted in the first significant capture of Imperial Navy sailors. Thirty-five *Hiryu* seamen were taken from one lifeboat, and other survivors from the cruiser *Mikuma* were also captured. Here the *Hiryu* sailors are landed at Midway to await transportation to Pearl Harbor, where they were interrogated by assistant fleet intelligence officer Robert E. Hudson. *(National Archives)*

At the battle of Santa Cruz (October 1942) an attempt to repeat the successful Midway tactic of flank attack on Japanese carriers miscarried. Here the *Enterprise*, maneuvering desperately, heels to port and loses an SBD dive-bomber over the side. The radio intelligence unit aboard the *Enterprise* would later enjoy the use of code materials and other documents from a crashed JNAF plane. *(National Archives)*

The American carrier *Hornet* dead in the water at the battle of Santa Cruz, October 26, 1942, with a destroyer alongside and the cruiser *Northampton* waiting to assist. Americans were unsuccessful in scuttling the *Hornet*, and late that night Japanese warships came upon the derelict. Admiral Kurita Takeo, commanding the Japanese battleships involved, may have recalled this incident in his later actions at Leyte Gulf. *(National Archives)*

Reports from observers on the ground were vital during the Guadalcanal campaign, and remained important throughout the war. These agents were called coastwatchers and used a simple alphabetical transposition code system, with a wheel device to generate garbled letters in place of plaintext. The U.S. Navy called its version of the code wheel the CSP-488; Army officers knew it as the M-94. This device is set to show the plaintext "Secret Officers Eyes Only" *(Author's Collection)*

The destroyer *Nagatsuki* beached on the shore of Kolombangara island, May 1944, a victim of the battle of Kula Gulf ten months earlier. Though specific Allied knowledge of *Nagatsuki's* "Tokyo Express" mission has yet to be shown, the way an Allied cruiser group intercepted the Japanese is highly suggestive. *(National Archives)*

As early as 1930, colleagues considered Lieutenant Commander Thomas H. Dyer one of the five or six most able U.S. Navy codebreakers. But Dyer's long service in shoreside intelligence posts penalized him with prewar promotions boards. *(National Security Agency monograph)*

Commander John S. ("Jack") Holtwick, Jr., among the most versatile of American intelligence specialists. A member of the first-ever mobile radio intelligence unit used in a maneuver at sea, Holtwick later designed a machine to work against one prewar Japanese code, and in 1935 he carried out a burglary of the apartment of a Japanese naval attaché to steal codes. *(National Security Agency monograph)*

Captain Joseph N. Wenger became one of the pioneers in radio intelligence. A close friend of Henri Smith-Hutton from the time both served in the Asiatic Fleet, Wenger would become deputy director of OP-20-G during the war, when Smith-Hutton headed the Navy's operational intelligence center in Washington. *(National Security Agency monograph)*

The intelligence nerve center of the Pacific war. Shielded by a security fence were the Joint Intelligence Center Pacific Ocean Area (JICPOA), at the center of this photograph, and the Fleet Radio Unit Pacific (FRUPAC), which together generated a great deal of U.S. knowledge of the adversary. Note the way the buildings are hidden behind the CINCPAC motor pool (Quonset hut in foreground), and all three are situated on the reverse slope of Makalapa Hill. *(Naval Historical Center)*

The Jade machine, one of the most sophisticated encryption devices built for the Japanese Navy, was used for messages between major bases. Jade had even more electric selector switches (twenty can be counted here) than Purple, yet was nonetheless solved by American codebreakers in 1943. *(Author's collection)*

Rabaul under attack by carrier aircraft on November 5, 1943, when intelligence enabled Admiral Halsey's South Pacific forces to arrive just hours after a powerful Japanese fleet entered the base. This photograph was taken by a plane from the *Saratoga*, and shows Japanese vessels fleeing at high speed. Burning brightly and stationary in the middle of Simpson Harbor is the cruiser *Maya*. *(National Archives)*

One of the Imperial Navy heavy cruisers to reach the open sea that day at Rabaul was the *Chikuma*, seen here through the gunsight camera of an SBD dive-bomber from the *Saratoga*. *(National Archives)*

The Marine crews of two PB4Y (maritime versions of the B-24 "Liberator") bombers, which flew the first photo reconnaissance mission over Truk, on February 4, 1944. The unescorted, twelve-hour flight covered two thousand miles from Bougainville and brought back the first pictures of the Combined Fleet base. *(National Archives)*

One of the Truk photographs taken on February 4: Dublon Island, site of Fourth Fleet headquarters, is at the lower left; in the center is the JNAF airbase on Eten. Two aircraft carriers are at anchor under the clouds at center right, and various other ships dot the harbor. The image of an oddly shaped ship in the corner of one of the marine photos turned out to be the first picture of the *Yamato*-class battleship, leading to extensive intelligence analyses of that type of ship. *(National Archives)*

Surigao Strait the morning after the battle became the scene of an extensive effort by U.S. PT boats and Filipinos to find and bring back Japanese survivors. A number of Imperial Navy sailors became prisoners this way, including the captain of the destroyer *Asagumo*. *(National Archives)*

The battle off Samar at Leyte Gulf, on October 25, 1944, represented Japan's best chance to break up an Allied invasion force, but a combination of circumstances, predisposition toward destroying carrier forces, and poor identification of adversary warships led the Japanese off on a tangent. Here the superbattleship *Yamato* maneuvers with a Japanese heavy cruiser, probably the *Haguro*, off her starboard quarter. This picture was taken by a plane from the U.S. escort carrier *Petrof Bay* during the first moments of the battle. *(National Archives)*

Fleet intelligence officer Captain Arthur H. McCollum attempts to explain what happened at Leyte Gulf to an audience of senior officers aboard the amphibious force command ship *Wasatch*, November 1, 1944. *(United States Naval Institute)*

Manila Bay, site of one of the great intelligence coups of the war: the recovery of priceless documents and equipment from the wreck of the *Nachi*, sunk after Leyte Gulf. Here salvagers use buoys to mark a wreck. The ship's masthead is visible just above the surface; the superstructure and stack of another wreck are seen at the center in the distance. *(National Archives)*

Office of Naval Intelligence team member James K. McNiece guides a diver, probably Joe Karnecke, toward the decompression chamber on the deck of the *Chanticleer* during the *Nachi* recovery operation. Behind them is a diving rig that lowered divers to the point from which they could descend by themselves. Intrigued by the items coming up from the sea, McNiece became a diver himself. *(James K. McNiece)*

There would be plenty to learn despite SOWESPAC's attitude, however. For example, in early 1944 a Lieutenant Commander Chisolm arrived from the United States to build Melbourne a machine to read the Imperial Navy Jade code. After several weeks' work Chisolm had a Jade machine up and running, and some of its decrypts proved very valuable to MacArthur. The machine could not have been built from purely local resources, FRUMEL reported; the staffers professed themselves glad that Chisolm had taken the trouble to prewire some components and assemble some of his materials before leaving the United States.

In actuality, almost every month through the first half of 1944 there was one or another product from Washington or Pearl Harbor that FRUMEL, if not the Southwest Pacific Command, acknowledged as a breathtaking advance. In turn SOWESPAC benefited from FRUMEL. One day Captain McCollum called up Commander E.S.L. Goodwin, officer in charge at FRUMEL, to ask if the Central Bureau could borrow a couple of language officers. Goodwin sent commanders Tom Mackie, of the Corregidor contingent, and Forrest Baird, who had arrived in November 1943 and been a radio unit chief at the Coral Sea battle. Later, U.S. Army authorities were saying Mackie's and Baird's work had shaved at least three months off the time it took to capture the Bismarck Archipelago.

In a way, Tex Baird happened to be lucky to reach FRUMEL without incident. Travel to Australia, even orders for it, could be difficult. Chief Johns, one of the Corregidor men being ordered to Washington, sat in Melbourne for months while the Navy issued three different sets of orders for him and FRUMEL and the Seventh Fleet mixed up the ones received. In other instances kana radio operators who reached Australia without orders that specified radio intelligence assignments were dragooned into general communications work. An incident that was by no means unique featured a radioman of whom FRUMEL could find no trace after being notified of his imminent arrival. Queries produced news of the kana man at various waypoints on the route; after a dozen FRUMEL appeals and *six months*, the operator had not been able to get farther than Guadalcanal.

San Francisco proved to be a key bottleneck. The travel office there had standing orders to permit passengers for Australia only on ships bound directly there (very rare) and not on vessels for intermediate destinations, such as Pearl Harbor, which were very frequent. This persisted despite the fact that air transport from Pearl Harbor to points south was quite available (the Air Transport Command moved 618,514 passengers across the Pacific). This kind of thing became a special headache for senior radio intelligence officers who were more or less expected to put in an appearance at Pearl Harbor when traveling to and from the continental U.S. Officers assigned to Australia found themselves begging for specific orders to make intermediate stops.

The fleet intelligence officer might have wished that more men made it to Australia because he would have had less difficulty keeping up with the mass of intelligence. Not only were there FRUMEL decrypts, the Fifth Air Force produced a great volume of aerial photography from its 6th and 71st Reconnaissance Groups, and the coastwatcher network peaked at about a hundred stations. A flow of additional personnel to the advanced intelligence center began in 1943 and swelled to significant proportions within a year. Yeoman James K. McNiece was one such man, who went to work for Seventh Fleet intelligence officer McCollum in early 1944. McNiece and his cohort had boarded ship in their Navy "blues"—heavy uniforms—for it had been cold then on the U.S. West Coast. When their transport arrived at New Guinea they were told to leave the same way they had come aboard, which meant throwing seabags off the side into bobbing landing craft below, then climbing down cargo nets in those same uniforms in the tropical heat. McNiece was sent south to Australia for special training, then returned to SOWESPAC headquarters. By then Captain McCollum's center was at Hollandia and Seventh Fleet had begun preparing to invade the Philippines. Yeoman McNiece was given the job of maintaining the card index of "marus," Japanese merchant shipping. He was amazed at how the intelligence enabled them to verify claims of sinkings of Japanese ships, based on actual longitude and latitude data from the Japanese themselves. The intelligence center could also tell when Japanese codes changed for then the stream of data would dry up, at least temporarily. Arthur McCollum would be spared the greatest bulk of the intelligence center's work, which came in 1945 with FRUMEL at full stride and aerial reconnaissance at 1,500 sorties or more per month. That was many times average rates of 1942 or 1943, and even double or more the numbers of 1944. By then, language officers Henri deB. Claiborne and Murray R. Stone had become fleet intelligence officer and deputy. The Seventh Fleet intelligence center ended the war with 184 officers and 226 seamen assigned.

There could be no doubt but that the Seventh Fleet and SOWESPAC enjoyed mountains of intelligence. In his time as fleet intelligence officer, Arthur McCollum would be a happy beneficiary, as he demonstrated one day for Allison Ind, the deputy controller of the covert-action unit at the Allied Intelligence Bureau. Ind knew McCollum as someone who always started by chewing out the AIB, then agreed to its proposals. In this instance the secret Z Force had just hit Singapore with frogmen, sinking Japanese ships by means of mines attached magnetically to their hulls. McCollum had just learned—through Chungking, London, then Washington—of the result. A number of vessels had been sunk and Captain McCollum called Major Ind into his office.

The fleet intelligence officer's fist hit the desk. "That's *joltin'* 'em!" McCollum exclaimed. "Good business. Didn't know what hit 'em! Come again when you want something."

Losses from limpet mines in Singapore were but one danger threatening the Japanese as a result of their poor intelligence performance. In fact, the Z Force commandos who hit Singapore had sailed thousands of miles through Japanese-controlled waters in a simple fishing boat without being detected. Japanese patrol planes had even overflew the boat on regular rounds with no effect. It may be surprising, but aircraft patrol happened to be one aspect of intelligence work to which the Imperial Navy devoted considerable attention. Even as the Japanese began to draw off increasing numbers of their combat aircraft to the meat grinder of the Solomons, they were careful to retain sufficient planes in the Netherlands East Indies and other places to fly regular searches for Allied submarines, raiders, and task forces.

Air officers and commanders of JNAF units calculated optimum distribution for search planes and flight routes. In view of the care devoted to this task it is perplexing that the Japanese did not make a greater effort to train aviators in accurate identification of friendly and hostile ships and aircraft. Already there had been identification problems at the Coral Sea, Midway, and Guadalcanal battles, yet none of this induced JNAF managers to pay concerted attention to the subject. In fact, the early errors were those of the JNAF at peak performance, and accuracy would thereafter deteriorate greatly, to the point where late in the war officers at the Naval General Staff would take every report from the front and divide by two or more to arrive at more reasonable approximations. Even then they would still be wrong.

The recognition problem owed much to the fact that training was left to local commanders. Before Pearl Harbor, aircrews practiced recognition diligently. Okumiya Masatake also reports that, in the Aleutians during the Midway campaign, pilots received training classes in recognition under a program devised by Lieutenant Commander Nakagawa Toshi. Admiral Obayashi Sueo, on the other hand, commander of carrier *Zuiho* and later of Carrier Division 3, noted that the only recognition material he received came in the form of loose sheets from the *joho kyoku*; these contained line-drawing silhouettes and performance data only. American pilots were typically shown similar items, but they were also given photographs taken from various angles, both of models and of actual Japanese equipment, and saw movies of Japanese ships and planes in action. Admiral Obayashi told interrogators that he saw no movies and in fact had no idea such a resource even existed. "We could not keep up with all developments," Obayashi said. "No regular recognition classes were held."

Pioneering the study of recognition in the Imperial Navy was Commander Nakagawa Toshi, a 1923 Etajima graduate with 1,500 hours of flying time who had dropped his bomb on a cruiser in the Pearl Harbor attack. Nakagawa was an instructor for dive-bombers and flying boats, and only came to the idea of a recognition course during flight training. He assembled material available from the Navy Ministry, the gunnery school, and the torpedo school. What he got was pictures from the 1941 edition of *Jane's Fighting Ships*, plus line drawings and performance statistics. Toward the end of the war Commander Nakagawa finally got wooden models and pictures on slides he could project on a screen. Nakagawa confirms that there were no movies or even movie facilities. About 250 students at a time sat for the recognition lessons as part of their training courses. Time spent amounted to one or two hours, sometimes up to half a day, at intervals of about two weeks over the space of a ten-month program.

Nakagawa's efforts to convey knowledge of Allied aircraft and ships were naturally constrained by Japan's limitations in terms of intelligence overall. Thus he had the best information on prewar weapons and systems, with knowledge progressively poorer as he tried to teach planes and ships introduced after war began. He illustrated certain classes of carriers, battleships, and destroyers, while aircraft taught included the P-40, F4F, F4U, P-38, P-51, B-17, B-24, B-26, the SBD and SB2C dive-bombers, the TBF torpedo bomber, and several types of seaplanes including the OS2U, PBM, PB2M, and PBY Catalina. Only toward the end of the war were the B-29 bomber and F6F fighter added to the course. In early 1943 Nakagawa began to assemble course materials into a two-volume recognition manual. For ships there were pictures from in front, overhead, and at a distance. The Naval General Staff printed 5,000 copies of the manual and distributed it to all aircraft carriers, air groups, fleets, and other major units. When copies ran out the recognition course was terminated.

Poor recognition skills might not have mattered so much if the Imperial Navy had been able to photograph Allied forces and targets and then analyze the results at leisure back at base. Here too, however, the Japanese lagged far behind their adversaries. Development of photography equipment and techniques was the responsibility of the Optics Section of the Naval Air Technical Arsenal at Yokosuka, a division of the Bureau of Aeronautics. The section developed a number of cameras, the best having lens apertures of fifty and twenty-five centimeters, with ten of the latter delivered in 1941 and again in 1942, and none of the fifty-centimeter models produced until 1943. In all, 575 of the larger and 326 of the smaller cameras were produced during the war, along with numbers of cameras that were much less capable or were intended for other applications.

These numbers suggest that camera supply was not the worst obstacle for Japanese Navy aerial reconnaissance. Instead, the key problems were aircraft and photographic interpretation. For a long time the Japanese did not have any specialized reconnaissance aircraft. The Imperial Navy seems to have decided during the Guadalcanal campaign that it needed not only more specialized planes, but pictures as well. Some Japanese Army KI 46 planes (which Allied intelligence called Dinahs) reached Rabaul and were taken over by the Imperial Navy to provide the necessary capability. In the spring of 1942 the Navy issued a specification calling for a fast, high-altitude scout plane, and one was in hand by mid-1944, but no more than two squadrons were ever equipped for the specialized photo function, one with the carrier fleet, the other in the North Pacific. That made a total of perhaps thirty-six first-line and a dozen reserve aircraft, and their serviceability rate often fell as low as 20 percent.

Photographic interpretation facilities and personnel were the next problem. All aircraft carriers had darkrooms and processing facilities, as did fleet headquarters, but carriers rarely had qualified personnel. At Yokosuka Lieutenant Commander Ezaki, who had studied photographic techniques with civilian experts in 1940, became the Navy's senior photo interpreter. With ten others Ezaki established a photographic interpretation school, developed the course, and wrote the teaching manual. The first class of interpreters completed training in late 1942. Five or six were sent temporarily to Rabaul, three stayed at Yokosuka as instructors, and the rest went to frontline air groups. There were between twenty and twenty-five interpreters in the second class, all of whom were assigned to Tateyama Air Group, a training command. A final class of thirty finished the course in early 1944, but there was little photography that required interpretation at the time and they were all reassigned to other duty. At the end of the war the Navy had a plan to have an interpreter with every air unit, so a hundred officers were in training, but the project never came to fruition.

As the system finally evolved, each of the specialized photographic reconnaissance units had its own interpreter who doubled as *hikoshi,* or assistant air officer. Pilots received thirty hours' special training in cameras and techniques, with most flights carried out at altitudes of 10,000 meters. At that altitude the fifty-centimeter camera produced pictures with a ground scale of about 1:20,000; the scale of twenty-five-centimeter photos was double that. These scales were roughly sufficient for aerial mapping or installation identification, but not for tactical planning. A few sorties produced pictures with scales down to 1:8,000, but these were the exception. For the United States, photos with a scale of 1:5,000 were standard for tactical planning.

Most Japanese photo interpretation was carried out at the unit level. In addition, the Japanese did not produce large numbers of copies of photographs and circulate them for reinterpretation by other commands. Instead each numbered fleet or air fleet would typically have a trained interpreter, but that officer merely responded to pictures sent to him. It was September 1943 before three photo interpreters arrived at Rabaul. On Guadalcanal and in the Netherlands East Indies in 1943, Japanese interpreters used photography to keep track of the pace of U.S. base construction, and this could be used for timing air attacks, but the pictures were not good enough to track Allied force levels, aircraft types, and so on. Decryption of Japanese message traffic showed that about half of scouting reports contained visual observation of ships or harbors. Only occasional messages referred to photography, and of those the overwhelming majority concerned construction and location of airfields.

Once again sophistication grew toward the end of the war. By 1944 the First Air Fleet, by then land-based, was making full use of photo interpreters, and fleet officers were beginning to take the initiative in requesting photo missions. Naval General Staff officers complained that they were unable to initiate missions, and such photography as flowed to NGS was often simply filed. Still, Commander Terai Yoshimori noted that photos arriving at the operations section were put to good use planning air strikes on Allied fleets off Okinawa. Commander Yokura Sashizo, an air intelligence officer with the joho kyoku, complained that most data came in the form of dispatches recording numbers and types of planes, rather than photos themselves. "I would have liked to have had more reconnaissance," said Yokura. "I would have liked to have known the number of planes at Saipan, for instance." Postwar investigation established that only four photo missions were flown over Saipan and just ten over Okinawa. On the other hand, Allied authorities noted more visual observation flights over their own ports of embarkation as the time neared for the final round of invasion operations. As a matter of fact, the last recorded Japanese aircraft shot down during World War II—on August 15, 1945—was a Myrt photo plane.

Another aspect of the Japanese effort, just as with the Americans, would be salvage and analysis. In the East Indies the Japanese salvaged several Dutch, British, and American warships up to destroyer size. They were then free to examine the foreign technology to their heart's content. More exotic was the use of divers from a salvage ship to examine the underwater wreck of British battleship *Prince of Wales,* which settled in relatively shallow waters in the South China Sea. The divers reportedly confirmed for the Imperial Navy that the British ship had had radar antennae. Similarly, at Penang during November 1943 divers from the *Kamishima Maru* raised important materials (not further identified) from a sunken British submarine. In April 1944 in Manila Bay the *Number 5 Kamikaze Maru* worked on the hulk of American submarine tender *Canopus.* During February and April the *Hokuan Maru* labored in Thai coastal waters on the wreck of an Italian vessel. Japanese divers seem to have been as intrepid as American.

Closely related to intelligence derived from recovery of items from sunken ships was what the Japanese learned from analysis of aircraft shot down or captured. American intelligence received a shock in the summer of 1945 when an aerial photo taken late that May over the Japanese base Tachikawa revealed a large four-engine bomber, dubbed the "Tachikawa Field 104." After the war investigators discovered the plane had actually been an

*American* B-17E Flying Fortress. The plane was a product of Japanese air technical intelligence. Tachikawa happened to be the location of the Army's Aviation Technical Research Institute. Yokosuka, of course, housed the Navy's 1st Air Technical Research Arsenal. Both units sent specialist teams right in behind the Japanese assault troops. From Clark Field the Japanese recovered the turbo-supercharger of a B-17 plus other kinds of spare parts. Eventually an entire B-17E was put together from the collection. Another would be recovered in the Netherlands East Indies, put together from the remains of fifteen B-17s wrecked on airfields there, and a third was found in pretty good shape in the same area. Designer Kikuhara Shizuo, who had originated the Emily flying boat, noted how impressed he was that the United States had perfected the B-17's subsystems to such a degree that a minimum of controls were necessary in the cockpit.

What the Japanese did with the B-17 they tried with many other planes, studying crashed aircraft, making photos and drawings, salvaging parts, and so on. This effort, like so many others, began as early as the China Incident, where the Japanese recovered a P-40E fighter and an A-20A twin-engine bomber. Within the JNAF these studies were conducted by the same people who did the design work for Navy planes. Thus, of 327 personnel at the Yokosuka main office of the Research Technical Arsenal and 186 at the branch office in Isogo, it has been estimated that roughly 10 officers, 10 civilian designers, and 150 enlisted men worked on studies of foreign aircraft.

Navy lieutenant Toyoda Takogo was one designer who worked in the foreign-technology program. He reports that the Japanese Army sent out most of the field teams, subsequently supplying the JNAF with copies of their reports and lending them aircraft as desired. The single team Takogo remembers the JNAF dispatching went to Burma to study a crashed British Mosquito light bomber. But the Navy center would be sent aircraft recovered in the Southern Area and would send teams to crash sites in the Empire area, including Okinawa, where an F6F Hellcat was recovered after raids in October 1944. British carrier raids in the Netherlands East Indies earlier that year yielded a TBM-1C Avenger. Yokosuka's specialists were surprised at its "extremely strong construction." When an F4U Corsair was captured near the Kasumigaura flight school, "we were surprised there were places on the wing covered with fabric." The JNAF recovered the flight manual for the B-24 Liberator in the summer of 1944, and flew a captured F6F Hellcat. The comparable Army unit also flew the Brewster Buffalo, the Hawker Hurricane, the B-17D and B-17E, and the PBM Mariner.

Flying experience and ground studies were used to compile reports on the foreign aircraft, but because the specialists were preoccupied by their own design work, the studies of foreign planes were fairly basic. Only very late in the war was a special section of three officers and twelve to fourteen men formed just to track foreign technology, first under Commander Nomura Suetsu, then under Iwaya Eichi. By way of comparison, the Office of Naval Intelligence in Washington had an equivalent section by 1942 and a much larger Technical Intelligence Center, jointly run with the British and the U.S. Army, soon thereafter.

Reports from the Air Technical Research Arsenal went to the 5th Section of the Naval General Staff—that is, to the American section of *joho kyoku*, where "Staff Officer D" was the air intelligence expert. According to Lieutenant Toyoda, *joho kyoku* staff "were not very interested in our reports because they were not technical[ly] minded." According to Commander Yokura Sashizo, who was Staff Officer D from January 1943 to June 1945, his difficulty was that technical intelligence at NGS remained a one-man show until the last months of the war, when Etajima graduates exceeded available assignments and a hundred or so were suddenly drafted into intelligence work. Commander Yokura worked hard to make sure all captured planes and equipment made it back to Yokosuka for study, and he appreciated the Research Arsenal reports. Yokura's primary intelligence sources were data from naval units afloat, observations of U.S. air attacks, radio reports from the United States, prisoners, crashed aircraft, captured documents and, lastly, reconnaissance. He believes that by the end of the war the Imperial Navy had very good understanding of aircraft types the Americans had been using in 1943. That was the size of the Japanese lag in technical intelligence.

As a one-man team, Staff Officer D had to do everything. He was responsible for air intelligence on both the British and Americans, for the Allied air order of battle, for technical material, and for recognition sheets to inform local commanders. Most of his work was statistical, Yokura relates, "and I got little information." There were some technical and tactical reports, which came by radio from the German General Staff, and the Imperial Navy occasionally reciprocated with lists of numbers and types of Allied aircraft believed to be in the Pacific. Yokura's best source on order of battle was shot-down planes, which had markings and often bore documents that yielded useful information. Prisoners sometimes divulged information about their own squadrons. Yokura also exchanged data with "Staff Officer C," Commander Imai Nobuhiko, who tracked fleet order of battle, and together they kept a good accounting of U.S. aircraft carriers, at least. In fact, one Third Bureau study on U.S. carrier task forces Yokura assembled in 1944 had U.S. authorities red-faced at how the Japanese could have derived such intelligence. The standard product, however, was periodic summaries of U.S. air strength printed on outline maps of the Pacific, circulated to all JNAF air groups and carriers.

The huge mass of work forced Commander Yokura to focus on the United States. Even there he had to specialize. For example, in contrast to the mountains of biographical data U.S. intelligence accumulated on Imperial Navy officers, Yokura's file on U.S. military commanders, which he assembled from radio reports, simply listed the top officers. When Yokura appealed for help to NGS chiefs and was merely given a few green young officers, he finally concluded that the Imperial Navy just was not going to develop *any* organization capable of handling air intelligence. He resigned and became a staff officer with the Third Fleet, then an aviation instructor.

Background information for *joho kyoku* appreciations came from the network of Japanese naval attachés throughout the world, but most especially in Europe. Latin American attachés, as already seen, provided Tokyo a certain amount of useful data, but the European attachés actually had a window on the other half of the world war. Existing accounts have focused almost entirely on the Japanese Army side, particularly on the role of General Baron Oshima Hiroshi, Tokyo's ambassador to Berlin. More attention needs to be given not only to Imperial Navy activities in Germany but also to attachés elsewhere in Europe.

Germany remained the senior ally, so Tokyo always put its largest contingent in Berlin. The naval attaché there in 1941 was Rear Admiral Yokoi Tadao, who doubled as chief technical inspector—that is, the official in charge of the kinds of engineering and scientific matters previously discussed in the prewar context. At that time there were three assistant attachés to gather information, one to act as paymaster, and one technical assistant. There were also a civilian expert and six officer technicians who acted as inspectors for shipbuilding, engineering, electrical developments, aircraft fuselages, aircraft engines, and torpedoes. Each officer had a civilian assistant. The civilian inspector functioned as the assessor of instrument technology. The inspectors visited German plants to solicit information and received reports, including translations of technical manuals, from local representatives of Japanese companies. Helping the Navy were the Mitsubishi, Okura, and Mitsui corporations; the Yokohama Specie Bank; Japan Bank; NYK Lines; and the Osaka Steamship Company. The inspectors received instructions from naval technical offices, the assistant attachés from *joho kyoku*. Within the embassy the naval attaché office was not very popular, a fact that reflected the Navy's opposition to the Tripartite Pact and the Army dominance that resulted from having a general for ambassador.

Beginning in early 1941, when a Japanese naval mission reached Germany by steamship into Lisbon, the naval attaché office was somewhat eclipsed. Traveling aboard the naval transport *Asaka Maru* were sixteen civilians and twenty-four officers, including such experts as Commander Otomo Hiroshi, an engineering officer previously assigned to the naval inspector's office in New York City, who had triggered ONI suspicions with a series of visits to U.S. aircraft plants in the Los Angeles area in 1936. Another member was pilot Commander Naito Takeshi, anxious to visit

Taranto, the site of the highly successful British carrier strike on the Italian Fleet.

Originally headed by an admiral who was an expert on engines for large warships, the mission was soon taken over by Vice Admiral Nomura Naokuni, an academy classmate of Kondo Nobutake and Takasu Shiro, among others, and a golfing partner of American admiral Thomas Hart during the time they had spent at Tsingtao in China. A submariner and torpedo specialist who had been on the delegation to the London Naval Conference of 1930 and had served two previous tours in Germany, Nomura was familiar with both the European scene and German technology. The admiral was also well qualified to observe war operations, having been chief of staff of the Combined Fleet in 1936 and chief of *joho kyoku* during the first years of the China Incident, as well as skipper in his time of the cruiser *Haguro*, the carrier *Kaga*, and the 2nd Submarine Squadron. In some ways Admiral Nomura seemed a better qualified representative of his service than was General Oshima for the Japanese Army.

The naval mission made extensive use of the attaché office in Berlin, and toured at length to examine Germany's technology base. Their original list of subjects for inquiry, which the Germans considered amounted to industrial espionage, included 115 technology subjects, 89 proposed factory visits, and 77 matters pertaining to German war experience. In March 1941 the Japanese officers were given an extensive tour of the battleship *Tirpitz*, then in final stages of completion (for reciprocity's sake, German attachés in Japan got a one-hour tour of the *Yamato*, which was, however, restricted to less important areas of the ship). Admiral Nomura's experts spent four days at the Junkers aircraft factory in Leipzig, three in Jena at the Zeiss optical works, six more days at the Messerschmidt plant in Augsburg, and so on. Somewhere along the line, the distinction between visiting mission and resident attachés was lost, and Nomura ended up as de facto naval attaché. He remained in Germany through the spring of 1943, doing things as unusual as going along on a U-boat war patrol, during which he assumed temporary command during the sinking of a British cargo vessel. It would again be by submarine that Nomura left Europe, for blockade-running submarines became the sole means of physical contact between German and Japanese allies.

Replacing Nomura in Berlin would be Rear Admiral Abe Katsuo, also a former chief of *joho kyoku*, and a War College instructor to boot. As a young officer Abe had been assigned to the United States, and he had commanded the cruiser *Tama* and the light carrier *Ryujo*. Abe was a 1912 graduate of Etajima, a class that included such Imperial Navy stars as Ugaki Matome, Yamaguchi Tamon, and Onishi Takijiro. Years later, on the 1940 Navy List, Abe ranked just behind the unfortunate Yamaguchi, and immediately ahead of Ugaki Matome. Admiral Abe came to Europe in the spring of 1941 as naval attaché in Italy, replacing Hiraide Hideo, who returned to Tokyo to become the Navy's bombastic official spokesman and propaganda adviser. The Japanese do not appear to have felt they could learn much from the Italian Navy, so when Nomura also returned to Japan, Abe, promoted to vice admiral, went to Berlin as Japanese naval representative to the Tripartite Military Commission, as well as chief of all Navy attachés in Europe.

The Tripartite Military Commission turns out to have been a weak reed insofar as alliance cooperation was concerned; it paled in contrast to the Allied institution of the Combined Chiefs of Staff. A volume containing the proceedings of the commission's weekly meetings during the last year of the war demonstrates that very few of its discussions dealt with strategy. Rather the sides used these meetings to present progress reports and exhort their allies. German representatives, for example, went into considerable detail regarding their counterattacks against the Normandy invasion and their hopes for V-weapons. Many of the same details appeared in German communiqués and propaganda broadcasts. Rear Admiral Kojima Hideo, who served in Berlin as naval attaché under Abe, commented that his boss had nothing to do on the commission except play bridge.

Kojima Hideo had no real background other than with *joho kyoku*. He was the closest thing the Imperial Navy had to a specialist intelligence officer—specialized, moreover, in German affairs. As a young language officer between 1923 and 1925 he had studied the history of the German Navy in World War I. Kojima returned to Berlin as naval attaché to Germany and Holland in 1937, and when he went home it was to head the German desk at *joho kyoku*. At the time of the Nazi-Soviet Pact, Kojima believed that Adolf Hitler had a true love for Japan, a special affinity for Japanese ideology, and was in effect an Oriental sage. Ordered back to Europe in the summer of 1943, Admiral Kojima left in the submarine *I-29*, which departed Penang on December 15, 1943, and reached Lorient on the Bay of Biscay on March 11, 1944.

Tokyo's primary source in Berlin was the information bureau of the Wehrmacht High Command (OKW). They were uniformly courteous and very free with material about the enemy, but quite reticent regarding submarine losses, German forces, strategic plans, and Luftwaffe data. The Germans would supply information about their own weapons once these were being used in battle, but not before, and they seemed very slow in developing new systems. The Navy Ministry asked for information on jet-propelled aircraft but made few other specific requests. They eventually received studies and blueprints of certain German aircraft.

The naval attaché also dealt with the Attaché Group of the German Foreign Ministry, and that sometimes provided useful information. With the spring of 1944, when OKW offices dispersed out of Berlin, it became harder and harder to reach them, and Kojima made fewer requests; he was now more dependent on the Foreign Ministry. He began to rely on British radio broadcasts, which he found quite accurate. German material he had to take on trust, but decided it was about 80 percent accurate. In cables to Tokyo, Kojima used no system for rating his intelligence but directly stated the sources and his evaluation of them.

Italy was the next most important post in Europe, at least during the time the Italians remained in the Axis. The naval office there consisted of three assistant attachés, one to deal in intelligence, one for finance, and a technical expert with five inspectors, respectively for mines and torpedoes, aircraft, fuses, guns, and boilers and pumps. The attaché office also employed a secretary, a typist, and two drivers.

The Italians exchanged three grades of information with the Imperial Navy: unclassified, secret, and most secret. Materials would be delivered in packets from the Navy Ministry by a sailor, either an ordinary seaman or a yeoman. For example, in November 1942 the news of the French scuttling their fleet at Toulon was graded "secret"; a typical "most secret" report would detail the composition of an American task force. The Italians never gave sources for the intelligence they shared, despite many Japanese requests, so naval attachés had difficulty evaluating it.

Several times a month the Imperial Navy attaché sent his intelligence to Tokyo by radio. His top collection priority was information on Allied intentions, followed by types and numbers of warships headed for the Pacific, with material on arms and armaments ranked next. Captain Mitsunobu Taro, the assistant attaché while Abe was in Rome, succeeded his boss when the latter left for Berlin, with promotion to rear admiral thrown in for good measure. Mitsunobu had direct contact with the Italian intelligence chief, Rear Admiral Franco Maugheri, head of the Servizio de Informazione Militare.

Mussolini's Italy left the war in the fall of 1943, though the Italian dictator would be rescued by German special forces and put in charge of a rump Fascist state in northern Italy. The Japanese naval attaché thereafter dealt with the rump state. In June 1944, returning from Merano, where he had gone to pay his respects to German theater commanders, Admiral Mitsunobu and three companions were murdered from ambush. Also killed were local representatives of the Mitsubishi and Mitsui corporations. Assistant attaché Captain Yamanaka Dengo escaped.

After the demise of its attaché Tokyo ordered Admiral Abe in Berlin to take on the Italian job in addition to his duties elsewhere. Abe in turn instructed Captain Yamanaka to act for him when he was absent, and made only one visit to northern Italy thereafter. Yamanaka Dengo became de facto naval attaché in Italy, communicating with Berlin and Tokyo several times a month.

Apart from these missions the Imperial Navy maintained attachés in Turkey, Vichy France, Spain, Portugal, Russia, Finland, and Sweden. There had been an attaché in Holland until 1940. An attaché worked intermittently in Rumania, and the case of the attaché in Moscow also proved anomalous. Germany attacked Russia in June 1941, of course, but Japan did not, and it maintained diplomatic relations with the Soviet Union. It was a boon for Tokyo to do so, for the Soviets had weekly flights to Stockholm, thus permitting Japanese couriers to move documents in spite of the ongoing war. The Soviets tightly regulated monthly transit across Russia to the Far East, and Japanese attachés in Moscow were even more restricted than those of the Allied powers—Captain Usui Yoshiro, the last Moscow attaché, was compelled to live in a small apartment and permitted to move only between it and his embassy—but Tokyo knew the value of the service.

Before the war there had been a kind of attaché roundtable, with the naval attaché in London recognized as the chief European representative of the Imperial Navy. Europe-wide conferences among Japanese naval attachés were held more or less regularly, for example at Lisbon in the summer of 1941. After Pearl Harbor, Berlin became the chief attaché office and the big conferences ended. Yamanaka Dengo reports meetings once a year, though Kojima Hideo recalls only attaché trips to consult with colleagues. These recollections are not mutually exclusive. In January 1943 an intelligence conference did occur in Berlin, but the attendees were almost exclusively Foreign Ministry and Army representatives. The Navy may indeed have gotten by with consultations.

As Germany went down to defeat in the spring of 1945 the Japanese naturally made some efforts to keep viable their attaché networks. Admiral Abe recommended that Captain Ogi Kazuto, one of his assistants, proceed to Sweden at the head of an expanded attaché office to include many from other European posts. Ogi was a member of the 1923 cohort from Etajima, a class that was a key in Japanese wartime intelligence efforts; it included not only his own Berlin colleague Captain Taniguchi Yasumori, but also Moscow attaché Usui, and even former Washington attaché Sanematsu Yuzuru. In any case, though the Navy appointed Captain Ogi to the post the Swedes denied him a visa. Ignoring such refusals, in the first days of May 1945 Ogi was among the group of twenty Japanese naval officers, including both Taniguchi and Admiral Abe, who fled to Sweden to be interned there. It is reported that despite internment Admiral Abe later participated in abortive peace feelers Tokyo put out toward the Allies.

Naval attachés in Europe, as had been the case in the Americas and at other posts, continued throughout the war to handle secret funds. During a five-week period in the spring of 1943, for example, $544,000 in Portuguese currency was transferred from the Japanese mission in Lisbon to the legation in Madrid. Specific information is available for secret funds in

Italy at the close of the war in Europe: The naval attaché expended ¥1,243 during the period March–April 1945 and had on account at the Bank of Rome about ¥32,500 plus 27,870 Swiss francs. Through the Tokyo Specie Bank branch in Berlin, during the first days of May the attaché office remanded to Tokyo its remaining funds, ¥127,164.31.

Although Admiral Abe in Berlin was senior Imperial Navy representative in Europe, there were subcenters of control. One was Turkey, where the mission spent the summer in Istanbul and wintered at Ankara. The Turkish mission controlled the arc of the Middle East, from Palestine right through Iran (then called Persia). The naval attaché after April 1940 was Commander Matsubara Akio. A major Japanese agent in this area, according to ONI and Office of Strategic Services files, was Enomoto Momotaro, the thirty-three-year-old Istanbul correspondent for the Tokyo *Nichi Nichi.* Enomoto made enough waves to be expelled from Turkey, after which he based himself in Sofia, Bulgaria. He was linked with German efforts to contact Indian nationalists, arrangements to get information out of Russia, and other intrigues. Enomoto later moved to Budapest, and in 1943 *Nichi Nichi* transferred him to Lisbon.

A major intelligence target for Japanese in Turkey was information on ships transiting the Suez Canal. No agents appear to have been recruited for this purpose, however, and Japanese intelligence was probably restricted to anything gleaned from certain German agents who operated in Cairo until the summer of 1942. As late as winter 1945 some officials at the intelligence center the Allies had in Cairo believed Japanese efforts in Turkey were still in a formative stage, but this does not accord with activities the Japanese actually carried out. According to one European attaché, for example, in early 1944 a delegation of Manchukuo diplomats accompanied by some Japanese actually reached home across Turkey and Persia to a probable sea rendezvous. There was also the case of Franz Mayr, Germany's most important agent in Iran until his expulsion by the British on August 15, 1943. Mayr's communications went over Japanese radio sets using a so-called Tokyo code, and the Japanese legation in Teheran handled his reports sent through the mail. These activities were in fact used as justification for ordering the Japanese mission to leave the country. In Syria (which then included Lebanon), the Japanese consulate in Beirut requested $4,950 in special funds for 1941; of that amount $2,400 was earmarked for intelligence procurement in Syria-Lebanon and $480 for Palestine. Later it was reported that Tokyo received reports in this area concerning Australian military movements, local defense works, and tribal disputes in Iran. An American counterintelligence report in the summer named two suspected Japanese agents. By 1945, hard-pressed German spymasters in Turkey were preparing to hand their own networks over to the Japanese.

Another key subcenter for Japanese intelligence was Lisbon, port of entry for neutral Europe amid a continent in flames. Lisbon reportedly controlled Japanese activities in Spain and, at one time, Italy. Since the Spanish represented Japan's interests in South America and elsewhere, Lisbon acquired even more importance. Enomoto Momotaro operated from here after August 1943, and worked on such projects as setting up a radio net connecting Stockholm, Madrid, Barcelona, and Vienna; or making communications arrangements for a prospective agent to be sent to the United States, where Enomoto himself had been in 1939 on his way to Europe. The journalist was also known to be in contact with Richard Klatt, alias Max, a notorious German spy who had tentacles running throughout the Balkans and into Russia.

American counterintelligence professed to have direct evidence of Japanese involvement, in this view directed from Lisbon, in political troubles in Bolivia during 1943. There the economy was dominated by tin exports, but price indexes remained flat and real value declined, even though Bolivia was America's main source for this mineral, which figured in the war effort. Labor problems in the mines at Potosí combined with political agitation, and a party formed with leanings toward fascism: the MNR, or Revolutionary Nationalist Movement in its English translation. Unrest culminated in a December 1943 coup which overthrew the government of Enrique Peñaranda, though without measurable improvement for the Bolivian economy. Another plot in Peru was aborted that New Year's Eve, when thirty-seven Japanese and five alleged German agents were arrested by authorities. "It would seem," concluded an ONI counterintelligence memorandum, "that the Pacific enemy has at least moderate capacity to wage an intelligence war without formal aid from another Power."

Beyond covert action, the Japanese in Lisbon also had standard collection requirements. Great importance attached to material on shipping in the North Atlantic, including shipbuilding and repair, data Japan shared with the Germans. Secret funds were used to procure British newspapers and such standard sources as *Jane's Fighting Ships* and *Jane's All the World's Aircraft*. For example, the Lisbon naval attaché indirectly acquired five copies of the 1942 edition of the former and two of the latter. These were forwarded to Berlin for analysis, and important extracts radioed directly to *joho kyoku*. Referring to Lisbon's role, the ONI memo just quoted also observed: "The importance of the city as an espionage 'post office,' if not readily apparent, has been disclosed repeatedly through censorship and internal security measures in both this country and Great Britain."

Given their hunger for intelligence and their lack of really well-placed spies, the Japanese were vulnerable to fabricators, spurious agents inventing reports to sell to the highest bidder. Lisbon (and Madrid) during the war were meccas for such "paper mills," as they are often called, and the Japanese did not escape. British counterintelligence in Lisbon identified one

Mario Soares Brandao as having sold data to Japan. When Brandao turned up in Philadelphia on a liner arriving from Portugal, U.S. immigration authorities detained him on contrived charges, while ONI worried that he had been enlisted as a Japanese spy.

For all his difficulties, Captain Muchaku Senmei, the Imperial Navy attaché in Lisbon, who also had supervisory authority in Madrid, managed to get off many reports, some of real value to *joho kyoku*. A Madrid report in early January 1943 identified convoys leaving San Francisco for the Aleutians; indeed, U.S. forces were moving from that port as part of the buildup for the May invasion of Attu. A Lisbon report later that year noted the June 19 launching of cruiser *Houston*, replacement for the valiant vessel sunk in the Sunda Strait; not only was the data accurate but within the month that new light cruiser would be joining the U.S. fleet. Another Lisbon attaché report gave details of the conversion of 10,000-ton tankers into "Woolworth aircraft carriers," the escort carriers American sailors familiarly called jeeps. A late 1944 report tabulated numbers of Allied ships in the Pacific and the number damaged since Pearl Harbor.

The Allies were not able to stop Japanese spies, but if there was no way to keep naval attachés from collecting data, at least the Allies tried to keep abreast of what was being reported. Lisbon is an excellent case in point. There is a story in the lore of espionage that OSS spies entered the Japanese mission in Lisbon to steal documents, after which the Imperial Navy changed its attaché codes, shutting out U.S. intelligence for more than a year. This tale is wrong at both ends—both on the penetration and on the codes.

Oddly enough the apocryphal tale from Lisbon appears to have originated in Washington, specifically from bureaucratic maneuvers by General George Strong, who headed Army intelligence and harbored intense dislike for the OSS. Strong charged that an OSS break-in during May 1942, amateurishly done, had caused the problem. In the ensuing investigation OSS chief Bill Donovan was able to show that there had been no break-in per se, rather that the OSS had recruited two Portuguese nationals, one a stenographer for the military attaché, the other a messenger for the naval attaché. These agents were only activated after Donovan applied to the Joint Intelligence Committee and that body approved the operation. The agents provided background data on personnel working for the Japanese mission and collected materials that came to them through the normal course of work. General Strong saw their reports and the Lisbon product and thus presumably knew that the charges he made were inaccurate.

Copies of the Lisbon material in ONI files clearly establish that the intelligence the OSS received, at least from the Japanese naval attaché, consisted of documents recovered from the wastebasket. The Portuguese agent in the naval attaché's office apparently photographed the discards before disposing of the waste paper. This fact also establishes that *no code material was involved;* the Japanese documents were plaintext copies of messages *prior* to encoding, and indeed may have been drafts that were never used. Even if Captain Muchaku had discovered the penetration his response would have been to tighten the handling of papers, not question the security of his codes.

The naval attaché code, which OP-20-G called Coral, actually *was* being read by Washington and without anything to do with Japanese antics in Lisbon. Coral was based upon an encryption device (which the Japanese knew as 97 Siki Romazi Inziki) using the same operating principles as the Purple diplomatic machines. This device was introduced in September 1939, and the Japanese had been careful about their communication security during its initial employment. There were no careless mistakes that allowed easy entry into the machine's design, which featured electric selectors to do the work of code wheels (the selectors had just twenty-five contacts, meaning the alphabet had more letters than the machine had points of output, so that a letter could encipher to itself, making the codebreaking job much more complex). The Coral machine also had a plugboard similar to the German Enigma, making the Coral machine, overall, more sophisticated than the German one. Moreover, at least until Pearl Harbor, the number of messages sent using Coral was limited, which further inhibited efforts to break into the system. However, Americans had uncovered the basic features of Coral when they broke Purple, and U.S. confidence increased further as the codebreakers solved the analogous Jade (also a 97 Siki machine) through 1943. Coral was first read by the Allies on March 13, 1944.

It turned out the vast majority of messages in Coral came from Admiral Abe in Berlin, not from Lisbon at all, and more than 5,300 of these, recovered and translated, eventually sat in OP-20-G files. Due to the nature of the business of the Tripartite Military Commission, which many of Abe's messages concerned, Coral turned out to be a prime intelligence source on *German* military operations. Abe, privately called "Honest Abe" in Washington, was determined to follow preparations to defend Europe against Allied invasion, and set himself up with a situation map on which he recorded German unit movements in northwest Europe. A duplicate map was maintained in Tokyo, to which he sent news of each change required. The Allies were thus able to follow German dispositions in detail, an important supplement to Ultra gained from the German Enigma machine.

In addition to a penetration of the Japanese mission in Lisbon and reading the naval attaché code, it has been reported that the Americans were receiving intelligence Roman Catholic Church officials passed up diplomatic channels to the Vatican. As if that were not all, the Americans had a source code-named Shark in the Japanese embassy in Turkey. The British, too, had a double agent in Turkey among spies the Germans planned to pass to

Japanese control. In sum, the Japanese gained from their networks in Europe; but what Tokyo learned would be little surprise to Allied capitals.

ALTHOUGH THE ALLIES HAD GOOD WORKING KNOWLEDGE OF THE INTELLIGENCE REPORTED TO Tokyo, they knew much less about what the Naval General Staff did with the information. In fact *joho kyoku* used the material to compile reports on key subjects as well as, evidently beginning in 1944, a weekly bulletin to which each branch of the Third Bureau would contribute notes on whatever was timely. A survey of Bureau products illustrates the kind of intelligence to which the Combined Fleet had access as the Pacific war approached its climax.

Several times a year the Third Bureau consolidated field reports and what it learned directly into studies of Allied shipbuilding. One report on February 1, 1943, for example, projected U.S. warship construction out to 1946. Included in the estimate were fifteen new fast battleships and six battle cruisers. The United States actually ordered seventeen fast battleships, of which it completed ten, and six battle cruisers, two of which actually joined the fleet. Of the fast battleships Washington planned to build, a half dozen were to be behemoths of 60,000 tons mounting twelve 16-inch guns. A *joho kyoku* naval construction estimate on July 1, 1943, noted that these ships, called the *Montana* class, would be canceled. In fact, the U.S. Navy canceled its *Montana*-class ships on July 21, 1943. The Third Bureau expected that 30,000-ton aircraft carriers would be substituted and in fact the United States did increase carrier construction, though Imperial Navy estimates did not have the exact details.

Another important question for Combined Fleet officers was the combat power of American warships, and the newest thing afloat on the U.S. side were the *Iowa*-class battleships. A *joho kyoku* report of April 15, 1943, gave details of armor and armament, a correct speed figure, dimensions, and so forth. Only the crew figure was wrong. The Third Bureau attributed its information to open sources, specifically *The New York Times*. A complementary report on April 13 from the naval attaché in Germany gave details of the anti-aircraft armament of the *Iowa* and a number of other classes of U.S. vessels.

A particular threat to submarine forces was the new class of warship termed a destroyer escort. *Joho kyoku* put out a report on the characteristics of these vessels on May 19, 1943. Here Japanese intelligence was wrong, but not by too much, on the general specifications of the ships.

Crucial to American projection of airpower across the Pacific would be aircraft carriers, not only big fleet carriers and light ones converted from cruisers, but the small jeep carriers that would be used for convoy escort and to support ground forces during amphibious landings. The Third Bureau issued a fairly detailed analysis of U.S. building capacity for escort carriers and their characteristics on May 31, 1943. The February shipbuilding projection included estimates anticipating that by 1946 the Americans would build six fleet carriers, thirty-four light carriers, and forty-one escort carriers. An intelligence projection of inventory (as opposed to construction rates) that the Third Bureau released on July 1, 1943, estimated that on January 1, 1946, the U.S. fleet would have thirty-seven large carriers and ninety escort carriers. In fact, through all the vicissitudes of program changes, cancellations when the end came in view, substitutions, and accelerations, before war's end the United States had launched twenty-three fleet carriers, ten light carriers, and seventy-six escort carriers. The inventory number in August 1945 for large (fleet plus light) carriers would be thirty-six, which compares quite favorably to the Third Bureau estimate of summer 1943.

Meanwhile, on August 8, 1943, *joho kyoku* came up with a report giving specifications for the B-29 bomber and predicting its appearance on the front sometime after autumn. A further report giving specifications appeared on January 31, 1944, and there were even more detailed reports on the B-29 issued on May 17 and July 15, followed by an analysis of the first B-29 raids on June 25, 1944, and a study of the 20th Bomber Command, the American unit that flew the B-29s, on September 16. Considering that the prototype B-29 first flew only in September 1942, that the plans for unit equipment were formulated in March 1943, and that plans for the plane's use in the Pacific were finalized only that December, Japanese intelligence did very well on this bomber. Initially the B-29s went to India, then China, to hit Japan from the rear as it were, and so the first move was sending engineer units to India to build the long runways needed by these big aircraft. That was November 1943, and the British command was not told until March 1944 that B-29s were coming to their war. The January 1944 Japanese report on the B-29 was already in Burma, where a copy of it was captured at Mawlu. Public release of news that B-29 "Superfortress" bombers were in India came only in June. The Japanese report predicted 40 to 50 B-29s in service by March, 100 in June, and 300 to 400 before the end of the year. In actuality there were 127 aircraft with the 20th Bomber Command as of July 29, 1944, and the number (including all U.S. forces) exceeded 400 sometime in March 1945.

Like Allied competitors, Japanese intelligence tried hard to anticipate the shape of things to come. In terms of projections on strength the Third Bureau performed fairly well. What the Japanese did not do so well was make specific predictions of proximate tactical operations, and evaluations of probable Allied intentions. The Imperial Navy's command system lacked any mechanism encouraging this kind of intelligence work. As the war reached full stride in 1943, *joho kyoku* was left behind by Allied intelligence units such as JICPOA, FRUPAC, FRUMEL, and ATIS. Instead the Third Bureau had to do everything itself, although its various sections were understaffed too. It was headed through 1942 by Ogawa Kanji, for most of 1943 and 1944 by Rear Admiral Yano Hideo, then successively in 1945 by Admirals Ono Takeji and Nakase Nobuo, followed by Captain Nagasawa Hiroshi; the decline of Japanese intelligence is mirrored in the fact that the last-named chief held the post concurrently with other NGS duties.

Takeuchi Kaoru, the captain (later rear admiral) who headed the 5th Section of *joho kyoku*, its American unit, replacing an aviation officer who went back to the fleet, told later interrogators that assignments with the bureau were most often given to older or sick officers slated for retirement or unable to serve more actively. Takeuchi himself, for example, came to *joho kyoku* in July 1942 from the Total Warfare Research Institute, where he had gone from a seaplane training unit because of dengue fever and slight hardness of hearing. His "Staff Officer A," Sanematsu Yuzuru, was something of an exception as a younger, vigorous officer.

For most of the war the 5th Section consisted of Takeuchi and only five other persons—an aide plus four staff officers. The A unit handled all aspects of American life and war production, including fleet operations in home waters; the B branch covered U.S. overseas territories and military operations, in effect America's Pacific Theater; the C unit was responsible for Latin America; the D unit, as already seen, handled air technical intelligence. The remainder of *joho kyoku* was equally understaffed, with just three officers in the 6th Section (China and Manchuria), five in the 7th (Russia and Europe) and four in the 8th Section (British Commonwealth). Finally, there were two more officers plus a deputy who worked directly for the chief of *joho kyoku*.

Contrasting Japanese practice with the proliferation of situation rooms and flag plots maintained by Allied intelligence is easy. "To make a chart showing positions of individual ships at any one time was beyond the competence of the 3rd [Bureau]," Admiral Ono said. "We did, however, try to decide which units of your fleet were in general large areas." That intelligence would be passed to the First Bureau, which relied upon it as being from a good source. Questioned on this point, Baron Tomioka replied that the most useful data from *joho kyoku* were weekly written estimates of Allied losses, strength, and locations; the oral information presented at the daily staff conference; and character analyses of Allied commanders. On the whole, Tomioka said, intelligence was "very poor, very haphazard."

Captain Ohmae Toshikazu, Tomioka's eventual successor as operations planner with NGS, remarked of the American intelligence:

> The 5th Section collects all information, checks it, makes their evaluation, throws out information which is unreliable. It takes the 5th Section

a long time to make an evaluation of most of the information. They then send their opinion to us. We also check it, and it may be a few more days before we are satisfied [enough] to use it. There were some difficulties.

In the summer of 1944, when additional manpower was finally assigned, *joho kyoku* outgrew offices at the Naval War College and was forced to move to Hiyoshi. That made data exchange especially difficult since telephone service often broke down. *Joho kyoku* began sending a liaison officer to NGS every morning to brief reports from the previous day, while Admiral Takeuchi came up twice a week. An officer on the operations staff—for Ohmae, it was Commander Miyazaki—was also charged with seeking any data needed from either Third Bureau or the Owada Group.

Admiral Takeuchi recalled that he was almost never asked to attend NGS planning conferences. "Anyone outside of the planning section during a planning phase was considered almost like the enemy and was not admitted at all to the deliberations or their plans," he said. Told that Commander Miyazaki remembered him sitting in quite often, Takeuchi countered, "They would call me in for perhaps ten minutes, give me the results of their considerations, then drive me out." Told that Ohmae gave him more credit than that, Takeuchi responded, "This is the first time I have heard of it. I never received information directly from the First Section."

Takeuchi also had difficulties with the Owada Communications Group. Since that unit was subordinate to the Fourth Bureau, its data went directly to the Naval General Staff, merely coming to *joho kyoku* for its information. Admiral Takeuchi remarked, "I felt that inasmuch as much of their information was intelligence in nature, it should be mine. Such was not the case. I received only occasional copies." Ironically, the U.S. Navy had had an identical struggle over whether radio intelligence belonged to communications or to ONI. In both navies the result was the same: Radio intelligence was subordinated to communications authorities.

Nevertheless *joho kyoku* did its best with whatever available. In addition to Owada Group reports, there were data from the Germans. "At first I thought the Germans underestimated your capabilities," Captain Sanematsu said later, "but just before the Normandy invasion I thought they had begun to overestimate your power." Newspapers and other open publications continued to be a very helpful source, analyzed by attachés in neutral lands with results cabled to Tokyo. Sanematsu believed that radio broadcasts were his single best source: "These were analyzed by us and after some experience we could distinguish between fact, fiction and attempts to mislead us." Prisoner interrogation was rated a poor source by a number of former Japanese officers, even though *joho kyoku* had had its own men in a Navy-controlled prisoner camp. Although the Japanese were no doubt disguising reality in an effort to elude war-crimes charges, general lack of emphasis on intelligence in the Imperial Navy suggests little attention to development of sophisticated interrogation techniques. That prisoners were not a good source may have been the truth.

Admiral Takeuchi has supplied an interesting vision of the methods he encouraged:

> We concentrated the efforts of the section in statistical study of all data received by the section, probably a result of peculiarity of my own experience, which included long study of American history, going back to the days of John Calvin. This was done in the belief that if enough data was sifted, as in diamond mining, enough data would result of value to make it worthwhile. In Japan there is a tendency to look on intelligence as synonymous with espionage. This does not agree with my view. The long term aspect of my work was concentrated on collection of all data over a period of time.

The pieces to a puzzle could be many and varied. Thus Captain Sanematsu, for example, observed that it was difficult to reconstruct the point in time when his branch of the 5th Section began to realize that the United States might be capable of producing 75,000 aircraft a year. Such assessments were slow because of the number of variables that had to be estimated. Raw materials, rate of building new factories, available manpower, coal production, the number of shifts being worked, were all factors in the calculation.

When additional personnel were drafted into *joho kyoku* it was Sanematsu's branch that was the main beneficiary. Soon he had two officers working on naval matters, four on policy and politics, five on ground forces equipment and production, and another five officers assessing manpower and military training. In all the A branch received almost half the thirty-seven reservists sent to intelligence. Sanematsu regarded this as an annoyance as much as a blessing, since none of the men had any special knowledge and he considered a year's training necessary to produce an adequate intelligence officer.

Commander Imai Nobuhiko, Staff Officer C in the 5th Section, also helps show how the Imperial Navy lost the intelligence war. The C branch was supposed to handle Latin America. "I was picked for my knowledge of Spanish," Imai said of the personnel bureau's decision, "but I have forgotten most of it." Seconded from Hong Kong, where he had been an adjutant on the staff of the 2nd China Expeditionary Fleet, in May 1943 Imai joined intelligence. Nine months later the B branch billet went vacant and Imai, the Spanish expert, suddenly found himself responsible for South America, Canada, Alaska, Hawaii, and all frontline intelligence to boot. Few of those personnel later added to *joho kyoku* were assigned to Imai. After the war, asked what could have been done to improve 5th Section performance,

Admiral Takeuchi unhesitatingly replied that the first thing he would have done would have been to add more officers with better skills to his B branch.

So the war continued, with *joho kyoku* increasingly outclassed. Says Captain Sanematsu, "I still think it would have lasted longer if we had handled the war properly." Of the Japanese, Commander Imai observed: "They are apt to start a battle without seeing the end." Errors and traits such as these led to the triumph of Allied intelligence, which began in the Solomons. There intelligence made up for missing the Japanese evacuation of Guadalcanal with a coup that did much to change the course of the Pacific war, a coup that led directly to the death of Combined Fleet commander Yamamoto Isoroku.

# EIGHTEEN

# "The Darkness Is Very Deep"

U GAKI MATOME MUST HAVE LOOKED TROUBLED, PACING HIS OFFICE DOWN IN ADMIRALS' country near the stern of the *Musashi*. When Ugaki became tense or upset, his teeth or gums would act up. The fifty-two-year-old admiral was beset by this affliction repeatedly through the war. His tension at the end of 1942, of course, flowed from the dilemma over evacuation of Guadalcanal. Admiral Ugaki had been aware of the problems there, and of the threat posed by the Australian-American counteroffensive that had begun in New Guinea. At the same time the Combined Fleet chief of staff had been looking forward to the recrudescence of Navy offensive capability as the fleet carriers returned with fresh air groups, which he expected in mid-January.

But war would not wait for the Imperial Navy. On December 13 Ugaki met with Lieutenant Funahashi Masatoshi, just returned from his assignment as gunnery observer on Guadalcanal. The young officer brought a note from Captain Monzen Kanae, senior Navy officer on the island, which said that hardships had gone beyond the limit. Funahashi could supply firsthand details. Just the day before, Ugaki had had to deal with a request that he release light carrier *Junyo* to help support a landing contemplated for Wewak on the north coast of New Guinea. In fact, Captain Okada Tametsugu's carrier would be tied up with the New Guinea campaign for over a month. Nothing seemed easy anymore, Ugaki felt, recording that the ambitious plans to smash the British, occupy Fiji and Samoa, and take other places had vanished like a dream.

The crisis the Japanese faced at the end of 1942 was no dream; the decision to pull out of Guadalcanal would be one of the toughest IGHQ ever made. We will never know whether Ugaki's toothache came back now—the section of his diary covering this period was later lost when senior staff officer Kuroshima Kameto left it on a train—but there *are* details of how Tokyo pondered what had to be done.

Japanese Navy and Army staffs resisted any evacuation decision. When they met together, Baron Tomioka suggested tabletop war games as a device for clarifying the options. Colonel Tsuji Masanobu, who had just returned from Guadalcanal and was well aware of the starvation, the lack of ammunition, the men perishing every day, insisted that this was no time to spend days canvassing the options. The exchange became heated when Tomioka got the idea Tsuji was questioning the bravery or skills of Navy officers. Admiral Fukudome Shigeru, chief of the operations bureau, mediated between the contending viewpoints. The option went right up to a liaison conference on New Year's Eve, which came to a more or less inevitable decision. Emperor Hirohito attended and posed some questions about how easily the Americans seemed to be able to create air bases. Admiral Nagano of the NGS found it difficult to reply. The Americans used machines, Admiral Nagano had to answer; the Japanese were obliged to rely on manual labor.

Following the decision to evacuate, Hirohito turned to the Army chief of staff, Sugiyama, whom he asked whether he should issue an imperial rescript in connection with the operation. The Army general thought not, but Hirohito insisted—had the Guadalcanal battle been victorious there would have been such a rescript, and surely one was now appropriate as well. Hirohito's pronouncement read:

> The Emperor is troubled by the great difficulties of the present war situation. The darkness is very deep, but dawn is about to break in the eastern sky. Today the finest of the Japanese Empire's army, navy, and air units are gathering. Sooner or later they will head toward the Solomon Islands where a decisive battle is being fought.

Despite the withdrawal, the rescript carried an undertone of aggressive action. Had American intelligence gotten wind of its wording, expectations of a Japanese attack would have been strengthened. The IGHQ directive that followed resolved to accelerate "present preparations for another offensive" as a means of preparing the evacuation more rapidly and to "facilitate the concealment of the plan."

The whole sequence of events was presented to the Japanese public in a very studied way. On February 9, as the last troops were leaving the Isle of Death, Tokyo's Information Bureau released a summary of operations at Guadalcanal that emphasized the losses inflicted upon Allied forces. Several days later the Domei news service put out a bulletin that coined a new word using the characters for "deployment" and "retreat." The evacuation thus became a backward deployment. "It was a Japanese word that had never been heard and above all never read," noted the French reporter Robert Guillain, still at large in Tokyo. "The Imperial general staff must have thought hard to come up with this strange, original, wily word."

What "deployment" suggested, as did Hirohito's rescript, was aggression. Admiral Ugaki put it explicitly in his diary, just before the New Year:

> If we can surprise an enemy's weak point at this stage, not only would it menace the enemy by showing him the existence of our fighting strength, but it would also result in diverting the enemy from this district. I believe it's necessary to plan for it promptly.

What Ugaki did not want was to stay in port, to be a fleet in being. "It will not be a good policy to keep all this strength at Truk," the chief of staff opined. "It will only result in lowering morale."

Admiral Ugaki was serious, and Yamamoto with him. They pulled out of Guadalcanal, but they planned the biggest conceivable offensive, a novel one like the Pearl Harbor attack, an offensive to be carried out entirely from the air. The Japanese hoped to hold MacArthur's ground forays in New Guinea, stabilize the Solomons front by reinforcing New Georgia and the northern islands, and then strike back with irresistible force.

IF THERE WAS GOING TO BE AN AIR OFFENSIVE, A VERY GREAT DEAL DEPENDED ON RABAUL AND its surrounding complex of bases. By early 1943 the Japanese were hard at work improving existing facilities and adding new ones, expending great energy on labor while enduring hardships unimagined before the war.

Rabaul. Americans' image of that place was a mixture of limited knowledge and sheer ignorance. Aerial photos showed that the Japanese had added ninety fighter and sixty bomber revetments to the airfield at Vunakanau, for example, but no photograph could show the hardships and privations behind those improvements. Malaria remained a huge danger to work crews, maintenance men, Japanese at large, even the natives. Admiral Tsukahara, the air fleet commander, had to be invalided home on account of sickness in December 1942. Commander Genda, the ingenious air planner, also caught malaria and went into the hospital. Lying flat on his back, he missed the Santa Cruz battle. Genda left for Tokyo in mid-November. Commander Ohmae, Southeast Area Fleet staffer, had his bouts with the disease, and fleet commander Admiral Kusaka Jinichi came down with dysentery. Disease felled many a Korean or Taiwanese laborer, and as late as 1945 malaria remained the leading cause of death among local people.

Japanese preparations were made despite obstacles and hardships.

Americans had difficulties too, but the Allies paid more sustained attention to their logistics support, and benefited from Japanese failure to threaten supply lines the way Americans obstructed those of the Japanese. Thus by early 1943 there were over 10,000 Imperial Navy aircraft maintenance men at Rabaul, including many of the best, but already streams of spare parts were drying up. Average serviceability rates for planes were falling to less than 50 percent. Covering the Guadalcanal evacuation the JNAF lost thirty-eight aircraft in three days without a major air battle. Effective strength of the Eleventh Air Fleet fell to about 150 planes.

Commander Ohmae keenly felt the problems of the air situation, and saw beyond maintenance bottlenecks to deterioration in pilot quality. "The land-based air groups at Rabaul were not effective," Ohmae recalled, "largely because there were only a few experienced pilots. We still attached considerable importance to the Solomons campaign and we had to have a better air effort." In February Ohmae pressed for carrier air groups at Rabaul, where they could fly from land bases without risking mother ships. Admiral Ozawa Jisaburo, recently appointed chief of the Third Fleet, the redesignated Kido Butai, rejected such arguments. Ozawa argued the carrier groups had to be kept together to improve training and ensure readiness for the next fleet action. Besides, the Japanese Army had finally contributed some resources to the campaign, setting up its 6th Air Division at Rabaul.

Hopes for the Army came to little in the end. Lieutenant General Itabana Giichi's 6th Air Division had arrived in Rabaul in December with several air regiments, a training brigade, and support units. It took over newly completed Rapopo Airfield, perhaps a dozen miles from Rabaul. But Itabana's aircrews proved to have no experience flying over water, and his planes (designed for service in continental Asia) had very short ranges, while Army mechanics at Rabaul were at the far end of a tenuous supply chain. The Japanese Army mounted its first fighter sorties over Buna on December 26–27. Desultory missions from Rabaul merely convinced JNAF officers that the Army would be of little practical value in the Solomons. When IGHQ renegotiated *nanyo* defensive arrangements, the Army air force would be allotted to New Guinea. Meanwhile, JNAF planners looking toward an air offensive were forced back to the option of carrier air groups to supplement land-based strength.

The debate might have gone on longer, but opponents were silenced by quite startling developments in the Bismarck Sea, the waters between Rabaul and New Guinea. Allied success would be a combination of new aerial tactics plus sterling intelligence performance. The occasion was the Japanese Army's attempt to reinforce New Guinea with its 51st Infantry Division, staging through Rabaul. The Imperial Navy moved the bulk of the unit in a single convoy, reminiscent of some Guadalcanal operations. The Southwest Pacific command expected such a move but did not know when

or how it might happen. General George C. Kenney's Fifth Air Force reconnaissance pilots produced the evidence at the middle and end of February of
extraordinary shipping concentrations at Rabaul. The Allies also detected
Japanese floatplane activities characteristic of preparation for convoy movement. A series of decrypts from radio intelligence supplied details; FRUMEL
produced one Japanese message stating an intention to run a convoy into
Lae in early March; OP-20-G decrypted another setting up a program of
convoys to New Guinea ports Lae, Madang, and Wewak, specifying that the
Lae convoy was delayed due to the need to strengthen its escort of destroyers; and the CINCPAC fleet intelligence bulletin added details of a reinforcement program that would move two additional Japanese Army divisions
(the 20th and 41st) to New Guinea as well. Later OP-20-G came up with a
translation of an Eleventh Air Fleet message regarding air cover for the convoy which detailed the Lae convoy's size and timetable. The gist of this information would be repeated in General Willoughby's SOWESPAC daily
intelligence summary in the form of suspicions drawn from aircraft reconnaissance missions. To disguise the sources, General Kenney, the air commander, laid on a pattern of searches that would permit aircraft to sight the
Lae convoy.

Ignorant of Allied intelligence developments, the Southeast Area Fleet
and Eighth Fleet went ahead with the convoy. Its escort numbered eight
destroyers under Rear Admiral Kimura Masatome, and there would be an
equal number of transports bearing about 6,900 troops altogether. Kimura
weighed anchor at Rabaul about midnight on February 28, leading the
Number 81 Convoy. Everything went smoothly until late the next afternoon, when a B-24 bomber saw the Japanese off New Britain. The next
morning they were again sighted, and a high altitude attack by B-17s followed, sinking one transport. Kimura detached two escorts to rescue 950
survivors and these ships pushed ahead to reach Lae after dark. These would
be the only Japanese to reach the planned destination. The remaining ships
were sighted once more on the morning of March 3; after a couple of hours'
delay due to adverse weather, Fifth Air Force bombers slaughtered the convoy, sinking all seven remaining transports and four of eight destroyers. The
other four ships recovered 2,427 men from the sea and fled to Rabaul.
Admiral Kimura had his flagship shot out from under him. General Adachi
Hatazo, the Army commander, had to be pulled out of the sea. Only
Commander Kanma Ryokichi's destroyer, *Yukikaze*, survived without a
scratch.

Several factors account for the carnage at Bismarck Sea. One is Kimura's
late time of departure from Rabaul, which placed him in a prime location for
Allied air attack. A sunset or even late-afternoon departure from Rabaul
would have meant that the first day's Allied search would have found
Kimura farther along on his track but still out of useful range for the bulk of

Allied aircraft, and with a second night to get closer to Lae before doom struck, close enough at a minimum for survivors to make their destination rather than return to the point of origin. A second difficulty had to do with air support. The Eleventh Air Fleet hoped to neutralize Allied air with a series of strikes coincident with the convoy's sortie, but weather precluded attacks and more than made up for inconvenience caused Allied airmen. The JNAF had also promised up to 200 fighters to cover the convoy movement, and that promise, too, proved impossible to keep. Instead the 21st and 26th air flotillas flew just about eighty sorties, and flights by Army planes of the 6th Air Division's 12th Brigade were rendered useless when it turned out that the aircraft and base units used incompatible radios. With Allied air strength at 207 bombers and 129 fighters, the Japanese had little chance, losing roughly half their planes.

A key factor contributing to Allied success was the new tactic of "skip" bombing, in which medium bombers approached their target at low altitude, and dropped 500-pound bombs in such fashion as to lob them into the sides of ships below. Unfamiliar with these tactics, the Japanese first thought themselves confronted by torpedo planes. The standard evasive maneuver in that situation, turning toward or away from the attacker, merely improved the target aspect for a skip bomber. The new tactics made a radical difference. In August 1942 Allied aircraft in the Solomons had dropped 434 bombs and obtained 19 hits, and the corresponding figures that September were 425 and just 9. At Bismarck Sea planes using skip bombing scored 28 hits out of 37 bombs dropped using this technique.

Finally, the Japanese were required to stay at sea longer than necessary because they had prearranged a time of anchorage at the destination, while Eighth Fleet desired to maintain secrecy by refusing to use radio. Fleet commander Mikawa Gunichi sadly concluded in his after-action report:

> In view of the incorrect estimate of the Allied air base strength on New Guinea, the plan to dispatch a convoy at the low speed of seven knots to Lae, where it was within effective attacking range for two days, proved ill-advised. The plan was started on the basis of a calculation that even in the worst situation about half of the troops would be able to land. It took into consideration the fact that a transport convoy had successfully anchored at Lae in January, and also the inactivity in the land operations on New Guinea after the withdrawal . . . in Buna. This operation ended in complete failure.

More succinct was the summary one survivor scribbled in his diary: "We are repeating the failure of Guadalcanal!"

Admiral Yamamoto remained determined to avoid such repetition, though daily increases in Allied strength made failure loom. One intelligence report filed at the end of January by Japanese troops on New Georgia estimated U.S. strength on Guadalcanal at three divisions with 200 aircraft on two fields, more than the Japanese could hope to best. Yamamoto pressed for offensive action before the Allies got even stronger; to assemble sufficient strength he was willing to commit carrier air groups. Admiral Ozawa Jisaburo of the carrier fleet supervised plans for the offensive even though he had opposed this use of his air groups.

While the Japanese began preparations, American forces in the South Pacific stole a march on February 21, when an amphibious force led by Richmond Kelly Turner landed 9,000 men in the Russell Islands northwest of Guadalcanal. Immediately behind the assault echelons came construction battalions, the fabled "Seabees," who began preparations for air facilities. Cruiser-destroyer groups of the South Pacific Command (SOPAC) were also active, with two major forces at sea, a heavy ship force, and a smaller support unit. On the night of March 6 one of the cruiser groups caught a two-destroyer Imperial Navy unit that had been sent to succor Vila on Kolombangara, where another Japanese airfield was almost ready for use. Both ships were sunk. "It looked like the 4th of July," Seaman James J. Fahey of the light cruiser *Montpelier* wrote in his diary. "The casualties on both Jap ships must be very high."

In fact some 174 survivors made it ashore to Vila, 49 of them from destroyer *Minegumo*. Her gunnery officer, Lieutenant Tokuno Hiroshi, took seven hours to complete the swim. Tokuno must have been appreciative that night of the endurance-swimming training given cadets at Etajima, where there was an annual 10,000-meter swimming race. Tokuno not only survived the loss of the *Minegumo*, he was promoted and posted to Mille as second in command.

This loss did not halt the Tokyo Express to Kolombangara. For example, Commander Iwahashi Toru's *Asagumo*, a destroyer that had barely made it through the Bismarck Sea debacle, was sent back out on the next Kolombangara run after just two days at Rabaul. Sailing with her were all three other destroyers that had survived Bismarck Sea. Due to the growing ferocity of Allied air attacks in The Slot, the destroyers went no farther than Shortland Island, where barges took over for delivery down south. Still, noted Ensign Nakamura Toshio of the *Asagumo*, his ship made no fewer than five transport missions to Shortland in the space of a month. On one voyage there was constant harassment by Allied airplanes, on another suspected magnetic mines, during a third an attack from a B-25 bomber. The pressure seemed constant.

After many successful interferences with Tokyo Express runs, on April 2 the CINCPAC fleet intelligence summary recorded yet again that destroyer transport missions were expected to Vila, Rekata Bay, and probably Munda. The same summary, and others too, betrayed some knowledge of Japanese intentions as regards aerial operations. Those intentions were about to become concrete actions.

In AFTER YEARS AN IMPERIAL NAVY SAILOR MIGHT NOT HAVE RECOGNIZED KIETA. THE INDIGE-nous people retained their Christian, primarily Roman Catholic, beliefs, but much else changed, the simple result of being thrown into a conflict among great powers wielding modern means of destruction. Brought perforce to an age of modernism, Kieta today has buildings of concrete, decorative façades, a cash economy in place of barter, citizens who pool their money to buy satellite dish antennas. Thinkers worry that people today ignore garden plots in favor of cash crops, consuming more and more rice and tinned fish, opening themselves to market forces.

The Kieta of 1943 seemed a simpler place, enough out of the way that Europeans fleeing the Japanese onslaught of the previous year had gone there believing they might not be found. Instead, attracted by the harbor at Faisi on Shortland Island, the Japanese occupied Kieta for security purposes and soon found it ideal for an airfield. Plantations, a few villages, a Chinese settlement, and a district office were the major features. The docks could take no boat larger than a pinnace so cargo vessels had to unload over the beach. A Marist Christian mission about three quarters of a mile east of the Chinese settlement stood in flat open terrain suitable for an airfield. The field the Japanese actually installed was a grass strip between the settlement and Kieta district office. The entire area, including Shortland Island, formed an integral part of the Japanese complex centered at Rabaul. Yamamoto's aerial offensive utilized Kieta as a waypoint between Rabaul and the bases at the southern tip of Bougainville.

Those southern Bougainville bases can be considered a subcomplex of the Japanese network. Installations at the tip or just off the coast at Shortland Island included the airfields Buin, Kahili, Ballale, and Faisi; a seaplane anchorage on Shortland; plus naval anchorages at Tonolei and Faisi. Excepting an intrepid Australian coastwatcher who maintained himself nearby, the Japanese had near total privacy—the entire Shortland area was inhabited by only about 1,300 people, mostly of Melanesian stock. On Bougainville as a whole there were just over 39,000, almost three times as many as lived on Guadalcanal. Behind their backs, as it were, the Japanese were about to make Shortland and Bougainville islands stepping-stones to major attacks in the Solomons.

In March 1943 the bulk of JNAF strength was at Buin, base of Captain Sugimoto Ushie's 204th Air Group and Captain Yamamoto Sakae's 582nd. The former was a fighter unit, the latter a mixed formation of fighters and carrier bombers. There were two more groups at Rabaul plus a reconnaissance unit, and another recon group arrived that month. All formed parts of the 21st and 26th flotillas of the Eleventh Air Fleet under Rear Admiral Joshima Takaji. Overall strength was nowhere near what was considered necessary, however. Not only would JNAF bring in carrier groups, to fly under Admiral Ozawa's Third Fleet command, but the 25th Air Flotilla came back from Japan to reinforce Joshima's force.

The ambitious plans caused major headaches for Commander Ikeda Masahiro, chief supply officer at Buin. Not only was it necessary to stock adequate fuel and spare parts, there were additional transfer problems because the Eleventh Air Fleet planned to return some units to Rabaul to enable the carrier air groups to operate as an integral force out of the Bougainville subcomplex. Similarly, air flotilla headquarters and a medium bomber group were to move from Rabaul to Kavieng. Admiral Ozawa's Carrier Division 1 planes plus those of Admiral Kakuta's Carrier Division 2 would fly down from Truk and, the day before initial attacks—planned for Guadalcanal—would advance to Bougainville. They would use Buin, Ballale, and Kieta. The Eleventh Air Fleet would fly from Buin, Buka, Rabaul, and Kavieng.

Admiral Yamamoto determined to personally supervise the conduct of his offensive, code-named I Operation. Along with chief of staff Ugaki and an assortment of assistants they left flagship *Musashi* at Truk and made the flight to Rabaul early in the morning of April 3. Over Kavieng they picked up an escort of three fighters for the final leg, arriving in time to confer with theater commander Kusaka Jinichi and tactical leaders Ozawa, Kakuta, Mikawa, and General Imamura Hitoshi, commander of the Eighth Area Army, the senior Army headquarters responsible for both the Solomons and New Guinea. A dinner with the guests, and then the Combined Fleet leaders climbed the hill just east of Rabaul town to sleep in the quarters of the Eighth Fleet commander. Though the day seemed auspicious, it ended on a sour note as Allied bombers hit Kavieng and caught cruiser *Aoba*, just returned from repairing damage at Cape Esperance. The new attack crippled her engines and inflicted internal damage.

Combined Fleet chief of staff Ugaki found the weather quite unfavorable for air operations. The initial attack was postponed a day, then another. Ugaki ordered the staff to look into the possibility of shifting the target to Port Moresby in search of better weather. He complained that staff planners were simplistic and inflexible. They finally came to tell him a change could be made, but only if ordered the previous night, so that April 6 would be the first opportunity to switch targets from Guadalcanal to Moresby.

On April 6 Yamamoto and Ugaki apparently decided to stick to the original target plans. They visited Lakunai Airfield to inspect the aircrews from *Zuikaku* of Carrier Division 1. That afternoon they went to Vunakanau to see off Vice Admiral Kakuta Kakuji and his Carrier Division 2 fighters, which

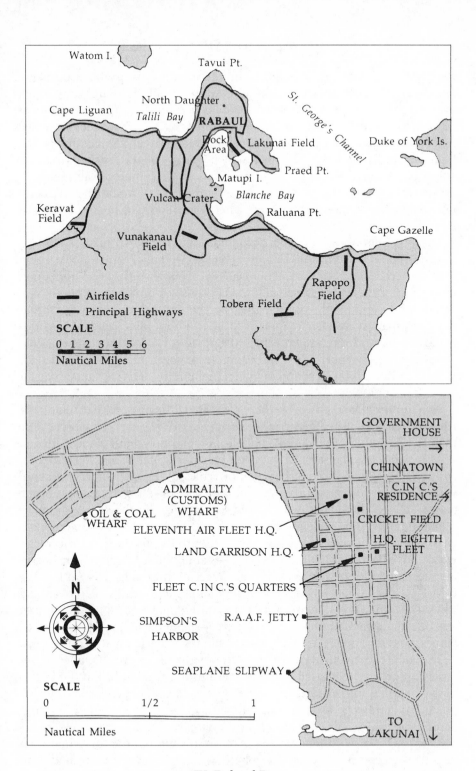

Watom I.

Tavui Pt.

North Daughter

Cape Liguan

*Talili Bay*

**RABAUL**

*St. George's Channel*

Duke of York Is.

Dock
Area

Lakunai Field

Praed Pt.

Matupi I.

*Blanche Bay*

Vulcan Crater

Raluana Pt.

Keravat
Field

Cape Gazelle

Vunakanau
Field

Rapopo
Field

Tobera Field

■■■ Airfields

—— Principal Highways

**SCALE**

0 1 2 3 4 5 6

Nautical Miles

GOVERNMENT
HOUSE

CHINATOWN

C. IN C.'S
RESIDENCE

ADMIRALITY
(CUSTOMS)
WHARF

OIL & COAL
WHARF

ELEVENTH AIR FLEET H.Q.

CRICKET FIELD

LAND GARRISON H.Q.

H.Q. EIGHTH
FLEET

FLEET C. IN C.'S QUARTERS

N

R.A.A.F. JETTY

SIMPSON'S
HARBOR

SEAPLANE SLIPWAY

**SCALE**

0                1/2                1

Nautical Miles

TO
LAKUNAI

IX. Rabaul Base

were to fly to Ballale. As rain picked up the volcanic ash in the atmosphere and deposited it on the roads from Rabaul town, the route to Vunakanau, over seventeen miles away, must have been a muddy mess. Commander Okumiya Masatake, Kakuta's air officer, marveled that Yamamoto seemed as comfortable as if he were at Tokyo headquarters. As Okumiya and Kakuta boarded their Betty bomber, which would lead the formation, the air officer pondered the incongruity of this scene, with Yamamoto and Ugaki in dress whites amid such forsaken surroundings. The Combined Fleet commander looked little different than when Okumiya had last seen him, at Hiroshima Bay.

The planes took off, leaving Yamamoto and Ugaki to inspect Captain Konishi Yukie's 705th Air Group, a medium-bomber unit. While being briefed there Ugaki saw the Carrier Division 2 planes return to Vunakanau one by one. They had not been able to get past the storm front between New Britain and Bougainville. Rather than postponing I Operation yet another day, the Japanese decided to time the attack an hour later, send off Kakuta's planes early, and have them refuel at Ballale then continue the mission. Ugaki received a report of an American cruiser-destroyer group headed for Munda or Kolombangara, and he noted them in his diary as "good prey for our attack tomorrow."

As a matter of fact, however, there remained little possibility of taking the Allies by surprise. Intelligence made the difference. As early as March 5 the CINCPAC summary noted movement from Japan to Rabaul of the 24th and 25th air flotillas. The same publication on April 2 mentioned that Admiral Ozawa in the *Zuikaku* might be south of Truk; so he was, ashore at Rabaul with the air group of that carrier and the *Shokaku*. These two pieces of the puzzle defined the available JNAF air strength, while the same summary remarked that "a possible attack on Allied units in the Central Solomons is envisioned for today or tomorrow." In the South Pacific the dates referred to would have been April 3 and 4; April 4—Yamamoto's birthday—had actually been the planned date for initial I Operation attacks. On April 4 the CINCPAC fleet intelligence summary commented "increased air activity expected soon." The same summary on April 6 contained a broad but precise outline of Japanese intentions: "Large[-scale] air action by land based planes, possibly supplemented by carrier planes, expected within one week."

The radio intelligence dovetailed with other sources. Allied planes began reporting greatly increased JNAF strength around Rabaul from the beginning of April. A massive fighter sweep by about sixty Zeros the same day left no doubt: Serious action impended. Reports of barge traffic out of Vila triggered more suspicions. Early-morning photographic missions for April 7 revealed (by American count) 114 aircraft at Buin, where there had been just 40 the previous day, and 95 planes at Ballale, where there had been none at all. Coastwatcher Paul Mason, whose local allies actually helped the

Japanese lay out their Buin airfield, had been driven away from that area, but he joined up with Jack Read in northern Bougainville and they reported Japanese planes as they flew past Buka. Japanese takeoffs from Buin and Ballale still were not missed since coastwatchers Nick Waddell and Carden Seton, on Choiseul just across the Bougainville Strait, reported these as they occurred. Captain William A. Read, a senior administrative officer on Guadalcanal with the staff of Commander Air Solomons (COMAIRSOLs), recalls that the coastwatchers' warnings came in at lunchtime. That proved the icing on the cake.

Yamamoto's subordinates launched seventy-one bombers plus 117 fighters toward Guadalcanal. With warning the Americans were able to get under way the cruiser group Ugaki had gloated over the previous night, which lay in Tulagi harbor. COMAIRSOLs also ordered seventy-six interceptors into the sky. Anti-aircraft went on alert; in fact, everyone was at Condition Red, and an unprecedented warning, "Condition *Very* Red," went out for the first time in the Pacific war. By 2:00 P.M. the Japanese were on radar. An aerial donnybrook followed as American interceptors and Japanese escorts mixed it up over the lower Solomons, while bombers broke through to sink destroyer *Aaron Ward,* a tanker, and a corvette.

One helpless witness to the bombing of the *Aaron Ward* happened to be a passenger on the landing ship she was accompanying, young Lieutenant (j.g.) John F. Kennedy, future president of the United States, then on his way to join a PT squadron on Tulagi.

The corvette that was sunk was the New Zealand ship *Moa,* vanquisher of the unfortunate *I-1,* the submarine disaster of such fateful consequence for the Imperial Navy.

Though there was a measure of retribution in the last-named action, this was not much to show in all. The results of I Operation attacks on New Guinea bases were similar. Oro Bay was hit on April 11 by 22 bombers and 72 fighters. Allied losses were a merchantman sunk, another beached, and a minesweeper damaged. Port Moresby was the target the next day. Japanese scouts reported 55 large planes and 80 smaller ones there, and the JNAF hit with a fighter unit of 55 planes, another 76 Zeros in an escort unit, and an attack force of 43 medium bombers. Allied sources admit loss of just 3 planes on the ground and 2 in the air. On April 14 the JNAF attacked Milne Bay with 37 bombers and 149 fighters. Again the losses seemed far less than warranted by the size of the forces employed—2 transports and 3 planes. For I Operation overall, the Allies had lost a destroyer, a corvette, a tanker, 3 transports, and about 25 planes. Japanese claims, on the other hand, amounted to the sinking of a cruiser, 2 destroyers, and 25 transports; and the downing of 95 planes for certain plus 39 probables.

Reviewing the results at Rabaul, Admirals Yamamoto and Ugaki, who saw only the JNAF claims, could have some reason for satisfaction. On the other hand, there was concern over Japanese air losses, which by Ugaki's count ran to more than a quarter of carrier bombers, 12 percent of fighters, and 18 percent of medium bombers. No JNAF formation could sustain such losses, in particular the precious carrier air groups. Having mounted 487 sorties by fighters, 115 by carrier bombers, and 80 by mediums, Yamamoto called a halt on April 16, declaring I Operation successfully concluded, ordering the carrier planes back to Truk.

The next morning Ugaki chaired a meeting at Rabaul to discuss the operation and its outcome. Commander Okumiya of Carrier Division 2 clearly recalls concerns by various officers over bomber losses. Just four missions had cost forty to sixty aircraft (depending on whose count is accepted as authoritative). Ugaki emphasized the necessity for new tactics, some means of countering heavy bombers, better reconnaissance. Insufficient airpower seemed the main reason for the deteriorating situation, and no significant reinforcement was in sight. Admiral Ugaki admonished everyone to do his very best. Air groups of the big carriers of Carrier Division 1 were to return to the Empire for reorganization and more training. Okumiya saw this as an admission that the Allies were now matching and exceeding the performance of the best JNAF planes. "The meeting concluded in a pessimistic air," he wrote, "we could anticipate only expanding enemy air strength and an ever-increasing drain o[n] our own."

Ugaki Matome was perhaps more caustic than he need have been. That afternoon a policy discussion among the most senior officers ended in a shouting match between Ugaki and Southeast Area Fleet commander (and host) Kusaka Jinichi. Even upon his arrival at Rabaul, Ugaki had been highly critical of the seeming unwillingness of top commanders to visit the front. He expressed a desire to inspect as far down the Solomons as Munda and Kolombangara, and dismissed General Imamura's account of how his own airplane had barely survived an American fighter attack during a flight to nearby Bougainville. To some extent it was Ugaki's job to be critical, and there is also a mitigating circumstance in that the Combined Fleet chief of staff was coming down with dengue fever (the day of the Rabaul conference his body broke out in fever pustules). Indeed, almost everyone at Rabaul was afflicted in one way or another: Kusaka had dysentery and could hardly keep anything down; Yamamoto picked a cucumber he tried to get the area chief to eat. As for Yamamoto, even people as far removed as air officer Okumiya noticed his physical decline. Ugaki noted that Yamamoto looked tired the day they first arrived. Medical analysts who have examined the evidence recently believe the Combined Fleet commander may have been suffering from beriberi, with swollen ankles and shaking hands, plus possible mental impairment. Yamamoto was said to be changing his shoes four or five times a day and getting vitamin C shots from his doctor.

Despite all obstacles Admiral Yamamoto was determined to support his air units in the field. Ugaki's criticisms of leaders who did not visit the front may have spurred him, and before the end of the I Operation the commander in chief decided he would fly to Ballale and Buin to congratulate his aviators personally. Commander Watanabe, who whiled away many evening hours at Rabaul playing *shogi* with Yamamoto, worked out the itinerary and sent it to the Bougainville bases. That turned out to be the beginning of disaster. The April 13 message was immediately intercepted by Allied radio intelligence.

Both Pearl Harbor and Washington worked on the Yamamoto trip message, which not only gave the timing of his flight but told how many planes would carry the staff and how many fighters would protect them. FRUPAC got out the first version of the decrypt, one that still had many unknowns; eighteen hours later, the Pearl Harbor unit scored again with a far more complete translation, followed by Washington just before 5:00 P.M. on April 14. The news featured in CINCPAC's Ultra bulletin of the fifteenth.

This account makes the exercise of decryption and translation sound so easy; in fact, it entailed mind-numbing work for hours at a stretch. Language officer Roger Pineau has supplied a firsthand recollection of the action at FRUPAC. In April 1988 Pineau related how the large number of addresses on the itinerary message had instantly drawn attention to it. Traffic analysts Tom Huckins and Jack Williams worked the address information. When an initial version clattered out of the IBM printer it went to chief linguist Major Lasswell.

"We've hit the jackpot!" linguist John G. Roenigk heard Red Lasswell say.

From his first worksheet on the message Lasswell knew it to be important, apparently about a plan to visit forward bases. Lasswell worked all night to recover relevant passages. The process was more complex for the Yamamoto itinerary because as a result of the *I-1* disaster, the Imperial Navy had introduced another JN-25 variant coincident with the start of the I Operation. That meant plenty of work for cryptanalysts Ham Wright and Tommy Dyer. Pineau recounts that they worked especially hard on the geographic area designators but Edwin Layton recalls this work being done by Jasper Holmes. Either way, it was Holmes's call to the fleet intelligence officer on their direct-line telephone that first alerted Chester Nimitz to what was up. It was left to the admiral to decide what to make of the intercept.

Red Lasswell was happy *he* didn't have to make the call on this one. Lasswell remembers the original message had been received by FRUPAC's own radio net, and that "I personally did the whole thing overnight." Though the incident perhaps seemed more noteworthy than Midway, "I didn't feel, somehow or other, the joy in [the Yamamoto decrypt] that I did in the other, because I sort of felt more of a snooper."

In Washington there was the same rush of interest. Petty Officer Albert Pelletier recalls Redfield Mason at OP-20-GY yelling to subordinates to double-check every date, time, and place in the message. Mason pronounced the result "good"—very high praise, coming from him. Linguist Edward Van Der Rhoer had the evening watch when the final version was completed; it was mild, and a hint of spring hung in the air. Van Der Rhoer recalls astonishment and mounting excitement as he read the message, which he saw primarily as providing the opportunity for setting out an ambush to shoot down Yamamoto.

Plenty of others saw the same potential. Back at Pearl Harbor, Lasswell and Holmes hand-carried the finished translation to Layton's office to make sure there was no error in transit to CINCPAC headquarters. Layton and Nimitz discussed whether there was anybody in the Imperial Navy capable of filling Yamamoto's shoes. Layton thought not. Nimitz sent particulars of the Yamamoto travel plan to South Pacific Command headquarters with instructions to Halsey to arrange an interception if he could.

Much has been speculated regarding the Yamamoto shootdown, both as to who approved it and which of the participating pilots actually got the bomber carrying the Japanese admiral. It is not necessary to enter these controversies here. Washington did consider the implications of the itinerary message, but President Roosevelt was out of town during the entire period and there is no indication in presidential records of his interest in this matter. Individuals in the South Pacific recall a message from Navy Secretary Frank Knox ordering the shootdown, mentioning the details of Yamamoto's travel plus the most suitable unit, the Army's 339th Squadron on Guadalcanal. Again no documentary record has been found. In connection with the same events, ONI analyst Ladislas Farago recalls doing a memorandum at the behest of Ellis Zacharias giving precedents for killing an enemy commander in war, a memo supposedly compiled specifically for Knox. On the other hand, Knox had no authority over Army air units, and it was strictly forbidden in U.S. security practice to put codebreaking information in an operational message. Nimitz did have command authority over the Solomons, and fleet intelligence officer Layton maintains that Nimitz made the sole decision. It is possible that the unprecedented nature of the mission led Secretary Knox to become involved, but most likely the nature of Knox's decision would have been to ensure Nimitz got a free hand, plus a hint as to Washington's desires in the matter.

In any case, Nimitz's orders to Bull Halsey made the Yamamoto mission concrete. As a result COMAIRSOLs called in his fighter chief and ordered preparations for the flight. It was clear to John P. Condon, the Marine operations officer for fighter forces, that even the P-38 did not have quite the range for the long flight to Bougainville. Extra wing tanks had to be flown up to Guadalcanal and installed on the P-38 fighters of the 339th Squadron the night before the mission. Only MacArthur's SOWESPAC had any of these tanks available. The logistical difficulties were considerable but they were overcome.

Major John Mitchell of the 339th led the mission, for which four top-scoring pilots were specifically selected as shooters and a dozen more P-38s went along to make sure they could get past the fighter escort. One was Captain Thomas G. Lanphier, Jr., of a different squadron but held over specially for this mission. Another was Lieutenant Rex Barber. These two officially share credit for the shootdown, and one of them actually did it. The P-38s reached the vicinity of Buin after a long overwater flight west of the Solomons, at least 500 miles by dead reckoning.

Ignorant of such American preparations, the Japanese went ahead with Admiral Yamamoto's trip. Captain Konishi chose two of his 705th Group pilots to fly Betty bombers on the mission. For security reasons pilots and crews were informed only after bedtime the night before the flight. Pilots of the six escorting fighters were told the same way. Subsequent accounts suggest that premonition about this trip was widespread. Yamamoto, though he had previously always flown in the same aircraft with his chief of staff, this time insisted that Ugaki travel in a different plane. Admiral Ozawa the carrier commander scoffed at the small escort, argued against the trip, then offered to bolster the escort with his own fighters. The offer was refused. At dinner the night before General Imamura told Yamamoto about his own experience the previous February, but the admiral did not take the point that there was a danger to him as well.

Perhaps the most ironic twist of fate came early on the morning of April 18, just before departure. At the last moment senior air officer Commander Toibana Kurio convinced staff favorite Watanabe to give up his place on Yamamoto's flight. Even though his deputy was going to Buin on Ugaki's plane, Toibana himself wanted to visit with the fliers in the front lines too.

Years before, Toibana had been the air officer in Shanghai who convinced his boss to delay warning JNAF units of the movement of the American gunboat *Panay*.

Here again, fate seemed to be exacting retribution.

Yamamoto and Ugaki, with other staff officers, mounted planes and took off from Lakunai field exactly on time. As a concession to security, and to permit the Combined Fleet commander to see something of his deployed forces, the flight path made its first landfall at the southern tip of New Ireland, then turned south along the east coast of Bougainville, past the Japanese bases at Buka and Kieta, then on to Buin, at a steady altitude of 6,500 feet.

Major Mitchell's covering force of P-38s jumped the JNAF escorts while Captain Lanphier's four-plane section of shooters went in from below. It was 9:35 A.M. local time by Tom Lanphier's watch as he dropped his belly tanks and moved to engage. Lanphier cut in behind the lead Betty while Rex Barber attacked the second; as they maneuvered for advantage and to evade the Zeros turning to defend their leaders, it is possible the targets became reversed. Petty Officer Hayashi Hiroshi, JNAF command pilot, flying the plane carrying Admiral Ugaki, recalled that the lead plane dived suddenly and his own began to suffer excessive vibration as he strove to maintain formation. Hayashi cutting his speed was probably what opened up the confusion of targets for the Americans. In any case, the first Hayashi knew they were under attack was when one of the escorting fighters zoomed over them to get in front of Yamamoto's plane.

Admiral Ugaki had been asleep until the moment of the attack. He ought not to have come along in his feverish condition, but now he awoke and intervened with an order to the pilot to stay behind Yamamoto's plane. Hayashi was surprised that the P-38s seemed to concentrate their attacks on the first plane, and soon they saw fires in both engines. Petty Officer Hayashi got his plane down close to the water, as close as he could get, and when his Betty was at last hit, it pancaked on the water and made a more or less successful crash landing. Admiral Ugaki fractured an arm and suffered a broken artery; fleet paymaster Admiral Kitamura and pilot Hayashi also survived. Assistant air staff officer Muroi Suteji apparently died from bullet wounds as American fighters attacked. There were no survivors from the Yamamoto plane. The admiral himself, decked out in a green tropical uniform he had never used, was found sitting in his flight seat, clutching his sword in classic fashion, except that the seat had been flung clear of the aircraft and rested against a tree.

Yamamoto's body was cremated on Bougainville, a marker placed at the crash site, and the remains taken first to Rabaul and then Truk, where they were placed in state aboard battleship *Musashi.* Among the visitors were Admiral Kakuta and Commander Okumiya, recent comrades in the I Operation, who had left Rabaul at the same moment and reached Truk just in time to learn of the loss. Kakuta had been handed the dispatch shortly after stepping onto the bridge of his flagship, light carrier *Hiyo.* After a short time at Truk the *Musashi* returned the commander in chief's remains to Japan, where an Imperial Navy farewell ceremony was held aboard the battleship on May 23, and a state funeral followed on June 5. Ugaki lay in the hospital, too ill to attend. Commander Watanabe, also sick at the time, left his bed to carry one of Yamamoto's medals in the cortège.

American codebreakers knew instantly of their success in getting Yamamoto, even though the Japanese government did not announce his loss until after the *Musashi* had reached Empire waters: Suddenly messages to the Combined Fleet were no longer addressed to the commander in chief but to his chief of staff. The implication was direct and obvious. Ironically, though this is not certain, the codebreakers may have made an error decrypting the original itinerary message, for they had identified Ballale as Yamamoto's destination. Both Petty Officer Hayashi and one of the fighter pilots who survived insist the destination was Buin and they had never heard anything about Ballale. In the end, it did not matter.

So Japan came to a last crucial turning that one day in April 1943. Imperial Navy officers agreed with the private opinions of American intelligence analysts that there was no one who could adequately replace Admiral Yamamoto. Japan had run wild for a time, just as he predicted before the war began, but that time had come to an end, and with Yamamoto's demise perished perhaps the Imperial Navy's best strategic brain. Japan had truly entered a valley of darkness.

# Full Circle

Y AMAMOTO'S SUCCESSORS DID NOT RISE TO HIS STATURE, NOT SIMPLY BECAUSE THEY WERE
not so capable as he, but also because they lacked opportunity. Yamamoto
had command at a unique moment in Imperial Navy history, when his service held the balance in the Pacific with commensurate superiority over all.
But the pendulum had already begun to swing before the Great Captain's
death, and none of Yamamoto's successors ever enjoyed his advantages. For
them command in the Pacific embodied the dilemmas of somehow creating
conditions under which the Combined Fleet could fight its cherished
Decisive Battle with some chance of success. As the balance swung further
in favor of the Allies, the question became even less one of engaging on
equal terms, and more of having any chance at all.

These were not ephemeral fluctuations in tactical conditions but basic
shifts in the war situation. As Admiral Ugaki had acknowledged at Rabaul,
the Japanese could not expect significant improvement at any early date. In
fact, in the months after the I Operation the war situation came full circle.
The transformation was first visible in the North Pacific where, in a single
year, the campaign cycled through Japanese offensive to stasis to defeat and
evacuation. The shift in the balance also became obvious in the Central and
South Pacific where, two years after Pearl Harbor, Allied forces were making equivalent onslaughts against similarly important Japanese bastions.
Intelligence continued to play a role in these operations. The campaign in
the North Pacific shows in microcosm the entire dynamic of this evolution
and thus furnishes a useful starting point.

. . .

For the Japanese the beginning had been all hope and optimism. Fleets moved forward in the North Pacific in conjunction with the advance to Midway. Though the Imperial Navy proved unable to decoy the Americans as intended, it nevertheless ended up with occupation forces in possession of the Aleutian islands Attu and Kiska, forward sentinels against Allied attack across to the Kuriles or northern Japan. Grasping for anything good to say after Midway, as well, Japanese officers seized upon successes here to put the best face on the campaign. Thus June 1942 marked the first Japanese success in the Aleutians; in fact this beginning was the high point of their effort.

Americans were hardly unaware of Japanese depredations in the Aleutians. Immediately following Midway, Admiral Nimitz ordered surviving American carriers north to counter the incursion. Vice Admiral Raymond Spruance, knowing his air groups were weakened in the wake of the battle, and realizing the hazards of flying aircraft in this region, had little stomach for the assignment. No doubt sensitive to the dangers faced by his few remaining aircraft carriers, Admiral Nimitz recalled the task force to Pearl Harbor, whence they would next appear in the South Pacific.

On the Japanese side, however, the exchange of American messages of high precedence here was overheard by the Owada Communications Group, which warned the fleet of the presence of an American task force. Vice Admiral Hosogaya Boshiro, commanding the Fifth Fleet in northern waters, asked for and received reinforcements for his next Aleutian cruises. These were intended to supplement the garrisons placed on Attu and Kiska and emplace seaplane units at the forward bases for air cover. An additional element of the force to be deployed to Kiska was a special midget-submarine unit with six subs, a hundred base personnel and 250 laborers.

Admiral Hosogaya's cover force reflected fears that American heavy ships were about. Rear Admiral Kakuta brought no less than four aircraft carriers: *Zuikaku*, *Zuiho*, *Ryujo*, and *Junyo*, partly led by him and partly under Admiral Hara Chuichi. Together the mobile forces and support groups included four battleships and six heavy cruisers. Perhaps it is not surprising that no surface naval opposition materialized, though the Americans did run submarines against Hosogaya's fleets. On July 5 *Triton* sank destroyer *Nenohi* off Agattu, making her the first Japanese warship lost in the Aleutians. Only twenty to thirty survivors endured the cold waters to be recovered by another vessel. Later that day off Kiska submarine *Growler* sank a second destroyer, *Arare*, while two more, *Kasumi* and *Shiranuhi*, were both badly damaged. This experience put the Japanese on notice that supplying their new forward bases would not be a simple matter.

Why anyone would want to fight a war in the North Pacific remained beyond comprehension, pretty much for the duration. This was the only theater where the weather was a bigger threat than the enemy, for both sides. Cold was merely one small part of this—after the jokes about the good parkas kept to wear *inside* the shelters, one had to deal with the problem. Long Arctic nights got on people's nerves; a typical example who became a statistic was Colonel Ronald A. Boone, former chief of the Far East Division of ONI, whose next posting was to Kodiak Island in the Gulf of Alaska. Boone committed suicide sometime thereafter. Even in daylight the acute angle of illumination from the sun played havoc with optical equipment. Magnetic anomalies complicated navigation; tremendous fogs closed in without warning and were very dangerous for planes attempting to land or ships trying to enter port. Even the best weather reports could have trouble with fog data. Radio reception often seemed quite good, but on occasion atmospheric conditions could play tricks on both radio and radar. In all, northern service remained difficult and, to a significant degree, miserable.

Aviators had special trials in the Aleutians, of which a good example is Captain Ito Sukemitsu's Toko Air Group, the first JNAF unit to reach Kiska. Six big Mavis patrol bombers of Ito's unit flew to the island a couple of days after it was occupied, with mechanics and shore personnel arriving aboard four cargo ships. Ito soon found that the fog hampered his reconnaissance flights, and to give the planes an extra margin of fuel he greatly reduced the radius of their normal flights. Nevertheless one of his flying boats found itself unable to land back at base and had to do so in the open sea, where it sank (though the crew were recovered); another plane disappeared in fog. Of the other aircraft, one was sunk and two were damaged beyond repair when U.S. warships bombarded Kiska in early August. A couple of weeks later Ito and his remaining plane returned to the Empire. At about that time seaplane tender *Kamikawa Maru* carried a dozen floatplane fighters of the 5th Air Group to Kiska, but the Japanese made no further effort to operate large aircraft in the Aleutians.

Imperial General Headquarters originally intended to evacuate Kiska and Attu altogether for the winter months, but the Japanese read the situation that fall as portending American invasion of Kiska, for which they prepared by moving the Japanese Army troops on Attu to the other island. Once IGHQ could scrape up additional reinforcements, these were sent to reoccupy Attu on October 30, 1942.

Intelligence remained a hit-or-miss proposition for both sides during the early days of the campaign. The Japanese went ahead with their invasion even though the aerial survey carried out beforehand from the seaplane tender *Kimikawa Maru* found Kiska shrouded in fog and impossible to photograph. As for the Americans, Japan's move occurred barely two weeks after the Joint Intelligence Committee in Washington predicted there would be no attack in the Aleutians. As already seen, moreover, early OP-20-G fears of just such an attack had figured in unwillingness to appreciate imminent

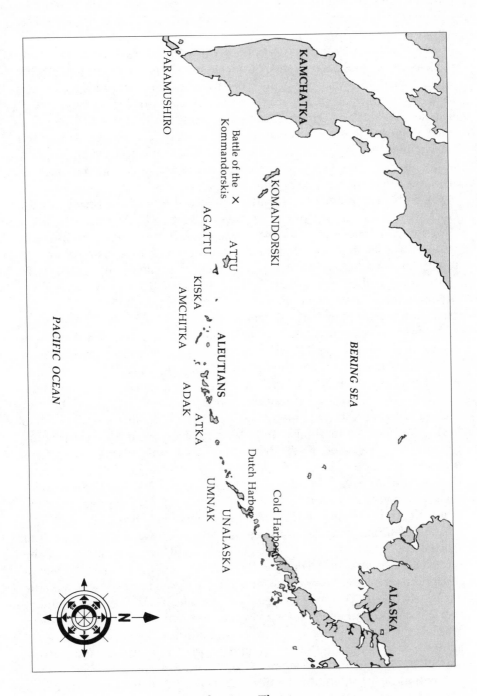

X. Aleutians Theater

Imperial Navy designs on Midway. Radio intelligence shortly thereafter contributed to preventing the development of what could have become a fleet action.

What followed became a war of posts and sallies, as it were, for many months. Admiral Hosogaya sailed from Ominato with his Fifth Fleet in early August when an American cruiser-destroyer group bombarded Kiska, and there was another sortie toward the end of that month after reports of a U.S. fleet near Atka Island. There actually were American ships at nearby Adak, and submarine *Ro-61* torpedoed seaplane tender *Casco*, damaging her, but the submarine was bombed and strafed by planes, then tracked and sunk by destroyer *Reid*. Five Japanese sailors were rescued and made prisoners of war, more grist for the interrogation specialists.

On both their islands the Japanese cleared ground for airfields but the work was maddeningly slow in the harsh climate. The American Eleventh Air Force responded with a program of repeated harassment by bombers. In various attacks on Kiska, planes sank submarine *Ro-65* (Japanese sources report this boat lost by accident), destroyer *Oboro*, and two cargo vessels. Destroyer *Hatsuharu* also suffered bomb damage off Kiska, losing her rudder, but managed to steer by engines alone the whole way home. At Attu, aircraft sank several more cargo or transport ships.

American landings at Adak put IGHQ on notice that the Japanese-occupied islands were endangered, but the sole alternatives were to get out of the Aleutians or reinforce them. Fearing that the Americans would jump ahead to the Kuriles, the island chain stretching north from Hokkaido, northernmost of the Home Islands, made reinforcement seem the best course. This reasoning supported reoccupation of Attu after its garrison had been sent to Kiska, and it also underlay a move to occupy the intervening island of Shemya in late November, when two cruisers and two destroyers escorted transports bearing 1,115 troops intended for that destination. Coincidental American bombing of Kiska again ignited fears of imminent invasion, however, and the Shemya occupation force diverted to Kiska, where the troops became one more reinforcement for a growing garrison.

Admiral Nimitz early on in the campaign had suggested use of the 2nd Marine Raider Battalion in the Aleutians, and in December 1942 he returned to the subject, recommending offensive action. Despite all difficulties, photo reconnaissance by now had built a good picture of developments at Kiska, where the Japanese seemed to be moving quickly on base facilities, and to have strengthened their garrison to as much as 7,500–10,000 men. This latter actually represented an overestimate, as Japanese forces on Kiska amounted to not quite 6,000 troops and laborers. In any case, Nimitz's recommendations encouraged a new offensive attitude and led directly to the occupation of Amchitka on January 12, 1943. By then Americans had a new naval commander in the islands, Vice Admiral Thomas C. Kinkaid up from SOPAC; one of his first actions was to propose an invasion of Kiska. Before long severely limited shipping and assault troops had transformed the idea into a plan for attack on Attu.

Meanwhile, the Japanese discovered from air reconnaissance on January 24 that the United States had occupied Amchitka. The noose was tightening around the Japanese-held islands as Kinkaid used his ships to interdict Imperial Navy supply lines while U.S. aircraft continued constant bombing raids. On February 5, IGHQ Directive Number 199 nevertheless ordered Japanese commanders to hold the western Aleutians at all costs and initiate preparations for defense of the Kuriles. On Kiska poor materials and rocky ground held up airfield construction (only half was completed even by April), while Attu's future airfield lagged even further behind. In late February American bombers began to fly from Amchitka, further tightening the blockade of the Japanese islands, a point driven home unmistakably on February 18 when American surface ships caught and sank cargo vessel *Akagane Maru*, bound for Attu. Another merchantman, following behind, saw the gun flashes of the cannonade and ran for home; a third made port at Kiska without incident.

The loss of the *Akagane Maru* effectively meant closure of the shipping routes to the western Aleutians. Admiral Hosogaya ordered a switch to submarine supply, but the Army objected and the Fifth Fleet commander was overruled at IGHQ. Hosogaya was told to try convoys, and the first of these reached Attu successfully on March 9. Just days after Hosogaya returned, an Army officer arrived from Attu by submarine to appeal for food and anti-aircraft ammunition.

Hosogaya Boshiro prepared another convoy for Attu but probably was not very happy about it. During the Midway campaign as well as his tours in central China, with Carrier Division 1, and in command of the 5th Destroyer Flotilla, Hosogaya had gotten used to having his way. Having graduated from the naval academy in 1908, Hosogaya was a classmate of such stalwarts as Nagumo Chuichi and Tsukahara Nizhizo, both of whom, already in this war, had had to perform under very great pressure. Like Nagumo, Hosogaya was a torpedo specialist; indeed, he had once headed the Navy's torpedo school. Now Admiral Hosogaya's own time of trial had come as the vessels of his main body weighed anchor at Paramushiro on the afternoon of March 23.

On the American side intelligence prepared the groundwork for what would become known as the battle of the Komandorski Islands. As early as March 11 the CINCPAC fleet intelligence officer had noticed unexplained air activity in the Kiska area and warned Aleutian units to be on the alert. The following day the intelligence summary, though admitting that details were not known, observed a possibility that the Japanese might be planning action. The daily summary on March 18 baldly noted, "There is growing suspicion the enemy may be planning a move in this area before May 1st."

To enforce the Aleutian blockade Rear Admiral Charles H. McMorris put to sea with a task group of a heavy cruiser, a light cruiser, and four destroyers which he disposed on a scouting line west of Attu. McMorris flew his flag in the vintage light cruiser *Richmond* although his heaviest ship was the treaty cruiser *Salt Lake City*. The latter, known to her crewmen as "Swayback Maru" for her superstructure and hull lines, happened to have been the most recent seagoing command of ONI's Ellis Zacharias. Now her captain was Bertram J. Rodgers, Annapolis class of 1916. The American destroyers were interspersed between the cruisers along the scouting line. Admiral McMorris spent nine days on this interdiction mission until, at dawn of March 26, his task group was located 180 miles due west of Attu.

In the meantime the Japanese convoy and its Fifth Fleet escort had left Paramushiro on March 24. Their initial messages were intercepted and one was processed at FRUPAC in Pearl Harbor. Portions of the message initially decrypted mentioned the convoy but said little about escort. Based on this notice, on March 25 Admiral Nimitz warned the U.S. northern Pacific commander, Rear Admiral Thomas C. Kinkaid, that a Japanese convoy was there for the taking. That same morning Kinkaid had recalled McMorris's blockade unit, but now the theater commander reversed those orders and gave McMorris authority to continue the patrol at his discretion. By the morning of March 26, after additional work on the intercepted Japanese message, FRUPAC had divined that the Japanese did indeed intend to escort their convoy to Kiska. Admiral Nimitz sent Kinkaid a clarification but by then it was already too late—"Soc" McMorris was fighting for his life.

The Japanese ships had sailed in several groups to favor two slower transports and a third cargo ship that sailed independently. Hosogaya set a rendezvous at sea, but stormy weather delayed it. He expected to meet his missing ships on the morning of the twenty-sixth. In all the Fifth Fleet commander had eight warships—heavy cruisers *Nachi* and *Maya*, light cruisers *Tama* and *Abukuma*, and four destroyers. Hosogaya also had a light cruiser (*Kiso*) and two destroyers that were not along on this cruise. One more destroyer accompanied the element of the convoy that had not yet joined up. At sunrise on March 26 Hosogaya's main force steamed north in line-ahead formation looking for the expected convoy element. Instead, one of his rear vessels sighted American ships. They were Admiral McMorris's task group.

Virtually simultaneously the American ships found the Japanese on their radar screens. The time was 7:30 A.M. According to the relevant ONI combat narrative, the range was 24,000 yards (the figure "14,000," which appears on charts in some accounts of this battle, is evidently a misprint).

Admiral McMorris expected a Roman holiday mopping up the Japanese convoy. He had no idea the Japanese covering force outnumbered and out-gunned his own fleet, and for some time the curvature of the earth hid *Nachi* and *Maya*, Hosogaya's biggest warships. For his part the Japanese admiral was under no illusions, and immediately ordered the convoy ships out of the area while he turned his battle line east, then south, to confront the Americans. About an hour after the initial sighting the Japanese opened fire. Captain Matsumoto Takeji's *Maya* was the first ship to be in useful range though at about the same time the flagship, Captain Soji Akira's *Nachi*, loosed eight torpedoes. Captain Rodgers's *Salt Lake City* commenced fire herself at 8:42 A.M.

Admiral Hosogaya estimated that the American fleet before him constituted the bulk of U.S. forces in the Aleutians, that his own force was superior, and that the Americans were so intent on pursuit of the convoy they were not initially aware of his movements. He planned to put his ships between McMorris and the convoy, then to get between the U.S. ships and their base—thus the turns east and south that he ordered. *Nachi* launched a floatplane to spot the fall of shot, and Hosogaya planned to keep the weather gauge by staying northeast of McMorris.

Despite Japanese advantages the Americans scored first with two hits on the *Nachi* at 8:50. One was a key strike—a direct hit on the starboard side just abaft the bridge; it damaged the electrical circuit for gunnery control, while killing eleven sailors and wounding twenty-one. The Japanese compounded this loss of director control by the power failure following an attempt to shift the generator to a boiler with low steam pressure. *Nachi*'s guns were left at full elevation and could not train. They were out of action for almost an hour, during which time she absorbed a third (noncritical) hit as well. Two other minor hits came later during the battle, including one shell that went right through the bed of a staff officer directly behind flag plot. Aside from the damage on *Nachi* the only ship to suffer damage—and that minor—was Captain Kanome Zensuke's light cruiser *Tama*. Virtually all significant damage was inflicted very early in the engagement. It is disputed whether the key hits were made by *Richmond* or *Salt Lake City*.

On the American side the strongest ship was *Salt Lake City*; if she were lost the rest of the task group would have little chance. Captain Rodgers did a superb job maneuvering his ship to confuse Japanese gun layers, sailing into the shell splashes, putting off aiming corrections. After the battle Rodgers would be decorated with the Navy Cross. Rodgers's archenemy during the interval when the Japanese flagship's guns were inoperative was Commander Futagami Enzo, gunnery officer of the *Maya*. While Rodgers would be very lucky for a long time (as naval battles go), Futagami scored serious hits on the *Salt Lake City* at 9:10 and 9:20. The ship would be hit four more times during a long stern chase of several hours (some credit should be apportioned to *Nachi* for the later hits). Finally the cruiser was forced to stop when she got water mixed into her last fuel line while counterflooding to correct a list. She was hidden by smoke screens as engineers made frantic efforts to correct the problem. To gain time the American destroyers dashed in for an attack, but only one got off any torpedoes before the weight of Japanese gunfire forced all to turn back. There were no torpedo hits. In about seven minutes "Swayback Maru" corrected her fuel feed problem and got under way again to the relief of all.

The Americans were lucky there were no Japanese torpedo hits. Very early in the battle, lookouts aboard the *Richmond* saw torpedoes pass under the ship's bow. Officers derided the report as an error—they decided the splash must have been that of a school of small fish swimming in a straight line. Two minutes later destroyer *Bailey* saw a torpedo breach the water off her starboard quarter. This report was dismissed because no one else observed it. In fact the *Nachi* records launching eight torpedoes at a time that fits very well with the time of observation of the torpedoes reported on the *Richmond.* It may be that only mistaken depth settings or some other malfunction saved the American flagship from grievous harm.

Although the *Nachi*'s chief torpedo officer was later wounded, that vessel would launch another eight torpedoes during the battle, and other Japanese ships thirty more. None hit. Admiral McMorris's task group seems to have been wholly unaware of any torpedo attacks.

Samuel Eliot Morison's account of these events suggests that McMorris remained throughout determined to get a crack at the Japanese transports and that he therefore conducted maneuvers designed to work around the flank of Hosogaya's fleet. This is highly unlikely. The situation was that the Japanese were between McMorris and his base with a force twice as strong as his. One did not have to be very sharp to draw appropriate conclusions from those facts, and McMorris was definitely smart—so smart his Navy nickname was "Soc," for the Socratic wisdom he seemed to project. The gunnery officer aboard flagship *Richmond,* Commander Ralph Millsap, writes much more convincingly: "After the initial phase of the battle, there is little doubt that Admiral McMorris's sole concern was saving his ships." McMorris possibly reasoned that by threatening a break toward the transports he might draw Hosogaya away from the blocking position the Japanese had assumed, enabling him to break for home.

Admiral Hosogaya in this instance threw away the most advantageous position an Imperial Navy surface force had held since Savo Island. Why? Both of his big ships had already fired most of their 8-inch ammunition (*Nachi* 707 rounds, *Maya* 904); his destroyers were reporting low fuel states. Hosogaya knew that considerable damage had been inflicted upon the Americans, but apparently his spotter plane did not report that the *Salt Lake City* was leaking oil and had stopped dead in the water. The latter was not apparent from the sea because the range was obscured by smoke screens.

Hosogaya may also have been impressed by the fighting spirit the American destroyers demonstrated in their own attack, and he certainly did not know that the American heavy cruisiser had expended 832 of her own shells as well. Ignorant of these factors, Hosogaya believed that the opportunity to achieve a decisive result had passed.

There was one thing Hosogaya *did* know, however, and that troubled him very much: Japanese radio intelligence told the admiral the Americans had launched a unit of "several score" aircraft at him from Amchitka. Judging from the *Salt Lake City*'s Combat Information Center (CIC) plot, which showed the range lengthening from 11:55 A.M. (while the ship herself was immobilized), Hosogaya must have ordered action broken off within about ten minutes of receiving this intelligence.

In actuality the air strike from Amchitka was delayed by a need to install auxiliary gas tanks and did not even get off the ground until 1:30 P.M. Even then only three B-25 bombers were involved. Another unit took off from Adak, 150 miles farther away, at 1:36; this strike comprised at least thirteen B-24s and eight more B-25s. Both these efforts were compromised by time and distance. Nevertheless, the fleet intelligence officer at Pearl Harbor expected Hosogaya to go on and complete his convoy mission following the Komandorski battle, and yet the Japanese gave up and returned to port. The probable explanation is the American air threat.

The surface battle would be followed by a propaganda fight. "Gunfire at long range was exchanged," reported the Navy Department's Communiqué Number 327. "When the engagement was broken off, the Japanese forces were observed heading westward." In other words, according to the U.S. Navy, the Japanese fled. A Tokyo news broadcast on March 30 report countered, "We had purpose in that our fleet went in [a] westerly direction in order to pursue [the] American fleet. There is only shock at such base means of propaganda taken by America." Admiral McMorris would be awarded the Distinguished Service Medal and became chief of staff to Chester Nimitz at CINCPAC, a post he held through the rest of the war. Admiral Hosogaya was relieved of command and put on the reserve list. Afterward he would be recalled, but merely to be governor of the South Seas region.

To ELUDE THE FEARED ALLIED AIRCRAFT, THE JAPANESE SHIPS MADE FOR THE SOVIET COAST OF the Kamchatka peninsula, followed it down to the Kuriles, and stopped momentarily at Paramushiro. The *Nachi* steamed on to Yokosuka to repair damage, spending about a month at the navy yard, though no dry-docking seems to have been necessary. By then events in the *nanyo* had led to Yamamoto's death. Those events brought in a new Combined Fleet commander in chief, much as the Komandorski battle led to designation of a new commander for the Fifth Fleet. Admiral Koga Mineichi would lead the Combined Fleet and Vice Admiral Kawase Shiro the Fifth. Events threw the two admirals into cooperation they never anticipated.

Kawase took over quietly enough; he was appointed from the immediate area, where he had been commander of the Ominato Guard District. Like his predecessor, Kawase rose as a torpedo specialist, sometime chief of two different flotillas as well as the school. He understood escort work and the need to move convoys to the Japanese-held Aleutians, and ordered the 1st Destroyer Flotilla, which the fifty-four-year-old Kawase had once led, to convoy a new shipment of floatplanes to Kiska.

The plan was for tender *Kimikawa Maru* to steam to a point perhaps 250 miles southwest of Attu then launch the planes to fly to Kiska. The seaplane tender would be escorted by flotilla flagship *Kiso*, substituting for the *Abukuma*, which was at Maizuru having radar installed, and two destroyers. Unbeknownst to the Japanese, they were about to stumble into the middle of the biggest operation yet seen in the Aleutians.

This operation was the invasion of Attu, an island Americans dubbed with the evocative code name Jackboot. Admiral Kinkaid led a task force comprising old battleships *Pennsylvania*, *Nevada*, and *Idaho*, three heavy and three light cruisers, one of the newfangled escort carriers, and nineteen destroyers. A suitable selection of transports carried 11,000 troops of the 7th Infantry Division. Two of the battle wagons were veterans of Pearl Harbor, while the amphibious-force commander was Rear Admiral Francis W. Rockwell, erstwhile boss of the unfortunate Cavite Naval Base at Manila. In a sense the Attu invasion was the first act of a long retribution that only ended in Tokyo Bay.

Initial warning of what was up came to the Japanese by radio intelligence: At 9:35 A.M. on May 12, their 51st Communications Unit picked up an American radio call sign on frequency 4385 kilocycles. Heavy ships began to bombard the shore about 11:00, and aircraft attacks started about 1:00 P.M. By that time American troops were ashore at several beaches, which had been reconnoitered for five days by submarines *Narwhal* and *Nautilus*. This day became the first of more than two weeks of bloody ground fighting during which, the official count held, 552 Americans were killed and 1,140 wounded, while Japanese losses amounted to 2,351 dead. There were only 28 prisoners. After one final suicide charge by the last of the Japanese garrison, the island was secured on May 29, 1943.

The Imperial Navy made its most immediate response by air. At this time the JNAF had its Twelfth Air Fleet in the Empire with the 24th and 27th air flotillas, each having three groups. Air fleet headquarters at Yokohama ordered formation of a strike force in the Kuriles, and the Japanese attempted their first attack with nineteen medium bombers on the morning of May 14.

Aleutian weather forced the bombers to turn back. The same thing happened to another nineteen-plane strike on the morning of May 23. Finally, on the twenty-fourth, a seventeen-plane formation made it to Attu only to be intercepted by American P-38s. Five JNAF planes were claimed downed as against no bombing damage.

At sea, meanwhile, the Fifth Fleet had its convoy en route to Kiska. That mission was immediately aborted and the *Kimikawa Maru* ordered back to Paramushiro alone; contrary to Morison, the senior staff officer of the 1st Destroyer Flotilla reports that the tender launched no aircraft to attack Attu (or fly to Kiska either). Rear Admiral Mori Tomeichi's escort ships were left to make a lightning surface attack on an invasion fleet that outnumbered them many times over. Rejecting daylight attack as simply giving the Americans too many advantages, Mori planned to make his naval assault on the night of May 13. Then calculations showed the distance was too far to cover in a night, even at full speed. Mori held position until Kawase, that night, ordered his return to Paramushiro. Admiral Kawase himself put to sea from Kataoka with cruiser *Maya* and destroyer *Usugumo.* Other Fifth Fleet ships were dispersed on various duties; he ordered them to join him as quickly as possible. Even with Mori's unit, however, Kawase knew he was no match for Admiral Kinkaid's invasion fleet, so he returned to base.

Submarines were the last chance for the Japanese. Kinkaid had warned that antisubmarine restrictions necessary to permit the pre-invasion activities of *Nautilus* and *Narwhal* were going to increase the submarine menace. His warning was right on target, but the restrictions stayed in place. When the invasion actually occurred, two I-boats slipped inside the American defenses. Commander Inoue Kikuo's *I-31* got off a torpedo that would have hit the *Pennsylvania* but for the alert the battleship received from a PBY orbiting overhead. Counterattacks by aircraft and destroyers forced Inoue's boat briefly to the surface, but he got away. Commander Yamamoto Hideo's *I-35* also missed on his attack and escaped pursuers.

At this juncture the new commander in chief of the Combined Fleet took a hand in the North Pacific. Admiral Koga appreciated that it was too late for Attu but wanted to catch a portion of the U.S. fleet if he could, thereby facilitating any subsequent Decisive Battle. Koga strengthened the Fifth Fleet with heavy cruisers *Myoko* and *Haguro,* and ordered a concentration in Empire waters, where he was already headed in the *Musashi*, bearing the urn with Yamamoto's ashes. Amid symbolic ceremonies for the mourned chief, Koga stopped for discussions at NGS, where his new chief of staff, Fukudome Shigeru, had recently been operations bureau chief. The result was IGHQ Navy Directive Number 246, issued on May 21.

The goal established by Directive 246 was "to create a sound strategic condition in the area and, at the same time, to contact and annihilate the main enemy fleet and to neutralize its plan of offense." Under the code name

Operation KE the fleet would feint as if attempting to recapture Attu, make every effort to evacuate Attu survivors, and bring off the garrison of Kiska in sequel and as soon as possible. If a sea battle flowed from this, Koga was to win it. The strategic importance of these northern operations is suggested by the fact that the Combined Fleet initiated air courier flights to Ominato—a service previously available only at Truk and Rabaul.

Imperial Navy forces concentrated in the Empire grew more formidable by the day. At Yokosuka-Tokyo under his own command Admiral Koga assembled the battleships *Musashi*, *Kongo*, and *Haruna*; carriers *Zuikaku*, *Shokaku*, and *Zuiho*; cruisers *Suzuya*, *Kumano*, *Agano*, and *Oyodo*; and eleven destroyers. At Hashirajima was Admiral Shimizu with battleships *Nagato*, *Mutsu*, *Fuso*, and *Yamashiro*, plus a screen of cruisers and destroyers. Also in home waters were light carrier *Hiyo* and cruisers *Tone* and *Chikuma*. In short, Koga had the bulk of the Combined Fleet.

Admiral Koga went to sea in late May. He told Fukudome that the Imperial Navy's sole chance for success lay in Decisive Battle. Japan had entered a new stage of the war, Fukudome later related, "and it was Admiral Koga's belief that it would not do . . . to rely upon passive defense plans, that we must take the offensive." But regarding actual operations Fukudome recalled only exercises in the Inland Sea.

Naval maneuvers off the Japanese coast were but a first step, however. Admiral Koga had to get the fleet accustomed to his methods, but he may have gone further. Movement records for flagship *Musashi* note the vessel at sea from June 9 to June 24 with a mission objective to "destroy the enemy." Records are not clear as to what the Japanese did, when, or why.

American intelligence was not entirely in the dark as to these activities, however. Edward Van Der Rhoer with OP-20-G writes that Rosie Mason's unit knew of Koga's fleet concentration responding to the Attu landings. At Pearl Harbor, the CINCPAC war diary for June 8 notes: "The bulk of the Japanese Fleet continues to hold extensive training exercises in Empire Waters. While this is believed to be designed to perfect defensive tactics, the fact that the Jap Fleet is capable of making a raid in force on our Pacific Island bases . . . cannot be overlooked." Nimitz answered with a bit of radio deception, and the war diary for June 19 reassuringly records that "it is indicated that our current RI [Radio Intelligence] deception plan is having the effect of causing the enemy to believe we are about to strike in the Eastern Mandates."

Americans in the islands were not so sanguine. Thomas F. T. Warren was one of the intercept operators at Johnston Island, part of FRUPAC's mid-Pacific radio net. He remembers the day the station commander called everyone in to give them a little talk: "Men, I have bad news for you. We have a fairly reliable report that a Japanese fleet is heading our way." There was no place to hide on the tiny island, and it was hardly possible to dig in because of the coarse coral sand and the fact that the water table rose to just six inches or so beneath the surface. There were suspenseful days before the alert was called off.

It was very much the same on Midway. Radioman Albert M. Fishburn was there on the anniversary of the big battle, and there was much talk about Japanese fondness for anniversaries. A U.S. carrier and her escorts lurked in the area while some B-17s and many B-24s flew in to augment air strength. "From beach to beach this stuff was a solid mass of armament," Fishburn said, "planes, tanks, and what have you." Submarines supposedly spotted the Combined Fleet north and west of Wake, headed toward Midway, but according to Fishburn the Americans "weren't sure whether they were coming back to actually bombard or strike or simply on maneuvers. We didn't know. I don't think the Navy knew at that time." The situation was further obscured because the Japanese introduced a new variant on their fleet code at the end of May.

American submarine activities make clear that either Koga moved the location of his maneuvers from the Inland Sea into broad Pacific waters, or that he moved to the Pacific with more than that in mind. In an excellent account of the U.S. submarine force, Joan and Clair Blair show that American skippers were told to look out for Japanese warships on the basis of Ultra decrypts. One submarine filed a contact report on June 9 of two carriers in Empire waters. Commander Roy Benson, who had narrowly missed Koga's fleet as it returned to Japan bearing Yamamoto's ashes, then saw the same Japanese carrier force on June 8, and got a chance to torpedo Captain Sumikawa Michio's light carrier *Hiyo* two days later. Sumikawa put his position at 300 miles off Yokosuka, so there can be no doubt Koga's fleet was truly at sea. The *Hiyo* eluded several torpedoes, one just a few feet in front of her bow, but three hit her (one failed to detonate) and one of those put her out of action, flooding two of *Hiyo*'s boiler rooms.

It may be that this evidence of U.S. subs active in Empire waters dissuaded Koga from his fleet offensive. Koga might also have been disheartened by what occurred at Hashirajima on June 8. There, the crews of the First Fleet had just been piped to lunch when tragedy struck Captain Miyoshi Teruhiko's battleship, *Mutsu*. Fujiyama Tsutae, fishing in the bay that morning, remembered how he could see the warship's silhouette only vaguely in the foggy, misty rain. Suddenly there was a tremendous explosion and he could see nothing except black smoke and water. When the smoke cleared there was only a mast that gradually disappeared beneath the waves. Another fisherman, Fujimoto Hisaru, found the sea covered with oil. For days blackened clothing and bodies washed ashore. Some 1,120 crewmen perished in the *Mutsu* tragedy. The ship's navigator, Commander Okihara Hideya, became the senior survivor. He was on deck walking toward the bridge when, the next thing he knew, he was in the water a good distance away grasping for a piece of flotsam.

According to comments First Fleet commander Admiral Shimizu Mitsumi made to a former subordinate, the internal explosion may have been caused by chemically unstable explosives in special high-power Mark 3 shells the *Mutsu* carried for her 16-inch guns. Shimizu was on his own flagship, *Nagato*, at the instant of the explosion, and from this nearby vantage point the blast had a color characteristic of a Mark 3 detonation.

It is a token of what is knowable and what is not in intelligence work that American intelligence continued to carry the *Mutsu* on its Japanese fleet order of battle for many months after the June 1943 tragedy. The ship was stricken from the order-of-battle lists only after information given by a prisoner interrogated in China.

In the meantime, Admiral Koga Mineichi wanted to conduct a naval offensive but was suddenly short by an aircraft carrier and a battleship before he had accomplished anything at all, and with U.S. submarines infesting Empire waters. Either Koga thought better of his original intentions, or he never went beyond the training phase. In the Aleutians, that left everything up to the local command, Kawase's Fifth Fleet, which made a last effort to slip supplies into Attu using *Abukuma* plus four destroyers, in part to evacuate the Navy radio intelligence chief, Commander Emoto Hiroshi, and his Army opposite number. The mission was aborted because the weather proved clear and the destroyer-flotilla commander worried about detection by Allied aircraft. Shortly afterward Japanese resistance on Attu ceased.

Despite success, Americans wondered about the Attu campaign, worried both about the ferocity of Japanese resistance and the quality of Allied intelligence. The following note, extracted from an Army G-2 report of June 19 and sent to an officer at OP-20-G, is worth quoting in full:

> Several conclusions are warranted with respect to the enemy's knowledge of our dispositions and operations in the Aleutians area as indicated by Japanese documents captured at Attu. It is probable that the enemy derived most of his information from visual observation of our shipping, analysis of our radio traffic and from carelessness in using the voice radio. Inasmuch as the captured documents reveal only fragmentary knowledge of our plans, it is probable our cryptographic system has not been broken, and that some of the enemy's intelligence, especially his conclusion that our attack of Attu would take place at Massacre Bay, was based on logical G-2 deductions. While belief was expressed that the enemy could have obtained only a very small amount of information from friendly planes downed in the vicinities of Kiska and Attu it is considered possible that markings, papers and documents gained from this source may have aided in establishing the identities of our air units. It is also considered possible that the immediate utilization of air communication codes carried by a downed bomber might have enabled the enemy to successfully intercept

operational messages during the period that these codes remained in effect.

Ruminations like these sparked American planning for the final step in the Aleutians, the invasion of Kiska. One problem of the Kiska planning was to project the likely scale of Imperial Navy reaction. Colonel Boone of ONI's Far East Division on June 12 estimated that the Kiska garrison would fight to the last man. The ONI projection also considered "not improbable" Tokyo Express–type runs with supplies by cargo vessels or destroyers, perhaps even submarines, and observed such efforts could be supported by a "fast striking group" of four heavy cruisers and other craft, a force the size of the Fifth Fleet at that moment. Moreover: "The probability must also be borne in mind that powerful, heavy Japanese forces could be capable of operating out of Yokosuka in a northeasterly direction." This intelligence appreciation was typical of those written during Kiska planning, and preparations for that invasion proceeded on the assumption it would be a knock-down, drag-out fight.

The Japanese had difficulties of their own, however. No surface ship had made it to Kiska since a destroyer in late February or early March, and submarine supply was inadequate for a large garrison. Evacuation by submarine was put in hand, but again the volume of the flow (one boat every other day) could not be made commensurate with the risks assumed by the submarine crews, especially once the Americans captured Attu and actually had a base in between Kiska and the garrison's home bases. Losses mounted steadily, including Commander Inoue's *I-31*. In addition on June 11, two days before Inoue's loss, the *I-9* was sunk near Shemya, while later in June the *I-7* was holed and beached as a result of destroyer gunfire at Kiska. About 820 Japanese were evacuated by submarine, but losses were clearly excessive.

Destroyers were the next and better alternative, but the operation was a difficult one, fraught with danger as well. American airpower meant the force would have to sail in the worst weather; that in turn magnified navigational problems and dangers. The danger of being caught in Kiska harbor also dictated that the evacuation force could not tarry there, so all loading would have to be accomplished in an absurdly short time. Rear Admiral Kimura Masatome, still smarting from the debacle at the Bismarck Sea, had been brought up to the North Pacific to take over the 1st Destroyer Flotilla. He would lead the evacuation fleet. On Kiska, Rear Admiral Akiyama Monzo prepared the garrison for a quick getaway. Men were to take their personal weapons and a few belongings, no more. Koga beefed up the Fifth Fleet with six extra destroyers to help carry the load, 5,200 soldiers of the Japanese Army and Navy.

In late June, Kimura held a dress rehearsal with almost all the ships that would eventually participate. He returned to Paramushiro and sortied for the actual evacuation on July 7, but as his force neared Kiska, Kimura found the fog lifting and was told there were indications of Allied planes about. He turned for home. Criticized for not pressing on, Kimura's senior staff officer, Captain Arichika Rokuji, requested that Admiral Kawase personally accompany them on the next attempt.

The diary of one Private Takahashi shows the way it was for the men awaiting the ships at Kiska. "It's unbearable day after day," Takahashi recorded on July 21. "I think it would be grand if our fleet would hurry and land. I am going mad." Part of Takahashi's entry for July 28 read: "Everyone is exhausted from the terrific bombing."

For once American intelligence was caught flatfooted—the fleet intelligence bulletin told of Japanese intent to mount an operation in the Aleutians on about July 25, and that could hardly be anywhere other than Kiska. Admiral Kinkaid sent a force of his own out to catch them, with three battleships the Japanese could not hope to match. On July 22 the Americans lashed out at Kiska with the heaviest bombardment it had yet seen, and they were in a blocking position on the twenty-fifth, when a PBY reported seven Imperial Navy ships near Attu. The blocking force missed these ships, but was only ninety miles away from Kiska on the night of July 25–26 when, almost an hour after midnight, five different ships picked up targets with their radars. Ironically, the night was clear, the sea calm, the sky cloudless, the barometer high and steady, and there was no fog. In a tremendous cannonade, the battleships and cruisers of the American force fired 1,005 shells at radar targets that never returned fire and that none of the destroyers present, or the heavy cruiser *San Francisco* either, could pick up at all. This wild engagement became known as the battle of the pips; the gun flashes were visible from Kiska. Japanese on the island wondered what was going on over the horizon and hoped it was not their evacuation ships being pounded.

Meanwhile the Americans compounded initial failure to regain contact with the Imperial Navy force the PBY had reported by pulling out two destroyers that had previously maintained a close blockade of Kiska. They sailed southeast to refuel, opening up exactly that quadrant through which Admiral Kimura's evacuation flotilla approached its destination.

Kimura had left base on July 21, marked time while waiting for fog, and refueled three times. Then he began a high-speed run to Kiska, where they followed the coast to the harbor, entered, and anchored. Boats moved back and forth from the shore carrying the garrison troops, whom Admiral Akiyama had already assembled. In the astounding period of just fifty-five minutes on July 29, Kimura's ships managed to load 5,200 men. Then they departed the way they had come.

The Japanese left explosives timed to detonate a few days later, leaving the impression that Kiska still had a garrison. According to Captain Arichika of the destroyer flotilla, only three dogs remained behind. Although no Japanese were on Kiska the Americans continued preparations for the planned amphibious assault. There were more surface naval bombardments, and, after a week of aborted missions, a good photographic cover was obtained on August 2. Kinkaid's intelligence officer wrote up a note saying that the pictures showed remarkable changes on the island, including destruction of twenty-six buildings (barracks, garages, the radio station). There was also the matter that Radio Kiska had gone off the air on July 28 and was not heard again, while pilots flying over the island suddenly encountered no anti-aircraft fire where it had been fierce before. More photo recon missions did not resolve the mystery of Kiska. The invasion forces went ashore beginning on August 15, 34,426 strong. They found only the dogs.

Aboard one of the ships offshore was General John L. De Witt of the Fourth Army, who had come to get a whiff of the "front." De Witt was the man who had excluded nisei from the Pacific coast and pushed for the internment of Japanese-Americans. It was ironic that now, at Kiska, some of those same nisei were among the invasion troops, energetically combing caves for documents left behind by the Japanese.

A second irony, one affecting the Japanese, flowed from the very success of the Kiska evacuation, in conjunction with certain other investigations. The Japanese monograph on naval communications assembled after the war notes quite openly: "From the success of the Kiska withdrawal operations and others it was concluded that the main codebook had not been broken." Perhaps it was not so bad after all that such an unprecedented sequence of errors precluded U.S. interception of Admiral Kimura's evacuation flotilla!

So ended the Aleutian campaign. The Japanese began it as a diversion but found it a millstone around their necks. Their units tied down in the North Pacific were not available for the crucial battlefields of the South Seas. The Allies were on the move—in the Solomons, New Guinea, the Central Pacific. Koga Mineichi hardly knew where to turn; soon he would hardly know what hit him. It all began with a brand-new plan for a Decisive Battle.

§UCH CONCLUSIONS AS IMPERIAL NAVY CODE EXPERTS DREW FROM EVENTS AT KISKA REPRESENTED the tail end of their investigation. The beginning of the trail lay in the lush tropical greenery of Bougainville, where Admiral Yamamoto's plane had gone down. Preliminary inquiry swiftly revealed the impressions of several survivors that the Americans had gone after the lead aircraft as if they knew who was aboard. Though the impression was mistaken, and the pattern of the attack entirely a coincidence, no more than suspicion was necessary to fuel investigations. Commander Watanabe knew very well what he had done to prepare the commander in chief's trip to Bougainville. Watanabe has stated his confidence in the security of Imperial Navy codes, but he feared that Japanese Army ones had been compromised. For this reason Watanabe had ordered that his message giving details of the visit plan was to be sent in Navy code only. As it turned out, someone made a mistake and the Yamamoto trip message went out in both service codes. Contrary to Watanabe's beliefs, it was the fleet code that the Americans were reading, while Japanese *Army* codes resisted efforts to unravel them right through 1943. Ignorance is bliss. The Japanese concluded that the Americans had learned of the trip from the dispatch mistakenly sent by Army radio.

Here is a further example of the vagaries of history, or at least of how American codebreakers had the luck of the Irish in this war against Japan: But for a mistake the Japanese would have had *no choice except* to consider their Navy code compromised. As it was, the Navy introduced new additives just to be on the safe side, but had they realized the cryptographic emergency that actually obtained, JN-25 might have become a thing of the past. This puts new light on the evacuation of Japanese troops from Kiska: The sequence of errors on the American side was accidental, but preservation of the ability to read JN-25 would have been worth permitting the escape of the Kiska garrison even as a deliberate action.

Commander Watanabe may have been concerned about this whole complex of issues but ultimately he did not bear the responsibility. The officer who did was the *joho sambo*, the Combined Fleet intelligence staff officer. That was Commander Wada Yushiro, who had an extra measure of responsibility as communications officer. It was the *joho sambo* who decided against pressing for replacement of the D Code (JN-25), and the same officer who gave Admiral Koga the information he needed to conduct operations. Combined Fleet apparently managed to get two days' warning on the occasion of the Attu invasion, and they did as well or better on some other occasions, as shall be seen presently.

Wada Yushiro had held the post of *joho sambo* for a long time, so a new assignment for him seemed reasonable. In addition, with the demise of Yamamoto there was major turnover of personnel on the staff. Before long Wada returned to Tokyo to work at headquarters where one of his academy classmates, Sanematsu Yuzuru, headed the U.S. section of the *joho kyoku*. The new man for *joho sambo* was Commander Nakajima Chikataka, previously communications officer for carrier commander Ozawa, southern operations commander Kondo, and the Naval General Staff.

Nakajima was considered one of the best communications officers in the Navy, and he was used to a certain amount of intelligence work since that went with his job, but before arriving on the Combined Fleet staff he had little idea of how much more important the function was at this command level. At the Combined Fleet level the intelligence job was both harder and more complex. It was harder because there was much more to do to keep track of Allied forces and operations. For example, Nakajima for the first time had to manage a small radio intelligence unit of his own, a group of three officers and six men directly under the fleet staff who monitored frequencies of interest to the fleet command, much like the mobile radio units the Americans sent with their task forces.

Intelligence work sucked up more and more of Commander Nakajima's time. When he arrived, most of his effort went into the communications side of the job, but within just a few months proportions had reversed. For intelligence purposes Nakajima had to read operational reports from the fleets and other units, the dispatch traffic, air reconnaissance and coastwatcher reports, traffic analyses of Allied communications, and messages and written reports sent by *joho kyoku* and the Naval General Staff. Subordinate commands were not required to file regular systematic reports, which was fortunate because if they had the paper flow that already threatened to submerge Nakajima would have washed over his head. Nevertheless, though reports were not required, the *joho sambo* had to ask for additional information whenever necessary, and Nakajima often made specific requests for aerial reconnaissance. He found they were only sometimes complied with, and mission photos rarely reached him. There were no photo interpreters assigned to the fleet intelligence staff.

In fact for several months there was no one at all (other than the radio monitoring group) on the intelligence staff. Commander Nakajima did a one-man job. He did not produce daily summaries like his opposite number at CINCPAC, Commander Layton; there was no situation plot; there were few written records of any kind. According to Nakajima, the only Allied fleet order of battle at Combined Fleet headquarters was "the one he kept in his head." Nevertheless, by February 1944 it was clear that fleet intelligence needed more manpower. Nakajima heard about a good officer and requested him by name. The man was assigned. Two additional officers joined the staff that October, and five more in summer 1945. All the latter men were selected by the Navy personnel bureau, were reservists, and had no particular intelligence skills or training. A few of the extra officers were good, others were poor analysts.

More than anything else, Combined Fleet intelligence would be systematized by the need to train these neophyte newcomers. Nakajima could keep the order of battle in his head, but his inexperienced assistants could not. The fleet intelligence officer made his helpers compile tables and charts to help them acquire the background necessary to become better analysts.

Coordination among commands remained nonexistent through most of the war. There were no meetings between Combined Fleet and subordinate fleet intelligence officers; Nakajima gave no thought to strengthening the capabilities of subordinate units by requesting more personnel for their intelligence staffs. Information from *joho kyoku* was fragmentary and very general. Urgent reports came by dispatch or on the telephone; news of a meeting of American commanders at San Francisco or Pearl Harbor might arrive as a note. *Joho kyoku* reports gave no source or evaluation of reliability and were difficult to use for that reason. For his own part, Commander Nakajima, who would remain fleet intelligence officer until the eve of the end of the war, sent very little information to *joho kyoku.* "My estimates did not always agree with theirs," he said.

Conditions improved slightly once the Combined Fleet staff moved ashore, but that was not until late 1944, when the fleet's strength had been almost expended. Finally the Japanese began to gather their different intelligence officers together once a week to share news and views. In April 1945 the Combined Fleet began exchange of data with the Army when they inaugurated weekly conferences. By then most of the fleet lay at the bottom of the sea.

"The whole system was weak," Commander Nakajima said of Combined Fleet intelligence. He ought to have known, since he himself remained the principal analyst. As the data came in, the fleet intelligence officer said, "I would think it over and come to some conclusion. It was not a very scientific method." Incalculables and imponderables made a large difference. For example, Nakajima thought the Combined Fleet did pretty well in assessing U.S. fleet composition because data could be drawn from American radio broadcasts. Yet, "if the broadcasts were false my estimates were bad." Despite such a realization, the Japanese seem to have paid little attention to American deception practices or psychological warfare techniques.

As Commander Nakajima put it, "With better intelligence we might have won the war."

Nakajima did the best he could, and passed his information along to the commander in chief, who would issue any orders necessary. That was where the buck stopped. The Combined Fleet commander was the ultimate audience for all the intelligence reporting. Admiral Koga Mineichi listened, but what he heard was the siren song of Decisive Battle. Much as had Yamamoto before him, Koga argued that the Americans would simply become stronger. The time to act was immediately. Koga told his chief of staff there was at least a 50 percent chance of success if a Decisive Battle could be made to happen in 1943. More than that, he said to Fukudome, "*the one chance* of success lay in" such an engagement (my italics). Rather than attempting to defend one or another key point, as various officers advocated, Koga wanted to risk everything in one massive confrontation.

Such views on strategy may seem out of character for Koga Mineichi, usually seen as a cautious, plodding commander. Assessing Koga for top naval officers, for example, ONI's Far East Division remarked of its report:

"The possibility is suggested that the appointment of an officer of Admiral Koga's temperament may be indicative of a change toward a more defensive naval policy." In the body of the report, after relating Koga's career history, the Far East Division observed:

> His position in naval circles has been a conservative one. Whereas Yamamoto was a bold and forceful innovator, to whom may be given credit for the building up of Japanese naval aviation, Koga's career has been orthodox, and his background one almost entirely concerned with ships.

*Time* magazine drew its assessment from Chinese sources: "They say he is 'extremely suspicious and careful' and lacks Yamamoto's ability to make quick decisions." Koga was considered taciturn, scholarly, and unpolitical. "In a race of unknown men," *Time* noted cattily, "he is an especial anonym."

In fact Koga, who achieved the rank of full admiral in May 1942, was held in high regard by the younger generation of Imperial Navy officers. He had long been considered a candidate for the Combined Fleet command and, far from being a hidebound reactionary, Koga had worked with the treaty faction during prewar days. He had favored the Washington Naval Treaty, had been a delegation member and active on technical matters in Geneva disarmament talks between 1927 and 1929, and had helped organize political maneuvers designed to help ratification of the London Naval Treaty the following year. Koga Mineichi had been a section chief in the operations bureau of the Naval General Staff in the early 1930s, and vice chief of NGS during the early years of the China Incident. Fukudome Shigeru had worked for him at that time and demonstrated skills Koga now wanted in his Combined Fleet chief of staff.

Born in Saga prefecture in September 1885, Koga Mineichi came from samurai stock and later developed connections with the Imperial Household. He graduated fourteenth in his class from Etajima in 1906. Attaining rear admiral's rank in 1932, Koga had never commanded an air unit or carrier, but he had been with technical inspectors' offices during some of the vital early years of Japanese aviation development. He had commanded the heavy cruiser *Aoba*, the battleship *Ise*, Cruiser Division 7, the Second Fleet, and the China Area Fleet (at the time of Pearl Harbor). Using the pen name Goho, Koga constantly exchanged letters with Yamamoto, both before the war and after it had started. Aristocratic, tall, and dapper with his goatee beard, Koga was amiable and courteous, of prudent disposition, well versed in international affairs. He was easy to work for.

Admiral Koga could be hardheaded and stubborn, but he was not inflexible. In the late 1930s, for example, he had persisted in arguing that aircraft posed no danger to surface ships because anti-aircraft defenses could always be augmented. The power air forces demonstrated following the advent of war in Europe showed the fallacy of that proposition, however, and as commander of the Second Fleet in 1940 Koga resisted proposals Ozawa Jisaburo made to concentrate the big aircraft carriers in a single unit, which would have removed Carrier Division 2 from Koga's force. Thus even before Pearl Harbor Admiral Koga wanted his ships to be protected by air cover furnished by carriers. Although Admiral Koga remained a battleship man at heart, his plans for the Combined Fleet held airpower in healthy regard. In fact, Koga became a motive force in the Imperial Navy's creation of a major new land-based air force to help in the Decisive Battle.

For security reasons, Koga's replacement of Yamamoto was handled in a very quiet way. Admiral Koga, then chief of the Yokosuka Naval District, left for the *nanyo* on what was ostensibly a mere inspection trip. Only after he arrived at Truk were the orders made known for him to assume command. One of his first actions was to issue an order of the day, on May 23, 1943, setting forth his view of where the Navy had been and was headed:

> On this occasion we pay our respects to the memory of a leader of the Combined Fleet, to a man whom we still remember. Yamamoto, the late Commander-in-Chief, died at the front. If we annihilate our stubborn enemy even at the cost of our own lives, we will know that his spirit lives on.
>
> During the past year and a half of this struggle, we have smashed the power of our great enemy and though we have, in the main, carried out our basic strategy, our enemy is striving for ultimate victory by expanding his preparations for offensive action and by devising plans for the strategic application of new weapons. Furthermore, taking advantage of the tide of the war in Europe, he is concentrating his main power in the Greater East Asia area and is preparing to launch a counter-offensive. No matter how many times the enemy may advance against us, we shall always welcome combat with him[,] and in exterminating him and assuring for ourselves the ultimate victory, we shall by united effort and perseverance forge for ourselves a greater and greater military power. At the same time that we manifest a relentless spirit of attack, we shall be prepared to meet the changing conditions of warfare with new strategies and new weapons, always keeping one step ahead of the enemy.
>
> The war is now at its peak. We defend what is ours and the task of meeting and striking the enemy must be the prerogative of the Imperial Navy. We shall defend ourselves to the last breath and shall totally destroy the enemy.

Invoking the spirit of Yamamoto, the new Combined Fleet commander exhorted Japanese sailors to unite with the soul of the former chief by devoting themselves wholeheartedly to the utter destruction of the Allies.

These were brave words, and Admiral Koga eventually backed them with detailed planning to match. The planning process suffered setbacks in his rush to react to American operations in the Aleutians; but after his return to Truk in July, work began in earnest, and by mid-August the ambitious scheme was complete. Koga's Decisive Battle concept would be promulgated in a set of four Combined Fleet directives issued on August 15, applying to the Pacific area, and two more orders covering the Netherlands East Indies and Indian Ocean theaters which appeared on September 25. In both contingencies the operational scheme would be similar. Because this became the basic Imperial Navy strategy for the next fleet engagement, it is worth examining in some detail.

As befitted an effort dedicated to triggering a Decisive Battle, Admiral Koga's plan distinguished between local activities and the major initiatives intended for the "third phase" of the war. In the southeast area, existing strength in the central Solomons would secure key points while major operations, for the time being, would be carried out by air forces including, "at a proper time," powerful concentrations to repeat the I Operation–type effort. Koga's orders observed that Allied operations made it clear that an attack on the "Inner South Seas" (the Mandates) was impending, and his measures were intended to defeat such an attack wherever it came. Each island base, Koga directed, would resist the superior enemy independently until reinforcements arrived, making it possible to free most fleet strength for the Decisive Battle.

The scheme for that engagement itself utilized a system of so-called interception zones. Each would have a designated advance base with a protected anchorage, anti-aircraft and antisubmarine defenses, and the wherewithal to support the Combined Fleet when it entered the local area to offer battle. In the eastern Pacific, for example, Koga divided his sea frontier between the Aleutians and the Marshalls-Gilberts into nine of these interception zones for what he termed Z Operations. (The later directives for Indian Ocean battles, code-named Y Operations, provided for four such interception zones.) For each zone, planners tried to derive an ideal position for the fleet to assume, and they designated this point in the sea by longitude and latitude. Beyond the nucleus of advanced bases and fleet positions would be a chain of bases in depth used to wear down the enemy. Air bases were to be located at intervals of no more than 300 miles, and each was to have several runways; underground aircraft, ammunition, and fuel storage; dummy runways and planes to divert the enemy; and other provisions.

Fleet operations would be conducted with the aid of submarines and a land-based air force. The orders provided that most Combined Fleet surface units would concentrate in the Inner South Seas (Truk) and participate in operations there and in the southeast area. "They will be prepared to counterattack with their entire strength should the Allied fleet attack," read Top

Secret Operations Order Number 40. It further provided that "a carrier striking force or interception force will attack and destroy strategic enemy key points and when the opportunity presents itself, contact and destroy enemy invasion units or fleets." A companion order, Number 41, provided that "enemy carriers will be neutralized by our massed air strength and after gaining air superiority, our main attack will be directed against the transport group. If the situation permits, the enemy fleet will be attacked. Depending upon the situation, the transport group may be attacked first." In all, the scheme anticipated that Allied invasion forces would be weakened at sea, then finished off before they could make landings.

For the first time in the history of the Imperial Navy, Admiral Koga's scheme gave official recognition to the emergent primacy of aircraft carriers. Top Secret Operations Order Number 43, also issued on August 15, 1943, provided basic fleet organization for Z Operations. In that organization, the carrier task force would be composed of groups, in very much the same style as the Americans' Task Force 58. One group would be built around the Third Fleet, the former carrier force. But that fleet was to detach one of its carrier divisions, which would be added to the battleship-heavy Second Fleet to form another carrier group. Significantly, Admiral Ozawa of the Third Fleet was to exercise tactical command of the carrier task force as a whole. The Japanese soon began to style this organization their "Mobile Fleet."

The creation of a full carrier task force in which battleships were subordinated to a carrier commander, only dreamed about in Yamamoto's day, was merely the first of the air innovations wrought by Koga Mineichi. A second was formation of a new JNAF air fleet specifically intended to work with the mobile fleet in the Decisive Battle. Together they would deliver a one-two punch or, as some saw things, the air fleet would be an anvil against which Allied fleets would be smashed by the hammer of the Mobile Fleet. This new formation would be known as the First Air Fleet. Emperor Hirohito personally presided over the investment of its commander, Vice Admiral Kakuta Kakuji. For chief of staff he would have Captain Miwa Yoshitake, formerly Combined Fleet air staff officer, who had been spared the Bougainville massacre because of the tropical dengue fever that invalided him home. Senior staff officer would be Commander Fuchida Mitsuo, the brilliant flight leader from Pearl Harbor and afterward. In a very real sense the First Air Fleet represented the Imperial Navy's attempt to recreate the winning combination of the early days of the war.

These things were accomplished at the instigation of Koga Mineichi or with his solid support. Admiral Koga made his plans and instituted organizational changes in spite of many voices insisting on parochial interests and objectives, whether demands to focus only on the central Solomons, or appeals not to override the traditional primacy of the battleship admirals.

Koga held out against the demands, and also saw quality in the ideas of such visionaries as Ozawa Jisaburo, with whom he sided in creating the new mobile fleet. Further, the inherent aggressiveness in Koga's fleet operations ran directly counter to the American image of him as a stodgy, cautious man of conservative bent. It is a mistake to perceive Koga this way. Americans would get a chance to see Koga's aggressiveness soon enough, but first there would be another round of fighting in the Solomons.

ONE JAPANESE LOCAL COMMAND CRYING OUT FOR ASSISTANCE WAS THE SOUTHEAST AREA Fleet in the Solomons. It did not matter that the Allies repeatedly delayed their offensive north of Guadalcanal (until late June in the final postponement). This afforded commanders at Rabaul more time to move their troops forward, but since resources were limited to start with, the difference was not all that great. In addition, moving reinforcements and supplies became constantly more dangerous due to growing Allied sea and air power. Besides, hidden behind more evident dangers were the effects of Allied advantages like Ultra and aerial photography.

An object lesson in the realities of the combat environment would be administered by SOPAC forces in early May 1943 off Vila. That place on Kolombangara Island had become a principal point in the Japanese supply system. Troops and equipment, rations and ammunition would be run through the Blackett Strait to Vila on Tokyo Express destroyers or in submarines, and there they would be transshipped to barges for the move to New Georgia and Munda, final terminus of the supply line. During the spring Admiral Halsey's forces tried to interdict the route with interceptions of Express missions or bombardments of Vila or Munda, but these were too risky to be repeated endlessly. Daylight permitted COMAIRSOLs planes to mount a pretty effective overhead blockade, but something also had to be done to win the night.

The answer was a tight little operation code-named Fifth Avenue. In early May, when CINCPAC identified an imminent Tokyo Express from intelligence, SOPAC mined the waters of Blackett Strait. Four converted destroyers laid a field of more than 250 mines during the night of May 6–7, covered by a cruiser-destroyer group. Within hours of the moment the last mine casing hit the water, a unit of four Japanese destroyers under Captain Tachibana Masao weighed anchor at Buka, bound for Vila. An experienced leader who had fought with his destroyer division at Midway, the eastern Solomons, and the Naval Battle of Guadalcanal, among others, Tachibana was familiar with the dangers of The Slot. He managed to avoid daytime air attack, then completed the run to Vila at high speed after dark on May 8. In Blackett Strait, three of his four vessels were mined as they left Vila after unloading. *Kuroshio* sank immediately; *Oyashio* was mined but survived long enough to be bombed the next afternoon, as was the *Kagero*. Destroyer *Michishio* crowded as many survivors aboard as she could and hightailed it to Shortland Island. Total losses amounted to nine officers and 183 men killed or missing, plus fourteen officers and ninety men injured. Tachibana would be reassigned to Port Arthur, Manchukuo.

Japanese commanders' frustration increased daily. Admiral Kusaka Jinichi apparently determined to accomplish what the I Operation had failed to do—neutralize Allied power in the lower Solomons. A series of medium- and large-scale air raids began about a week after Yamamoto's death. In mid-May Admiral Koga reinforced Rabaul with the 24th Air Flotilla, numbering fifty-eight fighters and forty-nine bombers. A series of big fighter sweeps—fifty to eighty planes at a time—was punctuated by bombing of a favorite old target, Henderson Field. On June 7 a huge air battle developed over the Russell Islands as a hundred Allied planes intercepted eighty JNAF fighters. On June 10 a convoy faced bombing off Guadalcanal, and on the 12th came another massive fighter sweep. The next day the Eleventh Air Fleet made an all-out effort against shipping in Ironbottom Sound, with the loss of almost all the twenty dive-bombers committed.

By mid-June aerial reconnaissance was reporting as many as 245 JNAF aircraft distributed among the fields of the Rabaul complex. The climax came on Wednesday, June 16, with a raid by 160 planes. Radio intelligence at Guadalcanal sounded the first warning, intercepting Japanese flight leaders as they netted in with each other. Coastwatchers picked up the formation as it flew south. In all, COMAIRSOLs had enough warning of what became known as "the big raid" to mount an interceptor force of 104 Allied fighters. The postwar Strategic Bombing Survey's study of the unit that evolved from COMAIRSOLs claims seventy-seven planes lost to fighters and seven more to anti-aircraft fire (other sources contain even higher claims); Japanese accounts admit losing about thirty aircraft.

Barely had Admiral Koga time to recall aircraft intended for the Marshalls when the Allies made their move against New Georgia and Rendova. The day of the attack there were eighty-three Zeros and sixty-six bombers at Rabaul. Eleventh Air Fleet as a whole had about 300 aircraft, but just 225 were serviceable. It happened that the vice chief of the Naval General Staff, Admiral Ito Seiichi, along with his Army opposite number, was visiting Rabaul when area fleet commander Kusaka received first reports of the Rendova landings. The officers quickly huddled and Kusaka sent out the largest air strike he could muster on such short notice: twenty-five torpedo bombers covered by fighters and preceded by a fighter sweep. With more waves later on, a U.S. Navy communiqué estimated that 110 JNAF aircraft had been involved, and a subsequent release stated that the real number must have been "substantially larger." The sole ship sunk, however, was command ship *McCawley*, flagship of the flotilla positioned off Rendova.

The Rendova–New Georgia landings, code-named Toenails, began a month of fierce fighting in the central Solomons. COMAIRSOLs dropped 778 tons of bombs that July and made a maximum effort against Buin. Tonnage exceeded that dropped during the four preceeding months. Vila, Munda, and Ballale were also targets.

Japanese supplies and reinforcements became crucial in the days and weeks following the landings. There had been about 7,000 troops in the sector, including the Yokosuka 7th and Kure 6th SNLFs. Not only were there Army appeals for supplies, the Navy had no wish to leave its own naval infantry out on a limb. Thus the Toenails landings triggered a series of surface engagements similar to those of the Guadalcanal campaign.

First blood went to the Japanese. Three destroyers were transiting Kula Gulf, the body of water between New Georgia and Kolombangara, on the night of July 5. They were outbound after landing reinforcements at Vila when Rear Admiral Walden L. Ainsworth's cruiser-destroyer group showed up to bombard positions in the area. One of the Imperial Navy tin cans put a Long Lance torpedo into destroyer *Strong;* that sank her, while the Japanese got away. The next night there was a sea battle in the same waters, reminiscent of Tassafaronga. Tanaka Raizo was gone—banished to Burma for protesting that Guadalcanal was not sustainable. In his place the night of July 6 was Rear Admiral Akiyama Teruo of the 6th Destroyer Flotilla. Sometime commander of naval barracks at Sasebo, a submarine base unit, and the light cruiser *Naka*, Akiyama was a thirty-year Navy man whose academy classmates included Tanaka, other destroyer leaders like Kimura Masatome and Hashimoto Shintaro, intelligence man Maeda Minoru, and radio intelligence expert Kakimoto Gonichiro. Of special interest is the fact that another of Akiyama's classmates was Rear Admiral Ota Minoru, commanding the naval infantry on New Georgia that the Tokyo Express was endeavoring to succor.

That night the American admiral, Ainsworth, was looking for trouble, his lost warship replaced for the occasion. No specific indication of intelligence knowledge of the Japanese sortie has yet been found. In any case, soon after midnight Akiyama's ten destroyers were already within the Kula Gulf, in the lee of a dark shore, when Ainsworth rounded the northern tip of New Georgia to enter. *Niizuki*, Akiyama's flagship, had been equipped with radar; the Japanese either detected Ainsworth that way or by eyeball, a full ten minutes before the Americans opened fire. The first salvo smothered *Niizuki*, killing Akiyama and sinking the ship, but two other destroyers answered with torpedoes that struck American light cruiser *Helena*. The first hit between her forward main battery turrets and just knocked her bow right off. Two more torpedoes impacted along the side and broke the ship's back, sending her to the bottom. Seaman Ted Blahnik, a 40mm gun director for some of the after anti-aircraft guns, remembers being mystified for a split second at the water washing into his gun tub: Forging ahead at over 20 knots, the bowless warship was gulping the water in but also generating huge waves over the deck. Many of the *Helena's* sailors saluted as they went over the side. "It wasn't necessary," says Blahnik, "but that's what we always did when we came aboard and that's what we did when we left."

Thus began an ordeal of many hours for sailors from the *Helena.* Several days passed before survivors were picked up by other ships or rescued by natives. Some drowned or were eaten by sharks infesting these waters. It was the same for Japanese survivors of the *Niizuki* and the *Nagatsuki,* the Imperial Navy combatants lost in this action. American records support the hypothesis that there was no foreknowledge of the Tokyo Express run. An entry in the CINCPAC war diary notes Admiral Ainsworth's initial report: "Enemy composition and losses unknown but he thinks he got all 7 ships except 1 or 2 cripples." Similarly, the ONI's Japanese naval activities summary for July 8 says: "On July 6, in Kula Gulf, at least 8 Jap ships, attempting to quit the area, were sunk by our surface forces." The Japanese task group was reported as consisting of three or four light cruisers and four or five destroyers. For some days Ainsworth insisted he had sunk cruisers in the battle, and it was due to the ability of U.S. radio intelligence to clarify the Japanese fleet order of battle that his impression could be corrected.

A week later Ainsworth would be in a second wild mêlée in the same area, a fight called the battle of Kolombangara. He had been given six more destroyers plus the New Zealand Navy light cruiser *Leander* to make good his losses. The Japanese would have light cruiser *Jintsu* and five destroyers in a combat group and four more acting as transports. Rear Admiral Izaki Shunji, a year behind Akiyama at the academy and a former skipper of the heavy cruiser *Mogami,* was on his guard as he made a delicate (and dangerous) approach direct to Munda. Even had he chosen not to consider Kula Gulf a warning, Sato Torajiro, flag captain aboard the *Jintsu,* was there to tell him about Tassafaronga. Both precedents were sinister.

Just as in a nightmare, the Americans were indeed on the prowl, and with a fleet superior to the Japanese. Not only that, they had the advantage of radar and of aerial sightings as Izaki's group steamed down The Slot. This time the Japanese did not even make it into Kula Gulf; Ainsworth intercepted them north of Kolombangara. However, Izaki benefited from a radar detector that showed him when his ships were being "painted" by radar waves, and which he somehow used to plot the bearing of the Allied fleet. Thus alerted, the Japanese launched a torpedo attack within two minutes of first sighting Ainsworth's warships. American torpedoes hit the water a few moments later.

Izaki turned to starboard; *Jintsu* lit her searchlight and began to shoot.

Not only was a light a vulnerable aiming point but also *Jintsu* was the biggest ship in the Japanese force and a natural target on all the radar scopes of Ainsworth's vessels. *Jintsu* was plastered but she may have been done in by a torpedo. Leading Seaman Toyoda Isamu, an Okinawan who had been with the ship since 1939, was at his messenger station near the cruiser's fourth stack when he felt a terrific explosion on the port side forward. The ship briefly listed to port, then rolled the other way, and within ten minutes she was sinking. Hits on the bridge evidently killed Admiral Izaki, Captain Sato, executive officer Kondo Issei, and most staff officers. Seaman Toyoda survived to be captured four days later.

Captain Shimai Zenjiro in the *Yukikaze* remained as the senior officer afloat with the escort unit. Little more than ten minutes after the start of the action, torpedoes tore into the *Leander* and the New Zealand ship went down. Shimai maneuvered his warships to repeat the torpedo attack, and about an hour later got in a very effective one, sinking American destroyer *Gwin* and damaging both Ainsworth's remaining cruisers, *Honolulu* and *St. Louis*. Some of these warships would be out of action for a very long time. Ainsworth reported damage to the Japanese as one cruiser and three destroyers sunk. He was right about the *Jintsu*, but the Imperial Navy lost no destroyers that night.

With South Pacific naval forces suffering constant attrition in these scraps in the central Solomons, SOWESPAC's Seventh Fleet agreed to send Australian cruisers *Hobart* and *Australia* to substitute for some of the ships Halsey had to send to the dry docks. *Hobart* had not yet even made it to Espíritu Santo when she was hobbled by a submarine torpedo. (Lieutenant Ichihara Rikinosuke's *Ro-103* had been in the area at the time, though Ichihara reported no successes by radio before being sunk himself on July 28.)

On July 18, an American destroyer unit reported a daylight engagement in Vella Gulf, between Kolombangara and Vella Lavella, with several Japanese tin cans. The following day, search planes reported sighting a Tokyo Express of three cruisers and six destroyers with two transports. Bombers followed and claimed results, but Japanese records show no ships hit in this area on this date. On the other hand, heavy air attacks on Shortland Island July 17 sank destroyer *Hatsuyuki* and damaged three others, mines at Kavieng damaged light cruiser *Nagara,* and air attacks in The Slot on July 20 hit heavy cruiser *Kumano* while sinking destroyers *Yugure* and *Kiyonami*. A third cruiser, *Yubari,* had been damaged by a mine off Buin earlier in July.

The Imperial Navy could not sustain such losses, and at Rabaul, Kusaka Jinichi knew it. The Japanese tried to maintain a very aggressive posture, but losses were demoralizing, tropical sicknesses did not help, and Kusaka was continually annoyed at the Navy's parsimonious attitude toward awarding medals or commendations. Kusaka, who had been president of Etajima at the time of Pearl Harbor, realized how important praise could be. Actually he had been on the point of retirement, and wished to retire on his birthday, December 7, the same day his daughter became engaged, in a celebratory burst of glory after thirty-two years in the Navy. He had gone to bed that night, woke up to be told that Pearl Harbor had been attacked, and so returned to his post as if nothing had happened. Now Kusaka found himself at Rabaul trying to make up for the deficiencies of the high command. As inducements in place of medals he took to handing out ceremonial swords, for example one to fighter ace Nishizawa Hiroyashi, another to destroyer skipper Hara Tameichi.

Admiral Kusaka remained perennially aggressive. Asked by inquisitors after the war whether he had planned another offensive following the loss of Munda and Vella Lavella, Kusaka replied, "We were always planning an offensive until the planes left for Truk." With the wisdom of fifty-three years, however, Kusaka realized the offensive had to be executed with the least risk to his forces. This was the rationale for Southeast Area Fleet Operations Order Number 10, which Admiral Kusaka issued on July 18. This directive provided for an effort to sweep the Allies from the New Georgia area and thus secure Munda and Kolombangara, then to be further strengthened, along with Bougainville, especially Buin and Shortland. The air force got orders for repeated group fighter attacks, with the standard to be surprise attacks at dusk or dawn or in the night, plus daytime reconnaissance and patrol. There should be special night attacks in Kula Gulf. The submarine force was to attack shipping in the New Georgia area, getting as close as possible to disrupt Allied supply activity. Most important, "Air units and surface units will cooperate with the submarine force, exerting every effort to cut enemy transportation lines, especially to prevent his unloading in the Kula Gulf area."

Kusaka's plan led to further Tokyo Express runs to Kolombangara, and on August 1 one of these ran into opposition from American PT boats. Captain Yamashiro Katsumori led the force from the *Amagiri* and expected to evade SOPAC forces by using Vella Gulf. Instead the *Amagiri* (Lieutenant Commander Hanami Kohei) ran down the *PT-109*, smashing that torpedo boat and leaving its skipper, John F. Kennedy, to rescue his crewmen as best as he could. Lieutenant (j.g.) Kennedy and his men would be aided by Australian coastwatcher Arthur R. Evans and indigenous tribesmen.

Back at Rabaul a couple of days later there was a plans conference for a further "rat" run to Vila led by Captain Sugiura Kaju. The plan was to repeat the successful formula of the previous mission, including its route. Another destroyer division skipper present, Captain Hara Tameichi, who had been on the earlier mission, objected but was overruled. Hara's destroyer, *Shigure*, wound up as the last ship in the formation. The destroyers carried 950 troops and fifty-five tons of supplies. Americans were ready this time, and aerial reconnaissance saw Sugiura coming. American tin cans pulled the trick Japanese ones had succeeded with so often: lining up against a dark shore, then torpedoing the passing enemy, opening gunfire afterward. Only the *Shigure* escaped; *Hagikaze, Arashi,* and *Kawakaze* were all sunk without much chance to fight. There were no American losses.

Aboard Lieutenant Commander Yanase Yoshio's destroyer *Kawakaze,* disaster struck so swiftly many crewmen thought they had been attacked by PT boats. Petty Officer Kawabata Shigeo, an anti-aircraft gun captain, felt a torpedo strike just under the bridge; the ship sank within five minutes. He believed Yanase and the bridge personnel must have been killed instantly. Another petty officer who worked in the ammunition room below thought they had been hit in the bow, but able seaman Masuda Tadao also believed the torpedo impacted under the bridge and added that the crew had barely reached battle stations when the *Kawakaze* came to her end. The loss must have come hard for Commander Wakabayashi Kazuo in Tokyo, the ship's previous skipper, who was now flag secretary to Navy chief of staff Nagano.

Expensive as was the defeat, the Imperial Navy went on to assign Captain Sugiura as commander of the heavy cruiser *Haguro.* This knowledge probably helped sour Hara Tameichi, who came to believe the Navy was trying to save face and disguise defeat by promoting men who had failed at the front.

AMERICAN INTELLIGENCE FOUND THAT THE CAMPAIGN OF 1943 BROUGHT UNDREAMED-OF opportunities as well as problems of unanticipated scale. One was the matter of prisoners. In all of 1942 only forty-nine prisoners had been captured in the Pacific Ocean area, most survivors of the cruiser *Mikuma.* They were taken care of on an ad hoc basis, with interrogation by Eddie Layton's assistant, Lieutenant Commander Robert E. Hudson. A fine language officer, Hudson had learned the Japanese people and their psychology best of all of them, and Layton had asked for Hudson by name when he got the job of fleet intelligence officer. Hudson did well with the limited number of prisoners taken at Midway, but no ad hoc method would suffice for the prisoners taken in the SOWESPAC area, of whom there were 1,167, including about 150 Koreans or Taiwanese, in 1942. In MacArthur's area the ATIS organization took the lead on interrogations.

True problems emerged for Pacific commanders in 1943 with actions like those in the central Solomons. Already holding Japanese sailors from the *Furutaka* and *Takanami,* sunk during the Guadalcanal campaign, SOPAC authorities suddenly acquired more Japanese, from the submarine *I-1,* the cruiser *Jintsu,* and the destroyers *Kawakaze, Minegumo, Yugumo,* and *Niizuki,* among others. The numbers overloaded SOPAC capacity. MacArthur's G-2 people sent a couple of their language officers over to Espíritu Santo that summer to assist in the interrogations, and another man plus three new linguists went from Hawaii or the United States, ultimately to join ATIS, but stopping on the way to do a little work for Halsey.

Hawaii also got the chance for some direct interrogation work after sailors were rescued from the Japanese submarine *Ro-61*, sunk in the Aleutians. It was the Central Pacific campaign that fall which really demonstrated the necessity for more facilities, however. Before the end of the year 522 Japanese prisoners had been captured in the Pacific and another 1,064 in the SOWESPAC area. In early 1944 the Joint Intelligence Center Pacific Ocean Area (JICPOA) set up a regular interrogation section for the first time, specifically putting two officers on this task, borrowing others as required. At that time there were approximately 450 prisoners in Hawaii, men who would be sent on to the mainland once interrogations were completed. The prisoners were kept in the Marine brig at the navy yard or at Camp Catlin, with seriously wounded Japanese sent to area hospitals. Later, Aiea Hospital opened up a prisoner ward, while a special stockade for prisoners was built at Iroquois Point, on Oahu. The stockade held 250 men at a time, although on one occasion it set a record by screening 2,066 prisoners in one day.

The workload grew enormously over time; during 1944 as many as 4,257 prisoners were taken by Pacific forces and another 5,122 in SOWESPAC. In the first two months of 1945 alone there would be 2,038 more Japanese prisoners. Since the Japanese were indoctrinated to prefer death to captivity, most prisoners were men who had failed somehow in attempts to die or, like oil-soaked sailors after a sinking, had had no choice in the matter. Paradoxically, since the stigma of captivity was so great for Japanese that they did prefer to die, the Japanese actually captured proved quite willing to talk, and a very great deal of intelligence information was imparted thereby.

The Office of Naval Intelligence made an effort to capitalize on this in a systematic way by setting up a Joint Interrogation Center. The camp opened up on December 15, 1942, at Byron Springs, California, with two language officers and seven civilian interrogators. One officer was later detached to Brisbane and the other to Pearl Harbor, although five more language officers plus two interrogators were added. The center interrogated sailors from the *Ro-61* and assembled reports on the *Mikuma*, *Furutaka*, and *Takanami*, but the stream of prisoner arrivals stateside remained so narrow that the center was deactivated in September 1943. That proved premature when the Marshalls-Gilberts campaign brought in the first large wave of prisoners. The center reopened at Tracy, California, in March 1944, at the request of CINCPAC.

One problem that persisted until almost the end of the war, limiting the quality of the center's interrogations, was that prisoners were moved without their files, so interrogators were unable to see what had already been learned from a man and what subjects ought to be followed up. The standard interrogation covered the subject's personal history, the chronology of his service, significant events in which he had participated, units to which he had been assigned, names of commanders or other personnel, particulars of ships or air units, details of equipment and armament, training and operations, communications, morale and propaganda, special recollections, and several other subjects. Much time was wasted plowing this ground over and over at different interrogation centers rather than pushing ahead to the most valuable information.

The highest-ranking Imperial Navy prisoner, taken at the apex of the war, and questioned in great detail, was not kept either in Hawaii or at the joint center, however, but sent to Washington. There Captain Okino Matao was housed at Fort Hunt, a portion of George Washington's original Mount Vernon estate that had been used as an army post in the Civil War and World War I. It reopened as an interrogation center some called "The Farm," and specialized in handling German prisoners. Senior counterintelligence officers from ONI and Army intelligence, plus substantive specialists from both organizations, plied the Japanese officer with questions and took the answers back to Washington to put to immediate use.

Like many others, this Japanese became a captive because he was helpless. Captain Okino had been on an airplane flight in China when the craft was shot down on January 18, 1944. Okino was captured in the wreckage south of Anking, with a crushed leg that had to be amputated. He was interrogated first by Chinese and then by a team from the Allied Southeast Asia Command; eventually he was passed to the Americans and moved to the United States. From a good family, married, with two children residing in the Shibuya section of Tokyo, Okino belonged to the 1919 class at Etajima. He had spent many years in China with fleet staffs or resident naval officers, and was at the time of his capture the resident naval officer at Hankow.

Thus Captain Okino had a unique perspective from the viewpoint of Allied intelligence. As a senior naval officer he could comment on the war situation on the basis of secret reports he had read, while, working for a bureau of the Naval General Staff, he could comment on the high command, and, as a representative of *joho kyoku*, on Japanese intelligence as well. An Etajima classmate of U.S. naval attaché Yokoyama Ichiro and Turkish attaché Matsubara Akio, not to mention combat commanders such as Solomons destroyer leader Yamashiro Katsumori, Captain Okino could furnish personality and biographical data. These subjects and others were very thoroughly covered in his various interrogations, including endless discussions of the intricacies of the Japanese high command and the organization of their secret services, in particular the Army's political-action unit, the *tomuku kikan*.

Of immediate relevance, from Okino the Allies received data on current strength and cumulative losses of the Combined Fleet, on the Japanese merchant shipping situation, on aircraft strength and losses, and other matters. The tabulation of battleship losses Okino furnished confirmed suspicions voiced in early 1944 that Japan had lost the *Mutsu* to internal explosion. As the war moved toward a conclusion, data from Okino helped American authorities prepare for the occupation of Japan.

Like prime intelligence sources from age immemorial, Okino was closely held. Foreign naval attachés in China, promised access to the senior prisoner, waited for months. The report from the Southeast Asia Command interrogation team also took a long time to wind its way to Washington. Once the attaché and British reports were available at ONI, the OP-20-G operational intelligence center had difficulty getting copies. As Bill Sebald of the center put it to Jasper Holmes at JICPOA, "The Okino interrogation report has finally reached ONI but despite all sorts of pressure I have as yet been unable to obtain a copy." Soon thereafter, however, both Sebald's unit (F-22) and JICPOA had the material, available to all senior Allied commands by about mid-1944. By then the struggle for the Solomons had ended in Allied victory. Japan was being pressed back to her innermost defenses.

Mᴜɴᴅᴀ ᴍᴀʏ ʜᴀᴠᴇ ʙᴇᴇɴ ᴀ ᴍᴀᴊᴏʀ ᴀɪʀ ʙᴀsᴇ, ʙᴜᴛ ɪᴛ ᴡᴀs ɴᴏᴛʜɪɴɢ ꜰᴀɴᴄʏ. ɪᴛ ᴡᴀs ᴀ ɢʀᴀᴅᴇᴅ dirt field, and its only shelters were revetments along a taxiway that wound behind the beach. A hill arose along the third side of the triangle formed by runway and taxiway, ideal for defense but not for base air activity. That hill and others west of it made Munda a very strong defensive position, too. American troops dared not invade Munda directly but rather landed at other points on New Georgia and tried to march overland. It became a slow slogging match.

Suspecting that New Georgia fighting might take a long time, and that there could be a better place for an airbase, COMAIRSOLs determined even before the invasion to send a covert scout mission to see if a better site could be found. This mission consisted of Air Solomons operations officer Stephen Jurika and another officer named Bill Painter, a civil engineer by trade. They were inserted quietly one evening by a PBY flying them up from Tulagi. Commander Jurika might have had a great respect for the local culture when he served in Tokyo as air attaché under Henri Smith-Hutton, but in the Solomons he went along with Americans who called the indigenous tribesmen "fuzzywuzzies" because they wore their hair straight up, twelve or even eighteen inches high. A number of "fuzzywuzzies" plus coastwatcher Donald Kennedy met the scout party when they landed at Segi Point, at the other end of New Georgia from the Japanese at Munda.

Kennedy was reputed to be carrying on a little private war with the Japanese; for a time Jurika became a part of it. The young language officer found Kennedy an able fellow, a very effective man. Indeed his private war, in which all imagined the coastwatcher to be hiding in the jungle as Japanese patrols passed by, was being carried out from a large house high atop a hill. The comfortable place had a wide, wraparound veranda, a corrugated tin roof, and a panoramic view of many miles of New Georgia and its coast. Kennedy affected always to wear khaki shorts and an Australian bush jacket. When Japanese patrols came too close, Kennedy's "fuzzy-wuzzies" simply wiped them out. In this fashion the coastwatcher created a de facto buffer zone protecting his Segi Point base.

Kennedy assigned half a dozen of his stouthearted tribesmen as escort and guides for the AIRSOLs surveyors, and had the whole group make a routine patrol to get acquainted with each other. Kennedy himself had been flown over New Georgia in an American aircraft to spot likely sites for an airfield. Jurika and Painter's job was to survey those places and select the best ones. They wore out their boots on the first dry-run patrol, which lasted just four or five hours in the bush, but they had extra boots and had brought fatigues dipped in coffee to make them very, very dark. Despite Japanese security patrols boating throughout the area, the survey party was able to get within just a couple of miles of Munda, where they quietly climbed one of the nearby hills and scouted the place. Watching the base routine they sketched locations of key facilities, barracks, the radio shack, and so on, and estimated whether the strip could take bombers and what size ships could enter the harbor. Then they went on to survey the other recommended sites, four or five of them, but there were problems with every one. Only when the exhausted party got back to Segi Point did Bill Painter realize that that place was itself the sole practicable alternative to Munda.

Thus the troops fighting through the jungle a few months later were after the one real installation of value on New Georgia. The SOPAC high command knew a base could be built by Seabees at Segi Point, and that actually became a key feature in the offensive plan, because the Army needed weeks to hack through the jungle fastness but the airfield had been cleared in just four days. Subsequently the field Jurika and Painter had found provided air support for the spearheads approaching Munda.

Jurika's was not the first scouting party to which Donald Kennedy had played host. A month earlier, three Marines under Lieutenant William P. Coultras of SOPAC naval intelligence had come in to reconnoiter the beaches used for the landings. Like Jurika, they were impressed with Kennedy, who invited them to sip Scotch on his veranda in the cool of the evening.

Kennedy's indulgences gave expression to coastwatchers' secret dreams: It remained the central object of their work to put themselves out of business. Donald Kennedy's war ended when Operation Toenails began. For

Allied and Japanese combat forces and intelligence units in the Pacific, however, the conflict raged with undiminished ferocity.

None of this surprised the Japanese on New Georgia. Not only did they have a general expectation that the Allies might come, but Lieutenant Yunoki Satoru, the SNLF intelligence officer at Munda, had specifically detected the SOPAC scout parties. American food cans were found in a hut near Munda while a letter to a young marine, torn into scraps but pieced together by Yunoki, came from a path only a half-mile from the base. Stephen Jurika reports that as his scouting party made its way back toward Segi Point they encountered signs of strong Japanese patrols searching for them.

After the warnings came invasion, then a long interval as the Allies fought the jungle and such harassing forces as Munda put into the field. Toward the end of July the American troops neared and pressure mounted; Japanese Army troops tried counterattacking on July 25, only to be forestalled by a more powerful American thrust. Rear Admiral Ota, the local SNLF commander, received orders to withdraw his men to a point from which they could be taken out by barge. Army forces eventually followed. Munda itself fell on August 4.

Given clear evidence that the Americans were strong enough to take Munda, there is no reason the Japanese could not have prepared for that eventuality. That is, much of the airfield and its installations could have been blasted, while material of intelligence value ought to have been destroyed. Instead the Allies found a treasure trove of materials at the fallen base. Among the documents recovered at Munda, for example, was one containing a list of the Japanese code designators used for geographic locations throughout the South Pacific, recovery of which had caused cryptanalysts headaches on many occasions, most recently in the Yamamoto shootdown. Now designators could be read off a list! Another retrieval was the Southeast Area Fleet directive previously quoted, which gave SOPAC details of the strategy the Japanese were following at that very moment. A third was minutes of a Southeast Area Fleet staff conference that had occurred at Rabaul in mid-June. Japanese information security was lax and remained so.

Next Admiral Halsey's SOPAC forces jumped ahead to Vella Lavella, bypassing Kolombangara, where the Japanese had expected to fight. They concentrated thousands on Kolombangara, but had only a handful of men on Vella Lavella, where there was a barge staging point at Horaniu. If the Americans could become established they could isolate the garrison on the other island. A brisk destroyer battle followed on August 17, a few days after the SOPAC landings, as Rear Admiral Baron Ijuin Matsuji led a unit south to cover barges moving troops to Vella Lavella. No ships were lost on either side, though the Japanese were unhappy with the performance of the radar on the *Hamakaze,* one of the few Imperial Navy destroyers so equipped at that time. It apparently mistook the barge group for an Allied naval force, inducing Ijuin to break off and run for Rabaul.

There were more trips to Horaniu over succeeding weeks, as well as cruises to Gasmata, Buin, and Rekata Bay. Shortland Island became a dangerous anchorage no longer a base; it was frequently subject to air strikes of 150 planes or more. Even Buka, quite close to Rabaul, was endangered. The Southeast Area command had become the province of many former NGS or Combined Fleet staff officers, and these men took the view that Bougainville's bases would be attacked directly, the way Munda had been, so that island needed frantic reinforcement. The difficulty was that virtually all Japanese Army forces entering the theater were being funneled to New Guinea to oppose MacArthur. With the Americans already halfway to isolating Kolombangara by taking over Vella Lavella, thoughts turned to the garrison of the bypassed island as a source of additional troops.

Imperial Headquarters agreed with the assessments made at Rabaul. On August 13, IGHQ Navy Directive Number 267 ordered all-out efforts to hold the central Solomons for the moment, but specifically foresaw a withdrawal "at the opportune time" to the "rear strategic positions." Then Admiral Nagano in behalf of IGHQ promulgated Directive Number 280 on September 30. That instruction ordained efforts to defend the Bougainville–Bismarck Archipelago area centering around Rabaul. Thus the Japanese recognized they were restricted to their regional base, and the orders suggested the severity of the situation by directing that an effort be made to destroy "the attacking enemy before he makes a landing." Envisioning stiff fighting in both the Solomons and New Guinea, Directive 280 also provided that shipments of large quantities of munitions to both places would be "speedily expedited."

In practice, the orders from Tokyo meant the abandonment of the central Solomons including Kolombangara, Rekata Bay, and Choiseul. From early October, Admiral Kusaka laid on "rat" and "ant" transport missions to all those places. Troops on Kolombangara were moved to Buin, those at Rekata brought back to Rabaul, and so on. There were 600 troops at Horaniu, so Kusaka sent Baron Ijuin with a destroyer flotilla to get them too to Buin. There were two groups of transports—one of three destroyers, the other of twenty barges—and six destroyers for escort. Off Vella Lavella on October 6 the Japanese blundered into six U.S. destroyers and fought a confused night action, losing the *Yugumo*. Commander Osaka Azuma's warship, which had had the good luck to survive the Bismarck Sea disaster, became the thirty-fourth Japanese destroyer sunk in the Solomons.

By now Bougainville's time had come. The Japanese expected attacks on the bases, but Bull Halsey had learned from New Georgia: This time the invasion itself simply seized the site for a prospective airbase. The plan (code-named Cartwheel) to reduce Rabaul was modified so airpower operating from such close-in bases would strangle the Japanese hub, itself left to wither. The point on Bougainville chosen for the invasion was Cape Torokina, at one side of Empress Augusta Bay. It was defended by 3,200 Japanese troops. In comparison, there were more than 6,000 at Buka, over 4,000 at Kieta, 15,000 at Buin, and almost 12,000 at Shortland Island and Ballale.

Admiral Kusaka countered with diligent efforts to maximize air strength. Directive Number 280 had ordered massive increases in aircraft under Southeast Area Fleet, a buildup to 216 fighters, 108 medium bombers, 45 dive-bombers, 18 torpedo bombers, 54 floatplanes, and 12 reconnaissance aircraft. At the time, serviceable strength of the Eleventh Air Fleet amounted to about 240 planes. Losses just around Rabaul numbered 9 that September but 55 the following month, and for the JNAF as a whole the corresponding figures for those months were 584 (of which 339 were noncombat losses) and 651 (459 noncombat losses).

The difficulties aviators faced in the Southeast Area can be illustrated by the saga of the 751st Air Group, known as the Kanoya Group before the JNAF reorganization of November 1942. A unit proud of its record, the 751st had been in on the sinking of the *Prince of Wales,* had fought with distinction through the early campaigns, and had come to the Solomons in the fall of 1942, where it based at Kavieng with a forward detachment at Rabaul's Vunakanau Field. It was about that time that the Allies began nightly harassment bombing of Rabaul, which they extended to Kavieng toward the beginning of 1943. This plus losses from its own long-range bombing wore out the 751st, which had to be sent to Tinian to refurbish. Under Captain Sada Naoshiro it returned to Vunakanau on August 13 after more than three months of rest and retraining. A dozen planes flew on to Buka to become a forward detachment. Though the policy was now to conduct mostly moonlight or night missions, Sada's complement of fifty-two bombers had been halved by the end of October. Even on the ground, pressure was intense because Air Solomons and MacArthur's Fifth Air Force were mounting a counterair campaign against Rabaul with Vunakanau as one of its main points of concentration.

At about this time the Commander Air Solomons, Admiral Marc Mitscher, was recalled to Pearl Harbor to assume a key carrier command. The new COMAIRSOLs was Major General Nathan F. Twining, a bomber pilot. Twining found he had 624 aircraft assigned. There was no way the JNAF Eleventh Air Fleet could match those numbers, even though Combined Fleet carrier air groups were beginning to make a new appearance at Rabaul. As SOPAC forces prepared to invade Bougainville, Twining was confident he could parry any punch the Japanese could throw.

All across the South Pacific, forces in motion brought a cataclysmic final battle for the Solomons. The climax astounded the Japanese with results they could not have anticipated. Intelligence would play a major role. But the stage was not yet fully set. Actions in the Central Pacific put the last props in place.

DURING THE MONTHS OF THE SOLOMONS CAMPAIGN, MUCH CHANGED IN THE CENTRAL PACIFIC. The innovative Admiral Inoue left, first replaced by Baron Samejima Tomoshige, former aide de camp to the Emperor. Then came Kobayashi Masahi, a prewar chief of American intelligence for *joho kyoku*. During most of this period the Fourth Fleet chief of staff was Rear Admiral Nabeshima Shunsaku. These officers presided over a gradual buildup of garrisons in the *nanyo*. Indeed, the most vital units in the sector at the time were construction units, comprising a total of 17,333 personnel in the Fourth Fleet's complement. Troops were coming out from the Empire—mostly Navy men at first, but a trickle of Army soldiers as well. In the last months of 1942 the Japanese placed significant numbers of men for the first time in the islands of the Marshall and Gilbert chains, as well as Ocean and Nauru with their valuable phosphate production.

Basic defense plans in the Fourth Fleet area were laid down in 1940, and were clearly outmoded by 1943. In one of his last actions before moving on to an assignment at Rabaul, Baron Samejima approved a new strategy, contained in his Inner South Seas Force Standing Order Number 21 of March 10. The order named specific islands in each group the Japanese should hold at all costs, and laid down a general scheme for attrition operations (*yogeki sakusen*) in conformity with the doctrine of Decisive Battle. Submarines would be stationed in the vicinity of likely invasion targets but far enough away to hit amphibious units at least a day before objectives could be reached. Local defense forces would patrol. Radio direction finding had an important role: "Communications forces, maintaining a close liaison among themselves, will quickly determine the operational plans of the enemy by intercepting and taking bearings on enemy communications." Advance attack forces would be guided by this intelligence to stand by in the right places, maneuver in seas where the JNAF had air superiority, then dash forward for night counterattacks. Carrier forces would operate alone or in cooperation to strike enemy carriers, make surprise attacks in support of land-based air, or reinforce forward bases as required.

The Marshall and Gilbert islands, which would become the focus of the first American invasion in the Central Pacific, were under command of the 6th Base Force at Kwajalein. The relevant operations order of this command provided that local defense forces must try to hold out while Army and SNLF reserves were brought to threatened islands by ships of Cruiser Division 14, the Fourth Fleet's main strength. Garrisons were to defend important points "to the death, rallying the full defensive strength when the enemy lands, and endeavoring to destroy him at the water's edge." In the contingency of a Marshalls invasion, available air strength was to concentrate at Taroa and Mille atolls before launching attacks.

As fleet chief of staff Nabeshima explained after the war:

> The Fourth Fleet would cooperate with the Combined Fleet in defending the Marshalls-Gilberts. Of course the Fourth fleet being small could not do much by itself. The general expectation was that you would attack either Nauru, the Gilbert Islands, or Wake. These points would be defended by troops on hand and by the Navy. Army troop reinforcements would be moved into the Kwajalein area and from there would be distributed where needed in the Marshalls for defense.

At the level of the Combined Fleet, these arrangements fitted well with Admiral Koga's plans for a Decisive Battle. The Combined Fleet rated the contingencies a little differently, however. Aboard the *"Musashi* hotel," as the flagship was familiarly known, the potential axes for the American offensive were from the Aleutians across to Hokkaido; through the Marshalls to the Carolines (i.e., through the Mandates); or by a middle route from Hawaii through Midway and straight across the Pacific, perhaps staging attacks on Wake and Marcus. According to Fukudome Shigeru, who headed the fleet staff, the latter option seemed most likely. By early June Koga had completed his arrangements by setting out the chain of command for possible operations. If there was an offensive in the Central Pacific the chief of his Advance Force would command both Fourth Fleet (and its air forces) and the submarine force. The plan to reinforce the Marshalls or Gilberts in the face of an Allied invasion was called Hei Number 3.

Precisely around this time Admiral Nimitz at Pearl Harbor reconstituted American carrier forces into an incredibly powerful task force. This unit benefited from the initial arrivals of a stream of newly constructed fleet and light carriers, the *Essex* and *Independence* classes respectively, which made possible formation of multicarrier task groups within the overall force. The carrier task force became a weapon of unparalleled flexibility and power, with each task group a powerful fleet in its own right, and the whole able to combine for blows of unprecedented strength, or separate to hit different targets or reduce vulnerability. Nimitz called his unit Task Force 58, forming it after arriving carriers had gained some experience in strikes on Marcus and Wake islands.

Rear Admiral Charles A. Pownall led the first of the units eventually to form Task Force 58. As the senior carrier commander in the Pacific, "Baldy" Pownall had the misfortune to be an obstacle to Nimitz's desire that the task force command go to the victor of Midway, Ray Spruance. Pownall also lost points for his unaggressive handling of his unit, Task Force 15, when his three carriers hit Marcus. A total of 275 sorties were flown. But the only intelligence Pownall had was whatever Bull Halsey had gotten when he struck the place shortly after Pearl Harbor, and Pownall was nervous even though the JNAF mounted no effective opposition. At midafternoon during a day of fully successful strikes, September 1, Baldy appeared on the bridge of flagship *Yorktown* and complained to her captain, J. J. Clark, "Why did I ever come to carriers?"

Pownall continued to lead Carrier Division 3 until early 1944, however, and after the Marcus strike he went back to sea with three different carriers to hit Tarawa and Makin on September 18 and 19. A significant innovation for which Pownall was responsible was the use of submarines stationed off the target islands for the purpose of rescuing downed aviators.

Pownall's Marshalls strikes alarmed Koga at Truk. The Japanese admiral, probably on the basis of radio bearings on Pownall's carriers, ordered preparation for sea, and the fleet sortied on September 18 as American planes were making their attacks. Koga sent two units, an Advance Force under Kurita Takeo with four heavy and a light cruiser; and a main body, under Ozawa with Carrier Division 1 (185 aircraft), two battleships, and four cruisers plus escorts. The Imperial Navy units set course for Eniwetok, the forward base designated by Koga's Z Operation for battle in this region of the Pacific. Koga himself remained at Truk with steam up ready to intervene with four more battleships if necessary. The forces at sea reached Eniwetok on September 20 but found the Americans had stopped their attacks in the Marshalls. Unable to discover Pownall's position, the Japanese remained until September 23, then reluctantly returned to Truk.

These activities at the front transpired simultaneously with an ambitious new round of strategic planning in Tokyo, which had not revised its general war strategy since the heady days of March 1942. Admiral Nagano of the NGS considered an American advance across the Central Pacific the most important threat to the Empire; his Army counterparts were mesmerized by the southeast theater, particularly New Guinea, and worried about Burma, where the British were clearly building for a counteroffensive out of India. The compromise, consecrated by formal conference in the presence of the Emperor on September 30, was to recast Solomons–New Guinea operations along lines detailed in Directive 280, already described, to hold Burma at all costs, and to adopt a new defense zone for the Central Pacific. This would be an inner line the Allies could not be permitted to breach, including the western Carolines, the Marianas, and the Philippines, among other objectives. Production and shipbuilding goals were also part of this plan but need not be covered here. More important is the fact that Japanese intelligence pulled no punches in projecting the scale of the threat: 12 aircraft carriers, 7,700 planes, and 35 divisions at the end of 1943; 16 carriers, 9,000 aircraft, and

43 divisions by mid-1944; 18 carriers, 12,000 planes, and 60 divisions by year's end. By the end of 1944, it was estimated, fully 7,000 of the 12,000 Allied aircraft would be fighting at the front. The Japanese wanted an ultimate battle against these forces, but to complete preparations it was of supreme importance that the inner sphere of national defense be held as long as possible.

Thus it was extremely upsetting to the Japanese command at this critical juncture that CINCPAC forces suddenly again threatened a direct advance on Japan by the mid-Pacific route. This occurred with another of those increasingly irksome carrier raids, now on Wake Island by Task Force 14, this time with no less than six aircraft carriers. In two days of raids, October 6 and 7, the Americans pounded Wake with 340 tons of bombs; a cruiser-destroyer group laid on another 3,198 rounds of naval gunfire. Eighty percent of buildings on the island were destroyed; a direct hit on the foundation of the old Pan American hotel instantly killed almost a hundred Korean laborers sheltering there. The raids put both of Wake's radars out of action and wrecked all four high-powered radios, as well as two of three Owada Group radio direction finders. So crazed did the Japanese become that in an interval between strikes the island commander, Rear Admiral Sakaibara Shigematsu, ordered his executive officer to execute all American prisoners there.* Almost a hundred fell before firing squads. Not only did that do little to compensate for Japanese damage and the 300 or 400 Japanese killed in the raids, but also Sakaibara and his executive were convicted and sentenced to hang for this atrocity after the war.

From Truk the initial reports looked as if a real invasion impended; Admiral Koga alerted his fleet to execute the Z Operation. But then American planes and surface action groups disappeared. That Nimitz hoped to trigger some Japanese action is suggested by this October 7 entry in the CINCPAC war diary: "Our attack on Wake does not seem to have caused a move of any major ships in the Mandates. It is increasingly evident that the enemy will not expose his fleet to battle." This observation was in fact incorrect. Koga Mineichi remained a very aggressive admiral merely awaiting an opportunity for battle. Just ten days later he thought he had it, after a plane from submarine *I-36* reconnoitered Pearl Harbor and reported that part of the American fleet was not there, while the Owada Group warned of possible major units in the Wake-Marshalls area once more. The Combined Fleet prepared for a sortie on October 16, and sailed at 9:40 the next morning.

This time Admiral Koga went to sea with his fleet, which he again ordered

---

*All the American prisoners on Wake by this point in the war were former construction workers employed in 1941 on the base facilities project. U.S. Marines and naval personnel had been evacuated from the island by the Japanese soon after the 1941 battle and sent to POW camps in China.

to Eniwetok. In company were Carrier Division 1 (194 planes), six battle-ships, eight heavy cruisers, and three light cruisers, plus escorts. Simultaneously, on October 16 the Imperial Navy changed its D Code; suddenly JN-25 was unreadable for the Americans. Once more, as so often happened at key moments in this war, radio traffic analysis saved the day. Duane Whitlock, a practitioner in Australia, put it thus: "Traffic analysis maintained the continuity of intelligence through the whole war because, when there were code changes, when our people weren't reading anything, [traffic analysts] were the guys that maintained the continuity. When they were reading something, we were . . . authenticating it. We tied it together; otherwise you just got separate translations of this message or that message."

In the case of the October Combined Fleet sortie, traffic analysis noticed that beginning on October 17 messages to Truk began to drop as addressees Koga, Kurita, and Ozawa—in other words, the key Japanese commanders who had gone to sea. On October 21 OP-20-G's daily radio intelligence summary observed increasing tactical radio traffic with overall volume higher than at any time since the crisis of the Rendova–New Georgia battles of early July. Moreover, "Traffic [deleted by U.S. authorities] associations for the 21st failed to clarify the locations of most major commands noted recently at Truk." By the following day the codebreakers were beginning to make new entries into JN-25 and noted fragmentary messages concerning certain operations that "suggest they are a series of defensive dispositions and measures to be adopted in certain eventualities in countering Allied offensive drives." The first hard information would be reported on October 25, when the Americans discovered orders for a series of strong antisubmarine sweeps, characteristic of efforts to protect a fleet, in a sea area north and east of Truk.

By that time Admiral Koga had actually become increasingly frustrated with the American ability to appear, make raids, then evaporate, and he ordered a final attempt to assume an intercept position by steaming to a point just 250 miles southwest of Wake, from which he directed air searches to the northeast of that island. Koga then brought the fleet back to Truk as the American codebreakers noted more evidence of a major antisubmarine sweep, which they saw as indicating the fleet's return to port, probably with aircraft carriers. Further,

it is believed that this force sortied from Truk sometime after 11 October and prior to 18 October and that its operations were coordinated with the recent defensive activities in the Wake-Marshalls-Gilberts area as a result of the Japanese belief that a strong U.S. task force had put to sea subsequent to 11 October. It is quite probable that the Japanese can be expected to take similar action if a U.S. attack in this area is suspected.

Before the end of October the American codebreakers had established positively that the Combined Fleet had been in the vicinity of Eniwetok and that the sortie had lasted from October 17 to October 26. In the daily summary the final words were cautionary ones: "The failure of radio intelligence immediately to detect the recent sortie from Truk of the Japanese fleets illustrates the limitation of this type of intelligence and the necessity for thorough and continuous reconnaissance by aircraft and submarine."

Meanwhile the Solomons were becoming increasingly important in Japanese communications traffic, and the codebreakers noted messages about some new operation or disposition. As Admiral Nimitz well knew, his forces in the South Pacific were about to invade Bougainville. Suddenly, "what appeared to be a short directive possibly modifying, cancelling, or putting into effect a prearranged plan or phase of operations, possibly as a result of recent Allied activity in the North Solomons, was originated by CinC Combined Fleet on 28 October to activities charged with the responsibility of frontier defense." In fact, Koga had ordered his carrier air groups to Rabaul to work with the Eleventh Air Fleet. The sparring had ended; the Solomons were about to witness a climactic battle.

THE SHORT TACTICAL MESSAGE AMERICAN CODEBREAKERS INTERCEPTED HAPPENED TO BE Koga's order to activate his RO contingency plan. Apparently finalized about the time of his cruise from Truk, Koga's RO operation represented an effort to counter Allied air superiority in the Solomons. Although his Decisive Battle concept required local commands to make do, in accordance with Imperial General Headquarters' new strategy Koga felt obliged to treat the Rabaul area as a strategic point to be reinforced on an emergency basis. At 4:30 A.M. on October 27 a search plane out of Rabaul glimpsed an Allied invasion flotilla deploying for a landing at Mono Island in the Treasuries, just south of the Bougainville coast. The emergency had come already.

Allied forces landed quickly in the Treasuries and pushed inland, with New Zealand infantry doing most fighting on Mono Island, and the American 2nd Marine Paratroop Battalion in Blanche Bay being guided by one of the ubiquitous coastwatchers. Another Marine Raider battalion made a diversionary landing on Choiseul. The main amphibious force under Rear Admiral Theodore S. Wilkinson closed in and lined up in Empress Augusta Bay on the western coast of Bougainville, where they put ashore 14,000 troops and 6,000 tons of supplies in a single day, clearing the bay before dark.

At Rabaul, in keeping with the new IGHQ policy of preventing invasions before they took place, Admiral Kusaka had already tried to disrupt this one. He had scraped together whatever naval units could be found and flung them out to intercept an American task force reported approaching Bougainville on Halloween night. The scratch force was uncommonly powerful for Rabaul at this time because a convoy had just arrived under escort by Cruiser Division 5 (Vice Admiral Omori Sentaro). That provided heavy cruisers *Haguro* and *Myoko*, light cruiser *Agano,* and a few destroyers to stiffen the thin resources of the Eighth Fleet. The latter could muster little more than light cruiser *Sendai* and several destroyers of Admiral Ijuin's flotilla. Under the circumstances Baron Samejima, now Eighth Fleet commander, appealed to Kusaka not to attempt this mission, but the theater commander remained obdurate.

Admiral Omori would be lucky, at least that night, for the reported American task force—Admiral A. Stanton (Tip) Merrill's cruiser-destroyer group—continued on to bombard Buka and the fleets missed each other. Wilkinson's invasion fleet also happened to be too far south for Omori during the time the Japanese were at sea. Just after they returned to Rabaul, however, Southeast Area Fleet learned of the invasion, which the Americans had code-named Cherryblossom. Admiral Kusaka and Admiral Tomioka Sadatoshi, the former NGS operations maven now at Rabaul, determined to carry out a counterlanding with fresh Japanese troops before the Americans consolidated the beachhead. On the night of November 1 Omori went out again with this mission to Empress Augusta Bay. On the way he received word that Tip Merrill's warships were already there. Vice Admiral Omori canceled the landing but resolved to attack with his surface ships.

Captain Hara Tameichi led the destroyers under Ijuin in one of Omori's columns. Hara was astounded at the lack of forethought in the plans. Omori with just two big cruisers was expected not only to fight his way into Empress Augusta Bay but also to destroy the amphibious shipping the Allies had used for Cherryblossom. It was more than Mikawa had accomplished at Savo Island, but with a smaller force that had never worked together. Hara quotes Omori Sentaro's comment in the gun room of flagship *Myoko* just before they sailed:

> We have never teamed together before, and this can be a dangerous detriment in battle. But Admiral Mikawa managed without a previously trained team, and so can we. I have firm trust and faith in the skill of each of you commanding officers and in the ability of your men. I believe we shall win.

As the meeting broke up, the 3rd Destroyer Flotilla commander, Baron Ijuin, spoke with Hara who joked back, "Let's be prepared for a swim and take along plenty of shark repellent."

Ijuin was in no mood to joke, but Hara's words would be more prophetic than he could have imagined.

Captain Hara would probably have lost his good humor had he known the American amphibious ships had already left Empress Augusta Bay with Ping Wilkinson. That former ONI chief did not have any specific warning the Japanese were coming but it was a good inference. Now only Tip Merrill awaited the Japanese fleet, with warships cleared for action, bristling with guns, and radars up and on line. Omori was entering the bay from the open sea, a neutral backdrop. Merrill steamed back and forth against the shore. His Task Force 39 had four light cruisers and eight destroyers; Omori had four cruisers and six destroyers. His advantages in torpedoes and 8-inch guns were, at a minimum, canceled by lack of cohesiveness in his own force and Merrill's radar and rapid-fire 6-inch armament.

The ensuing battle was a disaster for the Japanese. Omori entered the bay in separate columns thrown into immediate confusion once the Americans opened fire. Baron Ijuin's light cruiser *Sendai* turned to conform with the flagship only to narrowly miss colliding with Captain Hara's following destroyer. Avoiding that collision, the last two ships in the Japanese lefthand column actually did collide. Destroyer *Shiratsuyu* instantly lost any battle-worthiness she may have had. Meanwhile the very first American salvo hit the *Sendai*, soon shelled into oblivion: The American cruisers pumped out no less than 4,591 6-inch shells that night.

Omori's righthand column did even worse. Comprising light cruiser *Agano* and three destroyers, this unit charged ahead to no avail, then turned right into the path of heavy cruisers *Myoko* and *Haguro*. The flagship carried away part of the bow of *Hatsukaze* and the immediately following vessels in both center and right columns barely avoided collision. The hapless destroyer began settling and was later finished off by the Americans.

The next night the Japanese made their counterlanding and, on the basis of optimistic reports, Admiral Koga sensed an opportunity to smash the Americans at Bougainville. With his customary aggressive bent Koga ordered Kurita's Second Fleet cruisers south from Truk to hit the invasion area. Admiral Kurita put to sea from the big Japanese base on November 3. He had seven heavy cruisers and a light cruiser with a screen of four destroyers. Kurita Takeo had orders to pause at Rabaul to fuel, then hit the Americans off Bougainville. In a memoir Bull Halsey called this "the most desperate emergency that confronted me in my entire term" in the South Pacific.

Halsey's recollection makes good copy, sounds dramatic, and probably sold a lot of books. Because of what we know today, however, especially about intelligence, that version of events needs recasting. There was a threat to Americans at Bougainville, but only if their own countermeasures failed to work. The purported emergency should be seen as a trap—a trap for Japanese.

O̲N ONE OF THEIR DANGEROUS CRUISES DOWN THE SLOT CAPTAIN HARA ONCE ADVISED A COL-league not to return to Shortland, which he no longer considered a safe anchorage. The place had been bombed that very night. That time the destroyermen were lucky. During the predawn hours after the Empress Augusta Bay battle, Hara suddenly got the same feeling about Rabaul itself. This time there was no alternative. The battered Japanese ships staggered into Simpson Harbor. Once they had completed the ritual of return the commander of *Shigure* suggested that Captain Hara go over to *Myoko* and report to Admiral Omori. Hara acknowledged the suggestion but said he would wait first to see what happened in the dawn, and instructed vessels of his Destroyer Division 27 to remain poised to get under way instantly. Hara Tameichi's premonition served him well, for Rabaul's time had come.

General George Kenney of SOWESPAC's Fifth Air Force was the man who wanted to break Rabaul. Arrangements were such that COMAIRSOLs had focused entirely on the Bougainville operation. That was fine for Kenney; he rather preferred the glory of knocking Rabaul out all by himself, and he had gotten a start on the job early in October 1943. Promising that Rabaul would be "dead" by the twentieth, Kenney had sent a 349-plane raid on October 12 to smother the Japanese bastion, where photo reconnaissance just the previous day revealed JNAF with no fewer than 294 planes of their own. The raid laid down several hundred tons of bombs and damaged thirty ships, but only three were sunk and just fifteen planes destroyed. On October 18 the Fifth Air Force sent out an equally large raid but weather forced all except about fifty bombers to turn back. Raids of this size—forty to sixty bombers with fighter escort to match—hit Rabaul on four of the next ten days, but Halloween, and then All Souls' Day, provided an interval during which Fifth Air Force bases were socked in by bad weather, though between Rabaul and Truk the skies were clear enough that Admiral Ozawa was able to fly in with 173 of his Carrier Division 1 aircraft.

In any case, for November 2 the Fifth Air Force resolved to strike Rabaul heavily and sent out seventy-five B-25 bombers with an escort of eighty P-38 Lightnings. That morning, in addition to 114,000 tons of merchant shipping, Admiral Omori and Captain Hara were sitting in Simpson Harbor with their cruisers and destroyers. Hara got his tin cans in motion immediately and they were making way into the beginnings of sea swells at Simpson Harbor's entrance even as the fast low-flying B-25s flashed past into the anchorage. The planes seemed to fly right into the sights of his anti-aircraft gunners that day, and Hara believes his ships accounted for at least five bombers. U.S. official histories acknowledge the prowess of two Imperial Navy destroyers at this place and time.

There were propagandistic news releases from SOWESPAC headquarters, and some claims of getting Omori's heavy cruisers, but both *Myoko* and *Haguro* made it out of Simpson Harbor in good order and later left for Truk. Omori had escaped the shooting gallery; it was the next day that Kurita Takeo left Truk to enter it.

The day Admiral Kurita left was November 3. In his own memoir, Admiral William F. Halsey makes it appear as if he only became aware of these Japanese movements upon receiving an aircraft contact report on November 4. In fact, however, in a dispatch he marked "most secret," Bull Halsey *on October 28* told Nimitz: "Enemy forces now in Truk may move south in reaction to our present operations." Halsey asked to have an extra task force moved to where it could assist him. The authors of Washington's daily radio intelligence bulletin suspected by October 31 that Japanese carrier planes were being sent to Rabaul, and on November 1 noted that Kurita was no longer being addressed on messages of which he was usually a recipient although "no indications of larger Japanese surface units in this area were noted." Coincident with the Fifth Air Force attack on November 2, the daily summary observed that Japanese tactical message traffic levels were high, and half or more of the load consisted of high-priority items.

In the evening of November 2 CINCPAC sent Admiral Halsey a message that, as the Commander South Pacific (COMSOPAC) put it, "indicates reinforcements en route Rabaul against which forces now available to COMSOPAC will be at dangerous disadvantage." This exchange took place hours *before* Kurita left Truk. The OP-20-G radio intelligence summary for November 3 notes dryly, "CinC 2nd [Fleet—i.e., Kurita] is believed to have departed Truk on the 3rd for the South [i.e., Rabaul]."

Foreknowledge of the Second Fleet sortie from Truk would be vital for South Pacific forces. Time enabled Halsey to move Task Force 38 (Rear Admiral Frederick C. Sherman) with carriers *Saratoga* and *Princeton* to a position from which an attack might be mounted. This inkling of Allied knowledge also permits us to reinterpret the events that occurred northeast of New Ireland on November 4, when B-24 bombers north of Kavieng caught a convoy of three troopships escorted by two destroyers plus light cruiser *Isuzu*. It now appears likely the bombers were sent to prowl in hopes of finding Kurita. Indeed, his fleet passed that very location shortly thereafter, and Kurita detached heavy cruiser *Chokai* and a destroyer to tow ships damaged by the SOPAC Liberators. About noontime Kurita's remaining ships were spotted by another B-24 search plane. That plane's contact report made what followed credible to the Japanese without calling into question their communications security.

Admiral Sherman writes that he had to race through the night at his maximum practicable speed of 27 knots to reach a dawn launch position from which to strike Rabaul. Sherman sent out a deckload strike with every available plane: twenty-three torpedo planes; twenty-two dive-bombers; fifty-two fighters. Air cover for his own carriers was to be furnished by planes from land bases south of him. This daring operational concept deserved to be successful, and it was.

Admiral Kurita also steamed through the night, rounding the southern tip of New Ireland, then turning in to the St. George's Channel to enter Simpson Harbor. At 4:12 A.M. there was another aircraft contact. Cruiser *Suzuya*'s records show the force arrived at Rabaul at 5:58. In just a quarter-hour the first ships were already alongside oiler *Kokuyo Maru* taking on fuel. Later, others took their places. At 9:16 A.M. flagship *Atago* plus another heavy cruiser, *Takao*, were both oiling when Captain Aitoku Ichiro's *Mogami* first spotted a large mixed formation of bombers and fighters. Seconds later air-raid warnings began to go off all around Rabaul town. After that things happened second by second. It was Pearl Harbor all over again.

Aboard heavy cruiser *Atago*, Captain Nakaoka Nobuyoshi immediately ordered "AA Action," and cast off from the oiler as quickly as he could. *Atago* was barely under way at 9:20 when the planes seemed to begin dividing into groups, and within six minutes one of those groups had come up from behind the flagship. At 9:28 dive-bombers began to attack; half a minute later three near misses struck in the water slightly forward of the port beam. Splinters opened steam lines and set fire to the torpedo oxygen flasks; one shot across the bridge, where it tore out half of Captain Nakaoka's abdomen. The flag captain of Second Fleet was put on a stretcher and carried off the bridge. As he passed Admiral Kurita, Nakaoka shouted a final "Banzai!" A few minutes later he died.

The episode is said to have greatly affected Kurita. Nakaoka's death must also have affected certain of his Etajima classmates, including two right at Rabaul, Baron Tomioka and Rear Admiral Komura Keizo, chief of staff to carrier commander Ozawa. The man who would have to describe these events to the Japanese public, Rear Admiral Hiraide Hideo, the Navy's spokesman, also numbered among Nakaoka's classmates. Most poignantly another skipper, Captain Nakamura Katsuhira of the *Myoko*, one of Omori's cruisers, had been in this very place just days before, following the debacle at Empress Augusta Bay, and had escaped with his ship and his life. After hearing the fate of his classmate, Nakamura perhaps did not so much mind the exile into which he would be sent as resident naval officer in Nanking.

Another who must have been affected was Rear Admiral Baron Ijuin Matsuji. He and a handful of survivors from Empress Augusta Bay were fished out of the water by the *I-104*. Ijuin had been the previous captain of the *Atago*.

In the meantime, at Rabaul the *Atago* was fighting for her life. She opened fire with high-angle guns against more planes coming up from astern at 9:29, and there was a near miss to port at 9:29.5; within two minutes the ship had developed a list to port, not successfully corrected for almost an hour. A torpedo-plane attack at 9:35 could not touch the *Atago*, nor did a second-wave attack later.

Those moments around 9:30 seem to have witnessed the climax of Rabaul's destruction. For example, Captain Hayashi Shigechika had had his heavy cruiser, *Takao*, on the other side of the oiler when the attack began and he too got under way. Hayashi was racing for the entrance to Simpson Harbor at 9:30 when suddenly destroyer *Wakatsuki* tried to cut in front of his big cruiser. Hayashi ordered hard right rudder only to have the *Takao* turn into a bomb, which hit alongside the number two gun turret, putting both that and the number one turret out of action, killing twenty-three sailors and wounding an equal number. There was a torpedo attack, too, but the fish passed ahead and to port of Hayashi's ship.

Captain Aitoku's *Mogami* was just getting under way as American planes flew over Rabaul town and swung left in order to approach from the north-west. At 9:30, as the planes momentarily drew away, Aitoku opened fire with his main battery. But the attackers were upon him, and three minutes later *Mogami* suffered her first hit, a bomb, slightly to the right of centerline between the number one and number two turrets. Black smoke billowed from the ship. There were more close calls before 9:37, when *Mogami* reached the open sea, but almost immediately there was considerable leakage from splinter holes in the hull, and by 9:45 the magazines for the forward turrets were completely flooded. The second wave of Americans, Fifth Air Force bombers that arrived about 10:17 A.M., did not attack the *Mogami*.

There were similar stories all around Simpson Harbor that morning. On the *Mogami* nineteen sailors were killed and thirty-one wounded; losses to *Atago* included twenty-two killed and sixty-four wounded; on Captain Kato Yoshiro's *Maya*, whose engine rooms were set afire by a bomb right down her funnel, there were seventy men killed and sixty wounded. With assorted casualties or injuries on other ships, the human toll alone that morning in Rabaul was more than 136 killed and 203 wounded. Admiral Kurita's proud Second Fleet was a shambles, most of its ships crippled, unable to face an ocean swell, much less the American fleet. No ships were sunk, but some of the Imperial Navy's finest cruisers were going to be out of action for a while. The Japanese had put up resistance, of course, but there was no compensation for their own losses.* Of the attacking planes, the Americans lost

---

*The intensity of the battle is suggested by Japanese expenditures of anti-aircraft ammunition, which are recorded for the major warships present if not for the base as a whole. In their defense, Admiral Kurita's vessels alone fired 356 rounds of 8-inch ammunition and 128 rounds of 5.5-inch; 1,346 5-inch high-angle shells; 8,612 rounds of 25mm

just five bombers and five fighters. Victory was clear. There was just one act left in the saga of Rabaul.

THERE WAS A FURTHER CARRIER AIR STRIKE AT RABAUL ON NOVEMBER 11, AND ADDITIONAL Fifth Air Force attacks on the seventh and again the eleventh. Two of the carriers that participated in the November 11 attack, *Essex* (Captain Ralph A. Ofstie) and *Bunker Hill* (Captain John J. Ballentine), were commanded by scions of the prewar naval Attachés' Club in Tokyo. With Ping Wilkinson, who led the amphibious forces at Bougainville, also a former ONI potentate, and with intelligence having played such a special role in the Rabaul strikes, this climactic Solomons victory had special meaning for secret warriors.

Another commander who very much wanted the credit for the Rabaul action was General Kenney of the Fifth Air Force. He recalled the Rabaul air battle of November 2 as the toughest action the Fifth Air Force faced throughout the war, but he also claimed that never had anyone accomplished so much in so little time as in those attacks. Since Kenney was writing after the war, he knew when he penned this of the equally short and enormously effective carrier strikes a few days later, of the strikes on Japanese bases in the Central Pacific, of the atomic bombs. Without prejudice to the brave airmen who flew the Rabaul missions for the Fifth Air Force against the heaviest opposition it ever faced, Kenney's hyperbole became an obstacle to historical understanding.

The Fifth Air Force's own statistics for 1943 show Rabaul in *fifth* place among its major targets that year. The top target would be Cape Gloucester at the northwestern tip of New Britain, where SOWESPAC forces invaded on December 26. More than twice as many bomber sorties were flown against the top target as were flown against Rabaul; also ahead of Rabaul were Madang, Salamaua, and Wewak. The full Fifth Air Force campaign against Rabaul comprised 1,740 bomber sorties plus 504 by fighters, according to Fifth Air Force, but just 1,621 according to the Strategic Bombing Survey's postwar study of Rabaul. Moreover, the latter source clarifies that only 549 of the flights took place during November and December 1943. By way of comparison, COMAIRSOLs flew 1,262 sorties against Rabaul in January 1944 alone, and 2,043 in February, with a wartime total of 10,102 sorties. The Fifth Air Force was not the decisive factor in the reduction of Rabaul.

In another way, Fifth Air Force activities proved a positive detriment to the prosecution of the war. The Fifth Air Force's air intelligence reflected the

---

ammunition; and 17,239 of 13mm. Most of this expenditure occurred during a period of less than twenty minutes.

SOWESPAC predilection for generating results, or claims of results, without much concern for accuracy. It is well known, of course, that pilots overestimate and that debriefers often simply add up claims rather than try to verify which are real and which spurious. Air intelligence exists to correct that tendency, but at Fifth Air Force it did something different. Historian Lex McAulay, who has made the most detailed study of Fifth Air Force efforts against Rabaul, has found that combat claims alone total more than 600 JNAF planes downed, for overall losses over a thousand if calculations are made for ferry losses, accidents, the weather, and so forth.

The Strategic Bombing Survey estimated serviceable aircraft with the JNAF Eleventh Air Fleet at about 230 at the outset of the air campaign. We know that on November 1 Admiral Koga committed Carrier Division 1 with 173 aircraft. Finally, there are IGHQ records showing that at the point the carrier planes were withdrawn the combined strength of those units plus the land-based air units stood at 281 (including eighty-three damaged planes and twenty-eight reserves). Adding to the original estimate to account for aircraft under repair (JNAF serviceability rates stood at about 60 percent at this time), there could not have been more than about 550 JNAF aircraft involved in all. This means Fifth Air Force claims for a month of fighting over Rabaul amount to shooting down more than the entire Japanese air force, and almost twice that many if ground and other losses are included in the comparison.

To sharpen the point it can be noted that there were photographic covers by reconnaissance planes during the period. The initial set was taken on October 11—helpfully, the day before the Fifth Air Force began its campaign; it showed 294 Japanese aircraft. A cover on November 2–3 showed 259, and one of November 10 revealed 188 planes at Vunakanau and Lakunai alone, suggesting an overall strength of the same order of magnitude. The Fifth Air Force explanation was that the Japanese must be replacing every loss, not that something might be wrong with its methods of tabulating adversary losses. This judgment was advanced repeatedly in intelligence summaries; it was not a mistake made just once.

Moreover, the Japanese themselves were not solely occupied with the Fifth Air Force. The whole reason why carrier aircraft reinforced the Eleventh Air Fleet was to oppose Cherryblossom, the Bougainville invasion. A high-intensity air battle took place over the invasion area during the entire time the carrier planes remained at Rabaul, and losses in these air battles were considerable, increasing overall JNAF losses and calling Fifth Air Force claims into further question.

As an intelligence matter, accepting such claims across the Pacific meant supporting an estimate of Japanese aircraft production (and ability to replace losses) much greater than actually existed. When the kamikaze campaign began and brought with it constant mass air battles, estimates of aircraft production acquired unanticipated importance.

Meanwhile, as the sortie comparison between COMAIRSOLs (soon to become the Thirteenth Air Force) and Fifth Air Force suggest, South Pacific forces took the lead neutralizing Rabaul. By November 11 it was clear that the carrier air groups from Truk had exhausted themselves. On that date Koga ordered to Truk the fifty-two planes that were left. Emperor Hirohito issued an imperial rescript honoring achievements in the air battle, and Tokyo radio produced an amalgam of hopeful assertion and wild exaggeration. As recorded and translated by ONI, the gist of Radio Tokyo's perspective (as of November 19) was as follows:

> U.S. forces were perplexed by Japanese strategy, and the losses suffered by the U.S. Fleet are truly greater than those at Pearl Harbor. These great defeats have thrown MacArthur's Headquarters into a deep sense of insecurity and fear. . . . By conservative estimates, Tokyo places U.S. personnel loss at 18,000—counting the "instant" sinkings, deferred sinkings, and plane losses . . . and little or no damage [has been] suffered by Japan's side.

Somewhat more realistic was the assessment by Admiral Nomura Kichisaburo which Domei broadcast the same day: "Now the enemy's operations centering around the Solomons and New Guinea have suddenly become vigorous . . . we must take warning that hereafter America's counteroperations against Japan, with Anglo-American seapower as the root, will be hastened."

In fact Nomura was exactly right: The pressure against Rabaul built daily, especially once COMAIRSOLs took over the neutralization effort. In December 1943 the Japanese managed to get 400,000 tons of shipping into and out of Rabaul, landing precious cargoes of everything from food to uniforms, but the grind of daily strikes shrank that flow constantly. Rabaul had radar the Allies knew about, plus another secret installation, and there were Japanese coastwatchers at Buin and Empress Augusta Bay. The system provided an hour's warning of raids, on average. But fighter strength was constantly being worn down. The Eleventh Air Fleet was down to about 140 serviceable aircraft when MacArthur's troops landed at Cape Gloucester on New Britain. By the New Year the JNAF at Rabaul was down to 120–130 planes.

Naturally all the losses were not on one side; one of the more notable American ones came on January 2, 1944, when Major Gregory ("Pappy") Boyington was shot down over Simpson Harbor and was captured. The brash and swashbuckling commander of Marine Fighter Squadron 214, Pappy Boyington later was awarded the Medal of Honor for missions to Buin, and before his capture was top American ace in the Pacific, with twenty-six victories (this figure was later reevaluated and raised to twenty-eight).

American carriers raided Kavieng on New Year's Day and again on

January 4, while COMAIRSOLs put more than 230 aircraft over Rabaul on the seventh, when the JNAF scrambled seventy-four interceptors to meet them, and there were further large raids on January 14, 17, and 18. On January 23 an entry in the Imperial Navy's war diary notes, if one can believe such a thing, that the Rabaul raids were becoming more intense than ever.

Life at Rabaul amounted to daily crisis beneath a cascade of Allied aerial munitions. The Eleventh Air Fleet was just about burnt out, its 26th Air Flotilla worn by constant fights at long odds. Effective strength on January 19 stood at eighty fighters, thirty-two medium bombers, fifteen dive-bombers, and eleven torpedo planes, but 30 percent of the aircrews were sick, while rations had been cut back across the board, and no one at Rabaul was at peak performance. Once again Admiral Koga made the tough decision to commit carrier air groups to the maelstrom, this time simply for defense of Rabaul and to enable him to pull out the 26th Flotilla for rest and reorganization.

This time the candidates for the meat grinder were the men of Carrier Division 2. Their air officer was Okumiya Masatake, who had worked with the 26th at Buin the previous fall, and he hurried to visit his old friends after reaching Rabaul on January 25:

> The moment I passed through the door I realized something was wrong. Outwardly the staff personnel were the same. Nevertheless they had changed. Six months ago they were cheerful and hard workers, despite the rigors of life at Buin. Now they were quick-tempered and harsh, their faces grimly set. The fighting spirit which enabled us to ignore the worst of Buin was gone. The men lacked confidence; they appeared dull and apathetic. No longer were they the familiar well-functioning team.

Unlike the aircrew fighting every day at Rabaul, the Carrier Division 2 pilots had spent the past months training at Singapore, primarily Lingga Roads, the former British naval base. There had been no fighting, no worries about fuel; there was good food. As Americans might put it, the Carrier Division 2 pilots were full of piss and vinegar. But they had no combat experience, and Rabaul gave them no respite. The day after arrival Rear Admiral Joshima Takaji, commanding the unit, sent up ninety-two planes to intercept an American force over twice as large. On January 28 he sent up sixty-four fighters; on the twenty-ninth, sixty-three. So it went day after day.

The raids were incessant, day and night, from every direction and altitude. Okumiya soon learned exactly what had afflicted the flotilla staff his men had just replaced:

> It is one thing to know you have a mission to perform, but it is another to stay behind, at a desk, when the pride of Japanese manhood dies

because *you* have committed them to battle. Many of our top commanders would talk to no one for long periods of time; they could not help but reproach themselves for remaining alive at the expense of our young fliers.

And yet, absolutely nothing could be done to alleviate the situation. American air pressure increased steadily; even a momentary lapse in our air defense efforts might lose us Rabaul and our nearby fields. The endless days and nights became a nightmare. The young faces became only briefly familiar, then vanished forever in the bottomless abyss created by American guns. [Italics in the original.]

Not only Okumiya, but Joshima and Ozawa and Koga too realized that the sacrifice of the air groups could not go on, especially if the Imperial Navy wished to preserve anything of its carrier air arm. On February 20 remnants of the air groups evacuated to Truk. They were the last significant JNAF presence Rabaul would ever see. After February 1944 the vaunted Solomons bastion lay naked before American power.

Ironically it was only then, at the end perhaps, that Japanese staff officers began to understand the real cost of the challenge to the American giant mounted so blithely in 1941. Rabaul had become the post for many former NGS and Combined Fleet staffers who had roles in the earlier events. These men included Baron Tomioka, who rose to chief of staff under Kusaka Jinichi; Tachibana Itaru, *joho kyoku* spy; Sanagi Sadamu, NGS operations officer. There were others as well. Even Kusaka Ryunosuke, Jinichi's cousin and éminence grise to the commander of the Pearl Harbor strike, played a bit part at Rabaul on temporary duty under the Southeast Area Fleet commander. Some, like Baron Tomioka, would be recalled to the Naval General Staff or other posts, but 90,000 Japanese remained at Rabaul, beleaguered, right through the end of the war.

Kusaka Jinichi insists the morale of his Navy men never wavered. He kept them busy farming, to make Rabaul self-sufficient; training; fortifying; and producing munitions. Anti-aircraft ammunition became the worst problem and had to be carefully husbanded, but dud bombs were stripped to provide powder, and defective munitions could be repaired or ersatz anti-invasion weapons constructed. If captured explosives ran out, there was plenty of sulfur and carbon around Rabaul due to its active volcanoes; only nitrate remained scarce.

Imperial Navy men kept busy dreaming up schemes to help Japan despite their isolation. Kusaka had Radio Tokyo make certain broadcasts intended to challenge Allied forces to an invasion of Rabaul. At least one airfield was kept in commission until June 1945, and the fields were repeatedly used during the period. There were occasional transport planes from the Empire; on a number of occasions aircraft staged through Rabaul to scout places inaccessible from other Japanese bases; and the garrison themselves cannibalized wrecked aircraft at least twice to produce airworthy bombers. A floatplane from Rabaul made a night attack at Manus Island as late as August 1945.

A report to Tokyo in November 1944 stressed Rabaul's move underground to counter Thirteenth Air Force bombing. Storage areas were built fifteen yards underground, caves were opened (140 statute miles' worth) for everything from barracks to hospitals. The Japanese dug antitank ditches and improvised hand grenades and dischargers, mortars, mines, flamethrowers, and suicide boats. Training emphasis was put on close-quarter combat. Editors of a JICPOA intelligence publication introduced a translation of this report with the comment: "This document indicates that the CO at Rabaul is striking for a posthumous promotion."

In fact the Japanese at Rabaul were very much alive, and would remain so. But they would also be stuck for a very long time. Far from being the bastion of the South Pacific war, Rabaul became a backwater, left behind as the battlefront surged straight toward the Empire. Admiral Kusaka could do nothing about it. Baron Tomioka returned to the Naval General Staff but found that his Rabaul experience applied there as well: There was precious little he could do to turn back a ferocious Allied onslaught. For Japan the Greater East Asia war had come full circle.

# PART IV

## BY

## FORCE

## OF

## ARMS

T HE WAR ENTERED A NEW PHASE IN THE FALL OF 1943, IN WHICH AMERICAN INDUSTRIAL power made itself the engine of victory in the Pacific. Intelligence continued to be important, guiding Allied operations, preventing major disasters, and in particular providing marching orders for the submarine forces that brought the Japanese Empire closer and closer to the edge of the abyss. But intelligence no longer made the difference between victory and defeat. The armies, task forces, and air forces grew steadily stronger, and it was not long before they attained virtually unassailable strength.

These developments showed clearly in Admiral Chester Nimitz's campaign in the Central Pacific. It had been planned somewhat tentatively in early 1943 and begun with a certain confidence that fall; within a matter of months surging American strength enabled Nimitz to accelerate operations. Soon the task forces were challenging the very centers of Japanese power, while the momentum of the invasions became such that the Americans had to telescope their plans, abandoning objectives once thought important in favor of leaping even further ahead.

As the Allied offensive gathered momentum and strength, Japanese intelligence organs, inadequate as they were, acquired greater importance. Even poor intelligence provided crucial warnings that saved the fleet more than once, and prevented strategic surprise at the hands of the Allies in some of the biggest amphibious operations of the war. Intelligence alerted the Empire against the very heavy B-29 bombers, contributing so much to air defense that American authorities grew to suspect a leak and carried out their own investigations.

Ironically, the Japanese intelligence effort, becoming increasingly sophisticated by 1944–1945, was to a great degree squandered due to wastage in the fleet. Even perfect intelligence is useless without forces to take advantage of it, and the Imperial Navy was bumping up against the operational constraints imposed by losses it had suffered. Apart from the painful attrition of their biggest warships, the Japanese lost forty destroyers in the Solomons alone during 1942–1943. That amounted to a large fraction (two fifths) of prewar inventory and could not be made good by new construction, which totaled nine ships in 1942 and fifteen during 1943. The losses endangered every type of activity. A battle fleet that had stayed in port awaiting optimal conditions for Decisive Battle suddenly found itself gravely disadvantaged in such an engagement due to the weakness of its escort forces. Likewise, convoy movements, transport missions, and surface sorties had to be conducted with inadequate force at ever-increasing risk. Even submarine cruises were endangered by the combination of Allied intelligence and growing force.

Japan's progression to defeat acquired the inexorability of a swinging pendulum. Allied intelligence exacted virtual attrition from the Imperial Navy, frustrating its purposes and obstructing operations. Failure of conventional means then forced the Japanese into extraordinary measures. The use of destroyers and submarines for transport and supply missions—which had been an expedient for emergency situations in 1942—had become the standard mechanism for combat resupply by 1944. The increased use of these vessels in turn put them in greater peril, with Allied intelligence providing plentiful opportunities to extract an extra measure of destruction at every stage.

Ultimately the Japanese battle fleet, steaming into its long-awaited encounter, would itself be greatly hampered by the warships that were not there, by the missing legions of drowned sailors. As those sailors, ships, and planes expired in the nets cast by Allied intelligence, the Great Pacific War came to its climax.

# Hailstones and Hammerblows

T HROUGHOUT THE PROCESS OF PLANNING THE ALLIED ADVANCE ACROSS THE CENTRAL Pacific, intelligence remained at the fore. There was considerable concern about the strength the Japanese could build against prospective attacks in various theaters. One of the earliest of these intelligence projections, in October 1942, involved the Office of Naval Intelligence estimating the scale of Japanese air effort that might oppose an invasion of Burma. Naval intelligence estimated a number based on carrier-based and land-based JNAF strength, then cautioned that Japanese losses in other areas (principally the Solomons) made this scale of effort unlikely in Burma. By spring 1943 such reaction projections were being made for offensives into the Central Pacific as well as in the Philippine–Netherlands East Indies area.

Estimates for a Central Pacific campaign were thus appearing at the planning level months before there was any actual fighting in that theater. In late April the Far East branch of ONI projected Japanese reaction to an offensive under two contingencies: that Rabaul had already fallen, or that it had not. The ONI listed forces available in the area, both those that might arrive within a day or two, and those that could be expected four or five days after the beginning of the offensive. Since the Combined Fleet's base at Truk dominated the Central Pacific, for both contingencies most Japanese naval forces were already in the area, including five battleships, four aircraft carriers, ten cruisers, and an equal number of destroyers. Postinvasion reinforcement could provide up to seven battleships, six carriers, twenty heavy and light cruisers, and thirty-two destroyers a week or so after commencement of operations. If Rabaul had fallen already, additional light cruisers, destroyers, and submarines would become available since they would no longer be fighting with the Southeast Area Fleet. As for JNAF aircraft, roughly 200 carrier-based and about 300 land-based or seaplane aircraft were believed available in the area with much smaller numbers arriving later.

These theoretical estimates seemed to evaporate, however, when it became a matter of telling the planners exactly what the opposition would be. Responding to a request from the Joint Intelligence Committee, on May 31 ONI outlined Imperial Navy capabilities in the Marshalls and Gilberts, as well as the eastern Mandates, in very stark terms. The Far East branch noted that Jaluit was an important submarine base, usually with several I-boats being serviced and six to ten submarines on average in the area, while light cruisers *Kashima* and *Katori*, which traveled periodically between Truk and Jaluit, might be there too. The 6th Base Force, with command responsibility for the Marshalls and Gilberts, had a mere one or two destroyers plus the ancient (1899 vintage) minelayer *Tokiwa* and a number of converted patrol vessels. Air strength estimates given in another paper to the JIC amounted to forty-eight JNAF fighters, forty-two bombers, twenty-seven seaplanes, and ten patrol bombers, a force dispersed throughout the area and constantly shifting from one base to another.

The Far East branch did another reaction projection on June 12, in which it analyzed the contingencies of an Aleutian advance, one through Wake toward Eniwetok, a Marshalls-Gilberts operation, and an offensive staged from Rabaul directly into the Carolines. Necessary preconditions for the latter never existed, so that option can be bypassed, while the Aleutian advance was already in progress and would trigger Japanese retreat. Analysts at ONI believed an advance through Wake "would be resisted most vigorously," and Admiral Koga's fleet operations that fall bore them out. The ONI analysts also observed that "in all probability, the Japanese would consider the defense of the Marshalls of prime strategic importance," and predicted that JNAF aircraft would be brought from the Empire and elsewhere in Melanesia to augment local resources. A large fleet and air reaction was tabulated which, though it differed in detail from the April projections, was of similar magnitude.

None of the projections deterred Admiral Nimitz or his planners. By mid-July CINCPAC had a preliminary operations plan incorporating invasions of Makin and Tarawa, in the Gilberts, and the Marshalls. That same month an Anglo-American conference at Quebec accepted the Central Pacific advance as a next-stage operation, accelerating the schedule from 1944 to the fall of 1943. The speed-up in turn required use of troops from the South Pacific, so Major General Julian C. Smith's 2nd Marine Division was earmarked for the operation, which got the code name Galvanic. Intelligence projections show that the Navy always expected Galvanic to be hotly contested by the Japanese; therefore the targets cannot have been chosen because "the planners believed the operations would not be difficult."* Nor was planning rushed as others have maintained—the 2nd Marine Division began work on its tactical plans in the summer; the invasion forces had longer to prepare than had the invaders of Guadalcanal. Critics base the charge of rushed plans on later experience and hindsight, and ignore the fact that a lengthened planning process would have given the Japanese more time to reinforce and fortify the target atolls. In fact, there was enough planning to canvass a variety of objectives, and the Americans dropped an initial intention to make Nauru one of Galvanic's targets. That turned out to be helpful, because Combined Fleet intelligence expected a landing at Nauru, so the Japanese were increasing the defenses of that place.

Intelligence watched the Japanese carefully as the countdown to invasion proceeded. The picture that emerged would prove instructive.

As the planners cogitated, putting together an unstoppable invasion, naval officers at sea got on with the war. Some of the toughest but most productive activities were those of American submariners. Though still plagued by defective torpedoes, the subs were beginning to take a toll of Japanese shipping. They were especially assisted by radio intelligence, which was reading the Truk portmaster's code, as well as the merchant shipping code, and could furnish prospective locations of targets to subs on the basis of those codes and of messages sent in JN-25. Between May and July of 1943 radio intelligence enabled American submariners to make contact with Japanese fleet units eighteen times and attack eight of these contacts, damaging carriers *Hiyo, Unyo,* and *Taiyo,* as well as sinking the submarine *I-24.*

Admiral Nimitz at Pearl Harbor pressed strongly for long-range photo reconnaissance of the Marshalls and Gilberts, and submarines played an important role in the intelligence effort leading up to Galvanic. Details can be tracked in weekly estimates starting early in September by the intelligence unit soon to be renamed JICPOA. There were unusually large numbers of ships at Kwajalein, according to submarine reconnaissance on September 9, and six days later a scout sub reported two light cruisers and four destroyers there still. Submarine photographs of Makin and Tarawa were also of value to Galvanic planners.†

Radio intelligence remained the basis for most of the JICPOA weekly

---

*From the earliest of the JICPOA estimate series on the Marshalls and Gilberts, intelligence was projecting troop strength of 2,000–2,500 on Tarawa, including 1,500 SNLF infantry. The estimate increased to a flat 2,500 in the October 4, 1943, issue, and beginning on October 11, JICPOA raised that again to "possibly 3,500," a number still not exactly matching true Japanese strength.

†Although planners may have thought that pre-invasion scouting in the Aleutians by

reports, however. On September 13 the report noted Admiral Ozawa in the Truk vicinity with the major portion of Imperial Navy surface strength, and observed that he would have available only two big carriers and one light one. Three of the listed total of seven carriers in the Truk area "are quite definitely on plane ferry trips." The September 27 report, following the sortie by Ozawa and Kurita's forces, carried this timely observation: "It is believed that elements of the Japanese Striking Force were in the vicinity of Eniwetok early in the week. This force is believed to have been transient and to have returned to Truk." Subsequent weekly reports carried details of Japanese submarine activities in Hawaiian waters and of Imperial Navy response to the Wake Island carrier raids. The JICPOA weekly report missed Koga's fleet sortie in late October, but on November 1 noted his return to Truk, and on the eighth, with less than two weeks to go before Galvanic, helpfully observed: "The situation in the Marshalls-Gilberts appears to remain virtually unchanged. For the present the Solomons and New Britain appear to be absorbing most of the Japanese efforts." With one week left the word was, "It is believed there are no important naval units now in the Marshalls-Gilberts area other than several submarines."

The lead echelons of invasion ships left Pearl Harbor as early as October 21, while in the week prior to Galvanic B-24 bombers hit Tarawa and Makin every day. More than 200 ships carried 108,000 sailors and soldiers of the 2nd Marine Division and the Army's 27th Infantry Division. The landings came on November 20. Makin was overwhelmed in four days; Tarawa, tenaciously defended by 4,500 naval troops (including over 2,600 SNLF) under Rear Admiral Shibasaki Keiji, fell in three days of bloody combat. Only seventeen Japanese sailors were taken prisoner.* Contemplating the stiff losses the Marines suffered at Tarawa (1,027 dead, 2,292 wounded, 88

---

the submarine *Nautilus* and others posed impediments to antisubmarine activity, in fact their intelligence contribution proved so valuable that submarine reconnaissance became a standard technique. Richmond Kelly Turner asked for sub photos before leading the Galvanic forces to their targets, and *Nautilus* went out again. Lieutenant Commander R. B. Lynch, executive officer of the sub, happened to be a photo hobbyist, and ended up demonstrating to the boat's captain, Commander W. D. Irvin, that the purpose-built cameras they carried were not as good as his handheld Primarflex for periscope photography of shoreline objects. The Primarflex was a German-made camera and obviously impossible to procure during the war. The Navy ended up advertising in photography magazines for donations. Eventually ten Primarflex cameras were contributed by patriotic photographers and stored at PRISIC at Pearl Harbor, whence they were issued to subs headed out on reconnaissance missions. The *Nautilus* set the standard for subsequent efforts of this kind.

*The prisoners included two survivors of the submarine *I-35*, sunk off Tarawa by U.S. destroyers *Frazier* and *Meade* on November 22, as well as seven SNLF infantrymen and eight laborers.

missing), observers complain the Japanese were able to build up on Tarawa as a result of Colonel Carlson's Makin raid of August 1942. Comments of senior Japanese officers rejecting that assertion have already been noted. Here it is sufficient to remark that the bulk of Japanese combat strength on Tarawa, comprising the 7th Sasebo SNLF, was created and dispatched to the Gilberts only in early 1943. Further, a contingent of 2,300 Japanese Army troops, whose arrival at Kwajalein was highlighted in the JICPOA weekly estimates, never moved to Tarawa, as they might have had the Japanese taken warning from such things as the October carrier strikes on that atoll. The Army troops remained at Kwajalein as a strategic reserve for all the Marshalls and Gilberts, in consonance with Fourth Fleet invasion reaction plans, but when the invasion came they were not used.

In fact there was no question of activating preplanned schemes for meeting an American offensive in the Central Pacific. Fourth Fleet warships sailed to Kwajalein, where they could pick up the Army troops for a counterlanding; but before they even arrived at the intermediate point, Tarawa had fallen. Admiral Koga had also by this time expended his carrier air groups at Rabaul, so there was no committing Ozawa's striking force. Kurita's Second Fleet cruisers had been smashed by the air strikes on Rabaul too, so Combined Fleet's battleships had few other major vessels to constitute a balanced force.

When the Fourth Fleet transport element moved up to Kwajalein, Admiral Koga did support them with a cruiser force, but it was a shadow of the fleet Kurita had taken to Rabaul. This time Kurita had just three heavy cruisers—*Chokai, Kumano,* and *Chikuma*—plus six or eight destroyers. Had he met the Americans he could have done little other than run away. Instead, Kurita visited Kwajalein and Eniwetok on a cruise that lasted from November 24 to December 7. During that interval Fourth Fleet cruisers on "rat" runs transported extra troops to Mille and Maloelap atolls in the Marshalls north of Makin.

Koga's actual efforts to interfere with the American operation were limited to land-based aircraft and submarines. The JNAF sent up almost seventy extra planes from Truk over several days. According to Commander Matsura Goro, staff officer of the 22nd Air Flotilla in this region, the reinforcements were from the 24th Flotilla and flew down from Hokkaido and the Kuriles. Matsura recalls seeing Kurita's cruisers at Wotje, and remembers that the first warning of the approach of Galvanic forces came from Nauru-based search planes the day before the invasion. The first sighting of actual amphibious ships came only on the very morning of the landings. Prior to that, so far as the Japanese knew, the Americans might simply have come for another carrier raid.

The Japanese proved themselves adept at night torpedo attacks using light from flares dropped during an initial pass. Ozawa Jisaburo later told

Samuel Eliot Morison he had innovated these tactics as early as 1940. The Americans countered by setting up carrier air squadrons of night fighters (and later even whole groups), but these were as yet experimental during Galvanic. Sixteen torpedo bombers from Kwajalein and Maloelap delivered the counterattack the initial night of the invasion. Although carriers *Essex* and *Bunker Hill* emerged unscathed and half the attacking planes were shot down, light carrier *Independence* suffered damage enough to force her to withdraw for repairs. Several more attacks followed on subsequent nights, until a final futile effort on November 28. The relevant Japanese monograph puts the overall JNAF effort at 764 sorties (373 by medium bombers) between the time of Galvanic and the end of the year. The monograph puts losses at eighty-five; Captain Ohmae Toshikazu enumerates 152 aircraft lost during this period (sixty-one fighters, fifty-eight medium bombers, twenty-one dive-bombers, twenty scout planes, and a patrol bomber); Morison accepts the number 101. All these figures include planes lost defending other Japanese-held islands and those not returning from search missions as well as losses attacking the American fleet.

From cruiser *Katori*, Sixth Fleet flagship then at Truk, Vice Admiral Takagi Takeo ordered his submarines to form five different patrol lines. Some skippers thought the flow of messages confusing and counterproductive. In all eight I-boats and one smaller Ro-boat operated against the Galvanic forces, and six of them perished. One of the losses, *I-40*, on her first war patrol following shakedown at Kure, was commanded by Watanabe Katsuji. Commander Watanabe was the submariner who had been caught in a minefield off Pearl Harbor the first night of the war. This time he did not make it back. Though U.S. destroyer *Radford* is usually credited with sinking the *I-40* on November 25, Japanese sub skipper Orita Zenji believes it was the *I-19* that succumbed to the tin can. Orita does not give details of the *I-40* loss beyond noting she did not respond on December 3, when Admiral Takagi ordered all boats to report in.

The one significant accomplishment of the submarine force during Galvanic came in the early-morning hours of November 24, when Commander Tabata Sunao in the *I-175* torpedoed the escort carrier *Liscome Bay*. The ship sank with a loss of almost 650 American sailors. Tabata's I-boat was damaged by counterattacking destroyers, but she safely reached Truk.

Galvanic should be noted also for certain intelligence developments. During this operation JICPOA for the first time provided expert teams to accompany the assault forces, both for immediate interrogation of prisoners and to identify and preserve valuable documents. Each team consisted of a language officer, one officer from JICPOA's Enemy Bases section, a ground forces specialist, a photographer, and an enlisted man. One team landed right behind the assault forces on Makin, another on Tarawa. At the latter, experience showed that having just one language officer was insufficient since that man was constantly being diverted by field commanders' demands for tactical intelligence. The Tarawa team nevertheless was able to gather enough data from interrogations and documents, plus examination of the battlefield, to publish a study complete with sketches and photographs, classified "confidential," which JICPOA titled "Study of Japanese Defenses of Betio Island of Tarawa Atoll." Material from the study soon found its way into a new War Department field manual on Japanese forces and tactics.

At Makin the JICPOA intelligence team uncovered a treasure trove that again illustrated Japanese carelessness with respect to information security. Though the Japanese garrison numbered only 300 and its highest-ranking officer was merely a lieutenant, Makin proved a repository for baskets full of sensitive documents. Among the materials were copies of Fourth Fleet standing orders for resisting invasion, order-of-battle materials, supply data, diaries, and so on. An important document the JICPOA team missed was a Japanese codebook one sailor took as a souvenir, later to be discovered during a routine barracks inspection in Hawaii. Commander Dyer was mortified when he received the codebook, for the Japanese had continued using that code for several weeks during Galvanic but had retired it before the book came into his possession. In any case, Galvanic produced significant intelligence knowledge.

Those gains were only magnified by Flintlock, the next big amphibious operation. That would be to Kwajalein, although there had been interest in taking Maloelap and Wotje until Admiral Nimitz insisted on going right for the centerpiece of the Marshalls chain. There were 8,400 Japanese Navy and Army troops on Kwajalein's islets; the Americans landed 42,500 men of the 4th Marine and 7th Infantry divisions in one of the war's most successful amphibious assaults. The Japanese forces were eliminated at a cost of just 1,800 casualties while separate invasion forces also captured the atolls of Majuro and Eniwetok. By the third week of February the campaign was all over.

Once again there were advances made during Marshalls operations by intelligence practitioners of the traditional, not newfangled techniques. For Flintlock Admiral Nimitz strengthened the hand of the field intelligence teams by issuing instructions that reversed previous procedures: Rather than JICPOA depending upon items turned in by the combat units, now any item of captured equipment or any document or other item to be retained by a unit or individual had to be seen, approved, and stamped as approved by the JICPOA field teams. An extra officer and an enlisted man were added to each team to handle the additional workload.

Benefiting from arrangements made in the wake of the Gilberts operations to move captured documents immediately to JICPOA for translation and dissemination, by the time of Flintlock the system was well oiled. This proved fortunate, for JICPOA sources describe the flow of captured material from the Marshalls as a flood. Fortunately, too, Pearl Harbor had just received a contingent of thirty additional Japanese-language officers trained at Boulder who were pressed into immediate service with the Translation Section.

Of key import among documents captured in the Marshalls were several on Japanese radar equipment, techniques, and maintenance. One was an August 1943 secret manual on "electrical ranging technique," as the Imperial Navy called it, published by Yokosuka Naval Communications School. Another document JICPOA captured, translated, and published was a February 1943 reference manual on underwater sound gear from the Imperial Navy's mine school. This manual probably was on Kwajalein because of the atoll's previous status as principal Japanese submarine base. The volume, Mine School Reference Book Number 21, classified "very secret" by the Imperial Navy, contained specifications of Japanese antisubmarine warfare equipment, mathematical formulae underlying their principles of operation, and comments on desirable tactical methods. From this, American submariners could infer much about Japanese Navy antisubmarine warfare doctrine.

There were more gains from prisoner interrogation, as was becoming usual. Although 165 of the 265 prisoners taken on Kwajalein were Korean laborers, about fifty of the remainder were Imperial Navy sailors. Another sixty-four Japanese were made prisoners at Eniwetok. Of course senior Japanese officers were dead, among them Vice Admiral Akiyama Monzo, former defender of the Aleutians, come to Kwajalein to head the 6th Base Force in charge of both Gilberts and Marshalls. That formation came to its end with Flintlock.

The erstwhile diplomat and perceptive Japanese naval commentator Nomura Kichisaburo, in the face of Tokyo's wartime press restrictions, uttered the truth for all to hear. "They are searching the outer perimeter of Japan and trying to break down one corner of it," Admiral Nomura said just days before the Tarawa invasion. "This is the island-to-island, or the island leap-frog tactic." Reacting to the Flintlock operations in early 1944, Nomura noted in a Japanese newspaper that the South Pacific had really demonstrated American impatience, that the Central Marshalls were "the central route of advance."

The Japanese had not expected to be bypassed on such islands as Jaluit, Wotje, and Maloelap. They also did not expect to be hit the way they were by the now-mighty Task Force 58. Indeed, as the Americans mopped up the last defenders of Kwajalein, that carrier unit was already moving three of its four groups into the heart of the Mandates. The target—Truk—would have been unimaginable just a few short months before. In his newspaper article Admiral Nomura wrote that America's moves into the Marshalls compelled

Japan to consider "that the enemy will no doubt come with almost all his main strength in the Pacific participating." It is uncanny that at that precise moment Task Force 58 was preparing to assault the Combined Fleet's great base in the *nanyo*.

HAGIMOTO TOSHIO HAD JUST TWENTY DAYS IN THE NAVY AS A RESERVE SEAMAN WHEN HE and a hundred other sailors went aboard the crowded *Asakaze Maru* at Yokosuka one day in October 1943. Some of his equally inexperienced comrades joked about seeing Davy Jones's locker before their destination, but while passage was dangerous, going to sea had not yet become the terrifying experience of a year later. Their convoy was attacked, but it was another ship that was hit, and that one only damaged. *Asakaze Maru* towed the derelict to Saeki, then left again for the *nanyo* under escort by destroyer *Ikazuchi*. Hagimoto and others used to stay on deck late into the night, watching the stars and the phosphorescent jellyfish in the ship's wake. When they arrived at Truk, "we could see the fleet at anchor, a sight more impressive and magnificent than we had been prepared to see."

The fresh recruits reported to Dublon Island, in the Truk group, where Fourth Fleet headquarters was located. Their ship lingered at Truk ten days, then went on to the Marshalls, only to be sunk on the way by an American submarine. The sailors were separated into three groups for basic training. In January 1944, when Hagimoto completed this training, he was assigned to an anti-aircraft position on Fefan Island which immediately overlooked the fleet anchorage. He had only a few days to enjoy the sight of the Imperial Navy at anchor, however, because the warships began to disappear from Truk's lagoon.

Some movements were routine, such as the voyages of aircraft ferries leaving to pick up more planes for delivery to the front. Such warship activities were becoming increasingly dangerous as Allied intelligence used its mastery over Japanese codes to set up submarine attacks. During November and December 1943, for example, there were at least six torpedo attacks on major vessels of the Imperial Navy, in particular carriers, and the small carrier *Chuyo* was sunk. Even the *Yamato* was not immune—she had to give up a mission and return to Yokosuka after being hit in the bow by two torpedoes. By January 1944, though, the *Yamato*'s damage had been repaired and she was back at Truk. Carrier *Shokaku* underwent two torpedo attacks during a mid-January voyage from the Empire to Truk. Admiral Koga was undoubtedly on notice that his fleet base was threatened.

Threatened it was. As early as September 21, 1943, the CINCPAC war diary records Nimitz's planning groups at work on exploratory studies for capture of Truk. By October 16, notes the same source, the planners had completed detailed studies of Flintlock and switched to the view that Truk itself could be safely bypassed. The specific idea for a carrier raid on Truk, Operation Hailstone, was in hand by Halloween, although it was at first timed to occur between the Gilberts and Marshalls invasions. Task Force 58's carrier groups fully occupied themselves in support of the invasions, as it turned out, but after that they were free to execute Hailstone. Admiral Raymond Spruance, commanding the Fifth Fleet, of which Task Force 58 was the major striking element, issued his orders for the Truk raid on February 9, 1944. Flying his flag in the powerful new battleship *New Jersey,* Spruance left Majuro with a force comprising nine carriers, seven fast battleships, ten cruisers, and twenty-eight destroyers. Spruance exercised loose control over the fleet because Task Force 58 was in good hands under direct command of Rear Admiral Marc A. Mitscher.

Meanwhile, Japanese suspicions were kindled as a result of the Marshalls invasions. In part the losses the Owada Group suffered on the islands the Americans captured turned its attention to the area. On February 2 Owada temporarily assumed radio intelligence duties formerly assigned Kwajalein in the Japanese scheme, including reporting on activities around Hawaii. On February 4 the 1st Combined Communications Unit at Saipan, the main field command for intelligence, reported a need for at least one officer and fifteen additional radio operators to permit Wake and Nauru to take over the jobs previously done at Kwajalein.

A key indicator for Admiral Koga was an overflight over Truk the same day, February 4, by two American B-24 bombers, obviously photo planes. The aircraft, actually Marine planes from Bougainville, of Squadron VMD-254, were first seen from the *Musashi,* which opened fire unsuccessfully with anti-aircraft guns. The B-24s returned some of the first photographs of Truk taken since the start of the war, and at the upper end of one of them interpreters found the shape of the huge battleship. That picture ignited renewed debate over the tonnage and armament of the Japanese superbattleships,* but in the meantime the scout sortie furnished important information for Operation Hailstone.

In any case Admiral Koga took warning from activities in the Marshalls

---

*On February 25 the Truk photos were processed at PRISIC in Pearl Harbor; one picture showed the huge ship, obscured at the corner. The Office of Naval Intelligence brought ship-design experts into the discussion, concluding that the *Yamato* class must displace at least 60,000 tons. That also was the size experts thought necessary to mount 18-inch guns, but the same people argued that problems of stowage and propulsion, plus complications with docking and navigation, would render such a warship impractical. A Seventh Fleet intelligence officer was given this word just before returning to SOWESPAC, then passed through Pearl Harbor, where he talked to Eddie Layton. Previously a staunch defender of the proposition the *Yamatos* had only 16-inch weapons, Layton was by this time interrogating prisoner Noda Mitsuharu, former yeoman to Admiral

and the recon mission. He sent Kurita with battleships *Yamato* and *Nagato* plus units of the Second Fleet off to Palau on February 3. A week later Koga himself sailed for Japan in the *Musashi* together with a light cruiser and several destroyers. Koga's departure apparently followed key warnings from the Owada Group, for OP-20-G's radio intelligence summaries noted on February 10 a "sensational rise in the volume" of message traffic related to direction finding—28 percent of *all* Japanese Navy messages in the code system—following the preceeding day's levels, which had surpassed "all previous peaks ever recorded in this system"; meanwhile, tactical traffic was up only slightly and most other circuits showed little change. The summary remarked that there was no evidence that Second Fleet commander Kurita was still at Truk, though some associations placed him in its vicinity, while on the eleventh the report indicated evidence that Koga and *Musashi* had left too. This would be confirmed by an intercept reported on February 13.

During the final days before Hailstone the Americans remained in some confusion as to what prey they might actually find at Truk. Most notable were questions as to the presence of Admiral Kurita's Second Fleet. After doubting Kurita's presence, OP-20-G on February 11 again placed him at Truk together with cruisers *Haguro*, *Myoko*, *Naka*, *Oyodo*, and *Katori*, ten destroyers, and possibly light carrier *Zuiho*. On the other hand, JICPOA in Hawaii, which published a weekly "Estimate of Enemy Distribution and Intentions," maintained in its report of February 7 that there had been no "convincing evidence" of the whereabouts of Kurita or the Imperial Navy's battleship (First) fleet commander since the beginning of the month. Hawaii estimated on the basis of submarine reports that the battleships were en route to the Empire and specifically cited the aerial reconnaissance mission as showing "fewer cruisers and destroyers than expected." Significantly, JICPOA estimated that "the Combined Fleet Radio Intelligence unit has moved from Rabaul to Truk."

The last JICPOA estimate to appear before the execution of Hailstone came out on February 14. It projected both Combined and First Fleet commanders in Empire waters, Second Fleet unlocated, the carriers in the Empire. Only the Fourth Fleet commander was placed at Truk. Thus:

> Best estimates place all of the battleships and the majority of the carriers in the Empire. This estimate is based on incomplete information but is

---

Yamamoto. Noda repeated many jokes current in the Imperial Navy about the "special type" 16-inch guns of *Yamato*, converting Layton. Still, *The ONI Weekly* on August 30 carried a feature on Japanese naval guns discounting the possibility of the larger size for *Yamato*, and still listing her at 40,000 tons. The first reasonable accurate artist's conception of the appearance of the Yamato appeared in *The ONI Weekly* on September 20, based directly on the Truk photo.

believed to be fairly reliable. . . . This distribution is unusual. It might be explained by Japanese lack of confidence in the future security of Truk as a fleet base.

The estimate proved exactly correct on the broad outlines of Japanese activities though inaccurate on the details of warships in the Carolines, expecting three carriers, eight heavy and six light cruisers, and twenty-two destroyers. Actual numbers were much lower.

Both Washington and Pearl Harbor erred on the subject of Imperial Navy aircraft carriers at Truk. The mistake is a good illustration of the limitations of radio intelligence. Both American authorities placed at Truk ships of Carrier Division 2, no doubt because its air groups had been addressed in various messages. In actuality, as already seen, these air groups had been fighting on land at Rabaul and had just withdrawn to land bases at Truk. Radio intelligence could not distinguish Carrier Division 2 air groups from parent ships. Admiral Mitscher's pilots would soon learn the truth as they arrived over Truk.

The senior air commander at Truk was Rear Admiral Hasegawa Kiichi of the 22nd Air Flotilla, recently moved up from Tinian. Hasegawa was no slouch; he was an experienced air officer who had been a section chief at naval air headquarters, a training unit commander, a field commander in the northeast area, and skipper of carrier *Akagi* during the Pearl Harbor attack. Now Hasegawa came as close as anyone to unraveling the truth about the American codebreakers: According to a traffic analysis specialist at Melbourne, FRUMEL intercepted a message indicating suspicion the D Code (JN-25) had been broken. The suspicion was based on the way a certain tanker had been sunk right outside the entrance to Kwajalein after the Japanese had sent several messages related to her route. The message to Tokyo pointed out that the tanker's destination could have been revealed simply by reading headings on the dispatches. When FRUMEL specialists looked up the relevant traffic, the messages had indeed been intercepted and they had been reported out to the submarine force in exactly the way the Japanese admiral speculated.

Unfortunately for the Imperial Navy, Hailstone smothered Truk, preoccupying Hasegawa, and before he could make an issue of his suspicions the carrier raid killed him.

In the meantime Admiral Hasegawa's operations brought the Japanese the few successes they got from Truk during this period. On February 12 a half-dozen 22nd Air Flotilla patrol bombers from Saipan staged through Ponape to bomb the huge supply dump U.S. Marines had set up on one of Kwajalein's islets. Eighty percent of the supplies were destroyed in the resulting fire, along with several ships; twenty-five men were killed, and 130 injured. Marines were forced onto emergency rations for two weeks.

Hailstone itself would only be revealed the night of the attack when a search plane found Task Force 58 northeast of Truk. Hasegawa apparently got six bombers into the air to attack the intruders, but the planes never returned.

By that time much of Truk was a smoking ruin, for Admiral Mitscher had choreographed a day-long series of strong strikes, thirty in all, every one of them more powerful than the Japanese waves sent against Pearl Harbor. Leading off with a big fighter sweep to cripple opposition, the Americans pretty much had their way. Resistance was further hobbled because Hasegawa had his headquarters on one islet while the main fighter bases were on others. Moreover, the bulk of fighter strength belonged to the 26th Air Flotilla, which was at Truk for training and had never been subordinated to the local air command. The 26th Flotilla's own commander happened to be in Tokyo that day.

Truk boasted three well-maintained radars, but the American strikes came in at low level, only climbing to attack at the last moment. This tactic too no doubt owed something to intelligence, for it demonstrated fine appreciation of the operating characteristics of Japanese radar.

The first warning of attack was a white flare sent up from the comfortable tropical building which served as Fourth Fleet headquarters on Dublon Island. Seaman Hagimoto recalls that the anti-aircraft crews were at their places before dawn, since "word had already reached us of an enemy task force in the Caroline waters." The first wave of Americans—the sweeping fighters—was overhead within ten minutes of the flare warning. There are no surviving JNAF records, and estimates of the number of interceptors that actually got off the ground that day range from about twenty-five to sixty-six. Estimates of the number shot down range from twenty-five to thirty-four. American losses in two days of air attacks amounted to twelve fighters, seven torpedo bombers, and six dive-bombers, with eight of the total crashes or other noncombat losses.

Damage to shipping and bases was considerable. Light cruiser *Agano*, which had sought to escape ahead of the deluge, succumbed to a submarine. A destroyer, an aircraft ferry, sub tenders, auxiliary cruisers, six tankers, and seventeen merchantmen were sunk in harbor. Some accounts maintain that the bulk of the shipping caught at Truk was assigned to the Japanese Army and thus had not received Imperial Navy orders to vacate the base. Fourth Fleet headquarters, most of the communications center on Dublon, the majority of supplies, and the submarine base on Eten were all destroyed.

Meanwhile, Admiral Spruance had taken tactical control of a surface action group, including battleships *New Jersey* and *Iowa*, and was circumnavigating the atoll to bombard it and catch any ships attempting to flee. Spruance's staff desperately wished he would relinquish direct command, for the admiral had not handled ships in a long time and they wanted no part of the aftermath if he got a battleship hung up on some reef or stuck in a minefield. Attention shifted quickly to Truk's North Pass exit when light cruiser *Katori* and destroyer *Maikaze* emerged headed north. Both sank under a hail of gunfire, but not before *Maikaze* got off torpedoes that barely missed the American battleships, passing between the *New Jersey* and the following *Iowa.*

On the flag bridge of the *New Jersey,* Admiral Spruance turned to radio intelligence officer Gilven Slonim and said, "We better make sure that never happens again!"

The last Japanese victim was the destroyer *Oite,* sent out to recover survivors from the previously sunk *Agano,* bombed under before she could even clear the North Pass.

Imperial General Headquarters admitted the loss of two cruisers and three destroyers when it commented on the Truk attack in a February 22 communiqué. The release also put aircraft losses at 120 (more realistic than usual, though still far from U.S. estimates, which ranged from 230 to 280) and merchant ships lost at thirteen. On the other hand IGHQ claimed to have sunk an aircraft carrier, a battleship, and two cruisers, and also to have destroyed forty-five aircraft. In actuality the only American warship touched in the Hailstone battles was the light carrier *Intrepid,* which was put out of action for several months by a torpedo hit.

Seaman Hagimoto remembers the second set of Truk raids, on April 29–30, as beginning the morning after local commanders issued sake, beer, cigarettes, and sweets to celebrate the Emperor's birthday. Again the attacks were massive and all defending fighters were lost in the first hour of battle. The raids wiped out the last of two dozen fishing boats that had provided an important fraction of Truk's food supplies, while Army reinforcements that had swollen the garrison brought high manpower levels that began to threaten the supply of local foodstuffs—principally pineapples and breadfruit—and thus brought tensions with the local population.

Like Rabaul before it, Truk remained as a backwater post, no more important nor any better supplied than many other Japanese island garrisons left behind by the war. By then the Fourth Fleet commander had become Vice Admiral Hara Chuichi, left on the beach after his last job training fresh JNAF air groups. His deputy was Rear Admiral Sumikawa Michio, former boss of the 26th Air Flotilla. Ammunition expenditures plus losses forced Hara and Sumikawa to restrict the defensive efforts of their men. Only a single anti-aircraft gun was permitted to fire against the constant heavy-bomber attacks made against the base. American B-29 very heavy bombers actually used Truk as an experimental target, and the Fourth Fleet base suffered the indignity of an attack by *British* aircraft carriers in the summer of 1945.

King Kong Hara said, speaking of a possible invasion of Truk, "I believed that an attack was possible but not feasible. After the British carrier attack I thought one conceivable." Seaman Hagimoto's view was more down to earth. Hagimoto felt scandalized that Japanese leaders had expected to ward off attack with their skimpy forces, and thought irresponsible the prevailing sentiment that lack of equipment gave Japanese an opportunity to demonstrate superior valor. Hagimoto recalls weapons so primitive they were next to useless—refurbished 1914-vintage German guns captured in World War I to be used against modern aircraft. The chances of the Japanese remaining at Truk were perfectly expressed in the story of one young girl, a civilian who had been born there. She had never seen the Home Islands. As Truk seemed more and more dangerous, her family resolved to send the girl back, and she was put on one of the last merchant ships to leave. That ship was torpedoed almost as soon as it cleared the reefs. The young innocent did not survive.

THE EMPIRE'S ANSWER TO THE GREAT NEW AMERICAN TASK FORCE SLASHING ITS WAY ACROSS the Central Pacific was already in being, hard at work training on various bases in the Home Islands. This was the First Air Fleet, a brand-new formation and nothing like the unit of the same name created in 1941 for the Pearl Harbor attack. The new First Air Fleet was entirely land-based; it represented an effort to compensate for carrier losses by creation of a powerful land-based air force that could cooperate with the fleet in a Decisive Battle. The basic concept in Admiral Koga's fleet directives was that the First Air Fleet would deploy to that region of the Pacific selected as arena for the Decisive Battle and would then neutralize American carrier strength with powerful blows from the air.

While creation of the air fleet involved a certain expediency—carrier losses were being hedged, after all—the move was an imaginative initiative. Previous JNAF air fleets originated as administrative groupings and were combat commands only of necessity. The new First Air Fleet was specifically intended as a homogeneous combat unit of air groups that had flown and trained together for the stated purpose of winning the Decisive Battle. This was something new, and it was not an initiative of Admiral Nagano's Naval General Staff, which issued no directive pertaining to the air fleet until months after its creation. The Navy Ministry created the First Air Fleet with the encouragement of Admiral Koga and NGS both, and the latter exercised only the most general authority over the unit, similar to the supervision NGS gave other air groups involved in flight training.

The manner of creation of the First Air Fleet also signaled its distinction. Hirohito personally vested the command in Admiral Kakuta Kakuji, then sponsored a luncheon at which imperial officials fêted Kakuta and almost two dozen other officers assigned to the new formation. While the Emperor frequently presided over ceremonies presenting promotions or awards, his sponsorship of a luncheon was a mark of special distinction. Commander Fuchida Mitsuo, newly selected air officer on the First Air Fleet staff, prevailed upon Kakuta and his chief of staff, Captain Miwa Yoshitake, to visit Yamamoto's grave after the lunch. They paid respects to his spirit and swore to accomplish the mission.

Air officer Fuchida believed that if the new First Air Fleet could not win the Decisive Battle it could not be won. Navy Ministry personnel officers seem to have thought the same way. Consciously or otherwise the Imperial Navy was putting its first team into the First Air Fleet, perhaps in hopes of recreating the conditions that had brought success at Pearl Harbor. Fuchida's Etajima class (1924) and that of 1923 were heavily represented among air group leaders in the First Air Fleet—seven out of ten in the formation's main element, the 61st Air Flotilla. Even in the larger universe of twenty-four air groups that would eventually fly under First Air Fleet command, fourteen group commanders were 1923 or 1924 graduates. The old-timers—three members of the class of 1918—included Kamei Yoshio and Umetani Kaoru, men who had played important roles in the strike from Taiwan against Clark Field. Both of the two groups of hot *Raiden* and *Shiden* fighters were led by test pilots. Commanders of the 503rd, 523rd, and 755th groups had been air officers of (respectively) the *Akagi*, *Shokaku*, and *Soryu* at Pearl Harbor, while the leader of the 761st group had been air officer of the *Zuikaku* in the Solomons. Miyo Tatsukichi, commanding the Betty bombers of the 732nd Air Group, in 1941 had been the air staff officer on the Naval General Staff.

Commander Fuchida also requested and got top aviators for assignment to First Air Fleet. These included Commander Egusa Takeshige, the Navy's best dive-bomber pilot, who had led *Soryu*'s air group at Midway; Chihaya Takehiko, *Akagi*'s bomber leader at Midway and a scouting expert; and Furukawa Izumi, also an *Akagi* veteran, a premier horizontal bomber jockey. The basic concept was to rely upon the best leaders and the top fliers to train First Air Fleet crews up to a level at which they could be victorious in Decisive Battle.

This assignment proved more difficult than Fuchida Mitsuo might have thought at first. The Imperial Navy did not enjoy the position it had had in 1941, in terms of either aircrews or planes; in fact the gulf was considerable. When Admiral Kakuta and Commander Fuchida opened shop at Kanoya in July 1943 they started with just two air groups and found pilots coming to them with 120 hours in the air—a fifth of the average flight time of JNAF pilots in 1941. In every respect new pilots were worse off: Their training programs had been shortened (from a year to ten months for officers, from ten months to eight for enlisted pilots), their basic and intermediate flight training telescoped into a single stage, their training in combat tactics curtailed, and that in formation flying eliminated altogether. Limited aircraft production also restricted the planes available for advanced combat training and led the Navy to send the First Air Fleet pilots who had skipped this stage completely. Admiral Kakuta supported the practice because he knew he was getting the best 20 percent or so of the trainees and because the pilots would be able to log air time on actual combat aircraft types. Kakuta also argued that pilots coming directly to First Air Fleet would be unable to develop the bad habits they often acquired in advanced training. It is worth noting that the Japanese resumed obligatory advanced training for all pilots in the spring of 1944 because Kakuta's method consumed more aviation gasoline and led to excessive numbers of accidents and noncombat losses, and because new-generation JNAF aircraft could not be safely flown by novice pilots.

There was a material factor hidden from the outside that also affected First Air Fleet strength. This was the adverse trend in losses and production combined with that of combat demands. These trends particularly affected torpedo and dive-bombers—carrier-based attack planes—inventories of which had been almost wiped out during the big battles of 1942. In April 1943, it is estimated, the Imperial Navy had a total of just *ten* aircraft in service of both these types combined. Production in fiscal 1943 amounted to 1,820, but wastage took away 1,191. The carrier forces obviously had first call on the 639 such aircraft in inventory by April 1944. It is therefore not surprising that only eighty of 570 aircraft carried on the 61st Air Flotilla order of battle that June were carrier attack types. Even worse, attack types numbered just 120 of 1,250 JNAF aircraft under First Air Fleet command throughout the Pacific.

The trend in combat requirements made this problem impossible to solve. That is, the importance of regaining air superiority, or at least striving to do so, dictated first priority to fighter production. Growing qualitative inferiority crippled the combat effort; then continuing lack of success precluded subsequent shifts in production priority. The situation was somewhat better with respect to multi-engine medium bombers, of which First Air Fleet had 360 on its rolls in June 1944, but the net effect remained—even at full strength the First Air Fleet would have much less striking power than an equivalent-sized force a couple of years before.

These analyses presume that units are at full strength, and that too would not be the case when the First Air Fleet went into battle. For example, the Truk-based 22nd Air Flotilla had 380 planes on its rolls in June 1944, but the number established by postwar investigation, including those stationed elsewhere, was just 205. Finally, such analyses assume that aircraft are flyable and in good repair. This was less and less the case in the JNAF. Somewhere between 15,000 and 20,000 of the Imperial Navy's most experienced mechanics had been bypassed at Rabaul, and an equal number were left behind in the Marshalls and Carolines. More were lost in the Solomons

and Gilberts. Commander Ichinose Mitsukiyo, an expert on JNAF maintenance, confirms that performance in these areas had gone into decline by
the end of 1943. Maintenance men trained that year, about 27,300, barely
made up for the men at bypassed outposts, and of course the new ground
crews were inexperienced and facing more complicated new-generation aircraft. Demand forced the JNAF to relax test standards for promotion toward
the end of 1943 and, like flight training, the maintenance courses were
shortened. Again the net effect was to reduce combat capability in the First
Air Fleet.

Battle also required suitable air bases, and these would have to be found
and prepared before the fact, for Decisive Battle would be impossible without
them. Admiral Koga's orders (not those of the NGS) provided for base preparation, and led to a survey trip Commander Fuchida made in late 1943. The
initial plan was for the core unit, the 61st Air Flotilla, to move to the
Philippines, after which it would deploy to whatever front became the scene
of action. Fuchida selected a number of locations in the Philippines, then
more in the Marianas and Carolines, that would be improved to make way
for the air force.

A great deal of the preparatory work remained incomplete when the
Americans invaded the Marshalls and began their Hailstone carrier raids
into the Carolines. First Air Fleet crews were not yet up to training standards; airfields were not yet ready. Commander Fuchida estimated at least
two more months were needed. He would not get them. The Naval General
Staff in its Directive Number 327 of February 1, 1944, provided that the air
force could move to the front beginning in the middle of that month, while
another order accorded operational control to the Combined Fleet. Fuchida
went to Admiral Kakuta to protest the order, only to find that his boss did
not like it either, but felt they had no choice. The First Air Fleet was going to
war, and they had no idea how much U.S. intelligence knew about it.

In all likelihood the same factors that convinced Admiral Koga that the October
1943 American strikes on Wake Island presaged invasion of that place sufficed to convince Tokyo that powerful carrier raids on the Empire were
about to occur. It was one more demonstration of the continuing Japanese
sensitivity regarding their country's northeastern sea frontier. As a consequence, IGHQ Navy Directive Number 285, on October 14, ordered the First
Air Fleet to prepare to use its "attack mission strength" under Combined
Fleet command "for interception operations against the enemy fleet in the
east of the Japanese homeland."

No American carriers appeared in Empire waters; there was no repetition
of the Doolittle raid. This would have been merely another false alarm had

not Admiral Kakuta resorted to the airwaves to alert some units for operations. The most important result of Kakuta's action was in Washington, where the October 17 COMINCH radio intelligence summary noted that a formation designated the First Air Fleet "appears to be organizing naval air defense for Japan proper." This seemingly trivial incident thus brought American intelligence its first intimation of the existence of Japan's aerial strike force. A detailed study of JNAF organization issued by Pacific Fleet air forces in early August contained not a hint of the First Air Fleet; according to it, the Rabaul-based Eleventh constituted Japan's sole air fleet operating from land. Now the October 17 COMINCH report remarked that the First Air Fleet was "apparently a new command."

Precisely because American intelligence had an organic approach toward collection of information on a subject, the simple revelation of the existence of the First Air Fleet opened the door to disclosures much more harmful to the Japanese. Momentarily, however, those other revelations had to take back seat to another round of the Washington–Pearl Harbor dispute on intelligence.

It was at this time that the Joint Intelligence Center Pacific Ocean Areas (JICPOA) became the theater-wide advanced intelligence center its proponents had only dreamed of at the time of Midway. Now JICPOA produced intelligence, with FRUPAC, the old Station Hypo, as just one contributor. There were a variety of JICPOA publications, some taken over from previous units, and there were differences between Washington and Pearl Harbor as to which ones merely duplicated work being done at the other end. In Washington there were also differences over duplication of effort between Admiral King's COMINCH combat intelligence section and ONI's Far East Division. In late October analysts pointed out that their workload could be cut by almost two thirds by reliance upon JICPOA efforts, and also recommended that ONI be restricted to a mere library function, to service requests from combat intelligence and COMINCH operations planners.

Opposition to these proposals came from others who cited recent apparent errors in JICPOA reports. For example, several obsolete cruisers the Imperial Navy typically used for training or assigned to the China Area Fleet were being carried by JICPOA as newly commissioned heavy cruisers, and had been for five months. Similarly, JICPOA credited the Japanese with ten battleships (counting the *Mutsu* as sunk) while Washington believed there were eleven, and there were other differences in fleet order of battle as well. Differences in accounting Japanese Naval Air Force strength were highlighted that fall when various American and British intelligence authorities attended a conference in London specifically to discuss that subject. When, in early December, JICPOA deputy chief Jasper Holmes sent Washington an analysis of Japanese dive-bomber production based on identification plates on downed aircraft, the issue was joined in earnest.

In Washington by December 1943 there were 4,000 sailors and civilians working with OP-20-G; a staff of over a hundred with ONI's Far East Bureau; and a small but important combat intelligence unit (F-22) that worked directly for Admiral King but was housed administratively within OP-20-G. Indeed, the radio intelligence section had outgrown its quarters on the first deck of the Navy Department building and was soon to move uptown to a converted facility at Massachusetts and Nebraska avenues. King was not about to dismantle his apparatus, and the decision handed down through his intelligence chief, Captain Henri Smith-Hutton, was that both Washington and Pearl Harbor should continue steady on course.

The Washington–Pearl Harbor exchange did have the practical effect of bringing together experts from JICPOA and Washington, however. With his many years in the Japanese intelligence business, Smith-Hutton knew the value of keeping analysts on the same wavelength. Ostensibly as a device to discover whether the duplicative efforts of Washington and JICPOA were so superfluous they could safely be dispensed with, Smith-Hutton organized an exchange of visits. Captain Goggins of FRUPAC went to Washington, consulting mainly with OP-20-G but also visiting F-22. From F-22, Smith-Hutton sent reserve Commander William J. Sebald to Pearl Harbor.

Bill Sebald, it will be recalled, was the Japanese-language officer who, before the war, had left the service to become a lawyer for Westerners in Japan, and who had been brought back into intelligence by Arthur McCollum on the eve of Pearl Harbor. Sebald went on to become a stalwart of combat intelligence, a key section chief, and eventually boss. Sebald's first job returning to ONI had been to put together the intelligence available on the Japanese naval air force. "It was almost pitiful," he recalled, "how little information we had." Sebald visited U.S. Army intelligence authorities and found they had even less knowledge of the JNAF than had the Office of Naval Intelligence. It was an education.

Sent to Pearl Harbor in 1944, Commander Sebald was well aware of the whole air intelligence picture and of the progress made in the previous two years. At JICPOA, Jasper Holmes introduced Sebald to the center's resident Japanese air force expert, Harvard-educated Lieutenant Richard W. Emory, whose careful plotting of JNAF search patterns out of Truk provided the intelligence that enabled Task Force 58 to make its undetected approach to that Mandates base. Sebald flatly declared after the war that he felt CINC-PAC had had the better order-of-battle intelligence.

Both Emory and Sebald were alert when, on December 25, 1943, Tokyo sent a dispatch to Combined Fleet chief of staff Admiral Fukudome asking that rescue ships be provided for a move of a "First Air Fleet" to the Philippines. By late January COMINCH combat intelligence was on record with a memorandum analyzing the move, furnishing five possible reasons for it, and observing that it would be a most significant development.

American intelligence was wrong at that time about the composition of the First Air Fleet, speculating on the basis of the October information that it consisted primarily of training units. Then JICPOA weighed in on January 24 with a report hypothesizing, on the basis of the assignment of several light carriers and the antisubmarine Air Group 901, that the First Air Fleet was intended to control antisubmarine activities. Sebald responded on February 3 with an F-22 analysis questioning these conclusions. This piece accurately listed *nine of the ten* air groups in the First Air Fleet's major component and was wrong on only one other unit. It was clear that this was a combat formation, and U.S. intelligence also noted that fighters predominated in Kakuta's aircraft roster.

This was first-rate intelligence performance on a major unit that the Imperial Navy had not yet committed to combat and that, indeed, at the time the reports were written, had not yet even been deployed.

The explanation for the appearance of aircraft carriers associated with First Air Fleet became apparent in due course. These light carriers were to ferry aircraft units to locations in the Philippines and the *nanyo.* On February 11 the Japanese drew up schedules for *Chitose* to make three cruises while *Chiyoda* and *Zuiho* made two each to such destinations as Davao, Cebu, Saipan, and Guam. Naturally this whole plan changed with Task Force 58's Hailstone attacks on Truk and the follow-up forays into the Marianas, against which the Japanese sent their First Air Fleet on an emergency basis. Fuchida believed its commitment to battle at this time was a mistake. Just how big an error only gradually became evident.

IMMEDIATELY FOLLOWING THE AMBITIOUS CARRIER RAID UPON TRUK, ADMIRAL SPRUANCE detached the *Enterprise* and a few other ships for Majuro. He himself, circumnavigating Truk in a battleship force, made another unit. Carrier *Saratoga* he sent with several escorts to join Sir James Somerville's Eastern Fleet in the Indian Ocean. With two remaining groups Rear Admiral Mitscher set out to continue the raid, steaming into the Marianas after refueling from a service unit sent up to help him.

Spruance's operations had everything to do with intelligence. Even in the *New Jersey* off Truk, the Fifth Fleet commander had been concerned about what he could learn. When Spruance, who insisted upon exercising tactical command of the surface action group, was told of a radar contact on a Japanese patrol craft, he ordered that it be sunk in such a way as to ensure that prisoners were taken. The destroyer *Burns* sank the vessel without much trouble but had a much worse time getting the desired prisoners. Because they dived under the water each time the Americans approached, only six of the sixty Japanese sailors could be captured. The men were ultimately delivered to Spruance's mobile radio unit boss, Gilven M. Slonim, who had been with the admiral ever since Midway.

As for the Mariana Islands, they were a cipher asking to be unraveled. American planners were putting finishing touches on arrangements for Operation Forager, the anticipated invasion of those islands, yet many had hardly been seen since Japan received a League of Nations mandate, and even Guam had not been glimpsed since December 1941. The photographic covers of Saipan, Guam, and Tinian obtained were an important result of the February carrier raids on the Marianas.

A second result, hardly noticed though just as important or more so, was that the Imperial Navy was lured into premature commitment of its First Air Fleet. While it is true that the Japanese now had the short end of the stick in the Pacific both qualitatively and quantitatively, if the new force had deployed according to schedule it would have benefited from completed air-fields, radar installations, and crew training to the best standard the Japanese could manage by that point in the war. As it was, a number of the airfields remained incomplete, while a tour of the islands by the responsible Combined Fleet staff officer identified numerous shortcomings in such vital support functions as air warning and communications.

It was not only air staff officer Fuchida who had been aware of the need to complete the preparation phase. Combined Fleet intelligence officer Nakajima participated in countless meetings with Admiral Koga, who had revised the lineup of forces for his anticipated Decisive Battle most recently the previous September. Commander Nakajima remembered Koga saying, more than once, "In March of next year, we will carry out this program."

In any case, the original schedule provided for movements from late February through mid-April. For example, Seaman Inoue of the 761st Air Group, which fielded forty Betty bombers at Palau (plus an equal number at Tinian), arrived on February 28 aboard the *Chitose*. A Philippine ferry cruise by the *Zuiho* was slated to end as late as May 9. Instead, due to Mitscher's strikes only the earliest Central Pacific voyages were completed; the ferry ships (light aircraft carriers) were then recalled for fleet training with air groups. Much of the 61st Air Flotilla had to self-deploy as well as it could, with planes staging down through Iwo Jima and the Bonins or to the Marianas, or through Taiwan to the Philippines. Ground crews followed aboard slow transports. First Air Fleet headquarters was in place on Tinian by February 22.

At midafternoon that day a search plane caught sight of Task Force 58 still 420 miles due east of Saipan. For once the raiders had been found before reaching attack position. On Tinian, Admiral Kakuta and Commander Fuchida agreed the American planes were probably coming the next day. Aboard Task Force 58's carriers, Admiral Marc Mitscher told his two group leaders that the JNAF had been warned. That night Kakuta sent off twenty-seven medium bombers armed with torpedoes, accompanied by nine scout planes to illuminate the Americans. Commander Furukawa Izumi led the mission. None of the attack planes was ever seen again. The same thing happened to a strike of fifty-four dive-bombers that flew off next morning. Rear Admiral Frederick C. Sherman, who led Task Group 58.3 from the *Bunker Hill,* later wrote that he evaded the JNAF attacks by tracking their approach on radar and turning away at key moments, all the while firing only his big 5-inch anti-aircraft guns, which used flashless powder and thus did not give away the ships. Rear Admiral Alfred E. Montgomery's Task Force 58.2 used more conventional tactics, inflicting more losses but also subject to greater danger.

On February 23 the American carriers flew several hundred sorties at Tinian and commensurate numbers against Guam and Saipan. Airfields were cratered, installations destroyed, and, Samuel Eliot Morison wrote gleefully, the Japanese reported more aircraft destroyed than American pilots claimed.

Having secured needed reconnaissance photographs, Mitscher turned the fleet east and by the last day of February was securely anchored at Majuro.

The final act of Koga Mineichi's stewardship over the Combined Fleet began at Majuro, where Admiral Spruance's staff planned new carrier raids, this time at Palau. From SOWESPAC General MacArthur had also been agitating for Pacific Fleet carrier support, and a mission to strike targets near Hollandia in northern New Guinea would be added to Task Force 58's other objectives. Finally, from the Indian Ocean the British had some deviltry up their sleeves as well—Sir James Somerville planned to use the American *Saratoga* plus his own *Illustrious* to hit Japanese-controlled oil fields around Sabang off northern Sumatra.

Palau turned out to be the shortest-lived base the Combined Fleet ever saw. Kurita Takeo had gone there with his Second Fleet upon leaving Truk, and had then sent some ships on to Singapore, where they joined Ozawa and Carrier Division 1 at the Lingga Roads naval base. Admiral Koga reached Palau somewhat later, having gone to the Empire first for strategy discussions in Tokyo. Flagship *Musashi* entered the harbor on February 29 to find a force of heavy and light cruisers and destroyers. Koga's main strength consisted of air formations, units like Commander Matsumoto Naomi's 761st Air Group, whose arrival the previous day has been noted; Commander Urata Terujiro's 265th Air Group, which provided fighter cover for the base; and a detachment of ten reconnaissance planes of Commander Iwao Masatsugi's 121st Air Group.

The ninety planes stationed at Palau proved no match for Task Force 58's groups, but the Combined Fleet was not caught in base to witness that awful fact. A Combined Fleet intelligence dispatch on March 24 estimated that Allied attacks would be directed toward the Philippine area, along the New

Guinea coast, through the Carolines, featuring probable occupation of the Marianas. The generalized warning proved accurate enough, and the next day careful air searches to the east and south were specifically ordered for JNAF bases from Marcus to the Admiralties. Washington commented: "The tenor of the various dispatches suggests that the Japanese suspect an impending attack but are not sure of the direction from which it might come."

Persistence paid dividends. The Owada Group on March 26 recommended an alert for Central Pacific bases and noted appearance of radio call signs "Z1K" and "Z2T," previously used on the Honolulu broadcast circuit to address forces at sea at times U.S. carrier groups had been in motion, including before the Truk raid. Heavy and unusual radio traffic on the Honolulu circuit, Pearl Harbor's primary connection to forces in the field, was also noted. The afternoon of the same day a search plane out of Truk found a task force including aircraft carriers south-southeast of Truk, distance 600 miles. On March 28 OP-20-G observed of the Japanese: "Traffic reveals continued preoccupation with defensive measures in the Central Pacific in anticipation of a suspected imminent U.S. strike."

Major units steamed out of Palau on March 29. According to fleet intelligence officer Nakajima, Admiral Koga intended to use Kurita's ships if an opportunity presented itself for a surface action, so he sent them to a holding position northwest of Palau. To strengthen Kurita's striking power, Koga took his headquarters ashore, a move resisted previously, adding the *Musashi* to the five heavy cruisers and seven destroyers available. As she left the battleship encountered submarine *Tunny*, which days before had sunk the *I-42* in nearby waters, and which launched a six-torpedo spread at the *Musashi*. The flagship turned to avoid but took a hit in the bow, one that would confine her to a Kure dry dock for slightly more than two weeks. Destroyers *Urakaze* and *Isokaze* counterattacked the American sub, but it was left to a near miss from an American carrier plane to actually damage her.

Meanwhile Task Force 58 was sighted on its run in to the launch point. That night came another pyrotechnic display as scout planes dropped flares to illuminate the U.S. ships for trailing torpedo bombers. American radio intelligence picked up successive JNAF reports, of the attack begun, of torpedo action completed, of a large unidentified ship afire, of a battleship listing badly. In actuality, however, Admiral Mitscher's force suffered no damage whatever. A further attack the next day by forty more JNAF bombers also accomplished nothing.

Task Force 58 pounded Palau for two full days, much as it had Truk. The First Air Fleet tried to defend with fighters from Air Groups 201, 261, and 263. There were heavy losses. Twenty of twenty-three fighters launched by one unit did not return. Also lost were many planes that left Guam on an offensive search with Lieutenant Ibusuki Masanobu, senior pilot of the

261st. Seaman Inoue of the 761st Air Group recorded repeated attack efforts by his unit's medium bombers: nine planes on March 28, two attack units totaling twenty-four planes on the twenty-ninth, seven planes on the thirtieth even while Palau lay under attack. Eight more Bettys flew during the afternoon of the thirty-first, returning after nightfall, but were unable to find anything.

Commander Matsumoto's thoughts are not recorded, but Seaman Inoue was not very happy, except perhaps for the air-raid shelters, finally completed after two weeks' furious work. The entire garrison spent the last night of the raids in shelters or on lookout with steel helmets and gas masks. "The second attack unit planes seem entirely to have been destroyed by fire on the Peleliu airfield," Inoue recorded on March 30. "The planes of the first attack unit did not do so well either. The *Ryu* force [a special bomber formation] is utterly worthless." As for the First Air Fleet fighter units, after the strikes their pilots had to be evacuated to Saipan and the units rebuilt.

Reports and claims of Japanese aircraft lost in the strikes run as high as 150. American losses totaled twenty-five and most crews were recovered by alert guard submarines like the *Tunny*, attacked by mistake by U.S. aircraft. Naval losses included a patrol boat, four submarine chasers, an aircraft ferry, several tenders, and eighteen assorted merchantmen. Admiral Mitscher's carrier force went on to strike Yap and Woleai to finish out the series of raids, then withdrew southward, rearming and fueling before conducting more carrier raids around Hollandia in support of SOWESPAC's latest offensive.

In the meantime tragedy again struck the Combined Fleet. Having gone ashore from the *Musashi*, Admiral Koga and his staff were at Palau to see with their own eyes the power of the American striking force. Koga sent orders to First Air Fleet and Second Fleet to stimulate resistance and considered where to put his headquarters, rejecting Saipan and Guam in favor of Davao. Admiral Fukudome organized the fleet staff to move there in three flying boats on March 31 although communications facilities at Davao were not quite finished. On the afternoon of the thirty-first, the American air strikes slackened, but then a patrol plane reported that the U.S. fleet was actually closing in on Palau. Amid rising concern, chief of staff Fukudome and Admiral Koga decided to leave that night for safer haven at Davao. Commander Nakajima and others who advised waiting for daylight before flying were overridden. Ironically, it was later determined that the search plane mistook reefs and rocks east of Palau for the U.S. fleet.

Commander Nakajima would be left behind on Koror, and returned to Tokyo a week or so later. The third plane, delayed, did not get out of Palau until the morning of April Fool's Day, and reached Davao safely. The other planes took off as scheduled and flew into an eerie replay (sans American intervention) of the Yamamoto tragedy. Admiral Koga, who had mused to

Fukudome at one time that Yamamoto had been lucky to die at just the right point in the war, turned to his chief of staff before they boarded their respective airplanes and said, "Let us go out and die together."

Koga's plane took off and disappeared into the clouds. Neither admiral nor airplane was ever seen again. Also lost were all staff who accompanied the chief.

Admiral Fukudome, who must have felt like a true April Fool before this episode ended, took off in his own plane, which lost the other in a storm front. The pilot extended his course westward to get around the weather, then took a northerly heading toward Manila. Strong headwinds exhausted their fuel hundreds of miles short of the Philippine capital, and the pilot tried a water landing off Cebu. While descending he became disoriented, and Fukudome's own effort to regain control of the aircraft merely put it into a stall. There was a crash landing. The Kawanishi patrol bomber sank, but fortunately it had been at low altitude to start with; eleven of fourteen on board survived, including Admiral Fukudome, who hung on to a floating seat cushion and swam for about eight and a half hours before rescue. Also saved was Captain Yamamoto Yuji, an officer who had been with Fukudome off and on since both served with the Naval General Staff before the war. Several other staff officers perished. The other survivors were from the airplane's crew.

Now it happened that SOWESPAC's Allied Intelligence Bureau supported Filipino and American guerrillas in the Philippines, and in particular that the guerrillas had a presence on Cebu, known as Pony to the covert operations specialists at MacArthur's headquarters. Lieutenant Colonel James M. Cushing headed the Cebu Area Command, which dominated the hills west and south of Cebu City. Native fisherman loyal to the Pony guerrillas were the ones who rescued Admiral Fukudome and the other Japanese survivors.

What made the catch even more astounding is that Fukudome had been carrying a briefcase containing key documents, including Admiral Koga's Decisive Battle plan, most recently revised in early March, and an air staff study of carrier fleet operations. After the crash landing Fukudome kept the papers with him and only tried to get rid of them when he saw the rescuers and felt uncertain about them. The Filipino fishermen saw the briefcase and retrieved it before it could sink. The documents went with the prisoners to the Pony guerrilla command. The guerrilla 87th Regiment took charge of the captives at Balud, a small barrio outside Cebu City, virtually under the noses of a Japanese Army garrison. The prisoners were marched into the hills, with Fukudome, badly injured, carried in a hammock. Filipinos eventually misidentified him as Koga, giving rise to the legend that the guerrillas had captured the commander in chief of the Japanese fleet. The guard unit, led by young Lieutenant Salvador Varga, got word to Cushing of the prisoners and he in turn communicated with the Allied Intelligence Bureau (AIB) through Colonel Edwin D. Andrews on Negros. American submarine *Haddo* got orders to stand by for a pickup.

In the meantime the Japanese commander at Cebu, Colonel Onishi Seito, learned of the crash from a couple of survivors who escaped the Pony guerrillas. The imperial chain of command put plenty of pressure on Onishi for results, and it was not long before the local commander had three battalions in the hills ransacking every settlement in search of the prisoners. At length Cushing prevailed upon Fukudome to compile a message to the Japanese Army informing them that the guerrillas would release the prisoners if the Japanese would stop the slaughter of civilians begun in their search. Captain Yamamoto authored the note. Colonel Onishi agreed and the prisoners were conveyed to Cebu City. Fukudome rested there, left for Manila, then departed for Tokyo on April 20.

"Looking back on this experience," Fukudome told American interrogators later, "I believe that it was by miraculous luck that I was saved." A board of inquiry including Admiral Tsukahara Nizhizo examined the affair and cleared Fukudome, but it is not clear whether they knew Combined Fleet documents had been captured.

Picked up by an American submarine, possibly the *Haddo*, the documents swiftly appeared at the Allied Translator and Interpreter Section, a priceless bequest from AIB. Colonel Mashbir put his best people, two officers and two enlisted men, to work in total secrecy and only after-hours. The team included deputy director John Anderton, whose photographic memory for kanji characters had often been useful, Richard Bagnall, Faubian Bowers, and Yoshikazu Yamada. Later George K. Yamashiro played a key role in preventing certain translation errors from going forward. On May 23 ATIS published the first result, a limited-distribution translation of Koga's Z Plan, Combined Fleet Operations Order Number 73. Five days later followed limited-distribution publication of "A Study of the Main Features of Decisive Air Operations in the Central Pacific," a Combined Fleet staff report completed as recently as March 10.

The intelligence was exquisite. General MacArthur's chief of staff had copies flown to Pearl Harbor, where JICPOA prepared its own version for restricted circulation. The documents went to the fleet just as it moved out for Operation Forager, the Marianas invasion. It was too late to reach Task Force 58, which Admiral Mitscher had already led out of Majuro when the Japanese translations arrived. Copies for Mitscher had to be air-dropped to his flagship *Lexington* on the high seas. A PB4Y, the Navy version of the B-24, did the drop but *missed* the ship. The *Lexington* had to stop and put out a whaleboat, which recovered the documents. This intelligence arrived just in time to figure in the greatest carrier battle of World War II.

# Down to the Sea in Ships

ALLIED CODEBREAKERS WORRIED A GREAT DEAL ABOUT THE POTENTIAL SECURITY BREACH that occurred at Midway, but for most of the war they had little idea of what things the Imperial Navy really considered cryptologic emergencies. On one occasion, for example, a Fourth Fleet courier plane flying from Truk to Rabaul had developed engine trouble and jettisoned its cargo, which included codebooks tightly packed in one or more cases that the Japanese feared might be adrift upon the sea. Another time a submarine unloading supplies off Salamaua had been attacked and forced to submerge, while the deck cargo, including cryptographic publications, washed away. Then there was the time a box containing code materials being shipped from Kure to the Tsingtao Base Force was opened by seamen ignorant of its contents. Similarly, during the period of the big upsurge in Aleutian naval activity, a shipment of "crypto" materials was sent from the Yokosuka Naval District Library to the Ominato Ship and Ordnance Department. At the destination it was discovered that the lock on the freight car door had been removed, though the packages containing the code materials seemed intact.

On some of these occasions the Japanese added extra steps to regular encoding procedures or took special care in other ways. At other times they advanced the dates planned for the next regular additive list or codebook change. In all, between January 1, 1943, and the end of 1944 (including the *I-1* incident), Imperial Navy communications authorities discarded roughly 2 million copies of cryptographic publications in current or planned future use as a result of such emergencies. They also innovated a strip additive panel as an additional security measure toward the end of the war. The cautious attitude toward security is reflected in this statement in a postwar monograph: "The Japanese Navy could not obtain any actual proof whether the code was broken by the enemy, although it was presumed that some of the lost codebooks had fallen into enemy hands."

Such a careful attitude contrasts sharply with the repeated refusal of the Japanese to consider that their codes could have been compromised through other than physical means. During the period of Task Force 58's raids into the western Pacific and General MacArthur's latest advances in New Guinea, several more events called code security into question. One was the seemingly effortless sinking of a tanker, already related, off the entrance to Kwajalein. A second was the episode of the Take convoy, a disaster on the order of the Bismarck Sea debacle a year before. Submarines relying upon Ultra decrypts devastated a series of Japanese reinforcement convoys sent to Palau and western New Guinea during late April and May 1944 for a loss of over 3,900 men. While surviving ships and Japanese escorts rescued another 6,800 passengers from the Take convoy, these survivors, as at Bismarck Sea, arrived without their equipment.

The convoy disaster forced Vice Admiral Takasu Shiro of the Southwest Area Fleet to account for events leading to the loss. Staff officers met at Manila to retrace the fateful days of the Take convoy's cruise, and a breach of code security was one potential explanation for the disaster. Instead, some staffers theorized that the Allies had used traffic analysis for their essential intelligence, while others favored the view that the Philippine resistance had passed along information gleaned from workers on the Manila waterfront, where the convoy stopped during its voyage south. In fact the intelligence had come from both OP-20-G and U.S. Army solutions of Japanese communications.

A security breach of a type the Japanese understood better occurred during the battle for Biak, which MacArthur invaded with his 41st Infantry Division on May 27. A large island off the northern coast of Dutch New Guinea, Biak had been a key base for the 23rd Air Flotilla in the Japanese rear; then, during SOWESPAC's jumps up the New Guinea coast, it was suddenly in the front line. In an acceleration of his operations that began when Task Force 58 lent support to the early April landings at Hollandia, MacArthur made several additional invasions, leaving behind hapless Japanese garrisons, before landing at Biak. The garrison there was not hapless at all. Colonel Kuzume Naoyuki of the 222nd Infantry Regiment organized a sophisticated defense revolving around use of the numerous caves that dotted the island. He planned to defend the interior rather than the beaches, and ended up denying the Allies use of Biak's airfields right through late June, by which time the action had become ancillary to the huge fleet engagement taking place in the Philippine Sea.

Among the 10,000-odd troops on Biak were about 1,500 naval troops of

Rear Admiral Senda Sadatoshi's 28th Naval Base Force. The battle began well for them, since the JNAF put in a strong showing with early air raids on the U.S. landing forces, while Combined Fleet and IGHQ ordered substantial reinforcements for the 23rd Flotilla, once headquartered at Biak itself but since moved to Sorong. However, Allied combat power was enormous and the pressure on Admiral Senda's sailors unrelenting. He was forced to move his headquarters to a different cave complex. A section of the 28th Base Force's radio unit got instructions on June 8 to carry codebooks to the new location. On the way they ran into an American patrol and a firefight ensued, in the course of which the Japanese codebooks were lost. Out of mortification or otherwise (Imperial Navy communications authorities called it negligence), the loss was not reported to Tokyo for three weeks. By then Japan was fighting its long-awaited Decisive Battle.

The flap in Tokyo can be imagined. Communications experts made an immediate investigation of the Biak incident. They concluded (questionably) that only one or two minor codes could have been compromised in the fiasco; the Fleet Codes were held to be secure. Nevertheless, emergency measures were initiated both locally and on Navy-wide circuits, encoding procedures were partially altered, and the net result was a considerable slowdown in Imperial Navy communications. To be on the safe side, the Japanese introduced a fresh variant of the Fleet Codes as well. These changes hampered fleet communications at one of the most important moments in the history of the Imperial Navy.

"No MATTER HOW WE HIT ENEMY AMERICA," ADMIRAL TAKAHASHI SANKICHI TOLD A RADIO audience early in 1944, "it continues to attack us." A mover in the anti-arms-limitation faction before the war and regarded as one of the greats of the Imperial Navy, this was the same man who had once told a business magazine that the United States was merely a "patch quilt" of a country that would be thrown into confusion once its "slender hopes of victory" were denied. Now Admiral Takahashi remarked that the Americans aimed at Rabaul and other places as well. He said frankly, "Since last year we have given up to the U.S. the islands of Guadalcanal, Attu, Kiska, New Georgia, Kolombangara, Makin and Tarawa gradually, step by step. Very regretfully, it is a fact, and it can't be helped." To put a better face on things, the retired admiral emphasized American losses in all these operations, then offered a vision of future Decisive Battle: "Our Navy is . . . giving up these islands and is falling back, but on the other hand it is . . . coming nearer and nearer to the true aim of our ocean strategy."

That aim was very close at the moment MacArthur's forces landed at Biak, and it neared more every day. The Japanese had been prepared to defend Biak as a simple outpost, but when the battle began IGHQ's goals were suddenly more ambitious. Informed by FRUMEL, the AIB, and Central Bureau, MacArthur found a strong Japanese reaction no surprise. Admiral Thomas C. Kinkaid's operations plan of May 11 clearly noted that the Japanese were gathering powerful striking forces at anchorages west of the Philippines, notably Tawitawi in the Sulu Archipelago. As Kinkaid's fleet intelligence officer, Captain Arthur McCollum estimated that the Japanese might complete their concentration by the fifteenth and that their force would comprise most of the strength of the Imperial Navy. Units believed involved in the Japanese move totaled six battleships, five aircraft carriers, eleven heavy and three light cruisers, and twenty-five destroyers. All the warships, the report added, had been recently docked and had had radar fitted, and their anti-aircraft gun strength had been increased.

For their part, the Japanese had been monitoring the U.S. fleet, but seem to have lost track of Task Force 58, at least, by the middle of May. Then came the Biak landings. All of this occurred as the naval command was trying to reconstitute itself following the demise of Admiral Koga. At Lingga, Ozawa of the carrier fleet held tabletop war games on April 26–27 and May 6, and there was a conference to study the Decisive Battle plans on May 31; Ozawa issued a revised plan a few days later. In the meantime Admiral Toyoda Soemu was appointed new commander in chief of the Combined Fleet on May 1, while Kusaka Ryunosuke became his chief of staff. Toyoda modified the old Z Plan slightly to provide for a battle area in the western Carolines or Marianas, renaming it the A Operation with a directive issued a week after he took command.

The Imperial Navy had by then secured the return of former chief of staff Admiral Fukudome; given its concern for the physical security of codebooks, it is astonishing that the Japanese do not seem to have paid much mind to the capture of the Z Operation plans. It can only be conjectured that Japanese commanders considered the operational concept to be the only one practicable by that point in the war and therefore went ahead anyway.

Vice Admiral Ugaki Matome, who had returned to active service early in March as commander of Battleship Division 1, also voiced doubts about the plans when briefed with other senior officers at Tawitawi on May 19. Ugaki objected that the scheme did not allow for freedom of action in the event of loss of communications and that it did not allow for losses sure to occur. Ugaki also advocated incorporation of a provision for one element of the fleet to be sacrificed "if and when necessary for the sake of the main issue."

The outspoken Ugaki urged action when indications arrived of imminent invasion of Biak. Allied airpower on Biak would make it impossible to maintain Japanese air bases in western New Guinea, would eliminate the possibility of using those on Palau for the A Operation, and would threaten fleet operations west of Mindanao, again calling in question the practicality of the A plan. Alarmed at these prospects Admiral Ugaki ordered out *Yamato*'s launch in the middle of the night and had himself taken across to aircraft carrier *Taiho*, flagship of the First Mobile Fleet, Japan's answer to Task Force 58. Ugaki found that both the commander in chief, Ozawa Jisaburo, and his chief of staff, Komura Keizo, had already gone to bed. Rousting them out, Ugaki engaged the fleet commander in an hour-long midnight meeting. The next morning First Mobile Fleet recommended naval intervention to higher commanders.

Admiral Ozawa did not want to commit the entire mobile fleet, however, both because losses could be expected and because its state of training was poor. Admiral Takasu of the Southwest Area Fleet also weighed in with a recommendation that a counterlanding be attempted on Biak. Combined Fleet commander Toyoda at length issued Dispatch Operations Order Number 102, mandating a landing carried out by Rear Admiral Sakonju Naomasa's Cruiser Division 16. Battleship *Fuso*, two heavy cruisers, and a couple of destroyers would provide heavy cover. The initiative would be called the KON Operation.

The counterlanding proceeded well enough until the transport unit had picked up the troops intended for Biak; then, en route to that island, Allied aircraft found them very early in their mission. The Japanese had no idea the scout planes had been directed on the basis of Ultra intercepts. Admiral Toyoda suspended KON on the evening of June 3, but ordered it resumed a few days later. For the renewed effort Rear Admiral Sakonju shifted his flag to destroyer *Shikinami* while cruisers *Aoba* and *Kinu* and three destroyers supplied heavy escort. Ships of the transport unit each towed a large landing barge, possibly the first combat voyage for the Japanese-style LSTs, which had recently begun to enter service. Sakonju proceeded to Sorong, at the northwestern tip of Dutch New Guinea, which was as far as the reinforcement troops had gotten during the first attempt, and re-embarked them. This time an intercepted Japanese Army message tipped off the Americans that KON had resumed. Admiral Kinkaid ordered a cruiser-destroyer force under the redoubtable Australian vice admiral Sir Victor Crutchley to be off the Biak coast at the point previous Ultra decrypts had revealed as the Japanese destination, at the time now known to be Sakonju's intended time of arrival.

Crutchley made the rendezvous.

The Australian admiral well knew the Japanese were coming, again due to an aircraft that, vectored by Ultra, handily caught sight of the oncoming KON force. At 11:19:5 P.M. on June 8, American light cruiser *Boise* found the Japanese on her radar.

"Surface gadgets 290 distance 26,000," the *Boise* reported on the talk-between-ships (TBS) voice radio, signifying the Japanese were on the screen at 26,000 yards bearing 290 degrees, or west-northwest. A minute later destroyer *Fletcher* confirmed, "We have surface gadgets 293 distance 21,000."

Crutchley ordered his fleet to deploy on a northerly heading, and the warships were settling onto their new courses at 11:25 when Sakonju's vessels began to counter their maneuver, breaking up into formation elements. (Captain Shimanouchi Momochio of Sakonju's staff recalled, however, that the first Japanese sighting of Crutchley's ships was not until 11:40.) In any case the action turned into a stern chase, with the Japanese quickly working up to 32 knots on a northwesterly course. Torpedoes also forced Crutchley's cruisers into a turn, which delayed them critically. Finally only the Allied destroyers could match the Japanese speed.

Crutchley asked one of his destroyer leaders whether the Japanese had anything other than destroyers in their formation.

"All ships appear the same size," came back the answer on the TBS. "I am reasonably sure but not positive there is nothing heavier than destroyers."

It is just as well the Japanese ships were so fast; this saved the American and Australian destroyers from having to face heavy cruiser *Aoba* or light cruiser *Kinu.*

Rear Admiral Sakonju made good his escape, with destroyer *Shiratsuyu,* which received minor damage, the only ship on either side hit in the engagement. However, *Harusame* was sunk by aircraft attack and *Kazegumo,* which had figured in the first KON sortie, was sunk by submarine torpedoes.

One passage of Vice Admiral Crutchley's after-action report is worth quoting:

> It was a bitter disappointment. Why did the enemy turn then [at a moment when they were still 21,500 yards from his flagship, and in a night surface battle]? It was overcast at the time and there had been no visual sighting between surface forces. I am convinced that the enemy now has a surface warning radar nearly as good as ours.

Japanese technology was clearly improving.

Admiral Toyoda made one more effort to jump-start the KON operation. This time he determined to send the big boys, designating Vice Admiral Ugaki to command the operation and use both his superbattleships, *Yamato* and *Musashi,* plus three heavy and two light cruisers and seven destroyers. Ugaki raised anchor at Tawitawi on June 10 and steamed south to Batjan and Halmahera. The next day, as Ugaki continued on his way, a Central Pacific search plane found Task Force 58 headed toward Guam. A week before, the admiral had ruminated in his diary: "Whether one likes it or not the time for the battle upon which the rise or fall of the Empire depends is thus ripening." Now a communications officer suddenly handed Ugaki an alert order for execution of the A Operation. Americans were arriving at

Japan's inner perimeter; the battle for the Marianas was on. The day of Decisive Battle had arrived.

"THE BACKBONE OF THE REVOLUTIONARY CHANGES IN JAPANESE NAVAL STRATEGY IS THE TOR-pedo plane," Transocean Radio had broadcast from Berlin in November 1943. The radio feature waxed loquacious on how the JNAF had developed a "most secret technique" to "undreamed-of perfection," so that the JNAF became "a highly qualified, and not simply an auxiliary weapon in naval warfare." But even the Germans recognized that what had been true at one time no longer was. The feature also reported: "It speaks well for the wisdom of the U.S. naval command that it quickly adapted its naval strategy to the existence of such an effective Japanese naval air weapon. Successes of the Japanese torpedo airmen were in fact much handicapped by this careful employment of the U.S. Fleet."

This German broadcast provided a perfect sketch of the eclipse of the Japanese bomber force—which, as already seen, the JNAF was desperately attempting to reconstitute in the form of the First Air Fleet. Acutely aware of their difficulties, the Japanese put the best face on their situation, confident the islands would serve them in place of carriers. Rear Admiral Yano Hideo, who had commanded battleship *Nagato* at Midway, told a German journalist:

> If the U.S. believes that given sufficient number of aircraft carriers her forces can capture any island in the Pacific Ocean, they will have grave disappointments because they don't realize that every island now occupied by Japan is an excellent aircraft carrier in itself. From now on, American forces will face islands which for twenty years have been under Japanese control.

Of course Yano was referring to the Mandates, those fabled islands of mystery upon which American eyes had hardly lain since the League of Nations award. But Yano Hideo had to be speaking from his new interest, for he had been given a post in the Information Ministry. In reality, Rear Admiral Yano knew American strength, for he had just spent a year in charge of *joho kyoku* and moreover was a classmate of and had been close to America expert Ogawa Kanji, whom he had immediately followed on the Navy's promotions list when both were captains in 1940. Yano also knew the weakness of the Mandates in actuality, for at that same time he had been chief of the armaments section of the Navy Ministry's Military Affairs Bureau.

Now the crunch had come and First Air Fleet had been ordered to the islands. Then Task Force 58 had struck at a good half-dozen bases JNAF had been depending upon. With the carrier raids and New Guinea operations, the First Air Fleet's main flotilla had been reduced to barely 250 aircraft. Some of the expedients the Japanese resorted to in this situation truly mark their despair. In March, before Admiral Koga's death, the Combined Fleet studied the possibility that Ozawa's Mobile Fleet could make a surprise attack on Task Force 58's forward base at Majuro, concentrating in Empire waters, then steaming to a point northeast of Majuro where their strike would be coupled with an attack by torpedo-bearing amphibious tanks. At First Air Fleet in May, air officer Fuchida worked on a Majuro plan of his own, tentatively called Tan, under which twenty-seven torpedo planes led by Fuchida himself, plus an equal number of dive-bombers under Egusa Takeshige, would stage through Marcus, then Wake, and then hit Majuro from the rear.

To inform the Tan Operation leaders, reconnaissance expert Chihaya Takehiko took a couple of the new *Saiun* (Myrt) scout planes to Truk, then Nauru, judged the best place from which to scout Majuro. On the night of June 4, Chihaya overflew Majuro and saw at least a dozen carriers there; four were small, but there were plentiful targets for any raid. Fuchida wanted one last reconnaissance before his attack, and Chihaya was delayed a day by another U.S. air raid at Truk. On June 9 he scouted Majuro again. This time the anchorage was empty.

In efforts to rebuild the First Air Fleet, the Japanese meanwhile created a new 62nd Air Flotilla with as many groups as the 61st, but in spite of repeated requests by Admiral Kakuta the NGS would not permit the formation to deploy from Taiwan. A further air flotilla, which Kakuta wanted to do its training in the Philippines, much as his 61st Flotilla pilots had learned formation flying and combat tactics in frontline units, did not even leave Japan during this period. Raw aircraft strength recovered to former levels, but pilots were even worse trained, and the units that had already moved south were crippled by numerous crewmen on the sick lists with tropical maladies. An early May reorganization for the first time gave the First Air Fleet command status equal to that of one of the Imperial Navy's surface and submarine fleets. This removed the force from command of the Fourteenth Air Fleet, the air component of the Japanese Central Pacific Area Fleet.

Admiral Nagumo Chuichi now led the area fleet, and Kakuta's air fleet had been his biggest formation. Without it Nagumo had just a ragtag collection of patrol boats, base forces, and antisubmarine units. The so-called Fourteenth Air Fleet had but a handful of planes. It was a long way away from his proud command of the Pearl Harbor task force. For Rear Admiral Yano Hideo, sent out from Tokyo in March as Nagumo's chief of staff, reality was the antithesis of the confidence he expressed to the German reporter.

A reality test for life in the Mandates would be Nagumo's Central Pacific Area Fleet Secret Order Number 4, issued on April 4. The directive stated quite plainly:

In view of future military prospects, forces under the command of the Central Pacific Area Fleet will devise exhaustive methods for local self-support. To this end, local civilian agencies (henceforth this term will include the local population) will be utilized and directed to the utmost. At the same time each force will endeavor to produce supplies itself for its local self-support, using surplus manpower above defense requirements.

Saipan, Tinian, and Rota were told to raise foodstuffs for 100,000 persons. Guam, Yap, and Palau requirements were to be set by the local commander there, and Truk's by King Kong Hara. The operations plan, such as it was, would be set out in Secret Operation Order Number 1 of April 15, under which the main task was to "push forward at top speed the perfection of armaments and the development of combat potential," especially air bases. Nagumo insisted on strong scouting efforts with planes and picket boats to discover the oncoming enemy as early as possible. After that forces could "continue positive elastic operations, take the initiative and seize the opportunity to carry out surprise attacks, thereby lessening the enemy's strength and opening up opportunities for giving battle."

Antisubmarine activity, Nagumo declared, was especially important. He also wanted efforts, primarily by submarines, to replenish supplies on bypassed Marshalls atolls as much as possible. These were pious intentions, but tough to carry out.

Admiral Nagumo could issue any orders he wanted, but to whom did they apply? Command in the Central Pacific turned into a thorny question for IGHQ. Seduced by its continental war, the Army had never paid much attention to the Pacific until the end of 1943, when Allied advances into the Gilberts and Marshalls betrayed the beginning of the transpacific counteroffensive. Then the 31st Army was created under General Obata Hideyoshi specifically to reinforce the Central Pacific with main strength built around two infantry divisions. Obata arrived at Saipan on February 27, 1944, little more than a week after the first American carrier raids on Truk. His presence crystallized latent cleavages between Japanese Army and Navy. Taking his cue from the Army's traditional focus and its late commitment of forces to the Pacific, not to mention the Navy's responsibility for moving and supplying them, the Combined Fleet's Admiral Koga planned a unified defense under the responsible area fleet, which meant Nagumo. Army planners at IGHQ denounced the plan as irritating, inadequate, and vague. If combat were on land, the officers argued, command should devolve upon the Army.

General Obata felt the urgency of the situation and the need to get on with defensive preparations. He himself became the root of compromise in this matter, proposing a solution and advocating it within IGHQ. For this Obata was ideally suited; though he had transferred to the Army air force in recent years, he was originally of the cavalry, the Army's elite arm, and had spent many years, including the period immediately before his appointment to command in the Central Pacific, in the War Ministry or on the General Staff. Obata knew the corridors of power and convinced colleagues to accept an arrangement by which an island commander would be the senior officer present, regardless of service. General Obata and Admiral Nagumo met between themselves and reached an oral agreement to supplement the compromise. There would be no supreme command.

Now Owada Group warned that a powerful task force had departed Hawaii between May 11 and 17; in fact, the slowest echelon of Forager forces had left Pearl Harbor May 14. Admiral Raymond Spruance himself sailed aboard the *Indianapolis* on May 26, with a (now standard) mobile radio intelligence unit under Gilven M. Slonim. On June 6, as Allied troops stormed ashore in Normandy, France, Admiral Mitscher led Task Force 58 out of Majuro. Spruance joined him at sea. They had seven fleet carriers and eight light carriers, seven fast battleships, three heavy cruisers and seven light cruisers, and sixty destroyers—a huge armada. An intercept caught the urgent Japanese message on June 9 by the scout plane that found Majuro empty. The next day there was heavy aircraft radio traffic; some of the messages, given their signal strength, had originated nearby, but none was a sighting report. Then, on June 11, combat air patrol fighters shot down a Japanese *Army* search plane.

Because naval intelligence had always concerned itself primarily with the Japanese Navy, Imperial Army circuits were not routinely monitored by mobile intercept units like Slonim's and those that accompanied Mitscher and two of his task group commanders. No one heard whether the Army plane got off any report. However, later that morning Lieutenant (j.g.) Charles A. Sims, unit leader and language officer aboard Task Force 58 flagship *Lexington,* overheard a report that made it plain the Americans had been sighted. Official sources indicate this may have been a contact with American aircraft by a plane from Tinian, headquarters of the First Air Fleet. The Saipan seaplane base, plus air bases on Tinian and Guam, went on alert. Mitscher launched an offensive fighter sweep sooner than planned; attacks on Guam, Rota, Saipan, and Tinian followed.

North of Saipan, American carrier planes caught a convoy of a dozen merchantmen, accompanied by a torpedo boat and nine patrol craft, which had just left for Yokohama. The convoy was smashed, with ten of its cargo vessels sent to the bottom. It was the third important convoy broken up in the area, with a Truk-bound convoy having taken heavy losses in April and a Marianas one in May. Lost aboard his escort, *Iki,* during May was Rear Admiral Baron Ijuin Matsuji, one more Japanese sailor whose bravery proved inadequate to stem the tide of defeat.

June 11 began a long purgatory for Japanese in the Marianas. Every succeeding day brought more air strikes and, soon, bombardments by surface ships. The diary of Imperial Navy officer Nagata Kazumi, captured on Saipan, provides a glimpse of the tests the Japanese had to face. The first day there were few losses because the men retired to air-raid shelters, and after nightfall everyone except firefighters and lookouts retreated into mountain caves. Destruction of facilities began on the eleventh, however, and was already well advanced the next day. Our diarist notes: "Fought fire while maintaining lookout for enemy planes." Things were even more serious by Tuesday, June 13: "In keeping with the increasing severity of the bombing, lookouts and firefighting units today were kept on a stand-by alert. Air raid shelters were changed. . . . Strafing has become increasingly severe." The officer personally saw and counted several hundred American aircraft attacking. Ships closed in and began to shell them; by evening shells had begun to fall nearby, and Nagata had to lead the laborers of whom he had charge to yet another shelter, a few at a time to reduce their risk. With a few companions, on the veranda of the destroyed workers' quarters, "we who had stayed behind bolstered our spirits with five bottles of beer."

Then the bombardment, which had let up temporarily, began again. "It grew more and more dangerous for us where we were. There was no sense in our remaining." They arrived at their new site, a cave in the mountains, but "when we arrived at the cave we found it also to be vulnerable to naval gunfire," so they moved on again. On June 14:

> We were shelled all day long by naval guns firing at our valley. Very near us was a coast defense gun. I went up by myself on a hill from which I could see the Air Depot. Directly below were three enemy battleships, two heavy cruisers, and seven or eight destroyers. Far off shore were four carriers and a number of destroyers. It was like watching a [naval] review.
>
> During the night we moved again.

The next day American troops began to land on Saipan. The Japanese waited until after dark to bathe in a nearby stream, and Nagata took out a bottle he had brought with him: "There is something undescribable about a shot of liquor during a bombardment." That day he formed his men from the technical department and the depot into a makeshift combat unit including a machine-gun element. The lookouts had to be changed every hour to prevent their becoming completely terrorized. By dawn a hundred ships could be counted offshore.

Despondency set in quickly. On June 16, with U.S. troops ashore for just twenty-four hours, Nagata wrote: "There is nothing to do but be trampled under by the enemy tanks. There will be an attack when night comes." On June 17: "We had our first rice balls in a long time. We played cards while shells rained down about us, but the game did not arouse much interest. . . .

Was our training insufficient?" On June 18 the Japanese moved to yet another place of refuge. By then Commander Nagata knew Japan had already lost Aslito Airfield to the Americans, and only Airfield Number 2, which the Japanese called Banaderu, was left. It *had* to be kept in service to facilitate the Decisive Battle. Officers like Nagata, caught on the ground in the Marianas, could hardly know that the Decisive Battle was going on at that very moment.

SUFFERING ALONG WITH JAPANESE ON THE ISLANDS WERE JAPANESE ABOARD THE SUBmarines that were the first line of defense against any Allied invasion. Vice Admiral Takagi Takeo, whose headquarters had been successively driven from Kwajalein and Truk by American advances, had ended up on Saipan, where he continued to emphasize use of Sixth Fleet submarines on transport missions. Given perceived need, the Japanese were designing and beginning to construct specialized submarine transports, and Takagi defended himself against complaints of skippers tied down on missions by saying the I-boats would be restored to their traditional attack mission once transport boats began to emerge from the dockyards. Now Takagi himself and all the inner defense perimeter were suddenly threatened by the American Forager operation. When Combined Fleet issued orders for the A-GO Decisive Battle, Admiral Takagi got the opportunity to plan for a submarine operation following classic Imperial Navy doctrine. What happened once Takagi ordered that operation into effect simply demonstrated the degree of technical and tactical proficiency the Allies had achieved.

In essence, the Sixth Fleet's plans for the Decisive Battle had two elements; one, a force of submarines slated specifically for combat engagement; two, the general submarine force, diverted from its missions once the crisis arrived. Unfortunately for the Japanese, in a move roundly criticized later by such subordinate commands as the 7th Submarine Squadron, the plan also included a line of demarcation, drawn west of Saipan, past which no Japanese submarine was to attack. No doubt this rule was conceived to prevent mistaken attacks against the Imperial Navy's own mobile fleet, but since Task Force 58 maneuvered in precisely those waters through most of the battle which followed, the Sixth Fleet would be greatly hampered in its efforts to intervene.

A continuing weakness in Japanese submarine operations would also be built into Takagi's plan. As in earlier battles, the submarines deployed specifically for combat were placed on scout lines rather than (as was the U.S. practice) assigned patrol areas. This tied the submarines to specific points at sea and precluded them from responding flexibly to an evolving tactical situation. Problems with the method were demonstrated unmistakably by the *England* affair. In this instance the Japanese intercepted an American patrol plane's contact report which, it was quickly seen, had to pertain to the submarine *Ro-104*, part of what the Sixth Fleet called its NA patrol line. In a fatal move the Sixth Fleet immediately radioed orders to the entire NA line to displace sixty miles to the southeast, assigning specific positions in the message, which the Americans intercepted in turn and which quickly ended up at FRUPAC.

An incomplete version went to the JICPOA Estimates Section, where newly assigned submarine reports officer Lieutenant Bernice A. Johnson shared it with Jasper Holmes. The two were unable to make much of the data, but Holmes asked Joe Finnegan of FRUPAC to take a look at their map plot, and the latter was able to break out the entire set of submarine positions. An antisubmarine-warfare officer recently assigned to JICPOA, who had been grousing that the codebreakers didn't seem to help him the way they did U.S. submarine forces, was then given the intelligence, which he passed to a hunter-killer group composed of destroyer-escorts *England*, *George*, and *Raby*. The group proceeded to roll up the entire NA line, with the *England* making five kills in just twelve days plus sinking the *I-176*, which had been on a supply run. The feat was and remains unprecedented in anti-submarine warfare history.

Meanwhile Japanese radio intelligence intercepted American messages becoming more and more jubilant as the *England*'s score rose. Submariner Orita Zenji reports that some of these messages were decoded. At any rate the Sixth Fleet sent out a warning to its own boats, and *Ro-109* (Lieutenant Nakagawa Hiroshi) and *Ro-112* (Lieutenant Yuchi Toru) moved off the line and saved themselves. Submarine Squadron 7 stated in its battle experiences report:

> A formation in which a large number of submarines is arranged in a straight line, and in which each submarine occupies a fixed position, is very likely to be discovered if it is in the vicinity of enemy air bases which have been specially strengthened in anti-submarine devices. Once discovered, they receive a thoroughly neutralizing attack from the enemy and incur crippling damage. Therefore, there is considerable difficulty in organizing means of searching out the enemy, and in constructing barriers against the enemy.

Noteworthy also is that the Japanese supposed their patrol line to have been discovered by radio intelligence. In the next big fleet operation, that off the Philippines, the Japanese assigned their boats patrol areas.

Orita Zenji writes that the depredations of the Americans against the NA line, which lay to the south between the inner sphere and New Guinea and the Solomons, convinced Combined Fleet that the next blow would come from that direction. When the American fleet appeared from the east instead, Orita believes, the misapprehension resulted in a delay of several days before orders for any submarine concentration against the invaders.

In fact, on June 12 the only Japanese submarines in the Marianas were *Ro-36*, *Ro-43*, and *Ro-114*. Only one submarine, the *I-185*, was even as close as five days from the battle area, and she was en route to Wewak on a transport mission. Five other submarines were six to eight days away; seven were nine or ten; one, the *Ro-47*, still preparing to leave Kure, could not reach the area for eleven days.

Despite all difficulties the Japanese threw in every available submarine. Thirteen I- or Ro-boats were lost. The Japanese submariners thought they had achieved significant results. Lieutenant Ata Yoshihiro's *Ro-114* was credited with sinking an *Iowa*-class battleship that had been shooting at Guam. The boat herself was among those which did not return. Lieutenant Watanabe Hisashi's *Ro-115*, which did return, reported that she had threaded her way through a dense escort to fire torpedoes at an *Essex*-class carrier. Watanabe did not see the ship sink, nor did he detect visible damage, and he was driven away by escorts; but a radio intercept led the Japanese to credit the sinking. The success was attributed to Watanabe's attack thirteen minutes after sunset and in conjunction with air strikes putting great pressure on the U.S. fleet. Another radio intercept on June 21 reported the American carrier *Bunker Hill* (*Essex*-class) as sunk. American accounts not only do not confirm these sinkings, they do not even note any torpedo attacks from Imperial Navy subs.

Once American troops landed on Saipan there could be little question of Vice Admiral Takagi's continuing to direct Japan's submarine war. That function was assumed temporarily by the commander of Submarine Squadron 7, Rear Admiral Owada Noboru at Truk. Later the Sixth Fleet, after failing to evacuate Takagi by submarine, would be given a fresh chief in the Empire, Vice Admiral Miwa Shigeyoshi. About the only orders the subs were capable of carrying out effectively were evacuations, and as in Takagi's case, even these were not always successful. However, Lieutenant Commander Itakura Mitsuma with his *I-41*, to cite the opposite case, managed to get 106 airmen off Guam, taking them to Oita, where they could be incorporated into new units.

The greatest demonstration of the haplessness of the Imperial Navy submarine effort, however, would be the effectiveness of the American one. Ironically, in view of the Japanese doctrine of using submarines in fleet engagements, it was the American boats that proved deadly in just these circumstances. Just how deadly would be seen in the main fleet encounter of what has become known in American history as the battle of the Philippine Sea.

· · ·

THERE WAS A VERY SPECIAL SHIP, ONE ADMIRAL OZAWA MADE HIS FLAGSHIP, AMONG THE warships Japan was concentrating for its Decisive Battle. This was the aircraft carrier *Taiho*, ordered under the Imperial Navy's 1939 building program and laid down at the Kawasaki Industries yard at Kobe in July 1941. Captain Kikuchi Tomozo became her chief equipment officer, managing the complex process of fitting out the new fleet carrier with the myriad items intended to make her a functional man-of-war. *Taiho* sported a Type 13 radar, twelve medium and fifty-one light anti-aircraft guns, and space for seventy-four aircraft. On a displacement of 29,300 tons, innovative Japanese warship designers were able to achieve a fleet carrier that not only had a high aircraft capacity but could make great speed (33 knots) and had an armored flight deck able to withstand 1,000-pound bombs. Had the Imperial Navy had ships like this at Midway the outcome of that battle would have been very different.

As frequently happened in the Imperial Navy, when *Taiho* was commissioned on March 7, 1944, her erstwhile chief equipment officer became her first skipper. Captain Kikuchi's assistant, Commander Otomo Bunkichi, became executive officer. Otomo had served with Kikuchi previously, when the latter commanded *Zuikaku* in 1943, and, like his boss, was an aviator. Kikuchi, for his part, had been chief of staff of the Naval Air Training Command, commander of an air group on Taiwan, and a carrier commander. He had wide experience in JNAF billets.

The Japanese viewed the war situation so seriously that *Taiho* got little opportunity to work up in Empire waters—just a perfunctory couple of weeks for the most necessary shakedown. Then Captain Kikuchi took her south to join the mobile fleet at Singapore, where he arrived on April 5. Admiral Ozawa happily hoisted his flag in the new carrier to make her the fleet flagship.

At Lingga Kikuchi found many comrades from his Etajima class of 1917. Among them were Ozawa's chief of staff, Kimura Keizo, and such fellow carrier commanders as Matsubara Hiroshi (*Shokaku*) and Shibuya Kiyomi (*Junyo*). Captain Kobe Yuji of the *Nagato* was a classmate, as was Morishita Nobuei of *Yamato*. Naval academy contemporaries included Rear Admiral Obayashi Sueo (class of 1915), commanding Carrier Division 3, plus carrier captains Kaizuka Takeo of the *Zuikaku* (1918), and Yokoi Toshiyuki of the *Hiyo* (1918). Indeed, almost every major vessel in the roads at Lingga at this time was skippered by a graduate of the classes that left Etajima between 1917 and 1919. A couple had taught at the Naval War College. The only three exceptions were 1915 or 1916 graduates. A very fresh memory for all these men was the battle of Jutland, the World War I engagement that had *missed* becoming the Decisive Battle many had then hoped for. Young Imperial Navy officers could not help drawing conclusions from Jutland, just as did their American colleagues. Indeed, Admiral Ozawa himself, as a junior officer, had gone to Germany to make a special study of the German Navy and Jutland from their point of view.

A major criticism of Jutland, which has echoed down the years and began to be heard within months of the encounter, was that the British fleet failed to trap the German because it had not been aggressive enough in pursuit. This was the kind of argument Japanese officers could appreciate. The Koga plan for Operation Z, transformed by Toyoda into Operation A, was the embodiment of aggressive pursuit of a Decisive Battle, even by a fleet inferior to the adversary. Ozawa Jisaburo's task was to convert the generalized precepts of the scheme into a real operations plan.

Admiral Ozawa had one significant advantage, and he intended to utilize it to the fullest: Japanese aircraft had longer ranges than their American equivalents. Ozawa proposed to launch his strikes at full range, from a distance at which U.S. planes could not reach him at all. The concept fit very well into the overall scheme of Operation A: American forces would be discovered and weakened by the Japanese submarines, then battered by the First Air Fleet; Ozawa's carrier strikes would follow up with shuttle-bombing, hitting the Americans, landing to refuel and rearm at the Marianas' "unsinkable aircraft carriers," then returning to their ships while striking yet another blow.

Few Imperial Navy plans benefited from so much study and examination as this one. Vice Admiral Ito Seiichi of the Navy General Staff flew down to Singapore in March to hold detailed staff discussions with the operational commanders. Because the acute embarrassment of the Navy's repeated defeats forced Admiral Nagano Osami to resign after the Truk raids, and because his successor was Navy Minister Shimada, concurrently holding both offices, Admiral Ito effectively acted as naval chief of staff. Ito shared his results with incoming Combined Fleet commander Toyoda Soemu and chief of staff Kusaka Ryunosuke. The latter, along with other staffers, joined Admiral Toyoda without delay when the new commander in chief boarded flagship *Oyodo* at Kisarazu on April 30. Ito helped Shimada incorporate the plan into IGHQ Navy Directive Number 373, of May 3. War games and staff studies on the plans were held at NGS, aboard the *Oyodo*, aboard Ozawa's flagship, *Taiho*, and on a smaller scale on flagships of lesser units. Emperor Hirohito himself attended the critique of the Tokyo war games on May 2, a two-and-a-half-hour dissection in great detail and the first occasion during the war that the Emperor is known to have participated in a pre-operation planning session of this kind (at least for the Imperial Navy). Never had the Navy prepared such extensive and detailed plans.

Admiral Ozawa's primary concerns were the training of his air groups, on the one hand, and his fuel situation on the other. With poorer pilots but more sophisticated aircraft, accident rates were up; the JNAF could not even afford to fly its air groups out to their carriers when the vessels left port. Thus when *Shokaku* and *Zuikaku* sailed from Japan earlier that year, their aircraft had to be lifted laboriously onto the vessels' decks by crane at Iwakuni. The Singapore area was fine for fleet training but much too far from the battle area of the Marianas, leaving the Japanese without sufficient oilers to both sail to battle and conduct an engagement. Ozawa's compromise was to displace in advance to the forward base, in this case Tawitawi in the Sulu Archipelago. But Tawitawi had no completed airfields, and carriers had to leave the protection of the harbor to conduct flight training, with hazards that became more evident every day.

Through their codebreakers the Allies knew of the mobile fleet's move to Tawitawi. In fact, the April 30 edition of SOWESPAC's monthly summary of Japanese dispositions both noted considerable preparations at Tawitawi for basing naval units and predicted that Japanese naval forces at Singapore would shortly be moving up to base in "Southern Philippine waters." Both items were based on naval Ultra intercepts, but the monthly summaries carried a lesser classification than the radio intelligence itself. These and other items were later cited as security breaches in a survey of intelligence dissemination in this theater.

Much of Admiral Ozawa's mobile fleet arrived at Tawitawi only in mid-May. The Allies had sufficient time to concentrate submarines off the base, including Lieutenant Commander Sam Dealey's *Harder*. This and other subs became a thorn the Japanese could not loose. *Lapon* reconnoitered the anchorage on May 15, reporting the presence of six carriers, four or five battleships, eight heavy cruisers, and smaller vessels. Other warship movements through Davao, as well as the sortie of Japanese vessels for the abortive KON Operation, were all reported as they occurred. The *Gurnard* was credited with damaging a battleship, possibly *Kongo,* which for a time radio intelligence mistakenly thought might even have been sunk. Actually the *Kongo,* although in the stipulated area, does not seem even to have noticed the attack. Carrier *Chitose* and other Japanese vessels, on the other hand, recognized their luck in evading torpedo attacks made on them. Submarine *Harder* sank three of Ozawa's precious destroyers, and other boats dispatched two more in the Sulu Archipelago plus two in the Bonins. Ozawa's escort forces were reeling though battle had yet to begin.

Submarine commander Orita Zenji believes the spectacle of the massacre in southern waters induced Admiral Toyoda to expect the Allied invasion force from that direction, and that the resulting delay was fatal to Operation A. Fleet chief of staff Kusaka Ryunosuke describes Combined Fleet's reasoning differently: Some staff, most notably newly appointed air staff officer Fuchida Mitsuo, believed the land-based First Air Fleet would be the key to success and argued that Ozawa's Mobile Fleet should sortie simultaneously with the land-based air attacks. This dictated an immediate activation of the plans. Other staffers worried about fuel. If the fleet sailed prematurely and the Americans withdrew, or if the Americans were simply making another carrier raid, fuel would be expended needlessly while fleet forces and their invaluable tankers would be exposed to no purpose. In this view the actual U.S. invasion landings, by tying the American fleet up in protecting the troops on shore, would make the Japanese plan practicable.

Whatever his reasoning, in the afternoon of June 13 Admiral Toyoda ordered preparations to activate Operation A and followed with an execute order in the morning of the fifteenth when it was clear that the American landings had begun.

American authorities reacted instantly to the Japanese orders. On June 14 in his daily appreciation for Nimitz, fleet intelligence officer Layton argued that Admiral Toyoda saw U.S. activity in the Marianas as an invasion, not merely another carrier raid. In fact the CINCPAC bulletin explicitly referred to the Japanese Z plan, predicted that a modified form of that scheme would be carried out, and noted Japanese naval units already in motion. A prediction of Japanese battle strength of nine carriers plus six battleships with other vessels was exactly accurate. Commander Layton's report was wrong only on its prediction of the day battle might take place (CINCPAC thought June 17) and the route Ozawa might use transiting the Philippines (CINCPAC expected Surigao Strait; Ozawa actually took San Bernardino Strait). The intelligence, forwarded to the Fifth Fleet, enabled Admiral Spruance to determine that he had enough time left prior to battle to enable a portion of his force to raid Iwo Jima, smashing a vital refueling point for Japanese aircraft moving from Japan to reinforce the Marianas.

Daily radio intelligence summaries from COMINCH make it clear that the Japanese moves were neither unsuspected nor surprising in Washington either. On June 15 the summary stated that a Japanese plan to counter Forager appeared to have been put into effect on the thirteenth. Specifically: " 'A' Operations are believed to be a plan to counter any U.S. advance in the Central Pacific and to repulse raids by U.S. Striking Forces. While details of this plan are not known, it is probable that the bulk of the Japanese fleet will be committed." From traffic analysis the summary identified the cruiser *Oyodo* as Combined Fleet flagship. The OP-20-G report also commented on Japanese radio intelligence, noting that since late on June 12 there had been a steady stream of reports from the Owada Communications Unit, "possibly containing intelligence derived from the communications of U.S. task forces operating in the Marianas . . . possibly reflecting some success in exploiting the calls and frequencies belonging to units of these forces captured from a U.S. plane shot down over Saipan on the 11th."

The COMINCH summary returned to these issues the next day, noting continued indications of Japanese intent to commit the Combined Fleet. The June 16 report also indicated that a Japanese search plane from Marcus had seen the groups of Task Force 58 headed for Iwo Jima, and noted orders for planes at Iwo to attack the Americans. First Air Fleet continued to generate the bulk of Japanese tactical message traffic. On June 17 the COMINCH summary revealed that Japanese messages consisted almost exclusively of operational reports regarding the Marianas, that practically all of them were addressed to the "A Force"—that is, Ozawa's Mobile Fleet—and that the commander in chief of the Combined Fleet actively directed forces throughout the day. On June 18 the COMINCH summary reported continued strong evidence of a Japanese striking force approaching from Philippine waters, extensive aircraft reconnaissance, and, most important, a late-afternoon contact report by a plane that had sighted part of Task Force 58.

Actual Imperial Navy operations during these busy days were mirrored nicely in the U.S. radio intelligence. Ozawa had left Tawitawi on the thirteenth for Guimaras off the Philippine island of Panay. Upon receiving Toyoda's execute order he passed through the Philippines using the San Bernardino Strait, entering the Philippine Sea on June 16, where Admiral Ugaki joined him with units previously detached for the Biak operation.

Admiral Ozawa hoisted the battle flag used by the Imperial Navy's famous Togo Heihachiro at Tsushima. Ozawa also repeated to his fleet the words Togo had used in 1905, which Toyoda had just sent him to exhort a new generation of Japanese sailors in 1944: "The fate of the Empire rests on this one battle. Every man is expected to do his utmost."

While Ozawa steamed toward the fight, American submarines complemented the radio intelligence units. Submarine *Redfin* reported the Mobile Fleet leaving Tawitawi on June 13, while *Flying Fish* sent word when Ozawa exited San Bernardino Strait on the evening of the fifteenth. Twice on June 17 the *Cavalla* filed contact reports, first with one of Ozawa's oiler units, then while the fleet refueled in the Philippine Sea. It was clear the Japanese were operating just beyond the range of B-24s flying from Manus in the Admiralties.

Submarine *Seahorse* also reported Ugaki's KON force coming up from the south on June 15. This confirmed the information flowing into the intercept unit aboard Mitscher's flagship. Lieutenant Charles A. (Sandy) Sims had two positions manned continuously, assignment of which he left up to his chief, William Beltz. The latter kept one radio tuned to JNAF frequencies, while the other he switched around, often on Truk broadcast frequencies, sometimes on Japanese fleet circuits, sometimes Tokyo. The radiomen copied Ugaki's messages and, though Beltz only infrequently did direction finding, in this case his men found the transmissions coming up from the south. No one wanted to say anything because Sandy Sims was telling the radiomen, on the basis of Mitscher's copy of the actual Japanese operations plan, that the enemy fleet was going to be coming from the north, through the Philippines. Other submarines confirmed that, as did one radio fix Beltz

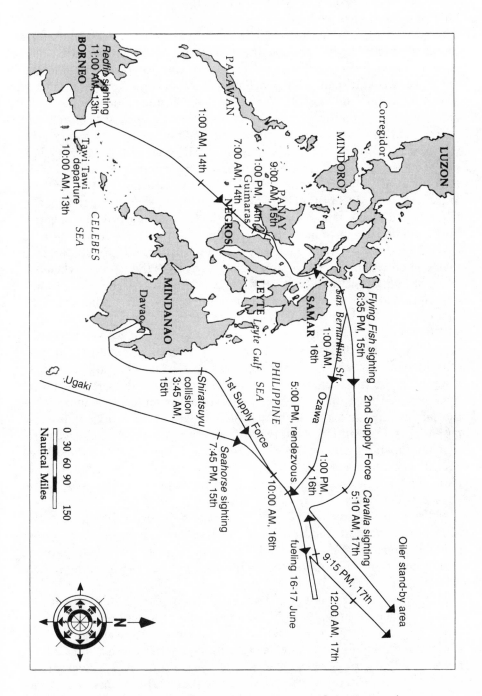

XI. Battle of the Philippine Sea (Approach to Contact)

got on the *Shokaku,* but it was nice to have the *Seahorse* report validate their other information as well.

Sandy Sims had a first-rate mobile radio intelligence unit, containing a number of men who had previously sailed under Gil Slonim. Now they benefited not only from experience but from the prior accumulation of intelligence. On Kwajalein, as it happened, marines had come upon a number of Japanese burning documents and had salvaged many, including a code-book, which had passed to Sims. The book was photographed before being sent to Pearl Harbor, with the consequence that at least one Japanese code was now being read directly on board the Task Force 58 flagship. As a language officer, Sims made immediate translations of messages and took them directly to Mitscher. On one occasion the practice got him in trouble. Mitscher's new chief of staff, Captain Arleigh A. Burke, was astonished to find a junior officer who often took the admiral aside for private conversations, and had access to him any time of day or night. When Captain Burke asked Sandy Sims why he talked to the admiral so much, the intelligence man politely responded he was not at liberty to reveal the subject of their discussions. Burke insisted, Sims sent him to Admiral Mitscher. Eventually, after approval from Pearl Harbor, Captain Burke would be initiated into the rites of Ultra.

When the time for battle came, the radiomen under Beltz and Sims would be able to provide vital intelligence. Beltz, who thought Japanese radio operators incapable of laying off their keys, was able to give warning even *before* a Japanese aircraft launch because he discovered radio operators testing their sets. Within minutes of such a launch, many aircraft would be doing the same thing, and that confirmed the intelligence. The huge volume of position reports sent by so many JNAF crews told the intercept specialists that the Japanese were inexperienced. Beltz believes their unit must have copied over a hundred different pilots and crews as the Japanese flew. And to top it off, by tracking signal strength the intercept unit could estimate the JNAF rate of closure.

Not even at Midway had a U.S. fleet had better intelligence support. At the Philippine Sea, however, that fleet, *with* its fine intelligence, was also markedly superior in aircraft numbers, in every category of warships other than heavy cruisers, and in such technological areas as radar and fighter performance.

Meanwhile, in air staff officer Fuchida's vision of the battle, which had much to do with reality, the fight was already being lost. For almost a week before the fleet engagement Task Force 58 and other U.S. warships had the run of the Philippine Sea. They used the time to batter those islands where Kakuta had his First Air Fleet planes. The Marianas themselves were hardest hit, but raids extended as far north as Iwo Jima in the Bonins. Losses sustained by the First Air Fleet included 110 aircraft in the Marianas plus the better part of those on Iwo, which then numbered more than 140. Equally important, the Marianas airfields would be neutralized by virtually continuous fighter sweeps.

One Japanese pilot to feel the effects of these actions would be Abe Zenji, who had flown from carriers at Pearl Harbor and the Aleutians and was back with a JNAF group. Sent to hit the invaders, Abe's dive-bomber was damaged, and he made for Guam. Far from carrying out a shuttle-bombing, Abe was marooned by the forced landing, and he spent the rest of the war hiding out on Guam. Except for the fact that he refused to surrender or participate in any desperate suicide attacks, his experience would be typical. Seaman Inoue of the 761st Air Group on Palau shows the way other JNAF bases were also reduced. Palau was hit on June 9 by B-24 heavy bombers, with damage and losses to every squadron in his group. The *Ryu* Force, considered the elite attack unit of the 761st, suffered sixty or seventy killed. Then came news of the Americans in the Marianas. "I guess Japan itself is really in danger now," Inoue wrote in his diary on June 15. "I am really very worried."

By drawing the venom from Admiral Kakuta's land-based air force before Ozawa's fleet made contact, the Americans defeated their adversary in detail and precluded whatever chance remained that good cooperation between the Japanese forces might overwhelm U.S. defenses. Two of the three prongs of Japan's Decisive Battle forces, land-based air and submarines, were thus exhausted before the initiation of the main engagement.

Saturday, June 17, was cloudy, becoming clear, opening with seven-tenths cloud cover. Ozawa groped for Admiral Spruance's American fleet, while the latter had Mitscher refuel two of Task Force 58's groups as the other two returned from the Iwo Jima strike. By evening Ozawa had fair intelligence on Spruance's dispositions. He expected battle the next day, and deployed a very heavily escorted advance group of three light carriers ahead of the remainder of the Mobile Fleet, which was divided into two more groups in much the same fashion as Task Force 58.

Sunday dawned clear, the best weather in several days, with Mobile Fleet pilots eager to match the supposed achievements of their land-based brethren, who had reported putting several U.S. fleet carriers out of action the previous evening (actually, only one ship, and she only an escort carrier, the *Fanshaw Bay*, had been hit, and with just one bomb). But extensive dawn searches proved negative. Meanwhile radio intelligence was active. As he left Tawitawi and then Guimaras, Ozawa benefited from radio deception in which land stations in the Singapore area assumed fleet call signs and maintained active traffic. The Owada Group reported long communications from U.S. submarines, however, so Ozawa knew he had already been spotted. In fact, on at least one occasion, the day he left Guimaras, the 3rd Combined Communications Unit supported Ozawa by jamming radio transmissions from a U.S. sub for over two hours. Mitscher's carriers seem to have been silent enough on the eighteenth, however, that Japanese special-duty groups could not alert Ozawa to their positions. Frustrated, the Japanese sent out a second search at noon, and this finally reported several groups of U.S. warships. Reports at midafternoon meant a dusk attack effort followed by the need to land at threatened airfields in the gathering darkness. Ozawa preferred to steam in a holding pattern and make his assault at dawn.

Rear Admiral Obayashi Sueo proved more impatient. Obayashi had been skipper of the light carrier *Zuiho* during Midway and at Santa Cruz, where an important lesson had been that rapidity of action was a key factor in battle outcomes. Now Obayashi launched as many planes as he could for immediate attack, and they were in the air when Ozawa's postponement reached him. The planes were recalled. One *Chitose* plane crashed upon landing. The battle lessons report drawn up after the engagement argues that immediate attack would have been the better choice.

Meanwhile Ozawa broke radio silence to describe his plans briefly in a message routed to subordinates, to Admiral Kakuta of First Air Fleet, and to Commander in Chief Toyoda. His message was necessary to ensure coordination of JNAF attacks the next day, but not so necessary as Ozawa imagined, since Kakuta's base air force already lay crippled and neutralized. A key error on the Japanese side is that Kakuta failed to apprise his colleagues of the actual state of the First Air Fleet, knowledge of which might have led Ozawa to turn away or Toyoda to terminate the A Operation. Ozawa's good coordination, on the other hand, was poorly repaid—an American land station intercepted his update message and got a close radio fix on the Mobile Fleet, which it passed promptly to Mitscher and Spruance.

The dawn broke fair but the day of June 19 would be partly cloudy with occasional squalls. American officers recorded cloud cover as seven-tenths—not enough to prevent Ozawa's dawn search from making very quick contact, however. Ozawa hurled attack groups at Task Force 58, but far from a Decisive Battle success, the aerial assault had very little impact on the Americans. Radio intelligence officers Gil Slonim, with Spruance, and Sandy Sims, with Mitscher, were alert, as were the teams on *Hornet* and *Yorktown*. The radiomen overheard when JNAF flight leaders gave their formations final pre-attack instructions. These were passed to Task Force 58's fighter interceptor officers, who also got data on the altitude and bearing of incoming strikes from ship radars. By 10:00 A.M., when the initial wave reached the Americans, they had already intercepted more than fifty messages.

Strong combat air patrols flying technically superior Hellcat fighters completed the winning combination the Americans exhibited that day. The action of June 19 has come down in American history as the "Marianas Turkey Shoot." The American achievement was remarkable, not only on the day of the Turkey Shoot but throughout Forager. Japan's First Air Fleet carried 1,644 aircraft on its order of battle. Of these only 1,188 would be available in the Forager area; Japanese naval historian Ito Masanori estimates that 500 of the land-based aircraft had been destroyed during the initial phase of Forager. Reduced serviceability due to poor maintenance, and airfield neutralization eliminated the First Air Fleet as a factor in the outcome. First Mobile Fleet then came to battle with 473 aircraft of its own, but they were now overmatched by the 956 planes Task Force 58 was capable of launching.

At the level of brass tacks, where it came down to encounters between aircraft over the Philippine Sea, comparison shows the JNAF even worse off. Ozawa launched a first wave of 129 planes, while Obayashi's carrier division launched 68 and Joshima Takaji's division another 49, in all 246 aircraft. A second wave of 82 planes went out late in the morning. Thus there were a total of 328 attack sorties, many of which were escort fighters with little attack capability. On its part, Task Force 58 put up a total of 413 combat air patrol fighters through the day. Interceptors actually outnumbered attack aircraft. Further, with the advantages of mobile radio units and radar, American fighter directors aboard the carriers were able to guide some 284 fighters to points of interception, so that CAP planes actually intercepting were almost as many as total JNAF sorties, and, given American technical advantages, superior.

American advantages loomed large in the overall results. Only one JNAF attack group reached a point of attack and sent the tactical message signifying it was proceeding to that action. Most other planes were met by American fighters when still fifty to seventy-five miles away from attack positions. Actual attacks on ships were sporadic throughout the day. Only 130 JNAF planes returned from their missions. If one adds in CAP, search, and antisubmarine sorties on June 19, the Mobile Fleet launched a total of 373 sorties for an overall loss of about 240 aircraft. Samuel Eliot Morison puts U.S. aircraft losses at twenty-three, and the more recent study by William T. Y'Blood finds just eighteen; these figures include noncombat losses. To complete the picture, the JNAF also lost about fifty First Air Fleet planes over the Marianas this day. One was a scout carrying the vaunted reconnaissance expert Chihaya Takehiko.

Ozawa suffered disaster even while his aircraft attacks were still on their way. Unknown to Captain Kikuchi of the spanking-new *Taiho*, as the ship completed launching her first-wave aircraft she was in the sights of American submarine *Albacore*. Lieutenant Commander James Blanchard fired six torpedoes at the speeding carrier, then went deep to avoid destroyer counterattack. Young Japanese pilot Komatsu Sakio, just taken off from *Taiho*, saw the torpedoes and dived into one of them, heroically saving the ship from that tin fish at the cost of his own life. That torpedo detonated just a hundred yards from the carrier, but Blanchard's number six fish hit home, impacting against *Taiho*'s port side, forward of the torpedo protection spaces, at a place where gasoline feed lines ran close to the hull. The ship's forward elevator, in the up position, fell about six and a half feet, while the elevator well began to fill with a mixture of seawater, gasoline, and fuel oil.

Captain Kikuchi reduced his speed by only one knot and stayed in formation while damage-control efforts began. The crew decked over the elevator opening. To rid the hangar spaces of gas fumes, doors and hatches were opened in hopes that fumes would be carried away, but the effect was to spread them throughout the ship instead. Now the Japanese paid the price for *Taiho*'s having been designed with fully enclosed hangars rather than ones with openings to the side, precluded due to low freeboard. Damage controllers tried to get rid of the fumes by operating every ventilation system on the entire ship, both feed and exhaust. Again the fumes were merely spread further through the vessel. At about 1:30 P.M. a spark ignited a vapor explosion that rippled throughout the carrier.

*Taiho*'s navigator, standing on the bridge, reported that the explosion appeared centered near the forward elevator. The armored flight deck split down the middle, hull bulkheads blew out on both sides of the hangars, and the heavy flight deck seemed to deflect downward the force of the blast. Engulfed in flames, the ship began to sink. Almost all the 500 or so survivors had been topside when the explosion occurred. The only engineering survivors came from the number two fireroom and escaped by climbing straight upward over masses of bent and twisted wreckage. *Taiho* listed to port, sank by the stern, and took with her thirteen planes and over a thousand sailors. Admiral Ozawa wanted to go down with his flagship but was prevailed upon instead to transfer to cruiser *Haguro*.

When Ozawa Jisaburo went over to the *Haguro* the Emperor's portrait went with him. In the confusion of the transfer, however, the very secret special codebook being used in the operation was forgotten. Thereafter Ozawa could not decipher the orders he was receiving from Combined Fleet flagship *Oyodo*. A considerable backlog of messages piled up before the *Haguro* was able to get a notice to this effect out to Admiral Toyoda. The special-duty group aboard *Taiho*, which had furnished valuable aid to Ozawa thus far, was also rendered useless by loss of their equipment and some radio operators in the disaster. The Japanese were thereafter assisted only by a smaller special-duty group aboard Vice Admiral Kurita's Second Fleet flagship, *Atago*.

In the meantime, before *Taiho* met her end the Japanese also lost another of their few fleet carriers, Captain Matsubara Hiroshi's *Shokaku*. This carrier became a victim of Commander Herman Kossler's submarine *Cavalla*, which had already done important scout work for the Americans. Kossler hit with four torpedoes (according to Clay Blair; most other sources credit three), and

*Shokaku* broke up and went down at midafternoon, with nine more scarce aircraft still aboard. *American* submarines had carried out the important function reserved for these ships in *Japanese* Decisive Battle doctrine.

The most controversial aspect of American actions at the Philippine Sea is the decision Admiral Spruance made to head east, away from Ozawa's fleet. This run took Task Force 58 away from the position it would have to reach to make an air strike on the Japanese. Spruance's maneuver was very much like what he had done at Midway the night of the big carrier strikes in that battle. In that instance, the Japanese had sent surface gunnery ships in an attempt to catch up to the U.S. fleet; at Philippine Sea it was again true that the strongest Japanese heavy ships, including *Yamato* and *Musashi,* were with the vanguard force, which was almost a hundred miles closer to Task Force 58 than the rest of the Mobile Fleet. Spruance was also responsible for the security of the Forager invasion flotillas, responsibility greater than he had had at Midway. His strategic decision was a conservative one but seems proper given circumstances.

On June 20 Task Force 58 headed back west at full speed and managed to get off a late-afternoon strike with 262 aircraft. As the sun set American planes caught Rear Admiral Joshima's Carrier Division 2 force, smashing Captain Yokoi Toshiyuki's light carrier, *Hiyo,* which the Japanese mistakenly thought had been dispatched by a coordinated attack by both aircraft and a submarine. Other aircraft secured hits on four carriers, battleship *Haruna,* and cruiser *Maya,* but these did not prove fatal. It was on the night of the twentieth that Ozawa actually did order a surface attack; but, unaware of Task Force 58's actual position, he countermanded the instruction after a couple of hours.

Admirals Mitscher and Spruance meanwhile faced the decision of what to do about recovering their planes returning in the darkness, and whether to head west in pursuit of Ozawa. Mitscher ordered Task Force 58 to head east, because that was the direction the pilots would be expecting, to use floodlights to illuminate the carriers, and to slow from 23 to 16 knots, giving the planes the least distance to fly. Aboard the *Indianapolis* Gil Slonim tried to convince Spruance to override Mitscher, arguing that the fleet ought to head west at speed and could still catch Ozawa that way. For the returning planes Slonim advocated leaving behind a couple of light carriers with appropriate escorts to do the recovery job. Spruance refused. The fleet devoted superhuman efforts to the dangerous night recovery, but nevertheless eighty-two planes were forced to ditch in the ocean, the biggest U.S. loss of the battle. Another six planes had been lost to anti-aircraft fire and eleven more to interception by the Japanese. The opportunity for pursuit was gone, the battle over.

The Mobile Fleet retired north, reaching Okinawa on June 22. Ozawa had six carriers remaining, but in all they could muster only thirty-five aircraft.

Every one of the carriers, plus the *Haruna* and the cruiser *Maya*, required either upkeep or damage repair. Ozawa's fleet had become a spent quantity.

Americans exploited their success when Rear Admiral Joseph J. Clark took his Task Group 58.1 up to hit Iwo Jima one more time, ably seconded as usual by the mobile radio intelligence unit under Lieutenant (j.g.) E. B. Beath. Coincidentally, the Imperial Navy forces on Iwo at this time were commanded by Captain Wachi Tsunezo, a radio intelligence maven in his own right, who considered it normal given his radars and radio monitors to get warning of an incoming raid when attacking aircraft reached a point 120 miles distant. Expert Zero fighter pilot Sakai Saburo, one of those who had been formed into a special unit of flight instructors in connection with the A Operation and sent to bolster First Air Fleet units at Iwo, reports that Jocko Clark's June 24 strike was detected at a range of only sixty miles. As many as eighty fighters still managed to take to the air, every one in Rear Admiral Matsunaga Sadaichi's 27th Air Flotilla. Clark's initial fighter sweep consisted of just fifty-one Hellcats. Despite adverse odds, the Americans downed thirty planes (Sakai reports forty fighters alone) against losses of only six F6Fs. With subsequent bombing attacks and defensive actions over Task Group 58.1, some sixty-six JNAF aircraft were no more.

The Iwo raid pretty much marked the end of the naval action. Ground combat went on in the Marianas, where Saipan was secured on July 9. By the fourth, according to Nagata Kazumi's diary, naval headquarters stood in the front lines of the Saipan fighting. Nagata already knew what would happen:

> The decision to make a final stand has at last been announced. . . . Only Japanese officers and men will fight under such hopeless conditions. The spirit of Yamato, however, is rendered powerless by the overwhelming strength and the heavy weapons of the enemy.
>
> The island of Saipan is too small. It is even difficult for me to hide myself and I am only five feet tall.
>
> Our last day will be here in a day or two. Nothing to regret, nothing more to do. . . . This is fate; it had to end this way.

Admirals Nagumo Chuichi, the Pearl Harbor attacker, and Yano Hideo, the naval intelligence chief, were suicides on Saipan, as was Takagi Takeo of the submarine service, once the proud victor at the Java Sea. On Tinian, where 4,000 naval troops under Captain Oya Goichi formed almost half the defense force, defeat also brought the suicide of air fleet commander Admiral Kakuta. Many more junior men participated in suicide attacks against the heavily armed American troops. Lost in battle for the first time were ground installations belonging to the Japanese radio intercept service, the 1st Combined Communications Unit. Of the Marianas defenders, only a few airmen and staff officers escaped by submarine. Tragically, many civilians jumped off cliffs into the sea.

Intelligence once again benefited greatly from the Forager captures. There were 1,780 prisoners on Saipan alone; this time, fewer than half of them were Korean laborers. Among the prisoners, captured after he was wounded and knocked senseless in an attack, was Petty Officer Noda Mitsuharu. Once scribe for Yamamoto, Noda had filled the same function for Nagumo at Central Pacific Area Fleet. He became a source of astonishing inside information on Japanese naval strategy and command practices, enlightening CINCPAC fleet intelligence officer Eddie Layton, JICPOA deputy Jasper Holmes, and others. As the front drew closer to Japan, counterintelligence officers too drew on Noda's recollections preparatory to the occupation.

Documents were another intelligence windfall of Forager, not to be measured this time in the tens, or hundreds, or even thousands. On Saipan upwards of *fifty tons* of documents passed into the hands of Allied intelligence. The take included a complete set of Imperial Navy administrative orders, from which fleet organization, command structure, leadership, order of battle, and even post office boxes could be derived. Then there was a very helpful digest of Japanese naval air bases, which contained actual diagrams of every JNAF facility in the Home Islands, soon to become a theater of war. Another item taken was a file of material on naval land forces that revolutionized JICPOA's understanding of this subject. Other documents seized included technical studies of novel anti-aircraft rockets, papers indicating Japanese interest in jet planes, a selection of area fleet and other directives, and the usual array of diaries and personal notebooks, which often contained highly valuable intelligence data.

Technical intelligence finds included specimens of several types of Japanese radio and radar equipment, whose characteristics were quickly analyzed and made the subjects of reports circulated by JICPOA. But there was one piece of equipment taken on Saipan that would be kept very quiet indeed—a Jade cipher machine. Marines entered a bunker to find a Japanese seaman with a hammer desperately trying to pound the machine into a pulp. He was working on the keyboard when the Americans shot him. The innards of the Jade machine were in perfect condition, and American cryptanalysts were able to verify their theories of Jade operation and perfect their entry into the system. That the Imperial Navy inevitably knew that Jade machines had been in the Marianas, and therefore vulnerable to capture, may have played a role in Japan's decision to discontinue Jade two months later.

One set of documents, which arrived too late to be of use at the Philippine Sea but would benefit the codebreakers during the next big naval battle, was the codebooks captured on Biak on June 8. Despite regulations requiring all captured papers to be reviewed by field teams, the Biak documents were held for days by persons unknown. They showed up at the Australian Central Bureau on the morning of June 19 and were immediately forwarded to fleet intelligence officer Arthur McCollum. He sent the code material on to FRUMEL, personally carried by one of his top aides in a special plane. The "swag" reached Monterrey Flats in the late afternoon, and the codebooks were photographed in order of their importance to the Allies. The first two films were carried to Brisbane by McCollum's aide the next morning, and started from there to FRUPAC and OP-20-G. Later copies went to British Station Anderson as well. FRUMEL had no explanation for the tardy receipt of the captured documents: "One supposes that more may trickle in later. Our diagnosis is—souvenir hunters."

Intelligence had helped win the Marianas battle. Its payoff was a new gold mine, a rich vein of fresh data and code material. Now the Allies enjoyed both unparalleled intelligence and considerable military strength. Suddenly Allied power seemed unassailable. Japan's last chance could only be a desperate venture. That is exactly what the Japanese planned for.

# "The Most Crucial Point
# Has Been Reached"

AS USUAL THERE WOULD BE MARKED DIFFERENCES BETWEEN THE PRIVATE AND PUBLIC faces Japan put on the events just transpired in the Philippine Sea. Publicly it had been a tough fight; though the claims were not of a victory, no defeat was conceded either. The respected naval historian Ito Masanori actually was fed material suggesting there had been *no* Decisive Battle. This induced him to write an article on "Japan's Fleet-in-Being Strategy" in which he remarked, "During the Saipan operation, the main body of the Japanese fleet remained inactive, for after due consideration of . . . factors, the probability of convincing success was found to be limited." Ito may have been hood-winked on the incidental details of the A Operation, but not even Imperial Navy propagandists could lead him astray on the basic strategic situation: "The question is whether the American Navy has strength enough to secure command of the fringes of Japanese shores . . . owing to the latest turn in the war situation, the United States has been favored with conditions suitable for conducting task force operations." Ito believed the Japanese fleet would soon emerge for a "decisive onslaught."

Imperial headquarters communiqués for the period of the A Operation claimed sinking or damaging nine aircraft carriers and five battleships. Japanese abroad were fed from this bowl, as for instance in Argentina, where attaché Rear Admiral Yukishita Katsumi (whose comments were promptly passed to U.S. intelligence) told another Japanese of the nine car-riers, admitting just two Japanese carriers sunk plus one damaged and taken to Taiwan. Yukishita frankly said that because Japan would need a year to replace the ten ships he thought lost, while the United States required only three months, the battle "may therefore be considered an American victory." Nevertheless, Yukishita did not object on July 1 when he heard embassy first secretary Omori Genichiro tell an audience of prominent Japanese residents that "the naval battle which took place around the island of Saipan was a Japanese victory." Omori inflated the claim for sunken U.S. aircraft carriers to thirteen.

A month later the *Mainichi* newspaper's Argentina correspondent, one Suzuki Saburo, expressed the view that what was happening was to Japan's *advantage:* "Japan welcomes the advance of American forces in the Pacific." The U.S. forces would concentrate on a few islands near Japan; then Imperial forces could choose their moment to knock out the Americans at one blow. The account sent to Washington would be amusing were not the issues so serious:

> Suzuki stated that he believes that the apparent Japanese reluctance to fight is lulling the Americans into a sense of false security now that they have taken Saipan and Guam, which is just the condition Japan desires. Suzuki pointed out that the Japanese are acting . . . in an attempt to attract an even greater concentration of American force so that the [Japanese] blow when it falls will thus be the more effective. Suzuki said that the Japanese Navy is not afraid, nor is it napping, nor are the Japanese pessimistic about American advances, but the Japanese are watching with the greatest of care for the proper moment to spring.

Such opinions were hardly restricted to naval historians or press commentators. Retired admiral Suetsugu Nobumasa, the former Combined Fleet commander, expressed himself quite similarly just weeks before the next great naval action. In an interview with the *Mainichi,* Suetsugu observed that the Pacific war would go on for a long time, with many air battles, "in the course of which the ripe moment will come for the Japanese forces to deal the final smashing blow to the enemy." The admiral referred to the Philippines, where a series of American carrier raids had just taken place, as a zone of destiny: "These operations indicate that the most crucial point has been reached in the war situation, presaging the most important fighting." The issue was "not a mere battle for the Philippines but one which will decide whether Japan can maintain or be cut off from her communication with the vital resources of the southern region." For that reason, Admiral Suetsugu opined, "the outcome of the Philippine operations will be of such a far-reaching nature as to decide the general war situation and I am certain it will be the greatest and most decisive battle fought."

FORMER COMMANDER IN CHIEF SUETSUGU'S PUBLIC REMARKS ACCURATELY REFLECT THE PRIvate views of the Japanese government and top planners of the Imperial

Navy. On June 21, at the end of the Philippine Sea battle, lord privy seal Marquis Kido's diary entry read: "The Navy, failing to grasp the best opportunity for a decisive battle, sustained considerable damage of airplanes and carriers. The result caused much anxiety and was most regrettable." Emperor Hirohito inquired of the Board of Generals and Admirals, his senior military advisers, what their plans for countermeasures were, and before long there were some quiet feelers as to how to bring the war to an end. General Tojo Hideki's cabinet fell as a consequence of the Marianas defeat. First Tojo tried to circumvent that development by inducing Admiral Shimada to give up his post as navy minister (though remaining as chief of the Naval General Staff), but that proved insufficient and Tojo himself was obliged to resign.

Incoming navy minister in the cabinet of General Koiso Kuniaki was Admiral Yonai Mitsumasa, a man who had resisted the push for war and was certainly amenable to peace moves. Yonai was entirely forthright in his speech to the Diet of September 9:

> The damage sustained by our side too must not be made light of. The unparalleled stubbornness with which the Japanese forces fought in the operations in the Marianas . . . [These] were truly actions which would make even the demons weep. In coordination with this, surface units of the Combined Fleet moved into Marianas waters, and with its smashing attacks, the enemy was about to be destroyed. Regrettably, however, the sending of the follow-up air power did not go as well as desired.

While telling Japanese legislators how poorly the A Operation had turned out, Admiral Yonai made private inquiries of Combined Fleet chief Toyoda Soemu. The commander in chief had been at General Staff offices for several days studying future operations when Yonai called him in for a little talk, asking right away about the naval situation.

Yonai wanted to know if the Imperial Navy could hold out through the end of 1944.

Admiral Toyoda replied that it would be extremely difficult to do so, and understood from this exchange that Yonai would use the fleet's weakness to argue for ending the war. Toyoda hardly felt himself as commander in chief to be in a position to engage in peace maneuvers, but the navy minister was in a different category.

Naval planners were well aware of the consequences of the Marianas defeat. Asked later what he thought had been the turning point of the war, Baron Tomioka Sadatoshi said simply: "The fall of Saipan. That gave you complete supremacy in our eyes on land and sea. In the south theater there was no suitable place where we had sufficient tactical reason to make a stand for a showdown. Saipan, however, was such a place. From there you could bomb the Homeland."

There can be no doubt the Imperial Navy's leaders knew exactly what chances they were taking. Looking back at the Philippine campaign after the war, Admiral Toyoda told interrogators, "Since, without the participation of our Combined Fleet there was no possibility of the land-based forces in the Philippines having any chance against your forces at all, it was decided to send the whole fleet, taking the gamble. If things went well, we might obtain unexpectedly good results; but if the worst should happen, there was a chance that we might lose the entire fleet." Toyoda simply said, "I felt that chance had to be taken."

The Combined Fleet commander's view would be accurately represented by Admiral Oikawa Koshiro, who replaced Shimada as chief of the Naval General Staff around this time. "I believe," Oikawa told the interrogators, "that the fleet authorities decided to take that step in the belief that they had a reasonable chance for success." Captain Takata Toshitane, Combined Fleet senior staff officer for part of this period and then an NGS planner, was also quite frank about the rationale for the plan that emerged after the Marianas defeat:

> By the time you had taken Saipan . . . we realized fully that it would be impossible for us to maintain a battle fleet in Japanese waters, subjected to bombing, and that when the American fleet did come in close to Japan that we would be unable to oppose it in any strength. Therefore, realizing that, we decided to commit our entire strength to the Leyte campaign . . . with the knowledge that we would lose most of it.

In Takata's view, Admiral Toyoda was resigned to that eventuality. His decision "was based on what happened to the Italian fleet in this war and the German fleet in the last war. Having seen those examples, he decided to use his operational strength wherever he could."

Actual Japanese preparations for the big campaign were rather more untidy than these quotes suggest. In fact, when Koyanagi Tomiji, chief of staff to Second Fleet commander Kurita, came back to Kure after a visit to Combined Fleet headquarters, he reported Tokyo in such a turmoil that hardly anything could be settled, while Combined Fleet itself was optimistically speculating about the potential for naval guerrilla warfare. Only reluctantly did NGS discard its plan for a relief expedition to Saipan. Gradually things came into focus. Without essential fuel supplies at home, the Japanese clearly needed to move the battle fleet to a base in the southern region, but because carrier air strength had been destroyed at the Philippine Sea those vessels needed to remain in Empire waters, at least for the present. Admiral Kurita took most of the surface forces to Singapore-Lingga in early July, his proud warships, even the superbattleships, reduced to transports for men and equipment on their way to Malaya. Subsequent strategy would be dictated by the bifurcated state of the fleet, its essential challenge being to devise a manner of getting the two very different elements to support each other effectively.

Because so much depended on this next operation, the war situation thrust Japanese intelligence even more to the fore. Given its limited effectiveness, however, Japanese intelligence missed Allied preparations for the invasions of Peleliu (in the Palau group) and Morotai, necessary stepping-stones to a Philippine campaign. Intelligence was also somewhat surprised when Task Force 38 began an extensive carrier raid into Philippine waters in September. However, the new Japanese battle plan accommodated a wide range of contingencies, and in the end intelligence furnished the desired warning.

Japanese staffs did their basic planning for the next battle in July and early August, while fighting continued on Tinian and guerrilla-style actions on Guam. The Japanese clearly appreciated that the blow might fall anywhere over a wide area, providing four distinct options ranging from the Kuriles and northern Japan through the main islands, to Okinawa and Taiwan and finally the Philippines. Their intent is suggested by the codename "Sho Go," or Victory Operation. The essential concept, prefigured in IGHQ Directive Number 431 of July 21, was to form a central reserve of air strength which could shift to the operational theater once the axis of Allied advance became apparent. At the same time fleet strength at Lingga "will be moved up to the Philippines or temporarily to the Nansei Shoto" (the Okinawa area) while that in Empire waters "will engage in mobile tactics as expedient . . . coordinating actions with base air forces to crush the enemy fleet and advancing forces." Opportunities to whittle down Allied strength would be grasped, while every effort would be made to scout out adversary intentions.

The areas within which Decisive Battle would be offered came into view within just a few days, when orders appeared for both the Army and Navy to build up defenses in the Nansei Shoto, the Bonins, and the Kuriles. Anti-aircraft and antisubmarine efforts were to be strengthened in a corridor connecting the Empire with the Philippines, while battle preparations were to be completed in the Empire by October and in the Philippines and the connecting area a month sooner. A joint Army-Navy paper drafted just after installation of Koiso's cabinet specified that "Decisive Battle will be waged against the advance of the main strength of the United States forces in the latter part of this year." Intended for discussion by a new body of top decision-makers, the Supreme War Direction Council, which would include the prime minister and some others, the July 24 proposal promised that "the enemy's plans will be smashed." In particular,

> when the enemy attacks one of the Decisive Battle areas, maximum air,
> sea, and ground strength will be assembled, the enemy carriers and trans-

•

port convoy will be sought out and annihilated on the spot, and, if a landing is effected, the enemy forces will be destroyed on land.

The Army section of IGHQ made an unofficial presentation of this new guidance to Prime Minister Koiso on July 27.

Meanwhile, a report from the chief of operations of the Naval General Staff arrived at Singapore on July 25. It warned that American admirals King and Nimitz had conferred in Hawaii with this conclusion: "The next enemy offensive will be directed at the Philippines and will be carried out shortly." The NGS was a couple of weeks late on the chronology of the COMINCH-CINCPAC meeting, but what is truly eerie is that Tokyo was making new decisions about Decisive Battle, with one focus on the Philippines, at the very moment when the Americans were making an identical decision, abandoning planned targets and timetables in favor of an invasion of Leyte in the central Philippines, known to the covert operators of the Allied Intelligence Bureau as Cyclone. The day before the NGS Philippine warning, in fact, President Franklin D. Roosevelt himself arrived at Pearl Harbor, where he met for several days with Admiral Nimitz and General MacArthur, in the only command conference at this level Americans held in the Pacific during the entire war. MacArthur argued for the Philippines invasion in preference to landings on Taiwan and the Chinese mainland. Nimitz eventually came to support this strategy. When a subsequent decision was made to accelerate the planned operation, Leyte became the target instead of Mindanao.

The Japanese continued their own preparations as well. On July 26, the eve of Roosevelt's Pearl Harbor meeting, IGHQ Directive Number 435 specified contingencies SHO-1 through SHO-4, linking each with one of the geographic regions already named. The Philippine contingency became SHO-1. That same day were revealed details of how JNAF and Army air units would be allocated to each SHO option. For the first time in the war, Army units (three air regiments) were placed under Navy operational control. Local commanders were enjoined to exercise initiative, disperse forces in depth, ensure maximum flexibility, and inflict losses on the adversary while conserving their own strength for the Decisive Battle.

General strategy in the war was the focus for the Supreme War Direction Council from its inception at the end of July. Officials were told the time had come for an end to wishful thinking. According to a senior Army operations planner:

> Japan's national power and war potential will gradually decrease, no matter how much effort Japan may exert, and, although she may be able to engage in a Decisive Battle before the end of this year, it will hardly be possible for her to counter any powerful attack during, and after, next year. The only way out of this difficulty is to check the enemy's advance.

The war council was offered four approaches, the last of which provided for almost all (70–80 percent) of Japan's remaining resources to be used in a proximate all-out effort. This option gained increasing favor. There were seven discussions between August 9 and 16, culminating in a joint service petition to the Emperor on the eighteenth, and a final decision in the presence of the Emperor on August 19.

By then the Imperial Navy's detailed plans for SHO were far advanced. Combined Fleet Top Secret Operations Order Number 83, on August 1, provided for cooperation with the Army "to intercept and destroy the invading enemy at sea in a Decisive Battle." As quickly as possible, air bases were to be prepared in the Philippines, of sufficient size and number to accommodate the aircraft of both the First Air Fleet and a newly formed Second Air Fleet. The Allied carrier forces were to be destroyed by air attack, and then surface and air forces would jointly combine to sink transport convoys. Should Allied troops succeed in landing, their amphibious shipping would become the principal target. Combined Fleet surface units were to sortie within two days of any invasion, and all-out air attacks would commence at least two days before the surface forces arrived at the target area. The separate Top Secret Operations Order Number 84 revised fleet organization for the anticipated engagement. Admiral Toyoda followed with additional revisions several days later, and he issued Order Number 87 to govern submarine activities on August 20. This instruction provided flexible operating areas and did away with attack restrictions: "Where penetration operations are being carried out by surface forces . . . [submarines] without adhering to prearranged deployment will make damaging attacks on the enemy. In such cases some confusion will be inevitable."

The Japanese labored with the urgency of men who knew their days are numbered. Admiral Toyoda later told interrogators that he had expected the Allied offensive against the Philippines to begin in August or September, while Imperial Navy preparations could not be complete before October or November. Replacing aircraft lost in the Marianas required at least four or five months, the Combined Fleet commander in chief noted.

Toyoda's chief of staff, poacher turned enforcer, was Rear Admiral Kusaka Ryunosuke, who had held the same job in the striking force during the heady early days of the war. Then Combined Fleet command had seemed an impediment, constantly obstructing the possibilities suggested by the field forces. Becoming Toyoda's second shortly before the Philippine Sea debacle, Kusaka began his new job confident that the Combined Fleet would triumph. In fact, when headquarters received the message that aircraft attack groups were on their way, Kusaka had been ready to celebrate by drinking a toast. Hopes dashed in that battle, the chief of staff now had a much finer appreciation of the Imperial Navy's decline in training standards and battle strength. Now Admiral Kusaka thought more of how unappreciative subordinates disrupted plans by resisting Combined Fleet orders.

There would be examples of this during planning of the SHO operation. On August 10 there was a meeting at Manila between operations officers and chiefs of staff of NGS, Combined Fleet, Southwest Area Fleet, and the principal operating forces. A Naval General Staff estimate predicted the next big Allied operation would come in the Philippines in late October. Then Combined Fleet staffers briefed the SHO plans. Efforts to discover oncoming Allied invasion forces at maximum distance (700 miles), and establish the intended objective, could be complemented by moving Admiral Kurita's Second Fleet forward to Brunei, on the north coast of Borneo, close to its fuel source and in position to rush out and attack the Allied flotilla while the air fleets took care of American carriers.

Admiral Koyanagi Tomiji, Kurita's chief of staff, was disturbed by the notion of simply throwing the surface fleet at an anchorage rather than using it directly for a Decisive Battle; he was steeped in the classic naval tradition, and warships seemed a more appropriate object of attack than transports and landing craft. Koyanagi raised the question of whether the surface fleet should try to attack aircraft carriers if such vessels were encountered. He recalls that Combined Fleet approved the suggestion. It would be a fateful exchange.

Koyanagi and his new senior staff officer, Captain Yamamoto Yuji, carried a copy of the SHO operations order back to Lingga with them. Senior commanders of Kurita's fleet were brought into the secret. War games were staged during the first days of September, the results studied, then new simulations held on September 14–15. The results favored Japan in the hypothetical battle, Ugaki Matome reasoned, because the Allies (called Red in the games) had tried to do too much, while JNAF forces had performed perfectly. "If it goes like this in reality," Ugaki wrote, "we shall have a chance to win and also be able to die satisfied even if we don't."

Admiral Ugaki did not feel satisfied a few days later, however, when Kurita's SHO operations plan was presented aboard flagship *Atago*. Koyanagi and Yamamoto seemed to lack answers to very basic questions about the scheme, and they still had none the next day, when Ugaki met privately with the senior staffers. He advocated attrition operations rather than some cosmic Decisive Battle, and believed that the fleet should seek an engagement with Allied surface forces rather than convoys. It is not clear whether Koyanagi told the battleship leader that as fleet chief of staff he had made almost identical objections.

In 1941, before Pearl Harbor, when Ugaki Matome had been Combined Fleet chief of staff and Kusaka Ryunosuke the chief of staff of the key field command, their reversed roles had played out in exactly the same fashion.

Other tabletop war games were held in Empire waters with interesting results. At Kure from September 1 to September 3, Admiral Ozawa held war games for his Mobile Fleet, now a rump force shorn of its principal surface strength. A fleet reorganization on August 10 recreated Carrier Division 1 with the newly built ships *Unryu* and *Amagi*, but there were no air groups and none would be ready, even for daytime-only operations, until the end of December. Carrier Division 3 now contained fleet carrier *Zuikaku*, the only large flattop currently battleworthy, and light carriers *Zuiho*, *Chitose*, and *Chiyoda*. A new Carrier Division 4 was added under Rear Admiral Matsuda Chiaki, comprising two unusual ships, battleships *Ise* and *Hyuga*, whose after gun turrets had been removed and replaced with partial flight decks to be used by floatplanes, twenty-two for each ship. Air groups for Carrier Division 3 would attain minimal competence in mid-October, those for Matsuda's hermaphrodite carriers in mid-November. Consequently, Ozawa's war games featured only a single air unit, that for Carrier Division 3, while Matsuda's warships sailed in their role as battleships.

The simulations showed that as a practical matter it would be impossible to effect a junction between Ozawa's carriers and Kurita's fleet from Lingga. The two forces would be too vulnerable maneuvering to rendezvous, and could be destroyed before they ever landed a blow. Because of the separation Ozawa himself could hardly exercise effective control over Kurita. Attempts to do so would merely duplicate the existing command structure, so Ozawa recommended that Combined Fleet exercise direct control over Kurita.

Ozawa's mission in both SHO-1 and SHO-2 was to divert Allied strength while also disrupting supply lines and rear areas. The war games showed this goal to be too ambitious. Ozawa recommended that his role be restricted to one of diverting the Allies. In addition, attacks by his battleships combined with Vice Admiral Nishimura Shoji's Fifth Fleet from northern waters, which were to be Ozawa's main device for inflicting losses, were judged to have very little chance of success. The Mobile Fleet commander recommended *reducing* his own force to the minimum necessary for its diversionary role and using units thus released in support of the Kurita fleet.

Finally, Admiral Ozawa judged from his war games that the Kurita force needed "directly cooperating air strength." Land-based air fleets "cannot be counted upon to provide any substantially effective direct cooperation." Without such help, "just as the Second Fleet command presently fears, there is great probability that [the Kurita fleet] will find itself carrying out its operations alone and unsupported." Ozawa recommended that his one functional carrier division plus escorting destroyers be attached to Kurita's fleet in mid-October when its air groups completed training.

This remarkable memorandum Vice Admiral Ozawa Jisaburo sent up to Combined Fleet without qualm. It is not often in any navy that a ranking commander advises that his own force be reduced, that the key elements of ·it be assigned to a subordinate, and that his mission be restricted to a subsidiary one, with command exercised at a higher echelon. Ozawa's advice was exactly this. It also happened to be quite prescient. A stronger Kurita fleet with organic air cover would have been even more resistant to Allied attacks. Had Ozawa's advice all been taken, the battle for Leyte Gulf might have turned out quite differently.

Instead the Combined Fleet command retained its basic scheme of maneuver. The northern force, Shima's Fifth Fleet, which despite its name amounted to only a couple of heavy cruisers, a light cruiser, and destroyers, would be detached from Ozawa, but its mission would be a haphazard one, its role never clear. No carriers were lent to Kurita, and that cost him dearly. Still the Combined Fleet had at least some kind of plan, and the seagoing forces had considered their parts in considerable detail.

All that remained was to see where the Americans would strike. Again Ozawa was on the mark, joining a growing chorus of Imperial Navy opinion, observing on September 10 that it was "most probable that the next operation will be SHO-1 from the south." The prediction found its echo from the Naval General Staff on September 21. That day IGHQ Navy Directive Number 462 was promulgated: "Execution of the SHO operation in the Philippine area . . . is anticipated." The Navy believed battle would come "in or after the last part of October." Forces were to prepare for SHO-1 with the highest priority.

One of the worst problems, as for all Japan at this stage of the war, was fuel. Two more scarce fleet oilers had succumbed to American aircraft at the Philippine Sea. During July and August, especially, available tonnage of shipping began to plummet as submarine sinkings hemorrhaged. Tanker losses had become so serious that the Combined Fleet no longer felt capable of operating more than 2,500 miles from its bases. Between the Kurita fleet and Leyte Gulf, along the route he would follow, the distance was approximately 1,700 miles. Shima's northern force would have to travel about 3,000 miles. The Philippines became the scene of a Decisive Battle waged at the very margin of the Imperial Navy's resources.

IN THE CRUCIAL QUESTION OF WHERE THE ALLIES WOULD STRIKE, INTELLIGENCE WAS THE KEY. Aerial reconnaissance has been discussed in some detail, but Japanese communications intelligence deserves more comment. It was the radio monitors who informed the fleet that the September carrier strikes on the Philippines were carried out by a considerable force; this is just one more illustration of how far these techniques had come since the days of the China Incident.

During the China hostilities the Navy's radio intelligence network had been minuscule, in all 23 large receivers and 13 radio direction finders (RDFs) on assorted frequencies. Each was limited by its particular antenna, sensitivity, location, and other factors. China was huge, of course, but though the Pacific was even larger, the Japanese network had also become a great deal more sophisticated. Empire-area resources were tied directly into nets controlled by the Owada Group, which by itself used about as much equipment as had been in the Chinese effort. Throughout Japan by 1944 the special-duty groups used 195 receivers, 80 monitors, and 115 direction finders. On Iwo Jima Captain Wachi had 3 RDFs, 4 receivers, and 3 monitors.

In the war theaters, transmission of results had become more difficult, though often still possible, and anyway results were of great value to local commanders. Until its fall Kwajalein had had the 6th Communications Unit with 10 RDFs, 14 receivers, and 4 monitors. At Truk the 4th Communications Unit had 13 direction finders, 8 receivers, and 4 monitors. Rabaul could still report intercepts and location fixes from the 8th Communications Unit's 6 RDFs, 22 receivers, and 4 monitors. At Wake, Marcus, Nauru, all across the Pacific and scattered in detachments throughout East Asia, the special-duty groups had an additional 81 direction finders, 216 receivers, and 3 monitors. In the Singapore-Lingga area was the 10th Communications Unit with 38 more receivers, 6 monitors, and 9 direction finders.

Active with the fleet were two additional units. Commander Nakajima as fleet intelligence officer of the Combined Fleet controlled the 25th, which had 3 direction finders, 10 receivers, and 3 monitors. With the Second Fleet there was also the 2nd Communications Unit, which used 2 RDFs, 10 receivers, and 2 monitors.

To centralize control of the far-flung detachments, the Imperial Navy created the 1st Combined Communications Unit for the southeast area and Pacific, and the 3rd Combined Communications Unit for the southwest, including the Philippines, the Netherlands East Indies, Malaya, and the Indian Ocean. The 3rd Combined had been activated in August 1943; the 1st dated from the beginning of the war and had been Admiral Kakimoto Gonichiro's command, but it had deployed forward to Saipan to better coordinate its network. Under Rear Admiral Ito Yasunoshin the 1st Combined Communications Unit had been one of the Imperial Navy formations overwhelmed in the defeat. Some of its documents figured among the material now in the hands of American intelligence. One such, a May 1944 network control plan, provided this description of the mission of the 1st Combined Communications Unit:

> In the present war situation, what is expected of the communication intelligence at Saipan is that we shall have prior intelligence of enemy offensive operations from the east or southeast against the Marianas, the Eastern Carolines, or even Japan, and from the southeast against the northern New Guinea area and even the Philippines.

Partial returns covering five detachments in the Central Pacific under the 1st Combined Communications Unit indicate an overall strength of twelve officers and 215 seamen. With deletion of areas just captured by the Allies, the unit's successors retained its basic mission.

Training for Imperial Navy radio intelligence people occurred at both Owada and the communications school at Kurihama (Yokosuka). The latter, an enormous complex including fifteen barracks and a large four-story concrete classroom building, instructed 12,000 sailors and 580 officers as of February 1944. Of the officers, 260 were specializing in radar operation and maintenance, 240 in communications, and fully 80 in radio intelligence and Allied codes. The course had been shortened to little more than two months. One trainee, who had gone through the Owada Group directly, was given six weeks to learn radio telephone procedure, foreign broadcast interception, and translation. Ironically, these hurriedly trained people could not be used efficiently precisely because the losses the Imperial Navy was suffering eliminated the assignments they might have been given. For example, the *entire* officer class Yokosuka graduated in May 1944 was then sent back to the school for forty days to await postings.

There were ironies, too, in the Navy's need for English-speaking trainees. Despite Japan's xenophobia, for example, the seaman just mentioned, who had trained at Owada, was selected because he had been born in Hawaii and spoke English. Another typical case was that of Kitayama Tadahiko, who before the war had passed the entrance exams for the naval engineering college and become a member of the forty-eighth class there. Kitayama soured on naval life and quit to attend the Tokyo School of Foreign Languages. There he studied English literature, specializing in poetry, and had worked his way up to fourth-year student when the Imperial Navy drafted him and promptly put him into radio intelligence. Kitayama served with a listening post on Taiwan on the eve of Pearl Harbor, with the 6th Communications Unit later, and was assigned to Kure toward the end of the war, about the time his family's home in Tokyo was bombed out.

Nerve center for all of the men and interception activities was at Owada, technically the Central Radio Intelligence Group. There 500 officers and men worked as intercept operators, as controllers for one of seven permanent RDF networks covering Empire waters, or in the codebreaking section. According to a 1946 commentary by American expert Joseph Wenger, only ninety to a hundred of the Owada personnel were directly involved in the codebreaking work. However, according to Ozawa Hideo, a member of the communications bureau of NGS, of which the Owada Group was officially the third section, the unit included ten reserve officers and 120 other personnel. Captain Morikawa Hidenari was assigned to head the Owada unit from August 18, 1944. Morikawa, a nephew of the Navy great Kato Kanji and one of the Navy's earliest codebreakers, had been active in China and had participated in break-ins before the war when American diplomatic codebooks were photographed. A 1922 graduate of Etajima, he was a classmate of Wachi Tsunezo, another radio intelligence specialist, as well as of Ohmae Toshikazu, now operations staff officer for Admiral Ozawa Jisaburo of the Mobile Fleet, and Otomo Bunkichi, who had been executive officer of the fleet flagship *Taiho*, lost so uselessly at Philippine Sea. The desire to make *something* work, finally, must have burned bright in them.

The Owada Group shared the codebreaking task with the 2nd Section of the NGS Communications Bureau, responsible for codebreaking research under Captain Endo Shigeru. Once communications officer aboard the *Mutsu*, Endo, too, no doubt labored furiously in an effort to reverse the fortunes of war. Lieutenant Commander Satake led the office working on American and British communications, and there were other offices for China and for Russia. Each had a few officers; a pool of student trainees shifted among them as the workload dictated. The section's paperwork was done by another pool of thirty typists. A messenger from Owada brought papers; the most urgent items could be telephoned directly. The 4th Bureau itself, headed by Rear Admiral Nomura Tomekichi, disseminated the intelligence to the rest of NGS, in particular the Operations Bureau, and to the Ministry. Daily and periodic summaries were sent. Information judged of interest to the Japanese Army was sent to the War Ministry, and specific codebreaking items to the Army's special section at Tanashi.

Commander Satake reports that the Japanese distinguished intercepted messages six ways: by call sign; by traffic volume; by code type; by priority; by signal procedures used; and by whether it was plain language. The volume was graphed against time, and the process was repeated for each geographic region, with message priorities displayed in color and total volume in black. This permitted the Japanese to infer a great deal regarding U.S. operations, especially once they put those data together with the addresses and date-time groups of individual messages, which were almost always recovered, even from coded messages. Codes the Japanese did read with fair regularity included U.S. weather codes and the Broadcasting Allied Movement Ships (BAMS) code for merchant-ship traffic. These sources added substance to the bare-bones analyses that came up from the Owada Group.

The Japanese fit puzzle pieces together fairly well. For instance, CINCPAC began using Admirals Spruance and Halsey as tandem commanders for the U.S. battle fleet, allowing one to prepare for the next operation while the other executed the current one. The force was known as the Fifth Fleet (thus Task Force 58) when Spruance had the command and the Third Fleet (and Task Force 38) when Bull Halsey was in charge. The Japanese first learned of such changes from press reports, but soon they could correlate with communications patterns: Halsey typically generated a much greater volume of message traffic than Spruance, whose communications officer got the reputation of being a better man. Another way to detect a command change was the easily noticeable interval of a month or so beforehand during which certain call-sign messages became dominant.

A kind of puzzle Satake frequently shed light upon with the warrant officer and twenty-six sailors who worked for him was the movement of invasion convoys. The Japanese solved about half the messages sent in the BAMS code, though frequently with such delay that subject ships would no longer be in the same area as when the message was intercepted. This robbed the traffic of utility for targeting submarine attacks, but invasion convoys were slow enough that a warning could be generated. In particular because the Japanese could identify the regular radio operators of a source once observed for a time, they could follow the progress of a convoy across the Pacific. Direction finding assisted this task. Japanese methods were not as satisfactory as the American, but analysis was the best that could be done. "Our whole analysis was based on probabilities," Commander Satake recalled. "There was nothing of a definite nature. There was not necessarily a great deal of urgency connected with our estimates. There were wide[ly] . . . varied opinions of the reliability of our estimates."

Commander Ozawa Hideo, who had been executive officer of the radio intelligence unit at Rabaul during the key year from February 1942 to 1943, agreed the Japanese could identify general target areas by detecting air-to-base transmissions and noting where radio silence was imposed. At Owada he kept in close touch with the *tokumu han,* the NGS codebreaking section, which was located in the Navy Ministry building until mid-1943, then moved to the third floor of the War College. Ozawa had a direct phone line to the *tokumu han,* which was fifty minutes away by car; he sent liaison officers there three times a day.

For all its shortcomings, Japanese radio intelligence had, and would continue to have, real impact on the prosecution of the war. A marginal intelligence capability combined with an increasingly marginal fleet, however, did not augur well for the final Decisive Battle.


CALCULATING JAPAN'S RESOURCES HAPPENED TO BE A PRIMARY TASK OF ALLIED INTELLIgence. Growing Imperial Navy tanker problems were one part of the whole Japanese shipping question. That had been a frequent subject for intelligence since the days of the Tokyo attaché, who had filled many diplomatic pouches with translations of Japanese shipping manuals, projections of merchant tonnage afloat, even illustrations of the spanker flags used by each Japanese shipping company. Tokyo's fuel-oil situation was another obvious intelligence problem; it, too, had drawn attention since attaché days. Air intelligence would also figure prominently in the Philippine campaign.

Esoteric as the subject might sound, Japanese shipping tonnage remained a key factor because Japan depended almost entirely upon imports for her war production. Coal and iron from Manchuria, rubber and tin from Malaya and Indochina, oil from the Netherlands East Indies, even phosphates from Nauru Island—without these and other raw materials Japanese production would grind to a halt. Production in and of itself was a problem of course, since the Empire could not hope to match American industrial might, but without such production levels as did exist, Japan would have declined even more precipitously. At the same time, the Japanese had created a Munitions Ministry for production, with ambitious plans to build as many as 50,000 aircraft. In 1944, therefore, available shipping tonnages were more important than ever.

According to one prewar attaché report, as of June 30, 1939, there were 4,029 merchant ships registered in Japan, including 1,101 of a thousand tons or more, with total tonnage in this category of over 4.8 million. A subsequent detailed study of Japan's economy at war gives the following inventories for 1940: more than 700 oceangoing freighters; 132 combination passenger-cargo vessels (49 of which could make 15 knots or more); 49 oceangoing tankers (20 capable of 16 knots or better). Roughly 20 percent of the big cargo ships had been completed since 1930, along with almost 30 percent of the passenger vessels and a whopping 65 percent of the large tankers. Colonel Hattori of the Army operations staff, whose figures can be considered semi-official, lists December 1941 merchant tonnage as 5.47 million. What happened to these ships and the new construction that supplemented them went a good way toward explaining what happened to the Empire in the Greater East Asian War.

American intelligence initially tracked Japanese shipping through the foreign-trade section of the Office of Naval Intelligence (ONI). This ONI section alone, in its 1941 reporting, did much to signal impending hostilities as apparent from shipping patterns. Among the trade section's fifty-two reports that year were ones indicating ships refueling far in excess of transit requirements, secret routings and acceleration of traffic on transpacific routes, hurried departures from Atlantic ports. When the United States froze Japanese assets there were already no Japanese merchantmen left in West Coast ports, and by October 10 ONI knew that a mere 14 Japanese ships were on the trade routes, as compared with a normal 110 to 150.

Building upon its prewar reporting, the trade section set up a system for recording merchant-ship losses of all flags once the United States was at war. The ONI trade section worked in cooperation with the War Shipping Administration and Army intelligence, but its reporting covered ground identical to that of the dissemination section (later renamed the statistical section) of the flag plot. Foreign-trade section reports were discontinued in January 1943.

The COMINCH combat intelligence unit created a system for tracking shipping casualties and submarine attacks that first gained notoriety in the context of the campaign against German U-boats but was applied equally in the Pacific war. Data from submarine reports were extracted and each listed attack noted on one file card by the name of the boat, on another by the date of the attack, on a third by claimed sinkings; there could be geographical or other additions. The system permitted rapid checking of intercepted loss reports or other sources against claims. As card-sorting machinery became more available, moreover, its use in this application enabled ONI to perform necessary correlations even more rapidly.

At Pearl Harbor a less precise system emerged with the prodding of Jasper Holmes, himself a former submariner. Some confusion arose with the two setups, but also some division of labor, as ONI used its records to publish periodic lists of Japanese merchant ships afloat, descriptions of new and existing types of ships, and summaries of the shipping situation. The first such shipping list was requested shortly after the Pearl Harbor attack, though afterward this work lost urgency in favor of support to the battle of the Atlantic. The wheel came full circle in 1943, however, as a focus on Japanese shipping became the statistical section's primary concern. These changes came at roughly the same time Pearl Harbor was developing its advanced intelligence center into JICPOA, and the organizational scheme would be further clouded by COMINCH's decision to have his radio intelligence unit, OP-20-G, officially administer Bill Sebald's combat intelligence unit, which contained the statistical section. As if that were not enough, in December 1942 General Marshall of the Army proposed that a joint committee be formed to make judgments as to the veracity of reports of damage or loss. A month later the Joint Army-Navy Committee on Assessment of Loss or Damage on Enemy Naval or Merchant Vessels would be formed; it was called JANAC for short. Thereafter the Navy's statistical section formed the core of its JANAC effort. Officers making important contributions to JANAC from the Navy include Commander James M. Andrews, Lieutenant W. W. Howells, and Lieutenant Gerrit P. Judd, who also supervised installation of the IBM card sorters applied to shipping casualty work. The section grew from an officer and two or three civilians to a peak strength of four officers, three civilian analysts, three enlisted personnel, and ten clerical workers.

Original officer in charge had been Jim Andrews, a Harvard anthropologist who came to this task in the spring of 1941 at his own insistence, instead of being placed in the ONI Far East Division. Andrews recruited E. C. Worman, a graduate student in anthropology, as a civilian analyst in early 1942. Will Howells had been an anthropology colleague of Andrews and was sent to the section upon commissioning in February 1943. Ensign Alice Mason, one of the best extractors of important data, had been a librarian in civilian life. Lieutenant Judd had been a graduate student in history.

Products of the unit included a monthly serial, "Japanese Merchant Marine Losses," which was graded "confidential," plus three secret quarterly tables: "Japanese Naval Losses," "Japanese Merchantmen Sunk," and "Causes of Japanese Tonnage Losses." Other parts of ONI and OP-20-G used the reports as raw material. For more than six months in 1944, the press of other work prevented JICPOA from compiling any list of vessels sunk. At that point Joe Rochefort, finally brought back into intelligence work in charge of a strategic studies unit under COMINCH, put out a fresh directory of Japanese merchant shipping. Jasper Holmes of JICPOA complimented the list as the best thing on the subject, but warned against using JICPOA's own "Maru Sunk" lists as sources. "It isn't worth it," Holmes wrote. "The 'Maru Sunk List' has never been reliable."

Pearl Harbor had neither man-hours nor available supervisory time to do the job right, and it had accepted without question submarine action claims that were approved by higher authority. Most data accumulated were thus of doubtful authenticity, hardly a credible source. This and other experiences induced both Bill Sebald and Joe Rochefort to try setting up something they informally called the Maru Intelligence Center, but getting approval proved an uphill struggle. By November 1944 Jasper Holmes found himself telling Sebald that such a unit had become urgent. From Washington the combat intelligence chief wrote, "It has been necessary to undertake a tremendous amount of missionary work around here in order to interest the various people in the proposition." Army intelligence opposed the move as impinging on its shipping section of JANAC. Rochefort eventually got a unit formed but by then it was the spring of 1945. Both ONI and JICPOA considered this a major step forward.

Despite confusion over the causes and numbers of sinkings, or claims of success by anxious skippers and pilots, the tonnage figures tell their own story. According to postwar JANAC (American) numbers, on December 7, 1941, Japan had 5,996,000 tons of shipping afloat. Between then and April 1, 1944 (Japanese fiscal years 1941, 1942, and 1943), Tokyo constructed 1,524,000 tons of ships and captured or salvaged 798,000 tons more. During the period through the Forager operation, however, 2,808,453 tons were sunk, leaving a merchant fleet of about 5.5 million tons.

The wartime U.S. intelligence figures are different, however. Intelligence estimates through July 1, 1944, postulate a cumulative total of 4,324,681 tons of losses. Amazingly, the figure Colonel Hattori provides for merchant sinkings through that date is 4,243,000 tons, leaving a fleet of about 4.1 million tons still available to Japan.

Regardless of the exactitude of numerical details, which appear pretty accurate, American intelligence had the overall picture in good focus, as indicated by this conclusion in a May 1944 ONI Far East Division summary:

> The enemy's shipping position from their standpoint is critical, and they are experiencing difficulty in maintaining their present lines of communication. This condition may well become a factor in softening their strategy, and force a decision to shorten their lines to a point where their operable tonnage can meet transport demands.

Since a minimum of 1.2 million tons of shipping was considered necessary to carry materials necessary for Japan's civilian economy, and military operations were drawing off another 3 million tons or so, precious few bottoms were left to convey the raw materials for war production no matter what the real number might be.

Although they may understate overall Japanese shipping losses, the JANAC figures (which were used by the Strategic Bombing Survey after the war) have the virtue of breaking out the data by cause of sinking rather than type of ship, and therefore permit some interesting observations as to the evolution of the war situation. Allied submarines were by far the leading agents of loss, even during the first two years of the war, in which there were palpable problems with submarine torpedo performance. Land-based aircraft took a steady toll of Japanese ships, though over the long haul losses so caused became a virtual background factor, eclipsed by carrier raids. The latter, almost wholly ineffectual until the beginning of 1944, suddenly exploded into a major factor, for example accounting for about 273,000 tons of shipping losses in February and March 1944, the months of the raids on Truk and Palau. In September, when Task Force 38 hit the Philippines, and again in January 1945, when there were extensive raids along the Indochina coast, carrier air outperformed the awesome Allied submarine force, even with its Ultra support. Mines accounted for some losses, but were almost equaled by simple accidents and storms. Surface attack became a negligible factor over the course of the war, although it had been one of the most effective during the months of the Japanese offensive.

The bottom line, as the Allies approached the Philippines in the fall of 1944, was that the Empire's merchant marine had serious difficulties and the Americans knew it. With the correction of torpedo trigger problems and the capable assistance of the codebreakers, Allied submarines were a weapon of great potency. Even as the Japanese resorted to larger convoys with heavier escorts the losses continued to mount. According to JANAC figures, submarines accounted for 195,000 tons in June, 213,000 in July, 245,000 in August, and 181,000 tons in September 1944. If the Allies captured the Philippines, shipping routes to the Empire would be so constricted they could be considered closed: yet another reason for the fierce battle about to erupt.

Estimating the Japanese shipping position, almost an anthropological problem to judge from the personnel assigned the task, remained conceptually similar to projecting aircraft production and combat strength, or estimating the Empire's oil situation. More will be said about shipping in connection with oil and tankers; but, looking ahead to the Philippine campaign, one key intelligence question would be Japanese aircraft strength.

Washington began to look at this question as early as the spring of 1944, when the Joint Intelligence Committee asked for estimates planners could use. Estimates were requested for Japanese aircraft in the Taiwan–Luzon–Hong Kong area, for an invasion at that time envisioned for Mindanao; the projections were to cover the span from two days before landings to twenty days afterward. Work on the general problem of the dimension of Japanese reaction to an invasion continued right up until Philippine operations began. Estimates ranged as high as 1,500 aircraft to start with, reinforced by another 1,405 within the interval of the projection. One or another aspect of the estimates would be criticized on several occasions by Lieutenant Aiken of Sebald's air section, as well as other experts.

In truth, air intelligence was in flux during the period these estimates were compiled. Serious questions on the table included Japan's rate of aircraft production, the size of the training establishment supporting the JNAF, and basic training and operating methods. Sebald's F-22 unit and JICPOA disputed whether Imperial Navy training air groups should be included in the numbers in order-of-battle estimates (a question clouded by the mistaken notion that JNAF's First Air Fleet was a training organization). The Navy, the Army, SOWESPAC, and JICPOA, not to mention the British, all had doubts regarding Japanese aircraft production rates, which were being revised upward through this period. Officials explained that the revision resulted from better understanding of the Japanese aircraft industry, not from actual production increases. For example, a paper for Army chief codebreaker Colonel Alfred McCormack used a range of subtle evidence to deduce that a certain factory in Manchuria contributed parts, thus adding to aircraft production. In actuality Japan's aircraft industry produced 28,180 planes during 1944, for a monthly average of 2,348. Japanese practice reflected the political power of the military services, and even though the JNAF was fighting the bulk of the air war, the Army allocation remained half of total production. As a matter of mathematics this amounts to JNAF average monthly production of 1,174 aircraft. It so happens that the assumption used for Japanese aircraft replacement in the Philippine invasion response estimates was 1,200 aircraft per month. A September 4 JICPOA estimate, on the other hand, gave a production estimate of 1,750 aircraft per month.

From SOWESPAC, air commander General George C. Kenney also expressed an opinion. Although the Army intelligence people still accepted Fifth Air Force claims at face value, Navy combat intelligence had adopted the practice of reducing claims of planes destroyed on the ground by 40 percent unless substantiated by photo reconnaissance. At any rate, in a September 17 letter Kenney said of the Japanese: "His airpower is in a bad way. He has a lot of airplanes—probably more than he had a year ago—but he has lost his element, flight, squadron and group leaders and his hastily trained replacements haven't the skill or ability or combat knowledge to compete with us. His mechanics are largely marooned and dead or dying in Bougainville, New Britain, New Ireland, the Carolines, Wewak, and parts of the NEI."

In this case General Kenney made a lot of sense.

As the planned invasion date approached CINCPAC began to prepare in earnest, dispatching Halsey and Mitscher with Task Force 38 to make a massive raid on the Philippines. Between September 9 and September 23 the carriers struck everywhere from Mindanao to Manila, sinking 213,250 tons of shipping and destroying over 300 aircraft. According to task group leader Frederick C. Sherman, the fleet believed the islands defended by 500 Japanese planes. But OP-20-G's estimate for September 7 stood at 368. Washington recorded JNAF strength peaking at 393 in the September 14 estimate, then falling to less than half that—185—in the report two weeks later. This intelligence estimate was accurate to within a couple of dozen aircraft of the actual strength of Vice Admiral Teraoka Kimpei's First Air Fleet in the Philippines.

Although Pearl Harbor may have had an exaggerated impression of the JNAF's production base, Captain Goggins and Commander Holmes and the rest of their analysts were remarkably in tune with Tokyo's essential strategy. The JICPOA "Estimate of Enemy Distribution and Intentions" of September 4 is worth quoting at length:

> It is believed that since losing the Battle of the Philippine Sea the enemy has undertaken an ambitious program of restoring his fleet and air forces for another all-out effort. . . . During the past few months losses have been unusually light. By avoiding heavy losses for several more months, the enemy should be able to assemble a larger air force than at any time heretofore. One new carrier (*Unryu*) has joined the fleet and two more (*Amagi* and *Katsuragi*) are expected to do so shortly. All but 7 submarines are refitting and training in the Empire. Destroyers present a serious problem for the enemy. A few are refitting in the Empire and 5 are expected to join the fleet within the next few months.
>
> There is every indication that the enemy's strategy is to avoid losses and not engage in a major action until the air forces and fleet are ready. At

such time as that occurs, probably not before December, the air forces and the fleet operating under the umbrella of its own shore-based air units will attempt an all-out decisive action. He plans to use his surface fleet to complete the destruction of our forces after the air forces have delivered a crippling blow and secured control of the air.

This estimate was on the money in terms of general Japanese intentions. Error arose from the timing factor—JICPOA assumed the Japanese would await full reconstitution of their air groups before emerging for battle. The Imperial Navy and JICPOA both agreed that December was the key date, but the Japanese had decided they could not afford to wait that long. Tokyo keyed its SHO plan instead to an *event* rather than a date, something the Japanese had never done before.

Meanwhile, Pacific authorities continued their reports, with a September 15 estimate of the Japanese situation correctly noting the separation of the fleet and the reason (to "improve the logistics situation with regard to oil"), though erroneously supposing that the movement consisted solely of heavy cruisers. From this the paper drew the conclusion that the Singapore forces would not attempt independent operations unless they had an unusual and unexpected opportunity and strong air support. Since much has been made of this conclusion it should be noted that the underlying reason for it—the absence of the Japanese battleships—would be corrected in further reports issued before the Philippine invasion.

Moreover, other aspects of the September 15 estimate correctly appreciated the Japanese air dilemma, noting that "the enemy is confronted with a definite shortage of trained air personnel." Further along, quite significantly, the report stated: "While the enemy might possibly be able to use the remnants of the old carrier groups for current operations, this is not considered a probable move. In any event, it is believed that not over one carrier division, totality not over 175–200 aircraft, are [*sic*] sufficiently trained to be used effectively in carrier operations."

In subsequent JICPOA weekly estimates, all of which appeared before the Philippine battle began, Pearl Harbor intelligence demonstrated knowledge of the existence of two "diversion attack forces" in addition to the striking force within the Combined Fleet, of the code name SHO, and of the preliminary movements of the Japanese fleet. There was also extensive discussion of fleet oilers, as will be seen presently. In fact an October 2 JICPOA estimate remarked that "fleet tankers continue to give the best indications of fleet intentions." Estimates erred on details of Japanese naval dispositions, with some battleships shown in Empire waters just days before they would be sunk in the Philippines, but the intelligence was not uniformly mistaken. A good deal of accurate perception appeared in the reporting too. Perhaps the real roots of American miscalculation at Leyte Gulf reside in the notion that

Japan's battle plan would center on its carriers rather than its gunnery ships. Since accumulated World War II experience amply demonstrated the primacy of the airplane, it was probably asking too much to expect intelligence to predict surface naval attack. Even there, however, JICPOA *had* correctly appreciated, seven weeks before the fact, the possibility of a surface attack coupled with a land-based air umbrella.

Allied officers worried about such an air umbrella. In contrast to conditions in the Marianas, moreover, there were over seventy airfields within flying distance of the Leyte invasion site. It seemed impossible to neutralize such a robust network. Instead the Americans would try to destroy Japanese aircraft, thus reducing the scale of any potential counterattacks.

Other aspects of the Japanese plan for Leyte Gulf were also anticipated by Allied intelligence, whether by JICPOA, Captain McCollum's Seventh Fleet intelligence center, or the British Station Anderson. For example, the Japanese intention to create a decoy force to fool the Allies had been discussed specifically in a Combined Fleet manual, "Striking Force Tactics." The manual had even illustrated this concept by mention of using hybrid battleship-carriers *Ise* and *Hyuga* as part of such a decoy unit. A copy of this manual was captured in the Marianas campaign and went to Pearl Harbor, where JICPOA translators rendered key passages into English. The translation circulated through the U.S. fleet during the summer of 1944, part of a series of JICPOA pamphlets titled "Know Your Enemy."

While a single reference to this decoy concept might have been dismissed as merely suggestive, there was specific intelligence available as a result of the sinking of Japanese light cruiser *Natori* by American submarine *Hardhead* off the Philippine island Samar on August 18, 1944. A young ensign and three seamen survived and drifted in a raft for three weeks until rescued by the U.S. sub *Stingray*. The survivors cleared up the confusion of *Hardhead*'s crew, who thought they had sunk a battleship, but the incident alerted Seventh Fleet intelligence that these Japanese were talkative. Intelligence sent two language officers plus Lieutenant Lawrence F. Ebb, responsible for tracking Imperial Navy movements, to meet *Stingray* when she docked at Darwin in early September.

Ebb and his cohorts discovered that the Japanese ensign possessed a wealth of information. He had been a member of a youth movement called the Navy Juniors and was an excellent sketcher, well informed, and an expert on ship and aircraft recognition in a navy that did not take those subjects very seriously. In his interrogation the Japanese spoke of the decoy role intended for *Ise* and *Hyuga* and also provided Americans with their first hard data on the postconversion appearance of the battleship-carriers. A sketch drawn by the ensign, remastered by American experts, was published on October 13 in a Seventh Fleet intelligence bulletin (number 15-44), appearing two days earlier in a memorandum (number 62A-44) and eventually also in the *ONI Weekly Review*. Clearly these data circulated widely.

At Seventh Fleet intelligence, the main elements of which moved aboard cruiser *Nashville* as the date for the invasion neared, Arthur McCollum translated his suspicions that the Japanese might oppose the invasion into intelligence to support General MacArthur. Washington, Pearl Harbor, and McCollum's own center basically agreed that the Imperial Navy had divided its strength between Empire waters and the Singapore area, although differences existed regarding the disposition of particular ship types. The JICPOA estimate of six to eight months between Japan's Philippine Sea defeat and new Imperial Navy major operations, conditioned by the need for the Japanese to train new air groups, was generally accepted. In late September, however, Captain McCollum argued in a staff memorandum that, at a minimum, Japanese surface forces in the Singapore area *would* be used to counter a Philippine invasion. McCollum, who retired in 1953 as a rear admiral, told an interviewer almost two decades later that there *had* been an inaccurate intelligence prediction before Leyte Gulf, but that it had been corrected in supplemental reports disseminated by radio. Thus he contradicted a study of the Leyte battle done by a Naval War College group including Captain Rochefort. That study maintained that "the Allied Naval Commander"—that is, Admiral Thomas C. Kinkaid of the Seventh Fleet—"did not believe that major elements of the Japanese Fleet would be involved in opposition to the Allied landings at Leyte." The War College study cited a notice by MacArthur's top air commander, issued the same day as McCollum's staff memo, declaring that "fleet action is less likely than ever." This prediction would be repeated as the Leyte invasion neared until, just days before the landings, MacArthur's own daily intelligence summary noted that "while [the Japanese Navy] may move in strength in and out of protected stations in home or adjacent waters, it is doubtful if it will seek any issue beyond the cover of land-based airplanes."

Samuel Eliot Morison's volume on Leyte Gulf agrees that intelligence prior to the battle had been "spotty and defective." But Morison appears to take this back with his comment that by the day of the invasion "it was beginning to be assumed that the Japanese fleet would offer battle." In fact, on October 20, with the Japanese fleet already on the move, MacArthur's headquarters issued an analysis of Japanese capabilities which did see the possibility of an Imperial Navy sortie, but even then expected the separate Japanese forces from Singapore and Empire waters to first rendezvous, probably in the South China Sea, before sailing around Luzon to hit the U.S. fleet. This analysis specifically ruled out any Japanese attempt to send their ships *through* the straits of the central Philippines because of "navigational hazards and the lack of maneuvering space which is vitally important when opposing a formidable concentration of carrier-based aircraft." Moreover, on October 21 MacArthur's intelligence summary observed "no apparent intent" on the part of the Imperial Navy "to interfere with our Leyte landings."

The predictions of intelligence units at Pearl Harbor and with MacArthur became highly controversial once a naval battle actually occurred during the invasion. Was Leyte an intelligence failure? The best answer seems to be that strategically, Pearl Harbor and Seventh Fleet each anticipated some things that would become elements of the Japanese plan, while not divining the Imperial Navy's actual intentions. However, as shall be seen presently, the codebreakers provided Ultra intercepts, primarily on the activities of Japanese fleet oilers, that should have afforded sufficient tactical warning to Allied forces to preclude surprise.

STRIKES TO DESTROY JAPANESE AIRCRAFT WERE NECESSARY TO CARRY OUT THE PHILIPPINE pre-invasion air strategy. So, much as Bull Halsey had raided the Philippines in September while Allied forces landed on Morotai and Peleliu, Task Force 38 now struck what the Japanese called their "connecting zone," the region of Okinawa, the Nansei Shoto, and Taiwan, which aircraft would have to transit when deploying from Japan to the Philippines.* Admiral Halsey planned to carry out his attacks in early October, shortly before the Leyte invasion of the Philippines.

Unbenownst to the Americans, the Taiwan-Okinawa area formed IGHQ's SHO-2 contingency. Halsey's raid automatically forced the Naval General Staff and Combined Fleet into considering activation of their plan. Moreover, this time the Japanese had a degree of forewarning. On October 2 the Owada Group reported the U.S. carrier force under way in the Marianas. In its estimate for that day JICPOA observed, "The enemy is jittery over the prospect of strikes by our carriers in the Bonins, Nansei Shoto, [Taiwan], and the Philippines." An intercept late the next day revealed the chief of staff of Japan's Southwest Area Fleet predicting attacks on the Philippines or Taiwan, and First Air Fleet considered attacks probable against the northern Philippines in a message sent at 11:00 P.M. on October 4. Taiwan was

---

*Many continue to dispute the necessity for Allied landings at Palau, carried out by the 1st Marine Division and Army 81st Infantry Division on September 15, 1944. In Nimitz's view the operation was to secure MacArthur's right flank as he landed in the Philippines, just as the latter's own invasion of Morotai on the same day would protect his left. Intelligence estimates by JICPOA credited Palau with Japanese strength as of July 31 of 20,000 Army, 6,000 Navy, and 3,000 construction troops, with overall personnel as high as 37,000–39,000. Postwar studies give Japanese strength of 10,500 on Peleliu itself and perhaps another 1,500 on Angaur, the 81st Division objective. American losses included 1,794 dead and about 8,000 wounded.

ordered cleared of shipping early the next morning. Further analysis by the Owada Group on October 6 specified that the Americans had sortied five days before, justifying an alert for the Philippines, Taiwan, and the Nansei Shoto. Based on these indications, as early as 9:32 P.M. on October 5, Southwest Area Fleet chief of staff Rear Admiral Nishio Hidehiko predicted a landing in the Philippines area. An anonymous codebreaker added the notation: "an astute conclusion."

From Pearl Harbor the JICPOA estimate of October 9 was able to state: "The Philippines–[Taiwan]–Nansei Shoto line has been under precautionary alert since about 4 October when Japanese radio intelligence anticipated carrier attacks in these areas."

All this happened before a single bomb dropped.

The bombs did drop, though, in great profusion, beginning on October 10, a day after a cruiser-destroyer unit bombarded Marcus Island again in an effort to make Tokyo believe in a threat from that direction. Relying upon their ample radio intelligence, the Japanese instead anticipated attacks on the connecting area. The week before the big battle, Taiwan's governor general, Admiral Hasegawa Kiyoshi, one of the Navy's most senior officers, flew to Japan to discuss with Prime Minister Koiso and others, according to the Domei news agency, "intensification of the island's contribution to Japan's war effort." In the opposite direction went Combined Fleet chief Toyoda Soemu, who met in Manila on October 7 with Vice Admiral Mikawa Gunichi, victor of Savo Island and now commanding the Southwest Area Fleet. Admiral Toyoda reviewed the SHO plans with Mikawa and a handful of key officers and inspected facilities in the Manila area. The commander in chief then traveled to Taiwan on October 9, en route to Japan, but was caught there at the moment Bull Halsey began to beat on the Japanese defenses of the Nansei Shoto.

At Yomitan Airfield on Okinawa, ground crews had just sent off the planes scheduled to fly to Taiwan the morning of the tenth and were sitting down to breakfast alongside the field when the air-raid warning sounded. Confused, Japanese at first presumed it must be their own planes returning. But whistling death ensued; 1,396 sorties loosed close to 600 tons of munitions. American pilots claimed sinking a dozen torpedo boats, two midget submarines, and four cargo ships, as well as downing 111 aircraft. Later studies reduce the score to eighty-eight planes destroyed, three quarters on the ground. Task Force 38 lost twenty-one planes, but all except five pilots and four aircrew were rescued. October 10 was the closest American ships and planes had come to Empire waters since the *Hornet* and *Enterprise* on the 1942 Doolittle raid. In reprise, the *Enterprise* came along for this trip too.

Panic ensued at Combined Fleet and the Naval General Staff. The Japanese had been on alert for the best part of a week but now faced an immediate decision as to whether or not to activate the SHO plan. To complicate matters, Combined Fleet was without its chief, at that moment marooned on Taiwan. In the absence of his commander in chief, but thinking that the strong Allied air attacks meant powerful invasion forces behind them, chief of staff Kusaka Ryunosuke issued a warning order for either SHO-1 or SHO-2 at 9:25 A.M. Combined Fleet Dispatch Order Number 1331 set in motion a fateful train of events. Filled with some notion of dazzling the Americans with a display of Japanese power, Kusaka made two fateful decisions: He unilaterally vitiated the detailed operational planning by alerting *only* air forces for SHO; and he stripped the Mobile Fleet of its air component by including its carrier air groups, just attaining proficiency, in the reaction force. On Taiwan Admiral Toyoda was asked for his opinion of an air-only SHO activation, but without access to the full picture at headquarters, Toyoda insisted the decision be made at Hiyoshi.*

At Oita Air Station on Kyushu, Mobile Fleet senior staff officer Ohmae Toshikazu was astonished to see that the alert order included Carrier Divisions 3 and 4. Captain Ohmae instantly went to a radiotelephone and contacted his counterpart at Combined Fleet, arguing that if the order were executed the Mobile Fleet would henceforth be unable to sortie against an enemy invasion force or otherwise play its allotted role in SHO operations. Combined Fleet refused to change the order. Ohmae then conferred with Vice Admiral Ozawa, who backed him in opposing the move, and they resolved to make Combined Fleet confirm its order before they would execute it. With telephonic contact interrupted, Ohmae hopped on a courier flight to Kure and went to Hiyoshi himself. Admiral Kusaka remained adamant.

Actual JNAF operations at this time were only preliminary, limited to extensive searching for Task Force 38 and concentration of forces. Vice Admiral Teraoka Kimpei's First Air Fleet, allocated 350 planes by the SHO plan, was at this time credited with just 211 planes by OP-20-G and only 175 by JICPOA. Admiral Fukudome Shigeru's Second Air Fleet, a new formation, had 510 planes on paper but would actually command many more when it was committed on Taiwan and Fukudome made air commander there. A Third Air Fleet had also been created in the Empire and assigned 350 aircraft for defense of the Home Islands. The paper allocations actually represented ideal strengths incorporating production aircraft not yet out of the factories; Fukudome notes that true figures were only about two thirds of the planned numbers.

Fukudome Shigeru had been Combined Fleet senior operations staffer under Suetsugu Nobumasa in the mid-1930s, a time when the latter

---

*Admiral Ozawa's planning included a contingency for using his carrier air groups without their mother ships, but overall plans both by Combined Fleet and the Naval General Staff lacked any such "air-only" provision.

became famous for his advocacy of rough-weather training. Fukudome avers that he planned maneuvers using the technique and championed it both in the fleet and later, when he went to the operations section of the Naval General Staff. Faced with growing U.S. superiority in the war, Fukudome returned to the notion of operations under adverse conditions, creating what was called the T Attack Force—"T" standing for the Japanese word for typhoon. This unit specialized in attacks by night and in bad weather, and Fukudome and fleet chief of staff Kusaka Ryunosuke both had high hopes for it. One of the first orders issued when Kusaka directed preparations for an air-only SHO was for the T Attack Force to concentrate at Kanoya, a timely assembly after dispersal to avoid losses. As with so much else, American radio intelligence intercepted that order and instantly concluded that the T Attack Force had to be some kind of elite unit.

Had this been 1942 the T Force might indeed have been an elite, but the year was 1944 and the JNAF was not what it had been. Under adverse weather conditions the need for the very best pilots and aircrews would be greater than ever; JNAF could no longer provide them. Unlike a ship which, barring unforeseen design problems, could at least keep the sea in stormy weather, airplanes would have intense navigational difficulties, both to target and back to base, plus horrific landing difficulties. Admiral Fukudome, who had been forced to resign as fleet operations officer after the torpedo boat *Tomodzuru* was lost with all hands in one of his rough-seas maneuvers, ought to have had a keen appreciation of the dangers. He knew better than most that aircrews assigned to the T Attack Force were far less capable than required.

The one officer who knew the score better than Fukudome had to be Captain Kuno Shuzo, commanding T Force. Kuno knew, too, that much of his strength comprised even less effective Army air units. As one of the early generation of JNAF pilots—he was a 1921 Etajima graduate—Kuno was steeped in a tradition that denigrated Army air capability. He had commanded air groups (including the 201st at Rabaul), instructed pilots, and worked for the Bureau of Aeronautics. Kuno's perspective must also have been affected by classmates on Combined Fleet staff, others who were senior staff officers to the carrier admirals at Coral Sea and Midway, and one who died on the carrier *Ryujo* when she went down off Guadalcanal. The predominant feeling seems to have been that while the T Attack Force might be a brittle tool, the necessity for results meant nothing else mattered.

During that day of October 11 the JNAF produced at least three contacts with the U.S. task force. *Joho kyoku* also weighed in with a six-paragraph top-secret dispatch that supplied considerable detail as to the composition of Task Force 38 during its September forays to Palau and the Philippines. The Third Bureau's intelligence was that the task force contained four carrier groups, each built around two fleet and two light carriers, generally resembling Task Force 58 of Marianas fame but with an additional large carrier. Japanese intelligence knew that Admiral Mitscher commanded, that the *Lexington* was his flagship, and that she formed part of Task Group 38.3. Auxiliary strength was given as eight to ten battleships, fourteen to eighteen cruisers, and sixty destroyers. The Japanese even knew that a unit of small escort carriers and other vessels typically followed behind the task force to resupply it at sea. Most important, "it is estimated that, as at the time of the Saipan attack, they are maintaining themselves in readiness for Decisive Battle at any time."

According to the U.S. Naval War College study of the battle of Leyte Gulf, "This is an extremely interesting dispatch and shows very clearly how accurate the Japanese information concerning [Task Force] 38 was . . . the information contained in this dispatch was almost entirely correct."

While Japanese commanders maneuvered air units, far to the south the first echelons of the massive invasion flotilla destined for Leyte— MacArthur's return to the Philippines—sailed from Manus in the Admiralties. At the same time Task Force 38 steamed toward Taiwan. Mitscher rendezvoused on his way with a replenishment unit that brought replacement aircraft to his carriers and refueled warships which needed it, just as in the *joho kyoku* report. A sixty-plane harassment strike flew off to attack Aparri in northern Luzon. After dark, night fighters from carrier *Enterprise* chased JNAF snoopers trying to identify Task Force 38. Edward Stafford, chronicler of the Big E's war history, captures the scene as one of her planes returned from destroying the JNAF scout: "Gary [*sic*; the pilot's name was Gray] flew back to *Enterprise* over the invisible ocean with its invisible task groups moving inexorably toward the morning launch point."

Despite night-fighter successes, several Japanese planes reported Task Force 38 during the night of October 11–12. That plus the Aparri attack convinced the Japanese that trouble loomed for Taiwan. The commander of the Takao Naval Guard District, the local area command, ordered an alert before dawn. Not long after, at 6:48 A.M., the leading American fighters began sweeping over Taiwan, initiating one of the biggest sustained air battles of the Pacific war. Both Combined Fleet chief Toyoda and Second Air Fleet boss Fukudome crouched under the bombs as the Taiwan airfields they happened to be at underwent assault from the sky.

Taiwan's trials continued for three days. Vice Admiral Kusaka continued in effective command of the Combined Fleet throughout that interval. He ordered execution of SHO-2 at 10:30 in the morning of the first day. He canceled sortie orders for Admiral Shima's Fifth Fleet and Matsuda's battleships, borrowed from Ozawa, but later reinstated the Shima mission when it seemed there was an opportunity to finish off Allied cripples. He also changed orders for the submarines of Sixth Fleet to provide for a concentration in Taiwanese waters to pick off Allied warships. Of the fifty-five submarines grouped in the Sixth Fleet on paper, only sixteen could be sent into action. Before any real concentration took place, MacArthur's Leyte landings began and the subs went there instead.

Minutes into the first attacks Fukudome's chief of staff suggested that as a morale-building measure, they continue to work at their offices in an administration building rather than moving to an air-raid shelter in a cave about two and a half miles away. Fukudome thought otherwise, especially since the shelter had just been improved to function as a command post. They moved. About an hour later an American bomb devastated Admiral Fukudome's aboveground office and the working spaces all around it.

At the beginning there were only 270 aircraft on Taiwan, and 200 of them were Army planes. Only sporadic and ineffective resistance could be offered. An after-action report by the Army defense command confirmed that "attacks against air bases were carried out with such persistence and thoroughness that installations at airfields suffered considerable damage." Admiral Mitscher's task force flew no less than 1,378 sorties on October 12, but only partial returns are available for the other days strikes were mounted. The task force claimed 655 Japanese planes destroyed; Fukudome asserts that losses totaled 329, including 179 planes that did not return from strikes sent against Task Force 38.

A novel element was inserted on October 13, when B-29 bombers flying from China cooperated with the fleet's raids from offshore. Japanese radio intercepts furnished advance warning of the raids, while American intelligence intercepted the Japanese messages warning their own forces of the incoming very heavy bombers.

Key to the outcome of the Taiwan battle would be the results of Japanese attacks on Mitscher's task force. Captain Kuno, Fukudome's senior executive agent in the Home Islands, staged groups of thirty or so of his T Attack Force planes through Okinawa every night to hit the U.S. fleet. There were special difficulties in communication between Army and Navy aircraft, a big headache for Kuno. Although the Army and Navy had made arrangements for communications during joint operations as early as 1943, these had never seemed satisfactory, and the Army air regiments attached to the 762nd Air Group for training in torpedo bombing had finally been taught Navy procedures instead. More than four months was required to attain acceptable proficiency among Army crews. The T Attack Force never attained results commensurate with the hopes vested in it or with the raw strength of its 186 aircraft.

Many Japanese daylight raids also staged through Okinawa, including the 101-plane strike on October 12. Already on Taiwan were 205 planes from training units and JNAF antisubmarine groups, but these were simply lucrative targets for keen Allied aviators. Ozawa's carrier aircraft, totaling 172 planes, reported in on October 12 and 13, permitting JNAF raids amounting to almost 400 sorties on the fourteenth. Final accretions to air strength included 31 aircraft drawn from units in China and 250 from the 51st Air Flotilla in northern Japan. Including 200 Japanese Army aircraft on Taiwan, in all some 1,425 aircraft were involved in the air battles and 761 offensive sorties were flown against Task Force 38.

This tremendous scale of effort resulted in no more than damage to American cruisers *Houston* and *Canberra.* Yet Japanese reports, annoying many when they were reflected in IGHQ communiqués, claimed sinking eleven aircraft carriers and damaging eight more, sinking two battleships and damaging two more, and so on. During the Taiwan air battle Japan paid the price for JNAF's lack of interest in a strong program of ship and aircraft identification during training. In an effort to exploit illusory results, Combined Fleet now committed more forces, including Vice Admiral Shima's Fifth Fleet, which reached Amami O Shima before the high command realized there was nothing to exploit.

Both Admiral Toyoda and air commander Fukudome applied sterile mechanical formulas to the pilot claims. Both were familiar with the tendency for aircrews to overestimate results. Toyoda automatically cut claims by half; Fukudome insisted that an elite unit like the T Attack Force ought to be credited with at least a third of what it claimed. As a consequence, both admirals underestimated U.S. strength at the instant the Imperial Navy embarked upon its last gamble. Barely was the ink dry on the propaganda claims concerning Allied losses when a Japanese outpost on Suluan Island began reporting American ships and landings. Suluan Island is at the mouth of Leyte Gulf. It was the moment of Decisive Battle, but now the Imperial Navy had already exhausted its air capability. It was a strange replay of the preliminaries to the battle of the Philippine Sea.

THE TAIWAN AIR BATTLE HAD REPERCUSSIONS ON BOTH SIDES OF THE PACIFIC. TOKYO HAD TO absorb the complaints of representatives abroad who felt shortchanged on reports from home. In Portugal, for example, the naval attaché planned festivities commemorating the supposed victory but had no information to impart other than the headquarters communiqués. The naval attaché complained in one message that he had received only plain-language rebroadcasts of the IGHQ communiqués, which he had already gotten from newspapers or radio days before. Another Lisbon attaché message broadened the complaint, contrasting his situation with that of the Army attaché, who reportedly had received detailed explanatory dispatches, embarrassing the naval attaché before the interested public. In a third cable the attaché, though fully realizing that IGHQ was preoccupied "with the increasing importance and aggravation of the war," still objected that as an official representative of Japan he needed more than "mere public pronouncements."

Washington had its own little tempest in the form of complaints regarding target intelligence for Taiwan. Commodore Arleigh Burke, chief of staff to task force commander Mitscher, made some pointed remarks while visiting headquarters a few weeks afterward. Burke told a U.S. Navy audience that pilots had been inadequately informed. Either there had been no target objective charts to give them, or these had arrived too late to be of any use. Bill Sebald of combat intelligence promptly relayed the gist of the charges to Jasper Holmes at JICPOA. Commander Holmes replied with a detailed enumeration of the intelligence JICPOA had produced for the operation, following a September 9 request from Bull Halsey for information on Taiwan and the Nansei Shoto. Over the next twenty days JICPOA had produced 18,750 air target maps in separate publications covering the Nansei Shoto, the Nanpo Shoto, and northern Taiwan; 750 target analyses of the Takao area, plus a similar number of air information summaries for northern Taiwan; 1,840 photographic mosaics of the Taiwan target area; and last, 62,500 photo prints of individual targets in the Takao area.

The intelligence material totaled roughly 30,000 pounds and was sent in care of two officer couriers by special aircraft to Ulithi. A typhoon prevented the planes landing there, and they diverted to Saipan, where the shipments were transferred to a destroyer and arrived at the Third Fleet anchorage on the night of October 5. Delivery was made to Halsey's flag secretary, Commander Harold Stassen. Material went directly to battleship *New Jersey*, the fleet flagship, and to two of the task groups; destroyers delivered packages of material to the two task groups that had already sailed.

In addition, as JICPOA quite correctly observed, the Taiwan operation formed part of a last-minute modification of strategic plans that created an entirely new axis of advance (to Leyte). A more timely intelligence production schedule was simply not possible. Commander Sebald dismissed the criticisms and told Holmes, "If [Burke] returns to Washington . . . I shall see that he has an opportunity to read what you have written." No more was heard of the matter.

The affair of the Taiwan intelligence illustrates quite nicely the depth and breadth of the intelligence support Allied forces were receiving in the Pacific. This represented the development of combat intelligence to new heights, based on aerial reconnaissance, radio intelligence, document translation and analysis, and prisoner interrogation. These pillars of intelligence enabled briefing officers not merely to point pilots at targets, but to inform them on the extent of aerial opposition, the best routes to fly to avoid hostile anti-aircraft fire, optimum altitudes to avoid radar detection, and so forth. Information pilots today consider to be routine was an unprecedented and exponential improvement in World War II.

For the land and sea forces the same held true. Using the pillars of intelligence, plus submarine reconnaissance, swimmer teams, and additional means, invasion forces were as well informed on their targets as humanly possible. Intricate latex models were even cast to furnish physical views of the lay of the land. The fleet, of course, benefited from radio intelligence revealing adversary movements and sometimes intentions. Only within a system as adroit as this, the system that actually existed in Washington and Pearl Harbor in 1944, can so esoteric a matter as the Japanese tanker situation have been a key indicator of the Imperial Navy's determination to emerge for its final Decisive Battle.

Referring to America's well-known secretary of the interior, Harold Ickes, senior Imperial Navy oil expert Rear Admiral Enomoto Ryuchiro remarked, "The trouble with the oil situation in Japan is that we had no Mr. Ickes." America had great home production plus access to Venezuelan and other imports. Japan had minuscule home production, averaging 260,000 tons a year, down from a prewar level of about 380,000 tons because equipment had been sent to the Netherlands East Indies to help restore production there after the battles of the conquest. Synthetic-oil production, in which program Enomoto had played a major role until mid-1942, only passed the 100,000-ton mark the following year and peaked at 135,000 tons in 1944. Under the weight of American bombing, production levels collapsed after that, while refining of synthetics for specialized uses, such as aviation fuel, lagged even more. By the end of the war Japan's entire synthetic-pine-oil program had produced just a few thousand barrels of aviation gasoline. Intelligence estimates projected aviation gas consumption in 1945 alone at about 6.5 *million* barrels, and for that and the preceding three years at roughly 25.9 million. Even draconian austerity measures left Japan's oil problem still intractable, with Netherlands East Indies oil the Empire's only hope.

There were two aspects to the question of reliance upon East Indies oil, production and transport, and both were subject to the vagaries of the rivalries between Japan's military services. All activities were controlled by an Army-Navy Oil Committee, composed of the vice ministers of both services along with relevant bureau chiefs and meeting periodically at the Army-Navy Club in Tokyo. Administrative arrangements in the East Indies also left the Army in charge of 85 percent of the oil production even as the Navy became the main oil consumer. The Imperial Navy had a few storage tanks at Singapore, but they were filled almost exclusively with Army oil. Under the Southwest Area Fleet the 101st Fuel Depot ran the oil fields at Tarakan and Sanga Sanga, while the 102nd had charge of the Balikpapan refinery.

Everything else belonged to the Army. This situation continually held potential for sharp feuds between the services.

Grand potentate in the oil business was Southern Area Army headquarters, its offices at Singapore. Admiral Enomoto was actually assigned to Singapore as naval attaché for fourteen months in 1942–1943, as if the Army were some foreign land. His specific job was liaison with the Army—getting production figures for Army oil fields to inform Navy officers on the Oil Committee in Tokyo, arranging oil supply for Navy forces in the Malaya–Netherlands East Indies area, expediting oil shipments to Japan. Through most of the war more oil was shipped directly to the forces in the field than to Japan, but supplies in the Empire were obviously critical to the war effort.

The Imperial Navy's hole card in the oil sweepstakes remained control of shipping. Army oil would be useless unless it reached field forces, and even Army-controlled tankers had to move under Navy orders as part of a joint pool. Once a month at Singapore, Navy and Southern Area Army representatives met to study Tokyo's latest allocations and decide on shipping and convoys. With the Army having the oil and the Navy the transport there was a basis for bargaining and cooperation to mutual advantage. "But for this fortunate state of affairs," observed Rear Admiral Asakura Bunji, chief of staff of the 1st Southern Expeditionary Fleet at the time of Leyte, "the Army would undoubtedly have left the Navy without oil." That would have been perilous indeed for a naval force that, according to a May 1943 estimate by the U.S. Office of Naval Intelligence, was consuming oil at a rate (excluding air operations) of 28 million to 47.5 million barrels per annum.

Moving oil required tanker bottoms. There had been 59 tankers displacing 2,000 tons or more in 1941, or 95 if one counts every ship bigger than 100 tons, for an aggregate tonnage of 556,000. During 1942, 13 more tankers of 46,000 tons were captured from the Allies or seized from the Vichy French in Indochina. According to Colonel Hattori, new construction added a dozen ships (46,000 tons) in fiscal 1942, then 95 (371,000 tons) during fiscal 1943. Of the total tanker pool only 39,200 tons were sunk or damaged prior to March 1943, but losses over the following year amounted to 369,100 tons, and during the months from April to July 1944 another 142,700 tons of tankers went to the bottom. Thus by August 1944, a time when the toll claimed by Allied submarines had begun to accelerate tremendously, and when the intensity of the war (and thus oil consumption) had increased greatly, the Empire's aggregate tanker tonnage had declined to roughly 468,000 tons.

American intelligence followed Japan's tanker situation from an early date. Estimates of Japan's shipping situation produced by ONI's Far East Division in March and December 1942 treated tanker tonnage as a separate category. By February 1943 the Far East Division already projected tanker tonnage down to 435,000, a shortage of 23,000 compared to ONI's estimate of the Empire's minimum requirements for this category. The supposed shortage worsened in subsequent estimates, with the aggregate projection reduced to 412,000 tons as of July 1, 1943, 399,000 tons on October 1, and 349,000 tons on February 1, 1944. Intelligence believed the Japanese were making good on their shipping requirements by altering freighters to carry oil in bulk or simply carrying drums of oil or bunkering ships to capacity, using double bottoms and unused compartments to carry fuel. Spurred by the hopeful intelligence, Allied submarine commands gave special priority to tanker attacks.

A detailed ONI study of Japan's shipping position as of April 1, 1944, issued in mid-May, substantially revised the estimates. The revision was based on new intelligence, which specified by name and tonnage the Japanese vessels in service as of December 1941. (This information was probably attributable to documents captured at Kwajalein.) By this time, too, ONI had a better understanding of problems in submarine attacks, such as faulty torpedoes. This ONI estimate observed:

> A considerable scaling down of tanker losses is revealed. This is the result of an intensive study by the Division of Naval Intelligence of loss assessments, the over-all results of which have made it prudent to reduce previous figures. Tanker losses are particularly difficult to estimate. Attacking forces find it difficult to distinguish tankers from other mer[chant] ships under certain conditions, and the question of correct tonnage assessment presents another complexity. Accordingly only those vessels now highly evaluated as tankers are included in our tanker loss category. The present loss estimate of 320,365 gross tons is believed to be on the conservative side.

As a matter of fact, ONI's assertion was indeed conservative: Hattori's figure for tanker losses over the period amounts to 408,200. The new estimate for aggregate Japanese tanker tonnage was 449,900. This represented a bigger tanker pool than U.S. intelligence had believed over a year before, but the new figure was much more accurate and, since Japan's war requirements had grown, the Empire continued to suffer a tanker shortage.

Increasingly effective attacks sharpened Japan's difficulties every day. The Empire lost significant tanker tonnage in the carrier raids on Truk and Palau, including three scarce fleet oilers at the former and five at the latter. Two more oilers went down beneath a hail of bombs in the Philippine Sea. Submarines accounted for two fleet oilers in June 1944, one that July, four in August, and two in September. By October 1 total Japanese tanker losses were estimated at 481,000 tons. Though the projection of Japanese aggregate tonnage was again revised upward, the mounting losses in fleet oilers posed serious limits for Japanese naval operations.

Radio intelligence contributed a good deal to the improvement of U.S. estimates during 1944. Starting to keep a weather eye on tanker messages, OP-20-G noticed in traffic names of ships that JICPOA listed as sunk. In July Pearl Harbor was asked about seven tankers whose names had appeared in messages decoded in Colombo, Melbourne, and Pearl Harbor, and at OP-20-G. A search of the files at Pearl Harbor showed that substantiation existed for some of the claims but not others. This helped lead to the October revision in the estimate of Japanese tanker tonnage.

Heightened interest in tankers also led to important combat intelligence. Appreciation of the Empire's oil problem helped the Allies understand the move of the Imperial Navy's gunnery ships to the Singapore area. The weekly JICPOA estimate of September 11, 1944, observed that "fleet logistics and anti-submarine actions continue to spotlight naval activity." A week later JICPOA noted, "The overall tanker movement picture is somewhat confusing insofar as determining fleet intentions goes, but it is apparent that large scale logistic preparations are in the making." On October 2 the report observed that several oilers were transporting fuel from Sumatra to Lingga, and that exercises in underway refueling had been scheduled.

After the Taiwan air battle the radio intercepts began to tell the story. On October 16, in a dispatch OP-20-G took a day to break, Combined Fleet chief of staff Kusaka assigned six oilers directly to the 1st Diversion Attack Force (tactical title for Kurita's fleet), ordered another to follow Kurita's orders, and designated two cargo ships to give up their fuel if Kurita required it. OP-20-G concluded: "This is the first indication of a possible sortie by [Kurita's fleet] which may comprise the bulk of the . . . units now in the Singapore area." The next day Americans intercepted more orders for the Kurita tankers plus one for a couple of Ozawa's fleet oilers to take on a full load of fuel at the Imperial Navy's main storage facility at Tokuyama. Americans discovered on October 20, upon decoding a message sent late the previous day, that two oilers standing by for Kurita at Hainan in the Tonkin Gulf were ordered to Coron Bay in the western Philippines. The ships were specifically directed to replenish Kurita's fleet, a clear indication that the Japanese admiral would arrive there presently.

Washington's radio summary of October 21 recorded intercepts pertaining both to a replenishment group working for the striking force (Ozawa's Mobile Fleet), and dispatch of tankers to refuel Vice Admiral Shima Kiyohide's Fifth Fleet, tactically known as the 2nd Diversion Attack Force, which had now been ordered to Philippine waters. Very significantly, the ships involved were Japanese Army tankers taken over by the Combined Fleet. The United States would not learn until after the war that these vessels had been subjects of heated argument in Tokyo, where the Navy's staff officers insisted they could not carry out the SHO operation without the tankers. As it was the ships were delayed in their planned arrival at the Pescadores, and Admiral Kusaka made inquiries as to their whereabouts.

They eventually arrived on October 22, a day the Americans intercepted more messages regarding the Japanese tankers sent to Coron Bay.

With information like this the JICPOA weekly estimate of October 23 was able to note the Kurita fleet arriving at Coron Bay for fueling, the Shima force believed to be arriving at Manila, and Ozawa's striking force, location uncertain, believed to be moving south from the Empire. All of this was based on "current sightings taken in conjunction with information on tanker movements." It was a fair approximation of the true situation. In Philippine skies and waters, battle was about to be joined.

# TWENTY THREE

# "The Enemy Task Forces Will Be
# Destroyed Tomorrow"

LIKE HITLER AND HIS GENERALS SPECULATING AS TO WHERE THE ALLIES WOULD LAND IN northwest Europe, the Japanese faced major intelligence dilemmas on the Philippine invasion. Timing would be a key factor in the SHO plan, which was predicated upon the Imperial Navy's gunnery ships striking the invasion convoys within forty-eight hours of a landing—in other words, before amphibious forces could fully unload. Since the Japanese fleet needed to move thousands of miles to effect such an attack, warning would be vital to success.

A wide variety of contact reports, battle notices, radio intelligence items, special intelligence from attachés, and the like flowed into the Naval General Staff and the Combined Fleet. Troops fighting at Palau or aircraft flying over the area, for example, supplied sighting reports on eight of the first ten days of October. The NGS Third Bureau, fabled *joho kyoku*, also learned that MacArthur's forces were beginning to use the airfield they had captured on Morotai. This news, in combination with the appearance of Task Force 38 off the Nansei Shoto, undoubtedly contributed to the feeling in Manila that an invasion was coming and the Philippines would be the target. *Joho kyoku* shared that impression, and predicted Allied efforts in the archipelago late in October or afterward.

At Combined Fleet headquarters opinion was mixed. Admiral Toyoda had thought the offensive would begin in August or September, but the Allies moved on Palau and Morotai at that time instead. By October Toyoda was uncertain but believed operations imminent; hence his visit to Manila to confer with Mikawa early in the month. Toyoda worried that if the fleet did nothing the Japanese public would lose faith in the Imperial Navy. His fleet intelligence officer, Commander Nakajima Chikataka, was of a different mind as to the threat. The *joho sambo* believed the Allies needed at least a month to recycle their amphibious forces following the battles on Palau and Morotai. Since the fight on Palau, at least, continued into October (and would not end until November), Nakajima expected the next invasion some-time in November.

On October 9 a key intelligence report appeared after an Army aircraft scouted the New Guinea coast. In harbor at Biak and Hollandia the plane reported over 250 transports of all sizes, many cruisers and destroyers, four battleships, and six aircraft carriers. Commander Nakajima realized then that action was imminent, but he still could not decide where. The forces seemed too large for a landing on Yap or the Talaud islands, but the timing was off for the Philippines; Nakajima expected another month or two before that invasion. He recalled, "We couldn't make up our minds as to your most probable objective."

Of course the *joho sambo* had access to the Southwest Area Fleet's astute message of October 8 foreseeing proximate landings. Then, at 11:23 P.M. on October 12, the Owada Group reported a large force about to sail from the New Guinea area. There were apparent communications tie-ins with the Admiralties and Pearl Harbor. The next night a further dispatch warned of a large-scale landing in the near future but did not hazard a guess as to objective. The Admiralties again, along with Saipan and Ulithi, appeared associated with the effort. Probably reacting to these reports, a JNAF plane scouted the Admiralties on October 15. It reported just twenty transports, along with a task group–size force of carriers and other warships; the Japanese did not know that an invasion convoy had already left Manus at the time of Task Force 38's Taiwan raid.

This day, Sunday, October 15, Admiral Halsey hit Manila with one of Task Force 38's groups. The Japanese were unaware of it, but their achieve-ment in the Taiwan battle had been to prevent Halsey from bringing all his four groups to bear on the Philippines on the first day as originally planned. Now the scale of attack would build more gradually. The Philippine Decisive Battle had begun, and the Japanese air force would fight it first.

WHEN BULL HALSEY'S CARRIERS BEGAN TO STRIKE MANILA ON OCTOBER 16 IT REPRESENTED A nightmare returned for First Air Fleet commander Vice Admiral Teraoka Kimpei. The Allied task force had already made one extensive foray against the Philippines, in September, just a month after Teraoka took command. By the middle of that month his serviceable aircraft were half the fleet's allo-cation. Once the Taiwan air battle began, these meager forces were supposed to join Fukudome's Second Air Fleet in annihilating the Americans. Now, not only had the enemy not been destroyed, but also the Army had issued an intelligence estimate that the invasion shipping seen off New Guinea could be carrying up to six full divisions, and the hated task force was hitting him again.

Admiral Teraoka did what he could. On October 12 he sent his chief of staff up to Clark Field to energize local leaders to get planes up against Task Force 38. No group was able to respond. "Having missed our opportunity through delay," Teraoka mused, "we were forced to swallow our anger and await the following day." That day Teraoka himself went up to Clark in a trainer piloted by his chief of staff, Captain Odawara Toshihiko. This time the air fleet made a major effort, putting up thirty attack planes escorted by seventy Zeros plus an equal number of Army fighters. All went well until the intermediate refueling point, where there were delays with the unfamiliar Army planes. Then clouds closed in over the Luzon Strait; the planes were unable to find anything or even to reach attack positions. The escort leader, Lieutenant Suzuki Usaburo, had engine trouble and was killed in a crash. Most of the planes were forced to land on Taiwan.

On October 14 Teraoka wanted fifty fighters to escort a strike by JNAF planes alone, but only twenty-eight were available. The best tactic possible under the circumstances was a "surprise attack" by two dive-bombers with eight Zeros to accompany them. That unit found nothing and made for Taiwan. Another bomber unit ordered to make a dusk attack could not complete preparations in time.

The admiral could perhaps be forgiven his frustration. Even the Japanese Army knew the score. In Manila during the period of preparations, Army and Navy staff officers worked together to an unprecedented degree. The planners became friendly and would go out together in the evenings. Lieutenant Colonel Nishimura, later killed, who was the 4th Air Army's chief liaison to Teraoka's command, made only positive comments about the JNAF's strategic planning. There were also no criticisms, either then or later, from the Army's theater command, Field Marshal Terauchi Hisaichi's Southern Army. Staff officer Murata Kingo of that command declared, "We all knew that the other arms were doing the best they could."

The searing intensity of the air battle was something new for Admiral Teraoka, who had spent most of the war in China, his news of the Pacific coming secondhand from officers like Koga Mineichi, who used to correspond with Yamamoto, or Kondo Nobutake, who came in December 1943 to take over the China Area Fleet. Teraoka had been first skipper of carrier *Soryu,* which he commanded in China waters in 1938, when his air officer was Odawara Toshihiko. Now Captain Odawara, who had later gone to the South Pacific as an air group leader, was with Teraoka once more. Odawara had also worked with the Bureau of Aeronautics; he was a well-known authority on aviation and flying. It fell to Odawara and Teraoka, in their present dire straits, to deal with suggestions for new tactics, aerial suicide tactics, that were to become one of the most feared and destructive techniques of the last phase of the war.

It was another of Teraoka's classmates, Vice Admiral Onishi Takijiro, who was the primary advocate of suicide tactics, which he pressed with the Navy Ministry and NGS in Tokyo. Suicidal maneuvers were not unknown in the Pacific, where wounded pilots occasionally crash-dived their planes to hit enemy ships, or outmatched bombers deliberately did this, or desperate men tried to down enemy planes by crashing into them. The novelty would be in using such suicide tactics systematically, in an organized fashion. During the September raids Rear Admiral Arima Masafumi, commanding Teraoka's 26th Air Flotilla and aware of Onishi's ideas, proposed "special attack" tactics to his boss. Teraoka refused to consider them unless there was a way for the pilots and crews on such missions to return.

There the matter stood until October 15, when search planes discovered Task Force 38 back off the Philippines. Teraoka was in Manila that day to confer with 4th Air Army commander Lieutenant General Tominaga Kiyoji; he received the report there early in the morning. An immediate strike was dispatched of six Zeros armed with bombs and nineteen more as escort; they actually managed to score superficial damage on the carrier *Franklin*, a hit on her deck edge elevator. While American planes riposted with an attack on Manila and Nichols Field, Teraoka and Tominaga put together a joint effort for the afternoon. At around noontime came a further contact report of two or three more U.S. carriers with another group. This report put the lie to claims of sinkings in the Taiwan air battle, since the Japanese knew Halsey had had sixteen carriers before that battle; if six or seven were now off Luzon, Japanese forces could not have accomplished the results claimed.

This development changed the whole complexion of battle, for the JNAF was hardly on equal terms with Task Force 38 if Mitscher's ships were at full or nearly full strength. At Nichols Field, headquarters of the 26th Air Flotilla, Rear Admiral Arima apparently drew this conclusion and decided to right the balance using "special attack" tactics, participating himself in the afternoon mission, which comprised three Bettys, ten dive-bombers, six Zeros with bombs, and an escort of ten Navy and seventy Army fighters. It was claimed that this attack damaged a cruiser and two carriers, as well as sinking an aircraft carrier, which, according to Teraoka, "blew up and sank in thirty seconds."

The Army observation plane that was the source for Teraoka's description of the afternoon air strike had been quite mistaken: U.S. fighters intercepted the attackers. No warship was even attacked that afternoon. Admiral Arima's sacrifice proved more than vain, however, because he set an example other Japanese increasingly sought to emulate. In the meantime, basking in supposed success, Teraoka received a congratulatory message from Combined Fleet and toasted with sake sent over by General Yamashita Tomoyuki, now commanding the 14th Area Army covering the Philippines. Admiral Teraoka was undoubtedly surprised on October 16, when planes searching out of Taiwan revealed no change in the strength of the groups attacked the previous day. More ominous still, a further report mentioned finding seven U.S. carriers near one of the other groups. If those reports were all accurate there could have been very few losses among Mitscher's Task Force 38. In fact there had been none.

Early in the morning of October 17 an observation post on Suluan Island at the entrance to Leyte Gulf reported the approach of Allied ships, and then landings on the island. This precursor landing by Ranger troops was to prevent Japanese interference with minesweepers and with the huge invasion convoys soon to enter Leyte Gulf. More carrier strikes hit Manila that day too. American radio intelligence intercepted the message when Combined Fleet chief of staff Kusaka, still acting in the absence of Toyoda, alerted the fleet for SHO-1. In his dispatch Kusaka referred simply to "S" operations, so an American analyst commented: "Meaning unknown. Suggest 'S' is basic [Japanese] plan to stem Blue attack on Philippines." This was amplified in OP-20-G's October 17 radio summary: "Yesterday's intercepted Japanese traffic reflected indications of a possible sortie, or preparations for a sortie, from Singapore by a Second Fleet task force. . . . U.S. landings on Suluan Island were reported, followed by the placing into effect of two operation plans, presumably to counter U.S. operations against the Philippines."

Admiral Kusaka issued the execute order for SHO in the evening of October 18; that, too, the Americans intercepted, along with at least ten other dispatches related to the Philippine fighting. Tanker movements, OP-20-G speculated, indicated preparations for sorties from both Singapore and the Empire, while submarine traffic suggested that I-boats were on their way to Philippine waters. Ultra provided American admirals an unparalleled advantage.

At Manila, air leader Teraoka noted on the eighteenth that "It has become obvious from this evening that the enemy is planning to land at Tacloban." That town was on the island of Leyte. In fact leading waves of American troops landed at 10:00 A.M. on October 20. Teraoka's fears for Leyte proved entirely accurate.

No longer would Leyte be Teraoka's problem, however. The day of the U.S. landings he handed over command to none other than Vice Admiral Onishi Takijiro, one more senior Japanese officer who had been caught by Bull Halsey's raids on Taiwan. Slated to lead the First Air Fleet, Onishi had left Tokyo on October 9, was at Kanoya when Task Force 38 began to bomb Okinawa, and tried to reach Taiwan by flying through Shanghai. He reached Takao just in time to be stuck there with Admiral Toyoda, who was coming from the other direction. Both were obliged to shelter in cellars during the days of the U.S. strikes. Onishi finally reached Manila on October 17, a few hours after it, too, had been bombed.

After working with distinction as staff chief of the old Eleventh Air Fleet, Onishi had spent most of the war in the Bureau of Aeronautics or the Munitions Ministry. Forced to comment from the sidelines, Onishi, always provocative, became increasingly acerbic. Amid the joyful early days, the air admiral told Navy planners that the *Yamato*-class superbattleships were no better than horse buggies in the automotive age; battleships should be scrapped and the materials recovered used to produce aircraft. Similarly, an Onishi paper toward the end of 1943 argued that it was wishful thinking to suppose there could be command of the sea without airpower. When the Aleutians fell, Onishi told friends that Japan should merely have bombarded the islands and gotten out, but instead had foolishly poured in men and matériel. Then, after the Saipan battle, Onishi, too, had been among those who wanted to stake everything on a naval relief expedition.

Now the air fleet under assault in the Philippines became the fifty-three-year-old Onishi's first combat command. It came at a key moment in the war, but one when his precious JNAF had already passed into eclipse. On October 17, when Onishi arrived at Manila, the First Air Fleet had declined to just ninety-eight aircraft. On October 20, the day he assumed command, the air "fleet" had a serviceable strength of no more than forty planes. Onishi had commanded more than that in 1940 when he led a composite air group.

Strength had fallen so far that the air fleet made no effort to launch standard searches on Onishi's first day in command. Even without searches, however, First Air Fleet managed no better than one strike with a couple of dive-bombers plus another using three fighter-bombers.

Admiral Onishi spent his first day at Manila closeted with Teraoka. Considering the rapidity with which Onishi subsequently took up the matter, their discussions must have touched on the "special attack" concept. Crash-dive tactics, soon to be called kamikaze in an allusion to the "Divine Wind"—violent storms—that had dispersed Mongol fleets in 1274 and 1281, offered some potential for reversing the strength disparities that had grown so huge. October 18 exemplified the gap. On that day the First Air Fleet managed to mount seventeen sorties against the Allies in Leyte Gulf, while the Americans put up 685 planes to strike Japanese targets, not counting close air support missions. It was a wonder the JNAF could accomplish anything at all.

Even before taking charge Admiral Onishi determined to use kamikaze tactics. One result of his talk with Teraoka may have been a decision to broach the subject with unit commanders first, rather than going directly to the pilots. As a consequence, on October 19 Onishi invited the commanders and air officers of the 761st and 201st air groups to headquarters in Manila.

Commander Maeda Kosei of the 761st came and was briefed on the kamikaze concept, which had undergone some discussion within the Naval General Staff as well, including talk between Onishi and Captain Genda Minoru. It is a measure of the growing impotence of the JNAF that the 761st Air Group, carried by JICPOA order-of-battle experts as the main offensive strength of the First Air Fleet, was revealed by Ultra to have only eight aircraft as of October 21.

That afternoon Admiral Onishi went up to Mabalacat, one of the fields of the Clark complex, for a meeting that has become a celebrated scene in Japan's kamikaze lore, in which pilots of the 201st Air Group volunteered for "special attack" (*"tokko"*) missions. According to a study of Leyte Gulf made by the U.S. Naval War College, the Mabalacat visit occurred simply because Captain Yamamoto Sakae failed to turn up at Manila as requested. Worried that the 201st Air Group commander might have been ambushed by guerrillas or that his car might have broken down, Onishi made the trip himself. As it turned out, Yamamoto *had* gone to Manila but in a plane—which, given the decline in JNAF maintenance, was perhaps as dangerous as facing guerrillas. The plane crashed with a faulty engine, sending Yamamoto to the hospital with a broken leg. He telephoned his executive officer, Commander Tamai Asaichi, deputizing him to act in his stead. Onishi convinced Tamai, senior pilots like Lieutenant Ibusuki Masanobu, and air fleet staff officer Commander Inoguchi Rikihei, to put the proposal to the pilots. Tamai did so, and the creation of the first "special attack" unit was the result. Lieutenant Seki Yukio, in Inoguchi's firsthand account, took only five seconds to insist he be allowed to lead the unit. The Shimpu Attack Unit, as it was christened, included twenty-three petty-officer pilots, divided into four sections, all of whom resolved to crash-dive Zeros armed with 550-pound bombs into Allied ships. New "special attack" units quickly formed all over the Philippines. Enthused pilots tried kamikaze attacks starting on October 21, but it would be four days before any met success.

In the meantime, when Admiral Onishi returned to Manila in his black limousine on the evening of October 19, he promptly went to Southwest Area Fleet headquarters, where ensued a long discussion among Onishi, fleet commander Mikawa Gunichi, chief of staff Nishio Hidehiko, and others—Captain Shibata Bunzo, the senior staff officer of Second Air Fleet, and Captain Hiramoto Michitaka, Navy liaison to the 4th Air Army. Onishi was wise to clear his plans with Admiral Mikawa, for the Philippine leaders that day received a Combined Fleet order designating Mikawa supreme commander of naval air units in the archipelago. That day, October 20, the Combined Fleet further determined to reinforce the Philippines with the bulk of the Empire-based Third Air Fleet and also designated October 25 as X-Day, the day of Decisive Battle. Toyoda had cast his die and now they were rolling.

With the choice of a target date for the Decisive Battle, the preparatory air

operations became absolutely crucial for the Japanese. While the senior officers were still in their Manila meeting, Second Air Fleet reported its plan to
make "Y-Day" major air strikes on the twenty-third, with a preliminary
night attack on the twenty-second. This offered the advantage of avoiding
an additional day of attrition to Allied action before the planned attacks, but
on the other hand the plan's drawback was to divorce Japanese air activity
from surface naval actions, reducing coordination as well as any support
value of the air attacks. The Second Air Fleet operations order for deployment forward to the Philippines went out on October 21; 350 aircraft were
to relocate and forty-eight longer-range bombers would remain on Taiwan.
At Pearl Harbor the Ultra monitors recorded the message, and codebreakers
had recovered the gist of it within eight hours.

Movement of the Second Air Fleet started at 9:00 A.M. with the T Force
and floatplane aircraft scheduled to execute the October 22 night attack.
Remaining units departed Taiwan later that day in such fashion as to arrive
in the Clark Field area about 5:00 P.M. By evening some 178 Second Air
Fleet aircraft had reached Clark, and if floatplanes arrived in the same proportion, the total of newly redeployed aircraft at this moment would have
been about 197. In addition Admiral Onishi's First Air Fleet had twenty-
four flyable planes. The 4th Air Army added more; General Tomonaga's air
army had had 105 aircraft on October 17; although that number declined
to thirty-seven by the twenty-second, another sixty-one aircraft arrived that
day, raising available Army air strength to ninety-eight planes.

Despite reinforcements, Japanese air plans fell victim to their weakness.
The precipitous decline of Admiral Onishi's command is one key factor in
this development—with just two dozen aircraft by October 22, Onishi dared
not order anything but search missions that day. His scant aircraft flew
comparatively few reconnaissance flights, so that by evening the Japanese
lacked active contact with the American task forces. As a result the attack
planned that night was canceled. By midnight the Second Air Fleet leader,
Admiral Fukudome, had reached headquarters in Manila. His found his
units already beginning to suffer attrition, with few targets plotted, and little sustainability, given that his maintenance crews and ground organizations had to move forward by sea.

On Y-Day the Japanese found themselves at continued disadvantage:
Their best contacts were those in Leyte Gulf itself. Strikes on the amphibious
forces were not going to be of much help in getting the fleet past the
American task forces, but the amphibious forces were the only available
target. The 4th Air Army flew against Leyte Gulf while naval air units left
Clark Field and swept the waters east of Luzon. Three strikes at Leyte added
up to about 150 attack sorties; MacArthur himself briefly felt a target when
bombers struck around flagship *Nashville*. But no major warships or even
transports were lost.

Outside the gulf the Japanese got their best results against Rear Admiral Sherman's Task Group 38.3. Two successive waves of forty to fifty planes were beaten off, but then a single dive-bomber put its 550-pound bomb into the flight deck of light carrier *Princeton.* The blast ignited the gasoline of planes on the hangar deck, which in turn detonated six torpedoes that had been slung on aircraft intended for use in *Princeton's* first attack of the day. Much as had happened to Japanese vessels at Midway, being caught with loaded aircraft proved fatal. Captain William H. Buracker and his crew fought the fires, and almost brought them under control with the help of light cruiser *Birmingham,* come alongside to permit her fire hoses to assist the stricken carrier. At midafternoon, as salvage efforts continued, a massive explosion ripped through the *Princeton,* also causing extensive damage to the *Birmingham,* with more than half the crew casualties. This was still not much to show for the 199 JNAF planes sent out from Clark that morning, of which 67 failed to return, and it certainly was nothing like the pilots' claims of a battleship, a carrier, and a cruiser left afire. The aerial arrow in the Japanese quiver had been expended swiftly, to too little effect.

THE LAST DAYS OF THE KURITA FLEET PASSED AMID A WELTER OF PREPARATION AT LINGGA. There were more war games aboard *Yamato,* now the flagship of Battleship Division 1, where results were minimal according to Vice Admiral Ugaki Matome, who felt hampered by the highly specific strictures of the SHO plans. Ugaki continued to advocate piecemeal operations, for want of a better term, to whittle away Allied strength, catching detachments of American fleets rather than seeking a decision against the whole. The concept had an obvious relation to attrition operations in classic Decisive Battle, and Ugaki again urged these ideas upon Captain Yamamoto Yuji shortly before the latter left for Manila to participate in the final eve-of-battle conference Admiral Toyoda had arranged. Many Japanese officers had soured on the whole notion of attrition during the bloody Solomons campaign, however, and Ugaki's proposals for alternate strategy went nowhere.

Somewhat more pleasing to the admiral was the arrival at Lingga on October 5 of his good friend Nishimura Shoji, commanding Battleship Division 2, who had brought his ships south from the Empire. Ugaki had not seen Nishimura since the latter visited while he convalesced after injuries in the Yamamoto shootdown. At Lingga aboard the *Yamato* Ugaki also learned of recent political developments in Japan from Nishimura and his flag captain, Ban Masami. Tojo's final days, Admiral Shimada's vain effort to retain a share of power from an NGS post, the coming of the Koiso cabinet, were vital developments.

Much time had to be devoted to hard work, but there was horseplay, too.

With facilities at Lingga rather limited, Admiral Kurita scheduled rest and recreation at Singapore for most of Second Fleet, battleships excepted. Between October 5 and 8 the heavy ships of Cruiser Division 5 and the vessels of 10th Destroyer Flotilla, all but Captain Tanii Tamotsu's 17th Division, would visit Singapore. They would be followed from October 8 to October 11 by Cruiser Division 4 and half the 2nd Destroyer Flotilla, while the other half visited the great Asian port with Cruiser Division 7 from the eleventh to the fourteenth. Sailors would have just one liberty ashore of only ten hours, however.

Battleships posed a special problem. The appearance and characteristics of the huge behemoths *Yamato* and *Musashi* were secret even within the Imperial Navy. Admiral Ugaki had therefore put an absolute prohibition on any Singapore visits by these warships; indeed, he disliked the potential for dissipation inherent in the port city and put Singapore itself off limits for *Nagato* too. That battleship instead went to Seletar, the former British naval base, which had ample recreation facilities. Vice Admiral Suzuki Yoshio also made Seletar the liberty port for the *Kongo* and *Haruna* of his Battleship Division 3. Though concrete evidence is lacking, the Japanese had just finished a series of improvements to the electronics suites of these warships and authorities probably did not want the vessels exposed to prying eyes.

As for *Yamato* and *Musashi*, they had to make do with transports to take portions of each crew for rest in shifts. But Admiral Ugaki also objected to the inevitable loss of readiness that entailed. The superbattleship crews were permitted only local recreation; they would have to grin and bear it.

One reason Ugaki could not afford to give up his crews was precisely because of the fleet's electronics upgrade. The Imperial Navy intended to use radar-controlled gunfire with its improved radars and antennas, and the warships, battleships in particular, needed to master the technique. Several gunnery exercises were held off Lingga in the weeks before SHO, and there were anti-aircraft and antisubmarine exercises as well. Local aircraft and submarines cooperated with the fleet, acting as mock attackers to be parried. Rear Admiral Hayakawa Mikio's 2nd Destroyer Flotilla held a special exercise against a Ro-boat as late as the afternoon of October 5.

In view of what was shortly to occur, a word about Japanese antisubmarine capability is in order. Losses among Imperial Navy destroyers were such that by October 1944 the fleet was torn between requirements for these ships in their different roles. The ships needed to be conserved for a fleet engagement, in which their torpedoes might prove decisive, but they were also vital as escorts. Considerable losses of destroyers to submarine and air attack through the summer of 1944 made skippers even more loath to engage submarines. At tactical conferences during that period, Japanese destroyer leaders went so far as to argue that their ships incurred too much risk in stopping to attack a submarine.

It had always been a weakness in Japanese antisubmarine warfare that escorts were inadequate in numbers, due to preference for "regular" combat roles rather than the defensive activity implied by antisubmarine warfare. This in turn militated against placing sufficient emphasis on submarine "kills," since escorts needed to stick with their flocks rather than play cat-and-mouse with enemy subs. So Japanese escorts tended to put down depth charges just long enough to get a surface unit past a point of attack. This simply encouraged aggressive Allied submarine commanders, which complicated antisub-warfare problems because more subs gathered to overwhelm the limited numbers of escorts. The Japanese had no way to determine the depth of a submarine, so their depth charges, which anyway had relatively small bursting charges (200–300 pounds), were given depth settings by prearrangement and percentage rather than positive contact and concrete data. A submarine could almost always escape by diving deep, and only toward the end of the war did the Imperial Navy introduce a deep-depth fuse for their charges. Finally, a Japanese destroyer carried ninety depth charges and would usually expend thirty-six in an attack on a hard contact. The need during a fleet sortie to conserve against a future contingency limited the degree to which a contact could be engaged. This would have disastrous effects for Admiral Kurita during the SHO operation.

Around midafternoon on October 16 Lingga received a warning message from Combined Fleet instructing the 1st Diversion Attack Force to prepare to sail. An amplifying dispatch from fleet chief of staff Kusaka explained: "Since it is recognized that such a sortie would vitally affect the fuel situation as well as future operations the final sortie order will be issued [only] if sortie appears necessary." It was the first order Kurita Takeo had received since the general SHO directives the fleet issued October 10. Admiral Kurita had begun from that time to prepare his force to take to the sea. By October 16 only cruisers *Aoba* and *Noshiro*, both still at Singapore, plus a number of floatplanes being serviced, were not yet combat-ready.

The next morning the Japanese on Suluan Island reported themselves under attack, and Combined Fleet issued its alert order for SHO-1. Kurita got the dispatch shortly after 8:00 A.M. At 11:28 the Second Fleet commander amplified his initial orders, telling the fleet to raise steam for 20 knots and be on twenty-minute notice for 24 knots—an early indication that he expected imminent battle. This order reflected Combined Fleet's further instruction that the 1st Diversion Attack Force proceed to Brunei. Having instructed his fleet to raise steam, and holding an order to proceed to Brunei, Kurita then remained in place until 1:00 the next morning, when his fleet actually departed Lingga.

Kurita's delay leaving Lingga was due to the submarine threat, which made it desirable to sail at night, and the need to get oilers to Brunei to refuel the fleet. The Japanese could have used the oil port Miri, also on Borneo, closer to their base, which would have obviated the tanker problem, but that happened to be an Army-controlled facility. Interservice rivalries here conspired to defeat Japanese plans.

In the evening before departure Admiral Kurita sent a dispatch to Hiyoshi that in a nutshell explained his subsequent actions. The message stated that his fleet would reach Brunei on October 20 and would be ready to sail on the morning of the twenty-second and provided options for subsequent moves. Planning to transit the Philippines by way of the San Bernardino Strait, Kurita pointed out that at a speed of 16 knots he would arrive there on the night of October 24 and his destroyers would have 60 percent of their fuel remaining, while at a 20-knot rate of progress he could arrive that morning but his destroyers would be down to 50 percent fuel, and thus would require refueling before returning to port. Since Kurita also observed that there was no time to get oilers into place for such a refueling, there was little question what course he had selected. Kurita's route would be to the west of Palawan, encompassing the shortest distance between Brunei and the San Bernardino Strait.

Meanwhile the Kurita fleet sailed as scheduled at 1:00 A.M., October 18. In contrast to usual Imperial Navy practice, destroyer flotillas made no antisubmarine sweeps off the harbors before the heavy ships exited. A search by floatplanes the previous afternoon was the sole measure taken at this stage of the sortie. Ten of these planes, newly equipped at Singapore with radar gear, would be key antisubmarine scouts for the fleet. Only at 6:30 A.M. did Kurita begin zigzagging; forty-five minutes later he instructed his ships to be ready to make 18 knots immediately and 20 with twenty minutes' notice. Fleet speed was set at 16 knots. Kurita sailed on, approximately one hour behind his planned timetable.

Around dinnertime that afternoon Kurita received an information copy of the Naval General Staff directive (number 476) that SHO-1 be carried out in the Philippines. The Combined Fleet execute order arrived shortly afterward. Imperial forces were in motion before the first American soldiers even stepped ashore on Leyte.

Aboard the *Yamato*, Rear Admiral Morishita Nobuei told the crew of their mission over the ship's public-address system. A hawk was seen to alight atop the main battery control director. The incident was considered an omen of good fortune. Enterprising sailors contrived to catch the bird, which was put in a cage and displayed on the bridge.

Some thought the hawk a baby since it seemed very small. All thought it very cute. Admiral Ugaki discovered that the bird was quite fond of beef, and he resolved to take good care of it.

There was another auspicious sign the night of October 19–20, when the horizon along the base course Kurita traveled appeared bathed in radiance.

Not all portents were so good, though. There was a submarine scare on

October 18, another the next day; on the nineteenth, one contact would be evaluated as a real sub. Considering that Kurita's fleet had a depth of twenty-four miles along its path of advance, so that an hour and a half was required to pass a given point, a submarine adversary could be especially dangerous. Just how dangerous remained to be seen.

By midnight of the nineteenth Kurita was 165 miles west-northwest of Brunei. He changed course for a final approach to the harbor. It was then that the Japanese were first seen by Americans, under conditions that had much to do with Arthur McCollum. The Seventh Fleet intelligence officer, worried for weeks about some move by Japanese surface craft from Singapore, had reasoned that they would have to refuel to reach Leyte waters. Brunei, on the north coast of Borneo and near the Miri oil fields, was the most obvious place to do that, and McCollum asked for a special watch on the port. His concern paid off on the morning of October 20, when a search plane saw what it identified as a battleship, three light cruisers, three destroyers, and six other warships off the north coast of Borneo. The Honolulu naval communications center later reported the Seventh Fleet message that noted this sighting, which had been discounted with the comment "type and size open to doubt." This key warning of Japanese action has dropped out of sight in subsequent accounts of Leyte Gulf, and McCollum himself once told an interviewer that the planes that covered this area never reported anything even though a good portion of the Japanese Navy passed right under them.

There was a definite sighting, however, and the Japanese knew it even if the Americans didn't. Within fifteen minutes of the time of origination of this message, battleship division leader Ugaki Matome recorded in his diary that radio operators aboard the *Yamato* had picked up a strong transmission from an American plane with the form of a sighting report. One of Admiral Kurita's primary escort units, Destroyer Squadron 10, reported that afternoon having overheard no fewer than *nine* sighting-type messages from just before noon to late in the day. Japanese sources also record overhearing the report being repeated by U.S. radio relay centers at Honolulu and in the Admiralty Islands. From then on the Japanese assumed the Allies were aware of their activity, and they were right, though for the wrong reasons, since it was Ultra that provided the necessary tipoff.

Meanwhile, at 9:18 A.M. on October 20 Kurita directed his units to proceed independently to anchorages in Brunei Bay, a measure he took early because the reefs stood a good forty miles from the berths. Most warships actually dropped anchor between noon and 12:30 P.M. Destroyers refueled from the heavy ships, while the big boys awaited the arrival of oilers due next day.

It was at this point, much as mobile fleet commander Ozawa Jisaburo had recommended, using his war-game studies of the original plan, that

Combined Fleet took direct control over Kurita's force. A dispatch from commander in chief Toyoda on October 20 directed Kurita to penetrate Leyte Gulf at dawn of the twenty-fifth, X-Day, and destroy Allied surface forces and then amphibious shipping therein. Kurita also received an unusual message from Kusaka Ryunosuke as he anchored. The Combined Fleet chief of staff suggested a *double* penetration of Leyte, with Kurita passing through San Bernardino Strait as planned, but detaching a unit to enter through Surigao Strait as well. Kurita had always intended to operate in concentrated fashion, and Japanese plans assumed his Second Fleet would do so. Ozawa had recommended that Kurita be reinforced even more strongly, while at another point Combined Fleet considered adding Shima's Fifth Fleet to Kurita's command. Kurita himself, when ordered to give up Cruiser Division 16 for independent support of an Army counterlanding, opposed the move as a dilution of his strength.

Most of the time Admiral Kurita spent at Brunei passed in considering the Kusaka proposal. Staff conferences continued through the afternoon of October 20 and the next day. Kurita told Captain Ohmae Toshikazu after the war that "since the chief of staff Combined Fleet had suggested that it would be preferable to let the Third Section operate separately and since this coincided with his [Kurita's] views he decided to divide his forces with rather an easy mind."

In effect, one key aspect of the approaching battle of Leyte Gulf would be a last-minute improvisation. This should be borne in mind when considering the eventual failures of coordination that occurred among forces assigned the subsidiary penetration mission.

Admiral Kusaka's improvisation proved much more successful in this case than in his "air-only" SHO. The mission of the so-called Third Section, which was Vice Admiral Nishimura's battleships, along with heavy cruiser *Mogami* and four destroyers, forced American commanders to defend Surigao Strait. Doing so created the potential for what finally occurred: a sequence of events that left Kurita unopposed except for aircraft. Admiral Mikawa at Southwest Area Fleet should also be given some credit; having been assigned control of the Fifth Fleet, he used it to augment the threat posed by Nishimura's rather limited force.

Most likely basing itself on interception of the aircraft contact report on the Japanese warships entering Brunei, at 11:29 P.M. on October 20 the Owada Group warned that it was highly probable the Kurita fleet had been sighted.

With refueling almost complete, at 5:00 P.M. the next afternoon Admiral Kurita assembled unit commanders and key staff officers in the wardroom of flagship *Atago* for a briefing that lasted several hours. Kurita presented the dual-penetration scheme as the approved plan, gave written orders to Vice Admiral Nishimura and a slightly different directive to his own subordinates, and had Army officers tell the group about the ground situation on Leyte. Toasts were drunk.

Kurita knew, because of intelligence and sighting reports received that very afternoon, that the Allies outnumbered him not only in the air but in battleships too. He and his chief of staff, Koyanagi Tomiji, also knew that many of their officers opposed the mission on which they had embarked. A number argued it would be more appropriate for naval chief Toyoda to join the fleet and lead it personally on this operation. Both Kurita on this occasion and Toyoda after the war referred to the awkwardness for the Navy if the fleet stood aside while the nation expired.

"The war situation is far more critical than any of you could possibly know," Admiral Kurita told his officers. "I believe that the Imperial General Headquarters is giving us a glorious opportunity. . . . What man can say that there is no chance for our fleet to turn the tide of war in a Decisive Battle?"

Most of all, Kurita declared, "You must all remember there are such things as miracles."


BY 5:00 A.M., OCTOBER 22, THE 1ST DIVERSION ATTACK FORCE HAD COMPLETED FUELING AT Brunei. Its chances would henceforward be critically affected by the interval of tactical warning available to the Allies to counteract its progress. Guided by its intelligence officer, Arthur McCollum, the Seventh Fleet had actually made elaborate preparations to detect any Japanese fleet sortie. After concocting his initial plan, McCollum went to operations officer Captain Richard Cruzen, who made a few changes and assigned forces for implementation. McCollum had figured that the Japanese would need a second refueling location in addition to Brunei, particularly for destroyers. The obvious possibilities were Malampaya Sound on the island of Palawan, or Coron Bay in the Calamian island group. In turn this suggested that the most likely Japanese approach route would be the Palawan Passage, though they might also choose to steam south of Palawan, through the Sulu Sea.

The American plan aimed to cover all these possibilities. Air reconnaissance was to be mounted from recently captured Morotai and from forward airstrips on Leyte as soon as they could be reopened. Air would cover the deep approaches, from northern Borneo to the Makassar Strait, and including both the Celebes and Sulu seas, as well as the southern end of the Palawan Passage. As a second means of detection, the Americans posted submarines to cover the sea approaches, including the Palawan Passage, Balabac Strait, and Sulu Sea; subs were also posted off Manila in case Japanese ships came down from the north. The submarines' orders were to search and report, not attack. A third safeguard would be Seventh Fleet's own search planes, as well as those of Halsey's Third Fleet, which would

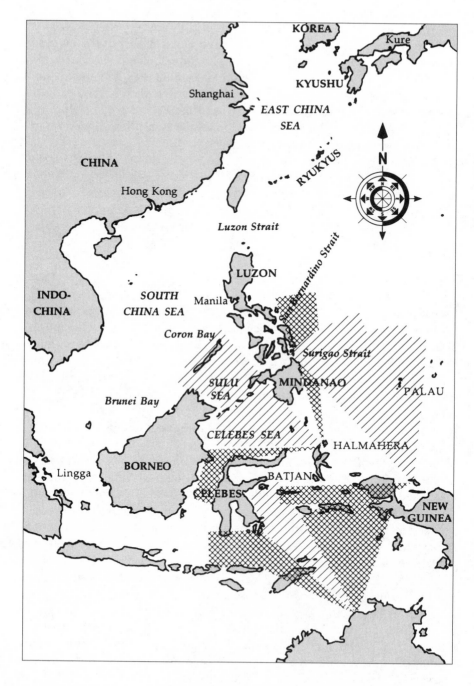

XII. Battle for Leyte Gulf (Allied Air Search Patterns, October 1944)

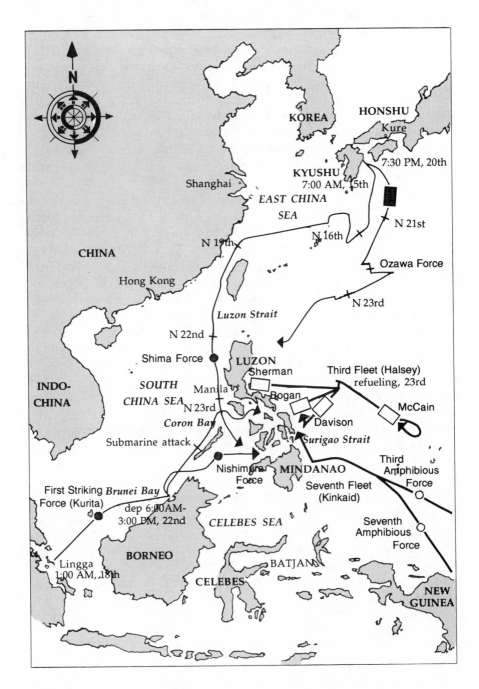

XIII. Battle for Leyte Gulf (Approach to Contact)

scout immediately adjacent waters. Then there was MacArthur's other air component, General Kenney's Fifth Air Force, which had plans to fly from Leyte within days of the initial landings.

In the event, every one of these detection mechanisms malfunctioned. As already seen, air-search reports off Borneo became lost in the communications system. Searches nearer Leyte on October 20 discovered a Japanese tanker, a repair ship, and a coast-defense vessel en route to Coron Bay, another potential tipoff. Seventh Fleet actually requested that the closest practicable air observation "with view of attack" be made of Coron Bay and vicinity, since this appeared "to be [a] highly likely concentration or fueling area for important elements [of the] Jap fleet that may attempt [a] strike against our Leyte forces."

Previous accounts fail to explain American surprise in view of the fact that the record contains not only a sighting of the Kurita fleet but specific anticipation of the use of Coron Bay by the Japanese. Actually, air operations did not match pre-invasion expectations. Aircraft flying from Morotai, base of the Eleventh Air Force, were at extreme range and had limited tracking time left once arrived in Philippine waters. They would be largely ineffective. Searches from the American carriers were shorter-legged and only found the Japanese much later. As for the Fifth Air Force on Leyte, its biggest airfield, required by the large B-24 bombers used for searches, was too muddy to use very much, while the smaller strip at Tacloban could not accommodate the B-24s. Night search by PBY Catalina planes from the Seventh Fleet would eventually prove to be the Americans' last chance to find Kurita's Second Fleet before it broke completely loose. Some of the PBY missions were preplanned and some set up on the spur of a moment by McCollum and Cruzen. On the night before the big battle a PBY flight was actually sent up the Samar coast and flew over the strait Kurita was about to enter. This plane, piloted by Lieutenant (j.g.) C. B. Sillers, happened to pass about an hour or so before the Japanese fleet arrived at the strait.

Only the submarines were left. When the Kurita fleet left Brunei and actually took the Palawan Passage route up toward San Bernardino Strait, U.S. subs duly saw and reported the Japanese. As shall be seen, they took off in pursuit, and although they achieved important results, the subs left their scouting post unguarded and *another* Imperial Navy surface group passed that way to the south, unreported. In effect, the elaborate detection plans went awry.

Admiral Kurita at Brunei knew none of this as his thirsty ships gulped down 15,800 tons of oil, enough to fill a superbattleship like *Yamato* several times over. With orders to enter Leyte Gulf at dawn on X-Day, what Kurita did know was that he had a coordination problem, because his planned route up the Palawan Passage through the San Bernardino Strait was considerably longer than the route through the Surigao Strait chosen for Nishimura's newly designated 2nd Diversionary Attack Force. Consequently Kurita instructed Nishimura to stay behind until the afternoon of October 22 while he got a head start on the SHO mission. It would be a desperate gamble, as Kurita personally knew from the Rabaul ambush. In the face of devastating Allied airpower, the Japanese fleet intended to force its way through the narrow seas of the Philippines, then the entrances to Leyte Gulf, to get at the shipping inside.

At 8:20 on October 22 the first section of Kurita's fleet got under way, heading upchannel toward the Brunei reefs. Admiral Kurita himself led this force, which included his own Cruiser Division 4, Vice Admiral Hashimoto Shintaro's Cruiser Division 5 (less the *Mogami*, now assigned to Nishimura's force), and Admiral Ugaki's battleships, all escorted by Rear Admiral Hayakawa Mikio's 2nd Destroyer Flotilla. After two hours the fleet began to clear the reefs and Kurita set his cruising disposition, to be followed by Vice Admiral Suzuki Yoshio, leading the second section of the fleet. Suzuki's force included his own Battleship Division 3, Vice Admiral Shiraishi Kazutaka's Cruiser Division 7, and Rear Admiral Kimura Susumu's 10th Destroyer Flotilla. In all the Kurita fleet possessed five battleships, ten heavy and two light cruisers, and fifteen destroyers.

One of Kurita's decisions at this stage was to send a number of his floatplanes ahead to San Jose on the island of Mindoro, leaving aerial antisubmarine patrol entirely in the hands of the shore-based 901st Air Group. A flat statement of this action appears in Kurita's after-action report for the battle, leading historians to criticize the admiral for stripping himself of this important organic capability at a critical moment. The rationale was that Kurita could not count on land-based support from Philippine-based air units, and to get any at all he wished to rely upon his own planes, which he could not be certain could be efficiently launched and recovered by the fleet under way.

Kurita's report does not tell the whole story, however. In fact there was a flurry of activity just before leaving Brunei wherein *Yamato, Musashi,* and *Nagato* exchanged floatplanes, and in some cases flight or maintenance personnel, leaving the first-named ships with a total of nine planes (including spares) and the *Nagato* with none at all. The fleet had a total of at least forty-one (and perhaps forty-five) aircraft, and it is impossible that all flew to San Jose; some of the battleships launched floatplanes during the X-Day battle.

Another key decision Kurita made at this time was in setting his cruising disposition. The formation adopted put his major vessels in two parallel columns, with destroyers to each flank and in between but no screening escorts in front. Zigzagging would be the sole means of frustrating submarines because formation speed was such as to impede effective sonar search by escorts. The arrangement also left a great deal to the G3M "Nell" patrol planes that flew in pairs from Miri to watch over the Kurita fleet.

During the afternoon Kurita issued two more orders setting standard procedures for which units would provide floatplanes to augment the antisubmarine patrols, furnishing more evidence that he had not in fact sent all his aircraft to Mindoro.

As darkness fell on October 22 Admiral Kurita was steaming northeast parallel to the coast of Palawan, maintaining a speed of advance of 16 knots and at antisubmarine condition two. Not only was his formation not good from an antisub-warfare standpoint, but also his speed was roughly 4 knots *slower* than the surface speed of an American sub; there were no aircraft out at night to keep those subs submerged; *and*, toward midnight, Kurita stopped zigzagging as he approached the Palawan Passage. This conformed to Imperial Navy doctrine for assuming base course prior to a scheduled turn, but it was risky in these dangerous waters when the Japanese were assuming that their operation had become known. Actually, light cruiser *Yahagi* had already made a sudden course change to port and fired a red flare shortly after 9:00 P.M. Moreover, at 6:00 P.M. and again at midnight Japanese radio intelligence intercepted nearby submarine transmissions, a total of three, plotting of which showed that one of the midnight calls was virtually on top of Kurita's course track. Another interception, at 2:00 A.M., when plotted showed an emitter possibly paralleling Kurita's track to the west.

Sure enough, disaster struck. The American submarine commander in Australia had deployed fully a dozen boats to track and report on Japanese movements. Two of the subs, *Dace* (Commander Bladen D. Claggett) and *Darter* (Commander David H. McClintock), started right off the tip of Palawan. McClintock was frustrated because the previous night he had detected several Japanese men-of-war at high speed (Cruiser Division 16 on its way to Manila) and had been unable to catch them. During the early-morning hours of October 23 both boats picked up the Kurita fleet and followed it off Palawan, reporting Japanese progress to the American command. McClintock's patrol report says it all:

> [We] sent out three contact reports, giving final estimate task force of eleven heavy ships. Tracking party said that gaining attack position was hopeless due to high target speed (initial estimate, 22 knots). We managed to average about 19 knots. Estimates of enemy speed began to drop until finally it was fifteen knots. We had them now! Did not attack in darkness, as it was considered vital to see and identify the force which was probably on its way to interfere with the Leyte landing. It was felt that there could be no radical dawn zig due to size of force and narrowness of Palawan Passage. Targets did not zig during night.

The *Dace* also tracked the Kurita fleet. Both subs were in position to attack at dawn.

Aboard battleship *Yamato*, radio operators picked up an urgent contact report sent by a submarine on the frequency 8470 kilocycles at 1:50 A.M. The signal strength was extremely strong, so the Japanese could only conclude that the sub lay very close by. Admiral Ugaki climbed to the bridge; skipper Morishita sent his ship to general quarters an hour before dawn. The battleship was just sliding into a port turn when, against the dawning eastern sky, explosions lit the horizon. At 5:34, flagship *Atago* was struck by four torpedoes in quick succession, and heavy cruiser *Takao* by two more. This was the *Darter*'s achievement; at 5:56, the *Dace* put four more torpedoes into cruiser *Maya*.

Pandemonium ensued among the Japanese. Fortunately the *Atago* took about twenty minutes to flood and sink, giving her radio unit enough time to destroy their code machine (probably Jade), lock up most other classified materials in a room below the waterline, and put certain key documents into weighted sacks to throw overboard. Destroyers *Kishinami* and *Asashimo* came alongside and took off the ship's skipper, Rear Admiral Araki Tsutau, forty-two other officers, 667 sailors, and two civilians. In his fine history of Japan at war, John Toland writes that Kurita and his staff swam to a destroyer (*Kishinami*), but available sources do not claim this, while the interval before sinking and the large number of survivors both suggest that the *Atago* was evacuated in an orderly manner. Sources also do not record whether Kurita had time to retrieve his archery set, well beloved, with which he used to practice aboard ship every day. In any case, Admiral Kurita spent nine hours on crowded *Kishinami* before being able to transfer to *Yamato*.

Another hidden but heavy loss in the *Atago* sinking was the equipment (at least) of the mobile radio intelligence unit that accompanied the Second Fleet.

Captain Oe Ranji's heavy cruiser, *Maya*, had few of the opportunities available to the crew of the flagship. *Maya* was hit by four torpedoes on her port side and capsized to port. She sank in four minutes according to Kurita's after-action report, eight by the reckoning of a postwar technical report. Her skipper and many of the crew were lost. Some survivors were put aboard the *Musashi*, where they helped work the anti-aircraft guns later that trying day and then were sunk again.

Heavy cruiser *Takao* was crippled by two torpedo hits but did not sink. She spent most of the day dead in the water off Palawan until her engineering officer, Commander Mori Eiji, was able to restore power to the screws. Kurita detached destroyers *Asashimo* (crammed with *Atago* survivors) and *Naganami* to escort her. Once under way, Captain Onoda Sutejiro took his cruiser back to Brunei, his escort later strengthened by torpedo boat *Hiyodori* and steamer *Mitsu Maru*.

At the risk of getting slightly ahead of our story, one thread of the submarine attack should be followed to its conclusion. Unknown to Captain Onoda, his *Takao* was almost attacked again while he worked to control her damage. Both *Darter* and *Dace* remained in the area, and both maneuvered to attack but evaded when Japanese destroyers approached them. Commander McClintock followed into the night of October 23–24 to try a surface attack on *Takao*, then making only 4 to 6 knots. Minutes after midnight, with a loud crash, *Darter* ran aground in poor visibility on a reef called Bombay Shoals. For hours McClintock and his crew tried everything they could think of to get their submarine off the shoal. The *Dace* broke off her own pursuit of *Takao* to assist. Finally the crew transferred to Claggett's submarine and tried to dispose of the *Darter* by demolition charges, then by torpedoing her, then shelling her, finally giving up to return to base with both crews on one submarine.

The *Dace* did not in fact give up until a Japanese patrol plane found both subs, identifying one as aground. The senior officer present was Captain Onoda of the *Takao*. Onoda had not been a naval attaché for nothing; once *Takao* had cleared the dangerous waters and had almost reached Brunei, at 8:00 A.M. on October 24 he sent the *Naganami* and *Hiyodori* back to the scene under command of the destroyer skipper to dispose of the sub and remove "any materials of operational value."

Here, in October 1944, was an incident to rival the notorious *I-1* affair. This time it was an *American* warship abandoned, its secrets available for the taking. *Darter* crew members insist that everything of value on the boat was destroyed before they crossed to the *Dace*, but formerly classified intelligence documents record losses noted below. The crew did get rid of its most sensitive materials, but the Japanese haul included radar material, radio and communications procedure documents, instruction books, ordnance items, and engine blueprints.

Even without code material, the radio and communication documents would be of value to the Owada Group, while the radar material likely helped the Japanese devise countermeasures to U.S. equipment. Japanese submarines had long been wanting more efficient engines, and blueprints offered the possibility of reverse-engineering American versions. Had the *Darter* incident occurred in 1942 instead of 1944, and had the Japanese been better organized to exploit technical intelligence, this loss might have greatly affected the progress of the war. The Americans proved very fortunate.

In the meantime the Kurita fleet pressed on. Admiral Ugaki temporarily assumed command from the *Yamato*, moving to evade what he concluded were four (not two) submarines. Captain Tanaka Jyo's *Chokai*, the only vessel left from Kurita's once proud Cruiser Division 4, was reassigned to Admiral Hashimoto's Cruiser Division 5. Kurita himself transferred from *Kishinami* to *Yamato* and hoisted his flag aboard her at about 3:30 P.M. By that time the fleet was beginning a circuit to the north and northeast to pass between Coron Bay in the Calamian group and Mindoro, and thence into the Sibuyan Sea. With a turn southeast after midnight, at 6:25 A.M. on October 24 the fleet was rounding the southern tip of Mindoro to begin its approach through the Sibuyan Sea to the San Bernardino Strait. Still, with the previous day's contact reports from the submarines to go on, Bull Halsey knew exactly what to look for. It was only 8:10 when Task Force 38's dawn search found the Japanese.

Rear Admiral Gerald F. Bogan's Task Group 38.2 made the first strike with a wave of planes launched at 9:10 that struck the Kurita fleet at 10:26 as it steamed into the Sibuyan Sea. After that, into the afternoon there were four attacks totaling more than 250 aircraft. *Yamato* and *Nagato* were each hit twice by bombs, but their capabilities were barely affected. One destroyer also suffered bomb damage. The heavy cruiser *Myoko* suffered a torpedo hit in her starboard after engine room, damaging two shafts and causing a list. Vice Admiral Hashimoto, obliged to shift his flag to Captain Sugiura Kaju's *Haguro*, detached the cripple to seek safety. The *Myoko*'s speed was further reduced by leaks, which contaminated the main feed water tank for the port after engine, forcing shutdown of the number one shaft. The damaged cruiser made Coron Bay on October 25 and left there for Brunei the next day, escorted by *Naganami*, fresh from her exploit uncovering the secrets of American submarine *Darter*.

Though these warships suffered from the air attacks, superbattleship *Musashi* was destined to perish under them. Rear Admiral Inoguchi Toshihira fought his ship bravely, assigning more than 700 *Maya* survivors on board to battle stations commensurate to their former jobs.* The first wave showed up on radar at about 10:00 A.M.; seventeen of the twenty-four planes went for Inoguchi's ship, making torpedo runs and simultaneously bombing from starboard bow and quarter. There were four near misses, one direct hit on an 18-inch turret roof, and a torpedo hit starboard forward of the beam. *Musashi* sprang leaks near the bow from near misses but the torpedo hit clearly inflicted the ship's first major damage. American aviators had never before seen one of the Imperial Navy's superbattleships at close

---

*The U.S. translation of *Musashi*'s detailed action report, and Yoshimura Akira's history of the ship (*Build the Musashi* [Tokyo: Kodansha International, 1991]), name the skipper as Captain Iguchi Toshihira. On the other hand such sources as the Naval War College study and John Toland in *The Rising Sun* give Rear Admiral Inoguchi Toshihira. Since it appears from internal evidence that Yoshimura utilized the after-action report, while translation was imperfect (as we have seen in this narrative), I do not rely upon these sources. John Toland, however, actually interviewed *Musashi*'s executive officer, who no doubt knew his boss's name very well. Toland's interview notes make clear that he accurately reproduced the name when finalizing his manuscript. The Naval War College study confirms this rendering, which I use here.

range. Even "artist's concept" drawings of the ships had appeared only recently in the *ONI Weekly*. Unerringly, however, they selected and attacked the target.

This torpedo hit so early in the engagement was a distinct setback for the *Musashi*, though she seemed visibly unimpaired. Commander Koshino Kimitake, the ship's gunnery officer, had already begun pressing the captain for permission to use high-capacity *sanshiki-dan* shells. Inoguchi resisted at first, because he wanted to save the big guns for the expected sea battle and as a gunnery expert he knew that just a dozen rounds of the special shells could damage the bores. But the torpedo hit resulted in a starboard list of about 5.5 degrees. Inoguchi and Koshino also knew that according to *Musashi*'s design parameters the main battery lost half its effectiveness when the list passed 4 degrees.

Damage control was the responsibility of the ship's executive officer, Captain Kato Kenkichi, who also happened to be a gunnery expert, having been chief gunner for the battleship *Mutsu* and cruiser *Nagara*, among others. Some of the crew thought Kato a robot, but he had been considered friendly enough to go along on Admiral Nagano Osami's 1932–1933 midshipman cruise to the United States, the one when the young officers had gone to lunch with the President of the United States. Kato had been present at some other key moments as well: He was executive officer of the *Chokai* when Admiral Ozawa narrowly missed a sea fight with the *Prince of Wales* and *Repulse* off Malaya; at Midway (which Kato considered a defeat despite the propaganda); and with Admiral Mikawa at Savo Island. This day on *Musashi* would be Kato's great crisis, and he began it by ordering Lieutenant Naito Masanao to correct the list by counterflooding.

Lieutenant Naito had what many considered the most advanced water-control system in the Imperial Navy. He directed forty or fifty men in three separate control rooms who could flood or pump out compartments throughout the ship. Naito and Kato were successfully adjusting the ship when, between 11:36 and 11:45, American planes scored three more torpedo hits on the port side amidships and forward. Naito believes the ship's speed increased his difficulties by magnifying the impact of the torpedo hits so they loosened rivets and caused cracks in the armor. So much water entered on the port side that even using all starboard stern tanks, balance could not be restored. The only thing left to do—emergency pumping—could not keep up with the flooding. Naito advised the skipper to consider flooding one of *Musashi*'s engine rooms. Inoguchi made that decision even though it meant that the men in another compartment along the ship's centerline would be trapped and unable to escape. *Musashi* lost speed but regained balance; if the leaks could have been stopped she would not have sunk.

Other damage proved crippling for *Musashi*, however. Bombs that hit during the same attack caused fires in one of the engine rooms, spreading to another and severing the main steam pipe, resulting in the loss of the number three propeller shaft. There were more near misses, and another torpedo hit at 12:17 put much of Ensign Suzuki Yakaku's damage-control party out of action, filling the forward sick bay with carbon monoxide. At 12:53 P.M. four torpedo bombers all scored hits, all in *Musashi*'s forward section, and the ship began settling toward the bow. Steaming forward only increased the water intake. Captain Kato was able to set up water barriers, but the ship was clearly in extremis. Admiral Inoguchi was wounded by a hit on the anti-aircraft control station that detonated on the bridge, also killing the ship's navigator, Captain Kariya Minoru, and a number of other officers. The Japanese believed that in this last attack, in midafternoon, they sustained no less than ten bomb hits and eleven torpedo hits, plus six near misses.

Maneuvering to evade the attacks, at 1:15 P.M. Admiral Kurita sent a dispatch to Mikawa at Southwest Area Fleet as well as to Ozawa with the carrier force, appealing for air support. Commander Yamaguchi Moriyoshi of the Second Air Fleet, Fukudome's operations staff officer, told interrogators after the war that he had provided standard fleet air support to Kurita—ten fighters overhead—but American pilots saw only four, and shot those down in short order. They were not ten aircraft on rotation, moreover, but ten planes that had to fly back to Clark Field periodically to rearm and refuel. At 3:30, with his own operations staffer, Commander Otani Inao, telling him the Americans could possibly mount three more air strikes before dusk, Admiral Kurita ordered a turn west. A 4:00 P.M. dispatch furnished the Combined Fleet this explanation:

UNDER THESE CIRCUMSTANCES IT WAS DEEMED THAT WERE WE TO FORCE OUR WAY THROUGH, WE WOULD MERELY MAKE OF OURSELVES MEAT FOR THE ENEMY, WITH VERY LITTLE CHANCE OF SUCCESS TO US. IT WAS THEREFORE CONCLUDED THAT THE BEST COURSE OPEN TO US WAS TO TEMPORARILY RETIRE BEYOND THE RANGE OF ENEMY PLANES AND REFORM OUR PLANS.

Admiral Kurita also ordered the *Musashi* to beach on a nearby island to become a stationary battery.

Here was a key moment in the saga of the Imperial Navy. At Hiyoshi the Combined Fleet headquarters had been on tenterhooks all day as reports flowed in of the greater and greater damage being inflicted on Kurita. At length commander in chief Toyoda sent a now famous order:

WITH CONFIDENCE IN HEAVENLY GUIDANCE, THE ENTIRE FORCE WILL ATTACK!

Toyoda later declared that his meaning was that retreating at this stage would not limit losses, so the Kurita fleet might as well advance.

Toyoda recalls that the Kurita message arrived about a half hour after his own dispatch went out. (This does not accord with the time-date groups on the messages, however.) Both he and Kusaka Ryunosuke note that headquarters was in a quandary over how to respond to Kurita. Kurita *was* an exposed force and was without fighter cover; but if SHO were stopped it would be almost impossible to restart the operation, and if the Japanese *did* smash the Leyte landing force it could mean holding the Philippines, which in turn would keep open the sea-lanes. In any case the whole plan had been premised upon throwing in all forces. Admiral Toyoda concluded that the policy should remain one of "advance even though the fleet should be completely lost. That was my feeling in sending that order; consequently I am safe in saying that the Second Fleet was not restricted in any way as to the damage it might suffer."

Examination led Hiyoshi to believe no response at all need be sent, because once Kurita received Toyoda's order he could not possibly maintain his westward course. In fact Kurita turned back eastward at 5:14 P.M., before receiving Toyoda's message. That morning, Kurita had already warned his fleet to have all torpedo crews ready for battle by the evening, and clearly expected to fight his way through the San Bernardino Strait. At 8:20 he informed Hiyoshi that he would pass through the strait, proceed along the east coast of Samar, and break through to Leyte Gulf after 4:00 A.M. October 25.

Astonishingly, no Allied ships blocked his way at San Bernardino. Other things seemed to go better as well. The *Musashi* was beyond pain, having sunk at 7:35 P.M., many of her seamen rescued. Japanese authorities also arranged to turn on the lighthouse providing a navigational point of reference at San Bernardino, which the Kurita fleet transited shortly after midnight. Reporting on plans for the morrow, including kamikaze special attacks, at 12:08 A.M. on October 25 Admiral Mikawa Gunichi of Southwest Area Fleet radioed Hiyoshi:

> TONIGHT EVERY EFFORT WILL BE MADE TO CARRY OUT REPEATED NIGHT ATTACKS, FOL-
> LOWING WHICH THE MAIN ENEMY TASK FORCES WILL BE DESTROYED TOMORROW.

THE COMING BATTLE WOULD BE ESPECIALLY HARD FOR MATSUDA CHIAKI. HAVING BEEN ONE OF the last prewar chiefs of the American section of naval intelligence, Rear Admiral Matsuda had warned of the power now crushing the Empire. At Midway, commanding battleship *Hyuga*, he had seen Japan turned away by successful application of airpower; then, commanding the *Yamato* in 1943, Matsuda had witnessed the transformation of the Combined Fleet from supple instrument of war to brittle, desperate collection of sailors and ships, intent on one final chance to blunt the enemy thrusts. Now Rear Admiral

Matsuda found himself in the position of leading warships into that final battle, not to smite the enemy but to be sunk by them in hopes other Japanese might yet break through.

Matsuda prepared his unit for combat but what he had was perhaps the oddest collection of vessels in the Imperial Navy. That was Carrier Division 4, which Matsuda took over in late May, when the hybrid battleship-carriers *Ise* and *Hyuga* were rejoining the fleet after completing their conversions. Less than a month later the Philippine Sea action decimated the Japanese carrier air groups; Matsuda not only heard the harrowing stories of having to send off fliers who never came back but was left to realize that he, a battleship man, would be on the front line with Ozawa's carrier fleet.

An August reorganization added to Matsuda's unit the large but light carrier *Junyo* and the very light carrier *Ryuho.* This gave Admiral Matsuda not only hybrid warships but a hybrid air group, since his JNAF 634th Air Group then comprised floatplanes as well as conventional ones. Halfway through training, the 634th flew off to destruction in the Taiwan air battle. Matsuda's light carriers lost all value. *Junyo* would spend the days of the big battle at Iwakuni or Kure; *Ryuho* circulated among various ports in Empire waters, staying nowhere as long as the two days she anchored at Sasebo. Without the light carriers or his planes, Admiral Matsuda was left with his two battleship-carriers, able to function only as gunnery ships. At least that was probably an easier role for the admiral.

Another admiral with an uncomfortable role was Ozawa Jisaburo. Komura Keizo, Ozawa's chief of staff, who left after the Philippine Sea battle to take over the 2nd Destroyer Flotilla, asserts that both of them knew before that battle had even ended that it was the death of the Combined Fleet. One can dispute this, but clearly the Turkey Shoot as a practical matter broke the power of the First Mobile Fleet, the newfangled, carrier-centered task force Ozawa and some others had long advocated. Vice Admiral Ozawa's recommendation that his own part in the SHO plans be reduced may have stemmed from realization that there was now no alternative save to give the gunnery ships center stage and devise some means to get them past airpower into shell range of the Allied fleet. Ozawa's Mobile Fleet doctrine provided a role for decoy operations, and even Yamamoto had used such tactics at Midway, the eastern Solomons, and Santa Cruz. It was not too far a jump to consider using the remnants of the carrier force in their entirety for a decoy mission, in particular since, having been an advocate, Ozawa knew the predominance carriers and carrier tactics had gained in the U.S. Navy.

Admiral Ozawa prepared for the decoy mission Combined Fleet had confirmed for him by fueling and positioning tankers, messages about which reached American intelligence as we have seen. Vice Admiral Shima's Fifth Fleet, originally intended to support Ozawa, had been drawn to the Taiwan area as a result of the air battles there, and Ozawa was not certain whether

Shima would be sent on to the Philippines to strengthen the gunnery attack forces or return to assist him. Admiral Ozawa and Combined Fleet headquarters also juggled destroyer assignments in Empire waters to furnish the Mobile Fleet with screen units, and when Toyoda moved fleet headquarters ashore he gave Ozawa his former flagship, light cruiser *Oyodo*. That ship entered the number four dry dock at Yokosuka Navy Yard on October 1 to overhaul engines and oil tanks, strengthen hull integrity and compartmentation, and fit ordnance and Type 3 Mark 1 radar gear. After final preparations *Oyodo* joined Ozawa's force on October 18. The SHO operation had already been activated.

Because he believed Kurita's gunnery ships required direct support by carrier aircraft, Vice Admiral Ozawa intended to take his Carrier Division 3 down to Singapore in about mid-November, when the aircrews would have acquired a little seasoning, but the Taiwan air battle nullified the advance planning. When Ozawa received SHO alert orders he knew he would have to operate from Empire waters, would not be able to provide air cover to anybody, and would only be able to operate as a decoy force.

Ozawa's paucity of experienced escort forces was such that the two fleet oilers assigned to him, precious though they were, would be covered by a single destroyer (assisted by four coast-defense vessels).

In his original planning Ozawa had considered three possible courses to the battle area. These he described for a conference of senior officers aboard *Oyodo* at Yashima anchorage on October 19. The decline of the Imperial Navy is visible in the fact that the *Zuikaku* was now the sole fleet carrier combat-ready with the fleet. With her were light carriers *Chitose*, *Chiyoda*, and *Zuiho*. The presence of the last-named ship is also significant because she had usually been considered so small as to be useful only for training, aircraft ferrying, or convoy or fleet air protection missions.

Next morning, as the Mobile Fleet prepared to sail, the carriers took on board the last pitiful remnants of the once proud JNAF sea eagles. For this last sortie carrier airpower consisted of fifty-two Zero fighters, twenty-eight Zeros rigged as fighter-bombers, twenty-five *Tenzan* torpedo bombers, four old Kate torpedo planes, and seven *Suisei* dive-bombers, plus two floatplane scouts on the *Oyodo*—in all, 118 aircraft. Another priority was preparation for radio deception. At 4:00 P.M. Ozawa's new chief of staff, Rear Admiral Obayashi Sueo, informed Combined Fleet that to carry out proper deception it might be necessary to detach Admiral Matsuda's *Ise* and *Hyuga* along with the *Oyodo*. Mobile Fleet noted the methods, frequency, call letters, and code that would be employed and asked that Tokyo Number One radio monitor their transmissions and report effectiveness.

Various warships left anchorages as necessary to rendezvous about 2:00 P.M. in the Inland Sea. *Zuikaku* and the carriers sailed from Oita, *Oyodo* from Yashima, where she had stayed after the commanders' conference. (Allied intelligence, incidentally, knew of the meeting from a decrypt translated this day.) Ozawa, apparently having flown from Yashima to Oita, was back in the *Zuikaku*. He set a number three radar watch and a speed of advance of 18 knots as his fleet, bearing the tactical title "Main Body," steamed toward the Bungo Strait. An antisubmarine sweep there was completed by 5:20. Ten minutes later, with the Main Body leaving the strait, Ozawa ordered a course change from his preplanned track and soon afterward began to assume an alert cruising disposition. The Main Body's after-action report maintains that the course change resulted from a submarine contact, but that, the first of several, occurred only at 5:45, when a shore-based aircraft saw something nine miles from the *Zuikaku*. The flagship herself detected a sub at 5:59 on a bearing indicating it must have been a different boat from that seen from the air; then, at 6:30 the *Chitose* reported radar contact with a submarine. Ozawa countered with a change of course, after which he switched to the second of his preplanned routes.

In fact all the contact reports had been false. Only one American sub, *Ronquil*, was in the Bungo Strait area at this time, and she lay southwest of the Japanese fleet. By midnight Ozawa's Main Body was over a hundred miles away, outdistancing any possible submarine moves.

During their first full day at sea, Ozawa and chief of staff Obayashi, along with senior staff officer Ohmae, studied the tentative plan Combined Fleet sent by dispatch on October 21. It became evident that the new scheme differed from previous SHO operations plans and from Ozawa's own tentative plan. Ozawa had intended to use Admiral Shima's 2nd Diversion Attack Force to decoy the Americans, then attack their flank with his own Main Body. Now Combined Fleet wanted Shima to help with counterlanding operations on Leyte; a potential detachment was still provided for in the orders, but of warships from Ozawa's own force (Matsuda's battleships plus destroyers) and only to mop up enemy derelicts following the decoy action. Admiral Ozawa advised Matsuda of the arrangement to enable him to make his own plans.

The day also demonstrated just how poor the JNAF had become. Between searches and antisubmarine flights, Ozawa put up a total of twenty-one airplanes on October 21; of those one crash-landed at sea, one *Chitose* plane crash-landed aboard the *Zuikaku*, and one plane crashed on takeoff. This represented a rather high rate of accidental losses.

As with the air forces, so too the surface fleet. The day began with the chief engineer informing Admiral Ozawa that the destroyer *Sugi*, one of the new smaller escorts (half the size of fleet destroyers), a brand-new ship completed only toward the end of August, had stopped all machinery and fallen out of formation because her oil filters had clogged overnight. Half Ozawa's slender escort of destroyers were of this new lightly armed type. The commander ordered all ships to ensure oil filters were clean. By 1944 many

Japanese warships were manned by sailors who simply lacked the experience and knowledge to run their vessels efficiently. The *Sugi* had occupied a key escorting position on the starboard quarter of light carrier *Chiyoda*, whose vulnerability increased substantially during the interval needed to get back in gear. Fortunately, there were no American subs around to take advantage. The two reports that day were both spurious: *Zuikaku* detected torpedo noise, necessitating an emergency turn by the fleet; and *Isuzu* claimed to have tracked a contact for almost an hour and a half.

The Main Body also refined its radio deception plans on October 21. Ozawa intended to transmit several lengthy dispatches to alert the Americans to his presence, insofar as possible each by different radios and call signs. There would also be ten or more signals sent regarding aircraft to divulge the presence of carriers, again using different codes and so on. Finally, a series of communications would be sent by *Oyodo* to one of Admiral Matsuda's battleship-carriers; if the Americans knew *Oyodo*'s call sign they might suspect the presence of the Combined Fleet command itself, since they could be expected to realize this cruiser had been fleet flagship.

Early in the morning on the twenty-second, Rear Admiral Nomura Tomekichi's *Hyuga* intercepted signals the Japanese interpreted as a group of four to six Allied aircraft carriers on a north-northwest course. At about the same time the 31st Base Force reported direction-finding fixes from the previous evening that could have been this or a similar U.S. force south of the Main Body. Plotting the positions made it clear that if the Americans steamed north, by afternoon they would be coming into aircraft range. Since that would trigger battle too soon—before X-Day—Ozawa ordered his ships to refuel during the afternoon while searching extensively for the Americans. He steamed directly east to lengthen his distance from the reported contact while maintaining position to quickly reach Philippine waters. The direction was determined by the need to steam almost into the wind to accomplish alongside refueling.

Again all the submarine contacts that day were false.

With the dawn Ozawa expected action of some sort. From Tokyo dispatches, he knew of the sighting report an American plane had sent of Kurita off Brunei on October 20. By the twenty-third it was entirely possible that, had it maintained the original schedule, the Kurita fleet might be coming inside Task Force 38 air range. Consequently this could be a key day for decoy action. Thus it was on October 23 that Admiral Ozawa ordered radio silence abandoned in favor of the deceptive measures previously planned to enhance his decoy role. That morning the Main Body prepared to make battle speed immediately; as time went on and nothing happened, the order was changed to steam for 24 knots with battle speed on twenty minutes' notice. By evening, when still nothing had happened, Ozawa resolved to cruise directly southeast, launch air searches and an immediate attack if anything was found, and, if not, detach the Matsuda battleship force as an advance guard to gain American attention in an unmistakable fashion. Clearly October 24, Y-Day, was going to be critical since none of the gunnery ships could make the schedule for penetrating Leyte Gulf without sailing through the archipelago on this day, under the very wings of U.S. airpower. Also, Ozawa's ships were beginning to run short of fuel, so that if no contact was made on the twenty-fourth he would have to begin detaching ships to fuel at Taiwan.

The northeastern tip of the Philippine island of Luzon is known as Cape Engaño, and the engagement involving Admiral Ozawa's Main Body would afterward be called the battle of Cape Engaño. That is peculiarly apt since *engañar* is Spanish for "to fool." Admiral Bill Halsey, Vice Admiral Marc Mitscher, and the other masters of Task Force 38 were going to be fooled by Ozawa, and how they reacted would make all the difference to the other Japanese forces. If Ozawa succeeded, the SHO plan might even work.

Worth noting is that Admiral Halsey was not known as "the Bull" for nothing. Always thrusting, and with a certain impatience, Halsey himself, after the great success of the September Philippine carrier raids, had recommended accelerating the tempo, a move that lead directly to the Leyte invasion. His orders for King II, the Leyte campaign, were to support the landings and prevent interference by the Japanese fleet. In response to criticisms of Raymond Spruance at Philippine Sea, however, Halsey's orders explicitly enjoined him to engage the enemy fleet as his primary task if such an opportunity existed or could be created. The latter stricture encouraged Bull Halsey's impatience.

On October 21, tiring of sailing back and forth east of the Philippines, Halsey radioed MacArthur:

MY PRESENT OPERATIONS IN STRATEGIC POSITION TO MEET THREAT OF ENEMY FLEET FORCES ARE SOMEWHAT RESTRICTED BY NECESSITY TO COVER YOUR TRANSPORTS. . . . EARLY ADVICE REGARDING WITHDRAWAL [of transports and other] SUCH UNITS TO SAFE POSITIONS . . . WILL PERMIT ME EXECUTE ORDERLY REARMING PROGRAM FOR MY GROUPS AND AT SAME TIME GIVE ME MORE FREEDOM FOR FURTHER OFFENSIVE ACTION.

Admiral Nimitz instantly asked Halsey to amplify what offensive operations he might have in mind, then sternly replied:

GENERAL PLAN AND TASKS ASSIGNED . . . CONTINUE IN EFFECT AND RESTRICTIONS IMPOSED BY NECESSITY TO COVER FORCES OF THE SOUTHWEST PACIFIC ARE ACCEPTED.

MOVEMENT OF MAJOR UNITS OF THE 3RD FLEET THROUGH SURIGAO OR SAN BERNARDINO STRAITS WILL NOT BE INITIATED WITHOUT ORDERS FROM ME. ACKNOWLEDGE.

General MacArthur also replied direct to Halsey:

BASIC PLAN FOR THIS OPERATION IN WHICH FOR THE FIRST TIME I HAVE MOVED BEYOND
MY OWN LAND BASED AIR COVER WAS PREDICATED UPON FULL SUPPORT BY THIRD FLEET.
. . . OUR MASS OF SHIPPING IS SUBJECT DURING THIS CRITICAL PERIOD TO RAIDING ENEMY
ELEMENTS BOTH AIR AND SURFACE. . . . I CONSIDER THAT YOUR MISSION TO COVER THIS
OPERATION IS ESSENTIAL AND PARAMOUNT.

The Bull was not going to be let off the hook. He meekly radioed CINCPAC
that his original message on the subject had been merely exploratory. As a
device to rearm and refuel his carriers, Halsey then began to shuttle one task
group at a time through the recently activated base at Ulithi.

Thus it was that on October 23, when initial submarine reports appeared
of the Kurita fleet as well as Admiral Mikawa's Southwest Area Fleet forces,
Halsey had only three task groups in place. These nevertheless contained
five fleet and six light carriers, six fast battleships, two heavy and seven light
cruisers, and forty-four destroyers. In itself the force available outnumbered
the Japanese in a number of key categories. That day Halsey received a dispatch from Admiral Kinkaid of the Seventh Fleet concerning those Japanese
forces already sighted:

I CONSIDER THE APPROACH OF THE ENEMY . . . TOWARD CORON BAY AS THE FIRST PHASE
OF THE BUILDUP OF MAGNIFIED TOKYO EXPRESS RUNS AGAINST LEYTE.

Halsey, who knew something of the Tokyo Express from Guadalcanal days,
knew that to be an instrument of harassment and counterlandings. Kinkaid,
though using that term, spoke of three "PROBABLE BATTLESHIPS" and of another
group of eleven warships "WITH MANY RADARS." That sounds like more than a
Tokyo Express. The gap in understanding that opened between the two
admirals would grow much wider.

Admiral Kinkaid wanted air strikes on Coron Bay and the ships approaching it, and warned that Japanese carriers might come down the *west* coast of
the Philippines from Taiwan, where he believed them concentrating. Halsey
made numerous strikes on the Kurita fleet on October 24, as seen already,
and also radioed that the Japanese carriers had yet to be located. Then, at
4:40 P.M. on the twenty-fourth, they were. Of course, Ozawa was *east* of the
Philippines, past Cape Engaño, not where Kinkaid thought at all. Bull
Halsey faced the crucial decision whether to seek out the carriers or attack
the Kurita fleet. Inadvertently that Japanese admiral helped the decision
along with his retreat away from the San Bernardino Strait, appearing
defeated with the loss of the *Musashi* and *Maya* and damage to other vessels.
In addition, if Kurita was only a "Tokyo Express," the threat from him could
not be all that serious. Halsey and other air-minded naval officers, on the

other hand, regarded carriers as the heart of the adversary threat, and he had explicit orders to make such "major" Japanese elements his primary target if they should appear. Naval officers were trained never to divide forces in the face of the enemy, militating against Halsey detaching any groups to guard San Bernardino Strait while he sought Ozawa. Halsey also knew how Spruance was already being criticized for not having pursued enemy carriers at Philippine Sea. In addition, if Halsey *did not* head for Ozawa, there was a chance he might be trapped between Japanese carriers and their land-based air in the Philippines.

Some fault Halsey because he used the immense power of Task Force 38 to go after a Japanese carrier fleet a pale shadow of its former strength. Analysts at ONI supposedly knew that Ozawa's Carrier Division 3 was the sole seaworthy Imperial Navy carrier formation. However, Lieutenant Edward J. Matthews, combat intelligence officer for Halsey's battleship commander, Admiral Willis A. Lee of Task Force 34, recalls that JICPOA was (erroneously) circulating reports that Japanese fleet carriers *Amagi* and *Katsuragi* were battleworthy. If so, they might be with Ozawa, making his Main Body a far more lucrative target. In fact, both ships were at Kure throughout this period, and *Katsuragi* had been commissioned only on October 15. Neither had an air group, nor did fleet carrier *Unryu*, lead ship of the class, which arrived at Kure in company with *Amagi*. The initial sighting report of Ozawa actually *did* specify three fleet carriers and one light one, rather than the true Japanese strength of one big carrier and three light ones.

According to Lieutenant Matthews, Admiral Lee tried to remind Halsey at least twice during the night of October 24–25 of the danger to San Bernardino by drawing his attention to reconnaissance reports from the Sibuyan Sea that showed Kurita again headed for the strait. Halsey's original operations plan, tentatively worked up that afternoon, provided for detachment of Lee. Halsey went to bed early that night, immediately after a staff meeting reviewing the latest developments. So did many others of the staff, including the plans officer, a Marine brigadier named Riley, and radio unit chief Gilven Slonim, both of whom expected Task Force 34 to be detached during the night and were stunned the next morning to see Lee's battleships still in the formation. Halsey's chief of staff, "Mick" Carney, had been left to make the final dispositions and had sent a dispatch at 8:42 P.M. ordering all three carrier groups north. For reasons never made clear Carney did not direct the separation of Task Force 34.

Bull Halsey took full responsibility for what happened at Leyte—it is by no means clear that Mick Carney's dispatches reflected anything other than his boss's intentions. In a postwar memoir and in articles later than that, Admiral Halsey remained adamant, asserting that given the decision to make over again he would have done the same thing.

Admiral Ozawa Jisaburo had an intelligence officer on his staff too—in fact, for the first time a specialist who did not also have to concern himself with the fleet's communications—but he was even more in the dark than Halsey. In the early morning of the twenty-fourth he received a First Air Fleet report of American carriers ninety miles from Manila, and fifty minutes later came a similar report from Air Group 901. When, at 11:15 A.M., one of his own scouts contacted a U.S. unit headed north just 180 miles from the Main Body, Ozawa determined that the time had come to act. At 11:45 he sent the largest air strike he could manage, thirty-four bombers and torpedo planes plus forty fighters. The Americans did not even notice their attack.

By midafternoon Admiral Ozawa had decided to draw attention to himself by activating Matsuda Chiaki's battleships as an advance force. It was about two hours later, when Rear Admiral Matsuda had reached a point about fifty miles farther south than the carriers, that the Japanese detected an American plane, overheard its contact report, and observed it drop "window" as an antiradar countermeasure. Two fighters scrambled to intercept the intruder but they did not bring it down, nor did ships' anti-aircraft fire.

In a strange sense Ozawa Jisaburo now found himself in a position very similar to, though the reverse of, that he had occupied in December 1941. Then it had been he with a naval covering force protecting an invasion landing while an unfortunate British admiral had been on the other side. Ozawa sent Matsuda's battleships ahead at Cape Engaño much as Tom Phillips had dashed forward with the *Prince of Wales* and *Repulse*. Then, as now, the crippling blows would be struck by aircraft. However, a key difference would be that at Cape Engaño the Japanese *wanted* Halsey to attack them, with the ulterior motive of sneaking Kurita's fleet into Leyte Gulf. Vice Admiral Ozawa handled his mission quite deftly.

American power remained paramount; and when Halsey struck off Cape Engaño on October 25 the result could only be described as a slaughter. As usual radio intelligence led the way, with Commander Gilven Slonim and his mobile unit aboard Halsey's flagship, fast battleship *New Jersey;* another detachment with Mitscher in the *Hancock;* and one on the *Essex* with Task Group 38.3. Only the previous afternoon Slonim's radiomen overheard for the first time the Japanese fleet circuit at 7910J kilocycles, copying map grid locations as JNAF scouts reported Halsey's position. On the twenty-fifth the radio units distracted Halsey somewhat from pursuit of Ozawa because they informed him of Japanese surface action in the seas behind him. Halsey pressed on still, and accomplished much of what he set out to do.

A series of five waves of attack aircraft pounced on Ozawa's fleet beginning at 8:00 A.M., continuing into the late afternoon. Mitscher's task force put up 527 strike sorties; 431 planes actually made attacks, and 153 pilots or crews claimed hits. Rear Admiral Matsuda had rejoined the Main Body early that morning following recall from the advance-guard mission, so his

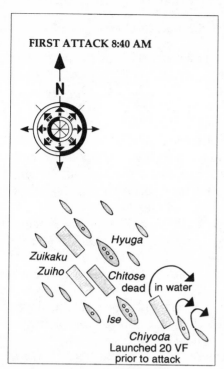

**FIRST ATTACK 8:40 AM**

N

*Zuikaku*
*Zuiho*
*Hyuga*
*Chitose*
dead in water
*Ise*
*Chiyoda*
Launched 20 VF
prior to attack

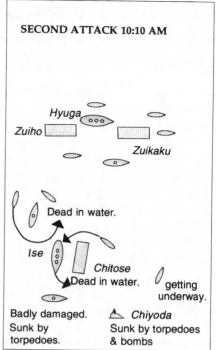

**SECOND ATTACK 10:10 AM**

*Hyuga*
*Zuiho*
*Zuikaku*

Dead in water.

*Ise*
*Chitose*
Dead in water.
getting
underway.

Badly damaged.
Sunk by
torpedoes.

*Chiyoda*
Sunk by torpedoes
& bombs

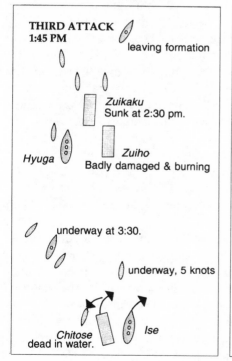

**THIRD ATTACK
1:45 PM**

leaving formation

*Zuikaku*
Sunk at 2:30 pm.

*Hyuga*
*Zuiho*
Badly damaged & burning

underway at 3:30.

underway, 5 knots

*Chitose*
dead in water.
*Ise*

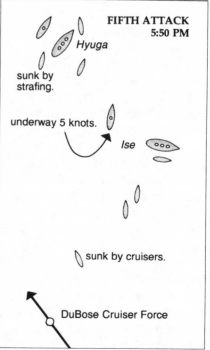

**FIFTH ATTACK
5:50 PM**

*Hyuga*

sunk by
strafing.

underway 5 knots.
*Ise*

sunk by cruisers.

DuBose Cruiser Force

XIV. Battle of Cape Engaño (October 25, 1944)

battleships contributed to Ozawa's fleet air defense. The *Hyuga* opened fire at 8:17, the *Oyodo* at 8:23; within seven minutes the first attack was over. Destroyer *Akitsuki* sank immediately, Captain Kishi Yoshiyuki's light carrier *Chitose* absorbed a number of bomb hits, three of them below the waterline; she was left crippled. Flagship *Zuikaku* suffered a torpedo hit, losing steering control and communications. The *Oyodo* came alongside at 9:52 to transfer Ozawa and the eleven officers of his staff, but a second attack forced her to withdraw temporarily. Admiral Ozawa managed to shift his flag at about 11:00 A.M., an emergency action that must have become distressingly familiar to him, since he had had to do the same at Philippine Sea.

Rear Admiral Kaizuka Takeo's *Zuikaku* dropped behind the formation along with Captain Sugiura Kuro's *Zuiho*, also damaged in the first attack. A single destroyer screened them. Captain Jyo Eiichiro's *Chiyoda*, fiercely afire and listing following the second-wave attack, was partially restored by Japanese damage control. Admiral Matsuda instructed Nomura of the *Hyuga* to take the vessel in tow, but the attempt had to be abandoned when a third wave of attackers struck after 1:00 P.M. Though the Main Body steamed north as quickly as it could, limited by the speed of the damaged ships, the Americans drew ever closer. By noontime the U.S.S. *Lexington* reckoned her position just over a hundred miles from the Ozawa force.

The American third wave attacked *Zuikaku*, once again damaged on her starboard side. She capsized to starboard in the early afternoon. Light carrier *Zuiho* also succumbed to additional damage in the third attack, though it took another two hours for her to flood enough to capsize, just about the time a fourth wave struck. The *Oyodo* screened as destroyers tried to rescue seamen from the doomed ships. By 5:00 P.M., when a small final attack planted seven bombs near Nomura's *Hyuga* without hitting her once, Ozawa's formation was tattered, to say the least. The *Hyuga* led, accompanied by a cruiser and a few destroyers. Miles behind, trailing oil, another light cruiser (probably *Tama*) followed. Nearby, Rear Admiral Nakase Noboru's *Ise*, with *Oyodo* and the last destroyers, were recovering survivors. Fully sixty miles south of the leading ships, the derelict *Chiyoda* was taken under fire by an American cruiser group.

In fact the battle of Cape Engaño ended as a gunnery action because Halsey got so close. Intending to detach "Ching" Lee's Task Force 34 to catch and shell Ozawa into submission, Halsey was stopped in mid-maneuver by the alarming news from Leyte. Embarrassed by the inquiries as to whether the battleships were guarding San Bernardino, as Kinkaid and some others mistakenly thought, Halsey was induced by a prod from Nimitz to order Task Force 34 back to the strait, and also to direct Vice Admiral John McCain's Task Group 38.1 to head that way as he returned from Ulithi. Another task group, Gerald Bogan's 38.2, also went south from the Ozawa chase. Lee's battleships would arrive at San Bernardino too late to block the strait, catching just a single destroyer Kurita had sent to recover survivors from the *Kumano*.

Task Force 34 also made little contribution to the destruction of Ozawa, except for a unit of three cruisers and nine destroyers Vice Admiral Lee left behind to pursue the Japanese on the surface. The unit, under Rear Admiral Laurance T. DuBose, eventually caught up with Ozawa's derelicts and it was his ships that finally sank the carrier *Chiyoda*, destroyer *Hatsuyuki*, and possibly light cruiser *Tama* as well. Jim Montgomery, a gunnery officer on one of DuBose's cruisers, remembers watching through the range finder as the Japanese cruiser was hit and stopped, moved off again, was hit and stopped again, and so on. Imperial Navy damage control had progressed considerably since Midway.

Meanwhile, Vice Admiral Ozawa learned from *Hatsuyuki* that American surface ships were engaging the vessels he had left behind. Gamely, Ozawa ordered Matsuda's battleships, flagship *Oyodo*, and remaining destroyers to turn back and support the cripples. Admiral Ozawa held to the southerly course until 11:30 P.M. before giving up and turning back toward Empire waters. The *Hatsuyuki* was never heard from again. Of all the tragedy of that day, this seems to have affected Ozawa the most. "It is a matter of regret," the admiral later told Americans, "that . . . when we immediately reversed course upon receipt of a report of an approaching enemy surface force . . . we were unable in the end to attain our objective."

ADMIRAL OZAWA, AFTER THE WAR, REGRETTED NOT ONLY HIS INABILITY TO HIT THE American cruiser force the night following the destruction of his fleet, but also Rear Admiral Matsuda's failure to close with Halsey the night before, just after American planes first found the Main Body. In truth that function, to sail as a surface action group in front of the fleet, had been intended for Vice Admiral Shima Kiyohide's Fifth Fleet, down from northern waters, which had exercised in that role. But when Ozawa sailed for Cape Engaño, Shima happened to be sitting in Mako (in the Pescadores, now called P'eng-hu) awaiting orders. Combined Fleet's handling of Shima's force, weak throughout the SHO operation, demonstrates the difficulties of coordinating at long distance the many disparate commands involved in this intricate plan.

Admiral Shima's odyssey began during the Taiwan air battle of early October. Wildly overestimating the effect of Japanese attacks, Combined Fleet ordered Shima to mop the sea clear of the hulks of Allied warships supposed to have been crippled in the battle. Shima sailed from Hiroshima Bay, paused briefly off Iwakuni, where he exchanged views with Ozawa, then left Empire waters via the Bungo Strait. With him were only three cruisers,

*Nachi, Ashigara,* and *Abukuma,* two of which made up Cruiser Division 21. Captain Hanada Takuo's light cruiser, *Abukuma,* was flagship of Rear Admiral Kimura Masatome's 1st Destroyer Flotilla, whose ships sailed separately from Kure and rendezvoused at sea. Not only did the Fifth Fleet find no enemies to mop up, it was seen by both submarines and aircraft and might very well have been destroyed had not the schedule for Philippine operations required Halsey to withdraw Task Force 38 to more southerly waters at this time. Rear Admiral Kimura, a master of operations under adverse circumstances, who had spark-plugged the Kiska evacuation, found himself at a disadvantage under 1944 conditions. He did no better than other Japanese escort leaders at Leyte.

Admiral Shima put in to Amami O Shima for fuel and there learned of the American landing at Suluan Island (at the mouth of Leyte Gulf), shortly followed by fleet chief of staff Kusaka's activation of SHO-1. On October 18 Combined Fleet headquarters sent orders that assigned Shima to Admiral Mikawa's Southwest Area Fleet. As Kusaka put it after the war, the idea at headquarters was not to try to dictate every activity of Shima's force, which was pretty small anyway (three cruisers and seven destroyers), but to let Mikawa use the Fifth Fleet for counterlanding operations. At the same time Hiyoshi headquarters detached Cruiser Division 16 from Kurita's fleet for the same purpose. Vice Admiral Sakonju Naomasa's cruiser unit, with heavy cruiser *Aoba,* light cruiser *Kinu,* and a single destroyer, headed for Manila, near which the *Aoba* was disabled by a submarine torpedo. Captain Yamazumi Chusaburo's heavy cruiser, which perhaps had been on the front line of the Pacific war more often than any other Imperial Navy major warship, would not be going to Leyte. The *Aoba* sought shelter at Manila, there to make temporary repairs.

Early on October 20 Admiral Shima arrived at Mako and again refueled; his ships were topped off before midnight. Half of Kimura's escorts were taken away from him when a destroyer division of the 1st Flotilla was ordered to Takao to pick up ground crews and base equipment of the Second Air Fleet, which had to get to the Philippines to rejoin the aircraft Admiral Fukudome was to deploy there. With the remainder of his force Shima planned to sail early next morning, but he encountered many difficulties. His mission for Mikawa was to make a counterlanding on Leyte with Army reinforcements, but the Southern Area Army was now saying it had not completed preparations for that move. Admiral Shima then sent Combined Fleet two messages recommending he revert to Ozawa's command, which he knew was about to leave Empire waters on its decoy sortie. There was no answer. Admiral Mikawa also radioed Hiyoshi with news of the Army's tardiness and advised that Shima ought to be attached to either Ozawa or Kurita.

Shima was an Etajima classmate of King Kong Hara; they were alike in certain ways. A direct and forceful man with a strong handshake, Shima Kiyohide thought his suggestions would be approved. Not only was it widely believed in the fleet that Decisive Battle required concentrated force but also the vice chief of the Naval General Staff, Ito Seiichi, happened to be another of Shima's classmates. The Fifth Fleet commander sent a further dispatch warning that fuel stocks were diminishing and the moment to seize the opportunity would soon pass. Shima was so certain of approval he called a captains' conference aboard flagship *Nachi*, gave departure orders, and drank toasts with sake the Emperor had presented to the ship.

Toward midnight a message arrived at Mako reconfirming Combined Fleet's order that Shima support a counterlanding attempt. The indignant subordinate, forced to cancel his sailing orders, sat in port. Stewing in his own juices, Shima perhaps recalled his days as resident naval officer in Manchuria (1933–1934), when Army hotheads had manipulated the nation into a march of conquest. A communications expert, once chief instructor at the Yokosuka Communications School, then director of that facility until his appointment to the Fifth Fleet the previous February, Shima was also upset at Combined Fleet's lackadaisical reluctance to respond to his dispatches. Leyte was going to be his first chance to get into the action since the early days of the war, when Shima had led Fourth Fleet task forces to occupy the Marshalls, Rabaul, and Tulagi. Now it looked as if he might miss the chance after all.

At Hiyoshi the Combined Fleet had not forgotten about the Fifth Fleet. Chief of staff Kusaka recognized that Vice Admiral Shima must have been extremely annoyed, but insisted that was inevitable given the circumstances. He conceded (in retrospect) inconsistent and extremely poor policy in the handling of the Shima force. Rear Admiral Takata Toshitane, by this time senior staff officer under Kusaka, later had this to say:

> Combined Fleet . . . took no action . . . due partly to the fact that [the Shima force], because of its slight strength, was not expected to be able to contribute significantly to the penetration operation. Further, it was feared that incorporation of [the Shima force] in [the Kurita fleet] at a time when the latter was most heavily occupied with sortie preparations, and especially when its operations plan had already been fixed, would throw the operation into confusion and at the same time necessitate increased radio traffic involving the risk of divulging our intentions to the enemy. A still further reason was that it was considered advisable to leave [the Shima force] under [Southwest] Area Fleet in anticipation of the eventual execution of counterlanding operations.

It should be pointed out in connection with Takata's observations that chief of staff Kusaka had not hesitated to improvise an air-only SHO at a time when the entire naval strategic plan had been fixed, or to ask Kurita under similar circumstances to divide his force to attempt a double penetration through both San Bernardino and Surigao straits. Actually, Combined Fleet did finally decide to assign Shima's force to Admiral Kurita's 1st Diversion Attack Force and so informed area fleet in the afternoon of October 21. Even then Admiral Mikawa did not receive a direct order but rather a message from Kusaka that Hiyoshi "concurred" in employing Shima to support Kurita's penetration of Leyte Gulf. Many hours had been wasted.

As the Leyte campaign developed, the Combined Fleet had thus ordered Shima's force into a surface action off Taiwan, then anticipated returning it to Ozawa's command, then assigned it to Mikawa, then delayed any decision, and now finally acquiesced in advice from subordinates. Hiyoshi gave Shima no actual combat orders.

Vice Admiral Shima had Mako radio Admiral Kurita for his views on the employment of the Fifth Fleet. The latter appears to have refrained from issuing direct orders too, instead merely informing Shima of his intentions and timetable. This left Shima to decide more or less on his own, merely on the basis of what his radios could pick up of the action around him. Since Ozawa was having communications problems on the *Zuikaku*, and many of his messages did not reach other Japanese commanders, and Kurita largely maintained radio silence, Shima's choice would be a difficult one.

Vice Admiral Shima's 2nd Diversion Attack Force weighed anchor at about 4:00 P.M. on October 21. He sailed south across the Luzon Strait and down the western side of that island, in part because of Mikawa's original orders to him to make for Manila. Three of Shima's destroyers were headed for that place with aviation personnel and it would be easiest for them to rejoin the Fifth Fleet west of Luzon. With orders to join Kurita, Shima now made for the Calamian Islands, where he expected to refuel at Coron Bay. To preserve radio silence he sent a floatplane describing these moves to Manila; there the information could be given to Captain Ishii Hisashi, who commanded the detached destroyers. The floatplane overturned in rough water inside Manila Bay, however, and the message never reached Ishii. His ships stayed under Southwest Area Fleet and performed only minor chores. Destroyer *Wakaba* was caught by U.S. planes and sunk west of Panay on October 24. The carrier *Franklin*, whose planes made the kill, was one of those ships supposed to have been destroyed by First Air Fleet attacks while Admiral Teraoka held that command.

Shima's ships supposed they would find tankers at Coron Bay, but they were disappointed. The admiral instructed his destroyers to refuel from the cruisers instead, an action completed just before midnight October 23. By then Shima had messages indicating that Vice Admiral Nishimura Shoji's Battleship Division 2 intended to penetrate Leyte Gulf through the Surigao

Strait. Reasoning that Nishimura's unit was much less powerful than the Kurita fleet, Shima resolved to support them.

What happened between Shima and Nishimura remains one of the most controversial aspects of the Leyte battle. The latter had been detached from the Kurita fleet to execute the Surigao penetration with his battleships *Yamashiro* and *Fuso,* the heavy cruiser *Mogami,* and four destroyers. It has been reported that Kurita selected Nishimura for this action because he was the next most senior officer in the force. Kurita supposedly feared that Nishimura's staff was fresh and not well prepared, and therefore unsuited to direct the entire fleet. However, this version conflicts with data showing that both Kurita's other battleship division leaders—Ugaki Matome and Suzuki Yoshio—in fact held pennants higher than Nishimura's. More likely, Kurita chose Nishimura's unit for conventional reasons: His Battleship Division 2 had joined only early in October, had little experience in common with the other units, had not exercised with them, and was composed of older, slower ships.

Nishimura sailed in company with Kurita to Brunei. It was there that Kurita suddenly picked Nishimura to carry out an independent operation. Battleship Division 2 remained at anchor after the rest of the Kurita fleet left, then departed at midafternoon on October 22. The detached unit, tactically known as the Third Section of the 1st Diversion Attack Force, made its way across the Sulu Sea toward the western side of the Philippines. On the morning of October 24 American aircraft saw Nishimura about to enter the Surigao Strait, and the search-strike group, in all twenty-eight planes, made its best effort. Rear Admiral Ban Masami's battleship, *Fuso,* sustained minor damage aft, and Commander Nishino Shigeru's destroyer, *Shigure,* received a hit forward that wrecked one of her 5-inch gun turrets. Thereafter Task Force 38 concentrated attacks on Kurita's force, and Nishimura steamed gamely into Surigao Strait. Well aware of his progress, American admiral Thomas C. Kinkaid moved to block the narrows with overwhelming force: six battleships; three heavy and six light cruisers; twenty-eight destroyers; thirty-nine PT boats. Kinkaid's dispositions resulted from warnings on the time of Japanese arrival and strength that he had had from Captain McCollum, fleet intelligence officer, who prepared a memorandum for the Seventh Fleet commander based on the intelligence available October 24.

In the final analysis Admiral Nishimura's challenge at Surigao Strait was not only a weak one, it would not have been much stronger even if he *had* been joined by Shima, something that did not happen. Why Nishimura and Shima did not join forces to maximize whatever chances they had will always figure among the mysteries of Leyte Gulf. American historians have argued that it occurred because the two admirals, Etajima classmates as it happens, had a little competition going, and Shima had six months' more seniority on the vice admirals' list. Thus Shima would have commanded any joint force, something Nishimura supposedly could not stomach. This argument assumes that the battleship commander was well apprised of Shima's intentions and movements, but in fact we do not know enough about the Fifth Fleet commander's dispatches to conclude that that was possible. We know Vice Admiral Shima was aware of Nishimura's general timetable, whereby the latter was to break through Surigao Strait at "dawn," but the record contains only one similar scheduling dispatch from Shima, sent before his arrival at Coron Bay. Since Shima was a communications expert, sensitive to the advantages of radio silence, there is reason to suspect he may not have sent any others. In postwar interviews Vice Admiral Shima mentioned no such messages, though he did refer to messages from Nishimura, and he explicitly stated his intention to support his classmate on the grounds that Nishimura's force was weak and had more need than the Kurita fleet.

Another possible explanation for the missed rendezvous is that none was intended, that Shima was to exploit Nishimura's results. Japanese ships and forces used Tokyo time wherever they might be. In a war fought over an expanse of nine time zones some such convention was necessary, but that meant the time of sunrise at any given locality might differ quite a lot from that of dawn in Tokyo. The Japanese convention was to take 4:00 A.M. as the time of "dawn." When Vice Admiral Shima received messages from Nishimura he saw that as the time of penetration and set his schedule accordingly. Shima planned to sail from Coron Bay at 2:00 A.M., October 24. What was objectionable about this arrangement was the notion that there could be an exploitation behind Nishimura's weak lead echelon at night, in the face of the enemy. Later, when halfway across the Sulu Sea and even entering the strait, Shima received Nishimura's progress reports and realized that the battleship admiral had actually accelerated his schedule. It was then too late for the Fifth Fleet to increase speed and reduce their separation.

This was a mistake Nishimura Shoji probably would not have made. Admiral Nishimura was a navigation specialist, a good man to get the best out of the old battleships *Yamashiro* and *Fuso*. He had spent virtually all his career at sea with the exception of the 1937–1938 period, when he had been a special student at the Naval War College. The fifty-nine-year-old vice admiral in his day had commanded the cruiser *Kumano* and the fast battleship *Haruna*, and at the time of Pearl Harbor had led one of the Japanese invasion forces on its way to the Philippines. A likely explanation for Nishimura's actions at Surigao Strait was that he felt the weight of responsibility heavily, in the same sense as those who were beginning to flock to join the kamikaze corps. It was a cultural trait that valued heroism amid tragedy, what some Western analysts have termed the "nobility of failure."

Indeed, tragedy seems to have dogged Nishimura through the Pacific war. His very first operation, convoying an invasion force to Vigan on

Luzon, was the only one of the initial round of Japanese invasions (other than the Wake operation) to suffer any losses. The loss had only been a minesweeper in rough seas, but the Imperial Navy prided itself on its ability to operate in bad weather. Commanding the 4th Destroyer Flotilla, Nishimura then shepherded invasion units on the main Luzon landing, at Lingayen Gulf, where transports were lost for the first time to U.S. subs. Days later Nishimura's only son, Teiji, who had graduated at the top of his class from Etajima, died at the other end of Luzon when his floatplane exploded on takeoff. Ugaki Matome, the admiral's good friend, who had also been one of Teiji's instructors, saw a death wish in Nishimura after that.

Tragedies then piled one upon another. Nishimura's poor handling of his destroyers off Balikpapan in February 1942 had left Japanese shipping unprotected while failing to challenge U.S. warships, making possible American victory in the Makassar Strait. At the battle of the Java Sea, Nishimura had been highly aggressive, quickly expending his torpedoes to no effect. Promoted to command Cruiser Division 7 off Guadalcanal, he had carried out one of those notorious cruiser bombardments of Henderson Field, but one so ineffective that the next day American planes rose to sink seven of eleven Japanese transports plus a light cruiser. In July 1943 Nishimura himself had been the target, during one of the endless Slot missions to Vella Lavella. He had found no U.S. ships to sink, but American planes found him, sinking a destroyer and battering his old command, the cruiser *Kumano*. Another destroyer left to rescue survivors would be sunk as well.

Ozawa Jisaburo, who had once been Nishimura's superior and did not suffer fools gladly, is said to have had high regard for Nishimura. Staff officers who had worked under him thought him perhaps too easily persuaded, a nice and gentle man who tried to avoid disputes. But Nishimura did not need to stay away from Shima to avoid coming under his command; rather the latter's single schedule message, once plotted on the charts, clearly showed that the Fifth Fleet intended no rendezvous at all, probably to avoid confusion in the dark. However, the message also revealed Shima's proposed timing to be so far behind Nishimura's pace that the two forces could hardly be said to be cooperating. There is no evidence that Nishimura contested this; instead he did the opposite, further accelerating his timetable. How could the competent Nishimura do this? Personal weakness or a death wish does seem to be the major potential explanation.

The battle of Surigao Strait became an ordeal for the Imperial Navy, a matter of surviving successive waves of Allied forces in a desperate effort to break into Leyte Gulf. The airplanes had been first; PT boats followed. On the American side there has been controversy in that the PT boats, like the submarines, were under orders to report Japanese movements, only attacking afterward. The stricture helps account for the PTs' meager results—almost

160 torpedoes damaged just a single ship. A letter Admiral Kinkaid sent to former PT officer Edward I. Farley almost ten years after the battle throws considerable light on the Seventh Fleet commander's reasoning:

> The disposition of PTs for the night of October 24 was carefully worked out by my staff and . . . the PT commander, and approved by me. Of course, we hoped they would be able to use their torpedoes with great effect, but their major role was to provide vitally important information, which they did. . . .
>
> To have concentrated 39 PTs at one point might have turned back Nishimura (do you really believe it?) but it also might have deprived [my tactical commander] of information he needed and of the opportunity to destroy Nishimura's forces. . . .
>
> Surely you would not have wanted the PTs to divorce themselves from the overall efforts of the Seventh Fleet and have a "little war of their own." . . . Though you may be disappointed at the lack of opportunity of the PTs to make a massed attack in the Surigao Straits, the service of information which they rendered was of extreme importance in the conduct of that action.

On the Japanese side the intelligence picture remained quite different. Nishimura had only the vaguest, most general notion of the strength ranged against him. Commander Nishino Shigeru of the *Shigure*, present at the conference at Brunei, recalled that the group was told the opposition might be two or more battleships, five or six cruisers, and ten or more destroyers. Amid the toasts and greetings, Nishino also recalled, Admiral Nishimura did not say much, as if he and his flag captain had already talked at Lingga and were determined merely to press forward. There is no record that the officers at Brunei were told anything about PT boats.

In the strait on the night of the twenty-fourth, everything was different. Darkness and danger were compounded by threatening weather that grew worse, according to Commander Shibayama Kazuo of destroyer *Asagumo*. Nishimura tried to cope with light fog and lowering clouds, and saw the PTs as he rounded the southern tip of Panaon Island. He ordered Captain Takahashi Kameshiro of Destroyer Division 4 to neutralize the PT boats, estimated at ten in number, then link up for the break-in. Takahashi thought he could engage the PT boats as a unit but kept running into more of them—partly because there were so many, but also because the first group of PTs discovered its radios were not working and had to make visual contact with another group to get out the necessary warning. The *Asagumo*'s commander perceived that the Japanese were inflicting no damage on the PT boats, but on the other hand the destroyers took no losses either. Nishimura radioed a report picked up by Shima, now about forty miles behind, that he had sighted several PT boats but the Allied situation remained unknown otherwise. Nishimura was going to advance into Leyte.

Captain Toma Ryo in the *Mogami* led one group of Nishimura's ships chasing PTs, then rejoined the main force. The destroyers took station ahead of the big ships, flagship *Yamashiro* immediately behind, then *Fuso*, while Toma's *Mogami* brought up the rear. They rounded Panaon about 1:40 A.M., making 18 knots almost due north. Commander Shibayama reports that the weather was so closed in, visibility was only about one and a half miles. Allied sources, in contrast, report a clear dark night, the sea absolutely calm, with visibility at two or three miles even without night glasses. The moon had set at 12:07 A.M.

Nishino's *Shigure* was the first to detect the newest attackers, different groups of smokestacks, first to port, then to starboard. Commander Nishino perceived the American ships approach, then turn away, but oddly had no idea they might have fired torpedoes. In fact ships of Captain Jesse G. Coward's Destroyer Squadron 54 had fired a total of forty-seven tin fish from both sides of the Japanese formation. Beginning about 3:08 A.M. the Japanese found themselves in torpedo water with virtually no chance to evade. Commander Tanaka Kazuo's destroyer, *Michishio*, was hit from port in her engine room. She sank in about ten minutes, taking Captain Takahashi down with her. Tanaka himself was thrown clear of the sinking vessel, lost consciousness, and was adrift for over forty hours until picked up by an American PT boat. (When he awoke he begged the PT crew to kill him. Instead he was sent to Australia as a prisoner to be interrogated by the Allied Translator and Interpreter Section [ATIS].)

Destroyer *Yamagumo*, also hit, became unnavigable, then blew up. Commander Shibayama's *Asagumo* would be luckier for a time. She, too, took a torpedo, in the port bow, but engineer Lieutenant Ishii Tokichi still managed steam for 12 knots, so the ship began to withdraw down the strait. Battleship *Yamashiro* also sustained a torpedo hit but continued to advance. Nishimura sent a dispatch warning of destroyers on both sides of the strait. More Allied destroyers, under Captains Roland N. Smoot and Kenmore M. McManes, also closed in for torpedo attacks. At 3:51 the Allied cruisers began to bombard Nishimura, followed two minutes later by the six battle-ships, five of which had been hit or sunk at Pearl Harbor but were now back to torment the Japanese. For twenty minutes the warships fired salvos at Nishimura's hapless vessels. In addition to his raw strength advantage, tactical commander Rear Admiral Jesse B. Oldendorf had the important advantage of "crossing the T," or being in a position broadside to the oncoming Japanese ships, from which he could use all his guns while Nishimura's vessels could reply only with their forward batteries.

Before very long the battle ended. Allied cruisers fired about 4,300 shells, the battleships almost 300 14-inch and 16-inch rounds. Vice Admiral

Nishimura went down with the *Yamashiro* when she capsized at 4:19. The *Fuso*, crippled in the torpedo action, had already broken up at 3:38. Captain Toma's *Mogami*, on fire at 3:56, still managed to launch torpedoes at 4:01. A minute later she caught multiple hits from a salvo probably fired by the heavy cruiser *Portland;* a shell exploded on the bridge, killing Toma, his executive officer, and everyone else there. Control of the ship devolved upon the gunnery officer. The *Mogami* fled the way she had come. *Shigure,* an older but lucky destroyer that had survived many close encounters in the Solomons, got away again. Commander Nishino's ship sustained a single 8-inch hit that disabled his radio and gyrocompass; later he lost steering control and had to spend a half hour repairing the rudder. While *Shigure* was doing that Shima's force passed headed into Surigao Strait.

The *Mogami* suffered a worse fate. Reeling from her damage, the heavy cruiser staggered back down the strait. She passed astern of the *Asagumo*, on which Commander Shibayama stood, the crippled destroyer that had lost her bow. Shibayama wanted to sail in company with the cruiser but could not match her speed. In fact, the *Mogami* was going too fast for her own good; as Shima proceeded north the distance was closing at a rate of almost fifty miles an hour. Steered from secondary control, the *Mogami* lacked proper visibility and was preoccupied with damage control. At the same time the Shima force was thrown into confusion by PT attacks, which finally scored—damage to cruiser *Abukuma.* Then Shima passed what seemed two fiercely burning battleships but were probably the halves of the shattered *Fuso.* Ahead a smoke screen came into view. Shima ordered torpedoes launched and turned to bring his broadsides to bear. Just then the *Mogami* appeared. Commander Mori Kokichi, Shima's torpedo staff officer, recalled that everyone aboard flagship *Nachi* was intent upon their torpedo attack and at first merely thought of the *Mogami* as another wreck. Only as they were turning away from their attack did they realize the *Mogami* was under way at about 8 knots and barely had steering control. Captain Kanoka Empei of the *Nachi* ordered his rudder hard over but collision could not be avoided. Kanoka, former *joho kyoku* officer and naval aide to Prime Minister Tojo, now among a growing parade of staff types given seagoing commands at the worst time of the war, was perhaps not fully prepared for emergency maneuvers in this situation. The *Nachi's* starboard bow was breached and the anchor windlass compartment flooded; the ship's speed fell to 18 knots. *Mogami* continued careening south only to be sunk next day by U.S. carrier planes.

Vice Admiral Shima recognized that very little could now be accomplished—against all those American ships he had but a single undamaged cruiser, the *Ashigara.* Unknown to him, the Allied fleet had begun to pursue south and would itself shortly emerge from the smoke screen. In any case Shima now thought discretion the better part of valor and began withdrawing, detaching destroyers to accompany the *Mogami* and also the damaged *Abukuma*. The latter ship sailed into a nearby bay to make temporary repairs enabling her to face the open sea, but she would be caught there by American planes. Jesse Oldendorf, leading his big boys down the strait in hot pursuit, came across Commander Shimayama's crippled *Asagumo*, which looked funny with just a single stack and no bow back to her number two turret. Light cruisers *Denver* and *Columbia* and destroyer *Bennion* finished off the ship and watched her sink. Commander Shibayama spent the day in the water before wading ashore on Panaon Island, where Filipino guerrillas captured him and handed him over to SOWESPAC intelligence officers. His chief engineer, Lieutenant Ishii, made it as far as Leyte and was captured a day later. They became subjects of ATIS interrogation.

At this key moment, with Allied heavy ships pursuing down Surigao, dawn bringing clarity to the situation, and American planes bearing down on the hapless Japanese, the radio intelligence group took a hand in the affair. Jesse Oldendorf turned away under pressure of the urgent necessity to bar the opposite entrance to Leyte Gulf, leaving only the planes. Aboard *Nachi*, a Hawaii-born radio intelligence lieutenant named Kameda sent a fake message that Japanese carrier planes were attacking, asking the Allied aircraft to return to their bases immediately. This ruse apparently worked well enough for Vice Admiral Shima to live another day, but not very long was left to the *Nachi*. That ship made for Manila where she, too, needed temporary repairs. There, on November 5, Shima went ashore to a morning meeting at Southwest Area Fleet headquarters. Returning to the docks, he had trouble finding a launch to take him out to the *Nachi*, moored off Corregidor. As Shima watched in horror through binoculars, two successive waves of planes from the U.S.S. *Lexington* sent his flagship to the bottom of Manila Bay.

The only Allied ship hit in the Surigao Strait battle, American destroyer *Albert W. Grant*, apparently was a victim of friendly fire. Still, all the Japanese losses might have seemed worthwhile if things had turned out better for the Kurita fleet.

WITH DAWN CAME THE DAY WHEN, ADMIRAL MIKAWA HAD PROMISED, THE ENEMY TASK forces would be destroyed. It could have happened. Kurita Takeo's fleet steamed down the east coast of Samar bound for Leyte, guns primed. Admiral Kurita led the biggest assemblage of gunnery ships in a single Japanese surface attack at any point of World War II, his sailors determined to avenge losses already suffered. Partly by accident, partly by design, the adversaries strong enough to stop Kurita were far away. Tom Kinkaid had his whole force off barring Surigao against Nishimura and Shima's somewhat inept efforts. Halsey had gone north to catch Ozawa because aircraft carriers were the new capital ships and the Bull was going to get them. The only things between Kurita and Leyte Gulf were a few bunches of "Woolworth aircraft carriers"—the tiny escort carriers—with the destroyers and destroyer-escorts supposed to protect them. If Kurita *had* reached Leyte Gulf he would have faced the dilemma of whether to follow the orders originally given—to attack the Allied amphibious shipping, a rather unheroic role for an Imperial Navy officer. Such an eventuality would also have involved a final surface action against the Seventh Fleet as Tom Kinkaid brought it back up from Surigao. These are huge imponderables, but what actually happened off the island of Samar was equally unlikely and just as fraught with drama.

As dawn approached Kurita ordered his fleet into battle formation. Sunrise on Wednesday, October 25, was recorded at 6:35 A.M. Minutes later light cruiser *Noshiro* and heavy cruiser *Chokai* both warned of planes aloft. Battleship *Yamato*, now Kurita's flagship in place of the cruiser torpedoed out from under him, had the planes on her radar within two minutes. Moments afterward lookouts saw the masts of ships. With four battleships and six heavy cruisers, Admiral Kurita had no fear.

All ready for a surface engagement, yet not expecting a fight until they entered Leyte Gulf, the Japanese encountered the American escort carriers almost by accident. It is difficult to establish who actually saw the Americans first. Assuming Japanese clocks were synchronized and after-action reports accurate, the honors seem to belong to Rear Admiral Kobe Yuji's battleship, *Nagato*, which reported masts at 6:41. Battleship *Kongo* saw masts at 6:45, as did *Yamato* and heavy cruiser *Tone* one minute later. Aboard *Yamato* the initial sighting was by a petty officer high up in the crow's nest. To avoid any error, fleet operations officer Commander Otani Tonosuke went up to see for himself. So did the staff gunnery officer, who climbed to gunnery control to report what could be seen through the optical range finder. On the flag bridge ensued discussion of whether the masts might be Imperial Navy craft exiting after passage of Surigao Strait, but all doubt vanished once Japanese observers spotted carrier flight decks. Before returning to the bridge, Otani personally saw two aircraft carriers.

Aboard heavy cruiser *Kumano*, gunnery control was manned by the ship's chief gunner, Lieutenant Hirayama Shigeo. He had been at his station all the previous day, during the big anti-aircraft battle, and through the night, when the fleet expected to have to fight its way through San Bernardino Strait. Exhausted, Hirayama had dozed off. He awoke to see an American torpedo plane off to the east. Hirayama wondered what the plane was doing there and ordered preparations for anti-aircraft defense. Then his lookout, too, reported carriers.

Light cruisers *Noshiro* and *Yahagi*, leading Kurita's destroyer squadrons, saw masts at 6:49 A.M., minutes after *Yamato*. Shortly thereafter *Yahagi* added that she could see three aircraft carriers. By then *Kongo* was reporting four carriers and ten other warships. *Haruna* became the last battleship to report seeing the Americans, at 6:50 A.M. It was early morning; a long day lay ahead. Although there were intermittent clouds and squalls, not ideal conditions for naval gunnery, the sea was moderately calm, making it easier to aim, and visibility ranged up to fourteen miles. Admiral Kurita laid a course to the east-southeast and ordered battle speed. Later he would write dryly in his after-action report that "masts were sighted to the southeast."

Here *seemed* opportunity for the Imperial Navy, opportunity unmatched in the annals of the Pacific war. A powerful surface fleet had aircraft carriers under its guns! By dint of tremendous sacrifice, accepting huge losses, the Japanese had turned the age of airpower at sea on its head. Previously Japanese admirals had only dreamed of such an encounter. At Midway, when the Imperial Navy suffered grievous blows to its own carrier fleet, commanders had ordered foolhardy tactical maneuvers in a vain effort to achieve this very situation. At Santa Cruz, Japanese battleships got close enough to actually *see* an American carrier, but that had been a derelict left behind as the opposing fleet retired. Off Samar on the morning of October 25 the opportunity was real, and an exact reversal of the war's strategic situation, in which the Allies enjoyed marked superiority. The Japanese arrived at this position despite all odds and in the face of American preparations to discover and combat them.

When news of Kurita's circumstances reached Combined Fleet headquarters in a dispatch, the report startled the assembled staff. Officers were "overjoyed," wrote chief of staff Kusaka Ryunosuke; the group "all but stood on its head." Headquarters waited breathlessly for news of combat. Now, in the twilight of the war, suddenly all seemed possible. Admiral Kurita held the fate of the Japanese Empire in his hands. Finally it would be the Decisive Battle, or at least the closest thing to one that the Imperial Navy achieved in the war.

This, too, was the way it looked on the flag bridge of superbattleship *Yamato*. The ultimate irony of Leyte Gulf is that the Imperial Navy's general lack of interest in intelligence, in particular ship identification, led to observers mistaking the American escort carriers for fleet carriers, the destroyers for cruisers, the destroyer-escorts for full-size destroyers. It proved an enormous error because it led Kurita Takeo, on the spur of a moment, to throw away Combined Fleet's long-prepared SHO plans.

Acts of rashness actually were unusual for Kurita, whose Navy reputation was as a cool-headed commander, aggressive but very conscious of the sailors under him, respectful of subordinates and staff. That did not mean the admiral was not competitive as well. Kurita was a sportsman, an avocation that was no façade; had he been an American naval officer Kurita would have played polo. In the Imperial Navy he played tennis and baseball when his ships were in port, and did archery wherever he was. Kurita liked his sake, did not smoke, and was very popular, being considered a very competent officer. He was marked in the Imperial Navy as one of those sea dogs good enough to attain high rank without ever passing the hallowed portals of the War College. He made captain in 1932, skippered cruiser *Abukuma* in Chinese waters during the "Incident," and as a junior rear admiral led a destroyer flotilla in the northern Pacific during the time of troubles with the Soviet Union.

Admiral Kurita's war record remained one of the most extensive in the fleet. He had led invasion groups and covering forces in the early Netherlands East Indies campaigns, had taken his Cruiser Division 7 raiding in the Indian Ocean, and more. Kurita had been at Midway, Guadalcanal, the Solomons campaign, the Philippine Sea. It had been his battleships, with Kurita on the bridge, that made the earth tremble at Guadalcanal on "The Night." It was Kurita again, aboard the *Kongo*, who at Santa Cruz had actually had an American aircraft carrier (the *Hornet*) under his guns. At the Philippine Sea, Kurita had been the only screen commander not to lose any of the carriers he was escorting. Leading the Second Fleet for over a year, Admiral Kurita was also well accustomed to the ships and subordinates under him, and carried easily the mask of command.

Perhaps by the same token, however, Kurita Takeo could be suspected of becoming a tad gun-shy. After all, he had been bombed and torpedoed more often than almost any other Japanese admiral, and only Ozawa Jisaburo had been driven off more ships flying his flag. Kurita might have yearned for the scholarly life of his grandfather, an authority on early Meiji literature, but his lot was to remain at sea. In the far-off days of the early war it had been Kurita who led the unlucky ships torpedoed off Java when the *Houston* and *Perth* made their desperate dash for the Sunda Strait. At Midway it was his cruiser, *Mikuma*, crippled by (another) collision with *Mogami*, that had gone down under a hail of American bombs and torpedoes. At Santa Cruz his flagship had been bombed by planes from the *Enterprise*. Kurita had led the cruiser force so brutally ambushed at Rabaul in November 1943, and over the following months the threat of carrier air attack had driven his fleet from Truk, then from Palau. On the morning of October 25, 1944, Kurita Takeo had just been through the slaughter of his personal command (Cruiser Division 4) by submarine attack, with his flagship sunk under him. Only the previous day, one of his most powerful battleships, a vessel thought in the Imperial Navy to be unsinkable, had succumbed to the weight of carrier strikes.

Admiral Kurita can be forgiven for believing aircraft carriers to be among his worst enemies. Now a group of them had appeared as if by magic right in front of him. Kurita and Koyanagi, his chief of staff, could not help being aware of the feeling among their subordinates against expending the Empire's last fleet to wreck mere invasion shipping. In many respects they agreed with these views. Their orders, like Bull Halsey's, contained an escape clause to the effect that enemy warships could be fought as necessary to gain entry to Leyte Gulf. Rear Admiral Koyanagi wrote that the apparition was "a heaven-sent opportunity" and "indeed a miracle." One senses that very little debate ensued as to whether or not to chase these aircraft carriers.

The Japanese commander had already made his first key error, however, and it could not be taken back. The previous afternoon, under pressure of all those air strikes, not knowing, due to communications problems aboard the *Zuikaku*, of Ozawa's success as a decoy off Cape Engaño, Kurita had made his turnaround in the Sibuyan Sea without informing his subordinate Nishimura. The latter consequently had never slowed his own fleet to conform to Kurita's timing. When Kurita finally sent a schedule dispatch, which was after Combined Fleet's fateful "divine assistance" message, Nishimura was already on his final approach and forged ahead anyway. Thus Kurita failed to coordinate with his subordinate, with the result that Kinkaid's Seventh Fleet was freed at an early hour to block the entrance to Leyte Gulf. It happens that Kinkaid's pursuit of the Nishimura-Shima remnants took him out of position to execute a quick blocking movement, but nevertheless Kurita's ideal would have been for the American admiral to be inextricably engaged at the moment the 1st Diversion Attack Force arrived off Samar.

Still, the situation at the instant of contact with the escort carriers offered the Japanese an unparalleled opportunity. For some hours before Kinkaid's fleet could come north or Halsey's south, Kurita could have his way. And the sportsman admiral had a big enough force to get his way, too. Despite the losses of the past days, Kurita still had four battleships, six heavy and two light cruisers, and ten destroyers. The Japanese had been preparing to change from the battle formation Kurita had assumed to fight his way through San Bernardino to a ring-shaped anti-aircraft defense for the final dash to Leyte, but the maneuver had not yet been executed. Thus, coincidentally, Kurita was already in battle order, with cruiser forces ahead and destroyer flotillas shielding his flanks (see Map 14).

Admiral Kurita was surprised to see American warships in front of him, but not as surprised as his adversaries. There were sixteen escort carriers in three groups; following American naval nomenclature the carriers were called units and all were part of the single "group" drawn from Task Force 77, the main strength of Kinkaid's Seventh Fleet. The escort carriers were Task Group 77.4. Furthest north was Task Unit 77.4.3, under Rear Admiral Clifton A. F. Sprague. "Ziggy" Sprague directly commanded escort carriers *Fanshaw Bay*, *St. Lo*, *White Plains*, and *Kalinin Bay*. Also attached was Carrier Division 26 (Rear Admiral Ralph A. Ofstie) with *Kitkun Bay* and *Gambier Bay.* Ofstie, one of the most experienced aviation officers in the U.S. Navy, also was a member of the prewar Tokyo naval Attachés' Club, having been air attaché from 1935 to 1937. He had gone up against Kurita before, as captain of fleet carrier *Essex* in the notorious Rabaul raids. For his part, Ziggy Sprague had been skipper of the oiler *Tangier* during those first desperate days of the war when the Wake Island relief attempt miscarried. These two admirals with their half-dozen Woolworth carriers, covered by three destroyers and four destroyer-escorts, became the main focus of Kurita's attention off Samar. Two more escort-carrier units, familiarly known as Taffys, 77.4.2 (Rear Admiral Felix B. Stump) and 77.4.1 (Rear Admiral Thomas L. Sprague), ranged farther to the south, escaped expeditiously. Some of the other Taffies carriers would be pursued by kamikazes, but Japanese warships only later became aware of them.

For Sprague and Ofstie of Taffy 3, however, it was another matter. They were the bull's-eye. Worse than that, their Woolworth carriers were 18-knot ships being chased by 32–34-knot Imperial Navy cruisers and 24–26-knot battleships, whose 8-, 14-, 16-, and 18-inch guns could wreck these unarmored ships with a single hit. The small carriers' planes might be able to inflict a certain amount of damage if the ships could survive long enough, for the planes aloft at sunrise were primarily fighters and scouts, and a strike against ships would have to be assembled and armed from scratch. Even then, however, Clifton Sprague could not hope to be as effective as any of Halsey's task groups, for his carriers had been armed for ground support and had neither strike aircraft in any great numbers nor antiship weapons such as torpedoes or armor-piercing bombs. Clifton Sprague's seven destroyers and destroyer-escorts could hardly hope to do more than delay the Japanese juggernaut.

The first intimation of danger came suddenly when Japanese voices were heard on the radio frequencies used to direct aircraft activities. Then sharp-eyed lookouts spotted puffs of smoke on the horizon that looked like anti-aircraft fire (Kurita's ships were shooting at the first planes they saw). After that, Ziggy Sprague's flagship, *Fanshaw Bay,* found ship returns on her radar scopes. It was 6:46 A.M. When Ensign Hans L. Jensen's Avenger, on routine antisubmarine patrol from the *Kadashan Bay* of Taffy 2, saw the Kurita fleet, it was one minute later.

Ziggy Sprague found it unbelievable that hostile ships would be in these waters and barked over *Fanshaw Bay*'s radio circuit that he wanted confirmation. William C. Brooks, a *St. Lo* pilot, confirmed that the warships had the pagodalike masts typical of Japanese vessels. Shortly afterward *Fanshaw Bay*'s lookouts could see that for themselves.

The Kurita fleet opened fire while still hull down at 6:58 A.M. A minute later shells began to pitch in the water close to Taffy 3 ships. The carrier sailors, unaccustomed to the chemical dyes used in large-caliber shells to distinguish fire from different ships, were surprised to see the pyrotechnics of danger. On the *White Plains* a sailor called out, "Hey, they're shooting at us in Technicolor!"

Two crucial decisions Admiral Kurita made at the very outset may be closely related to the mistaken identification of Taffy 3's ships. The first was Kurita's order for a southeast course. Often overlooked in favor of criticizing the fleet commander's tactical order, the course selection was made despite the fact that the wind was blowing from the east. This meant that as Japanese warships fired, and as they went to battle speed, their funnel and gun smoke would inevitably blow out between the various columns of Kurita's ships, obscuring their range and making gunlaying much more difficult. Even resort to radar-controlled gunfire ("Gunnery Method *Otsu*"), which Kurita was soon to order, did not eliminate this difficulty, particularly for torpedo craft. By contrast, had Kurita ordered a southwest course, in effect turning inside the U.S. ships rather than trying to work around them, the targets would have lain on the unobscured side of Kurita's fleet (and he would have been on the direct course for Leyte Gulf). It is very likely that Kurita ordered the course he did in an effort to hem in fast carriers before they could turn into the wind to launch aircraft, unaware that Taffy 3's slow escort carriers really did not pack that much punch. Against this threat, the direct course was preferable to reduce the range as quickly as possible, improving gunnery control and the probability of critical hits.

Admiral Kurita often receives criticism for his tactical order to make a "general attack," in effect releasing subordinate units to operate independently. This too has something to do with mistaken identity. The advantage of these tactics was that they permitted rapid combat action, desirable if the Americans were fast carriers that could outsteam the Japanese but not otherwise. In actuality the Woolworth carriers could not have escaped the Imperial Navy even if they had been fueled with nitroglycerin. In hot pursuit, Kurita's fleet quickly lost cohesion and became a more or less disorganized mob, not a disciplined force.

Hot-pursuit tactics meant the Japanese could not use the Long Lance torpedoes, one of their best weapons. Against fast carriers, chief of staff Koyanagi recounts, there would have been no point to torpedoes; numerous practice exercises had shown that fleet carriers could easily evade torpedo attack. Accordingly Kurita's orders relegated his flotillas to a passive role, following behind the racing cruiser divisions and battling behemoths. In reality the slow escort carriers were not very maneuverable and would have been easy victims for the speedy Japanese torpedoes, freeing Kurita's fleet to attack the next Taffy.

Mistaken identity also contributed to decisions made independently by gunnery officers on the Japanese ships which helped Taffy 3 survive the shock of combat. Figuring they were facing fast carriers, one or two battle-ships, and cruisers, many of the Japanese ships loaded armor-piercing shells, not high explosives. In more than one case, such shells actually hit American ships and went right through them without exploding, their fuses not activated by the thin skins of the targets. The Japanese believed in the big force, however. Even after the war, when he was in a position to know the truth, Rear Admiral Koyanagi wrote of an adversary with four or five fast carriers, one or two battleships, and at least ten heavy cruisers. Commander Otani Tonosuke, the fleet's operations staff officer, recalls that the battleships were first mentioned in the fourth or fifth update report by *Yamato*'s gunnery control. After that everyone was convinced such ships were really out there. Interrogated after the war, Koyanagi admitted that he himself never saw them.

In any case, battle had come and Taffy 3 would have to take its chances. Ziggy Sprague ordered his destroyers and escorts to lay smoke and his carriers to launch planes as quickly as possible, to harass the Japanese if not sink them. Planes flew off with whatever they were armed with—small bombs, rockets, even machine guns. At 7:07 Sprague radioed that he was under attack at a point eighty miles northeast of the entrance to Leyte Gulf, repeating the information fifteen minutes later with the addition of strength estimates for the Japanese and the news that they seemed to have divided into two units. Admiral Kinkaid instantly repeated the information to Halsey's Third Fleet.

The Kurita fleet meanwhile opened fire and began its chase. Lookouts aboard *Yamato* saw Taffy 3 turn away at 6:53, and Koyanagi followed by ordering Battleship Division 1's own course change. As the engagement became generalized, Kurita's chief of staff abandoned the Imperial Navy standard procedure of having the fleet commander personally direct the unit in which he was embarked. Vice Admiral Ugaki, who had become superfluous once the fleet commander transferred to his ship, was given back maneuver control of the division. Ugaki thought the initial response of the fleet had been slow due to uncertainty over Taffy 3's identity; now he tried to make up for lost time. The *Yamato*'s gunnery officer, Commander Nakagawa Toshio, opened fire at 6:59. Three minutes later Nakagawa confirmed the presence of six carriers, but at 7:09 they disappeared into a squall.

Aboard the other ship of Battleship Division 1, Rear Admiral Kobe Yuji's *Nagato*, preparations for a daytime action began almost an hour before. At 6:54 Kobe broke out the Imperial Navy battle ensign; three minutes later he warned the ship would engage to her port side. Gunnery officer Commander Inouye Takeo trained the ship's main battery out 25 degrees to that side; Inouye commenced fire at 7:01 with the range at more than 36,000 yards. Three minutes later he observed a hit on a carrier, but already the American destroyers were laying a smoke screen, and at 7:12 came the first of what became incessant air attacks. Three minutes after that the *Nagato* loosed a 16-inch salvo at a mere destroyer. Commander Inouye then ordered the ship's secondary guns to stand by for surface engagement.

Starting perhaps a mile to port of Ugaki's ships were the two vessels of Vice Admiral Suzuki Yoshio's Battleship Division 2. Leading his column was Rear Admiral Shimazaki Toshio's *Kongo*, which at 6:59 received *Yamato*'s flag signal to form Number 10 Battle Disposition, followed two minutes later by "Close enemy carriers and attack!"

At 7:00 A.M. precisely, according to *Kongo*'s action report, Kurita sent his first dispatch to Combined Fleet: "We are engaging enemy in gun battle."

At precisely the same moment, *Kongo* received her first air attack of the morning. Commander Noguchi Yutaka, gunnery officer, attempted to keep track of the surface targets and the air action at the same time, commencing fire at 26,500 yards after the battleship had settled onto an easterly course. Aircraft carriers seemed to disappear into a squall at 7:05. Fifteen minutes later a strafing aircraft disabled *Kongo*'s ten-meter rangefinder, and shortly after 7:30 Admiral Shimazaki would be forced into a port turn to evade torpedoes.

Rear Admiral Shigenaga Kazue's *Haruna* opened fire at 7:01, just a minute behind *Kongo*. Gunnery officer Commander Gondaira Masao used radar ranging, the first time this technique had ever been employed in combat by the Imperial Navy. Between smoke, squalls, and American air attacks (which began on the *Haruna* at 7:08), Gondaira checked fire after five salvos. Following almost twenty minutes of silence, *Haruna* resumed fire at 7:31 with secondary armament at a "cruiser," then a destroyer. Gondaira's 14-inch main battery opened again at 7:48 but got off just two salvos before the range was obscured. At 7:54 a report from *Kumano* gave a position for the Americans, and *Haruna* was able to pick out another "cruiser" as a target, again to starboard, loosing a 14-inch salvo at 8:02. Evidence suggests *Haruna*'s target at this stage may have been among Felix Stump's Taffy 2 warships.

Action by Japanese heavy cruisers also figured in the battle of Samar, as this segment of the Leyte engagement has come to be called. There were two heavy ships in Vice Admiral Hashimoto Shintaro's Cruiser Division 5, *Haguro* and *Chokai*. In Vice Admiral Shiraishi Kazutaka's Cruiser Division 7 were four vessels: *Kumano*, *Suzuya*, *Tone*, and *Chikuma*. These ships mounted a total of fifty-six 8-inch guns, their 5-inch secondary armament was as good as anything on Ziggy Sprague's escorts, and they had torpedoes too. Equally significant, unlike the Japanese battleships, these cruisers were just as fast as destroyers—they had the best chance to work around and cut off Taffy 3.

When the battle began, Shiraishi's 7th Division formed the wing of the

Japanese scouting force closest to Taffy 3 and consequently took the lead in the easterly chase that began. It was the luck of the draw that this admiral now led the pursuit, with Hashimoto falling into line behind him, for the latter had been an aggressive leader of flotillas while Shiraishi had made his mark as a staff type—as early as the 1920s he had been flag lieutenant to a senior admiral visiting Australia. When the war opened and right on through the Guadalcanal debacle, Shiraishi had been chief of staff to the Second Fleet commander. His last known seagoing command had been in 1940 as skipper of the cruiser *Kako.* With a cruiser division Shiraishi returned to the fleet to see the display of Allied power at Philippine Sea. Crossing the Sibuyan Sea just the day before this Samar battle, his flagship *Kumano* had been subjected to attack. Now the trapping of Taffy 3 depended upon this fifty-two-year-old native of Nagasaki who was a denizen of the hallways of power, not the quarterdecks of warships.

Division flagship *Kumano* under Captain Hitomi Soichiro was doing 24 knots at 6:55 A.M. when the cruisers first spotted the Americans. Engineer Commander Horiyama Sakae was ready to increase to 28 knots immediately and on twenty-minute notice for full speed. Admiral Shiraishi set a course to southeast, then south, then back to the southeast, warning his cruisers that the gunnery targets were carriers, ordering speed of 31 knots. The cruisers watched as the Japanese battleships successively opened fire; at 7:03 the *Yamato* signaled: "Cruiser divisions attack!"

Feverish preparations ensued. At 7:05 Shiraishi in succession radioed his cruisers: "We are closing enemy," then "Intend to engage to starboard." A minute later Kurita ordered destroyer flotillas to the rear. Shiraishi by now was headed almost due east at a recorded speed of 35 knots. The urgency of the affair is apparent in the fact that 32 knots was considered the standard for maximum practicable formation speed in the Imperial Navy.

At 7:10 the cruiser commander signaled his ships to open fire. Range to the Taffy 3 carriers was then measured at 20,000 yards. Almost simultaneously American planes began to harass the Japanese cruisers and hover around them like gnats around a horse. Shiraishi communicated with Hashimoto for the first time at 7:11, when the admiral told the other leader that Cruiser Division 7 had gone to maximum battle speed and was headed southeast. Captain Hitomi's ship observed an aircraft carrier on fire at 7:16, just after Sprague emerged from a squall. The observation was in error as no U.S. ship was hit in this stage of the action. By radio two minutes later Shiraishi ordered fire shifted to enemy light carriers that were making smoke. The *Kumano's* identification of the adversary as "light" carriers at 7:18 is the first time in the Japanese records that anyone seems to have realized the Americans were anything other than a task group of fleet carriers. Shiraishi never signaled this crucial information to Kurita, even though he was closest to the U.S. fleet, had been placed in the van for scouting purposes, and knew the value of such reports from his time on Second Fleet staff.

Destroyer flotillas were also accepted scouting forces in Japanese naval doctrine, and they, like Shiraishi's cruisers, had enough speed to close and see the Americans better. Here is revealed Kurita's folly in keeping his destroyers out of the engagement. It may well be that the fleet commander was influenced in this regard by the extent of attrition already suffered by the escort available. The years of destroyer losses facilitated by Allied intelligence had come home to roost. When Decisive Battle finally occurred, Japanese destroyer forces had become so weak they were incapable of conducting it.

Admiral Hashimoto's Cruiser Division 5 also had had its share of tribulations. In the Sibuyan Sea the day before, Hashimoto had lost his flagship. Transferring to *Haguro* he would have had but a single heavy cruiser left except that the slaughter of Kurita's own unit by submarines had orphaned the *Chokai*, which Kurita promptly attached to Hashimoto. That morning these cruisers' attention was first taken up by airplanes, but then they, too, saw masts on the horizon. Hashimoto went to 24 knots at 6:52, then ordered 26 two minutes later, and 30 at 6:57. Aboard *Haguro*, Captain Sugiura Kaju prepared to shoot at surface targets beginning at 6:54, received Kurita's orders to close and attack a few minutes afterward, and raised his battle ensign at 7:02.

The *Haguro* commenced fire at 7:05 with range estimated at 18,700 yards. Observers on the bridge thought the very first round scored a hit; like Shiraishi's lookouts, they may have mistaken ships making smoke for the effects of shell fire. In any case the cruiser quickly pumped out five salvos with twenty shells trying to straddle the Taffy 3 ships. American planes were on the *Haguro* in an instant, harassing her at every opportunity. American ships took a hand at 7:13 when a destroyer began to shoot at the *Haguro*, which was forced to rig for starboard gun action, only beginning to reply after two minutes, when Sugiura's main battery opened at 13,500 yards. There were heavy squalls, and *Haguro*'s gunners were hampered by a narrow field of vision, but they believed they saw hits beginning with the third salvo. Twenty-eight shells sped toward the target before a "cruiser" and another destroyer suddenly began firing too. The first target was thought to be damaged in her after section and listing sharply. The entire exchange took no more than five minutes.

According to Theodore Roscoe, historian of American destroyers at war, it was 7:20 when Commander Ernest E. Evans's ship, *Johnston*, made a dash at the Kurita fleet, loosing a full salvo of torpedoes. A cyclone of Japanese shells fell around as Evans kept up his fire, at ranges as short as 5,000 yards. Given the times that appear in Japanese records, it must have been *Johnston*'s torpedoes that smashed Shiraishi's flagship, *Kumano*. At 7:24 lookouts spot-

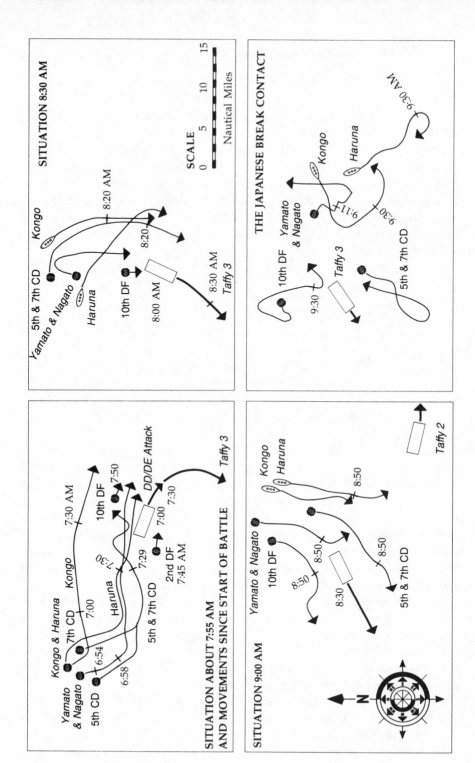

XV. Battle of Samar (October 25, 1944)

ted three torpedo tracks off the starboard bow. It was too late to evade. One torpedo hit, just forward of the number ten frame, severing the bow section of the cruiser. Though her engines remained entirely undamaged, Captain Hitomi's ship was instantly reduced to a mere 14 knots. Admiral Shiraishi ordered Captain Teraoka Masao's *Suzuya* to come alongside and take him aboard, but that cruiser's after fuel tanks had been ruptured by near misses from aircraft, contaminating 800 tons of fuel and limiting her speed to 24 knots. *Suzuya* would not be fully adequate but Shiraishi felt he had little choice. About 8:00 A.M. he went over on a cutter together with four officers, two attached officers, and two petty officers of his staff.

Meanwhile, with *Kumano* crippled and *Suzuya* told to stand by, Shiraishi ordered Captain Norimitsu Saiji of the *Chikuma* to assume temporary command of Cruiser Division 7. The most senior captain in the unit, though he happened to be in the third ship of the formation, Norimitsu quickly ordered remaining ships *Chikuma* and *Tone* to fire on destroyers to the southeast. Captain Mayuzumi Haruo's *Tone*, which had been engaging to starboard since 7:13, was already doing exactly that. Mayuzumi had one harrowing experience, which illustrated the dangers the Imperial Navy accepted in exchange for the superior performance of its oxygen-powered torpedoes. Immediately after he ordered a launch to starboard, a near miss ignited the oxygen flasks connected to the center and inner tubes of number three torpedo mount, setting fire to them. A young petty officer saved the ship by instantly launching the affected torpedoes before they could detonate. Moderately wounded, Mayuzumi was one of the *Tone*'s hundred casualties; the 419 rounds the main battery fired wore out half the ship's gun barrels and disabled both her radars and the sonar, all of which would have to be replaced.

Mayuzumi was among the luckier ones; Captain Norimitsu never came back. As the morning wore on the Japanese warships were increasingly subjected to air attacks, which became fiercer as the Americans dug into their magazines for proper antiship ordnance. The *Tone* eventually reached Brunei with a shell hit but four from bombs, plus three near misses to boot. Norimitsu's *Chikuma* completely disappeared, not to be heard from again; postwar records showed that Halsey's planes had sunk her as Task Force 38 raced back toward San Bernardino Strait. Crippled *Kumano* was attacked again and again, and at one point later in the day became unnavigable, but damage-control measures held up; she made it to Coron Bay, and then steamed to Manila at 10 knots. Admiral Shiraishi's last flagship, the *Suzuya*, never rejoined the formation; aircraft attacked her, too, so incessantly that the cruiser sank that afternoon. Destroyer *Okinami* rescued 415 sailors including Captain Teraoka, a submariner who ended up holding this command for less than two months, and Admiral Shiraishi, who was not again employed in a seagoing capacity.

The *Johnston*'s attack would quickly be followed by others. Destroyer-escort *Hoel* sallied toward the Kurita fleet a few minutes after her sister, and shortly thereafter Ziggy Sprague issued orders for all escorts to make smoke and form up for torpedo attacks. Roscoe credits *Hoel* with the hits that damaged *Kumano,* but this does not seem possible from comparison of the time she launched with the Japanese records. Historians generally credit the hit to *Johnston.* Destroyer *Heermann* made her sortie at 7:54, aiming torpedoes at both a cruiser and a battleship. Destroyer-escorts *Raymond* and *Dennis* also went toe-to-toe with the Japanese during the first critical hour of the surface engagement, saving their torpedoes until about the time *Heermann* launched hers.

Effects of the brave actions of the Taffy 3 escorts are evident. Cruiser leader Hashimoto's flagship, *Haguro,* repeatedly engaged American destroyers, "cruisers," even a presumed "heavy cruiser" during this period. On the latter target the main battery commenced fire at 7:46, when the American was at 10,400 yards on an opposite course, loosing four almost complete salvos (thirty-eight shells). *Haguro* claimed one or two hits on the last salvo, then more when she resumed fire later. Captain Sugiura's gunners claimed to have straddled a destroyer on the first salvo at about 7:55, and to have scored hits on a couple of carrier targets. But American shells hit the *Haguro,* setting afire the port-side launch, and then at 7:57 the cruiser observed two torpedo tracks passing astern.

Battleship *Haruna* engaged a "cruiser" at 7:34 and a destroyer a little over two minutes later, even using two salvos from her fourteen-inch main battery. Gunnery officer Gondaira found another "cruiser" target at 7:58 and resumed 14-inch fire. The *Haruna* was startled to record this *Yamato* signal at 7:56: "Watch out for torpedo tracks!"

Battleship *Nagato* actually saw them. Rear Admiral Kobe Yuji's vessel had been preoccupied by aircraft attacks, so much that anti-aircraft crews were authorized to fire at will. Then a sharp-eyed lookout saw three torpedo tracks to starboard. Admiral Kobe ordered the rudder hard over to port and had just enough time to evade them. The torpedo tracks passed along the starboard side of the *Nagato.* Six minutes later she began firing with both main and secondary batteries on a "cruiser" target at 9,400 yards.

On the flag bridge of *Yamato* the atmosphere had been very confident as the engagement opened. Asked afterward if commanders had thought the American force could be eliminated, fleet operations officer Otani replied, "We didn't think we'd have much trouble. We were very powerful." But confusion continued as to the identity of the Americans. Commander Otani and others were at first convinced they faced fleet carriers, but what they could see did not correspond to the photographs in their identification books. Some speculated the Americans must be auxiliary carriers, but that did not accord with the seeming inability of the Japanese warships to catch up, from which senior officers concluded the Americans must be retreating at 30 knots. In addition, there were doubts as to strength—gunnery control reported a second group of U.S. ships (Taffy 2) beyond the first, but those on the bridge could see nothing of it. Otani also complained, "We had poor communication with our cruisers and couldn't see what they were doing."

Again and again the bridge and Commander Nakagawa's optic range finder on the ship's fighting top differed in their assessments of the opposing fleet, the persistent attacks of American escorts, and the damage done to Taffy 3's Woolworth carriers. This was not only true of the *Yamato*. Every Japanese battleship and many of the cruisers repeatedly claimed hits, damage, and even sinking of American escort carriers long before 7:50, when escort carrier *Kalinin Bay* incurred the first known hit on any of the small flattops. Smoke laid by the American ships played a big part in Japanese confusion. "The smoke was made very quickly," Otani recalled, "and the use of smoke was skillful." Admiral Kurita made an exception to Japanese naval practice because his chief of staff, Koyanagi, was not familiar with handling large gunnery ships in combat. Kurita therefore asked Ugaki to direct both the movements and fire of his Battleship Division 1.

It was Admiral Ugaki in control, therefore, when torpedo tracks were sighted to starboard at 7:54. That triggered *Yamato*'s torpedo warning, which also helped save *Nagato*, and the flagship heeled under hard left rudder, combing the torpedoes. The choice of direction was exceedingly poor, however, since it put the *Yamato* on a course parallel to the torpedoes and unable to deviate though she was headed directly away from the Americans. With torpedoes parallel to her on both sides the *Yamato* did not dare turn back south. This went on for a full ten minutes. Turning toward the torpedoes rather than away from them, which would have put *Yamato* in hot pursuit of her quarry, or reducing speed temporarily to let the tin fish outrun the superbattleship, would have been far preferable tactical choices. Ugaki Matome's diary reveals him as outspoken in his criticism of other officers' tactics, but his actions at the battle of Samar put his own skills in a very poor light.

Once the fleet flagship was able to come around to the south-southeast, *Yamato* found herself over 30,000 yards from the American ships, with the latter invisible behind smoke and squalls. The flagship lost even more time by stopping to launch her number two floatplane in an effort to regain contact. Such scouting, of course, was futile in airspace dominated by desperate American aircraft, and after less than twenty minutes radio messages from the plane ceased, never to resume.

Small wonder Kurita Takeo, despite his fleet's superior surface capability, had even less understanding of the situation an hour into the engagement than he had had at the beginning of it. Determined to achieve results in the face of the enforced idleness of his flagship, as the *Yamato* wore around to the north Admiral Kurita sent a single message, first by radio, then by flag signal. The result was to scatter and disorganize his fleet even more. Kurita signaled: "Attack!" An American translator later noted that the same ideograph could be rendered as "Charge!"

PLENTY OF PEOPLE LISTENED THAT DAY, COMMANDERS TO THEIR RADIOS, ENEMIES TO THEIR radio intelligence experts, trying to learn what had happened off Samar. Radio conditions, coincidentally, were very good, and a number of the messages that passed between Kinkaid and Halsey, or between Kurita and Combined Fleet, also informed others on both sides. On the American side the information went straight up the chain of command to President Roosevelt's Map Room at the White House. Interested bystanders at the Navy Department included Secretary of the Navy James S. Forrestal, Navy chief Ernest J. King, and the men and women of OP-20-G. At Pearl Harbor Admiral Nimitz and all his staff, including JICPOA, awaited the outcome breathlessly, as did Japanese naval staffs at Tokyo and Hiyoshi.

Mobile radio units were perhaps the first to learn anything useful. The 7910J radio circuit was active from very early in the morning, and at 8:03 A.M. (Philippine time) monitors overheard a Kurita order: "Crudiv 5 and Crudiv 7 attack!" The intelligence was of obvious importance to sailors of Taffy 3. On Guam, where Nimitz would soon move with a CINCPAC advanced headquarters and where a large new radio facility was being set up to support that command, radiomen also listened in. Albert M. Fishburn was one, having been moved up from Midway to Kwajalein, now to Guam. The day was unusual because the intercept station, about to relocate from temporary to permanent quarters, tried to remain in action nevertheless. Thus Fishburn found himself manning a radio working off batteries in the back of a big Marine truck. It was unnerving because Japanese soldiers left over from the island battle were still conducting guerrilla actions. Even though the radiomen carried carbines, here they were being asked to work completely in the open. The truck was like an oven, too. Fishburn worked the 7910J circuit that day. "It just operated all day long," he recalled. "It was just one ship after another."

Intelligence reports from Guam and the frontline fleet units provided grist for the mills of JICPOA and OP-20-G. Traffic analysis at FRUPAC on October 24 showed Ozawa, Shima, and Kurita all in Philippine waters. Other specific intercepts solved that day or the next included news of Kurita under air attack, cruiser *Kumano* unable to make way (with position conveniently provided), sighting reports on Taffy 3, and positions of Japanese submarines in nearby seas. There was also a mistaken report associating cruiser *Ashigara* with Kurita's fleet. Jasper Holmes at JICPOA found CINCPAC staff following the action tensely. "On the morning of the twenty-fifth," he later wrote, "I eagerly searched the Estimate Section's copies of these messages, reading victory in every dispatch, until I encountered the escort carriers' astounding report of being under gunfire from Japanese battleships."

Commander Holmes telephoned fleet intelligence officer Layton to ask the whereabouts of Task Force 34, Admiral Lee's mighty battleship unit of the Halsey fleet. Holmes assumed that Bull Halsey had left Ching Lee behind to guard the San Bernardino Strait. Captain Layton felt that unless Third Fleet had sent some message to that effect, Halsey had done no such thing. Their conversation paralleled others at CINCPAC headquarters. Admiral Nimitz knew Halsey had issued a battle plan that provided for detaching Task Force 34, but there was nothing to indicate Halsey had actually done so. Some officers argued that Admiral Halsey might have sent his execute orders out on short-range TBS radio, but when emergency appeals began to arrive from Kinkaid, doubts soared at Pearl Harbor. Nimitz resisted sending any message that might be construed as interfering with his tactical commanders' handling of their forces, but as the appeals kept coming, and particularly after Halsey signaled that he was sending McCain's Task Group 38.1 to help while he fought Ozawa with his other groups, Nimitz concluded that the battleship unit could not be anywhere near Samar or Halsey would have ordered it to attack.

Deputy chief of staff Captain Bernard Austin suggested that Halsey simply be asked where the battleships were. Nimitz finally approved. A dispatch with this simple question went to Jack Redman's communications apparatus, where a radioman caught the emphasis on the question by repeating its operative phrase. Finally the ensign who encoded it added "padding"— words at beginning and end that were designed to frustrate cryptanalysts. In this case the wording, possibly drawn from Alfred, Lord Tennyson's poem "The Charge of the Light Brigade," set during the 1853–1856 Crimean War (the charge had also occurred on October 25), sounded too much like an integral part of the message. When the dispatch arrived aboard Third Fleet flagship *New Jersey* it was handled just that way, and read: WHERE IS REPEAT WHERE IS TASK FORCE THIRTY-FOUR. THE WORLD WONDERS.

Admiral William Halsey was incensed that his tactical judgment should be questioned in this fashion. The Bull tore the baseball cap from his head and threw it on the deck with a few choice words. He had begun activating the battleship unit to pursue Ozawa, but responded to the implied criticism by ordering Ching Lee back to Philippine waters with carrier groups to follow. That move permitted the escape of Ozawa's remaining warships.

Had Halsey known who else was listening he might have been more resigned to the actions he had to take. In Washington, copies of most of these operational cables routinely went to the White House, where they were scanned for important news by officers at the Map Room. At about dinnertime of the twenty-fourth (Washington time) the Map Room heard about a most unusual message sent to Halsey in *plain language,* not encoded in any way:

ENEMY FORCES ATTACKING OUR [escort carriers] COMPOSED OF FOUR BATTLESHIPS, EIGHT CRUISERS AND X OTHER SHIPS. REQUEST LEE PROCEED TOP SPEED COVER LEYTE. REQUEST IMMEDIATE STRIKE BY FAST CARRIERS.

Though Map Room officials wrongly assumed the originator of this dispatch to be Vice Admiral Daniel Barbey, the amphibious landing commander, not Seventh Fleet commander Kinkaid, they instantly felt that President Roosevelt would want to know. The message was retyped as part of a briefing note to FDR—a very unusual procedure for a president who most often took oral reports or was simply handed message flimsies.

President Roosevelt was interested enough to have further briefing notes prepared as the night wore on and reports reached Washington. Some briefing notes were never sent up to FDR because he had already scanned the messages on which they were based. The Map Room also prepared a summary chronology of events culled from the message traffic of October 22–26. Again, this was highly unusual reporting.

FDR made no public statement on these private reports.

At the Navy Department there were also observers breathlessly awaiting the reports. Japanese translator Edward Van Der Rhoer of OP-20-GZ, the translation section of the staff, remembers that his unit had begun to chart the progress of the various Japanese naval forces on a map as they neared Leyte. The codebreaking unit had now grown so large (about 4,500 in Washington alone) that it had had to move to the converted Mount Vernon Seminary at the confluence of Nebraska and Massachusetts avenues in the northwest section of the city. There, behind double fences and stringent security precautions, Japanese and other codes were broken. Redfield Mason continued in charge of the GZ translation section, and decrypts completed there formed the basis for the COMINCH daily radio intelligence summaries. These suggest that knowledge in Washington cannot have been as complete as is claimed by Mason's subordinate Van Der Rhoer. The October 25 summary reads:

> Intercepted Japanese traffic reflected widespread U.S. aircraft, surface, and submarine attacks against Japanese forces. Counter-measures by Japanese surface forces against U.S. forces were also indicated, but details are few. Contact with U.S. forces off Luzon apparently was maintained throughout the day.

Summary language in the October 26 report shows the battle to have already passed:

An extraordinarily heavy file of operational traffic on the major Japanese fleet channel, which began about [3:00 P.M., October 24], continued to dominate intercepted Japanese traffic throughout the 25th. Traffic reflected numerous aircraft sighting reports of U.S. surface forces and at least one report indicated that a Japanese surface force was under air attack near the entrance to Leyte Gulf on the morning of the 26th. Details of actions continue meager, although some new damage to Japanese forces is indicated.

Tanker watching had served OP-20-G and JICPOA very well in the run up to Leyte, providing indications of Imperial Navy movements and concentration for battle, but radio intelligence did not do as well during the engagement itself as it had in some other Pacific battles.

The big difference in October 1944 was that the U.S. fleet had become so strong it could win through despite the intelligence, in the face of surprise and Japanese determination. Rosie Mason may not have been able to tell Ernie King exactly what was happening, and COMINCH would also be plagued by garbled and incomplete reporting in operational channels, but the Navy felt confident enough that Admiral King appeared with Secretary Forrestal the afternoon of the Samar battle for a press conference to mark a major defeat for the enemy.

Tokyo's picture would be somewhat the reverse. As already noted, the Combined Fleet had been greatly hampered by Admiral Toyoda's trip to Manila, forcibly extended when he was caught on Taiwan by Halsey's carrier raids. Even afterward, returning to headquarters proved much more difficult than anticipated. Bad weather forced Toyoda's plane to land on Kyushu, short of his goal. He took off from Omura Air Base before dawn on October 20 and reached Hiyoshi about 9:00 that morning. His thirteen-day absence prevented Combined Fleet from adhering to a consistent policy—witness the difficulties over employment of the Shima force. Intelligence reports continued spotty, and operational reporting once the Japanese forces began battle became as bad, as Toyoda averred under interrogation after the war: "At the time I did not have and Combined Fleet Headquarters did not have information regarding the details of the engagement."

As at Pearl Harbor, Hiyoshi became rapt with excitement when, early in the morning of the twenty-fifth, a 1st Diversion Attack Force dispatch announced the sighting of masts of ships off Samar. A few minutes later Kurita added that he was opening fire at three aircraft carriers. Hiyoshi was delirious—Kusaka remembers staff officers all but standing on their heads. It seemed a golden opportunity, the true Decisive Battle; this was the largest adversary force drawn into a surface battle since the beginning of the war. Such a view was possible only because of mistaken identification, a direct consequence of the larger Japanese failure to emphasize or utilize their intelligence effectively. Admiral Kurita did nothing to dispel the pipe dreams at

7:30, when he reported being engaged against six aircraft carriers, three of which he classed as "regular carriers." Other reports before 8:00 claimed sinking of an American "cruiser" and one of the carriers. Additional information came from the Owada Communications Group, of which more presently.

In truth the hour between 8:00 and 9:00 would be the closest the Americans came to "defeat" at Leyte Gulf. During this hour the Kurita fleet began to make good on its speed advantage, and toward the end of it the flotillas were ordered into action. Once it was over Ugaki's Battleship Division 1 would be only about a dozen miles from Taffy 3, and Hashimoto with the remaining heavy cruisers barely more than five. Battleships *Kongo* and *Haruna* even took off in pursuit of Rear Admiral Stump's Taffy 2.

The evolution of the situation can be glimpsed quite graphically in the increasingly frenzied tone of Kinkaid's dispatches. At 7:35 A.M.:

UNDER ATTACK . . . ENEMY COMPOSED OF FOUR BATTLESHIPS, EIGHT CRUISERS, MANY DESTROYERS SPLIT IN TWO FORCES . . .

At 7:39:

FAST BATTLESHIPS ARE URGENTLY NEEDED IMMEDIATELY AT LEYTE GULF.

Then, at 8:29:

MY SITUATION IS CRITICAL. FAST BATTLESHIPS AND SUPPORT BY AIR STRIKE MAY BE ABLE PREVENT ENEMY FROM DESTROYING [escort carriers] AND ENTERING LEYTE.

If Kinkaid had not chased the Nishimura-Shima forces down Surigao Strait he would not have been in quite so serious a position, although Taffy 3 remained at risk regardless, since it would necessarily take a certain amount of time for Task Force 77 surface forces to debouch from Leyte Gulf. Kinkaid's battleships were at further disadvantage because they held low inventories of armor-piercing projectiles (less useful than high explosives in beach bombardments) and had expended many of those at Surigao Strait. The net effect was that there was no heavy cover for the Taffy units. Admiral Ernest J. King held this against Kinkaid afterward, seeing him, even more than Halsey, as responsible for Kurita's passage through San Bernardino.

Whether the error was Kinkaid's or Halsey's, it was the Taffy that paid the price. Kurita's charge bore down relentlessly upon them. At 8:05, according to *Kishinami*'s report, destroyers of the 2nd Flotilla at last were close enough to fire. A half hour later the ships of 10th Destroyer Flotilla joined the fray. The *Haruna* opened up at almost 36,000 yards when she saw Taffy 2 to the southeast at 8:10. Both Admiral Suzuki's battleships subsequently chased the new target formation. The *Kongo* and *Yamato* both claimed sinking one of Taffy 3's carriers a quarter hour later, with *Kongo*, in another of those misidentifications that plagued the Japanese, calling the vessel an *Enterprise*-class (fleet) carrier. Between 8:42 and 8:52 Captain Sugiura's heavy cruiser, *Haguro*, also claimed sinking a carrier with seventy-eight rounds of shell fire. The target first listed sharply to starboard; then the Japanese cruiser's sixteenth salvo hit the bow, amidships, *and* the after section, upon which the carrier virtually disintegrated.

Though not precisely accurate, Japanese log entries do convey the flavor of the event. Admiral Clifton Sprague published an account of the battle a few months later with the apt title "The Japs Had Us on the Ropes." In fact after 7:50, when the *Kalinin Bay* suffered her first hit, Imperial Navy gunners more and more often got the range and scored, while Taffy 3's escorts had expended their torpedoes, their best weapon against the more numerous, more capable adversary. *Fanshaw Bay* took four 8-inch hits and had two more near misses. *Gambier Bay*, first hit at 8:10, was so battered she had to be abandoned forty minutes later. She was most likely the carrier referred to in *Haguro*'s report. A photograph of *Gambier Bay* under attack shows a big ship on the horizon which looks very much like the *Haguro*. The Woolworth carriers *Kitkun Bay* and *St. Lo* were remarkably lucky—repeatedly straddled by Japanese salvos with spreads as narrow as twenty-five yards, neither ship was hit at all. Also very lucky was *White Plains*, lightly damaged by a miss early in the action that turned out to be the worst she got. Among the escorts, destroyers *Hoel* and *Johnston* were sent to the bottom and destroyer-escort *Samuel B. Roberts* sank from damage a few hours later, while most of the other Taffy 3 escorts were hurt to a greater or lesser degree.

Thus, by 9:00 the future looked very bleak for Ziggy Sprague and Task Unit 77.4.3. The combat power of his escort forces had peaked and was in decline, his little carriers could go no faster than before, and the Japanese were catching up at last. Sprague's auxiliary carriers had begun to accumulate damage; their chances were diminishing by the minute. At 9:05 the Takao Communications Unit in Taiwan intercepted a plain-language transmission, repeated by Allied radios in the Admiralties appealing for help, a message very similar in content to Kinkaid's 8:29 dispatch. This transmission was also picked up by the Owada Group, which circulated it among Japanese receivers at 9:24. It did look as if Taffy 3 was on the ropes after all. Help from Kinkaid's battleships remained hours away, while Vice Admiral Lee's Task Force 34 was even farther away than that.

At 9:11 Vice Admiral Kurita recalled all units, ordering them to re-form on the Battleship Division 1 column, which he turned due north. Kurita now headed *away* from Leyte Gulf and permitted the escape of Taffy 3.

Of the many controversies that swirl around the Leyte battles, that over Kurita's decision is probably the sharpest. Kurita's orders went out as the fleet was on the verge of success. For example, Rear Admiral Kimura's 10th Destroyer Flotilla, after its leader *Yahagi* shot up the *Samuel B. Roberts*, had begun maneuvering for a torpedo attack on Sprague's remaining escort carriers. When the regrouping order came, Kimura decided to go ahead and execute the attack, which he did between 9:15 and 9:23, launching at least sixteen torpedoes from four destroyers. (The exact number is not known because one of them, *Nowake*, would be sunk the next day by American cruisers mopping up after the big battle.) The *Yahagi* reported one "regular carrier" sunk and one damaged. Others thought they saw three carriers and a "cruiser" enveloped in black smoke and sinking. In fact there were no results at all. Kimura's perseverance seemed commendable in one respect, but it would have adverse effects as well.

One element in Kurita's decision may have been the persistent American aircraft attacks; they had been going on throughout this period, but the planes were now arriving armed for combat against heavy ships. Shortly before 9:00 the *Chikuma* lost her rudder to a torpedo-plane attack, and *Chokai*, too, suffered a torpedo hit, which disabled her engines. Both heavy cruisers would be in Davy Jones's locker before the day was out—the *Chokai* scuttled because she could not be towed, the *Chikuma* finished off by U.S. aircraft as she fled the scene. These cruiser losses (even though the ships remained afloat at 9:11 A.M.) may have demoralized Kurita, who had suffered numerous losses on his way to Leyte and had had *Suzuya* and *Kumano* already put out of action that morning. Misidentification may have played a role, too, since Kurita was acutely aware of his own losses, while the repeated reports of American "cruisers" began to make it seem that Taffy 3 could be as strong as he was. (At 8:22 the *Yamato* herself had recorded seeing a "battleship.")

What was happening to Kurita's cruisers also put the admiral on notice that the numerous reports of sinking American "regular carriers" did not seem to be leading to any diminution in the air attacks. If anything the raids were growing in ferocity and strength.

Rear Admiral Koyanagi offers additional perspective on Kurita's crucial decision. The long interval during which the Kurita fleet had continued a stern chase of the Americans suggested that Ziggy Sprague's ships were indeed making high speed—the 30 knots of fast carriers, not the 18 knots of Woolworth carriers. Since *Japanese* fuel supplies were limited, such a high-speed chase could not be continued indefinitely. Moreover, the *Nagato* was only capable of 24 knots, so if the Americans really could make more speed than that, there would be no catching them. It was not until after the war that responsible Japanese officers learned there had been no fast carriers off Samar on October 25, 1944.

Recounting these events, Koyanagi wrote:

> Giving up the pursuit when we did amounted to losing a prize already in hand. If we had known the types and number of enemy ships, and their speed, Admiral Kurita would never have suspended the pursuit, and we would have annihilated the enemy. Lacking this vital information, we concluded that the enemy had already made good his escape.

This reasoning does not account for the fact that the identity of the Taffy 3 carriers, as least as far as type was concerned, was readily available to observers trained in ship identification. Koyanagi's analysis really stands as an indictment of Japanese naval intelligence. His conclusion—"In the light of the circumstances, I still believe that there was no alternative to what we did"—obscures the intelligence failure.

Admiral Kurita himself referred specifically to air attacks in telling interrogators why he broke off contact at 9:11 A.M. The small raids by one or a few planes seemed to have dropped off, Kurita recalled, so "I . . . thought that there would be later on—perhaps an hour later—a large formation attack. Therefore I ordered the formation to close." Kurita intended to head back southwest and enter Leyte after re-forming. However, he could as easily have reconstituted his formation while heading *toward* Leyte, and in fact a northerly heading meant it would take longer for certain ships, such as *Yahagi* and her destroyers, or the remaining cruisers, or *Kongo* and *Haruna*, to rejoin. Moreover, Kurita held to the northerly course even after 9:40, when he learned from Southwest Area Fleet of the plain-language distress calls broadcast by the Americans.

When interrogated after the war, Kurita himself made no mention of the fuel argument. That objection was directly met by fleet operations officer Otani. "We were low on fuel," Commander Otani declared; "*this was not critical* but we were low." (My italics.) Otani put the fuel issue last on his list of reasons for the turn away from Leyte. Others were the Japanese beliefs that considerable results had already been achieved and that the Kurita fleet was much delayed on its schedule; the fear that the fleet would be subjected to land-based air attack inside the gulf; the probability of a surface attack there from Kinkaid's fleet; the expectation of a reinforcement unit approaching from the Halsey fleet; and the thought that by this time most amphibious ships would have escaped.

A sighting report from Southwest Area Fleet then furnished Kurita a new target, a supposed task force to the southwest, and he maintained that heading. In one of the mysteries of Leyte Gulf, Kurita chased a phantom task force and even claimed at one point to have seen masts on the horizon. During this interval he received the Owada and Takao units' intercept reports on the American emergency messages, which did not deter him from his new object. This was the estimate of the situation in Kurita's after-action report:

> Until about [noon], we were determined to carry out the plan to pene-trate into Leyte Gulf in spite of repeated enemy air attacks. . . . The enemy was . . . concentrating its carrier-based air strength at Tacloban and together with its surface task force, was disposing itself to counter the pen-etration into Leyte which it anticipated. Its preparation to intercept our force apparently was complete whereas we could not even determine the actual situation in Leyte Gulf. Moreover, in view of what happened to the [Nishimura force], it seemed not unlikely that we would fall into an enemy trap, were we to persist in our attempt at penetration. The wiser course was deemed to be to cross the enemy's anticipation by striking at his task force which had been reported in position [slightly east of north] distance 113 miles from Suluan light at [9:45]. We believed that [to] turn about, proceed northward in search of this element would prove to be to our advantage.

So at 11:50 A.M. Admiral Kurita set out after the phantom task force, for-mally abandoning the Leyte plan at 12:36. Kurita informed Combined Fleet that he had sunk three or four aircraft carriers and two heavy cruisers.

In an interview with Japanese naval historian Ito Masanori after the war, Admiral Kurita remarked that he had come to question his decision to aban-don the SHO mission. "My mind was extremely fatigued," Kurita related. "It should probably be called a 'judgment of exhaustion.' I did not feel tired at the time but, under great strain and without sleep for three days and nights, I was exhausted both physically and mentally." Accustomed to making his own choices once staff assembled the facts, Admiral Kurita held no meeting prior to these decisions. Soon after 1:00 P.M., reasoning that any effort now to close in on an alerted carrier task force would prove futile, Kurita aban-doned his new objective and set a course to pass through the San Bernardino Strait.

At Hiyoshi and Tokyo there could have been intervention to set Kurita back on track. After all, something like that had been done just the previous day. Hiyoshi, convinced that Ozawa's decoy maneuver had succeeded, also did not believe Halsey's Third Fleet could move back in time to obstruct Kurita. And the high commanders were well aware of the Owada Group's reports, which gave a vivid impression of Allied desperation. Like Nimitz, however, Admiral Toyoda did not wish to interfere in tactical commanders' business. Toyoda did not think he could make good decisions for a localized battle area thousands of miles from fleet headquarters. Another argument Toyoda makes in his memoirs—that he did not consider Leyte such a large naval engagement anyway—was clearly for public consumption. Chief of staff Kusaka was more forthright, admitting that he wished Kurita had rushed into Leyte, but also that Hiyoshi was ignorant of the local situation. Thus despite the Owada intercepts, Combined Fleet hesitated to send orders. It finally composed a dispatch that more or less merely reminded Kurita of the mission (to penetrate Leyte "if possible"), but by that time it was too late.

Kurita sent one dispatch reaffirming an intention to penetrate the gulf, but then advised of his desire to seek out the phantom task force. Late that afternoon Naval General Staff chief Admiral Oikawa Koshiro sent a morale-building dispatch reporting Emperor Hirohito's deep satisfaction at the battle results, specifically including those of the Kurita fleet. The next morning Admiral Toyoda ordered ships capable of repair at Singapore to head for that place, while heavily damaged vessels should make for Empire waters. If necessary, emergency repairs could be done at Hong Kong or Keelung.

In public statements the tone would be very different. The newspaper *Asahi Shimbun* commented on October 26:

> The fact that the United States Navy has suffered two successive defeats of the greatest magnitude in less than two weeks . . . indicates either [that there is] a complete lack of ability and recklessness . . . or [that] some factor other than strategic is dictating the conduct of the enemy's recent operations.

Radio Tokyo had fulsome praise for the Japanese Navy:

> The Imperial fleet, which patiently held back its desire to engage in battle in order to pile training upon training, had finally been given the chance to manifest its power. The Imperial fleet saw an opportune moment to deal a death blow upon the enemy fleet and boldly and fearlessly sailed out to challenge a battle with the main strength of the enemy fleet.

That much of the broadcast was actually correct, but then the announcer continued: "Japanese forces now have complete air and sea superiority on and around Leyte." Japanese soldiers and sailors, under fierce air attacks while trying to run convoys into Ormoc on Leyte, must have been surprised to hear this. The truth was that the battle of Leyte was over and Japan had lost it. What followed would be nothing less than the final destruction of the Imperial Navy.

# The Last of the
# Imperial Navy

A N END TO JAPANESE AMBITIONS AT LEYTE GULF DID NOT HALT THE PHILIPPINE CAMPAIGN, which had just begun and would become a fearsome maelstrom. Sailors with the fatally delayed Imperial Army counterlanding project, airmen with the new kamikaze units, and other surface and submarine sailors kept struggling, perhaps harder than ever, but fighting a kind of broken-backed war. This was not immediately apparent, especially to the fired-up kamikaze pilots at Mabalacat, Cebu, and Davao, who added to the Leyte Gulf toll on October 25 by finishing off escort carrier *St. Lo* and damaging others from both Ziggy Sprague's and Felix Stump's task units. In the first flush of success the special attack corps redoubled its efforts. Kamikaze attack became a staple of the Philippine and subsequent campaigns.

Misidentification continued to bedevil the Japanese, not least the kamikazes. During the course of the campaign, special attack units claimed sinking five fleet carriers, two battleships or cruisers, and five (positively identified) cruisers. According to U.S. records only two escort carriers and three destroyers went down. The second of the Woolworth carriers, *Ommaney Bay*, hit on January 3, 1945, did not actually sink but was so badly damaged the Americans scuttled her the next day. Indeed, damage remained the most frequent end result of kamikazes which struck their targets (only a small proportion did so). Vessels damaged included seven fleet, two light, and thirteen escort carriers; five battleships; three heavy and seven light cruisers; and twenty-three destroyers, plus other ships. Kamikaze claims were accurate on the numbers of damaged cruisers and battleships, but greatly *understated* damage to carriers and destroyers. In the

Philippine campaign the Japanese sent out 421 planes on special attack missions, expending 378 of them, while 137 of 230 fighters sent to escort kamikazes also failed to return.

The Japanese submarine effort bears mention. The Sixth Fleet formed available subs into three groups for operating areas in the Philippine Sea. Boats *I-26, I-45, I-54,* and *I-56* had all left Kure before October 15. Admiral Miwa Shigeyoshi rushed to ready more for sea, and especially to equip them with radar sets, newly available in the submarine force. Despite the equipment, losses were heavy: Half the boats sent out failed to return. This included four of the five boats stationed closest to Leyte Gulf. One of them, Lieutenant Commander Kondo Fumitake's *I-41,* claimed credit for sinking an *Essex*-class carrier, for which she was nominated for first-class battle honors, but she had actually merely damaged light cruiser *Reno.* Though submariner Orita Zenji maintained that Kondo's sub was lost in Ormoc Bay on November 28, Japanese records list the *I-41* as not heard from after November 13, and other U.S. records hold that the boat was sunk by aircraft and a destroyer-escort cooperating east of Samar on November 18.

The other sub nominated for first-class battle honors during this period would be Commander Morinaga Masahiko's *I-56,* which sailed from Kure on October 15 and returned November 4. Assigned a patrol area east of Mindanao, Morinaga, a destroyer man who had switched to submarines, was like a shepherd turned poacher. He reported getting in among a convoy to sink a large transport on October 24, sinking an escort carrier (correctly identified as "*Island*-class") and a destroyer on October 25, and three medium transports two days later. Though right about his target, the *Santee* of Taffy 1, Morinaga erred on his result. The *Santee* proved very resilient that day, for she was hit not only by Morinaga's torpedo but by a kamikaze. Despite all the damage, she was making almost her full speed just a couple of hours later. William T. Y'Blood, who has made the most detailed study of the escort carriers, reports that *I-56*'s torpedo glanced off the ship's side before exploding some distance away. That may have saved the *Santee.* Morinaga himself immediately came under attack by a destroyer and aircraft. Pilots claimed to have seen the submarine explode, but Morinaga in fact lived on to become chief of staff of Japan's postwar navy, the Maritime Self-Defense Force.

Of the four Sixth Fleet subs stationed off northern Samar and the San Bernardino Strait, waters frequented by Task Force 38, none reported any battle result and all returned safely—three to Maizuru, the other to Kure. By mid-November, Admiral Miwa believed the Sixth Fleet had accounted for three aircraft carriers, seven destroyers, and at least five cargo ships. American records confirm only the *Santee* and *Reno* damage plus the sinking of destroyer-escort *Eversole* on October 28.

Meanwhile plenty of other Japanese sailors were trying to get away from the Leyte area just as quickly as possible. Many did not make it. American aviators finished off cruisers *Suzuya* and *Noshiro* of the Kurita fleet, plus *Mogami* and *Abukuma* of the forces that had been in Surigao Strait. The *Nachi* reached Manila, only to be caught there by aircraft on November 5. Admiral Kurita returned to Brunei. The *Haguro* went to Singapore, joined there later by *Ashigara*, to reinforce the *Takao* of the 3rd Southern Expeditionary Fleet. Vessels in good condition concentrated there or at Camranh Bay in French Indochina; cripples made their painful way to Empire waters.

A particular fate would be reserved for Captain Kato Kenkichi of the *Musashi* and 1,275 other seamen who survived the end of that superbattleship. To plunk all these sailors down somewhere risked a breach of the secrecy surrounding the big ships, not to mention disclosure of the sinking of the *Musashi*, which would be a blow to the morale of a navy that regarded her as unsinkable. The solution? The survivors were segregated on Corregidor and formed into something called the Kato regiment, a naval infantry unit. One contingent, 420 in number, was put aboard a transport for Taiwan in late November, but a U.S. submarine torpedoed the vessel en route; only 370 *Musashi* survivors survived the second sinking. In Japan they were placed in virtual imprisonment on a small islet in the Inland Sea. Another group of 200 technical specialists went aboard light carrier *Junyo*, freshly repaired after damage at Philippine Sea. American submarine *Redfish*, acting on Ultra information, torpedoed *Junyo* east of Nagasaki several days into her cruise. The *Junyo* was towed to Sasebo, where she moored, inactive and unrepaired, through the end of the war. The *Musashi* crewmen immediately moved to Kure and were sequestered in the barracks of the naval paratroop regiment. Back in the Philippines, 146 men of the Kato unit were sent to help defend Manila; 117 of them perished or went missing in action.

Counterlandings on Leyte were a feature of the Japanese effort which, as at Guadalcanal, *had* to work if the battle was to be won. The original counterlanding had entangled Combined Fleet plans for the SHO operation, but eventually went forward anyway. In anticipation of a troop escort mission, Rear Admiral Sakonju Naomasa brought his Cruiser Division 16 up to Manila. Just before entering the bay flagship *Aoba* was torpedoed, forcing Sakonju to shift the command pennant to Captain Kawasaki Harumi's light cruiser *Kinu*. Next day Admiral Mikawa ordered Sakonju to escort Army reinforcements to Leyte, and organized a convoy of five transports. Sakonju sent one of his staff officers ahead to make arrangements to join up with the transports.

The operation proceeded without a hitch until the troops landed at Ormoc, on the opposite side of Leyte from where the Americans were going ashore. Completing the unloading shortly before dawn, October 26, the convoy cleared harbor and headed for Coron Bay. Soon after sunrise, however, two American patrol planes showed up and began to track the Japanese ships. Admiral Sakonju's evasive maneuvers were ineffectual, though nothing happened for the moment, probably because Allied forces were temporarily preoccupied with strikes on other Japanese naval forces. Before noon, though, about fifty American planes arrived and pasted the convoy. Many of the planes set upon destroyer *Uranami*, holed by five bombs that hit nearby, with another twenty impacting within a hundred yards or so. Captain Kawasaki momentarily avoided damage in *Kinu*, but an attack an hour later wrecked steering control, and after that destruction was just a matter of time. Kawasaki's ship suffered eighty-three killed and fifty-one wounded, on top of forty-nine casualties taken in a strafing attack in Manila a few days before. The captain, who in 1940 had ranked just behind Teraoka Masao of the *Suzuya*, survived to discover that his friend and fellow cruiser commander had disappeared at Leyte Gulf. Kawasaki, Sakonju, and other survivors were rescued by Transport *No. 10* and conveyed to Manila. Their unit no longer had any ships, so the Imperial Navy abolished Cruiser Division 16.

This "Tokyo Express" had obviously been rather expensive, but the Japanese Army considered it quite successful since three battalions moved from the Visayas had deployed without loss. Army authorities promptly slated the elite 1st Infantry Division for commitment, and before the campaign had ended would land some 45,000 troops and 10,000 tons of supplies on Leyte, in the face of increasing losses as the U.S. Fifth Air Force began flying from Tacloban and Dulag airfields and the escort carriers kept up their considerable scale of effort. A postwar Fifth Air Force study estimated that the Japanese sent a total of 22,000 tons of supplies to Leyte in convoys or later "ant" runs, though their estimate that just 15 percent of this amount arrived cannot be accurate. Still, at no time did the Japanese Army have more than about 1.5 division-equivalents of effectives in the field or enjoy support from more than twenty-five to thirty guns of medium caliber or larger. By November 10, when Leyte supply runs were about to be halted, fewer than ten artillery pieces remained in service. The Japanese resistance that made Leyte such a fierce fight happened in spite of great inferiority in strength. To a considerable degree the Imperial Navy deserves credit for Japanese ability to wage this battle.

A more or less standard unit of six destroyers, four escorts, and four transports ran convoys with 1st Division troops into Ormoc on October 23 and 25 and then every night until the thirtieth. American fighter-bombers from Tacloban (averaging 44 planes available daily after October 28) and B-24s from Morotai attacked without discernible impact until early November, when losses began to mount. After November 3 aircraft available on Leyte averaged 73, rising to 119 after November 10. Dangers to Japanese shipping increased commensurately. The Australian Number 6 Wireless Signals Unit monitored the radio frequencies used by Japanese aircraft that provided air cover for their Ormoc convoys. During the Leyte campaign the Australians would be credited with furnishing initial intelligence on seventeen Japanese ships sunk on the Ormoc route.

By this time Rear Admiral Hayakawa Mikio's 2nd Destroyer Flotilla had begun providing escorts for Leyte. Hayakawa had been detached from the Kurita fleet after accompanying it to Brunei and assigned to Mikawa's Southwest Area Fleet. Having been Mikawa's flag captain at the battle of Savo Island, when he skippered *Chokai*, Hayakawa remained on comfortable terms with his new boss. Leyte would be traumatic for many Japanese sailors, and Hayakawa was no exception; he had been driven off his flotilla leader, the *Noshiro*, which was sent down by air attack as Kurita's remnants tried to escape. Admiral Hayakawa then raised his flag on the *Shimakaze*, a destroyer of experimental design and the fastest ship in the Navy, lead ship of Captain Shiraishi Nagayoshi's Destroyer Division 2. The bright side for Hayakawa was that he would be returning to a unit he himself had commanded in 1940. Also, Shiraishi was an ordnance and technical expert able to furnish good advice on operational matters. For example, at Manila before sailing with the Leyte convoys, Hayakawa had the destroyers unload their (explosive) oxygen-driven torpedoes. It turned out to be a wise precaution.

Japanese Army commanders were pleased to get most of the 1st Division into Leyte with few losses and had resolved to follow with the 26th. Mikawa and Hayakawa created an ambitious plan to get the troops to Leyte: Two convoys would sail from Manila twenty-four hours apart, each with a few escorts. The lead convoy would unload, and as it headed back its destroyers would join the second-echelon convoy to increase its protection. To test the waters, as it were, the lead convoy carried bulky supplies (6,600 tons as against 2,000 men) while the second embarked most of the troops (10,000 soldiers). As befitted the second echelon's status as the more vital convoy, Admiral Hayakawa sailed with it.

Had this been a one-shot deal it might just have come off. The lead echelon, with intelligence of American submarines all around them, made haste through the Sulu Sea. Approaching Leyte the night of November 10, the ships were attacked by Fifth Air Force planes. Still the convoy held on, closed Ormoc, quickly unloaded, then headed back to sea. As planned, the three destroyers in the escort joined Hayakawa, giving him a total of seven destroyers, a minesweeper, and a sub-chaser, a screen of unprecedented strength for the Japanese. To preclude interference, the JNAF put several dozen fighters over the convoy as it neared Leyte.

The precautions did not matter. Kamimura Arashi, chief engineer of the *Shimakaze*, heard that a single American plane had found the convoy almost as soon as it left Manila. The aircraft made no effort to attack, but merely tracked them hour after hour. Kamimura figured they were marked for death. The night before they were scheduled into Ormoc, Kamimura heard furious battle sounds topside; he thought it must be a PT-boat attack, but in fact the Fifth Air Force had returned to the fray. Next morning, with the transports barely a mile from Ormoc docks, Bull Halsey put three task groups into a concentrated attack, launching 347 planes. Japanese fighters were shot down or brushed off, every one of the five transports was sunk, and the escort suffered grievous losses. The only reinforcements to arrive at Leyte were those men who swam to shore.

Not even Lieutenant Kamimura in his engine room belowdecks and below the waterline was safe from the hail of bullets and bombs. Cannon shells or heavy-caliber machine-gun bullets pierced the side of the ship and killed the sailor standing right next to him. Water gushed into both sides of the ship, the steam pipes ruptured, and *Shimakaze* lost power. The skipper ordered his crew to prepare to abandon ship, so Kamimura climbed up to the bridge. He saw no trace of the five transports. Admiral Hayakawa lay dead, two bullet holes in his chest. Captain Shiraishi desperately gripped the compass stand; he was pale, his left leg hit, and he was unable to move from a sitting position. The senior staff officer was wounded in the right shoulder, the navigator lay on the floor dying, the gunnery officer was dead. It was not a pretty picture. The destroyer *Asashimo* came alongside to take off survivors, only to be driven away several times by marauding aircraft. Also among the victims this day at Ormoc was *Naganami*, proud flagship of the same flotilla in the victory at Tassafaronga. Two more destroyers sank as well, and two of the three that escaped, plus light cruiser *Kiso*, perished at Manila on November 13, when Task Force 38 renewed its raids on that Luzon port. Only the *Asashimo* lived to fight another day.

The debacle of the TA Operation, as the Ormoc convoys had been known, ended the "Toyko Express" to Leyte. Barely fifty survivors of the destroyer unit made it to join friendly troops ashore. Radio Tokyo never announced the death of Admiral Hashimoto. At least five more destroyers plus heavy cruiser *Kumano* sank in Philippine waters through the rest of November, and though several more convoys were sent to Leyte, the Japanese Navy hesitated to risk destroyers again until December 12, when two went south with orders to bring back naval personnel stranded on Leyte. Lieutenant Kamimura and his companions hustled aboard the ships, which promptly weighed anchor. Everyone knew Leyte was on its last legs—the Americans themselves had by now made an assault landing at Ormoc. The destroyers moved quickly, but not quickly enough to escape two American PT boats, which sank the *Uzuki*, and with her half the survivors of the 2nd Flotilla. Typically, observers identified the American warships opposing them as destroyers. While the Leyte sailors went to Manila to be sent home, forces were already gathering for one of the Imperial Navy's last offensive surface attacks.


THEIR MINDORO SORTIE, WHICH THE JAPANESE CALLED THE REI OPERATION, WAS ANOTHER action demonstrating the fundamental difference in outlook between the Imperial Navy and Army. Having won on Leyte, the Allies were preparing to invade Luzon, where they would land at Lingayen Gulf. They needed airfields closer to that place than Leyte. Its northern tip barely seventy miles from Manila and only about 200 from Lingayen, Mindoro seemed the ideal place. The Japanese Navy agreed. Having made its own Philippine invasion at Lingayen in 1941, the Navy read the portents well. In addition, the Japanese recognized that Allied aircraft flying from Mindoro would extend the adversary's reach over the South China Sea, making even more dangerous the sea-lanes to the East Indies. For its part the Imperial Army hardly cared. Allotting troops to Mindoro merely reduced forces available on Luzon. Shifting into final defensive formation, with Southern Army headquarters evacuating to French Indochina, the Army had no intention of mounting a serious defense of Mindoro. The Army garrison deployed there amounted to *two companies* of infantry, plus a company of survivors sunk on their way to Leyte, in all 375 men.

Japanese scouts reported the Allied invasion flotilla at eighty vessels when it transited Surigao Strait on December 13. The invading force totaled 27,000 men of the so-called Western Visayas Task Force, among them 11,878 combat troops. The rest were service and construction men and air-unit ground elements. It was clear that the Allies intended to win—indeed, the ground outcome was a foregone conclusion. Mindoro would be transformed into an air bastion with great rapidity.

The JNAF remained the first arrow in the Japanese quiver. Admiral Fukudome now led the combined remnants of both the air fleets in the Philippines. He estimates that the JNAF was able to maintain a strength of up to 600 aircraft through about mid-December and expended something on the order of 3,000 planes through the entire Philippine campaign. Captain Ohmae, on the other hand, puts losses at 350 through December 1, with 200–300 replacement aircraft brought in by then, and current strength of 250. Captain McCollum and Seventh Fleet intelligence put JNAF December air strength at 405. According to Ohmae that would be the peak month, when despite replacements of 300 aircraft, strength still declined to just fifty planes by January 1, 1945. The Mindoro defense proved an important source of that decline.

As soon as the invasion force was sighted the Japanese geared up for powerful attacks. That day roughly 150 sorties hit the invasion fleet, including the Army bombers of Colonel Ogawa Kojiro's 5th Air Regiment, who had all pledged themselves to make special attacks. Cruiser *Nashville* and destroyer *Haraden* were both damaged. The next morning Task Force 38 and Leyte-based air suppressed much of the Japanese air effort. The 186 sorties planned degenerated into fewer than seventy planes which actually took off, half of which were caught by fighter sweeps, while the others achieved no results since there were no good contact reports that day.

The Mindoro invasion took place on December 15. That day JNAF hit with fifteen kamikazes; on the sixteenth there were fourteen Navy aircraft in the attack, plus four from the Army. Fukudome asked Taiwan for reinforcements, and about 150 aircraft flew down. During succeeding days the 4th Air Army made 128 sorties against Mindoro, and the First Air Fleet seventy-four. It was significant that the total air effort mounted for Mindoro, upward of 350 sorties, was about the same as that eventually opposing the Luzon invasion itself, roughly 400 sorties. At Mindoro the results amounted to four LSTs and a PT boat sunk and one cargo ship damaged.

Naval commanders, sparked by Fukudome, wanted to mount an immediate bombardment mission. Admiral Mikawa gave the job to Destroyer Division 43. The mismatch of task and resources is evident in that this unit mounted a total of nine 5-inch guns in three light destroyers. It was essentially an antisubmarine formation. The ships gamely withdrew to some reef islands west of the Philippines from which to make their surprise raid, but had trouble finding sufficient fuel for the mission. The *Matsu*-class destroyers also suffered from engine problems, so their raid was canceled and the vessels withdrew to French Indochina.

Admiral Mikawa thereupon assigned the task to Vice Admiral Shima's 2nd Diversion Attack Force. Shima had the hybrid battleships *Ise* and *Hyuga* at Camranh Bay, plus two cruisers and six destroyers at Cape St. Jacques (Vung Tau). New fleet carrier *Unryu* was headed into the area, carrying planes to Taiwan, but she was sunk by submarine *Redfish* in the East China Sea on December 19. In any case, Shima remained ashore and delegated the mission to Rear Admiral Kimura Masatome, his destroyer leader. Indicative of the chances Kimura gave his hopefully titled "penetration unit" is that he chose to sail in fleet destroyer *Kasumi* rather than either of his big ships, heavy cruiser *Ashigara* or light cruiser *Oyodo*. The remainder comprised two more fleet destroyers and three light ones. Matsuda Chiaki's battleships stayed behind, leaving for Singapore a few days later. Admiral Kimura weighed anchor at 9:00 A.M. on Christmas Eve. Kimura had planned to make his raid an hour before midnight on Christmas Day but delayed a day due to bad weather.

As usual, Allied commands were not completely in the dark regarding Japanese intentions. Two submarines in the Indochina region separately filed contact reports on parts of Shima's force two days before Kimura sailed.

On the morning of December 23 (Philippine time), CINCPAC released a message specifically suggesting the reports might indicate buildup of the 2nd Diversion Attack Force to "act as a bombardment and covering force for counterlanding on Mindoro." On Christmas, FRUPAC broke an earlier message sent by Shima's staff regarding refueling, again associating that force with active operations. These indications came despite the Japanese having changed their code additives as of December 16. As at Leyte Gulf (the fleet had previously changed its additive lists on October 2) the security measures did not prevent the Allies from gathering useful intelligence.

Perhaps advance indications should be regarded as suggestive rather than conclusive, since Admiral Kinkaid's Seventh Fleet did not organize any response until after 6:00 P.M. on December 26, when a PB4Y search plane piloted by Lieutenant Paul F. Stevens saw Kimura's ships beneath him. Stevens, who went on in the Navy to retire as a captain after commanding units of carrier-based nuclear-armed bombers, recalled that from above ships always seem bigger and faster than they are. He reported Captain Miura Hayao's cruiser *Ashigara* as the superbattleship *Yamato*. To make sure someone got the message, he landed at San Jose Airfield on Mindoro to tell the local commander.

Within two hours the 310th Bombardment Wing on Mindoro put up every available plane, both B-25s and fighters, altogether ninety-two fighters and thirteen bombers plus a number of P-61 "Black Widow" night fighters. First to be attacked would be destroyer *Asashimo*, the lucky survivor of Ormoc, at about 8:45 P.M. Once again she emerged unscathed. About a half hour later destroyer *Kiyoshimo* went down. The destroyer unit commander, her skipper, and 210 sailors were later rescued, and a message to that effect would be among those decoded by American intelligence. In postwar American accounts, *PT-223* shared credit for the sinking. Lieutenant Stevens himself bombed a cruiser he believes was *Ashigara*. At 9:24 a plane crashed aboard Captain Miura's *Ashigara*, and minutes later another plane, possibly a fighter, crashed into the after smokestack of light destroyer *Kaya*. In the face of opposition from eleven PT boats on a patrol line, an equal number of less seaworthy PTs inshore, and the air attacks, Admiral Kimura engaged what he identified as a convoy, then bombarded San Jose and environs for twenty minutes. Next day lucky *Asashimo* reported being bombed twice more, *and* being attacked by a surfaced submarine, but suffered no damage.

Meanwhile the Seventh Fleet assembled a scratch reaction force under Rear Admiral Theodore E. Chandler, with two heavy and two light cruisers plus eight destroyers, but Chandler was hundreds of miles away. Flagship *Louisville* had been sending parties of sailors ashore for recreation since Christmas, and no doubt other vessels were doing the same. It took time to prepare for sea; and at 1:27 P.M. on December 27 the force, Task Unit 77.14, had reached a point still almost fifty miles from Mindoro. At midafternoon Chandler formed column and swept the waters off the island. There was nothing to be seen. At 6:00 P.M. he halted alongside *PT-80* to take aboard Japanese prisoners for interrogation. A half hour later but 700 miles away Kimura's warships entered Camranh Bay.

In the REI Operation the Japanese lost the *Kiyoshimo*, suffered damage to other ships, and had 139 sailors killed or missing plus 74 wounded. Admiral Kimura claimed sinking two medium transports, two small cargo ships, and a PT boat, and shooting down seven airplanes. Fleet intelligence officer McCollum, who describes Mindoro as something of a surprise, remembered the damage as a tanker sunk. Samuel Eliot Morison put the damage at a single cargo ship damaged, a PT boat sunk by friendly aircraft, and twenty-six aircraft lost, most to crashes as they attempted to land in the dark. The raiding party of a hundred Japanese troops with whom the naval sortie was coordinated accomplished nothing whatever.

American forces quickly developed Mindoro and went ahead to launch their Luzon invasion. There were few possibilities for Japanese victory, as recognized by General Yamashita Tomoyuki, who withdrew his troops to the hills and began an extended battle of attrition that continued through the remainder of the war. Though Yamashita conceded Manila, ordering it not to be defended, Rear Admiral Iwabuchi Sanji of the 31st Base Force thought otherwise, and fought to the last with about 16,000 sailors, turning Manila into a very bloody battle in which an estimated 100,000 Filipino civilians died while the Allies suffered 6,500 casualties. Another 6,000 or so Japanese, mostly sailors and naval infantry, manned Corregidor and the Manila Bay defenses under Captain Itagaki Akira. His command included the *Musashi* survivors, sixty-five of whom now manned the heavy guns of the artificial battleship called Fort Drum. These positions were captured in February and early March 1945.

By then the Japanese air force had left the Philippines for good. Just before the Lingayen landings, unable to withstand the suppressive raids from Allied airpower, the Japanese pulled out. Army air was first to leave, followed days later by the JNAF. Fewer than fifty planes made the flight to Taiwan. Some essential personnel also left. When the invasion came only two planes remained at Clark Field, both transports, and a few more key men said good-bye. Ground crews and even pilots from a number of JNAF groups stayed behind to form ad hoc infantry units and fight alongside Yamashita in the hills of northern Luzon.

Naval men left behind were not simply superfluous nobodies but included officers and seamen vital for the war effort, for security, or both. The *Musashi* sailors are a case in point. In fact, that particular security nightmare crystallized despite all precautions when, on April 13, 1945, the Americans captured a twenty-seven-year-old lieutenant, Kojima Kiyofumi. On Luzon as a code officer with the 26th Air Flotilla, Kojima had previously served aboard the *Yamato*—in fact, among the bridge personnel of that superbattleship. His interrogation proved an intelligence bonanza for JICPOA. Another intelligence windfall, probably in June, would be the capture of Commander Yoshioka Chuichi, a renowned aviator in the JNAF, who had been Fuchida Mitsuo's assistant air officer in preparing the Pearl Harbor attack. He was now an aide to Admiral Onishi. "How many months can we live on tapioca?" Yoshioka asked his diary at one point. "I want to meditate on why Japan acted so foolishly." A few days later: "Relying on America and England to rebuild Japan is the far-sighted national policy. It is impossible to think that a nation will perish simply by losing one war." The thought mirrored one Yoshioka had had in April: "If we depend on America, our national policy will be perfected. Flowers will bloom and spring will come." The words were prescient.

Among the Japanese Navy men left behind in the Philippines was Captain Sata Naohiro. This man had been air officer of the *Kaga* at Pearl Harbor and subsequently fought at Rabaul and with the First Air Fleet during A-GO and Leyte. Like Sata, other air group commanders and senior pilots were marooned as well.

The Philippine campaign must not be left behind without recounting one last intelligence coup, one of such magnitude as to dwarf perhaps any other single score of the Pacific war. This is the *Nachi* affair. Soon after subduing Captain Itagaki and the other naval troops on Corregidor, Seventh Fleet moved up the submarine rescue ship *Chanticleer*. This vessel joined up at Subic Bay with an ONI field team drawn from Seventh Fleet headquarters, including an intelligence specialist, a language officer, a photographer, and a yeoman, James McNiece. The team had traveled by PT boat, then outrigger canoe, and had been one of the first American units into Cavite, then had helped on Corregidor. The *Nachi*, former flagship of Japanese Vice Admiral Shima, had been sunk off Corregidor in the aftermath of Leyte Gulf. Now she lay in fairly deep water, a little over a hundred feet, on the Bataan side of the island.

Divers from Lieutenant Luther Tyndall's *Chanticleer* began exploring the *Nachi* wreck on April 14, immediately after the ONI team went aboard the rescue ship. Senior diver Joe Karnecke found Japanese secret documents in the *Nachi*'s charthouse; after that Americans dived almost daily, exploring the inside of a wreck containing many dead crewmen along with rapidly multiplying marine life. Jim McNiece had the job of preserving the documents and equipment recovered until they could be taken away for intelligence analysis. Papers he tried to dry out, pieces of machinery he often smeared with grease and put back underwater so they would not be exposed to salt air. An aircraft shuttled the items to the fleet intelligence center at Hollandia.

The most exotic thing recovered from the *Nachi* was Shima Kiyohide's vice admiral's flag, which is today displayed in the museum of the United States Naval Academy at Annapolis. But this very real exploration of Davy Jones's locker yielded immensely valuable revelations. Because *Nachi* had been flagship of the Imperial Navy's Fifth Fleet, and because of the Japanese practice of distributing secret documents rather widely, the ship's closets and desks (*Chanticleer* divers joked that the ship's safes contained only rice bowls) were stuffed with a much greater array of material than might otherwise have been the case. It may well be that this particular salvage project was selected specifically on the basis of knowledge from radio intelligence that *Nachi* had been a fleet flagship until sunk.

The mother lode of intelligence treasure from the *Nachi* began with a copy of Yamamoto's November 1941 strategic war plan. There was also a wide array of orders and plans originated at different times by the Combined Fleet, Second Fleet, Fifth Fleet, 1st Mobile Fleet, 1st and 2nd Diversion Attack Forces, and Naval General Staff. The plans covered subjects ranging from Japanese operations during the initial offensive phase of the war to Koga's Z Operation, and the SHO plan. Also included were Mobile Fleet, Combined Fleet, cruiser division, and Diversion Attack Force doctrine manuals and standing orders, which were of more than historical import; and there was a copy of the Navy Ministry's 1944 regulations on identification of friendly units, which remained in force so far as known. The *Nachi* documents contained further valuable material detailing mine fields and force allocations in northern waters, which would serve the Allied submarine effort immediately and Allied forces as a whole in case of a naval campaign in connection with any invasion of Japan. Some fruits of the effort began to appear within a couple of months in the JICPOA bulletin titled *Weekly Intelligence,* in the form of articles on Japanese naval strategy based for the first time on true data. The material kept a posse of ATIS translators busy for weeks.

In addition to documents, the wreck of the *Nachi* yielded specimens of Imperial Navy equipment useful to Allied technical intelligence. These include the first known samples of Japanese shipborne radars, radar search receivers, and certain ordnance items. Divers working the *Nachi* also found infrared and ultraviolet signal lamps which, until the *Chanticleer* salvage effort, were completely unknown to U.S. intelligence. The rapidity with which the Allies attempted to widen these breaches in the Japanese security shield is suggested by the fact that Lieutenant Kojima, the prisoner who had been a communications officer on the *Yamato,* was being questioned regarding the infrared signal lamps within weeks of their discovery.

This extended intelligence project, quite akin to the process of mining a lode, became possible as Japanese were progressively defeated in the Philippines, driven away from the Manila area, and posed less of a threat. For example, during the third week of March, only eleven to fourteen

Japanese air sorties were reported throughout the SOWESPAC theater, with a high point on March 22, when two Japanese planes were seen to bomb Biak and four to seven appeared in the Lingayen area. Data like these make it clear that the Philippine campaign was effectively over from an aeronaval standpoint. Its outcome proved a disaster in every respect for the Imperial Navy. Japan's lifeline had truly been cut.

THE JAPANESE HIGH COMMAND HAD NO ILLUSIONS REGARDING THE OUTCOME OF LEYTE GULF. Notwithstanding the optimistic public posture of IGHQ, or valiant efforts to keep up the fight in the Philippines, the sea lords knew exactly how deep the failure had been. There was now little question of preserving the sea-lanes to the Southern Area, whence resources came. The second section of the NGS operations division, responsible for defensive measures such as creation of sea-lanes, was soon to lose an important facet of its work. Rear Admiral Hori Yugoro, chief of the Southern Naval Sea Route Department, who did much of the actual convoy assignment work, might as well close up shop. The carriers were without air groups, the land-based air flotillas were decimated; the battle fleet was mostly sunk or damaged, and most of what was left of it remained in the Southern Area, thousands of miles from Empire waters.

Strategically, the direction of Allied advance was clear. It was not to the Netherlands East Indies or Malaya that they would go, save for localized operations by former colonial powers, but direct against the Empire. The need to re-form the fleet was paramount. Admiral Oikawa of NGS ordered damaged ships to return to Japan, along with some escorts and light craft, figuring that the repaired vessels could become the nucleus of the fleet while combat-ready ships already in the south opposed Allied operations there.

The orders reached Brunei in mid-November, where the shattered remnants of the Kurita fleet still lay. Simultaneous with Combined Fleet movement orders came Naval General Staff instructions reorganizing the fleet. Superbattleship *Yamato*, among the damaged warships slated to return home, became the separate flagship of the Second Fleet. The *Nagato* was regrouped into Battleship Division 3 with the *Kongo*, also to make the voyage, though sister ship *Haruna* for the moment remained in the south. Light cruiser *Yahagi* and four destroyers provided escort. It is a measure of the hard times that had befallen the Combined Fleet that three key battleships, the strongest warships left to the Navy, would be hazarded with such skimpy cover. They sailed from Brunei in the afternoon of November 16 after that place had been hit by a strike force of forty B-24s with P-38 cover. The Japanese were leaving just ahead of the reaper.

It is a measure of *why* the Combined Fleet had fallen upon the hard times it had that American bombers just happened to visit hours before the departure. Similarly, submarines in intervening patrol areas received Ultra warnings to expect Japanese battleships. In the East China Sea on November 21 the *Sealion* found two battleships and two destroyers visible through her periscope. Identifying both the big ships as *Kongo*-class, and apparently not seeing the others, *Sealion* put four torpedoes into Rear Admiral Shimazaki Toshio's *Kongo*. The ship seemed damaged, albeit not mortally so, but then before *Sealion* could complete preparations for a renewed attack, the battleship suddenly erupted into flames and exploded. Neither Shimazaki nor Vice Admiral Suzuki Yoshio, division commander, was among the 237 sailors rescued later. The other Japanese vessels escaped.

Barely a week later, in Empire waters, American submarine *Archerfish* torpedoed the just-completed supercarrier *Shinano* outside Tokyo Bay. Captain Abe Toshio drove his ship on, headed for Kure, believing her damage not sufficient to sink her. A destroyer man and torpedo expert, without much time in big ships, Abe mistakenly believed the *Shinano* had more watertight integrity than in fact she did; in many respects the new carrier remained a construction project even at the moment of her demise. Abe went down with his ship.

These two cases had an interesting fallout in Allied intelligence circles. American intelligence had earlier carried the *Kongo* as sunk when she was very much alive. This time they correctly chalked up the tally to the submarines and took the ship off the order-of-battle lists. The carrier, however, remained a subject of error for months. *Archerfish* was credited with having sunk *Katsuragi*, another new Japanese fleet carrier to be sure, but hardly in the *Shinano*'s class. In January 1945 JICPOA experts revised the lists to reflect *Shinano*'s loss, but even then classed her as a light carrier converted from a cruiser, not as the behemoth she was. Examination of the sinking claims by the JANAC unit ultimately awarded the *Shinano* credit to *Archerfish* but listed the Japanese vessel with less tonnage than she actually displaced. Even the best intelligence systems are hardly ever perfect.

Meanwhile, Ultra remained on the job while the Philippine campaign wound to its inevitable conclusion. One Japanese emergency measure was to send Admiral Matsuda Chiaki's hybrid battleships south to act as transports, shuttling troops among minor garrisons, like the Paracel Islands in the South China Sea, to places where they could be sent to the Philippines. The *Hyuga* and *Ise* departed Sasebo on November 11, and within days Ultra began warning subs to look out for them. In fact the ships broke through the increasingly tight submarine blockade and arrived at Lingga on November 21. Three weeks later they sailed to French Indochina, where they docked at Saigon for a few days, then spent the rest of December at Camranh Bay. As already recounted, the local senior commander refused to use these ships for the REI raid against Mindoro.

The Mindoro mission, incidentally, proved a morale-booster at home, and a certain embarrassment to the Americans. Both the desire to respond and the hope of catching Matsuda's battleship-carriers contributed to plans for Gratitude, Admiral William Halsey's cruise off the Indochina coast with Task Force 38. The Bull had just completed a series of attacks on Luzon and Taiwan, designed to support the Lingayen Gulf invasion, when he entered the South China Sea on January 10, 1945. Leading with Bogan's group (38.2) and a new ad hoc task group with the carrier fleet's two night combat–trained air groups, Halsey hoped to draw the venom of any kamikazes in Indochina, then paste the place with full-strength air strikes. Instead there was practically no air reaction at all. Admiral Bogan insolently sailed his carrier group within fifty miles of Camranh Bay itself. Strong air strikes were flown against Saigon, Camranh, and Da Nang (then called Tourane), with photo recon flights over such later famous localities as Hanoi and Haiphong. Halsey claimed forty-one ships sunk for 127,000 tons; JANAC later posted results of forty-four ships totaling 132,700, including fifteen naval vessels and a dozen tankers.

The success proved considerable, but not untouched by disappointment. First was the inability to really touch the Imperial Navy. Admiral Shima was gone and so was Matsuda, who left for Lingga with his battleships on New Year's Day. American pilots scoured the bays up and down the coast from Camranh, hoping to find battleships lurking under camouflage, but there was nothing to be seen. Among the claimed results were French ships, both merchantmen and warships demilitarized by the Japanese, which added to Halsey's tonnage figures but did nothing to diminish Japan's war effort. Only one major warship would actually be sunk during this operation, the light cruiser *Kashii*, indeed a very "light" cruiser, which had been used at various times as a training ship and a submarine headquarters, and was now in use as flagship of a convoy escort unit. The results were so meager that Halsey's subordinates, who knew he planned more days of air attacks, advised him to call off the whole program, including strikes on Hong Kong. Halsey agreed, terminated the mission, took Task Force 38 back to Ulithi, and handed over command to Admiral Spruance, who would be in charge of the restyled Task Force 58 for the planned invasions of Iwo Jima and Okinawa.

Convoy losses off French Indochina were the most significant outcome of Operation Gratitude. Commander Kuwahara Tadao, an Imperial Navy reserve officer (rare) commanding one of the escorts with the convoy Halsey had struck, recalled that his escort group had taken a unit of Army troop-ships to Taiwan for forwarding to the Philippines, then brought tankers and freighters to Saigon, from where the former sailed on to Singapore to load oil. Just three days before, they had started for Japan with a new convoy, including two loaded tankers. The larger tanker and some other vessels were sunk along with the *Kashii*, while the other tanker and cargo ships were forced to beach.

Disasters like this would put out of business a convoy system at last hitting its stride. An index of the seriousness with which the Japanese were beginning to take the shipping war was the effort to use radio intelligence more coherently in the process, much as Americans and British did in the Atlantic. The Japanese reactivated a direction-finding unit at Samah in the Pescadores, strengthened the 11th Communications Unit at Saigon and the 10th at Singapore, and established a relay point at Takao (headquarters of the 1st Surface Escort Unit, later the Grand Escort Fleet), all to strengthen the convoy effort. Beginning in March 1944 the Japanese started using mobile radio intelligence teams, groups of a petty officer and three seamen assigned to escort carriers and to flagships of important convoys. Later the 1st Surface Escort Unit and all the naval districts (save Maizuru) each got a half-dozen such teams to distribute as necessary. The teams achieved considerable results, but ship commanders were unable to fully exploit them because throughout the war the Japanese mounted only low-frequency direction finders aboard ships, on the theory that polarization and turbulence phonemena made use of high-frequency units on ships impossible. It remained extremely difficult for seagoing radio teams to coordinate with land-based direction-finding units. Since American subs used low-frequency radio only for things like talk-between-ships voice transmissions, by the time Japanese radiomen got bearings on such signals it was often too late to avoid attack.

The Grand Escort Fleet used the results of the radio intelligence to form the basis for daily summaries, special warnings of enemy movements, and an overall submarine intelligence report issued at ten-day intervals. Japan's rising index of frustration is again evident in the fact that the fleet gave up making the periodic reports in 1945, thereafter restricting itself to spot warnings for dispersal or withdrawal of large convoys or predictions of air attacks.

With the Allies closing in, the Japanese well knew their convoys would not last much longer. Emergency measures were attempted. Allied intelligence had known for some time that the Japanese were getting extra oil home by loading simple drums of it on freighters. Now the Japanese tried doing the same with warships. Aircraft carriers were especially well suited because they had large areas of unobstructed deck space built sturdily to take the weight of planes. Several carriers for which there were no air groups were run in and out of Singapore at intervals. Admiral Matsuda's *Hyuga* and *Ise*, departing Lingga for the last time on February 10, were similarly loaded. The last actual tanker convoy that sailed from Singapore for the Empire left on March 19, 1945. Due to such measures, despite considerable losses off Indochina in January (to aircraft) and February (to submarines), Japanese oil imports actually rose for the first quarter of 1945. After that the Empire was on its own.

During this final phase of the war, the defense of fortress Japan, radio intelligence again proved of great value to the Imperial Navy, this time in air defense. Japan underwent massive aerial bombardment from the American B-29 force, now established on Marianas bases. The B-29s had the range and bomb loads to devastate Japan as never before. They worried about Japanese air defenses, though, and high-altitude raids commenced on November 24, 1944, when eighty-eight B-29s attacked the Tokyo area and dropped about 220 tons of bombs. On the night of November 29–30 came the first night mission, with navigation by radar and dead reckoning. Both methods put a premium on weather conditions over the target, and precursor aircraft were often sent to render last-minute reports on local conditions. Throughout the war the Japanese had great success with Allied weather codes, including American, and this proved the case with the B-29 campaign in particular. In the same fashion as the Japanese managed to come up with advance warning of the Taiwan B-29 raid during the great carrier air battle there, they repeatedly predicted the incidence and targets of B-29 missions.

A special delegation of codebreakers, Army personnel in this case, was sent to the headquarters of the XXI Bomber Command, the B-29 force, in March 1945 to investigate this situation. They found that the Japanese had identified the frequencies and most call signs of the XXIst's air-to-ground communications net, that from observation of those communications they were able to make accurate estimates as to the strength of B-29 forces in the Marianas, and that for a time in November and December they had also been able to intercept radio transmissions between planes and the control tower, thus discovering major takeoffs. Procedures were tightened, visual signals substituted for radio contact with the control tower, and other measures taken.

This was but the latest incidence of code security becoming an issue with the B-29 force. Questions arose as early as the spring of 1944, when the B-29s were still in India and requested access to decrypt material on the Japanese Navy. The request resulted in a visit to XX Bomber Command (then the top B-29 command) by the OP-20-G veteran Commander Jack Holtwick. Rather than simply giving the bomber boys the radio intelligence, the Navy preferred to attach a naval liaison officer to the command who could furnish reports to the air intelligence staff. The issue was apparently resolved in favor of bomber command, for a later list showing authorized Ultra recipients at XXth headquarters names air staffers and code-room personnel as if the intelligence were flowing directly to the Army Air Forces.

In the fall the B-29 command extended its requests to include data on the Japanese air order of battle. The bomber force wanted information in great detail, right down to the composition and identities of individual Japanese air units. In the Navy the practice at combat intelligence was to assemble a weekly table with estimates of Japanese air strength in each geographical area, but not with unit information. Local commands like CINCPAC and SOWESPAC maintained their own inventories of Japanese units and their strengths. This service would be extended to the B-29 command, and on October 6 Captain Sebald of COMINCH combat intelligence also compromised on the matter of detailed order of battle to the extent of furnishing data on JNAF air fleets, their associated flotillas, tactical titles, and operating areas. The intelligence was forwarded the next day by the War Department's Military Intelligence Service.

Simultaneously with the air-order-of-battle question arose an issue over whether XXI Bomber Command officers who were recipients of Ultra material were flying combat missions against the Japanese. Everywhere on the globe the regulations regarding handling of code material were identical: Persons privy to such intelligence were not permitted in circumstances under which anything that happened to them could compromise the secret to the enemy. Dwight Eisenhower and Winston Churchill, no less, were prevented from visiting frontline units for precisely this reason. Press reports had it that bomber commander General Curtis LeMay and his intelligence chief had gone along on combat missions, which would have been prohibited if they were Ultra recipients. Liaison officers responsible for Ultra at both XXI Bomber Command and theater headquarters told Washington that neither man was in fact an Ultra recipient.

The B-29 force mounted twenty-two major missions during its initial operations, which lasted through March 1945. Most were midday raids from high altitude; the November night attack was deemed unsuccessful and not repeated. On average, missions flew every four to six days. It was on one of the earliest raids, even before the Marianas bases came into use, that one of the B-29s crashed in Ariake Bay, providing an object for analysis by Japanese air technical intelligence experts.

Costs of the B-29 attacks were relatively high even at the altitudes of 28,000 to 31,000 feet; on several missions the raiding forces found themselves opposed by as many as 200 to 300 Japanese fighters that might make 500 individual attacks. The bombing program limited XXI Command's selection of targets (and the aircraft's range), enabling the Japanese to concentrate their defending fighters. A typical B-29 during December 1944 could expect to have to face an average of 5.1 fighter attacks during its flight, and the average rose to 7.9 in January. But the Japanese did not develop a centralized air defense headquarters with authority to commit all fighters of all services, though they did expand the coastal radar network to provide fairly comprehensive coverage. Fighters assigned to air defense stood at about 375 during this period, and thirty-seven B-29s were shot down between December and March.

Allied strategy now attempted to isolate Japan and fully capitalize on the Philippine victory. Part of the work would be done by submarines, squeezing the sea-lanes tight shut. Part would be the very heavy bomber campaign, directly crushing the Japanese war effort from overhead. Japanese air defenses stood in the way of a fully developed air campaign, however. The air generals felt an acute need for island bases closer to Japan, as places where navigation beacons could improve their accuracy, where damaged or malfunctioning aircraft could recover instead of crashing, and where fighters could be based to escort the bomber raids and negate the Japanese air effort. From these needs flowed the rationales for two more island invasions, the biggest of the war. One, at Iwo Jima, would be accompanied by Admiral Spruance's Task Force 58 attacking Japan itself. The other, at Okinawa, brought on the biggest kamikaze battle of the war and the last sortie of the Imperial Navy.

IT WOULD BE RAYMOND SPRUANCE WHO LED OFF THIS NEW PHASE OF HOSTILITIES. BEHIND him, the Fifth Fleet commander knew, was an immense invasion force set to put ashore Marine troops to wrest Iwo Jima from Japanese control. Just 600 miles from Japan, Iwo's four airfields would become a perfect landing place for ailing B-29s and any other aircraft in trouble in Japanese waters. As had become standard doctrine, Admiral Spruance was to put his carriers up against the largest concentrations of Japanese airpower in position to interfere with the invasion. Geography dictated that those concentrations were Admiral Ugaki's Fifth Air Fleet, newly formed on Kyushu, and Admiral Teraoka's Third Air Fleet in the environs of Tokyo on Honshu. The American carrier force would mount strikes on Japan itself for the first time. There was also an element of retribution involved, for Americans wanted to get back for the kamikaze attacks off Taiwan in January which had damaged fleet carrier *Ticonderoga*.

Marc Mitscher led the fast carrier task force under Spruance. He had five task groups, for Halsey's device of a group with night-fighting air units now became permanent. In all, Task Force 58 went to sea with five light and eleven fleet carriers. Other anti-kamikaze innovations included greatly increasing the proportion of fighters in each air group (to roughly 70 percent), having orbiting CAP fighters already out some distance from the warships, and covering different zones of the circumference of a circle around the fleet. Mitscher selected a launch point for February 16 raids on the Tokyo area that was a mere sixty miles off the coast of Honshu. Despite rain, high winds, and even light snow, Mitscher's carriers put up 2,761 sorties (many of them for the purpose of CAP), including 738 attack sorties. Aircraft struck airframe and engine plants in the Tokyo area plus military bases and airfields throughout the Kanto Plain. Not until late afternoon did Japanese snoopers discover Task Force 58. Though Mitscher stuck around for a second day of strikes to polish off his targets, no effective riposte was forthcoming.

On February 19, following a concentrated three-day plastering by battleship and cruiser guns, aircraft, and everything else that could be brought to bear, the Americans landed on Iwo Jima. That began a five-week-long battle that was one of the bloodiest yet waged, more costly in overall ground casualties than the entire five months of Guadalcanal. In contrast to that campaign, and for that matter the ongoing Philippine fighting, little naval action occurred around Iwo. Despite Iwo Jima's proximity to the Home Islands, and its status as headquarters of Rear Admiral Ichimaru Toshinosuke's 27th Air Flotilla, the Japanese made little effort to support the defense from the sea or air. The exception came during the first few days of the battle, with a spate of kamikaze attacks. These kamikazes came on February 21 and were from Admiral Teraoka's Third Air Fleet, most likely elements of Air Group 601. This group, under Captain Sugiyama Riichi, was the formerly carrier-based heart of the JNAF and continued to have better morale than other naval air units. In any case the planes broke through all opposition to sink escort carrier *Bismarck Sea* and damage fleet carrier *Saratoga*, putting her out of action for over three months. The latter loss proved especially painful, since *Saratoga* was one of the two specialized night-fighting carriers in Task Force 58.

As significant as the attacks on the Americans right off Iwo were those on the newly activated Allied anchorage at Ulithi. Japanese submarines were the first to patrol there, and submarine-conveyed special attack weapons called *kaiten* became the first to attack. The *kaiten* were essentially torpedoes piloted by humans—basically, simpler versions of the two-man midget subs used early in the war at Pearl Harbor, Sydney, Diego Suarez, and elsewhere. Before the A Operation the Japanese had had a plan to combine air and special attack weapons (amphibious tanks) in an assault against an American fleet anchorage. That had never come to fruition. The Sixth Fleet carried on alone, and on November 20 a more practical *kaiten* attack was conducted by five *kaiten* carried by boats *I-36* and *I-47*. Inside Ulithi one of the *kaiten* sank an oiler full of aviation gas. Submarine *I-37* was sunk en route to make a coordinated *kaiten* assault on Palau.

A group of six submarines called the Kongo mission was to carry out the next set of *kaiten* attacks, in mid-January. Five of the subs survived, and fourteen human torpedoes went into action, but no results were achieved, though the Sixth Fleet seems to have persisted in the belief the *kaiten* were scoring one for one in their attacks. After the Iwo invasion several *kaiten* missions sent to strike that vicinity or the sea-lanes leading there were unable to get past Allied escort forces, and unable even to initiate attacks.

Meanwhile, at the moment the Allies attacked Iwo, Admiral Ugaki had been about to make an aerial special attack on Ulithi called the Tan

Operation. Masterminded by Commander Nomura Ryosuke, a pilot risen to the staff after leading the fighter unit aboard *Soryu* and fighting in the East Indies campaign and at Rabaul (during the half year after the loss of Guadalcanal), the scheme had the support of senior staff officer Captain Miyazaki. A highly aggressive officer himself, Admiral Ugaki bought the plan with enthusiasm. As with the *kaiten* strike previously, the object was to catch Allied warships at anchor. A Saiun ("Myrt") scout plane flying from Truk on March 9 confirmed that heavy ships were actually at Ulithi. The next day, preceded by a patrol bomber to check weather and four medium bombers to scout, a main force of two dozen twin-engine *Ginga*s, guided by four more flying boats, would make the attack. The planes took off but were recalled when a premature report arrived indicating that only a single carrier lay at Ulithi. A later report clarified the assessment (accurate) that all of Task Force 58 lay at anchor. The Fifth Air Fleet repeated the strike on March 11. More than half the planes had to abort with engine problems, but eleven aircraft reached the target after nightfall and successfully damaged fleet carrier *Randolph*, though not so seriously as to prevent another scout from Truk reporting next day that there were no damaged carriers at Ulithi.

Japanese intelligence put in its best performance ever in connection with the Allied invasion of Okinawa, the island that dominated the Nansei Shoto, just 350 miles from the southern tip of Kyushu and governed as a metropolitan prefecture of Japan. In early March 1945 *joho kyoku* noted a high-level strategy conference just held in Washington. These, according to Japanese experience, usually preceded offensive upsurges by twenty to thirty days. The Owada Group's careful plotting of daily messages in the BAMS merchant-ship code reached a peak after which volume of traffic began to fall off. Japanese experience led them to expect an attack once traffic volume passed the top of a curve. In addition, the Japanese assembled scattered radio and search data into a profile indicating an assembly of shipping in the Marianas larger than that before the Iwo Jima landing, an assembly capable of carrying three or four divisions at least. Army intelligence listed seven divisions in the Marianas and two or three in the Philippines available for a new operation. Finally, Allied submarine activity surged in the Nansei Shoto while air attacks on Taiwan and aerial recce flights over Okinawa increased markedly.

*Joho kyoku* concluded that Okinawa would be invaded next and the landing would come in late March. This intelligence was passed to the Naval General Staff, as confirmed by Captain Ohmae, now an operations staff officer there; Commander Miyazaki, an assistant; and Baron Tomioka, returned to NGS to head the operations bureau. In fact, while the main landings occurred on April 1, ancillary efforts to take outlying islands did begin in March. Commander Nakajima Chikataka, fleet intelligence officer with Combined Fleet, reports that in November 1944 he predicted an Allied axis of advance that would take it to Okinawa, and projected the actual invasion ten days in advance.

Given forewarning NGS was able to plan a defense of Okinawa. The Army, too, collaborated on this "Ten" (or "Heaven") plan, but its mission would be ashore, opposing the invaders. The Navy intended to hurl Admiral Ugaki's special attack units from the Kyushu area in a series of massive kamikaze attacks called *kikusui* ("floating chrysanthemums"). There would also be special attacks launched by suicide boats from the shore, two squadrons of which were transferred from Haha Jima to Okinawa shortly before the invasion. There they formed part of a 7,000-man naval contingent under Rear Admiral Ota Minoru, whom Americans had last met defending New Georgia in the Solomons. Ota planned a last-ditch ground defense of naval installations. The Naval General Staff also contemplated a surface naval sortie, which might or might not get in among the Allied invasion fleet but which, given the strength left to the Imperial Navy, amounted to a suicidal enterprise. In effect the Ten Operation became a massive special attack, invoking the heavens, as it were, to move the earth. According to Commander Miyazaki of the NGS operations staff, main elements of the plan were put in place at the end of January and into February. Miyazaki and other officers like Commander Imai Nobuhiko, the *joho kyoku* American section chief, considered that intelligence had been right on the money for the Iwo Jima invasion, but in fact there would be no surprise at Okinawa either.

When the invasion came as predicted it became clear the Allies meant business. Like the massive invasion of the Philippines, Okinawa was an army-size operation, code-named Iceberg, in which the invasion fleet put ashore 16,000 troops in the first hour and 50,000 on the first day, eventually building up to hundreds of thousands. Supporting fleet forces were immensely powerful as well: 3,025 ships, including eighteen light and fleet carriers with Task Force 58. Japanese planners were realistic in believing that conventional attack methods could not succeed against such force.

In contrast, opposing Imperial Navy surface forces remained pathetically weak. Admiral Ota's suicide boats managed only four attacks, which smashed a landing craft converted to a gunboat. Second Fleet forces in the Empire amounted to *Yamato* plus the 2nd Destroyer Flotilla. There were other battleships and cruisers at anchor, but none ready for sea; supplies of oil to fuel a sortie were quite limited. *Yamato* herself was scheduled for drydocking to augment anti-aircraft armament, scrape the bottom, make minor repairs, and add radar equipment. Instead the superbattleship quickly got under way from Kure to the Navy's huge oil depot at Tokuyama.

By this time the Second Fleet was under command of Admiral Ito Seiichi, formerly vice chief of NGS, who took over in December when Kurita left to become president of Etajima. The latest staff officer sent to the fleet, Ito represented the high priests of the staff. He had been with the Naval General

Staff since before Pearl Harbor, had preceded Ugaki as chief of staff of Combined Fleet, and before that headed the personnel bureau at the Navy Ministry. Ito had been an attaché in the United States when Yamamoto was there, attending Yale, and chief of the midshipman corps at Etajima when Nagano was president of the academy. It was Nagano who had asked Ito to serve under him as vice chief on the General Staff. Otherwise Ito, then a relatively junior rear admiral, would have had little chance for the post. Though Ito opposed war with the United States, he played a prominent part in the decision over when to present the infamous fourteen-part message effectively declaring war. As late as 1944 Ito told a colleague's wife that Japan was too small to combat a foe like the Americans. By then, at least at the high-command level, the facts were clear. Ito himself, who had paid some attention to the problems of increasing production of aircraft and escort vessels, knew them well. He had the reputation of a deep thinker but struck some, like Fukudome Shigeru, who had been a year behind him at the academy, as lacking the heart of a fighter.

If so it is doubly ironic that Ito commanded the surface fleet in the Ten Operation, for it is precisely with arguments about fighting spirit and the way of samurai that he stilled the objections of the combat-experienced captains around him, who denounced as folly the plans for the *Yamato* sortie. Admiral Ito is said to have opposed the scheme on an intellectual level, and there is evidence on both sides of the question of whether he favored special attack tactics in general. Rear Admiral Komura Keizo, looking ahead to the defense of the homeland, advised deactivating the Second Fleet and moving its men and weapons ashore, both limiting losses and contributing to ground defense. Ito is supposed to have been on the verge of proposing this course to Combined Fleet when the Ten contingency arose. At length Hiyoshi stopped sending Ito messages on the subject of the sortie and sent Kusaka Ryunosuke to convey the orders personally. Admiral Kusaka, who had been visiting the Fifth Air Fleet, coordinating the massive *kikusui* attacks, was angered at news of his assignment because Toyoda had made the decision without reference to him. Ito was also an Etajima contemporary, one year behind him, so personal feelings intruded as well. According to Kusaka, Ito heard the orders with a smile on his face and no hint of anxiety. Kusaka must have felt relieved.

In part the decision depended upon Emperor Hirohito, and that is why Toyoda made it without his chief of staff. At an audience on March 29, when NGS chief Oikawa told Hirohito of the Allied moves in the Nansei Shoto, the Emperor inquired as to what actions the surface fleet would take. Considered a criticism of Navy inaction, this remark impelled planners to order the *Yamato* sortie. There were also planners who worried that the Second Fleet had to be used before it was sunk in harbor or the fuel supply dwindled. As Rear Admiral Takata Toshitane said of the *Yamato*'s mission:

"That was the very last possible sortie we could have made from a viewpoint of fuel, personnel, and so on, that was our last gasp."

This is an appropriate point to shift attention to the Allied codebreakers. From March 26, when Ultra included a decrypt of the execute order for Operation Ten Number 1, the codebreakers carefully monitored Japanese activity. The operation, codebreakers remarked in an April 2 summary, "seems to date, to have been more sound than fury." A decrypt from diplomatic traffic, specifically a German naval attaché report on March 29, gave considerable insight into Imperial Navy plans:

> Having used only part of its air strength in the last [task force] attack, the Jap navy is determined to use its remaining strength in conjunction with the army air force for a decisive blow at the next opportunity, probably the Okinawa landings. However the opinion of naval officers is greatly divided on the success of such an action.

The April 4 summary included commentary on a good half-dozen messages which supplied details of JNAF plans for the first *kikusui* raid, including a twenty-four-hour postponement that revealed the date as April 6.

So far as the *Yamato* is concerned, the key dates for radio intelligence are April 5 and 6. The JICPOA summary for April 5 lists two Ultra items that all but gave the game away: a message that Ito's 1st Diversion Attack Force would pass the Bungo Strait at a certain time and wished to fuel at Tokuyama and then, a few hours later, this: "Second Fleet will arrive in the area E[ast] of Okinawa at dawn of the 8th." The summary notes further that a message from Admiral Spruance originated at 12:30 A.M. on the sixth, briefly telling his carrier and battleship commanders: "You take them on!" This was about fifteen hours *before* the *Yamato* and her consorts at Tokuyama even weighed anchor.

As continued to be the bane of America's radio intelligence war, Washington wanted the credit for the *Yamato* decrypts. A memo Joe Wenger wrote the day after the big aeronaval action reports that OP-20-G sent CINCPAC a dispatch at 2:21 P.M. on April 6 informing Nimitz of the Tokuyama refueling of Yamato, and that this was followed an hour later by news that the surface force would sortie through the Bungo Strait, and later yet by a time of sortie and a route and schedule. Washington erred on the date, initially reporting that Admiral Ito would attack at dawn on April 9, but later corrected this mistake. "Although situated 8,000 miles from the scene of operations," Captain Wenger argued, "the Washington unit participated actively in those operations by supplying timely intelligence." This all sounded wonderful, except to those who knew that a dozen hours before the OP-20-G warnings Admiral Spruance had already sent orders for dealing with the Japanese sally based on FRUPAC decrypts of the same messages.

On April 6, in fact, the day OP-20-G achieved its first solutions of the *Yamato* sortie messages, the JICPOA daily summary contained notice of four more Ultra decrypts containing last-minute changes in Admiral Ito's lineup and itinerary, and instructions for Air Group 951 to strengthen antisubmarine patrols at the exit of the Bungo Strait. An important intercept on April 7 revealed that the JNAF planned fighter cover over Ito's fleet only between 6:00 and 10:00 A.M. The JICPOA comment: "They quit too soon."

As had happened at the Philippine Sea, submarine reports picked up where radio intelligence left off, sighting Ito's little fleet right outside the Bungo Strait. A couple of hours behind his itinerary given the JNAF, Ito complicated his own problem of how to get near enough to do damage by choosing the longest of three proposed course tracks, one that consumed miles and valuable time in attempting to deceive possible observers as to the fleet's destination. The inexperienced Ito rejected protests by more seasoned skippers that Japanese disadvantage was such that the best course was the most direct one. Ito also rejected Komura Keizo's suggestion that the few warships might achieve much more if they simply acted like commerce raiders, breaking into single-ship units and steaming independently to the objective.

The Komura alternative would at least have given Task Force 58 headaches in finding and tracking all the different Japanese ships. As it was, Spruance and Mitscher knew Ito's objective and had plenty of time to arrange air searches to conveniently "find" the Japanese. Historians who have written about doubts allegedly entertained by Spruance and/or Mitscher were working without benefit of the Ultra record and on the basis of misleading accounts of senior officers, like Arleigh Burke, who wished to conceal the use made of radio intelligence in the war. There was no uncertainty, no gamble. Mitscher had three task groups available, enough potential sorties to bloody a fleet much larger than Admiral Ito's.

To have sailed fast and directly south-southwest, instead of following the westerly course he took for a good seven hours on his last day, could also have served Admiral Ito better. The Second Fleet made good roughly 350 miles at the speed Ito ordered. Had that distance all been south-southwest the *Yamato* would have reached a point east and south of Amami O Shima. In fact, Ito's midday position for April 7 would have been very close to that shown for Task Force 58 at that time. Mitscher would no doubt have withdrawn before Ito rather than run alternately northeast and northwest, as he did, and the *Yamato* would still not have reached Okinawa, but at least this last sortie might have posed a real threat instead of a merely hypothetical one.

As it was, Admiral Ito's little force was promptly found, at 8:23 A.M. on April 7, by an *Essex* search plane. Two PBM Mariner flying boats took over. The after-action report of the 2nd Destroyer Flotilla notes recognition of carrier-based planes at 8:40, and of flying boats at 10:14. At that very moment Task Force 58 was launching its strike aircraft, 386 in all, including ninety-eight torpedo bombers. Mitscher's strike orders were simple: The groups of Admirals Sherman and Clark, a little farther to the north, were to concentrate on the *Yamato;* Radford, coming up after sending fighters to cover Okinawa, was to start with light cruiser *Yahagi.* After dealing with those targets, all units would go after the destroyers.

Escort commander Komura's flotilla report notes sighting a strike wave of 150 planes about twenty-eight miles away at 12:32 P.M. The *Yamato* formation went to 24 knots two minutes later, stopped zigzagging, and opened fire. Individual evasive maneuvers began at 12:37. There were no heated discussions on the bridge of *Yamato,* as there had been aboard *Musashi* at Leyte Gulf, about whether to use the *sanshiki-dan* beehive shells, whose poorly machined bore guides could tear up gun barrels. Rear Admiral Ariga Kosaku did not oppose it; gunnery officers went ahead.

On the bridge of the *Yahagi,* Rear Admiral Komura also knew planes were coming. He and Captain Hara Tameichi, the "miracle captain" destroyer leader of Solomons days, now at sea once more after training torpedo-boat crews, had heard of passing aircraft from a lookout station on Amami O Shima. The ship was ready but there was not very much to fight with. At 12:43 the *Yahagi* first glimpsed five torpedo planes turning to attack from port, then three torpedo tracks; then there was a torpedo hit on the port side, forward. "It is hard for me to believe to this day the occurrence of the next event," Hara wrote afterward. "*Yahagi* stumbled crazily for a few minutes and then shuddered to an abrupt and horrifying halt! It was inconceivable that a speeding warship of her size could be brought so suddenly dead in the water by just one torpedo."

Aboard the *Yamato* there was an American-born Japanese, a nisei, Ensign Nakatani, employed for obvious reasons monitoring American voice radio transmissions. Nakatani sat calmly copying reports while his ship absorbed more and more damage. A comrade saw him later, dead, still sitting in front of the radio, earphones over his head, as if concentrating on the ether. Commander Hayashi Shikiro controlled the elaborate counterflooding system of the huge battleship. American planes in the first wave scored at least two and possibly three torpedo hits on the port side, and several amidships compartments flooded. Hayashi coped gamely with the consequences for over an hour, but halfway through another series of attacks he reached the point where engine rooms would have to be flooded to correct the list. Two torpedoes struck on the starboard side—almost a favor, helping counter massive flooding from five to seven torpedo hits to port. Four bombs struck the upperworks. Lieutenant Commander Kawasaki Katsumi, commanding the anti-aircraft guns, learned that some of his men on the port side had become trapped by the rising water. Compartments could no longer be opened. Then the bombs wiped out one of the damage-control stations. Admiral Ariga ordered the bow brought around to point north, into the waves: better for abandoning ship, but a final admission of futility.

Ariga and Ito stayed with the ship until the end. The list grew to an incredible 35 degrees; the ship's speed was down to a mere 7 knots. The *Yamato* eventually rolled over on her beam ends, and some magazines exploded as she did so. Yoshida Mitsuru, the ship's young radar officer and chronicler of her last minutes, saw Ito, aloof and silent throughout the battle, leave the bridge for his day cabin below, and Ariga climb up to the anti-aircraft control station and lash himself to the binnacle there. It was just as well, perhaps, that Ariga did not survive, for he would be wanted in connection with the interrogation and murder of certain American aviators taken prisoner at Midway.

Like the *Yamato*, light cruiser *Yahagi* came to her end. So did four of the eight destroyers escorting the pair, among them lucky *Asashimo*, which had survived Ormoc Bay on Leyte and the tip-and-run raid on Mindoro. Some 1,187 officers and men were lost from the destroyer flotilla, and 3,063 of the personnel aboard *Yamato*. Only 269 sailors were pulled from the sea. American losses amounted to ten planes and a dozen aircrew.

In 1985, following a seven-year search, a deep-sea submersible found the wreck of the *Yamato* in 1,100 feet of water. The hulk of the superbattleship had split into three sections from the force of the final magazine blasts. Members of the former crew and relatives of the dead held a Shinto ceremony on a ship floating over the site. Akiyama Minoru, an official of the committee that had organized the search, simply remarked: "We wanted to console the spirits of the dead crew."

Their spirits might have been pacified, or perhaps avenged, had the *kikusui* operations been better organized and conducted. If the *Yamato* sortie was going to have *any* tactical effect at Okinawa, it would be to draw off a large fraction of American airpower for the interval necessary to smash the Ito fleet. To have an impact, therefore, the sortie ought to have been launched in conjunction with air operations. As already noted, Admiral Ugaki's Fifth Air Fleet had prepared a massive air attack called *kikusui* after a request from the Naval General Staff on April 3. The planned *kikusui* was war-gamed the next day and briefed on April 5, but it is not clear why there was a twenty-four-hour postponement. The weather, at least, was good on the day the *kikusui* was originally to have been carried out. It would have been easy enough to delay an extra day to coordinate with Admiral Ito's fleet. Ugaki's diary demonstrates that he was aware of *Yamato*'s special attack mission by April 5, early enough to make cooperative arrangements. Also, Fifth Air Fleet learned the ground forces were being asked to make attacks north on April 7 toward the airfields the Americans were starting to use. Again, a delay would have enabled the *kikusui* to strike while some

Allied forces were preoccupied with the land offensive. Ugaki sent no such order. Instead he went for a long walk in the afternoon and did some hunting.

BY THE SPRING OF 1945 THE *TOKKO* TACTICS HAD BECOME THE NORM, NO LONGER THE exception, to be progressively adopted by every branch of each of the Japanese services. Kamikaze air attacks were as common as orthodox ones. By American count the Japanese air forces would take at least 3,000 combat losses during the Okinawa campaign, of which roughly 1,900 aircraft were expended on kamikaze flights. In all, including repeated carrier raids on the Empire and the fighting over the Okinawa beachheads, some 7,000 Japanese aircraft would be destroyed. For the first time, the Imperial Navy and Japanese Army conducted a joint operation on a large scale—Army planes flew under Navy command, primarily that of Admiral Ugaki's Fifth Air Fleet. The campaign began with Task Force 58 bludgeoning the Home Islands, then proceeded through a succession of ten major *kikusui* mass air raids. It is astonishing that in spite of careful preparation for an air offensive, when the time came to coordinate this with the *Yamato* sortie the JNAF failed to do so.

The campaign began not at Okinawa but at Ulithi, where Spruance and Mitscher took their carrier task force to sea in mid-March. There would be no surprise this time, however, for a JNAF reconnaissance plane staged through Truk instantly sighted Task Force 58, reporting it at sea on March 14. This time the fleet had embarked five mobile radio units, and there was another in the amphibious force headed directly for Okinawa. Top intelligence boss was Marine Bankston T. Holcomb, recently returned from China, where he had helped get another radio intelligence unit up and running. Now a lieutenant colonel, Holcomb was spelling Gil Slonim, who was getting some rest after the tough campaign Halsey had waged.

Intercept conditions were poor the first few days, so for once the Americans seem to have missed receiving the earliest JNAF contact report; but thereafter they copied many messages sent on March 16 and 17. Caught flatfooted, the radio intelligence men evaluated the traffic as airborne communications drills. In fact Admiral Ugaki, who had been out hunting pheasants on the seventeenth, returned to his hotel to find Nomura, his operations staff officer, bearing a *joho kyoku* warning that Task Force 58 was under way and coming north. Night scouts made the first actual sightings, messages this time intercepted by Holcomb's monitors, along with transmissions from a picket boat. An American destroyer sank the picket, which got off one final message, also intercepted.

Colonel Holcomb took the plain-language emergency report to Admiral

Spruance's chief of staff to warn that surprise had been lost. Though it was only about 9:00 P.M., Spruance had already turned in for the night, and his staff chief was reluctant to disturb him.

"Holcomb," said the officer, "you go and wake the admiral and tell him."

The marine made his way to admiral's country, knocked on Spruance's cabin door, and waited. Spruance, a very calm person, answered. When he saw his mobile radio man he asked, "Yes, Holcomb, what is it?"

A message flimsy quickly changed hands. Spruance glanced at it, then looked up, "Well, is Admiral Mitscher aware of this?"

"Yessir," Holcomb replied, "I am sure he is, because my man is over there, and I am sure he got the same message."

"All right, then, thank you very much," Spruance said. "I'll let Admiral Mitscher handle this." Spruance turned over and went back to sleep.

Ashore at Kanoya, Admiral Ugaki was under orders to preserve air strength for the Ten Operation, but could not stand to have his forces caught on the ground, and decided to order a full-scale attack. The first planes were already taking off when headquarters decoded specific directives to avoid combat. Ugaki believed himself already committed and even sent orders to prepare one of his best special attack units, but they proved too dispersed to react in time. Fifty planes were lost that day, against damage to the *Yorktown* and *Intrepid* and a dud bomb hit on *Enterprise.* The fight continued on March 19, when the carrier *Franklin* suffered such heavy damage that only incredible luck and great effort saved her, while *Wasp* also sustained some injury. On the twenty-first, carrier *Enterprise,* covering the crippled *Franklin,* which was escaping Empire waters under tow at just a few knots an hour, suffered damage from fires ignited by friendly anti-aircraft shells. The unfortunate group now suffered the first attack by Japan's latest secret weapon, a rocket-powered kamikaze called the *ohka.* The 721st Air Group, specially formed to fly the strange new weapons, had already been frustrated in getting into combat. Its first stock of the murderous rocket-bombs had been aboard the *Shinano* when she sank. Later a second shipment bound for the Philippines had gone down with the *Unryu.* The *ohka* pilots were desperate to get into action, and fifteen of them went on this first mission, each slung beneath a mother plane, with three medium bombers as leaders and a direct cover of thirty-two fighters. Many escorts dropped out with malfunctions, especially clogged fuel pumps. Another formation did not join up. Scouts reported that the Americans had no combat air patrol, but that proved illusory. About fifty interceptors jumped the strike unit at a point still short of the American fleet. Some Bettys jettisoned their *ohkas* to try aerobatics; others were shot down with the bombs still attached. Only four bombers survived, none still bearing its payload. The crippled American carriers continued on to Ulithi to begin repairs.

In all, during this latest round of strikes on the Empire the JNAF lost 161 of 193 aircraft committed, while American reports claimed a total of 528 destroyed in the air or on the ground. Ugaki claimed his sea eagles had sunk five carriers, two battleships, and three cruisers. Instead Mitscher's task force had suffered only the damage noted, and went about its pre-invasion strikes in the Nansei Shoto and on Okinawa. Contrary to Ugaki's prediction, the Iceberg landings were not delayed at all.

Vice Admiral Maeda Minoru watched with growing horror as the Americans carried each of their operations to its inevitable conclusion. The former *joho kyoku* chief was leading the Tenth Air Fleet under Ugaki's over-all command. Maeda had returned from China, where he had been resident naval officer at Nanking among other posts. Having led land-based JNAF air at Midway, he had witnessed the turning point; now he would see the final debacle.

Units of the Sixth Air Army plus Ugaki's and Maeda's forces combined to carry out *kikusui* Number 1 on April 6 and 7. Scouts contacted four task groups in waters off Amami O Shima plus the invasion shipping off Okinawa. As Bankston Holcomb averred, however, Task Force 58 radio intelligence now possessed a priceless advantage: The round of air battles off the Home Islands had tipped off radio crews to the latest JNAF communications procedures. After the first couple of attacks, monitors knew what frequency JNAF used for special attack messages. Ugaki's flight leaders, with their own close escorts, would report once airborne and estimate their time of arrival at the target. The first time it happened, Holcomb and Charlie Sims, still heading Mitscher's radio unit, saw how the system worked. After that it was no mystery; the Japanese never varied frequency or procedures. As soon as the flight leaders went on the air, Holcomb would go to Spruance with estimated times of arrival and the latter would order the fleet to maneuver. Holcomb recalled, "He always listened as soon as I told him what I heard on the radio." Task Force 58 monitors intercepted three such arrival calls in the early morning, plus orders to deploy for attack in both morning and afternoon, all in addition to numerous contact reports.

As a result of the fine performance of radio intelligence the *kikusui* Number 1 operation proved far less devastating than might otherwise have been the case. Admiral Ugaki mounted an impressive effort—699 sorties (355 by kamikazes), one of the largest Japanese air attacks of the war. For all that just two destroyers were sunk, although there was damage to many more warships.

On April 8, the day Admiral Ito's *Yamato* would have arrived off Okinawa had she survived, radio intelligence detected nothing and even radar spotted only two search planes in the late afternoon.

A second *kikusui* had already been planned. The Japanese hoped for better results with their all-time first team, the 343rd Air Group under the redoubtable Captain Genda Minoru. Genda! The air pioneer moved over from his staff job to lead this unit of highly experienced pilots flying the hot *Shiden* fighters. Genda's pilots averaged 500 hours of flight time, far higher than the typical JNAF experience level. From flying in defense of Japan against the B-29s they deployed to Kanoya on April 8. Over the next five months Genda would lose a hundred planes and pilots, including all his unit commanders. He recalled: "I was on the verge of assuming command in the air myself and expect I would have been killed had the war lasted another month."

The second *kikusui* had been scheduled for April 10, but bad weather forced postponement to April 12. *Ohka* bombs participated, symbolically bringing Genda together again with 721st Group leader Captain Okamura Motoharu, one of his daredevil comrades from Flying Circus days. The operation achieved little beyond sinking a destroyer, though again many vessels sustained damage, including Spruance's flagship—the battleship *New Mexico*—and carrier *Enterprise*, a task group flagship. On May 12, aboard the *New Mexico*, Gilven Slonim's unit suffered a fatality: A radioman was killed when a kamikaze hit the ship's smokestack, near the radio shack. The man's post was right next to Slonim's, who would also have been killed except that he had gone below to deliver a message to the admiral. The damage forced Spruance to shift his flag to another vessel, the second time he had had to do so. Soon afterward Bull Halsey returned to spell Spruance in the fleet command.

Fighting would be fierce during the prolonged Okinawa campaign, but only once after the first *kikusui* would the Japanese manage more than 150 special attack sorties in a day. Thirty-four warships sank, the largest a destroyer. Another 368 were damaged, including eight carriers, four escort carriers, ten battleships, five cruisers, and sixty-three destroyers. The toll among destroyers was especially painful and reflected the new defense technique of posting these ships as radar pickets, far out from the main fleet, to get additional warning time. Sailors on the pickets were guaranteed a harrowing time since Japanese aircraft often attacked them instead of pressing on to the main anchorage.

Though the kamikazes did not actually sink so many ships, they justifiably became the major fear for Allied commanders during the final phases of the war. Many, many vessels were damaged, and the damage was appalling. Casualties among crews had never been higher. The terror of the kamikazes boring in to die in the face of all the fire that could be concentrated on them unnerved many an Allied sailor. There was great concern during the final months, as the Allies looked ahead to an invasion of Japan, regarding the damage kamikazes might do then. In fact, the Japanese reserved as many as 5,000 aircraft, collecting an aviation-gas reserve sufficient for three to five loads per plane, to fight the battle for the homeland, Operation Kettsu. It would have been monumental carnage.

Kamikazes naturally became a prime subject, one suited for manipulation by the propaganda section of the NGS, at this time headed by Captain Shiba Katsuo. His program tried to instill a fear of the *tokko* corps and convince the Allies that Japan would fight to the last man. Watching the kamikazes day after day, Americans had little difficulty believing both propositions. Intelligence reports offered tactical and technical tips on meeting the kamikaze threat but could suggest no perfect solutions. Nevertheless, Allied combat power had become even more predominant. Even the British now had a full carrier group–size force in the Pacific. The American fleet had been bloodied but hardly beaten. What hope had Japan of winning?

W HATEVER EXPECTATIONS ONE ENTERTAINED FOR A BATTLE FOR THE HOMELAND, ALLIED strength and intelligence advantages meant that much would depend upon new weapons. Of these the one offering the most potential clearly was the atomic bomb, while a most novel instrumentality would have been a "death ray." More prosaic, but at least in the field already, were various types of *tokko* weapons including rocket-powered bombs, explosive boats, even man-pack underwater attack gear. While public exhortations proclaimed that victory would come from unity, from every heart beating as one, from civilian participation in the last battle, more than a few senior officers put their hopes in new weapons and *tokko* tactics. When the battle of Okinawa drew to a close in June 1945, attention began to focus on the coming battle for the Empire. Whether new weapons would be ready for the struggle became a matter of considerable importance.

Development of an atomic bomb offered a literal quantum jump in destructive power. Western readers are generally aware of Anglo-American progress on such a weapon through the Manhattan Project, but Japanese interest is almost unknown. While it is true that Japan did not complete such a weapon during the war, this does not mean the Japanese were not aware of the possibility, or indeed that they had no atomic-bomb research program. Both the Japanese Army and the Imperial Navy had such projects, but our focus here will center entirely on the Navy effort.* At the outset, nevertheless, we must note that it was the Army that initiated atomic research in Japan, funding investigations at the Rikken Institute beginning in 1940.

*The interested reader may consult the work of the Pacific War Research Society, *The Day Man Lost* (Tokyo: Kodansha International, 1982). Also useful is an article by Deborah Shapley, "Nuclear Weapons History: Japan's Wartime Bomb Projects Revealed" (*Science*, vol. 199, no. 4325 [January 13, 1978], pp. 152–57). A full-length account in English is Robert K. Wilcox, *Japan's Secret War* (New York: Morrow, 1985).

The Imperial Navy came to the subject by a different route, being interested in the possibilities of atomic power for driving large machines such as
the engines of battleships. Physicists collaborating with naval officers at
early stages were aware of the weapons application but did not think it practical enough. In the spring of 1942 the Naval Technological Research
Institute agreed to support study of nuclear physics, a program to be known
as B Research. An account by the Pacific War Research Society quotes the
project document:

> The study of nuclear physics is a national project. Research in this field
> is continuing on a broad scale in the United States, which has recently
> obtained the services of a number of Jewish scientists, and considerable
> progress has been made. The objective is the creation of tremendous
> amounts of energy through nuclear fission. Should this research prove
> successful, it would provide a stupendous and dependable source of power
> which could be used to activate ships and other large pieces of machinery.
> Although it is not expected that nuclear energy will be realized in the near
> future, the possibility of it must not be ignored. The Imperial Navy,
> accordingly, hereby affirms its determination to foster and assist studies in
> this field.

Of course, if one considers wartime A-bomb work in terms of a race, it is
clear the Japanese Navy's start was late and tentative. The Manhattan
Project focused directly on a weapon. With President Roosevelt's approval,
investment in the project was massive from the start, and key physics experiments were conducted in 1941–1942, so that research engineering on an
actual weapon began in the summer of 1942 when the Manhattan Project
opened its facility at Los Alamos, New Mexico. It was about this time that
the Imperial Navy sponsored what it called the Physics Colloquium, intended
to explore the possibilities for both atomic power and weapons.

Members of the committee included leading figures in Japanese science
and industry, ranging from Nishina Yoshio, a key figure in the Army atomic
program, to Sagane Ryokichi, whose father had trained Nishina and who
himself had worked at the Radiation Laboratory Ernest O. Lawrence created
at the University of California. Nishina was elected chairman, but it was
Sagane who posed the central question: Could Japan manufacture a bomb,
and if so, how soon? The group pondered these mysteries for about a year,
convening monthly, concluding there was little chance for a scientific
breakthrough. B Research came to a halt.

That did not end naval atomic research, however, even though physicists
took a dim view of the possibilities. Instead the Naval Ordnance Bureau took
over as sponsor of what would subsequently be known as F Research, and
initial grants were made to a group under Arakatsu Bunsaku, a former pupil

of Einstein who had also worked at Cambridge's well-known Cavendish Laboratory. Under Arakatsu were scientists like Yukawa Hideki, who in 1949 would become the first Japanese ever awarded the Nobel Prize in physics. Just as in the West, however, some physicists refused to work on an atomic bomb, among them Sagane. Arakatsu himself later wrote a memoir in which he maintained that his main object in trying to interest the Navy in an atomic program was to keep talented young physicists out of the draft. In any case the Navy's funding level, initially just a few thousand yen, proved entirely inadequate to the task. Physicists like Sagane, who involved himself in Japanese radar research, considered their work more practical.

Uranium stocks, ore, and enrichment swiftly became the major concerns of the atomic program. When the Navy made a ¥600,000 grant for atomic matters in mid-1943, just about half went to Arakatsu and his physicists. The rest subsidized prospecting and geological studies, mostly in Korea and Manchuria. Many of these were also being conducted by the Army, including efforts by the Geological Institute of the South Manchurian Railway. Both the director and deputy, Sakamoto Takao and Sasakura Masao, discovered certain deposits themselves and were instrumental in mining ventures.

Meanwhile the physicists worked on a cyclotron at Kyoto University. Arakatsu labored on a part-by-part inventory of pieces for such a machine. Had he been willing to join the atomic-bomb effort, Sagane Ryokichi would have been vital, for he had worked on Ernest Lawrence's cyclotron in California as well as Japan's first installation of this type. Necessary parts were rationed and merely dribbled out to the F Research project. Uranium separation by centrifuge was a goal of the Kyoto physicists, but the design for the machinery had barely been completed by the end of the war. The F Research project attained high priority only around the time of Leyte Gulf, further frustrating the physicists since sea transport was becoming impossible and the uranium sources were mostly abroad. Lieutenant Commander Kitagawa Tetsuzo of the Navy's chemical bureau went to Kyoto as a full-time liaison officer, contracts were let for centrifuges and other technical equipment, and as late as April 1, 1945, naval offices were issuing lists of chemicals necessary for extraction; but time had passed Japan by.

The Arakatsu laboratory ended up as a source of such theoretical speculations as "Research on Fission of Uranium Bombarded by Thermal Neutrons," a paper actually issued days after Japan's surrender. Notebooks and folders of graphs and mathematical formulas, some dating to August 1943, were seized by Allied intelligence officers at the end of the war, deposited in a U.S. repository, and translated by a predecessor to the Central Intelligence Agency. A scientific intelligence survey conducted in Japan at war's end established that Japanese atomic research remained at a preliminary stage. Since the Japanese Army stood relatively much further advanced in this area than the Imperial Navy, the latter's achievements can only be construed as minimal.

Another exotic weapon the Japanese worked on was a Velikhovsky-style "death ray." It was conceptually sound enough; studies began in 1940 with the observation that mice and groundhogs suffered injury when placed between condenser plates through which electric currents were passed. This led to the notion that very-short-frequency radio waves focused in a high-power beam might cause physiological effects in mammals. During 1943–1944, when Admiral Kusaka Ryunosuke led the Yokosuka Air Group, a major center of Navy research and development, he found subordinates keenly interested in this project, while the fleet looked askance at the idea. Still, a weapon capable of incapacitating Allied aircrews would have been an invaluable addition to Japanese air defense.

Given the ambitious aims of the program, Japan committed ¥1 million to "death ray" research as late as 1945, at a time when the nation was in desperate straits. This amounted to half the total expenditure on this program throughout the war. The apparatus consisted of a high-power shortwave oscillator fed by several magnetrons wired in parallel for a total output of 250–300 kilowatts. Calculations were that given the antenna and focus, this output would be sufficient to kill a rabbit at 1,100 yards' distance within ten minutes once a new higher-capacity vacuum tube had been developed. Experimental results included rabbit deaths (at about a hundred feet in ten minutes) and groundhog deaths (in twenty minutes). Allied scientists who considered the Japanese experiments as reliable indications of potential believed that a ray apparatus that would be capable of killing unshielded human beings at ranges of five to ten miles was possible.

Less exotic and much better known was the balloon-bomb program. As in both the other programs, Army authorities committed more resources than the Navy did, centering efforts around a variety of high-strength paper created for baseball gloves and permitting a lightweight balloon. The Navy balloon was instead made of rubberized silk, which was heavier and could not carry quite as much payload. Rear Admiral Naneko Kichisaburo of the Sagami Naval Arsenal pioneered the Navy effort, whose actual head was Technical Lieutenant Commander Tanaka Kiyoshi. The services' different programs were consolidated in March 1944, and operational launchings began that November—symbolically, on the birthday of the Emperor Meiji. The balloons were supposed to ride the jet stream east to the United States, where time detonators ignited their hydrogen lifting gas, dropping their eleven- to thirty-three-pound bomb loads. These were not very substantial payloads and results were minimal. In all some 9,300 balloons were launched prior to April 1945, when operations were terminated with perhaps another 1,000 still in storage. American sources record just 285 balloon incidents, ranging from fires and explosions to fighter interceptions at altitude.

On May 5, 1945, Mrs. Archie Mitchell, wife of a minister from Bly, Oregon, and five teenage children became the only known fatalities from the balloon-bomb program. A bomb detonated after they found it in a field.

Obviously there is no comparison between pinpricks like these and the B-29 campaign against Japan. In the Tokyo raid of March 10, 1945, in which LeMay's bombers used incendiaries to start a fire that gutted much of the Japanese capital, 130,000 persons died by the official estimate. Six more major bombings made Tokyo a ruin, and that was just one city; many more were hit. The B-29s also dropped aerial mines in Japanese waters to interdict coastal shipping, bombed industrial and transportation targets, and did their best to suppress defenses. Allied submarines competed with the bombers in a campaign of strangulation. Controversy continues as to whether the isolation of Japan rendered unnecessary either the planned invasion of the Empire or the atomic bombings of Hiroshima and Nagasaki.

The Japanese expected invasion, of course, and their appreciations of where it might come and in what force tallied rather closely with actual Allied plans. The Imperial Navy and Army husbanded their last resources for the final battle, which would have been truly cataclysmic. Including its training establishment the Navy had over 7,000 aircraft still, with an equal number of pilots, 1,422 more training on Kyushu, and a further 800 in hospitals. Every one was ready to make kamikaze or conventional attacks on an invasion fleet. Nineteen destroyers were still in fighting trim, and were to be used to transport *kaiten* to the attack area, then throw themselves into suicidal attacks to cover the torpedo approaches. Land-based naval attack weapons included a hundred small (five-man crew) submarines called *koryu*, 300 *kairyu* two-man subs, 120 *kaiten*, and about 4,000 explosive attack boats. There were also suicide frogmen called *fukuryu* ("crouching dragon") who would use underwater-breathing apparatus to get underneath Allied ships, then attack them with lunge mines. The frogmen were trained at the Yokosuka Mine School and at Kawatana, and 1,200 had graduated before the end of the war; another 2,800 remained in various stages of training.

An idea of the thoroughness with which the Japanese prepared the last battle can be gleaned from plans to set up "strongpoints" *inside* sunken ships from which the *fukuryu* frogmen could sally to attack. Similarly there were plans to concentrate *ohka* rocket-bombs inside caves from which they could be launched to strike the Allied fleet. Allied planners were by no means mistaken in believing that the battle of Japan would have been a bloodbath. One measure of the new reality of Japanese strategy was selection in May of Admiral Onishi Takijiro as vice chief of the Naval General Staff. Admiral Toyoda simultaneously replaced Oikawa as chief of staff, while Ozawa took over as commander in chief of the Combined Fleet.

Meanwhile the naval attaché system performed its final wartime service for Japan. Lieutenant Commander Fujimura Yoshio was attaché in Bern,

Switzerland, and well aware of the role of Allen Dulles, in that city as local chief of station for the Office of Strategic Services (OSS), a major U.S. intelligence agency. Fujimura himself could have been in no doubt that Japan was beaten—he had served in all kinds of warships, including aboard the *Akagi* with Genda Minoru, and was familiar with superships like the *Yamato* in his professional capacity as a big-gun expert, in which he had shown such excellence as to be awarded a sword by Emperor Hirohito. An assistant attaché in Berlin before the war, then a Combined Fleet staff officer, Commander Fujimura had his eyes wide open. Less than a month after the sinking of the *Yamato*, he initiated quiet contact with Dulles through a German intermediary. The OSS chief quickly asked Washington for a set of terms that could be given the Japanese. Washington not only approved but used its codebreakers to read the dispatches subsequent exchanges produced. For weeks, framed by the fall of Nazi Germany, contacts continued in Bern with some hope, but Tokyo remained suspicious. Navy Minister Yonai proved amenable to sending a high-level plenipotentiary when that was suggested in June, but the Army intended to continue fighting. The Fujimura channel closed.

Much maneuvering continued in Tokyo, more or less in tandem with preparations for battle. Admiral Takagi Sokichi allied himself with Yonai, Hoshina Zenshiro, and others in a peace faction, while Onishi and Toyoda seem to have agreed with top Army officers that continued fighting was preferable. The Potsdam Conference among Allied leaders, warning Japan to surrender unconditionally or face destruction, strengthened the hand of diehards who saw no willingness to compromise. Japanese officers wished to preserve the titular and practical authority of the Emperor as head of state, but Allied authorities made no concessions. For the moment it looked as if the issue would be settled on the battlefield.

Two events combined to break the deadlock. One was Russia's entry into the Pacific war on the Allied side. Renouncing their nonaggression pact with Tokyo, the Russians burst into Manchuria and mounted invasions of the Kurile Islands. Tokyo thus learned that no power was left which might intercede with the other Allies, while the Army simultaneously lost its last remaining source of forces capable of coming to the aid of the Home Islands.

The second shock to Tokyo's resolve came from the atomic bombing of Hiroshima on August 6, 1945, then Nagasaki on August 9. This awesome display of combat power tore illusions to shreds. Tokyo had no idea whether the Americans had more such bombs, and no doubt what they were. Physicist Sagane Ryokichi quickly traveled to Hiroshima and confirmed the awful truth. Not even the utmost bravery and resourcefulness counted much against ultimate weapons. Hirohito determined to stop the bloodshed and took a hand in political maneuvers to end the war. Even with the Emperor's support, however, the government of Suzuki Kantaro had to survive an attempted military coup by Army officers and an abortive revolt by naval aviators before the decks were cleared for surrender.

On the military side the war ended as it had begun, with aircraft and submarine strikes. On July 24 and again four days later at Kure, Task Force 38 (the carrier fleet had again come under Halsey's command) finished off many of the vessels remaining to the Imperial Navy. Among the ships sunk in shallow water, à la Pearl Harbor, or so badly damaged as to be useless were battleships *Haruna*, *Ise*, and *Hyuga*; aircraft carriers *Amagi*, *Katsuragi*, and *Ryuho*; and cruisers *Tone*, *Aoba*, and *Oyodo*. The cruisers were of symbolic importance, since one had been at Pearl Harbor, one had fought everywhere beginning at Wake Island, and one had served as flagship of the Combined Fleet. For their part the Japanese also struck one final blow, on July 30, when Commander Hashimoto Mochitsura's submarine, *I-58*, encountered the heavy cruiser *Indianapolis*, recent bearer of atomic-bomb components, on the high seas. Hashimoto had been running *kaiten* missions for months, but this time he attacked with torpedoes and sank the American vessel. In a metaphor for the viciousness of the war, sharks consumed the majority of the 800 or so sailors who survived the sinking (the ship took several hundred more down with her). Only 316 *Indianapolis* seamen were recovered, many in shock after several days of exposure during which they saw their buddies eaten.

With tragedy on all sides, Emperor Hirohito broadcast to the Japanese people that the nation would sue for peace. The Emperor had never made a national address; most Japanese had never heard his speaking voice, much less the ceremonial tones Hirohito used in this radio talk. After he spoke there remained no question of going on with the war, but even then there were some who could not accept this outcome. Onishi Takijiro penned a farewell poem and greetings to his wife, then committed ritual suicide. Ugaki Matome mounted an airplane and flew away on a final kamikaze mission, a flight to oblivion. Ugaki headed south for Okinawa; but no attack was recorded there, nor were any Japanese planes intercepted. Some think that wreckage found years later on a small rock outcropping was what was left of Ugaki's plane. Throughout the war Admiral Ugaki had mourned his recently deceased wife; many times he had thought of appropriate times and places to die. On August 15, 1945, he got his chance and seized it with both hands.

# Hungry Ghosts

I N SEVERAL ASIAN COUNTRIES IT IS CUSTOMARY TO MAKE OFFERINGS TO THE DEAD, IN PAR-
ticular flowers and little bits of food. Those who die where their bodies cannot be interred, those who cannot be honored by ritual, are called hungry
ghosts. The Great Pacific War ended with veritable legions of hungry
ghosts—not only those lost on ships from the *Arizona* to the *Yamato*, but
those expired on death marches, in firestorms, laboring on railways to
nowhere, mopping up island garrisons, starving among island garrisons,
and so on. There were heroic battles, but hopeless ones too, ranging from
Japanese banzai charges to Americans defending Corregidor to Dutchmen
fighting for Java. There are many kinds of lessons to be drawn from this war.
Though it has been fashionable of late to talk about race and class, to decon-
struct the mythology of hatred—a rather advanced stage of analysis—
historians have yet to exhaust the classical historical lessons, particularly
those pertinent to intelligence and organizational behavior. This cannot
exorcise the hungry ghosts but in a small way it can help give their sacrifice
meaning.

It is worth noting that this war, prosecuted with such ferocity and brutal-
ity, ended with scarcely a whimper. On August 19 two Betty bombers from
Kisarazu carried sixteen persons to Ie Shima, near Okinawa, where they
transferred to an American C-54 aircraft for a flight to the Philippines. There
the plane landed at Nichols Field and the delegation, led by General Kawabe
Torashiro, proceeded to Manila. The Imperial Navy's component consisted
of six individuals, led by Rear Admiral Yokoyama Ichiro, aide to the minister but previously Tokyo's last naval attaché in America. Another member,

Captain Ohmae Toshikazu of the NGS operations bureau, had once figured in ONI's list of Japanese Navy spies. A third, Mizota George Chuichi, happened to be a nisei who had helped Imperial Navy intelligence. With Mizota as interpreter the officers found themselves quietly arranging modalities of the surrender.

Allied fleets came to Japanese waters, paratroops and marines landed to secure key objectives, and Halsey's Third Fleet anchored in Tokyo Bay. Senior officers of the Allied Powers assembled on the battleship *Missouri* for the formal surrender, which took place September 2. The day was surprisingly cool for that time of year, and gray clouds hung low in the sky. Sidney Mashbir, the ATIS translation maven who had done much for intelligence in the Southwest Pacific, had thought the Japanese in Manila to be practically dying in their chairs when they first saw the draft surrender document. Now, in Tokyo Bay, Mashbir was on the launch that took the nine-member Japanese delegation from shore to a destroyer that conveyed them to the *Missouri*. Mashbir perhaps exaggerated his role in these events for history, but there were plenty of men who stood on the deck of the *Missouri* that day who did exactly the same thing. Baron Tomioka Sadatoshi, among the Imperial Navy delegates, no doubt appreciated the kind of intelligence support that Mashbir's ATIS organization had furnished the Allied war effort. Here indeed is a starting point in that World War II in general, and the Pacific War in particular, proved an important milestone in the evolution of intelligence.

THE DIFFICULTY IN EXPLAINING THE PACIFIC WAR LIES NOT IN DESCRIBING HOW ALLIED FORCES did so well, but in detailing how Japan fared so poorly. The Imperial Navy was almost entirely annihilated. Just a few ships, such as battleship *Nagato*, were even in good enough condition to be sent to Bikini Atoll for atomic-bomb tests that would spell their demise. More common by far were ends like that of heavy cruiser *Haguro*, which survived Leyte Gulf, holed up at Singapore and Lingga, was sent on a voyage to the Andaman Islands, and became the hapless victim of British destroyers. The primary reason the *Haguro*'s fate was far more common than that of the *Nagato* was Allied intelligence. In fact, intelligence remains the missing piece in the puzzle of explaining the Pacific war.

Even analysts of intelligence have traditionally focused upon Pearl Harbor, where it all began, or on the Midway battle, where much hung in the balance. But these early engagements form just a small part of the story. The true achievements of intelligence in the Pacific war lie in the day-to-day accumulation of a fund of knowledge regarding the adversary. Cryptography, traffic analysis, aerial photography, prisoner interrogation, document capture and translation, and technical intelligence each became pillars of an overall effort greater than the sum of its parts. Based on the firm foundation of language officers and attachés trained in Japan before there ever was a war, and on the bedrock of knowledge accumulated in the face of a closing society, the intelligence effort made the difference during the critical early phase of the Pacific war.

This is by no means to say that force was not important. The fight for the Malay Barrier illustrates beyond all else that good intelligence remains useless in the absence of sufficient force to exploit it properly. Intelligence without force is sterile; force without intelligence, however, is often wasted. During the early phase of the Pacific war Allied intelligence provided a basis for eluding the worst Japanese blows while preparing a trap that helped equalize the odds. In the Solomons campaign, when both sides were in rough balance, Allied intelligence advantages permitted the infliction of such losses on Japanese logistics units that the latter were forced into reliance on combat forces for logistics purposes. This virtual attrition of Japanese forces effectively reduced combat power even without actual losses. At the same time the Japanese were forced to use their combat forces in such fashion as to make them more vulnerable, and this in turn accelerated losses among those forces. When Imperial Navy forces went to sea for the long-desired Decisive Battle, they suddenly found themselves without the escort units and defenses that might have enabled them to fight effectively.

During the later period of the war, when Allied force had become preponderant, intelligence was still important. Many were the occasions when Japanese defenses were outfoxed, garrisons left behind, impending operations broken up, or activities frustrated, due to foreknowledge provided by intelligence. The Rabaul raids of November 1943, and the decimation of Japanese submarine patrol lines wrought by the escort named *England* in May 1944, are examples of achievements that would have been impossible, or at least highly unlikely, except for intelligence. The ambush of Admiral Yamamoto above Bougainville is the obvious case. What is not so well known, but demonstrates that the potential of intelligence had not diminished, was that Japanese admiral Yamagata Seigo perished as a result of an exactly similar aerial ambush along the China coast on March 17, 1945. In that case Yamagata actually survived the crash but killed himself when faced with capture by Chinese guerrillas.

It was Allied force, not intelligence, that obliged the Japanese to adopt kamikaze tactics, but even there intelligence provided an extra margin of warning that often made the difference between being damaged or being sunk. Without intelligence advantages like the codebreakers and the mobile radio intercept units it is entirely possible that Japan's novel tactics might have blunted the Allied offensive once it reached the Philippines and Okinawa. Even with *both* intelligence *and* force, expectations were for a bloodbath off Japan, one that could only have been more costly had Allied knowledge been poorer.

Intelligence came of age in an important way during this war. Accumulation of knowledge, and inquiry into secondary and even tertiary factors capable of influencing a situation made it possible to predict behavior in unprecedented ways. A certain way of framing intelligence questions for analysis, leading to intelligence estimates and analyses of great scope and depth, is an important legacy of World War II. Intelligence estimates have become much more sophisticated in the era of the Central Intelligence Agency and other such postmodern organizations, but this war gave the practice a jump-start. By 1945 Washington was producing intelligence estimates that would be recognized as such by present-day analysts. This was especially true of Captain Joseph Rochefort's unit under COMINCH and of the Research and Analysis Branch of the OSS. Even standard order-of-battle analysis achieved a high level of competence. Only such careful and considered intelligence work could have enabled analysts, like some at JICPOA in October 1944, to predict a Japanese naval offensive merely from the activities of tankers.

A cautionary note flows from the intelligence competition that existed among centers in Washington, Pearl Harbor, and Melbourne, and with the British Eastern Fleet. Of course competition is healthy to a degree, and cooperation was also possible, scrubbing and otherwise improving the intelligence product. Concern regarding who received the credit for important intelligence achievements was only human. Unfortunately it resulted in real drawbacks to the intelligence effort. The banishment of Joe Rochefort after Midway is the most prominent example but not the only one. Allied intelligence proved fortunate in that the synergistic improvements brought about by increasing flows of several types of data minimized adverse effects on the pillar of radio intelligence.

On the other hand, the "hungry ghosts" metaphor has a certain peculiar suitability to intelligence. The pillars of intelligence and their synergism succeeded beyond anyone's prewar imagination—the Pacific war was not opaque. Insofar as the "fog of war" is susceptible of being eliminated by intelligence, it was in the Pacific. That sort of knowledge proved costly, however, and grew ever more costly after the war, when the machine spies became more expensive and more widespread. The hungry ghosts of intelligence soaked up every dollar as soon as it was proferred. Radio listening posts proliferated, photography became much more capable, language programs were the norm rather than the exception. But the masses of raw data became oddly unconvincing, as if, past a certain point, hard intelligence fails to convey surety. Today the mavens long for old-fashioned spies. Perhaps that is the hungry ghosts' revenge.

·   ·   ·

The war consumed many of those who fought it, and not only by death. In intelligence, where the work was so secret and the benefits to the Allied cause so huge, secrecy mitigated against proper recognition of accomplishment. Ironically, it was the careerists, precisely the horn-blowers and flag-wavers who scrambled for the credit, who prospered from the war. Officers—including some of the most brilliant—who kept their mouths shut and did their work competently received scant recognition.

Joe Rochefort is the paradigmatic case. Though ending the war in a responsible position as chief of a strategic intelligence unit directly under COMINCH, Rochefort was placed on the retired list in 1947. Recalled several years later to assist with Pacific Fleet evaluations, then Naval War College studies of Pacific battles, Rochefort was a senior analyst on the college's massive Leyte Gulf report. On that study the budget (conveniently) was allowed to run out just as analysts were about to deal with the engagements at Cape Engaño and off Samar, including critical actions by Halsey and Kinkaid. Rochefort ended up working for the Federal Civil Defense Administration, living above the beautiful beaches of Torrance, California. He was twice denied the Distinguished Service Medal for which Nimitz had recommended him; when an energetic campaign finally resulted in its award, Rochefort had been nine years dead.

Admiral Donald M. Showers, a leader of the effort to get Rochefort the recognition he deserved, rose to director of naval intelligence from his start as a junior officer at Station Hypo. He and Captain Roger Pineau, the former language officer who became general factotum for Samuel Eliot Morison's research and for many fine studies of the Pacific war, represented the best traditions of intelligence. There were others too. Tom Dyer, Tom Mackie, Joe Finnegan, Ham Wright—all went on to shuttle between the codebreaking Naval Security Group and what became the National Security Agency. All plied their trade through the Korean War to retire as captains. The Central Intelligence Group (later the Central Intelligence Agency) would be graced by JICPOA chief Roscoe Hillenkoetter as director and FRUMEL linguist Rufus Taylor, much later, as deputy. Less exalted but quite valuable CIA people who were Pacific intelligence alumni included William B. Goggins (JICPOA) and Arthur H. McCollum (ONI). William J. Sebald, energetic COMINCH combat intelligence leader, went on to be a diplomat and ambassador to Australia. Henri Smith-Hutton, who left COMINCH just before Leyte Gulf for a destroyer unit command in the Pacific, later was skipper of light cruiser *Little Rock* and air attaché to France. He retired as a captain in 1952.

Among those who attained flag rank, McCollum retired in 1953 but continued as a consultant to the CIA for over a decade. Edwin T. Layton twice headed the naval intelligence school, did a further tour as Pacific Fleet intelligence officer, and headed the intelligence unit of the Joint Chiefs of Staff before he passed away in 1984. Ellis Zacharias commanded the battleship *New Mexico* and did war propaganda work before retiring in November 1946. Until his death in 1961 he lived in Jacksonville, Florida. Redfield Mason retired in 1966 after command of the naval district that includes New York. The acerbic Mason, whom few would accuse of being friendly, was decorated for improving the Navy's image, by helping city officials during the massive power failure that blacked out New York City on November 9, 1965. Joseph N. Wenger became deputy director of the National Security Agency and, in addition to the Distinguished Service Medal he received for World War II service (the same decoration denied Joe Rochefort), received this nation's highest award for intelligence work, the National Security Medal, of which he became the second recipient. Wenger's career ended in collapse and emergency hospitalization. He was placed on the retired list in February 1958. Jack Redman retired in October 1957, the same time Wenger entered the hospital. Though also a rear admiral, Redman retired in the rank of vice admiral. This was on the strength of a Gold Star to his Legion of Merit, gained as skipper of battleship *Massachusetts*, which bombarded Japan during the last days of the war.

For the most part these officers were lucky enough to escape the controversy over intelligence at Pearl Harbor. Those who did not were ruined by it, starting with Laurence Frye Safford, founder of OP-20-G. The whole mess about who ought to be held responsible for the surprise at Pearl Harbor, as if someone *had* to be responsible, embroiled Captain Safford in deepening quicksand. Despite truly notable achievements inventing cryptographic mechanisms, Safford was never again promoted, and retired in grade in 1951, though actually kept on active duty for two more years. Swirling controversy over whether there was a conspiracy to conceal intelligence about Pearl Harbor, over the "Winds" code messages, and so on, engulfed Safford along with Captain Alwin D. Kramer, the OP-20-G translation-section chief. The Pearl Harbor investigations broke Kramer, who retired in the fall of 1946 to have nothing more to do with the Navy or intelligence. Admiral Ping Wilkinson, the ONI chief at the time of Pearl Harbor, suffered the saddest fate of all: he died in 1946 when his automobile unaccountably rolled off a ferry near Norfolk, Virginia. Some suspect that Wilkinson's death was related to the controversies over Pearl Harbor. Perhaps that death assuaged the hunger of the ghosts.

The deaths of Daniel Callaghan and Norman Scott off Guadalcanal, and of Theodore Chandler at Lingayen Gulf, were tragic but isolated; these three were the only American admirals to die in combat in the Pacific. Some would add Wilkinson as a casualty of war also. Either way, the losses were very few. Not so for the Imperial Navy, in which dozens of admirals expired in combat. They, indeed, constitute a number of the hungry ghosts. Some Australian, British, Dutch, American, and other ghosts may have been assuaged by the imprisonment or execution of admirals and lower-ranking officers after the war-crimes trials held in Tokyo, Rabaul, Jakarta, and elsewhere. At the big Tokyo trial, guilty verdicts and life sentences were meted out to Admiral Shimada, former navy minister, and Admiral Oka Takasumi, ministry bureau chief for military affairs. Admiral Nagano Osami of the Naval General Staff was a defendant too, and was posthumously declared guilty, but avoided imprisonment or worse by dying of pneumonia and a heart attack at sixty-five years of age. Illness struck down Nagano at Sugamo Prison after a day in court, and he died at the U.S. 361st Station Hospital on January 5, 1947. Admiral Shimada went to prison; he was paroled on account of poor health in 1955, but lived another twenty-one years.

By the time Shimada was released from prison, the purge of former Japanese officers had ended and the enmity between the United States and Japan had been transformed into friendship. Where former Imperial Navy officers had been scorned—one admiral, for example, scratching out a living as a manual laborer for a railroad—suddenly they were again respected. Kusaka Jinichi, the Rabaul air admiral, and Watanabe Yasuji, Yamamoto's favorite staff officer, became Buddhist aspirants, though Watanabe later entered business to become a corporate director. Fuchida Mitsuo, the Pearl Harbor flight leader, became a Christian missionary.

Others returned to their former profession once it again became acceptable. Former Admiral Shimada and NGS planner Baron Tomioka both served on commissions studying Japan's new self-defense forces. An early head of the Maritime Defense Force was Nagasawa Ko, of Java Sea and Coral Sea fame. Genda Minoru, airman extraordinaire, returned to military service from the shipbuilding industry and became a general and commander in chief of the defense forces from 1959 to 1962. He died in 1989 on the anniversary of Japan's surrender, outliving Fuchida by thirteen years. Submarine ace Morinaga Masahiko rose to become chief of staff in the defense forces, while Okumiya Masatake joined the Air Self-Defense Force and became lieutenant general and chief of operations. Pilot Abe Zenji continued on to colonel in the Air Self-Defense Force, and Hashimoto Toshio, another air force colonel who had been a pilot in the Pearl Harbor attack, would be a senior aide to Genda in 1961. Submarine man Hashimoto Mochitsura, who sank the *Indianapolis* just before the war's end, retired from the Maritime Self-Defense Force to a Shinto shrine.

Of former *joho kyoku* personnel, Ogawa Kanji went on to collaborate in editing the diaries of Admiral Ugaki Matome. Also to become a writer was Sanematsu Yuzuru, now the author of several important books on the Pacific war. On the other hand, Terai Yoshimori, in 1941 Japan's assistant naval attaché for air in Washington, went to the Maritime Self-Defense Force, from which he retired as a vice admiral.

These men's careers did not calm the ghosts perhaps, but they did show there remained a future after the past, and in that future Japan became stronger than ever.

Many thousands of Japanese served in the Imperial Navy during the period of this narrative. Personnel rose from 97,000 in 1937, to about 250,000 in the summer of 1942, to as many as 1,660,000 by July 1945. Though it is paradoxical that naval personnel figures grew even as the fleet became smaller and weaker, what is most significant in all this is that the history of the Imperial Navy (and Army too) amounts to one of our most detailed case studies of Japanese organizational behavior. Students of Japan, businessmen, and curious readers have been much interested in the Japanese art of management, corporate style, organizational skills, and the like. The Imperial Navy in World War II existed in a social milieu somewhat different than the Japan of today, but general principles of conduct and standard operating procedures are very much alike. The story of the Imperial Navy can speak to observers today, much as it did to intelligence analysts at the time.

Like the Japanese corporation, the Imperial Navy remained at all times a highly disciplined and close-knit group. This had certain advantages in adversity, for sailors in many situations pressed ahead in the face of almost certain death and with the knowledge that the opponent's strength or technical capability exceeded their own. In the postwar business environment single-mindedness and strength of purpose have gained Japan many advantages, especially with advanced products. The opposite side of the coin, however, has been that determination is the determination to make do. Again and again during the war, when the situation changed quickly, Japanese discipline stood in the way of flexibility. At a tactical and technical level, this obstructed innovation, in particular the adoption of improvisations across the entire force. There were many instances of individual initiative during 1941–1945, from submarines trapped in mine fields off Pearl Harbor to special maneuvers destroyers could make in torpedo actions, that were not reflected in general practice until long after, if ever. Kamikaze or *tokko* tactics are probably the boundary case because the Japanese switched almost entirely to them, while adopting them so late in the war, even though the technical balance had shifted against Japan much earlier.

Imperial Navy experience reaffirms the value of peer groups, whether these be Etajima classes, staff college cohorts, flight school units, or management trainee groups. Much of the Navy's more delicate and crucial business was transacted by officers using connections of one sort or another. Informal links were often as vital as official lines of authority. The Rabaul mafia, if one could call it that—the group of officers who held key positions during the Solomons campaign—was far more central in the conduct of the Leyte and Philippines campaign of 1944–1945 than is usually realized. One can say the same about the Pearl Harbor mafia in relation to the entire first phase of the war, until perhaps the summer of 1942.

Tight discipline did not mean unquestioned authority, however. It is highly significant that the Naval General Staff lost control of the Combined Fleet as Japan moved toward war. The fleet commander in chief eclipsed the General Staff because of his apparent triumph at Pearl Harbor and in other early operations, then held his new stature even as the war situation changed. The high command reasserted itself toward the end of the war, during preparations for defense of the Empire, but it is instructive that by that time the fleet had, for all practical purposes, ceased to exist. One may postulate that senior leadership in large Japanese organizations may be threatened by successful subordinates yet becomes more unassailable than ever as conditions worsen.

The role of intelligence in the Imperial Navy's war bears certain important implications. Japanese operation plans and field efforts often seemed to work from the notion that forces and weapons operate independently of the war situation. Thus every attack could "annihilate" the enemy regardless of strength, or the sea could be "controlled" despite a superior opposing fleet. Intelligence was useful if it gave confidence that such aims could reliably be attained, but was discounted otherwise. This seems to be an area in which Japanese have learned from the war. Market conditions and other items of what would be considered intelligence were the subject a military one, now play a much greater part in the decision-making of large organizations than was the case in 1941–1945. Managers may still be outfoxed, but no longer haplessly.

Fixed ideas, on the other hand, seem ingrained in the psyche. During the Imperial Navy's war the cult of the Decisive Battle held sway, as has been recounted at considerable length. This fixed idea, which almost had the force of cargo cults in some traditional societies, had adverse effects on aviation, on submarine tactics, and on the use of fleet forces for sea control. Certain management maxims and production techniques seem equally enshrined in Japanese business practice today, making for a Japan that can easily say no. But just as the fresh doctrine that won Tsushima lost at Midway, the fixed idea is always a danger.

Some of the problems emerge more concretely if we consider the fixed idea in the context of research and development, as important to the Imperial Navy of World War II as to the large corporation afterward. The idée fixe of Decisive Battle meant *Yamatos* and not *Shinanos*, range finders not radars, small-scale rather than mass aircrew training. Research and development of advanced aircraft, exotic weapons, and the like were affected adversely. The Japanese knew going into the war that they had a smaller production base, which made it all the more important to have the higher-quality forces, weapon for weapon and man for man. Here again the Japanese have learned from wartime experience and are today known for especially strong research efforts.

Some senior Imperial Navy officers remarked after the war (and the charge was repeated as late as 1958 by Samuel Eliot Morison) that Japan lost the war due to "victory disease"—that is, by arrogance instilled by the initial successes in the war, which led the Japanese to ignore defensive strategy. As applied to the Imperial Navy this criticism distorts Japanese war plans and doctrine. In fact, Decisive Battle doctrine was always defensive in nature, and Imperial Navy war plans always assumed a defensive period following an initial offensive. Claims about victory disease hide more fundamental flaws. Arrogance flowed more properly from the notion of spiritual superiority, the "Yamato spirit," which fed the propensity to ignore intelligence. Centering strategy around a Decisive Battle proved disadvantageous when, in part due to the consequences of that very cult, conditions for such a battle evolved in a direction favoring Japan's adversaries. Between Pearl Harbor and Leyte Gulf Japanese admirals labored mightily to bring about a Decisive Battle, and finally succeeded under very adverse conditions. It is symptomatic of the more fundamental flaws in Imperial Navy practice that when the Kurita fleet turned the tables on Taffy 3 off Samar the weakness of Japanese intelligence helped rob Kurita of his opportunity.

After Leyte, of course, Decisive Battle in the traditional sense was no longer possible. Kamikazes achieved great results but were not capable of winning the war because they could not carry the battle to the enemy. The *tokko* tactics proved in essence a defensive, last-ditch weapon. Even if the Allies had been fought to a standstill off Okinawa and the Home Islands, the submarine blockade, the B-29 bombers, and the atomic bombs would still have ended the war on Allied terms.

These historical events provide yet more food for thought for hopeful two-minute managers. The fact is that Japanese officers and technologists exhibited greater flexibility and innovation on the verge of defeat. Perhaps this phenomenon is more general, since one can very well argue that Allied soldiers, sailors, and airmen also exhibited great inventiveness under duress. Perhaps the lesson is that the last moments before victory are always the most dangerous; a desperate adversary is willing to try anything, in marketing as much as in war.

Looking back over the years one might argue that American generals (and managers) succumbed to victory disease also. That is, they failed to draw lessons from World War II experience that could have helped in the postwar economic competition. That foreign assistance helped rebuild Japan's economy with the most modern production technology only compounded the error. This ultimate irony may be just the thing to appease Japan's legions of hungry ghosts.

# N O T E S

ABBREVIATIONS USED IN THE NOTES

| | |
|---|---|
| CF | Confidential File |
| COD | Counterespionage: Oriental Desk |
| EMP:NAT | Estimates of Military Potential: Naval Attaché Tokyo |
| FDRL | Franklin D. Roosevelt Library, NARA |
| MRF | Map Room Files |
| MR | Map Room |
| NARA | National Archives and Records Administration |
| NHC | Naval Historical Center |
| NSA | National Security Agency |
| NSG | Naval Security Group |
| NSGC | Naval Security Group Command |
| NWC | Naval War College |
| ONI | Office of Naval Intelligence |
| OPNAV | Office of the Chief of Naval Operations |
| PSF | President's Secretary's File |
| PW:NAT | Probability of War: Naval Attaché Tokyo |
| RJN | Records of the Japanese Navy and Related Translations |
| SRH | Special Research History |
| SRMD | Cryptologic Agency Discrete Records of Historic Import |
| SRMN | U.S. Navy Discrete Records of Historic Cryptologic Import |
| SRN | Japanese Navy Message Individual Translations |
| SRNS | Japanese Naval Radio Intelligence Summaries |
| USC | United States Congress |
| USMC | United States Marine Corps |
| USN | United States Navy |
| USNI | United States Naval Institute |
| USSBS | United States Strategic Bombing Survey |
| WDC | Washington Document Center |

Chapter 1: "Your Message, Affirmative"

8 "Your message, affirmative": Ellis M. Zacharias (with Ladislas Farago), *Secret Missions: The Story of an Intelligence Officer.* New York: G. P. Putnam's Sons, 1946, p. 20.

18 "He was not only gracious": Captain Stephen Jurika, USNI Oral History, v. 1, pp. 336–37.

20 "it is the policy of the Navy": Naval Attaché Tokyo, Report 46-37, February 27, 1937. FDRL: PSF: CF, b. 68, f. "Probability of War—Naval Attaché Tokyo, v. 1." Hereafter cited as PW:NAT.

20 "treaty-less period": Naval Attaché Tokyo, Report 52-37, March 1, 1937. Ibid.

21 "the Japanese Navy declares without reserve": Naval Attaché Tokyo, Report 149-37, May 22, 1937. FDRL: PSF: CF: b. 66, f.: "Estimates of Military Potential, Naval Attaché Tokyo, v. 1." Hereafter cited as EMP:NAT.

21 "Japan now has under construction" et. seq.: Naval Attaché Tokyo, Report 15-38, January 20, 1938. FDRL: PSF: CF:, b. 68, f: PW:NAT, v. 1.

23 "spy wagon": James R. Young, *Behind the Rising Sun.* New York: Doubleday, Doran & Company, 1941, pp. 185–86.

### Chapter 2: Watching the Japanese

28 "naval infiltration": Naval Attaché Report 24-39, February 6, 1939. FDRL: PSF: CF: b. 68, f.: PW:NAT, v. 1.

30 German reports on Japanese strategic policy: John W. Chapman, translator and editor, *The Price of Admiralty: The War Diary of the German Naval Attaché in Japan 1939–1943.* Ripe (E. Sussex, England): Saltire House, 4 vols., 1982–1989.

33 Popular writers: Fletcher Pratt in *Sea Power and Today's War* (1939) and in *Secret and Urgent* (1939); William D. Puleston in *The Armed Forces of the Pacific* (1941).

33 Arthur Marder: See his *Old Friends, New Enemies: The Royal Navy and the Imperial Japanese Navy, I: Strategic Illusions, 1936–1941.* Oxford, England: Clarendon Press, 1981.

33 actual physical standards: "Special Translation No. 49: Naval Aviation Training," CINCPAC/CINCPOA Bulletin 35-45, February 10, 1945. NHC: Microfilm JP-22.

33 "accidents at training stations": Naval Attaché Report 176-39, August 9, 1939. FDRL: PSF: CF, b. 66, f.: EMP, NAT, v. 2.

33 "a commercial product of Junkers": Naval Attaché Report 310-37, November 30, 1937. See Report 173-37 as well. FDRL: PSF: CF: b. 66, f.: EMP:NAT, v. 1.

34 "have not designed, by themselves": Report 173-37, op. cit.

35 "some haste in getting over the station": Naval Attaché Report 62-37 March 17, 1937. Ibid.

37 "other types follow the Western fashions": *U.S. Naval Institute Proceedings,* June 1941, p. 882.

39 "It is most unfortunate": Rear Admiral Henri Smith-Hutton, USNI Oral History, v. 1, p. 78.

### Chapter 3: "Four Years on a War Footing and Unlimited Budgets"

41 "expedited" et. seq.: Quoted from paper "Policy Measures Toward China,"

September 23, 1936. Reprinted in James W. Morley, ed. *Japan's Road to the Pacific War: The China Quagmire.* New York: Columbia University Press, 1985, pp. 193–94.

42 "fully prepared to engage": quoted in ibid., n. 67, p. 454.

42 "the situation in Shanghai": quoted in ibid., p. 266.

46 "security measures in Central and South China": U.S. Armed Forces, Far East (Military History Section), *Japanese Monograph No. 144: Political Strategy Prior to the Outbreak of the War, Pt. I.* NHC: RJN, Monograph Series, b. NA, f.: No. 144.

46 "Navy air strength," etc.: ibid., Appendix No. 8.

48 "if we had sent an air group ashore": Smith-Hutton Oral History, op. cit., v. 1, p. 78.

49 "Peaceful beneath us lay the rich river valley": Okumiya Masatake with Roger Pineau, "How the *Panay* Was Sunk," *U.S. Naval Institute Proceedings,* June 1953, pp. 587, 590.

50 "I had been working for five years": Joseph C. Grew, *Ten Years in Japan: A Contemporary Record.* New York: Simon & Schuster, 1944, p. 234.

51 "We were all impressed": ibid., p. 237.

51 "stepping stone to war": Nomura Kichisaburo, "Stepping Stones to War," *U.S. Naval Institute Proceedings,* September 1951, pp. 927–31.

52 "We could not do the job": Clarence P. Taylor, Naval Security Group Oral History, pp. 13–14. Hereafter cited as NSG. The 4th Marines were evacuated from Shanghai aboard two chartered liners in the autumn of 1941.

53 "It was a great bunch of people": ibid., p. 17.

53 "In the winter": Roy Sholes, NSG Oral History, p. 5.

54 "Almost instantly": Naval Attaché Report 152-38, July 11, 1938. FDRL: PSF: CF: b. 68, f.: PW:NAT, v. 1.

54 "The Japanese Navy has been engaged": Naval Attaché Report 236-38, November 28, 1938, ibid.

54 "Where, before the war": ibid.

55 "a first rate air power": William M. Leary, "Assessing the Japanese Threat: Air Intelligence Before Pearl Harbor," *Aerospace Historian,* December 1987, p. 28.

55 "I believe": Admiral Oikawa Koshiro, USSBS Interrogation No. 494, p. 5. NHC: RJN; USSBS Series, b. 73.

56 "The Army may be bogged down": Hugh Byas, *The Japanese Enemy.* New York: Alfred A. Knopf, 1942, p. 11.


## Chapter 4: Like an Athletic Competition

62 "Monday, Monday": Rear Admiral Hirama Yoichi, "Japanese Naval Preparations for World War II," *Naval War College Review,* Spring 1991, p. 66.

62 For U.S. fleet problems, see E. B. Potter and Admiral Chester W. Nimitz et

al., eds., *Seapower: A Naval History*. Englewood Cliffs, N.J.: Prentice-Hall, 1960, 636–37.

63 Chihaya Masataka: See his manuscript "The Judgment of the Japanese Navy on the War with the United States," 1946. NHC microfilm.

63 "If the United States–Japan war": Commander Matsuo Kinoaki, *How Japan Plans to Win* (trans. Kilsoo H. Haan). Boston: Little, Brown, 1942. This book appeared in Japan two years earlier.

64 "You are not the usual sort": quoted in Arthur Marder, *Old Friends, New Enemies*, v. 1, pp. 128–29.

65 "the condition and capabilities": Japanese Navy Ministry, Naval Inspector's Office, "Matters for Which Investigation Is Requested in 1940," March 1, 1940, p. 35. NARA: RG-38: Office of Naval Intelligence, Far East Section, Translations series, b. 5, f.: Translation No. 125.

72 "I felt in my guts": *Newsweek*, November 25, 1991, p. 37.

83 "We had them pretty well covered": Robert L. Dormer NSG Oral History, p. 6.

## Chapter 5: "The First Time It Flies I Want to Be on Board"

87 "surprise attack fleet": Matsuo Kinoaki, *How Japan Plans to Win*, op. cit., pp. 282–84.

87 "Through Ticket to Manila": Edward S. Miller, *War Plan Orange: The U.S. Strategy to Defeat Japan, 1897–1945*. Annapolis, Md.: Naval Institute Press, 1991, pp. 35, 86–99.

91 "Any time you worked": Jeffrey M. Dorwart, *Conflict of Duty: The U.S. Navy's Intelligence Dilemma, 1919–1945*. Annapolis, Md.: Naval Institute Press, 1983, p. 34.

92 "the natives were savage head-hunters": Willard Price, *Japan's Islands of Mystery*. New York: John Day Company, 1944, pp. 27, re Palau p. 109, re Truk pp. 183–84, re Ponape p. 191. According to the observations of visiting Imperial Navy air staff officer Okumiya Masatake, by way of contrast, the airfield at Truk was not completed until 1941, and by late 1942 still remained the only airfield at that place.

93 "The information gathering side": Dorwart, *Conflict of Duty*, p. 165.

95 "no evidence is found anywhere": Naval Attaché Report 183-38, August 1938, p. 6. FDRL: PSF: CF: b. 66, f.: EMP:NAT, v. 2.

96 "the only way to get the information": Henri Smith-Hutton, USNI Oral History, v. 1, p. 304.

96 "I don't think you'll make it": Stephen Jurika Oral History, USNI Oral History, v. 1, p. 339.

96 "Fine . . . The first time it flies I want to be on board": ibid., p. 337.

97 "If you pick up every rumor": Rear Admiral Arthur H. McCollum, USNI Oral History, v. 1, p. 151.

97 "deranged mercenary": quoted in Dorwart, *Conflict of Duty*, p. 97.

98 "I must tell you": ibid.

98 "A lot of people in the Navy Department": Arthur McCollum, USNI Oral History, v. 1, p. 153.

### Chapter 6: "We Have a Chance to Win a War Right Now"

104 "You know, we make them yell": quoted in Arthur McCollum, USNI Oral History, v. 1, p. 117.

106 "closest to the war faction": Fujiwara Akira, "The Road to Pearl Harbor," in Hilary Conroy and Harry Wray, eds., *Pearl Harbor Reexamined.* Honolulu: University of Hawaii Press, 1980, p. 154.

107 "Prussian son of a bitch": JICPOA Estimates Section Appreciation, May 29, 1945. NARA:RG-457:NSA Records: "Identifications, Locations, and Command Functions of Significant Japanese Army/Navy Personnel," SRH-102.

108–110: All the quotations on these pages are drawn from surviving records of the Imperial Conferences, edited and translated by Ike Nobutaka and published as *Japan's Decision for War* (Stanford: Stanford University Press, 1967). These, and further quotations in later passages, will be identified in these notes by the date of the meeting and the page in *Japan's Decision* on which they appear. It should be noted that the conference transcripts in Ike are based on Japanese Army records; Navy records of the same meetings were destroyed during the war. All source texts purport to be direct quotes.

108 "We must build bases": June 11; Ike, pp. 50–51.

108 "not refuse to risk": June 12; Ike, p. 51.

108 "How about making": June 16; Ike, p. 56.

108 "I believe that . . . our Empire": July 2; Ike, p. 81–82.

109 "According to Navy reports": July 12; Ike, pp. 102–103.

111 "As for war with the United States": July 21; Ike, p. 106.

111 "He is of the opinion": Kido Koichi, *The Diary of the Marquis Kido, 1931–1945: Selected Translations into English.* Frederick, Md.: University Publications of America, 1984, p. 297.

112 "We are getting weaker": September 3; Ike, p. 131.

112 "We hope that the enemy will come out for a quick showdown": ibid.

112 "By the latter half": September 6; Ike, pp. 139–40.

113 "We will carry diplomatic negotiations": September 6; Ike, p. 150.

113 "To his mind Japan": from Konoye memoirs, cited by Herbert Feis, *The Road to Pearl Harbor.* Princeton, N.J.: Princeton University Press, 1950, p. 266.

113 "All the seas, everywhere": quoted in John Toland, *The Rising Sun: The Decline and Fall of the Japanese Empire, 1936–1945.* New York: Bantam Books, 1971, p. 113.

114 "If I may express": Letter, Admiral Yamamoto Isoroku–Admiral Nagano Osami, September 29, 1941; in Conroy and Wray, eds., *Pearl Harbor Reexamined,* p. 154.

114 "There is no longer time": October 4; Ike, p. 180.

115 "we will be all right in the beginning": October 24–25; Ike, p. 188.

115 "I think it would be easier": November 1; Ike, pp. 201–202.

115 "Nagano . . . is clearly determined": Ike, p. 207.

116 "Hereafter we will go forward": November 5; Ike, p. 224.

116 "We are, therefore, confident": Ike, p. 233.

116 "minute study": Cordell Hull, *The Memoirs of Cordell Hull.* New York: Macmillan, 1948, v. 2, p. 1069.

116 "We do have enough time": November 29; Ike, p. 261.

117 "most serious crisis": December 1; Ike, p. 272.

117 "There is no time for that": December 4; Ike, p. 284.

**Chapter 7: "So Long as I'm CinC We Shall Go Ahead"**

120 "it is quite unlikely": quoted in Commander Seno Sadao, "A Chess Game with No Checkmate: Admiral Inoue and the Pacific War," *Naval War College Review,* January–February 1974, p. 32.

122 "no Western commentator": Johannes Steel, *Men Behind the War.* New York: Sheridan House Publishers, 1942, p. 354.

122 "I met . . . Yamamoto": Willard Price, "America's Enemy No. 2: Yamamoto," *Harper's,* April 1942, p. 449.

122 "I wanted to return": ibid., p. 451.

125 "hairy barbarians": ibid., p. 450.

125 "When I entered his apartment": Zacharias, *Secret Missions,* p. 93.

126 "the most important ship of the future": *National Geographic,* July 1942. Cited in Richard Hough, *The Death of the Battleship.* New York: Macfadden Books, 1965, p. 65.

126 "As I see it": quoted in Edward Behr, *Hirohito: The Man Behind the Myth.* New York: Villard Books, 1989, pp. 174–75.

126 "elaborate religious scrolls" . . . "These battleships": quoted in John Deane Potter, *Yamamoto: The Man Who Menaced America.* New York: Viking Press, 1965, p. 30.

127 "Admiral Yamamoto maintained": quoted in Captain Inoguchi Rikihei and Commander Nakajima Tadashi (with Captain Roger Pineau), *The Divine Wind.* Annapolis, Md.: Naval Institute Press, 1958, p. xiii.

127 "It is agreed": quoted in ibid., p. xiv.

127 "Personally, I feel": quoted in Agawa Hiroyuki, *The Reluctant Admiral: Yamamoto and the Imperial Navy* (John Bester, trans.). Tokyo: Kodansha, 1979, p. 192.

127 "I can raise havoc": quoted in Potter, *Yamamoto,* p. 41.

127 "If it is necessary": quoted in ibid., p. 43.

128 "Should hostilities once break out": quoted in James A. Field, Jr., "Admiral Yamamoto," *U.S. Naval Institute Proceedings,* October 1949, pp. 1105–1106.

128 "It is a mistake": quoted in Captain Roger Pineau, "Admiral Isoroku Yamamoto," in Michael Carver, ed., *The War Lords.* Boston: Little, Brown, 1976, p. 397.

128 "What a strange position": quoted in Potter, *Yamamoto*, p. 129.

129 "We have no hope": quoted in Pineau, p. 397.

129 "There is no means": quoted in Fukudome Shigeru, "The Hawaii Operation," in David C. Evans, ed., *The Japanese Navy in World War II* (2nd ed.). Annapolis, Md.: Naval Institute Press, 1986, pp. 7–8.

130 "It's better to have a Decisive Battle": quoted in Gordon Prange, with Donald M. Goldstein and Katherine V. Dillon, *At Dawn We Slept*. New York: McGraw-Hill, 1981, p. 15.

131 "We will make a storming assault": quoted in Tsunoda Jun and Uchida Kazutomi, "The Pearl Harbor Attack: Admiral Yamamoto's Fundamental Concept," *Naval War College Review*, Fall 1978, pp. 86–87. The family of former staff officer Fujii Shigeru also discovered among his papers a copy of a draft, apparently of this memorandum, which was published in 1966 (Prange et al., *At Dawn We Slept*, n. 16, p. 742).

135 "In Japanese tactics we are told": Captain Watanabe Yasuji, USSBS Interrogation no. 65; *Interrogations*, v. 1, p. 65.

136 "national death": Admiral Fukudome Shigeru interview, *Newsweek*, December 11, 1961, p. 67.

136 "Opposition to the operation": Fukudome, "Hawaii Operation," p. 11.

137 "If only the development of the aircraft carrier": Admiral Baron Tomioka Sadatoshi, quoted by Stephen E. Pelz at round table discussion, "Pearl Harbor After Fifty Years," conference of the Society of Historians of American Foreign Relations, George Washington University, June 19, 1991.

141 "Are you suggesting": quoted in Agawa, *The Reluctant Admiral*, p. 229.

141 "We are undoubtedly in the most serious crisis": quoted in Captain Hara Tameichi, Fred Saito, and Roger Pineau, *Japanese Destroyer Captain*. New York: Ballantine Books, 1961, p. 44.

144 "I originally agreed": Admiral Nagano Osami, IMTFE Interrogation, March 26, 1946; reprinted in Hans L. Trefousse, *What Happened at Pearl Harbor*. New Haven: College & University Press, 1958, p. 256.

144 "On what day": quoted in Agawa, *The Reluctant Admiral*, p. 214.

144 "We also consider": ibid.

144 "cornered Japan": Emperor Hirohito oral history, recorded by Terasaki Hidenari, published in *Bungei Shunju*, November 1990; reported by David E. Sanger, "In a Memoir Hirohito Talks of Pearl Harbor," *The New York Times*, November 15, 1990.

146 "My favorite viewing place": Ensign Yoshikawa, quoted by Ron Laytner, "Japan's Pearl Harbor Spy," *The Washington Post*, December 10, 1978.

146 The terms "inside" and "outside" appear in Ladislas Farago, *The Broken Seal*. New York: Bantam, 1968, pp. 139–40.

147 "at least one third": Memorandum, "Japanese Intelligence Network in the United States," May 21, 1941. NARA: RG-38: ONI: COD, b. 1, f.: "Japanese Intelligence Activities U.S./General."

148 "We devoted much *sake* and *sukiyaki*" et. seq.: Captain Wachi Tsunezo, USSBS Interrogation No. 423. NHC: RJN: USSBS series, b. 72.

149 "There is also a plan": ONI (OP-16-F-2), Memorandum, "Japanese Espionage System in the United States and Suggested Counter Policy," June 11, 1941. NARA: RG-38: ONI/COD, b. 1.

155 "Now don't be alarmed": quoted in Fuchida Mitsuo, "The Air Attack on Pearl Harbor," in Evans, *The Japanese Navy in World War II*, p. 40.

156 "absolutely necessary for operational reasons": quoted in Frederick D. Parker, "The Unsolved Messages of Pearl Harbor, *Cryptologia*, October 1991, p. 305.

157 "Good luck on your mission": quoted in Fuchida, "The Air Attack on Pearl Harbor," p. 43.

157 "May God help us": quoted in Prange, et al. *At Dawn We Slept*, p. 426 (italicized in the original).

## Chapter 8: Who Slept at Dawn?

158 "Our task force has entered western longitude": Admiral Ugaki Matome, *Fading Victory: The Diary of Admiral Matome Ugaki 1941–1945* (trans. Chihaya Masataka, eds. Donald M. Goldstein and Katherine V. Dillon). Pittsburgh: University of Pittsburgh Press, 1991, p. 33. Hereafter cited as Ugaki Diary with date and page number. This entry is for December 2, 1941.

159 "Climb Mount Niitaka 1208": quoted in A. J. Barker, *Pearl Harbor*. New York: Ballantine Books, 1969, pp. 82–84.

159 "send false messages": CINCPAC/JICPOA, *Weekly Intelligence*, v. 1, no. 22, December 8, 1944, p. 9, from Annex to Combined Fleet Top Secret Operations Order No. 1, November 5, 1941. Reprinted USC (79/1) *Hearings Before the Joint Committee on the Investigation of the Pearl Harbor Attack* (1946), Pt. 13, p. 715. Hereafter cited as Pearl Harbor Hearings.

160 "I was never really satisfied": Captain Fuchida Mitsuo USSBS Interrogation No. 603, p. 15. NHC:RJN:USSBS series, b. 73.

161 "There were those among us": Vice Admiral Hara Chuichi, USSBS Interrogation, p. 10. USSBS Field Team No. 3 Supplementary Report: Interrogations of Senior Naval Commanders at Truk, No. 20. NARA: Microfilm Publication M1655, Roll 311.

163 "Japan's navy": Naval attaché report of March 12, 1941, quoted in "Summary of Possibility of Outbreak of War," p. 23. FDRL: PSF: CF:, b.66, f.: "Summaries, Tokyo."

163 "In this event attack southward": Naval attaché report of November 17, 1941, ibid., p. 33. Note: The report is undated on this particular copy of the summary list but is clearly dated in a more detailed version of the list held in ONI files (see NARA: RG-38: ONI series, b. 22).

168 "Right Tender": Ralph T. Briggs, Oral History, p. 5. NARA: RG-457: SRH-051.

169 "The only thing I know": Kenneth A. Mann, NSG Oral History, p. 5.

169 "there was something way over my head": Jacob J. Mandel, NSG Oral History, p. 2.

171 "The news on the 9 P.M. wireless": John Ferris, "From Broadway House to Bletchley Park: The Diary of Captain Malcolm D. Kennedy, 1934–1946," *Intelligence and National Security*, v.4, no.3, July 1989, p. 440.

171 Eric Nave Recollections: James Rusbridger and Eric Nave, *Betrayal at Pearl Harbor*. New York: Summit, 1991. Since publication, Nave is said to have retracted some of the assertions made by lead author Rusbridger.

172 "The fleet observed strict radio silence": Fuchida Mitsuo, "I Led the Air Attack on Pearl Harbor," in Paul Stillwell, ed., *Air Raid Pearl Harbor*. Annapolis, Md.: Naval Institute Press, 1981, p. 4.

173 "conquest" and "insidious": Thomas A. Gilmore, NSG Oral History, p. 6.

173 "it was quite slack just before the war": Frank W. Hess, NSG Oral History, p. 12.

173 "We were aware": Thomas A. Gilmore, NSG Oral History, p. 5.

174 "All my experience": Elmer H. Frantz, NSG Oral History, pp. 27, 28, 24.

176 "This was just lousy": Captain Joseph J. Rochefort, USNI Oral History, p. 112.

177 "Do you mean to say": quoted in Edwin T. Layton et al., *And I Was There*, p. 244.

177 "it wouldn't be a surprise to me": Brigadier General Bankson T. Holcomb, NSG Personal History Tape, p. 8.

177 "They're Japanese aircraft": quoted in Layton et al., *And I Was There*, p. 313.

## Chapter 9: Air Raid, Pearl Harbor

178 "the silent struggle with nature": Kuramoto Ike, "The Southern Cross," in Pearl Harbor Hearings, Pt. 13, p. 514.

179 "the treasure of the Japanese navy": quoted in *Newsweek*, December 12, 1966, p. 38.

179 "All right, all the plans are made": Captain Fuchida Mitsuo, USSBS Interrogation No. 603.

179 "as a Japanese": Yokota Shigeki Interrogation; ATIS No. 230, Interrogation Report No. 148, August 16, 1943. Pearl Harbor Hearings, Part 13, p. 623.

179 "Our sea eagles": Kuramoto, "The Southern Cross," op. cit.

180 "All the way we were flying": quoted in *The Washington Post*, December 6, 1991, p. D2.

180 "It was lovely": quoted in *The Washington Post*, December 7, 1981, p. A1.

185 "TO . . . TO . . . TO . . .": Fuchida, "I Led the Attack on Pearl Harbor," in Stillwell, *Air Raid Pearl Harbor*, p. 10.

185 "TORA . . . TORA . . . TORA": ibid., p. 11.

185 "We had to avoid smoke": quoted in *The Washington Post*, December 6, 1991, p. D1.

186 "Nobody returned fire" quoted in *The Washington Post*, December 7,
   1981, p. A18.
187 "AIR RAID, PEARL HARBOR": Stillwell, *Air Raid Pearl Harbor*, passim.
188 "About three hundred yards away": Captain Thomas H. Dyer, USNI Oral
   History, p. 219.
188 Hone: Thomas C. Hone, "The Destruction of the Battleline at Pearl
   Harbor," *U.S. Naval Institute Proceedings*, December 1977, pp. 49–59. Cf.
   John F. De Virgilio, "Japanese Thunderfish," *Naval History*, Winter 1991,
   pp. 61–68.
189 "commander, carrier divisions": Pearl Harbor Hearings, Part 23, p. 683;
   cf. Part 24, p. 1593.
190 "RADIO BEARINGS INDICATE": Dispatch, Com16-OPNAV, 080333, December 8,
   1941 (Priority). FDRL: MRF: b. 38, f.: "MR no. 36: Japan-Formosa (1)."
193 "We may then conclude": Fuchida, "I Led the Attack on Pearl Harbor," in
   Stillwell, *Air Raid Pearl Harbor*, p. 12.
193 "We should retire as planned" et. seq.: quoted in John Toland, *The Rising
   Sun*, p. 255.
194 "sneak-thievery" . . . "I would be prepared": Ugaki Diary, December 9,
   1941, pp. 47–48.
196 "Pearl Harbor shone red": ONI (OP-16-FE), Captured Document: "Report
   of I-69's Operations off Pearl Harbor," no. 41–43, April 14, 1943, p. 2.
   NARA: RG-38: ONI Reports series, b. 2, f.: "1943 F-14 Serials."
196 "a date which will live in infamy": "Roosevelt Speech Text," *The New York
   Times*, December 10, 1941.
197 "One can search military history in vain": Samuel Eliot Morison, *Rising
   Sun in the Pacific* (vol. 3), p. 132.
197 "We won a great tactical victory": Admiral Hara Chuichi, in
   Supplemental USSBS Report, Interrogations Truk, p. 26.
197 "The Japanese Naval General Staff": Hugh Byas, *The Japanese Enemy*, op.
   cit., p. 103.


**Chapter 10: Wings Across the Water**

198 "Where is Pearl Harbor?": quoted in *Newsweek*, December 12, 1966,
   p. 42.
199 "Look at the face of the old man": quoted in Henry S. Stokes, "Ex-
   Chauffeur for Japanese Premier Recalls War and Intrigue," *The New York
   Times*, October 4, 1981, p. 14. This article reports highlights of a Japan
   Broadcasting Corporation television documentary.
199 "great news of our successful attack": Kido Diary, December 8, 1941,
   p. 323.
199 "express personally my appreciation": Togo Shigenori, *The Cause of Japan*.
   New York: Simon & Schuster, 1956, p. 215.
200 "I told him that my Ambassador": Henri Smith-Hutton, USNI Oral
   History, vol. 1, pp. 328–29.

200 "emphasized in solemn terms": John Chapman, ed., *The Price of Admiralty*, vol. 4, December 8, 1941, p. 751. One historical mystery which analysts have recently attempted to resolve by postulating Japanese-German naval cooperation is the disappearance of the Australian cruiser H.M.A.S. *Sydney* on November 26 following a battle with a German merchant raider. Some argue that the *Sydney* was sunk by a Japanese I-boat during or shortly after the engagement.

201 "farewell visit": ibid., p. 752.

201 "The only answer I got": Robert Guillain, *I Saw Tokyo Burning*. Garden City, N.Y.: Doubleday, 1981, p. 5.

202 "Japan has done her utmost": quoted in Otto Tolischus, *Through Japanese Eyes*. New York: Reynal & Hitchcock, 1945, p. 146.

205 "All the men were restricted": Sakai Saburo with Martin Caidin and Fred Saito, *Samurai*. New York: Ballantine Books, 1965, p. 47.

206 "The American pilots were amazing": ibid.

207 "My orders were explicit": quoted in Major General Courtney Whitney, *MacArthur: His Rendezvous with History*. New York: Knopf, 1956, p. 13.

208 "We still could not believe": Sakai et al., *Samurai*, p. 51.

213 "I didn't know that ships communicated": Robert E. Dowd, NSG Oral History, p. 11.

214 "The conclusion that must be drawn": quoted in Duane L. Whitlock, NSG Oral History, p. 17.

214 "sat there hour after hour": Robert E. Dowd, NSG Oral History, p. 15.

215 "was very hard to believe": Edward Otte, NSG Oral History, p. 33.

216 "I shall do everything possible": quoted in Tsuji Masanobu, *Singapore: The Japanese Version* (Margaret E. Lake, trans.). Sydney: Ure Smith, 1960, p. 60.

218 "We are off to look for trouble": quoted in Arthur J. Marder, *Old Friends, New Enemies*, vol. 1, p. 420.

218 "Patrol duty was an unpleasant experience": quoted in Commander Okumiya Masatake and Horikoshi Jiro with Martin Caidin, *Zero: The Story of Japan's Air War in the Pacific: 1941–1945*. New York: Ballantine Books, 1957, p. 63.

218 "What is most worrisome": Ugaki Diary, December 6, 1941, p. 38.

220 "chain of disaster": Major General S. Woodburn Kirby, *Singapore: The Chain of Disaster*. New York: Macmillan, 1971.

## Chapter 11: Islands in the Sun

225 "The present situation": captured notebook of a junior officer (JICPOA Item #4986), p. 67. Pearl Harbor Hearings, Part 13, p. 611.

226 "GUAM DESTROY ALL": OPNAV Dispatch 042356, December 4, 1941; reprinted Pearl Harbor Hearings, Admiral Thomas Hart testimony, Exhibit 21, Part 10.

227 "Oh, this is Radio Agana": Stewart T. Faulkner, NSG Oral History, p. 19.

228 "sharp operators": Markle Smith, NSG Oral History, p. 8.

229 "They did not even notice": quoted in SOWESPAC, ATIS, "Enemy Publications No. 6, Hawaii-Malaya Naval Operations," p. 34. NHC: USN Microfilm no. A-5.

231 "I feel I have done a very sorry thing to him": quoted in Prange et al., *At Dawn We Slept*, p. 574.

231 "It's like asking a junior sumo wrestler": quoted in Agawa, *The Reluctant Admiral*, p. 266.

233 "IN VIEW INDICATED INCREASED AIR ACTIVITY": Dispatch, CINCPAC-OPNAV 210147, December 21, 1941. NHC: CINCPAC War Diary (aka "Graybook"), microfilm reel no. 1, p. 72.

234 "ENEMY ON ISLAND—ISSUE IN DOUBT": quoted in Commander W. Scott Cunningham and Lydel Sims, *Wake Island Command*. Boston: Little, Brown, 1961, p. 133.

237 "land of eternal summer": Kuramoto Iki, "The Southern Cross," p. 5. Pearl Harbor Hearings, Part 13, p. 518.

238 "After experiencing defensive weakness ourselves": Ugaki Diary, February 1, 1942, p. 81.

239 "our carelessness in being ignorant": ibid., p. 82.

### Chapter 12: "Great Speed, Grim Determination, and Taking All Risks Is Necessary"

246 "But I don't believe": Charlie Johns, NSG Oral History.

247 "These fellows amazed me": ibid.

249 "taken special care": *U.S. Naval Institute Proceedings*, March 1938, p. 438.

249 "open secret" . . . "make but a poor showing": ibid., July 1938, p. 1062.

249 "the Dutch . . . have prepared": ibid., December 1941, p. 1793.

251 "AN IMPORTANT REASON": Dispatch, COMINCH-CINCAF 182035, January 18, 1942. FDRL: MRF: b. 38, f.: "MR no. 46; ABDA Area."

255 "a fine type of fighting sailor": Samuel E. Morison, *The Two-Ocean War*. New York: Ballantine Books, 1972, p. 76.

255 "some Dutch naval commanders": Morison, *Rising Sun in the Pacific*, p. 310.

257 "THERE ARE SIGNS": Dispatch, ABDACOM No. 01864, February 21, 1942. FDRL: MRF: b. 38, f.: "MR no. 49: ABDACOM Information Bulletins (1)."

257 "I am afraid that the defense": quoted in John Connell, *Wavell: Supreme Commander*. London: Collins, 1969, p. 194.

257 "I AM CONCENTRATING EVERYTHING": Admiral Conrad Helfrich, Cable ABDACOM (W) 83, February 24, 1942. FDRL: MRF: b.38, f.: "47A ABDA 'W' Series—Wavell Personal."

258 "Ripple free as floating oil": Kuramoto, "The Southern Cross," Pearl Harbor Hearings, Part 13, p. 520.

259 "Suddenly . . . men were no longer tired": Walter G. Winslow, *The Ghost That Died at Sunda Strait*. Annapolis, Md.: Naval Institute Press, 1984, p. 111.

259 "followed haughtily" and "following us": Hara Tameichi et al., *Japanese Destroyer Captain*, pp. 73, 76.

261 "Japanese gunnery appeared to be extremely accurate": Winslow, *The Ghost That Died at Sunda Strait*, p. 115.

264 "a sudden squall came up": Chief Petty Officer Kawabata Shigeo, SOPAC Interrogation no. 377, p. 11. NHC: RJN: SOPAC series, b. 11.

264 "It is simple": quoted in John Toland, *But Not in Shame: The Six Months After Pearl Harbor.* New York: Random House, 1961, p. 253.

270 "with one eye for food": quoted in "A Brief History of U.S. Naval Pre–World War II Radio Intelligence Activities in the Philippine Islands," SRH-180, p. 72. NARA: RG-457.

### Chapter 13: West, South, or East?

272 "which entail considerable risk": quoted in Arthur J. Marder, Mark Jacobsen, and John Horsfield, *Old Friends, New Enemies.* Vol. 2: *The Pacific War 1942–1945.* Oxford: Clarendon Press, 1990, p. 109.

273 "increased activity in Singapore": Com14 Radio Digest, March 14, 1942. SRMN-008, "CINCPAC-Com14 CI Bulletins/Radio Digests 1 March– 31 December 1942." NARA: RG-457.

274 "Movement west from Malaya": Com14 Radio Digest, March 16, 1942.

274 "increasing indications": Com14 Radio Digest, March 19, 1942.

274 "an air unit or units": Dispatch, Admiralty ULTRA 212000, March 21, 1942. FDRL: MRF: b. 43, f.: "MR no. 63; Japanese Intelligence Reports (Com14)."

274 "In the Indian Ocean": Kuramoto Iki, "The Southern Cross," Pearl Harbor Hearings, Part 13, p. 522.

274 "Indications remain strong": Dispatch, CINCPAC 260315, March 26, 1942. FDRL: MRF: b. 43, f: "MR no. 63."

274 "continued indications of offensive": Dispatch, Com14 260303, March 26, 1942. FDRL: MRF: b. 43, f: "MR no. 63."

277 "an enemy bomber unit": Carrier *Hiryu*, Battle Report no. 5 (March 26, 1942–April 22, 1942). NHC: RJN, Washington Document Center series, b. 37, f.: "WDC 160647."

277 "did no more harm": Kuramoto, "The Southern Cross," Pearl Harbor Hearings, Part 13, p. 523.

279 "There will be no security": quoted in Henry P. Frei, *Japan's Southward Advance and Australia: From the Sixteenth Century to World War II.* Honolulu: University of Hawaii Press, 1991, p. 166.

282 "further indication of impending": Dispatch, Com16, 041228, March 4, 1942, in SRMN-005, "OP-20-G File on the Battle of Midway," p. 263. NARA: RG-457.

283 "very confident": Orita Zenji with Joseph D. Harrington, *I-Boat Captain.* Canoga Park, Calif.: Major Books, 1976, p. 52.

284 "That sounds like the real thing": Thomas Dyer, USNI Oral History, p. 239.

285 "I wonder how much longer": *Hyuga* seaman's diary, SOPAC Captured Document Translation no. 1037. NHC: RJN: SOPAC Translations subseries, b. 5.

286 "to a certain extent": Naval Attaché Report 42-41, March 12, 1941. FDRL: PSF: CF: b. 66, f.: "PW/NAT, v. 2."

**Chapter 14: Incredible Victories?**

295 "I made only a few important reports": Captain Atsuo Shigehiro USSBS Interrogation no. 422. NHC: RJN: USSBS series, b. 72.

299 "there is a great possibility": JICPOA Item no. 4986, p. 31. Pearl Harbor Hearings, Part 13, p. 572.

301 "numerous indications": Station Hypo notice, April 3, 1942, in "The Role of Radio Intelligence in the American-Japanese Naval War," vol. 1, p. 213. NARA: RG-457: SRH-012.

301 "PART OR WHOLE OF FIRST AIR FLEET": Dispatch, Admiralty 131720, April 14, 1942. FDRL: MRF: b. 64, f.: "MR 63 Japanese Intelligence Reports (Com 14)."

302 "Already the new focal point": ONI, "Japanese Naval Activities," April 17, 1942. FDRL: MRF: b. 64, f.: "MR203, Japanese Naval Activities March 7–July 31, 1942."

305 "now underway": Com14 notice, May 1, 1942. SRH-012, p. 239. NARA: RG-457.

307 "Scratch one flattop": quoted in Stanley Johnston, *Queen of the Flat-tops.* New York: Bantam Books, 1984, p. 149.

309 "We will join battle with the enemy in the west": quoted in Layton et al., *And I Was There*, p. 399.

311 "Never in all my years": quoted in James H. Belote and William M. Belote, *Titans of the Sea.* New York: Harper & Row, 1975, p. 95.

311 "A dream of great success": Ugaki Diary, May 7, 1942, p. 122.

318 "Now you guys be sure": quoted in Duane Whitlock, NSG Oral History, p. 27.

319 "a brilliant piece of work": Thomas Dyer, USNI Oral History, p. 244.

319 "my strong right arm": Colonel Alva B. Lasswell, USMC Oral History, p. 17.

319 "All I knew": ibid., p. 36.

320 "I have a difficult time": quoted in E. B. Potter, *Nimitz.* Annapolis, Md.: Naval Institute Press, 1976, p. 83.

322 "The approaching battle": quoted in Lieutenant Frederick Mears, *Carrier Combat.* New York: Ballantine Books, 1967, p. 60.

324 "Well, . . . you were only": quoted in Potter, *Nimitz*, p. 93.

324 "The enemy is accompanied": ONI, *The Japanese Story*, p. 7.

326 "Unable to help" et. seq.: Captain Fuchida Mitsuo and Commander Okumiya Masatake, *Midway: The Battle That Doomed Japan.* New York: Ballantine Books, 1968, p. 157.

326 "We goofed!": quoted in Gordon W. Prange, Donald M. Goldstein and Katharine V. Dillon, *Miracle at Midway.* New York: McGraw-Hill, 1982, p. 265.

327 "That is the way": Admiral Kusaka Ryunosuke, USSBS Interrogation no. 530. NHC: RJN: USSBS series, b. 75.

328 "Admiral, follow me": quoted in Alva B. Lasswell, USMC Oral History, p. 35.

330 "White clouds": Prisoner Statement, "Admiral Yamamoto's Yeoman's Story, 'Action at Midway,' " n.d. (1944), p. 1. NHC: Morison Papers, b. 22, f.: "No. 4: The Battle of Midway." Though the prisoner is unidentified, Noda Mitsuharu was Yamamoto's yeoman at the time, was captured in 1944, and did in fact provide extensive debriefings to U.S. intelligence. This source is cited below as "Noda."

330 "The members of the staff": ibid.

331 "The indescribable emptiness": ibid.

331 "We, the engineer crew": *Hyuga* Seaman Diary, SOPAC Captured Document Translation no. 1037. NHC: RJN: SOPAC Translations Subseries, b. 5.

332 "the sound of the wind": Noda Statement, p. 3.

332 "There is nothing else we can do": Noda Statement, p. 3.

332 "We cannot sink the Emperor's warships": quoted in Prange et al., *Miracle at Midway*, p. 320.

333 "I am the only one": quoted in Fuchida and Okumiya, *Midway*, p. 188.

335 "He looked as if he felt": Noda Statement, p. 4.


## Chapter 15: "The Most Imperative Problem at Present"

336 "the most imperative problem": Ugaki Diary, June 9, 1942, p. 159.

340 "Our fliers flew directly": Taguchi Risuke, "Naval Operations, First Year, Greater East Asia War," IGHQ Release, December 10, 1943, p. 8. NHC: Morison Papers, b. 21, f.: "Taguchi, Risuke."

341 "The place was shaking": Arthur McCollum, USNI Oral History, vol. 2, p. 472.

351 "somewhat" Edwin O. Reischauer, *My Life Between Japan and America.* New York: Harper & Row, 1986, p. 91.


## Chapter 16: Chrysanthemum and Cactus

359 "In the Fire Department": quoted in Constance Babington-Smith, *Air Spy.* New York: Ballantine Books, 1957, p. 107.

366 "Isle of Death": Kato Matsuo, *The Lost War.* New York: Knopf, 1946. Cf. Toland, *The Rising Sun*, p. 439.

368 "We didn't attach much importance": Admiral Fukudome Shigeru USSBS Interrogation no. 503; *Interrogations*, vol. 2, p. 527.

370 "slightly the favorite to date": Pacific Fleet Intelligence Summary, August 6, 1942. "CINCPAC Fleet Intelligence Summaries June 22, 1942–May 8, 1943," NARA: RG-457: SRMN-009, p. 53.

370 "unless ORANGE radio deception": ibid., August 21, 1942, p. 69.

370 "employment in the Bismarck-Solomons area": CINCPAC War Diary, August 10, 1942, p. 823. NHC: Microfilm, CINCPAC War Diary, Reel 1.

370 "it is not at all certain": ibid., August 17, 1942, p. 829.

371 "It now seems most probable": ibid., August 21, 1942, p. 831.

371 "No positive info as to presence of carriers": Dispatch, COMSOPAC-CTF 61 et al. 180916, August 18, 1942. CINCPAC War Diary, Reel 1, p. 655.

371 "INDICATIONS POINT STRONGLY": Dispatch, COMSOPAC-CTF 61 220910, August 22, 1942. CINCPAC War Diary, Reel 1, p. 808.

373 "ON NIGHT OF 4TH AND 5TH SEPTEMBER": Dispatch, New Zealand Naval Board T.O.O. 1834M/10, September 4, 1942. "Royal Australian Navy Support to USN Through Australian Commonwealth Naval Board Summaries/Translations of Japanese Messages, February–December 1942." NARA: RG-457: SRMN-006, p. 183.

381 "indicating the possibility": Japanese Naval Activities, October 19. 1942. "CNO Summaries of Intelligence." NARA: RG-457, SRNS-189.

389 "It is believed": Japanese Naval Activities, October 23, 1942. NARA: RG-457: SRNS-193.

390 "considerable success was attained": Japanese Monograph No. 118, *Operational History of Naval Communications, 1941–1945*, p. 304. Hereafter cited as "Naval Communications". NHC: RJN: Monographs series, b. 95, f.: "A-118, Idem."

390 "A strong enemy task force sailed": ibid., p. 300.

390 "All indications": Fleet Intelligence Summary, November 6, 1942. "CINCPAC Fleet Intelligence Summaries," NARA: RG-457, SRMN-009, p. 173.

390 "Predict an enemy all out attempt": Summary, November 9, 1942. ibid., p. 178.

391 "with news that another enemy offensive": Admiral William F. Halsey and J. Bryan III, *Admiral Halsey's Story*. New York: McGraw-Hill, 1947, p. 124.

391 "We want the big ones": quoted in Toland, *The Rising Sun*, p. 472.

393 "This is far from my aim": Ugaki Diary, November 15, 1942, p. 275.

393 "My only regret": Dispatch, CINCPAC-Radio Intelligence Units 170139, November 17, 1942. "OP-20-G Exploits and Commendations, World War II," NARA: RG-457: SRH-306, p. 58.

395 "A major action in this area": Pacific Fleet Intelligence Summary, January 31, 1943. NARA: RG-457: SRMN-009, p. 278.

## Chapter 17: "You Don't Have to Be Crazy, but It Helps!"

400 "They brought the communications documents down to us": Philip H. Jacobsen, NSG Oral History, pp. 30–31.

401 "It was very useful to have": Thomas Dyer, USNI Oral History, p. 272.

402 *"everything of any nature":* OPNAV (OP-16-F-9), Serial 01226416, May 11, 1942, reprinted in Navy Department Bulletin, June 1, 1942, p. C-6.

NARA: RG-38, ONI: Counterespionage series: Oriental Desk, b. 1, f.: "Japanese Intelligence Activities, U.S. (General)."

404 "I've heard that you've been talking": Arthur McCollum, USNI Oral History, vol. 1, pp. 362–63.

406 chicken tracks: Ralph Cox, NSG Oral History.

407 "Death was the only excuse": Elmer Dickey, NSG Oral History.

408 "You don't have to be crazy": Wilfred J. Holmes, *Double-Edged Secrets: U.S. Naval Intelligence Operations in the Pacific During World War II.* Annapolis, Md.: Naval Institute Press, 1979, p. 54.

410 "I refused to accept that": Joseph Rochefort, USNI Oral History, p. 256.

411 "The only probable explanation": W. J. Holmes, *Double-Edged Secrets*, p. 116.

418 "ten campaigns": Sidney Mashbir, *I Was an American Spy.* New York: Vantage Press, 1953, p. 223.

424 "That's *joltin'* 'em!": quoted in Allison Ind, *Allied Intelligence Bureau.* New York: David McKay Company, 1958, p. 258.

425 "We could not keep up": Rear Admiral Obayashi Sueo, USSBS Interrogation no. 310. NHC: RJN: USSBS series, b. 71.

428 "I would have liked": Commander Yokura Sashizo, USSBS Interrogation no. 250. NHC: RJN: USSBS series, b. 70.

429 "we were surprised there were places": Lieutenant Toyoda Takogo USSBS Interrogation no. 384. NHC: RJN: USSBS series, b. 72.

430 "were not very interested": ibid.

430 "I got little information": Commander Yokura Sashizo, USSBS Interrogation no. 250. NHC: RJN: USSBS Series, b.70.

437 "It would seem": ONI (OP-16-B-7-0), Memorandum for File, "Japanese Collaboration with Other Axis and Certain Neutral States in Intelligence Activities," February 3, 1944. NARA: RG-38: ONI: Counterespionage series: Oriental Desk, b. 8, f.: "Intelligence Organizations, Japanese Government (December 1940–August 1944)." It should be noted that some historians attribute the Latin American troubles entirely to German manipulations, while others go so far as to find the cause in maneuvers by *British* and F.B.I. officers attempting to create a World War II casus belli on a par with the notorious "Zimmerman Telegram."

437 "The importance of the city": ibid., p. 4.

438 "Woolworth aircraft carriers": Imperial Navy Attaché, Lisbon, Draft Dispatch no. 235, n.d. (ca. November 1943). NARA: RG-38: Counterespionage series, Oriental Desk, b. 17, f.: "Japanese Activities in Lisbon, 12 July 1943–17 March 1944." Recovered by O.S.S., this message was returned to the United States, translated, and made available to ONI on March 10, 1944.

442 "To make a chart showing": Rear Admiral Ono Takeji, USSBS Interrogation no. 246. NHC: RJN: USSBS Series, b. 70.

442 "very poor, very haphazard": Rear Admiral Tomioka Sadatoshi, USSBS Interrogation no. 355. NHC: RJN: USSBS series, b. 71.

442 "The 5th Section collects": Captain Ohmae Toshikazu, USSBS Interrogation no. 350. NHC: RJN: USSBS series, b. 71.

443 "Anyone outside of the planning" et. seq.: Rear Admiral Takeuchi Kaoru, USSBS Interrogation no. 410. NHC: RJN: USSBS series, b. 72.

443 "I felt that inasmuch": ibid.

443 "At first I thought the Germans" et. seq.: Captain Sanematsu Yuzuru, USSBS Interrogation no. 421. NHC: RJN: USSBS series, b. 72.

444 "We concentrated the efforts": Rear Admiral Takeuchi Kaoru, USSBS Interrogation no. 222. NHC: RJN: USSBS series, b. 69.

444 "I was picked for my knowledge": Commander Imai Nobuhiko, USSBS Interrogation no. 236. NHC: RJN: USSBS series, b. 70.

445 "I still think it would have lasted longer": Captain Sanematsu Yuzuru, USSBS Interrogation no. 421. NHC: RJN: USSBS series, b. 72.

445 "They are apt to start": Commander Imai Nobuhiko, USSBS Interrogation no. 236. NHC: RJN: USSBS series, b. 70.

### Chapter 18: "The Darkness Is Very Deep"

447 "The Emperor is troubled": quoted in Edwin P. Hoyt, *The Glory of the Solomons.* New York: Stein & Day, 1983, p. 21.

447 "present preparations": Supplement no. 2 to IGHQ Navy Directive 184, January 4, 1943. IGHQ Navy Directives, vol. 1, p. 85. NHC: USN Microfilm J-27.

448 "It was a Japanese word": Robert Guillain, *I Saw Tokyo Burning,* p. 80.

448 "If we can surprise an enemy's weak point": Ugaki Diary, December 29, 1942, p. 316.

448 "It will not be a good policy": ibid.

449 "The land-based air groups": Captain Ohmae Toshikazu, USSBS Interrogation no. 495. NHC: RJN: USSBS series, b. 73.

451 "In view of the incorrect estimate": Eighth Fleet, After Action Report, March 3, 1943 (WDC 16269-B); received ATIS April 10, 1946. NHC: Morison Papers, b. 27, f.: "Battle of the Bismarck Sea, 1943–1946."

451 "We are repeating the failure": ATIS Enemy Publication no. 7, Bismarck Sea Operations, part 2, November 29, 1943, p. 67. This comprised translated documents from three briefcases and a map case recovered on Goodenough Island, March 8, 1943. The "take" included both the Japanese Army operations order and Admiral Kimura's basic convoy order. Cited in Morison, *Breaking the Bismarcks Barrier* (vol. 6), p. 60.

452 "It looked like the 4th of July": James J. Fahey, *Pacific War Diary, 1942–1945.* New York: Zebra Books, 1963, p. 27.

456 "good prey for our attack tomorrow": Ugaki Diary, April 6, 1943, p. 323.

456 "a possible attack on Allied units": Pacific Fleet Intelligence Summaries, April 2, 4, 6, 1943. NARA: RG-457: SRMN-009, pp. 341, 343, 345.

458 "The meeting concluded in a pessimistic air": quoted in Okumiya and Horikoshi, *Zero,* p. 176.

459 "We've hit the jackpot": Captain Roger Pineau, quoted in R. Cargill Hall, ed., *Lightning over Bougainville.* Washington, D.C.: Smithsonian Institution Press, 1991, p. 42.

459 "I personally did the whole thing": Alva B. Lasswell, USMC Oral History, p. 40.

460 "good": Captain Roger Pineau, quoted in Hall, *Lightning over Bougainville,* p. 42.


**Chapter 19: Full Circle**

469 "There is growing suspicion": Pacific Fleet Intelligence Summary, March 18, 1943. SRMN-009, op. cit., p. 325.

472 "After the initial phase of the battle": Commander Ralph H. Millsap, "Skill or Luck?" *U.S. Naval Institute Proceedings Supplement,* n.d. (March) 1985, p. 84.

473 "several score": Japanese Monograph no. 89, "Northern Area Naval Operations," p. 32. NHC: RJN: Monographs series, b. 93.

473 "Gunfire at long range": Navy Department Communiqué no. 327, March 28, 1943. *Communiqués 301 to 600,* U.S. Navy: Office of Public Information, 1945, p. 9.

473 "We had purpose": quoted in Samuel Eliot Morison, *Aleutians, Gilberts, and Marshalls* (vol. 7), n. 21, p. 35.

475 "to create a sound strategic condition": IGHQ Navy Directive no, 246, May 21, 1943. NHC: IGHQ Navy Directives, USN Microfilm J-27.

476 "and it was Admiral Koga's belief": Admiral Fukudome Shigeru, USSBS Interrogation no. 503. *Interrogations,* vol. 2, p. 512.

476 "destroy the enemy": Battleship *Musashi,* Tabular Record of Movement (WDC 160624), p. 6. NHC: Tabular Records of Movement of Japanese Battleships and Cruisers, USN Microfilm JT-1.

476 "The bulk of the Japanese fleet": CINCPAC War Diary, June 8, 1943, p. 1567. NHC: Microfilm, CINCPAC War Diary, Reel 2.

476 "it is indicated": ibid., June 19, 1943, p. 1574.

476 "Men, I have bad news": Thomas F. T. Warren, NSG Oral History.

477 "From beach to beach this stuff": Albert M. Fishburn, NSG Oral History.

478 "Several conclusions are warranted": extract from G-2 Periodic Report no. 77, June 19, 1943, attachment to Memorandum, ONI-OP-20-G, July 7, 1943. NARA: RG-38: Counterespionage series, Oriental Desk, b. 1, f.: "Japanese Intelligence Activities, U.S. (General)."

479 "not improbable": Memorandum, ONI (OP-16-FE)-Joint Intelligence Committee, June 12, 1943. NHC: Naval Security Group Command: World War II Intelligence Documents series, b. 1, f.: "SA/35SP: Reports on Jap Fleet and Intentions."

480 "It's unbearable day after day": Anonymous, "The Diary of Takahashi," *U.S. Naval Institute Proceedings,* July 1980, p. 76.

481 "From the success of the Kiska withdrawal": Japanese Monograph no. 118, Naval Communications, p. 91.

483 "the one he kept in his head": Commander Nakajima Chikataka, USSBS Interrogation no. 309, p. 2. NHC:RJN: USSBS Series, b. 70.

484 "My estimates did not always agree": ibid., p. 5.

484 "The whole system was weak": ibid., pp. 7, 4, 5, 7.

484 "*the one chance* of success": Admiral Fukudome, *Interrogations*, v. 2, p. 512.

485 "The possibility is suggested" et. seq.: ONI (OP-16-FE), Intelligence Report 66-43, May 25, 1943. NARA: RG-38: Naval Operations series, ONI Reports subseries, b. 2, f.: "1943 F-14 serials."

485 "They say he is 'extremely suspicious'": *Time*, November 8, 1943, p. 30.

486 "On this occasion": Admiral Koga Mineichi, "Address no. 4 to the Combined Fleet," 232003, May 23, 1943. Pearl Harbor Hearings, Part 13, p. 612.

487–8 "third phase" et. seq.: Combined Fleet, Top Secret Operations Orders numbers 40–41, August 15, 1943. ATIS Limited Distribution Translation no. 39, Part VIII. NHC: USN Microfilm A-2.

491 "substantially larger": Navy Department Communiqué no. 429, July 1, 1943. *Communiqués 301 to 600*, p. 52.

492 "It wasn't necessary": Dan Bauer, "Torpedoes at Sea," *Military History*, April 1991, p. 34.

492 "Enemy composition and losses unknown": CINCPAC War Diary, July 5, 1943, p. 1616. (This is an east longitude date.) NHC: Microfilm, CINCPAC War Diary, reel 2.

492 "On July 6": ONI, "Japanese Naval Activities," July 8, 1943. FDRL: MRF: b. 65, f.: "MR 203(3) Japanese Naval Activities (7)."

494 "We were always planning an offensive": Admiral Kusaka Jinichi, USSBS field team interrogation no. 1, in USSBS Study no. 75, *The Allied Campaign Against Rabaul*, p. 47.

494 "Air units and surface units": Southeast Area Fleet Operations Order no. 10, July 18, 1943. NHC: RJN: SOPAC translations series, b. 3, f.: "No. 730."

498 "The Okino interrogation report": Memorandum, Commander W. J. Sebald–Commander W. J. Holmes, June 9, 1944. NARA: RG-457, "JICPOA/F-22 Administrative Correspondence," SRMD-009.

501 "at the opportune time": IGHQ Navy Directive no. 267, August 13, 1943. IGHQ Directives, USN Microfilm J-27.

501 "the attacking enemy" et. seq.: Ibid., IGHQ Directive no. 280, September 30, 1943.

503 "Communications forces": Fourth Fleet, Inner South Seas Force, Standing Order no. 1, March 10, 1943. NHC: NSGC: World War II Documents series, b. 1, f.: "5-A/70, Misc. Organizations and Doctrine."

504 "to the death": Ibid., Fourth Fleet, Marshalls Area Defense Force, Operations Order no. 5.

504 "The Fourth Fleet": Rear Admiral Nabeshima Shunsaku, USSBS Interrogation in Idem., v. 2, p. 411.
505 "Why did I ever come to carriers": quoted in Admiral J. J. Clark with Clark G. Reynolds, *Carrier Admiral.* New York: David McKay, 1967, p. 125.
506 "Our attack on Wake": CINCPAC War Diary, October 7, 1943, p. 1670. NHC: Microfilm, CINCPAC War Diary, reel 2.
507 "Traffic analysis maintained": Duane L. Whitlock, NSG Oral History, p. 26.
507 "Traffic [deleted]": COMINCH Summary of Radio Intelligence, October 21, 1943. NARA: RG-457: SRNS-0556.
507 "suggest they are a series": ibid., October 22, 1943. SRNS-0557.
507 "it is believed that": ibid., October 26, 1943. SRNS-0561.
508 "The failure of radio": ibid., October 27, 1943; SRNS-0562.
508 "what appeared to be": ibid., October 29, 1943. SRNS-0564.
509 "We have never teamed together": quoted in Hara et al., *Japanese Destroyer Captain,* p. 230.
510 "the most desperate emergency": Halsey and Bryan, *Admiral Halsey's Story,* pp. 180–81.
512 "most secret": Dispatch, SOPAC-CINCPAC 280643, October 28, 1943. In CINCPAC War Diary, p. 1819.
512 "no indications of larger Japanese surface units": COMINCH Radio Intelligence Summary, October 31, 1943. SRNS-0566.
512 "indicates reinforcements en route": Dispatch, SOPAC-CINCPAC 030100, November 3, 1943. In CINCPAC War Diary, p. 1822.
512 "CinC 2nd": COMINCH Radio Intelligence Summary, November 3, 1943. SRNS-0569.
517 "U.S. forces were perplexed": ONI (OP-16-B-7-0), Intelligence Digest 43-13, "Pacific Area News," November 23, 1943, p. 2. NARA: RG-38: COD series, b. 19, f.: "Reports for CINCPAC."
517 "Now the enemy's operations": ibid., Digest 43-14, November 29, 1943, p. 2.
518 "The moment I passed through": Okumiya Masatake et al, *Zero,* pp. 222–23.
518 "It is one thing to know": ibid., p. 224.
520 "This document indicates": JICPOA Bulletin 107-45, May 14, 1945, p. 19. NHC: USN Microfilm JP-30.

## Chapter 20: Hailstones and Hammerblows

526 "would be resisted most vigorously": Memorandum, ONI (OP-16-FE)–Joint Intelligence Committee, June 12, 1943. NHC:NSGC: World War II series, b. 1, f.: "5A/35SP, Reports on Jap Fleet and Intentions."
526 "the planners believed": Harry A. Gailey, *Howlin' Mad vs. the Army.* New York: Dell Books, 1987, p. 71.
528 "are quite definitely on plane ferry trips": JICPOA, "Estimate of Enemy

Strength in the Marshalls, Gilberts, and Adjacent Areas," September 13, 1943. NARA: RG-457, "Estimate . . . [idem.] 6 September–27 December 1943," SRMN-021. This became the first of several series of special estimates that focused on Japanese strength in various areas as the Allied offensive progressed. The Carolines-Marianas, Philippines, and Empire approaches all were subjects of subsequent estimates.

528 "It is believed that elements": ibid., September 27, 1943.

528 "The situation in the Marshalls-Gilberts": ibid., November 1, 1943.

528 "It is believed there are no important naval units": ibid.

531 "Study of Japanese Defenses on Betio Island of Tarawa Atoll," JICPOA Special Publication, n.d. (1943).

531 baskets: Ladislas Farago, *War of Wits*. New York: Paperback Library, 1954, p. 64–66.

532 "They are searching the outer perimeter": ONI(OP-16-B-7-0), Intelligence Digest: "Pacific Area News," no. 43-14, November 29, 1943, p. 2. Op. cit.

532 "the central route of advance": *ONI Weekly Review*, vol. 3, no. 5, February 2, 1944, pp. 390–91. NHC: World War II Command File: CNO File: *ONI Intelligence* Review, b. 180.

533 "that the enemy will no doubt come": ibid.

533 "we could see the fleet at anchor": Hagimoto Toshio, "Sorrow and the Southern Cross," in Soka Gakkai, ed., *Peace Is Our Duty*. Tokyo: The Japan Times, 1982, p. 164.

535 "sensational rise in the volume": COMINCH Summary of Radio Intelligence, February 10, 1944. NARA: RG-457; SRNS-0668.

535 "convincing evidence": JICPOA, "Estimate of Enemy Distribution and Intentions," February 7, 1944. NARA: RG-457, "JICPOA Estimates, April 1943–August 1944 (pt. 1)," NARA:RG-457; SRMD-010.

535 "Best estimates place all": ibid., February 14, 1944.

537 "word had already reached us": Hagimoto, "Sorrow and the Southern Cross," p. 168.

538 "We better make sure": Gilven M. Slonim Interview.

538 "I believed that an attack was possible": Vice Admiral Hara Chuichi USSBS field interrogation, Interrogations of Senior Naval Commanders at Truk, no. 20. NARA Microfilm Pub M16, Rd1 311.

542 "attack mission strength": IGHQ Navy Directive no. 285, October 14, 1943. USN Microfilm J-27.

543 "appears to be organizing": COMINCH Radio Intelligence Summary, October 17, 1943. NARA: RG-457; SRNS-0552.

543 "apparently a new command": ibid.

544 "It was almost pitiful": William J. Sebald, USNI Oral History, p. 254.

546 "In March of next year": quoted in Commander Nakajima Chikataka, USSBS Interrogation in Idem., vol. 2, p. 435.

548 "The tenor of the various dispatches": COMINCH Radio Intelligence Summary, March 26, 1944. NARA: RG-457; SRNS-0713.

548 "Traffic reveals continued preoccupation": ibid., March 28, 1944, SRNS-0715.

549 "The planes of the first attack unit": Inoue Diary in JICPOA Bulletin, Translations and Interrogations no. 18, Item no. 13,833, p. 50. NHC: USN Microfilm JP-21.

550 "Let us go out and die together," John Toland, *The Rising Sun,* op. cit., quoted p. 544.

551 "Looking back on this experience": Admiral Fukudome Shigeru, USSBS Interrogation, in *Interrogations,* vol. 2, p. 521.


**Chapter 21: Down to the Sea in Ships**

553 "The Japanese Navy could not obtain": Japanese Monograph no. 118, "Naval Communications," p. 90.

554 "No matter how we hit enemy America" et. seq. (except "patch quilt" and "slender hopes"): ONI (OP-16-B-7-0), Intelligence Digest: "Pacific Area News," 44-4, January 24, 1944, p. 1.

554 told a business magazine: quoted in Otto Tolischus, *Through Japanese Eyes,* p. 111.

555 "if and when necessary": Ugaki Diary, May 19, 1944, p. 373.

556 "Surface gadgets 290": quoted in G. Herman Gill, *Australia in the War of 1939–1945: Royal Australian Navy, 1942–1945.* Canberra: Australian War Memorial, 1968, p. 431.

557 "All ships appear the same size": quoted in ibid., p. 432.

557 "It was a bitter disappointment": quoted in ibid., p. 435.

557 "Whether one likes it or not": *Ugaki Diary,* op. cit., June 3, 1944, p. 385.

558 "The backbone of the revolutionary changes": ONI (OP-16-B-7-0), "Intelligence Digest: Pacific Area News," 43-13, November 22, 1943. This source reports a Berlin Transocean broadcast on November 14, interestingly enough, shortly after U.S. authorities revealed the success of their Rabaul strikes.

558 "If the U.S. believes": ONI Intelligence Digest 44-4, Ibid.

560 "In view of future military prospects": Central Pacific Area Fleet, Secret Order no. 4, April 3, 1944. JICPOA Item no. 8889, June 27, 1944. NHC: NSGC: World War II Intelligence Documents, b. 5, f.: "7000s–8000s."

560 "push forward at top speed": Central Pacific Area Fleet, Secret Operations Order no. 1, April 15, 1944. (JICPOA Item no. 8883, June 29, 1944. Ibid.

562 Our diarist notes: Diary of Nagata Kazumi, June–July 1944. JICPOA Bulletin 116-45. NHC: USN Microfilm JP-32.

564 "A formation in which": Battle Lessons of the Greater East Asia War, vol. 7: Submarines, p. 31. Enclosure A to U.S. Naval Technical Mission to Japan, Target Report S-17/18: Japanese Submarine Operations, February 1946. NHC: USN Microfilm JM-200-I.

569 " 'A' Operations are believed to be": COMINCH Daily Radio Intelligence Summary, June 15, 1944. NARA:RG-457; SRNS-0794.

570 "The fate of the Empire": quoted in Samuel Eliot Morison, *New Guinea and the Marianas* (vol. 8), p. 231.

573 "I guess Japan itself": Diary of Seaman 1/c Inoue, June 15, 1944. JICPOA
   Item no. 13,833 in JICPOA Bulletin 22-45, USN Microfilm JP-21.
578 "The decision to make a final stand": Nagata Diary, July 4, 1944. USN
   Microfilm JP-32.
580 "One supposes that more may trickle in": Fleet Radio Unit Melbourne,
   FRUMEL News, June 27, 1944, p. 5. NARA: RG-457: "OP-20-G File of Fleet
   Radio Unit, Melbourne, 28 June 1943–2 September 1945," SRH-275,
   p. 91.

### Chapter 22: "The Most Crucial Point Has Been Reached"

581 "Japan's Fleet-in-Being Strategy": Ito Masanori, idem., *Contemporary
   Japan*, vol. 13, nos. 7–9, July–September 1944, pp. 643, 639.
581 "may therefore be considered": U.S. Army, G-2 Division, Military Attaché
   Report, Argentina no. 11242, June 29, 1944. NARA: RG-38: COD, b. 18, f.:
   "Japanese Intelligence Activities, Latin America January 1944–August
   1945."
582 "the naval battle which took place": ibid., no. 11261, July 4, 1944.
   NARA: RG-38: COD, b. 18.
582 "Japan welcomes the advance": Department of State, Central Information
   Office Report no. 15694, August 12, 1944, NARA: RG-38: COD, b. 18.
582 Suetsugu observed: Admiral Suetsugu Nobumasa in Domei Radio
   Broadcast. Quoted in *ONI Weekly Review*, October 11, 1944, p. 3220.
583 "The Navy, failing to grasp": Marquis Kido Diary, June 21, 1944, p. 385.
583 "The damage sustained by our side": Admiral Yonai Mitsumasa Diet
   speech, *Contemporary Japan*, p. 851.
583 "The fall of Saipan": Baron Tomioka Sadatoshi, USSBS Interrogation no.
   355, p. 7. NHC: RJN: USSBS series, b. 71.
584 "Since, without the participation": Admiral Toyoda Soemu, USSBS
   Interrogation, in *Interrogations* vol. 2, p. 317.
584 "I believe . . . that the fleet authorities": Admiral Oikawa Koshiro USSBS
   Interrogation no. 494, p. 12. NHC: RJN: USSBS series, b. 73.
584 "By the time you had taken": Admiral Takata Toshitane USSBS
   Interrogation no. 276, p. 3. NHC: RJN: USSBS series, b. 70.
585 "will be moved up to the Philippines" et. seq.: IGHQ Navy Directive no.
   431. Reprinted USSBS, *Campaigns of the Pacific War*. Washington, D.C.: U.S.
   Government Printing Office, 1946, pp. 292–93.
586 "The next enemy offensive": Ugaki Diary, July 25, 1944, p. 436.
586 "Japan's national power": Colonel Hattori Takushiro, *Complete History of
   the Greater East Asian War* (U.S. 500th Military Intelligence Service Group
   trans.), WDC 78436, Part 8, p. 271. Copy at Naval Historical Center.
   Original published Tokyo: Hara Shobo, 1966.
587 "to intercept and destroy": Combined Fleet, Top Secret Operations Order
   no. 83, August 1, 1944. MacArthur Historical Report, vol. 2, part 1, p. 329.
587 "Where penetration operations": Combined Fleet, Top Secret Operations

Order no. 87, August 20, 1944. ATIS: Limited Distribution Translation no. 39, part 8. NHC: USN Microfilm A-2.

588 "If it goes like this in reality": Ugaki Diary, September 15, 1944, p. 455.

589 Admiral Ozawa judged: First Mobile Fleet Memorandum, "Tactical Organization," September 10, 1944. NHC: RJN: Leyte Series, b. 33, f.: "Intelligence."

590 "most probable that the next operation": ibid.

590 "Execution of the SHO": IGHQ Navy Directive no. 462, September 21, 1944. MacArthur Report, vol. 2, part 1, p. 353.

591 "In the present": "Know Your Enemy: Japanese Radio Communications and Radio Intelligence," JICPOA Bulletin 5-45, January 1, 1945. NHC: USN Microfilm JP-19.

594 "Our whole analysis": Lieutenant Commander Satake T., USSBS Interrogation no. 431. NHC: RJN: USSBS series, b. 72.

597 "It isn't worth it": Memorandum, W. J. Holmes–Joseph Rochefort, August 14, 1944. NARA: RG-457: SRMD-009, JICPOA/F-22 Administrative Correspondence.

597 "It has been necessary": Letter, W. J. Sebald–W. J. Holmes, November 9, 1944. Ibid.

598 "The enemy's shipping position": ONI (OP-16-FE), "Estimate of Japan's Shipping Position," Serial 11-44, April 1, 1944. NARA: RG-38: ONI Reports series, b. 5, f.: "1944 F-16 Serials."

600 "His airpower is in a bad way": Letter, General George Kenney–General Hap Arnold, September 17, 1944. NARA: RG-457: "Papers from the Files of Colonel Alfred McCormack," SRH-141, part 2.

600 "It is believed": JICPOA, "Estimate of Enemy Distribution and Intentions," September 4, 1944. NARA: RG-457: SRMD-010, Part 2.

601 "improve the logistics": CINCPOA (Fleet Intelligence Officer), "Estimate of Enemy Situation," September 15, 1944. NHC: Morison Papers, b. 93, f.: "CINCPOA Estimate." Also subsequent dates as noted.

603 "the Allied Naval Commander": Naval War College, *The Battle for Leyte Gulf, October 1944: Strategical and Tactical Analysis*, vol. 1. Newport, R.I.: Naval War College, 1953, p. 22. Hereafter cited as "Naval War College Study," with volume number.

603 "fleet action is less likely than ever": quoted in Morison, vol. 12, p. 72.

603 "may move in strength": Message, SOWESPAC GHQ–SOWESPAC Forward, 171536 October 1944. Naval War College Study, vol. 1, pp. 22–23.

603 "spotty and defective": Morison, vol. 12, p. 71.

603 "it was beginning to be assumed": ibid., p. 160.

603 "navigational hazards": SOWESPAC Estimate, October 20, 1944. In Naval War College Study, vol. III, p. 6-A.

604 "The enemy is jittery": JICPOA, "Estimate of Enemy Distribution and Intentions," October 2, 1944. NARA: RG-457: SRMD-010, Part 2.

605 "an astute conclusion": JICPOA, "Summary of Ultra Traffic," October 6, 1944. NARA: RG-457: SRMD-007, Part 1.

605 "The Philippines–[Taiwan]–Nansei Shoto line": JICPOA, "Estimate of Enemy Distribution and Intentions," October 9, 1944. NARA: RG-457-SRMD-010, Part 2.

605 "intensification of the island's contribution": quoted in *ONI Weekly Review*, vol. 3, no. 40, October 4, 1944, p. 3220.

608 "it is estimated": Third Section (NGS): Dispatch 111255, October 11, 1944. (Drawn from Destroyer Squadron 10, Detailed Action Report no. 13). NHC: RJN: Leyte Series, b. 30, f.: "Miscellaneous Orders and Dispatches."

608 "This is an extremely interesting": Naval War College Study, vol. 1, p. 281.

608 "Gary . . . flew back to *Enterprise*": Edward P. Stafford, *The Big E*. New York: Ballantine Books, 1974, p. 404.

609 "attacks against air bases": Imperial General Headquarters, Battle Experience Report no. 47, December 19, 1944 (captured on Iwo Jima). JICPOA Bulletin 107-45, May 14, 1945, p. 89. NHC: USN Microfilm JP-30.

610 "with the increasing importance": Office of Strategic Services (OSS), "Translation: Imperial Japanese Navy Publicity on Battle off Formosa—Criticism of," December 16, 1944. NARA: RG-38: COD series, b. 8, f.: "Japanese Activities Lisbon 2 October 1944–11 May 1945."

611 "If [Burke] returns to Washington": Letter, W. J. Sebald–W. J. Holmes, November 23, 1944. SRMD-009, JICPOA/F-22 Administrative Correspondence. NARA: RG-457.

612 "The trouble with the oil": Rear Admiral Enomoto Ryuchiro, USSBS Interrogation no. 172. NHC: RJN: USSBS series, b. 69.

614 "A considerable scaling down": ONI (OP-16-FE): "Estimate of Japan's Shipping Position April 1st 1944, Including a Special Report on Shipbuilding," serial 20-44, May 19, 1944, p. 1. NARA: RG-38: ONI Reports series, b. 5, f.: "1944 F-16 Serials."

615 "fleet logistics": JICPOA, "Estimate of Enemy Distribution and Intentions," September 11, 1944. SRMD-010, JICPOA Estimates of Enemy Distribution. NARA: RG-457, Part 2.

615 "The overall tanker movement": ibid., September 18, 1944.

615 "This is the first indication": COMINCH, "Summary of Radio Intelligence," October 17, 1944. NARA: RG-457: "Japanese Radio Intelligence Summaries 1944," SRNS-0918.

616 "current sightings": JICPOA, "Estimate of Enemy Distribution and Intentions," October 23, 1944.


**Chapter 23: "The Enemy Task Forces Will Be Destroyed Tomorrow"**

618 "We couldn't make up our minds": Commander Nakajima Chikataka, USSBS Interrogation, in *Interrogations*, vol. 1, p. 145.

619 "Having missed our opportunity": Admiral Teraoka Kimpei Diary, October 12, 1944 (from Diary Extracts 10–20 October, U.S. Navy translation). NHC: RJN: Leyte Series, b. 30, f.: "Senior Officer Comments."

619 "We all knew": Colonel Murata Kingo, USSBS Interrogation no. 171, p. 1. NHC: RJN: USSBS series, b. 69.

621 "Meaning unknown": JICPOA, "Summary of ULTRA Traffic," October 17, 1944. NARA: RG-457: "JICPOA Summary of ULTRA Traffic 11 September–11 December 1944," SRMD-007, Part 1, p. 108.

621 "Yesterday's intercepted Japanese traffic": COMINCH, "Summary of Radio Intelligence," October 17, 1944. NARA: RG-457: SRNS-0918.

621 "It has become obvious": Vice Admiral Teraoka Kimpei Diary Extract, October 18, 1944. NHC: RJN: Leyte Series, b. 30, f.: "Senior Officer Comments."

627 "Since it is recognized": quoted in Naval War College Study, vol. 1, p. 421.

629 "type and size open to doubt": Message, Com7thFlt 210721 October 1944 (Honolulu Repeat October 22/0130). FDRL: Map Room Files, b. 95, f.: "MR 300, Warfare Pacific (Section 10)." This message indicates that the aircraft report was first sent on October 21, but that must result from garbling, because the time of origination at Seventh Fleet is some hours earlier than the time of sighting given in the dispatch itself.

630 "since the chief of staff": quoted in Naval War College Study, vol. 3, Part 1, p. 192.

631 "The war situation": quoted in Edwin P. Hoyt, *The Battle of Leyte Gulf.* New York: Pinnacle Books, 1973, p. 13.

634 "with view of attack": Message, Com7thFlt 210526 October 1944. FDRL: Map Room Files, b.95, f.: "MR 300, Warfare Pacific (Section 10)."

636 "[We] sent out three contact": "Submarine *Darter* Patrol Report," in Theodore S. Roscoe, *Pigboats.* New York: Bantam Books, 1967, p. 339.

638 "any materials of operational value": Cruiser *Takao*, Detailed Action Report, Leyte Gulf (WDC 160641), p. 2. NHC: RJN: Leyte Series, b. 31, f.: "Destroyer Squadron 10."

641 "UNDER THESE CIRCUMSTANCES": First Diversion Attack Force, Battle Summary Operation "SHO," USSBS, *Campaigns of the Pacific War*, p. 301.

641 "WITH CONFIDENCE": Combined Fleet, Dispatch SMS 241813, October 24, 1944. In ibid.

642 "advance even though the fleet should be completely lost": Admiral Toyoda Soemu, USSBS Interrogation in Idem., vol. 2, p. 317.

642 "TONIGHT EVERY EFFORT WILL BE MADE": Southwest Area Fleet Dispatch 250008, October 25, 1944 (Mikawa-Toyoda). NHC: RJN: Leyte Series, b. 30, f.: "1st Striking Force (2)."

647 "MY PRESENT OPERATIONS": Third Fleet, Dispatch 210645, October 21, 1944 (Halsey-MacArthur). FDRL: MRF, b. 95, f.: "MR no. 300, Warfare—Pacific (10)."

647 "GENERAL PLAN": CINCPAC Dispatch 211852, October 21, 1944 (Nimitz-Halsey). Ibid.

648 "BASIC PLAN FOR THIS OPERATION": Cable, MacArthur-Halsey 211200 October 1944. Ibid.

648 "I CONSIDER THE APPROACH": Seventh Fleet, Dispatch 230142, October 23, 1944 (Kinkaid-Halsey). Ibid.

653 "It is a matter of regret": Admiral Ozawa Jisaburo Comments, "Postwar Impressions of the SHO Operation," n.d., Far East Command, Headquarters Special Collection (item 22, Footlocker 5, SWPA Series vol. 2). NHC: RJN, Leyte Series, b. 30, f.: "Senior Officer Comments."

655 "Combined Fleet . . . took no action": Captain Ohmae Toshikazu, "Research Report on Questions Relating to the SHO Operation," n.d. (c. April 13, 1953), p. 7. NHC: ibid.

658 "nobility of failure": Ivan Morris, *The Nobility of Failure: Tragic Heroes in the History of Japan.* Rutland, Vt.: Charles E. Tuttle, 1982.

660 "The disposition of PTs": Edward I. Farley, *PT Patrol.* New York: Popular Library, 1962, pp. 109–110.

665 "masts were sighted to the southeast": Vice Admiral Kurita Takeo, USSBS Interrogation, in *Interrogations,* vol. 1, p. 41.

665 "overjoyed": Admiral Kusaka Ryunosuke, *The Combined Fleet: Memoirs of Former Chief of Staff Kusaka.* Tokyo: Mainichi Shimbun Sha, 1952. Translation of excerpts by U.S. Navy, p. 9. NHC: RJN: Leyte Series, b. 30, f.: "Senior Officer Comments."

667 "a heaven-sent opportunity": Rear Admiral Koyanagi Tomiji, "The Battle of Leyte Gulf," in Evans, op. cit., p. 367.

669 "Hey": quoted in William T. Y'Blood, *The Little Giants.* Annapolis, Md.: Naval Institute Press, 1987, p. 160.

671 "Close enemy carriers": Battleship *Kongo,* Detailed Action Report, Leyte Gulf, WDC 161637, p. 6. NHC: RJN: Leyte Series, b. 31, f.: "BatDiv 3."

671 "We are engaging": ibid.

672 "Cruiser divisions attack" et. seq.: Cruiser Division 7, Detailed Action Report, Leyte Gulf WDC 161005. NHC: RJN: Leyte Series, b. 31, f.: "CruDiv 7."

676 "Watch out for torpedo tracks": quoted in Battleship *Haruna,* Detailed Action Report no. 2 (WDC 161637), p. 6. NHC: RJN: Leyte Series, b. 31, f.: "BatDiv 3."

676 "We didn't think": Commander Otani Tonosuke, USSBS Interrogation no. 437, p. 7. NHC: RJN: USSBS series, b. 72.

677 "We had poor communications": Commander Otani, Interrogation in Idem., vol. 1, p. 173.

677 "The smoke was made very quickly": ibid.

678 "Crudiv 5 and Crudiv 7": quoted in Ronald H. Spector, ed., *Listening to the Enemy.* Wilmington: Scholarly Resources, 1988, p. 95. (Condensed from NARA: RG-457: SRH-289. Cf. "Pacific Ocean Mobile Radio Intelligence Unit Reports, 1944," SRH-314.)

678 "It just operated all day": Albert M. Fishburn, NSG Oral History.

679 "On the morning of the twenty-fifth": W. J. Holmes, *Double-Edged Secrets,* p. 192.

679 "WHERE IS REPEAT WHERE IS": quoted in E. B. Potter, *Nimitz,* p. 340.

680 "ENEMY FORCES ATTACKING": Map Room Briefing Note, n.d. (October 24, 1944, Washington date). FDRL: MRF, b. 95, f.: "MR no. 300 Warfare—Pacific (10)."

680 "Intercepted Japanese traffic": COMINCH, "Summary of Radio Intelligence," October 25, 1944. SRNS-0926, NARA: RG-457 "COMINCH Summary of Radio Intelligence."

681 "An extraordinarily heavy file": ibid., October 26, 1944. SRNS-0927.

681 "At the time I did not have": Admiral Toyoda, in *Interrogations*, vol. 2, p. 317.

682 "UNDER ATTACK": Seventh Fleet (TU 77.4), Dispatches 242235, 242239, 242329, October 24, 1944; all quoted from CINCPAC War Diary, p. 2246. NHC: Microfilm Idem, reel 2.

685 "Giving up the pursuit": Koyanagi, p. 368.

685 Admiral Kurita himself referred: Admiral Kurita Takeo, USSBS Interrogation Idem., vol. 1, p. 42.

685 "We were low on fuel": Commander Otani, USSBS Interrogation no. 437.

686 "Until about": First Diversion Attack Force, Battle Summary, p. 304.

686 "My mind was extremely fatigued": quoted in Ito Masanori with Roger Pineau, *The End of the Imperial Japanese Navy.* New York: Jove Books, 1984, p. 178.

687 "The fact that": Asahi and Radio Tokyo commentaries October 26, 1944. Digested in *Contemporary Japan*, vol. 13, nos. 10–12, October–December 1944. Portions or all of the same commentaries are in *ONI Weekly Review*, vol. 3, no. 44, November 1, 1944, p. 3488.

## Chapter 24: The Last of the Imperial Navy

696 "act as a bombardment": JICPOA, "ULTRA Traffic Summary," December 23, 1944. SRMD-007, p. 310.

698 "How many months" et. seq.: Quoted from an article, "Japanese Naval Officer's Diary Reveals Concern About Future," in U.S. Army, Pacific (Counterintelligence Corps), *C. I. Bulletin* no. 63, August 15, 1945, pp. 1–2. NARA: Microfilm Publication M-1652, reel 38.

711 "That was the very last": Rear Admiral Takata Toshitane USSBS Interrogation no. 276.

711 "seems to date": JICPOA, "Summary of ULTRA Traffic," April 2, 1945. SRMD-007, Part 3, p. 4.

711 "Having used only part": ibid., p. 7.

711 "Second Fleet will arrive": JICPOA, "Summary of ULTRA Traffic," April 5, 1945. Ibid., p. 12.

711 "Although situated 8,000 miles": Joseph N. Wenger Memorandum, "C. I. Contributions to Operations 6–7 April 1945," April 9, 1945. NARA: RG-475: SRH-306, p. 105.

712 "They quit too soon": JICPOA, "Summary of ULTRA Traffic," April 7, 1945. SRMD-007, Part 3, p. 19.

713 "It is hard for me to believe": Hara Tameichi et al., *Japanese Destroyer Captain*, p. 292.

714 "We wanted to console the spirits": quoted in John Burgess, "Wreckage of Huge Battleship is Found," *The Washington Post*, August 14, 1985, p. A18.

716 "Holcomb, . . . you go and wake": quoted in Bankston T. Holcomb, USMC Oral History, p. 53.

717 "He always listened": ibid., p. 57.

718 "I was on the verge": Captain Genda Minoru USSBS Interrogation no. 479. NHC: RJN: USSBS series, b. 73.

720 "The study of nuclear physics is a national project": Pacific War Research Society, *The Day Man Lost: Hiroshima, August 6, 1945* (no translator given). Tokyo: Kodansha International, 1981, quoted p. 26.

# B I B L I O G R A P H Y

## DOCUMENTARY SOURCES

**National Archives and Records Administration (NARA):**

Records Group 38: Office of the Chief of Naval Operations: Operational
Records Series

Office of Naval Intelligence (ONI): Far East Division:
Captured Japanese Documents Series (1942–1946)

ONI: Far East Division (OP-16/OP-23): Translations
Series

ONI: Far East Division: Serial Reports Series

ONI: Far East Division: Reference Material Series
(attaché reports)

ONI: Counterespionage: Oriental Desk

Records Group 80: Department of the Navy (selected records)

Pearl Harbor Liaison Office Series

Records Group 226: Office of Strategic Services

Records Group 457: National Security Agency (Note: In past years some
writers have taken to referencing the titles and
identification numbers of each item consulted. This is
the equivalent of listing file titles in other document
collections. As in other collections, some of these files
are many boxes long; others have just a few pages. As
with other collections, here will be listed only the
broad categories of records, the "series." Interested
readers may consult the notes for leads to specific
documents or folders.)

SRH: Special Research Histories

SRMD: Joint Service Discrete Records of Historic
Cryptologic Importance

SRMN: U.S. Navy Discrete Records of Historic Cryptologic
Importance

SRN: Japanese Navy Message Translations

SRNA: Japanese Naval Attaché Message Translations

SRNM: Miscellaneous Records

SRNS: Japanese Naval Radio Intelligence Summaries

**Franklin Delano Roosevelt Library, NARA:**

President's Secretary's Files: Confidential File Series
 Safe File Series
Map Room File Series
John Toland Papers: Series I, Series V

**Harry S. Truman Library, NARA:**

President's Secretary's Files: Subject File
 Intelligence File

**Naval Historical Center, United States Navy:**

World War II Command File: Chief of Naval Operations Intelligence File
 Commander Air Solomons File
 Commander Air South Pacific File
 Commander-in-Chief Pacific File: War Diaries
 Assorted Microfilms
Records of the Japanese Navy and Related Translations:
 Washington Document Center Series
 North Pacific Translations Series
 South Pacific Translations Series
 Allied Translator and Interpreter Section Series
 Leyte Series
 Japanese Monographs Series
 Japanese Original Document Series
 Miscellaneous Series
Naval Security Group Command: World War II Intelligence Documents Series
Samuel Eliot Morison Papers

## ORAL HISTORIES AND INTERVIEWS

For a subject increasingly embedded in the past we are fortunate indeed to benefit from oral histories compiled by several institutions and the armed services, from interviews by historians such as John Toland, and from interrogations performed during and after the war by intelligence units and the United States Strategic Bombing Survey. This history has made considerable use of these resources, as the notes will attest. Here I list individuals in one of three categories. First are those who furnished interviews or gave oral histories. I performed a few of these interviews, but most were collected by the oral-history programs of the U.S. Marine Corps, U.S. Navy and Columbia University, the United States Naval Institute, or the Naval Security Group (NSG). A few Japanese interviews are listed, which do not fit easily in the large set collected by Toland or in the interrogations in our third category. In each case interviewees are listed with the highest rank they are known to have attained. Sources of the interviews are indicated in parentheses. Sources of interrogations are explained separately in a note that accompanies that listing.

### Interviews

Cdr. Joyce M. Barker (NSG); William Beltz (NSG); LCdr Gordon I. Bower (NSG); Seaman Ralph T. Briggs (NSG; also John Toland); Nicolas Caravakis (NSG); LCdr Kenneth E. Carmichael (NSG); Ralph Cox (NSG); Elmer Dickey (NSG); Capt Thomas H. Dyer (USNI); LCdr Robert E. Dowd (NSG); Robert L. Dormer (NSG); Granville Esch (NSG); CPO Bernard J. Evans (NSG); Albert M. Fishburn (NSG); Lt Elmer H. Frantz (NSG); CWO2/c Thomas E. Gilmore (NSG); Raymond G. Hagen (NSG); David A. Hatch (Prados); Frank Hess (NSG); BrigGen Bankston T. Holcomb (USMC; also NSG personal history statement); Virgil Houck (NSG); Jack E. Ingram (Prados); LCdr Phillip H. Jacobsen (NSG); LCdr Carl Jensen (NSG); Lt Charlie J. Johns (NSG); Capt Stephen Jurika (USNI); Capt Homer L. Kisner (NSG); Capt Jackson L. Koon (NSG); Col Alva B. Lasswell (USMC); RAdm Edwin T. Layton (USNI); LtCol Stephen Lesko (NSG); Capt George W. Linn (NSG); RAdm Arthur M. McCollum (USNI); James K. McNiece (Prados); Jacob J. Mandel (NSG); RM1/c Kenneth A. Mann (NSG); Lashley H. Mann (NSG; also NSG personal history statement); RAdm James L. Montgomery (Prados); Robert G. Ogg (NSG; also John Toland); LCdr Elliot Okins (NSG); PO Omi Heichiro (Walter Lord); Edward Otte (NSG); Lt Larry L. Paxson (Prados); James Pearson (NSG); Capt Albert J. Pelletier (NSG); James J. Perkins (NSG); Capt Roger Pineau (Prados); Thomas Powell (Prados); John Quesenberry (NSG); CWO Charles G. Quinn (NSG); Capt Francis A. Raven (John Toland); Capt Joseph J. Rochefort (USNI; also Percy Greaves); Lt Meddie Royer (NSG); RM1/c Raymond A. Rundle (NSG); Capt Sanematsu Yuzuru (John Toland); Henry F. Schorreck (Prados); Capt William J. Sebald (USNI); Roy Sholes (NSG); Capt Gilven M. Slonim (Prados); Capt William R. Smedberg (USNI); Capt Henri Smith-Hutton (USNI); VAdm Roland N. Smoot (USNI); Lt Paul Stevens (Prados); Clarence P. Taylor (NSG); VAdm John S. Thach (USNI); Robert Throckmorton (NSG); CPO Howard Troup (NSG); Thomas F. T. Warren (NSG); Capt Watanabe Yasuji (Walter Lord); Capt Duane L. Whitlock (NSG; also NSG personal history statement; also Prados); LCdr Theodore J. Wildman (NSG).

### John Toland Interview Series

All interviews were compiled for Toland's book *The Rising Sun.* Lt Abe Heijiro; Ens Aoki Yasunori; Lt(jg) Asami Wahei; Civilian Fujimoto Hisaro; Capt Fujita Masamichi; Civilian Fujiyama Tsutae; VAdm Fukudome Shigeru; Capt Genda Minoru; Lt Hirayama Shigeo; PO Hosoya Shiro; Capt Ikeda Sadae; Lt Iki Haruki; Capt Kamimura Arashi; Capt Kato Kenkichi; RAdm Komura Keizo; LCdr Koyama Choichi; RAdm Koyanagi Tomiji; Lt Kuhara Kazutoshi; VAdm Kusaka Jinichi; VAdm Kusaka Ryunosuke; Lt Matsumura Hirata; VAdm Mikawa

Gunichi; Capt Miyo Kazunari; Lt Mori Juzo; VAdm Nagasawa Ko; Lt Naito Masanao; Cdr Nishino Shigeru; Y2/c Noda Mitsuharu; Capt Nomura Jiro; RAdm Obayashi Sueo; Capt Ohmae Toshikazu; Capt Oi Atsushi; Y1/c Omi Heijiro; CPO Oshita Mitsukuni; Dr. Sagane Ryokichi; PO Saima Haruyoshi; Gen Sanagi Sadamu; Cdr Sata Naohiro; Lt Shiga Yoshio; VAdm Shima Kiyohide; Ens Shimoyama Fukujiro; Capt Suzuki Eichiro; Adm Suzuki Suguru; RAdm Takagi Sokichi; Lt Takahashi Katsusaku; Ens Takahashi Kiyoshi; LCdr Tanaka Tomonobu; Cdr Terauchi Masamichi; RAdm Tomioka Sadatoshi; CPO Tomokane Hisao; Capt Wachi Tsunezo; Capt Watanabe Yasuji; Lt Yamamoto Heiya; PO Yamazaki Toshiiwa; Ens Yoshizawa Takeo; PO Yunoki Akira.

## Wartime and Postwar Interrogations

Interrogations form invaluable basic sources for Pacific war history. The best-known repository of these data is *Interrogations of Japanese Officials*, a two-volume compilation released by the U.S. Strategic Bombing Survey (USSBS) in 1946. However, that collection includes fewer than 120 of the more than 600 interrogations conducted by USSBS. This study has made an effort to go beyond the published collection. Not only were there hundreds of additional indexed interrogations, but USSBS field teams conducted dozens of *further* interrogations that are nowhere indexed. In what follows I attempt to furnish a usable reference that shows not only which interrogations were consulted but identifies their location in USSBS or other sources. Names that appear followed by a number (prefixed "#") are to be found in the body of USSBS interrogations other than those published. Names with a "v" number are interrogations in those volumes of the USSBS published collection, sometimes more than one per volume. Names followed by an "M" number are interrogations that appear only in the referenced USSBS subject monograph. Several names appear with an "MP" number and then a further number with the prefix "R." These were senior officers interrogated at Truk after the war, the interview reports being kept among background documentation for the USSBS Truk monograph, which was never published. The notations here refer to the reel number of a National Archives microfilm publication. Among wartime interrogations, "I&T" refers the reader to the "Interrogations and Translations" issues of the JICPOA Bulletin; "NHC:MP" refers to the Samuel Eliot Morison Papers collected at the Naval Historical Center; "NHC:SOPAC" refers to the South Pacific series translations and interrogations of the Historical Center's collection of Japanese Navy Documents and Related Translations.

INTERROGATIONS: Capt Abe Tokuma (v. 2); Capt Amagai Takahisa (v. 1); Capt Aoki Taijiro (v. 1); Capt Arichika Rokuji (v. 2); Capt Arita Yuzo (#219); Lt Asaii Masaaki (M-74); Capt Asayama Toshio (M-75); Capt Atsuo Chigehiro (#422); Lt Chiba Kenjiro (M-74); Cdr Chihaya Masataka (v. 1); Col Chikabari Shigeharu (M-74); Cdr Doi Yasumi (v. 1; v. 2); RAdm Enomoto Ryuchiro (#172); Capt Fuchida Mitsuo (v. 1; v. 2; #603); VAdm Fukudome Shigeru (v. 2; #524); LtCol Fujii Kazume (v. 2); Cdr Fujimori Yasuo (v. 2); Capt Fujita

Masamichi (v. 1; v. 2); Cdr Fukamizu (v. 1; v. 2); Maj Furuki Hidesaku (M-76); Lt Futa Kyoshi (M-76); Capt Genda Minoru (v. 2; #479); Cdr Hanada Nikichi (#433); VAdm Hara Chuichi (MP-1655/R311); Capt Hara Michio (#242); Cdr Hashimoto Shigefuso (v. 1); LCdr Hirata Kozo (M-76); Cdr Hori Tomoyoshi (M-75); RAdm Horiuchi Shigetada (v. 1); Capt Ihara Mitsugo (v. 1); Cdr Imai Nobuhiko (#236); Gen Imamura Hitoshi (M-75); Capt Inoguchi Rikihei (v. 1); Capt Inouye Isamu (v. 1); RAdm Irifune Naosaburo (M-75); Cdr Isawa Yutaka (v. 1); Capt Ishihara Kawakita (v. 1); Cdr Ishikawa Yasutaro (M-75); Civilian Kabayama Sukehide (#443); RAdm Kamada Shoichi (M-76); Capt Kamide Shunji (v. 2); Capt Kani Kurotaro (v. 1) Col Kaneko Rinsuke (v. 2); Civilian Kanzaki Chojiro (M-76); Lt(jg) Kasao (M-76); Capt Kato Kenkichi (v. 2); LtGen Kato Rimpei (M-75); RAdm Katsumata Seizo (v. 1); CPO Kawabata Shigeo (NHC:SOPAC); LtGen Kawabe Torashiro (v. 2); Ens Kawachi Mamura (M-76); Capt Kawaguchi Susumu (v. 1); Capt Kijima Kikunori (v. 2); RAdm Kojima Hideo (RG-38:ONI:COD); RAdm Kojima Hitoshi (MP-1655/R311); Lt Kojima Kiyofumi (I&T); Capt Komoto Hirouchi (v. 2); RAdm Komura Keizo (v. 2); Capt Koyama Tadashi (v. 2); RAdm Koyanagi Tomiji (v. 1); Seaman 2/c Kurihayashi Kumasabara (M-74); Lt Kurihara Akio (M-75); VAdm Kurita Takeo (v. 1); VAdm Kusaka Jinichi (M-75); Cdr Kuwahara Tadao (v. 1); WO Mashima Ryoji (M-76); RAdm Matsuda Chiaki (v. 1); LCdr Matsumoto Midari (M-75); Cdr Matsuura Goro (v. 1); RAdm Matsuyama Mitsuharu (v. 1); RAdm Matsuzaki Akira (v. 2); Capt Minami Rokeumon (v. 1); Cdr Miura Kintaro (v. 1); VAdm Miwa Shigeyoshi (v. 2); Cdr Miyamoto Tadeo (v. 1); Cdr Miyazaki I. (#369); Cdr Miyazaki Takashi (v. 2); Cdr Mizutani Katsuji (v. 2); LCdr Mori (M-75); Lt Morikawa (M-75); Lt Morikawa Shigeru (M-76); Ens Motomura Harusai (M-76); Cdr Mukai Nifumi (v. 1); Lt Murashita Guinicha (M-76); LtCol Murata Kingo (#171); RAdm Nabeshima Shunsaku (v. 2); Adm Nagano Osami (v. 1; v. 2; #498); LCdr Nakagawa Toshi (#425); Cdr Nakajima Chikataka (v. 1; v. 2; #309); LCdr Nakamura Achiro (M-76); Lt Nakazato Hisao (M-74); LCdr Nishikawa (v. 2); Cdr Nishino Shigeru (v. 2); Adm Nomura Kichisaburo (v. 2); LCdr Nomura Ryosuke (v. 2); RAdm Obayashi Sueo (#310); Capt Ohara Hisashi (v. 1); Capt Ohmae Toshikazu (v. 1; v. 2; #350); Capt Oi Atsushi (v. 1; v. 2); Adm Oikawa Koshiro (#494); Col Oishi Chisato (M-76); LCdr Okamoto T. (v. 1); Capt Okino Matao (RG-38:ONI:COD); LtGen Okumiya Masatake (v. 1; v. 2; #329); Lt(jg) Okuno Y. (v. 1); VAdm Omori Sentaro (v. 1; v. 2); RAdm Ono Takeji (#246); Cdr Otani Taisuke (v. 1; #205); LtCol Oya Kokuzo (#364); Cdr Ozawa Hideo (#208); VAdm Ozawa Jisaburo (v. 1); RAdm Sakaibara (M-74); Lt Sakuda Sawaaki (M-76); Lt Sakurai Jiro (M-76); Capt Sanematsu Yuzuru (#421); Cdr Sano Sumio (M-76); Capt Sasaki Akira (v. 2); Capt Sasamoto Kenji (M-76); LCdr Satake T. (#431); Cdr Sekino Hideo (v. 1); Capt Shiba Katsuo (#330); Capt Shibata Bunzo (v. 2); Capt Shibata Otokichi (v. 1); Capt Shiki Tsuneo (v. 2); Cdr Shimada Koichi (v. 1); Maj Shimada Masuda (v. 2); Capt Shimanouchi Momochiro (v. 2); LCdr Shintome Sanjuro (M-76); Seaman 1/c Shirata Kimeo (M-74); VAdm Shiraishi Kazutaka (v. 1); Lt Sinohara Takeji

(M-76); Cdr Sogawa Kiyoshi (v. 2); RAdm Soji Akira (v. 2); Civilian Sone E. (#442); Capt Sonokawa Kameo (v. 2); Col Sugita Ichiji (v. 2); RAdm Sumikawa Michio (MP-1655/R311); Capt Suzuki Mitsunobu (#411); LCdr Tachibara Soichi (M-74); Cdr Tadenuma Saburo (v. 1); Capt Takahashi Chihaya (v. 1); Capt Takahashi Kameshiro (NHC:MP); RAdm Takata Toshitane (v. 1; #274); RAdm Takeuchi Kaoru (#222; #410); Cdr Takita N. (#374); Capt Tamura Kyuzo (v. 1); LtCol Tanaka Ryoji (v. 2); Lt Tanaka Tatsuhiko (M-76); WO Tanaka Toshimoto (M-76); Ens Tanaka Yuska (M-76); Ens Tasaki Tadashi (M-76); Cdr Terai Yoshimori (v. 2; #291); Maj Toga Hiroshi (v. 1); Lt Tokuda Sutemitsu (M-74); LCdr Tokuno Hiroshi (v. 1); RAdm Tomioka Sadatoshi (#355); Lt Tomita Ryoji (M-76); Capt Toyama Yasumi (v. 1); Seaman1/c Toyoda Isamu (NHC:SOPAC); Adm Toyoda Soemu (v. 2); Lt Toyoda Takogo (#384); Lt Tozawa Hiromi (M-76); Capt Tsuda Hiroaki (v. 1); Capt Wachi Tsunezo (#423); WO Wakamatsu Minoru (M-76); LCdr Watabe Masamichi (M-75); Lt(jg) Watanabe (M-76); Capt Watanabe Yasuji (v. 1); VAdm Paul Wennecker (v. 1); Cdr Yamaguchi Moriyoshi (v. 1; #365); Cdr Yamamoto Tadashi (v. 2); RAdm Yamamoto Yoshiyo (#210); RAdm Yamanaka Dengo (RG-38:ONI:COD); Capt Yamaoka Mineo (v. 1); LCdr Yasumoto Shisei (v. 1); LCdr Yatsui Noriteru (v. 1); RAdm Yokoyama Ichiro (#445); Cdr Yokura Sashizo (#250); Adm Yonai Mitsumasa (v. 2); WO Yonemoto Saichi (M-76); RAdm Yoshimi Nobukazu (M-76); LCdr Yunoki S. (v. 1).

## PUBLISHED SOURCES

### Official Histories and Documents

Australia. *Australia in the War of 1939–1945.* Series 2:
  G. Herman Gill, *Royal Australian Navy 1942–1945.* Canberra: Australian War Memorial, 1968.

United States:
*United States Army in World War II: The War Department*
  (All volumes in the series were published in Washington by the Office of the Chief of Military History on the dates indicated.)
  Robert W. Coakley and Richard M. Leighton. *Global Logistics and Strategy 1940–1943* (1955).
  Richard M. Leighton and Robert W. Coakley. *Global Logistics and Strategy 1943–1945* (1968).
  Maurice Matloff and Edwin M. Snell. *Strategic Planning for Coalition Warfare 1941–1942* (1953).
  Maurice Matloff. *Strategic Planning for Coalition Warfare 1943–1944* (1959)
*United States Army in World War II: The War in the Pacific:*
  Louis Morton. *Strategy and Command: The First Two Years* (1962).
  Louis Morton. *The Fall of the Philippines* (1953).

John Miller, Jr. *Guadalcanal: The First Offensive* (1949).
John Miller, Jr. *CARTWHEEL: The Reduction of Rabaul* (1959).
Philip A. Crowl. *Campaign in the Marianas* (1960).

United States Army Air Force: *The Army Air Forces in World War II* (7 vols.)
William F. Craven and James L. Cate. Chicago: University of Chicago Press,
1948–58.

United States Army Air Force: Assistant Chief of Staff for Air, *Mission
Accomplished: Interrogations of Japanese Industrial, Military and Civil Leaders of
World War II*. Washington, D.C.: Government Printing Office, 1946.

United States Congress (79th Congress, 1st Session). Joint Committee on the
Investigation of the Pearl Harbor Attack. *Hearings*. Washington, D.C.:
Government Printing Office, 1946 (39 vols.).

United States Department of Defense. *The Magic Background of Pearl Harbor*.
Washington, D.C.: Government Printing Office, 1978 (8 vols.).

United States Department of Defense, National Security Agency: *United States
Cryptologic History: Series IV, World War II, vol. 5, A Priceless Advantage: U.S.
Navy Communications Intelligence and the Battles of the Coral Sea, Midway, and
the Aleutians* (by Frederick D. Parker). N.p. (Fort George G. Meade, Md.):
Center for Cryptologic History, 1993.

United States Department of Defense, National Security Agency: *United States
Cryptologic History: Series IV, World War II, vol. 6, Pearl Harbor Revisited:
United States Navy Communications Intelligence, 1924–1941* (by Frederick D.
Parker). N.p. (Fort George G. Meade, Md.): Center for Cryptologic History,
1994.

United States Office of Strategic Services, Research & Analysis Branch. *Japanese
Analyses of the Causes of Defeat*. Washington, D.C.: OSS Report, 1945.

United States Navy: *Navy Department Communiqués* (3 vols.). Washington,
D.C.: U.S. Navy, 1943–1946.

United States Navy: Naval Historical Center: John C. Reilly, Jr., *Operational
Experience of Fast Battleships: World War II, Korea, Vietnam* (2nd ed.).
Washington, D.C.: Naval Historical Center, 1989.

United States Naval Operations in World War II: (All volumes are by Samuel
Eliot Morison and were published by Little, Brown on dates indicated.)
vol. 3: *The Rising Sun in the Pacific* (1954).
vol. 4: *Coral Sea, Midway, and Submarine Actions, May 1942–August 1942*
(1949).
vol. 5: *The Struggle for Guadalcanal, August 1942–February 1943* (1954).
vol. 6: *Breaking the Bismarcks Barrier, 22 July 1942–1 May 1944* (1954).
vol. 7: *Aleutians, Gilberts and Marshalls, June 1942–April 1944* (1951).
vol. 8: *New Guinea and the Marianas, March 1944–August 1944* (1953).
vol. 12: *Leyte, June 1944–January 1945* (1958).

vol. 13: *The Liberation of the Philippines, 1944–1945* (1959).
vol. 14: *Victory in the Pacific, 1945* (1990).

United States Naval War College:

*The Battle of the Coral Sea: Strategical and Tactical Analysis: May 1 to May 11 Inclusive, 1942*. USNWC, 1947.

*The Battle of Midway Including the Aleutian Phase: Strategical and Tactical Analysis, June 3 to June 14, 1942*. USNWC, 1948.

*The Battle of Savo Island, August 9, 1942: Strategical and Tactical Analysis*. USNWC, 1950.

*The Battle of Leyte Gulf: Strategical and Tactical Analysis* (4 vols.). USNWC, 1953–1958. (Note: The planned final volume of this series, never written, would have covered the battle of Cape Engaño and that off Samar.)

United States Navy, Office of Naval Intelligence, Publications Branch. Combat Narratives and Operational Monographs:

*Early Raids in the Pacific Ocean* (February 1943).

*The Java Sea Campaign* (July 1943).

*The Battle of the Coral Sea* (March 1943).

*The Battle of Midway* (March 1943).

*Solomons Islands Campaign II/III: Savo Island, 9 August 1942; Eastern Solomons, 23–25 August 1942* (November 1943).

*Solomons Islands Campaign IV/V: Cape Esperance, 11 October 1942; Santa Cruz, 26 October 1942* (November 1943).

*Solomons Islands Campaign VI: Naval Battle of Guadalcanal, 11–15 November 1942* (February 1944).

*Solomons Islands Campaign VII/VIII: Tassafaronga, 30 November 1942; Japanese Evacuation of Guadalcanal, 29 January–8 February 1943* (March 1944).

*Solomons Islands Campaign IX: Bombardments of Munda and Vila-Stanmore* (June 1944).

*Solomons Islands Campaign X: Operations New Georgia Area* (June 1944).

*Solomons Islands Campaign XI: Kolombangara and Vella Lavella* (Oct 1944).

*Solomons Islands Campaign XII: The Bougainville Landing and the Battle of Empress Augusta Bay* (June 1945).

*The Aleutians Campaign* (May 1945).

*The Assault on Kwajalein and Majuro, Part 1* (August 1945).

United States Navy, Office of Naval Intelligence:
*ONI Weekly Review.*

United States Navy, Office of Naval Intelligence, Publications Branch: *The Japanese Story of the Battle of Midway*. OPNAV P32-1002, June 1947.

United States Armed Forces Far East, History Division, Japanese Monographs Series (cited are only those actually consulted):

No. 88: *Aleutian Naval Operations, March 1942–February 1943.*

No. 89: *Northern Area Naval Operations, February 1943–August 1945.*

No. 99: *Southeast Area Naval Operations, II: February–October 1943.*

No. 100: *Southeast Area Naval Operations, III: November 1943–February 1944.*

No. 118: *Operational History of Naval Communications, December 1941–August 1945.*

No. 139: *Outline of Operations of the Navy's South Seas Force: December 1941–March 1942.*

No. 144: *Political Strategy Prior to the Outbreak of War, Part 1.*

No. 161: *Inner South Seas Area Naval Operations, I: Gilbert Operations.*

United States Armed Forces Far East: Supreme Commander Allied Powers: *Reports of General MacArthur: Operations in the Southwest Pacific* (2 parts); *Japanese Operations* (2 parts). Washington, D.C.: Government Printing Office, 1966.

United States Strategic Bombing Survey, Pacific Division, Reports:

No. 2: *Japan's Struggle to End the War.*

No. 15: *The Japanese Aircraft Industry.*

No. 44: *Japanese Naval Ordnance.*

No. 46: *Japanese Naval Shipbuilding.*

No. 48: *Japanese Merchant Shipbuilding.*

No. 49: *Chemicals in Japan's War.*

No. 50: *Chemicals in Japan's War: Appendix.*

No. 51: *Oil in Japan's War.*

No. 52: *Oil in Japan's War: Appendix.*

No. 54: *The War Against Japanese Transportation.*

No. 61: *Air Forces Allied with the United States in the War Against Japan.*

No. 62: *Japanese Air Power.*

No. 63: *Japanese Air Weapons and Tactics.*

No. 64: *The Effects of Air Action on Japanese Ground Army Logistics.*

No. 66: *The Strategic Air Operation of Very Heavy Bombardment in the War Against Japan (Twentieth Air Force).*

No. 67: *Air Operations in China, Burma, India in World War II.*

No. 68: *The Air Transport Command in the War Against Japan.*

No. 69: *The Thirteenth Air Force in the War Against Japan.*

No. 70: *The Seventh and Eleventh Air Forces in the War Against Japan.*

No. 71: *The Fifth Air Force in the War Against Japan.*

No. 72: *Interrogations of Japanese Officials* (2 vols.).

No. 73: *Campaigns of the Pacific War.*

No. 74: *The Reduction of Wake Island.*

No. 75: *The Allied Campaign Against Rabaul.*

No. 76: *The American Campaign Against Wotje, Maloelap, Mille and Jaluit.*

No. 77: *The Reduction of Truk.*

No. 78: *The Offensive Minelaying Campaign Against Japan.*

No. 97: *Japanese Military and Naval Intelligence.*

Also consulted were published and unpublished supporting documents and interrogations.

United States Naval Technical Mission to Japan:
Final Report and Subject Reports.

## Books

Abend, Hallett. *Ramparts of the Pacific.* Garden City, N.Y.: Doubleday, 1942.

Agawa, Hiroyuki. *The Reluctant Admiral: Yamamoto and the Imperial Navy.* John Bester, trans. Tokyo: Kodansha International, 1979.

Allen, Louis. *Singapore 1941–1942.* Wilmington, Del.: University of Delaware Press, 1977.

Argyle, Christopher J. *Japan at War, 1937–1945.* London: Arthur Barker Ltd., 1976.

*Army Times* Editors. *Pearl Harbor and Hawaii: A Military History.* New York: Walker & Company, 1971.

Ballantine, Duncan S. *U.S. Naval Logistics in the Second World War.* Princeton, N.J.: Princeton University Press, 1947.

Ballard, Geoffrey. *On ULTRA Active Service: The Story of Australia's Signals Intelligence Operations During World War II.* Richmond, Victoria, Australia: Spectrum Publications, 1991.

Barber, Noel. *A Sinister Twilight: The Fall of Singapore.* Boston: Houghton Mifflin, 1968.

Barker, A. J. *Midway: The Turning Point.* New York: Ballantine Books, 1971.

———. *Pearl Harbor.* New York: Ballantine Books, 1969.

Barnes, Harry Elmer, ed. *Perpetual War for Perpetual Peace.* New York: Greenwood Press, 1969.

Barnhart, Michael A. *Japan Prepares for Total War: The Search for Economic Security, 1919–1941.* Ithaca, N.Y.: Cornell University Press, 1987.

Beach, Edward L. *Submarine!* New York: New American Library, 1952.

Beard, Charles A. *President Roosevelt and the Coming of the War, 1941: A Study in Appearances and Realities.* New Haven: Yale University Press, 1948.

Beesly, Patrick. *Very Special Intelligence.* Garden City, N.Y.: Doubleday, 1978.

Behr, Edward. *Hirohito: The Man Behind the Myth.* New York: Villard, 1989.

Bell, Roger J. *Unequal Allies: Australian-American Relations and the Pacific War.* Melbourne: Melbourne University Press, 1977.

Belot, R. de. *La Guerre aeronavale du Pacifique, 1941–1945.* Paris: Payot, 1957.

Belote, James H., and William M. *Corregidor.* New York: Playboy Press, 1980.

———. *Titans of the Sea: The Development and Operations of Japanese and American Carrier Task Forces During World War II.* New York: Harper & Row, 1975.

———. *Typhoon of Steel: The Battle for Okinawa.* New York: Bantam Books, 1984.

Benedict, Ruth. *The Chrysanthemum and the Sword.* Boston: Houghton Mifflin, 1946.

Ben-Zvi, Abraham. *Prelude to Pearl Harbor: A Study of American Images Toward Japan 1940–1941.* New York: Vantage Press, 1979.

Bergamini, David. *Japan's Imperial Conspiracy.* New York: Pocket Books, 1972.

Blair, Clay, Jr. *Silent Victory: The U.S. Submarine War Against Japan.* Philadelphia: J. B. Lippincott, 1975.

Blair, Clay, Jr., and Joan Blair. *Return from the River Kwai.* New York: Simon and Schuster, 1979.

Bond, Brian, ed. *Chief of Staff: The Diaries of Lieutenant General Sir Henry Pownall,* Vol. 2: *1940–1944.* Hamden, Conn.: Archon Books, 1974.

Bosworth, Allan R. *America's Concentration Camps.* New York: W. W. Norton, 1967.

Bowen, John. *Undercover in the Jungle.* London: William Kimber, 1978.

Boyd, Carl F. *The Extraordinary Envoy: General Hiroshi Oshima and Diplomacy in the Third Reich, 1934–1939.* Washington, D.C.: University Press of America, 1980.

Brown, Cecil. *Suez to Singapore.* New York: Random House, 1942.

Browne, Courtney. *Tojo: The Last Banzai.* New York: Holt, Rinehart & Winston, 1967.

Bryan, J., III. *Aircraft Carrier.* New York: Ballantine Books, 1966.

Buell, Thomas B. *Master of Sea Power: A Biography of Fleet Admiral Ernest J. King.* Boston: Little, Brown & Company, 1980.

———. *The Quiet Warrior: A Biography of Admiral Raymond A. Spruance.* Boston: Little, Brown, 1974.

Burlingame, Burl. *Advance Force Pearl Harbor: The Imperial Navy's Underwater Assault on America.* Kailua, Hi.: Pacific Monographs, 1992.

Burns, Richard D., and Edward M. Bennett, eds. *Diplomats in Crisis: United States-Chinese-Japanese Relations, 1919–1941.* Santa Barbara, Calif.: Clio Books, 1974.

Butow, Robert J. C. *Japan's Decision to Surrender.* Stanford, Calif.: Stanford University Press, 1954.

———. *Tojo and the Coming of the War.* Princeton, N.J.: Princeton University Press, 1961.

Byas, Hugh. *Government by Assassination.* New York: Knopf, 1942.

———. *The Japanese Enemy: His Power and His Vulnerability.* New York: Knopf, 1942.

Bywater, Hector. *Seapower in the Pacific: A Study of the American-Japanese Naval Problem.* Boston: Houghton Mifflin, 1921.

Caidin, Martin. *The Ragged, Rugged Warriors.* New York: Ballantine Books, 1966.

———. *A Torch to the Enemy: The Fire Raid on Tokyo.* New York: Ballantine Books, 1960.

———. *Zero Fighter.* New York: Ballantine Books, 1969.

Carpenter, Don, and Norman Polmar. *Submarines of the Imperial Japanese Navy.* Annapolis, Md.: Naval Institute Press, 1986.

Carter, Wallace Reed. *Beans, Bullets and Black Oil: The Story of Fleet Logistics Afloat in the Pacific During World War II.* No publication data (from format and foreword, appears to have been produced by the U.S. Government Printing Office, ca. 1952).

Chambliss, William C. *The Silent Service.* New York: New American Library, 1965.

Chapman, John W. M., ed. *The Price of Admiralty: The War Diaries of the German Naval Attaché in Japan 1939–1943.* Ripe, England: Saltire House Publications Society. Vol. 1: 25 August 1939–23 August 1940 (1982); vol. 2: 23 August 1940–9 September 1941 (1984); vol. 3: consolidated with vol. 2; vol. 4: 10 September 1941–31 January 1942 (1989).

Chihaya Masataka. *The Judgment of the Japanese Navy on the War with the United States.* Unpublished ms., 1946. Naval Historical Center copy.

Clagget, John. *The U.S. Navy in Action.* Derby, Conn.: Monarch Books, 1965.

Clark, Joseph J., and Clark G. Reynolds. *Carrier Admiral.* New York: David McKay, 1967.

Clark, Ronald. *The Man Who Broke Purple: The Life of Colonel William F. Friedman, Who Deciphered the Japanese Codes in World War II.* Boston: Little, Brown, 1977.

Clarke, Thurston. *Pearl Harbor Ghosts: A Journey to Hawaii Then and Now.* New York: William Morrow, 1991.

Coffey, Thomas M. *Imperial Tragedy: Japan in World War II, the First Days and the Last.* New York: World Publishing Company, 1970.

Cohen, Jerome B. *Japan's Economy in War and Reconstruction.* Minneapolis: University of Minnesota Press, 1949.

Cohen, Stan. *Enemy on Island, Issue in Doubt: The Capture of Wake Island, December 1941.* Missoula, Mont.: Pictorial Histories Publishing, 1983.

Collier, Richard. *The Road to Pearl Harbor: 1941.* New York: Athenaeum, 1981.

Congdon, Don, ed. *Combat: Pacific Theater—World War II.* New York: Dell Books, 1958.

———. *Combat: The War with Japan.* New York: Dell Books, 1962.

Connell, John. *Wavell: Supreme Commander, 1941–1943.* Michael Roberts, ed. London: Collins, 1969.

Conroy, Hilary, and Harry Wray, eds. *Pearl Harbor Reexamined: Prologue to the Pacific War.* Honolulu: University of Hawaii Press, 1990.

Cook, Haruko Taya, and Theodore F. *Japan at War: An Oral History.* New York: The New Press, 1992.

Coox, Alvin D. *Anatomy of a Small War.* Westport, Conn.: Greenwood Press, 1977.

———. *Japan: The Final Agony.* New York: Ballantine Books, 1970.

———. *Nomonhan: Japan Against Russia, 1939.* 2 vols. Stanford, Calif.: Stanford University Press, 1985.

Coox, Alvin D., and Hilary Conroy, eds. *China and Japan: Search for Balance Since World War I.* Santa Barbara, Calif.: ABC Clio Press, 1978.

Corbett, P. Scott. *Quiet Passages: The Exchange of Civilians Between the United States and Japan During the Second World War.* Kent, Ohio: Kent State University Press, 1987.

Costello, John. *The Pacific War.* New York: Rawson Wade Publishers, 1981.

Craig, William. *The Fall of Japan.* New York: Dial Press, 1967.

Croizat, Victor J. *Across the Reef: The Amphibious Tracked Vehicle at War.* London: Arms and Armor Press, 1989.

Cruickshank, Charles. *SOE in the Far East.* New York: Oxford University Press, 1983.

Cunningham, W. Scott, with Lydel Sims. *Wake Island Command.* Boston: Little, Brown, 1961.

D'Albas, Andrieu. *Death of a Navy: Japanese Naval Action in World War II.* New York: Devin-Adair, 1957.

Davis, Burke. *Get Yamamoto!* New York: Random House, 1969.

———. *Marine: The Life of Chesty Puller.* New York: Bantam Books, 1984.

Davis, George T. *A Navy Second to None: The Development of Modern American Naval Policy.* New York: Harcourt, Brace & Company, 1940.

Day, David. *The Great Betrayal: Britain, Australia and the Onset of the Pacific War 1939–1942.* New York: W. W. Norton, 1988.

Deacon, Richard. *A History of the Japanese Secret Service.* London: Frederick Muller, 1982.

Denlinger, Sutherland, and Charles B. Gary. *War in the Pacific: A Study of Navies, Peoples, and Battle Problems.* New York: Robert McBride & Company, 1936.

De Toledano, Ralph. *Spies, Dupes and Diplomats.* New York and Boston: Duell, Sloan & Pearce with Little, Brown, 1952.

Devereux, James P. S. *The Story of Wake Island.* New York: Bantam Books, 1989.

Dickson, W. D. *Battle of the Philippine Sea.* London: Ian Allen, 1975.

Dingman, Roger. *Power in the Pacific: The Origins of Naval Arms Limitation, 1914–1922.* Chicago: University of Chicago Press, 1976.

Donovan, Robert J. *PT-109: John F. Kennedy in World War II.* Greenwich, Conn.: Fawcett, 1962.

Dorwart, Jeffrey M. *Conflict of Duty: The U.S. Navy's Intelligence Dilemma, 1919–1945.* Annapolis, Md.: Naval Institute Press, 1983.

———. *The Office of Naval Intelligence: The Birth of America's First Intelligence Agency, 1865–1918.* Annapolis, Md.: Naval Institute Press, 1979.

Drea, Edward J. *MacArthur's ULTRA: Codebreaking and the War Against Japan, 1942–1945.* Lawrence, Kans.: University Press of Kansas, 1992.

Dull, Paul S. *A Battle History of the Imperial Japanese Navy, 1941–1945.* Annapolis, Md.: Naval Institute Press, 1978.

Dunlop, Richard. *Behind Japanese Lines: With the OSS in Burma.* Chicago: Rand McNally & Company, 1979.

Duus, Masayo. *Tokyo Rose: Orphan of the Pacific.* Paul Duus, trans. Tokyo: Kodansha International, 1983.

Emerson, John K. *The Japanese Thread: A Life in the U.S. Foreign Service.* New York: Holt, Rinehart & Winston, 1978.

Enright, Joseph F., with James W. Ryan. *Shinano! The Sinking of Japan's Secret Supership.* New York: St. Martin's Press, 1987.

Evans, David C., ed. *The Japanese Navy in World War II.* 2nd ed. Annapolis, Md.: Naval Institute Press, 1986.

Fahey, James J. *Pacific War Diary 1942–1945.* New York: Kensington Publishing, 1963.

Falk, Stanley L. *Decision at Leyte.* New York: Berkeley Books, 1966.

———. *Palaus.* New York: Ballantine Books, 1974.

———. *Seventy Days to Singapore.* New York: G. P. Putnam's Sons, 1975.

Farago, Ladislas. *The Broken Seal: "Operation Magic" and the Secret Road to Pearl Harbor.* New York: Bantam Books, 1968.

Farley, Edward I. *PT Patrol: Wartime Adventures in the Pacific and the Story of PT's in World War II.* New York: Popular Library, 1962.

Feifer, George. *Tennozan: The Battle of Okinawa and the Atomic Bomb.* New York: Ticknor & Fields, 1992.

Feldt, Eric A. *The Coast Watchers.* New York: Ballantine Books, 1966.

Feis, Herbert. *The Road to Pearl Harbor.* Princeton, N.J.: Princeton University Press, 1950.

Ferguson, Ted. *Desperate Siege: The Battle of Hong Kong.* Garden City, N.Y.: Doubleday, 1980.

Field, James E., Jr. *The Japanese at Leyte Gulf: The Sho Operation.* Princeton, N.J.: Princeton University Press, 1947.

Foot, M.R.D., ed. *Holland at War Against Hitler: Anglo-Dutch Relations 1940–1945.* London: Frank Cass Ltd., 1990.

Forrestel, E. P. *Admiral Raymond A. Spruance, USN: A Study in Command.* Washington, D.C.: U.S. Government Printing Office, 1966.

Francillon, Rene J. *Japanese Aircraft of the Pacific War.* New York: Funk & Wagnalls, 1970.

———. *Japanese Carrier Air Groups 1941–1945.* London: Osprey Publishing, 1979.

Frank, Benis M. *Okinawa: Touchstone to Victory.* New York: Ballantine Books, 1969.

Frank, Pat, and Joseph D. Harrington. *Rendezvous at Midway.* New York: Paperback Library, 1968.

Frank, Richard B. *Guadalcanal: The Definitive Account of the Landmark Battle.* New York: Random House, 1990.

Frei, Henry P. *Japan's Southward Advance and Australia: From the Sixteenth Century to World War II.* Honolulu: University of Hawaii, 1991.

Friend, Theodore. *Between Two Empires: The Ordeal of the Philippines, 1929–1946.* New Haven: Yale University Press, 1965.

Fuchida Mitsuo and Okumiya Masatake. *Midway: The Battle That Doomed Japan.* Annapolis, Md.: Naval Institute Press, 1955.

Fukui Shizuo et al. *Japanese Naval Vessels at the End of [the] War.* Tokyo: Second Demobilization Bureau, Administrative Division, 1947.

Gailey, Harry A. *Howlin' Mad vs. the Army: Conflict in Command, Saipan, 1944.* New York: Dell Books, 1987.

Galvin, John R. *Air Assault.* New York: Hawthorne Books, 1969.

Garfield, Brian. *The Thousand Mile War: World War II in Alaska and the Aleutians.* New York: Ballantine Books, 1969.

Glines, Carol V. *Attack on Yamamoto.* New York: Jove Books, 1991.

Goldstein, Donald M., and Katherine V. Dillon. *The Way It Was: Pearl Harbor, The Original Photographs.* Washington, D.C.: Brassey's, 1991.

Goldstein, Donald M., and Katherine V. Dillon, eds. *Fading Victory: The Diary of Admiral Matome Ugaki 1941–1945.* Chihaya Masataka, trans. Pittsburgh: University of Pittsburgh Press, 1991.

Goralski, Robert, and Russell W. Freeburg. *Oil and War: How the Deadly Struggle for Fuel in World War II Meant Victory or Defeat.* New York: William Morrow, 1987.

Gordon, Gary. *The Rise and Fall of the Japanese Empire.* Derby, Conn.: Monarch Books, 1962.

Grattan, C. Hartley. *The Southwest Pacific Since 1900: A Modern History.* Ann Arbor: University of Michigan Press, 1963.

Grider, George, and Lydel Sims. *War Fish.* New York: Pyramid Books, 1959.

Gray, Edwin. *Operation Pacific: The Royal Navy's War Against Japan, 1941–1945.* Annapolis, Md.: Naval Institute Press, n.d. (1991).

———. *Submarine Warriors.* New York: Bantam Books, 1990.

Grenfell, Russell. *Main Fleet to Singapore.* New York: Macmillan, 1952.

Grew, Joseph C. *Report from Tokyo: A Message to the American People.* New York: Simon & Schuster, 1942.

———. *Ten Years in Japan: A Contemporary Record Drawn from the Diaries and Private Official Papers.* New York: Simon & Schuster, 1944.

Griffith, Samuel B., II. *The Battle for Guadalcanal.* New York: Ballantine Books, 1963.

Guillain, Robert. *I Saw Tokyo Burning: An Eyewitness Narrative from Pearl Harbor to Hiroshima.* Garden City, N.Y.: Doubleday, 1981.

Hall, R. Cargill. *Lightning over Bougainville: The Yamamoto Mission Reconsidered.* Washington, D.C.: Smithsonian Institution Press, 1991.

Halsey, William F., and J. Bryan, III. *Admiral Halsey's Story.* New York: McGraw-Hill, 1947.

Hamill, Ian. *The Strategic Illusion: The Singapore Strategy and the Defence of Australia and New Zealand.* Singapore: Singapore University Press, 1981.

Hansell, Haywood S., Jr. *Strategic Air War Against Japan.* Montgomery, Ala.: Air War College, Airpower Research Institute, 1980.

Hara Tameichi, Fred Saito, and Roger Pineau. *Japanese Destroyer Captain.* New York: Ballantine Books, 1961.

Harries, Meirion, and Susie Harries. *Sheathing the Sword: The Demilitarization of Japan.* London: Hamish Hamilton, 1987.

———. *Soldiers of the Sun: The Rise and Fall of the Imperial Japanese Army.* New York: Random House, 1991.

Harrington, Joseph D. *Yankee Samurai: The Secret Role of Nisei in America's Pacific Victory.* Detroit: Pettigrew Enterprises, 1979.

Hashimoto Mochitsura. *Sunk.* E.H.M. Colgrave, trans. New York: Holt, Rinehart & Winston, 1954.

Hata Ikuhito and Izawa Yasuho. *Japanese Naval Aces and Fighter Units of World War II.* Annapolis, Md.: Naval Institute Press, 1989.

Hattori Takushiro. *The Complete History of the Greater East Asia War* (U.S. Army, trans. 1953). Published in Japan by Hara Shobo, 1966.

Havens, Thomas R. H. *Valley of Darkness: The Japanese People and World War II.* New York: W. W. Norton, 1978.

Hayashi Saburo, with Alvin D. Coox. *Kogun: The Japanese Army in the Pacific War.* Westport, Conn.: Greenwood Press, 1978.

Hayes, Grace Person. *The History of the Joint Chiefs of Staff in World War II: The War Against Japan.* Annapolis, Md.: Naval Institute Press, 1982.

Heinrichs, Waldo. *Threshold of War: Franklin D. Roosevelt and American Entry into World War II.* New York: Oxford University Press, 1988.

Hess, William N. *Pacific Sweep: The 5th and 13th Fighter Commands in World War II.* Garden City, N.Y.: Doubleday, 1974.

Hilsman, Roger. *American Guerrilla: My War Behind Japanese Lines.* Washington, D.C.: Brassey's, 1990.

Hitchcock, Walter T., ed. *The Intelligence Revolution: A Historical Perspective.* Washington, D.C.: Office of Air Force History, 1991.

Hoehling, A. A. *December 7, 1941: The Day the Admirals Slept Late.* New York: Kensington Publishing Corp., 1991.

———. *The* Lexington *Goes Down: The Last Seven Hours of a Fighting Lady.* Englewood Cliffs, N.J.: Prentice-Hall, 1971.

Holmes, Wilfred J. *Double-Edged Secrets: U.S. Naval Intelligence Operations in the Pacific During World War II.* Annapolis, Md.: Naval Institute Press, 1979.

———. *Underseas Victory.* 2 vols. New York: Zebra Books, 1979.

Honan, William. *Visions of Infamy: The Untold Story of How Journalist Hector C. Bywater Devised the Plans That Led to Pearl Harbor.* New York: St. Martin's Press, 1991.

Horikoshi Jiro. *Eagles of Mitsubishi: The Story of the Zero Fighter* (Shindo Shojiro and Harold N. Wantiez, trans.). Seattle: University of Washington Press, 1981.

Hough, Frank O. *The Island War.* New York: J. B. Lippincott, 1947.

Hough, Richard. *Death of the Battleship: The Tragic Close of the Era of Seapower.* New York: Macfadden-Bartell Books, 1965.

———. *The Fleet That Had to Die.* New York: Ballantine Books, 1960.

Howarth, Stephen. *The Fighting Ships of the Rising Sun: The Drama of the Imperial Japanese Navy, 1895–1945.* New York: Athenaeum, 1983.

———. *To Shining Sea: A History of the United States Navy, 1775–1991.* New York: Random House, 1991.

Hoyt, Edwin P. *The Battle of Leyte Gulf: The Death Knell of the Japanese Fleet.* New York: Pinnacle Books, 1972.

———. *Blue Skies and Blood: The Battle of the Coral Sea.* New York: Pinnacle Books, 1975.

―――. *Closing the Circle: War in the Pacific, 1945.* New York: Avon Books, 1987.

―――. *The Glory of the Solomons.* New York: Stein & Day, 1984.

―――. *Guadalcanal.* New York: Jove Books, 1983.

―――. *Japan's War: The Great Pacific Conflict, 1853–1952.* New York: McGraw-Hill, 1986.

―――. *Leyte Gulf: The Death of the* Princeton. New York: Avon Books, 1987.

―――. *The Lonely Ships: The Life and Death of the U.S. Asiatic Fleet.* Los Angeles: Pinnacle Books, 1976.

―――. *The Marine Raiders.* New York: Pocket Books, 1989.

―――. *Raider Battalion.* Los Angeles: Pinnacle Books, 1980.

―――. *To the Marianas: War in the Central Pacific, 1944.* New York: Avon Books, 1983.

―――. *Yamamoto: The Man Who Planned Pearl Harbor.* New York: McGraw-Hill, 1990.

Huber, Thomas M. *Japan's Battle for Okinawa.* Leavenworth, Kans.: U.S. Army Combat Studies Institute, Leavenworth Papers no. 18, 1990.

Hull, Cordell. *The Memoirs of Cordell Hull.* 2 vols. New York: Macmillan, 1948.

Humble, Richard. *Japanese High Seas Fleet.* New York: Ballantine Books, 1973.

Hynd, Alan. *Betrayal from the East: The Inside Story of Japanese Spies in America.* New York: Robert McBride & Company, 1943.

Ichihashi Yamato. *The Washington Conference and After: A Historical Survey.* New York: AMS Press, 1969.

Ienaga Saburo. *The Pacific War: World War II and the Japanese, 1931–1945.* New York: Pantheon, 1978.

Ike Nobutaka. *Japan's Decision for War: Liaison and Imperial Conference Records, March–December 1941.* Stanford, Calif.: Stanford University Press, 1967.

Ind, Allison. *Allied Intelligence Bureau: Our Secret Weapon in the War Against Japan.* New York: David McKay, 1958.

―――. *A Short History of Espionage.* New York: David McKay, 1963.

Inoguchi Rikihei and Nakajima Tadashi with Roger Pineau. *The Divine Wind: Japan's Kamikaze Force in World War II.* Annapolis, Md.: Naval Institute Press, 1958.

Iriye Akira. *Across the Pacific.* New York: Harcourt, Brace & World, 1967.

―――. *After Imperialism: The Search for a New Order in the Far East, 1921–1931.* Cambridge, Mass.: Harvard University Press, 1965.

―――. *Power and Culture: The Japanese-American War 1941–1945.* Cambridge, Mass.: Harvard University Press, 1981.

Isely, Jeter A., and Phillip A. Crowl. *The U.S. Marines and Amphibious War: Its Theory and Practice in the Pacific.* Princeton, N.J.: Princeton University Press, 1951.

Ito Masahi. *The Emperor's Last Soldiers.* New York: Coward McCann, 1967.

Ito Masanori with Roger Pineau. *The End of the Imperial Japanese Navy.* Andrew Y. Kuroda and Roger Pineau, trans. New York: Jove Books, 1984.

Jacobs, G. F. *Prelude to the Monsoon: Assignment in Sumatra.* Philadelphia: University of Pennsylvania Press, 1982.

James, D. Clayton. *The Years of MacArthur.* Vol. 2: *1941–1945.* Boston: Houghton Mifflin, 1975.

*The Japanese Air Forces in World War II: The Organization of the Japanese Army and Naval Air Forces, 1945.* New York: Hippocrene, 1979 (reproduction of a 1945 British intelligence handbook).

Jensen, Oliver. *Carrier War: Task Force 58 and the Pacific Sea Battles.* New York: Pocket Books, 1945.

Jentschura, Hansgeorg, Dieter Jung, and Peter Mickel. *Warships of the Imperial Japanese Navy 1969–1945.* Anthony Preston and J. D. Brown, trans. Annapolis, Md.: Naval Institute Press, 1977.

Johnson, Chalmers. *An Instance of Treason: Ozaki Hotsumi and the Sorge Spy Ring.* Stanford, Calif.: Stanford University Press, 1990.

Jones, Ken, and Hubert Kelley, Jr. *Admiral Arleigh (31-Knot) Burke: The Story of a Fighting Sailor.* New York: Bantam Books, 1985.

Kahn, David. *The Codebreakers: The Story of Secret Writing.* New York: Macmillan, 1967.

Karig, Walter, et al. *Battle Report.* 5 vols. New York: Rinehart & Company, 1944–1949.

Kase Toshikazu. *Journey to the* Missouri. New Haven: Yale University Press, 1960.

Kato Matsuo. *The Lost War.* New York: Knopf, 1946.

Kawahara Toshiaki. *Hirohito and His Times: A Japanese Perspective.* Tokyo: Kodansha International, 1990.

Kecskemeti, Paul. *Strategic Surrender: The Politics of Victory and Defeat.* New York: Athenaeum, 1964.

Kelly, Terence. *Battle for Palembang.* London: Robert Hale, 1985.

Kennedy, Malcolm. *A History of Communism in East Asia.* New York: Frederick A. Praeger, 1957.

Kennedy, Paul V. *Pacific Onslaught: 7th December 1941–7th February 1943.* New York: Ballantine Books, 1972.

———. *Pacific Victory.* New York: Ballantine Books, 1973.

Kent, Graeme. *Guadalcanal: Island Ordeal.* New York: Ballantine Books, 1971.

Kerr, E. Bartlett, *Flames over Tokyo: The U.S. Army Air Forces' Incendiary Campaign Against Japan, 1944–1945.* New York: Donald I. Fine, 1991.

———. *Surrender and Survival: The Experience of American POWs in the Pacific 1941–1945.* New York: William Morrow, 1985.

Kerr, George H. *Formosa Betrayed.* Boston: Houghton Mifflin, 1965.

Kido Koichi, Marquis. *The Diaries of Marquis Kido, 1931–1945: Selected Translations into English.* Frederick, Md.: University Press of America, 1984.

Kimmett, Larry, and Margaret Regis. *The Attack on Pearl Harbor: An Illustrated History.* Seattle: Navigator Publishing, 1991.

Kiralfy, Alexander. *Victory in the Pacific: How We Must Defeat Japan.* New York: The John Day Company, 1942.

Koginos, Manny T. *The Panay Incident: Prelude to War*. Lafayette, Ind.: Purdue University Press, 1967.

Korotkin, I. M. *Battle Damage to Surface Ships During World War II*. Leningrad, 1960. Joint Publications Research Service, trans.; republished by David Taylor Model Basin, 1964.

Kurzman, Dan. *Fatal Voyage: The Sinking of the USS* Indianapolis. New York: Atheneum, 1990.

Kusaka, Ryunosuke. *The Combined Fleet: Memoirs of Former Chief of Staff Kusaka*. Tokyo: Mainichi Shimbun Sha, 1952. Excerpts translated by U.S. Navy.

Kuwahara Yasuo and Gordon T. Allred. *Kamikaze: A Japanese Pilot's Own Story of the Suicide Squadrons*. New York: Ballantine Books, 1957.

Laffin, John. *ANZACs at War*. London: Abelard-Schuman, 1965.

Langer, William S., and S. Everett Gleason. *The Undeclared War 1940–1941: The World Crisis and American Foreign Policy*. New York: Harper & Brothers, 1953.

Layton, Edwin T., with Roger Pineau and John Costello. *"And I Was There": Pearl Harbor and Midway—Breaking the Secrets*. New York: William Morrow, 1985.

Leckie, Robert. *Challenge for the Pacific*. Garden City, N.Y.: Doubleday, 1965.

———. *Strong Men Armed: The United States Marines Against Japan*. New York: Bantam Books, 1963.

Lee, Bradford A. *Britain and the Sino-Japanese War 1937–1939: A Study in the Dilemmas of British Decline*. Stanford, Calif.: Stanford University Press, 1973.

Lee, Robert E. *Victory at Guadalcanal*. Novato, Calif.: Presidio Press, 1981.

Lenton, H. T. *Royal Netherlands Navy*. Garden City, N.Y.: Doubleday, 1968.

Lenton, H. T., and J. J. Colledge. *British and Dominion Warships of World War II*. Garden City, N.Y.: Doubleday, 1968.

Leutze, James. *A Different Kind of Victory: A Biography of Admiral Thomas C. Hart*. Annapolis, Md.: Naval Institute Press, 1981.

Lewin, Ronald. *The American Magic: Codes, Ciphers, and the Defeat of Japan*. New York: Farrar, Straus & Giroux, 1982.

Lockwood, Charles A. *Sink 'Em All!* New York: Bantam Books, 1984.

Lockwood, Charles A., and Hans C. Adamson. *Battles of the Philippine Sea*. New York: Thomas Crowell, 1968.

Lockwood, William W. *The Economic Development of Japan*. Princeton: Princeton University Press, 1968.

Loomis, Vincent V., with Jeffrey Ethell. *Amelia Earhart: The Final Story*. New York: Random House, 1985.

Lord, Walter. *Day of Infamy*. New York: Bantam Books, 1963.

———. *Incredible Victory*. New York: Pocket Books, 1968.

———. *Lonely Vigil*. New York: Pocket Books, 1978.

Lorelli, John A. *The Battle of the Komandorski Islands, March 1943*. Annapolis, Md.: Naval Institute Press, 1984.

Lott, Arnold. *Most Dangerous Sea*. New York: Ballantine Books, 1959.

Louis, William R. *British Strategy in the Far East, 1919–1939.* Oxford, England: Clarendon Press, 1971.

Lundstrom, John B. *The First South Pacific Campaign: Pacific Fleet Strategy December 1941–June 1942.* Annapolis, Md.: Naval Institute Press, 1976.

————. *The First Team: Pacific Naval Air Combat from Pearl Harbor to Midway.* Annapolis, Md.: Naval Institute Press, 1984.

MacArthur, Douglas A. *Reminiscences.* Greenwich, Conn.: Fawcett Books, 1965.

McAulay, Lex. *Into the Dragon's Jaws: The Fifth Air Force over Rabaul.* Mesa, Ariz.: Champlin Fighter Museum Press, 1986.

McCarthy, John. *Australia and Imperial Defense 1918–1939: A Study in Air and Sea Power.* St. Lucia, Queensland, Australia: University of Queensland Press, 1976.

McCune, Shannon. *The Ryukyu Islands.* Harrisburg, Penna.: Stackpole, 1975.

Macintyre, Donald. *Leyte Gulf: Armada in the Pacific.* New York: Ballantine Books, 1969.

McIntyre, W. David. *The Rise and Fall of the Singapore Naval Base.* Hamden, Conn.: Archon Books, 1979.

McLachlan, Donald. *Room 39: A Study in Naval Intelligence.* New York: Athenaeum, 1968.

Manning, Paul. *Hirohito: The War Years.* New York: Dodd, Mead, 1983.

Marder, Arthur. *Old Friends, New Enemies: The Royal Navy and the Imperial Japanese Navy.* Vol. 1: *Strategic Illusions, 1936–1941.* Oxford, England: Clarendon Press, 1981.

Marder, Arthur, Mark Jacobsen, and John Horsfield. *Old Friends, New Enemies: The Royal Navy and the Imperial Japanese Navy.* Vol. 2: *The Pacific War, 1942–1945.* Oxford, England: Clarendon Press, 1990.

Mashbir, Sidney Forrester. *I Was an American Spy.* New York: Vantage Press, 1953.

Mason, John T., Jr., ed. *The Pacific War Remembered.* Annapolis, Md.: Naval Institute Press, 1986.

Matthews, Tony. *Shadows Dancing: Japanese Espionage Against the West 1939–1945.* New York: St. Martin's Press, 1994.

Matsuo Kinoaki. *How Japan Plans to Win.* Kilsoo K. Haan, trans. Boston: Little, Brown, 1942.

May, Ernest R., ed. *Knowing One's Enemies: Intelligence Assessment Before the Two World Wars.* Princeton, N.J.: Princeton University Press, 1984.

Mayer, S. L., ed. *The Japanese War Machine.* Seacaucus, N.J.: Chartwell Books, 1976.

Mears, Frederick. *Carrier Combat.* New York: Ballantine Books, 1967.

Merglen, Albert. *Surprise Warfare: Subversive, Airborne and Amphibious Operations.* Kenneth Morgan, trans. London: Allen & Unwin, 1968.

Merillat, Herbert C. *Guadalcanal Remembered.* New York: Avon Books, 1990.

Middlebrook, Martin, and Patrick Mahoney. *Battleship: The Sinking of the Prince of Wales and the Repulse.* New York: Scribner's, 1979.

Mikesh, Robert C. *Broken Wings of the Samurai: The Destruction of the Japanese Airforce.* Annapolis, Md.: Naval Institute Press, 1993.

————. *Japanese Aircraft Code Names and Designations.* Atglen, Penna.: Schiffer Publishing Ltd., 1993.

————. *Japan's World War II Balloon Bomb Attacks on North America.* Washington, D.C.: Smithsonian Annals of Flight Monograph No. 9, 1973.

Mikesh, Robert C., and Tagaya Osamu. *Moonlight Interceptor: Japan's Irving Night Fighter.* Washington, D.C.: Smithsonian Institution Press, 1985.

Miles, Milton E., with Hawthorne Daniel. *A Different Kind of War: The Unknown Story of the U.S. Navy's Guerrilla Forces in World War II China.* Garden City, N.Y.: Doubleday, 1967.

Miller, Edward S. *War Plan Orange: The U.S. Strategy to Defeat Japan, 1897–1945.* Annapolis, Md.: Naval Institute Press, 1991.

Miller, Thomas C., Jr. *The Cactus Air Force.* New York: Bantam Books, 1981.

Millot, Bernard. *The Battle of the Coral Sea.* Annapolis, Md.: Naval Institute Press, 1974.

————. *Divine Thunder: The Life and Death of the Kamikazes.* New York: McCall Publishing Company, 1970.

Minear, Richard H. *Victor's Justice: The Tokyo War Crimes Trials.* Princeton, N.J.: Princeton University Press, 1971.

Monks, John, Jr. *A Ribbon and a Star: The Third Marines at Bougainville.* New York: Pyramid Books, 1966.

Monsarrat, John. *Angel on the Yardarm: The Beginnings of Fleet Radar Defense and the Kamikaze Threat.* Newport, R.I.: Naval War College, 1985.

Montgomery, Michael. *Who Sank the Sydney?* New York: Hippocrene, 1983.

Morgenstern, George. *Pearl Harbor: The Story of the Secret War.* New York: Devin-Adair, 1947.

Morley, James W., ed. and trans. *Japan's Road to the Pacific War.* Selections translated from *Taiheiyo senso e no michi: kaisen gaiko shi,* all published in New York by Columbia University Press as indicated:

————. *The China Quagmire: Japan's Expansion on the Asian Continent 1933–1941* (1983).

————. *Japan's Advance into Southeast Asia, 1939–1941* (1980).

————. *Japan Erupts: The London Naval Conference and the Manchurian Incident, 1928–1932* (1984).

Morris, Ivan. *The Nobility of Failure: Tragic Heroes in the History of Japan.* Rutledge, Vt.: Tuttle, 1982.

Morrison, Wilbur H. *Above and Beyond, 1941–1945.* New York: Bantam Books, 1986.

————. *Point of No Return: An Epic Saga of Disaster and Triumph.* New York: Playboy Press, 1979.

Morton, William F. *Tanaka Giichi and Japan's China Policy.* New York: St. Martin's Press, 1980.

Mosley, Leonard. *Hirohito: Emperor of Japan.* New York: Avon, 1967.

Muir, Malcolm. *The* Iowa-*Class Battleships:* Iowa, New Jersey, Missouri, *and* Wisconsin. Poole, Dorset, England: Blandford Press, 1987.

Murakami Hyoe. *Japan: The Years of Trial, 1919–1952.* Tokyo: Kodansha International, 1983.

Musicant, Ivan. *Battleship at War: The Epic Story of the U.S.S.* Washington. New York: Harcourt, Brace, Jovanovich, 1986.

Myers, Ramon H., and Mark R. Peattie, eds. *The Japanese Colonial Empire, 1895–1945.* Princeton, N.J.: Princeton University Press, 1984.

Naito Hasuho. *Thunder Gods: The Kamikaze Pilots Tell Their Story.* Ichikawa Mayumi, trans. New York: Dell Books, 1990.

*Navy Times* Editors. *They Fought Under the Sea.* Derby, Conn.: Monarch Books, 1962.

Neumann, William H. *America Encounters Japan: From Perry to MacArthur.* Baltimore: Johns Hopkins University Press, 1963.

Newcomb, Richard F. *Iwo Jima.* New York: New American Library, 1965.

————. *Savo: The Incredible Naval Debacle off Guadalcanal.* New York: Bantam Books, 1963.

Nish, Ian H. *Alliance in Decline: A Study in Anglo-Japanese Relations, 1908–1923.* London: Athalone Press, 1972.

————. *Japanese Foreign Policy, 1869–1942: Kasumigaseki to Miyakezaka.* London: Routledge & Kegan Paul, 1977.

O'Callahan, Joseph T. *I Was Chaplain on the* Franklin. New York: Macmillan, 1957.

O'Connor, Raymond G. *Perilous Equilibrium: The United States and the London Naval Conference of 1930.* New York: Greenwood Press, 1969.

Ogaka Sadako. *Defiance in Manchuria: The Making of Japanese Foreign Policy 1931–1932.* Berkeley: University of California Press, 1964.

Okumiya Masatake and Horikoshi Jiro with Martin Caidin. *Zero: The Story of Japan's Air War in the Pacific, 1941–1945.* New York: Ballantine Books, 1957.

O'Neill, Richard. *Suicide Squads of World War II.* New York: Military Heritage Press, 1981.

Orita Zenji with Joseph D. Harrington. *I-Boat Captain.* Canoga Park, Calif.: Major Books, 1976.

Owens, William D. *Eye-Deep in Hell: A Memoir of the Liberation of the Philippines, 1944–1945.* Dallas: Southern Methodist University Press, 1989.

*Pacific Islands Year Book, 1944.* 5th ed. Suva, Fiji: Pacific Publications, 1944.

Peattie, Mark R. *The Rise and Fall of the Japanese in Micronesia, 1885–1945.* Honolulu: University of Hawaii Press, 1988.

Pelz, Stephen E. *Race to Pearl Harbor: The Failure of the Second London Naval Conference and the Onset of World War II.* Cambridge, Mass.: Harvard University Press, 1974.

Popov, Dusko. *Spy-Counterspy: The Autobiography of Dusko Popov.* Greenwich, Conn.: Fawcett Books, 1975.

Potter, E. B. *Admiral Arleigh Burke.* New York: Random House, 1990.

————. *Bull Halsey.* Annapolis, Md.: Naval Institute Press, 1985.

————. *Nimitz.* Annapolis, Md.: Naval Institute Press, 1976.

Potter, E. B., and Chester W. Nimitz, et al., eds. *Sea Power: A Naval History.* Englewood Cliffs, N.J.: Prentice-Hall, 1960.

Potter, John D. *The Life and Death of a Japanese General.* New York: New American Library, 1962.

————. *Yamamoto: The Man Who Menaced America.* New York: Viking Press, 1965.

Prange, Gordon W., with Donald M. Goldstein and Katharine V. Dillon. *At Dawn We Slept: The Untold Story of Pearl Harbor.* New York: McGraw-Hill, 1981. *December 7, 1941: The Day the Japanese Attacked Pearl Harbor.* New York: McGraw-Hill, 1988.

————. *God's Samurai: Lead Pilot at Pearl Harbor.* Washington, D.C.: Brassey's, 1990.

————. *Pearl Harbor: The Verdict of History.* New York: McGraw-Hill, 1986.

————. *Target Tokyo: The Story of the Sorge Spy Ring.* New York: McGraw-Hill, 1984.

Prange, Gordon W., Donald M. Goldstein, and Katharine V. Dillon. *Miracle at Midway.* New York: McGraw-Hill, 1982.

Price, Alden, ed. *Sea Raiders.* North Hollywood, Calif.: Challenge Books, n.d. (ca. 1962).

Price, Alfred. *Instruments of Darkness: The History of Electronic Warfare.* London: MacDonald & James, 1977.

Price, Willard. *Japan's Islands of Mystery.* New York: John Day Company, 1944.

Quigley, Harold S. *Far Eastern War 1937–1941.* Boston: World Peace Foundation, 1942.

Radford, Arthur W. *From Pearl Harbor to Vietnam: The Memoirs of Admiral Arthur W. Radford.* Stephen Jurika, Jr., ed. Stanford, Calif.: Hoover Institution Press, 1980.

Rearden, Jim. *Cracking the Zero Mystery: How the U.S. Learned to Beat Japan's Vaunted World War II Fighter Plane.* Fairfield, Penna.: Stackpole Books, 1990.

Reid, Anthony, and Oki Akira, eds. *The Japanese Experience in Indonesia: Selected Memoirs of 1942–1945.* Ohio University Monographs, Southeast Asia Series, No. 72. Athens, Ohio: Ohio University Press, 1986.

Reischauer, Edwin O. *My Life Between Japan and America.* New York: Harper & Row, 1986.

Reynolds, Clark G. *The Fast Carriers: The Forging of an Air Navy.* Huntington, N.Y.: Robert E. Krieger, 1978.

Robertson, John, and John McCarthy, eds. *Australian War Strategy, 1939–1945: A Documentary History.* St. Lucia, Queensland, Australia: University of Queensland Press, 1985.

Rohwer, Jurgen, and G. Hummelchen. *Chronology of the War at Sea 1939–1945.* 2 vols. New York: Arco, 1972–1974.

Romulo, Carlos P. *I Saw the Fall of the Philippines.* Garden City, N.Y.: Doubleday, 1942.

Roscoe, Theodore. *United States Destroyer Operations in World War II.* Annapolis, Md.: Naval Institute Press, 1953.

———. *United States Submarine Operations in World War II.* Annapolis, Md.: Naval Institute Press, 1949.

Roskill, Stephen. *Naval Policy Between the Wars.* 2 vols. London: Collins, 1968–1972.

Rout, Leslie B., Jr., and John F. Bratzel. *The Shadow War: German Espionage and United States Counterespionage in Latin America During World War II.* Frederick, Md.: University Press of America, 1986.

Rusbridger, James, and Eric Nave. *Betrayal at Pearl Harbor: How Churchill Lured Roosevelt into World War II.* New York: Summit Books, 1991.

Russell, Lord, of Liverpool. *The Knights of Bushido.* London: Corgi, 1958.

Rutherford, Ward. *Fall of the Philippines.* New York: Ballantine Books, 1971.

Sakai Saburo with Martin Caidin and Fred Saito. *Samurai!* New York: Ballantine Books, 1965.

Sakaida, Henry. *Winged Samurai: Saburo Sakai and the Zero Fighter Pilots.* Mesa, Ariz.: Champlin Fighter Museum Press, 1985.

Sayer, Ian, and Douglas Bolting. *America's Secret Army: The Untold Story of the Counterintelligence Corps.* New York: Franklin Watts, 1989.

Schultz, Duane. *The Last Battle Station: The Saga of the U.S.S. Houston.* New York: St. Martin's Press, 1985.

———. *Wake Island.* New York: Playboy Press, 1979.

Sekigawa Eiichiro. *Pictorial History of Japanese Military Aviation.* London: Ian Allen, 1974.

Sergeant, Harriet. *Shanghai: Collision Point of Cultures, 1918–1939.* New York: Crown Publishers, 1990.

Seth, Ronald. *Secret Servants: A History of Japanese Espionage.* New York: Paperback Library, 1968.

Sherrod, Robert. *History of Marine Corps Aviation in World War II.* Washington, D.C.: Combat Forces Press, 1952.

Sherman, Frederick C. *Combat Command: The American Aircraft Carriers in the Pacific War.* New York: Bantam Books, 1982.

Shiroyama Saburo. *War Criminal: The Life and Death of Hirota Koki.* John Bester, trans. Tokyo: Kodansha International, 1977.

Sigel, Leon V. *Fighting to a Finish: The Politics of War Termination in the United States and Japan, 1945.* Ithaca, N.Y.: Cornell University Press, 1988.

Silverstone, Paul. *U.S. Warships in World War II.* Garden City, N.Y.: Doubleday, 1968.

Sims, Edward H. *Greatest Fighter Missions.* New York: Ballantine Books, 1965.

Slackman, Michael. *Target: Pearl Harbor.* Honolulu: University of Hawaii Press and *Arizona* Memorial Association, 1990.

Smith, S. E., ed. *The United States Navy in World War II.* New York: William Morrow, 1966.

Smith, Stan. *The Battle for Leyte Gulf.* New York: Belmont Books, 1961.

———. *The Battle of Savo.* New York: Macfadden-Bartell, 1962.

———. *The Destroyermen.* New York: Belmont Books, 1966.

Soka Gakkai Youth Division, ed. *Peace Is Our Duty: Accounts of What War Can Do to Man.* Tokyo: Japan Times, 1982.

Spector, Ronald H. *Eagle Against the Sun: The American War with Japan.* New York: Vintage, 1985.

———. ed. *Listening to the Enemy: Key Documents on the Role of Communications Intelligence in the War with Japan.* Wilmington, Del.: Scholarly Resources, 1988.

Spurr, Russell. *A Glorious Way to Die: The Kamikaze Mission of the Battleship Yamato, April 1945.* New York: Bantam Books, 1983.

Stafford, Edward P. *The Big "E": The Story of the U.S.S. Enterprise.* New York: Ballantine Books, 1976.

———. *Little Ship, Big War.* New York: Jove Press, 1985.

Stanley, Roy M., III. *Prelude to Pearl Harbor: War in China, 1937–1941: Japan's Rehearsal for World War II.* New York: Scribner's, 1982.

———. *World War II Photo Intelligence.* New York: Scribner's, 1981.

Steel, Johannes. *Men Behind the War: A Who's Who of Our Time.* New York: Sheridan House, 1942.

Stephan, John J. *Hawaii Under the Rising Sun: Japan's Plans for Conquest After Pearl Harbor.* Honolulu: University of Hawaii Press, 1984.

Stewart, Adrian. *The Battle of Leyte Gulf.* New York: Scribner's, 1979.

Stewart, William H. *Ghost Fleet of the Truk Lagoon, Japanese Mandated Islands: An Account of "Operation Hailstone."* Missoula, Mont.: Pictorial Histories Publishing Company, 1982.

Stillwell, Paul, ed. *Air Raid, Pearl Harbor: Recollections of a Day of Infamy.* Annapolis, Md.: Naval Institute Press, 1981.

Stripp, Alan. *Codebreaker in the Far East.* London: Frank Cass, 1989.

Swinson, Arthur. *Defeat in Malaya: The Fall of Singapore.* New York: Ballantine Books, 1970.

Takagi Sokichi. *Memoir of the Termination of the War.* Tokyo: Kobundo, 1948 (this translation is to be found in the Franklin Delano Roosevelt Library, John Toland papers).

Tansill, Charles Callan. *Back Door to War: The Roosevelt Foreign Policy, 1933–1941.* Chicago: Regnery, 1952.

Taylor, Lawrence. *A Trial of Generals: Homma, Yamashita, MacArthur.* South Bend, Ind.: Icarus Books, 1981.

Taylor, Theodore. *The Magnificent Mitscher.* Annapolis, Md.: Naval Institute Press, 1991.

Theobald, Robert A. *The Final Secret of Pearl Harbor: The Washington Contribution to the Japanese Attack.* New York: Devin-Adair, 1954.

Thomas, David. *Battle of the Java Sea.* London: Pan Books, 1971.

Thorne, Christopher. *Allies of a Kind: The United States, Britain, and the War Against Japan, 1941–1945.* New York: Oxford University Press, 1978.

————. *The Issue of War: States, Societies, and the Far Eastern Conflict of 1941–1945.* New York: Oxford University Press, 1986.

————. *The Limits of Foreign Policy: The West, the League, and the Far Eastern Crisis of 1931–1933.* New York: Capricorn Books, 1973.

Thorpe, Elliott R. *East Wind Rain.* Boston: Gambit, 1969.

Togo Shigenori. *The Cause of Japan.* New York: Simon & Schuster, 1956.

Toland, John. *But Not in Shame: The Six Months After Pearl Harbor.* New York: Random House, 1961.

————. *Infamy: Pearl Harbor and Its Aftermath.* New York: Berkeley Books, 1983.

————. *The Rising Sun: The Decline and Fall of the Japanese Empire, 1936–1945.* New York: Bantam Books, 1971.

Tolischus, Otto D. *Through Japanese Eyes.* New York: Reynal & Hitchcock, 1945.

Tolley, Kemp. *Yangtze Patrol: The U.S. Navy in China.* Annapolis, Md.: Naval Institute Press, 1971.

Toyoda, Soemu. *The Last Imperial Navy.* Tokyo: Sekaino Nippon Sha, 1949. USN translation of excerpts at Naval Historical Center.

Toynbee, Arnold. *Survey of International Affairs, 1936.* London: Oxford University Press, 1937.

Trefousse, Hans L. *What Happened at Pearl Harbor: Documents Pertaining to the Japanese Attack of December 7, 1941, and Its Background.* New Haven: College and University Press, 1958.

Tregaskis, Richard. *Guadalcanal Diary.* New York: Random House, 1943.

————. *John F. Kennedy: War Hero.* New York: Dell Books, 1962.

Trenowden, Ian. *Operations Most Secret: SOE, The Malayan Theater.* London: William Kimber, 1978.

Tsuji Masanobu. *Singapore: The Japanese Version.* Margaret E. Lake, trans. New York: St. Martin's Press, 1960.

Tuleja, Thaddeus V. *Climax at Midway.* New York: W. W. Norton, 1960.

————. *Statesmen and Admirals: Quest for a Far Eastern Naval Policy.* New York: W. W. Norton, 1963.

Utley, Jonathan. *Going to War with Japan, 1937–1941.* Knoxville: University of Tennessee Press, 1985.

Vader, John. *New Guinea: The Tide Is Stemmed.* New York: Ballantine Books, 1971.

Vandegrift, Alexander A., with Robert Asprey. *Once a Marine: The Memoirs of General A. A. Vandegrift, United States Marine Corps.* New York: Ballantine Books, 1966.

Van Der Vat, Dan. *The Pacific Campaign, World War II: The U.S.-Japanese Naval War, 1941–1945.* New York: Simon & Schuster, 1991.

Van Oosten, F. C. *The Battle of the Java Sea.* Annapolis, Md.: Naval Institute Press, 1976.

Vespa, Amleto. *Secret Agent of Japan.* Garden City, N.Y.: Doubleday, 1941.

Warner, Denis, and Peggy Warner with Seno Sadao. *Disaster in the Pacific: New*

*Light on the Battle of Savo Island.* Annapolis, Md.: Naval Institute Press, 1992.

————. *The Sacred Warriors: Japan's Suicide Legions.* New York: Avon Books, 1984.

Warshofsky, Fred. *War Under the Waves.* New York: Pyramid Books, 1962.

Watts, A. J. *Japanese Warships of World War II.* Garden City, N.Y.: Doubleday, 1967.

Watts, A. J., and Brian G. Gordon. *The Imperial Japanese Navy.* Garden City, N.Y.: Doubleday, 1971.

Wheeler, Gerald E. *Prelude to Pearl Harbor: The United States and the Far East, 1921–1931.* Columbia, Mo.: University of Missouri Press, n.d. (1963?).

White, W. L. *They Were Expendable.* Cleveland: World Publishing Company, 1944.

Whitehouse, Arch. *Squadrons of the Sea.* New York: Modern Library, 1962.

Whitman, John W. *Bataan: Our Last Ditch, The Bataan Campaign, 1942.* New York: Hippocrene Books, 1990.

Whitney, Courtney. *MacArthur: His Rendezvous with History.* New York: Knopf, 1968.

Wilcox, Robert K. *Japan's Secret War.* New York: William Morrow, 1985.

Wilds, Thomas. *Japanese Forces in the Gilbert Islands, 10 December 1942–November 1943.* Monograph ms., n.d. Washington, D.C.: Naval Historical Center: USN Microfilm J-3.

Wilhelm, Maria. *The Man Who Watched the Rising Sun: The Story of Admiral Ellis M. Zacharias.* New York: Franklin Watts, 1967.

Williams, Peter, and David Wallace. *Unit 731: Japan's Secret Biological Warfare in World War II.* New York: Free Press, 1989.

Willmott, H. P. *The Barrier and the Javelin: Japanese and Allied Pacific Strategies, February to June 1942.* Annapolis, Md.: Naval Institute Press, 1983.

————. *Empires in the Balance: Japanese and Allied Pacific Strategies to April 1942.* Annapolis, Md.: Naval Institute Press, 1982.

Winslow, Walter G. *The Fleet the Gods Forgot: The U.S. Asiatic Fleet in World War II.* Annapolis, Md.: Naval Institute Press, 1982.

————. *The Ghost That Died at Sunda Strait.* Annapolis, Md.: Naval Institute Press, 1984.

Winton, John. *The Forgotten Fleet: The British Navy in the Pacific, 1944–1945.* New York: Coward-McCann, 1969.

————. *Sink the* Haguro! London: Archon Books, 1978.

————. *Ultra in the Pacific: How Breaking Japanese Codes and Cyphers Affected Naval Operations Against Japan 1941–45.* Annapolis, Md.: Naval Institute Press, 1993.

Wohlstetter, Roberta. *Pearl Harbor: Warning and Decision.* Stanford, Calif.: Stanford University Press, 1962.

Woodburn Kirby, S. *Singapore: The Chain of Disaster.* New York: Macmillan, 1971.

Woodward, C. Vann. *The Battle for Leyte Gulf.* New York: W. W. Norton, 1965.

Yardley, Herbert O. *The American Black Chamber.* New York: Ballantine Books, 1981.

———. *The Education of a Poker Player.* London: Jonathan Cape, 1979.

Y'Blood, William T. *The Little Giants: U.S. Escort Carriers Against Japan.* Annapolis, Md.: Naval Institute Press, 1987.

———. *Rising Sun Setting: The Battle of the Philippine Sea.* Annapolis, Md.: Naval Institute Press, 1981.

Yokota Yutaka with Joseph D. Harrington. *The Kaiten Weapon.* New York: Ballantine Books, 1962.

Yoshida Mitsuru. *Requiem for Battleship* Yamato. Richard H. Minear, trans. Seattle: University of Washington Press, 1985.

Yoshimura Akira. *Build the* Musashi! *The Birth and Death of the World's Greatest Battleship.* Vincent Murphy, trans. Tokyo: Kodansha International, 1991.

Young, James R. *Behind the Rising Sun.* New York: Doubleday, Doran & Company, 1941.

Zacharias, Ellis M., with Ladislas Farago. *Secret Missions: The Story of an Intelligence Officer.* New York: G. P. Putnam's Sons, 1946.

## Articles and Papers

Aldrich, Richard J. "Conspiracy or Confusion? Churchill, Roosevelt and Pearl Harbor." *Intelligence and National Security,* July 1992.

Andradé, Ernest, Jr. "The Cruiser Controversy in Naval Limitations Negotiations, 1922–1936," *Military Affairs,* July 1984.

Andrews, E. M. "The Broken Promise—Britain's Failure to Consult Its Commonwealth on Defence in 1934, and the Implications for Australian Defence and Foreign Policy," *Australian Journal of Defense Studies,* November 1978.

Anonymous, "The Diary of Takahashi," *U.S. Naval Institute Proceedings,* July 1980.

Anzai Jiro. "From Copenhagen to Coventry—A Hypothetical Attempt at Solving the So-called Pearl Harbor Riddles," *Otemon Gakuin University Faculty of Letters Review,* no. 14 (1980).

Baldwin, Hanson W. "Saga of a Ship—The *Houston,*" *The New York Times Magazine,* March 3, 1946.

Ballendorf, Dirk A. "Earl Hancock Ellis: The Man and His Mission," *U.S. Naval Institute Proceedings,* November 1983.

Barde, Robert E. "Midway: Tarnished Victory," *Military Affairs,* December 1983.

Bartlett, Donald. "Vice Admiral Chuichi Hara: Unforgettable Foe," *U.S. Naval Institute Proceedings,* October 1970.

Beatty, Frank E. "The Background of the Secret Report," *National Review,* December 13, 1966.

Bledsoe, Albert M. "The Japanese Naval Academy," *U.S. Naval Institute Proceedings,* March 1949.

Bratzell, John F., and Leslie B. Rout, Jr. "Research Note: Pearl Harbor, Microdots, and J. Edgar Hoover," *American Historical Review*, December 1982. (See also Letters & Replies, *American Historical Review*, October 1983.)

Breslin, Thomas A. "Mystifying the Past: Establishment Historians and the Origins of the Pacific War," *Bulletin of Concerned Asian Scholars*, October–December 1976.

Brower, Charles F. "Assault vs. Siege: The Debate over the Final Strategy for the Defeat of Japan." Paper presented at conference, "The United States and Japan in World War II," Hofstra University, December 5, 1991.

Brown, G. M. "Attitudes to an Invasion of Australia in 1942," *Journal of the Royal United Service Institution*, March 1977.

Brooke, G.A.G. "Singapore 1942: Gallantry and Disaster," *Army Quarterly and Defence Journal*, January 1992.

Bruce-Briggs, B. "Another Ride on Tricycle," *Intelligence and National Security*, April 1992.

Brugioni, Dino. "Naval Photographic Intelligence in World War II," *U.S. Naval Institute Proceedings*, June 1987.

Burns, Richard D. "Inspection of the Mandates, 1919–1941," *Pacific Historical Review*, spring 1968.

Bywater, Hector. "The Coming Struggle for Sea Power," *Current History*, October 1934.

Campbell-Smith, Roy. "Seapower and the Japanese Empire," *U.S. Naval Institute Proceedings*, November 1946.

Cant, Gilbert. "Bull's Run: Was Halsey Right at Leyte Gulf?" *Life Magazine*, November 24, 1947.

Castle, Alfred L. "Ambassador Castle's Role in the Negotiations of the London Naval Conference," *Naval History*, summer 1989.

Chapman, John W. M. "Japanese Intelligence 1919–1945: A Suitable Case for Treatment." In Christopher Andrew and Jeremy Noakes, eds., *Intelligence and International Relations, 1900–1945*. Exeter, England: Exeter University Publications, 1987.

———. "Pearl Harbor: The Anglo-Australian Dimension," *Intelligence and National Security*, July 1989.

———. "Tricycle Recycled: Collaboration Among the Secret Intelligence Services of the Axis States, 1940–41," *Intelligence and National Security*, July 1992.

Chihaya Masataka. "Mysterious Withdrawal from Kiska," *U.S. Naval Institute Proceedings*, February 1958.

Coffin, C. E., Jr. "Effects of Aerial Bombardment in China," *U.S. Naval Institute Proceedings*, September 1938.

Cohen, Jerome B. "The Japanese War Economy 1940–1945," *Far Eastern Survey*, December 4, 1946.

Coles, Michael H. "What the Japanese Learned from Taranto," *Military History Quarterly*, spring 1991.

Coletta, Paolo E. "Prelude to War: Japan, the United States, and the Aircraft Carrier, 1919–1945," *Prologue,* winter 1991.

Condon, John P. "Bringing Down Yamamoto," *U.S. Naval Institute Proceedings,* November 1990.

Conroy, Hilary. "Japan's War in China: Historical Parallel to Vietnam?" *Pacific Affairs,* spring 1970.

Coox, Alvin D. "Flawed Perception and Its Effect upon Operational Thinking: The Case of the Japanese Army, 1937–1941," *Intelligence and National Security,* April 1990.

———. "Japanese Military Intelligence in the Pacific Theater: Its Non-Revolutionary Nature." In Walter T. Hitchcock, ed., *The Intelligence Revolution.* Washington, D.C.: Office of Air Force History, 1991.

———. "Repulsing the Pearl Harbor Revisionists: The State of Present Literature on the Debate," *Military Affairs,* January 1986.

———. "The Rise and Fall of the Imperial Japanese Air Forces." In Alfred F. Hurley and Robert C. Ehrhart, eds., *Air Power and Warfare.* Washington, D.C.: Office of Air Force History, 1979.

Cowman, Ian. "An Admiralty Myth: The Search for an Advanced Far Eastern Fleet Base Before the Second World War," *Journal of Strategic Studies,* September 1985.

Cressman, Robert J. "Desperate Battle at Unalaga Pass," *Naval History,* fall 1990.

———. "To Retrieve Our Initial Disaster," *Naval History,* summer 1992.

Davis, Frank. "Operation OLYMPIC: The Invasion of Japan, 1 November 1945," *Strategy & Tactics,* August–September 1974.

Dean, Ralph J. "Eta Jima: Hallowed Halls," *U.S. Naval Institute Proceedings,* March 1983.

De Virgilio, John F. "Japanese Thunderfish," *Naval History,* winter 1991.

Doerr, Paul W. "The Changkufeng/Lake Khasan Incident of 1938: British Intelligence on Soviet and Japanese Military Performance," *Intelligence and National Security,* July 1990.

Dodd, Norman L. "The Crown Colony of Hong Kong," *Military Review,* October 1976.

Dorny, Louis B. "Patrol Wing Ten's Raid on Jolo," *U.S. Naval Institute Proceedings Supplement: The U.S. Navy Yesterday,* March 1985.

Drea, Edward J. "Defending the Driniumor: Covering Force Operations in New Guinea, 1944," *Leavenworth Papers,* No. 9 (1984).

———. "The Development of Imperial Japanese Army Amphibious Warfare Doctrine, 1890s–1941." Paper presented at the Society for Military History meeting, Fredericksburg, Va., April 10, 1992.

———. "Missing Intentions: Japanese Intelligence and the Soviet Invasion of Manchuria, 1945," *Military Affairs,* April 1984.

———. "Nomonhan: Japanese-Soviet Tactical Combat, 1939," *Leavenworth Papers,* no. 2 (1981).

———. "Reading Each Others' Mail: Japanese Communications Intelligence, 1920–1941," *Journal of Military History,* April 1991.

Esthus, Raymond A. "President Roosevelt's Commitment to Britain to Intervene in a Pacific War," *Mississippi Valley Historical Review*, June 1963.

Fearey, Robert A. "Reminiscences: My Year with Ambassador Joseph C. Grew, 1941–1942: A Personal Account," *Journal of American–East Asian Relations*, spring 1992.

Ferris, John. "From Broadway to Bletchley Park: The Diary of Captain Malcolm D. Kennedy, 1934–1946," *Intelligence and National Security*, July 1989.

Field, James E., Jr. "Admiral Yamamoto," *U.S. Naval Institute Proceedings*, October 1949.

Fishel, Edwin C., and Louis W. Tordella. "FDR's Mistake? Not Likely," *International Journal of Intelligence and Counterintelligence*, n.d. (summer 1992).

Frank, Richard B. "Guadalcanal: The Pivotal Campaign," *U.S. Naval Institute Proceedings*, August 1992.

Fuchida Mitsuo and Okumiya Masatake. "Prelude to Midway," *U.S. Naval Institute Proceedings*, May 1955.

Fujita Nobuo and Joseph D. Harrington. "I Bombed the USA," *U.S. Naval Institute Proceedings*, June 1961.

Fukaya Hiroichi. "A Japanese Soldier in Andaman," *Army Quarterly and Defence Journal*, July 1991.

Fukaya Matsuo. "Japan's Wartime Carrier Construction," *U.S. Naval Institute Proceedings*, September 1955.

Fukuda Teizaburo. "A Mistaken War," *U.S. Naval Institute Proceedings*, December 1968.

Fukudome Shigeru. "Hawaii Operation," *U.S. Naval Institute Proceedings*, December 1955.

Gallicchio, Marc. "After Nagasaki: General Marshall's Plan for Tactical Nuclear Weapons in Japan," *Prologue*, winter 1991.

Genda Minoru. "Tactical Planning in the Imperial Japanese Navy," *Naval War College Review*, October 1969.

Gordon, Gilbert. "The Royal Navy and the Japanese Threat." Paper presented at conference, "The United States and Japan in World War II," Hofstra University, December 6, 1991.

Gordon, John, IV. "The Navy's Infantry at Bataan," *U.S. Naval Institute Proceedings Supplement: The U.S. Navy Yesterday*, March 1985.

Grace, Richard J. "Whitehall and the Ghost of Appeasement," *Diplomatic History*, spring 1979.

Grajdanzev, A. J. "Formosa (Taiwan) Under Japanese Rule," *Pacific Affairs*, December 1942.

Grasselli, Albert A. "The Ewa Marines," *Naval History*, spring 1991.

Grattan, C. Hartley. "Those Japanese Mandates," *Harper's Magazine*, December 1943.

Graybar, Lloyd J. "American Pacific Strategy After Pearl Harbor: The Relief of Wake Island," *Prologue*, fall 1980.

Grover, David H. "Night Attack at Shanghai," *Naval History*, winter 1991.

Haggie, Paul. "The Royal Navy and the Far Eastern Problem, 1931–1941," *Army Quarterly and Defence Journal,* October 1976.

Haight, John McVickar, Jr. "FDR's Big Stick," *U.S. Naval Institute Proceedings,* July 1980.

Hall, Cary. "After the Seventh," *Naval History,* winter 1991.

———. "Was It a Surprise: Battleship Readiness Conditions at Pearl Harbor," *Shipmate,* December 1979.

Hammond, Ralph. "On the Road to War," *Naval History,* winter 1991.

Hirama Yoichi. "Japanese Naval Preparations for World War II," *Naval War College Review,* spring 1991.

Holmes, Charles A. "A Sky Gunner's Battle for Wake," *Naval History,* April 1987.

Hone, Thomas C. "The Destruction of the Battle Line at Pearl Harbor," *U.S. Naval Institute Proceedings,* December 1977.

Hosoya Chihiro. "Miscalculations in Deterrent Policy: Japanese–U.S. Relations, 1938–1941," *Journal of Peace Research,* summer 1968.

Howard, Warren S. "Japan's Heavy Cruisers in the War," *U.S. Naval Institute Proceedings,* May 1950.

———. "The Kongos in World War II," *U.S. Naval Institute Proceedings,* November 1948.

Inoguchi Rikihei. "The Kamikaze Creed," *U.S. Naval Institute Proceedings,* February 1973.

Isby, David C. "CA: Tactical Naval Warfare in the Pacific, 1941–1943," *Strategy & Tactics,* May 1973.

Ito Masanori. "Japan's Fleet in Being Strategy," *Contemporary Japan,* July–September 1944.

"Japan's Uncompleted Atomic Bomb," *Kaizo* magazine Special Edition, November 15, 1952.

Junghans, Earl H. "Wake's POWs," *U.S. Naval Institute Proceedings,* February 1983.

Kahn, David. "The Intelligence Failure of Pearl Harbor," *Foreign Affairs,* winter 1991–1992.

———. "Pearl Harbor and the Inadequacy of Cryptanalysis," *Cryptologia,* October 1991.

———. "Why Weren't We Warned?" *Military History Quarterly,* autumn 1991.

Kamps, Charles T. "Singapore: The Campaign for Malaya, 8 December 1941–15 February 1942," *Strategy & Tactics,* March–April 1981.

Kawakami Kiyoshi. "Unsolved Naval Problems of the Pacific," *Pacific Affairs,* October 1931.

Kelly, Jerry R. "Sheathing the Emperor's Sword: The Assassination of Admiral Isoroku Yamamoto." Paper presented at conference, "The United States and Japan in World War II," Hofstra University, December 6, 1991.

Kent, Tyler. "The Roosevelt Legacy and the Kent Case," *Journal of Historical Review,* summer 1983.

King, Cecil S., Jr. "Asiatic Fleet Odyssey," *Naval History,* winter 1991.

Kiralfy, Alexander. "Japanese Naval Strategy." In Edward M. Earle, ed., *Makers of Modern Strategy,* New York: Athenaeum, 1966.

Lanphier, Thomas G., Jr. "I Shot Down Yamamoto," *Reader's Digest,* January 1967.

Layton, Edwin T. "Rendezvous in Reverse," *U.S. Naval Institute Proceedings,* May 1953.

Leary, William M. "Assessing the Japanese Threat: Air Intelligence Prior to Pearl Harbor," *Aerospace Historian,* winter 1987.

Le Compte, Malcolm A. "Radar and the Air Battles of Midway," *Naval History,* summer 1992.

Lowman, David D. "Rendezvous in Reverse (II)," *U.S. Naval Institute Proceedings,* December 1983.

———. "The Treasure of the *Awa Maru," U.S. Naval Institute Proceedings,* August 1982.

Loxton, Bruce. "Three Cruisers, Three Destroyers, Two Seaplane Tenders . . . ," *U.S. Naval Institute Proceedings,* August 1992.

Lundstrom, John B. "Frank Jack Fletcher Got a Bum Rap," *Naval History,* summer 1992 and fall 1992.

MacDonnell, Francis. "The Search for a Second Zimmerman Telegram: FDR, BSC and the Latin American Front," *International Journal of Intelligence and Counterintelligence,* n.d. (summer 1992).

McIntosh, Kenneth A. "Revenge at Coral Sea," *Naval History,* summer 1990.

McPoil, William D. "The Development and Defense of Wake Island, 1934–1941," *Prologue,* winter 1991.

Marks, R. Adrian. "America Was Well Represented," *U.S. Naval Institute Proceedings,* April 1981.

Martin, James M., and Bertrand P. Ramsay. "Seamines and the U.S. Navy," *Naval History,* fall 1989.

Mason, Robert. "Eyewitness," *U.S. Naval Institute Proceedings,* June 1982.

Massie, Robert K. "The 1921 SALT Talks—And You Are There," *The New York Times Magazine,* October 6, 1977.

Matsumoto Kitaro and Chihaya Masataka. "Design and Construction of the *Yamato* and *Musashi, " U.S. Naval Institute Proceedings,* October 1953.

Matthews, Edward J. "Bombarding Japan," *U.S. Naval Institute Proceedings,* February 1979.

———. "What Ship Is That?" *U.S. Naval Institute Proceedings,* July 1976.

Messegee, Gordon H. "Death Is a Lonely Sound," *Naval History,* fall 1989.

Miles, Sherman. "Pearl Harbor in Retrospect," *Atlantic Monthly,* July 1948.

Millsap, Ralph H. "Skill or Luck?" *U.S. Naval Institute Proceedings Supplement: The U.S. Navy Yesterday,* March 1985.

Miner, Deborah. "Policy Makers and Their Critical Assumptions: United States Thinking About Southeast Asia, 1940–1941." Paper presented at meeting of the American Political Science Association, September 1977.

Miranda, Joseph A. "DOWNFALL: The American Invasion of Japan, 1945," *Command*, March–April 1990.

Mooradian, Moorad. "He Only Won Once," *U.S. Naval Institute Proceedings*, November 1990.

Morton, Louis. "The Japanese Decision for War," *U.S. Naval Institute Proceedings*, December 1954.

———. "Japanese Policy and Strategy in Mid-War," *U.S. Naval Institute Proceedings*, February 1959.

———. "War Plan Orange: Evolution of a Strategy," *World Politics*, January 1959.

Naske, Claus M. "The Battle of Alaska Has Ended and . . . the Japs Won It," *Military Affairs*, July 1985.

Nish, Ian H. "Japanese Intelligence, 1894–1922." In Christopher Andrew and Jeremy Noakes, eds., *Intelligence and International Relations 1900–1945*. Exeter, England: Exeter University Publications, 1987.

Nomura Kichisaburo. "Japan's Demand for Naval Equality," *Foreign Affairs*, January 1935.

———. "Stepping Stones to War," *U.S. Naval Institute Proceedings*, September 1951.

Noyer, William L. "Last Ship out of Manila," *American History Illustrated*, May 1985.

Ohmae Toshikazu and Roger Pineau. "Japanese Naval Aviation," *U.S. Naval Institute Proceedings*, December 1972.

Okumiya Masatake. "For Sugar Boats or Submarines?" *U.S. Naval Institute Proceedings*, August 1968.

———. "How the *Panay* Was Sunk," *U.S. Naval Institute Proceedings*, June 1953.

———. "The Japanese Perspective," *Naval History*, winter 1991.

———. "Lessons of an Undeclared War," *U.S. Naval Institute Proceedings*, December 1972.

Omi Heijiro. "The Combined Fleet and My Memoirs of the Navy," ms., May 31, 1966. Ms. in John Toland Papers, FDR Library.

Parker, Frederick D. "The Unsolved Messages of Pearl Harbor," *Cryptologia*, October 1991.

Peattie, Mark R. "Akiyama Saneyuki and the Emergence of Modern Japanese Naval Doctrine," *U.S. Naval Institute Proceedings*, January 1977.

Peattie, Mark R., with David C. Evans. "Sato Tetsutaro and Japanese Strategy," *Naval History*, fall 1990.

Pfeiffer, Omar T. "Planning for War," *Naval History*, winter 1991.

Pineau, Roger. "Admiral Isoroku Yamamoto." In Michael Carver, ed., *The War Lords*. Boston: Little, Brown, 1976.

Potter, E. B. "Arleigh Burke Buries the Hatchet," *U.S. Naval Institute Proceedings*, April 1990.

———. "The Crypt of the Cryptanalysts," *U.S. Naval Institute Proceedings*, August 1982.

————. "The Japanese Navy Tells Its Story," *U.S. Naval Institute Proceedings*, February 1947.

Prados, John. "Planning the Pacific War: To the Malay Barrier," *Strategy & Tactics*, March–April 1984.

————. "The War Against Japan, 1941–1945," *Strategy & Tactics*, November–December 1977.

Pratt, Fletcher. "Americans in Battle, No. 1: Campaign in the Java Sea," *Harper's*, November 1942.

Pratt, Sir John. "On Criticisms of British Far Eastern Policy," *Pacific Affairs*, June 1943.

Price, Willard. "America's Enemy No. 2: Yamamoto," *Harper's*, April 1942.

Quynn, Allen G. "The Capture of Amoy, China, by a Japanese Naval Landing Force," *U.S. Naval Institute Proceedings*, June 1939.

Reber, John J. "Pete Ellis: Amphibious Warfare Prophet," *U.S. Naval Institute Proceedings*, November 1977.

Reynolds, Clark G. "The Continental Strategy of Imperial Japan," *U.S. Naval Institute Proceedings*, August 1983.

————. "Remembering Genda," *U.S. Naval Institute Proceedings*, April 1990.

————. "Taps for the Torpecker," *U.S. Naval Institute Proceedings*, December 1986.

Robinson, Walter L. "*Akagi*, Famous Japanese Carrier," *U.S. Naval Institute Proceedings*, May 1948.

Rusbridger, James. "The Sinking of the 'Automedon,' the Capture of the 'Nankin': New Light on Two Intelligence Disasters in World War II," *Encounter*, May 1985.

Russett, Bruce M. "Pearl Harbor: Deterrence Theory and Decision Theory," *Journal of Peace Research*, summer 1967.

Ryan, Paul B. "The Thunder of Silence: General Marshall's Moral Dilemma," *Armed Forces Journal International*, August 1983.

Rychetnik, Joseph S. "Defiance Rewarded," *Military History*, June 1989.

Sanger, Grant. "Freedom of the Press or Treason?" *U.S. Naval Institute Proceedings*, September 1977.

Sekine Gumpei. "Japan's Case for Seapower," *Current History*, November 1934.

Seno Sadao. "A Chess Game with No Checkmate: Admiral Inoue and the Pacific War," *Naval War College Review*, January–February 1974.

Sesser, Stan. "Logging the Rain Forest," *The New Yorker*, May 27, 1991.

Shapley, Deborah. "Nuclear Weapons History: Japan's Wartime Bomb Projects Revealed," *Science*, January 13, 1978.

Shrader, Grahame F. "U.S.S. *Colorado*: The 'Other' Battleship," *U.S. Naval Institute Proceedings*, December 1976.

Sprague, Clifton. "The Japs Had Us on the Ropes," *The American*, April 1945.

Stankovich, Mike. "The Hardest Choice," *Naval History*, winter 1988.

Stewart, R. A. "Assault on Timor," *Marine Corps Gazette*, September 1974.

Stokes, C. Ray, and Tad Darling. "Yokosuka Naval Air Base and Japanese Naval Aviation," *U.S. Naval Institute Proceedings*, March 1948.

Stripp, Alan. "Breaking Japanese Codes," *Intelligence and National Security*, October 1987.

Stuart, Harry A., and R. G. Tracie. "Oil for the World's Navies," *U.S. Naval Institute Proceedings*, July 1941.

Tanabe Yahachi and Joseph D. Harrington. "I Sank the *Yorktown* at Midway," *U.S. Naval Institute Proceedings*, May 1963.

Tanaka Yuki. "Poison Gas: The Story Japan Would Like to Forget," *Bulletin of the Atomic Scientists*, October 1988.

Tanetsugu Soh-sa. "War in Southern Pacific," *Contemporary Japan*, January 1944.

Taylor, Blaine. "Ambush in Hostile Skies," *Military History*, August 1988.

———. "Fight Left Unfinished," *Military History*, December 1987.

Taylor, Telford. "Day of Infamy, Decades of Doubt," *The New York Times Magazine*, April 29, 1984.

Thach, John S. "Butch O'Hare and the Thach Weave," *Naval History*, spring 1992.

Thomas, Norman. "The Fate of the Japanese in North America and Hawaii," *Pacific Affairs*, March 1943.

Tillman, Barrett. "Hellcats over Truk," *U.S. Naval Institute Proceedings*, March 1977.

Torisu Kennosuke with Chihaya Masataka. "Japanese Submarine Tactics," *U.S. Naval Institute Proceedings*, February 1961.

Trumbull, Robert. "World's Richest Little Isle," *The New York Times Magazine*, March 7, 1982.

Tsunoda Jun and Uchida Kazutomi. "The Pearl Harbor Attack: Admiral Yamamoto's Fundamental Concept with Reference to Paul S. Dull's *A Battle History of the Imperial Japanese Navy (1941–1945)*," *Naval War College Review*, fall 1978.

Urwin, Gregory J. W. "The Defenders of Wake Island and Their Two Wars, 1941–1945," *Prologue*, winter 1991.

Vogel, Bertram. "Some Notes on Japan," *U.S. Naval Institute Proceedings*, May 1946.

Wang Shi-fu. "Naval Strategy in the Sino-Japanese War," *U.S. Naval Institute Proceedings*, July 1940.

Ward, Robert E. "The Inside Story of the Pearl Harbor Plan," *U.S. Naval Institute Proceedings*, December 1951.

Wark, Wesley K. "In Search of a Suitable Japan: British Naval Intelligence in the Pacific Before the Second World War," *Intelligence and National Security*, May 1986.

Warnecke, G. W. "Suetsugu's Fence—Key to Pacific Strategy," *Pacific Affairs*, December 1942.

Whiting, John. "Predictions of War," *Naval History*, winter 1991.

Wilds, Thomas. "The Admiral Who Lost His Fleet," *U.S. Naval Institute Proceedings*, December 1951.

————. "How Japan Fortified the Mandated Islands," *U.S. Naval Institute Proceedings*, April 1955.

Wood, F.N.L. "New Zealand in the Pacific War," *Pacific Affairs*, March 1944.

Wyatt, Lee T. "Casualty Estimates and the Invasion of Japan." Paper presented at conference, "The United States and Japan in World War II," Hofstra University, December 5, 1991.

Yokoi Toshiyuki. "Thoughts on Japan's Naval Defeat," *U.S. Naval Institute Proceedings*, October 1960.

## Periodicals

These sources contained news material of value published either contemporaneously or subsequently.

*Contemporary Japan*
*Newsweek*
*The New York Times*
*Time*
*U.S. Naval Institute Proceedings*
*The Washington Post*

# I N D E X

Netherlands East Indies, 16, 121, 122,
169, 203, 209, 216, 235, 260, 416,
591, 595, 612, 666
campaign for, 245, 248–49, 251–56
Netherlands Foreign Intelligence Staff
(NEFIS), 416
*Nevada*, 189, 474
New Britain, 235
New Georgia, 498–500
New Guinea, 236, 239–41, 281, 299, 302,
356, 394, 416, 448–49, 501, 505,
553
*New Jersey*, 534, 537–38, 545, 611, 650,
679
Newman, Jack B., 267, 420, 422
*New Mexico*, 718, 731
*New Orleans*, 175, 189, 394
Newton, J. H., 190
*New York Times*, 21, 56, 149, 197, 201,
296, 341, 343, 440
New Zealand, 217, 343
*Nichi Nichi*, 201, 348, 436
*Niizuki*, 491–92, 495
Nimitz, Chester W., 232, 274, 284, 302,
305, 315, 316, 318, 324, 329, 356,
380, 382–84, 403, 407–8, 410–12,
421, 459–60, 468, 470, 473, 476,
504, 506, 508, 512, 523, 526–27,
531, 569, 586, 647, 652, 678–79,
686, 711
FDR-MacArthur meeting with, 586
fusion intelligence idea and, 404–5
Layton's Midway analysis and, 320–22
Nine Power Treaty (1922), 13
19th Minesweeper Division, Japanese, 232
901st Air Group, Japanese, 545, 635, 650
951st Air Group, Japanese, 712
Nishida Masao, 391
Nishimura, Lieutenant Colonel, 619
Nishimura Shoji, 252, 258, 260, 263–65,
275, 589, 625, 630, 635, 656–64,
667
Nishimura Teiji, 659
Nishina Yoshio, 720
Nishino Shigeru, 657, 660, 661, 662
Nishio Hidehiko, 605, 623
Nishizawa Hiroyashi, 493
*Nitta Maru*, 145, 148
Noda Mitsuharu, 139, 142, 191, 330–31,
332, 335, 337n, 534n–35n, 579
Noguchi Yutaka, 671
Nomura Kichisaburo, 28, 51, 64, 72,
104–7, 109, 114, 116, 117, 165,
197, 348, 517, 532–33
Nomura Ryosuke, 708, 715
Nomura Suetsu, 430, 433
Nomura Tomekichi, 593, 646, 652
Noonan, Fred, 93
Norimitsu Saiji, 675
*North Carolina*, 19, 298, 383

North Pacific campaign, 465–81
Attu operation in, 474–78, 480
battle of the pips and, 480
Decisive Battle doctrine and, 475, 476
intelligence and, 466–68, 469, 476–77
JNAF and, 474–75
KE Operation and, 475–76
Kiska invasion and, 479–81
Komandorski Islands battle and,
469–73
OP-20-G and, 478–79
*Noshiro*, 627, 664–65, 690, 692
*Nowake*, 394, 684
Noyes, Leigh, 166
Nuboer, J.F.W., 247
Number 11 Squadron, British, 276

Obata Hideyoshi, 560–61
Obayashi Sueo, 425, 566, 574, 575, 644,
645
Odawara Toshihiko, 619–20
Oe Ranji, 637
Office of Naval Intelligence (ONI), U.S., 8,
17, 18, 21, 24, 27, 53, 66, 87, 104,
375, 381, 382, 430, 525, 543, 544
Boone report of, 301–2
Central Pacific intelligence estimates of,
525–26
Code and Signal Section of, *see* OP-20-G
Combat Intelligence Branch of, 352–54
and fortification of Mandated Islands, 89,
91, 95, 96, 98
*I-1* intelligence windfall and, 401–3
Japanese codes and, 76–77
Japanese naval aviation and, 32–34
Japanese oil estimates of, 613–14
Japanese shipping tracked by, 595–98,
613–14
Joint Interrogation Center of, 496
Jurika's Zero fighter report and, 39
language officer project of, 7–10, 23
"Long Lance" torpedo report and, 31–32
manpower of, 70
*Nachi* affair and, 698–99
Pearl Harbor planning and, 147, 149
racial, cultural bias of, 33–35
Yamamoto as interest of, 125–26
Ofstie, Ralph A., 32, 35, 37, 515, 668
Ofusa Junnosuke, 201–2
Ogan, Joseph V., 29, 104
Ogawa Kanji, 66, 139–40, 148n, 150–51,
166, 298–99, 442, 558, 559
Ogawa Kojiro, 695, 732
Ogg, Robert G., 172
Ogi Kazuto, 435
Ogimoto, Lieutenant, 389, 395
O'Hare, Edward H., 240
*ohka* weapon, 716, 718, 723
Ohmae Toshikazu, 43, 67–78, 359–60,
361, 365, 377, 442–43, 448, 449,

# A B O U T   T H E   A U T H O R

JOHN PRADOS is the author of seven previous books, including *Keepers of the Keys: A History of the National Security Council from Truman to Bush*. His most recent military study, written with Ray W. Stubbe, is *Valley of Decision: The Siege of Khe Sanh*. He holds a Ph.D. in International Relations from Columbia University. Prados lives with his family just outside Washington, D.C.

## A B O U T   T H E   T Y P E

This book was set in Photina, a typeface designed by Jose Mendoza in 1971. It is a very elegant design with high legibility, and its close character fit has made it a popular choice for use in quality magazines and art gallery publications.